Esquire's ENCYCLOPEDIA OF 20TH CENTURY MEN'S FASHIONS

Esquire's ENCYCLOPEDIA

McGRAW-HILL BOOK COMPANY

NEW YORK / SAN FRANCISCO / ST. LOUIS
DÜSSELDORF NEW DELHI
JOHANNESBURG PANAMA
KUALA LUMPUR RIO DE JANEIRO
LONDON SINGAPORE
MEXICO SYDNEY
MONTREAL TORONTO

20 of TH CENTURY MEN'S FASHIONS

O. E. SCHOEFFLER
AND WILLIAM GALE

Staff for McGraw-Hill

General Editor	**Leonard Josephson**
Editing Supervisor	**Tobia L. Worth**
Art Director/Designer	**Edward J. Fox**
Directors of Production	**Gerard G. Mayer, Stephen J. Boldish**
Copy Editor	**Beatrice E. Eckes**

Original fashion illustrations by
Harlan Krakovitz

**Esquire's Encyclopedia of
20th Century Men's Fashions**

Copyright © 1973 by McGraw-Hill, Inc.
All Rights Reserved.

Schoeffler, O. E., and Gale, William
    Esquire's Encyclopedia of
    20th Century Men's Fashions.

ISBN 07-055480-3   72-9811

Contents

Founding Editor's Note

When we began planning *Esquire* in the early thirties, and even before that, in the late twenties, when we were concerned with its predecessor publications, we constantly had a *beau idéal* in mind: the man of taste, with a sense of style and a respect for quality. We reported as fashion the things he wore, and they became fashionable largely because he wore them. Even the occasional apparent exception—the Basque fisherman's shirt, the Scandinavian peasant's sweater, the Spanish workman's sandal—became fashionable only after he adopted them for casual wear.

Our aim was the establishment of a standard of masculine elegance, and a bizarre aim it must have seemed in an era when Presidents were photographed fishing in derby hats and "Jimmy the well-dressed man" was a comedian's gambit and a surefire figure of fun.

But the fact is that there have always been men of taste, with a sense of style and a respect for quality, through good times and bad, through periods of upheaval and tranquillity alike, and they have always stood out like so many weather vanes in the swirling winds of fashion.

Some of them had names that are still evocative—Lord Chesterfield, Richard Brinsley Sheridan, Beau Brummell, on down to men so recently gone as Anthony Drexel Biddle and the late Duke of Windsor (best remembered as the Prince of Wales). Others are still around—men like Fred Astaire and Cary Grant.

But there were, and still are, many others whose names nobody would recognize but whose positions made them central to the ebb and flow of fashion trends, and it has been the job of our fashion editors, from the beginning, to find them and "tail" them, like so many detectives, and now and then simply to collate the totals and averages of their preferences. These men have a breedy look, and your impulse would be to say that on them almost anything looks good, but probably only because if it weren't they wouldn't wear it. Such men are relatively easy for the specialist to spot, though the essence of their elegance is that they would never stand out in a crowd. That's why becoming such a specialist is relatively hard. Partly it's a matter of having an eagle eye for crucial trifles. That can be trained, of course, but it helps to have the initial aptitude that responds most readily to training.

In any case, we had the specialists from the start. There were Captain Murdocke in London and John Starbuck over here, from the very beginning in the twenties; and even in the early days of *Apparel Arts* there turned up a most unlikely recruit named Henry Jackson, who became the first fashion editor of *Esquire;* and Kay Kamen, our specialist in boys' fashions (he and Jackson were both killed in the same plane crash); and George and Jacques Meyer. And then, from 1939 for the next thirty years, there was Shef.

O. E. Schoeffler had the eye, and he had the knack of inculcating it in others. Over the years he trained virtual squads of young lieutenants, and many of them have since gone on, at least in part on the impetus of his indoctrination, to posts of command far afield. He left our fashion forces far stronger than he found them, and the fashion pages more of a mainstay of the magazine than ever. Today, behind those pages are a woman, Rachel Crespin, and a man, Kenneth Fish, and their overall look was never more knowing. Now photography is the rule and a drawing the exception, whereas in the old days the reverse was true. Some of the fashion artists were formidable fashion experts in their own right, notably Laurence Fellows and Robert Goodman (the former gone at a great age and the latter at a tragically young one) and the inimitable Leslie Saalburg, who is alive and well and living in Paris. As some of the examples reproduced in this book show, their pages had an imperishable flair and look as fresh today as the day they came off their easels and drawing boards, long years ago.

Of course, if it was all so simple as I make it sound, looking back over the years, then how to account for this book's enormous size and panoramic scope? Well, for one thing, don't forget that Oscar Schoeffler and Bill Gale have been working on this one volume for over three years. Shef is nothing if not thorough, and he and Bill Gale have not only checked each other but have cross-checked with batteries of experts in all the many fields and processes involved in the total coverage of the subject. The subject, though approached from the viewpoint of forty years of *Esquire* fashion coverage, represents far more than that in its totality. We are dealing here, after all, with one of the three essentials

of life, the one that comes after food and ahead of shelter. And the aim has been to leave no reasonable question about men's clothing unanswered.

The result, obviously, is to tell you more than you could conceivably care to find out, at least at one sitting, about any one of the many aspects of twentieth-century fashions for men. But this being the age of man-made fibers and such manufacturing miracles as permanent-press and double-knitting, it also had to be anticipated that at least some of your questions might be technological, and that has meant recourse to a host of technicians, to assure you of brief and simple explanations of many extremely complicated processes. Further to reduce the awesomeness of the sheer volume of information retrieval that this book inevitably comprises, it has been deemed humane to present it in glossary as well as encyclopedic style, with the result that you can get a short answer when you have neither the time nor the need for a long one.

Since this book already carries an Introduction, the temptation must be resisted to cover too much here. But it seems remiss, after citing the work of the editors and artists involved in the fashion pages, to omit all mention of the wordsmith's function. The fashion copy, which has been quoted frequently in the course of the narrative, has been the work of too many hands over the years to permit much exact attribution; but over recent decades it has been, more often than any other, the voice of George Frazier that has intoned the monthly lesson out of the *Esquire* fashion dogma, and never has it been more felicitously expressed. In fact, were this the occasion to hand out three golden apples among those who have worked on the fashion side of *Esquire* over the years, for typifying most fully, though each in his highly individual way, that *beau idéal,* the "man of taste, with a sense of style, and a respect for quality," one would have to go to George Frazier, another to Leslie Saalburg, and the last, which should also be first, to Oscar Schoeffler, whose monument this book really is.

ARNOLD GINGRICH

vii

Introduction

As its title clearly indicates, *Esquire's Encyclopedia of 20th Century Men's Fashions* is an encyclopedia. It is also a social history, for the clothes men wear tell us not only a lot about the men who wear them but a lot too about the climate of the time in which they live: the social, economic, and political conditions that influence the way a man dresses. This, then, is a lavishly illustrated encyclopedia that, in seminarrative style, covers in detail every item of apparel worn by the American man of this century while exploring the society of which his clothes are a reflection. And since fashion is an overall look and attitude, this book also considers twentieth-century man's luggage and leather goods, perennial status symbols; the styling and care of his hair; and his toiletries, which have always been a measure of his self-pride. Each category of apparel is covered chronologically, decade by decade, so it is possible, by reading what is written and illustrated about each category for any one decade, to create the *total* look for that period.

The reader will find that some categories are covered at greater length than others. What determined the coverage given each category by the authors was the duration of its life-span plus its degree of fashion importance. Sportswear, for instance, is tremendously important today; yet its story does not cover as many pages as suits, for the practical reason that sportswear did not achieve any degree of fashion importance until the 1920s.

Esquire's Encyclopedia of 20th Century Men's Fashions also takes the reader behind the scenes, to the mills where the fabrics are made and to the plants where the clothes made from these fabrics are manufactured. Every step of every process is described in detail.

Since this book deals with eight decades of fashion, it offers the reader a uniquely panoramic view of men's fashions in the twentieth century. Beyond the treatment given each category of apparel, it discusses the dominant fashion colors and color combinations, as well as the various influences that, under certain circumstances, can convert a fashion foible to a fad and then, on occasion, catapult it to the status of a bona fide fashion, at which point it becomes subject to the visible and invisible currents that are rather loosely termed "fashion cycles." It is at that stage in the life of any fashion that a guidebook is essential if one intends to follow its progress. For that reason the authors of this encyclopedia have included a comprehensive Glossary that runs the gamut from A (Aberdeen socks) through Z (zoot suit and Z-twist).

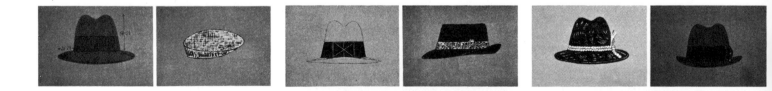

The reader will also find here a wealth of anecdotal material (rare in an encyclopedia), in recognition of the fact that fashion is and always has been intensely personal. We have, on one hand, the fashion authorities—designers who create the fashions and editors who observe and evaluate the fashion cavalcade—and, on the other, the fashion elitists—the socialites, athletes, and entertainment personalities, among others—who lead the fashion cavalcade. All three groups come alive in these pages to give the reader a very real picture of the particular contribution each makes singly and in tandem toward the creation of fashion as we know it.

And because the "name" designer is a phenomenon of the so-called Peacock Revolution of the 1960s, the biographies of eighty internationally famous menswear designers are included along with their photographs and some illustrations of their work.

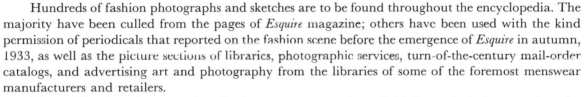

Hundreds of fashion photographs and sketches are to be found throughout the encyclopedia. The majority have been culled from the pages of *Esquire* magazine; others have been used with the kind permission of periodicals that reported on the fashion scene before the emergence of *Esquire* in autumn, 1933, as well as the picture sections of libraries, photographic services, turn-of-the-century mail-order catalogs, and advertising art and photography from the libraries of some of the foremost menswear manufacturers and retailers.

The publication of an encyclopedia is a gargantuan task, and this is particularly true when the encyclopedia is the first of its genre. This book would not have been possible without the cooperation of the many who generously contributed their expertise to this project: periodicals, professional organizations, museums, libraries, fashion artists, and the *Esquire* staff. We are particularly indebted to Stanley J. Capelin, president of Capelin Associates, for writing the chapter "Evolution of Apparel Manufacturing."

And our special thanks to: Abercrombie & Fitch Co., After Six, Inc., American Cyanamid Co., American Enka Co., American Footwear Manufacturers Association, Inc., American Optical Corp., American Silk Mills Corp., American Tourister, American Wool Council, Aquascutum of London, England, Arrow Co. Division of Cluett Peabody & Co., Inc., Ashear Brothers, Inc., Atlantic Products Corp., Baltimore Luggage Co., Beaunit Corp., Better Vision Institute, Botany Industries, Inc., British Woollens, British Wool Textile Industries, Brooks Brothers, Burlington Industries, Inc., Buxton, Inc., Camp & McInnes, Inc., Canterbury Belts, Ltd., Celanese Corp., Cisco, Inc., Clothing Manufacturers Association of the United States of America, Cone Mills Corp., Cotton Incorporated, Crown-Metro, Inc. (Cravenette), Daily News Record, Dan River, Inc., H. Daroff & Sons, Inc., Deansgate, Inc., Deering Milliken, Inc., Delton, Ltd., Du Barry Division of Warner-Lambert Co., E. I. du Pont de Nemours & Co., Eagle Clothes, Inc., Eastman Chemical Products, Inc., Ericson Co. of Sweden, Esquire Fashions for Men, L. B. Evans Son Co., Inc., FMC Corp., Fox-Knapp Manufacturing Co., Fragrance Foundation, Fur Information & Fashion Council, Inc., Goodstein Bros. & Co., Inc., L. Greif & Bro., Hammonton Park Clothes, Handcraft, Inc., Hanley Industries, B. W. Harris Manufacturing Co. (Zero King), Hart Schaffner & Marx, Haspel Brothers, George W. Heller, Inc., Hercules, Inc., Hickey-Freeman Co., Inc., Hickok Slacks, Inc., Leonard Hyde, Hystron Fibers, Inc., International Silk Association, Interwoven Socks Division of Kayser-Roth, Irish Linen Guild, Jantzen, Inc., Jaymar-Ruby, Inc., Jockey Menswear (division of Cooper's, Inc.), H. Kauffman & Sons Saddlery Co., Inc., William B. Kessler, Inc., Knothe Bros. Co., Inc., B. Kuppenheimer & Co., Lakeland Manufacturing Co., Roger Laviale, Ltd., H. D. Lee Co., Inc., Levi Strauss & Co., Londontown Manufacturing Co., Luggage & Leather Goods Manufacturers of America, Inc., McGregor-Doniger, Inc., Manhattan Shirt Co., Man-Made Fiber Producers Association, Mark Cross Co., Ltd., May Optical Co., Men's Fashion

Association of America, Inc., Men's Tie Foundation, Inc., Men's Wear, Michaels Stern & Co., Modern Textile Dictionary, Monsanto Company, National Association of Men's Sportswear Buyers, National Outerwear & Sportswear Association, Inc., New England Shoe & Leather Association, Onondaga Silk Co., Inc., Palm Beach Company, Gino Paoli, Phillips Fibers Corp., Phillips–Van Heusen Corp., Pompeii Tie, Rochester Button Co., S. Howard Rosenthal, Louis Roth Co., Samsonite Corp., H. E. Seisenheimer Co., The Shoe & Leather Lexicon, J. P. Stevens & Co., Inc., The Stevens Fabricopedia, Leonardo Strassi, Ltd., Swank, Inc., Talon Division of Textron, Tioga Textile Associates, Inc., A. R. Trapp, Inc., Union Carbide Corp., Uniroyal, Inc., United Carr Division of TWR, Inc., United Luggage Co., Inc., Van Baalen Heilbrun & Co. Inc., Bernard Weatherill, Inc., Weldon, Inc., Wool Bureau, Inc., Woolrich Woolen Mills, Yardley of London, Inc.

It is our hope that each and every one of them will conclude that this, the finished product, is worthy of their time and talents.

THE AUTHORS

Esquire's
ENCYCLOPEDIA
OF 20TH
CENTURY
MEN'S
FASHIONS

Suits

Although the Victorian era barely lasted into the twentieth century, it had a decisive influence on men's fashions in the first decade of the century. Men's suits had a stuffy, conservative look that at times resembled an extension of the upholstered look of the Victorian furniture popular in American homes of the period. Men's suits were actually oversize, the suit of a man of average size requiring 5 yards of cloth.

The double-breasted suit with high lapels and a rounded front was in favor in patterned heavy fabrics in 1899, as shown in the Sartorial Art Journal *supplement.*

1900–1910

A new century had begun, and the United States was busy building its industries and cities. In the nineteenth century Americans had been occupied in opening frontiers and struggling for survival in a climate that was not always friendly. Life was physical and often dangerous. Now, in the first decade of the twentieth century, the descendants of the pioneers were living urban lives and were preoccupied with the comforts of home. Their clothing, like their furnishings, was generously upholstered. Both sexes used clothes to cover and decorate their bodies and to establish subtly the fact that they were no longer obliged to pit themselves against the elements. Clothes were a status symbol, although the term was then unknown.

Suit coats were long, loose-fitting, and buttoned high. The shoulders were heavily padded and appeared even bulkier than they were because the lapels were tiny and notched. Sleeves were cut full to the cuffs, which often were turned back and sometimes were buttoned at the wrist. Trousers were pleated at the waist and cut large and loose about the hips and thighs, tapering to very narrow bottoms. This exaggerated trouser style was called "peg-top." Trouser cuffs were unknown at the turn of the century except to men wealthy enough to have their suits custom-made on Savile Row, in London. (Britishers attending race meets and other country sporting events had long since acquired the habit of turning up the bottoms of

The walking frock suit fashionable around 1900 combined a jacket having short lapels and a waist seam with trim-cut trousers. [HART, SCHAFFNER & MARX]

The four-button jacket having patch pockets and very short lapels with matching trim-cut trousers was an outstanding fashion in 1900. [HART, SCHAFFNER & MARX]

their trousers in an attempt to keep them clear of mud and moist turf.) By 1905, however, cuffs were becoming numerous in the United States. Legend has it that an English nobleman, on his way to a wedding in New York on a rainy day, turned up his trousers to avoid their being splattered and, arriving late at the church, forgot to turn them down. Fashion-conscious men noticed him, and the fashion for trousers with cuffs began.

Vests, or waistcoats, as they were known more formally, were essential to a man's suit. In one vest pocket he would carry his heavy gold watch and in another his watch fob, a gold chain extending across the vest to connect the two. All vests were adaptations of the English postboy waistcoats of the 1870s, being cut high under the armholes and fashioned of wool front and back in order to keep the wearer warm.

Sack suit. If a man had only one suit, it was a dark blue serge. And if

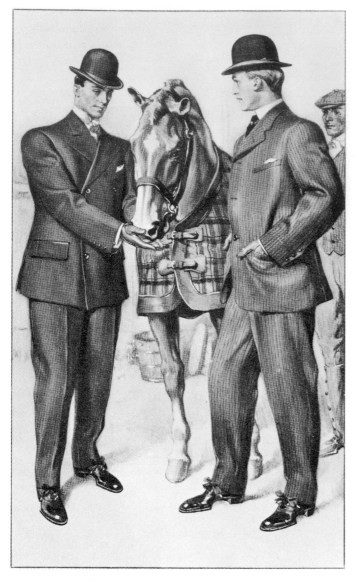

In 1905 high-roll lapels distinguished both single- and double-breasted suits, shown here with high-crown derby hats. [HART, SCHAFFNER & MARX]

The walking frock suit remained in fashion in 1905, as did the very long chesterfield overcoat. [HART, SCHAFFNER & MARX]

he had an eye for fashion, it was a dark blue serge sack suit, the shapeless jacket of which accounted for the name. Broadly speaking, the sack was any coat without a waist seam, the body and skirt being cut in one piece.

A single-breasted three- or four-button model with tiny notched lapels was by far the most popular sack suit, but three-button double-breasted suits with wide, shapely lapels were available (short or stout men were advised to avoid them). The man who could afford several suits might have, besides his sack suit of serviceable serge, sack

suits of sturdy worsted and luxuriously soft vicuña. The more adventurous dresser took immediately to the sack suit whose coat had the new soft-roll lapels. By 1907, in fact, the sack suit had risen above the restrictions imposed by its name, and both single- and double-breasted models were beginning to show slight shaping at the waist and hips, which gave them a more youthful, trimmer appearance.

The goal of the well-dressed man in this decade was to look genteel, prosperous, and athletic in the broad-chested fashion of Theodore Roose-

velt. A sack suit of dark blue, dark gray, or black all but guaranteed this look.

English walking coat suit and cutaway frock coat. An adaptation of the English cutaway or walking frock suit, the English walking coat suit was an attempt to produce a suit that would be acceptable for business hours and dressy enough for more formal occasions. As a manufacturer of the period, American Fashions, put it, "The English Walking Coat Suit—becoming to most men, especially those of heavy build—is as much favored by business men as by professional men, because it gives one a distinguished appearance and may be worn with propriety at afternoon functions, if made of dark-toned fabrics." The coat extended to the knees and had a sharply cutaway front; unlike the sack coat, it had subtle shaping. The business frock suit, as it was sometimes called, was most popular in black or oxford gray vicuña and in plain or striped gray sharkskin worsted.

Considerably more formal was the cutaway frock coat, worn with striped trousers. The coat was usually of black or oxford gray worsted, and the two-tone striped trousers of light or dark gray worsted. Worn with a high silk hat, spats, and a walking stick, the cutaway frock coat was immensely elegant and was much in favor with banking executives.

Although the English walking coat suit and the cutaway frock coat won only limited acceptance with the

Long jackets dominated the fashion scene in 1907: (left) a double-breasted model with an overplaid design; (right) a square-front jacket with two buttons set low, worn with a pinned stock and a hat with the brim turned up at the side. [HART, SCHAFFNER & MARX]

the wearer a rumpled, unkempt look. The fashion-conscious men of the North preferred to suffer the heat in suits made of heavier, more wrinkle-resistant fabrics.

At fashionable summer resorts white flannel trousers worn with a dark serge suit coat were practically a uniform. For informal weekend wear, a flannel suit with fancy outing stripes in gray, blue, brown, or olive was also admired. A man wearing a suit of this type with a cool-looking panama hat or a straw skimmer was every inch a fashion plate. Young men and those who thought of themselves as young were partial to three-button single-breasted outing suits made of tropical-weight worsteds, cheviots, serges, and flannels. By 1907 the trousers of these suits had belt loops and cuffs.

1910–1920

The climate of war never fails to affect men's fashions. This is true not only immediately after a war but also

In 1905 the full-shouldered sack suit with four buttons, very short lapels, and a square front was featured in Scotch cheviot with matching tapered trousers. [L. GREIF & BRO.]

American man of this decade, they were perhaps the first indications that he was getting ready to accept a suit that would be less bulky and be fashioned along more natural lines. Oddly enough, it was the college student of the period who clung most tenaciously to the oversize suit. By 1910, in fact, this suit had become a symbol of the Ivy Leaguer and was popularly known as the "rah-rah" suit.

Summer suits. Air conditioning was far in the future, and in the hot months of this decade the American man had to cope with rising temperatures as best he could. He consigned his serge, cheviot, and worsted suits to mothballs and changed to suits of flannel and linen. The all-white suit was especially popular, for it not only looked cool but clearly signified that the wearer was not of the blue-collar working class. In Southern cities suits of seersucker or light English worsted were often worn, but for the most part these were poorly tailored and gave

An outfit suggested for wear in Palm Beach in 1910 consisted of a light-color suit with a shaped jacket, a waistcoat, and 3-inch cuffs on the trousers, a wing collar, a bow tie, and a straw hat with a puggaree and the brim turned down. [COURTESY OF CULVER PICTURES, INC., NEW YORK]

The cane-carrying man in this illustration wears a double-breasted jacket, with one button to fasten and slanting welt pockets, and peg-top trousers with extremely deep cuffs (1910). [HART, SCHAFFNER & MARX]

Fashions for the university man in 1910 included a double-breasted jacket, peg-top pants with deep cuffs, a bow tie, a starched collar, and a small-shape cap. [HART, SCHAFFNER & MARX]

in the period just preceding the conflict. The tempo of a nation quickens as the military atmosphere heightens, and the young, whose lives will be most deeply affected, become a focal point. The nation appears to be rejuvenated on many levels. Such youth-conscious periods never fail to produce dynamic changes in the clothes men wear.

The fall of 1912, when the unmistakable sound of saber rattling came from across the Atlantic, saw a radical change in color, with purple suddenly the most advertised color for men's suits. This was a short-lived fad, but after a decade of navy blue, banker's gray, and sedate brown, it was an extraordinary forecast of the fashion

freedom that would come later in the decade.

Very early in the decade suits had lost their oversize proportions. Whereas a barrel-chested physique with massive arms and Herculean thighs was the ideal of the previous decade, the new ideal was to be youthfully lanky and slim as a whippet. Suits were made to emphasize this look where it existed and to create the illusion where it did not. As early as the fall of 1911, in fact, suits were being tailored along trimmer, more youthful-looking lines. Jackets averaged 30 inches on a size 40 suit, and fronts were straight with only a slight opening at the bottom. Shoulders were becoming more natural, and many

retailers advertised that their new suits had no padding. Sleeves were narrow and had a new feature, four buttons set well up from the edge of the cuff. Even semipeg trousers had almost disappeared, being replaced by modified London trousers that were cut narrower at the waist and ended just at the ankles, often showing a bit of brightly colored socks. These trimmer trousers were not only cuffed but creased front and back, an innovation introduced a few years earlier in London by King Edward VII, a portly but extremely fashion-conscious man. The three-button jacket was still the national favorite, but the return of long-rolling lapels (though still only $2\frac{3}{4}$ inches wide) often made it resemble

In 1911 very long jackets with a high closure were worn with high-water peg-top trousers, reaching only to the ankles. [HART, SCHAFFNER & MARX]

The suit for fall, 1911, had a close-fitting jacket with natural shoulders, a matching vest, and cuffless trousers. With it were worn button-top shoes. [HICKEY-FREEMAN CO.]

a two-button model. By 1914 the natural-shoulder suit dominated the fashion scene, and its jacket had lost another inch, now measuring only 29 inches on a size 40 suit, for in the period just before World War I it was smart to look as leggy as one of the sketches of Joseph Leyendecker, the most renowned fashion artist of the day, whose men were so elongated as to resemble stick figures.

By the spring of 1915 a full-page advertisement in the *Saturday Evening Post* reflected the effect World War I had already had on American men's clothing: "A crisp and definite new note is struck," said the copywriter. "Take it point by point in its style details: The natural shoulders inno-

cent of padding. The shaped body with *military high-waist effect.* The five-button waistcoat, worn with the top button open, giving a decided effect as it rolls back from a rich scarf and a background of neat shirt pattern."

This youthful styling, which had appeared even before America's entry into the war, became increasingly popular with the return of servicemen to civilian life after the war. Having grown accustomed to the facile lines of his military uniform, even the least fashion-conscious young veteran was determined to look and feel equally comfortable in his civilian clothes. For the first time since the start of the century young men were unwilling to dress like their fathers: they were in-

sisting on more natural styling and were more than willing to experiment with new fashions. The returning soldier, anxious to shed the drabness of his military wardrobe, received a spirited welcome home and an assurance from apparel manufacturers that he would now have a chance to express his individuality with clothes that were youthful but not freakish.

As suits became softer and more comfortable, so did related items of apparel. The high starched shirt collar gave way to the soft collar, and the high-buttoned shoe was replaced by the oxford. The younger man also showed a preference for the wristwatch, which had first appeared in 1914, and the resulting decline of the

the following year this look reached its peak with the introduction of a waist-seam coat cut extremely sharp and high under the arms. The most popular version of the new coat was a one-button jacket with its solitary button set precisely on the waist seam and a straight front falling to square or blunted corners without an opening. A smart, clean-cut silhouette that emphasized youthful vigor and aggressiveness, it was highly appropriate for a nation about to enter an era of "flaming youth."

Country suits. During a decade that saw the young begin to exert an extraordinarily strong influence on the American life-style, the nation became increasingly sports-minded. London was still the men's fashion capital, and Americans looked to the British for guidance on what to wear for active and spectator sports.

The norfolk suit was inspired by the

The dandy of 1911 at the Belmont races wore a gun-club-check walking frock suit with two flapped pockets and turned-back cuffs on the sleeves, a high collar, and a roll-brim hat and carried a cane. [NEW YORK PUBLIC LIBRARY PICTURE COLLECTION]

heavy gold watch and fob made a vest less important. The younger man now judged a vest strictly on its fashion appeal. As early as the fall of 1914, fancy vests (advertised as "high-falutin vests") had made their appearance. These vests were smartly fitted at the waist, and many of them had graceful, long-rolling lapels. Cut high, they showed well above the opening of a suit jacket.

This tradition-toppling decade ended on a note of unparalleled prosperity. After the restrictions imposed by a global war, America felt reborn and optimistic about the future. By 1918 men's suits clearly expressed these youthful high spirits. A high-waisted look was dominant, and by

(left) In 1912 the Hickey-Freeman Co. featured a modification of the full English model with close-fitting lines and long-roll lapels. (right) The norfolk style with pleats and a yoke, suggested as "suitable for horseback riding, golf and other outdoor sports."

BANTAM   OXFORD

hunting jacket worn by the Duke of Norfolk in the early eighteenth century. In England at the time it was the custom for men to wear country jackets associated with their districts. The jacket of the Duke's hunting suit, which became known as the norfolk jacket, was worn by men in the county of Norfolk with matching trousers. The distinguishing features of this jacket, faithfully reproduced in an American copy almost two centuries

later, were two box pleats down each side in front and two down each side in back. Long a favorite with the English country squire, the norfolk suit was advertised for the first time by American stores in the fall of 1911 as a golf suit. By the middle of the decade the American copy of the norfolk was immensely popular and had become the preferred costume not only for golf but for bicycling and croquet as well, with the jacket doing double duty in

the wardrobe of the horseman.

The norfolk jacket's flapped lower patch pockets extended to the box pleats. At the chest were vertical slit pockets beneath the pleats. Some models had side vents, but others had none. The first American copy had a belted back, and soon models with all-around belts appeared. Often the jacket was worn with knickers, heavy woolen knee hose, and a tweed cap to make an outfit that was acceptable whether the wearer was actively engaged in a sport or was simply watching from the sidelines. Worn with or without a vest, and with matching trousers of Harris or Donegal tweed, the norfolk jacket was presented as a serviceable suit for men who were young in years or in heart and who preferred to be well dressed even in their casual activities. Despite its English countryside origin, the norfolk jacket, worn with white flannel trousers and a straw skimmer, also became a proper summer weekend outfit at even the most sophisticated American resorts.

Also adapted from English suits, though considerably less popular than the norfolk suit, were the suffolk and Sunningdale country suits. As the name suggests, the suffolk was worn by men in the county of Suffolk. Like the norfolk, the suffolk jacket had two box pleats down each side in front and patch pockets with flaps, but a single box pleat ran down the center of the back. Some models had side vents, and others no vents at all.

The Sunningdale, originally a golf suit named in honor of the renowned English course, had a series of pleats running vertically from the top of the back to about $2\frac{1}{2}$ inches below, spaced approximately 3 inches apart. Similar pleats were repeated across the waist. The purpose of rows of pleats across the one-piece back was to provide ample fullness through the shoulder blades for free-swinging action. While the Sunningdale had been designed originally as a golf suit, American men wore their American-made copies for all sports or simply as unusually comfortable, smart-looking country suits.

(left) An essentially young man's outfit for spring, 1912, comprised a suit with long lines and deep cuffs on the trousers, a small-knot tie, a starched high collar, a low-crown derby, and pointed shoes. (right) A version of the norfolk style with a two-button front, designed for men "who are young either in years or in spirit." [HICKEY-FREEMAN CO.]

TECK

STRAND

The norfolk jacket of 1917 had a square front with three buttons. The matching deep-cuffed trousers were worn over a pair of high-button shoes. [HART, SCHAFFNER & MARX]

Style that's right

YOU needn't pay extra to have your clothes right in style; but you'd better be sure of the maker's ability to create style. There are plenty of clothes makers, but very few style makers.

At the left is a good waist-seam suit with welt seams at the back. The second young man from the right wears a Raglan overcoat; the young man at his right, a two-button military sport suit.

In 1918 the waist-seam suit with a deep center vent was a favorite with young men. [HART, SCHAFFNER & MARX]

Natural-shoulder suit. This decade saw the natural-shoulder look accepted universally. By 1914 and 1915 most major suit manufacturers were advertising "natural, easy, distinctive styles." The new look featured natural shoulders, a soft front, body tracing, and patch pockets. The single-breasted suit with a center vent was the most popular model, although even a six-button double-breasted model had the same softly tailored styling. In 1916 the look was enhanced by a snugger-fitting waist. The silhouette was slim, trim, and close-fitting in both coat and trousers. Softly tailored shapeliness was what the fashion-conscious American man wanted. Yet, oddly enough, he was still wearing a high starched shirt collar with his new softly tailored suit.

In the fall of 1917, after the United States had entered World War I, the federal government instructed clothing manufacturers to stop making items that used excessive amounts of cloth. One of the first "casualties" was the belted pinchback jacket that had become prominent only the previous spring. At first a sports coat, the jacket had been adapted for general wear by very style-conscious younger men, some of whom went so far as to favor a belt running three-quarters of the way around. Vertical slash pockets began to replace the popular patch pockets. Not only did they require less cloth, but they were very much in keeping with the snug-fitting suit. From a purely economic standpoint, the biggest victim of wartime restrictions was the two-pants suit. There is

no record of when the two-pants suit was first introduced. In some quarters, it is believed to have been introduced by a New York City retailer in 1912; in others, by a Chicago retailer in 1916. In any event, the two-pants suit disappeared during World War I and was reintroduced after the war. By 1927 it accounted for 38 percent of American suit production, maintaining its popularity through 1941 and the entry of the United States into World War II.

By 1919 youth completely dominated the fashion scene. Rare indeed was the manufacturer who admitted that he designed for the older customer. Men grew up, not old. At least that was the stance of an industry that perceived, and correctly so, the American male's belief that in his dress and life-style he could stay the advance of years. It was not surprising to see elderly gentlemen depicted in advertisements wearing bow ties, skimmers, and three-button suits or a senior citizen attired in a single-breasted, high-waisted model with lean, facile lines, a carnation in his 4-inch lapel symbolizing the youthfulness with which he had put his wardrobe together.

With the war over and clothing restrictions relaxed, generously proportioned patch pockets were back and became more popular than ever. The snug-fitting natural-shoulder suit with a center vent was so popular by the end of the decade that some manufacturers ruled out this fashion for the man with a paunch, contending that only a slim, trim figure could carry the one-button model with aplomb.

In view of the emphasis on youth, it was not surprising that the attractive natural-shoulder suit should have been bastardized into what eventually became known as the "jazz suit," in which the natural-shoulder line was nipped away for a tight, pinched look. The jacket, which had three closely spaced buttons, was extremely tight-waisted, and the center vent of its long skirt was 12 inches long. The trousers were short and as skinny as pipestems. In its own way, the exaggerated jazz suit was as freakish as the outsize suit of the previous decade. As it became more popular with some young men, cheaper, poorly made versions were produced, until by 1923 the jazz suit, by then a caricature of itself, vanished from the fashion scene.

It would be unfair to suggest that the dance craze that swept the nation during the decade 1910–1920 was solely responsible for the jazz suit. In the years leading up to American involvement in the war, when the young American dance team of Irene and Vernon Castle were doing lively new dances like the bunny hug and the turkey trot, an informal dance suit had evolved. With its one-button jacket, wide lapels, and vertical pockets, it had a slender, leggy look that, unlike that of the jazz suit, was tasteful and flattering.

Although this decade saw the natural-shoulder line tampered with and made temporarily less attractive in the process, the authentic natural-shoulder suit had become a sartorial classic and, like a true classic, would endure long after such mutations as the jazz suit were forgotten.

1920–1930

If the young had had an impact on the national scene in the previous decade, their influence in the twenties was positively incendiary, for this was the era of flaming youth. America's youth was both literally and figuratively in the driver's seat, since by 1923 there were 15 million cars on the road. After a war young people grow rebellious, as though to punish their elders for having created a world where war is possible. And the young flaunt their youth during these times, wearing it like a merit badge. The flaming youth of the twenties appeared to make a fetish of their youth, and sometimes they seemed to be pushing themselves to the limit, perhaps not only to prove how young they were but how old everybody else was. The Charleston and the black bottom were the favored dances, and many extroverted young couples climbed on tabletops to exhibit their skill at these new jazz dances that demanded a maximum of agility and endurance. The whole nation, in fact, was dance happy, and marathon dances, a particularly grotesque form of entertainment, quickly developed into a kind of indoor sport.

When youth becomes a cult, the young use fashion to declare their independence of the older generation. Furthermore, a unisex look never fails to evolve from the camaraderie felt by the rebellious young of both sexes. When to this is added the fact that, owing to World War I, for the first time in modern history there was a surplus of women, it is understandable that the girls of this decade strove to look as boyish as possible.

In 1920 women were finally granted the right to vote, and the liberated female, the now irrepressible "flap-per," flaunted her new equality by bobbing her hair, discarding her corset, and smoking cigarettes in public. She considered herself the equal of any man and did not see why she should not look it. Her favorite hat, a cloche, was in fact an imitation of a soldier's tin helmet. She flattened her bosom to achieve a boyish figure and wore an exact duplicate of her escort's yellow slicker coat, decorated with copies of drawings by John Held, Jr., of slick-haired sheikhs and knobby-kneed flappers. When winter came and he bundled himself into an ankle-length raccoon coat, she did the same. Early in the decade, the flapper had ripped the skirt off her swimsuit, but her boy friend had not as yet doffed his top. As a result, their beach costumes were so similar that *Men's Wear* wrote: "It is difficult to separate the lads from the lassies at the beach this summer" (July 8, 1925).

This new spirit of equality between the sexes also revealed itself in clothes that were exclusively masculine. In consequence, the broad-shouldered, broad-chested look in suits was a thing of the past. The man of this youth-oriented decade wanted to look boyishly slim, and the snug-fitting, understated natural-shoulder suit that had become so popular in the previous decade was carried over into the "roaring twenties."

The jazz suit of the previous decade managed to survive until 1923 or 1924, mainly because of its acceptance by sharp dressers in the theatrical profession, who even copied its extreme silhouette for their tuxedo suits. Always anxious to be noticed and eager to adopt the latest fad, the vaudevillians who congregated outside the Palace Theater in New York (the home of two-a-day vaudeville) were particularly partial to the latest innovation in the jazz suit, a seam running around the jacket from front to back, mildly suggesting the belt on a military uniform. By this time jazz clothing had gone about as far as it could without falling into the theatrical costume category. That it lasted as long as it did was extraordinary.

In 1921 a recession curtailed spending and sent many small businesses into bankruptcy. Although it did not last long, it had a long-lived effect on menswear retailers, who in the mid-twenties attempted to attract customers with easy-payment plans and storewide reduction sales. Yet, despite the subsequent upsurge in the national economy, the retail value of clothing declined by 21 percent from 1923 to 1929. As some retailers began to favor unbranded lines that gave them bigger profits, brand-name manufacturers resorted to newspaper and magazine advertisements, as well as the new medium of radio, to ask the customer: "Is it price or clothes value you seek?"

By 1924 Ivy League students vacationing abroad were, like their fashion-conscious fathers, coming under British fashion influence. But unlike their fathers, who shopped in Savile Row, they found their inspiration at Oxford University, where students, not being permitted to wear knickers to class, had devised the solution of Oxford bags, voluminous trousers measuring about 25 inches around the knees and 22 inches around the bottoms that could easily be slipped over the forbidden knickers. The Ivy Leaguers adopted this style, and soon New Haven tailors were making natural-shoulder suits with trousers measuring from 18½ to 22 inches around bottoms that billowed out over the wearer's Scotch-grain shoes. This new natural-shoulder suit with wide-bottom trousers, worn with a button-down shirt, a regimental-striped necktie, and colorful argyle socks, constituted the Ivy League uniform of the mid-twenties.

The college man's dream was to go dressed like that to meet Constance Bennett under the clock at the Hotel Biltmore in New York. The blonde actress daughter of the actor Richard Bennett was one of the most popular flappers in New York, and it was a status symbol to be seen tea-dancing with her at the Biltmore, the Della Robbia Room of the Hotel Vanderbilt on Park Avenue, or the Plaza Grill on Fifth. Small sandwiches and slivers of

In spring, 1926, the straight-hanging university-style jacket with rounded-notch lapels was combined with full-cut trousers.
[SCHEYER-TAILORED FOR OGILVIE & JACOBS]

cake were served, and eventually the Ivy Leaguer who frequented tea dances was referred to as a "cake-eater," and his natural-shoulder suit with wide-bottom trousers was called a cake-eater's suit.

While the collegians of this decade were copying the fashions of their British cousins at Oxford, their fathers, who were making money on Wall Street, were patronizing the leading West End tailors of London, who by now were tiring of the natural-shoulder silhouette and favored a bolder, more assertive look, expressed in a double-breasted suit with a greater breadth of shoulder and wider lapels. (These lapels, which measured 3¼ inches, even appeared on single-breasted suit jackets.) Most significant was the fact that this new look was

favored by the young Prince of Wales, who by this time was the undisputed men's fashion leader of the world. A relatively small number of Eastern college men copied this style, but the majority of college men and middle-class businessmen remained loyal to the natural-shoulder suit with its straight-hanging jacket.

There was one thing both the fashionable father and his son had in common, and that was knickers, another style borrowed from the British. The father wore them for golfing, and his son wore them on campus. In the process, knickers became so popular that soon both British and American manufacturers were turning out knicker suits. The new odd pants called slacks also became popular during this decade, and men of all ages wore them with 2-inch-wide belts for sports and leisure wear, white flannel being the most favored fabric.

During this period, when men were becoming increasingly conscious of the comfort and practicality of their clothes, the summer suit made modest but definite progress. In 1920 a three-button sports suit appeared in cartridge cloth, a silk fabric previously used only to hold powder charges for big guns. Cool and attractive, it was a forerunner of the lightweight summer suit. During the decade engineers at the Goodall Worsted Company succeeded in producing the first successful all-white suit of a cotton-and-mohair blend, which was named the Palm Beach suit. By the late twenties Goodall, determined to ensure that its new fabric be properly tailored and priced, began to manufacture its own suits at a set price. By this time it was fairly obvious that summer would soon be the third season in the men's clothing field. Meanwhile, most of the tropical worsted suits worn during the summer months were fashioned of a loosely woven, crisp woolen called "Fresco." Since the fabric weighed 13 ounces to the yard, it was scarcely lightweight, and it was Fresco's porosity rather than its weight that accounted for some degree of coolness.

The menswear business became increasingly imaginative in its selling and display techniques. Some lower-priced stores created momentary sensations by substituting live men for wax dummies; their faces made up to resemble wax heads, these men had mastered the trick of holding a pose for several minutes before "coming to life" before the startled gaze of window shoppers. By 1925 even the bona fide dummies had taken on a more natural look, and shop windows had begun to use new methods of display. More and more often glass replaced heavier, more ornate stands, credit for this trend going to the Paris Exposition of 1925 that had launched an *art moderne* look that was startlingly simple and uncluttered. The most sophisticated stores now preferred to show less merchandise but to show it with style. This often meant just one suit of clothes on display, with related accessories draped over an antique chair and a wrought-iron candelabrum.

The advertising of men's clothes increased substantially during this decade, and on December 3, 1927, the *Saturday Evening Post* ran the first four-color double-page spread of menswear. The H. B. Glover Company advertisement showed brightly colored men's pajamas under a headline that typified the twenties' preoccupation with youth: "Eternal Youth Lights a Conflagration of Color." *Esquire* magazine was still in the future, but David Smart, its dynamic founder, had already entered the menswear field with *Gentlemen's Quarterly,* a syndicated haberdasher booklet sold to retailers, which made its publishing debut with a Christmas, 1926, issue.

This decade, which had opened on a high note of prosperity with many workingmen wearing $20 silk shirts, ended with a crash when the bottom fell out of the stock market on October 29, 1929, and tycoons and factory workers alike lost their shirts.

Natural-shoulder suit. With wartime memories rapidly fading into the background, the high-waisted military look in the natural-shoulder suit, which had been popular at the end of the previous decade, gave way in the

In the spring of 1926 the fashionable suit had a double-breasted jacket with wide lapels, two sets of buttons, and welt pockets and full-cut trousers with pleats below the waistband. [SCHEYER-TAILORED FOR OGILVIE & JACOBS]

twenties to a jacket with straight-hanging lines. The single-breasted model was the most popular, possibly because it enhanced the long, lean look that was still the ideal. Lapels in the early twenties were short and quite narrow, measuring $2\frac{3}{4}$ inches or sometimes only $2\frac{1}{3}$ inches in width. In 1921 and 1922 a size 40 suit had a $30\frac{1}{2}$-inch jacket. If it was a three-button model, all three buttons were fastened, giving the wearer a fashionable high-buttoned, short-lapeled look. Some men chose a four-button model, bringing the natural-shoulder look to its limits, although the two- and three-button styles remained the leaders. While the collegian, inspired by the Oxford bags, wore trousers measuring from $18\frac{1}{2}$ to 22 inches or more at the

bottoms, the businessman kept his trouser bottoms at $17\frac{1}{2}$ inches.

By 1925, however, some of the most affluent American men were copying the new British look with its bolder proportions. Still, most American men remained faithful to the natural-shoulder silhouette, although wider lapels, sometimes measuring $3\frac{3}{4}$ inches, were not uncommon. The most popular suit fabrics were striped cheviots and worsteds that weighed about 15 ounces to the yard, producing a rather hefty suit.

It is significant that, as Wall Street prospered and even elevator men and errand boys were trading stock tips, the average American man was becoming noticeably more conservative in his dress. There was nothing dull about his appearance, however. Wearing a felt hat, perhaps turned down on one side in the fashion of Mayor James J. Walker of New York, or one of the new wide-brimmed derbies and the new wing-tip shoes, the well-dressed man in his natural-shoulder suit was best described as dapper.

As this softly constructed suit with its minimum of shoulder padding gained popularity, an increasing number of stores began to specialize in catering to the men who wore it, with Brooks Brothers becoming a leader among them. For younger men with fashion sense but little money, small stores that sold natural-shoulder suits with vests for a modest $29.50 began to appear.

The natural-shoulder silhouette changed very little during the decade, and innovation came in the guise of color. While the mature man still preferred his natural-shoulder suits in navy blue, medium gray, or one of the new shades of brown, in 1927 the Ivy Leaguer switched his allegiance to new pale colors such as tans, grays, blue grays, and gray blues. And what made the new "ice-cream suit" particularly newsworthy was the fact that it was most popular in a husky diagonal tweed fabric. The effect was incongruous but smart-looking. Still, the suit enjoyed only a brief popularity for the good reason that the pale colors soiled easily and the tweeds were scratchy.

Many socially correct Ivy League students resented being called cake-eaters, particularly when that bit of Jazz Age nomenclature was extended to include a class of noncollege youth. For just as the jazz suit had become a caricature during the previous decade when the new natural-shoulder suit was taken up by more flamboyant dressers, so the natural-shoulder suit with the wide-bottomed trousers favored by the Ivy Leaguer soon had its less attractive copies and these, too, were referred to as cake-eater suits, although they were cut in a much more extreme style. This young noncollege group evolved a style that featured a narrow, slope-shouldered jacket, more snugly shaped at the sides and back and trimmed with skinny peaked or notched lapels. The trousers were narrow to the calf and then billowed out into bell bottoms. Whereas the Ivy Leaguer favored his brightly striped school tie, the noncollege cake-eater chose a dark tie that was usually no more than an inch wide and looked properly pinched when worn with a high soft collar. This rakish look was topped with a flat cap. The noncollege man further demonstrated fashion independence by eschewing the ice-cream tweeds of the collegian for hard-finished worsteds, which more often than not were pinstriped.

Perhaps sharing the cake-eater name with a noncollege group of sharp dressers was partly responsible for the change that took place in the wardrobes of some college men in 1925. Always eager for a fresh new promotion, manufacturers and retailers turned to this new collegiate look, which owed much to the British suits the Ivy Leaguer's father had custom-tailored in London. The new style was a sharp departure from the straight-hanging natural-shoulder suit, being broad at the shoulders and snug at the hips. The suit jacket was approximately 29 inches long on a size 40, with a rounded front and with buttons and pockets placed rather low. Sleeves were full, and lapels broad and curv-ing. There were either no vents or a very short back vent. Vests, an essential part of this suit, boasted six buttons and were cut high. Trousers were cut straight from the knee to the bottom. Widely advertised as the new college look that was suitable for the mature man as well, it did enjoy some popularity but never replaced the classic natural-shoulder suit. In 1928 the dominant college suit was still the three-button natural-shoulder suit, which by that time had $3\frac{1}{4}$-inch notched lapels that rolled to the top button.

British influence. During the twenties and early thirties no man wielded greater fashion influence than the Prince of Wales. For almost two decades he was a source of inspiration and income to menswear manufacturers and retailers on both sides of the Atlantic. At the peak of his power his influence was so extraordinary that a wealthy Chicagoan left standing orders with Scholte, the royal tailor at the time, for a duplicate of every suit the Prince had made. His visit to the United States in 1923 raised the morale of British trade and aroused the interest of fashion-conscious American men.

Red ties were considered effeminate until the Prince of Wales chose to wear the reddest red tie he could find. Brown suede shoes were considered vulgar until he wore them. Single-handedly, he relieved a depression affecting Fair Isle, in the Shetland Islands, when he chose to appear on the golf links wearing one of the fine hand-knit sweaters made there. In short order, Fair Isle sweaters were selling in American shops for as much as $35 each. When the Prince turned up at Belmont Park, Long Island, wearing a big panama hat of a type that had not been seen in the United States for a decade, almost overnight the panama hat was back in fashion. More than any other individual, he made London the men's fashion capital of the world, and during the prosperous twenties, when increasingly large numbers of affluent Americans traveled abroad, British influence affected the wardrobes of American men as never before.

A new style called the "English look" became prominent in the spring of 1923, was promoted by the more expensive American stores, and reached its peak in the fall of 1924. The suit jacket had broader shoulders, and its relatively loose lines draping from the shoulders obliterated the waistline. Lapels measuring $3\frac{1}{2}$ inches in width rolled to the top button or just below it. In many models the jacket had no vents. By the following year this silhouette had assumed a more honestly British character. Retail advertisements that autumn were featuring the English look under varying names. Essentially, however, they were all describing a single-breasted suit with broad shoulders, a deep chest, a defined waist, and snug hips. To the masculine, athletic American this was an attractive look and found instant acceptance. Waist suppression was the chief change, but American manufacturers settled for an only moderately defined waist. The trousers had pleats at the waistband and measured $17\frac{1}{2}$ inches at the bottoms.

In the mid-twenties flannel became a markedly popular fabric, in another tribute to the fashion impact of the Prince of Wales, who during his 1923 visit showed a partiality for double-breasted gray flannel with a white chalk stripe and lapels measuring $3\frac{3}{4}$ inches in width. Worn with a wide-knot tie (a four-in-hand that became known as the Windsor knot) and a widespread collar to accommodate it, the suit had a bold but well-bred look. The glenurquhart plaid suit, which was to become a great favorite with American men in the thirties, first came into prominence in the United States when it was worn by the visiting Prince in a single-breasted style, with a snap-brim felt hat and cocoa-brown buckskin shoes, the kind of shoes that until then few American men would have thought suitable for wear with a town suit.

While the vest was no longer a functional necessity since the demise of the pocket watch, it remained in vogue during the twenties particularly since the two-button single-breasted suit gave a vest so much exposure. The fashionable man bypassed the conventional model for the double-breasted vest with pocket flaps.

Knicker suit. College men vacationing in England discovered plus fours, knickers that hung 4 inches below the knee. For years the English, Irish, and Scots had been wearing knickers, baggier versions of the knee breeches of English court dress, on their country estates and on the golf course. But it was the Ivy Leaguer who was responsible for bringing them to the United States in the early twenties, when the vast popularity of golf made the very comfortable knickers practical as well as fashionable. Until then the knickers worn by American golfers had been rather close-fitting. Now they grew longer and baggier by the year, until besides plus fours there were plus sixes and plus eights.

By 1924 white linen knickers were the vogue at the fashionable summer resorts, although knickers were turning up in every fabric from flannel and tweed to gabardine, whipcord, and the new Palm Beach summer fabric of cotton and mohair. When the Prince of Wales wore knickers while touring the cattle ranches of South America in the late twenties, their popularity rose still further. One Argentinian millionaire sailed for London and ordered 20 knicker suits from Scholte.

Manufacturers in the United States and England proceeded to introduce the knicker suit to the general public. The British saw it as comprising a rather simple tweed jacket with a pair of matching knickers. The Americans were more ambitious and introduced a four-piece suit consisting of a jacket, vest, matching trousers, and knickers that proved to be very practical. With the trousers, the jacket and vest made up a suit that could be worn to the office. Then, by substituting the knickers for the trousers and slipping into a pair of golf hose, the wearer was suitably dressed for sport. However, few American men chose to wear the knickers with a jacket when playing golf, much preferring a cardigan or pullover sweater.

The most popular fabrics for the knicker suit were tweed and cheviot. In the spring of 1927 gray and red brown were the most popular colors, with small checks and diamond effects the most popular designs. The college man's knicker or golf suit was invariably in the ice-cream shades he preferred, a color choice he carried over to the Fair Isle sweater he wore beneath his jacket in place of a vest.

The February, 1928, issue of the *International Tailor* forecast the model golf suit for the coming spring-summer season as follows:

"Two-button single breasted model. Coat length $29\frac{1}{2}$ inches; shoulders normal, lapel, 11 inches to upper button hole; notch on lapel and collar, $1\frac{1}{2}$ inches each way.

"Width of lapel at widest point, $3\frac{1}{4}$ inches. Back finished with belt running from side to side seam with knife pleats running from shoulder to belt. Four outside patch pockets.

"Knickers fit easy over hips and of moderate width and length. They have one or two pleats and are finished at the bottom with strap and buckle."

Since golf was still a rich man's game, the knicker or golf suit selling for about $80 in fine stores was limited to the more affluent sportsman. It retained its popularity and snobbish appeal in the next decade, when slacks began to supplant knickers on and off the golf course. As late as 1936 the former Prince of Wales, now King Edward VIII, turned up on the golf links in new-style plus fours that were cut like an Indian army officer's slacks with the material turned up and sewn into the lining instead of being attached to the leg with a buckle. "The shape and tailoring of the new garment are more interesting," noted one fashion reporter, who hoped that "this summer will see fewer men disporting themselves on golf courses in unsightly long trousers." His wish did not come true as the knicker vanished from the fashion scene.

Not until 1970 did the knicker suit show signs of regaining a measure of popularity, and then it was seen not on the golf course but on city streets, where it was worn by the more avant-garde youth of both sexes.

1930–1940

In 1931 *Vanity Fair,* then the most sophisticated American magazine, played a game called "Who's Zoo?" Albert Einstein was likened to a French poodle, and John D. Rockefeller, the billionaire with a pocket full of shiny new dimes, to a sluggish loris. A profile of Herbert Hoover, the nation's beleaguered President, next to an English bulldog carried the following jingle:

> Mr. Hoover is not worried,
> Unlike this pet,
> Whose brow is furried.
> The tireless watchdog
> Of our nation,
> He has a firm grip
> On the sitchee-ation.

But Mr. Hoover's grip slipped, and early in 1933 a radio-locked nation

A double-breasted gabardine suit was a good foundation on which to build a summer wardrobe in 1934. Worn with it was an optimo panama hat. From Esquire, *June 1934.*

The natural-tan gabardine suit was regarded as a campus uniform in 1935. The typical model had a three-button single-breasted jacket with patch pockets. From Esquire, *May 1935.*

The checked cotton seersucker suit with a double-breasted jacket was an example of the trend toward lightweight clothing in the thirties. From Esquire, *June 1935.*

heard Franklin D. Roosevelt, its new President, say "We have nothing to fear but fear itself."

Grim as they were, the Depression years were not entirely without their rewards. As always in a time of national disaster, people moved closer to each other, drawn by a sense of camaraderie that is second nature to Americans. Together they took cheer wherever and whenever they could. It was a time of extremes, of fads and fanatics. There were college boys swallowing goldfish and the not-so-young climbing flagpoles in imitation of the champion flagpole sitter Shipwreck Kelly. Meanwhile, the marathon dances of the twenties became big

business, attracting many contestants with cash prizes. As the Depression continued, folk heroes seemed to grow more heroic, more charismatic. Babe Ruth was not just a great baseball player: he was the Home-run King. The heavyweight champion Joe Louis was the Brown Bomber. The motion-picture star Jean Harlow was not merely a blond: she was a platinum blonde.

In a period when the song "Brother, Can You Spare a Dime?" captured the temper of the times, Americans showed they were still capable of thinking big. Everything American was still big or biggest: the Empire State Building, Radio City Music

Hall, King Kong, the big apple. It was the era of the big dance bands: Sammy Kaye, Kay Kyser, Benny Goodman, and the Dorsey brothers. And in the autumn of 1933, a low point of the Depression, *Esquire*, a man's magazine, made its first appearance at what was then a phenomenal newsstand price of 50 cents.

While the have-nots of this decade outnumbered the haves by a crushing majority, they not only did not seem to resent those who still had money but appeared eager to read about the glossy world of the rich and famous. Perhaps this contact with a still-unscarred part of the world was like a light at the end of a tunnel, an assurance that everything would soon be right and bright again and that after all the whole world was not utterly bleak.

Newspapers and magazines covered Barbara Hutton's lavish debut at a ball in the Ritz Carlton Hotel in New York and chronicled the party activities of Elsa Maxwell, who was restoring the fancy dress ball to an eminence it probably had not enjoyed since the days of Marie Antoinette. While veterans of World War I were staging a bonus march on Washington, socialites were boarding pullmans for Palm Beach, taking along their own sheets and pillowcases of silk moiré and sable throw rugs.

The opening of the Chicago World's Fair in 1933 brought out the city's moneyed people in full regalia. A year later, in an introduction to the society photographer Jerome Zerbe's book *People on Parade,* the writer and dandy Lucius Beebe recalled the evening:

I still recall the occasion of the opening of the World's Fair where Mr. Zerbe had been commissioned to record in imperishable bromide of silver the abandon of the Palmers and Armours. The climax of his professional activities was reached at the launching of an arrangement known as the Streets of Paris one chill Illinois evening, and an ocean of plug hats and imperial sable tipits was cascading down the stairs impeded only by a cross current of persons smelling vaguely of Guerlain's Shalimar and Four Roses whisky who were going to one of the seventeen bars. Mr. Rufus Dawes had waggishly entwined a lady's corsage of orchids about the brim of his chapeau claque and was pretty good camera news. An unidentified youth had set fire to his dinner jacket and was extinguishing himself with a seltzer syphon. Two bands were playing "Pomp and Circumstance" out of tune in honor of the arrival of Mrs. Potter Palmer. Jack Pierce, the playboy of Astor Street, had released a handful of cockroaches down the back of an unidentified marquise. A third band was getting into the hotter stretches of "The Bells of Saint Mary's." Ernest Byfield was commanding champagne wine in pails. Mrs. Henry Field was being transported from table to table in a gold lamé rickshaw. Approximately a million celebrities were falling on their faces or kissing the wrong people, and Mr. Zerbe had the screaming meemies with excitement. He had shinnied to the top of a

bogus Doric column and the light of his bulbs was as incessant as heat lightning. They were unquestionably the social world photographs of a generation, since nothing like this Walpurgis night in the madhouse had been staged in America's least reticent city since the fire.

Motion pictures, of course, were the great escape vehicle. The screen was called the silver screen, and 85 million Americans managed to scrape together enough change to take in a double feature once a week. The motion-picture theater coaxed them inside with bank and dish nights, plus a steady fare of amusing films affectionately called "screwball comedies," in which beautifully gowned women were pursued by handsomely tailored men, implausible beings completely untouched by the Great Depression. Screen stars were never before or after so glamorous or so influential as fashion innovators.

Fashion survived during the thirties despite the appalling condition of the economy. Business was so bad that it challenged the imagination and resourcefulness of manufacturers and retailers alike, who were in a mood to do anything to generate sales. *Apparel Arts,* forerunner of *Esquire's Gentlemen's Quarterly* magazine, made its debut with a Christmas, 1931, issue, and menswear stores seized upon it, using it as a counter catalog from which to sell.

Not surprisingly, the Depression returned fashion to the hands of those who could still afford it: F. Scott Fitzgerald's "very rich rich." The privileged few who still had the money to dress well dared to improvise and break fashion rules. Their clothes reflected their inborn feeling of security. Slowly but surely, as these fashions began to trickle down to the man in the street lucky enough to have the price of a new suit of clothes, this air of casual elegance began to leave its mark on the American wardrobe.

The look was decidedly British, for the rich American of the thirties was the same man who had shopped Savile Row in the twenties. He took at once to the new English drape suit that

American manufacturers had borrowed from the London bespoke tailors—a style destined to influence men's suits and coats for the next two decades. With its broader shoulders, waist nipped in at the front and sides, and high-waisted, full-cut, double-pleated trousers, it was, in the words of *Esquire,* "the way to dress if you are so sure of yourself under the New Deal that you are unafraid of offering a striking similarity to a socialist cartoonist's conception of a capitalist. Since a good appearance is about all that is left to the capitalist anyway, why not go ahead and enjoy it?" (February, 1934).

The Depression saw the decline of the youth cult, as the mature American man once again assumed fashion leadership. Sons now copied their fathers, who maintained an elegant look even on the sports field. The idea of correct clothes for every occasion prevailed, and society chroniclers followed fashionable Americans everywhere, photographing them at work and play.

Esquire captured the almost offhand elegance of this decade in June, 1934, when it listed "the most prominent birthplaces of style":

1. Westbury, Long Island: Where the polo-playing set spend a great deal of time.

2. Rye, New York: Where the Biltmore Country Club is one of the most important style centers in the U.S.

3. New York Stock Exchange: The real birthplace of New York styles.

4. Yale: The undergraduate, often with a Wall Street career in his future, already acts and dresses like the young broker type who haunts New York's financial district.

5. Southampton, Long Island: The watering place where sands are made of platinum and the waters of sapphire.

6. Newport, Rhode Island: Has a decidedly high social caste that originated with the 400 in the Gay Nineties and has lasted down through the thrilling thirties.

7. Park Avenue: Where young brokers live and play, in the after-dark twin of Wall Street.

8. Palm Beach, Florida: To try to express the fashion significance of Palm Beach is like trying to explain the beauty of a woman.

9. Princeton: Where a large portion of the student body are some of the top-

The gray flannel suit with a blue overplaid, made with a two-button peaked-lapel jacket, was regarded as an international fashion in 1936 when augmented with a white linen waistcoat and a black homburg hat. From Esquire, May 1936.

The herringbone Shetland suit with a three-button jacket on the man at right was popular in fall, 1936, at Eastern university centers. With it was worn a knitted tie in a solid color. From Esquire, September 1936.

rankers in American social, financial and diplomatic circles. They spend their vacation abroad and in general reflect the younger generation's version of what is being worn and what is being done in the smart world of their elders.

It was the cosmopolitan life-style of the rich and socially impeccable American that inspired the new fashions that American manufacturers were busily creating. This "partnership" of the American millionaire and the menswear industry proved immensely profitable, for it was this clothes-conscious man's insistence that he look and feel elegant and comfortable at all times which inspired the

mixed suit of the early thirties that eventually evolved into the ensemble of sports jacket and slacks, the truly lightweight summer clothing that finally launched the third season in the men's clothing field, the colorful sports shirts that soon became major items of merchandise, and the clothes specially designed for each of the sports being played by the increasingly sports-minded Americans.

Finally recovering from the Depression, the decade concluded on a grand note in 1939 with world's fairs in both New York and San Francisco. That same year witnessed the world premiere of *Gone with the Wind*, the biggest

and costliest motion picture of the decade. And that September the biggest and costliest war of the twentieth century began. So the decade ended as it began, with disaster.

English drape suit. A businesslike inventory of the American interpretation of the English drape suit read as follows:

Jacket. Broad shoulders with no padding. Soft front, full across chest and shoulder blades. Tapered sleeves with full sleevehead finished with tiny tucks at the shoulder. A decided suppression at the waist and close fitting at the hips. Single- and double-breasted models, with single-breasted made in two- and three-button

The man at left wears a British blade suit, the jacket of which has fullness across the chest and shoulder blades. The younger man at right has on a double-breasted British blade suit with long-roll lapels. From Esquire, February 1938.

Front and rear views of the British blade suit. The rear view gives an idea of the fullness across the shoulder blades and shows the side vents. From Esquire, February 1938.

styles, with top button (placed at waist-line) worn buttoned, lower button left unfastened. Jacket is either side vented, or more often, ventless. American inter-pretations eliminate the tiny tucks or pleats found at the top of the sleeveheads of the British models. Breast pocket of jacket is expected to be a boon to fancy handkerchief business.

Waistcoat. Worn with drape jacket, it is designed to carry out English silhouette. A short, high-waisted style to conform with silhouette of jacket, with six button front. The one button at the bottom is set on a "V" opening and designed not to be fastened.

Trousers. Full cut and very high-waisted with two pleats at the waistband on either side. Wide across the hips . . . so full that trousers hang straight from the waist in front and back. Pleat at top of the crease of the trousers is 1½″ wide. Width of cuffed trousers around the bottoms is 19 inches—a full inch wider than the non-drape suit. Without belt loops, trousers must be worn with suspenders or, as the British call them, braces.

Fabrics. In worsteds, with plain twills, herringbones and small patterns. In the small all-over patterns, some of the most attractive color combinations are black and white, gray and white, tan and white, two shades of brown, grayish blue and gray, bluish gray and blue, and some multi-color effects. Pin dots, fine checks and miniature geometrical designs are also well-adapted to this drape suit style.

Best customer. Fairly tall man of medium weight. Not for the stubby fat man. (*Men's Wear,* Apr. 20, 1932)

At first salesmen in the retail stores found a certain amount of resistance to the drape suit, for most Americans believed that a properly fitting suit jacket should be perfectly smooth across the chest and back. The drape suit, owing to the extra fullness on the chest and over the shoulder blades that was designed to permit free action of the arms, had vertical wrinkles between the collar and the sleeve head. Women accompanying their husbands were especially critical of these wrinkles. Eventually, however, this planned fullness for the sake of comfort and ease was accepted and became a selling point, although as the

The double-breasted jacket with long-roll lapels was worn in 1938 in checked tropical worsted fabrics for summer and in heavier-weight worsteds for winter. From Esquire, *June 1938.*

their French cuffs to accommodate this trimmer sleeve.

The drape silhouette soon was adapted to topcoats and overcoats and even to the new sports jacket with a belted back that was being popularized by well-dressed film stars. Not until the late thirties, however, was the drape shape adapted to summer suits, most manufacturers believing that lightweight fabrics did not lend themselves to draping. As the drape gained popularity, it also gained new names. In some stores it was advertised as the British blade, while others referred to it as the British lounge or lounge suit. It sold for approximately $45 to $50.

The drape suit first appeared in worsted and sharkskin and subsequently in flannel, cheviot, saxony, and tweed. Immediately popular in solid colors, it was also seen in stripes of all widths as well as in plaids. Blue, medium gray, and gray blue were the leading suit colors during the last half of the decade, although by 1939 greenish shades, which in 1935 had accounted for only 1 percent of suit sales, were preferred, accounting for 28 percent of the suits sold.

Glen plaid (glenurquhart) suit. "Be prepared for the coming of glens," wrote a fashion reporter in *Men's Wear* in July, 1930. Glen plaid suits, he predicted, were on their way to national popularity, "not just for the man who has a half dozen or more $50 and up suits in his wardrobe, but with a lot of the one-suit-a-season young and middle-aged men who pay $22.50 and up for their suits." He cited the number of boldly defined glen plaid suits being worn by graduates and undergraduates at the Yale-Harvard crew race and reminded his readers that the Prince of Wales was particularly partial to this plaid. Derived from the tartan of Urquhart, the design had been woven in woolen and worsted fabrics in England for university and business wear during the latter part of the nineteenth century.

Certainly the 1923 appearance of the visiting Prince of Wales in a double-breasted glenurquhart suit with wide peaked lapels had made the

drape suit became more popular and inevitably was modified, the fullness at the chest and shoulder blades was reduced.

By 1935 the sleeve shape of the drape suit was changing. The straight sleeve was being replaced by one that tapered to a cuff measuring 10 inches around. This tapered sleeve created some problems of its own, for a French shirt cuff was invariably too wide to fit easily inside it. The drape was so popular, however, that shirt manufacturers quickly narrowed the width of

clothes-conscious American aware of its possibilities. That it did not become immediately popular on a national scale was perhaps due to the fact that the fabric must be cut and tailored precisely so that the horizontal lines of the plaids match at the center seam in the back of the jacket and on the legs of the trousers. This kind of impeccable tailoring was not to be found in the less expensive suits that were the best the average man could afford in the Depression. The more affluent man (socialite or film star) quickly took up the glen plaid suit, appreciat-

ing its lively good taste, and soon this bold plaid was being seen in sports jackets and the new lightweight summer suits. A single-breasted white linen jacket worn with glenurquhart slacks, for example, made a very elegant summer-weight "mixed suit." The motion-picture star Douglas Fairbanks, who often appeared to be strongly influenced by the style of the Prince of Wales, preferred a double-breasted glen plaid, which he wore with a striped shirt, a checked necktie, a homburg hat, and a red carnation in the $4\frac{3}{4}$-inch lapel of the jacket. This use of pattern on pattern was a striking example of the new freedom with which the well-dressed man of the thirties assembled his wardrobe.

The first and still the most generally accepted of all suit plaids, the glenurquhart has often had its name applied erroneously to other bold plaids.

Summer: the third season in the men's clothing field. It was ironic that in a decade when the struggle for survival was paramount the summer suit should finally evolve. Coping with summer heat, after all, was one of the less pressing problems facing the American man. Nevertheless, the summer suit as we know it today, and which had been on the verge of appearing for years, finally emerged in the mid-thirties when manufacturers and retailers were working overtime to stay in business. The timing could not have been better.

In 1933 only a little more than a million summer suits were sold. Production had increased to 1.6 million by 1935, not including the tropical worsted suit, which accounted for approximately 40 percent of the total volume. By 1936, with the New Deal beginning to breathe life into the economy and a measure of optimism into the man in the street, the summer suit season was firmly established. Until then American men had taken on a kind of regional look with the coming of summer, as they attempted to adjust to the climate in the various sections of the country. Most men in the Northern cities preferred to sweat it out rather than look rumpled in

seersucker, while their Southern counterparts were more than willing to sacrifice a crisp crease for the sake of comfort. Now in 1936 summer suits, lighter than ever and capable of retaining their good looks, were available in the $26.50 to $29.50 price range, at a time when many men were once again feeling prosperous enough to invest in a new summer suit.

In fact, the year 1936 saw what in the trade was called "the battle of the fabrics." The choice of summer-weight suit fabrics was big and was getting bigger all the time. There were new

A bold plaid was used in 1939 in the suit with a paddock-model jacket having two highly placed buttons. The pattern was the authentic red Mohr, a red, black, and gray check worn originally by men of this district in Scotland. From Esquire, *October 1939.*

The paddock model was adapted to summer clothing in 1939. A single-breasted style with two buttons placed high, it was seen in such fabrics as pale linen, tropical worsted, Palm Beach cloth, gabardine, and fiber blends. From Esquire, *August 1939.*

A three-button suit with soft-rolled lapels, cut on the slim lines in vogue for young men in 1914. [L. GREIF & BRO.]

A young man's suit of 1919 had a jacket indented at the waist with a slight flare over the hips. [HICKEY-FREEMAN CO.]

The jacket of this youthful 1920 suit was snug-fitting. It had welt pockets, rope shoulders, a soft front, and link cuffs. [HICKEY-FREEMAN CO.]

A tan lightweight worsted suit for spring and summer wear in 1923. It had an easy-fitting two-button jacket with wide notched lapels and a matching vest. [HICKEY-FREEMAN CO.]

Suits

In 1939 a degree of restraint was achieved with this outfit, consisting of a pencil-stripe black worsted suit, a white shirt with a starched spread collar, and a gray geometric-design tie. The double-breasted jacket had long-line lapels and cuffs on the sleeves, and the trousers were cuffless. The waistcoat was omitted. From Esquire, *November 1939.*

tropical worsteds weighing only 8½ to 9 ounces to the yard, as compared with earlier tropical worsteds that weighed 10½ to 12 ounces to the yard. Then there was rayon, the first of the synthetic, or man-made, fibers. Originally called "artificial silk," it was given the name "rayon" by Kenneth Lord of Galey & Lord in 1924, when the fabric was being used most extensively in the

sports shirt industry. While the all-silk suit remained an aristocratic garment favored by only top-level manufacturers and custom tailors, the production of rayon rose from 127 million pounds in 1930 to 300 million in 1936 and suits of 100 percent rayon became available in all colors. There were also smart-looking summer suits made of blends of worsted and rayon, woolen and rayon, cotton and rayon, and acetate and rayon. An outstandingly successful blend of 50 percent acetate and 50 percent rayon developed in 1934 by the Dan River Mills produced a summer fabric weighing only 6½ ounces to the yard. Suits of this new blend were available in a range of solid colors, stripes, and many other patterns. The classic Palm Beach suit, a blend of cotton and mohair, was enormously popular in both its original shade, called "oatmeal tan," and in white as well as in biscuit and shades of gray.

The popularity of American summer suits in this decade can best be illustrated by the fact that they were now being exported to England, where the public quickly learned to appreciate the fact that a cool-looking and well-tailored Palm Beach suit, for example, weighed merely 2 pounds, 9 ounces, as compared with a normal-weight suit of 4 pounds, 7 ounces. This was an ideal suit for a British official stationed in a colonial outpost where he had had to rely on overhead fans and gin and tonic for respite from the steamy temperature.

Oddly enough, seersucker, a cotton weave that was one of the coolest and most inexpensive summer fabrics, remained popular largely in the South during this period, although Princeton undergraduates, then recognized as fashion innovators, had started wearing it in the 1920s. In Northern cities seersucker's crinkled look was considered a drawback. It was another decade before men in such cities as New York and Boston would venture to wear it, although F. R. Tripler & Co., on Madison Avenue in New York, kept seersucker suits in stock for men secure enough or avant-garde enough to wear

what everyone knew was an inexpensive suit.

Gabardine, in contrast, became one of the most admired summer fabrics of the decade despite the fact that a ready-made suit of this fabric sold for about $40, or about $15 more than the average summer suit. Furthermore, gabardine, at 12 to 13 ounces to the yard, was considerably heavier than most other summer fabrics. Yet, it was this extra weight that made the fabric tailor so well, and despite its weight, gabardine felt as cool as it looked. Both college men and their fathers took to single- and double-breasted suits of gabardine in shades of tan, gray, blue, navy, and brown. Many men favored the gabardine suit with red cotton threads woven on the back (called "red-back gabardine"), assuming that these red threads filtered the heat rays. How effectively they worked was debatable, but the faint glints of red that appeared on the front of the cloth created an attractive sheen that suggested coolness.

Linen, long one of the most preferred summer fabrics despite its weight, also enjoyed a new surge of popularity in fresh shades of blue and brown. Pinwale corduroy, a lighter-weight corduroy, was publicized as a summer corduroy and achieved a measure of acceptance in slacks and sports jackets of navy, brown, and blue gray, particularly among preparatory school students and university undergraduates.

In keeping with the pinched budgets of the thirties, summer suits in the early years of the decade had been made with patch pockets, which were the most economical kind to make. Patch pockets stayed in style long after their budgetary appeal was of no consequence but disappeared in 1942 when War Production Board (WPB) regulations eliminated them from suits. Although summer suits in the early thirties were not tailored in the drape style, by the late thirties at least one summer suit in this style was in the wardrobe of any man who considered himself even modestly clothes-conscious.

1940–1950

The Depression was over. Defense spending buoyed the previously sagging economy, and a boom was on, although the period was far from carefree. United States involvement in the European conflict was, after all, only a matter of time. Yet, despite the grim outlook men's interest in fashion had not declined. On the contrary, it was more lively than ever, perhaps stimulated by the nagging thought that soon the fashion-right colors would be khaki and navy blue. And after a decade of deprivation, the average American was prosperous again, with money to spend on clothes. As the conflict in Europe continued, however, the tendency of most men was to dress in a simpler and more subdued style.

The now-celebrated English drape suit was carried over into the new decade, with its wrinkles and breaks modified and with most men regarding this shape as the ultimate in comfort and ease. Slowly the terms English or British drape, British blade, and British lounge, all names for the same silhouette, fell into disuse. What remained was the term "lounge suit," a fitting and proper appellation for a casually elegant style.

The infatuation with youth that marked the years immediately before the United States entry into World War I did not emerge in the period before American involvement in World War II. The country was sadder and wiser, with many World War I veterans on hand to remind people that war really is hell. Also, the country had survived one global war only to be sunk into a depression, and now another and far more threatening war loomed on the horizon. All this had a sobering effect on the nation and, in turn, was reflected in the clothes worn by both sexes.

Women's fashions featured a "hard" silhouette with padded square shoulders and short skirts. Once again, as women were about to cope with a relatively manless society, their clothes appeared to have become masculinized. Men's fashions, which had become increasingly colorful toward the close of the previous decade, now became less colorful and more conservative. Darker blues and grays became more popular, and even the glenurquhart plaid suits were less bold. Dark blue worsted and banker's gray flannel with chalk pinstripes were the choices of many well-dressed men.

As suit colors grew muted, however, styling features became more assertive. The double-breasted jacket had a new lapel that rolled to the bottom button,

A summer suit calculated to be cool in 1941. The fabric was a tropical worsted that weighed 8½ ounces per square yard and was porous to admit the breezes. The three-button jacket had welt pockets. From Esquire, *June 1941.*

revealing an expanse of shirt front. "White is right," said *Esquire* in June, 1941, showing the all-white suit, a casualty of the Depression years, now back not only in lightweight worsted flannel and Palm Beach cloth but also in blends of man-made fibers such as acetate and rayon.

This suit, illustrated in 1942 during World War II, conformed to the fabric-conserving regulations of the War Production Board. The WPB specifications included a maximum length of 23¾ inches for a size 37 jacket, no waistcoat with a double-breasted jacket, and trousers measuring 22 inches at the knee, 18½ inches around the bottom, and 35 inches at the inseam for a size 32 waist. No cuffs, pleats, tucks, or overlapping waistbands were permitted. From Esquire, *June 1942.*

The usual prewar preoccupation with physical fitness appeared, and there was new emphasis on looking taller and slimmer. Fashion editors drew guidelines for the short man to follow: "Never cut yourself in two by pattern, model or color. Emphasize the up and down lines. Stretch yourself out—start at the shoulder to build yourself up. We don't mean you should look as though you had put your coat on without removing the hanger, but we do mean select your jacket with the shoulders squared. Avoid stubby or short or high roll lapels. If it's a double-breasted suit you favor, try rolling the lapels to the lower button. Watch the length of your jacket. If it's too short it will tend to saw you in half. If too long, it will shorten the appearance of your legs. In fabrics, choose vertical stripes and narrow herringbones" (*Esquire*, April, 1940, p. 103).

In the spring of 1941 the military influence on men's clothes was obvious. Americana colors began to appear on college campuses. The theme of red, white, and blue could be seen in suits, sportswear, and related accessories. Air blue, inspired by the U.S. Army Air Force color, was seen in faintly chalk-striped worsted both on and off the campus. Khaki-colored suits in worsted, a civilian adaptation of the cavalry twill used in army uniforms, had a strong appeal for the undergraduate. The growing popularity of covert cloth suits was understandable, too, for this sturdy twill weave had a military air, particularly in shades of tan and olive brown. Tailors and retailers in the Ivy League areas reported steadily increasing sales of covert suits, especially in the new cloth that weighed merely 12 to 13 ounces to the square yard, or 6 ounces lighter than the cloth used in covert overcoats. Gabardine suits, particularly the red-back gabardine with its faintly reddish glints, were also immensely popular on and off campus.

With the entry of the United States into the war in December, 1941, the menswear industry prepared to retrench. The War Production Board was established. Its first official act, in March, 1942, affected all suits containing wool, and the government estimated that the new regulations would effect a fabric saving of 26 percent. In June, 1942, *Esquire* called the new pared-down suits "streamlined suits by Uncle Sam" and stated: "WPB regulations will speed up general acceptance of men's authentic fashions." The editors concluded: "All in all, more men will dress in accordance with good fashion standards as a result of these rulings."

Further WPB regulations affecting men's suits were announced that year, and it became clear that the prewar movement toward simplicity had been well advised. Wartime casualties included trouser cuffs, vests, two-pants suits, and the zoot suit. (The zoot suit was important only as one of the first examples in the twentieth century of a style that originated at the bottom of the social ladder.)

The long-awaited invasion of Europe came on June 6, 1944. The following spring Franklin D. Roosevelt died during his fourth term of office. Nazi Germany collapsed in May, 1945. Atomic bombs were dropped on Hiroshima and Nagasaki, and on August 14, Japan surrendered. The great war was over.

This was the signal for women, tired of manning the home front, to dress in an ultrafeminine way again and for men to revel in the colorful, assertive clothes that always have a magnetic appeal after the anonymity of uniforms. In the fall of 1947 women embraced the "new look" of the French couturier Christian Dior, a very feminine silhouette with puffed sleeves, a pinched waist, padded hips, and a voluminous skirt. The next year, in its October issue, *Esquire* discussed its new "bold look" on this patriotic note: "The American male is a member of the greatest country in the world—and he's beginning to look the part!" The look was a bold concept that coordinated color, design, and shape, affecting everything a man wore from the line of his suit to the border on his pocket handkerchief. It was a signal for the man weary of military uniformity to declare his individuality with what *Esquire* described as "a self-confident look . . . as distinctive as it is distinguished . . . as virile as football—as masculine as the Marine Corps—as American as the Sunday comics."

One of the few benefits of military service appears to be the comfort of the uniforms provided the military man. Manufacturers had, for example, made tropical worsteds for the United States government that weighed only 9 to 10 ounces to the yard. So the returning serviceman was more determined than ever to overcome hot weather in style, and manufacturers were quick to give him what he wanted: light summer suits that held their crisp good looks.

Nylon cord suits weighing a mere 6 to 8 ounces per yard became important in 1949. Suits that blended nylon with rayon and cotton were advertised by Haspel Clothes (*Men's Wear*, Oct. 7, 1949) as having a "crisp, new-as-tomorrow look." Two-trouser suits of seersucker cord were promoted as "iced-up and spruced up—light as a fig leaf—with trim-tailored shape that stays neat in the heat," thanks to a crease-resistant finish, and retailed for only $18.75. For an additional $9 the well-dressed man could invest in a two-trouser suit of rayon in one of the "deep freeze tones" of gray, blue, tan, or brown, with a surface of alternate light and dark fibers that gave a "flake effect similar to the frost on a window pane." By the end of the decade, cotton and rayon cords, rayon, and rayon blends were displacing tropical worsted as the leading summertime fabrics.

In the autumn, gray suit colors predominated, with conservative charcoal gray the leader. This decade, which began between the end of a depression and the start of a global war, ended on a note of cautious optimism. The "man in the gray flannel suit" was waiting just around the corner.

War Production Board regulations. The first official act of the Board affected all suits containing wool. En-

Jackets with buttons set low were accepted by men conscious of the subtleties of fashion. The suit illustrated here had a double-breasted jacket with low buttons and long lapels to accentuate height. The summer fabric was a blend of cotton, mohair, and rayon. From Esquire, May 1945.

tirely eliminated were two-trouser suits, full-dress coats, cutaway coats, double-breasted dinner jackets, patch pockets, fancy backs, belts, and pleats. The vest suffered only a partial eclipse, for while it was forbidden with a dou-ble-breasted suit, it was judged optional with the single-breasted model. The WPB also restricted the length of the inseam of trousers to 35 inches on a size 32 regular and eliminated cuffs, but bottom and knee lengths were curtailed only slightly. These orders took effect on March 30, 1942, but custom tailors were granted an extension until May 30.

In the autumn of that year, the WPB laid down further rules for manufacturers and custom tailors, and as a result the American man found himself with narrower trousers and a shorter jacket. The WPB ruled that all trousers be cut narrower and cuffless: trousers with a 32-inch waist, for example, would now measure only 22 inches at the knee and $18\frac{1}{2}$ inches at the bottom. A size 37 suit jacket could be no longer than $29\frac{3}{4}$ inches. Patch pockets, belts, pleats, tucks or yokes, and vents were outlawed on suit jackets, and pleats, tucks, and overlapping waistbands were banned from trousers. A special ruling permitted cuffs on slacks and flaps on the pockets of garments made of corduroy.

These streamlined suits would, in the opinion of *Esquire*'s fashion department, create no particular hardship, since fashion-conscious men were already indicating a preference for simpler suits. "Patch pockets are out," noted O. E. Schoeffler, *Esquire*'s fashion editor, in the June, 1942, issue. "Well turned out men had already indicated a preference for regular welt pockets. Fancy frills were outlawed, and a good thing too. Belts, tucks and similar ornamentation on jackets have held little interest with men who give fashion leads, so no radical changes along these lines may be anticipated. Plain backs rule.

"The required narrower trousers without cuffs conform to a good standard of dress. These have been noted and illustrated in the fashion pages of *Esquire,* particularly in connection with the Return of Simple Elegance.

"The two-piece suit, without waistcoat, becomes obligatory if a double-breasted jacket is worn. This, too, has been stressed in these pages. Odd waistcoats of cotton or cotton and rayon mixture may take on new significance with men who still like the idea of wearing a waistcoat.

"Soft fabrics, including Cheviot, flannel, Saxony, tweed and Shetland, will be emphasized to a greater extent. This parallels the trend toward semi-sports clothes.

"All in all, more men will dress in accordance with good fashion standards as a result of these rulings."

Good fashion standards were maintained when the WPB banished the zoot suit as a glaring example of wasteful manufacture. Nor was it a surprise when teen-agers throughout the country registered their outrage, for the zoot suit, in the opinion of some psychologists, was more than a fad. It was a sign of "the rebellion of the young men of less fortunate class against everyday environment."

The reaction of this segment of American youth to the government charge that the continued manufacture of the zoot suit would interfere with the war effort startled many people who looked with despair at the bizarre fashion. Repellent to traditional and conservative observers was the garish coat, heavily padded with as much as 6 inches of stuffing, styled with boxy shoulders and a tapered waist, and reaching almost to the knees. Slash pockets and pegged sleeves were other distinguishing features of the zoot suit jacket. There was little wonder that the WPB took strong exception to such a generous use of fabric. The trousers were jacked up by suspenders almost to the chest. The knees were full (32 inches), and the cuffs (12 to 15 inches) were better suited to bicycling than to dress wear.

The first zoot suit of record had been ordered in 1939 from a store in Gainesville, Georgia, whose owner was so startled by the purchase that he had the suit photographed. The purchaser, a busboy, paid $33.50 for the suit that two years later would be referred to in the *Reporter* as "the badge of the hoodlums." Credit or blame for inspiring the zoot suit with its pleated and draped shape generally goes to the cartoonist Al Capp, whose Lil' Abner traded in his too-small, too-tight suit for one cut full and roomy because to him the excess cloth was a sign of affluence.

The psychological implications of the zoot suit were explored in the wake of the WPB ban. J. V. D. Carlyle wrote: "The boys who were quick to take up the Zoot Suit wanted, first of all, to express themselves. And they found the Zoot Suit a perfect medium for doing so. The Zoot Suit was different; it was colorful; it had definite character. The Zoot Suit and Zoot accessories marked the wearer as the young man of taste, distinction and dash. The Zoot Suit enabled each young man to definitely express his personality; to show that he was in the know. In the writer's opinion, it is extremely unfortunate that the Zoot Suit became a sign of disorder in the eyes of certain sections of the trade. If nothing else, the Zoot Suit showed the concern of the young man for clothes and fashion—no matter what the fashion might be. The Zoot Suit also showed the possibilities of developing native and sectional fashions in this country" (*Men's Reporter,* winter, 1948).

The zoot suit had a short but highly controversial career and an abrupt and farcical demise.

Bold look. As introduced by *Esquire* in the spring of 1948, the bold look was a natural reaction to the austerity that always characterizes war years. In the opinion of the magazine's fashion department, it was a look that American men had been approaching during 1946 and 1947 with their approval of the Windsor knot and the spread collar. In effect, the bold look took these authoritative accessories and built on them to offer men their first completely planned outfit with colors, shapes, and designs coordinated to achieve what the editors, in April, 1948, called "a look of self-confident good taste."

"Remember," *Esquire* editorialized, "the first thing you notice about a well-dressed man is the man himself; then you notice his dress." The bold look was a new look, and *Esquire* dissected it as follows: "American men wear their clothes with assurance and self-confidence, and the clothes reflect the men who wear them. That's the spirit of the Bold Look. It's the way you wear your clothes as much as it is the clothes themselves. But clothes are important, for they're part of your over-all appearance. The newest styles that are appearing wherever the leaders of fashion gather exemplify the Bold Look."

It was a look that actually depended more heavily on accessories than on the suit, and in October, 1948, *Esquire* fashion artists illustrated how a suit could be given a new look of self-confidence and authority by means of a new shirt with the widespread "command collar" and bigger buttons, a boldly patterned or aggressively striped tie with a Windsor knot, the new snap-brim hat with prominent binding on the underside, the new socks with wider ribbing and broader clocks, the new pocket handkerchief with a wide border, the new hefty thick-soled blucher shoes, the massive cuff links, wider tie clasps, and heavy gold-link key chains. "Even the gray flannel suit lends itself to the Bold Look," observed *Esquire,* "when it's worn with a blue broadcloth 'command collar' shirt and a widely striped yellow-and-blue rep tie. The cinnamon brown snap-brim hat accents the grey of the suit, too, thanks to its black band and grey binding. The brown is carried through in the husky bluchers." The influence of the bold look was carried over into 1949 as the American man, made more aware of a coordinated fashion look, gave new fashion impetus to the designers of rainwear, suspenders, belts, and sweaters.

In its April, 1949, issue *Esquire* urged its readers to show their "true colors" when choosing their suits, and guided them as follows: Brown-haired men were told that they could choose from a range of complementary colors, but gray was deemed the most flattering. Gray-haired men were cautioned to be meticulous in their choice of colors and told that their most flattering was dark blue. The black-haired man was told he would look best in dark gray, while the blond-haired were directed toward suits of gray blue.

For the summer of 1949 the bold look was epitomized in a suit whose

The "bold look" in suits was characterized by broad shoulders and wide lapels, and in accessories by positive designs. From Esquire, *April 1948.*

fabric weighed 10 ounces to the yard, or a little more than tropical worsted. A fabric of this weight in the dominant checks, glen plaids, and stripes of the bold look was considered heavy enough to be worn ten months of the year.

Although the bold look lost momentum early in the next decade as a spirit of conservatism swept the nation, its impact on the wardrobe of the American man remained constant. He now chose his shirts, ties, hats, and other accessories not as single items of apparel but for what they could contribute to his overall appearance. He saw himself now in a full-length mir-

ror, and henceforth he would be a much more sophisticated and demanding shopper.

Lightweight suits for year-round wear. Now that the problem of dressing for summer had been solved to general satisfaction, certain manufacturers and retailers, in the autumn of 1949, began promoting lightweight fabrics for year-round wear. Rayon suits retailing for $35 were the subject of an impressive series of advertisements run by the American Viscose Corporation in *Time,* the *New Yorker,* the *Wall Street Journal,* and the *Journal of Commerce.* "Rayon has been adapted for year-'round men's suit," announced one advertisement, while another read, "The quality $35 suit is back!" The fiber was described as "wonderfully springy" and "wrinkle-resistant." In most instances, the fabrics were 100 percent rayon, although others were blends of rayon and wool identified as "predominantly rayon." "Practically as satisfactory as a worsted at a much lower price," promised one enterprising manufacturer, who was geared to produce a two-pants all-rayon suit of a fabric weighing only 13 to 13½ ounces to the yard for less than $30 (*Men's Wear*, Sept. 9, 1949).

An article in the issue of *Men's Wear* of September 9, 1949, expressed a certain skepticism regarding this aggressive advertising campaign: "Some people in the trade have the feeling that American Viscose is running the advertisements in the hope that they will stimulate curiosity. If a customer drops into your store to inquire about the year-'round all-rayon suit, you may get the impression that there is a demand for suits of this type. If you talked to your cutter, and he talked to the mill—well, the subject might snowball into something big for year-'round rayon suits." The article concluded with this commentary: "*One could get confused:* The subject is receiving much comment in the trade—for instance, the paradox: After spending years to convince the public that rayons are lightweight and cool, ideal—almost a specific—for summer-weight clothing, mills are telling the customers that rayons are warm and suitable for wear throughout the cold weather."

In that same issue, the editors noted a new combination, wool plus nylon, and observed: "The magic appeal of nylon has hit the woolen industry." This was a new blend of 80 percent wool and 20 percent nylon staple, resulting in a doeskin fabric with the feel of cashmere that was stronger and more durable than a pure wool, testing up to a tensile strength of 55 pounds. It had been developed by the Cyril Johnson Woolen Company after months of research, experimenting,

and testing, with the cooperation of Du Pont nylon experts.

The new blended fabric was being made in eleven plain solid colors weighing 9 to 10 ounces per yard and in a medium-size herringbone pattern in twelve shades weighing 8 to 9 ounces. The colors included tans, browns, blues, grays, and greens. Although it was announced that suits of the new fabric would be in the stores retailing for about $55 the following spring, *Men's Wear* believed that "due to the tight situation in the nylon market today and the tremendous demand for this fiber, it is expected that the production of this blended fabric will be quite limited." It was not until 1966 that the term "welterweight" was applied to such medium-weight fabrics.

1950–1960

The feeling of peace after years of depression and war was so welcome that Americans quite understandably wanted to hold onto it forever. By 1953, when a smiling general moved into the White House to a national chorus of "I like Ike," for a time at least the nation did seem cloaked in security. And so did the American man as he slipped into a new "uniform" of charcoal gray flannel. This single-breasted natural-shoulder suit with straight-hanging lines was called the "Ivy League look," but at Brooks Brothers it was still referred to as the "Number One Sack Suit," the true Brooks Brothers designation. Brooks did not suggest that it had been instrumental in popularizing the Ivy trend but implied that popular taste had simply and sensibly gravitated to what it had been doing for the past six decades.

The aggressive optimism that had created the bold look in 1948 gave way to this more conservative, almost cautious look as the political climate of the fifties assumed a tense and wary air. American troops were fighting an undeclared war in Korea, while in Washington television cameras recorded Sen. Joseph McCarthy's hunt for

The trend away from the broad shoulders of the 1948 bold look is underscored by the lessened width and straight-hanging lines of the Mr. T style of 1950.

Communists in government. Except for colorful casual clothes and a penchant for fancy vests, the American man in the first half of this decade dressed down. Perhaps President-elect Dwight D. Eisenhower signaled this preference when he refused to wear the traditional cutaway and top hat to his inauguration in 1953, settling instead for a short jacket, striped trousers, and a homburg.

In October, 1950, *Esquire* introduced "Mr. T," a new trim look with 1 inch whittled from the shoulders of a suit jacket and ¾ inch from the lapels. The straight-hanging lines of his natural-shoulder suit gave Mr. T an up-and-down look. The era of the Windsor knot, bulky shoes, and wide-brimmed hat—the accessories of the bold look—was over; the new trim look demanded accessories of smaller, narrower proportions. Ties were obligingly narrowed, and so were shoes and the brim of the tapered-crown hat. "His clothes are in PERFECT TASTE," said *Esquire* of Mr. T, noting that the "old Superman effect" was a thing of the past. Whereas the bold look appeared to say "Look at me," the new trim look seemed to say "Accept me." A pink button-down shirt was almost its only "daring" fashion statement. Even the collegians of the decade dressed down, with chino pants, a skinny black knit tie, and moccasins the standard campus fashion. Temporarily, at least, the Ivy Leaguer ceased to be a fashion innovator.

In the spring of 1952 there was a trend toward checks—small checks. *Esquire* welcomed the change, its fashion editors applauding the advent of pattern and detail as an antidote for the plain grays and solid blues that had long predominated.

The lounge suit so popular in the forties steadily lost ground as more and more men joined the Ivy cult. Suit jackets dipped to 30¾ inches on size 40 of the popular three-button Ivy League suit. In August, 1955, *Apparel Arts* described the modified Ivy look favored by the more mature man in this manner: "Suits feature slightly narrow shoulders, having less width but built up a trifle with a minimum of padding. Front of the jacket is slightly suppressed at waistline while back is straight-hanging. Lapels, especially on single-breasted jackets, are of correspondingly less width. Both sleeves and trousers are tapered."

As the decade progressed, most American troops left Korea, Senator McCarthy faded from the nation's television screens, and the American man began to dress up again. By the mid-fifties man-made fibers were the big news, with stores throughout the country offering a wide variety of blends, many of which had the added appeal of being washable. All-rayon fabrics and rayon blends were more popular than ever, and in the new Palm Beach cloth cotton was eliminated to make room for tough, durable nylon. The vogue for silk shantung, first imported into the United States from Italy soon after World War II, helped bring the silk suit within a price range the middle-income American could afford, and it also began a trend toward other nubby fabrics. Soon even the man in the gray flannel suit could find a flannel that had been heightened by slubs and nubs.

As Americans regained some of their innate optimism, color again became apparent in men's suits. Two and even three colors were introduced in the nubs to enliven the usually staid gray, brown, or blue suit.

In the summer of 1954 the summer suit aroused new excitement. Apparently determined to compensate for the decades spent sweltering in heavy suits, some American men adopted a three-piece suit consisting of trousers and a pair of walk shorts in the same lightweight summer fabric as the jacket. This was a revolutionary idea, particularly in a decade noted for conservatism, but it failed to survive, largely because by then air conditioning performed flawlessly.

By the late fifties an extreme version of the Ivy League look, called the "jivey Ivy," had evolved; it featured a four-button jacket with narrow shoulders and snug-fitting trousers. This was a sure sign that it was time for a new suit silhouette to appear and challenge the supremacy of the Ivy.

The "Continental look" emerged in 1956. A fresh new concept inspired by an Italian model, within the next two years it was being interpreted by American manufacturers seeking to make it conform more flatteringly to the taller, more athletic American physique. "Dressy . . . very smart . . . suave," said *Gentlemen's Quarterly* in its spring issue, predicting that the shorter, more shapely Continental suit would produce a vogue for bolder, more colorful accessories. "Who can wear this new silhouette?" asked the magazine and promptly answered its question by stating that almost anyone would look well in the Continental suit, with the exception of the man "who has a bay window," since the jacket with its rounded, cutaway front would "mercilessly expose his avoirdupois."

Stylists discussed the question of whether the Continental suit would replace the Ivy League model, while many Continental adherents debated whether to choose a Continental suit with peaked lapels or the new shawl collar that offered a softer lapel line. Still, a survey made early in 1958 by the Clothing Manufacturers Association of the United States of America showed a slow but gradual increase in Ivy models. Meanwhile, knitted suits tailored in the Continental style made headlines, although at that time they were more newsworthy than practical.

For the first time in the twentieth century London's fashion leadership was challenged, as the Continental look gained popularity and vacationing Americans returned from Italy with shirts, sports shirts, ties, and shoes purchased in shops on the elegant Via Condotti in Rome. While the Continental and Ivy factions were contending for fashion supremacy, however, a fashion revolution was brewing in a London alley called Carnaby Street, just a short walk from Savile Row. As the decade moved to a close, no one could have predicted the incredible impact the flamboyant clothes of Carnaby Street combined with the new sounds of a Liverpool group called the Beatles would soon have on American social and fashion mores.

"Miracle" fabrics. The fifties were the decade of the new synthetic fibers, the years 1950–1952 marking a high point in the development of man-made fabrics. In 1950 alone three new fibers, Dacron, Dynel, and Vicara, were introduced, and in 1951 limited numbers of the first all-Dacron suits were in production.

In its July, 1952, issue (pp. 57, 59, 61, 105), *Esquire*'s *Apparel Arts* magazine gave retailers the complete story of the discovery and development of the "miracle" fabrics, along with their problems and possibilities, under the title "Synthetics: What Do They Mean to You?" The writer noted, "Many quarters of the synthetics industry believe that the new textiles have now passed through their first phase—a period of introduction and early development," and added, "This was the period of achievement for the scientist who could point to fabulous new fabrics, created entirely through scientific methods, without the use of natural fibers." It was observed, however, that during this introductory period the retailer generally moved cautiously: "In many cases, he preferred to 'wait and see' and test consumer reaction. Nylon, for example, had to be sold harder to the trade than to the consumer. On the other hand, many stores sensed the promotional possibilities, and sold it hard."

Apparel Arts went on to note: "The second phase of synthetic development, now underway, promises the stability in which the average men's wear retailer can operate confidently and profitably. This is the period of refinement and improvement, with synthetics gradually finding their own niche in the apparel fields. Instead of a widespread, general use of each synthetic in garments of all kinds, its use is being confined to fabrics where its advantages will be most practical. In this new phase, blends promise to play a major role, with producers combining the characteristics of several synthetics or a synthetic and a natural fiber to produce a fabric engineered for a specific end-use.

"Thus far, with the more spectacular synthetics only a few years old, the 'man-mades' have had a healthy effect on men's retailing. They have created interest wherever they were sold and promoted. They have resulted in more promotion, better promotion, increases in store traffic and added sales.

"The new fabrics offer the average men's wear retailer many merchandising advantages: first, here is merchandise that will interest today's cus-

tomer, the type of clothing he has long wanted—lightweight, spot resistant, crease resistant, holds a press, durable. Secondly, here is new and daring merchandise, the type of item that gives a smaller store a substantial jump on his chain store competition, always notoriously slow to move. In addition, extensive publicity material and the basics for imaginative ads and windows are available and ready to be put to use. It all adds up to opportunity for increased volume and a general enlivening of the retail operation.

"These new fabrics with the amazing properties obviously are the work of no one man or even one company. They are the result of the work of large organizations able to combine huge research staffs, a great deal of money and a willingness to gamble on the American public's desire for their product. Years of research and huge expenditures went into each fiber before it was marketed. Nylon, for example, represented a total investment of $27,000,000 and Orlon $25,000,000 before the public saw it in any quantity. Today, total sales in the synthetic industry amount to more than one billion dollars, with 50 plants owned by 28 companies. Raw material purchases alone amount to $500,000,000 a year."

A bright future was predicted for the synthetics, but there were major problems of supply, price, and color still to be dealt with, and *Apparel Arts* called on the vice presidents of three corporations active in the development of man-made fibers to discuss these problems candidly:

Arthur Witty, vice president, Witty Bros. Consumer acceptance of men's apparel made of Du Pont's 100 percent Dacron was much greater than anticipated in 1952. Despite the fact that six times the number of garments were made than in 1951, consumers' demands could not be met.

This season, about 16,000 men will have the opportunity to buy 100 percent Dacron suits. Last year, our company had only enough for 200 suits. These suits were sold through 250 retail outlets in key cities throughout the country. Although garments of Dacron are still being produced on an extremely limited basis, we are

looking forward to 1953 with an optimism regarding the possibility of increased amounts of piece-goods and additional pattern work.

Clinton Smullyan, vice president in charge of sales, Phillips-Jones Corporation. Prices of nylon shirts are now lower than they have been in previous years, and it is very likely that by 1953 or 1954, Orlons will cost less than at present.

Whether these synthetic garments will eventually constitute, say, half a man's shirt wardrobe, and the remainder cottons, is a matter of conjecture. The question cannot be definitely answered until the synthetic fabrics that are manufactured have all the advantages of cotton. Obviously, the present prices of nylons and Orlons should not limit sales by retail stores, be they large or small. Proper promotion is a major factor in selling any garment regardless of fiber content.

W. G. Helmus, vice president, Fair Lawn Finishing Company. Few people realize that these newer fibers are produced with little or no information available pertaining to the dye or dyeing procedures. Dye chemists and dyers have done an excellent job in a short space of time in obtaining satisfactory results, almost as fast as the volume of yarn comes from the mill. Nylon, for example, can now be dyed in almost any shade with fastness similar to, and sometimes better than, older and better known natural and synthetic yarns. Orlon, manufactured in two types, presents more of a problem, as each type of Orlon fiber requires unusual methods of dyeing. Vicara and Acrilan are being dyed successfully in a complete range of colors. Dacron can be dyed in most shades but seems to take dye more favorably in light and medium shades.

To the problems of supply, price, and color were added problems of pressing and washability with some of the synthetics. Discussing the pressing problem, *Apparel Arts* urged retail salesmen to advise customers to observe the following rules: "Don't expose to intense heat; use the pressing machine as cool as possible and at lowest practical pressures. If hand steam iron is used, apply for short intervals using a light touch. Iron over a press cloth or with cloth-covered steam presshead to prevent shininess."

The problem of washability concerned not shrinkage but stretching. Furthermore, some synthetic fabric linings tended to warp or stiffen. It was only a matter of time, however, before commercial laundries installed new machines to solve these problems. The synthetic fabrics and blends used in the wash-and-wear suit presented still another problem: laundrymen claimed that dry-cleaning processes left a substance on fabrics that reacted disastrously when brought into contact with laundry solutions. After further research it was conceded that a wash suit should be either dry-cleaned or washed for life, but never both.

On the problems of price and color, *Apparel Arts* had this to add: "Here's how to handle the price problem. Some synthetics do cost more but tell your customer about the convenience and low upkeep which 'more than makes up the difference.' Mention laundry and dry cleaning savings. Use phrases like 'cheaper in the long run,' and 'it pays for itself in the end.' Give him reasons to justify the price. A key point: don't spotlight the price; mention price and then go on to list the product's features.

"Be ready when your customer complains about the lack of varied colors in some lines. Show him how he can change color in his outfit through the use of bright accessories. Have the latter right at hand to show him and so build an extra sale. Wear the product your store is advertising. Personal experience makes for sincerity, a powerful sales weapon. Remember the basic point: a synthetic is best when it has all the qualities which make a natural fiber successful, and then has some extra important characteristics which the natural fiber can never have."

Apparel Arts maintained that old techniques were not suited to selling the new fabrics and urged salesmen to learn the fabrics' properties and use imagination to sell their customers, reminding them that "synthetics have special appeal for several special types of customers. Stress the easy-to-pack easy-to-carry advantages. Bachelors, students, hotel dwellers will like the easy laundering, non-ironing properties of some synthetics. The vacationer or traveler can be impressed by crease-resistance. The hard-on-clothes customer can be advised of the tough-

ness imparted by many synthetics or blends. Learn to study each customer, to pick out these 'types' and sell them with the right approach. Wherever possible, get action into the sales pitch by demonstrating the product's advantages as you talk about them."

Ivy versus Continental. On November 22, 1954, *Life* magazine noted: "The 'Ivy League Look' identified with determinedly inconspicuously dressed New England males for over 50 years and with Madison Avenue advertising men for the past 10, has now got out of the Eastern hands and is making its way across the country. It has also got away from upper-

The traditional, or natural-shoulder, suit of 1957 and other years accented straight-hanging long lines. By fastening the top and middle jacket buttons, the wearer emphasized the elongated look. A herringbone weave was favored in worsted fabrics.

bracket tailors and into the hands of cut-rate clothiers like S. Klein."

Later, George Plimpton, writing in *Gentlemen's Quarterly* in 1959, summarized the evolution of the Ivy look in an article titled "Fashion Is a Tradition at Brooks Brothers," in which he stated: "The coat and trousers which go under the unprepossessing name of 'Number One Sack Suit' is the true Brooks Brothers trademark: three buttoned and single-breasted, with natural shoulders and straight hanging lines, the suit has remained relatively unchanged for over half a century. It is only since the war that the natural shoulder style has come into national prominence under the title 'the ivy league look.'"

Esquire had anticipated this look when, in October, 1950, it introduced Mr. T, its new trim look, which in retrospect its fashion department decided might more accurately have been called the "natural look." The Ivy League look that followed so closely on its heels and went on to sweep the country to become a new male uniform was in its purest form a three-button single-breasted model with wide button spacing, narrow small-notched lapels, welt edges, flaps on the pockets, and pleatless trousers. Like any immensely popular style, however, the authentic Ivy model underwent certain modifications in order to increase its acceptance. A modified Ivy model, retaining the essential features of the original, was cut on patterns designed to flatter the more mature man, and it was to be anticipated that the extreme jivey Ivy, with a four-button jacket and very narrow trousers, would evolve, too. Regardless of which model a man chose to wear, however, the effect of an Ivy suit was neat and narrow. It was indeed a uniform look that honestly reflected the understatement of a decade in which the nation's collegians were referred to as the "silent generation." Yet, as the decade approached its climax, an entirely fresh and unexpected new concept entered the picture: the Continental look.

Unlike the Ivy, the Continental sil-

The Continental look of 1958 drew attention to the short jacket, broad shoulders, shaped waistline, slanting besom pockets, sleeve cuffs, short side vents, and tapered cuffless trousers. Clear-finished worsted fabrics, especially in small designs, were associated with this fashion.

houette lacked authenticity. A shorter, shaped suit, the model introduced in the United States in the spring of 1956 was itself a modification of the Italian-borrowed design. Pictured for the first time in a periodical in the winter, 1957, issue of *Gentlemen's Quarterly,* it drew this prediction from the editors: "Every manufacturer will interpret this fashion in his own way. Those who wish all the Continental refine-

ments can find suits with no chest pocket, cuffs on the sleeves."

The Continental model shown at the convention of the International Association of Clothing Designers (IACD) had the three-button jacket favored by the Italian man: a rather square-shouldered coat with a width of approximately 18 inches in size 40, a more closely fitted front waist, slightly fitted side seams, and short side vents. The lapels were semi-peaked, the shorter jacket had a curved cutaway front, and the tapered trousers were cuffless. Clothing manufacturers present at the convention expressed the opinion that versions of the Continental look would eventually appear even on Ivy suits.

By 1958 there were one-, two-, and three-button variations of the Continental look, the two-button version being preferred by most American men. A Trans-America style approved by the IACD's one-hundredth semi-annual convention had notched lapels on a three-button model and semi-peaked lapels on a two-button model. The shoulder line of the jacket was straight but not square, as on the authentic Continental, and while the front was open, there was less of a cutaway effect. That year, in its October issue, *Gentlemen's Quarterly* showed still further variations of what its editors considered to be "a dressy, very smart suit." Under the heading "New Approaches to the Continental in Lighter Spring Shades," it depicted a one-button suit of silver-gray sharkskin with angled peaked lapels, crescent-shaped welt pockets, and side vents; a three-button natural-shoulder wool plaid suit with semipeaked lapels, slanted welt pockets, and side vents; a two-button air-vented wool suit with square shoulders, a shaped waist, higher lapels and button placement, horizontal welt pockets, no vent, and single-pleat trousers; and a two-button version in a black wool flecked with silver that had angled welt pockets, semipeaked lapels, sleeves with stitched cuffs, and no vent.

"The advent of the Continental suits and topcoats has raised the ques-

tion in some quarters, 'Will the Continental Replace Ivy?'" noted *Men's Wear* on February 20, 1959. "Ivy, the most discussed and most influential, if not the most widely-worn fashion since the days when the then Prince of Wales was the men's wear fashion arbiter of America, has been joined by a relatively fast starting newcomer, the Continental."

As early as October, 1958, *Gentlemen's Quarterly* showed a Continental suit with a shawl collar like those worn on dinner jackets. "Why all these innovations?" asked the editors. "Only to find something new. Why should men have to see and buy the same thing in a clothing store year after year, from their first suit to their dotage? It isn't just a woman's prerogative to want something different once in a while." The Continental suit was that "something different." It not only lured many men away from the understated look of the Ivy but forecast the shaped, or contour, suit with which Great Britain would soon reassert its fashion influence. In the contest between the Ivy and the Continental, however, there was no clear-cut winner. The coming fashion revolution would see to that. In the decade ahead, an era of intense individuality, no one look could rule.

Silk and silk-looking suits. The first silk suit, made of pongee, appeared on the American fashion scene in 1910. From the beginning the silk suit with its natural glossy beauty and superior draping qualities was a status symbol, and suits of this luxury lightweight fabric were made only by the most prestigious custom tailors and manufacturers in the country. Then, in 1952, a representative of Saks Fifth Avenue brought back handloomed silk shantung from Italy. An irregularly textured fabric weighing only 10 ounces to the yard, silk shantung achieved almost instant popularity, and since it could be adapted to power looms, soon practically every manufacturer of consequence was producing silk suits. The resulting competition worked effectively to lower the price of the silk shantung suit, so that by the mid-fifties silk was no longer a rich man's fabric.

In the early 1950s single-breasted three-button suits of silk shantung in beige, brown, blue, and elephant gray were being seen everywhere. By 1953 suits of black and gold silk shantung were a leading fashion—an early indication of the Italian influence that would become more pervasive as the decade progressed. With the development of yarn dyed fabrics that permitted the use of multiple colors in a single piece of cloth, the silk suit became increasingly colorful and noteworthy in an era otherwise marked by understatement. Soon silk, silk blends, and silklike weaves began to appear in dinner jackets, sports jackets, slacks, and robes. The trend was what *Esquire* referred to as the "silk sequence," with consumer and retailer interest reaching a peak.

"Silk," observed *Apparel Arts*, in its spring issue, "is cool, crisp, lightweight, porous and resilient. Moreover, the variety of surface effects and weaves in silk are so varied that they lend themselves to all types of clothing at almost every price level. In regular suitings, for instance, there are shantung and honan effects that have a frosty, lustrous finish, also seven ounce weight tropical suitings. Aside from their texture interest and coolness, further interest is added in some of these suitings by the introduction of pin stripings."

Since this was the decade of the miracle fabrics, silk-looking suits made of rayon, rayon and cotton, rayon and acetate, and mohair blends soon cropped up. (It is interesting to note that rayon had been known as the artificial silk until 1924.) The vogue for both silk and silk-looking suits lasted until early in the sixties, but silk shantung continued to retain a measure of popularity thereafter through its use in dinner jackets and dress trousers as well as in a wide range of colors for slacks.

Seersucker suit. "Why should the very cheap remain the province of the very rich?" asked *Esquire* in August, 1966, rejoicing in the fact that in the

The shaped British look of 1959 combined broad shoulders and shaped body lines. Lapels were peaked, as shown, or notched. The back view shows the shapeliness of the jacket and the deep side vents. Worsted fabrics predominated.

previous decade the sorely neglected seersucker suit had finally been accepted by the general public. American seersucker, a cotton variation of the Calcutta silk seersucker worn by the British in India, had long been rejected by men who thought it looked too blatantly what it was, a remarkably inexpensive summer fabric.

"I have been wearing coats of the material known as seersucker around New York lately, thereby causing much confusion among my friends," the columnist Damon Runyon wrote on July 28, 1945. "They know that seersucker is very cheap and they cannot reconcile its lowly status in the textile world with the character of Runyon, the King of the Dudes. They cannot decide whether I am broke or just setting a new vogue" (quoted in *Esquire,* August, 1966). Still, the rumpled-looking seersucker suit was a kind of status symbol; Runyon once remarked that a man wearing a seersucker suit with aplomb could cash a check anywhere in New York with no questions asked. The rationale, he felt, was that any man self-confident enough to wear one of these suits must be affluent. A poor man would not make his poverty so apparent.

The Princetonians of the twenties, among the young fashion innovators of that decade, wore seersuckers both on and off campus. In the majority of the fashionable country clubs during the thirties and forties the seersucker suit was almost commonplace, but most Americans would have nothing to do with it, regarding it as a poor man's suit. It took the introduction in the early fifties of a synthetic seersucker that was both washable and uncrushable to effect a change in the public attitude. Certainly no new fabric was ever launched with such extemporaneous showmanship. As the story goes, Joseph Haspel, one of the founders of Haspel Brothers, the New Orleans firm that pioneered in making washable seersucker, attended a business meeting in Florida wearing a seersucker suit of the new Orlon-and-cotton blend. When some observers were openly skeptical of his claims for the suit's wash-and-wear qualities, he walked into the ocean wearing the suit. That night he turned up at a board of directors meeting, cool and elegant, still wearing the same suit.

From then on, no reasonable man could afford to overlook seersucker. Once the fabric had been accepted by the average man, it was no longer a symbol of the rich or the socially secure, but there soon proved to be a new way of perpetuating seersucker's status: by 1960 a custom-made seersucker suit could cost as much as $225. By the late sixties the once *déclassé* American seersucker fabric had been adopted by some of the foremost European tailors, who were styling it in summer suits that reflected the Nehru and military influences so popular at the time among fashion-conscious men on both continents.

1960–1970

The sixties were a tradition-toppling decade in almost every field from fashion to art, from romance to religion. At the outset America put its first Catholic President in the White House and his fashionable First Lady on a pedestal, and before the decade came to a close it put a man on the moon. In the years between, the nation quaked to the tremors of a cultural revolution, a youth quake. Since the clothes men wear are a barometer of the world in which they live, a fashion revolution was a natural by-product. And as time-encrusted male and female stereotypes were scrambled and, in some instances, totally discarded, the American male emerged in the late sixties looking younger, fitter, and more colorful than ever before. From the gray flannel cocoon stepped a peacock.

Oddly enough, the start of the decade showed little indication of the coming Peacock Revolution. Americans knew all about Carnaby Street, "the birthplace of swinging London" and already a London tourist attraction, where cluttered shops blaring forth rock music and operating on the concept of instant fashion sold flashy clothes that were sometimes obsolete within a season. London's fashion aristocrats on Savile Row were outraged, but most Americans were amused. After decades of British fashion dictatorship, perhaps Americans thought it was time the elegant Britishers had their composure shaken by a band of scruffy, long-haired teenagers in bright-colored body shirts, low-rise trousers, and Chelsea boots. In any case, in the United States in the spring of 1961 young men were still well mannered and clean-cut—traditionalists down to the third buttons of their natural-shoulder suits.

"An elegant man in the summer is like an ice cube on a platter of hot tamales," observed *Esquire* in August, 1962, when it appeared that every man had at least one wash-and-wear suit in his wardrobe now that these suits were available in every silhouette.

The Continental suit silhouette was fading away, however, and people no longer referred to the still-popular natural-shoulder silhouette as the Ivy League look. Meanwhile, in the fall of 1960, a new silhouette had appeared. This time it was a "British look," or "London line," inspired by Savile Row. Presented in the October, 1961, issue of *Gentlemen's Quarterly*, it featured a lightly padded jacket with a flare to the skirt, wider lapels, pronounced side vents or a healthy center vent, a moderately cutaway front, and slanting pockets, as well as plain-front trousers. The new suit appeared to be better adapted to the rangy American physique than the Italian Continental look had been, and *Gentlemen's Quarterly* stated: "Having scored victoriously in last year's trans-atlantic crossing, the British Look continues its wardrobe-invading triumph." The most style-conscious Americans chose this flattering high-fashion suit in one of the new vibrant shades of blue that had just replaced charcoal gray as the leading color.

In October, 1962, *Gentlemen's Quarterly* advised its readers to complement the British look with widespread-collar shirts, "often striped," traditional shoe styles cut on the high side, striped and neat-patterned ties, and hats with upcurled brims. Summing up, the magazine said: "The over-all look is manly and mature, tailored rather than loosely casual, simple, non-gimmicky and sophisticated."

American manufacturers lost little time in producing their version of the British look, favoring an only slightly traced jacket with square normal shoulders, and christened it the "American silhouette." Meanwhile, in Paris Pierre Cardin, the first of the farsighted women's couturiers to begin designing for men, was updating his version of the British look, with the shaping on his suit jacket starting at the armholes.

Yet, most American men in the early sixties were still conservative dressers. In 1961, for instance, the one-button suit was considered "avant-garde, perhaps, but sensible."

It was newsworthy when Brooks Brothers launched a two-button model on which it had been working for two years, its success owing much to the fact that John F. Kennedy, the newly inaugurated President, had a predilection for the two-button style, which exposed a more than fair expanse of shirt front and gave a man the appearance of big-chestedness. Featuring a new Brooks Brothers two-button suit with a matching vest in its February, 1962, issue, *Esquire* noted: "The resultant model does not vary in the Brothers' penchant for natural shoulders, notched lapels, flap pockets, center vent. But the longer roll to the lapels, plus slightly more waist suppression, gives the suit a trimmer and more tailored appearance than Brooks' conventional models." In short, the well-dressed man that year was still very much the traditionalist, give or take a button.

A year later, the understated look was still the dominant one when the fashion writer George Frazier wrote in *Esquire:* "What is so nice about men's clothes is that their obsolescence is never obligatory. That is the reassuring thing—that they do not go out of style very swiftly. It is not that they never change, but, rather, that they change so gradually, so almost imperceptibly, that only in retrospect does one realize that there has been change." In retrospect, that statement sounds innocent and smug. But in 1963 what man of sound mind and a feeling for the proper order of things would think to look down the social ladder and expect to see a fashion revolution creeping up? What mature man could imagine that his wardrobe would be turned inside out by the aggressively colorful, antiestablishment gear of young rebels?

Just as the British at first regarded their long-haired Carnaby Street shoppers as renegades of no particular fashion influence, so Americans were about as well prepared for the Peacock Revolution as they had been for Pearl Harbor. The first tremors came with the hippies, who burst upon the national scene in a kaleidoscope of color

and with cries of "flower power" proceeded to drop out of society, but not before their antimaterialistic philosophy and classless, often genderless clothes affected a new generation of young Americans. Soon a Rockefeller scion would be telling a journalist, "Sure I think my father's a success, but being the president of a bank isn't necessarily my idea of success." A subsequent survey among youth in the seventeen to twenty-three age bracket would show that more than 90 percent were convinced that business was obsessively profit-minded and too little concerned with the public welfare.

Suddenly, or so it seemed, youth was no longer a cult. By 1965 it was a bona fide subculture. Idealistic and fiercely critical of the older generation, the young raged against a world they had not made and decided that no one over thirty was to be trusted. On the defensive and perplexed, the mature American abdicated his traditional role of leadership, and youth took over. Their clothes, hair, and music showed their independence and rejection of the establishment. Carnaby Street's "mod look," a potpourri of Edwardian elegance, the American West, and military garb, was combined with the hippies' passion for "doing your own thing" to give this new breed a new look that would soon affect even the wardrobes of the conservative over-thirty American.

"The whole point of fashion today is to be sexy," noted the British designer Hardy Amies, as men on both sides of the Atlantic began to dress up instead of down. The shaped suit predominated, and lapels grew wider, ties grew wider and bolder, and shirt collars spread to complement this more youthful silhouette. As had been the case thirty years earlier, the youth syndrome prevailed. Sociologists vied with each other in analyzing America's "new" life-style and imputing its orientation to the young and the young-minded.

To be young and committed was even more important. Civil rights and the war in Vietnam became the twin issues that brought millions of Ameri-

cans out on the streets and campuses to march, protest, pray, and burn. The country's social conscience, pricked by its youth, grew sharper, and confrontation politics became the order of the day. The blacks demanded equality. The American Indians demanded equality. The American women demanded equality. The homosexuals demanded equality. And manufacturers of campaign buttons became prosperous by turning out slogan-carrying buttons for militant activists of every persuasion. The clothes of many American college students became increasingly classless (blue jeans and work shirts) as the students empathized with the country's disadvantaged minorities.

The pill became a reality, and there

Jackets with narrow lapels were popular in 1964. At the same time they had less fullness and width across the chest. Smooth worsted-polyester blends were well adapted to this style.

was new sexual freedom. Fashions became more body-conscious, with miniskirts for women and brightly colored body shirts for men. Unisex clothes evolved, and with them see-through clothes for both sexes. As members of the women's liberation movement called for "inoffensive plainness," women's fashions became more masculinized and men's more colorful and newsworthy. By the late sixties the pantsuit for women was commonplace. Thigh-high boots and gaucho hats prompted fashion editors to label the "now" woman's fashion point of view "tough chic." Lustrous-looking suits for men became popular, and *Bonnie and Clyde,* a gangster film, brought a revival of gangster-striped suits and shirts reminiscent of the thirties.

The American man, who once considered anything beyond an after-shave lotion and talcum effeminate, now chose from a collection of more than 400 colognes. Barber shops became hair-styling parlors, and with new emphasis on youth and masculine sex appeal the manufacturers of hairpieces and hair dyes became prosperous. Books on diet and exercise were on the best-seller lists, and middle-aged men took to jogging before breakfast. For the ideal masculine figure had changed, too: brawn was out of style, and a slender, well-proportioned body was in fashion. The youthful new clothes demanded it.

By 1966 the leading women's fashion designers in both the United States and Europe were beginning to work in the menswear field as well. Their labels sewn inside suits and accessories had "name" value. It was clear that changes in men's fashions would now be just as frequent and dynamic as those of the distaff side, leading more than one fashion columnist to observe that much of the innovation in fashion and breaking of new ground was coming in the men's field. In 1968 *Esquire* sponsored the First International Designers' Conference, and that year saw the conventionally tailored suit threatened in turn by the velvet Edwardian jacket, the safari suit, the

Nehru, the waistcoat suit, and the knitted suit. Surveying the fashion scene toward the end of this decade, social critics were impressed by the manner in which men were discarding the somber, drab appearance that had prevailed for more than a century and a half and returning to their former peacocklike status.

In 1969 the miniskirt was threatened by the midi and maxi lengths, and the national economy by inflation. As the Dow-Jones industrial average declined seriously in 1970, pessimistic forecasters recalled 1929, when hemlines dropped and the stock market crashed simultaneously. But the nation's astrologers, a new power elite, explained that the decade's turmoil was to be expected. This was, after all, the age of Aquarius, a time of worldwide unrest and experimentation.

White suit. Since the beginning of the twentieth century the popularity of the all-white summer suit has varied widely, remaining constant only in the South, whose clothes-conscious men apparently have always agreed with *Esquire*'s contention that the white suit is as romantic a garment as any man ever put on his back. That it survived years of neglect to become an established fashion leader in the late sixties is a tribute to its durability as well as to the ripening good taste of American men.

Prior to World War I only the more affluent could afford the upkeep of a garment so easily soiled. The smart dresser who could, suffered willingly through steamy summers in a cool-looking but heavy white flannel or linen suit. In the prosperous twenties the white suit gained popularity and appeared in cities and towns across the country. When F. Scott Fitzgerald's Jay Gatsby, one of the most sartorially resplendent characters in twentieth-century fiction, appeared in his blue gardens, where "men and girls came and went like moths among the whisperings and the champagne and the stars" (*The Great Gatsby,* New York, 1925, chap. 3), he wore a spotless white flannel suit. By 1936, with the

first synthetic fabrics a reality, a truly "air-conditioned" white suit capable of retaining its crisp good looks was available to any man who had the price, but the pinched economy of the Depression dictated more practical, darker colors, and the white suit became principally a "fun suit," with Princeton undergraduates wearing house painters' white jackets and overalls and calling the outfit a "beer suit."

In 1941 *Esquire* advised its readers that "white is right" in lightweight worsted flannel, Palm Beach cloth, and blends of man-made fibers such as acetate and rayon. The entrance of the United States into World War II, however, cut short the comeback of the white suit in that decade. In 1956 the return of the white suit was announced once again, this time in a trim silhouette with very narrow lapels. Then, in July, 1962, *Esquire* asked its readers to "reconsider, gentlemen, the classic white suit." The *Esquire* classic was a heavy yet aerated Moygashel linen, updated with lean contemporary lines. The two-button ventless jacket had slightly built-up shoulders and a noticeably suppressed waist. Not until the summer of 1967, however, did the white suit begin to appear in numbers on Northern city streets. (Unlike Gatsby, who wore a silver shirt and a gold-colored tie with his white flannel suit, the 1967 man wore a dark shirt and a printed silk tie with his white suit of lightweight textured wool twill.)

Since 1967 the white suit has settled comfortably in its rightful place high on the list of smart and practical summer suits. In 1968, for example, in the cruise and resort collection shown by Antonio Cerruti, an Italian textile manufacturer turned designer (a collection that won the praise of the international fashion press), three of the most photographed suits were made of a new wrinkleproof white fabric, a blend of silk, wool, and linen, that had been created in Cerruti's own mill. That year, with the Nehru suit at the peak of its popularity, a New York custom tailor reported that he had made more than thirty Nehrus in white gabardine having mother-of-pearl buttons with 14-carat gold centers, at a price of $395 each. At *Esquire*'s Second International Designers' Conference in 1969, the young British designer Peter Golding showed a knitted shirt suit in pale ivory worn with a hip-slung leather belt. By 1970 the all-white linen suit, crisp and correct as ever, had been rediscovered by leading designers in the United States and Europe. There were shaped double-breasted suits of Irish linen, safari suits with the longer, shaped jacket, a tie belt, and button-flapped pockets, and cocktail suits of heavy white cotton brocade worn with see-through cotton lace shirts and white nubby silk ties.

The comeback of the all-white suit is now a matter of record. Its character may have been too assertive in the decades when conformity ruled men's fashions and men dressed down, but today it is a peacock suit perfectly attuned to the dramatic new silhouettes that are evolving and strong enough to carry the most boldly colorful accessories. The new white suit is a recognized classic and deservedly so.

Mod Influence. "Mod Discovers America!" *Gentlemen's Quarterly* headlined a fashion story in September, 1966, the text of which began, "Mod is the mode at the moment." Although that moment was brief, much of the best of the mod mode, reinterpreted for the American figure and way of life, worked its way comfortably into the American wardrobe. Insofar as the mod movement as a whole was concerned, it had a comparatively brief popularity in the United States and then faded away, for the good reason that, in the rush to capitalize on it, much poorly designed and shoddily produced merchandise was introduced and aggressively promoted as authentic mod fashion.

Mod fashions began in 1957, when John Stephen, who opened a closet-size shop at 5 Carnaby Street, started, in his own words, "a crusade to brighten men's clothes. When one is young and one feels everything is gray and drab, you *know* they want some-

The Regency double-breasted jacket of 1969 had three sets of buttons in parallel arrangement and high-roll lapels. The shapely back showed deep side vents. Chalk-stripe fabrics of a medium or light weight were used for this type of suit.

thing new and exciting. It wasn't a matter of being in the right place at the right time. I made it happen. When I started I had to fight to sell our clothes. People laughed at pink and red slacks. Frilly shirts. They said they were clothes for women and were effeminate. Word of mouth really made us. Some boy would buy a colorful shirt or tie and some friends would see it and ask, 'Where'd you get it?'" (*Gentlemen's Quarterly,* February, 1966).

The youngsters who wore the colorful Carnaby Street garb were, in the main, members of a motor scooter group called the Mods. And the Mods were mod, short for "modern." Beginning with shirts and ties, Stephen proceeded to design and manufacture entire wardrobes for his mod clientele, and often they unwittingly told him what they wanted. It became a kind of silent partnership. "For instance," Stephen recalled in 1966, "when I saw customers trying on trousers and pushing the waistband down, I knew they wanted hipsters. But at that stage they didn't know it themselves."

British youth of all classes soon began dressing mod, John Stephen became a millionaire, and Carnaby Street, a mere 125 yards long, became a tourist attraction. For the first time fashion was starting at the bottom of the social ladder and working upward, and, what was all the more extraordinary, it was happening in class-structured Britain. Suddenly the back alley became famous, even causing the prestigious London press to take notice. The spectacle of somewhat stuffy, highly conservative publications hailing Carnaby Street for having put the city on the map was amusing. With effusive prose they described the Carnaby influence as having ignited a desiccated, old-fashioned industry and producing new sparks of fashion interest in Great Britain and throughout the world.

American tourists visiting London brought mod clothes home with them, and by 1965 Carnaby Street had come to Main Street with high-buttoned double-breasted jackets, colored body shirts, floral ties, wide belts, and low-rise trousers. By the end of 1966, however, much unattractive merchandise that was advertised as "Carnaby Street-inspired" appeared in stores and failed to move, and retailers became disenchanted with mod fashions.

By 1967 the mod craze had faded away, although its most attractive styles had left an indelible impression on the wardrobes of American men of all ages. Carnaby Street, however, despite predictions that it was nearing the end of its run of success, continued to prosper, packed with colorful boutiques and with camera-carrying shoppers and tourists estimated to number 15,000 on an average day.

Nehru suit. Fashion reporters, looking back on this dynamic decade, concluded that it was a time when clothes for both sexes often became costumes and when costumes became acceptable as clothes. Perhaps that explains the meteoric rise of Nehru styling in men's suits and jackets. This was a kind of

magnificent experiment that caught fire late in 1966 and misfired less than two years later.

The Nehru suit, worn for years by men in India and glamorized for the American and European taste by the handsome appearance of Prime Minister Jawaharlal Nehru, first appeared on the international scene when salesmen in Adam, the Paris shop of the designer Pierre Cardin, took to wearing gray flannel Nehrus soon after a trip Cardin made to India. The jacket, an exact copy of the Indian original, was close-fitting with a shaped back, a buttoned front, and a 1½-inch standing collar. The trousers were slim and tapered. Soon afterward the Nehru suit, or simply the jacket, was being seen in London, then in New York and other principal American cities. Versatile, it lent itself to a variety of fabrics. It was styled for business in gray, dark blue, brown, and tan flannel and twill woven worsted. For summer, the jacket looked handsome in such lightweight fabrics as cotton, linen, and man-made fiber blends, most often in tan or white. For evening wear, a Nehru jacket of a sumptuous acetate brocade or velvet was worn with dark formal trousers. There were also Nehru evening suits of colorfully brocaded silk.

Lord Snowdon wore a black Nehru dinner jacket with a white satin turtleneck shirt, and his photograph appeared in almost every major American newspaper. *Life* magazine did a full fashion spread on the Nehru as worn by men in all walks of life. Johnny Carson appeared on television wearing a businessman's Nehru jacket with a turtleneck sweater, and within a day retailers throughout the country reported a phenomenal increase in Nehru suit and jacket sales. Soon Nehru styling was adapted for knitted zipper-front sweaters and sports shirts, and by 1968 some men's fur coats featured the Nehru collar. The Nehru also inspired a new kind of jewelry for men: linked chains carrying large metallic pendants worn about the neck. Some younger men wore beaded necklaces with their Nehru jackets.

Then, as suddenly as it came into prominence, the Nehru began to pall, and the man in the gray flannel Nehru suit began to wonder how he could convert the jacket to another style. But the distinctive look that first attracted him to the style made conversion impossible, and the Nehru in his closet became a fashion antique.

Edwardian suit. As the Nehru was fading from the scene, Edwardian-inspired suits and jackets were reaching the peak of their popularity. Distinguished by longer, multibuttoned double-breasted jackets with waist suppression and deep center vents, Edwardian styling, when seen in the more opulent fabrics such as brocade and velvet, had a theatrical flair that appealed especially to many younger men. Naturally, a brocade or velvet Edwardian jacket with a greatcoat collar required something more romantic than a conventional shirt and tie, and shirts with lace jabots and lacy cuffs spilling over the wrists became the vogue.

Edwardian suits for spring and summer daytime wear featured six or eight buttons highly placed and closely spaced, angled flap pockets, and tapered trousers. With or without a greatcoat collar, the Edwardian daytime suit in a cotton twill or one of the man-made fiber blends was too avant-garde a style for a man with a less than perfect figure. Like the Nehru, the Edwardian suit had a brief but very colorful career.

Unconstructed suit. "Unconstructed suit" was an umbrella term for a collection of controversial suits which evolved in the last years of the decade and which were a sharp departure from previous twentieth-century suit silhouettes. In this category were the waistcoat, or vest, suit, the tunic suit, and the shirt suit. The basic characteristic of all unconstructed suits was the absence of shoulder padding and hand tailoring.

The waistcoat suit was sleeveless and in general single-breasted and closed with three or four buttons. The waistcoat ended at the waistline or, in the case of a double-breasted style, at

The shaped suit of 1970 had wide lapels and patch pockets with inverted pleats. The pattern of the worsted fabric was known as parquet because it resembled the design of inlaid flooring. The jacquard-pattern shirt had a big collar, complemented by a wide tie.

mid-thigh. The trousers were pleatless and flared slightly at the bottoms. The waistcoat suit was styled in corduroy, flannel, worsted, and lightweight tweed and was particularly adaptable to knitted fabrics. It was usually worn with a long-sleeved shirt or a turtleneck of a contrasting color. Many waistcoat suits were designed for formal wear in such lustrous fabrics as black mohair. Decorated with beaded embroidery, they were worn with a silk shirt and black mohair trousers.

The somewhat less popular tunic suit had sleeves, a fairly long jacket that usually measured 31 or 32 inches, and a three-button or slide-fastener closure. It was worn most often with a wide belt. The tunic suit was available in most of the same fabrics as the waistcoat suit.

The shirt suit, perhaps the most avant-garde of the unconstructed suits, was worn invariably with a very wide leather belt. The choice of fabric and color determined its versatility. A shirt suit of a dark crushed velvet, for instance, might be worn in the daytime and then converted to formal evening wear by simply substituting for the body shirt a long, lustrous shirt in white or a pastel shade to be worn outside the trousers. A velvet shirt suit could be worn day or evening without change. In 1968 Pierre Cardin introduced a version of the shirt suit in black leather, consisting of a shirt jacket with a laced V neck and close-fitting trousers.

The easy suit, a more conventional type of unconstructed suit, was regarded in some quarters as one of the major concepts of 1969–1970. Unlike the unconstructed suits mentioned above, it was lightly padded, although it, too, lacked hand tailoring. In November, 1968, *Esquire* predicted the "discovery" of the easy suit, explaining that in this case "easy" meant "easy to interchange," that is, a suit that could be worn as easily with a turtleneck in the country as with a shirt and tie in the city. In fact, the easy suit was derived from a quest for a suit that, at least superficially, would resemble a conventional suit but would be more in keeping with the late-sixties trend toward clothes with a casual feeling and fit.

The 1968 *Esquire* spread showed a collection of easy suits designed in Europe, ranging from a Regency-inspired diagonal wool knit to a collarless jacket of tweed with matching trousers. The easy suit concept was a sophisticated one and certainly was not expected to have instant mass appeal. Unfortunately, some American manufacturers seized upon the con-

cept as an excuse to make cheaper suits of clothes. The fit of such hastily made suits was often fitful rather than casual, and they did nothing to enhance the image of a "new wave" garment that was meant to be casually elegant. Furthermore, instead of adhering to the idea of an unconstructed suit, these manufacturers, in their attempts to reach a mass market, produced suits with varying degrees of construction, thus making the term

The knitted suit of the seventies caused a rapid shift in the textile and apparel industries. Shown here is a diamond-pattern knitted wool suit in the favored wide-lapel style.

The suit with an action-back jacket became popular in the seventies. The front was finished with wide lapels, and the patch pockets had buttoned flaps. The back, as sketched, had pleats at the sides and an inverted-pleat vent. The fabric was an Art Deco design, seen in both knitted and woven types.

ing attitudes of major corporations toward more colorful clothes for male employees, found that while the pantsuit for women had achieved practically national acceptance in even the most conservative business firms, waistcoat, vest, and tunic suits were still barred except in the advertising agency field and that even there they were acceptable only in the creative departments.

Knit suit. "If one thing more than any other characterizes clothes in these times, it is the astonishing increase in comfort. The creativity of chemistry has wrought wonder fabrics undreamed of in all the eras of elegance that have gone before." This statement, which appeared in the October, 1970, issue of *Esquire,* paid homage to the miracle fabrics of the fifties and sixties and, in particular, to the knits that had recently become a fashion reality. By the late sixties knits had ceased to be a novelty. Flexible and wrinkle-resistant, with all the difficulties finally overcome, they had become designers' favorites.

Several knit suits were shown at the Second International Designers' Conference in 1969, each illustrating the functionalism, simplicity, and lightness of design found in knits. There were shirt suits of a heavy knit fabric, two-piece 100 percent knit suits with tremendous stretch in the back, and a double-breasted knit coat with elbow patches and snap fasteners. In October, 1970, *Esquire*'s fashion pages displayed double-knit suits of Dacron and Fortrel worn with long-sleeved V-neck knit shirts. Eminently practical, the knit suit represented years of research and development, coming as it did half a decade after the all-wool stretch suit, which had been heralded as the most revolutionary innovation in men's fashions owing to its resilience at pressure areas. In August, 1962, *Esquire* had devoted a spread to the then-new stretch suit. The following excerpt from that spread will serve to give some small indication of the work that preceded the emergence of the successful knit suit of the late sixties:

"easy suit" a confusing one for the buying public.

In December, 1970, the *Daily News Record* maintained: "People are no longer sure what Easy Suits are . . . not even the people who are making them." Still, the editors believed that no matter how the easy suit concept

had been mistreated, it was accomplishing one thing: "It is opening the doors to a marketwide investigation of new production methods that might be more adaptable to today's fabrics and today's comfort requirements."

An article in *Gentlemen's Quarterly* in March, 1971, reporting on the chang-

The recovery after each stretch kept the suit looking freshly tailored, free of wrinkles and sag. Until now, it would have been lunacy to expect all this from a suit. Manufacturers have been experimenting with stretch material for quite some time, and there are now three basic types in production. Helanca got things going ten years ago with the development of stretch nylon. They started with raw nylon yarn, twisted it, heat-set it, and then untwisted it. This left it limp and lifeless but gave it a "torque" so that, after being knitted or woven into cloth and exposed to moist heat, it contracted into millions of microscopic curls and coils. The fabric could be stretched, but it would always spring right back. Stretch socks are made entirely of this material, and they expand in every direction. Various other effects, however, can be obtained by subtle uses of stretch nylon in combination with other fibers. For instance, nylon might be woven horizontally on a vertical warp of wool so that only the wool shows. This creates a seemingly pure wool fabric with the added advantage of a horizontal stretch. (Ski pants, casual footwear and special hats are now made of blends like this: and suits will be, too, in a year or so.) The next significant development came several years later when an ingenious method was devised for imparting stretch properties to pure wool. The process called for a highly twisted yarn, which was woven wider than usual, mechanically shrunk and then set with heat and chemicals like a "permanent wave." This crimped the yarn, or gave it a zigzag, much like the curls in the Helanca nylon. Timely Clothes brought out a whole line of stretch suits, sport jackets and slacks; and Kuppenheimer Clothes, working on its own variation called Kupp-eez, plans to introduce a selection in the major cities this fall. Again, this cloth can "give" and then recover. Wrinkle-resistant, no sagging, and it's all wool. The Raeford Worsted Company, a division of Burlington Industries, discovered how to give wool elasticity without chemically changing the molecular structure of its fibers. The system they use is so new that a patent is still pending and for the moment the details are not available.

By every indication, the stretch suit is on the move. Stretch cloth can be made in all weights, colors and types of weave; and it tailors easily. At last a man can sit, stand, kneel, crouch or cross his legs without worrying about the crease in his trousers or the smoothness of his suit. The stretch suit always keeps its shape, always fits perfectly and remains comfortable whatever the position.

The stretch suit was exciting news in 1962, but certain problems stood in the way of its becoming a major fashion breakthrough. Despite the feeling that it could be made in all colors, the only stretch cloth available in large volume was dark blue, and this was a disappointment at a time when the American man was growing increasingly color-conscious. Furthermore, many other minor production problems arose. The time was ripe for fashion innovation, and soon the Peacock Revolution would divert consumer attention elsewhere.

By the late sixties the knit suit offered the American man what the stretch suit had promised, and by the early seventies it was well on its way to becoming an integral part of his wardrobe. In fact, in its September, 1971, issue, *Gentlemen's Quarterly* heralded "The Return of the Gentleman": "A gentleman of adaptable elegance, whose suit can find its way in any ambience—sophisticated urban to casual country." On the editorial page of that issue Bernard J. Miller, the publisher, noted that the costume party was over and that the male population at large was abandoning the excesses of the fashion revolution. Once again, he wrote, taste and discrimination were "the crucial common denominators of the well-dressed man." It was significant that the model on the cover wore a patterned double-knit suit. Should the reader have any lingering doubts of the fashion significance of the knit suit, the writer Paul Roth called knits "the newest and most exciting development in men's suits, sport coats and pants," foreshadowing a fresh era in menswear. Roth concluded: "Knits have brought back the gentlemanly look, but in a comfortable, convenient way. The elegance is all there—only the stuffiness has been removed."

Designer influence. By the end of the sixties some of the most original and exciting men's suit designs could be traced to men who were or had been designers in the women's fashion field. Pierre Cardin was the first famous couturier to see the design possibilities in menswear. As early as 1954 he opened Adam, his Paris boutique for men. Stocked primarily with accessories, Adam was so successful that soon Cardin began to design and manufacture men's apparel as well. In 1962, with the opening of a Cardin boutique for men in Bonwit Teller, New York, until then exclusively a women's store, Cardin designs for men came officially to the United States.

Hardy Amies, dressmaker to Queen Elizabeth II and sometimes described as "the archetype of the haughty dressmaker, Anglo-Saxon breed," began designing neckties in 1957. In 1961 he contracted to serve as design consultant for Hepworth's, British men's tailors with a chain of nearly 400 retail shops. In 1966 he signed a five-year contract with Genesco as men's design consultant, thus entering the American market.

John Weitz, a fashion designer for women and children, entered the menswear field in 1964, becoming the first American name designer to create styles for men. He was soon followed into the field by Oleg Cassini, whose designs for Mrs. John F. Kennedy had won him international fame, and by Bill Blass, who launched his menswear career with his total look for the American male.

This invasion of the menswear field by designers of women's wear provoked much resentment on the part of men's tailors and manufacturers in both the United States and England. Savile Row tailors, already piqued by international press attention to Carnaby Street, now had to contend with competition from well-publicized name designers. Speaking at the annual dinner of the Master Tailors' Benevolent Association, Teddy Watson, tailor to the Duke of Edinburgh, attacked "the weird and gimmicky garments which have emerged from these people trained and raised in women's dressmaking, applying their often absurd ideas to men's tailoring." The American designer Francis Toscani, a past president of the International Association of Clothing Designers, struck out at the industry's fascination with the designer influ-

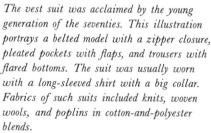

The vest suit was acclaimed by the young generation of the seventies. This illustration portrays a belted model with a zipper closure, pleated pockets with flaps, and trousers with flared bottoms. The suit was usually worn with a long-sleeved shirt with a big collar. Fabrics of such suits included knits, woven wools, and poplins in cotton-and-polyester blends.

The belted Cardin suit of 1970 marked a trend toward a more casual appearance. The tunic-style jacket had lower pockets with flaps and slanting upper pockets.

ence. His attack questioned how hard couturiers worked and how they could find time to travel extensively, promote their fashions, and still be true to their craft. He labeled them promoters and peddlers and deplored the adulation being heaped upon them.

Since those days of heated debate the designer label has steadily gained in influence. ("People today want a name on their clothes," maintains Hardy Amies.) Although there are some well-known designers who have spent their entire careers in menswear, the majority of the best-known names belong to men whose prestige was first built in women's wear. The International Designers' Conference, sponsored annually since 1968 by *Esquire*, has made it possible for the most important and inventive American and European designers now creating for men not only to show their fashions but to elaborate on their fashion philosophies. Their highly individual approaches to the subject of men's clothes can indicate the direction men's fashions will take in the future. The following excerpts are from speeches made at the *Esquire* conference or from personal interviews:

Pierre Cardin. I do not pretend to design for everyone, because habits are difficult to change. So I started with young people; in life, you must always start with the young, because they can wear anything. That is why I always look to the future, and not behind me. I like always the new life; for me, fashion must be tomorrow, not yesterday—so I aim my designs for youth.

Now life is changing, and change is always more interesting. A new suit may seem extreme and impossible to wear but it is possible to wear anything somewhere in the world. People dress the same in New York and Paris, but differently in Brasilia; it is not possible to wear the same clothing with the same lines in an old city and in Brasilia, too. The men must look like new men, because life is always new. You must prove that you are *now,* not in the 19th or 18th or 17th century.

Hardy Amies. I was once asked, "For whom do you design? What are you thinking of?" It is an ideal man that we are working for. He is a decent citizen, pays his taxes. He is well aware of all that goes on around him. He reads the *Wall Street Journal,* but he also knows his way around the Museum of Modern Art. He is 39 long. He can be of any age; he looks forty-five but his bank balance is that of a man of seventy.

I am a student of past fashions, and I think of future fashions. The suit, as we know it today, is about one hundred years old. But I feel that there is still a tremendous opportunity for skillful design within the quite restricted sphere of a jacket and trousers to produce clothing which is right for people to wear today. I design to sell, and I have an immense respect for the man's suit. It never fails to fascinate me, because it can be used as a disguise of old age. A sweater and pants can't do that. But with a suit you conceal and reveal. I put fluidity into my suits. The pants flare so they move. But you have rigidity where you want it, and so you appear to have good shoulders even if you don't. And with a suit you have all the excitement of adding the proper tie and shirt. The suit is by no means finished.

The whole point of fashion today is to be sexy. Manufacturers are frightened of this, but sexuality in male dress is generally desired, even if subconsciously.

By 1977, it's highly possible that there will be two very different schools of fashion each with its own followers. The very functional Space Age clothes that reflect the hard, brash industrial life of today, and the romantic clothes in extravagant fabrics that draw their inspiration from the romantic eras of fashion history.

John Weitz. I design for the busy, modern man. He wants featherweight, crush-resistant, easy-to-pack clothing with pockets that he can reach and a minimum of extra buttons and clutter. He is the man of today—not of yesterday nor of 2000 A.D. He fancies himself neither as a Regency buck nor as Buck Rogers. He wants his clothes to be part of himself, a comfortable, tasteful, supporting part—no more, no less. He believes that brains make the man, not clothes. He wants to be supported by his appearance. He shuns eccentricity. He considers foppery juvenile. He can be introduced to new ideas when they make sense—in clothes, cars, houses, decorations, or any other part of his environment. Show him that it works and he will buy it.

Oleg Cassini. There are several potential new markets, one of which is the market of the man who wants to be a swinger.

Now, a swinger doesn't have to worry about his age. A swinger is a man who wants to get out of the corporate world into the young, "mod" world without losing dignity. He wants young clothes, well-fitting clothes, clothes that make a significant change in his attitude and in his personality.

What makes Americans what they are? I am trying to prove—I hope satisfactorily—that Europe has borrowed from us almost as much as we have from them. The first man, to me, who became elegant and functional at the same time was the American cowboy. The cowboy realizes instinctively that form-fitting clothes are both elegant and functional, as are his use of beautiful belts, buckles and boots.

Bill Blass. I believe that the 60's and the 70's will go down as one of the most romantic periods in dressing ever. You all know that if your wife is going to be an Indian maharani one night and a Victorian Gibson Girl the next, you cannot keep wearing that gray flannel suit. So I got into this thing quite logically: through the medium of what the girls are wearing and what men should wear to complement them. After all, the whole thing is based on sex. We want to look more attractive to them. The only way to do it is to dress and to look better.

Although, theoretically, the clothes I make are for what I feel is the decidedly neglected man of over thirty, there is no doubt that the young are the inspiration for clothes today. The other inspiration that I take my theory in designing from is the fact that there are two ways of dressing men to make them more attractive to the opposite sex, make them more powerful, make them feel better. One has to do with sports—polo, golf, tennis, swimming. Anything that smacks of sports makes a man look great. The other influence undoubtedly is the military. Throughout history the military has dominated the picture as a most attractive way for a man to dress.

I feel that the rather casual or even sloppy look is preferable to one of great neatness.

Sports Jackets

The sports jacket as we know it today—that is, a special jacket and not simply a suit jacket worn with a pair of odd trousers—was literally nonexistent at the turn of this century. Tracing its family tree is a frustrating experience for the fashion historian, but it would seem that an immediate ancestor was probably the long, bulky greatcoat, which, having proved to be a hindrance to the country squire who needed to leap hedges, climb stiles, and ride to hounds, was eventually cut off below the hip. That is, a shorter coat was achieved but not a sports jacket; still man was at least inching his way toward a more comfortable and practical garment.

1900–1910

In 1900 a bona fide sports jacket was only a gleam in the eye of the well-dressed man who perhaps secretly hankered for something sartorially more exciting than the suit jacket of dark blue serge he wore with white flannel trousers—the "uniform" seen at fashionable summer resorts. Like the serge suit jacket, even his white flannel trousers may have been doing double duty, since they might have been simply the bottom half of an all-white flannel summer suit. Yet the average American man of this decade was much too devoted to the formal look in clothes to think in terms of something as informal as a sports jacket; he was quite willing to put up with any number of petty and not-so-petty discomforts (high starched shirt collars, for example) to maintain a look of gentility. He simply had not progressed to the point where he expected comfort from his clothes.

1910–1920

Before the sports jacket could emerge, men's suit jackets first had to evolve a more natural-looking silhouette, which in fact they began to do

The Victorian velvet smoking jacket and checked trousers may be regarded as a forerunner of sports jackets and slacks combinations. [THE BETTMANN ARCHIVE, INC.]

now cut narrow. By 1914–1915 the natural-shoulder suit with a military, high-waisted effect dominated the fashion scene, and the long suit jacket had been cut down to a short 29 inches on a size 40 suit. World War I had exploded in Europe, and, as always,

The dark blue double-breasted coat and white trousers were worn in 1900 with a high starched collar, a small tie, and a soft felt hat. [HART, SCHAFFNER & MARX]

In 1910 the double-breasted jacket of a suit doubled as a sports jacket when worn with white trousers and buckskin shoes.

very early in the second decade of the century. As early as 1911 suits were being tailored along trimmer, more youthful lines. The once heavily padded shoulders were fast giving way to more natural shoulders, and sleeves—once cut full, even to the cuffs—were

men's clothes reflected the new military atmosphere even though United States involvement was several years in the offing. This youthful styling naturally enough became even more popular with the end of the war and the young serviceman's return to civilian life. Insistent on more natural styling in his clothes, this younger, sports-minded American was psychologically ripe for a bona fide sports jacket.

The norfolk jacket of 1918 might be called the first American sports jacket, although it too was borrowed from the norfolk suit of Harris or Donegal tweed that manufacturers of this youth-conscious decade advertised as "a thoroughly serviceable suit for men who are young, either in years or in spirit, and who wish to be distinctly well dressed, even on their outings." The norfolk jacket worn with white flannel trousers and a natty straw skimmer constituted a summer outfit that passed muster at even the most snobbish vacation resorts. As one fashion writer observed in 1918, "The Norfolk seems to be an extra jacket to be worn with odd knickers or flannel trousers." Although the norfolk jacket now loomed as a smart new leisure fashion, its roots extended back to eighteenth-century England, when it was the custom for men to wear country jackets associated with their districts. The norfolk, copied from the jacket of the Duke of Norfolk's hunting suit, was worn by the men in the county of Norfolk; its distinguishing features were two box pleats down each side in front, two box pleats down each side in back, lower patch pockets with flaps that extended to the box pleats, vertical slit pockets at the chest, and side vents or no vents at all. The first American copies, though faithful to the British original, also featured a belted back, and before long all-around belts were also used.

Reporting on fashions at the more elegant winter resorts of the South, a writer noted the predominance of norfolk jackets worn with odd knickerbockers that fastened with strap and buckle below the knee. By now the high starched shirt collar had been replaced by the soft collar, and with a norfolk jacket and knickers the well-dressed man, at, say, the Gulf Club in Palm Beach, would most likely favor a shirt and collar of white silk with a bow tie or a striped four-in-hand.

"Life and color exist because the war is over," a *Men's Wear* reporter decided as he observed prominent society men vacationing at Aiken, South Carolina, in 1919. "On the golf course and at the stands where the clay birds were being 'killed,' I tired in endeavoring to enumerate the assortment of Norfolk suits. These were mixed suits in nine out of ten cases. As I have explained before, the jacket is different from the knickerbockers, but the effect is a harmony rather than a contrast." In support of this point, the writer called to mind a Mr. Cyril Barclay who had appeared in a brown jacket and taupe-color knickers, brown stockings, brown-and-white shoes, pink silk shirt and collar, and a green-and-brown tie. "There is a craze at present," the writer continued, "for these clothes to be made of American homespuns. The wool may come from Mr. Gardener's sheep, Mr. Tafft's or Mr. Somebody's else. It is dyed and woven by the Biltmore weavers and the finished product seems very wonderful. I can state candidly and with enthusiasm that I have never seen as clear and as beautiful colorings in the foreign homespuns."

An English writer reporting in *Men's Wear* (Nov. 15, 1919) on a weekend spent at a country estate in the Northeast was impressed by the ease with which the affluent American man had adapted to the casual country clothes one was accustomed to seeing "at great houses in England in long past autumns." He also noted a predominance of shades of blue and decided that, added to what he heard from England, all indications pointed to their continued and greater use in sporting and lounge wear the following summer.

Despite the newfound pleasure in colorful and imaginative casual wear, the terms "sports jacket" and "sports coat" were still not used. And although the more affluent American man was building a most impressive wardrobe of norfolk suits and odd knickerbockers that he could mix and match, at the end of this decade the bulk of the male population still preferred to wear the jackets, and often vests, of their business suits with white flannel trousers and white shoes. It was a long-time habit, and one that would last a few more years before being abandoned. In fact, not until 1923 would even the fashion-conscious Ivy League undergraduate actually accept the idea of a planned jacket or sports jacket fashion.

1920–1930

By 1923 the best-dressed men seen at such fashionable resorts as Palm Beach had taken up the sports jacket to such an extent that *Men's Wear* felt obliged to publish an analysis of their preferences. The most popular model that year was the coat with a pinch-back or belted-back effect. Running a close second, however, was the three-button plain-back model, and in a rather weak third spot was the two-button plain-back. At the very bottom of the list was the norfolk jacket, which now accounted for a mere 4 percent of the sports jackets seen at Palm Beach, which was generally acknowledged to be the winter social center of America. Gray was the most popular sports jacket color, with gabardine tan, brown, and blue the runners-up respectively. The notched lapel was seen on 91 percent of the sports jackets, almost three-quarters of which were ventless.

The following year Palm Beach was reported to be having the most successful season in its history, attracting more American and European notables than ever before. A report published in *Men's Wear* in January, 1924, attempted to analyze the burgeoning popularity of Palm Beach and the reason for its formidable fashion influence, and it is interesting as a commentary on this period of prosperity

The belted high-waisted jacket of a jazz suit of 1920 was often used as an odd jacket with separate trousers. [THE BETTMANN ARCHIVE, INC.]

as well as on the life-style of the very, very rich, which, in *Palm Beach* at least, has changed little during the intervening decades. The report said:

"During the present season there are two classes of sojourners, one consisting of those who have been spending their winters at Palm Beach for many years and the other made up of the people who have heard so much about the famous resort that they are curious to know what it really is. Because of the presence of this 'rubber-neck' or 'imitator' class those of the 'old guard' are doing their utmost to be exclusive and away from the masses.

"In order to be secluded more and more society folk are acquiring beautiful and luxurious villas which are surrounded by well planned gardens abundant in tropical growth. A short time ago several sales of estates varying in cost from $100,000 to $300,000 were reported. One impression that nearly everyone has of Palm Beach is that it is an expensive resort. Some people say that it is the most costly of all resorts in America, which may be true when one considers the expenditure for several cars, a speed boat, a yacht, membership and dues of the various clubs, entertainment, servants, high-priced jewelry and extras. There is apparently no limit to the amount one can spend.

"The natural surroundings of Palm Beach are ideal, for a few minutes after bathing at the beach the pleasure seeker can skim in a speed boat over the quiet waters of Lake Worth, which is less than a mile from the ocean. Golf, tennis, fishing, and the other sports help to while away the idle moments. When the season is at its height the many parties are so tiring that the more fortunate cruise to Nassau or some other nearby point for a rest. The social life is very strenuous.

"The presence of the social leaders has made Palm Beach the winter fountainhead of women's style representatives. Women's magazines and papers have been reporting for several years fashions that later became popular with the masses. A similar position is held in the men's wear field, for

along with the increased interest in men's styles generally has come the enhanced significance of Palm Beach as a source of style information. Progressive men's wear shops have been sending their experts and buyers to Palm Beach to study the apparel worn and to utilize the results in buying and merchandising. According to reports of the stores the men who visit Palm Beach are becoming more fastidious than ever before. The customer will buy nothing but the latest styles."

An analysis of apparel worn by 300 of the best-dressed men at Palm Beach during the daytime revealed that 38 percent preferred a three-button sports jacket with medium lapels and medium shoulders, buttons placed somewhat lower, and a well-rounded front. The belted jacket accounted for 22 percent; it had three buttons and a half belt in the back and was seen mostly in gabardines and lightweight fabrics. The two-button jacket, which was favored by 17 percent, was similar to the three-button model except that it had wider lapels and much broader shoulders. Two- and three-button double-breasted jackets, which together accounted for 18 percent, showed broad shoulders, very wide lapels with a long roll, and buttons placed very low. Jackets with vents were favored by 56 percent of the Palm Beach socialites, and medium gray, blue, medium brown, blue-gray, light brown, and tan gabardine were the leading colors, in that order of preference. All-white flannel trousers, white flannels with stripes, and knickerbockers (of the same fabric as the sports jackets) were the most popular, with the flannel trousers preferred by 57 percent and the knickerbocker suit by 8 percent.

The unbridled prosperity of this decade was for some a cause for concern. One fashion reporter stopped off at Newport, Rhode Island, one of the most moneyed if not *the* most moneyed resort in the nation at the time, and came away disappointed, remarking, "I saw nothing worthy of special comment. The place is too filled with 'new money' and there is no display. 'New

money' is fearful of making mistakes in the stilted realms of that historic town, so it doesn't venture beyond its Te Deum for what is given" (*Men's Wear*, Aug. 6, 1924).

The same writer was alternately cheered and worried at the thought of the international polo match that would take place at Westbury, Long Island, early in the fall. He was certain it would be a fashion show, ". . . but how the crowds who will want to see the games are going to be accommodated I can't for the life of me appreciate. When 'the days' arrive there'll be a wonderful rush for seats, and mark me, they will bring any figure the speculators may ask for them. The original price was thirty dollars plus tax for the three games, but many of the seats, especially those in the main stand, and near the club enclosure where the Prince of Wales is to be, will bring a hundred dollars and probably more apiece for each day. Remember, old dears, the heir to the British Empire is to be there with all the grand seigniors of this America. If you are introduced to His Royal Highness, do not forget that it will not be necessary to address him as 'Sir' or stand in his presence, because he is coming incognito as Baron Renfrew, so you may meet him as you would any nice old dear. But regardless of this charming youth I feel sure that those three days of international polo will bring together the most brilliant displays of fashion in multitude that this country has ever known."

The influence of the Prince of Wales, incognito or otherwise, all but defied description. The yellow-haired heir to the throne was, with little or no effort at all, the greatest traveling salesman the British menswear industry had ever had. His visit to the United States in 1924 was front-page news, and photographers trailed him from the Long Island estates of America's wealthiest families, where he weekended, to the White House, where he lunched with President Calvin Coolidge—with detours to the races at Belmont Park and the polo matches at Meadowbrook. And wherever the Prince traveled, what he wore was a matter of deep interest. Before he had even stepped ashore, he was snapped on the bridge of the S.S. *Berengaria*, wearing a black-and-white glenurquhart jacket and cap, with gray flannel trousers. It was even considered news to report that the only article of jewelry worn by the Prince was a medium-size plain gold signet ring on the little finger of his left hand.

The royal visitor's fashion influence on American men was analyzed as follows in *Men's Wear* shortly after his arrival here: "More and more each day since the arrival of H.R.H. The Prince of Wales in this country has it become apparent that this young man is looked upon and accepted by the people of America as one of the most interesting human beings in the world today, and more numerous and more convincing are the evidences that he is the leader in the realm of fashion. It is quite true that there are many Englishmen—and perhaps a goodly number of Americans—who are just as well dressed as this captivating young heir to the British throne, but the significant fact is that there is no other single individual in all the universe whose clothes attract anything like as much consideration and admiration as his do. There is a genuine psychological appeal to almost everybody in the story of what the Prince of Wales does, what he says, where he goes and what he wears. Whether he is the best dressed man in the world or not is not exactly the point. The most important thing is that the average young man in America is more interested in the clothes of the Prince of Wales than in the clothes of any other individual on earth" (Sept. 10, 1924, p. 36).

Single-handedly, the Prince of Wales returned prosperity to depressed Fair Isle, off the Scottish coast, when he appeared on the golf links wearing one of the hand-knit sweaters made there. Almost overnight Fair Isle sweaters were selling in American shops for as much as $35 each, and the immense popularity of these sweaters focused attention on the Fair Isle tweeds, which, in 1924, were fast gaining popularity too. A golf jacket and plus fours made of Fair Isle tweeds formed a sporting outfit seen at the best English clubs and one that American fashion writers were predicting would be picked up by the affluent, pace-setting Americans. This jacket had a two-button front and a long rolling lapel, and was designed to be worn with trousers of the same material as well as to do double duty with the plus fours. The back, though quite plain and without a vent, had a great deal of width across the shoulders, while the plus fours were very loose and baggy and finished at the knee with a band and buckle.

Although the norfolk had lost ground with the mature man of fashion by the mid-twenties, the clothes-conscious collegian had discovered it as a separate sports jacket as well as a part of a suit, even if in many instances the term norfolk was used rather indiscriminately and the jacket in question simply had some of the features of the authentic norfolk, such as the box pleats down each side. In any event, the norfolk plus a penchant for Harris Tweed finally won the American college man over to the concept of the sports jacket, and from the mid-1920s on any collegian who fancied himself a sharp dresser would see to it that he had a wardrobe of sports jackets.

The British influence on American men's fashions steadily gained momentum during this decade. Reporting from Oxford, a *Men's Wear* fashion writer analyzed the Britisher's approach to his apparel: "Britishers do dress—as no other men in the world. A glance at the gorgeous creatures strolling in London's West End suffices to prove that. Like the honor of one's wife, attire is treated as a sacred thing, to be taken for granted, not to be discussed more lightly nor openly. An enterprising British tailor relates indignantly that American university students are allowing their photographs to be used in connection with clothing advertisements. Try to imagine a graduate of Oxford or Cambridge lending himself to the same purpose and you will mentally crystallize the psychology of two nations" (Dec. 1, 1926, p. 70).

During the summer of 1924 fashion reporters covering the Henley regatta were filing stories eagerly read by American manufacturers and retailers who looked to England for the upcoming trends that would be picked up by the more affluent Americans and then later by the mass market. They were told that the blazer was "a garment enjoying an extraordinary popularity in England this season," though the days of the old multistriped model were obviously numbered because smartly dressed British men were favoring their flannel jackets in more somber self-colors such as navy, golden brown, chocolate, indigo, and gray. The most popular model seen at the Henley regatta proved to be a double-breasted navy blue bound with white, carrying four buttons, long soft-rolling lapels, a plain back without a center seam, and either patch or welted pockets. This style owed much to the original blazer, a jacket first worn aboard the H.M.S. *Blazer*, a sailing vessel of the 1860s. The captain, noting that his men were a disreputable-looking lot, had ordered them to wear dark blue jackets on which were sewn the British Navy buttons. They were, as a result, uniformly dressed, and the captain felt their appearance had been vastly improved. Some years later this nautical jacket was adopted by British civilians in a slightly different form, but still dark blue with metal buttons, and it then became known as the blazer. Despite its lowly origin, the blazer worn with very loose white flannel trousers was a dashing though conservative outfit that had undeniable appeal for the wealthy American of the 1920s who, being extremely class-conscious, adopted it as yet another means visually to divorce himself from the masses.

By 1925, only a year later, the blazer vogue had spread to the West Coast. One fashion writer noted that the blazer was "spreading up and down the California coast like wildfire.

Oxford Model

In 1926 the allover tweed sports jacket with a belted and yoked back, four patch pockets, and a cap to match was worn with an odd pair of plus fours and argyle stockings.
[FASHION INSTITUTE OF TECHNOLOGY]

. . . Now it is fairly certain that the vogue has gained sufficient impetus to carry through the winter. Those in a knitted fabric of subdued coloring are popular, but the growing favorite is the flannel jacket in stripes of lively hue." One accompanying photograph taken at the Del Monte tennis tournament showed a prominent young tennis star garbed in a flannel blazer of purple and white, and another concentrated on a spectator who wore a blazer jacket of a closely knitted fabric in two shades of brown with biscuit flannel trousers.

A reporter covering the international tennis matches at Newport wrote that blazers were being worn extensively and that most were double-breasted, in navy blue, dark brown, or pastel shades, trimmed with brass or pearl buttons. Lapels on jackets were getting wider, and more men wearing sports jackets with side vents were observed. Some members of the visiting Oxford-Cambridge tennis team were sketched wearing tight-fitting double-breasted jackets, extremely wide flannel trousers, and cocoa-brown snap-brim hats. A survey of styles worn by 300 well-dressed men at Newport that summer of 1925, however, revealed that 46 percent still preferred the three-button single-breasted plain-back jacket. But the more avant-garde dressers of the younger set were beginning to adopt the double-breasted model worn by the English tennis team.

In 1926 among the outstanding items of interest at Palm Beach in men's apparel was the gabardine sports jacket. The following excerpt from a fashion report appearing in *Men's Wear* was filed from "the garden spot of the world": "Beyond any shadow of a doubt the gabardine sports jacket is going to be enormously popular throughout the entire United States. There is no doubt of this. Its increase here at Palm Beach on all types and classes of men from all parts of the United States is startling." The writer also noted: "Belted coats for sport have come back with a bang. And tan, of various shades, is the outstanding color for sports jackets as sure as I am a foot high. Plain tan, or tans with an overplaid, or tans with a pronounced pattern. But it is tan! tan! tan! and don't you forget it. I am speaking now of sports clothes other than the gabardine, which of course is also tan." To illustrate these fashion points, this report provided sketches of a socialite wearing a belted gabardine jacket with flannel trousers in a wide block stripe, including two back views of the jacket in order to show the variation of the pleats. At the end of the season the fancy-back gabardine jacket was just as popular as ever, with tweed and Shetland in second and third places respectively. The three types of backs of gabardine jackets seen at Palm Beach that winter were the bellows effect with seams; pivot shoulders with buttoned effects at the waist; and the belted back with bellows in back. It was also reported that fully 13 percent of all the single-breasted jackets observed were belted.

In 1928 *Men's Wear* once again surveyed Palm Beach as a center of fashion, reporting as follows:

"Palm Beach literally outdid itself this season, 'fashion-ly' speaking. More brilliant than ever before, this greatest American winter resort has furnished this year enough style ideas to keep the ambitious merchant and manufacturer busy for several months devising ways and means of converting them into cash. No longer need Palm Beach be called the American Lido, or Biarritz, or Deauville. Americans need no longer borrow those hitherto more dazzling names in describing a resort which outshines the best that the Old World has to offer. Palm Beach stands alone and in its own right as one of the world's greatest playgrounds for wealth, luxury, and the blue blood of this land.

"In order to be properly attired at the different sports and social functions which he attends, a man at Palm Beach must have at least five different types of apparel. Rivaled only by the brilliance of the social affairs and second in importance only to the ensemble is the great variety of color that had made its appearance this year in men's dress. Odd jackets for wear with flannels or parts of suits have become brighter in hue and more sporty in appearance.

"Second in importance to the color development is the more marked trend toward English style in and out of the garment and the sharper line that is part of the development. Also, the increase in the popularity of the double-breasted jacket must be carefully considered. Among the single-breasted jackets, two styles stand forth pre-eminent, one being the three-button jacket with peaked lapels. The other is the two- or three-button, single-breasted jacket with notched lapels of a stubby character, as made by many English tailors and some of the best Fifth Avenue tailors."

Concentrating on the sports jackets worn by these men of wealth, the writer was most impressed by the tremendous variety in colors, adding, however, that these colors were confined for the most part to flannel, with worsteds and tweeds having more somber tones:

"Off shades of blue and shades with a bluish cast will be in demand for summer wear. The standard dark blue that has been so long associated with jackets for wear with white flannels has been overshadowed by the brighter, gayer shades of blue. Blues that are as light as robin's egg blue were worn by well dressed men. Prussian blues, deep medium blues, and blues with a suggestion of purple were worn also. Blue grays were also in evidence to a small extent, and there were combinations of blue and brown.

"Next in importance were the brown shades. Many of these were of a rich cocoa shade with a tinge of red, and the shadings ran as far as a cream colored tan. While many browns were seen in the flannels, this color was confined for the most part to the tweeds and a few to worsteds.

"The fact that the plain grays still lead all other colors must not be lost sight of, however. This light color was the most popular in both worsteds and flannels.

"Green is the newest note for men's jackets, and was seen in all the materials that men use for their jackets with the exception of linen and similar materials. It was most popular in flannels, and gabardine was next in order. However, green will be sold only in small quantities during the coming season and the popular greens will be mixtures with other colors. A light grayish green was seen on the very best dressed men, and the Lovatt shades in general were those that the style leaders had accepted. These Lovatts are mixtures of green with neutral grays, blues, tans and browns. Pure green will not arrive as a color for men's suits until the greenish shades of other colors have established themselves, which will take at least a year to develop significantly, and will require

careful promotion of the authentic shades by men's wear organizations.

"For the manufacturer of sports wear it is interesting to note that several of the smartest dressed men were wearing white flannel jackets to match their trousers. White linen suits were also worn by some of the men, and linen in the natural shade was utilized in the odd jackets of some.

"Flannels form the bulk of the materials used in the jackets of these men of wealth and there has been an increase in this material over the percentage of last year. Patterns are entirely absent in this popular fabric. Worsteds also show a marked increase, and the new note is the predominance of sharkskin or pick and pick weaves. These are in black and white for the most part, although a few were seen in various shades of brown. The black and whites are combined to make all shades of gray, from a silver gray to a dark oxford shade, the most popular being the medium shades.

"The tweeds present the only patterns with the exception of the sharkskin worsted, and these are all faint. Small all-over diamond patterns predominate and it is interesting to note the similarity between these patterns and the neckwear patterns. A wave of small designs seems to have swept over men's wear of all sorts, including neckwear, tweeds, and golf hose. Even in the tweeds, however, the majority are in plain diagonal weaves or plain small herringbones.

"Gabardines have received a setback due to the increasing popularity of the flannels and worsteds, but this material is still worn by some of the smartest dressed men at Palm Beach.

"The question of the cut of jackets has been left until this point, since it is of secondary style importance to the jacket colors. The double-breasted jackets have increased in popularity over last year. The most popular of these is the American type with natural shoulders, but notice that the English styles with broader shoulders, when combined, outnumber the American style.

"In the single-breasted jackets the

American natural shoulder jackets are far more popular than the English jackets, but one of the most important styles is the three-button peaked lapel jacket. Second to this is the two-button American jacket of the type produced by the leading Fifth Avenue tailors. Particular attention should be given to the small notch of the lapels, the soft rolled front, and the natural wrinkles at the shoulders, indicating no padding and extra material to allow freedom of movement. The English peaked lapel jacket, in contrast to this, has the padded shoulders and a straighter line. These two are the jackets that will become popular in this country, and already have been selling well in some places."

Fashion photographs accompanying this impressive feature included those of a three-button double-breasted fine-striped flannel jacket with patch pockets and white pearl buttons, worn with white flannel trousers; a navy blue two-button jacket with notched lapels, worn with fine-striped white flannel trousers; a two-button light tweed jacket with patch pockets, worn with narrow-striped flannel trousers; and a three-button light gray flannel jacket, with white Shetland trousers.

The campus of Princeton University was rightly regarded as the site of some of the most fashionable young men in the country, many of whose fathers were among the best-dressed men wintering at Palm Beach. Therefore, no survey of collegiate fashion trends would be considered complete without polling the Princetonians, and often these impeccably garbed Ivy Leaguers constituted an entire fashion study by themselves, one to which aggressive retailers never failed to give full attention. One such report, appearing in *Men's Wear* in 1928, focused on the fashions Princetonians displayed at a house party weekend that began with a late Friday evening dinner, moved on next day to the Yale-Princeton polo match (where many of the sports enthusiasts made airplane flights while waiting for the match to begin), a Saturday night dinner dance, late Sunday breakfast, and an early dinner. The fashion report proved how quickly the Princeton men adopted the fashions of their elders, those American innovators who, in their turn, were adopting the fashions of their British counterparts. As a result, much of what was seen in Palm Beach only a matter of months before was now being worn at Princeton, although the Princeton man often took his summer vacation abroad and absorbed the British fashion influence firsthand.

The report began: "One of the significant features of this year's house parties, from the sartorial angle, was the greater individuality in dress of the students. One played a peaked lapel jacket, another a two-button jacket, a third a double-breasted jacket, still another the regulation three-button New Haven coat, and others belted back jackets. In addition to this distinctiveness of attire, the English influence was more evident than ever before.

"The newest style development this season is the belted back gabardine sports jacket. Although only six of these coats were seen during the entire weekend, the wearers were of the type who set the styles. In contrast with the tan gabardines of the men at Palm Beach, the prevailing color at Princeton is a shade of walnut brown. One of the students wore a belted back jacket of this color and had knickers to match.

"The acceptance of this gabardine style is undoubtedly due to the influence of brokers, bankers, and other business men who are fathers or friends of these men at Princeton, and who play golf at the most exclusive country clubs in the metropolitan district, spend their winters at Palm Beach, go to Newport, Southampton, or other resorts in the summer time, and are men of the world. They are the men who establish standards of dress for the country and recognition of this position is evidenced by the acceptance of the gabardine jacket by the Princeton students. This indicates that styles at Princeton are influenced to some extent by what is worn by the

alumni and successful men" (*Men's Wear,* Nov. 21, 1928).

Another example of this mature influence was the wearing of club blazers at Princeton, which, in turn, was yet another example of the British influence on the mature American man. The 1928 Princeton survey noted that the club men were wearing blazers of navy blue with brass buttons, having club insignia, piping, and club colors on the breast pocket. The report concluded with the observation that on weekends fewer knickers were worn, abandoned for flannel trousers.

Student pictures used to illustrate the Princeton study showed such outfits as a tan tweed jacket, an apple-green pullover, and white flannel trousers; and a belted-back, walnut-color gabardine jacket with matching knickers and solid-color golf hose. In this category of fancy-back jackets, one of the most popular was a combination of a puckered yoke and belted back on a ventless jacket. The effect was one of ripples below the yoke and above the belt, thus giving the wearer more ease of motion. This style was equally at home with matching trousers and with knickerbockers.

By 1928, a fashion survey of sportswear worn by college men throughout the nation revealed Harris Tweed to be a favorite fabric. "A good many of the students are wearing jackets in Harris tweeds, gabardine and shetland," the survey showed. "These usually have belted backs and patch pockets. The newest style, the chamois jacket with three-button front and belted back, has been taken up by a limited number of Yale students and it is believed that this style will spread.

"One of the most interesting sportswear developments in the south is the odd Harris tweed jacket at the University of Virginia. One of the leading firms there is showing an English importation, a single-breasted Harris tweed jacket with three buttons set rather close together and a small notched lapel. The popularity of this jacket at this southern style center may have an early effect at other southern institutions.

"Under the heading of sportswear come leather jackets, which are quite popular with students attending middle western universities, and at Illinois the vogue for the corduroy jacket continues. Retailers at Champaign, Illinois, are selling extremely short, heavy wool jackets in navy blue. Suede jackets in tobacco brown and light grey were popular at the University of California" (*Men's Wear,* Nov. 21, 1928, p. 71).

Fashion illustrations accompanying this report showed a chamois jacket with a belted back worn with a crewneck pullover and a felt hat; and a Harris Tweed knicker suit of a light brown checked tweed.

Now that sportswear had finally arrived and was being accepted by the most fashion-conscious men in America, comfort rapidly became a main factor in the cut of every garment and even in sports shoes. As a fashion reporter noted in a 1928 report on fashionable dress for country and golf, "Natural shoulders with an indicated waistline, softness of fronts and that tendency for drape confront us in every jacket, plain or belted. The slacks and knickers express the same ease, and in the shoes, whatever their fashion, an obvious breadth in width of toe is to be seen that is not a part of more formal footwear."

In the winter of 1929 President-elect Herbert Hoover visited Palm Beach just before his inauguration, and though he received a respectable amount of attention from the nation's press, insofar as the fashion writers were concerned he was virtually nonexistent among the Palm Beach regulars in their bright plumage.

"The acme of perfection in fit, comfort and style is especially noticeable in the odd jackets worn by these wealthy men," wrote one reporter, surveying the scene at the beautiful Bath and Tennis Club. "Although they are all the same in their luxuriousness, they all have enough individuality to give them that indefinable something known as 'style.'

"What trends will be seen spreading from Palm Beach to Main Street?

"In the first place with regard to jacket models, there are two exceptionally outstanding points in the prevalence of the belted back, and in the return to society of the longer jacket with the vent. Last year approximately four-fifths of the single-breasted jackets had plain backs, while this year, the percentages show three-fifths in the opposite direction." And to demonstrate this point, there was an accompanying illustration of a jacket whose back fullness was achieved by small tucks and pleats.

With regard to the longer jacket, the writer reported: "As long as the masses of men in this country are wearing short jackets, it is natural that the leaders of fashion should take up longer models. The cream of Palm Beach's social and sartorial dictators have dropped the shorter type and have adopted jackets ranging in the neighborhood of thirty or thirty-one inches in length, according to their height. These jackets are shapely and have a flare over the hips."

While gray was the leading sports jacket color, accounting for 26 percent of those glimpsed at the Bath and Tennis Club, brown jackets had more than doubled in number over the past year and now accounted for 25 percent of the jackets. Rich tones of deep, pure brown, such as tobacco and chocolate, were preferred. Tan accounted for 20 percent of the jackets worn at Palm Beach, while blue had dropped off slightly, and hardly any smartly dressed men were seen wearing the conventional navy blue.

Flannel, long the most popular jacket fabric, moved to second place, and tweeds and Shetlands became the favorite. "This increase," noted the fashion writer, "goes hand in hand with the increase in browns, for a great many of them are of this color. In contrast to the Fair Isle type of tweeds of a few years ago, those worn this year are of small diamonds and modest designs."

Mindful of retailing interest in the Palm Beach scene, the writer ended his report with a few pungent predictions: "With an increase in belted back jackets, it was only natural to expect a like growth in popularity of gabardine. This fabric should be a big seller for summer wear. The best shades are plain light tan, reddish tan, greenish tan, bluish grey and walnut. Cream color silks are also worn with these belted back jackets.

"A style that will have mass popularity, in the light of observations made in Florida during this past season, is the camel's hair sports jacket. These jackets come in natural tan shade and follow the other single-breasted garments in having a belted back.

"Play up these sports jackets. It is a big field, and has been grossly overlooked by retailers throughout the country. There are huge profits that have not been exploited to their fullest possibilities. The average man needs at least one sports jacket for his summer wear, and you can sell that one or more to him by promoting them with the proper style appeal. Tell him that Palm Beach men wore more sports jackets this year, and that there are fewer suit jackets worn with flannel trousers than ever before. This foreshadows a tremendous national popularity and a record breaking sportswear business—if you promote it intelligently!" To the reporter this meant featuring sportswear as "THE LATEST FROM PALM BEACH, thereby getting the men to come to your shop and setting yourself up as an authentic style leader."

All this business advice seemed sound, but one factor was unaccounted for: the Depression that was to rumble across the nation following the crash of the stock market in October, 1929. Neither the reporter hero-worshiping the rich Palm Beachers nor the rich Palm Beachers worshiping the tropical sunshine were prepared for that considerable inconvenience.

1930–1940

The economic depression wiped out many great fortunes, but Palm Beach, which had survived a hurricane only a few years earlier, also managed to survive the economic squeeze without sacrificing any of its panache. "This fount of perpetual youth," as one writer called it, was, in 1931, still the most fashionable American winter resort. It appeared, in fact, that the Depression had worked to its advantage, sweeping out the "new money" and putting control back into the hands of the "old money."

"Conditions this year," wrote a reporter as the season neared its conclusion, "were not the same as they were during that fantastic era two years ago, when getting a new motor car, yacht, or even a home merely meant placing an order for a good-sized block of a favorite stock and selling it a few days later. Anyone who did not know Palm Beach in those days would still be impressed with the extravagance this season. Persons who have always had money still have big bank accounts and are entertaining very elaborately. One retired banker maintains his place, as in former seasons, with a skeleton force of 34 servants and an additional crew for big luncheons and dinner parties. There are many others in a similar position. It will take more than fluctuations in security prices to interfere with the pleasures of the real set, which has been escaping the snow and slush of northern winters and basking in the tropical sun for years.

"There is still a lot of money in circulation at this resort. It seemed there were never as many smart automobiles as were seen speeding up and down County Road this year. Specially built foreign and domestic motors with new color schemes were about as plentiful as dented fenders on Sunrise Highway. Anyone looking for new ideas in cars could have found as many in Palm Beach as in any other part of the country.

"The same holds true for anyone in search of new sartorial style trends. For a fashion to get a right start, it must first be seen worn by the right persons. After that it is only a matter of time until it spreads to wider circles. General business conditions this year did the work of the thresher by eliminating the chaff, or men who do not count

Two sports jackets for weekend wear in 1936: (left) a diamond-pattern Shetland, worn with a foulard muffler; (right) a dark green flannel blazer with club insignia on the chest pocket, worn with a silk foulard neckerchief. Both were combined with plain flannel slacks. From Esquire, *July 1936.*

A campus civilian fashion during World War II consisted of a striped Shetland jacket in blue, brown, and gray and tapered gray flannel slacks. From Esquire, *January 1943.*

Mr. T's sports jacket was a three-button mid-tone brown tweed, worn with a metal-buttoned tartan waistcoat. From Esquire, *November 1950.*

A double-breasted blue blazer with long roll lapels was combined with a tan turtleneck pullover and tan slacks in 1969.

Sports Jackets

Mr. "T"
Esquire's New Trim Look takes to the Turf

There's a race or two left at Belmont, then the United Hunt Meet, and a month of running at Jamaica. Or if you prefer the sound of cleats to horseshoes, there's football in the air everywhere. Mr. T's Turf wardrobe is designed to have you on the right track for any fall sporting event. If the weather's living up to tradition around Indian Summer, you'll be best dressed in the outfit at the left. Our man wears a tapered crown pork-pie hat, black band for contrast in tan felt. His jacket is a Mid-tone brown tweed, three-button, single-chested with center vent. Authentic Scottish Tartan waistcoat has metal buttons. Brown foulard tie with shield design arranged in that tall, Mr. T, terraced pattern. Rounded collar shirt is held

in the sartorial scheme of things, and leaving the kernels, or men of established positions in finance and society. Styles first favored by this last-mentioned group in previous years later became popular with the proletariat with a high degree of regularity. And now this set is leading the way to adopting new ideas in warm weather apparel" (*Men's Wear,* April, 1931).

A survey of Palm Beach fashions that season showed gray to be the leading sports jacket color, with grayish green, green, and bluish gray also prominent. (A particularly outstanding outfit was a gray sports jacket

Two examples of patterns in sports outfits of 1934. The standing figure combines a checked tweed jacket having bellows pockets with solid-color slacks, while the seated man brings together overcheck slacks and a solid-color wool jacket with bellows pockets, two pleats at the shoulder seams, and a center vent.
[HART, SCHAFFNER & MARX]

of flannel or Shetland worn with biscuit-color flannel slacks.) White jackets in linen, flannel, and Shetland were also popular; not surprisingly, a year later the white sports jacket was taken up by other fashion-conscious though somewhat less affluent Americans. There was a rise in the percentage of men wearing double-breasted jackets as well as in the proportion of men wearing single-breasted jackets with belted or fancy backs of some kind. Vented jackets were seen in considerable numbers, and some of the jackets tended toward greater length.

A review of the Palm Beach scene never failed to make the Depression seem a boorish intruder, yet often a trade paper made practical use of the extravagant tastes of the Palm Beach habitués. In 1931, for instance, a *Men's Wear* writer credited the men seen on the patio of the Bath and Tennis Club with making the American public more and more sportswear-conscious, and he urged retailers to merchandise the Palm Beach look to the maximum: "The men who set the styles for a good portion of the male population in this country have given their approval to this idea of greater variety in sporting clothes. Now, if you are able to sell two or three pairs of flannel trousers or other articles to customers who ordinarily buy only one, you can increase the volume of your business. These extra garment sales are a source of enlarged revenue. To make a customer buy additional articles of sports apparel, and in turn have a larger total at the bottom of the sales check, the salesman has to present intelligent reasons. One method of developing this end of the business is to stress the advantages of having more than one jacket, pair of trousers or pair of shoes.

"Two odd jackets and three pairs of flannel trousers may be assembled into six different ensembles. For example, if the jackets are grey and brown and the trousers are plain white, grey and biscuit, the wearer has a variety of mixed suits. The three pairs of trousers are correct for wear with either of the jackets. By adding one or two pairs of

narrow striped trousers it is possible to give greater variation to the outfits. By coordinating the window displays, promotion matter and sales effort along this line, it is highly possible that interest in sports apparel will be stimulated and sales increased. This idea applies not only to jackets and trousers, but to shoes, hats, neckwear, shirts and accessories as well" (Apr. 8, 1931, p. 52).

For prime examples of the results to be gained by this mixing of colors and fabrics, the writer turned to some of the outfits photographed at Palm Beach that season:

With grey jackets. Grey is one of the most popular jacket colors . . .
Grey flannel jacket, pink and white striped shirt with tab collar, grey and blue figured tie, grey striped trousers and white buckskin shoes.
With blue jackets. There has been an increase in the number of bright blue jackets seen at this famous southern spa this season . . .
Blue vicuna jacket, white oxford shirt with button-down collar, red, green and black figured foulard tie, grey flannel trousers and black and white saddle strap shoes.
With tan jackets. Tan continues to be an important color for sports jackets . . .
Tan gabardine jacket, cream color shirt with a pinned collar, red and grey figured foulard tie, grey flannel trousers and brown and white straight tip shoes.
With brown jackets. Brown jackets are expected to have widespread consumer acceptance this season . . .
Brown Glen Urquhart tweed jacket, cream color shirt with pinned collar, green and white figured tie, white trousers and white straight tip shoes.
Blue-grey jacket ensembles. Another smart shade in jackets is bluish grey, which is becoming to most men . . .
Blue-grey shetland jacket, green chambray shirt with pinned collar, yellow and blue striped tie, light bluish grey trousers and all-white buckskin shoes.
Greenish jacket combinations. Greenish cast jackets were more popular this season . . .
Green flannel jacket, blue and white shirt with pinned collar, red, green and white figured linen tie, greyish green trousers and brown buckskin shoes.
The white jacket. White is much worn in linen, flannel and shetland jackets and suits . . .
White shetland jacket, white oxford shirt, red, black and white figured cotton

tie, chamois color trousers and white buckskin shoes.

By 1932 white as a color for sports jackets had become a strong fashion and was particularly popular for wear with dark or brightly colored slacks—a fashion that was to retain its popularity for the remainder of the decade. In 1932 a double-breasted white linen jacket worn with brown linen slacks was a combination often photographed at smart resorts. In 1937 it was a lightweight white linen norfolk jacket with an all-around belt, worn with yellow beach slacks. And in 1939 white still reigned, in a double-breasted, brass-buttoned white cotton blazer worn with cabana-red beach slacks.

The English drape jacket had come to the fore by 1932 and was already reported to be selling best in the higher-price range. It was quickly adapted to topcoats and overcoats as well as the popular belted-back sports jackets. Despite its quick acceptance by the more affluent set, before the English drape style could trickle down the social scale to the so-called man in the street, who despite the Depression just might have the price of a suit or sports jacket, it would have to overcome a certain amount of sales resistance. After all, for years the American man had been conditioned to expect smooth-fitting clothes, and now here was a high waisted style that actually had wrinkles—between the shoulder points and collar and at the sleeve head. It was enough to induce Simon Ackerman to run an advertisement that offered the customer three versions of this style (*Men's Wear*, Apr. 20, 1932):

ABOUT THE "DRAPE" MODEL

The Drape Model, of English origin, has arrived. The authentic model calls for a snug-looking but easy-fitting garment. The whole garment must have a soft, comfortable appearance.

Hand tailoring is vital to the correct expression of this model. Only sensitive human hands can stitch the necessary combination of drape and mould. Our suits are "hand-tailored" and are clearly marked as such. We use that term in its strictest sense. We are not just tossing the words around.

You will find three versions of the Drape Model on view in our stores.

Every type of garment is produced in all proportions, so that no matter what your size, we can accurately fit you.

Apparently every retailer promoting the English drape style realized he had certain psychological blocks to overcome and evolved his own technique for dealing with them. One West Coast retailer, for example, insisted that the customer stand about 25 feet from the mirror in order to get the overall effect before scrutinizing the artfully planned wrinkles.

Depression-squeezed retailers seized upon the new style and aggressively promoted it. When Macy's department store in New York took it up, there was no question but that the English drape had achieved mass appeal. In fact, competition was rife between various factions, each claiming to have been the first to introduce this British style to these shores. *Men's Wear* wrote: "An interesting phase in the development of the English drape this spring is the apparent jealousy that has been aroused among both retailers and manufacturers. Some merchants are so insistent in their claims to be the first to have shown this model that they are willing to fight in defense of such claims. Counter claims and contradictions, charges and challenges are flying right and left in this little battle to settle the question as to who was the first to display this style or to advertise it or to sell it. It perhaps makes no difference who rightfully deserves this credit; the fact remains that this controversy is helping materially to establish the English drape style on the market" (Apr. 20, 1932, p. 42).

In 1933, despite the growing rate of unemployment, winter resorts still flourished and the man of means was as clothes-conscious as ever. The following excerpt from *Men's Wear* shows the optimism which the writer was attempting to pump back into a deflated industry:

"Sailfish in the Gulf Stream, turquoise blue water and sunbaked sands along Florida's famous shores, the rolling green fairways of California's seaside golf courses, and festive social affairs in the tropics, are but a few of the things that lure the fashionables to warmer climes at this time of the year, and prior to a sojourn in either of these far-famed resort centers, the well dressed cosmopolitan man pays a visit to his tailor, shirtmaker, bootmaker and other outfitters, to make sure that his wardrobe is in 'resort-shape.' New York shops catering to this class of trade report that customers are not nearly as numerous as they were in '29. Yet there are still many men whose preferences for certain styles or niceties in attire distinguish them from the 'pack,' and interviews with some of these leading outfitters reveal that their customers are still at the head of the fashion procession, purchasing things that will be the cynosure of all eyes in February at such places as Palm Beach, Miami and some of the Pacific resorts" (Jan. 25, 1933, p. 26).

And in this Depression year of 1933, what was the man who was affluent enough to afford a vacation at a top-notch winter resort buying? Very likely an English drape sports jacket of Shetland or tweed, single-breasted and belted, or an adaptation of a norfolk jacket in a houndstooth check, with an all-around belt and box pleats at the pockets. (Belted models were popular that year.)

In the spring of 1934 trade reporters were looking ahead to a fall when business might be "merry and bright." One writer felt that there was much glamour in the new styles, noting that belts, buttons, gadgets, pleats—boxed and inverted—and easy swing backs were "the rule rather than the exception in jackets, topcoats, and overcoats. The merchandise is attractive to the eye. It has pep and zip and go and punch. The reviewing buyer will feel his mouth begin to water when he considers the exploitation possibilities that are presented to him" (*Men's Wear*, May 23, 1934, p. 30).

The double-breasted sports jacket of 1934 was either a separate sports jacket or the jacket of a suit. The tan jacket sketched here may have been gabardine, flannel, or shantung for wear with pale gray flannel slacks. From Esquire, *June 1934.*

Peering ahead into the uncertainty of a future still clouded by the Depression, the trade press was nevertheless positive and optimistic:

"A decided tendency toward longer jackets is apparent. Vents are being used more frequently. The sway is away from excessively broad shoulders to more natural widths. Details like the taper of sleeves are being given more attention. Soft-fronted jackets are fast replacing the stiff, boardy variety. Double-breasteds continue strong. The belt-pleat influence of sports jackets is making itself felt in top and overcoat models. These are the highlights in the model situation for Fall.

"What with the pleats, belts and bellows pockets, loud huzzahs should begin to rise from the camp of the piece goods men before many blue moons have passed, for all of this belting and pleating and bellowsing means more cloth per garment. And a great many of these jackets that are not pleated and belted are double-breasted, some lines even containing jackets that are both double-breasted and belted.

"The problem becomes one of selection of best-sellers. Many and varied are the models that pass before the eyes of the buyer as he scans the lines before making his commitments. A number that continues to have a magnetic effect on the merchant is the belted back style with bellows shoulders. This jacket, measuring about 29 inches in length, is two-buttoned and has medium width notched lapels. The shoulders are unpadded and the sleeves, full at the head, taper to medium width cuffs. The back has a stitched-on belt placed right at the waistline, with four tucks above and none below. The deep bellows pleats at the sides extend from the belt to the shoulder seams. A vent from the belt to the bottom of the jacket has the practical advantage of making this a comfortable jacket. There is a choice of plain or leather buttons for this type jacket and more and more of the latter are being used. Another idea in the way of fancy back jackets has all the features of that described above but also has a yoke shoulder with four tucks below the yoke. This gives the back of the jacket an abundance of cloth with consequent freedom of movements. Both of these jackets are of soft construction throughout the fore part and have inside pockets for cigarettes, etc. The patch pockets have flaps.

"A plain-back sports jacket, designed to appeal to merchants seeking new style thoughts to augment their stocks of belted back models, has a three-button front which is soft and pliable. The notched lapels are of medium width and the bottom of the coat is cut away slightly in front. The medium width shoulders are finished with two tucks at the shoulder seams. Buttons of horn, a six-inch vent on each side and a change pocket are distinctive features. This garment, while decidedly of high-style inspiration, should capture the fancy of the young man who wants something 'different.'

"In plain back, single-breasted jackets, the so-called Brooks type is contained in many lines. This is a three-button model with short notched

The biswing belted-back jacket of 1934 allowed free action. It appeared mainly in Palm Beach cloth, linen, and other fabrics in a natural tan shade with a pair of gray flannel slacks. From Esquire, *July 1934.*

lows pockets. Washable jackets appeared here and there. White linen was the usual choice, in either single or double-breasted, the former with belted back. Very smart and cool looking were ecru colored shantungs" (*Men's Wear,* June 20, 1934, p. 20).

Brown proved to be the favored sports jacket color that autumn, and tweeds were extremely popular. In the cheering section at a big football game in the East, a fashion photographer observed more tweed suits and odd tweed jackets than he had seen for some time. *Esquire* fashion pages showed a brown single-breasted Shetland jacket, in a diamond pattern with leather buttons and bellows pockets, worn with black-and-white herringbone tweed slacks; a single-breasted tweed Shetland jacket with a longer center vent, worn with narrow cavalry twill trousers; and a two-button tan

The combination of a brown jacket and gray slacks, which originated in Oxford and Cambridge in 1930, had grown in importance by 1931. Shown here is a brown Shetland jacket with an overplaid and side vents, worn with gray flannel slacks. From Esquire, *October 1934.*

lapels. The shoulders are medium width and the body of the jacket tends toward straight lines. Measuring $29\frac{1}{2}$ inches, the back has a six-inch center vent. A soft, pliable front is the outstanding characteristic of this hardy perennial" (*Men's Wear,* May 23, 1934, p. 31).

It is significant to note that, as early as June 1 that year, socialites at the United Hunts Meet on Long Island were in fact offering a preview of the styles predicted for the fall. "In and out of the betting ring strolled one after another of Long Island's wealthy sportsmen wearing checked Shetland or tweed jackets many of which were

made up in three-button, plain back models, some with center vents, others side-vented." Fashion reporters at the meet also noted an abundance of gabardine jackets, with tan the favorite color and reddish tan in second place. Despite the appearance of the new plain models, belted-back jackets were still numerous, some with bellows pleats and others with inverted center pleats between the yoke and belt. "One of the newest and smartest models seen in gabardine had a row of vertical seams spaced about an inch and a half apart across the shoulders and another row at the waistline. It was finished with side vents and had inverted bel-

linen jacket with a belted back, center vent, and biswing pleat, worn with blue-gray flannel trousers—an outfit, the editors claimed, a man could wear morning, noon, and night at a summer resort, for all but formal evening occasions.

With all the interest being shown in belted jackets, the norfolk attained a fresh spurt of popularity. As early as 1933 some trade writers were expressing great optimism about its possibilities, and in discussing it managed to give a version of its pedigree too:

"Mentioning a Norfolk jacket to most persons in the clothing industry brings to mind a very definite style, a jacket with an all-around belt, two long vertical box pleats in front and a single box pleat down the middle of the back. However, to a good many others the Norfolk means any style of jacket with a half- or all-around belt. The model with the box pleats and all-around belt was originally, and still is, used quite extensively for shooting. According to sources considered reliable, Coke of Norfolk, Earl of Leicester, had something to do with introducing this style of garment. On his 43,000 acre estate in Norfolk, England, containing many beats where the Prince of Wales, later King George IV, and other members of nobility were invited to shoot partridge and other game birds, he and some of the peers adopted the belted jacket with box pleats and very large patch pockets. The reason that these men liked a belt was that it made the jacket fit snugly at the waist and kept the cold air out. Fashion plates of many decades ago show both the model with the single box pleat in back and the one with two box pleats were worn. This type of jacket is called the Norfolk because it was first worn in the Norfolk district in England."

Since its inception there have been many variations of the authentic norfolk jacket. For instance, in the thirties one prominent New York tailor made a norfolk with two box pleats in front and one in back but added a yoke in front and back. The sleeves of this jacket had buttons and cut-through buttonholes so that they could be rolled back. In common with all norfolk jackets, this model had vertical chest pockets under each pleat.

Keen observers of young fashions as seen on the style-conscious campus of Princeton University were quick to note a small but promising number of norfolk jackets in Harris Tweed, and one New Haven retailer said he thought he would sell more norfolks that spring than he had during any recent season. Less optimistic retailers regarded the stylish norfolk as a means of selling both suits and odd jackets of this type on a style basis. As it turned out, the norfolk did gain a respectable amount of popularity, and early in 1934 *Esquire* recommended for cruise and Southern fashions a natural linen norfolk—a style that was to remain popular for the next several seasons—and, for winter sports, a semi-norfolk jacket of a heavy gray tweed.

Despite the tendency of the best-dressed men to prefer a plain-back

The heavy tweed jacket in a blue-and-gray glenurquhart plaid was taken up by Eastern sportsmen in 1935 in combination with a blue turtleneck sweater and gray flannel slacks. From Esquire, *March 1935.*

sports jacket, the fancy back retained its leadership in 1935 for the second year. "Considered from the viewpoint of mass distribution, the second year is always the biggest for any given style, and this is going to hold true for fancy back jackets," one trade publication had accurately predicted in the fall of 1934.

The shirred-back jacket, with one piece of material between the yoke and belt and a long vent, was the biggest-selling style. Shops carrying clothing in the top price brackets were expected to make a stronger feature of the plainer types of models, but ever since the film star Clark Gable had walked across the screen wearing a shirred-back jacket, this style was on its way to becoming an all-time best seller. For this was the fashion heyday of the Hollywood personality, a fact celebrated in print by *Apparel Arts* in the winter of 1938–1939 in an article titled "The Hollywood Halo." Illustrated with photographs of such screen luminaries as Gable, Gary Cooper, Cary Grant, Robert Taylor, and Errol Flynn, the article called them "the Pied Pipers of Hollywood who play a pleasant tune for their fun-loving followers—and there's business along the path they pursue. The duration of their dynasty no one dares predict." World War II took most of Hollywood's pied pipers out of their shirred-back jackets and put them into khaki or navy blue, but while it lasted, the fashion influence of the handsome, well-tailored Hollywood leading man was a factor to be reckoned with. It helped to bring California style into every city and town in the country.

By the mid-1930s many sports jackets showed the influence of riding-clothes styling through extreme fullness at the shoulder blades on each side, slanting flap pockets, 10-inch side vents, and a noticeable flare to the skirt. This was a London innovation, and *Esquire,* aware of its acceptance by the majority of the best American tailors, sketched this model in a checked tweed, accessorizing it with a ribbed turtleneck sweater and a checked cap. This jacket was a veritable masterpiece of freedom and comfort, a forerunner of the roomy, comfortable sports jacket that was to evolve within the next few years.

Retail-clothing merchants of the Depression period were desperate, hence more than willing to try anything to stimulate business. *Apparel Arts* reminded them of the new opportunities the winter migrations to Southern and Northern resorts offered for "*suggestive selling,*" based on the practice of merchandising for the occasion. "Selling for the occasion is an art and a science," wrote the editor, "and selling for the occasion is an opportunity frequently neglected and often muffed by the otherwise shrewd and wide awake merchant. It is important, therefore, for the merchant and sales staff to know something about the occasions for which they are selling apparel. The clever salesman, of course, will not stop there. He will use his knowledge to suggest items of apparel in keeping with the various climates, environments, social activities, and sports which will be met with during the vacation" (vol. 5, no. 2, 1934).

The clever salesman would know that Palm Beach, for example, was "ablaze with blazers," as a *Men's Wear* fashion reporter declared. In what he termed a "Southern garden of fashion . . . a man-made paradise," this reporter considered the spontaneous revival of the flannel blazer to be the biggest style development in clothing during the 1935 season. "Absent from the well dressed man's wardrobe for many years, the blazer has again become fashionable at Palm Beach. Every one seen is in a solid shade. French and royal blues and a dark brown are the three most favored colors. The two-button double-breasted model is a trifle more popular than the two-button, notch lapel, single-breasted. Both have plain ventless backs and brass buttons are used more frequently than white pearl. With the blue blazers pale blue trousers are usually worn. Pale beige trousers have the same contrasting, yet harmonizing, effect with the brown

(*left*) *A sports jacket of black-and-brown glen plaid with an overplaid sets off a brown suede postboy waistcoat; the gray slacks serve as a neutralizer. From* Esquire, *September 1935.*

flannel blazer. The other choice is grey flannel for slacks, which is worn with any of the blazers. This sportswear ensemble is going to be taken up quite generally this coming season, just as many other styles in the past which have appeared first at Palm Beach have spread throughout the country. Plans should be made immediately for selling these blazers" (Mar. 20, 1935, p. 23).

And they were. For the remainder of this decade, the blazer jacket remained extremely popular. *Esquire* suggested a dark flannel single-breasted blazer with white flannel trousers as the ideal outfit for weekending in the country—appropriate

By 1938 the plain-back sports jacket had replaced the fancy-back in popularity. That summer colorful Shetland jackets with center vents and solid-color flannel blazers without vents were being worn by most of the well-dressed socialites vacationing at fashionable Southampton, Long Island.

In fact, the classic single-breasted Shetland jacket, which had been popular for about twenty years, adapted perfectly to the new trend toward easy, natural styling. In the same styling was *Esquire*'s fashion of the month for July: a single-breasted lightweight Palm Beach jacket in a deep hemp color, with a plain back, patch pockets, and nickel buttons. The only fancy backs seen that summer were in tan gabardine. Sports jackets for the fall were longer (30 inches), full-chested, plain-back, easy-fitting models. Taking a long look at the back-to-college wardrobes of the well-dressed young men that year, *Esquire*'s O. E. Schoeffler commented that the four-button jacket, after an absence of many years, was being seen everywhere, adding that "the last time there was a run on four-button jackets, more than a decade ago, they succeeded the three-button model. And at the moment, almost everything is three-button, with a plain back." The sturdy cavalry twill covert, the latest fabric added to the undergraduate's wardrobe at Yale and Princeton that semester, was seen in both slacks and sports jackets, with olive tan the favorite color. But no matter what the fabric, sports jackets were of simple lines, roomy and comfortable.

The following year the fashion leaders at Princeton University were sporting the four-button sports jacket with slanting flap pockets and flapped breast pocket. Made of all types of tweeds—Shetlands, Harris, and Irish homespun—this revival of an old college fashion, when worn with a striped silk crochet tie or ribbon-shaped bow tie, oxford button-down shirt, flannel slacks, and wing-tip brogues, became a uniform for many of the well-dressed men at the leading Eastern universities.

(left) Leather patches at the elbows of a sports jacket served primarily to prevent the wearing away of the fabric. With the gun pad at the shoulder, they set a fashion in 1938. The Irish tweed jacket was combined with covert cloth slacks. From Esquire, *September 1938.*

for standing around the perimeter of a tennis court or coming down to the breakfast table; a single-breasted notched-lapel blazer of boldly striped terry cloth with a matching muffler, worn with light blue beach slacks, for relaxing at Eden Roc at Cap d'Antibes, "one of the world's most fashionable swimming holes"; and a double-breasted dark blue flannel blazer with brass buttons, worn with cream-color gabardine shorts, for lounging around a beach club in the Bahamas.

A country note as of 1939. The jacket, in a basket-weave Shetland that has a self-check effect, was made with a three-button front, a flap on the chest pocket, and a deep center vent in back. With it were worn corduroy breeks, crepe-sole chukka shoes, a flannel tattersall-check shirt, and a cashmere tie. From Esquire, *April 1939.*

Toward the end of the decade Palm Springs, a new and exciting desert resort, firmly established itself as if to celebrate the fading away of the economic depression that had gripped the nation for so many years. "The whole atmosphere is geared to throw troubles to the wind," wrote one reporter. "In such a setting it is natural that those who cater to the clothes ideas, idiosyncrasies and needs of the visitors must catch the spirit of the resort." Early-season business at Palm Springs in 1938 was reported at 25 percent above the same period the preceding year. Two of the resort's most sumptuous hotels, the Desert Inn and El Mirador, opened in the fall. Suede and chamois jackets, ideal for the cold desert evenings, were sold in soft, languorous colors indigenous to the desert atmosphere. Other widely popular sports jackets included a stylized navy pea jacket of fine-quality rayon pile, worn

with flannel, linen, or gabardine slacks; and a collarless linen jacket with tucks in the back to give it a semifitted appearance. The colorful and highly distinctive fashions created for and seen in Palm Springs, often on the person of a famous film star, gave the already justly famous California look added appeal.

As sports clothes became increasingly casual and comfortable, it was only natural that the convenience of the so-called wash fabrics for summer should arrive before the end of this decade. Summer sports fabrics for 1939 were reviewed as "the most attractive ever shown. Mills and converters have developed colors that might have been snatched from a gor-

This loud plaid for jackets made a lasting impression on the undergraduates of Eastern universities in 1939. The classic Prince of Wales plaid, it had red-and-white checks with blue plaid border lines. The three-button jacket, worn with the two top buttons fastened, had side vents. With it were worn gray flannel slacks, wool socks in the Prince of Wales plaid, and brown reversed-calf shoes. From Esquire, *September 1939.*

geous Mediterranean sunset or lifted from delicate shadings in a limpid mountain lake and applied them to the most diversified aggregation of 'wash' fabrics for men's wear ever to have been presented to a public grown definitely more sportswear-, summer-wear-, color- and comfort-conscious than in any previously recorded period in sartorial history" (*Men's Wear*, Jan. 11, 1939).

While all these cloths could be classified as wash fabrics, the constructions ranged from an all-cotton fabric on through blends of cotton and rayon; cotton and worsted; and cotton, rayon, and worsted. The "miracle" synthetics were years away, and in war-clouded 1939 these wash fabrics were a singular bit of optimistic fashion news.

1940–1950

America had no sooner emerged from the Depression when it was face to face with another war. Understandably enough the average man, who finally had some spare money in his pocket, was not in a mood to dress up. When he went shopping, he moved toward more conservative-looking clothes. And when it came to sports clothes, ease and informality were the keynotes.

Shetland and tweed proved more popular than ever. While the four-button single-breasted jacket with elbow pads and long side vents was still being seen, the three-button notched-lapel model was the favorite; more often than not it was worn with a pair of natural covert cloth slacks that reflected the new military influence. Nowhere was this influence more apparent than on college campuses, where striped Shetland jackets, in the words of *Esquire*, loomed "as heir apparent to plaids." All shades of tan were popular, and even the porkpie hat of the undergraduate was now usually khaki-color. (The varsity cap was often in a fawn or dune color.) Gabardine suits and sports jackets were still popular since they fitted so well into the smart but relatively inconspicuous fashion picture that

In 1940 striped Shetland jackets loomed as successors to plaid jackets. The one at left, in three shades of brown stripings, was combined with covert cloth slacks and saddle-strap shoes. From Esquire, May 1940.

added up to standard good taste. Even the button-down shirt was most often in a tan or ivory color.

In the summer of 1940 the newest men's fashion color was called sandune, a fashion find of the Southern resort season. One of the main features of this new and neutral shade was its affinity for practically any color, a point *Esquire* proved by outfitting a model in a pair of sandune slacks and a green-checked lightweight two-button Shetland jacket with soft, long-rolling lapels. This outfit was topped with a greenish-tone hemp hat with a blue puggaree band for an ultracasual look, and *Esquire* assured its readers that the washable sandune slacks would go equally well with a blue, brown, gray, or tan sports jacket. The editors also asked the reader to

notice the length of the jacket, which was "indicative of the current and rather pronounced trend toward long jackets." It was as though the man living in the shadow of military service was unconsciously doing his best to look natty but not too conspicuous.

The War Production Board (WPB) regulations of 1942 served to emphasize this dressed-down look by eliminating from jackets patch pockets, fancy backs, pleats, belts, and vents. With wool now a strategic material, soft fabrics like Shetland, tweed, and flannel were emphasized more than ever. An *Esquire* fashion sketch that year, of a double-breasted navy blue flannel blazer worn with lightweight washable sandune slacks, reflected the military spirit. So did a fashion sketch of another, more mature, and obviously draft-free male in a Harris Tweed jacket with side vents and a pair of neutral covert cloth slacks.

By 1943 *Esquire* fashion pages fairly bristled with the military influence in both art and copy. One showed an undergraduate obviously only a few steps away from army induction: The copy read, "So before he whips into the Olive Drab number, let's make with the orbs on his solid set of threads, for those uniform desires don't bar him from one last fling at the tweed and gabardine garb"; and his outfit consisted of a striped Shetland jacket, gray flannel slacks without cuffs (a WPB ruling), a grayish tan oxford button-down shirt, a V-necked natural tan sweater, and, over his arm, a tan worsted gabardine raincoat. It was evident from this outfit that this neatly turned-out stripling was already psychologically prepared for olive drab.

When the war was over, however, the first piece of apparel to reflect a sense of celebration was the sports jacket. The young, sports-minded American was back in mufti, and he apparently had no intention of having his sports jacket mistaken for a suit jacket. One of the smartest sports jackets of 1945 was photographed in the November issue of *Esquire:* a charcoal-and-gray striped blazer of

soft Shetland tweed cut on easy lines, with a plain back and patch pockets. Within the year the bush jacket—forerunner of the safari jacket of the late 1960s—and the range, or stockman's, jacket gained acceptance. The hip-length bush jacket was usually of a tan cotton twill with bellows, belt, and pleated pockets; the waist-length ranch jacket was often of wool gabardine and had a zippered front and pockets. More and more, stylish Americans showed a partiality for

The blue-on-brown plaid jacket was popular in 1940 at many of the leading universities. The twill and intricate weave of brown-and-natural Shetland set off the simple blue plaid markings. The two top buttons of the straight-hanging jacket were fastened. Accessories included a striped crochet tie, an oxford shirt, a stitched rough felt hat, striped wool socks, and seamless-top shoes. From Esquire, *October 1940.*

This leisure jacket, a California fashion in sandune (tannish yellow), presents a light tone against deep harbor-blue slacks. From Esquire, January 1942.

These two sports jackets were made of distinctive fabrics in 1942: seersucker and Shetland. The pipe smoker's jacket had the traditional tan-and-white stripes in the puckered cotton material. The seated man wore a plaid Shetland jacket and cotton drill slacks and held the big, soft straw hat called the "peanut vendor." From Esquire, June 1942.

Bold sandwich stripes in rough Shetland set the standard of fashion in 1942. The neutral brown-and-natural tone of the jacket blended with the brownstone color (a mixture of brown and gray) of the flannel slacks. From Esquire, April 1942.

The weave of this undergraduate's jacket of 1942 formed a self-overplaid design in brown and natural, typical colors of Shetland fabric. His olive-drab felt hat conditioned him for his future military service. From Esquire, October 1942.

jackets of India madras worn with walking shorts or flannel slacks and a foulard scarf.

Since his military uniform had combined smart styling with comfort, the ex-serviceman would settle for nothing less in his civilian clothes; so it was natural that the casual clothes of the California designers should come to the foreground at this time. *Esquire* showed a soft tweed jacket boasting

The bush jacket, which had been out of fashion for several years, staged a comeback in 1943. In tan cotton gabardine, lightweight and washable, it had the traditional four patch pockets with box pleats and button flaps and the all-around belt. From Esquire, August 1943.

three patch pockets and loose casual lines, calling it a stylish product from "the land of sunshine, movies and planes." As the decade progressed, California designs proceeded to grow more casual and more colorful. A collarless blazer and a wide variety of leisure jackets originating on the West Coast became popular across the country, most often in solid-color fabrics such as gabardine, twill, and flan-

The casual jacket, a well-established fashion in California in 1944, quickly moved to all parts of the country. Typical was the sharkskin jacket (right) in blue and white with a red overplaid. The bicycle rider's shirt was a rayon with an overplaid pattern. From Esquire, September 1944.

In 1945 the collarless flannel blazer, a strong fashion in California, was made in Balboa blue, a deep shade named after the West Coast yachting center. The slacks were a flannel-finish rayon in a lighter tone of blue. From Esquire, August 1945.

nel. These leisure jackets sometimes combined a solid-color front with plaid or checked sleeves and back. A much-photographed leisure jacket of 1947 was a belted model with a yoke front and back as well as extra roomy patch pockets.

In the spring of 1948 the American man formally declared his independence of the restrictions the war had imposed and eagerly picked up *Esquire*'s "bold look." Pictured by the magazine's editors as "a look of self-confident good taste," it designated the first completely planned outfit for men, with colors, shapes, and designs neatly coordinated. The bold look affected everything in a man's wardrobe from the wider width of his lapels to the shape of his hefty, thick-soled bluchers. His sports jackets were broad-shouldered and dynamically patterned. The overall effect of the bold look was one of exuberant self-

confidence, and it was no mere accident that, at the same time, the clothes of the American female—thanks to the "new look" of French couturier Christian Dior—emphasized her femininity with puffed sleeves and padded hips. For, after all, the war was over, men were back in the mainstream, and life was back to normal; and quite rightly the fashions of both sexes celebrated this happy fact.

The bold look carried over into 1949. Nylon cord suits and jackets for summer were big fashion news. Crisp and lightweight, nylon cord and seersucker gave the American man the ease and informality he wanted from his summer clothes and, when boldly striped, the look of "self-confident good taste" that had attracted him to the bold look in the first place. From all indications it appeared that the American man, more fashion-conscious than ever, was determined to

wear clothes that would express his new, optimistic outlook. Apparently no one could have predicted the conservatism that would mark men's apparel in the next decade and spawn the "man in the gray flannel suit," which was as much a state of mind as it was a suit of clothes.

1950–1960

Esquire gauged the trend toward more conservative apparel when, in February, 1950, it reported on the fashion preferences of America's outstanding men of achievement. "They represent an American aristocracy of accomplishment," wrote the editors, "and so it is not surprising that in the absence of a playboy ruling class, their ideas on dress as well are seriously observed by other men." Exactly what were these style setters of 1950 looking for in their clothes? According to *Es-*

quire's survey it was "Ease and Naturalness . . . No Exaggeration . . . Distinction without Drabness . . . and Comfort via lighter weight apparel." As an example, the editors chose a maroon cashmere sports jacket, asking the reader specially to note the simple cut and patch pockets. With this jacket the model wore a yellow sheer-linen shirt, a polka-dot foulard bow tie, gray lightweight gabardine slacks, and white buck-wing shoes with black soles.

The next month *Esquire* elaborated on this theme under the fashion banner "American Informal": "With this issue, we explore the greatest trend to date in men's fashions: American Informality built right into your dress and 'formal' clothes. Nothing to do with a crystal ball. Nothing dreamed up by a guy with a clothing dummy and a tape measure and time on his hands. But this is Fashion getting in step with the needs of American men, noting their insistence on comfort, on the easy, non-exaggerated . kind of clothes that combine our natural casualness with a pleasure in feeling and looking right. Added together now, at long last, you can dress to the hilt, and not feel like a candidate for the wax museum. Color, comfort, casualness, correctness: demand it, now, because it's the big style." Accompanying fashion sketches showed the correct outfit for practically every occasion, from spectator sports (a brown plaid lightweight tweed jacket with a pleated back and deep center vent, worn with dark gray flannel slacks) to winter resort (a linen jacket and yellow linen slacks) to university campus (a single-breasted tweed jacket, covert slacks, and white bucks).

The new soft-constructed natural-shoulder line was correct, said the editors, "for young men of all ages. Let the acrobats have hourglass waistlines. And leave the hulking shoulder pads on the football field. For city and campus alike, naturalness is the answer—no frills, nothing superficial." Translated into fashion specifics, that spelled natural-width shoulders, slight shaping in front, a straight-hanging

back, and soft-roll lapels. Such a silhouette, *Esquire* decided, "mirrors the restraint and good taste of the men who wear it." It also mirrored the tense and wary political climate of the period, the by-product of an undeclared war in Korea and Senator Joseph McCarthy's widely publicized congressional investigations. At a time like that, small wonder the American man was dressing with restraint.

Expressing this understated look still further, *Esquire* in the fall of 1950 introduced "Mr. T," a new trim look that whittled 1 inch from jacket shoulders and ¾ inch from lapels. Mr. T's ideal sports jacket was a three-button mid-tone brown tweed with a center vent. With it he would most likely wear tan gabardine slacks, a Scottish tartan waistcoat, and a tapered-crown porkpie hat.

In this period of muted colors and narrower proportions, tartan designs were a veritable oasis of color. The innovation of authentic tartan designs in campus clothes was fashion news in 1950, and a three-button tartan flannel blazer or a small-patterned tweed jacket with a tartan lining was a welcome flash of color in an otherwise charcoal gray world. The mature man, on the other hand, usually confined his penchant for checks to a tattersall waistcoat. The most popular fabrics for sports jackets in 1952 were Shetland, flannel, homespuns, tweed, gabardine, and cashmere. And the lighter the weight, the better. That year the new man-made miracle fabrics rated fashion headlines, and new words like Dacron, Orlon, and Arnel entered the vocabulary of every menswear salesman. A typical sports jacket advertisement featured a three-button style with flap pockets and side vents, made of "the sensational new blend, Dacron and wool." Impressive advertising campaigns extolled the virtues of the new synthetics and blends, and praise for their ease of care was peppered with such claims as "little ironing," "laundry safe," "resists wrinkles," and "the final word in wash-and-wear." All-rayon fabrics and rayon-and-acetate blends became more pop-

ular than ever, and cotton was eliminated from the new Palm Beach cloth to make room for nylon.

Yet despite the new miracle fabrics, lightweight Shetlands were still considered *the* fabric for spring, 1953, the lighter-weight synthetics and blends being reserved exclusively for warm-weather wear. "For the man who is seeking a minor change, the two-button jacket might give him what he's looking for," advised a trade writer. Considered advance styling that year was the side-vented, three-button model with flap pockets and ticket pocket—"an excellent model for the fellow who can wear it and feel perfectly at ease. But don't force it on your customers."

This air of conservatism eventually led to a trend toward calmer sports shirts. A survey of fashions seen at Southern resorts during the winter season of 1953 prompted *Men's Wear* to see "strong evidence that there is in progress a revolt or call it what you will—against over-designed, obvious, and ill-considered patterning. This is being felt in high fashion circles and shows every sign of spreading fast." And if Southern resort observations could be relied upon, the writer felt that this might mean that the major pattern interest would move to sports jackets, shorts, and slacks. Palm Beach socialites were already showing a strong preference for India madras jackets in bold patterns as well as for jackets with extroverted checks and fancy windowpane effects. It was felt, therefore, that "odd jacket sales should be way up this spring and summer—in all fabrics: silks, linens, cottons, lightweight woolens, blends, and synthetics. Looks like an odd jacket season ahead—providing they are light in weight and have texture interest. Watch for close harmonizing of odd jackets and slacks—a monochromatic look" (Mar. 20, 1953, p. 74).

Meanwhile, the vogue for silk shantung had sparked a trend toward other nubby-type fabrics, and in the spring of 1953 the feel of fabric was all-important—a fact that was not lost on manufacturers of synthetics, with many an advertisement referring to "opulence in look and hand." *Esquire* devoted a spread to "The Nubby Touch," editorializing as follows (April, 1953, p. 92):

"The big shift in men's fashions this spring is toward apparel made of fabrics with soft, irregular textures. It is all crystallized in three words—THE NUBBY TOUCH—and is destined without a doubt to fly high and far. Nice part about it is that it fits in texture-wise with one of the primary moves in men's apparel, which is the matter of design and strictly the natural look.

"The N.T. swings into its natural pace when it comes to sportswear. The N.T. is no more nor less than that— crinkly, relaxed kind of fabric which you'll see popping up on all sides, quickly recognizable by the little threads or slubs—deliberately planted to give it that let's-take-it-easy-air. Look for it in lightweight woolens, flannel, blends of man-made fibers."

Accompanying fashion sketches included those of a nubby lightweight woolen sports jacket, a rough tweed jacket, and a pair of homespun jackets with coarse textures. Even the accessories with these nubby-touch jackets had the correct feel: roughish silk ties, rough felt hats, and brushed leather shoes. *Esquire* completed this fashion roundup with a bit of advice: "Warning: don't nubbify yourself into a porcupine, just major in the nubby look, but contrast it with smooth-finish items for emphasis. The result . . . good taste."

Silk and silk-type fabrics continued to show an upward trend in suits, sports jackets, and slacks. "So strong is the fashion significance of the silk character," wrote a *Men's Wear* reporter from Palm Beach, "that it is strongly influencing most all other fabrics from cotton, linens and man-made fibers. Newest addition to the silk fabric group is silk tweed. . . . The silk suit and silk odd jacket seem to provide the 'dressy' suit and jacket men have needed. Navy blue is the best color for both daytime and evening. Natural and white follow close

behind. These colors, plus a few novelty colors, are seen in odd jackets ranging from bright red, pink, maize and rust" (May 20, 1953, p. 80). But the so-called novelty colors were thought to have "limited high fashion position—and probably limited sales." Accompanying photographs taken at Palm Beach showed one golf spectator in a silk shantung jacket with linen slacks and another, squinting over a golf score, looking expensively casual in a navy silk noil jacket.

The summer of 1953 saw the light-weight summer sports jacket finally come into its own. *Men's Wear* reported that "the fabric styling is new and different and will appeal to men in search of something out of the ordinary. These jackets will do something both to and for the wearer, something which will arouse his pride in ownership." Cited among the most attractive types were the new slub and nub effects, the shantungs, the thick-and-thins, the fleck cords, and the fluff-weave blends. All were made with a minimum of lining. *Men's Wear* illustrated its article with photographs of a three-button jacket of rayon-and-cotton blends; a two-button blend of rayon, acetate, and nylon; a three-button blend of rayon and silk in a linen-type weave; and a two-button of very lightweight rayon in a slub, or splash, effect.

Among vacationing collegians that summer the rayon-nylon cords were by far the top choice, in light gray, light tan, and light blue. In tropical worsteds, however, the college man of the fifties, dubbed a member of the "silent generation" by the press, remained loyal to the very conservative charcoal gray. Walking shorts had made their appearance on campus that spring, and the college man continued wearing them through the summer months, a pair of cotton shorts and a single-breasted cord jacket adding up to a very lightweight and very comfortable combination.

Knits joined the expanding family of sports jacket fabrics, leading one trade writer to decide: "Now, you haven't enough fingers on your hands

or toes on your feet to count all the various fabrics of which sports jackets are made. They include pure natural fibers, 100 percent synthetic fibers and numerous blends of both, in light-weight, medium weight and heavy weight cloths. Interesting among the newer things are the wool jersey jackets . . . very light in weight, quite porous, and the natural elasticity of the knitted fabric makes them flexible and easily adjustable to the normal movement of the body. Their texture closely resembles that of fine woven fabrics but on the body—well, the wearer feels nothing on his body" (*Men's Wear,* June 15, 1953, p. 83). Photographs illustrating this article showed a navy blue wool jersey jacket in a blazer model with brass buttons, and a knitted wool jersey in a tweed pattern that looked like a woven tweed.

The Princeton man, that ultrasmart dresser, was returning to campus wearing medium dark gray flannel. His natural-shoulder jacket had little or no padding, and his suit trousers and slacks were cut straight and never pleated. In the opinion of many fashion savants, the Ivy Leaguer of this period had all but abdicated fashion leadership in favor of falling in line with the conservative trend that had already engulfed the more mature man of fashion.

During the last half of the decade, however, color returned to sportswear and the emphasis on the feel of fabric continued. *Esquire* celebrated the return of color by splashing a cotton jacket—blue stripes on red—across an ocher-color page. The doldrums were past. Most American troops had left Korea, and Senator McCarthy had faded from the nation's television screens. Relieved Americans were feeling optimistic again and in a mood to dress accordingly. "Rare and opulent fabrics are the solid substance of The Elegant Air," *Esquire* stated in 1957, devoting pages to suits, outercoats, and sports jackets of vicuña, cashmere, and llama fleece. Outstanding was a subtly tailored sports jacket of checked cashmere, a nap of luxury.

In subsequent issues of *Esquire* that year a lightweight wool challis in a red hand-blocked print was displayed against a red paneled wall, and film star Alan Ladd sported a camel-color suede jacket with narrow lapels, a center vent, and leather buttons—a stellar example of the broad-shouldered California style. A shapelier-than-customary sports jacket was shown featuring only two buttons ("Who uses the nonexistent third one, anyway?"), lapels slightly shorter than usual, and "further revved up by slanted pockets." This jacket showed the undeniable influence of the "Continental look," a shorter, shapelier Italian-inspired suit silhouette that had emerged in the spring of 1956 to offer the natural-shoulder Ivy League look its first serious competition. Of course, a high fashion like this called for high color and bold patterns, and *Esquire* photographed one such example, terming it an "incendiary blazer"—a wool jacket with ombré stripes graduating from gray to brown. While the shorter, shapelier cut of the Continental look often proved less than attractive on the rangy American physique, the penchant for high colors and bolder patterns it had sparked was carried over even into sports jackets cut along the more relaxed Ivy League lines.

Textural excitement continued to run high during the remainder of the decade. Rugged textures were more or less dominant in the fall of 1957. Narrow-striped corduroy jackets with leather buttons and slightly slanted flapped pockets were coupled with slacks of fine-wale corduroy. Crisp-textured woolens with leather trim were a recurrent theme, and *Gentlemen's Quarterly* in a salute to the rugged textures photographed a checked tweed jacket—a four-button model—featuring leather collar, cuffs, buttons, and elbow patches.

During the late fifties there was a positive boom in checks and plaids. Two- and three-button jackets with side vents and slanting pockets turned up in houndstooth checks and glenurquhart plaid. The vogue for extremely lightweight sports jackets con-

tinued, and it was a proud retailer who could boast a screen-plaid cotton that weighed only 1 pound.

India madras, the colorful lightweight plaid fabric that had attracted some attention in the latter half of the forties, became a high-ranking fabric for summer and resort wear during the colorful last half of the fifties. O. E. Schoeffler, on a photographic tour through the Southern vacation resorts for *Esquire,* reported seeing multicolored India madras jackets everywhere: as a beach coat with a white terry cloth lining and trim, worn with boxer shorts; as a sports coat, worn with matching walk shorts or solid-color slacks. Predominantly red and soft green, the India madras plaid was most often a three-button jacket with one button on the cuff of the sleeve.

By 1959 the sports jacket had become one of the most colorful and imaginative items in the American man's wardrobe. For although, as *Gentlemen's Quarterly* observed at the time, "he is reluctant to support radical changes in his suits, our man likes a sporting look in his leisurewear, and currently favors the plaid in his sports jacket." As proof *Gentlemen's Quarterly* showed a natural-shoulder worsted jacket in a "faded tartan" of grayish

India madras in many different plaid color combinations was worn in sports jackets in the sixties. From Esquire, *July 1963.*

green and gray, with a red-and-white overcheck; a jacket in a textured worsted, with a design reminiscent of a stained-glass window; and a lightweight wool challis jacket in a broad paisley design judged to be "a brilliant, logical idea for the natural shoulder citizen."

Although suits certainly gave little indication of the sartorial revolution that was to erupt in the decade ahead, these brilliantly colored, imaginatively patterned sports jackets—many with modified Continental touches—strongly hinted at the peacock implicit in every fashion-conscious man. It was only a matter of time before that colorful bird would step out in full plumage.

1960–1970

Sportswear in this decade started with a burst of color. *Esquire* fashion editors predicted, "This summer a bright, bold parade of pattern and color will take over the smartest resorts," and as a kind of preview promoted the golden tones in casual clothes, calling the brilliant yellows, deep mustards, and paler sand colors "canyon golds." A spread in the April, 1960, issue included a lemon-color sports jacket of a cotton fishnet-weave cloth from Italy, worn with slacks that blazed in stripes of canyon gold and green, fashioned in bleeding India madras. While this particular jacket was cut along very casual, natural lines, many sports jackets in 1960 showed touches of Continental styling: a slightly cutaway front, waist suppression, slanted pockets, and side vents. Saluting the international élan of a visiting British actor, for instance, *Esquire* photographed him in a small-check medium-weight worsted sports jacket of a soft gold tone whose styling was identified as "modified Continental design."

Ivy Leaguers that year, however, remained loyal to the natural-shoulder sports jacket with straight-hanging lines, showing a marked preference for tweeds overplaided in lively colors and wool flannel blazers in camel shades

The trend toward double-breasted jackets was unabated in 1967: (left) a dark blue denim blazer of Arnel and rayon with double rows of white stitching at the edges; (right) a giant multicolor plaid cotton with a high front closure. The slacks were of the durable-press type. Both outfits were worn with mock turtleneck pullovers. From Esquire, *May 1967.*

continued strong, with California designers tailoring it big-shouldered and full-cut.

By the mid-1960s silk was being seen increasingly in sportswear. Green was a prime color in the summer of 1964, and a particularly handsome jacket in bottle green was fashioned of handwoven silk that had a distinctive interweaving of black threads. The next summer *Esquire* showed a jacket of striped cotton, rayon, and silk, while *Gentlemen's Quarterly* featured silk tweeds, noting that nubby silk was simulating the look of tweed, the proof being a jacket of a tweedy wool-and-silk blend that the editors felt achieved a combination of country forthrightness and urban suavity.

In 1966, while college campuses were full of bold-plaid tweed sports jackets in bright, beefy colors, *Esquire* was heralding the fact that "Pierre Cardin, for years a leading men's fashion designer in Europe and in many ways the precursor of mod fashions, has at long last established roots in the New World." It predicted that the innovations of couturier Cardin, who had shown his first men's collection in 1962, would "undoubtedly become a staple of the American man's wardrobe." Certainly, once Cardin fashions became available in the United States, the Peacock Revolution had begun in all seriousness. The first designer successfully to defy the prevailing Ivy League style in suits, Cardin brought the same shapeliness and bold cut to his sports jackets.

Simultaneous with the arrival of Cardin merchandise in the United States was the revival of interest in the double-breasted jacket—in blazers, suit jackets, and outercoats. Since the 1930s little had been seen of double-breasted blazers, but in 1966 they were being worn by the more fashionable men and *Esquire* was on hand to photograph a group of them: a bottle-green India madras with white pearl buttons and side vents; a dark navy in a basket-weave fabric of Dacron and worsted; a green glen plaid in a blend of worsted and silk; and a medium blue of Dacron and linen.

with brass buttons and deep, 10-inch center vents. But by autumn the more avant-garde were moving in the direction of jackets that combined the natural shoulders, three buttons, and notched lapels of the traditional with the cutaway, slanted pockets, waist shaping, and side vents of the Continental. And grape—a warm, earthy color—complemented perfectly the sporty personality of this new hybrid fashion. The popularity of the so-called vineyard colors continued for the next few seasons, and in the spring of 1963 *Esquire* printed a color photograph of a lovely blonde model wearing culottes and her escort wearing a wool-and-Orlon pebble-weave sports jacket in "pale dry Sauterne," which happened to be only a shade or two away from her hair color.

In spite of the new passion for color, that same year rough, tough tweeds, bold Shetlands, and hairy-faced cheviots—vying with smooth worsted sports jackets for first place—were being seen in such muted shades as oatmeal, soft grayish tan, and camel. As it turned out, this proved to be nothing more than a detour on the road to brighter and better colors. The flattering and colorful India madras

Slightly-wider-than-usual lapels and deep side vents attested to the Cardin influence.

Born on London's Carnaby Street and christened mod fashion, the shaped suit jacket had been refined and made more acceptable to mature men by Pierre Cardin, whose jackets achieved their shapeliness through high armholes, waist suppression, and flare. Not every manufacturer abandoned the more conventional styling, however, and as late as 1968 the natural-shoulder sports jacket was still prominent. *Gentlemen's Quarterly* that year reflected that, in spite of the fumes and soot of modern city life, white suits and jackets had made steady headway, and selected a group to illustrate the point. Among them was a healthy sprinkling of both styles, along with others that, sartorially speaking, straddled the fence: a double-breasted all-white jacket of rayon, cotton, and acetate that featured square shoulders, a traced waist, and side vents; and a natural-shoulder crepe-woven silk patterned jacket of blue-bordered stripes in black, with pearl buttons, modified shoulders, and deep side vents. *Esquire* countered with illustrations of two jackets the editors felt could not be more *au courant:* a large windowpane plaid with natural-shoulder styling and a shaped Dacron-and-wool hopsack. But no matter which style he preferred, the American man wanted it colorful. "By and large," said *Esquire,* "the male of the species is more flamboyant than the female, his tastes running to vivid blues, flaming greens, chrome yellows." Henceforth, "peacock" would be a fashion writer's synonym for this "new wave" man.

The man in the gray flannel suit had left, but now returned looking pounds lighter and years younger. He now used a men's cologne, and a hair dye if he felt like it, and was more aware than ever of the importance of his clothes. "The whole point of fashion today is to be sexy," said British designer Hardy Amies, who, like Cardin, had achieved fame in the women's fashion field before designing

for men. "You must prove that you are *now,* not in the 19th or 18th or 17th century," said Cardin. And the new wave peacock agreed with both gentlemen and chose his sportswear accordingly. Still loyal to the blazer, he wore Cardin's double-breasted twill-weave wool model with its high-button closure, peak lapels, flap pockets, deep side vents, and six brass buttons that carried the Cardin name—and, of course, the waist shaping that started at the armholes. And a plaid in butter gold and turquoise. And a blend of linen and cotton in what *Gentlemen's Quarterly* described as "Technicolor-toned, Cinerama-sized paisleys," as well as "a rousing eight-gold-buttoned double-breasted coat whose Chicago-fire-red background is smashingly tartan-plaided."

The sports jacket's determination to

solve its identity crisis—never to be confused with a suit jacket—was solved now once and for all. As evidence *Gentlemen's Quarterly* showed a colorful collection of shaped sports jackets that included a nylon-and-acetate jacket in a decorative floral-diamond print; a six-button double-breasted white polyester jacket with lemon-yellow stripes; an exuberantly plaided wool, with notched lapels, angled flap pockets, and side vents, that was shouldered and shaped; a one-button hopsack-woven jacket of pale blue Dacron, wool, and mohair whose gently curving dark-blue–stitched lapped seams joined up with angle-patched lower pockets; and an emphatically shaped crushed-velvet jacket worn with a silk scarf, a crepe shirt, flared suede slacks, and boots.

"This fall campuses will be as riotous

The tweed norfolk jacket with box pleats in front and back, patch pockets with flaps, and a buttoned all-around belt was a 1968 version of a model of the early twenties.

with colors as with cranky confrontations," Esquire predicted in 1968, also taking note of a collegiate trend toward pattern-on-pattern mixtures as well as a return of the bold tartans. Meanwhile, off campus many an affluent, trend-setting alumnus was wearing one of the star-size–plaided sports jackets.

Pierre Cardin, whose name had by now become synonymous with a lifestyle, was continuing to make fashion headlines month after month. As samples of his creativity and craftsmanship, *Esquire* presented a short self-belted jacket with industrial zippers on the side and on the pocket; and a four-button single-breasted jacket with a patch pocket on the chest, a deep, Western-style yoke, inverted action pleats, and a waist-high center vent.

Gentlemen's Quarterly in March, 1970,

introduced what it called "the soft line sports coats." After the riotous, robust prints, Broadway-bright checks, and exuberant plaids, the editors reasoned that the time had come for a soft, quiet look: "These past few years casual wear has been brash, colorful and a little too much for many men to feel 'casual' in. Things have settled down, however, and wearability, coupled with a softer, more subtle eye appeal characterizes sports coats for spring. The coats are fitted—but comfortably, allowing freedom of movement. An easy, flowing style is evident and the long-point short collar makes the open neck more attractive. Patterns can still be bold and intricate, but they're presented in softer colors and shades, making them palatable even to the most reticent of dressers." As an example the editors chose a three-button

jacket with a "rolled-under" top button, natural shoulders, a moderately shaped waist, straight flapped pockets, and a center vent—"soft and easy."

This softer approach, said *Gentlemen's Quarterly*, stressed design subtleties in unexpected places, such as in a plum-hued cord knit jacket whose roped shoulders added squared-off lines that flowed smoothly into the shaped waist and whose vented cuffs repeated the slant of the flapped pockets. How many styling innovations could go into a sports jacket and still stay within the bounds of the soft, quiet look? *Gentlemen's Quarterly* photographed an answer—a four-button, single-breasted, windowpane-plaided jacket with wide peaked lapels, an angled welt pocket (in line with two lower ones), and a center vent.

Nineteen seventy-one was a big year for fabrics, and knits were the big news in both men's suits and sports jackets. A decade earlier, in August, 1960, *Gentlemen's Quarterly* had saluted the knitted sports jacket as a "wonderful wardrobe addition; it is light, resilient and comfortable; it always springs back to shape—just as sweaters do—and is perfect for travel; and a knit coat is different enough from a suit jacket to make you relax and forget the world of business." But, as it turned out, knits needed development before they could realize their full potential. In 1969 *Gentlemen's Quarterly* had again touted the knits, this time secure in the knowledge that perfection had been attained: "After years of experimentation, manufacturers this fall present men with an impressive collection of tailored knit clothing—an event comparable to the introduction of man-made fibers. The advantage of these new knits? For openers, they are lighter in weight. They are able to expand and contract with the body's movement, which insures not only shape-retention and a virtually wrinkle-free garment but jump-for-joy comfort" (September, 1969, p. 123). Illustrating this article were photographs of a two-button shaped sports jacket of polyester double knit with a ticket pocket and

This tan corduroy bush jacket has two chest pockets, two lower patch pockets with flaps, and an all-around belt (1968).

a deep center vent; and a waist-shaped suit of striped double-knit polyester.

Manufacturer enthusiasm was great, and one sports jacket specialist, showing a blazer of a double-knit fabric weighing a mere 11 ounces, declared he had such faith in the fabric that he was taking an in-stock position on the blazers for fall. As to the future of knit sports jackets and blazers, he said, "I see knits growing substantially, because they fit in with today's way of life." Still another manufacturer credited the double knit with being "the first 100 percent sports jacket." Maintaining that until the advent of the double knit materials used for sports jackets had not allowed complete freedom of movement, this manufacturer's full-page advertisement explained that, unlike other materials, a double knit is actually three-dimensional: "So when your body bends or arms lift, the double-knit actually uncoils. Stretches."

Fancy-back sports jackets made a comeback in the seventies, and *Gentlemen's Quarterly* featured a four-button model of Irish linen that created a new look in fancy-back styling by outlining the yoke and half belt with contrasting double stitching. Inverted pleats, yoke to belt, added extra comfort. Double-stitching became newsworthy styling in 1971, and *Gentlemen's Quarterly* showed a shaped three-button sports jacket boasting a new effect in double stitching that was achieved by tracing the yoke front with contrasting color. Sleeve cuffs, edges, pockets, belt, and back were all double-stitched to match the yoke front.

Blazers and blazer suits gained even more popularity in the seventies, many of them featuring fancy backs. A two-button single-breasted model, for example, had box-pleated pockets with scalloped flaps and a half-belted back. A three-piece blazer suit acted like a whole wardrobe: a blazer and sports slack ensemble plus a separate sports slack. An action-back double-breasted blazer had a military flair: an inverted pleat and flap button-through patch pockets in the front, and a half belt, gusset back, and higher

Tartan blazers in single- and double-breasted models were worn by members of Esquire's *college board. From* Esquire, *September 1970.*

center vent in the rear.

The bush, or safari, jacket reappeared too, and with even more dash than it had shown in previous years. Two fine examples were a belted mid-wale corduroy with flapped pockets and epaulets, lined with plush pile; and a gabardine with oversize collar and lapels, Western yokes front and back, large flapped patch pockets, contrasting leather buttons and

leather trim with contrasting saddle stitching throughout the jacket, a high center vent, and saddle stitching in back running from yoke to wrist. But without a doubt the ultimate safari jacket was a camel-color knit.

As noted before, fabrics were the big fashion news in the early seventies. Sports jackets were fashioned of camel suede, 100 percent cotton canvas, brushed denim, printed corduroy, and

A sports jacket of 1971 had buttoned flaps on the pockets and an action belted back with an inverted-pleat vent. The boldly striped fabric was a blend of wool and polyester.

The clearly marked black plaid on a white background lends itself to the shaped body of this two-button sports jacket with wide lapels and a deep center vent (1971).

imported pigskin. And a shaped jacket of French tapestry worn with low-rise double-knit trousers and a French knit shirt was a very "now" outfit. In another vein but equally contemporary was a shaped four-button jacket with a lay-down bal-type collar, a center vent, a sewn-on belt, and stitched tracing that ran from the shoulder blade to the top of the belt.

Adaptations of the classic norfolk jacket made the fashion scene in all-wool fabrics in 1970. Very much in the norfolk tradition was a model with shoulder yokes, vertical panels front and back, framed patch pockets with button-through scalloped flaps, and an all-around self-belt with buckle.

The so-called unconstructed suit was an umbrella term for a collection of highly individualistic suits that evolved in the late 1960s and were unlike any suits previously known in this century. In this category were the waistcoat, or vest, suit; the tunic suit; and the shirt suit. The basic characteristics they shared were the absence of shoulder padding and the lack of hand tailoring. And, with the exception of the shirt suit, they in one way or another embodied the concept of the sports jacket of the seventies, for the top, usually sleeveless, could be

This knitted wool jacket in a geometric jacquard design, 1971 style, is worn with boldly striped knitted wool slacks with a flare line, a figured tie, and a striped shirt.

featuring two patch pockets belted in the middle. Similar matching vest sets were made in crepes and velvets. Certain styles of the vest, or waistcoat, suit more closely resembled the styling of the avant-garde sports jackets of the seventies. Among them were a double-breasted, slightly tapered vest suit of Dacron and rayon with eight buttons, flap pockets, and a half-belted back; and a corduroy sleeveless, belted tunic suit with two patch pockets with tunnel looping.

The "easy suit," or "nonsuit" as it was sometimes called, was a more conventional form of unconstructed suit. Unlike the other unconstructed suits, it was lightly padded, although it too did not have hand tailoring. It was called "easy" because this design was so readily interchangeable. In short, it was a suit that could be worn just as easily with a turtleneck in the country as with a shirt and tie in the city, and as a result it came closer to the accepted concept of a bona fide sports jacket than did the other unconstructed suits. Although the terms easy suit and nonsuit confused much of the buying public, in many quarters the easy suit was regarded as one of the more important concepts of 1969–1970 because it reflected so well the new decade's trend toward clothes with more casual fit and feel.

Among some of the more imaginative easy suits of the early seventies were a fully lined, padless, softly constructed garment of 100 percent texturized Fortrel polyester mini-bone weave, the jacket of which resembled a military campaign jacket; and a color-coordinated uncut corduroy outfit consisting of a two-piece single-breasted tunic suit with a 32-inch-long matching outercoat that featured front yokes, two outside patch pockets, hanging loops with an all-around belt, and a leopard lining.

And so it developed that, after having finally established an identity independent of the suit jacket, the sports jacket—like the suit—had become a subject of fashion experimentation. Ironically, it appeared that eventually the sports jacket and the

A knitted jacket with wide lapels, deep pocket flaps, and contrasting stitching. It is worn with diamond-design knitted slacks with a flare and two-tone blucher shoes (1971).

worn with bottom-flare slacks of a contrasting fabric in much the same manner as a conventional sports jacket.

In some instances, the two matching pieces might be sold separately and the outfit not given the designation "suit." An example of such an outfit was a vest set of cotton corduroy in a bandanna print of brown and royal blue on pumice, the sleeveless jacket

suit jacket just might come to resemble each other more than anyone could ever have anticipated. Meanwhile, with a shorter workweek predicted within another decade, the resulting increase in leisure time combined with the sports-oriented personality of the American man suggests that the sports jacket is on the threshold of what is certain to be its most dynamic period in this century.

Pantology:

Slacks, Knickers, and Shorts

In the first decade of the twentieth century fashions, like the life-style, were far from casual. After the dynamic and often boisterous times of the nineteenth century, Americans were intent on becoming urbanized, and their clothes, like their home furnishings, were formal and substantial-looking. There was an almost self-conscious quality about the gentility of Americans living in the rapidly expanding cities. In adjusting to the confinement of urban living, they were growing increasingly status-conscious, and their clothes were status symbols. The more affluent, fashion-conscious man at the turn of the century was perfectly willing to forfeit comfort if in so doing he looked more the prosperous and proper citizen.

The American man's wife was generously padded and corseted, and he himself wore suits that were heavily padded and actually oversize, giving him a stuffed appearance. Even in periods of relaxation his wardrobe was quite formal-looking. White linen or flannel trousers worn with the jacket of a business suit, most often a dark blue serge, were the most acceptable casual outfit during the summer months. The sports jacket was as yet unheard of, and the linen or flannel trousers were the bottom half of a summer suit. The American life-style would have to become somewhat fluid before a man's wardrobe could accommodate more casual clothes. Fortunately, Americans have always been flexible, and despite the decade's outward preoccupation with propriety the American man was not destined to spend many more years wrapped inside a loose-fitting, high-buttoned suit. In fact, by 1907 the sack suit began to take on some semblance of shape. A global war and the inevitable preoccupation with youth that accompanies war would, in the next decade, accelerate the trend toward more

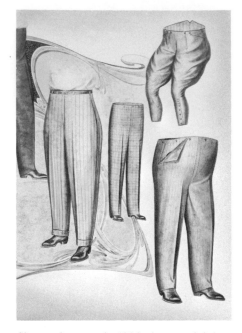

Shapes of trousers in 1906. At upper left is partly visible a pair in which the bottom slopes from front to back. The next pair tapers from the hips to narrow cuffed bottoms, in a forecast of the peg-top style. Next are straight-hanging styles, one with turned-back pockets, and a pair of riding breeches. [NEW YORK PUBLIC LIBRARY PICTURE COLLECTION]

imaginative and comfortable clothes. Once the trend was established, odd pants would come into their own.

1910–1920

Although most fashionable men continued to wear business suit jackets with their white linen or flannel trousers, by 1911 the outfit had considerably more dash, for suits were being tailored along trimmer, more youthful lines. Jackets were shorter, shoulders more natural, and sleeves narrower; and trousers, cut more trimly, were cuffed and creased front and back. A fashion photograph of 1911 shows a

The close-fitting knickers worn for golf in 1895 showed the influence of earlier court breeches. [HART, SCHAFFNER & MARX]

handsome young man in a four-button, double-breasted dark blue serge jacket with long rolling lapels and trimly cut, deeply cuffed trousers of white linen, with a straw skimmer tucked under his arm. The caption reads: "Here is a typical scene at one of the polo games in Potomac Park, Washington; these games are quite a society affair."

The massive look in men's suits was fast disappearing, and by 1914 the preferred silhouette featured natural shoulders in a short jacket (29 inches on a size 40 suit) with a high-waisted effect that reflected the military atmosphere of the time. As American involvement in World War I grew near, the country became increasingly youth-oriented, and so did men's clothes. Joseph Leyendecker, the most famous fashion artist of the period, sketched lanky, leggy young men wearing clothes that looked shaped and youthful. This was a look that would become dominant by 1918, when the returning soldier, more physically fit than ever before, would insist that his clothes look and feel both stylish and comfortable.

America remained youth-conscious during the postwar era, and the mature man of affluence and style, the sartorial leader of his day, began to dress up for what were commonly known as the "idle hours." The norfolk country suit, an adaptation of the British suit of the same name, was a great favorite, and the jacket was often worn as an odd jacket with white flannel trousers or knickers. Baggy versions of the knee breeches of English court dress, knickers had been worn for generations by English, Irish, and Scots on country estates and golf links. Now well-dressed Americans wore them on the golf links of elegant resorts as well as for casual country life and spectator sports. The dark blue suit jacket worn with white trousers was still immensely

popular, however, and duck and Palm Beach cloth joined linen and flannel as the most favored fabrics for trousers.

A fashion report of 1918 covering the scene at Palm Beach for *Men's Wear* devoted much space to odd knickers and knickerbocker suits. One man was photographed at the Gulf Club wearing a norfolk jacket with a belted back and knickers of rough herringbone silk fastened with straps and buckles below the knees. The ex-serviceman insistent on comfort in his clothes had aban-

Close-fitting knickers of two types were worn in the early twentieth century by Earl Howe and King Manuel II of Portugal at Gopsall, Lord Howe's Leicestershire seat. [THE BETTMANN ARCHIVE, INC.]

doned the high starched collar, and with his norfolk jacket and knickers the man of fashion now most often wore a shirt and collar of white silk with a bow or four-in-hand tie. A fashion writer noted "a craze" for knickers and knickerbocker suits of American homespun woolens, and he said that he had never seen such clear and beautiful colorings in foreign homespuns (*Men's Wear,* Apr. 19, 1919, p. 90).

1920–1930

The twenties were the era of "flaming youth," and never before had the American man been so willing to try the new and different. Since he was now extremely sports-minded, it was natural that much of this experimentation would involve his sports clothes. By the early twenties, therefore, odd trousers were an essential part of every well-dressed man's wardrobe. An analysis by *Men's Wear* (Apr. 11, 1923, p. 90) of the sports trousers worn by 300 of the best-dressed men at Palm Beach broke down as follows: white flannel, 38 percent; white flannel with a stripe, 14; white linen knickers, 14; white linen plus fours, 10; knickers in the same fabric as the coat, 9; plus fours in the same fabric as the coat, 6; trousers in the same fabric as the coat, 6; gray flannel, 1; gabardine knickers, 1; and checked knickers, 1.

By this time odd trousers had taken on enough fashion importance to warrant a spread devoted to their "romance and history" that included such miscellaneous data as: "The oldest pair of pants in existence—found at Thorsbjerg, Denmark, where it was worn some 2,000 years ago. Note the interesting loops showing that the garment was held in place by a string or belt." "A pair of trousers was literally a pair until the XIVth century, as each leg covering was separate without being sewed together" (*Men's Wear,* May 6, 1925).

Knickers continued to be newsworthy throughout the decade. By 1924 white linen knickers dominated the fashion scene at the more elegant resorts, and when the influential Prince of Wales wore knickers while touring the cattle ranches of South America, their long-range popularity was assured.

In June, 1925, *Men's Wear* reproduced two retailing advertisements that the editors judged to be examples of good "say something advertising"; both featured knickers. One, for pure Belgian linen knickers ($3.45), included a line drawing of the knickers, with dotted lines pointing to various styling features, and body copy backing up the store's contention that "every golfer should have at least three pairs—one in the locker, one at home, one in the laundry." The other advertisement promoted four-piece suits, knickerbocker suits with a vest and a pair of long trousers. The body copy stressed the suits' "soft, flexible construction—designed for comfort." The knickerbocker suit, first taken up by the wealthy man of fashion, was now accepted by the general public.

Knickers were seen in every fabric from flannel and tweed to gabardine, whipcord, and the new Palm Beach summer fabric of cotton and mohair. While the first knickers worn by American golfers had been plus fours, the enthusiasm of Ivy League students for knickers resulted in their growing longer and baggier. Plus sixes and even plus eights were not uncommon on golf courses and around smart resorts.

Having succeeded in giving knickers a baggier look, Ivy League students were ready to adopt something even baggier, the Oxford bags worn by Cambridge and Oxford students, who used them to camouflage their knickers, which had been banned for classroom wear. In 1925 these voluminous trousers, which measured about 25 inches around the knees and 22 inches around the bottoms, had been brought home by the vacationing American students and were attracting widespread publicity. Advance notice had been given Americans in *Men's Wear* the previous year, when writers covering such fashionable events as the Henley regatta cabled word of "the very loose flannel trousers worn." Visiting American journalists reported in 1925 that the bags were so popular with upper-class British students that most of them had three pairs, one of silver, one of biscuit, and one of either lavender or powder blue.

In the spring of 1925 John Wanamaker introduced the Oxford bags in New York in a full-page newspaper advertisement that read:

First in America
Redleaf-London OXFORD BAGS
The trousers that have created such a furore in England. Originated by the students at Oxford, they are worn in many places by young men of fashion. 20 to 25 inches wide at foot.
Almost as wide at the knee. Fashioned after the English style with high-cut waistline, and pleats in front. May be worn with braces, but equipped with belt loops and side straps and buckles as a concession to the American habit.
In plain color flannels: Biscuit . . . Silver Grey . . . Fawn . . . Lovat . . . Blue Grey . . . Pearl Grey. $20 a pair. (Quoted in *Men's Wear,* Sept. 23, 1925)

To publicize their Oxford bags, which had been made within a stone's throw of Oxford University, Wanamaker's dressed several salesmen in them and directed them to stroll about their Redleaf-London Shop, a department that specialized in British clothing and furnishing ideas. Since British fashion influence was at a high point and the Ivy League student was the fashion leader among American youth, the Oxford bags scored a great success. They affected the suit silhouette of many young Americans, who, inspired by the bags, favored natural-shoulder suits with trousers that measured from $18\frac{1}{2}$ to 22 inches around the bottoms. By the autumn of 1925 the fashion press reported that the Oxford bags had become popular with city dwellers as well as collegians. A story headlined "Oxford Bags Arrive on Coast" went on to report:

"Women may giggle hysterically . . . men stop in their tracks to swear harsh and lusty western oaths, the Oxford Bags have arrived—and are doing very nicely indeed, thank you—in San Francisco and on the University of California campus.

Knickers were full-cut in 1925 and often were worn with a crease in front and in back. [HART, SCHAFFNER & MARX]

The plus fours of 1927 carried two pleats on each side beneath the waistband. [HICKEY-FREEMAN CO.]

"It was more than half expected, by even the most dubious members of the trade, that the college extremists would pounce with joyful cries upon the bags. And why not? Their 25-inch width is scarcely more radical than the 22-inch flannel and corduroy slacks so widely worn at present. Thirty-five inches is a different matter but only one of degree; although the writer cannot vouch for the statement personally, it has been reported that even the latter measurement has been recorded by Berkeley observers. This to the distress of city stores, who fear such extremes will kill the style around town" (*Men's Wear,* Sept. 23, 1925).

Since extremes of any kind inevitably lead to a swing in another direc-

tion, the trade press that year noted that menswear designers were already decreeing narrower trousers for the fall and winter suits of 1926. In the meantime, reporters covering fashionable summer resorts noted that knickers for wear off the golf links were disappearing. "Plain white flannel trousers, white flannels with pencil, chalk and block stripes, biscuit and pale blue flannels have taken their place, and much to my surprise trousers are even wider than they were last year" (*Men's Wear,* July 8, 1925). Fashion sketches accompanying this article showed a Wall Street broker in a gabardine jacket, very full white flannel trousers with brown stripes, and a pair of buck shoes trimmed with tan leather; a

young man in a pale china-blue jacket with white pearl buttons, white flannel trousers, and white buck shoes trimmed with tan leather; and a mature man of fashion wearing a white linen jacket, gray flannel trousers, and a pair of white buckskin shoes with heavy black soles.

Another writer decided in 1929: "Good taste has nicked the knicker. This garment, which was primarily intended for the golf links, has been relegated to its proper place as an article for sporting wear, and well dressed men are wearing knickers only when chasing golf balls over the countryside. Flannel trousers have replaced them entirely. These trousers, though a little more full than those for town wear, show no signs of exaggeration" (*Men's Wear*, Apr. 10, 1929, p. 16).

By 1929 the popular flannel trousers were, in the words of the *Men's Wear* journalist, "a rhapsody of brilliant hues." Examples cited at Palm Beach included a reddish tan gabardine jacket with light brown block-striped flannels, a Prussian-blue flannel jacket and blue-and-gray striped flannels, and a tobacco-brown flannel jacket with sunburn-tan flannel trousers. What did this harmony mean to the menswear retailer? The writer said:

"In the first place, it means that you can sell at least three pairs of flannel trousers where you formerly sold one pair to a customer. This does not mean that just because they are favoring variety in Palm Beach your customers are going to start walking into your shop from now on and ask for three pairs. It is up to you to train your salesmen to recommend certain styles of trousers for certain styles and colors of jackets, using the fashion news from the Florida playground as a guide.

"The big new style in flannel trousers at Palm Beach this past season was solid colors in light, bright tones. Last year only one out of ten men wore solid color flannels, but this year it is one out of six. Then last year, only tan, grey and green were to be seen, and those in the regulation shades; while this year, the colors seen were almost all new. Such ones as pale blue, lemon, sunburn tan, metallic greys, pale green, tobacco brown, and pale blue-greys show that the variety is infinite. If you do not have these in stock, get them at once. Tell your customers the history of this style, how it is being worn by the best dressed leaders of society and finance in the country. If you are the first to register this style in your community, it will be another stone in the foundation of your style leadership" (Apr. 10, 1929, p. 14).

While striped flannel trousers had dropped in popularity, the writer suggested that the retailer should not conclude that he was going to stop selling stripes in the future. He assured him that stripes would still be very popular that summer on both white and colored grounds, with no one type the favorite: "Variety is the spice of the season, and men can show their individuality of dress in this field." An accompanying chart showing some of the most popular and smartest patterns in striped flannel trousers indicated, however, that alternate block stripes were leading other patterns, although in group-striped effects there was already a marked tendency toward closer stripes. The *Men's Wear* survey of flannel trousers being worn in Palm Beach that season revealed the following data: white, 54 percent; block-striped, 18; pinstriped and cluster-striped, 11; gray, 8; biscuit and brown, 4; pale blue, 2; pale yellow, 2; and pale green, 1.

In December, 1929, *Men's Wear* took certain retailers to task for not responding with sufficient enthusiasm to the modern man's willingness to accept the new and different: "Merchants of menswear, their salesmen, their window dressers and advertising managers should suppress their personal ideas on the subject of dress and conform their attire to the 'new' and 'correct' in men's apparel and NOT to their own ideas on the subject. Why wait for fashions to become popular before you wear or display them?" Such a fashion was the new shorts that some golfers had taken up. Members of the Los Angeles Country Club, among them the singer Al Jolson, posed for photographers in their new khaki shorts. Meanwhile, in Chicago executives of Hart Schaffner & Marx reported a gratifying response to the shorts they were offering for immediate delivery. Made of the same fabric as their 26-inch Oxford bags, the shorts were constructed in almost the same manner as the upper portion of regulation trousers and had pleats at the waist. Worn with knee-high hose and a pullover or sleeveless sweater, shorts carried the decade's desire for comfort to its limits.

1930–1940

The buoyancy went out of the nation's economy with the collapse of the stock market in October, 1929, but the Americans who could still afford to play golf played, and in June, 1933, they traveled to the Thirty-seventh Annual National Open Tournament in Glenview, Illinois. More than 10,000 spectators were on the links, and they "probably set a new record for the amount of new lightweight summer ensembles at a golfing event," according to a *Men's Wear* reporter covering the tournament. He went on to describe the scene:

"For the third successive year the open was staged during a severe heat wave and the players again experimented with various types of apparel in an effort to keep cool. A combination which appeared particularly refreshing and which caused some comment amongst both golfers and non-golfers was a grey broadcloth shirt with either grey cotton or flannel slacks or knickers.

"That trousers and slacks are continuing to cast a shadow over knickers was one of the striking observations at the 1933 Open. Less than one-third of the golfers were attired in plus fours. The remainder preferred slacks and odd trousers with the former most favored. In this connection it was noted that a surprisingly large number of the knickers worn were constructed with features previously confined to slacks, such as clasps at the side. Knickers seemed to be cut less full than previously, there being no plus sixes in evidence and the plus fours were more fitted than the full cut garments of yesteryear.

"In their endeavors to resist the sun's torrid rays, the players showed a preference for lightweight materials and it was quite obvious that they have been paying attention to the promotion of linens, cottons, and lightweight woolen and worsted materials by leading menswear merchants. Linen led in caps and showed an increase in trousers. Cottons jumped to the fore and mesh cotton found some adherents. In fairness to wool it must be said that flannel took first place amongst trousers and knicker materials.

A resort uniform of 1935, worn by the man at right, was composed of full-cut gray flannel slacks with deep pleats, an extension waistband, and adjustable side tabs, a knitted blue polo shirt, and two-tone shoes. From Esquire, *June 1935.*

During the resort season of 1935 American visitors at Nassau borrowed the British fashion of shorts for warm-weather wear. The man at left wears a pair of tan gabardine shorts; his companion, a pair of brown glenurquhart slacks in a lightweight fabric. From Esquire, *July 1935.*

"Stripes were of consequence only in trousers and knickers. Most of the cotton slacks, as well as whipcords and some flannels were striped, the markings on the whole being narrow and placed rather close together. More dignified stripes were those on whipcord trousers and slacks. Those on cottons were varied, often two and three colors having been used.

"Solid colors stayed in front of the trouser and knicker fields. Solid grey was especially popular, principally in flannels. Even in wools, plain weaves were most accepted, although small self patterns were quite prominent. Fancy weaves, combining two or more designs of herringbone, twill, diagonal, diamond or check, were observed for the most part in the new cottons.

"The preponderance of light and medium shades of grey emphasized rather conclusively that this color will be on the increase at golf courses in various parts of the country before long. There were greys in flannels, in soft wool fabrics, in lightweight worsted, and even in cottons.

"Gabardine and poplin, while not important for mass acceptance, were preferred by several of the best dressed men, chiefly for knicker wear. Practically all of the slacks were with two side straps. Bottoms were mostly about 19 and 20 inches. That slacks, as they have been produced, are not ideally made for the golfer was evidenced by the large number of players who turned up the cuffs, as one would on a rainy day" (June 21, 1933, p. 16).

A writer-photographer team covering the Florida scene noted that the flannel trouser vogue continued among well-dressed golfers, while knickers had all but vanished: "Grey in medium to dark tones is easily the best color. Gabardine slacks are becoming more popular. Both grey and tan are seen to a considerable extent. White is worn not only in flannel and gabardine but in wash materials as

Shorts for boating, golf, and tennis were recommended in 1936. The man at right wears a pair in tan gabardine with an elastic cord belt, a knitted shirt, a yachting cap, and espadrilles. From Esquire, *January 1936.*

(left) The fashion of the slacks suit, consisting of slacks with a matching shirt, was imported from the French Riviera to American resorts in 1936. (right) The gray flannel slacks of this period were full-cut and cuffed. From Esquire, *August 1936.*

well. Small check trousers, particularly in bluish green, though observed only occasionally, are extremely smart looking. All trousers are made high-waisted and have pleats at the waistband. The knicker situation is about the same—few are seen" (O. E. Schoeffler, *Men's Wear,* Feb. 23, 1935). Photographed on the links at Palm Beach, the motion-picture star Douglas Fairbanks wore a blue acetate yarn shirt, gray chalk-stripe flannel trousers, brown reversed-calf shoes, and a coconut-brown straw hat.

Even during the Great Depression the so-called horsey set flourished, and in its October, 1935, issue *Esquire*

showed a correct costume "for horsey folk to wear at early fall point to point meets." The model wore a shepherd's-check cap, a houndstooth jacket, a turtleneck sweater, medium-dark flannel slacks, and brown blucher brogues with plain uncapped toes.

Although fashionable Americans had apparently abandoned knickers by the mid-thirties, a visit by members of the fashion press in 1936 to the British Open Championship, always acknowledged to be one of the most significant fashion events of the season, showed that knickers were worn by 70 percent of the players and spectators. "There were not the exaggerated plus

fours, sixes or eights, of past seasons," reported a writer in *Apparel Arts*, "but instead they were very sensible and well-proportioned garments. Practically every type of tweed was in evidence, with cheviot tweeds especially popular.

"The new knickers introduced are entirely different from the old type in other ways than their general cut. Old fashioned models were all of the button or buckle types, while in the newest knickers there is a string or cord at the knee band and this cord is just wrapped around the leg once and then twisted under itself. This is a great advantage over the buckle, since it holds in place securely, the material isn't pulled, and the tension above the calf of the leg is practically eliminated.

"An interesting combination worn by many of the better dressed golfers and spectators was a lightweight cheviot tweed jacket of Glen Urquhart check and knickers made of the material and color but carrying a small hound's tooth check" (vol. 6, no. 3, 1936).

The writer observed that the more meticulous golfers in the East were following the lead of the British and once again favoring the use of knickers. Besides their obvious fitness for golf, he maintained that they had many other uses: "They are the sensible and practical garment for winter sports, such as skating and tobogganing, and are also suitable for hunting or any kind of general rough country usage."

Esquire in its March issue that year also predicted a "homecoming for the prodigal knicker" in an article that stated: "The knicker got into bad company some years back and had itself banished by the best dressed golfers as a result. It was really the white knicker with its leering suggestion of absent-mindedness on the part of the hurried dresser, which got the whole blooming family into Fashion's dog house. But Fashion is both fickle and short of memory and here comes the knicker back with a bang and with a British accent in the way of a cord that wraps once around the leg and then tucks in under itself, in place of the old time buckle at the cuff."

Yet despite these optimistic fashion reports as well as photographs of the Prince of Wales on the golf links wearing the new-style knickers, there was no revival of interest in knickers in the United States. They were not to be seen again as a significant fashion until 1970, when they would be worn by the more avant-garde fashion innovators of both sexes. This was one of the very few times when the fashion-conscious, still economically solvent American of the Depression thirties showed his independence and refused to follow the lead of the well-dressed Britisher, who in this decade exerted an immense fashion influence on both sides of the Atlantic.

If anyone doubted the predominance of slacks, he had only to attend the National Open Championship in New Jersey that year, where nine out of ten men competing for the highest honor in golf favored slacks—a higher proportion than had been recorded in fifteen years. The materials and colors of the trousers were considered by the attending fashion press to be the chief points of style interest. Worsted gabardine, generally in plain weaves, ranked at the top of the scale. Tan outstripped all other colors, with gray and bluish gray as not very close second and third choices. Flannel in white, gray, and beige was still immensely popular, and very fine tropical worsted slacks were well regarded for both comfort and smart appearance. For the most part, the style of the slacks was uniform, featuring two front pleats, a high waist, and full-cut legs. The few knickers that appeared were cut surprisingly full, as though the wearers were in a mood to make a bold fashion statement. Gene Sarazen, who had worn only knickers for many years, chose baggy gabardines. As one reporter noted, "The very few men who wore knickers have been consistent wearers of them for the past several years, never having switched to slacks."

In the meantime, Ivy Leaguers and their fathers wore suit jackets and sports jackets in the British drape style. An outfit combining a gray flannel drape sports jacket, white cricket cloth slacks, a tab-collar shirt, a guards tie of the Royal Artillery, and a snap-brim hat added up to a very proper British look.

Popular all through this decade were slacks of covert cloth, which first gained acceptance with undergraduates at Yale and other Eastern universities, who wanted a sturdy, rugged type of slack fabric. New Haven tailors met their requirements with a covert cloth that had the right look and rugged quality, but it weighed 15 to 17 ounces to the yard and resulted in uncompromisingly heavy slacks, which were not suited to a decade that tended toward comfortable, lightweight fabrics. Eventually a covert cloth was developed that weighed only 11 or 12 ounces to the yard, and the popularity of covert slacks was assured.

Flannel slacks never suffered even a temporary dip in popularity. *Esquire* in June, 1935, offered what it considered to be practically a resort uniform: a navy blue polo shirt, gray flannel slacks, and black-and-white sports shoes. A white silk handkerchief worn loosely knotted at the neck and a blue beret completed the outfit. That spring, *Esquire*'s fashion staff suggested that the early-season boating man slip into a heavy crew-neck sweater, gray flannel slacks, and a white sailing cap. For the June, 1937, issue the magazine sketched at Palm Beach an outfit that the editors were certain would be worn by "hundreds of well dressed men throughout the country in June and July and by thousands in August and September": rum-color flannel trousers with a wide belt, a half-sleeve alpaca sports shirt, and crepe-soled sports shoes.

Ivy Leaguers returning to their studies in the autumn of 1936 wore gray flannels with their three-button Shetland sports jackets, crew-neck sweaters, and white elk shoes with black saddles.

The new emphasis on lightweight slack fabrics affected flannel, too, and a new fabric weighing 10 or 11 ounces to the yard was quite different from the heavier-weight doeskin that had been the traditional flannel slack material. Gabardine, extremely popular in suits and sports jackets during this decade, appeared in a slack fabric that weighed only 9 or 10 ounces to the yard. Lightweight cotton corduroy made slacks that were considered ideal for both beach and lounging, and in 1937 *Esquire* featured a full-cut pair in brown with a shirt copied after the tropical bush shirt first seen in the Bahamas and worn coat-style outside the slacks. For deep-sea fishing, *Esquire* recommended light and comfortable corduroy worn with a lightweight shirt

The plus-four suit in the thirties sustained the fashion for knickers. The one on the man at right was in brown-checked cheviot with an overplaid design. From Esquire, *March 1938.*

(center) Cavalry twill, a sturdy fabric associated with the hard wear of military service, appeared in 1938 as a classic in narrow-style slacks for country wear. From Esquire, *March 1938.*

of cotton or flannel. For yachting, it suggested white flannel trousers to be worn with a double-breasted blue serge coat, in an echo of the serge jacket–white flannel trousers summer costume seen at the turn of the century.

Slacks for resort wear during the last half of the decade were invariably highly colored, full-cut, lightweight, pleated, and beltless, with a tab and button adjustment at the sides and no belt loops. In February, 1938, *Esquire* showed seaweed-color beach slacks distinguished by a 4-inch waistband with self-straps and buckles, worn with a mocha linen-and-cotton beach shirt, and red beach slacks worn with a

bright yellow basket-weave cotton shirt.

Esquire's fashion director visited Palm Beach in the winter of 1937–1938 to get a preview of the following summer's styles. He reported in January, 1938, that the most striking change was the increasing popularity of combinations of sports shirts and slacks:

"These outfits show up on all sides, whether at the Everglades or Bath-and-Tennis Club, the Alibi, latest fashionable place for luncheon and cocktails, or any of the hotels or beaches. Every man appears to have several of these outfits.

"These shirts and slacks range from

neutral to vivid shades. The natural linen tone—described as bamboo, putty, and others—is by far the most generally accepted. Some of the shops underestimated the demand for it and their stocks have been inadequate. The newest shade, naturally observed to a much lesser extent, is really a companion tone—faded silver grey. Another refreshing and smart hue is bluish green. Blue, of course, is very strong in navy, light navy and marine. Reds, both wine and rust, are noted, but rate as the less popular shades. Yellow is in the running again.

"The texture of the fabrics is coarse. Linen, which leads, has an irregular surface, produced by the nubs, sometimes in a herringbone weave. The cottons are of similar character. Some are nubbed, others in loose weave with heavy thread. Rayons reflect the same theme of styling. Probably the only exceptions are gabardine and sharkskin rayon. None of these fabrics have the appearance of being neatly pressed; rather, wrinkles seem to be desired.

"The slacks are full-cut. The legs are wide all the way to the bottom. A self belt appears above the two pleats on each side.

"Three models of sports shirts are getting the play. The pullover and jacket types are about equally popular. The latter has pearl, wooden or nut buttons and patch pockets. It may be worn tucked inside the trousers, but usually hangs outside. The pullover model has one button at the neckband and two below, and a medium-size collar. The third contender, seen less often, is the bush shirt with all around belt and four patch pockets."

That summer *Esquire* featured in its July issue color photographs of several of the new shirt and slacks combinations, among them a linen beach suit consisting of an open-front shirt with half sleeves and matching slacks in red, a Côte-blue beach suit with a half-sleeve open-front shirt and matching trousers of a lightweight washable linen-and-cotton mixture, and a crew-neck half-sleeve lisle shirt with contrasting border, neck, and sleeves, worn with matching blue cotton beach slacks. There were two opinions on the self-belts of these shirt and slacks ensembles. Belt manufacturers maintained that the self-belts were flimsily constructed, whereas the manufacturers of the ensembles argued that the self-belts were more comfortable and neater-looking.

Walk shorts made rapid progress as a direct result of the British influence in Nassau and Jamaica. Shorts were sometimes paired with sports shirts of a matching fabric and color, such as a two-piece set, featured by *Esquire* in July, 1938, that consisted of linen-and-cotton pleated shorts worn with a lighter-weight shirt of the same material that had a high-set collar, a four-button front, half sleeves, and two patch pockets. An equally cool and comfortable resort outfit consisted of gabardine shorts and the popular bush shirt of cotton poplin.

Like beach slacks, walk shorts for sailing, fishing, or club wear were often beltless, having instead a 4-inch waistband. In linen or flannel, they were especially popular in deep blue and light or medium gray. When worn with a double-breasted blue flannel blazer, crew socks, blue sneakers, a silk scarf, and a white-top sailing cap, the gray flannels were considered particularly stylish for informal sailing or knocking around a boat club. The classic walk shorts of natural-tan twill cotton worn by many smart Britishers who frequented the Caribbean resorts were the first to be taken up by style-conscious Americans. They retained a certain popularity especially with the college student, who complemented his with a colorful striped belt and enhanced the West Indies look with a native coconut hat with a striped club band.

Lightweight India madras fabric was another popular Caribbean fashion import in the late thirties, being used in sports shirts, swim shorts, and walk shorts. The bright colors ran, but they were supposed to, and so that did not dampen the well-dressed man's penchant for this "guaranteed to bleed" fabric. The actual fashions, however, were made up by West Indian natives.

In 1939 "breeks" (English schoolboy slang for breeches) gave a new direction to the cut of slacks. The full-cut trousers popular throughout the decade were now being challenged by new narrow trousers of heavy cord fabric that *Esquire,* in its April issue, guaranteed would "defy burrs, thorns and such country hazards."

1940–1950

The more fashionable business suits at the start of the forties were most often cut in the English drape style of the thirties, a casually elegant style that no doubt many a man wished he could adopt as a life-style. For it was not easy for even the most elegant man to feel casual about life as he stepped into this new decade, which, with a long depression recently ended, was marked by the start of World War II. Defense spending had revitalized the national economy, and money was again plentiful, but few Americans felt in a mood to celebrate. The war had already begun in Europe, and only the most dogged optimist (or incurable escapist) could believe that the United States would not become involved. Men's clothes reflected this mood of watchful waiting. Even sports jackets, which had become very colorful in the thirties, were now mostly single-breasted models in shades of brown, worn with natural covert cloth slacks—a monotone outfit which suggested that the man wearing it had already conditioned himself to a uniform of army khaki. Resort wear, in contrast, had lost none of its color, and here the male peacock still showed his plumage.

In its February, 1940, issue, *Esquire* offered "a collection of paint pot fashions guaranteed to enliven any Southern resort setting—all part of the current trend that makes the rainbow the limit in beach apparel. This season, more than any other, the sun will be smiling down on miles of striped, checked, plaid and Paisley shore lines." In a fashion situation like this, it was to be expected that the California influence would be strong, and the West Coast inspired a casual sports jacket that definitely enhanced the fashion significance of slacks. Practically a shirt jacket, it had set-in sleeves, a roll collar of the shirt type, a four-button front, and two lower pockets. Especially popular in wool, sharkskin, camel's hair, and gabardine, it called for slacks in such lush colors as russet, bright yellow, gold, and blue green. Unlike the beltless slacks of the thirties, with their very wide waistbands, these slacks had short belt loops and narrow belts.

Notable fashions seen at fashionable resorts during the winter of 1940 in-

Ease and informality were the keynotes of the country outfit in the foreground, which included thick-wale corduroy breeks, the trim-fitting slacks of 1940. From Esquire, *May 1940.*

top, in striking contrast to Bahamian coral slacks.

The next year, however, the military atmosphere that was rolling over the country like a fog left its imprint on all types of sportswear. And by April, 1942, *Esquire* took note of the GI influence and showed a model wearing a rough Shetland sports jacket and well-cut cavalry twill slacks, cuffless in accordance with War Production Board regulations. By autumn slacks were pared down still further as pleats, tucks, and overlapping waistbands were eliminated.

Throughout the war years flannel and gabardine slacks and shorts were popular in gray, gray blue, dark brown, and a darkish gray brown, understated shades that had more than a casual kinship with the colors of military uniforms. *Esquire*'s fashion department decided that covert cloth slacks also had "plenty of snap and showed the military influence." A September, 1943, fashion sketch showed an about-to-be inducted college student in a striped Shetland jacket and cuffless gray flannel slacks. His plain-toe brown shoes revealed the influence of army officers' shoes on civilians' choice of fashions.

In May, 1944, *Esquire* featured a resort outfit consisting of a pair of tan cotton shorts (a frank adaptation of the shorts worn by the Army in the tropics) and a cotton shirt in stripes inspired by the hues of American service ribbons.

Victory gardens were an important part of the wartime landscape and also affected the fashion picture, as *Esquire* noted in July, 1944, in a feature titled "Summer Truckin' Clothes": "If all the pole beans in Victory gardens were tied end to end, we don't know where they'd reach. Certainly the 22,000,000 gardeners in this country put *Jack and the Beanstalk* to shame. We don't want to get involved in a mathematical discussion because after all we are interested in the clothes these two are wearing. The bean pole tier's shirt is a lightweight cotton with blue and white plaid on a red ground. It is worn outside the slacks for coolness. His

cluded a cabana-striped cotton mesh beach shirt worn with washable rust slacks; an open-front boating shirt with vertical strawberry stripes and three-quarter sleeves, worn with shorts to match the stripes; a Bermuda suit consisting of matching jacket and shorts of colonial-tan lightweight suit- ing, worn with knee hose, an India madras polo shirt, and a native straw hat with a vibrantly colored hand-tied band; a lace-stitched pullover of brown plaid on a white ground, worn with Nassau green shorts; a dark blue knitted lisle pullover with raglan shoulders and white stripes across the

slacks of blue denim are up to any rough work in the garden and are easily laundered. The little scarecrow at the lower right is made of the actual fabric of his outfit."

The fall of 1945 saw the college man returning to classes after military service, and *Esquire* observed in its September issue that the traditional loud clothes formerly seen on the campus had been replaced by more subdued shades: "While definite plaids are still around, a new seriousness is reflected in clothes as well as in the classroom." Slacks of flannel and gabardine were still popular, but most noteworthy was the appearance of chino, the military cotton twill fabric (a summer work type of fabric) that had been carried over into civilian life and was now accepted for general wear. Chino slacks in olive drab remained popular on campuses through the rest of the forties and well into the fifties.

Although the military influence clung to men's fashions even after the conclusion of the war, the American man eventually shook himself free of olive drab and regained his fashion individuality. In the spring of 1948 *Esquire* successfully introduced the "bold look," a concept that coordinated color, design, and shape and affected virtually every item in his wardrobe. Once again uninhibited in fashion, he seemed anxious to make up for the years of conformity that war had imposed. A direct result of this new assertiveness was the sudden surge in popularity of walk shorts, which in 1949 were being seen on campuses and at smart resorts in everything from solid colors to eye-catching plaids, dominant checks, and bold stripes. A survey led *Men's Wear* to state:

(*right*) *The natural shade of corduroy was a favorite fabric for narrow-cut slacks in 1941. From* Esquire, *October 1941.*

Shorts are Sensational! This has been a big year for men's walking shorts. They have now come to be considered a major item in sportswear.

For the past two or three seasons walking or play shorts have been worn by well dressed men at such noted resorts as Southampton, Palm Beach and top places in the Bahamas. By last spring, walk shorts had taken Princeton and Yale by storm and showed every indication of developing into one of the most important style stories of the year. From different parts of the country have come reports of a big jump in sales of shorts this summer, with prospects of still further increases next year. Best selling fabrics, lengths, colors, etc., are indicated in the following round-the-country reports.

Boston. Walk shorts have blossomed out in greater numbers than ever before, with men's stores pulling from 30 to 60 per cent more business on this item than a year ago.

Most quality men's operations found Bermuda walking shorts (those that come to just a little over the knee) their best sellers. Generally, the extreme heat over the long two-months period this summer was regarded as instrumental. Most retailers feel that next year will see walking shorts coming in for even greater attention. This, because men are getting over their fear of them and because of the popularity gained this season.

Most stores report that $10 was about the price level where walking shorts received the greatest acceptance. Generally, all stores carried them in a number of fabrics, including faded blue denim at $6.50, chino or khaki and sail cloth at $9 to $10, and flannel at $18. Others also carried them in Palm Beach fabric, in corduroy and in worsted gabardine.

Minneapolis. Best selling was the above-knee-length short in rayon gabardine with tan the leading color. Browns and navy tied for second place. Best prices: $5.95 and $7.95.

San Francisco. Gabardine walking shorts, priced $12.50 and $6.95, were best sellers in the Bay Area specialty shops and departments. Where treated as a specialty item, with some luxury gabardines and other imports running as high as $35 per pair, success beyond expectations was reported. Sales are sharply divided into two brackets: The middle aged man who uses them for patio lounge wear; and the young tennis enthusiast for sport.

Philadelphia. Until recently limited almost exclusively to the college trade, now the older business man likes them for plain loafing purposes, or for cutting grass. With the influx of older buyers, there appears to be a trend toward the more expensive wool gabardines, identified as Bermuda shorts and retailing for $10 and $15 a garment.

However, the best seller is a natural tan in cotton twill or cotton gabardine, retailing at $5. White is a close second.

Detroit. Sales of walk shorts have just about tripled at the J. L. Hudson Co. There might have been a steeper sales climb if inventories had not been virtually cleaned out by the end of July. The $5.95 cotton gabardine short rang up the highest unit sales, followed by items at $4.95 and a rayon short at $7.50. Good sales were made in the $8.50 and $12.50 brackets, too.

Chicago. Marshall Field & Company reports that walking shorts have sold way ahead of 1948. Washable cottons mostly, preferably with an 8½ inch inseam. The 11½ inch inseam, as in Bermuda type, is considered a little too long.

Carson, Pirie, Scott plan to feature walking shorts strongly again in 1950. Gabardines in natural and white at $12.50 for worsteds, and other fabrics at $6.95 have been very good, with the latter price the most popular. Denims in sand and natural at $5.95 were excellent. The 8½ to 10-inch inseam most popular.

Madison, Wis. Four shops here—MacNiel & Moore, Olson & Veerhusen Co.,

Stephan & Thorsen and C. W. Anderes Co.—all report excellent business in Bermuda-length gabardine shorts. Gabardine is the most wanted fabric, chiefly cotton, in tan, brown, grey and blue. (Sept. 9, 1949. p. 66)

1950–1960

After World War I, men's fashions were transformed in color and style under the influence of youth, who so dominated the postwar period that it became known as the era of flaming youth. In contrast, in the post-World War II period, save for the excitement of the bold look of 1948 (which retained some measure of its impact during the next year), the American man adopted a type of understatement in his clothes that is best summed up by the tag "the man in the gray flannel suit." As much a state of mind as it was a suit of clothes, it matched the mood of the fifties. Youth, the fashion catalyst of the twenties, abdicated its customary role, clung to a "uniform" of chino slacks and button-down oxford shirts, and earned itself a reputation as the silent generation. The United States was embroiled in an undeclared war in Korea, and on the home front Sen. Joseph McCarthy was a man to be reckoned with; it was a time of caution and conservatism.

Reporting on the fashion preferences of some of the nation's outstanding men in its February, 1950, issue, *Esquire* summarized their fashion philosophy as follows: ease and naturalness, no exaggeration, distinction without drabness, and comfort through the use of lighter-weight fabrics. Accompanying this report was a sketch showing a maroon cashmere sports jacket worn with lightweight gray slacks. That autumn, *Esquire*'s fashion department introduced a new trim look, called "Mr. T," that removed 1 inch from jacket shoulders and ¾ inch from lapels. The softly constructed natural-shoulder line, recommended for men of all ages, appeared in Mr. T's three-button brown tweed sports jacket, worn with a pair of tan gabardine slacks.

The slim slacks favored by university men and other wearers of natural-shoulder jackets in the fifties had a back strap and buckle but no pleats at the waistband.

In November of that year, *Esquire* gave fashion's new conservative mood a name, "American informal," and declared it to be "the greatest trend to date in men's fashions." It was, said the editors, a sign of fashion's getting in step with the needs of American men, noting their insistence on comfort, on easy, nonexaggerated clothes that combined natural casualness with a pleasure in feeling and looking right. Fashion sketches accompanying this feature showed a predominance of tweed jackets worn with slacks of covert and flannel.

In July, 1952, *Apparel Arts* gave its readers a full account of the new man-made fabrics, "fabulous new fabrics, created entirely through scientific methods, without the use of natural fibers." The previous year, a limited quantity of the first all-Dacron suit had been produced. Now it was only a matter of time before slacks of these new fabrics would be on the market, too. Then manufacturers of slacks made of a blend of wool and a synthetic could boast that they would hold their press and shape longer, and the advertisements for such blends as Dacron and gabardine would boast that they could be worn for weeks without pressing, despite heat and humidity, and would recover without wrinkling even when folded and packed, as well as totally resist bagging at the knees and seat.

That summer, fashion writers were enthusiastic over new lighter-weight rayon slacks in novelty weaves and a wide range of colors, as well as pure silks and pure linens and some rayons that closely resembled silks and linens. As one trade reporter reminded retailers, "The selling goal in summer slacks this year is a complete summer slacks wardrobe—a variety of fabrics, weights and colors to go with various sports jackets, thereby offering a wide selection of ensembles. Remember, sportswear is steadily growing more popular all the time and emphasize the fact that counting Saturdays, Sunday, holidays and weekday evenings, the average man has more hours in which to wear sports slacks" (*Men's Wear,* June, 1952).

In the autumn of 1952 flannel slacks were still considered the first choice for dress-up occasions with sports jackets, but one trade paper reported that both flannel and worsted gabardine were being outsold by rayon and rayon-and-wool blends, primarily because of the price advantage.

New slack waistbands, some with self-fabric belts and others designed to be worn without a belt, occasioned controversy in the early fifties similar to that of the late thirties when shirt and slacks ensembles were being made with self-belts. *Men's Wear,* noting that waistband fitting was now a selling

The Continental shapes had an impressive influence on the slacks worn by American men in 1952 and later years. Slacks of this type tapered to cuffless bottoms.

feature of tremendous importance in slacks, attempted in February, 1952, to clarify the controversy:

PRO: Among the slack makers comment ranges from the flat prediction that in a few years most or all better grade slacks will be in self-belt or beltless models, to the contention that the new models are "extra" business, and as such do not hurt belt sales.

Producers using self-belts insist that the old complaint of flimsy construction does not apply to the present product. They add further, that the self-belts do not represent sales being "thrown away," but rather "plus" selling points for which a premium is charged on the wholesale price and regained in added mark-up.

CON: Aside from questioning the quality of self-belt construction, belt makers warn that retailers who go along with the new trend unnecessarily hurt a department that has consistently turned out a profit virtually unimpaired by the periodic mark-downs common to the business.

They argue that even though mark-up on slacks now being shown to be worn without regular belts may in some cases be as much as the combined mark-up on a pair of slacks and a separate belt, past experience has proven that this practice won't stand long in the face of competition . . . a more difficult selling period.

The controversy continued the next year, and fashion pages were full of gabardine and synthetic-and-wool flannel slacks made with self-belts and continuous waistbands.

By the mid-fifties the war in Korea was over, the political climate at home had brightened with the censure of Senator McCarthy, and the American man was again in the mood to dress up. American designers, manufacturers, and retailers were more than eager to give him the new clothes he wanted, and so were a group of creative men in Rome. This decade saw the emerging fashion influence of Italy on the American man's suits, shirts, ties, and sportswear, particularly slacks. In April, 1954, *Esquire* focused on the new tapered slacks that were being seen in Rome:

"Ever since women have taken up wearing slacks and bell bottoms have ceased to be something belonging exclusively to the Navy, there has been a lingering threat to man's most triumphant symbol of his estate—his pants. So it's nice when something good comes along to help him reassert what is rightfully his.

"Here are some new slacks that are turning up all over Rome—very handsome in their smooth fit, narrow cut and tapered legs. The effect is a Continental version of that long-legged look that cowboy pants give our native croupiers.

"There's a new move in pockets here. They are tilted forward and finished off with flaps that button down—a neat precaution when scaling the Colosseum with a light meter in your pocket. They accent the slacks'

India madras walk, or Bermuda, shorts, which lacked pleats at the waistline (1956).

unusual slimness, and a further good point is that they add to a man's appearance of height. Another surprising innovation is the elastic inset at the back which makes them comfortable to wear in hot weather. For all their casualness, these slacks look as suave on a bar stool in the Rupe Tarpea as they do strolling around the ruins.

"Roman designers are turning out these slacks in lightweight cottons, but you'll soon see American adaptations in Orlon and wool blends, gabardines, linens and mixtures of Dacron and acetate. If our guess is right, they'll show up in everything from black to bright red. Corded and solid-color slacks are good companions for your plaid or check shirts; black makes a

good neutralizer for your loudest prints, and the light-blue slacks go well with either dark or bright plain colors."

Also from Italy came hand-loomed silk shantung, and the resulting competition among American manufacturers to produce garments of this lightweight, irregularly textured fabric so lowered prices that by mid-decade silk was no longer a rich man's fabric. Soon silk, silk blends, and silklike weaves began to appear in slacks, sports jackets, dinner jackets, and robes as well as in business suits. "Silk," wrote *Apparel Arts* in April, 1954, "is cool, crisp, lightweight, porous and resilient. Moreover, the variety of surface effects and weaves in silk are so varied that they lend themselves to all types of clothing at almost every price level." Silk-looking suits and slacks made of rayon and blends of rayon and cotton, rayon and acetate, and mohair were soon on the market in a wide range of colors.

By the mid-fifties cuffless slacks that tapered sharply to 17½ inches at the bottom were the dominant style, and the cotton pants of the college man bore no resemblance to the baggy chino pants of the early fifties. Tailored with a back strap and tapered legs, twill slacks brightened with hairline stripes set ⅛ inch apart were the big fashion news on campus. Tight pants were in style. In 1956 *Esquire* hailed Pierre Cardin, the French couturier, as a new figure in men's fashions, noting that Cardin trousers were smartly tapered, too. In fact, looking at London, Paris, and Rome, *Esquire* offered this composite picture:

"Trousers have lost their pleats, sometimes gained a buckle and backstrap, and have taken on a slimly tapered line entailing less width at the knees than heretofore, even less at the cuff. The fashion began in Rome, and has raced around the world in everything from twill sportscar breeks to formal business wear.

"This is pleasant news for most men, since this has a slimming effect on your overall appearance. The difference between your old trousers and this new

cut is marked enough to feel lighter as you wear them. Men who are pretty solid characters find themselves much lighter, getting compliments for being strong-willed dieters, and in general enjoying the more youthful appearance these natural lines seem to produce" (March, 1956, p. 63).

A subsequent issue of *Esquire* devoted a page to Italian-cut trousers in various widths of corduroy, from extra wide wale to a fireman-red pinwale with tunnel belt loops.

As predicted in 1949, walk shorts became a fashion staple in this decade. By the summer of 1954, in fact, some American men had adopted a three-piece suit consisting of jacket, trousers, and walk shorts. This was a revolutionary idea that attracted considerable press attention, but it failed to become more than a passing fad, not because of modesty but because modern air conditioning had made so abbreviated a summer outfit unnecessary.

In August, 1954, and again in August, 1956, *Esquire* devoted color pages to "the shorts story." In the earlier coverage the fashion writer observed: "Shorts are moving into focus for every informal event on your weekend calendar, accompanied by bright shirts and colorful rise stockings." Using a strobe effect, the photographer showed his model ready for a morning game of golf attired in cotton shorts, *après-golf* in a pair of Australian-cut shorts of cotton twill, ready for luncheon in lightweight linen shorts, and ready to drink a late-afternoon martini in lightweight flannel shorts— "dignified, in deference to the martini, by black moccasins and a cotton bow tie." The shorts story of 1956 began by informing the reader: "The shorts story is longer than ever before, in terms of style and fabrics. Time was you could find one store in town had a pair in grey flannel. Now look them over: in cotton, pleatless front; India madras; short cords for action; candy-striped seersucker; cotton tartan wash and wear; blend fabrics in stripes; natural poplin; light weave linen; Glen Urquhart plaid in cotton."

The reader was cautioned: "Don't forget to wear them knee length so that you don't look like a fugitive from a baseball game. With them you'll want knee-length socks in contrasting designs. The shoes of course should be moccasins or sports styles. And wear these shorts with a swagger, lads. This is a fashion with the comfort men have been waiting for so long, and now—in its many forms—it has entree anywhere."

The next year, sports jackets were shorter than usual (28 inches), and the shorts worn with them were shorter, too. But, as in the case of any fashion that reaches its peak of acceptance, there were alternatives so that a man could choose what was most flattering to his physique. In May, 1958, by way of illustration, *Esquire* showed longer, thinner stovepipe shorts to give a man a slimmer look than conventional Bermudas. The stovepipe model covered the wearer's knee and came close enough to being full-length trousers, said the fashion editors, to warrant a matching jacket. The accompanying fashion sketch showed a pair of Belgian linen, "soft, shaggy, elegant textured. The jacket is lined with silk. The ensemble walks out of the informal realm of sportswear into the world of high fashion for suburban weekends or country clubs, any time up through the cocktail hour."

As early as September, 1954, *Esquire* honored "the well-knit man," observing that knitted slacks and sports jackets, relaxed and easy-feeling, were "the most exciting newcomers in years." Knitted slacks in rib-knit or jersey became popular, but shape retention remained a problem. Consequently, in this decade knitted slacks accounted for only a minor share of the total volume of slacks sales. The great knit revolution was still approximately a dozen years in the future.

Color became increasingly popular as the decade progressed, and by 1958 fashion writers were referring to colorful resort-wear slacks as "fancy pants." In February that year, *Esquire* showed a half dozen, urging the reader to let his wildest impulses be his guide: "The brighter the trousers, the better to relax in a holiday mood." The fancy pants shown were a houndstooth check in cool blue-and-white woven cotton, foulard-pattern cottons, an outsize version of India madras plaid, a district check in Dacron and cotton, another India madras, "this time on a less astonishing scale," and a printed paisley cotton, "the most original idea of all." As a footnote, the writer added: "No sand-catching cuffs!"

Despite the penchant for color, however, white slacks were featured in the late fifties. For the February, 1958, issue *Esquire* photographed a pair of impeccable white flannel and paired them with a hot-red flannel blazer of lightweight wool and cotton. White slacks were judged practical as well as handsome when fashioned of an Acrilan blend that dried fast and smooth. Tapered, cuffless, and worn with a classic blazer in fine Italian silk, they formed half of an ideal hot-weather outfit.

1960–1970

Tapered slacks remained an integral part of the new trimmer silhouette of the sixties, so much so, in fact, that in 1962 *Esquire* devoted two pages to "A Compendium of Pants," noting that in the change from full, double-pleated trousers and slacks to slim, tapered ones some confusion was inevitable. Readers were writing to ask "how much taper is correct in their trousers, whether the cuffless trend has faded with the passing of interest in Continental models, whether everybody can wear pleatless trousers, when the new low-rise slacks can be worn." To answer some of these basic questions, the editors decided to summarize their current thinking about the look of a man's clothes below the belt, "for nothing can more quickly spoil the total effect of a man's outfit than trousers that sag at the waistline, pull through the abdomen, spill over into the shoes, or bag throughout." And so *Esquire* tackled the subject of pants:

Cuffs. The rule here depends on several things: suit style, fabric, and—when you come right down to it—preference. British-oriented tweed or a soft flannel looks better cuffed; hard-finished worsteds can take a razor-sharp crease that one may not want to break with a cuff. "Weighting" lightweight summer trousers with cuffs helps them retain their shape. Narrower bottomed trousers are more apt to go cuffless, while the true natural-shoulder traditionalist would never dream of de-cuffing his trousers. Leaving off cuffs lengthens the line of trousers, helps make a short man look taller. Degree of dressiness is no criterion—sport slacks can go cuffless (why have dirt catchers on the golf course or picnic grounds?). About the only general statement that can be made is that softer and heavier goods look better cuffed; whether or not you choose the more advanced look of cufflessness for your smooth-finished fabrics depends, of course, upon your own taste.

Pleats. Trouser fronts are either plain-fronted or single- or double-pleated; the double-pleat is, for the most part, limited to tradition-preserving custom tailors. While the single-pleat is still, by far, the most popular, the trimmer look of pleatless trousers is continually gaining favor and is *de rigueur* for the younger man and the natural-shoulder enthusiast. Sport slacks, especially, are going the way of no pleats (though the less-confining pleated models are preferred by many active sportsmen: e.g., golfers). While pleats—contrary to popular conception—will not hide a "pot," they will give a heavier-set man more room through the front. The choice, therefore, depends on comfort and the "look" a man wishes to achieve.

Rise. The rise of a man's trousers is that space from the crotch seam to the top of the waistband. In the past few years, slacks with a dungaree-type low rise, usually featuring an extension waistband and side tabs, have found enthusiastic popularity, especially with younger men. These trousers, naturally, fit lower at the waistline, resting on the hips. A slim man who likes the casual effect of such sport slacks, can wear them; a heavier man should avoid a low-rise trouser since a stomach bulging over the top of one's trousers looks most unflattering.

Taper. With the whittling down of clothing to trimmer proportions, all trousers have begun to be more emphatically tapered (decreased gradually in width from top to bottom): from a 23"–19" knee-to-bottom ratio of not too many seasons ago, the average pair of trousers today measures 21"–18". Some sport slacks and young men's suit trousers measure 17"—and even narrower—at the bottom. *Esquire* feels that the extreme taper of pipestem trousers deserves no more place in the wardrobe of the well dressed man

Flared denim slacks having patch pockets with buttoned flaps (1968).

cording to age and personality type: "Mature man likes single-pleats, true, but now more plain-fronts (and inside waistband supports) . . . in his proportions. Traditional man still wants belt-loop models, but eyeing more beltless versions . . . in his dimensions. Teen man will get super slims (13–14 inch bottoms) to more moderate proportions . . . also super selection of pockets. Fabrics: whipcord (heathers), clear-finished worsteds, heather tweeds, basketweaves, dark-to-light sharkskins, twists, bengalines, parquet weaves, lighter weight import wools." That year the fashion press agreed almost unanimously that all slacks should be tapered and that "the magic numbers for the cuffs are 15-, 16- and 17-inches for the teen, traditional or mature man" (*Men's Wear,* May 10, 1963).

In April, 1963, *Gentlemen's Quarterly* featured sketches of wash-and-wear slacks with slightly angled front and back pockets and an extension waistband that could be adjusted by side buttons and tabs, while noting that the younger man often preferred extremely tapered, hip-riding, low-rise slacks without cuffs and with novelty treatments at the waist and pockets. Clearly, waistband and pocket details were important styling features.

In 1964 slacks manufacturers were advertising that press, crease, and smoothness were set in slacks for life through "the revolutionary new Permanent Press Processes." There were permanent-press walk shorts, too, in flashy colors, iridescent fabrics, and patterns such as madras plaids and wide seersucker stripes.

Stretch slacks were now considered a basic fashion. Stretch was, said *Men's Wear,* "the hidden extra that can mean added year-round business" (Nov. 13, 1964, p. 64). And, of course, there were different kinds of stretch slacks for different uses. To be specific, there were two basic kinds of stretch fabrics: action stretch, with 30 to 50 percent give, for sports; and comfort stretch, a new concept for fabrics with 15 to 30 percent give, allowing for adequate freedom of body movement in ordi-

Allover-figured slacks with flared bottoms (1970).

nary daily use. Either kind was used in slacks, depending on the direction and degree of stretch required. Vertical stretch fabrics were used for action wear, and horizontal stretch fabrics were favored for comfort. The amount of vertical and horizontal stretch differed according to the garment's use. In short, there were no set standards, but a built-in stretch of 25 to 35 percent in width was deemed desirable for comfort and proper recovery. In casual or dress pants about 13 percent stretch was said to be needed at the knee and about 5 percent in the seat, and the fabric required considerably more stretch to prevent bagging and sagging.

than the baggy look of yesteryear. Trousers must also be proportioned to a man's build—more taper will help a shorter man look taller, but will only exaggerate the height of a tall, slim man.

Length. Proper length for trousers follows an absolute rule: they should just touch the tops of the shoe—with only the barest suggestion of a break, if at all. (There should certainly be no break at all at the time of the fitting, since trousers will inevitably sag a bit.) The very-high fashion trend of ankle-length trousers is a skimpy look that goes along with tight pants—the tight pants that are worn by many young men, but which are no more advisable for the well dressed man than the too-long trousers that slop over the shoes. (April, 1962, pp. 94–95)

In its issue of May 10, 1963, *Men's Wear* divided the slacks market ac-

Knitted slacks with a button-through fly, patch pockets angled at the bottom, a big buckle, and a wide belt (1970).

1964. Fat pants have become slim slacks and in so doing have added height, reduced weight of the wearer. Shape and unlimited fabrics have added style and sales appeal. Today, slacks are a major part of all men's wardrobes . . . with special emphasis on the young men and teen men markets. Today we have suit pants, dress slacks, active sports slacks, spectator sport slacks, country slacks, play slacks, work slacks, at-home slacks, cut off slacks (shorts) and even formal slacks. The general mood in dress today is casual—in all degrees. Therefore, the occasions for slacks wearing are almost limitless.

Bell bottoms, reminiscent of the pants worn by college students dancing the Charleston in the 1920s, first appeared as resort wear in 1966. In its June issue *Esquire* hailed them as an important addition to the sporting man's wardrobe and showed denim, cotton duck, and cotton hopsack bell bottoms and, finally, "the real article, a pair of white-cotton regulation Navy bell bottom pants." Now, for the first time in several seasons, tapered slacks had fresh competition. The Peacock Revolution had exploded in the United States, and individuality was its credo. From this point on the fashion-conscious man would pick and choose, selecting clothes that could help him make a fashion statement. Tapered slacks? Bell bottoms? Belt? Beltless? The choice was his, for clothes as a means of self-expression were now considered the prerogative

of every man. Nowhere was this attitude more apparent than in sportswear.

In September, 1968, *Esquire*'s roundup of campus fashions showed a pair of close-fitting glen plaid knickers. A year later, after a visit to Capri, its fashion editors featured a see-through shirt and pants of self-embroidered cotton as well as short pants that ended some 3 inches above the ankle. Flare-bottomed beach slacks were in style, reported *Esquire* after a trip to the Greek isles and showed a selection of them in awning stripes and geometric, floral, and Indian prints, some with drawstring waistbands and others with wide belt loops and Western pockets. Meanwhile, resort slacks were evolving still another look in the United States: the straight-leg style, snugly fitted in the seat and wide in the legs to achieve a straight line. Some models had wide waistbands and others wide belt loops, but practically all the straight-leg pants had high-set front pockets, and a few featured a "double-breasted button fly."

At the same time, jeans, a durable example of Americana for generations, suddenly rose in popularity as American teen-agers claimed them for their own. Described in the *Dictionary of American Slang* as "a pair of stiff, tight-fitting, tapered denim cowboy work pants, usu. blue, with heavily rein-

In 1964 fashion writers generally credited the growing fashion importance of slacks to fabrics and their new characteristics: wrinkle resistance, spot resistance, stretch, and wash-and-wear. It was decided that the "leg look" set the pace for the total look contributed by other sportswear items. In fact, the leg look was so important to fashion that *Men's Wear* ran candid photographs of men in slacks in 1940 and 1964 and acclaimed the superiority of the latter-day look in extravagant terms:

1940. Remember when slacks were little more than leg coverings? Big seats. Wide legs. Broad hips. Choice of fabrics was limited to gabardine and flannel.

Baggies.   *Straight-leg slacks.*   *Elephant bells.*   *Flares.*

forced seams and slash pockets," the first pair was cut in 1850 by Levi Strauss, who used the same canvas material he sold to Western miners for tents and wagon covers. Shortly afterward, Strauss switched from canvas to a tough cotton fabric that came to be known as denim. In the 1860s a Nevada prospector who insisted on carrying rock specimens that ripped his pants inspired a major change in the pants that had become known as Levi's: copper rivets at all points of strain. For the next 100 years, jeans were worn around ranches and farms and enjoyed a fluctuating popularity with high school and college students of both sexes. Then, in the late sixties, American teen-agers rediscovered jeans (many of them regarded jeans as

Smooth-fitting cuffless knitted slacks with an extension waistband, angled pockets, and slight flare (1971).

a means of antiestablishment protest), and suddenly these work pants became runaway best sellers. After more than a century of standardization, they appeared in a great variety of shapes (standard, tapered, bell bottom, straight-legged stovepipe), fabrics (denim, twill, corduroy, cotton, suede, hopsacking), and colors (plaids, solids, stripes, checks, psychedelic prints, tapestry). Sales were so large that pants-only and jeans-only stores were opened throughout the country. By 1970 jeans sales, growing at more than three times the rate of slacks sales, accounted for almost half of the $3 billion pants market, and American manufacturers were selling them in forty countries throughout the world. On July 4, 1970, *Business Week* treated jeans in a three-page story titled "Country Pants Take Over the Town." On November 6, 1970, *Men's Wear* predicted: "The real sales explosion is still to come." The *Daily News Record* reported on April 23, 1971, that work clothes sales to retailers were shifting from matched sets to jeans, the youth market being judged responsible for the shift.

"Knit," however, was the truly magic word of fashion in the early seventies, serving as a tonic for the $20 billion men's apparel industry. As early as the late sixties knit slacks were causing excitement in solid colors, and by 1971 patterns were plentiful and the knit fever was spreading. Surveys revealed that retailers throughout the United States regarded knits as the most exciting development in the industry in years:

"We're buying what we can get in knits. No one can get enough stock."

"Knit slacks have changed my buying pattern—I'm buying every 30 days."

"Knits dominated our slacks sales this past year . . . up to 75 percent to 80 percent of our volume."

"We're placing advance orders for fall in knit slacks, sport coats, shirt and slack sets, shirt suits—all in double knits."

"Knits, naturally will be the most important thing in men's wear this fall."

"Knits will help make clothing sell."

"I suppose eventually 50 percent or more of our clothing stock will be knits."

"When you sell a knit to one fellow, his friends come and ask about them."

In the *New York Times Magazine* "Report on Men's Wear" of April 18, 1971, knits dominated both advertising lineage and editorial space. The flexible fit of knits was the big news of the season. "In complete harmony with today's feel for comfort and style," said an Eastman advertisement for Kodel, showing a pair of red-and-white barber pole–striped double-knit slacks with flare legs, wide belt loops, and Western pockets. "The big news is knits—lightweight and agreeably easy to move around in," wrote

Diagonal rib-knit slacks with a two-button extension waistband of elastic material (1971).

the editors of this fashion report.

"The knit fever is spreading into a new direction: JEANS," announced the *Daily News Record* on April 9, 1971. "It finally links up two front-running concepts with slacks makers skimming off the best of two worlds to pull this one off." The reader was cautioned, however, not to expect too many model changes: "A jean still has to look like a jean to make it . . . but now knits double the promotion punch." And the list of knits included bonded jersey, sweater knits, raschels, polyester double knits, and tricots.

Yet, despite the excitement caused by knit jeans, *Men's Wear* asked as early as November 20, 1970: "What's next for the jeans generation?" Leading the list of possibilities were hot pants (short shorts), followed by knickers and overalls (streamlined in long-leg or shorts models). All three were reportedly already capturing regular denim jeans business, selling briskly on an immediate or nearby basis that, in this writer's opinion, confirmed the fact that fast cycling was the rule in the casual slacks market. A little later the *Daily News Record* published this front-page story:

"Youth oriented slacks manufacturers are turning to knickers and shorts to generate plus business for the pants market.

"Interest in regular slacks and jeans has been stabilized for some time at the basic flare model, with fashion excitement being generated up top or through fabrics like knits, brushed treatments and corduroy. So manufacturers are turning to more unusual looks, like knickers and shorts to add interest to the leg. Manufacturers are careful to explain that this does not mean the demise of long pants: it is simply the introduction of two items they feel will become volume looks in the future" (Jan. 20, 1971).

In the meantime, theatrical nostalgia had helped generate fashion nostalgia, as the revival of *No, No, Nanette*, a Broadway musical of 1925, brought back the tap dance, the soft shoe, and the fashions of the Jazz Age, among them knickers worn with hand-knit

(*top left*) Pleats at the waistband of slacks in 1972 appeared mainly on elephant bells and baggies. (*top center*) High rise (rise is the distance from crotch to waist) and a wide waistband were related fashion features of 1972. (*top right*) The narrow waistband, 1 to 1½ inches wide, has belt loops and requires a narrow belt. (*bottom left*) Low-rise slacks of 1972, which lacked a waistband, fitted tightly, resting on the hips; they were higher in back than in front. (*bottom center*) The tab closure, a variation of the extension waistband, was used on all types of slacks in 1972. (*bottom right*) Western blue jeans, America's oldest fashion, are finished with two scoop pockets and a small watch or change pocket.

sweaters in brash colors and geometric patterns. Also returning on this wave of nostalgia were pleated pants with the high waist and full-cut legs popular during the thirties, although now they more often than not had one pleat rather than two pleats. This time they proved to be mainly an attraction for the very young man who had never worn such pants before. These full pants were very clearly at odds with the shaped jackets of the seventies, and so they were seen mostly with the Art Deco pullovers that were suddenly in vogue again too, after a fashion eclipse of several decades. Although these Harold Teen–style pants received much publicity, they were worn by relatively small groups in the youth market. Flared trousers, on the other hand, had by the early seventies become so important that to complement them a shoe with a blunt toe had been designed.

While manufacturers of jeans and overalls were reported to be enjoying almost boom conditions in a slow economy, there were rumors that in Paris men's fashions were returning to tailored clothing with a look described as "Contemporary chic." And flared pants had already given way to pants that were wide but fell straight. "What is out is glaring exaggeration," read one report. "It's a return to classicism," read another (*Gentlemen's Quarterly*, January, 1970).

Regardless of what shape pants may take in the future, in the seventies they ceased to be regarded as strictly masculine apparel, as millions of American women began wearing pantsuits, hot pants, slacks, jeans, and knickers. It was apparent that the inevitable wave of imaginative new pants designs for women would encourage the male peacock to accept more avant-garde designs for himself. There was no question but that some of the most dynamic fashion changes in menswear during the final quarter of the century would begin with pants.

Topcoats and Overcoats

The oversize suits of the turn of the twentieth century demanded outercoats that would complement their prosperous, well-fed look. Ranging in length from 42 to 52 inches, the overcoats of the first decade of the century usually extended well below the wearer's shinbones and, in some instances, ended only a couple of inches above the bottoms of his cuffless trousers. The longest and dressiest overcoats were sometimes called "paletots," a term that had been used in France some years earlier to designate overcoats of various styles.

An ulster overcoat of vicuña ("the acme of luxury in wearables," as a contemporary advertisement described this ultrasoft fleece), melton cloth, whipcord, heavy tweed, or unfinished worsted was more than compatible with a sack suit so full that it required 5 yards of cloth. There was an almost voluptuous quality about such a greatcoat, with its broad collar and lapels, deep pockets, whole or half belt, and double-breasted closure that reflected the decade's preference for a frankly upholstered look in clothes and decor. The ulster took its name from the Irish province of Ulster, a region where moist, cold winds necessitated sturdy protective garments. Already a popular fashion in the nineteenth century, the ulster then was made of heavy frieze, a double woolen cloth of a twill construction. An authentic ulster had a detachable hood or cape, or both, offering still further protection from inclement weather, but in twentieth-century America they seemed superfluous, and so heavy a coat fabric was no longer deemed necessary. As a result, the ulster of 1900 was made of a lighter-weight fabric that, at 32 ounces or more to the yard, was nevertheless heavy enough to maintain the stalwart look that was the ulster trademark. The semiulster, or ulsterette, a slimmer version, would become popular in the next decade.

Raglan overcoats with very full, loose backs were also fashionable. The sleeves were set in the shoulders, eliminating the need for seams across the shoulder points. As a result, the coat had a particularly graceful appearance. When given a silk velvet collar, the raglan was an elegant coat pre-

(left) The short covert cloth topcoat, sometimes called a benny, was one of the extreme styles of 1900. (right) The velvet-collared chesterfield with a fly front and the high silk hat typified the formality of turn-of-the-century men's apparel. [HART, SCHAFFNER & MARX]

ferred by the finest custom tailors and manufacturers of expensive coats.

For men who preferred a more understated look, there was no coat more aristocratic than the chesterfield. Already a favorite with well-dressed men in the Victorian era, the classic chesterfield (a sartorial compliment to the Earl of Chesterfield, a fashion leader of the 1830s and 1840s) was a fly-front, semishaped coat with a vel-

The text for the advertisement in which this illustration appeared in 1902 read: "Do you walk much? If you do, the topcoat is almost a necessity. It does not restrain one's freedom in walking, which is a very important advantage, and it is a stylish overgarment."
[HICKEY-FREEMAN CO.]

vet collar and a back vent. In 1860 the chesterfield was knee-length. By 1875, it had dropped to about 3 inches below the knee, and by 1878 to mid-calf. By 1890 it was short again, stopping only a few inches below the knee. Yet no matter how the length of the coat varied, it maintained a popularity that carried over into the twentieth century, in the first decade of which a more generously cut version was preferred. A dark blue or oxford gray chesterfield with a velvet collar could be handsomely adapted to formal occasions, when the fashionable man about town wore it with a silk opera hat and white kid gloves.

The box coat, which evolved from the chesterfield, had a sturdy air that appealed to men who admired the husky, broad-chested look of Theodore Roosevelt. A double-breasted model in a clearly marked herringbone weave sold particularly well. Perhaps one of the chief attractions of the coat was the fact that it could be made of a lighter-weight fabric and still, because of its boxy silhouette, give the wearer the appearance of the ideal athletic physique of the period.

The English walking frock suit, with its subtle shaping and sharply cutaway front, influenced a trend toward the formfitting overcoat that gained momentum during the last half of the decade but did not take hold until the period just before World War I, when men's suits assumed trimmer lines. The more avant-garde version of the formfitting overcoat was single-breasted with the bottom button at waist level. This style was knee-length, but versions of a more conventional length had fly-front closures and sweeping skirts.

The topcoat, much lighter in weight than the overcoat, made its appearance each spring as a luxury garment bought by men of fashion affluent enough to enjoy a coat designed to be

In 1905 men preferred their overcoats to be cut very long and to be made of heavy fabrics.
[HART, SCHAFFNER & MARX]

The short topcoat and the double-breasted suit were important styles in 1905. Also shown are round-crown derbies, wing collars, gloves, and canes. [COURTESY OF CULVER PICTURES, INC., NEW YORK]

use of lower-priced cotton-mixed fabrics caused considerable debate among coat and suit manufacturers, prompting the following editorial in the *Hart Schaffner & Marx Style Book* under the title "The Question of Quality":

"You ought to be more particular about the quality of your clothes this season than ever before; the clothing market is full of fabrics that look a good deal better than they are, and that will cost you a good deal more than they're worth. They are mixtures of wool and 'mercerized cotton,' made to look like wool and silk; like all imitations they're inferior.

"For many years wool has been preferred to cotton in clothing fabrics; a preference based on experience not on sentiment; we want all-wool in our clothes instead of cotton or cotton mixtures, because wool is better than cotton; wears better, looks better. Quality in clothes is an economy; it costs less, not more.

"Cotton-mixed fabrics are not a new thing in clothing; such clothes have been made for years, and sold to people who either don't know any better or who think they can't afford to be well dressed. But a new class of cotton-mixed fabrics has appeared, called 'mercerized cotton worsteds'; they look so good that they deceive even experts; they are nothing but the old 'cotton cheat.'"

The consumer soon decided in favor of all-wool fabrics, and it would be several decades before the development of synthetic fibers would pose a dynamic new challenge.

1910–1920

The military atmosphere that dominated most of this decade had a revolutionary effect on men's clothes even some years before the United States entered World War I. As early as 1910 Harvard undergraduates were wearing ankle-length side-buttoned dusters with doughboy collars. Born of the motor age, the duster coat was part and parcel of owning one of the new open cars. Invariably white, pale tan, or lemon color, dusters were made of

worn for a relatively few weeks each year. It therefore had a snobbish appeal that certain manufacturers stressed in their advertising, often referring to "an artistic spring topcoat" and emphasizing its "grace of outline . . . beauty of finish." Always knee- or fingertip-length, as though to make it immediately obvious that this was a topcoat and not an overcoat, it was made of covert, vicuña, whipcord, Bedford cord, or worsted. Among the most popular topcoats was a fly-front chesterfield that barely reached the knee. The choice of colors was wide and handsome: tan, brown, olive, black, and light, medium, and dark shades

of gray. The most expensive models were usually silk-lined throughout and more often than not had silk velvet collars and silk-covered or buckhorn buttons. Retail prices for topcoats ranged from a low of $14 to a high of $25, which was quite expensive if one considered that a practical all-wool overcoat could be had for about $12. Yet, despite the cost and the fact that early in the decade rainwear fabrics showed such improvement that in some quarters it was predicted that the raincoat would make the topcoat obsolete, the topcoat not only survived but shortly attained mass appeal.

As the decade came to a close, the

gabardine, twill, duck, or Palm Beach fabric.

In 1910 overcoats still were heavy garments made of fabric weighing 32 or more ounces to the yard. Full-cut raglans and single-breasted chesterfields were the most fashionable, along with the new ulsterette, which had a narrower collar and slightly narrower lapels than the ulster of the previous decade. The inverness, which was of the same type as the ulster, appeared and gained a limited popularity. More correctly known as the inverness cape, it was a large, loose, dramatic-looking overcoat that reached to or just below the knee and had easy sleeves and a deep cape that fell from a fitting collar to a point between the elbow and the wrist. Some extreme versions of the inverness had a double cape, with one just covering the shoulders while the other extended the length of the arm. The inverness took its name from the Scottish seaport, located north of the Great Glen on either side of the Ness River. Like Ulster, the area was known for rain and cold that dictated the need for a coat that would shed water and provide warmth. The popularity of the coat spread throughout the British Isles during the latter half of the nineteenth century. The inverness was made of an extra heavy woolen or tweed patterned in bold plaids or checks. The French adopted the inverness, too, preferring it in dark solid colors and calling their version *le paletot,* which in reality was an umbrella term used for overcoats of various styles. (The English picked up the term and applied it to some of their easy but semifitted coats, and, as noted, during the first decade of the twentieth century Americans applied the term "paletot" to seam-waisted overcoats that were 52 inches long and flared to sweeping skirts.) Toward the close of the decade, the black inverness with a velvet collar attained some acceptance as an evening coat, but the inverness was too flamboyant a style for most American men, who were now showing a new interest in clothes that had a more natural fit and were easy to wear. The inverness seemed out of step with current trends.

As early as 1911 and 1912 suits were being tailored along slimmer, more youthful lines, and the high-waisted, natural-shoulder suit was soon to take over and establish fashion leadership. Custom tailors and coat manufac-

The shapely overcoat of 1910 had three buttons set close together on its single-breasted front. [HART, SCHAFFNER & MARX]

The influence of the automobile on overcoats in 1910 was apparent in the convertible military collar, deep side pleats, and extreme length. [HART, SCHAFFNER & MARX]

The generous proportions of these overcoats were clues to accepted fashion in 1911: (left) a long model made in a heavy fabric with a high-fastening military collar; (right) a coat of the ulster type. [HICKEY-FREEMAN CO.]

turers, aware of the growing trend toward suits with less padding, predicted that overcoats would soon follow suit. The distinguished tailor shop Brandegee, Kincaid & Co., in advertising in the *Chicago Apparel Gazette–Men's Wear* the readiness of its clothes for the autumn-winter season of 1912, took care to mention "the remarkable fitting qualities which characterize the neck and shoulders of our models, whether they be suits or overcoats. While this feature is not new with us, the prevailing modes demand a per-

fect 'hug' of neck and poise and proportion to the shoulders."

Writing from London that year, an American fashion correspondent who had been present at the main event of the steeplechasing season at Liverpool observed in the *Chicago Apparel Gazette–Men's Wear:* "The most noticeable thing seen was the trend in the direction of covert cloth—the revival is very great. Of course, it must be taken into consideration that sportsmen have always been rather fond of covert as a material for a racing coat, but for

a few years this particular make of cloth seems to have died away, and it seems 1912 is going to see a big revival. The coat most fashionable was one which reached to the knees—just a loose sack coat, one which will slip on over a dress suit and not hug it anywhere."

The trend away from the bulky overcoat affected even the fur-lined coat. A *Men's Wear* fashion writer was particularly enthusiastic about "a greatcoat for country wear, for rough wear—one that was lined with fur and yet had no fur showing." This coat was of handwoven Shetland wool lined with Manchurian sable, and the writer applauded its warmth, luxury, and lightness. In the same article he described two coats that illustrated the public's growing awareness of the military and the effect this was having in the design of more shapely and more dashing overcoats. One, a hussar's coat of dark blue melton, double-breasted and shapely, was lined and trimmed with Persian lamb on the collar, deep cuffs, and peaked lapels and featured military frogs. The second coat was observed on a famous operatic virtuoso entering the Ritz-Carlton: "A double-breasted and shapely blue chinchilla army coat, with narrow belt at a short waistline and inverted pleat hanging to about four inches below the knee. This coat was lined with baby seal. The belt gave a decided waist effect, and there was a pronounced flair to the skirt."

Chinchilla, a closely woven, curly-textured fabric, became one of the most discussed overcoat fabrics in the fall of 1912. Long a favorite in England, chinchilla in twentieth-century America was a fabric in steady but comparatively limited demand for little boys' overcoats and the smaller sizes of misses' and children's coats. Then, in 1912, chinchilla overcoats for men suddenly became fashionable. The demand for chinchilla was so unexpected that it prompted the *Chicago Apparel Gazette–Men's Wear* to review the history of the fabric:

"Years ago, as everyone has heard lately from the 'old-timers,' the chinchilla overcoating was the standard and staple fabric. How the chinchilla lost its prominence as the principal fabric in the men's overcoat business, and gave way to the diagonal, the kersey, the fancy cheviot and the cassimere-faced cloth, are all matters of recent history and not necessary to recall here. Two things, however, must be remembered. First, that the gradual change to lighter weight of cloth, for both overcoats and suits, had much to do with the displacement of the bulky and heavy goods of those days. Modern steam heating, and a popular tendency to resisting the weather, instead of shrinking from it, have had much to do with the change. It is the pride of many today that they seldom or never wear an overcoat, although pneumonia has removed some of these people from our midst.

"The second matter to be remem-bered is that several mills of high standing have kept in the business of making chinchillas all these years; have kept their standards for their respective qualities without deviating from them, and are to-day the leaders in supplying the new demand, to the satisfaction of both their customers and themselves.

"Nothing has been seen in years like this demand, trailing over from the past winter, and bursting upon the woolen trade without notice, asking for chinchillas at all or any prices of all possible shades, and in an endless variety of fabrics, for the winter season of 1912."

The writer ended his article with a word of caution for retailers: "Whether the demand for the fabric itself will equal the early prophecy is another and serious question in itself. The American people certainly are prone to 'crazes,' but whether this one is well based and founded on good judgment will not be known till the cold weather comes. But one thing certain, no buyer should go heavily into the purchase of chinchilla garments unless he does so with eyes wide open. It is not a fabric that can be produced in good quality at a low price."

The cold weather came and went, and although the chinchilla overcoat for men proved to be more in demand during the 1912–1913 season than it had been for some years, it did not then establish itself as an important fashion. A decade later, it would make a comeback and be photographed on Wall Street and at the Long Island polo matches, but for one reason or another this was one fashion that did not move down the social scale and attain mass popularity. The chinchilla

Both snug and easy lines appeared in overcoats in 1915: (left) a small snug-waisted, double-breasted overcoat with wide lapels; (right) an easy-fitting chesterfield with a fly front. [HICKEY-FREEMAN CO.]

Natural proportions in the shoulders and flared fullness over the hips comprised the fashion formula in overcoats for young men in 1915. [HICKEY-FREEMAN CO.]

Topcoats and Overcoats | 99

Overcoats for Young Men

That is to say: Overcoats for men who are young in years and men who are young in spite of them.

The very spirit of Winter is incarnated in these three youthful overcoat styles. They have the snap and sparkle of frost and snow. They look crisp and capable. There is that assurance in their lines which seems to say, *the harder they come the better we like it!*

The *Princeton* is moderately snug, with rope shoulder, vertical pockets, and lines that are stylish and individual.

The *Poole* (in the center above) is a straight hanging box effect, swinging from the shoulders in easy, graceful lines.

The *Plymouth* is a big, blustering storm coat, with stitched-on belt in back, vertical muff pockets, and an insolent disregard for the weather.

They look good in a show case—better in a show down!

Overcoat styles designed especially for young men in 1918 included (left to right) the snug-fitting rope-shoulder type, the straight-hanging box coat, and the roomy storm coat with a belt stitched on in back. [HICKEY-FREEMAN CO.]

Overcoats That Excel!

Between an overcoat that fits you and one that merely goes around you there is all the difference that there is between home and a furnished room.

If all you want is to be covered up, any old overcoat will do; but if you want genuine style, any one of these Hickey-Freeman models will give you all that you can ask of an overcoat—and then some! For it is a principle of Hickey-Freeman-Quality workmanship that to exceed customers' expectations is the surest foundation for increased success.

The *Byron* is our standard model. In black or Oxford fabrics. A staple garment, but individual in spite of it.

The *Belmont* is an extra long double-breasted storm coat, with buttoned-on belt at back and a convertible cyclone collar.

The *Penbury* is a loose, liberal skirted model, spoiling for rough weather; with Raglan shoulders, and combination collar.

They are as perfect as human ingenuity can make them!

Three overcoats praised as excellent in 1918: (left to right) the basic model; the extra long storm coat; and the loose, wide-skirted raglan type. [HICKEY-FREEMAN CO.]

overcoat faded from the scene early in the thirties, although it returned and enjoyed some popularity in 1949.

One reason for the failure of chinchilla to be widely accepted during this decade was the increasing interest in fleece-lined overcoats of lightweight fabrics. By 1918 overcoat fabrics weighed only 22 to 24 ounces to the yard; the bulky overcoat had vanished. Yet despite the trend toward outercoats of lighter weight and the high prices prevailing for furs toward the end of the decade, more men were buying fur coats than ever before. One trade paper noted: "The fur coat is fast becoming the choice of so many

thousands of people that it is quite a common garment. And this is true in spite of the high prices of skins and furs, in which an advance of at least two hundred per cent has been recorded since the beginning of the war. The fact is that when the average person buys a fur coat, he looks upon it in the nature of an investment and expects to, and generally does, secure from three to eight years of wear, depending upon the quality of the garment" (*Men's Wear*, Feb. 5, 1919, p. 74).

The youthful styling that influenced so much of men's clothing in the postwar period was also much in evidence

in the fur coats of 1919, which were often referred to as "the new young men's models." Whereas the average fur coat had once been long and baggy, now manufacturers were making fur coats with the flattering lines of cloth coats. Formfitting fur-lined coats with belted backs were immensely popular, as were the fur-lined ulster and ulsterette in lengths of 46 to 48 inches. Among outstanding examples were a marmot-lined belted-back coat of Irish frieze cloth with a beaver collar and a mink-lined ulsterette of dark oxford gray with an otter collar. Raccoon continued to be the favored fur for motoring, but even this staple fur had increased tremendously in price since the beginning of the war.

Men's Wear observed that while the collection of furs was increasing every year, the fur coat was not as great a vogue in the East as it was in the West (Feb. 5, 1919). Nevertheless, the fur industry was optimistic and for good reason: the demand exceeded the supply. "There is a shortage of furs at the present time and no relief is anticipated in the near future," said one fur overcoat manufacturer quoted in *Men's Wear*. "The labor shortage is extremely bad and, with the strike for shorter hours and advance in wages on the part of operators, there is small

chance of any reduction. Prices for 1919, in my opinion, will be considerably higher for all fur garments than they were in 1918." Still the fur or fur-lined coat was a status symbol, and in this prosperous postwar period many a man considered one indispensable to his wardrobe. If his budget was tight, he could at least invest in a fur-collared coat, for after the privations of the war years the American man was in a mood to dress up.

1920–1930

The military influence so evident in men's coats and suits immediately

after World War I was still prevalent at the start of the era of "flaming youth." Nowhere was it more apparent than in the formfitting, lightweight overcoats of 1920. Typical of this trim look was a single-breasted, British-inspired coat with a fly front and a sewn-on belt running around the high waist. The belt was so firmly stitched in back that when the wearer tightened it in front, the back had an extremely waisted appearance. Another popular formfitting model was a single-breasted waisted chesterfield with long double-breasted lapels rolling down to the waistline, where they were held by a link button. The back view

Warmth and style were the selling points of the double-breasted overcoats shown at the left of this 1920 advertisement. Both coats have slash pockets. [L. GREIF & BRO.]

I TS time to look to your Fall clothes needs. And we're especially ready to serve. Your wardrobe can be an expense or an investment. Its the latter only when it combines good looks with long service. And its the "investment" character of GRIFFON CLOTHES that has earned their wide popularity. You may be always sure of right style—careful, thorough tailoring—and the kind of service that makes you congratulate yourself on your choice.

THE STANFORD Overcoat shown to the left above,

is one of the attractive double-breasted ideas for Fall— it has both warmth and style.

THE FIAT belted Overcoat has that impression of "bigness" so much sought in the coat for rough weather wear.

THE STRAND (in the center) has the right touch for the man who wants to be well but not conspicuously dressed.

THE BENTON (at the right) has the "style atmosphere" younger men will favor.

had a V look, for the skirt hugged the hips and exaggerated the coat's broad-shouldered effect.

Such shapely coats were not created with the portly man in mind. For him there was a single-breasted chesterfield that, while appearing extremely shapely, hung entirely free from the body. Also British-inspired, it was a kind of preview of the softly draped "English look" suits that well-dressed Americans would be wearing in the spring of 1923. In fact, the popularity of these suits that year would usher in the semiformfitting outercoat, for there was no question that London ruled the men's fashion world. It was a simple statement of fact when a *Men's Wear* correspondent wrote, "London is more famous in the sartorial world than it has ever been since pre-war days" (Feb. 7, 1923).

The affluent, trend-setting American kept his eye trained on London, and the shrewd manufacturer and retailer did the same. When John David, owner of a chain of men's stores in New York, visited London in the fall of 1923, he noticed that the better-dressed men were wearing blue overcoats. Upon returning home, he vigorously promoted blue overcoats in full-page newspaper advertisements. His introductory headline, "London Applauds; Paris Approves and New York Adopts Blue," made it clear where men's fashions originated, and the copy exploited the fact:

"Since mighty few of us are Apollos or Romeos—and no sensible man wants to be—the trick of dressing smartly is not to put on 'what I like,' but what 'I look best in.' There is a certain color that harmonizes particularly well with all types of face and figure, and that color is blue.

"Just home from London, where I went to study English styles at their source, it was my observation that the best dressed men, from Prince's Gate to Piccadilly, wore blue. Blue is not only the most becoming and richest-looking color in overgarments, but it is the smartest color as well this season. Age is honorable, except when applied to eggs or fashions. There's nothing

like a young style-tip, just off the ship" (quoted in *Men's Wear*, Nov. 21, 1923, p. 60).

The following excerpt from a *Men's Wear* article offers a picture of the smart Americans of the period who were the first to adopt the newest fashions from London:

"Masses of fashionably dressed humanity packed the trains and jammed the roads to the polo field of the Meadowbrook Club on Long Island to see the first of the long anticipated matches between the Argentine and American teams for the world's polo championship. The rumble of hoofs, the click of mallet against ball, the speed and spectacular playing of these poloists of worldwide fame exerted an appeal that drew thousands of the best-dressed people of America to the scene of strife. The gaily colored bunting that waved in the breezes offered no competition to the bright hues which the assemblage sported in the ensembles in which they gambled against the ever-threatening downpour.

"If one knew the worth of only a small fraction of the men who promenaded behind the stands during the intermission, the figures would be stupendous. A great many nations could well have used the cars parked in the surrounding fields to aid them in paying off the war debts. Rolls Royces, Packards, Pierce Arrows, Hispano Suizas, Isotta Fraschinis and all the other types associated with wealth and luxury were jammed in rank upon rank. A large percentage of all the millionaires in America, and about all of those in the east, shouted themselves hoarse as Hitchcock and Lacy galloped over the turf making polo history every minute.

"But these moneyed people do not require mere dollars upon which to rest their fame, for their reputation and renown is built on generations of tradition. The majority of the family names are not known to the present-day and time alone, but were equally well known when the horse cars rumbled up Broadway and the pigs and chickens dined on Madison Avenue. They have the background of good

taste, and therefore one need not be afraid that the clothes they wore are the expression of nouveau riche originality. Their very upbringing has culture as its foundation, and there is little wonder that they blaze the trails which Fashion follows throughout the country. Information as to what they are wearing at the present moment is information as to what will prevail throughout America some months hence."

What kind of overcoats were being worn in the winter of 1923–1924 by these fashion leaders? According to a *Men's Wear* analysis of overcoats worn by 500 well-dressed Wall Street men, 24 percent were wearing single-breasted chesterfields; 19 percent, single-breasted box coats with broad shoulders; 16 percent, single-breasted box coats with narrow shoulders; and 14 percent, raglans. Considerably less popular and listed in the order of their importance were single-breasted semiformfitting overcoats, double-breasted guards coats, double-breasted chesterfields, double-breasted semiformfitting overcoats, and doublebreasted ulsters. The favorite overcoat colors of the group were black, gray, dark brown, blue, and black-and-white and brown-and-white herringbone.

The researchers made a particular note of the fact that 9 percent of the men had "again taken to herringbones. Last year it was like looking for the proverbial haystack needle to find a herringbone. When the 'masses' took to herringbones the 'classes' dropped them like hot irons. Now that the masses have turned the cold shoulder to herringbones, the classes, or at least 9 per cent of them, have taken them up again" (Nov. 21, 1923). The motion-picture actor Adolphe Menjou, generally acknowledged to be one of the best-dressed men of the period, put it more succinctly: "When people overdo things, the smartly dressed people shy to the other extreme."

In this time of prosperity Americans were becoming increasingly sports-minded, and the most prestigious sporting events never failed to attract the fashion press in its search for

Overcoats in 1925 had narrow shoulders to conform to the narrow shoulders of contemporary suit jackets. The model at left had a big ulster collar and lapels and sleeves with cuffs. [HART, SCHAFFNER & MARX]

The British influence on overcoats in 1925 was seen in wide peaked lapels and shapely body lines. The appearance of canes in many illustrations during the early part of the century reflected their fashion significance. [HART, SCHAFFNER & MARX]

trends. Department stores throughout the country, eager to establish themselves as fashion headquarters in their respective cities, often used their newspaper advertisements to report on what influential and well-dressed men were wearing. J. L. Hudson in Detroit, for instance, headlined one advertisement "Here Is What the Well Dressed Men Wore at the Steeple Chase Saturday" (*Men's Wear,* Nov. 21, 1923, p. 58).

The year 1923 saw the eclipse of the jazz suit, a narrow, tight-waisted exaggeration of a natural-shoulder suit that had emerged after World War I, but not before it influenced the styling of a topcoat with an all-around belt, raglan sleeves, a broad, curving collar, and enormous patch pockets. A theatrical-looking coat inspired by a theatrical-looking suit, it appeared in a Shirek and Hirsch advertisement in a rear view in which the wearer, clutching the leash of a Russian wolfhound, faced the miragelike scene of a palm-shaded desert encampment over which the word "Alluring!" hung like a sunburst (*Men's Wear,* Apr. 11, 1923).

Not surprisingly, the fashion leaders on Wall Street were not poking the stems of their boutonnieres through the lapels of jazz topcoats. Their favorite topcoat in 1925 was a single-breasted fly-fronted model with broad shoulders and notched or peaked lapels, particularly in a black-and-white or brown-and-white herringbone

tweed. The younger fashion leaders, the undergraduates at Princeton University, who were the fashion innovators of the Ivy League, preferred a single-breasted natural-shoulder topcoat having three buttons and notched lapels with blunted corners. Very light shades attracted Ivy League undergraduates that year, and a *Men's Wear* analysis of the topcoats worn by 300 of the best-dressed Princetonians showed a marked preference for very light gray, very light gray blue, and very light brown. While the Wall Street man wore a derby with a narrow curled brim, the Princetonian preferred a soft felt worn with a smart center crease. One coat popular with both the broker and the college student was the raccoon. As *Men's Wear* observed, "The man who would advertise his wealth and social position must have a coon coat in his wardrobe, even if he never wears it except to the three or four football games that he attends in the late fall."

Many of the most sophisticated men of fashion had at least one fur-lined overcoat in their closets, but some men objected to fur or could not afford it. For them the next best thing was a greatcoat made long enough and heavy enough so that it was almost as warm and opulent as any fur-lined coat. A 1928 model was a double-breasted, fly-front, easy-hanging chesterfield of dark blue chinchilla with a velvet collar, turned-back cuffs, half-peaked lapels, and a slightly noticeable waist effect. Chinchilla, considered an impractical fabric by some contemporary fashion experts, who decried the fact that it gathered and held dust, was one of the few British-endorsed fashions that most American men were slow to accept. By 1928,

Trim lines and wide lapels were features of overcoats in 1925. The buttons on the double-breasted model were widely spaced in both directions. [HART, SCHAFFNER & MARX]

however, chinchilla had made headway among the elite, and at the polo matches that year photographers focused on well-dressed young men wearing guards coats of chinchilla, a fashion that would establish itself with fashionable men of all ages early in the next decade. A double-breasted coat with a half belt and an inverted pleat in back, this British classic would become so popular among affluent men of the Depression era that its style would be adapted for topcoats of a lightweight blue material.

In the winter of 1928–1929 soft coat materials were used more often than they had been in years, and there was such a variety of styles that one fashion editor said, "Really, there are so many styles I can't begin to give them all." So he simply summed up the collection with this observation: "The tendency will be for an expression of grace in all overcoats, which entails a decided leaning to ease of hang with evidence of drape not only in the full garments but in the shapely as well" (*Men's Wear*, Sept. 5, 1928).

In 1928 the four leading overcoats were judged to be the chesterfield, the shapely fly-front overcoat, the camel's hair coat, and the fly-front box coat. The reasons for their popularity were summarized in *Men's Wear*:

Chesterfield overcoat. This style of coat, which has for many years been a favorite with well dressed men both here and abroad, goes hand in hand with the current derby vogue, and is a popular style with both business men and university men this fall for day and evening wear.

Shapely fly-front overcoat. This particular style of coat, of English origin, is quite a favorite with men who wear the single-breasted peaked lapel jacket suit. It is preferable in the tweed fabrics of the darker shades and is much in evidence at fashionable places.

Camel's hair coat. By sheer force of fashion appeal, this coat has become a favorite garment in the wardrobe of many thousands of well dressed men. Though it predominates in the natural camel's hair color, darker shades and patterned effects are now being introduced.

Fly-front box coat. This is one of the most popular styles with well dressed university men. It is rather loose and straight hanging, and is usually made in tweeds and

fleeces, including the entire range of the more acceptable colors. In its correct length it is 46 to 48 inches long. (Sept. 5, 1928)

No other coat had the fashion impact of the camel's hair polo coat in this decade. It was introduced to the United States by members of the English polo team who came to play in the international polo matches on Long Island and tossed camel's hair coats around their shoulders while they relaxed between chukkers. Undergraduates at Princeton and Yale began wearing the camel's hair polo coat in 1926, and the style promptly spread to leading Eastern and Midwestern university campuses. (Until the double-breasted polo coat with a half belt arrived, university men had shown a marked preference for single-breasted overcoats and topcoats.) By the late twenties a polo coat, a fly-front chesterfield with a velvet collar, and a reversible coat (Harris Tweed on one side and tan processed cotton on the other) were three coats the clothes-conscious Ivy Leaguer was almost certain to have hanging in his closet.

So many polo coats were seen and photographed during the United States–Argentina polo matches in the fall of 1928 that fashion reporters were unanimous in assuring retail merchants that they could not overemphasize the fashion importance of tan polo coats. One article stated: "While the vogue of this style with the best dressed men of the world is indisputable, it is only getting started, so far as national popularity is concerned. By promoting this style for fall and next spring in the medium weight material, which is really an all year round proposition, merchants will not only increase profits, but enhance their style prestige" (*Men's Wear*, Dec. 5, 1928). Although the six-button double-breasted model with a half belt was the classic polo coat, variations were seen at the polo matches, too, among them a single-breasted box coat, a four-button model with raglan shoulders and an all-around belt, and a wraparound style with no buttons and a tied belt. Should a retailer doubt the relevance of polo coats at polo games to his business, *Men's Wear* did its best to assuage his doubts:

"What difference does it make to you that Mr. So-and-So, noted member of eastern society, wore a camel's hair coat at the recent International polo matches on Long Island? None at all, in so far as your interest in Mr. So-and-So goes, but a great deal in that he is a member of the set which sets the styles for the rest of the American people. If he were the only one who wore a polo coat there would be no need mentioning it, but the fact that a number follow him in favoring this garment means that this imitation will be carried on, and that it should be a big factor in stocking your goods for the future. That this process is continually taking place and that the fashionable members of society who attend these great polo games influence the sartorial trends throughout the United States, has been proved time and time again and the very repetition of it, combined with the additional proofs that are being given should be enough for you to notice and to prepare yourself for future demand" (*Men's Wear*, Apr. 10, 1929, p. 86).

The following autumn, camel's hair coats outnumbered raccoons at the Yale-Princeton football game. Almost as popular as the camel's hair was the navy blue chesterfield with a velvet collar; undergraduates chose a fly-front model, while alumni preferred a double-breasted coat. Just behind the chesterfield in popularity was the fly-front single-breasted box coat in tweed or fleece. But it was the camel's hair coat in a variety of styles that dominated the sartorial picture at the game, although it was noted that the double-breasted coat with a plain back, an almost classic polo coat, appeared to be the favorite camel's hair style.

A survey in 1928 of Midwestern and Southern universities showed the strong fashion influence of Ivy Leaguers on the wearing apparel of collegians throughout the country, but it also established the fact that cli-

matic conditions and variations in life-style produced some marked differences in overcoat and topcoat preferences. The following excerpts are taken from *Men's Wear*, which reported this survey under the headline "Long, Dark Grey and Blue Overcoats Lead at Mid-Western and Southern Universities."

These analyses are of the overcoat styles of 800 of the best dressed men at the Universities of Wisconsin, Michigan, Ohio and Illinois, and of topcoat models and colors worn by a similar class of students attending the Universities of Virginia, Washington and Lee, Duke, North Carolina and Georgia. Careful observations and accurate checking reflect the style situations in these parts of the country.

The outstanding style features disclosed by the survey of mid-western styles are as follows:

1. There is a marked tendency toward a shorter overcoat on the part of the better dressed students; that is, a coat from 46–47 inches in length with fly-front.

2. Many well-dressed students are indicating a preference for softer-finished or fleece overcoatings rather than the hard-finished fabrics on which the bulk of the business has been done this season.

3. The tendency toward the velvet-collared chesterfield is quite marked.

In the south the salient features are:

1. Long, single-breasted topcoats, 48 to more than 50 inches in length, in navy blue and oxford gray tweeds, prevailed and will be leading styles next season.

2. The tendency toward the shorter, 46 to 47 inch, fly-front topcoat was noted at the University of Virginia. This model will be more important at this university next fall and will affect the styles at the other universities slightly.

3. More and more raglan topcoats in Harris, Fair Isle and reproductions of these tweeds will be favored during the winter of 1928–29 at Virginia, but at the other universities this style will appear in only small numbers during that time.

Considering first the mid-western styles, it must be emphasized that the tendency toward the shorter fly-front coat is indicative of the style trend and not suggestive of a merchandising feature. These shorter coats will continue to be in the minority but will be worn by the best dressed students. It will take more than one season for this model to supplant the long topcoat and dominate the situation.

A similar condition prevails in regard to fleece fabrics. Though these softer-finished materials are important factors with the student bodies of these

The long straight lines of the topcoats of 1928 achieved a tubular effect and provided roomy comfort for the wearer. [HICKEY-FREEMAN CO.]

universities, they are still in their incipient stage and will account for only a small percentage of the total business.

The double-breasted overcoats included in this analysis were either not new coats or were purchased from stores away from the university campus, for hardly a retailer serving this important class of trade has sold any double breasted models this year. The men now wearing this style will replace them with a long, single-breasted button-through coat in oxford gray or navy blue, the typical university style in this section of the country.

The widespread popularity of the derby in the middle west points to a greater vogue next year as well as a continued demand for dark colored overcoats. The wardrobes of most of the boys contain only one overcoat, which garment is selected with the idea of serving not only for general campus wear, but for "formal" occasions as well. This custom, no doubt, explains the almost universal acceptance of dark oxford gray and navy blue overcoats and also accounts for the slowness with which the chesterfield overcoat has been taken up by these men. This style is too dressy for general wear; therefore, the purchases of velvet-collared coats have been confined largely to the wealthier boys who have at least two overcoats. The currents of style from Princeton and Yale to other universities will bring greater acceptance of the chesterfield coat, but by no means will it be the leader.

The longest overcoats were found at the University of Illinois, where it is expected next year this same style will continue and the shorter coat will be less in evidence than at Wisconsin and Michigan. The men at these latter universities will buy the shorter fly-front coat with greater avidity.

It is estimated that from 25 percent to 35 percent of next fall's overcoat business at middle western university centers will be done on the single-breasted, fly-front coat of approximately 46 to 47 inches in length. As was previously mentioned, this is the style of coat favored now by the best dressed men and their influence will be exerted over the remaining numbers who will gradually accept the shorter style of coat.

It is forecast that the remaining 65 percent to 75 percent of the volume of business will be accounted for by the long, single-breasted model with button-through front. Although the students in this section of the country are highly style conscious, it takes some time for a style to be universally adopted, or in other words, the transitions from one style to another require from one to two seasons or more, so next season the big style will continue to be the long coat. These predictions make no allowance for double-breasted models, which merchants appealing to the university trade are advised not to stock or promote yet.

In the south the predominance of long, single-breasted topcoats in navy blue and oxford gray was the most impressive style note gleaned. The vast majority of the coats were the button-through style, and the tweeds were of self-diagonals, herringbones, diamonds and checks. The difference between these topcoats and the average coat worn at northern institutions is that the double faced or through-and-through finish of the fabrics of southern coats are heavier than the single thickness of the northern coat materials. In other words, the winter outer garment of the southern university men is a lightweight overcoat or a heavyweight topcoat.

The small percentage of brown coats seen reflects the limited possibilities of this color for overcoat fabrics.

Based on the numbers of shorter fly-front coats seen at the University of Virginia, it is a safe prediction that this style will be of greater importance next year. The styles at other universities will be affected slightly by this influence, for the student body of the University of Virginia is the best dressed group of any of these southern universities.

Raglan coats in Harris, Fair Isle, and reproductions of these tweeds were in favor at the University of Virginia. Stevens-Shepherd Company at Charlottesville, Va., reported that 50 percent of their business was done on single-breasted fly-front coats and the remaining half on raglan coats of Harris tweed. The leading shades were medium and light brown mixtures and gray mixtures.

Only a few velvet collared chesterfields were seen worn by students on southern campuses, but because this style is not designed for general campus wear, it was only natural that limited numbers were observed. At Yale or Princeton chesterfield overcoats are not worn about the campus for general, but for dress-up occasions.

Only one tan polo coat was seen on this trip but the fact that Stevens-Shepherd Company, Charlottesville, Va., and Brooks, Durham, N.C., are giving this style prominent positions in their displays undoubtedly will influence the men to buy these coats next season. Polo coats are in a similar situation in that neither is the choice of a "one coat" man.

Coonskin coats and pony and dogskin coats were favored by only a small number of men. Only one fur-lined coat with black shell appeared at Washington and Lee.

A second survey that year reported on the overcoat, suit, shirt, collar, neckwear, and shoe styles seen along Broadway, and *Men's Wear* took care to remind the retailer that fashions worn there were relevant to his operation:

"In your town, Mr. Merchant, you probably have an element among the younger generation that resembles to a larger degree the Broadway type. They may spend the evenings in the drug stores and pool parlors, or else they may pass their spare hours in making a round of the homes of their fair young lady friends in rickety Fords or shining Packards. But still they have this desire to spice up their dress, and if you count upon their patronage to supply you with your daily bread and butter, it is necessary that you be progressive, and keep up with the latest styles in this gaily lighted district of Manhattan, for here the trend of styles is determined for all parts of the country among this class of men. You may not find that the styles arrive next week or the week after, but they will come and come hard, and if you are not fully prepared with the necessary articles to fill the latest prescriptions of Dame Fashion you will find your clientele will move away to some other place where they can obtain what they want when they want it" (Dec. 5, 1928).

This survey showed that one of every two theatrical men passing along Broadway favored the three-button double-breasted overcoat. Adapted from an English style, this theatrical version had a few notable changes: buttons were placed lower, and while the back was shapely, the narrowest part hardly ever came at the natural waistline, where it appeared in the English original. The coat was most often seen in dark blue and oxford gray, although it was noted that many younger Broadway men preferred medium gray and tones of brown in glenurquhart, herringbone, and other designs. The chesterfield was very popular in blue and dark gray, although here, too, many Broadway men preferred this formal outercoat in brown or gray tweed. The raglan style so popular in topcoats was equally popular in overcoats.

In the spring of 1929 topcoats of camel's hair, tweed, and covert were making fashion news. Raglans, reported to be increasing in popularity, were judged to be better adapted to tweeds and rough fabrics. "The topcoats of the well dressed men seen at the New York Stock Exchange are chiefly tweeds," wrote a *Men's Wear* reporter, who went on to include leading Broadway actors among the men whose clothes influenced apparel sales throughout the country. "The Broadway decision counts for something these days," he commented. "Broadway has a huge sartorial following throughout this country, and its strong endorsement of color will be felt from coast to coast. This color range is being felt in topcoats as well as in all the other articles of apparel." Along with the Wall Street broker, the Broadway celebrity chose tan as his favorite topcoat color that spring; this choice was no doubt influenced by both men's strong preference for the camel's hair coat, which had been accepted so widely by this time that a double-breasted style with a toga drape in back could be thrown over formal summer wear.

"If you want to feature a style with an appeal to the man who has more than one topcoat in his wardrobe," this writer remarked, "play single-breasted fly-front tan covert topcoats. Men who control the financial destinies of American commerce are showing a great preference for these coats. It is strictly a high style idea and will stamp your shop as knowing what's what with the leaders of fashion" (Apr. 10, 1929, p. 98).

Still, the range of topcoat styles that spring was particularly varied, as the selection offered at F. R. Tripler & Company in New York demonstrated. Among distinctive styles were a semi-shaped fly-front coat with peaked lapels, a broad-shouldered coat with a wide panel, a loose-fitting raglan coat, a shapely fly-front coat, and a fly-front raglan.

A fashion reporter's review of the overcoats scheduled for the winter ahead noted: "A decided preference on the part of the smartest dressed men for the skirted coat, the coat in which the skirt shows plenty of drape. That is the only distinct tendency, variety prevailing in fabrics, patterns and colors" (Men's Wear, Mar. 6, 1929).

The popularity of the raglan style was enhanced when, in 1929, the Prince of Wales arrived at the Epsom racecourse for the start of the Derby wearing a dark gray worsted raglan. A fashion maverick, he also wore what a Men's Wear writer described as a "racy flat brimmed tall hat; in other words, he wore that model which one would expect to see with hunting and riding kit, and not the conservative hat which he usually wears in London or with formal clothes" (July 10, 1929). Fashion innovation was not confined to the Prince, for that day his brother-in-law, Viscount Lascelles, wore a raglan overcoat of a dark gray

covert, and the fashion press remarked that it was unusual to have a double-breasted front on a smart raglan coat.

Only a short time after the Prince of Wales appeared at the Derby, prices on the New York Stock Exchange collapsed. It might have been expected that the Crash would threaten the bond that linked the fashion-conscious, trend-setting American with his British counterpart, but it proved to have just the opposite effect.

1930–1940

Reports of the Great Depression of the thirties sometimes leave the impression that it was a social leveler, whereas in reality it had quite the opposite effect. For although the middle class joined the have-nots, there were Americans who maintained their fortunes. They were in a decided minority, but that fact in no way diminished their influence. Fashion photographers followed them, photographed them at work and play, and filled newspapers and magazines with their pictures. During the twenties these men had looked to London for fashion leadership, and in this decade they continued to do so. Furthermore, despite the worldwide Depression London had no intention of abdicating its fashion leadership. In the struggle between style and the Depression, style was judged the victor, as the following excerpt from a fashion writer's report, filed in London in 1932, clearly indicates:

"Here in England one hears of drastic price cuts and other efforts to create business, yet all the time there is in London a set of tailors and shirtmakers who are busy supplying the needs of those men who, despite the adverse financial effect of reduced dividends, realize they have a certain role to play and that by maintaining their reputation as style leaders in the true sense of the word they are helping trade and keeping for London her name as the fashion centre of the world.

"I am writing this after reading various references in American newspa-

pers to the battle of Style versus Depression. Most emphatically do I say that the retailer and manufacturer who throughout these trying times keeps the flag of style flying will come out on top in the end. Notwithstanding his drastic price reductions and other efforts to attract business, he will create in the minds of his customers that respect which can only be paid to style. They will know that he has the right goods when there is money to spend; they will continue to patronize his shop; and later on when times become more normal he will benefit from the foundation he has so well and truly laid" (Men's Wear, Mar. 23, 1932).

The Prince of Wales was still a step from the throne, but insofar as the affluent, clothes-conscious American was concerned, he was the King of Fashion. What he and other well-dressed Englishmen wore was inevitably adopted by both Americans and Britishers who were still in a position to be fashionable.

For years smartly dressed Britishers

A big plaid of the horse-blanket type appeared in this roomy tweed ulster made for a frosty afternoon at a stadium. From Esquire, *November 1934.*

had been wearing the dark blue guards coat, inspired by the uniform coat of the Grenadier Guards, and for almost as many years farsighted American fashion editors had been predicting that this handsome style would soon be adopted by smartly dressed men in the United States. The prediction finally came true in this decade. The double-breasted guards coat had the casually elegant look that the still-affluent American of the early thirties coveted. For winter it was made of dark blue chinchilla. For spring the guards coat was of dark blue cheviot weighing about 18 ounces to the yard. Regardless of the season, the fashion features remained constant: wide lapels rolling to the middle of three pairs of buttons, with the upper buttons spaced slightly apart, an inverted pleat running almost all the way up the back to the collar instead of stopping between the shoulder blades, and a stitched-on half belt loose enough to accommodate deep folds on either side of the pleat.

Fashion reporters covering the fashionable United Hunts Meet at Belmont Park, Long Island, the traditional close of the New York racing season, commented on the number of well-dressed sportsmen wearing the guards coat, which by 1932 had become, in the words of a *Men's Wear* reporter, "very definitely a key garment in the well dressed men's overcoat wardrobe this season. In dark blue, the coat as worn by the best dressed men has broad shoulders, is shapely at the waist and drapes to the bottom with deep folds in back. In selling overcoats this season, this flash from America's racing capital might well be used to advantage in convincing a doubtful customer of the high position of this style in the world of fashion" (Nov. 23, 1932).

At the Princeton-Yale football game in 1932 the raccoon coat appeared to have graduated to the alumni class, while undergraduates shunned it in favor of greatcoats in short-nap pile or fleece fabrics. "Heavy weight coats were seen in greater number than they have been in recent seasons," noted

Men's Wear in the same issue. There was also a generous collection of double-breasted chesterfields in smooth-finish fabrics, although the classic velvet collar appeared to be less popular than it had been at the Princeton-Yale game of the previous year. The tan camel's hair coat was so popular "that a view of the Princeton side of Palmer Stadium revealed a distinctly light tannish cast to the crowd." Unlike the chesterfield, now without its velvet collar, this fashion perennial had not changed at all. The classic double-breasted model with a half or all-around belt was still the favorite, even if some raglan shoulders were also reported. The newest fashion, however, was the reversible coat, which was popular with both undergraduates and alumni. The Harris Tweed reversible was seen most often, with hundreds of men of all types wearing it. The usual tweed with a leather lining was photographed. The popular acceptance of the reversible coat was credited with having aroused and maintained interest in raglan models of all types during this decade. *Apparel Arts* in 1936 gave its approval to a black raglan-sleeved dress coat with a military collar, "the first new evening coat fashion in many years." Once regarded as limited to sports or country wear, the style had come a long way.

The self-assured Briton's casual way with bold patterns was copied by well-dressed Americans, and at the autumn United Hunts Meet at Belmont Park coats of aggressive plaids and checks vied with double-breasted camel's hair and fly-front covert cloth models. A relative newcomer also showing the British influence was the short-warm coat, a sporty model that measured 44 inches in length and had a decided flare not only to the sides but to the front and back of the skirt as well. A prominent East Coast sportsman who posed for photographers that day wore a leather-buttoned short-warm coat of tan melton, a brown derby, a brown cheviot suit, brown wing-tip shoes, and a white cashmere muffler with black

figures. He looked properly British, which was undoubtedly what he intended.

No one in this decade was indifferent to the fashion influence of the Prince of Wales, whose name appeared in *Esquire* with such regularity that in April, 1935, the fashion editors simply referred to him as "the P. of W.," adding "We hope you can't penetrate this incognito because every month we swear off mentioning his name in these pages again." Yet it would have been impossible to write of men's fashions without mentioning him, and the next month *Esquire* was the first to admit it: "Every third or fourth issue we swear off mentioning the Prince of Wales, getting sicker, if possible, of talking about him than you are of hearing about him. But it seems you can't keep him out of a discussion of the origin of new fashions as they come along. And the way we feel about these discussions of origin is that it is better for you to hear it from us than from the other boys out on the street corners."

The British look gathered momentum with a buttonless topcoat in bold district checks. Particularly popular with students at Oxford University, this style won considerable acceptance in the Eastern part of the United States and was eventually taken up by some of the more clothes-conscious American motion-picture actors, who had tremendous fashion influence during this decade. It was not surprising, therefore, when *Men's Wear* observed that "London and Hollywood gave the clothing industry the wrap model overcoat" (May 23, 1934). This roomy, loose-fitting coat was usually seen in either camel's hair or a soft, fleecy fabric that utilized llama fibers. The wraparound was considered an ideal coat for the man behind the wheel of an elegant open roadster. It was widely advertised, often in copy aimed at the younger man with a "natural flair for swank."

The wrap model was important in the overcoat lines of 1934. Three of the most photographed styles were a polo type of coat incorporating the popular bellows pleat of the contemporary sports jacket, with pleats at the side extending from the shoulders to the belt and down to the bottom of the coat; a camel's hair wraparound with three belt loops and two generous pleats adding fullness to the skirt; and a raglan-shouldered model with a new low-dip collar, a full back with inverted pleats, and a scalloped yoke. The wraparound's generously proportioned collar was usually worn turned up, and the belt was casually tied. The overall effect was so casual as to seem almost careless, and it gave the man who wore it well a certain dash.

In the meantime, the camel's hair topcoat was not neglected. In May, 1934, *Esquire,* after noting that the camel's hair coat had been in college longer than the stupidest undergraduate, added: "Since its first appearance, the model has been changed many times, but the fabric seems to be as much of a campus fixture as the buildings and grounds department. First, if you remember, it was a long and full affair, either half or full belted, bedecked with white buttons, and obviously deriving its inspiration from the coats of the international polo players. Today, the model is changed beyond recognition, and while the older types do survive, this one is the ranking favorite at the moment." The accompanying fashion sketch showed a coat cut rather short, with a full skirt and slashed pockets, a three button single-breasted front, and relatively narrow notched lapels.

The cotton-backed knit coat, popular in the twenties, gained still greater acceptance. The soft, fleecy fabric with its bulk and loft had an elegant sort of boldness rarely associated with a knitted fabric. The single-breasted model of the coat was a particular favorite and could be had in light, medium, and dark shades of gray, blue, and brown. It was so much in demand by 1932 that it was advertised as the largest-selling coat in the world. The semiulster was as popular as ever, particularly in imported Scotch fleece, and was advertised as strong, soft-textured, soft-looking, and amazingly warm. The soft density of fleece fabric was ideally suited to the opulent lines of the semiulster. When worn with a glenurquhart suit (a favorite of the Prince of Wales), a plaid wool muffler, and a rough felt homburg, the semiulster was one of the status symbols of the time.

A grandiose country coat was a glenurquhart semiulster of heavy fleece or Harris or Shetland tweed. For those who could afford it, it was available with a collar trimmed with mink, otter, or opossum. In May, 1934, *Esquire* recommended what it called a "town ulster" fashioned of a soft, rough mixture of cheviot and Shetland that was worn with a bowler, a dark blue suit, a checked shirt with a round starched collar, and a striped rep tie. Double-breasted with four buttons to button, this coat was most readily identified by a breast pocket that carried a flap, as did the regulation side pockets. Although there was a very slight suggestion of a waistline, the shape was more along straight, boxy lines. Sketched on a very tall man, it looked particularly dashing, but *Esquire* assured the reader that the town ulster was becoming to all but very short men. "It is relatively long and tends to give the illusion of added height," explained the editors, "assuming that you are of medium build, and not too roly-poly to begin with. Don't be misled by the word ulster—these coats are not unduly heavy."

Despite the popularity of these generously cut coats, there was also a marked trend toward shorter coats, a trend noted very early by *Esquire.* In its October, 1934, issue, under the heading "Outercoats Are Shorter This Season," the magazine showed a double-breasted topcoat of covert cloth that came only 2 inches below the knees. The reader was asked to note the blue cornflower boutonniere and was reminded that "you don't *have* to wear a breast pocket handkerchief with your topcoat if you don't feel like it. That is a passing vogue." In September, 1935, *Esquire* showed a short racing topcoat of covert made by a famous sporting tailor in London. It carried five rows of stitching and hardly came below the knees. Worn with a bowler and a red carnation boutonniere, it was, admitted the editors, "an outfit somewhat confined in its appeal, its present acceptance being limited strictly to that advance guard of the fashion trends, the horsey set you see at race meets."

By 1936, however, *Apparel Arts* considered the knee-length topcoat "front page fashion news. Ideal for town or country, the garment may be worn in any type of weather and is, in effect, a sport coat, dress coat and raincoat all in one. It is seen primarily in the single-breasted fly-front model with peak or notched lapels, although the double-breasted model is sometimes worn. The accepted fabric is natural colored covert cloth, with whipcord and melton also used. Reminiscent of the garments worn in the old coaching days, this coat still retains details that have a horsey touch, such as the stitching at the bottom, on the cuffs at the sleeves, and on the pocket flaps. The seams are all raised or strapped."

The knee-length covert topcoat had four rows of stitching, sometimes called "railroad stitching," with the rows spaced about $\frac{3}{8}$ inch apart. A double-breasted racing model with strapping down the center of the back carried five rows of stitching. Worn with a flat narrow-brimmed derby, the natural-tan covert coat was a requirement for the wardrobe of a man who considered himself to be well dressed. In August, 1937, covering the wardrobes of young men returning to college, *Esquire* showed a single-breasted, fly-front, notched-lapel knee-length coat of covert cloth with five rows of stitching.

Coats with fur linings or collars, or both, appeared to refute the fact that the country was still in the grip of a depression. Lined with mink or some less expensive fur that spread out over the big collar and wide lapels, the most luxurious of these coats resembled a fur ulster and extended well below the knees. A slimmer version was shown in the November, 1935, issue of

An oversize glenurquhart in a fairly heavy tweed appeared in this true British raglan with slash pockets and leather buttons. From Esquire, *March 1935.*

Two ulsters in fashion in 1936: (left) a gray checked tweed with a maroon overplaid; (right) a brown tweed with a fur collar. From Esquire, *November 1936.*

Esquire, in which the writer tackled the problem of selling an expensive coat during the Depression era: "It would be silly to infer that an outfit like this can be had for a song. The outlay is practically operatic. But if you're the kind who can afford a coat like this, then this is the kind of coat to get. However cold the winter, the worst that can happen to you, wearing this, is to be caricatured by the *New Masses.* Speaking of the revolution, this model's swagger military lines were inspired by the great-coats of the Czar's staff officers. The fabric is tweed and the lining is fur. The otter collar is cut in a new manner, combining the best features of the notch and peak lapel types. If the coat is buttoned up to the throat, as it may be, the collar stands up about your ears. The tapered sleeves, slanted pockets and the slight waist suppression combine to take away that fat Mandarin look that was once the curse of all coats with fur linings."

Even college students took to fur-lined coats, and among the most popular was a diagonal-weave Harris Tweed ulster with rabbit fur lining and a raccoon shawl collar. For what *Esquire* called "sit-down football, that arduous sport," the fashion department in November, 1937, recom-

mended this coat and a derby hat, a combination it thought represented a compromise, or even a sort of coalition, with the coonskin of former years, for "these are indeed the saddened and wisened late thirties and not the giddy and goofy early twenties." Meanwhile, the raccoon had won back the approval of the undergraduate, who now preferred the coat with a shawl collar, a wool lining, and large leather buttons.

While not attaining the level of acceptance of the knee-length topcoat, the fingertip coat enjoyed some popularity with what *Men's Wear* liked to call the Wall Street–Ivy League fashion axis. In 1937, *Apparel Arts* editors noted that for two years they had been showing the fingertip coat for various informal occasions. "This was no original idea on our part," they said, "but a result of our observations at leading fashion centers in England and America. Originally we introduced the short fingertip raincoat with side slits that was first seen in Scotland at the golf matches. Many claimed that it was not practical because it did not protect the trousers; but giving the wearer less weight and an added amount of freedom when walking, it was gradually accepted by undergraduates and sportsmen for on-campus and informal country use.

"This past spring at Princeton University the fingertip-length coat with military collar and raglan sleeve, which was introduced through *Apparel Arts* last summer from London, met acceptance by well dressed undergraduates for on-campus wear. Made of various types of gabardine and whipcord fabrics, this coat also carried side slits."

Reporting on university fashions, *Esquire* in its August issue that year included a gabardine fingertip-length field coat with raglan sleeves, a military collar, and side vents, recommending it for campus, motoring, and country wear.

With an eye still trained on London, *Apparel Arts* reported on the incredible popularity of the glenurquhart among smart Britishers, many of whom showed a preference for a dynamic new double-breasted and shaped glenurquhart overcoat with broad shoulders and extremely wide lapels. In fact, this bold plaid, then reaching the height of its popularity, left its mark on even the camel's hair coat. In 1936 a glenurquhart camel's hair coat appeared that was cut along the generous proportions of a semiulster. In the fall of 1936, *Apparel Arts* devoted a double-page spread to what it called "the Prince of Wales topcoat," recounting its adoption by the Prince, which automatically meant its subsequent adoption by his affluent admirers in England and the United States:

"He simply saw the original garment in the window of a retail store in Edinburgh, liked it and went inside and bought it. The Prince first wore the coat in London a year ago and others were not slow in taking up this fashion. The coat was originally made up in a llama type fabric and it is a short, loose-fitting raglan sleeved single-breasted fly-front topcoat with a blunt, stubby peak lapel. At the time the Prince of Wales first wore the coat, it was shown both in *Apparel Arts* and *Esquire* and many younger men, particularly undergraduates at the Eastern universities, adopted this fashion. Since then the garment has gained a much greater measure of acceptance.

"The coat seen in the accompanying photograph, worn by a well known American turfman who is considered one of the best dressed men in this country, is identical in model to that worn by the Prince of Wales. It too is a single-breasted fly-front raglan sleeved coat with slash pockets and double-breasted lapel.

"This garment is especially appropriate for young men, but by no means need it be reserved for university and country wear. It may also be worn in town with a snap brim or derby hat. Although the garment should be made up in tweeds, since this fabric imparts the desired effect and swagger to the lines of the model, it should be remembered that it is still fashionable to wear tweed or semi-country clothing in town. A recent cable from London states that men of all ages are wearing a similar coat in bold pattern with raglan sleeves, fly-front and double-breasted lapel in town as well as in the country."

A second double-page spread in this issue gave front and side views of the Prince of Wales topcoat along with exact specifications and swatches showing three of the various alternative choices of fabric. For a size 37 regular, the coat length was 44½ inches; the width of the cuff, 2½ inches; the widest part of the lapel, 4½ inches; and the length of the lapel from tip to first button, 10½ inches. A postscript called attention to "the

very natural raglan shoulder with loose-fitting armhole, the self cuff, the flare at the bottom of the coat, the vertical slash pockets and the blunt peak lapels. This model has all the characteristics of the true raglan with narrow, natural shoulder, and should come only an inch or two below the knee." The fabrics of the three swatches were a cheviot tweed in a shadow check, a district-plaid cheviot in a large, colorful glenurquhart pattern, and a large houndstooth-check Harris Tweed. Among other coats featured in this issue were a fly-front knee-length overcoat with slanted pockets; a semiulster with four buttons to button, slant pockets, and set-in sleeves; and a double-breasted blue guards coat with a half belt and a full skirt.

In 1937 the loden cloth coat was as popular in the United States as it was in Europe. A soft fleece fabric originating in Austria, loden cloth was made of a raw wool taken from mountain sheep and was sometimes called a grease wool, since its natural oil content was so high. The original loden coat from Austria, in a forest green, was a fairly long coat with set-in sleeves, slash pockets, a button-through front, and a military collar. But the American man preferred his loden cloth in a fingertip-length raglan style, although *Esquire,* reporting on the Tyrolean influence in men's fashions in its September issue that year, showed an authentic Tyrolean model "worn by sportsmen in the Tyrol for years for shooting, walking and driving." On the same page, the editors showed the extent of Tyrolean influence with sketches of Tyrolean-motif suspenders, reversed-calf shoes in the Tyrolean manner, Tyrolean acorn-pattern cuff links, a green wool tie with Tyrolean flowers, a cotton flannel plaid shirt from the Tyrol, a lightweight wool muffler with Tyrolean shooting figures, and a hat identified as London's interpretation of the black Tyrolean hat for informal town or spectator sports wear.

It is interesting to note that as the decade came to a close and the coun-

The man at right wears a fingertip-length racing coat of covert cloth. From Esquire, *March 1939.*

try began to emerge from the Depression, coats tended to be more practical. With enough money to start buying clothes again, the average American was going to be a more discriminating shopper. In the winter of 1938–1939, the eminently practical reversibles and removable-lining coats were competing with the pace-setting double-breasted raglan for leadership. The next winter a full-page advertisement by C. B. Shane Corporation of New York (*Esquire,* November, 1939) promoted "2 Complete Coats in One." Under four small sketches the respective first-person copy read:

"It's the perfect topcoat. Just the weight I want these crisp days.

"When the frost comes, I need more warmth, so I take the lining, pull a single fastener and . . .

"With one simple motion, I attach the body and sleeve lining neatly and snugly.

"My coat is entirely transformed. Now it's the perfect overcoat, warm in the coldest weather."

For $25 a man could buy a coat of Alpagora that, according to the advertiser (Stratburg, Galion, Ohio), gave 38 percent longer wear and 25 percent more warmth while weighing 2 pounds less than the average overcoat. "Scientifically moth-proofed and shower-proofed, Alpagora is a knitted blend of soft lustrous Alpaca plus rugged mohair and fine protective wool" (*Esquire,* November, 1939).

The dark blue coat became enormously popular in 1939, in a not unexpected reaction to World War II, which had long been threatening and had now begun. This fashion trend had first been noted in November, 1938, by *Esquire* fashion editors reporting on the revival of the navy blue coat of melton cloth, a rugged fabric first worn in Melton Mowbray, the hunting area in England. "Drastic surgery on an old favorite, " is the way *Esquire* viewed the revival:

"What appears on the surface to be a new fashion in men's clothing is often merely the return of an old favorite on which a fashion operation has been performed—the elimination or addition of details which do not alter the underlying characteristics of the garment. Such a fashion is the navy blue coat of Melton cloth. Originally a coaching coat with narrow shoulders, in length it descended somewhere to the region of the calf, and had as much opening at the lapels as is noticeable in a baseball catcher's chest-protector. Young men in this country and abroad who accepted covert cloth in topcoats are now adopting the Melton coat for winter wear, in its revived version. Shoulders are broad, but natural, and the coat has been shortened to about knee length, with roomy pockets and wide flare to the skirt. The chest-protector

A melton coat reminiscent of coaching days appeared in 1939 with set-in sleeves and flapped change and chest pockets. From Esquire, *November 1939.*

type of front opening has been lowered, pockets have been lowered and, reminiscent of coaching days, they are roomy and flapped. A long center vent permits the maximum of comfort when walking. Collar, lapel, front of coat and all pockets carry welt seams, and the sleeves have three rows of stitching at the cuffs."

The sketch accompanying the report showed a model wearing his melton cloth topcoat with a hard-finished worsted suit ("a grey-blue shade now popular in London"), a bowler with a full crown and a narrow brim, and a racing umbrella—all very correct and very British. The decade ended as it had begun, with British fashion influence dominant.

1940–1950

The transition from the Depression of the thirties to the war of the forties had a sobering effect on Americans that naturally affected the clothes and colors they wore. The dark blue coat that became popular in the fall of 1939 continued to gain acceptance in 1940. In November of that year *Esquire* devoted a page to a silver-haired model wearing a narrow-panel overcoat made of a navy blue cheviot of an exceptionally close weave, "making it a dress-up type of coat and one that does double duty as a perfectly harmonious outergarment for wear with evening clothes."

The article continued: "The moral here is that overcoat models are undergoing a change. For one thing, the buttons on double-breasteds used to be spaced far apart, both crosswise and lengthwise, but now it's smarter when the buttons are set relatively close together. The effect is that of a narrow panel and that, of course, is where this model gets its name. The general idea of the narrow panel overcoat was introduced at the close of the racing season last year and has since been perfected and popularized to a point where it constitutes the acme of correct fashion in town overcoats." Pointing out that the coat's shorter length, only an inch or two below the knee, was also in keeping with the current trend, *Esquire* turned its attention to the rest of the model's wardrobe, which had an overall look of substance and dignity: a gray homburg hat, a red silk scarf with a white circle pattern ("relieving the dark-blue tone of the overcoat and adding a slapdash of color"), gray mocha gloves, a blue suit in a clear-face worsted, and black straight-tip shoes. But it was the narrow-panel coat that was the fashion news and a silhouette that would remain popular through most of the decade.

In this conservative climate the chesterfield in muted shades was quite at home, although it had a few styling changes that were traceable to the military atmosphere that pervaded the country. The velvet collar gave way to a self-collar, the peaked lapels took on added width, and the coat assumed flared lines. Navy blue continued to rise in popularity. Even the more assertive semiulster overcoat, with its half belt, convertible collar, and slash pockets, became most fashionable in navy blue. Finally, the luxurious town coat with a fur lining settled for this shade of blue.

Tweed overcoats were in demand, but the well-dressed man was expected to discriminate between the tweed coat that was proper for town wear and the tweed coat that was strictly for country wear. In the November, 1940, issue, *Esquire* pointed the way:

"The man at the left is wearing a very commendable business outfit . . . a blackish-brown Shetland overcoat with fly-front and peaked lapels. For the rest, a Tartan cashmere muffler, brown hat worn with center crease only, pigskin gloves, brown worsted suit, tan shoes.

"The other overcoat, you will note, reaches only to the knees; it has three pairs of buttons with the lapel rolling to the top pair. The bluish diagonal tweed is a countrified fabric. The rough-textured felt hat is in keeping with the coat, as are the natural woven cashmere muffler, knitted gloves to match, grey cheviot suit, brown shoes."

In the spring of 1941, the shorter coat predominated. The English short-warm coat, or British warm, as it was often called, enjoyed a resurgence of popularity, particularly in Harris or herringbone tweed. Ending just above the knee, with rows of stitching around the bottom and at the sleeves, it had the military air and easy leg movement that men were now seeking. Not surprisingly, the fly-front raglan short coat with a military collar sold well.

As colors grew more conservative and the bold patterns of the thirties were replaced by herringbones, plain diagonals, and simpler effects, the styling features of both coats and suits grew more extroverted. Double-breasted suit jackets in 1943 featured a new lapel that rolled to the bottom

The single-breasted navy-blue coat at left, with peaked lapels and a fly front, vied with the bulkier checked tweed ulster for national fashion honors. From Esquire, *January 1940.*

leading spring colors showed the American man's readiness to forget navy blue. One, a subtle blending of blue and green called lovat green, was especially attractive with the new soft tweeds. The other was a warm brown popular in an overchecked tweed. A conspicuous topcoat silhouette was the raglan coat with set-in sleeves, notched lapels, adjustable tabs on the cuffs, and slash pockets, which were almost a requirement for raglan styles.

Brown continued to be an important coat color for fall, but this time it was loam brown, which had gray overtones. Dark blue made a comeback, but now it was marine blue, a shade lighter than navy. In the winter of 1946–1947 buttons in two pairs and the long roll lapel were still features of the dressy double-breasted overcoat, but now the buttons had been moved upward so that, instead of rolling to the top button, the lapels extended to the bottom button and there was only one fastening.

During 1947 it almost seemed as if the American man could not get enough color in his wardrobe. Fabric designers began to weave together brown, tan, blue, and green to achieve a multiple-color effect, the blue being used in the overplaid and the other colors being interwoven as a background. The effect was particularly attractive in a generously cut single-breasted raglan coat of tweed.

In March, 1949, dark blue cashmere was adapted to the "bold look" in a double-breasted polo-type coat with a half belt, set-in sleeves, patch pockets, and stitching set back ⅝ inch from the edges. Worn with a muffler having doubloon coin dots, a snap-brim hat, and the new hefty, thick-soled blucher shoes, it was the epitome of what *Esquire* called "a look of self-confident taste."

In the fall of that year, the man tall

button, and double-breasted overcoats carried a big roll lapel.

The strict regulations issued by the War Production Board affected menswear for the duration of the war, but in 1946, with the war over and the young veteran back in mufti, the industry picked up again. That spring, topcoats showed a preoccupation with more youthful styling: the middle button was moved below the natural waistline, and coat lapels were of the long roll type, accentuating a slender line. Coats ended at the knee, and the

(opposite) Plaids and checks constituted the fashion formula for spring in these sporty tweed topcoats. From Esquire, *March 1940.*

some in checks

Hᴇʀᴇ's a right smart collection of checked tweed topcoats—forerunners of the sports trend for spring. All are correct for wear in town or country, as well as for traveling. At upper left is a single breasted fly front peak lapel tweed coat in two-button style with lapel rolled to the waistline. This is a brown cheviot with colorful Glen pattern, and comes only two inches below the knee. It is worn in town with semi-sports clothes, reverse calf shoes and either the Cavalier, Homburg or bowler hat. The left hand figure of the center group shows a single breasted, button-through, raglan sleeve, tweed topcoat in large tan Glen pattern, with leather buttons, flapped pockets, ticket pocket and a wide flare to the skirt. It is especially appropriate for country wear with Lovat tweed suit, reverse calf "gummies" and sports hat. The man in the center wears a three-button, notch lapel, single breasted Harris tweed coat with set-in sleeves and leather buttons, monk front shoes and semi-sports hat. The man at the right wears a Harris tweed balmacaan topcoat in large blue, grey and white check, a favorite with college men. It has slash pockets, military collar and raglan shoulders, and is worn here with a pork pie hat, striped flannel suit and brown brogue shoes. At lower right is a knee length single breasted fly front grey Glen Urquhart topcoat with set-in sleeves. Although shown here with town accessories, it is equally correct for spectator sports.

(For answers to all dress queries, send stamped self-addressed envelope to Esquire Fashion Staff, 366 Madison Ave., N. Y.)

types of topcoats

Here we have not only four topcoats, but four complete outfits to describe, so we get to the business at hand without delay. Fabrics, colors, and designs determine the purpose for which topcoats are most appropriate. Specific types for town may be differentiated easily from those for country. The covert cloth topcoat worn by the executive at the **top left** has all of the ingredients of correct fashion for wear to business. The olive-tan shade goes well with most suits and has become a favorite. Closely allied is this trim fly-front model with rows of stitching around the bottom and at the cuffs. The rest of his outfit consists of a brown turned-up brim hat, maroon and white Macclesfield tie, white broadcloth shirt, starched collar, glen plaid suit, brown shoes. At the **top center** is the ardent sportsman rigged out for country in the green and brown Harris tweed coat patterned after the British Warm. Its shortness guarantees free leg action, and it carries stitching around the bottom and the sleeves. With it he wears a pork-pie lightweight green felt hat, foulard tie, oxford shirt, diagonal weave tweed suit, brown reverse calf sandan boots with crepe rubber soles. The man at the **top right** is wearing another type of topcoat commendable for sportswear. It's a blue-on-brown plaid tweed, signifying a basic color trend. This raglan model coat with military collar has slash pockets. His brown felt hat, a slope-crown model, is gaining in popularity. The printed foulard tie is backed up by a Sandune shirt with attached collar, and the sky-grey flannel slacks blend with the rest of the outfit. The plain toe shoes of reverse calf have rubber soles. The fellow at the **bottom** brings us back to town in a brown Shetland topcoat with peaked lapels, fly-front, and change pocket. It's tops for fashion. The Americana striped silk tie is in good company with the porcelain-blue broadcloth shirt and white starched collar. His suit is chalk-striped grey unfinished worsted and the shoes are brown calf.

(For answers to your dress queries, send stamped self-addressed envelope to Esquire Fashion Staff, 366 Madison Ave., N. Y.)

enough to carry it well preferred a broad-shouldered overcoat with long roll lapels of great width, the low-set V opening serving to frame such bold look fashions as a widespread collar and a decisively striped tie with a Windsor knot. Covert cloth and diagonal-weave tweeds were ideal fabrics for wide-shoulder, wide-lapel overcoats now that lighter-weight clothes were returning. Dunbrook—the Ohio Overcoat Company, advertising a big, roomy raglan tweed overcoat, headlined its advertisement "Take a Load off Your Shoulders" (*Esquire,* October, 1949).

The tall, broad-shouldered silhouette introduced by the bold look evolved into the "tall-T effect," which *Esquire* illustrated in October, 1949, with two topcoats it deemed "fitting companions for the new charcoal worsted suits." One, a double-breasted tweed chesterfield, had peaked lapels and buttons that were placed higher. The other, a covert cloth, was "suit-weight and roomy." Both coats hung some inches below the knees.

The overcoat story of the decade ended on a strong note of elegance with the introduction of a new model, the Chester, a double-breasted style designed for the big man. Its shoulders and lapels were wide, and the back showed a half belt and an inverted pleat that extended from a point between the shoulder blades to the bottom. In dark blue or dark gray cashmere, the Chester was an eminently stylish coat.

The fashion outlook seemed bright. The Depression was a decade in the past; the war memories were slipping into history. The bold look, an expression of new vitality and optimism, had

In 1944 this attaché-case carrier was wearing a brown herringbone topcoat with set-in sleeves and the slash pockets usually associated with raglans. From Esquire, March 1944.

proved a tonic for the menswear industry and a fashion lesson for the consumer. Yet in the fall of 1949 charcoal gray was the dominant suit color; it proved to be a harbinger of the middle-of-the-road character of the coming decade.

1950–1960

The fifties were a conservative decade, and for the first half the password was restraint. The bold look of the late forties had taught the American man the importance of a coordinated look, and now he proceeded to build his wardrobe around a look of understatement. In its February, 1950, issue *Esquire* began the new decade by polling the sartorial preferences of several hundred of the nation's outstanding men and passed on the results to its readers:

Ease and naturalness. Never extreme, the top executive dresses to express his own individual tastes and talents. Self-confident, natural, his appearance accents the *man.*

No exaggeration. Where restraint is the password, no one needs shoulders like a weight-lifter or hips like a halfback. The heavy work is done with the brain.

Coordination. The man of affairs thoughtfully selects his accessories with his suit as the basis of the outfit. The effect is refined, personal, and unobtrusive.

Distinction without drabness. It takes a bold man to finally arrive at the head of a conference table and he wouldn't be expected to be timid when it came to color. Instinctively, he chooses patterns and shades that are notable for their restraint and good taste.

In this period of conservatism, when men sought distinction without drabness, there was nothing smarter for a country weekend than a tan polo cloth British warm coat with leather buttons. In March, 1950, *Esquire* sketched one on a model who also wore a porkpie hat and brown brushed-calf shoes with crepe rubber soles.

In 1950 the magazine introduced Mr. T, a new trim look. The straight-hanging lines of his natural-shoulder suit gave Mr. T a vertical look, which in turn required accessories of more modest proportions than those of the bold look. The trim look was carried over to his coats, and easy-fitting tweeds with a high military bal collar, straight-hanging lines, slash pockets, and notched lapels more than met the demand. The tweed fabrics were all-over weaves of small proportions marked with deftly designed overplaids. Fly-front topcoats of silk-soft gabardines and coverts were favored, too, both being the kind of smooth, lighter-weight fabric that complemented the trim look. Wanting warmth without weight, many men chose an overcoat that combined a woolen shell with a pile-fabric lining. The bulky overcoat had been completely superseded.

In the springs of 1951 and 1952 patterns and checks were popular in both coats and suits, but in keeping with the conservative Ivy League character of the period, they were

(left) The ulster came to town in 1934. A double-breasted coat in a rough-textured combination of cheviot and Shetland, it had good length and a flapped chest pocket. From Esquire, *February 1934. (center) The knee-length covert topcoat, revived in 1936, had raised seams at the edges. It was worn with a plaid or other patterned suit. From* Esquire, *March 1936. (right) The dark blue chesterfield with peaked lapels was popular in spring, 1937. From* Esquire, *March 1937.*

Three types of tweed overcoats popular in 1938: (left) a brown plaid double-breasted coat; (center) a diagonal-tweed raglan; (right) a fingertip-length coat with raglan shoulders and side vents. From Esquire, *November 1938.*

(left) Navy blue was widely favored in 1939 for both double-breasted and single-breasted overcoats. From Esquire, *November 1939. (right) The low-opening coat, shown for spring wear in 1940, bridged the gap between the heavy overcoat and the lighter topcoat. From* Esquire, *March 1940.*

(left) The tan fleece British warm was above knee-length and had a flapped chest pocket. From Esquire, *November 1941. (right) The fly-front topcoat in brown-and-natural herringbone Shetland had a trim appearance. From* Esquire, *October 1945.*

Topcoats and Overcoats

small patterns and checks. Even double-breasted overcoats and topcoats with fairly wide lapels and collars adhered to the straight-hanging lines and natural shoulders of the Ivy look. A representative overcoat of 1951, for example, was a raglan of small houndstooth checks with a bal collar, a button-through front, and slash pockets. A year later, a new model, the split raglan, made its appearance and was judged to be even more in keeping with the natural-shoulder Ivy League look. This new-style raglan had set-in sleeves, and the shoulder seams extended down to the cuffs. The lapels were notched, the pockets were patch-style, and the stitching around

Nubby tweed, strong in all apparel of the time, added a distinctive note to this raglan coat in 1955. The coat had a bal collar, leather buttons, tabs on the sleeves, and slash pockets.

the pockets was set back about ½ inch from the edge. Flaps were set within the frames of the pockets, and so the style was called a "frame patch pocket."

By the mid-fifties, as more and more Americans moved to the suburbs that ringed the large cities, overcoats and topcoats reflected a less urban lifestyle. Nubby tweeds in plain weaves, small checks, or contrasting tones became fashion news. In the words of *Esquire*'s fashion department in October, 1955, "Tweed's been around the track before, but never with such a thoroughbred look . . . all carrying less weight and, consequently, more dash." A handsome example was a full-sweep single-breasted tweed topcoat worn with a velour Tyrolean hat and a tweed suit. The full-cut raglan coat with slash pockets that had been so popular in the forties was still a best seller in the tweed category. A year later, in October, 1956, *Esquire* was still declaring a tweedy year, giving its approval to "a lofty type of tweed flecked with colorful nubs and light in weight to conform to the current trend in topcoats."

By mid-decade, the American man began to dress up instead of down and showed a readiness for more colorful clothes. In short, he was prepared to emerge from his gray flannel cocoon. Two or even three colors (multiple or compound colors) were introduced in the nubs to give new life to gray, brown, and blue suits. Similar effects were achieved in tweed outercoats with such mixtures as two shades of gray with blue, gold, and red nubs. Soft, fleecy fabrics shared in this colorful trend, and there were handsome solid colors and heather mixtures, particularly the lovat shade of soft greenish blue, as well as brown-and-gold blends.

The natural-tan shade of covert cloth was as much at home in town as at a sporting event, with a velvet collar on a fly-front coat lending covert an elegant note of formality for town wear. Gabardine topcoats, many with zipped-in linings, proved ideal for air travel, which was becoming in-

creasingly commonplace for many Americans. The water-repellent worsted gabardine with a zipped-in lining was publicized as an all-season coat; the prevailing model was a single-breasted raglan. Silk and silk-looking suits and sports coats were popular by mid-decade, and this lustrous look soon influenced topcoats. Single-breasted styles in blends of silk and wool were soon being seen in small diamond patterns, geometric designs, and solid colors.

The last half of the decade saw a revival of old favorites and the introduction of exciting new fashions. In November, 1956, *Esquire* welcomed the revival of the blues: "Fashion has changed its tune, and the blues are back in full swing, arranged for suits, sportswear, topcoats and accessories, and improvised in many keys for day and evening wear." An elegant example was a new four-button double-breasted blue suit worn with an all-weather dark blue gabardine topcoat.

In 1957 the buttonless topcoat with a wraparound belt that had been popular in the thirties made a comeback, this time with a brightly colored lining. The following year, bright linings were used in all styles of coats of all colors and became a major fashion influence.

Colors and patterns that had almost vanished from the fashion scene at the start of the decade reappeared before it was over. Revivals included the district-check topcoat, in a raglan style with flap pockets, a bal collar, and a button-through front. Among other coats were a woolen bal topcoat in a shepherd's check of gray, black, and white with a red overplaid, lined with red wool; a lovat-green topcoat mottled with black in a soft, distinctive herringbone wool tweed with pearl buttons, raglan sleeves, and slash pockets; and a very lightweight waterproof and windproof raglan coat that featured the newest development in outerwear construction, a nylon exterior fused to an all-wool plaid lining by a process that formed air cells to prevent condensation and provide insulation.

Natural-tan cashmere, this time of a curly texture, aroused considerable fashion interest in a two-button double-breasted overcoat with a half belt. Antelope suede in its natural soft tan color was a new material for an outercoat with set-in sleeves, slash pockets, an all-around belt, and a convertible collar that could be fastened at the top or rolled to a lower point.

In 1959 a new styling concept appeared in overcoats based on a triangle shape: natural shoulders with a decided flare from the waist to the bottom. One of the most distinctive coats in this new shape was made of an unfinished flannel in a diagonal weave, the top half being lined with gold satin and the bottom half with a herringbone cashmere.

The shaped Continental suit that challenged the Ivy League look in the spring of 1956 led to the Continental topcoat of 1959, a knee-length coat with broader shoulders, a shaped body, and semipeaked lapels. The favorite fabrics for this dressy topcoat were patterned cheviots and worsteds. The favorite topcoat color that spring was a burnished brown, an ideal shade for the Continental style. Very early in the next decade a more subtly shaped British silhouette, more in harmony with the rangy American physique than the Continental look, would dominate men's suits, and by the end of 1959 it was beginning to affect the general silhouette of overcoats.

1960–1970

The Peacock Revolution was the leading fashion news of the sixties, affecting almost every item in the American man's wardrobe. It started with shirts and ties, moved on swiftly to suits, and next affected outercoats. Yet in the first years of the decade overcoats and topcoats were still in the process of reclaiming the fresh colors and bold patterns they had lost during the early fifties. There was little to suggest that a full-scale fashion revolution would occur in this decade. As late as 1965, in fact, the most popular

outercoats were still the stylish staples: the short guards coat, the camel's hair, the British warm, and the covert and melton cloths.

The year 1960 saw worsteds in gun-club checks and glenurquhart plaids, both ideally suited to raglan and split raglan coat styles. This was fashion progress, but it was safe and predictable, giving no indication of the fashion upheaval to come. Patterns continued to be popular in the topcoats of 1961, with a dash of unconventional colors for added interest. For example, an olive glen plaid with split raglan shoulders and a flapped chest pocket might be accented with wine and gold-color stripings, and a brown-and-white checked raglan of velour-textured wool might be flecked with touches of green.

In 1962 the suede leather outercoat arrived from Europe. When shown in a double-breasted trench coat style, it was particularly attractive to the young American peacock. Although it had only limited appeal that year, by 1968 leather jackets and outercoats would be important fashions. But in 1963 the fashion writer George Frazier observed in *Esquire,* though for the last time: "What is so nice about men's clothes is that their obsolescence is never obligatory."

The knee-breaker outercoat appeared in 1963, and in its November issue *Esquire* gave it three full-color pages, commenting: "There is much to be said for a fashion concept that combines style and convenience." "Knee breaker" was an umbrella term coined to include topcoats, overcoats, and outercoats of all kinds that broke at the knee or slightly above. "They have," said *Esquire,* "a neater, more flattering line and their shorter length makes them ideal for unencumbered walking." A representative group of that season's knee breakers included an updated version of the polo coat in a blend of camel's hair and wool with a natural-beaver shawl collar and a full muskrat lining; a classically styled coat of luxurious baby-antelope suede with a pale beige mink lining that buttoned in for extra warmth; a

The split raglan coat of 1961 had a set-in-sleeve effect in front and raglan seams in back.

multicolor Irish tweed having a one-piece raglan sleeve with a button-tab cuff; a double-breasted dark brown corduroy coat that ended 3 inches above the knee; a conservatively styled topcoat of imported French wool broadcloth in what was then a new color for topcoats, vicuña; an all-wool weather coat in a bold black-and-white houndstooth check with a split raglan sleeve, a bal collar, and a button-through closure; and a conservatively dressy black double-breasted wool coat with a herringbone weave on the outside and a plaid weave on the inside.

Besides appearing in the new shorter length, the topcoats that year began to evolve a new silhouette which owed much to the British warm coat that had first won American acceptance in the thirties. This new model had shoulders and lapels of medium width, shapeliness at the waistline, a bottom

The double-breasted coat of 1963 had a convertible collar, three sets of buttons, slash pockets, and a clearly defined plaid pattern.

flare, and two pairs of buttons, with the upper pair at the waistline. Still, the college man remained faithful to the classic British warm with three sets of buttons in a double-breasted closure. However, the number of buttons did not matter; what counted in 1963 was that the coat be a knee breaker.

Brooks Brothers, the home of the Ivy League look, had started a small revolution of its own when, early in 1962, it introduced a two-button suit with slightly greater waist suppression. By 1963, the popularity of the two-button suit, helped immeasurably by the fact that President John F. Kennedy favored this style, resulted in the two-button, single-breasted topcoat. Unlike the two-button suit, the topcoat did not attract much of a following, and in the fall Ivy Leaguers returned to college with British warm

coats having such new styling features as a convertible military collar, flaps on both the lower pockets and the chest pocket, and side vents.

Overcoats in the winter of 1964–1965 acquired new luxury with fur collars and fur linings, once again the ultimate in elegant winter wear. But fur, no matter how expensive, was not the important news. Shape was—a concept carried over from the new shaped suits that had made every clothes-conscious American man also diet-conscious. The close-fitting topcoat with broad shoulders, waist suppression, a two-button closure, peaked lapels, and slanting flap pockets was a dramatic expression of the new youth culture that had swept across the United States by the mid-sixties. To be young was considered vitally important, in the view of the nation's sociologists, and the shaped topcoat said the same thing in fashion terminology.

The fitted box coat designed for sportswear was one of the new shapes. In November, 1964, *Esquire* featured a double-woven, double-weight woolen with a suppressed waist created by Datti of Rome: "The dominant feature is a boxy shape. Side panels give it a geometric look. There is an exaggerated welt seaming throughout, a high center vent, a flare to the bottom, a square front yoke which extends around the button closure." Although this style was accepted by only a few men, the shaped back and raised seams were to have a noticeable effect upon the styling of coats for the rest of the decade.

Knee breakers in white with extraordinary linings were shown in *Gentlemen's Quarterly* in November, 1964. According to the editors, the most colorful coat that winter would be white. To prove their point they showed a double-breasted coat of white napped mohair that had white leather buttons, pointed and buttoned flap patch pockets, a split shawl collar, epaulets, side vents, and a red quilted lining; and a white Angola leather trench coat with a black leather buckled all-around belt, stitched-down

shoulder flaps, slash pockets, and a black acrylic pile lining. These were hardly coats for every man, but they made a strong fashion statement that left no doubt that the Peacock Revolution was not a passing fad and that from now on changes in menswear would be as dynamic and dramatic as they were in women's clothes.

With the American peacock ready to strut, *Gentlemen's Quarterly* wondered in November, 1967, if a detachable cape might not be a likely addition to his outercoat. "We have been showing capes since our first issue, ten years ago," wrote the editors in 1967, "but frankly, nobody has cared very much. In the past few months, however, their dash and swagger have caught the fancy of London's swinging young blades and Parisians on the Rue de la Pompe have acclaimed them as *le der-*

The dressy-looking overcoat of 1964 was a two-button double-breasted model with a shaped body and slanting pockets. It was favored in navy blue.

nier cri. Stateside, too, the mood may at last be ripe for their resurgence."

In the same issue, *Gentlemen's Quarterly* showed a thigh-high coat inspired by the British officers' warmer: a double-breasted coat of putty-shaded wool with waist suppression and flare, a flapped chest pocket, angled lower flap pockets, and a deep center vent. Worn with a jaunty cap and a long, boldly striped wool scarf, it foreshadowed the military-inspired coats to come.

"With outercoats having reached almost jacket brevity, it is a pleasure to have a conspicuously longer (42″–46″) garment that is high-waisted and shaped to a bold flare," observed *Esquire* the following June. This conspicuously longer garment was named the "maxi-greatcoat," an aristocratic-looking coat that appeared to have stepped out of the Napoleonic Wars. Among the maxis photographed were a dark navy wool melton with black brass military buttons, lined in red wool; an emerald-green tweed with a deep inverted back pleat, flap pockets, and a half belt in back; and a salmon-color heavy wool twill.

The following autumn, the maxi-greatcoat appeared in a great variety of fabrics and colors. The French designer Pierre Cardin offered one in brown Donegal tweed that, like the Cardin suit jackets, was shaped from the high armholes to the pronounced flare at the bottom. Cerruti in Paris produced a maxi in double-faced diagonal-weave cashmere and wool, and another European-made maxi was in a vicuña-shade wool with a brown Persian lamb shawl collar.

Now that the Peacock Revolution had reversed the line of command and fashion was starting at the bottom of the social ladder and working upward, leather, once considered the almost exclusive property of motorcycle toughs, became respectable. In November, 1968, *Esquire* decided that of all materials used in men's clothing leather had the most personality. "As a matter of fact, it is because of this that it experiences such fluctuations in personality," the editors concluded. "A

The maxi coat of 1968 was a very long, shaped double-breasted coat with a big collar, wide lapels, and huge slanting flapped pockets. Twill was the favored fabric.

few years ago, for instance, leather's lot was not a very lucky one. This was strictly a case of guilt by association. The sight of leather on Brando and his wild ones as they roared into town on their motorcycles gave it an inimical image, hinting of anarchy and atrocities. But the point about leather is that it always survives such misfortunes. It is not for nothing that it is often referred to as the most masculine of all materials. It is also one of the most romantic, the most glamorous, summoning up, by the mere mention of its name, the vision of the American cowboy—his saddle, his jerkin, his boots, and so on. And it also suggests fliers in the First World War. The very word reminds you of somebody like Buddy Rogers or Richard Arlen or Gary Cooper as he gets into the cock-

pit, a lady's white silk scarf around his neck, and always he is wearing that leather jacket as he pulls the goggles down over his eyes and gives that gallant little wave. And of course leather was the uniform both of SS troops and Montgomery's Desert Rats. And, finally, leather is a smell—one of the richest and most meaningful smells in the world, suggesting not only cowboys and World War I aviators, but also club chairs and the volumes in a university library. This winter would be a lot less elegant were it not for what a number of esteemed designers and manufacturers have been achieving with leather."

What they were achieving included such fashions as a three-quarter-length antiqued-leather coat with a belt, a center vent, lower flap pockets, a detachable pile lining, and a front zipper that veered off to give a diagonal closure at the top; an eight-button trench coat in a palomino naked leather that had epaulets, lower slash pockets, a notched collar, and a zip-out pile lining; and a six-button double-breasted coat of antiqued leather with a Regency-style collar, wide lapels, angled pockets, a deep center vent, a full back yoke, and a half front yoke. The following year swaggering double-breasted fur coats trimmed with leather were high fashion news.

By the end of the decade, coat lengths had been stabilized at 44 or 45 inches (midi) and 47 or 48 inches (maxi). There was still the knee breaker, but it was fast losing ground. The question was, which length would prevail? In 1970, the length of men's outercoats was as controversial a topic as the length of women's dresses. "The mini, the midi, the maxi—but mostly the maxi," decided *Esquire* editors in February, 1970, adding that "the growing acceptance of the maxi marks a distinct sign of men's clothes beginning to blend fashion and functionalism. After all, if outercoats are intended to provide warmth, it would seem sensible that they do so at full-length." To illustrate the point they showed a supermaxi, almost a floor sweeper, in a horse-blanket plaid. Yet

Fur-collared overcoats represented an impressive trend in 1969. This black double-breasted coat had its lapels and collar covered with luxurious fur.

on another page *Esquire* fashion director Chip Tolbert showed a wrapped coat that stopped several inches above the knee, for as Tolbert explained, "the sensible shape of the Seventies is upon us. What seems to me especially encouraging is that it imposes no strict conformity. And variety is the spice of the new designs, enabling modern man to meet the need for the flexible wardrobe required in the swift Seventies."

Before the end of the sixties, many an American man had happily adopted fur. The American man had grown fur-conscious again in the mid-fifties, when fur hats imported from Sweden and the Middle European countries enjoyed a vogue. Yet except for an occasional fur-collared overcoat worn with a fur hat, fur was considered a woman's pleasure until the latter half of the sixties, when men's fur coats in mini, midi, and maxi lengths suddenly appeared in large numbers. Their styles ran the gamut from a mini mink with a half belt and a center vent to a midi of natural muskrat with a buckskin belt and brass buttons and a supermaxi of black curly lamb, double-breasted and shawl-collared. No fur was too dramatic or unusual to attract customers, as coats of Brazilian leopard, zebra-stenciled calf, and kangaroo proved.

By November, 1969, *Gentlemen's Quarterly* was referring to fur as "man's second best friend," predicting that "if there was a flurry of fur for men last winter, there will positively be a pelting of pelts during the frigid—and fashionable—months ahead." The writer went on to give the reader an account of the history of man as a fur wearer. "The sanctioning of fur for red-blooded males is not, of course, an innovation of the Age of Unisex: ermine was a highly prestigious symbol of purity for medieval cardinals and ermine spotted with black astrakhan paws (the number of paws signifying rank) was an early favorite of English nobility. Even before that there were the fur-clad cavemen, and skins held high appeal for Greek warriors and Roman nobles. But for the average man familiar with tweeds, flannels and permanent-press, the world of furs is still an alien planet on which, like the moon, he is about to take his first small tentative steps."

To give those first small tentative steps the spring of confidence, *Gentlemen's Quarterly* editors offered the following guide to furs: "The Fur Products Labeling Act, passed by Congress in 1952, requires that every fur selling for over $5 must have the following information stated on labels, sales slips and in advertisements:

"The true English name of the animal from which the fur has come. (No other name is permitted to appear.)

"The name of the country of origin of all imported furs.

"The proper information as to whether the fur has been 'treated,' i.e., bleached, dyed, tip-dyed or in any way artificially colored. (These processes are often used to enhance the beauty of the fur and are not necessarily indicative of inferior pelts.)

"Disclosure as to whether the garment is entirely, or even partially, composed of paws, sides, flanks, gills, tails or waste fur. (These would be used for less expensive garments: in most cases, the best fur comes from the back of the animal.)

"If the furs are used, second-hand or reconditioned, and whether the coat contains any damaged furs.

"In sizing up a fur, look for these features:

"Pelts that are lustrous and bright, as well as silky in texture.

"Garments that use well-matched furs.

"Skins with uniformity of color and pattern.

"High density, as well as uniform density.

"On bushy furs, make certain that the long top hairs (or 'guard hairs') are plentiful.

"Soft, pliable skins that are also firm. (Stiff, brittle skins are indicative of old age or poor processing.)"

Just one year later, in 1970, *Gentlemen's Quarterly,* with every other fashion magazine of stature, reversed its position on fur coats. Ecology had entered the vocabulary of concerned Americans, and in the light of burgeoning ecological awareness *Gentlemen's Quarterly,* in an article titled "The Fur Furor," decided: "O.K. Everybody makes mistakes. Which isn't to say that humanity can't reverse itself and stop making them, however." In its November issue, when the magazine was accustomed to showing an array of the latest men's fur styles, it stated: "Short of outlawing the fur trade, the best way of conserving fur-bearing animals may be to persuade the public that wearing furs is arrogant, ecologically unsound and, in general, pretty rotten."

Still, the editors admitted that opinions about the fur scene were sharply divided and that partisans were very articulate, "loaded with statistics and determined to project an image of holy rectitude." The search for truth, they decided, could be confusing. To prove how confusing it was, the editors polled scores of famous persons for their opinions, of which the following excerpts give some indication of the passionate feeling on both sides:

Walter J. Hickel, Secretary of the Interior. The important issue is not whether the fur or skin of an animal should be used as an article of clothing, but whether this use is at the terrible expense of obliterating a species or endangering its survival.

Dr. Leslie Glasgow, Assistant Secretary for Fish and Wildlife and Parks, Department of the Interior. When a wildlife can be managed so that a harvestable surplus is produced, then there is nothing wrong in harvesting the extra animals. It is irrational to let a species destroy or overcrowd its range, for nature will resort to such remedies as disease or starvation to reduce the population.

H.R.H. Prince Philip, the Duke of Edinburgh, president, British National Appeal, World Wildlife Fund. The appalling disregard for the fate of wild animals and plants in almost every country in the world is a discouraging reflection on the selfishness and lack of consideration of mankind. Howls of protest go up if one dog or one monkey goes into space, but not so much as a whisper is heard when a rare species becomes extinct owing to man's so-called progress.

Johnny Weissmuller, formerly Tarzan. Fur coats, I love them. They're beautiful. But I wouldn't want to have one if it meant the animal is going to become extinct. I don't own a fur—the loin cloth I wore as Tarzan was antelope cloth.

Tom Seaver, pitcher, New York Mets. I chose mountain lion for a fur coat because it has an air of masculinity, and it's very warm. As for conservation, there are bounties on mountain lions in six states—Arizona, Colorado, California, Montana, Oregon and the state of Washington.

Cary Grant, actor. More and more men are wearing fur, and more power to them.

The man-made furs (pile fabrics) had a strong appeal in 1970 in coats such as this roomy double-breasted model with sturdy leather buttons.

I know about the great fur conservation controversy, and I certainly agree that furs on the danger list should not be used in fashion. But for those that aren't, why not? I've seen some of the simulated furs and they're really great looking.

Alice Herrington, president, Friends of Animals, Inc. We do not align ourself with the fake fur movement. Aside from the fact that many fake fur garments are trimmed or lined with the real thing, the wearing of fake fur still tends to glorify the wearing of dead animals, a fashion we are striving to make unfashionable.

More men, however, apparently shared Cary Grant's view of simulated furs, and soon they were buying real-looking fakes at reasonable prices, thus salving their consciences while wearing coats that often seemed so nearly genuine that only an expert could detect their fakery. Printed Orlon, for instance, looked like tiger, and a lush silvery gray pile imitated chinchilla. Black Orlon so closely resembled black seal that only a seal would notice the difference, and viscose rayon dyed in an off-white shade was akin to pony skin. Now the luster and status of a pelt were within the reach of every man, and even a dedicated ecologist could wear one without feeling compromised.

In the early seventies the practicality and comfort of knitted suits, jackets, and slacks led to the knitted outercoat. Both flat knits and fuzzy, lofty knits of wool and wool-and-polyester blends were used in single- and double-breasted styles. Moving up the fashion scale with knits were coats of pile fabrics, made of lustrous yarns in dark shades of blue, brown, gray, and black. Youth's stress on the sense of touch was opening the door to fabrics with a strong tactile appeal.

With the end of the sixties, the most revolutionary decade in the history of the menswear industry, the concept of instant fashion continued into the seventies. Clothes were designed for the moment. Never before had men's clothes been so vivid a form of self-expression, nor had the American of the twentieth century ever been so aware and so proud of his physical presence. It sometimes seemed as if the Peacock Revolution were just beginning.

Casual Outerwear

There was little if anything that was casual about the outerwear worn by men in the first decade of the twentieth century. Working hours were long, and the workingman had little leisure time. Moreover, the affluent American of the period was far too preoccupied with the propriety of his dress to influence the development of more casual attire. The advent of casual outerwear would have to wait until the last vestiges of the Victorian era disappeared and the American man developed a taste for more informal living. During this decade, therefore, outerwear might more correctly be called "work clothes," for it was the man who earned his livelihood working outdoors who had a need for the special kind of sturdy, serviceable clothes that, in years to come, would often serve as a model for apparel that would be called "casual outerwear." Meanwhile, it was the work clothes manufacturers who provided the clothes worn by the men whose skill and muscle were helping to build the United States: the railroad worker, the construction worker, the telegraph lineman, the lumberjack, and the driver of the horse-drawn truck.

Materials for work clothes were selected for durability, warmth, and low price. Canvas, duck, corduroy, and leather rated high when judged on this scale. Corduroy, for instance, sold for 5 to 10 cents per yard, and leather for about 5 cents per square foot. The styling of this category of outerwear was, of course, completely utilitarian. Was it warm enough on winter days when the wind bit into a man's hide? Was it roomy enough to permit him to do the physical labor he had to do? A double-breasted coat of corduroy or leather with a wool blanket lining met these qualifications. Often worn below such a coat was a sheepskin vest, another item of apparel that provided a workingman with the proper insula-

tion. Made of suede leather and lined with wool, this vest was fastened with sturdy metal buckles similar to those used on contemporary galoshes. The price was about $3 retail, which was rather high in view of the fact that an interlined work coat of cotton duck cost the same.

1910–1920

An important work coat at the start of this decade was a leather-and-corduroy reversible in a double-breasted style that sold for $7, a sum that was not inconsiderable at the time. However, it was well worth the price, since leather and corduroy had proved to be two of the most practical fabrics a workingman could hope to wear.

Heavy woolen garments naturally were important. A heavy wool shirt known as the "stag coat shirt" was popular with fishermen and lumber camp workers. Made of a herringbone fabric weighing 20 ounces to the yard, it had a double yoke front and back. The laboring man also showed a marked preference for woolen work shirts of bold buffalo checks in red and black or green and black. Equally bold and colorful were the Indian-blanket plaid mackinaws that, in the years ahead, would retain their popularity as casual outerwear for men who no longer used their brawn to earn a living. In rainy weather lumberjacks wore oiled and waxed cotton jackets and pants, which soon earned the nickname "tin pants," for the good reason that they were so stiff that they stood up even when there was no man inside them. Heavy woolen pants became the trademark of the iceman, who carried pounds of ice from truck to customer, for heavy wool was the only material that could take the inevitable soaking and still keep him comfortable.

Sheepskin lining became widely used in work clothes, particularly in coats of corduroy and cotton moleskin that were now available in lengths that reached anywhere from the waist to below the knee. Like the Indian-blanket mackinaw, these coats retained their popularity and eventually became standard equipment for football players for wear on the bench as well as before and after play.

World War I had a profound effect on men's clothes. The returning soldier, who had grown accustomed to the functional ease and style of his uniform, now demanded as much from his civilian clothes. He had little patience with the grave formality of the bulky suits and starched collars his father wore. Furthermore, the ex-serviceman was physically fit and extremely sports-minded. To all this was added the fact that the country had become an industrial power, with more and more men finding the kind of employment that called for agile minds rather than strong muscles. In short, the United States was finally ready for more casual living and more casual clothes. This readiness was fortunate for the federal government, which at war's end had an enormous surplus of leather jerkins, long sleeveless vests that buttoned high to the neck and were backed with khaki woolen cloth, which had been worn as body warmers by men in the trenches. Made available at surplus outlets, they quickly sold out, thus signaling the birth of the Army-Navy store.

It was soon apparent, however, that if the jerkin had sleeves it would sell even faster and at a higher price. So

sleeves were sewn in, and a merchandising lesson was learned. Now, though there was still a vast market for work clothes, modifications of this sturdy apparel found a market among men who wanted casual clothes for the hours when they were simply relaxing. As a result, the outerwear industry expanded to include modifications of military apparel, and the category of casual outerwear as we know it today was established.

32 BROOKS BROTHERS

16C05 16C06 16C07 16C08 16C09

16C05 Norfolk Jackets of un-dressed leather or suède, un-lined, very light and warm

16C06 Jackets of undressed leather or suède, without collar, patch pockets, satin lined

16C07 Odd Chester Jackets of Stockingette

16C08 Napa Tan Leather Waist-coats, without collar, flaps on pockets, lined with red flannel

16C09 Napa Tan Leather Double-breasted Hunting Coats, buttoned up to neck, lined with red flannel

Suede and smooth-finish cabretta-type leathers appeared in 1915 in norfolk and other coats as well as in waistcoats. [COURTESY OF BROOKS BROTHERS, NEW YORK]

1920–1930

By the 1920s college students who would never swing an ax or drive a truck had discovered that casual outerwear, most often adaptations of the work clothes that may have been worn by their grandfathers, had considerable panache. This was particularly true in the West and Midwest, where winters were more severe than in the East. On campuses in these sections of the country double-breasted coats of corduroy, canvas, or cotton moleskin with wool or sheepskin linings were immensely popular. So were single-breasted black leather jackets with beaver or wombaton beaver collars.

The mackinaw had retained its popularity, and of equal importance was the double-breasted Hudson Bay coat, a thick, heavy woolen coat that, like the mackinaw, was of fingertip length (although the term was not used at the time). The Hudson Bay coat was usually in white or a light color with two or three broad stripes running horizontally around the bottom. By the late twenties a 36-inch mackinaw was introduced in a shawl-

The double-breasted man's skating jacket of 1920 was made in a heavyweight fabric. This reefer type with an all-around belt had a big collar and huge pockets. [THE BETTMANN ARCHIVE, INC.]

This sports blouse of 1926, made of red-and-black wool weighing 22 ounces per yard, had a heavy knitted waistband and adjustable cuffs. [WOOLRICH WOOLEN MILLS]

collar style and in a wool that weighed approximately 40 ounces to the pound. Sometimes a variation of the mackinaw would appear and be called a "coat shirt." An example of this, about 1924, was a coat shirt made of all-wool felted cloth doubled over the shoulders halfway down the front. It had a full double back with large game pockets that buttoned under the double front, as well as two large front pockets with storm flaps.

The stag coat shirt of the previous decade was now an important casual outerwear fashion that was often seen on the ski slope or the skating pond, usually in a red-and-black plaid or in multicolor checks with a bold overplaid. A popular style featured a four-button fly front, a cape back, two large breast pockets with button-through flaps, adjustable-tab cuffs, and a convertible collar with a wide, soft roll. A stag hunting coat had also evolved by the late twenties. Made with a military collar and a stag body, it had a five-button fly front with a

(opposite) The moleskin coat with a sheepskin lining, a practical outerwear garment, was very popular with men in 1927. From the 1927 Sears, Roebuck and Company catalog.

Bigger Value Than Ever!

We've Improved the Coat

We've Lowered the Price

and We've Waterproofed It Too!

Full 36 inch Length

Now Only $7.98

Heavyweight Moleskin Cloth, Sheep Lined

Over 100,000 satisfied customers have worn and been pleased with our extra big value Sheep Lined Moleskin Coat. It is known from one end of the country to the other. It is made specially for us and sold only by us. It is made to our rigid specifications, under our direct supervision and carries our broad guarantee to satisfy you perfectly. The splendid materials are capable of the utmost in wear. The sturdy workmanship, the very unusual roomy comfort of this coat and its practicability will satisfy you thoroughly.

Now! A Better Coat for Less Money—and Waterproofed, Too!

We have always been way below the market in price for a coat of this quality, but now you actually pay less money than ever before—it's a bigger value than ever! On top of that you get a coat which protects you absolutely from wind, rain, sleet and snow. Because, fine as this coat has been, we have done the other thing necessary to place it above all other sheep lined coats in its class—we have treated the heavy moleskin cloth with a special process (no rubber used) to make it waterproof. Weatherproof! That's the word. It is proof against any and all kinds of bad weather.

Six Outstanding Features

The sheepskin lining is carefully selected from the finest to be had, generously soft, thick, woolly — warm! Soft knit worsted wristlets fit snugly around the wrists.

Heavy strips of leather reinforce the pocket corners, preventing them from ripping and tearing.

The armholes are specially reinforced to give longer wear and to permit free movement of the arms without ripping or tearing.

A seemingly small, but highly important, improvement are the guard buttons which, on the inside of the coat, back up every big button. No more buttons pulling off. Note the illustration of some of these features at the right.

The price is possible only because of the enormous quantities we buy. We believe confidently that no one but Sears can possibly give such genuine quality for so little money.

Sizes, 36 to 46 inches chest. Length, 36 inches. State chest measure taken over vest. Shipping weight, 7¼ pounds.

41K552 — Genuine Sheep Lined Waterproofed Drab Moleskin Coat. **$7.98**

Guard buttons—keep buttons from coming off.

Genuine moleskin cloth specially processed—water proof.

Big, extra wide roomy swinging pockets between inside and outside lining—weatherproof — stormproof.

Real leather tacked at each end of pockets to prevent ripping and tearing.

Reinforced armholes prevent tearing of sleeves.

Knit worsted wristlets grip the wrists snugly.

Genuine Leather — Wool Lining

Big Price Reduction on U. S. Army Jerkins

Wonderful for Warmth and Long Wear

THIS SEASON'S PRICE $2.19

There is nothing quite equal to this Genuine U. S. Army Jerkin for wear and protection against wind and cold. Made of heavy selected quality tan leather. Soft and pliable and lined with heavyweight all wool melton cloth. It is an absolute defense against the elements, whether worn over or under your coat. And wear! Seems as if it never would wear out! Ask any army man or any other man who has ever worn one. We bought a huge lot of these jerkins at a fraction of their cost to the government. This saving we pass on to you. A splendid bargain. All first quality jerkins. All have passed the rigid government test.

Sizes, 36 to 46 inches chest measure. State chest measure. Shipping weight, 2¼ pounds.

41K5627—Tan Leather Only.................. **$2.19**

cape, a large game pocket from seam to seam in back, and two large patch pockets with button-through flaps. An advertisement maintained that it was "soft, pliable and beautiful in appearance, yet it will wear like iron." Also eminently wearable was the lumber jacket in a bold plaid. Made of a wool weighing from 24 to 30 ounces to the yard, it was a single-breasted jacket with generously sized lower pockets of either the slash or the flapped patch type and a knitted elastic waistband for maximum warmth.

With the flapper and her sheikh typifying an era of "flaming youth," it was to be expected that even casual outerwear would sometimes go to extremes. An example of fashion gimmickry was a three-way zippered coat of gabardine with a zip-out lining that could be worn as a collarless separate coat. Another conversation piece was a golfing jacket that rolled up into a zipper bag.

1930–1940

This decade started under the weight of a national depression. In a difficult period casual outerwear bore echoes of happier, more prosperous times, and it also cost less than a new suit or overcoat. For the unemployed man as well as for the still-affluent sportsman casual outerwear, particularly outerwear in the winter sports category, continued to have great appeal. It was warm, comfortable, and practical.

A 1931 catalog for fur, sheepskin, and leather outer apparel seemed to ignore the Depression and filled its pages with genuine leather coats, sheepskin-lined coats, suede leather jackets, horsehide and suede coats, and, on its last page, "men's high grade fur coats." Among them were a double-breasted coat of lambskin with a notched collar and turnback cuffs; a coat of selected natural China dog skins ("closely resembling raccoon") with a large collar and deep cuffs; a raccoon lined with a woolen skirt and a satin yoke, having a shawl collar and turnback cuffs; and a coat of Austral-

(left) The tweed short-warm coat with a fur collar and a fleece lining was accepted in 1934 for cold-weather spectator sportswear. From Esquire, February 1934.

ian wombat with a long-roll shawl collar.

The American man still showed a penchant for the leather jacket, and on April 24, 1935, Men's Wear reported that the best sellers were near replicas or at least adaptations of prevailing models in tweed. The shirred back, for example, was particularly noteworthy. "A higher premium is placed on little details of the jacket," said the article. "Two-way cuffs, convertible Cossack collars, slanting pockets, golf tee holders are some of the features which are of major importance. Suede leathers still dominate the total volume of business, but the demand for smooth leathers in the upper price brackets is increasing. Leather and wool are combined more frequently than heretofore, the former being used as a lining. Extremely light shades, like natural chamois and cream, are rising in favor coincidentally with a wider use of dark browns."

The front of the jacket was getting as much attention as the back, and the reporter noted: "Buttoned models are far more numerous than they were last year. The majority have three buttons with an additional one under the convertible collar. Patch pockets are being used more profusely, and the inverted bellows or military kind show up on a greater number of jackets than heretofore, another detail reflecting the sport coat influence in leather goods.

"Are they going for long or short jackets? That's a query heard quite often by producers of leather jackets. Jackets measuring 29 inches, the length of an ordinary suit jacket, are getting a good deal of attention. Probably the most popular length is around the 26–27 inch level. The short blouses, which are about 22 inches long, are being taken up more and more, particularly in the South and Far-West.

"Suede is still the best-selling material. Capeskin in particular is liked, and imitation pig is being bought to a considerable extent, running chiefly to the natural shade. The perforation idea, inspired by perforated shoes and started on the Pacific Coast, is gaining some headway. This is strictly a style idea and seems to be a paradoxical one at that. Leather jackets came into fashion originally because they stopped the winds. Now, holes are punched into them to let the breezes through. The perforated jacket might well become the garment for mild weather wear.

"There seems to be no middle-of-the-road policy in leather colors. They're either very light or quite dark. Champagne, cream and chamois tones are strong. Dark brown is being used extensively. Light grey seems to be showing more life than it did last year.

"There is some experimenting being done with fancy skins and grained effects. This is partly due to the beginning call for smooth grain leathers and something may be laid to the tendency to 'ventilate' leather jackets by means of perforations. Ostrich skin with its comparatively large holes lends itself to this type of treatment and while it cannot be said that there has been a stampede on the part of the public to equip itself with ostrich, there has been some response to the idea. At any rate the fancier-finish smooth leathers will bear watching."

Even in the mid-thirties there were many rich men (the so-called quality trade), for whom a leather jacket was strictly a sports item. These men found time to dash off to St. Moritz for a ski holiday, and it is interesting to note that many of the snow fashions worn in 1935 later became casual wear for men who had yet to put on a pair of skis. It is also of interest that in 1935 much of the handsome ski apparel worn by fashionable sportsmen was referred to as "workmanlike," as if to remind them that many of these fashions could be traced back to the working clothes worn at the turn of the century.

A *Men's Wear* reporter that year photographed the motion-picture actor Buddy Rogers, handsomely dressed, and posed at the top of a slope in St. Moritz. The accompanying article described in detail the highly specialized apparel worn by the experienced skier set for a day's run through the woods:

"In the first place, he has found from actual experience that ski-running is hard, hot work, that he will get into a first-class perspiration before he has covered a mile and that the exercise will keep him in a glow. His shirt will likely enough be of wool, in light weight, and over this he will have a blouse, a jacket, or a parka of gabardine or one of the windproof cotton materials which have reached such a high degree of lightness and resistance to cold and wet.

"To start with the volume item first, his jacket matches the trousers in blue melton. It has a buttoned or slide-fastener front and a belt or an elastic at the waist which, when fastened, will allow the jacket to blouse all around.

(center) A gabardine coat with a pile fabric lining and collar insulated the wearer fashionably in 1937. From Esquire, February 1937.

The overcoat of 1937 combined fabric (Harris Tweed in a herringbone weave) and fur (a raccoon collar and a rabbit fur lining). From Esquire, November 1937.

The two distinctive types of outerwear in 1938: (left) a fingertip-length covert cloth coat with a deep vent; (right) a tweed field coat with rows of stitching around the bottom and on the sleeves. From Esquire, *October 1938.*

The same style jacket is made and will be called for in both gabardine and cotton, in dark blue, in tan and less frequently in white.

"To jump from the low to the high, one of the smartest of the ski jackets, which has Austrian inspiration although made in this country, is in appearance not unlike a mess jacket or a tailless dress coat, except that it is double-breasted and folds completely over, has wide lapels, is ex-

tremely form fitting, has padded shoulders and is well tailored.

"Less ultra than the jacket described above is one with a short-waisted effect, having a fitted back with two rows of tucks at each side of the waistline. These tucks are held in shape by an elastic which aids in the snug fit. Still another jacket, of the bloused variety again, has two inverted pleats in the back.

"The parka jacket, as its name implies, is a derivation of the Eskimo parka, or hooded coat. This garment fits loosely, hanging from the shoulder, and in some of the models being shown there is a novel arrangement at the waist. The skirt of the garment is finished in two layers. The inner layer is tucked in under the pants while the outer layer falls outside the pants, making a perfectly snowproof joint. Usually these parkas are made of some lighter material, but are windproof, the cotton ones being particularly effective. They are made to slip over the head and have a slide fastener at the throat. The hood may be worn over the head or hanging down the back. It has a draw string so that it may be drawn as closely about the face as the wearer wishes" (Aug. 21, 1935, p. 18).

During the last half of this decade, the styling of garments of leather and wool (often of combinations of the two materials) appeared to be moving farther from what a *Men's Wear* writer called "their original keynote, as sounded in lumber camps and hunting field, and edging closer to current ideas in sportswear and regulation clothing." In short, in the process of being adapted to casual outerwear, the work clothes of earlier years were losing more and more of their original identity. This change had already been noted in the trend of leather jackets' taking on styling features of tweed sports jackets. Now it was the turn of other garments: "The lumberjack or mackinaw has been considerably refined and high styled in such features as detailing of lapels, tailoring of sleeves, single-needle work leaving inverted pleats almost invisible, careful matching of plaids and attention to sizing, fullness and length.

"In quality garments, the selling points of better-grade mackinaws are 100 percent wool content, bright pattern, and the garment's roominess and unskimped cut. An oversize coat gives a more striking impression of quality.

"An example of how mackinaws and other winter sportswear pick up ideas from regular clothing is the number of notched lapels," noted this writer, quickly moving on, however, to give the reader this warning: "Informed clothiers know that to form the collar and lapel of a lounge suit properly, considerable hand-felling is necessary. As this cannot be done in a mackinaw, nor is it expected by the customer, watch closely when buying mackinaws with notched lapels to see that the points lie flat. A split collar helps it hug the neck" (Mar. 23, 1938).

In the last years of the decade, the sheepskin-lined coat, long a staple of the laboring man, was taken up by the New York City motorcycle police, who wore a three-quarter-length double-breasted coat of blue broadcloth with a collar and lining of dyed baby lamb.

An example of a garment that moved from the category of general outdoor sportswear to casual outerwear was the Cravenette raincoat, which in March, 1936, *Esquire* hailed as new, observing that it had first been introduced in England for riding, fishing, and general sportswear and worn with trousers to match. On *Esquire*'s fashion page, however, it was worn with an old tweed suit, a porkpie hat, and buckskin shoes by a Yale undergraduate who probably knew little if anything about the origin of his knee-length raincoat.

Meanwhile, some handsome coats were seen in the grandstands at Ivy League football games, and in November, 1937, *Esquire* sketched quite a few, among them a Harris Tweed ulster with a rabbit-fur lining and a raccoon collar at the Yale Bowl. An outstanding coat in any year, it was especially noteworthy in a year when the Depression still lingered.

By 1939 the mackinaw had added

2 inches, for a record length of 38 inches, and earned the name "railroad mackinaw." This had been a fight-for-survival decade for most Americans, and a long mackinaw, a seemingly indestructible garment, seemed an appropriate note on which to end one of the most difficult periods of this century.

1940–1950

Sports outerwear continued to take on the look of regulation clothing and, as a result, began to be worn more and more frequently as weekend casual outerwear. Examples were a double-breasted wool-lined leather jacket that was originally restricted to the skating pond; a native-pattern long-sleeved wool ski sweater; and a double-breasted tan cotton knee-length coat with a fur collar and a fleece lining, which was ideal for spectator sports and now was doing double duty as a car coat. By 1945 *Esquire* would show a zipper-front version of this coat in twill in a city setting, worn with a business suit, a button-down shirt, and a soft felt hat.

The GI influence soon made itself apparent in civilian casual wear, primarily in an adaptation of the battle jacket. The civilian version had the same roominess at the chest and across the shoulders and the same generous-size pockets, fly front, and buttoned waistband as the original.

Warmth and durability were key selling points during the World War II years. Outerwear manufacturers reminded their retailers that many United States homes were going to be very short of oil for heating, which meant that retailers were going to have great opportunities to sell such body-warming garments as sweaters with large reinforced pockets and windproof cuffs; warm sports vests with knitted backs; waist-length jackets of genuine capeskin inspired by the U.S. Army Air Corps flying coat, with windproof knit wristlets and bottoms, completely lined with a water-repellent windproof poplin; and full-length all-purpose coats of water-

repellent gabardine with alpaca-pile shawl collars and linings and sleeves lined with leather for wind protection and warmth.

In 1948 *Esquire* launched the "bold look" and promptly moved the American man away from his wartime stereotype. Bold patterns and extroverted colors characterized this look, and soon outerwear manufacturers took the hint and added styling features to their garments that gave them boldness. Many surcoats took on a more aggressive character (the surcoat was inspired by the tunic worn over a suit of armor, and the name was loosely applied to practically any coat of an in-between length during the 1940s). A typical bold look surcoat of the late forties was a zipper-front model with

Corduroy was in fashion in outerwear in 1940. An example, on the man at right, was the fingertip-length coat with raglan shoulders, big pockets, and railroad stitching around the bottom. From Esquire, *October 1940.*

The sturdy outercoat on the seated man was designed to ward off cold winds. It was made of cotton twill with a wombat collar and a sheepskin lining. From Esquire, *February 1941.*

(right) The military influence on civilian apparel during World War II appeared in a waist-length jacket of processed cotton with big chest pockets. From Esquire, *May 1945.*

an all-around belt, saddle pockets, and wide stripes around the bottom.

During this period the suede jacket lost practically all of its laboring-man character as the Western influence asserted itself. The motion-picture actor Ray Milland modeled this more sophisticated version: a generously long leisure jacket with front and back shirring, a swagger tie belt, man-sized patch pockets, and custom-padded shoulders.

Coats and jackets once seen only in the most rural settings now appeared in more urbane surroundings. Among such garments were a big, burly ulster of all-wool worsted covert with a mouton collar and a 100 percent alpaca-pile lining and a wool polo

coat several inches above the knee, with a full belt, leather buttons, a full rayon lining, and three colorful stripes below the waist and above the cuffs.

In some instances one jacket might have three distinct personalities. A man might start with a wool-lined jacket for blustery weather and then flip off the outer jacket and have a collarless wool jacket for casual indoor or outdoor wear. Or he might decide to wear the unlined outdoor jacket for mild-weather wear. In short, this was a three-way coat made possible with a flip of the zipper.

On August 26, 1949, *Men's Wear* illustrated a collection of casual outerwear under the heading "The Outer Man," and each of the garments

showed the influence of the bold look. Among the styles shown were a lightweight corduroy surcoat 31 inches long with a mouton collar, bellows pockets, a shirred elastic waist, a two-piece front belt, slash breast pockets, a quilted lining, and fully lined sleeves; a 26-ounce wool surcoat 31 inches long with a full belt, saddle pockets, a zipper front, and a colored sheepskin yoke and collar; a 31-inch wool surcoat, a streamlined version of the old mackinaw, in gray green and brown, cut from one piece of cloth and featuring a shirred yoke, an elastic waistband, and a half belt; a jacket of heavy wool with a mouton collar, elastic side snubbers, two-way flap patch pockets, and a quilted lining;

and a brown capeskin jacket with a removable lining of rabbit fur.

1950–1960

Fashion never fails to mirror the social and political climate of a period, and the 1950s proved to be an age of conservatism and caution. The "man in the gray flannel suit" prevailed, and *Esquire* immortalized him when, in 1950, it introduced "Mr. T," the new trim silhouette. However, casual outerwear, like sportswear, managed to retain its independence and its colorful character. In fact, casual outerwear became one of the most imaginative fashion categories of this decade as the new synthetic fabrics gave it an exciting new dimension.

The bush coat, an adaptation of the classic big-game hunter's coat, became so popular in the early fifties that some considered it the favorite of all surcoats. A particularly popular model was of doeskin, gabardine, or a new blend of nylon and rayon gabardine, with a zipper front, a yoke, two flap pockets on the chest, and two lower big flap pockets. Often available in ten colors, the bush coat, with or without a pile lining, continued the bold look of the previous decade. The immense popularity of the bush coat led in turn to a norfolk-type surcoat with an all-around belt, pockets with flaps, and a quilted lining.

The jerkin, by now a rather traditional garment recalling the origins of authentic casual outerwear, reappeared with a zipper side opening. Worn with a pair of gabardine, flannel, or covert slacks, it foreshadowed the vest suit that would make its appearance toward the end of the next decade.

Esquire proved that a gentleman could be dressed for warmth and still conform to the tall, trim Mr. T lines when it photographed a full-length double-breasted coat with a mouton collar, a pile lining, and a tweed shell for its November, 1950, issue. It also pointed out that until Mr. T arrived, pile-lined coats had plain gabardine shells. The new coat was the ideal coat

"whether bucking the crowds at the big game or battling winds on the way to the commuters' special."

Corduroy was as popular as ever. *Esquire* fashion editors noted in September, 1950, that "nothing takes a beating and keeps coming back for more like a corduroy sports jacket. The new twist is the use of patterns (printed corduroy) that are similar to tweed sport coat designs."

Outerwear continued to acquire a more jaunty, youthful look with such styles as the duffle, or toggle, coat that originated in Austria. An all-purpose coat of 100 percent wool or fleecy loden cloth, it had a hood and two enormous patch pockets and closed with rope loops and wooden pegs. There were also the pea coat in a heavy dark blue melton cloth, adapted from the naval uniform coat, with three or four sets of black buttons on a double-breasted closure; and the Eisenhower type of blouse with a zipper front and adjustable side tabs.

On May 9, 1952, *Men's Wear* published an outerwear report based on surveys taken in the major markets. This first report revealed that in 1950 outerwear accounted for 25 percent of men's clothing sales for the average store, while by 1951 outerwear's share had risen to 27 percent. It also showed that woven alpaca was the favorite lining. In storm coats the most significant style trend was toward the single-breasted coat with a small fur collar, tailored along topcoat lines and featuring either raglan or set-in sleeves. There was also considerably more emphasis on shorter coats (36 to 40 inches long) that employed such high-fashion features as fly fronts covering hidden zippers and fluid shoulder lines with alpaca collars. Surcoats had a neater look that was more of the spectator type (this was generally true of all jackets), owing to their fly-front, raglan-sleeve, and hidden-pocket styling. For strictly cold-weather and utility wear, in contrast, the report concluded that there was a swing in the other direction, with bulkier-looking quilted garments that were lightweight but had the appearance of

heaviness in their quilted outsides. Such heavier jackets were most often seen in solid colors and hard-wearing staple fabrics such as cavalry twills, wool-and-rayon gabardines, and olive-drab sateens.

In 1953 *Men's Wear* published an outerwear market report that touched on surveys taken in nine of the principal markets. A capsule summary reads as follows:

Minneapolis–St. Paul. Storm coats continue important, also some alpaca linings.
Milwaukee. Good demand for leather jackets of all kinds.
New York. Linings and inside features highlight. Three-way coats in wide variety.

This tan gabardine storm coat had a pile fabric collar and lining, an all-around belt, slanting pockets, and set-in sleeves (1950).

The toggle, or duffle, coat of the early 1950s, of a tan melton fabric, had a cord-and-toggle closure, big patch pockets, and an attached hood. It was 38 inches long.

Chicago. Self collars replacing fur collars. More wool shells shown.

Los Angeles. New styles in leather jackets. Three-way knits still strong.

Boston. Trend to longer length jackets, wool shells. Leather garments big.

St. Louis. Forecasts more use of leather.

Portland. Dropped shoulder line catching on.

Seattle. Insulated surcoats as best sellers for fall.

The report covered the highlights of some of these markets in greater detail:

Minneapolis–St. Paul. Storm coats with the overcoat look are shown by more houses. This means a self-collared coat (some add a detachable mouton collar) and continuance of the alpaca-lined body and fancy shell. The single-breasted raglan-sleeved storm coat with club alpaca or mouton collar has been growing steadily each year and in some lines overshadows the old favorite—the double-breasted, notch-collared coat.

Fashionwise, the popular surcoat has emerged as a leading contender for outerwear dress honors. It is particularly effective in the fancy shells styled with raglan sleeves, fly fronts, and worn straight hanging. (Three piece belts are included for conversion to fitted silhouette, if desired.) Also important is the steady gain of the fingertip to 40-inch coat. One firm patterns the latter after the British Bobby Coat with detachable alpaca lining and detachable mouton collar.

Lightweight, high fashion leathers, soap and water washable or saddle soap washable and resistant to non-oily stains, present excellent merchandising possibilities for next season. In greatest representation are suedes, kidskins, cowhide, and some horsehide.

Milwaukee. Manufacturers expect to capitalize on the popularity of leather by making a great many garments in a wider variety of colors. New suede shades this year include charcoal, sand, navy, champagne and cork. Horsehides are being shown in new shades of palamino and lighter tans.

Manufacturers this fall use suede in waist length jackets, jerkins, 26-inch blouses, sport coats and 31-inch jackets. The longer jackets have detachable belts and patch pockets. Some of the shorter jackets and sport coats are designed primarily for leisure wear. This fall suede is also shown in combination with wool knit trim.

In cloths the surcoats in 31- and 34-inch lengths lead in popularity. The waist length bomber-jacket is expected to be big for early selling.

Rayon's the most used synthetic for fall outerwear in combination with wool and in combination with nylon. Orlon acrylic fiber appears in a 32-inch jacket, while there's some use made of washable white Dynel for trim.

In this market, alpaca's still rated as the most popular lining for the cold climates. However, firms are placing equal stress on quilted nylon, quilted rayon and rayon metal insulated. Also shown is a new 60-40 wool-rayon lining.

New York. Linings have been given more attention than ever before, with the result that in a great many coats and jackets the inside is more important than the outside. And some of the insides are really terrific, so colorful, in fact, that the wearers will want to display them at every opportunity. Alpaca in both linings and collars has almost completely disappeared from outerwear in this market. Quilted wools are far bigger than ever before, and quilted nylon is used in all types of garments by a few of the larger manufacturers.

One of the biggest features in New York lines for next fall are the three-way coats in which there is a wide variety of shells and of inner garments. These three-wayers constitute a small outerwear wardrobe in themselves and the idea seems to be catching on more and more each season, accelerated by the changing and uncertain weather of the last few seasons.

Los Angeles. Perhaps the most significant development leather-wise is the return of glove goatskin to the field. This supple skin is again to be had in quantity and manufacturers are optimistic it will return to high favor. It is particularly handsome in three-way knit jackets.

As for western jackets, along with the usual fringed and contrasting yoke styles made primarily for rodeo and dress in the Far West, designers have brought forth models with subdued grains which retain the Western flavor but make the garments less restricted in their use.

The national significance of this survey was then discussed as it pertained to a review of the merchandise itself—the kind that sold best and the types that were in the ascendancy and those on the downgrade:

Use of synthetics grows. There has been considerable interest in the industry, all the way from the mills and converters, through the manufacturers and to the retailers, over outerwear garment shell fabrics, and this interest is not likely to show any abatement so long as the synthetic fibers continue to excite the situation. Alone and in blends with the natural fibers, they are contributing a large share of the success that is accruing to the outerwear industry. Their future in this field is not yet an open book. New excitement has been created by the entrance of the so-called "miracle" types, Dacron and Orlon, not in general use yet awhile but definitely on their way and fast. Retailers apparently like them and mention them frequently throughout their comments in answers to the survey questionnaire.

The biggest single classification of shell fabrics sold last season are the various blends of rayon, acetate and nylon, totaling 54 percent of the unit sales of coats and jackets. Some of these were rayon and acetate only but a large majority of them were rayon, acetate and nylon. This time the survey attempted to break down this general classification of synthetic fiber shell into the various blends produced by the mills and converters, but found this practically impossible because of the retailers' uncertainty as to just what composed the shells of their garments, that is, whether rayon and acetate, rayon and nylon or rayon, acetate and nylon. This may have been partly due to the confusion caused by the government edict distinguishing between rayon and acetate and specifying that henceforth each be listed separately on labels and content tags. Retailers long had been in the habit of including both under the general name of rayon. Thus these are all included in the 54 percent reported here and suffice it to say that most of them are the blend of rayon, acetate and nylon. This is confirmed by the largest mills making this type of outerwear shell fabrics. A year ago, the rayon and acetate and rayon and nylon blends totaled 49 percent, 5 percent less than this last season's 54 percent.

Wool shells decline. The most noticeable change in shell fabrics occurred in wools. In the season just past, all-wool shells dropped to 19 percent of the total unit sales from 30 percent the season before. This was probably due to the high price of woolen and worsted fabrics. These were divided 62 percent gabardines, 38 percent tweed types. At this time it looks as though the use of woolen fabrics for outerwear shells is on the rise again, several manufacturers having increased the number of woolen shell garments in their new lines for next fall, as reported in the market reviews on other pages in this issue.

The blends of rayon-and-wool and rayon-acetate-and-wool totaled 13 percent this past season as compared to 15 percent a year ago. Next in the shells-content chart, volume-wise, was cotton, 7 percent, making a big jump from about one percent in the previous season. All-nylon shells were pegged at 4 percent, a rise of 1 percent from the Fall of '51.

All other synthetic blends showed a total of 3 percent last season and these included all those cloths containing various percentages of Dacron, Orlon and Acrilan. This looks small now, but better keep your eye on these fabrics in the future. They are finally in the outerwear picture and their star is likely to grow brighter as the seasons roll by.

Lining preferences. As indicated in the market reports on other pages, outerwear linings are now attracting more attention than are the shells of the garments, for in a great many cases, here is where the warmth-giving qualities of the coat or jacket are to be found. Furthermore, because of the kind of weather that has prevailed the last few winters, there is a growing demand for zip-in or removable linings, which turns the spotlight on the inside of the coats. Retailers were asked what type of linings they think will sell best next season in coats and jackets of

predominantly synthetic or cotton shells, and here is the way they rank them:

First, quilted linings; second, alpaca; third, rayon; fourth, wool cloth; fifth, shearling; sixth, fiberglas; seventh, Orlon fleece; and eighth, metal-insulated linings.

In coats and jackets of predominantly woolen shells, here is the way the retailers think the various types of linings will sell: First, quilted linings; second, alpaca; third, rayon; fourth, wool cloth; fifth, Orlon fleece; sixth, fiberglas; seventh, metal-insulated linings; and eighth, shearling.

In the strictly quilted linings, here is the way the retailers list their preferences: First, by a wide margin, all-wool batting; second, fiberglas; third, synthetic fiber and wool batting; fourth, part wool, part cotton batting; fifth, all-synthetic batting; sixth, other vegetable fibers; and seventh, cotton. For next season there are some new insulations that were not included in last season's list. The all-synthetic batting listed here as fifth will include nylon. The rayon listed third in the types of linings will include the rayon fleeces.

Call for leather jackets rises. To the question, "Is the demand for leather jackets, other than suede, increasing or decreasing compared with a year ago?" 57 percent of the retailers participating in the survey said "increasing," 23 percent said "decreasing," and 20 percent reported "no change." Last year these respective percentages were 38, 36 and 26.

In answer to the same kind of question regarding suede jackets, 86 percent of the retailers replied "increasing," 5 percent said "decreasing," and 9 percent found no change up or down from the previous season. A year ago these respective percentages were 68, 15 and 17, for comparative purposes.

As to the types of leather jackets in greatest demand, the retailers ranked horsehide first by a wide margin, goatskin second, capeskin third and cattlehide fourth, which was about the same way they rated them a year ago. For next season suede is being extensively used along with woolen fabrics.

The wanted lengths. Coat and jacket lengths show only minor changes in the over-all picture, except that full length coats declined sharply in sales last season from the previous fall, down to 15 percent of the total sales of outerwear from 26 percent in the Fall of '51. The surcoat stays at the top as first choice length, accounting for 33 percent of the outerwear sales, with jacket lengths at 27 percent last season, hip length 22 percent and the three-quarter length bringing up the rear at 3 percent.

Storm coats, stadium coats, ulsters or whatever you choose to call them took a

tumble from the position they used to occupy in retailers' estimates. For next fall only 18 percent of the retailers consider the outlook for these coats good. About 37 percent say the outlook is poor and 45 percent describe the outlook for storm coats as "fair." These undiscourageables will give them another chance next fall in the hopes that the old-fashioned cold, snowy winters of the past will return. A large number of merchants, however, declare that they "have had enough" and will not gamble any further with these garments. (May 8, 1953, pp. 95–103)

The annual convention of the National Outerwear and Sportswear Association in 1954 focused on the World War II veteran who had learned to "live casually . . . without restrictive influences." Casual clothes suited his more relaxed life-style, and the NOSA convention theme proclaimed that outerwear was now "a 12-month business."

Esquire in November of that year turned to the new man-made fibers: "Their properties are startling: the fabrics are as warm as they look, yet they feel light as a puff of smoke and all are washable." Photographed amid a collection of laboratory beakers and alembics were a jacket of Orlon fleece ("a marvel of softness, porous enough for easy wear"), a cognac-color nylon jacket, and a high-pile fleece jacket of knitted Orlon with knit cuffs and waistband. "No one can resist pile linings of Orlon," advertised Du Pont. No matter how often a jacket or surcoat was washed or dunked, it was claimed that the lining of Orlon acrylic fiber stayed soft.

Gentlemen's Quarterly in 1955 showed, along with a trio of short blouses in suede imported from New Zealand, a pair of suburban coats: a 22-ounce nylon-fortified melton cloth with a multicolor nub, horn buttons, and a high-count satin-finish lining backed by heavy wool quilting; and a 100 percent tweed with a center vent, horn buttons, a pile lining, and a quilted skirt, gussets, and sleeves. One outerwear manufacturer chose to call his fingertip coat an "English walking coat." The Buck Skein Brand Company called its waist-length jacket of rugged sheen gabardine a "power

This seat-length zipper jacket of 1955 was made of a fabric of 65 percent polyester and 35 percent cotton, processed for water repellency and stain resistance. It had a yoke front and a nylon fleece lining.

steering jacket . . . never binds or restricts when driving, golfing, gardening or working at your particular do-it-yourself project" (*Esquire*, May, 1956).

In October, 1956, *Gentlemen's Quarterly* noted: "More and more Americans are driving to work and to weekends in sleek, low sportscars. One wonders what manner of clothes will evolve for these high horse-power moderns." The wondering led *Esquire*, in cooperation with designers at the Ford Motor Company and General Motors, to create some sportswear fashions of the future that proved to be a kind of preview of the space age jump suits that would evolve in the following decade. One design was a two-button white leather jacket

trimmed in red and fully lined in red satin, worn with a pair of black cashmere pants. Another design was a zipper-front one-piece gabardine garment with a yellow corduroy front and a stitched all-around belt, worn with bush boots and a crash helmet.

In the same issue *Gentlemen's Quarterly*, noting that leather outerwear was continuing its advance in popularity and styling, observed that the luxury look of leather was providing "a flock of dramatic and inventive variations on classic styles, as well as many totally new fashion conceptions. Combinations make news; leather and suede jackets and coats receive accent touches of tweed, knits and rich pile fabrics. One self-contained combination creating excitement is suededback shearling. New tanning techniques are producing leathers with softness, luster and draping qualities never before possible. Suede has a finer nap, more pliant hand, resistance to spotting. New colors of fashion import include soft greys, champagne, turquoise blue and vivid red." Accompanying this feature were photographs of a hip-length, pile-lined white leather jacket with a zipper on one side creating a double-breasted effect and a black leather jacket with slanted flap pockets and triple-stitch edging adding dress-up touches.

Esquire's fashion department collected some logs, sank a hatchet in one, and, using that as a backdrop, photographed for its October, 1956, issue some handsome apparel, including a suede jacket with knit trim and a car coat of suede leather with a lining of alpaca and plaid wool. Among the accessories shown were a brushed shrunken-calf cap with a concealed visor, an alligator belt, a leather tie, and a pair of bear-hide moccasin shoes.

Jackets and coats now were often being promoted as the basis of a complete wardrobe, which in turn was said to be regarded by some class-conscious Americans as a symbol of quality. Fine clothes, like fine cars and homes, had become a status symbol.

In 1956 *Esquire* devoted a page to

a feature based on the fact that outerwear had emerged as "a distinct category rather than as just a mass of stuff you bundled up in when you went outdoors.

"Not too long ago, 'outerwear' was made up of leather jackets, mackinaws, heavy sweaters, and father's old overcoat. But with skiwear heightening the outdoor scene, and the styling of Army uniforms—notably the Eisenhower jacket—getting a solid masculine but jaunty air about the stuff, outerwear has finally come into its own. Here's a bit about some of its main characteristics:

"One classification is the so-called waist-length, which is the influence of the Eisenhower jacket. As implied, this is waist-length; jacket with set-in sleeves; usually blouse-type, with slanting pockets and zipper closure. The intermediate-length coat, which measures about thirty-two inches for a man of average height, is just a trifle longer than the conventional jacket of a business suit. Next is the thirty-five to thirty-six-inch-length coat, generally described as the suburban coat. Reversibility is a consideration on certain types of coats of this length, with the soft fleecy type fabrics on one side and the smooth, water-repellent fabric on the reverse.

"Many of the fabrics are specially developed for coats of this same type. Brushed wool fleece and tweeds are widely accepted. They have a loftiness which provides warmth with a minimum of weight. Similarly, tweeds are extremely strong because their roughish surface connotes sports types of apparel. Man-made fibers play a significant role in this fashion development. Some of the brushed wools and tweeds are blends of Orlon or Dacron with wool. Filament nylon is woven into sleek, smooth-finished fabrics and adapted for certain types of coats, particularly the waist-length and the thirty-two-inch styles. Gabardine continues to be in the line-up in all worsted or blends of worsted with man-made fibers or others. Poplin, the closely woven fabric, is also much in the picture. Nylon and Orlon fleeces are used not only in the shell, or outer part of the coat, but also for linings.

"Leathers and plastic materials have their proponents in outerwear. Many of the leathers, either the smooth finish or the suede surfaces, have a softness which makes them adaptable for these jackets. One of the interesting notes about the leather jackets is the surge to varied colors as well as the conventional shades. With such a rising cycle, plastics, including vinyl and others, are rugged and bound to be satisfactory to the wearer.

"The colors of the jackets fall into three general classifications. These are the soft tones, which include such shades as greys, tans, blues and greenish effects. Next are the bright tones which have vivid accents, such as red with grey, bright yellow, green or others, either alone or in combinations with a neutralizing shade. Next are the very deep tones, the browns, blacks and deep greys and blues which are related to the colors of sports jackets and slacks. One note in this matter of color is the use of sharp contrasts. For example, navy blue with white trim, turquoise with black, very dark brown with beige.

"The inside of the jacket is just as important from the fashion point of view as the outer appearance. Lustrous satin of man-made fibers is used freely in bright shades either to harmonize or contrast with the color of the coat. Quilted effects with science fibers provide satisfactory insulation against the cold and are decorative at the same time. Nylon fleece has gained in popularity because it performs the function in insulation, has eye appeal and is washable. Wool, including alpaca, shows up in woven fleece types and in the pile fabrics. Blends of fibers have wide usage for the interior of the coat. Shearling or lamb's wool is used in natural shades or colored effects.

"Details of the models of the coats give emphasis to the fashion significance of outerwear. Many of the suburban coats are in the four-button model. Leather-covered and bone or plastic buttons are used in relationship with the color of the body of the

jacket. Some are fly-front coats. The zipper shows up repeatedly in the coats of the three different lengths. The toggle and loop closure is noted on specially styled models" (January, 1956, p. 96).

By the late fifties loden cloth was appearing more and more frequently in outerwear, a fact *Esquire* acknowledged by sketching a suburban coat of blue loden cloth ("blues are back in full swing") in 1956 and photographing the television star Dave Garroway in a bush jacket of a newly lightweight loden with a shirt-style collar and an action back with a yoke and pleats for extra fullness in 1959. *Gentlemen's Quarterly* declared in its winter, 1957–1958, issue: "Loden cloth makes news for fall in new reversible treatments as well as in the expanding trend toward distinctive stylings with a European accent." Illustrating this feature were photographs of a camel-color loden cloth outercoat with a wraparound yoke and a brown loden lining; and a reversible coat of oxford gray loden on one side and oyster poplin on the other, with slanted pockets and braided loop fasteners.

For the college student, a double-breasted sheepskin coat with two big pockets was being featured in 1957, to be worn fleecy side in and suede side out. *Esquire* in September of that year suggested a "gallant sweep of cape styled for the stadium (grandstand, not bench)" of fleecy, pure wool melton cloth with roomy inside pockets, side slits, and a rough-weather hood. "Bold new lines for the man with the Elegant Air" was the opinion of *Esquire*'s fashion writer.

Fur hats for men made an impression in the late 1950s. Once the American man had accepted fur, he was in a mood to want more, and in November, 1957, *Esquire* encouraged him with a presentation of "Winter Wraps to Warm the Outer Man." "They're all yours, men—fur coats, fur collars, fur hats, plus the practical luxury of all the new science fibers, as well." The editors made their point by showing "what is probably the world's most elegant dress coat—a fleecy blue mix-

A double-breasted checked wool outercoat with two slanting upper pockets, two flapped lower pockets, and a pile fabric collar and lining (1959).

ture of beaver fur and Dynel fiber, lined with pure nutria, which also forms the collar." They also added a short coat of Dynel pile for everyday suburban wear and a new Italian-cut cotton coat lined with deep pile and collared with raccoon.

"Looks like fur," said *Gentlemen's Quarterly* of a collection of sporty winter coats in suburban and jacket lengths. Among those shown were a double-breasted alpaca pile in three-quarter length with a full iridescent lining, flap and ticket pockets, and tab-and-button sleeves; a double-breasted coat of an Orlon-and-Dynel fabric resembling seal, with slash pockets, a convertible collar, and a full faille lining; a double-breasted shorter-length suede coat fully lined with Orlon pile backed by Arnel; and a champagne-color African cabretta leather suburban coat fully lined with Orlon pile and topped with a brownish gray Dynel shawl collar.

"Brilliant, flamboyant red brightens the sportswear picture for fall," observed *Gentlemen's Quarterly* in November, 1958. "Dazzling when used by itself, hot red also serves notably as a dramatic ground color for bold patterns in black or charcoal, or as peppery accents." The editors proceeded to prove their point by peppering three pages with such fashions as a hot-red ski sweater of heavy wool worsted, featuring a bold design of accordion-rib side panels in black running down the front and back, with a black placket collar that could be converted to a modified turtleneck; a soft, fleecy surcoat, a blend of 90 percent wool and 10 percent cashmere, with a box check in black on a hot-red ground and a stand-up collar, cuffs, and slash pockets trimmed with black knit; and a polished-cotton shirt of interlaced hot red and black.

By 1959 the Continental influence, which had been strong for several years in men's suits, had affected outerwear, too. In a fingertip-length coat of gray flannel, for example, it was apparent in deep, slanted flaps on the pockets. This decade, which had begun conservatively with the man in the gray flannel suit, ended with the restoration of fashion individuality, gray flannel having been adapted for casual wear. Even sheepskin had a suave new look owing to an electrified glazed finish.

1960–1970

O. E. Schoeffler, *Esquire's* fashion director, traveled to Squaw Valley, California, site of the 1960 winter Olympics, and reported in the January issue on the internationally inspired fashions in outerwear he observed there. They included a fleece jacket with a satin-lined attached hood and two set-in pockets; a thigh-length sheepskin coat with leather straps and buttons and a colorful wool plaid lining; a hip-length coat, cloth on one side and colorful wool plaid on

This short outercoat of the early 1960s, an adaptation of the British shooting coat, had large pockets with flaps. The fabric was a sheen rayon-and-wool gabardine. The body was lined in pile fabric, and the sleeves in quilted rayon.

the reverse side, with a bulky-knit collar; an authentic Eskimo parka of Orlon pile with a one-piece hood, fox-fur trim, and a sloping-shoulder one-piece construction providing complete freedom of movement; a double-breasted corduroy coat with leather shoulder patches, knitted cuffs, and an alpaca lining; a bold wool plaid blouse with a bulky-knit collar, sleeves, and bottom band; a hip-length jacket in cabretta leather with an astrakhan-framed shawl collar and lining; a 40-inch double-breasted gabardine coat with a shawl collar of mouton and an alpaca lining; and a chubby parka of furlike Orlon. Meanwhile, *Esquire* editors decided that the newest developments in parkas were the hood that disappeared, quilting

used as decoration, and multicolor abstract prints.

Hot red had been fashion news in the late fifties, but in the early sixties it was blue that was red-hot, a fact *Esquire* illustrated in October, 1961, by a close-up of a wool outercoat in a giant blue plaid, with a detachable hood and leather buttons concealing a zipper.

"Outerwear goes ski," declared *Men's Wear* on April 27, 1962, commenting on the profusion of quilted parkas in waist, hip, and thigh lengths. "The new direction for fall-winter outerwear is ski," said the editors. "It's loaded with new colors . . . new models . . . new reasons to promote this news-making category. Take it in two shifts, if you will: Active-ski . . . and after-ski."

In November of that year *Esquire* devoted four pages to "The Progress of

A black cabretta leather coat with an astrakhan shawl collar and lining, set-in sleeves, leather-covered buttons, and slanting pockets (1962).

the Parka," observing that "Eskimos have distinguished themselves by virtue of two timeless contributions to society: rubbing noses and wearing parkas. The nose trend hasn't caught on much below the Arctic Circle, but it's been a different story with the parkas. They've not only found acceptance; they've taken over. Practically all skiing jackets are now designed after the parka, and the rest of fall and winter outerwear, attempting to incorporate a 'ski look,' has adopted the style too." Illustrating this feature were a full-length coat of blue denim laminated to Curon foam and lined with a bright red virgin wool, which had much of the sportiness of a parka because of its oversize zipper concealed by a fly front, snap toggles, and detachable center-zipped hood; and two jackets influenced by the parka design, one a hip-length style of Vycron-and-

This 1963 corduroy outercoat was designed for campus, stadium, and suburban wear. It had a deep heavy-knit wool collar, leather buttons, buttoned-tab side vents, and a tartan lining.

cotton gabardine with a drawstring hood, diagonal pockets, bulky-knit cuffs, and high-luster Orlon pile and the other a slightly longer model of all-cotton medium-wale corduroy with an attached hood, set-in sleeves, and an extra deep yoke, fully lined in deep pile of 100 percent Orlon.

Men's Wear welcomed what it called "a new breed of outerwear. Call it the commuter, the suburbanite, or what you will. It's the knee-length coat (sometimes an inch or so longer) that dresses up or down for fall-or-winter weather. It can come in wind-shielding cotton-plus blends or downright dressy wools. It may be single- or double-breasted, have a shawl or notched collar" (Apr. 26, 1963).

In 1963 the impact of the ski parka

A suede leather coat with a curly pile fabric shawl collar, a yoke front, and slash pockets (1963).

resulted in a new coat length, a 32-inch length that was popular in zipper fronts and button fronts and in most every fabric available. By then almost as many parkas were seen on high school grounds as on the ski slopes: longer, belted parkas with tricky shoulders or shoulder-to-waist welting, all in brisk colors and prints. In 1964 the parka was credited with influencing the styling of reversible coats; almost a prototype was a man-size wool glen plaid that reversed to corduroy.

In the early sixties suedes were favored in all lengths and all shapes. A particularly popular model was a 39-inch single-breasted coat with a notched collar, a double-stitched yoke, flapped hacking pockets, a button-off back belt, and a zip-out acrylic-pile lining. In November, 1963, *Gentlemen's Quarterly* said that designers of suede coats would go to any length "to prove how persuasive [suede] can be to the man who seeks the special in his outerwear." To illustrate this contention, the magazine showed a fingertip-length coat in tan suede, shawl-collared and fully lined in a rich brown Orlon pile. In 1964 the rush to suede continued, with quilted suede providing a new point of interest.

The British influence in outerwear was apparent during the early sixties in such fashions as an adaptation of the safari coat in a polyester–pima cotton blend with a lining and collar of Orlon pile; a 40-inch coat, inspired by the British riding mackintosh, in a blend of Orlon and wool jersey lined with cotton check; a 29-inch coat, a weatherized combed-cotton shell, in a bold glen plaid that featured raglan sleeves, a stand-up knit collar, and side vents with adjustable straps; an adaptation of the traditional English shooting coat in a blend of cashmere and wool, with suede shoulder patches; and a 28-inch coat of all-wool camel melton, inspired by the original British duffle coat, with traditional cord loops and wooden pegs, smartly lined with an authentic Royal Stuart cotton tartan.

"Outerwear is a 12-month busi-

A zipper jacket made of a diamond-patterned polyester-and-cotton fabric with vertical pockets and a knitted wool collar (1964).

stretch details or in stretch fabrics. Latest addition to outerwear beach cover-ups: It's outerwear that spans another season—often a ski parka take-off that's lighter, brighter and vinyl-coated—to spend a new season under the sun. These are the kinds of outerwear that your customers know. They are basics, functionally designed to do a day-in-day-out job. Why not consider the profitable possibility of showing . . . promoting . . . and selling ALL outerwear on a WARD-ROBE basis. In exactly the same way that the ideal suit wardrobe includes a dressy blue, a business herringbone, a Saturday cheviot suit, etc., help your customers build a year-round outerwear wardrobe" (*Men's Wear,* Nov. 8, 1963).

Sketches accompanying this article and illustrating this wardrobe concept included:

Commuter outerwear. A knee-length coat with a zip-out pile lining and a button-on pile collar, worn with a herringbone cheviot suit.

Dress outerwear. A natural-shoulder sports jacket with a wool turtleneck and a felt cap.

Ski outerwear. A quilted nylon stretch parka, "as much at home on campus with a change of sweater and slacks."

In-town outerwear. A British warm in camel-color wool with a genuine fur collar, worn with a glen plaid flannel suit and a British-type raw-edge lightweight felt hat.

Stadium outerwear. A long corduroy coat with a pile lining that extended onto the collar, worn with a bold Shetland sports jacket, a button-down shirt, and Norwegian-type moccasins.

Action outerwear. An unlined golf jacket with motion and comfort detailing.

Beach outerwear. A summer parka in a vinyl-coated madras with a hood and push-up sleeves.

Indoor-outdoor outerwear. A suede-and-alpaca-knit coat ("dressy enough for a cocktail party in the suburbs or a day in the country") worn with a sports shirt and ascot.

Red returned to fashion with oxblood, cranberry, and burgundy shirts,

ness," the NOSA convention of 1954 had stated, and the fashion writer Stan Gellers echoed this thought in a 1963 article titled "The Outerwear Wardrobe":

"Outerwear is a 12-month busines," Gellers began. "Now, there's the right item for every activity . . . the right weight for any season . . . the correct functional design built into the fabrics, the findings and the models. Consider the assortment of 12-month outerwear at hand to sell this way: For zero-and-below days: Long coats with

warmth on the inside via pile or quilting. For ski (active or spectator): Shorter or longer authentic parkas. For outdoor-indoor wear: Lightweight dressy jackets with sport coat details and the rugged appeal of outerwear. For the commuter and the man-on-the-move: Double-the-purpose coats with collars and linings that come off, shells that can take a beating. For in-town use: A new and dressy breed of outerwear with rich fur collars, true outcoat lines. For fall or spring action: Sportsman-like jackets with

sweaters, and patterned wools. *Esquire* reported in October, 1963: "With the probable exception of hot-rodders (who find red slightly annoying) and bullfighters (for whom it is occupationally hazardous), most men are donning red sports clothes." Four models on laminated red stools set on a red patent-leather floor wore respectively a red blazer, a red nylon zippered jacket with black cotton rib-knit cuffs and collar, an imported English knit vest of 100 percent red wool and a red-and-white tapered block-check cotton shirt, and a zippered red wool jacket with black knit banding styled along the lines of a West Point jacket.

Corduroy was back in outerwear news, this time because of a smart new way of cutting this traditional fabric. It was available in wide, wide wales, thick-and-thin wales, high-and-low ribs, formed panels, man-size herringbones, and multicolors.

A Western influence asserted itself in outerwear during the Presidency of Lyndon B. Johnson. There was, said *Men's Wear*, "nothing cowboy about this ranch look that's seemingly made for a man of means" (Apr. 17, 1964). *Esquire* honored this newest fashion influence in its October, 1964, issue with a full-page, full-color photograph displaying a Western-style casual coat in a pale tan Angola leather with a notched collar, a zip-out lining, and split raglan sleeves; and a black leather jacket styled like a crew-neck cardigan, worn with leather slacks stitched to hold the center crease. Even corduroy was adapted to the new Western look in a ranch jacket with an acrylic "shearling" lining, a notched collar, a stitched yoke, and a button front. Popular, too, was a rib-knit sweater of 100 percent wool with leather lacing.

While campus and stadium coats continued long (38 to 40 inches), a short-length bicycle coat (short enough to leave the legs free) evolved. College men astride motor bicycles wore 32-inch coats of loden cloth, leather, wide-wale corduroy, and vinyl.

The pea coat and the bush jacket popular in the 1940s came back in the mid-sixties, but with some important differences. In the pea coat style were a brown double-breasted rawhide jacket, lined in acrylic pile and embossed with brass buttons and a luxurious kangaroo-fur collar; and a rich thick- and thin-wale corduroy with epaulets, a chest pocket with a flap, angled lower pockets, and bold embossed brass buttons. Reminiscent of the bush jacket were a lamb suede jacket with a two-way zipper closure, a deep back yoke, patch pockets with wooden buttons, and an Orlon pile lining and collar; and a natural-shade moderate-wale corduroy with leather buttons and epaulets and sleeve tabs and belt finished in a suede-type material.

In 1966 *Esquire* showed a shaped walking coat in a beefy diagonal-weave tan wool—an offshoot of the new shaped suits that were being worn by the more fashion-conscious men. In November, 1968, it introduced its readers to a new look in leather, observing that of all the materials used in clothing leather had the most personality. In the new jacket and coats *Esquire* showed, leather had been treated as though it were a light and supple fabric, with the result that the apparel had a swashbuckling sort of elegance.

What had happened to leather garments was also happening to virtually everything in the well-dressed man's wardrobe: a dash of fresh, uninhibited imagination showing a new awareness of the relationship between a man's personality and his clothes. In short, the Peacock Revolution had arrived, and a trench coat of golden-tan naked leather with epaulets, slash pockets, and a deep center vent was simply one of the new head-turning styles that announced that fact. It was not surprising, therefore, when *Gentlemen's Quarterly* stated in November, 1969, that the swaggering double-breasted fur coat was now the ultimate in elegant winter wear, "whether the pelt is genuine or fake." Fur, said the magazine, was "man's second best friend."

By 1969 leather was seen in trench

The casual look in sportswear is demonstrated in this outfit, consisting of a pullover shirt with a pleated patch pocket and side vents, a double rope belt worn over the hips, giant-overcheck slacks, and shiny white moccasins.

coats, midi coats, maxi coats, car coats, jerkin-length vests, flight jackets, and norfolk jackets and as trim on fur coats. What had started as a Western look for fringed-vest wearers was now being seen on the streets of cities throughout the country. In March, 1970, *Esquire* introduced "the look of leather à la Cardin," considering "Cardin" to be the name of a new lifestyle. Among the Cardin designs displayed was a short self-belted jacket with industrial zippers on the side and pocket, a pullover with a Western-style

A belted suede leather jacket with a big zipper and an alpaca fleece collar and lining (1971).

with jeans and casual slacks, and this is the way they're selling in boutiques. They're also the obvious put-togethers with vestsuits, shirtsuits, safaris and battle jackets."

This concept of "second skin" sent many a mature man rushing to a gymnasium, particularly when he aspired to wear the new knits that by 1970 were no longer a novelty but an integral part of a fashionable man's wardrobe. Many of the "new wave" nonsuits were knits, but no matter what they were made of, they had no place for a man to hide even an incipient paunch.

Gentlemen's Quarterly in April, 1970, presented a large collection of casually suited men wearing such styles as a collarless natural-shade cotton vest suit; a norfolk-inspired suit of belted brushed denim with a military collar, box-pleated pockets, and a snap-front closure; a splashy printed corduroy vest suit equipped with a shawl collar, a snap-fastened front, and four concealed pockets; and a belted knit shirt suit with a buttoned front, a chest pocket, and side vents.

By 1971 the jeans generation on college campuses and high school grounds had a jacket to call its own. It was a slim bomber-type jacket, most often seen in leather, corduroy, denim, poplin, and double knits. Some models had furlike collars, metal tab accents, and authentic cowboy detailing. Denim emerged as a fabric for both business and casual wear. A blue cotton denim suit, for example, with a fully lined jacket, pleated buttoned pockets, leather buttons, and an action back, was now acceptable for city wear. And denim knits were popular in both business suits and unconstructed suits. Denim sportswear, meanwhile, gained in popularity. Sueded denim, with the bulk of ship's canvas and the hand of soft leather, was fashioned into jackets and slacks with lacing grommets and T-bar zippers.

In the early seventies a quilted look appeared in both men's and women's outerwear. The *Daily News Record* (Apr. 21, 1971) regarded it as "another ex-

laced placket, and Cardin's interpretation of a classic style, a two-button jacket with wide peaked lapels and a bold curve to the cut. That year leather was generally accepted as a most desirable body covering for all seasons, age groups, and occasions.

Turtlenecks came back, but as one fashion reporter put it, "any resemblance to those launched three years ago is coincidental. This time the dimensions are different. Today's turtleneck is skinny, body-hugging with the same profile that young customers are

snapping up in Wallace Beery, tank top and dress shirt looks in knits. Bodies are slim . . . arms are slim . . . armholes are higher . . . and the neck folds over to produce a deep four-inch (or more) 'cuff.' Lengths are either waist high or like long tunics to take overbelts. Today's turtleneck is engineered for young customers and the boutiques. The fit follows the concept of 'second skin,' and the mood goes along with the current splurge on easygoing sportswear accessories. Today's turtlenecks are built to be worn

ample of a European look quickly moving to the U.S." It showed fashion sketches of the quilted look in several categories, among them a battle jacket of brushed cotton twill with suede shoulder patches and a furlike collar. Western-style slacks and fine-wale cor- duroy slacks both got the quilted treatment, too, from the knee to the bottom.

Probably no other category of fash- ion is so well attuned to the life-style of this youth-oriented era as casual outerwear. Rooted in the work clothes of past generations, it has a special appeal for today's classless society. So it appears inevitable that in the last quarter of the century casual outer- wear will have an increasingly impor- tant influence on the styling of even regulation clothing.

Fur Coats

There are undoubtedly many members of the under-thirty generation who believe that fur coats for men first came into prominence in the late 1950s. But a glance at the family album, toward the front of the book, will show that the fashionable man at the turn of the century often wore a double-breasted coat of, say, natural brown muskrat or coonskin. For in those years of white winters, fur and fur-lined coats were in the wardrobe of any man who could afford them.

Early in the second decade of the century men's suits were being tailored on slimmer, more natural lines, and soon there was a move away from bulky overcoats. This trend toward lighter-weight clothing, combined with military influence in the years just preceding World War I, produced increasingly shapely and dashing overcoats, many of which were luxuriously lined with fur. A New York fashion writer in 1912 was enthusiastic about "a greatcoat for country wear, for rough wear—one that was lined with fur and yet had no fur showing." This coat was of handmade Shetland wool lined with Manchurian sable.

(below left) In 1915 the double-breasted reversible ulster, with wool fabric on one side and fur on the reverse side, was made to individual order. (below right) Shawl-collared fur coats of generous length were among the outercoats available that year. [COURTESY OF BROOKS BROTHERS, NEW YORK]

While the fur coat per se lost ground in the 1920s, a raccoon coat was the pride of the college man, and the stands at any Ivy League football game were clogged with long, generously collared coonskin coats, not all of them worn by students. As a *Men's Wear* journalist of the period observed: "The man who would advertise his wealth and social position must have a coon coat in his wardrobe, even if he never wears it except to the three or four football games that he attends in the fall." Soon even junior-grade clerks coveted raccoon coats as status symbols, and a popular song of the period contained this line: "Raccoon coats don't care who's wearing 'em./ Hall room boys will soon be sharin' 'em./To do the raccoon!"

The coonskin coat remained popular through the twenties and into the early thirties, but as early as December 5, 1928, *Men's Wear* noted that at the Princeton-Yale football game the camel's hair coat had made its way to first place with Ivy Leaguers. And by the Princeton-Yale game of 1932 the raccoon coat appeared to have graduated to the alumni class, while un-

(below left) Fur coats for sporting wear, fur trim on wool-lined coats, and lap robes for comfort in cars were among the luxuries available in 1915. (below right) Coonskin and black dog coats had a special appeal for university men who drove Stutz Bearcats and other sporty cars after World War I. [COURTESY OF BROOKS BROTHERS, NEW YORK]

In the thirties furs for men were used mainly in collars and linings. This tweed overcoat had an otter collar and lining. From Esquire, *November 1935.*

The big collar and lapels of this dark blue ulster provided ample space for Persian lamb. The lining was of luxurious mink. From Esquire, *February 1936.*

dergraduates shunned it in favor of heavyweight coats in short-napped pile or fleece fabrics. But three years later *Men's Wear* reported: "The raccoon coat is back in fashion. More were seen at the climax football games in the East this season than at any time in the past ten years. The best style, worn by undergraduates and alumni alike, is very dark in color, has a shawl collar and usually hefty leather buttons" (Dec. 18, 1935). What was the story behind its surprising comeback? The reporter concluded: "This change is attributed to a renewed fashion interest in fur coats for men and to a betterment in economic conditions." It was also noted that the

cloth coat with a fur lining, though greatly outnumbered by the raccoon, was also gaining in popularity.

Unfortunately, the nation was no sooner out of the Depression than it was in the grip of World War II, and the vogue for the fur coat went into a decline from which it did not begin to rally until the last half of the 1950s, when growing prosperity and the new synthetic fibers brought the luxury of fur into the reach of the middle class. The movement back toward fur began with fur hats imported from Sweden and soon extended to fur and fur-lined coats.

"They're all yours, man—fur coats, fur collars, fur hats," said *Esquire* in

November, 1957, showing "what is possibly the world's most elegant dress coat, a fleecy blue mixture of beaver fur and Dynel fiber, lined with pure nutria, which also forms the collar." Not surprisingly, the comeback of the fur look brought with it raccoon, this time in big 1920-ish collars on Continental-styled cloth coats lined with deep pile.

Coats in new fibers that looked like fur made an impression, and *Gentlemen's Quarterly* photographed a collection of them in 1958; outstanding among them was a shorter-length double-breasted coat of Orlon and Dynel fabric resembling seal, with slash pockets, a convertible collar, and a full faille lining. Uncommon furs were appropriated for pre- and post-ski coats, and for its December, 1960, issue, a *Gentlemen's Quarterly* photographer trained his lens on a collection that included a short, bulky black-and-white-striped skunk coat with a stand-up collar and a parka of natural brown hair seal with an attached hood, a concealed full-length–zipper front, and two inside zippered pockets. All-fur coats "for the daring few" is the way *Gentlemen's Quarterly* put it in December, 1961, reminding its

The fun image of a raccoon coat was underscored by the maxi length and the large matching hat. From Gentlemen's Quarterly, *November 1970.*

readers: "In medieval Europe fur was almost exclusively a male prerogative. One's social position could be judged by the amount and type of fur worn on his back. In the modern world men have been limited to fur as headwear, linings, and collar trim. But now the man who has the courage and the purse to be resolutely avant-garde can do an all-fur coat."

All this was intended to ease the man with the courage and the purse into the costliest fur coats that were designed for men in the years just preceding the Peacock Revolution. Among them were a white mink ("A rare first for men!"), a three-quarter double-breasted coat with a shawl collar, slash pockets, and black silk lining that was priced at $2,200; a knee-length black Persian lamb with a shawl collar ($795); and a full-length double-breasted black Alaska seal ($2,000). When the football star Joe Namath wore a full-length mink in which he posed for photographers, resistance to fur melted. Fur coats for men were in fashion, and no newspaper or magazine story on the Peacock Revolution failed to include fur.

In November, 1968, *Esquire* showed a fur coat that attracted attention for several reasons. First, it was in the new maxi length. Second, it was a shaped, six-button double-breasted model with a sprawling collar. Third, it had a large glen plaid pattern stenciled on grayish brown Chinese marmot, an effect, said the caption writer, that would have been impossible in the fur technology of a few years earlier.

By this time fur and furlike coats for men were so widely accepted that designers created increasingly dramatic styles with which to keep interest alive. *Gentlemen's Quarterly* photographed a maxicape of brown-and-white guanaco fur from South America, with arm slits at the sides and a chain across the neck. In November, 1968, *Esquire* showed two impresario-styled coats modeled by piano virtuosos: a long, flared black coat of Swiss viscose pile with a huge mink collar and a waist-high inverted pleat in back; and a shaped double-breasted coat of Alaska

The popularity of fur outerwear reflected the prosperity of 1970. This double-breasted style is shown in hair seal, but it appeared in many other furs. The fur hat complemented the coat.

seal with a collar of black Persian lamb.

Gentlemen's Quarterly continued to promote fur and encourage still-hesitant men. For the November, 1968, issue its photographer went to Finland, for pictures of models in high-fashion furs: a turtleneck Alaska seal parka with angled slash pockets and button-cuffed sleeves; a six-button double-breasted coat of white unsheared nutria; an eight-button double-breasted coat of blond Persian lamb with a full collar, lapels, and a deep center vent; a dramatic Persian lamb cape collared, bordered, and epauleted in darker fur; and a Nehru-collared coat of natural sheared leopard with a frog closure at the neck and a fly front widely trimmed in brown calf. A trip to Boston with furs designed for Boston Brahmins produced a spread of double-breasted coats of such furs as black-dyed mink,

dark Swakara lamb, and navy blue hair seal in November, 1969. In the same issue *Gentlemen's Quarterly* focused on fake fur, ". . . because fake fur apes the genuine article so well and the low cost of these synthetics puts them within reach of anyone who fancies them." It showed a printed Orlon that looked like tiger, a thick silvery-gray pile that imitated chinchilla, a black Orlon that resembled seal, and viscose dyed to an off-white shade similar to pony skin.

Esquire in November, 1969, called its biggest fur-coat feature to that date "The Fur Side of Paradise." The article stated, "The renaissance of the fur-bearing male, who had been in retirement in the discreet decades since the coonskin coat was part of our collegiate culture, becomes more emboldened every blustery day." Illustrating the article were color photographs of such avant-garde fur fashions as a double-breasted kangaroo trimmed in brown leather; a black-and-white russet broadtail coat with a natural fox collar; a thigh-length deep brown African Swakara; a white zebra-stenciled calf coat; a double-breasted unplucked nutria coat resembling a pea jacket; a shaped double-breasted blazer of Mexican mountain lion; a black-dyed broadtail maxi evening cape with a red silk lining; a sleeveless tunic of moon-silver muskrat with leather piping and a brass-buckled buckskin belt; a tunic-style zippered coat of natural muskrat; and a motorcycle jacket of unplucked nutria with leather trim and brass buttons.

By 1970, however, many ecologically oriented persons had begun to oppose the fur coat for both sexes.

Opulence in outerwear: (foreground) Givenchy showed what could be done with mink for men in a big-collared double-breasted coat; (right) a generously cut double-breasted unplucked nutria coat; (upper left) Givenchy's use of Brazilian leopard cat in a maxi coat with matching knickers. From Esquire, *November 1970.*

How did this shift in public opinion affect the fashion magazines that had been showing the latest fur styles? "It's conceivable to now ask where the magazine's conscience was," granted the editors of *Gentlemen's Quarterly,* one of the first magazines to confront the issue, in November, 1970. "Did the showing of Alaskan seal, for instance, imply *GQ*'s condoning the questionable practices surrounding the animal's death? Times change, as do people and their attitudes. But the one thing a fashion magazine cannot do is compel its readers to wear—or, for that matter, not wear—a particular item. What we can do is display the evidence. *GQ* feeling is that while wearing furs from animals bred for that purpose is reasonable, the indiscriminate slaughtering of animals solely to enable their furs to grace someone's back is not, especially when the practice results in the animal's extinction. But the ultimate decision, obviously, lies with the wearer and his conscience." The magazine then proceeded to show alternatives: a fake raccoon that sold for $135 and prompted the caption writer to observe: "Financially and ecologically, fake furs are clearly ahead of the genuine article"; an above-the-knee fake seal coat with a big-notched collar and a price tag of about $45; a black mink coat that sold for $3,500 ("Mink is bred solely for its fur"); a fake mink wrap costing about $170; a real Persian paw trimmed and lined with dyed nutria ($900); and a fake Persian paw ($175).

In November, 1971, *Esquire* photographed a collection of fur coats many of which reflected the wave of nostalgia that was then sweeping over the nation. Reminiscent of the twenties were three raccoon coats shaped for the seventies, with big leather patch pockets. The caption writer noted that "this season's furs are non-endangered species" and that the coats from these ecologically approved pelts looked like fur coats designed for men. Those shown included three sturdy double-breasted coats: a belted black-dyed mink paw, a natural Canadian sea otter, and a sash-belted processed-goat coat with a sea otter collar. But nothing, said the caption writer, could be more masculine, more swagger, than the fur greatcoat: "It is, so to speak, the Mounties after their man." The article showed three greatcoats of midcalf length with oversize collars and lapels, one of coonskin and two of wolfskin. "And always in the Seventies, there is, of course, the maxi, a length that makes much sense on days when the wind blows free," commented *Esquire* in introducing a display of "practical, protective" maxis of dyed Persian lamb paws, dyed Spanish Tigrado lamb, and black-dyed goat.

A series of reverses affected the fur industry in the early seventies. The New York State Mason Act, which went into effect in September, 1970, made it illegal to sell or offer for sale tiger, cheetah, vicuña, red wolf, polar bear, mountain lion, jaguar, ocelot, margay, and three kinds of leopard. Then, the economic recession that began in 1969 carried over into the seventies and worsened. Fake furs continued to sell well, however, prompting *Business Week* to observe on November 20, 1971: "As conservationists bite deeply into their business, fake furs gnaw away at what's left." And while the sale of women's fur coats declined seriously, men's fur coats enjoyed a minor boom. *Business Week* noted: "Two years ago, only a couple

This midcalf-length wolfskin coat, by Bill Blass for Revillon, had an oversize collar. From Esquire, *November 1971.*

of manufacturers were making furs for men; now, well over two dozen are involved." Taking cognizance of the sales still being generated by furs for men, a leading New York department store attempted to lure back female customers by means of "his and her" raccoon coats.

In the early seventies it was the fur-bearing peacock that was the mainstay of the beleaguered fur industry, and the prognosis was good as retailers aggressively advertised and promoted fur for men. One New York retailer summed up the general feeling when his advertisement in the *New York Times* stated that he wanted every man to wear fur.

Rainwear

The proverb "Everybody talks about the weather but nobody does anything about it" is not true, of course. Rainwear manufacturers have been doing something about the weather for generations, in response to another adage, "Necessity is the mother of invention"—necessity in this case being the fact that there is an average of 122 rainy days in twenty-eight of the largest American cities every year.

1900–1910

By today's standards the rainwear produced in the first decade of this century seems more utilitarian than stylish. It was created with protection as its prime aim—with all seams double-stitched, and often strapped and cemented as well, in order to keep water from penetrating inside. A fashionable look was very much an afterthought.

The concept of rubberized fabric for rainwear, so popular in this decade, was created by Charles Macintosh, a Scotsman, who in 1823 perfected, and patented, a method of molding rubber between two layers of fabric. Indeed, as late as 1900 almost any raincoat was still referred to as a mackintosh. Since the purpose of rainwear was protection of the clothes worn underneath, almost all raincoats were long enough to reach a man's ankles. A box-coat style in navy blue or black was the most popular, in both single- and double-breasted models, with a velvet collar sometimes added for a touch of fashion.

Some coats were actually made of rubber, although they were rarely if ever referred to as rubber coats. In this category some attempt at a fashionable look was made by adding a fancy plaid back. The double-breasted coat dominated, and the prevailing style had six pairs of buttons, of which the top pair fastened close around the neck and just below a short collar. Since waterproofed coats kept out not only the rain but air, too, some rubber coats were designed with a patented ventilated epaulet shoulder in an at-

FOR FIELD, STREAM AND CAMP

This array of water-repellent garments for the sportsman, shown in an R. H. Macy & Co. advertisement of 1909, includes an oilskin coat and hat, patch-pocket khaki coats, a hunting outfit in army khaki cloth, a khaki shirt, and corduroy and army khaki cloth norfolk coats and matching trousers. [NEW YORK PUBLIC LIBRARY PICTURE COLLECTION]

tempt to compensate for this drawback. Oil slickers were also guaranteed to be waterproof, and they too were most uncomfortable in warm weather. Available in either black or a bright shade of yellow, the slicker had eyelets fastened with zinc buttons and, like the rubber coat, buttoned high at the neck.

The somewhat more stylish rainwear of this period included the heavy melton coat with a fancy plaid twilled lining and a deep buttoned slit or vent in the back; and a coat of English covert cloth in light tan, with a very wide velvet collar, plaid lining, and a deep slit up the back that could be buttoned if the wearer so desired.

1910–1920

A page from the 1915 Brooks Brothers catalog reports the following rainwear: "Raincoats of gabardine, covert cloth and waterproof tweeds. Mackintoshes and rubber coats, lined and unlined. Oilskin jackets and trousers for golfing, etc., in the rain"— conservative and eminently serviceable rainwear. But a giant step forward in the category of rainwear came with World War I and the need

(left) The newest type of raincoat for spring, 1910, had a fly front and was extra long. (right) A lightweight overcoat. [HICKEY-FREEMAN CO.]

(left) Lightweight overcoat with patch pockets. (right) Long fly-front raincoat with a convertible collar. [HICKEY-FREEMAN CO.]

Gabardine, covert cloth, waterproof tweed, and rubberized coats were shown in 1915 in single- and double-breasted styles. [COURTESY OF BROOKS BROTHERS, NEW YORK]

for an all-weather coat that would also provide foul-weather protection for the doughboy fighting in the trenches. In response to this need, Thomas Burberry of England created the trench coat of a fine twill cotton gabardine, a yarn-dyed fabric chemically processed to repel rain. Since this processing did not in any way affect the porous quality of the fabric, the trench coat permitted ventilation. In short, it was a water-repellent coat but not a waterproofed coat. However, under normal rain conditions the wearer would remain dry.

The trench coat very quickly became the official coat of the Allied fighting men, and soon Aquascutum Limited, an internationally famous London firm established in 1851, was turning out trench coats for military personnel. Although the style has altered somewhat over the intervening years, the trench coat has never lost its appeal.

During the war years of this decade, the trench coat was a four-button double-breasted style with shoulder or gun flaps, straps on the sleeves, an all-around belt with brass rings (to hold a water bottle and hand grenades), a convertible collar, and a deep vent with an inset of fabric fastened with a button. The coat had a buttoned-in lining of wool with sleeves, and this lining was also interlined with an oiled fabric. All in all, the trench coat was a great success as a military coat, and since it was stylish as well, its postwar success was practically assured.

1920–1930

The waterproofed oil slickers of 1900–1910 were now being seen on most college campuses. The college man eschewed the black in favor of the bright yellow and often wore with it a sou'wester hat of the same material and color. Since the slicker came almost to the ankles, and since he wore black galoshes as well, it's safe to assume that the college man of the 1920s was the driest man in the country on rainy days.

By 1928, however, reports from the highly fashion-conscious campuses of Yale and Princeton indicated that the trench coat or the French aviation coat (very similar to the trench coat) was about to displace the slicker in popularity. Some of these Ivy Leaguers preferred a trench coat of a rubberized fabric lined with flannel, while others chose a gabardine with flap pockets. The aviation coat, on the other hand, particularly admired at Yale, was most often a double-breasted raglan-sleeved gabardine lined with one thickness of oiled silk and one of a lightweight, brightly plaided wool, a combination that made the coat both waterproof and warm. These aviation coats featured all-around belts and straps of gabardine at the ends of the sleeves, and they could be worn unbuttoned or fastened snugly at the neck. Like the trench coat, the aviation coat was being worn on even the sunniest days, thus giving promise of becoming an all-weather coat too. One observer at Yale and Princeton reported that students starting off for spring vacation often carried these coats on their arms despite the fact that they were wearing topcoats.

Men's Wear, discussing the popularity of the aviation coat, noted: "The current of style from Princeton and Yale to other parts of the country is the same now as it was five or six years ago, only today styles move more rapidly. These young men, who were photographed as they were leaving New Haven and Princeton, were taking the French aviation coats to their homes in all parts of the country. To their friends and members of their sets, the style will be absolutely new, and immediately other boys of their social standing will wonder where they can buy these coats, and they will try to get them at their local retailers. If the retailers are on the job, they will have these coats in a short time and tell the history of the coat . . . because the young men know that these coats are the ones favored by the students at Princeton and Yale" (*Men's Wear—Chicago Apparel Gazette,* Apr. 25, 1928, p. 77). And just in case there were still some retailers who questioned the fashion authority of the Ivy Leaguers, *Men's Wear* listed the customers of New Haven's leading tailor, who specialized in the English type of clothing favored by Yale men—a long, impressive list headed by F. W. Pershing, son of General Pershing.

The trench coat and the aviation coat were expensive garments (often priced as high as $100), well beyond the reach of the average workingman who quite often ordered his rainwear from the pages of the Sears, Roebuck catalog, which, in 1927, offered "Absolutely Waterproof!" coats and rain suits that sold for about $5. "Let it pour!" boasted the Sears, Roebuck copywriter as he added the following fashion descriptions:

Practical two-in-one reversible. Waterproof coat. Soft and flexible. One side is dull finish black rubber surfaced, other is cotton Asia cloth. Double back. Deep slash pockets and firmly cemented seams. 52 inches long. $4.98.

Black rubber coat. Soft and pliable. Dull finish black rubber surfaced waterproof coat. Lined throughout body and sleeves with good quality white sheeting. Has vulcanized one-seam back, two lower flap pockets and ventilated eyelets under arms. 48½ inches long. $3.79.

Waterproof slicker coat and pants. Shoulders, elbows and fly front of jacket are triple thickness. Large cape and back. Pants made apron style with triple seat and triple front. Average length of jacket, 30 inches. Jacket, $2.89. Pants, $2.89. Worn with waterproof slicker hat with chin strap and ear flaps. Stitched down brim. Soft cotton flannel lining.

The catalog also sold Slicker Oil Compound for recoating and preserving oiled slicker clothing. A 1-pint can cost 28 cents.

In 1929 Jack Murdocke, covering the Derby Day races in England, wrote that never before had he been "so impressed with fashions from the point of view of mackintoshes, waterproofs, raincoats and tall hats. Furthermore, the coats were standardized, for the man about town, the smart Englishman who goes racing, finds it's necessary to wear the right kind of coat for battling against the English climate, even though he patronizes the more exclusive members' stands and enclosures at Epsom and Ascot. Hence rubberized materials supersede the lightweight coverts and raglans" (*Men's Wear—Chicago Apparel Gazette,* July 10, 1929). Accompanying this report was a photograph of the Marquis of Londonderry wearing a military waterproof with his morning coat, trousers, and top hat.

In England, where the raincoat and rolled umbrella are as complementary to each other as whisky and soda, the man of fashion had long been determined that rainwear need not be unimaginative to be utilitarian, and in the next decade his American counterpart, traditionally an Anglophile in matters of fashion, would also learn how to defy the elements without sacrificing style.

1930–1940

American fashion reporters were now focusing more and more attention on well-dressed Britishers, whose fashion impact was greater than ever. And, naturally enough, a great deal of attention was given to British rainwear. After all, a *Men's Wear* writer put it: "In England, where rain is taken not as a dispensation of Providence but rather as routine weather, the raincoat is an integral part of the wardrobe and is worn on all occasions, including the most formally dressed outdoor affairs, such as the race meetings held at Ascot. Judging from the clothing style trends and from high style advices from abroad, it is pretty safe to predict the belted raincoat is a swanky and tempting garment to almost any man. When such a coat has a swing and a swirl to it, there is all of the romance clinging to its skirts that is to be found in the Highland kilt. Generally speaking, the cut of the better grade coat for Fall will be looser, with fuller skirts and more 'drape.' This is in conformity to the greater informality and 'sporty' aspect of men's clothing.

"Weight and ventilation being always a factor in the rubberized fabric groups, considerable attention is being given to the development of rubberized materials with a base of lightweight silk, either real silk or a substitute. Some of these silk base, three-ply fabrics are finished in tweed effects, some in suede finishes.

"Cotton gabardines are being styled for those who like a smart as well as a serviceable garment at a fair price. The lighter weights are unlined, or else have skeletonized linings, but there is also a decided set in this grouping toward the 'reversible' type. Some of these 'reversible' coats may actually be turned inside out and worn with either face outside; others are double thickness, but are not designed to be worn on both sides, although their full lining is of the same material and the coat is finished practically the same on both sides. A novelty in the reversible style is a cotton gabardine made in two tones, one a tan the other a deeper tone, and this coat may be worn with either side out, two coats in one.

"Oiled cottons, because of their lightness, their lack of bulk, their durability and real water-shedding properties, are favored by those who want a raincoat for service. Such a coat is ideal for the sportsman or the city man who is forced to face inclement weather in large gobs. An innovation in model is a new coat designed primarily for sport wear, which opens to the waist with a slide fastener and is donned by the pull-over route. This coat has raglan sleeves and sufficient fullness across the chest and through the body to be worn over a shooting coat or sweater and still allow perfect ease of movement. It also has a hood which will protect the back of the head and neck and which also projects well over the forehead, the hood being held in place by strings at the throat, which also serve with a snap fastener to secure and close the body of the coat after the slide fastener has been drawn shut. There are sleeve tabs and a tie belt at the waist and large, squarish,

The fashion emphasis in rainwear in 1934 was on white. Important features in the double-breasted style were the big collar, which could be turned up for good protection, and lapels that could be buttoned high. From Esquire, *March 1934.*

useful pockets. Being wide-skirted, there is nothing to impede the sportsman's movements either above or below, as it were."

In fact, the wide-skirted, loose-hanging coat was *the* American raincoat of the mid-1930s, favored in the words of this writer "by those who really know. There is a multiplicity of good reasons for the full-skirted coat. In the first place, the full, loosely draped coat is actually a better medium for keeping off the wet than a coat which fits tightly, the reason for which is that most of the untreated or lightly treated fabrics are not entirely waterproof. They are only water-shedding because of their particular weave-construction or surfacing. A certain amount of moisture will seep through. A coat is like a tent. An ordinary tent of canvas will not leak in a driving shower, as long as you do not touch or scrape its under side. Touch the underside and the water will begin to seep through instead of shedding off. The same principle applies to a loose fitting coat. The loose coat does not rub, is not so likely to be stretched taut across the shoulders for instance, and therefore will not allow the water to seep through as readily as a tight-fitting coat of the same material" (*Men's Wear,* July 25, 1934). Furthermore, the full coat with wide skirts had scope and sweep—true bravura style.

Meanwhile, patterns were starting to replace solid colors in British raincoats. These patterns were made up in a cotton fabric with a rubber back and had a decidedly sporty appearance that very soon would affect American designs. Most of these new coats had raglan sleeves, a great fullness in back, and a center seam and vent. But for those Britishers who were still wedded to solid colors there were gabardine coats in all shades of green, navy, greens and blues shot with purple, and rust tones. Never before had there been such a variety of styles and colors. As one writer put it, with typical British understatement, "It must be admitted that style is entering into the mackintosh end of the business."

Back in the United States, swagger

raincoats clearly showing the British influence held sway on the opening day of the 1934 autumn racing season at Belmont Park, Long Island. A fashion journalist covering the event that drizzly day wrote: "One of the most fashionable looking coats that passed in review in the paddock was the fly-front raglan style, extremely full cut in the skirt, borrowing somewhat from the toga mode. This model made its appearance in whitish grey rubberized cotton and tan worsted gabardine of fine texture, the latter draping beautifully. Some of the polo players who turned out for the races wore very light-weight rubberized coats in raglan style with button-through front. Belted double-breasted coats that had a noticeable flare to the bottom were worn in worsted and cotton gabardines and rubberized cotton. The regulation trench coat was seen, and a few smartly dressed men wore single-breasted belted raglan coats, usually in rubberized cotton. Some who came through the general admission gate were wearing oiled cotton coats" (*Men's Wear,* Sept. 19, 1934).

At the Yale-Columbia football game played in the Yale Bowl during a steady downpour in October, 1934, the cheering section on the Columbia side was filled with every sort of water-repellent garment, even rubber ponchos. On the more fashion-conscious Yale side, however, there were predominantly the reversible coat and the gabardine raincoat. Insofar as the spectators were concerned, there were trench coats galore as well as rubberized coats, both coated and rubber-backed. Yet it was the Yale man's preference for the reversible and gabardine coats that counted most in fashion circles. (And it was also noted that many a Yale undergraduate arrived at the stadium with a terry cloth towel draped around his neck like a muffler. It was judged a practical rainy-day accessory, and in view of the Yale man's fashion leadership, merchants and designers were encouraged to follow his lead and bring out towels styled after popular muffler patterns.)

Esquire that year trained its sights on

two new British-inspired rainwear fashions: the white raincoat and the shorter raincoat with full sweep: "The term 'white raincoat' is really a misnomer, as the smart shade that is indicated by this general designation is an oyster color. Pure white raincoats are still reserved for the on-duty wear of dairymen and traffic cops. The model that is sketched here is the roomy double-breasted type with raglan sleeves and a convertible collar which, when buttoned up, is strongly reminiscent of wartime pictures of the Crown Prince. For wear in really dirty weather, the sleeves are provided with extra tabs which may be buttoned over." As for the new raincoat—short but with full sweep, a favored fashion in England—it had very wide lapels and two enormous flap pockets and came only a few inches below the knee.

At the same time *Men's Wear* correspondents in key cities filed reports on the most popular rainwear fashions currently being worn and on those styles retailers expected to be selling most in the months ahead. The following excerpts have been taken from those reports:

Buffalo. From a style viewpoint, retailers look for greater acceptance of the oiled balloon cloth coat in double-breasted model with an all-around belt, priced to sell close to $10. This type of coat, rainwear buyers believe, will sell equally well in styles with either raglan or set in sleeve. . . . When it comes to the higher-priced novelties, some retailers will place considerable emphasis upon the cotton gabardine trench coat with a detachable camel's hair lining priced close to $20 or $22.50. This will be a raglan with full belt, slash pockets and leather buttons. . . . From a color viewpoint the light tans will predominate, with some darker tans and the deeper shades of green.

Cleveland. The demand has been largely confined to a limited number of styles. Oiled cotton and silk coats have been most popular in virtually all the stores at prices from $7.50 to $13.50. Deep green and brown seem to be slight color favorites. . . . Buyers believe that some heavier types may enjoy an improved demand as cooler weather sets in next Fall. One of these is the new wrap-around gabardine trench coat, which experienced a flurry in sales here early this Spring. One buyer said that a new lightweight raincoat made of waterproofed acetate and viscose yarns,

which is transparent like the better oiled silks, promises to sell well during the coming months at about $5. Of the rubberized types, the black coat with a frosty sheen, selling at $5, leads the demand.

Boston. Lightweights in all fabrics and grades were more in demand than heavier goods, especially the gossamer fabrics that can be folded into a handful and tucked into a car door pocket. A new imported coat expected to sell by one store which prides itself on the variety and size of its raincoat stock is of oyster color rubberized cloth, with fly front, patch pockets, and convertible collar, in raglan style. Another leading clothing store has been very successful with a lightweight coat of fine rubbercoated silk, gabardines in the better grades and suede finish coats for younger men.

Atlanta. Oiled cotton and silk raincoats in light weights, selling at prices between $5 and $15, have proved most popular with Atlanta retail clothiers this summer and will probably continue to lead raincoat sales this coming fall. Blue and deep sea-green have been the most popular colors. . . . In local shops catering to the "advance style" trade, it is reported that more tweed type raincoats will be purchased for fall business than formerly, and that sports styles will predominate. The greatest objection to heavier raincoats is that they are too hot for summer and do not offer protection enough in the winter season. . . . Development of a poncho for men was suggested by another merchant. "I can see no reason," he said, "why the cape, made longer and camouflaged with the name poncho, should not be made a popular rain garment in the south; it would have everything—light weight, protective qualities and convenience."

Chicago. Some buyers expect that the white raincoat will become more important in the fall. Certain quality men's stores report that during the latter part of the spring they sold these coats, and indications are that the better-dressed men will favor them. Medium price volume establishments feel that domestic garments made of rubberized materials in dark colors will have the big call, while popular price department stores feel their customers will continue to demand raglan trench coats for rainwear. . . . As general business conditions improve higher-priced raincoats will be bought, some buyers say. One quality store reports its best selling price has been $6.50 for a rubberized, single-breasted, raglan raincoat, whereas some seasons back its best selling price was $10. Other popular numbers in this store, which does one of the best raincoat jobs in the Middle West, are a double-breasted British coat with set-in sleeves at $8.50, and a Belgian suede coat at the same

price. Another big distributor of raincoats says $15 is its best seller, this being for a domestic balloon cloth coat, with $7.50 its next best price. Several prominent stores say the big demand has been for raincoats at around $3.50, but they believe with improved conditions coats at $5 to $10 should be in greater favor.

St. Louis. From a style standpoint, there was a noticeable demand for the double-breasted coat in the lightweight, oiled fabric, which is expected to continue in favor among the young men returning to college. Blues, browns, and sea greens have been the leading colors. The popular price garment in this material is $7.50, although quite a few of the higher-priced coats are sold. . . . The leading coat is the tan trench coat in a wide range of prices, from $3.95 to $7.50 in the popular price sections of the department stores, to $5 to $12.95 in the better stores, with $6.95 as the best seller. . . . Economic reasons are given for the popularity of the trench coat. During the last few years, this type of garment has been made to do double duty, being worn as both a topcoat and a raincoat. Retailers expect to see a continuation of this trend next season. (*Men's Wear,* July 25, 1934)

In 1935 *Men's Wear* observed that silk was making "great strides in masculine esteem as a lightweight rain shedder. Like the cotton coats, the great majority of these silk garments are made in the balmacaan model, many to button through, but some of the fly-front variety. Inasmuch as the objective is usually lightness, single-breasted are the rule. Some of the cloth is treated and some of it is rubberized, and it is reported that retailers are more and more interested in the silk raincoat when accompanied by an envelope to match so that the garment may be carried conveniently in travel or may be left in the pocket or compartment of an automobile."

Men's Wear also advised that, in those rarefied heights where men were willing to pay $45 or more for a raincoat, "attention should be paid to the new leather reversible coat which is rainwear, stormwear, blizzard-wear, all in one. The outside is of the softest tanned sheepskin, smooth, of course, and the inner fabric is worsted gabardine. Again the style is balmacaan. It would seem that the battle is joined between the balmacaan and the trench coat." In 1935 the trench coat

Shown at a point-to-point race, the man in the center wore an oyster-color fly-front raglan raincoat with a full skirt, a gusseted back vent, large patch pockets, and wrist tabs. From Esquire, *March 1935.*

Two rainwear fashions of 1937: (left) a generously cut processed gabardine coat with raglan shoulders: (right) a rubberized coat with a sweeping skirt, a style favored in England. From Esquire, *April 1937.*

Coats in two fabrics popular for rainwear in 1940: (left) an oyster-color cotton twill, processed for water repellency, with a high-fastening bal collar, worn with rubbers in the design of wing-tip shoes; (right) a processed worsted gabardine in a belted style. From Esquire, *November 1940.*

The man at right wore a raincoat with set-in sleeves and broad shoulders to accommodate a wide-shouldered jacket. From Esquire, *November 1943.*

Rainwear

still had a loyal army of admirers who regarded it as more than just a coat and were willing to pay $100 and more for an import, the styling of which had undergone virtually no appreciable change since it was introduced twenty years earlier. Another survey made that year revealed that the oiled-cotton raincoat was the leader in countrywide sales, with cotton gabardines in second place. Prices ranged from $5.50 to $10.50.

About this time some trade writers were criticizing certain retailers for their failure to merchandise rainwear more aggressively and imaginatively. "Too many merchants," said one writer, "content themselves with placing a few rainwear garments hurriedly in their show windows at the first sign of rain, possibly a display near the front entrance, while others merely paste a sticker on their windows bearing the legend 'Raincoats,' and let it go at that" (*Men's Wear,* July 24, 1935).

One prominent New York retailer, however, had the proper promotional spirit, which, in the opinion of this writer, other retailers might emulate: to promote rainwear in its class—rainwear for town, for country, for work, and for play. In short, any raincoat would not do for any purpose. "Women have already been made keenly style conscious about rainwear," the writer stated, "and there is no earthly reason why men should not also know and feel that they cannot afford not to be as smart when they are wet as when they are dry. A progressive merchant who worked well should be able to sell a prospect at least three coats where he is now buying one, emphasizing style, health, efficiency and utility."

The writer also reminded retailers that although "no one doubts that rain is the best stimulant for selling waterproof clothing, some of the best business in some stores is done on clear days. One drenching is usually all the average man needs to remind him of his wet weather clothes requirements. Save him the drenching and urge him to get a raincoat before it rains."

Esquire had already made a practice of pinpointing certain raincoats for specific wear. In its November, 1935, issue, for instance, it showed "a new short raincoat with side vents for country spectator wear"; and a few issues later, "the short raincoat of imported gabardine with side vents for wet weather in the country."

A raincoat survey in 1936 revealed that the two leading types of raincoats, from the point of view of volume of sales, were the oiled cottons and the processed cotton gabardines—the leaders for the second time. Suedes, however, showed considerable strength in the East and Middle West, selling fastest at $5. The best-selling model was the double-breasted style, chiefly the belted raglan, representing 46 percent of sales throughout the country. Second to it was the single-breasted button-through raglan, which accounted for 21.4 percent.

When retailers were asked what they found to be the best waterproofing process, it was found that the pattern of sectional choices in types of garments was pretty closely followed. In the East, where cotton gabardine was the leading fabric, the retailers chose Cravenette as their favorite; in the Middle West and South, where oiled-cotton raincoats sold best, the retailers designated oiled fabrics, and on the West Coast virtually all favored the Cravenette process.

Whipcord raincoats retailing about $50 increased in popularity during the last half of this decade. Their weight made them practical topcoats as well as raincoats. Tan was considered the best shade, and the majority of these coats were fly-fronted balmacaans.

The family of rubberized coats became increasingly diversified during this period. There were rubber-covered garments, rubber-backed garments, and some that had a layer of rubber between the outer and inner layers of cloth in accordance with Charles Macintosh's concept. Coats were shown in rubberized silk, rubberized poplin, and rubberized tweed as well as in rubberized jersey and rubberized gabardine; rubberized gabardine had been treated so that to all intents and purposes it appeared no different from regular gabardine cloth. The rubberized silk coat, which retailed for about $10, often weighed no more than 12 ounces.

Coats with all-around belts were as popular as ever and in the better-grade raincoats were being made broader in the body, to allow more efficient ventilation and to reduce perspiration on warm days. During the late 1930s inside pockets of many of the new styles featured waterproof slide fasteners, and most pockets were of the slash type.

Although the reversible coat was generally regarded as being more in the topcoat class than in the rainwear class, it had become so popular by the mid-thirties that no discussion of rainwear would be complete without mention of the tweed-and-gabardine reversible. There were, of course, many different kinds of reversible raincoats: the higher-priced coats of a tweed or Shetland shell backing a worsted gabardine, and others of a very fine cotton gabardine or twill.

An L. Fellows drawing of 1938 shows the man at left wearing a full-sweep raglan coat with a fly front and an all-around belt. From Esquire, April 1938.

Rainwear for the back-to-college wardrobe of 1938: a green oiled-cotton raglan coat that represents an improvement over the slicker of earlier years. From Esquire, *August 1938.*

The popularity of oiled-cotton fabrics continued in 1938, with worsted gabardine a prime favorite in the upper price brackets (many of the gabardines were made with an iridescent effect). Poplin and plain twill cottons were reported very popular on college campuses and were appearing at fashionable races and hunts as well. Linings were also very much in the news that year, with the cotton twill or poplin of the coat also being used for the lining. It was claimed that the main virtue of this particular construction was the added protection of the second layer of processed cotton.

The removable lining was also a strong selling point. And rubber-coated fabrics were being shown most frequently with the rubber on the inside of the coat. Double-breasteds, which had once dominated the fashion scene, were by 1938 overshadowed by the single-breasted styles.

By the end of this decade waterproof blouses were growing increasingly popular with golfers and sportsmen. These were raglan-shouldered cotton blouses with a slide-fastened front and bag pockets, roomy through the body but snug over the hips. Some of these blouses also featured elastic-band cuffs.

The problem of finding a truly protective raincoat light enough for comfortable wear in the warmer months had been solved by 1938. The leading styles that year included a tan worsted gabardine topcoat with a 77-inch sweep to the bottom; a pale tan cotton twill with white pearl buttons covered by a fly front; a green oiled-cotton coat; a self-lined poplin coat with an

A gabardine raglan coat of fingertip-length with side vents. From Esquire, *August 1938.*

inside cash pocket; a rubbe gray silk; and a slide-fastene twill. The same year John Wa of New York promoted its n count cotton fabric raincoa the name "Duckweather," customers to come in and water on the fabric. War pima cotton cloth had 540 t the square inch (the genera raincoat fabrics had appre 120 threads), and in additior so closely woven, the su Duckweather was slightly su

A survey questionnaire s tailers in key American citie produced some very interes lights:

. . . Although it represent small percentage of sales, the coacher coat (a knee-length mc front and wide lapels) showec the most significant change e the next season—going from of sales to 2.7 per cent. (This in the next year would serve door to even shorter-than-kne

. . . Vented raincoats were increase from 58.9 to 59.2 per

. . . Slash pockets were a favorite over horizontal pocke

. . . The number of stores ca with slide fasteners were exp crease from 10 per cent last per cent next season.

1940–1950

In its November, 1940, i decided: "No one gets use wet—that is, as opposed to That's why it pleases us to on you in this discussion of This is precisely what the ceeded to do, using sketc handsome raincoats as illus terial:

"The raincoat at the lef colored cotton twill, is espe essed to repel moisture. E been tinkering with waterp for years, and the most rece are virtually impervious ments, even retaining the after a round trip to the d A combined touch of fa practicality is the fly front which, due to the smooth e

sented, sheds raindrops like anything. Also leading a double life are the military collar, slash pockets, tabs and buttons at the cuffs and the generous sweep at the bottom of the coat. Incidental accoutrements are the lightweight brown felt hat with silk ribbon and striped blue worsted suit.

"The other raincoat is of processed worsted gabardine. It has raglan shoulders, slash pockets, and buttons and tabs on the sleeves; the all-around belt adds to the military effect of the double-breasted front, as do the lapels rolling to the top button. The soft greenish mixture hat and the Lovat colored cheviot suit serve to make an excellent combination."

Esquire that year maintained that raincoats are as individual in appearance as any item of apparel, running a full page of "rainbeaters" with this footnote: "You won't be interested in this page if you're the type who enters a store and says, 'Give me a blue suit!'"

At the top of the page was a pipe-smoking collegian wearing a knee-length bone-colored poplin-weave cotton university raincoat with raglan shoulders, fly front, balmacaan collar, and stitching at the bottom and cuffs. Below, a very British-looking gentleman, complete with derby, polka-dot silk scarf, and rolled umbrella, wore a full skirted, single breasted, fly-front rubberized cotton hunting raincoat with an all-around belt, large flap pockets, and a convertible collar. Next to him stood an ultracosmopolitan type wearing a worsted gabardine balmacaan with a fly front, raglan shoulders, a military collar, and slash pockets. But by far the most colorful chap on the page was the Ivy Leaguer wearing a sports jacket, sweater, slacks, a checkered cap, and a brass-buttoned coaching-type coat in a green oiled-cotton fabric similar to the old-fashioned slicker. At the bottom of the page were two more youthful pipe-smokers in earnest conversation: the man on the left, with a giant golf umbrella tucked under his arm, wore a fingertip-length waterproofed cotton rain jacket with a convertible collar,

side slits, and matching trousers; his companion wore the popular short raincoat of cotton gabardine, with side vents, fly front, and convertible collar—a coat that *Esquire* deemed ideal for university and country.

The year 1940 also saw one prominent rainwear manufacturer announce an "amazing new process" that would, it was promised, revolutionize raincoat making. The raincoats were advertised as follows: "Korosealed by Goodrich! This process is your guarantee of the 100% water-proof extra-long-wearing raincoat that will *never* stick, stiffen, or harden. Sun-proof, grease-proof, stain-proof, and mildew-proof. Absolutely odorless. Contains no oil or rubber. Complete protection in shower or torrent!" Accompanying this advertisement was a sketch of a shin-length raincoat, which, when packed in its handy envelope container, weighed a mere 5 ounces.

Lightweight protection was the chief advertising claim for rainwear of the early 1940s. Both sexes wanted it in a coat that would also stay soft and pliant. For by then smart styling was taken for granted.

Esquire in 1941 advised its readers to "repel rain in fashion" and repeated the happily obvious: "Coats that keep out the rain have graduated from the strictly utilitarian category to an established fashion plane. Coincident with this progress has come betterment in the methods of treating the fabrics to resist the elements." To illustrate this point, the fashion editor showed a tan processed cotton gabardine coat with raglan shoulders, a military collar, a fly front, and slash pockets; and a coat of tan processed cotton showing the military influence in its epaulets, buttons at the covering lines, and all-around belt—according to the fashion copywriter, a removable wool lining made this coat suitable for cold days.

By 1941 undergraduates had become the leading advocates of raincoat wear, and light-colored coats were just as popular on clear days as they were on rainy days. *Esquire* liked an oyster cotton coat in a three-quarter-length model, "which despite its shortness has

met with a wide acceptance"; and a green oiled-cotton coat with wide sweep to the bottom.

A full-page raincoat advertisement in *Esquire* in October, 1941, demonstrated the wide range of choices open to the man wanting to buy an under-$20 raincoat. Among the models photographed were a fingertip-length reversible of a soft, water-repellent velvet corduroy on one side and a bleached-bone gabardine showerproofed by Cravenette on the other, featuring slash pockets and railroad stitching; a fly-front fingertip-length reversible of covert cloth on one side and bleached-bone gabardine on the other (both sides showerproofed by Cravenette), with slash pockets and set-in sleeves, a deep yoke, and railroad stitching on the cuffs and bottom; and a balmacaan-style gabardine with a fly front, deep yoke, and sleeve lining.

By 1943 the knee-length raincoat had taken over despite some criticism that it was impractical. *Esquire* showed a handsome example—a fly-front processed coat with set-in sleeves that, according to the editors, offered a variation from the conventional raglan effect, making the shoulders look broader and bringing the outergarment into conformity with the lines of the jacket for neater fit.

The following year *Esquire* sketched a coat of natural-tan worsted gabardine that was based upon the newest scientific developments in military garments. "The same philosophy of protection, that of layers of fabrics in military uniforms, is applied to the civilian coat," the writer explained. "The buttoned-in removable lining is not silver, but well worth its weight in wool. Set-in sleeve goes well with broad-shoulder jackets and slash pockets open through for convenience."

Esquire showed little patience for the "curious illogic" of those men who, in 1944, were still giving little thought to the rainwear section of their wardrobes: "A man will trade in last year's model topcoat with scrupulous regularity, but any old raincoat will do—after all, it's raining, isn't it?" Hoping

to break such men of this bad habit, the fashion department showed a raincoat "about as unpretentious as any garment well can be, but its air of utility by no means detracts from its good looks. The coat is of ivory colored processed cotton in a single-breasted model with fly-front, raglan shoulders and slash pockets."

Demonstrating once again that civilian garb was profiting from military research, *Esquire* in 1945 noted: "One improvement in raincoats consists in a processing of the fabrics that causes them to retain water repellent properties when dry cleaned." Just such a coat was a conventional raglan with a fly front, slash pockets, and tabs at the sleeves. "Cagily tagged as 'shower-proof' it repels a 'reasonable' amount of rain."

Esquire's "bold look" of 1948 carried over into the following year and inspired what the editors called a "valiant raincoat—husky all over—big pockets, big lapels, big buttons, and a wide sweep. Set-in sleeves and square shoulders make you look like an ex-fullback." In the color of a palomino pony, this bold raincoat extended several inches below the knees.

1950–1960

According to *Esquire,* in 1950 a college man's requirements, indoors and out, were comfort and casualness; tweed was the fabric that best suited his frame of mind. For a rainy day on campus he chose a fly-front raglan raincoat of processed cotton poplin— "one fabric with a high rainproof rating"—and with it he wore a processed rain hat in the same fabric.

The see-through vinyl plastic raincoat, touted by some rainwear manufacturers as lighter, tougher, smarter, and 100 percent waterproof, made news in the early years of this decade. "Complete waterproof protection with stitchless electronically sealed seams," advertised one firm, illustrating its ad with photographs of a man in a balmacaan model that folded into a convenient packet; and of a zippered rain jacket with slash pockets and a de-tachable hood that included a handy carrying pouch for use as a golf club cover. And for children there were plastic raincoats with Western decorations, matching helmets, and Western boots.

Men's Wear in 1952 predicted: "Rainwear for Fall and Winter will continue to combine practicality and styling. All-weather, water-repellent raincoats made of wool and synthetic blends are bound to go over big with men who want to have a coat which can be worn rain or shine. . . . Not to be underestimated in any consideration for rainwear for Fall and Winter is the finer quality cotton coat, also treated with a water repellent. In touring the market we found that manufacturers had made the most of cotton in fashioning their garments. Incidentally, don't be surprised if the cotton, knee length coacher coat and the cotton-wool reversible turn out to be 'sleepers!'"

One of the nation's leading rainwear manufacturers announced the "first major improvement in plastic rainwear," in a *Life* magazine advertisement previewed in *Men's Wear* (Feb. 20, 1953). The exclusive features of this embossed gabardine-textured vinyl coat included plastic buttons electronically heat-sealed to become part of the coat ("no more loose or lost buttons"), 20 gauge reinforced heat sealed buttonholes, a new and wider stand-up "protection" collar, free-action raglan sleeves, large seep-reinforced pockets, 100 percent electronically heat-welded seams, and reinforcement at each point of strain.

Plastic rainwear failed to capture a dominant position, however, for two reasons. First, lacking porosity, it was decidedly uncomfortable to wear during the warmer months; and second, before this decade was over the American man, who was using apparel more and more as a means of self-expression, wanted rainwear that showed more color and imagination than see-through vinyl plastic. As a result, by the early 1970s plastic rainwear was all but extinct, used chiefly as a kind of emergency rainwear.

The year 1953 saw a major break-through in rainwear fashions with the introduction of the raincoat made of 50 percent polyester and 50 percent cotton, a processed fabric both water-repellent and washable. It was brought out in two styles: the single-breasted raglan and the double-breasted, belted trench coat. This new coat (later to be christened the "London Fog") was first seen at Saks Fifth Avenue in New York City, and soon after retailers in all sections of the country were highlighting it. By this time a third style had been added: a single-breasted trench coat with set-in sleeves, an all-around belt, a zippered sleeve pocket, and a change pocket.

In February of that year, *Men's Wear*

A double-breasted raglan coat in a processed sueded cotton with a glen plaid design has slanting pockets and adjustable sleeve tabs (1958).

observed: "Among the newer raincoats that are guaranteed to be 100 per cent water-proof is an all-nylon garment, light in weight, neat, good-looking, completely protective. An older style which seems to retain its popularity is the all-combed cotton gabardine trench coat with processed cotton lining. This style is bought as much for its cut as for its utility appeal.

"The most important development in raincoats, however, is the trend toward so-called rain topcoats, the garment that serves both purposes. Most of these are made in the regulation topcoat models, single-breasted button-through, with either set-in sleeves or raglan shoulders, and usually of cloths simulating woolens or worsteds, always water-repellent processed. Many of the newer coats in this category are made of blends of synthetic fibers or these fibers combined with wool or cotton. Others are made exclusively of the natural fibers, such as the plain worsteds and the checked cottons. The three-quarter length coat is gaining."

Illustrating this feature were a rain-topcoat of a new blend of rayon, acetate, and Acrilan with a cashmere-like hand in a two-color miniature check pattern, with raglan shoulders; a military model of combed-cotton gabardine with a processed-cotton lining; and a 100 percent nylon coat guaranteed to be completely waterproof. "All meet the 'light weight' test," noted the caption writer.

The black raincoat took on fashion impetus in 1955, incorporating a scarlet yoke that gave the coat an aura of elegance as a raincoat for formal occasions as well as for informal wear. In Dallas, for example, where there is little rainfall, these black coats were promoted as lightweight topcoats ideal for chilly days.

The coacher coat, which in a 1938 survey had been singled out as a possible "sleeper," also came into its own in this decade. And smooth, silky gabardine continued to attract the man who was in the mood to spend a little more money for a more luxurious raincoat. A tightly woven gabardine

made from a blend of rayon and Dacron was hailed as a fine all-weather coat, while a more expensive gabardine—of a 50 percent Dacron, 50 percent wool blend—was judged to be ultra-water-repellent as well as wrinkle-resistant and long-wearing.

This decade saw the introduction of various water-repellent processes. Of special note is "Aqua Five," Aquascutum's exclusive process for impregnating fabrics for raincoats, which penetrated every fiber so completely, according to the advertisements, that it became part of the fabric.

1960–1970

After dropping to a three-quarter length in the 1950s, raincoats crept back up above the knees in the early 1960s. *Men's Wear* commented on this: "Lengths continue to get shorter in the style items, particularly in those models slanted toward the Young Man Market where 38-inch coats are not unusual. Novelty treatments rate well in that group, too." And since no decade since the 1920s catered to the young with such fierce determination, the shorter raincoat became the dominant style for all ages.

Men's Wear in 1962 noted: "While the split-raglan models continue to be very strong in all grades, some producers of top-quality coats see the beginning of a swing toward full raglans with the classic stand-up bal collar. Look for many more fancy pile liners in stripes and tweedy effects." Illustrating this feature story (captioned "Youth has its fling") was a shipboard photograph in which lively young models wore various types of raincoats: a short one of denim on the outside, corduroy on the inside, with oversize flapped pockets; a belted, double-breasted model in a bold houndstooth check with a scalloped yoke; and a 39-inch-long trench coat of black loden cloth.

The following year *Gentlemen's Quarterly* sent a group of models to the Casbah in Tangier, where it proceeded to photograph them in a collection of foreign-made raincoats: a short, off-

white cotton coat with leather-edged upper slash pockets, roomy lower patch-flap pockets, a shoulder and pointed front yoke, a curved back yoke, peak lapels, leather buttons, a full belt, and diamond-shaped leather buttonhole trim; an iridescent tan cotton, single-breasted, with an angled yoke, front panels, brown-leather-edged angled pockets, peak lapels, button-tab sleeves, allover stitched trim, and an inverted back pleat joining a center vent; a box-pleated light gray cotton, leather edged and buttoned, with slash pockets, a full belt, a yoke and an inverted pleat in back, and blue corduroy lining; and a bal-collared cotton coat from Spain with leather-edged buttonholes, oversize bone buttons, angled and buttoned flap pockets, triple-stitch trim, and cuffed sleeves. Also photographed on the mosaic walk outside a sultan's palace

Above-knee-length Continental-style raincoat of processed cotton with a yoke front and back, an all-around belt with rows of stitching, and buttoned tabs at the side vents (1960).

was a clay-colored double-breasted worsted gabardine coat, raglan-shouldered and peak-lapeled, with straight flap pockets, cuffed sleeves, and a half belt in back. At the gate to the Casbah the *Gentlemen's Quarterly* photographer snapped some classic bal-collared all-weather coats including a black cotton with raglan-back sleeves that reversed to a full raglan in off-white; a putty-colored Dacron-and-cotton fly-front model; and a short rainproof in a natural shade, made of Dacron and Zantrel and lined half in black, half in gold.

In 1963 *Men's Wear* observed that in fall rainwear lines gabardines were being shown in several versions, which included blends, all-cottons, and some pure worsteds; and laminated foam liners were still another feature. The writer predicted: "In fashion colors, black will still be among the best as black-browns, blue-grays, olives, and black-olives all jockey for the follow-up position. Obviously, the naturals, sands, tans and oysters will account for the mass of business done in staples. However, a new shade—or rather a revived shade—seems to have a powerful potential. It is called 'London Tan' and is variously shown as a plain color and as an iridescent. Opinions on iridescents generally vary from one firm to another. Most, however, believe that they will still sell well" (Apr 12, 1963). Accompanying this forecast were photographs showing, among other styles, a new short trench coat model, 40 inches long, in a deep olive color; and an all-cotton raglan model in London tan with a one-piece sleeve and a new broad collar.

A 1964 *Men's Wear* article titled "Fabrics and Finishes" stated that there were 138 separate operations in the making of a single well-made raincoat, not including the pressings. Nine of these operations were photographed with the following captions:

. . . In order to get a smooth, flat laying chest in a split-raglan model, the interlining facing runs all the way up the front, as usual—but also continues across the front to the sleevehead to achieve this smooth effect without buckles or ridges.

. . . Matching plaids: Patterned coats should be matched from the collar seam down. Patterns should not "V" toward bottom. This takes extra goods in the cutting. Of course, plaids should match at all seams.

. . . Clean lining seams are used even in concealed areas to prevent ravelling. All lining seams should be "serged" or lock-stitched.

. . . Buttons should be permanently attached to a well-made raincoat. Some use elasticized thread, others an injected plastic coating on button thread to prevent breaking off.

. . . On fly-front construction the inside layer of the fly should be indented or offset from the front of the fly to provide easier access for fingers as well as to prevent wearing-out of the back fly. Where buttonholes show, most good coats use simulated hand-made buttonholes.

. . . Railroad stitching on collar "stand" will anchor interlining to prevent curling and add firmness.

. . . An open bottom lining, usually secured by a strap, will "hang" better than a closed lining. Closed linings also often conceal sloppy interior work.

. . . When an interior yoke of contrasting color is used, the top-stitching thread should match the color of the yoke where visible. To achieve this, a "stitch and turn" sewing operation is used.

The highly informative text for "Fabrics and Finishes" reads as follows:

Blends of polyester and cotton are the most popular fabrics used in rainwear today. Most of these are in poplin weaves and the percentages of each of the fibers used in the blends have many variations. However, the percentages of cotton and polyester used in the cloth are not a measure of the cloth's quality. Much depends on the cloth's construction, the number of picks and ends used in its weaving and the finishing of the fabric, as well as the type and quality of those yarns.

Obviously, two-ply yarns are superior to "singles," but the information is not indicated by the fiber content.

Blends of acetate and cotton and polyesters, acrylics and cottons are often used in the weaving of iridescent cloths and there are nylon-cotton poplins, too.

All-cotton fabrics can be found both in luxury grade coats and the lowest price rainwear. Here, too, the quality of the yarns and the construction and finish of the cloth is more indicative of the quality than the fiber content.

Pure worsted gabardines are in the process of making a limited comeback, this time in sporty casual models as well as in staple styles.

Woolens, used alone as well as in blends, have acceptance in proofed patterned coats and corduroys with water repellent finishes bridge the outerwear-rainwear categories.

Among the novelty fabrics used in rainwear are some plastic coated cottons made to resemble leather and, of course, the plasticized cottons used in the "wet look" garments that have scored some degree of success.

Stretch fabrics containing polyesters, cotton and Lycra have been successfully merchandized in some higher-priced coats, not so much for their stretch qualities as for their silky hand, lightness in weight and according to their makers, their very high degree of water repellency.

Warmers. Several types of warmers (zip-in or button-in liners) are used in rainwear. Among these are the pile fabrics made of alpacas and acrylics (the alpacas are more costly and are considered superior), the woven woolen fabrics both plain and patterned, and in the luxury grades—cashmeres, fancy mohairs and real furs. While most of the pile warmers are in solid shades of black, olive, red, gold and brown, some of the better grades are made in subtle cross-dyes. The wools, too, vary from solid shades to patterns. Some are heavy while others are comparatively light.

Finishes. Modern rainwear finishes fall into two major classifications: Durable water resistant; and durable oil and water resistant. The latter finishes, Zepel, Scotchguard and Ranedare-S, due to their oil-resistant abilities, will also repel oil and fat based spots and soiling. Among the durable finishes that will repel water but are susceptible to oil and fat staining are Sylmer, Zelan, No-Rane, Phototex, Permel-Plus and Cravenette. In trade parlance, "Durable" indicates the ability to retain its power to perform after repeated washings and dry cleanings. However, few if any of these finishes retain 100 per cent of their effectiveness after dry cleaning and/or washing, losing a small percentage of their original abilities with each of the first three or four cleanings or washings. Other factors also affect the performance of these finishes. First, of course, is the cloth to which they are applied. Next is the efficient application of the finish and third is the manner in which the garment is rinsed after washing and the fluids used in dry cleaning. Obviously, any and all of those factors can determine the durability of "Durable."

In the fall of 1966 *Gentlemen's Quarterly* sent a collection of what the edi-

A wide napoleon collar and lapels are features of this double-breasted coat of tan processed cotton gabardine. It has set-in shoulders and is just above knee-length (1968).

This double-breasted maxi-length coat has buttons set on converging lines, a big collar, wide lapels, a shaped body, and flared lines (1969).

with a zipper-concealed chest pocket, buttoned-and-flapped lower pockets, epaulets, buckle-and-strap sleeves, and a full belt; the other a single-breasted of tan cotton, all-around belted and leather-buckled, with wider epaulets, a right-shoulder flap, buttoned slash pockets, buttoned sleeve straps, a back yoke, and a center vent.

The fall of the following year *Gentlemen's Quarterly*, taking heed of the military take-over of rainwear, sent a crew to Ecuador to photograph the following swashbucklers: a natural-color double-breasted cotton coat with a buttoned shoulder yoke, epaulets, buttoned-and-pointed slash pockets, strap-and-buckled seams, a center vent, an all-around belt, and mohair lining; a natural-toned cotton with all-around double-stitched trim, a bal collar, leather-piped buttons, a center vent, an all-around leather-buckled belt, extra large framed pockets, and a detachable wool lining; a burly wool tweed houndstooth-checked double-breasted trench coat with six leather buttons, raglan sleeves, epaulets, a gun flap, a yoked back, and a deep center vent; a sand-colored double-breasted cotton poplin all-weather coat with a full belt and bal collar, buttoned shoulder epaulets, large flapped patch pockets, a side vent, and tartan plaid lining; and a thigh-high double-breasted coat of putty-shaded wool inspired by the British officers' warmer, with waist suppression and flare, a flapped chest pocket, angled lower flap pockets, and a deep center vent.

The Peacock Revolution, born on Carnaby Street, triggered the mass movement of famous women's wear designers into the menswear field, and since it originated in London, it was only a matter of time before England's Hardy Amies, the Queen's couturier, was selling his designs in America along with such other "name" designers as Pierre Cardin of France and John Weitz of the United States. *Gentlemen's Quarterly* focused attention on Mr. Amies's short tan poplin jacket, lapeled as well as lined in black-and-brown checks, with a set-in front, rag-

tors called "young-in-spirit shower-proofs" to the Netherlands. There, at Kampen, an important medieval trade center, the *Gentlemen's Quarterly* photographer snapped a tobacco-colored hip-length cotton waterproof, leather-buttoned and double-breasted, with an all-around belt, buttoned epaulets, and a deeply notched collar; a gold-tan cotton with a button-down shoulder cape, slash pockets, button-tab sleeves, and a full belt; a short-length raglan-sleeved scooter coat of tan cotton, with slash pockets, a center vent, and inside-buttoning straps to encircle the legs and prevent the coat from flapping; and a mod-inspired double-breasted striped cotton with an Edwardian-size collar, buttoned epaulets, and angled piped pockets.

Moving on to Amsterdam, the *Gentlemen's Quarterly* photographer posed the models at night against the backdrop of street lamps reflected in canals and casting shadows across the facades of sixteenth-century buildings. In this mood setting the camera registered a reversible all-weather coat with a set-in front and raglan-back sleeves—one side in black-and-white checked cotton, the other in navy blue—creating contrasting lapels for both sides; and a Dacron-and-cotton coat of gray plaid, with a set-in front and raglan-back sleeves, a center vent, and a collar and lining of black alpaca. In the gardens of the thirteenth-century castle at Muiden, the camera caught a pair of trench coats: one a tan leather-buttoned Dacron-and-cotton

lan-back sleeves, chest-placed flap pockets, and slashed lower pockets.

The British fashion influence, now revitalized by the Peacock Revolution, showed up in raincoats-with-capes that echoed the days of Sherlock Holmes. In 1967, noting that it had been showing capes since its first issue, ten years before, *Gentlemen's Quarterly* rejoiced in their acceptance at long last by showing the following models: a short waterproofed and side-vented off-white cotton with a detachable cape, both lined in blue; a bal-collared gold cotton coat, side-vented with slash pockets, whose cape fell over an eight-buttoned double-breasted front; and a black, brown, and white houndstooth-checked coat with an all-around buckled belt, four patch-flapped pockets, and a detachable matching cape that could be reversed to its black cotton poplin side.

Esquire in 1968 observed: "Inevitably, the vogue of the shaped suit has influenced the styling of this spring's outercoats." To illustrate this, the editors chose three examples, "two of them, incidentally, from ancient and august British firms": a tan polyester-and-cotton weave with set-in sleeves, a fly front, slanted pockets, slight waist suppression, and a 20 inch vent; a tan shaped raincoat in poplin weave; and a shaped, water-repellent, semiraglan checked cotton with slash pockets, button-through front, and tabbed-and-buttoned sleeves.

In 1969 *Gentlemen's Quarterly* flew a crew to India to photograph a collection of raincoats in a setting of mosques and bazaars. Among the rainwear were a six-buttoned double-breasted lime-shaded cotton waterproof, with an outsized collar, a tunnel-looped belt, generous buttoned-flap pockets, a deep center vent, and stitched edges; an alpaca-lined, cape-backed off-white Dacron-and-cotton, with a fly front, an all-around belt, belted cuffs, a chest flap, a deep inverted center vent, and stitched trim; a shorter-length single-breasted coat of off-white cotton and polyester, with a gold Borgana collar, lapels, and lining, angled zippered chest pockets, lower flapped pockets, and an all-around belt; and a slash-pocketed coat of double-breasted cotton and polyester, collared, lapeled, and lined with brown Orlon pile.

Reminding its readers that one of the pleasures of the Peacock Revolution is its lack of preachments, *Esquire*, in February, 1969, declared that the length of a man's raincoat was now a purely personal matter. "Men's raincoats no longer need be knee length which is all to the good since there are downpourish days when maxi length seems mandated." Then, to demonstrate the new do-your-own-thing fashion credo, *Esquire* presented a full-page color photograph of a noted French singer and composer wearing a tan ten-button double-breasted Edwardian-shaped coat of Dacron and pima cotton that was even shorter than knee-length.

In the same issue of *Esquire*, the fashion pages were almost exclusively covered with a collection of rainwear proving that the range of styles and materials was extensive enough to enable any man to find what was most becoming to him. Among the coats photographed were an off-white Dacron-and-cotton with wide-welt slashed pockets; a shaped Napoleon-style coat of cotton canvas; a cotton poplin Spanish import with an off-center industrial zipper flanked by appliqued brass-studded strips for a double-breasted look; an off-white twill of Dacron and cotton with angled pockets and a deep inverted pleat; a cognac-colored, twelve-button double-breasted Edwardian of polyester and combed cotton, with stitched welt seaming, wide-welt slashed pockets, a deep back yoke, and a vivid yellow multicolored plaid lining; a maxi-length, ten-button double-breasted of cotton gabardine with an Edwardian collar, angled flap pockets, and conspicuous shaping; and an imported tan poplin with a full belt, two envelope pockets, a waist-high inverted pleat, front tab closures, sleeve trim, and oversize button-on epaulets.

By the fall of 1970 rainwear manu-facturers had, in the opinion of *Men's Wear*, pulled out all stops for the spring of 1971. The important elements of the fashion picture as seen by this publication were:

. . . Belts appear everywhere, from sashes to half-belts, from mini-pocket belts to belts on sleeves and shoulders.

. . . Double-breasted are still the predominant style, many with new blazer button treatments or bias cuts. The d-b trend coincides with more shape than ever before.

. . . Lapels are wider, intended to stand up and be noticed.

. . . Canvas leads the new fabric pack in both industrial and 50/50 cotton/polyester blends. Repellency-treated knits and texturized polyesters are looming boldly on the horizon, forecasting the eventual demise of poplin.

. . . Lengths will fall at the 40-inch level for most manufacturers, but most also plan to include at least one 43-inch to 44-inch length in their lines.

. . . Surface interest, both in the form of beefier fabrics such as canvas and upholstery cloths and contrast stitching, is prevalent everywhere. Leather, both real and imitation, is being used extensively for trimmings as well as entire coats.

. . . French blue, fawn brown and off-whites are expected to be among the hot colors of the season.

Rainwear manufacturers expressed their enthusiasm for double knits, and in 1970 many stated that they expected double-knit raincoats to account for 20 percent of their models for the following spring, predicting they would play an even larger role in the fall. One major house felt that the knits represented "the industry's future"; still another, that knits were "headed for phenomenal success and have a great future." A trade magazine, however, believed the only apparent drawback to knits for rainwear was that "most manufacturers have had to resort to using a waterproof interlining for sufficient repellency. They also point out that knits are still expensive and are not yet being produced fast enough to satisfy demand."

The vinyl raincoat, first seen in the fifties, made a comeback in the seventies, and so stylishly that one would hardly associate it with its forebears. *Esquire* showed one of the eye-catching "wet look" vinyls, double-breasted and well shaped, with a cape yoke and full belt, and worn with a matching wet look hat. Maintaining that the maxiraincoat was the only kind that really made sense, *Esquire*'s fashion department showed a maxi with trench coat detailing and the wet look achieved through the application of a plastic coating. In the same issue the editors also photographed a wet look rain suit in natural-color coated raw silk, worn with a matching sou'wester-style hat. But vinyl—the smooth glossies or the duller crinkles—had more impact on women's outerwear than men's, and by the late 1960s the vinyl fad had passed, although while it lasted it resulted in some extraordinarily effective-looking garments.

Proving that the length of a man's raincoat was still a matter of purely personal choice, the *New York Times Magazine*'s "Report on Men's Wear" for spring, 1971, showed a collection

The trench coat of the seventies has traditional storm pockets, epaulets, and gun flaps. New features are a wider belt, a bolder two-way collar, and added length [AQUASCUTUM LTD., LONDON]

of rainwear that ran the gamut from a deep-vented above-the-knee double-knit showerproof of camel-colored twilled polyester to a midi-length of tan cotton with an ultrahigh center vent.

Also in 1971, *Men's Wear* observed: "The rainwear industry is taking a no nonsense approach to the fall season. The frills, and even some of the manufacturers of the past few seasons, are gone. Instead the industry is banking on basic fashion." And the *New York Times* noted that, after several seasons of rapid change, "Fashion has sensibly settled down."

As *Men's Wear* viewed the picture, the prime elements for the fall of 1971 were shaping up as follows: "Lengths are down in both volume and high fashion lines . . . knits are coming on stronger to provide plenty of consumer excitement. . . . Warm-Looks are everywhere, evolving from both fabric and color combinations to pile linings and collars." The article continued: "The new lengths are significant. While they vary in inches, they represent a unified direction being taken by the industry. Volume makers have gone down to kneelengths, making 40 to 40½ inches the new standard. The high fashion and boutique lines are all mid-calf starting at the 43-inch level and going all the way down to 47 inches in some of the imported models.

"Knits are equally important. Primarily they are targeted to coincide with the excitement being generated by knits in all areas of apparel this fall. Yet they also represent a new counteroffensive to outerwear and topcoats in a more popular price range. For while they appear as parts of rainwear lines, double knits thus far have not been able to stand up to accepted water repellency tests.

"To overcome the repellency problems, several manufacturers have resorted to non-knit yokes and lines. While this increases repellency it has the negative effect of removing the stretch factor and comfort of knits.

"Instead, most manufacturers, who predict knits will account for from 10 per cent to 15 per cent of fall volume,

expect to promote knits as a new type of outercoat to compete with higher-priced topcoats and outerwear.

"The warm-looks are a third, yet equally important, ingredient in fall rainwear. They include a host of new fabrics and colors destined to connote warmth and all-weather practicality. They represent not only a counterattack against the inroads that outerwear has been making on the rainwear industry, but also are an attempt to regain some of the fashion incentive that outerwear has garnered for the past few seasons.

"In the boutique and high fashion area warm-looks come through in quilted cottons, felts, cotton suedes and polyurethane leathers as well as synthetic fur linings and collars. In the volume lines, warmer-toned colors, darker checks and plaids and fur collars also abound to connote all-weather practicality.

"Combine all these elements and add a growing tendency towards slight shaping and continued importance of double-breasteds as well as fly fronts in the volume lines, and the rainwear picture may be as bright as the industry is hoping it will be. Industry members sum up their feelings by saying that basic fashion will be the volume producer, but in view of today's ingredients this definition has undergone a change for the better."

The trade press that year predicted a new rainwear look on the horizon: coat suits. It was generally felt that the coat suit principle coincided with the growing separates concept developing in menswear. One leading rainwear house reported: "Our customers don't necessarily want to wear jackets under their outerwear. They are turning towards a fashion look that's complete with turtle-neck and matching jean-style pants" (*Men's Wear*, Mar. 17, 1971).

Meantime, the rain-topcoat was gaining in popularity during the early 1970s—in both blends and double knits, and in longer lengths, fancy patterns, and plaids.

By the 1970s the unisex look already apparent in the casual suits for men and pantsuits for women had established itself in rainwear. It was a look that *Esquire*'s fashion camera captured one rainy day in Norfolk, England, with film stars Julie Christie and Alan Bates wearing identical gold-colored double-breasted raincoats of Terylene polyester-and-cotton gabardine with a back yoke, epaulets, raglan sleeves, and a high inverted center pleat.

"Rainwear has become an item business, selling on a three-season basis and may soon move to four seasons," said the marketing director of a major rainwear house in a trade journal interview in 1970. And certainly the concept of a rainy-day wardrobe for every season is becoming more and more of a reality as the younger man discovers the inherent romance of rainwear. To him, the ultimate peacock, it is like a second skin that sheds water—essential, practical, and, best of all, extravagantly stylish.

For rainwear, once put-it-on-take-it-off apparel whose sole reason for being was the unpredictability of the weather, has now become high fashion, with the happy result that a sunny day and a dashing raincoat are now thoroughly compatible. In fact, the styling of men's raincoats during the third quarter of this century has proved so extraordinary that the raincoat per se has assumed a strong personality.

Formal Evening Wear

The business suit of the first decade of the twentieth century was heavily padded, loose-fitting, and buttoned high; it was formidable-looking rather than elegant. For a look of elegance, a man turned to formal evening clothes, specifically the tailcoat, which had a measure of shapeliness. The lapels of this handsome black coat were of medium width, and the tails

extended to just below the break in the knees. All in all, the tailcoat appeared to have little in common with the business suit except for one thing: heavy fabric that weighed 16 to 18 ounces to the yard. Comfort had nothing to do with style, night or day.

The rest of this formal outfit consisted of a stiff-bosom white shirt with matching cuffs that might or might not be attached and a detached high standing collar. The two most popular collar styles were the poke, a high band collar with a very slight curve of the corners in front, and the wing, which had a folded-back tab on each side. A white tie in piqué, linen, or cotton matched a single- or double-breasted waistcoat. The shirt stud or studs were usually pearl, often large, and mostly white, though sometimes black, with cuff links to match. Black silk hose, black patent-leather high-buttoned shoes with cloth tops, and a high silk hat completed this admirable ensemble.

Some men, however, preferred the tuxedo, or dinner jacket, which first appeared on the scene in 1886, when a fashion maverick named Griswold Lorillard wore it to the Tuxedo Park Club's white-tie-and-tails autumn ball. Traditionalists adopted a condescending attitude toward the innovation, regarding it as semiformal evening attire, but it was not without its admirers. The tuxedo came in two styles, with a shawl collar and satin-faced lapels, and with peaked lapels. Some men straddled the fence sartorially and with their dinner jackets wore the stiff-bosom shirt, high standing collar, white tie, and waistcoat that normally accompanied the tailcoat.

Whether the man of fashion chose to wear the elegant tailcoat or the somewhat more businesslike tuxedo, over it he wore a formfitting black overcoat that was far more stylish than the customarily loose and bulky over-

(*above*) *A long-roll shawl-collared dinner jacket and a shapely tailcoat were offered in 1901 by the Hickey-Freeman Co. Readers of the company's brochure were advised, "The finer grades are silk-lined throughout."*

(*above*) *In 1900 white bow ties, starched standing and turned-down collars, stiff piqué and pleated-bosom shirts, white double-breasted waistcoats, and high-button evening shoes were worn with dinner jackets: (left) a black shawl-collared jacket with satin facings; (right) a white peaked-lapel style.*

(*left*) *In 1905 evening clothes were presented by the Hickey-Freeman Co. in "fabrics fine-class, dressed and undressed worsteds and llama Thibets."*

coat of the period. Frequently the evening coat was made of vicuña or cashmere and had a military collar and a short cape that extended just over the shoulders. The fly-front velvet-collared chesterfield with a back vent was another popular coat, especially since it was appropriate for both day and evening formal wear.

1910–1920

As early as 1911 business suits began to be tailored along trimmer, more natural lines, but formal evening clothes remained constant, for they already had a slim look. After World War I, however, when Americans were in a jubilant mood and ready to dress up and celebrate, formal attire needed updating. The soldier was back in civilian clothes, and fashion was anxious to satisfy his desire for easier-to-wear clothes. His 1918 business suit had natural shoulders and a higher waist, and so, without upsetting tradition, manufacturers also made the tailcoat and tuxedo available in the natural-shoulder style. For young men who had a fondness for the "jazz suit," which was nothing but a vulgarization of the attractive natural-shoulder business suit, an adaptation of this suit, too, was available in the tuxedo, with jacket buttons set close together at the waistline, a wide flare over the hips, and an exceptionally deep center vent. The trousers of the jazz tuxedo were cut along the lines of its daytime counterpart, either straight and trim or tapered with a peg top.

Some men now preferred the pleated-bosom evening shirt with a turndown collar to the conventional stiff-bosom shirt with a high standing collar. An avant-garde minority wore the black inverness overcoat, a frankly theatrical-looking velvet-collared garment with a deep cape that extended to somewhere between the elbow and the wrist. The inverness had only limited popularity, since it was too substantial a coat for a time when younger men wanted clothes with a more natural fit.

The last two years of this decade

Elegance in formal evening wear in 1917: a luxurious fur-collared overcoat, a high silk hat, a high poke collar, a white tie and waistcoat, and a black tailcoat. [HICKEY-FREEMAN CO.]

were lively and prosperous and seemingly were dedicated to making the returning soldier glad to be home. The welcome included formal dances and balls, which prompted much formal-wear advertising on the part of the more aggressive retailers.

1920–1930

The tuxedo was conspicuous by its absence at the gala opening of the Metropolitan Opera Company season in 1920. A fashion reporter covering the event wrote: "During the inter-

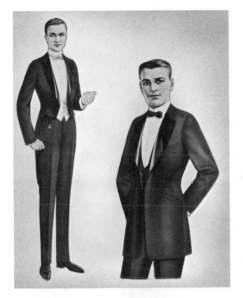

(*left*) *The evening tailcoat of 1920 had satin-faced lapels and was worn with trim-cut trousers.* (*right*) *The dinner jacket had narrow shoulders and shaped body lines.* [FASHION INSTITUTE OF TECHNOLOGY]

missions I made my way from the box corridors to the club room. There loitered what one might call fashionable men from everywhere and I cannot say I found anything that would jolt one, or I could not expect it, for while among them were elegants of the world, their dress was that of gentlemen of the world. I made notes from hats, etc., down to the shoes of these men" (*Men's Wear*, Dec. 1, 1920, p. 113)

Among the outfits the reporter noted were a tailcoat and trousers of black herringbone cheviot with lapels silk-faced to the edge, bone buttons, broad put-on cuffs with three buttons, a simple large white pearl in the shirt, cuff links to match, patent-leather low boots, and white double-breasted piqué waistcoat, shirt, collar, and tie; a tailcoat and trousers of deep blue vicuña with the shawl collar on the coat faced to the edge with deep blue satin, silk buttons, sleeves with turned-back cuffs, two black pearls in the shirt, cuff links to match, white double-breasted linen waistcoat, shirt, collar, and tie, and varnished low boots; and a tailcoat and trousers of

plain black undressed worsted with collar and lapels faced to the edge with satin, bone buttons, broad turned-back cuffs with three buttons, a single-breasted five-button small-diamond-figure piqué waistcoat with short rounded points and a rolled collar, a single pearl in the shirt, cluster pearl cuff links, and varnished low boots.

British fashions continued to attract style-conscious Americans. One of the best examples of the well-dressed Englishman was Jack Buchanan, an actor-singer-dancer who was starring on Broadway with Gertrude Lawrence and Beatrice Lillie in *Charlot's Revue*. Like many other self-confident men of the twenties, Buchanan had both a tailcoat and a tuxedo in his wardrobe. His tailcoat was worn with a white double-breasted waistcoat that was so narrow at the waist it gave the suggestion of being only a belt. His one-button peak-lapeled tuxedo had an almost corsetlike effect at the waist of the jacket, much like that of the popular snug-fitting business suit. With it he wore a stiff-bosom shirt, a wing collar, a black butterfly bow tie, a white double-breasted waistcoat cut straight across at the waistline, and pleated trousers.

Reporting from London to *Men's Wear* (Apr. 23, 1924, p. 51), a fashion journalist commented on new waistcoat designs favored by the best dressed men: a double-breasted evening waistcoat with an oval opening, a double-breasted waistcoat with a square opening, and a single-breasted model with a soft roll collar. As he saw it, the white evening waistcoat, particularly the new backless model, was now accepted in London as correct for wear with the tuxedo since such trend setters as the Prince of Wales and Lord Louis Mountbatten had taken it up. What was good enough for the Prince was more than good enough for fashionable Americans. This report had scarcely been printed when smart New Yorkers were wearing full-collar double-breasted waistcoats with their dinner jackets. The complete formal evening outfit for a summer night on the town in the last half of the twenties

included a stiff white shirt with a single pinkish pearl stud, cuff links with small pink pearls in the center, a black satin bow tie, a straw boater with a club band, and laced patent-leather shoes.

A *Men's Wear* survey of summer evening-dress styles seen at fashionable New York places in 1928, however, revealed that while most men favored bold wing collars and stiff-bosom shirts, many of the younger generation were wearing negligee shirts with soft attached collars. "This style," noted the survey report, "mirrors the quintessence of informality, in fact, these men could hardly adopt any other more radical style and still be 'properly' dressed. This trend toward greater informality is emphasized by the increase in popularity of double-breasted dinner jackets which are usually worn without waistcoats" (Aug.

In 1923 the dinner jacket for both undergraduates and alumni had rounded notched lapels and was worn with a wing collar, a black bow tie, and a white waistcoat. [FASHION INSTITUTE OF TECHNOLOGY].

The tailcoat, finished with wide lapels, was worn in 1926 with a single-stud piqué dress shirt, a bold wing collar, a butterfly bow tie, and a double-breasted white waistcoat. [SCHEYER-TAILORED FOR OGILVIE & JACOBS]

22, 1928, p. 77). According to the survey, there had been a slight decrease in the popularity of bold wing collars while the number of men wearing fold collars had increased from 24 to 30 percent of the total. Long bow and butterfly ties were still the leaders, although there was a marked preference among the best-dressed men for the pointed-end bow. White pearls were the dominant choice for studs, both those worn in sets and the larger ones worn singly. Black pearls were of less importance, and only 4 percent of the men wore gold studs.

Another survey earlier that year covered 200 of the best-dressed men at Palm Beach (*Men's Wear*, Mar. 21, 1928). It revealed that 89 percent of these men wore the plain-front low

patent-leather evening shoe, and 66 percent favored the bold wing collar. But the soft fold collar was making inroads in Palm Beach, too, accounting for 4 percent of the collars worn in 1928. In shirts there was slightly more variety than had been observed the previous year, but it was the plain white linen shirt with a starched bosom and two studs showing that the majority of the best-dressed men preferred. Butterfly and batwing bows had declined in popularity, and the straight-end tie showed a slight increase. It was not so much in the cut of the tie that the change was seen as in the length. Bows worn by the most elegant men were elongated to such an extent that they sometimes protruded a full inch beyond each wing of the collar. The survey takers predicted that the coming style in dinner jackets was the single-breasted one-button jacket with silk facings on its peaked lapels and collar, the style worn by Jack Buchanan a few seasons earlier.

As this easy, more informal decade drew to a close, a trend toward increased formality in evening attire was noted among Ivy League students, prompting *Men's Wear* to decide that this meant that "very soon young men all over the country—influenced by college styles—will be demanding the tail coat from their local retailers." At a dance held at Princeton in 1928, for example, the tailcoat had been worn by 19 percent of the best-dressed undergraduates, inducing the writer to decide: "Greater formality is the order of the day. From this start there is no doubt that within the space of a few years the tailcoat will become nationally popular" (Apr. 11, 1928, p. 84).

In the meantime, peak-lapeled dinner jackets had risen in popularity, with 42 percent of the Princetonians wearing them. Also noted was a growing fondness for the wing collar, the bold wings having increased by about 5 percent. As for the formal shirts seen at Princeton that year, "even a casual observer could not help but notice the great prevalence of stiff bosom shirts. These were worn by 19 out of every 20 men, almost always with but one

Wide peaked lapels with satin facings appeared on the fashionable dinner jacket of 1926, which was worn with a wing collar, a black butterfly bow tie, a piqué shirt, a white waistcoat, and patent-leather plain-tip evening shoes. [SCHEYER-TAILORED FOR OGILVIE & JACOBS]

or two studs showing, the type with three showing being so scarce as to be a rarity. Flat set studs were far more popular than the single black or white pearl, and the plain patent leather shoe with fairly pointed toe was still the mode among the students."

1930–1940

In the twenties the single-breasted dinner jacket had been the vogue, but by 1932 the double-breasted jacket, the least formal style, was steadily gaining in popularity. It had, of course, been preferred for several seasons at Palm Beach as well as in Europe by such fashionable men as the actor-playwright Noel Coward and King Alfonso XIII of Spain.

Meanwhile, certain features unmistakably identified the fashionable tailcoat for fall, 1932. These were styling details that were traceable to the current English drape style in business suits. (The drape suit, which had extra fullness on the chest and over the shoulder blades in order to permit free action of the arms, formed vertical wrinkles between the collar and the sleeve head. Eventually, this planned fullness was accepted and became a sales point.) A fashion commentator wrote in *Men's Wear* (Sept. 7, 1932, p. 29):

"Shoulders are quite broad, waistlines high, shoulder blades and chest full cut, showing intended wrinkles, sleeves are tapered and tails tend toward points as against the square-cut effect of years ago. This is the style of tail coat in great favor with cosmopolitan men. Not all men, however, will go for this style, so the next most fashionable type is a coat with natural shoulders, fairly high waistline, pointed tails and without the ample fullness across the chest and shoulder blades. Both styles have high arm scyes and both coats are cut to fit snugly on either side in the back so that the garments stay in place no matter what position the arms are in or what the posture is.

"Two features distinguish the style that is commonly called the English model from the so-called American custom tailor type. These are the openings in front and the breadth of shoulders. The American model has natural shoulders and the front of the coat is cut so that a fairly broad expanse of shirt front is shown, while the British style is quite broad shouldered, has short lapels and the front is cut so that much less of the shirt front is visible. Of late, the former style has been gaining considerable headway in London and on the Continent, as well as in this country. Practically all the evening coats turned out by tailors in this country have dull silk facings on the lapels, although some of the stores carrying clothes ready-for-wear sell coats with shiny satin facings. A feature of the fashionable coats worn by well dressed men is the cloth button,

which is supplanting the bone button so popular at present."

In dinner jackets, too, drape-style features were present:

"The soft construction, fairly broad shoulders, fullness across the chest and shoulder blades, and suppression at the waist identify this fashionable and comfortable model. Peaked lapels are most generally used and these, in the majority of cases, have dull silk or grosgrain facings. The least formal of all evening jackets, the double-breasted, is fast becoming an outstanding style. In this model, there are two prevailing types, the English with its wide lap or button stand, and the American with its narrow lap. The former is cut so that only a small area of the shirt front is in view, while the latter, with curved lapels, shows a generous amount of shirt front. This is a two-button model, the lower button to button, while the English jacket, with buttons placed higher, is made to button either the upper or lower button."

Among accessories for wear with the tailcoat and dinner jacket the bold wing collar was the favorite: "The most fashionable style has large wings and a decided dip in front, which features a more natural neckline and at the same time adds to the comfort of the collar. The neckband of the dress shirt to go with this type of collar has to be cut with the same dip forward. The stiff bosom shirt with two studs showing is the mode of the season for both informal and formal evening wear. Fine marcella and bird's wing design pique is favored over other types of shirt bosom fabrics. The open back model is gaining in popularity, and some very smartly dressed men prefer to have cuffs in plain linen instead of the fabric to match the shirt front."

The fashionable waistcoat to be worn with the tailcoat was made from the same material as the shirt bosom: "The single-breasted models show either a V opening with soft roll lapel or a semi-V opening, the former being popular in three- or four-button styles and the latter only in the four-button model. Moderate length points char-

acterize both models. In double-breasteds, the styles with fairly narrow band effects are enjoying the greatest popularity. All waistcoats are high waisted to conform to the new silhouette. The white waistcoat is, of course, correct for wear with the tail coat or the dinner jacket, but the black is proper only with the dinner jacket and is in the best of fashion when the fabric matches the facing on the lapel of the jacket. Modestly patterned black silks only are used, well turned out men never wearing any gaudy jacquarded effects."

The prevailing shapes of ties were the butterfly of moderate width, the straight club, and the pointed-end style:

"For wear with the tail coat the tie may match the shirt and waistcoat,

The dinner jacket for young men in 1931 had wide peaked lapels with satin facings, broad shoulders, and the London body line. [HICKEY-FREEMAN CO.]

whereas the tie to go with the dinner jacket may be of the same cloth as the lapel facing or in a similar plain weave.

"Plain white or black pearl studs and links to match are preferred by smartly dressed men in London and in New York. However, some well groomed men go in for jewel and onyx sets, the latter and similar dark tone effects being worn only with the dinner jacket.

"Black silk or lisle hose, either plain or with clocks, adorn the ankle of the well dressed man in the evening, and his shoes are of either patent leather or black highly polished Russian calf low evening shoes or pumps. Pumps are showing definite signs of staging a comeback in a substantial way, while the favoritism for black Russian calf evening shoes is one of the significant footwear developments in fashionable circles. These shoes, when properly groomed, have such a lustre that they are hardly distinguishable from patent leather and, of course, are comfortable and do not crack.

"Nothing can mar the effect of an otherwise comfortable evening ensemble more than an improper hat. The tall silk hat is the correct style for either tail coat or dinner jacket. Of late, the opera hat has become extremely popular with the young man attending fashionable debutante parties and similar affairs. In London and in New York, the black Homburg is frequently seen worn by sophisticated gentlemen in informal evening dress."

The broad shoulders and easy fit of the evening overcoats of this period also showed the influence of English drape styling:

"The overcoats in favor with men who set the standards of dress in this country are usually in some luxurious cloth like cashmere. While the variety of evening overcoats is great, the majority of men favor either the easy fitting single-breasted style with dull silk-faced lapels, cloth collar and fly front, or the plain double-breasted Chesterfield, probably with plain cloth collar. While usually made up in black, coats of these types are fre-

quently seen also in dark oxford grey or midnight blue.

"Supplementary accessories include white silk crepe scarf with fringed ends or knitted silk muffler. These scarfs or mufflers are worn either choker style or simply draped around the neck.

"White kid gloves usually cover the hands of men in evening dress, white buckskins in slip-on or snap fastener style being the alternative."

In 1933 white was encouraged for evening wear through the short-lived popularity of the mess jacket, which resembled a tailcoat cut off at the waistline and was not becoming to all physiques. Made in white linen or cotton gabardine and worn with high-waisted lightweight black dress trousers, a stiff-bosom shirt, a narrow cummerbund in black, bright red, or dark blue, a wing collar, and a black butterfly bow tie, the mess jacket soon faded from popularity (not too soon in the opinion of *Esquire,* the editors calling it a "ridiculous craze"), but not until it had opened the door to the white dinner jacket for formal summer wear.

Esquire observed in January, 1934, that new little touches in formal dress were things of consequence: "You realize this when you compare the attire of the two figures in this sketch. The older man is wearing an outfit which, while perfectly suitable for one of his years, is dated considerably . . . in comparison with the modish turnout of the younger man in the foreground. The latter figure can be taken as an example for anyone under sixty. (Older men ought, and probably will want to, wear a gardenia or white carnation in place of the clove red carnation which is affected by the younger element, but with this one exception, the outfit in the foreground is both correct and becoming for all men, including those well along in middle age.) The coat lapels are of dull silk. The trousers are full cut and, to give the right effect, ought to hit you just a bit below your lowest rib. The brief waistcoat comes down to the corners of the coat front, and shouldn't miss. If it fails to come down that far,

the high waisted effect is overdone, and if it comes down below that point, you'll be suspected of having rented the outfit. Don't pay any attention to rotogravure pictures of dukes in evening dress with underslung vests that protrude below the coat front—you've got to be a duke yourself to get away with that, and it's still wrong anyway. These waistcoats are usually backless—that is, with no back save a strap which is drawn in snugly to hold both shirt and waistcoat permanently in place. Oldsters may retain the high silk topper, but the collapsible opera hat in dull grosgrain is preferred by younger men, and is considered smarter."

A new version of the tailcoat was featured in the November, 1934, issue of *Esquire:* a style that, according to the editors, seemed to have been influenced by the tailor who made evening clothes for the British royal family. Notable among its styling features were short, stubby lapels of dull ribbed silk, false cuffs on the sleeves, and the absence of an outside breast pocket. The brevity of the lapels made the waistline seem higher although the front of the coat had not been shortened. The trousers carried a heavy single braid and were pleated. With this tailcoat the *Esquire* fashion model wore a dress shirt of plain white linen with a two-stud open front and single square-cornered cuffs; the wings of his collar extended beyond the modified butterfly bow tie. The double-breasted white piqué waistcoat had short but sharp points, and the reader was asked to note that its buttons were black while the shirt studs were white. An opera hat and a navy blue guards coat, said the editors, would complete this outfit for wear outdoors.

In January, 1935, *Esquire* again commented on the fact that fashions in formal evening clothes change very little ("For it is usually a period of ten or eleven years before any radical changes become noticeable"), but reminded readers that changes do occur and, "slight though most of them may be, they are all part of the fashion picture." For example, backless waist-

The formal evening coat of 1934 had wide lapels covered with dull grosgrain silk. Also worn were a stiff-bosom piqué shirt, a wing collar, a butterfly bow tie, a white waistcoat with a shawl collar, patent leather evening shoes, a collapsible opera hat, and a black overcoat. From Esquire, January 1934.

For midsummer nights at the country club in 1935 appropriate formal wear was either a midnight-blue tropical worsted evening suit with a shawl-collared double-breasted jacket (center) or a washable white single-breasted shawl-collared model (right). From Esquire, July 1935.

coats were practically the only ones being sold in London in the mid-thirties, and the editors noted that the trend was moving in the same direction in the United States:

"The newest of these waistcoats have a black elastic strap replacing the one of white material. The reason for this is that the elastic gives a much snugger appearance to the waistcoat, since the black does not appear conspicuous against the dark trousers. The three-button single-breasted V-front model with square corner lapels, although still in favor, is being replaced in London by the double-breasted model with the same opening, the same lapels and pointed corners.

"Shirt studs and cuff links are very small and are made in flat white enamel and small white pearls while plain crystal studs are still preferred by many. A departure is the fact that waistcoat buttons, which in the past have been white to preserve the 'all white front,' have taken to black, gold, wine, blue and other dark colors to contrast with those worn in the shirt front and cuffs.

"Although oxfords are most widely favored, opera pumps are gaining in popularity. The smart patent leather oxfords have five eyelets, a graceful tapered toe and are without toe caps.

The correct pump follows the shape of the patent leather oxford and has a dull ribbed silk bow.

"While the opera hat is popular in London, the ribbed silk crushable hat is most frequently worn in this country. Both are correct. Black hose are the only kind that may be worn with tail coats. The red carnation always adds a tasteful finishing touch to the formal evening ensemble."

An indication of the tremendous popularity and elegance of the formal wear of this decade can be found in a 1935 column written by Lucius Beebe for the New York *Herald Tribune:* "A well-attired New York gentleman was worth $4,975 on the hoof after six in the evening," maintained Beebe, drawing up a list that specified the cost and kind of clothes and accessories he felt such a man would require during this Depression decade. The list included a mink-lined evening greatcoat ($2,500), a diamond and platinum dress pocket watch and chain ($1,500), either an opera or a high silk hat ($30), gold garters ($150), silk socks and underwear ($20), and, on the far end of the watch chain, a *fouet* ($300), a gadget designed to eliminate carbonation from champagne. Most men of fashion, of course, managed to be extremely well turned out for a fraction of Beebe's $4,975.

In the thirties the fashionable college man had both a dinner jacket and a tailcoat in his wardrobe. For the preparatory school student *Esquire*'s fashion department in October, 1935, illustrated the salient points of prevailing evening-wear fashions for the very young: a midnight-blue double-breasted dinner jacket, worn with a shirt with a turned-down attached collar and a club-shaped bat tie; a midnight-blue tailcoat with a double-breasted waistcoat and, over the wearer's arm, the new military-collared silk-lined coat for evening wear; a shawl-collared single-breasted midnight-blue dinner jacket with a bold wing collar, a black butterfly tie, and a maroon breast-pocket handkerchief. An alternative to the military-collared evening coat was the navy chinchilla guards coat. (Except for this single note of navy, it was obvious that midnight blue was the preferred shade for evening wear.)

Since the opening of the horse show at Madison Square Garden was the effective start of the season of tails and toppers, *Esquire* was in attendance and in its November, 1935, issue, brought back a description of the newest in formal outerwear: a fly-front, raglan-shouldered coat with a military collar and a lining of dull ribbed silk. With it a fashionable gentleman wore an opera hat, a white silk crepe scarf, and white string knit gloves. When he removed his coat, he was seen to be

wearing the latest version of the midnight-blue tailcoat with a single-breasted waistcoat of a new wide-ribbed piqué.

In January, 1936, *Esquire* noted a major change in tailcoat styling, prefacing the details with this observation: "Tail coats used to be like Fords—it was a point of pride that the model was seldom changed." Now even a cursory glance at the new tailcoat proved that it varied markedly from the prevailing design. The tails were both shorter and wider, the waistline natural, and the chest undraped. Like the prevailing design, the old-fashioned waistline seam had been preserved; sleeves carried false cuffs; and there was no breast pocket. (Tailors said that the coat hung straighter with the breast pocket eliminated, and many men who wore a boutonniere felt that the addition of a breast-pocket handkerchief made them look too much like a Christmas tree.) "At least an inch of white shirt cuff should show below the sleeve," advised the fashion editor, who also noted that the changes in tailcoat styling could be credited to the Prince of Wales ("At any rate, they're the last word from London").

More trend-setting news was reported from London in that issue: a new green dress tie, "a believe-it-or-not item that has the loftiest sponsorship from London" and one that, the editors said, might be adopted for cruise wear with a silk dress shirt and a double-breasted dinner jacket.

Meanwhile, the dinner jacket had not remained unchanged. The latest style was the more formal single-breasted model with ribbed-silk lapels, in contrast to the shiny facing of the double-breasted coat that had been the favorite for the last few seasons. It was worn with a stiff shirt, a wing collar, a black waistcoat, a semibutterfly tie, and plain gold studs. Either patent-leather pumps or oxfords were suggested. With the less formal double-breasted dinner jacket, men continued to wear the soft collar-attached shirt and a satin tie to go with the satin lapels.

By 1936 summer white and cream-color dinner jackets were so popular with fashionable men in both single- and double-breasted styles that they vied with black and midnight blue for leadership. In Palm Beach cloth, linen, silk tropical worsted, and a new blend of mohair and worsted, the white dinner jacket paved the way for color in summer formal clothes, with plum, dark green, wine, bright blue, light navy, and gray being worn on the moonlit patios of Palm Beach. Color coordination was the next logical development. Dark red was the important note in bow ties and cummerbunds, and black hose often had red clocks. Red and cornflower-blue boutonnieres lent a final dash of color.

Esquire marked the trend toward cool summer white in 1936 with praise for lightweight fabrics, which the magazine clearly regarded as an overdue fashion change:

"There are many late spring and summer functions, such as Saturday night parties at country clubs, where the women are comfortable in evening dresses that bulk up to little more than nothing and the male population perspires in an evening kit or the combination of odd jacket and flannels. The white mess jacket was last summer's answer, but smart men have abandoned it because it became a universal jazz band uniform. This year, the big swing is to single- or double-breasted dinner jackets, collar and self lapel facings. These are worn with tropical dress trousers, patent leather oxfords or pumps, a white, soft shirt with either soft or laundered collar and a black dress tie. Midnight blue, calculated to look blacker than black after nightfall, is also an acceptable shade for the trousers. For that matter, trousers of the same material as the jacket are also correct" (August, 1936, p. 150).

With the decade's increased emphasis on formality, *Esquire* from time to time offered its readers a few ground rules, as in November, 1936: "Strict propriety calls for a white tie when there are ladies in the evening, but during the early part of the social season—say as long as your summer's tan lasts—you won't be noticeably out of step if you wear a dinner coat for dinner, dancing and the theatre. If you want to make a slight gesture in the direction of formality you might wear a wing collar with the dinner jacket rather than the turnover collar that is now virtually standard for informal wear. In general the dinner coat is proper on shipboard, in the tropics, for dinner parties at home, theatre parties and club and stag affairs. With it wear either the black or midnight blue Homburg. It is correct also (but very uncommon in this country) to wear a silk hat with dinner clothes. But don't, under any circumstances, wear a derby with a dinner jacket. Better to go bare headed or wear a checked cap or an immigrant's shawl!"

In January, 1937, *Apparel Arts* also took cognizance of the fact that the white tie and tails held an important place in the wardrobe of well-dressed men. There was no doubt that standards of formality in after-dark apparel had stiffened in recent years: "The tail coat is an absolute requirement for scores of social functions." *Apparel Arts* also noted new ideas in the design of waistcoats being made in London. Most of the new waistcoats were single-breasted with roll collars and very sharp points. The magazine reported that a major trend in tailcoats was toward a lower front with a natural waistline. The coats had lower waistline seams in back, allowing them to fit more snugly; the tails tapered gracefully but not too abruptly, coming a fraction of an inch below the knee. The most popular tailcoat color was still midnight blue, and lapels were no longer short and stubby but rolled with an easy naturalness in a graceful curve. Trousers in most cases carried two narrow braids set closely at the sides.

Throughout the last half of the thirties *Esquire* continued to show the impact that white and color were making in tropical worsted or washable dinner jackets. A note of caution was added in June, 1937: "When dressing in town the black or midnight blue dinner jacket is preferable." But once the editors had made this statement, they endeavored to show exactly how liberated summer evening dress had become. The India madras cummerbund, for example, had replaced the waistcoat for many men. Red silk foulard and blue polka-dotted handkerchiefs were being worn in the breast pockets of white or midnight-blue dinner jackets. Vivid silk hose was being worn with a patent-leather monk-front shoe that until recently had been seen mainly at sporting events, and boutonnieres made of feathers were introduced in red, gold, blue, and white.

In 1939 the most fashionable overcoat still had a fly front and raglan shoulders, but the military collar had been supplanted by peaked lapels and a breast pocket with a flap had been added. Proper boutonnieres for white tie and tails, said *Esquire* in February, were the blue cornflower, coral carnation, white gardenia, and clove-red carnation.

"What do you know about formal fashions?" asked *Esquire* with just one month left of the decade. This question accompanied a question-and-answer quiz illustrated with a sketch of the horse show at Madison Square Garden. "For the edification of a quiz-conscious public, we are converting the usual description of this illustration into a questionnaire on formal fashions. If you answer all you're quite a get-arounder; if half, you're pretty good; if none, you should read *Esquire* more carefully."

Question. What single feature of this tail coat strikes you as being obviously different from conventional models?
Answer. The black satin shawl collar. This is the first time this has been shown for full evening dress since before the War.
Question. Is there anything unusual about the patent leather shoes?
Answer. Yes; they are dress brogues, with punching across the instep and around the side of the shoe. They were recently introduced by George VI for dancing, and are the most comfortable evening shoes known.
Question. What is the proper length of the tails?
Answer. The tails should extend a fraction of an inch below the bend of the knee in back.

Question. What is the proper length of the front of the tail coat?
Answer. It should come below the natural waistline so that no part of the waistcoat extends below it.
Question. Why is the watch fob worn on the left side?
Answer. For the same reason that a man once carried his sword on the left side—it's easier to get at with the right hand.
Question. Name four of seven other significant details of this evening turn-out.
Answer. The two-stud open front dress shirt; the high, wide wing collar with broad tabs; the white butterfly tie which is a shade shorter than the wing collar; the white linen waistcoat with roll collar and black buttons; the small white pearl shirt studs; the tail coat buttons of checkered silk; the false cuff at the sleeve, with plenty of white linen cuff showing. (November, 1939, p. 130)

1940–1950

Esquire offered further tips on formal evening wear in January, 1940: "Rules of formality are as strict as those governing a young ladies' finishing school with the possible exception of a curfew hour. The 'dos' and 'don'ts' are based largely on tradition. Rugged individualists who depart from the beaten path will find themselves either unable to break through a stag line or else mistaken for bandmasters, a tribe noted for wasp waistlines, barn-broad shoulders and Himalayan high rise trousers." Among the rules offered were the following:

Don't shove the opera hat to open—just tap the brim on your palm. To close the topper press the crown against your chest, but never close it unless necessary for packing.

Trousers with tail coat always carry double braid and break above instep.

For hose you may wear lightweight black wool as correctly as silk. Take your choice.

Always wear the waistcoat snugly and be sure your starched shirt front is short enough so that it doesn't dive into the tops of your trousers or extend at the sides under your suspenders.

The midnight-blue dinner jacket arrived in tropical worsted that year, and most men preferred the double-breasted model with four brass buttons and satin shawl lapels. Worn with dress trousers of equally airy material,

Evening clothes were varied in 1941: (left) a single-breasted peaked-lapel dinner jacket and a black homburg hat; (center) a double-breasted dinner jacket with long-roll lapels; (right) a midnight-blue tailcoat with dull grosgrain silk facings on the lapels, a collapsible opera hat, and patent-leather pumps. From Esquire, *January 1941.*

a soft white silk shirt, a satin tie, silk hose, and patent-leather pumps, it formed, in *Esquire*'s opinion, "a formal outfit with flair."

Esquire introduced another fashion feature in August, 1940, as follows: "Listen, my children, and you shall hear exactly what to wear for a midsummer night's formal, R.S.V.P. We can't tell you the whole story here but if you pay attention to what we do have to say, you'll get by with enough to spare. Attention, class!"

Two impeccably groomed figures were shown. Figure A wore a lightweight midnight-blue evening suit with black satin lapels rolled to the top button of the double-breasted model. ("Smart in every respect, it may not look quite as cool as a breeze; the fabric, however, is a tropical worsted and the lining and padding of the jacket are at a minimum, insuring adequate comfort.") The reader was asked to note that the trousers draped slightly over the low-cut patent-leather evening shoes, the butterfly bow tie was of satin, and the soft-bosom dress

shirt carried an attached collar with a fairly wide spread between the points. The white linen band of the coconut palm hat placed it in the correct evening category, although a sennit straw would have been a correct alternative choice of headwear.

Figure B wore a single-breasted shawl-collar white jacket. The trousers were of midnight blue with a single braid down the side, and a midnight-blue cummerbund was also worn. "The shirt," wrote the copywriter, "is something new. In the fly-front model, there are two eyelets instead of buttonholes, calling for the use of studs. The fly-front portion of the shirt is below the bottom eyelet and is fastened with a concealed pearl button, while the tab at the bottom holds the shirt front down. Originally seen in England where the shirt was invariably made-up in silk, it has been copied here in both silk and cotton." Other accessories were a black ribbon-shaped silk tie, patent-leather pumps, and silk dress socks. Separately sketched were an elastic-mesh garter and clocked dark blue silk socks, completing the list of essentials with the exception of such incidentals as pocket handkerchiefs and boutonnieres.

"Black + White = Evening Dress" was the fashion-wise arithmetic *Esquire* offered its readers at the outset of a decade during which many men would consign their formal wear to mothballs while donning military uniforms. In a sense, therefore, this refresher course on the correct details for evening dress was a kind of end-of-the-term crash program. The following paragraphs gave the reader all he needed to know on the subject:

The wing collar and the neckband of the dress shirt should have a forward slope. This slant not only gives a flattering neckline but contributes to greater comfort around the neck.

Shirt bosoms should be short enough so that they do not extend below the waistband of the high-rise trousers to prevent them from bulging. Less width will also help to preclude ballooning bosoms.

Pleated bosom shirts are becoming more popular for wear with the evening jacket. The latest trend is toward many narrow pleats on each side. Those first to set a fashion are wearing shirts of this type.

Stiff bosom shirts always have stiff cuffs. Pleated bosom shirts, correct only with dinner jacket, carry double cuffs. Sleeves should be long enough to show ½ inch of the shirt cuff below coat sleeve.

White butterfly bow ties are correctly worn in front of the collar wings with the tail coat. The black or blue silk club-shape bow tie is gaining favor for wear with the dinner jacket.

The backless waistcoat, tailored either in white pique, black or midnight blue silk, has become an established fashion simply because the absence of extra fabric in back makes it much more comfortable than those with backs.

Grosgrain silk facings on lapels have widest acceptance for tailed coats and dinner jackets. The more lustrous satin-faced lapels, though less popular, have gained high fashion rating.

The white knitted or woven silk muffler, invariably worn throwover fashion, may have an embroidered monogram as a personal note. Most widely used are the oblong shaped mufflers.

White gloves are obligatory for formal and for semi-formal evening wear. White kid or mocha are acceptable with the tail coat; white mocha good taste with the dinner jacket.

Black woolen socks with white clocks are authentic alternates with clocked black silk or lisle socks for accenting evening clothes, formal or semi-formal.

The pleated cummerbund in black, midnight blue or maroon silk may be substituted for the black, midnight blue or white waistcoat with the evening jacket; either the midnight blue or white being acceptable for resort wear.

Pleats of trousers for tail coat or dinner jacket should have the folds opening toward the center. This gives proper fullness for appearance and comfort.

The tail coat should be long enough to cover the waistcoat. In other words, the waistcoat should be short enough to be concealed by the sides of the tail coat.

The Homburg hat in black or midnight blue felt is proper with the dinner jacket. The derby correctly worn for business or country is never acceptable with evening clothes.

The shiny high silk or grosgrain silk collapsible opera hat are the only two formal hats of established tradition to top off the tail coat.

Trousers should be long enough to break slightly over the instep. A single silk braid down the sides is acceptable; double braid with a tailcoat, optional.

The dark blue or oxford grey overcoat is expressive of evening formality. Other colors are definitely not in keeping with either the dinner jacket or tail coat. (November, 1940, p. 106)

During World War II, War Production Board regulations permitted only the single-breasted dinner jacket. In January, 1945, *Esquire* showed one that merited WPB approval: a midnight-blue unfinished worsted with peaked lapels and grosgrain facings worn with a midnight-blue waistcoat, bow tie, and black studs. Since dress shirts with bosoms were another wartime casualty, a man had to make do with the shirts he had or depend on his favorite shop's supply.

Esquire's "bold look," introduced in 1948, made the American man happy to be back in mufti again. Its component parts for formal evening wear comprised a dress shirt with a wide center pleat and a soft, widespread collar; a broad-shouldered dinner jacket with broad satin-faced peaked lapels; and a more virile edition of the butterfly bow, its lower ends having a longer, more rakish flare than the top ones. For summer formal wear in the bold look style *Esquire* judged in August, 1948, that white was right: "There's nothing like white to make a suntan (the healthiest-looking color a man could have) seem even tanner, healthier, handsomer." It was the wide, rolling peaked lapels of the new white double-breasted dinner jacket that gave it the bold look, that lent the chest and shoulders the appearance of added breadth. Completing this outfit were midnight-blue lightweight worsted trousers with a broad silk braid down each side, a white rayon twill cummerbund, wide but thin all-elastic white braces, a white breast-pocket handkerchief, studs and cuff links of dark red stones, a dark red bow tie, and a red carnation. There was very little to indicate the conservatism that would soon dominate men's apparel for both day and evening.

1950–1960

Esquire's "Mr. T" symbolized the new conservative silhouette of the early fifties, and his midnight-blue single-breasted dinner jacket included all the natural, trim characteristics that dominated his daytime wardrobe. The jacket had a narrow shawl collar, narrower shoulders, and straight lines, and with it Mr. T wore a narrow bow tie and a dress shirt with two studs.

Single- and double-breasted evening jackets were enjoying equal popularity, however, and in August, 1950, *Esquire* recommended either one in black or midnight blue for semiformal evening wear. But for summertime, said the editors, "you'll like to wear lightweight white for comfort's sake." Since comfort was a prime consideration during this decade, even formal-wear worsted had lost some ounces and now weighed about 10½ ounces to the yard.

This was a conservative, cautious period, and men seemed more concerned than ever with the correctness

The return of the natural-shoulder dinner jacket in 1950 marked the beginning of a long-lasting trend. The illustration shows a single-breasted model with a narrow shawl collar, worn with a narrow Mr. T bow tie. From Esquire, *November 1950.*

The french-blue double-breasted dinner jacket in a worsted mohair blend, shown at left, was popular for tropical wear in 1950. It had a single set of buttons. The red-and-blue plaid bow tie had pointed ends. The man in the center wore a single-breasted white dinner jacket. From Esquire, February 1950.

of their clothes. *Esquire,* in 1952, aimed to satisfy them by producing a time-table for correct dress around the clock in town and country. The after-six pointers read as follows:

For the formal evening.

Jacket. The worsted tail coat in midnight blue or black has no substitute, no compromise. It should be tailored to fit your figure flawlessly.

Waistcoat. Choose either the single- or double-breasted type. Either is correct.

The fabric is a white pique, and is patterned with a V-front.

Trousers. Naturally, of the same fabric as the tail coat. And, as in the coat, the fit is all-important. You'll find braid at both outer side seams.

Shirt. White, with a starched white pique bosom. The cuffs are single and extend slightly beyond the jacket sleeve. Wear a bold wing collar.

Necktie. Bow tie, of course. Of white pique, and it can match your shirt bosom and waistcoat. And it's easy to tie, so wear it that way.

Hose. Your colors are limited to black or midnight blue, depending on the coat color. Many nylon, wool or lisle types are available—all are good.

Footwear. Your shoes should be low-cut patent leather or long-vamp patent leather pumps. The type depends on your taste but patent it is.

Hat. Either of two varieties; the high silk kind or the high collapsible opera. The former is more formal, the latter is a bit more convenient.

Gloves. Spotless white kid, mocha or chamois. Chamois, you know, is washable, and the others are readily cleaned. They all last for years.

Outercoats. You've a color choice: black, oxford grey or dark blue. If you prefer the single- to the double-breasted, look for the fly-front styles.

Accessories. First, you need white braces. Then a white scarf, white handkerchief. Finally, a white or red carnation on your jacket lapel.

Jewelry. Studs of pearls or precious stones for your shirt bosom, with cuff links to match. You'll wear a pocket watch and a good key chain.

For semi-formal evening wear.

Jacket. Single- or double-breasted dinner jacket in black or midnight blue. In summertime, you'll like to wear lightweight white for comfort's sake.

Waistcoat. Can be either single- or double-breasted and in black or midnight blue. Wear the cummerbund with your lightweight summer jacket.

Trousers. Of the same fabric as the jacket, and with conventional braid at sides. If your jacket is lightweight, and white, choose midnight blue trousers.

Shirt. Here you have a choice. Either a white pique with single cuffs, or a pleated bosom shirt with double cuffs. Collar style can be either wing or fold.

Necktie. A bow tie, naturally. Midnight blue or black, butterfly or narrow (that's up to you). Try maroon with your summer jacket for more color.

Hose. Depending on the color of your trousers, wear black or dark blue. The fabric choices are many: see what you prefer in nylon, wool or lisle.

Footwear. Formal and semi-formal footwear are interchangeable. Either occasion requires the low-cut patent leather shoe or patent leather pump.

Hat. The Homburg is the hat, no 'buts' about it. Wear it in midnight blue or black. And if the weather is warm, choose a suitable straw hat and band.

Gloves. They are always essential for evening wear. And for a semi-formal evening, you'll want a pair of grey mocha, chamois or buck, button or slip-on.

Outercoats. All three colors are acceptable: black, oxford grey, and dark blue. In single- as well as in double-breasted. The fly-front style is optional.

Accessories. You will require a white scarf around your neck, white handkerchiefs, a red or white carnation in your lapel, black and white braces.

Jewelry. Wear a watch, pocket or wrist. Your studs and cuff links of mother of pearl, enamel, gold or colored stone. Also, a key chain and lighter. (March, 1952, p. 80)

The fashion news for 1953 was the feel of fabric: the nubby touch of a

Dusk gray for evening wear made news in 1954. The man lighting a cigarette wore a peaked-lapel dinner jacket while the smoker's jacket had a shawl collar. Both men wore patterned gray bow ties and matching cummerbunds. From Esquire, January 1954.

fabric with a soft, irregular texture. The iridescent look and nubby touch of silk shantung made it an ideal dinner jacket fabric for cruise and resort wear.

By the mid-fifties the political climate had relaxed to some extent, and men's semiformal attire was shown in welcome colors. "Parfait colors" *Esquire* called these fashion-fresh tones and gave them a double-page spread

in February, 1955, photographing combinations of jacket, shirt, tie, and cummerbund or cummervest (a wide type of cummerbund) with appropriate jewelry. There was, for example, a black-walnut dinner jacket with a crushed-raspberry tie and cummerbund and red cuff links and studs; a crushed-strawberry jacket with a cummervest and tie of gray silk shantung and gray pearl jewelry; a jacket the

The shawl-collared mess jacket, known as the Janeiro jacket, was introduced in a gold nubby synthetic fabric. The buttons were metal, and the sleeves had turned-back cuffs. From Esquire, *February 1957.*

color of French vanilla ice cream, with a cummervest and tie of gold shantung and blue-and-gold jewelry; and a crushed-blueberries jacket with accessories in a modified version of the same tone. All the jackets were of silk and Orlon, a texture that, according to the caption writer, matched the colors in its smooth richness.

This color cycle continued through 1956, when bright red and bold tartan dinner jackets became popular, often in blends that mixed wool with the still relatively new easy-to-wear, easy-to-care-for synthetic fabrics. Since nothing was cooler or easier to care for than seersucker, this fabric was enjoying a revival of popularity for daytime

wear in both town and country. By the mid-fifties seersucker was being used for dinner jackets.

Meanwhile, a new daytime silhouette called the "Continental look" had entered the picture. Its dominant features were a shorter, shapelier jacket and peaked or semipeaked lapels. In November, 1959, *Gentlemen's Quarterly* praised it as "a dressy, very smart suit." Inevitably, this dressier suit silhouette and the lustrous fabrics in which it was made affected evening clothes, and vice versa. In 1958, for example, *Gentlemen's Quarterly* had shown a Continental business suit with a shawl collar like those worn on dinner jackets.

The Continental look dinner jacket gave evening clothes a more cosmopolitan appearance. The mohair dinner suit with peaked lapels and satin piping and braid was a striking example of the new style. In black or silver gray with piped cuffs and waist suppression, combined with trousers with matching silk or satin side stripes, the Continental-styled dinner jacket marked a new period of evening elegance. Accessories took on a richer look. There were matching sets of bow ties and cummerbunds or cummervests in jacquard, checkerboard, and honeycomb designs and fancy-bosom dress shirts with fine tucked pleats, embroidered lace fronts, and lattice-type venetian-blind effects. Even evening overcoats showed the Continental influence. Although *Gentlemen's Quarterly* conceded that any black coat of more formal fabric and design was correct for evening wear, it suggested in November, 1959, that "the man who is the recipient of many invitations to dress affairs will want one formal evening coat in his wardrobe" and that preferably it should be of mohair. As an inducement, the magazine showed two luxurious black mohair examples: a coat with slash pockets, cuffed sleeves, a center vent, and a velvet inset on a bal collar; and one with a satin shawl collar and cuffs and a white silk lining. The fifties, a decade that had begun in so conservative a mood that it was sartorially

inhibited, ended on a note of incomparable elegance.

1960–1970

The opening years of the sixties, a decade that brought great changes in men's fashions, began quietly, with little indication of the Peacock Revolution that would soon pass through the American man's wardrobe. The Continental look was being replaced by the "British look," a flattering high-fashion silhouette better suited to the American physique. The new look featured a lightly padded jacket with a flare to the skirt, wider lapels, pronounced side vents or center vent, a moderately cutaway front, slanting

The Regency double-breasted dinner jacket of the sixties and seventies had three sets of buttons in parallel arrangement and satin-faced high lapels. Shown here in a velvet fabric, it was worn with a pleated-bosom shirt and a satin butterfly bow tie.

pockets, and plain-front trousers. Soon adaptations of this look appeared in formal wear, in a major step in the direction of the shaped suit.

By 1965 the Peacock Revolution reached the United States with the colorful "new wave" fashions earmarked for the young, but it had little if any impact on formal wear. In 1966 for example, *Esquire*'s feature "Fashion Guide for All Occasions" hewed to the traditional.

"Lord Chesterfield was emphatic on the subject of proper dress," it began, "and he always wrote copious letters to his son about it. In one such note he said, 'Take great care always to be dressed like the reasonable people of your own age, in the place where you are; whose dress is never spoken of one way or another as either too negligent or too much studied.' In other words, dress well but don't go overboard. And that, here and now, two hundred years later, is one of *Esquire*'s abiding concerns.

"What it all adds up to, of course, is the contemporary look of today's well dressed man. The new shaped silhouette, wide bold ties, knee-length topcoat, double-breasted blazer and the trim-fitting, slim-line trousers."

As for semiformal dress, the fashion department advised the reader: "There is very little leeway here. The concepts of formality are narrow indeed and tradition is practically binding." Illustrating this statement was a black peaked lapel dinner jacket with satin facing on the lapels but not on the collar. It was worn with a white pleated-bosom shirt, plain smoked-pearl removable buttons, a black bow tie, plain-toe black patent-leather oxfords, and a white pocket handkerchief. Alternative accessories included a very pale natural-color silk shirt and plain pearl studs, a black wide-flared bow tie, black onyx studs with metal borders, and a black four-button single-breasted vest with a straight-cut bottom. The outfit was tasteful and flattering but scarcely revolutionary.

Then, late in 1966, the Nehru jacket enjoyed a meteoric rise, influencing menswear for both day and evening.

The black mohair and worsted dinner jacket worn by this celebrant of New Year's, 1967, was a double-breasted model with two sets of buttons and a satin shawl collar. The coat carried over the arm was made of the same kind of fabric as the jacket. From Esquire, *1967.*

The jacket, an exact copy of the Indian original popularized by the handsome appearance of Prime Minister Jawaharlal Nehru, was soon adapted for formal evening wear in sumptuous brocade or velvet. A photograph of Lord Snowdon wearing a black Nehru dinner jacket with a white satin turtleneck sweater appeared in newspapers throughout the United States. The Nehru actually had a limited fashion career, but while it prospered, it attracted great publicity.

As the Nehru fad died away, the Edwardian appeared. A theatrical look for day or evening, it was distinguished by a longer double-breasted jacket with waist suppression and a deep center vent. Evening opulence in black, brown, royal blue, ruby red, or emerald green velvet or brocade was incompatible with a conventional or even a fancy-bosom dress shirt, and the Edwardian dandy of the late 1960s wore a lace-jabot shirt with lacy cuffs spilling over his wrists. Like the Nehru, the Edwardian dinner suit had a brief but colorful career. It left its mark on formal attire, inspiring *Gentlemen's*

Two styles of formal evening clothes for men in 1971: (left) a black mohair suit with velvet facing on the wide peaked lapels and flared trousers, by Oscar de la Renta; (right) a mohair suit with a satin border on faille notched lapels, by Robert Don Paulo for After Six Formals.

ple, not only survived but acquired fresh interest with black stripes or piping. And a new wave all-white maxi-length evening coat expressed its vigor without a single black button. A waist-shaped, six-button double-breasted model with a deep center vent, it had flaring peaked lapels, lower flapped pockets, and a white satin lining. Beneath this maxicoat the model wore a more or less conventional black dinner suit, but his hat flaunted tradition. In place of a homburg, he wore a large white fedora with a wide black band.

The Edwardian influence lingered as late as 1969. What remained was the best part of the look, which, combined with the traditional, produced dinner suits of uncommon attractiveness. In November, 1969, *Esquire* displayed many of these longer, leaner-looking dinner suits. A particularly handsome example was a six-button double-breasted Edwardian model of black velvet ("elegant without being outre") with velvet-covered buttons, slanted flap pockets, and wide satin lapels, worn with velvet trousers featuring Western pockets and side stripes of satin braid. The rest of the ensemble included a natural-color silk shirt with a tucked-pleat front, an outsize black satin bow tie, lion's-head cuff links and studs in white enamel and 18-carat yellow gold with ruby eyes, and square-toed black patent-leather evening shoes with a gold chain buckle ornamenting the instep.

Knits, too, were adapted for evening wear, and for its April, 1969, issue *Esquire* photographed a one-button black polyester dinner suit with a satin shawl collar and an almost indiscernible jacquard pattern. The model wore a widespread-collared white dinner shirt with a crossover black tie, its two untied ends held in place in the center by studs. Meanwhile, the silk dinner jacket in such colors as eggshell and citron continued to be seen everywhere, often with an evening shirt of still another color. Color also appeared in formal shoes of blue, brown, and burgundy.

Designers, many of whom had made

Quarterly to note in November, 1969: "The peacock has replaced the penguin and once-sacrosanct traditional formal wear has been assailed by startling—but more elegant than ever—fabrics, designs and colors."

"Startling . . . more elegant than ever" formal fashions were shown in *Gentlemen's Quarterly* in November, 1969. Despite the color craze, black proved to be still elegant as well as beautiful. Illustrating this fact was a satin-buttoned black mohair tailcoat collared in satin-edged black velvet, worn with matching trousers and a

white piqué waistcoat; a black mohair dinner suit ("as spirited as it is formal") trimmed in wide black satin, with angled piped pockets and a deep center vent; and a square-shouldered, deep-vented, cardigan-style evening suit of satin-edged black mohair, without buttons or chest pocket or either one, worn with an outsize black velvet bow tie and a velvet-striped shirt.

Notwithstanding the Peacock Revolution and its color, simple black and white was far from outmoded. The classic white dinner jacket, for exam-

their reputations in women's wear, brought their imagination and skill to men's formal wear. A young-spirited trend in formal-wear trousers began in 1970 with patterned trousers. In its April issue *Gentlemen's Quarterly* showed several pairs with solid-color dinner jackets and such extravagant dress shirts as a flare-bottomed red-and-blue check with a white windowpane overcheck, embellished with black satin side stripes, and a tapestry paisley design in blue and magenta with a flared bottom and curved pockets. Among other innovations of the early seventies were a sleeveless jump suit, an at-home outfit that was acceptable as semiformal attire when worn with a dinner jacket; and a battle jacket converted to formal wear in velvet with the addition of a satin collar.

Yet a man could dress to please himself, and next to these mavericks might stand the author, editor, and professional daredevil George Plimpton in traditional black and white. Permissiveness was one of the most persuasive points in favor of the new sartorial freedom, and there was no rule against simple black and white. In fact, as the seventies continued, black and white became increasingly popular. Designers who confined themselves to the penguin colors succeeded in making the classic contemporary through an imaginative use of new and unusual fabrics and subtle refinements of tried-and-true silhouettes. One of the best examples appeared in *Esquire* in February, 1970: a shaped six-button evening suit of black panne velvet with wide lapels, side vents, and covered buttons. It was not freakish but simply high fashion.

So tradition was not dead after all. This was true particularly of the formal evening wedding, at which the white-tie-and-tails outfit was still re-

This black mohair dinner jacket with wide peaked lapels was worn with a one-piece jump suit that resembled waistcoat and trousers and served as an at-home evening suit without the jacket. The ruffled shirt was complemented by a satin bow tie cut straight across the top and flared at the lower sides (1971).

quired for the groom and wedding guests. And the copy for a full-page *New York Times* advertisement by Saks Fifth Avenue on November 4, 1970, showed that tradition in formal evening wear was more than a "remembrance of things past": "For a festive black-tie dinner or one of those special evenings when white tie is in order. . . . We feel evening clothes should be as beautifully tailored as any suit you own, with particular attention to the silhouette, careful shaping of luxurious dark fabrics in traditional black, deep blue or newly favored dark brown. And when it comes to correct evening furnishings, we keep track of current etiquette." The illustration showed a dashing young man with fashionably longer sideburns, wearing white tie and tails and a luxuriously lined opera cape and holding an opera hat. His white tie was rather large, his lapels broad, and his tailcoat handsomely shaped. The outfit was a perfect example of the classic made contemporary, blending respect for the old with a lively interest in the new.

Today formal evening wear has ceased to be a status symbol. It is simply the kind of clothing a man likes to put on when he wants to look and feel his handsomest. One might have thought formal wear would be swept away by the Peacock Revolution, which, like most revolutions, started at the bottom of the social scale and moved upward. That did not happen because the revolution was a *Peacock* Revolution: formal evening wear not only survived but, with an injection of fresh ideas, flourished. One of the happiest aftereffects has been the ability to inspire the independent young to respect the part tradition plays in formal dress. In fact, it seems that many young men derive a special pleasure and reassurance from formal evening wear; in this rapidly changing, technological society it is one corner where tradition still counts. So, in ways other than pure fashion, formal evening wear is an expression of today.

The formal day apparel shown for a wedding in 1936 remained a classic fashion in subsequent decades. Included were varying styles of cutaways, waistcoats, striped and patterned trousers, ascot, four-in-hand, and bow ties, and fold and wing collars. From Esquire, *June 1936.*

The Arrow Collar man was used to display formal evening wear in the second decade of the century.

Formal evening attire in 1939: (left) a blue raglan evening coat, worn with a high silk hat and a cream silk scarf tied in ascot fashion; (center) a tailcoat with narrow lapels, worn with a colored boutonniere; (right) a side view of the same style of tailcoat; (below) white waistcoats with, respectively, a rolled shawl collar and angled lapels. From Esquire, *January 1939.*

Summer evening fashions of 1937: (upper left) a midnight-blue double-breasted dinner jacket with satin lapels; (upper right) a white cotton-drill dinner jacket with peaked lapels and, to its right, a Windsor-shape bow tie; (center) a silk dress shirt with a center box pleat, an India madras cummerbund, and a strap-and-buckle patent-leather dress shoe; (lower left) a shawl-collared dinner jacket in tan tropical worsted or a blended fabric; (lower right) a double-breasted shawl-collared dinner jacket in a washable white fabric. From Esquire, *June 1937.*

A cool-blue dinner jacket with an angled shawl collar, made in a blend of Dacron and Orlon that was automatic wash-and-wear. From Esquire, *June 1961.*

Formal Day and Evening Wear

WHITE TIE AND TAILS

AT THE left is the new evening paletot, made single breasted with fly front, peak lapels, raglan shoulders, slash pockets, and flap on the breast pocket. With it is worn a silk top hat, cream color silk scarf, white evening gloves and a dress suit. In the center is the new tailcoat with the long, rolling narrower style lapels. Accessories include a two-stud open front shirt, bold wing collar, thistle shape white tie, roll collar single breasted white evening waistcoat, and coral studs and cuff links. At the right is a side view of the same tailcoat, showing the false cuff and the lengthening effect of the coat. Below are two versions of the waistcoat, one with roll collar, the other a single breasted model with square lapels. Proper boutonnières comprise the blue cornflower, coral color carnation, white gardenia, and the above red carnation.

(For answers to all dress queries, send stamped self-addressed envelope to Esquire Fashion Staff, 366 Madison Av., N. Y.)

Summer Evening Dress

Dinner Jackets for warm weather are correctly worn at country large parties in the country and aboard ship. When dressing in town the black or midnight blue dinner jacket is preferable.

The new one button peak lapel singlebreasted cotton drill dinner jacket with self buttons in the town worn by well-dressed Englishmen at Nassau.

Summer dress shirts of silk or broadcloth with plain, pleated or stiff bosoms are correct. The majority of well-dressed men prefer turn over collars, either starched or soft, to match shirt. The various shape of dress ties shown here are those most popular.

Doublebreasted midnight blue silk dinner jacket with black satin lapels.

A new silk dress shirt with four inch crescent bar. Originated in London and worn at Nassau.

India Madras cummerbund replacing waistcoat for warm evenings.

Patent leather monk front dress shoe originated by Englishmen in the West Indies.

Singlebreasted color dinner jacket,

(For answers to all dress queries, send stamped self-addressed envelope to Esquire Fashion Staff, 366 Madison Av., N. Y.)

The morning, or cutaway, coat of 1926 was an oxford-gray cheviot with peaked lapels, worn with a gray double-breasted waistcoat, striped gray trousers, a black ascot held with a pearl stickpin, a white shirt, a wing collar, a high silk hat, gray mocha gloves, black shoes, and gray spats. [SCHEYER-TAILORED FOR OGILVIE & JACOBS]

successor, was being challenged by the single- or double-breasted dark gray jacket worn with striped trousers. And the new fold collar, a soft collar, was finding favor with many younger men who no longer wanted anything high and starched around their necks. Yet a reporter covering the Easter finery worn by fashionable New Yorkers in 1926 was optimistic about the future of correct dress:

"Eliminating all those who are not in the fashionable set, one salient note of the appearance and attire of the men was that the increasing number of young men who wore formal day dress clothes foreshadows that we are entering an era of fastidious and cor-

rect dress. These scions of fortunes and future captains of wealth will fill nobly their positions, at least as far as appearances go.

"Their high silk hats, which showed considerably bell-shaped tops, most frequently were worn at a rakish angle. Medium wing collars and white shirts usually formed backgrounds to silver gray or black and white ties of self or modest figures. Four-in-hand ties were much in the majority.

"Their cutaway coats reflected no eccentric characteristics, but had those lines of correct style that leading tailors attain in their garments. One or two buttons in front, with notch or peak lapels, the former predominating but the latter a bit 'swankier,' were the styles. Braided edges continued to be quite popular. Various stripings of trousers included the black ground with white stripes spaced three-quarters of an inch apart, block stripes, and groups of various widths of stripings.

"One detail that indelibly marked the details of the clothes was the wearing of linen or 'canvas' spats in white, biscuit, or grey. That an increased interest in dress prevails is evidenced by the vogue of these things. Waistcoats usually matched the jacket and no reason other than the cold day can account for the few washable waistcoats that were seen.

"Chesterfield coats, either single-breasted style with notch lapel, fly-front and velvet collar, or double-breasted with self collar, were the only accepted models for wear with the cutaway. Black, oxford or navy blue were the colors.

"With the older generation the clothes were more or less as of yore. It seems that they do not vary the style to any great extent as to color or pattern, and if there is a change it is only a slight widening of the lapel, or other minor change.

"Silver grey continued to be the tone of neckwear and trousers. Alternate stripes and white stripes with generous spacings on black grounds played important parts in patterns of trousers.

"A distinguished foreigner, who was seen on Park Avenue, showed a preference for grey cashmere trousers, the shading of which gave a wide striped effect. His cutaway was rather shapely and carried only one button. The edges showed a braiding. His black patent leather shoes had straight tip toe caps and tan uppers. This play of colored uppers was noticed as a very important item with the best dressed men.

"Mufflers worn with Chesterfields and cutaways on Easter Sunday were usually knotted 'choker' style. One gentleman on Park Avenue whose white silk scarf was tied this fashion had the black monogram showing at the opening of his overcoat. Most of the men carried either a crooked handle, or the straight-shaft malacca cane" (*Men's Wear*, Apr. 21, 1926, p. 63).

A reporter covering the Fifth Avenue Easter parade two years later did not seem quite so optimistic about the future of formal day wear. He commented: "The dress of one of the old school is a decided contrast with the styles of today!" And he noted that one of the growing vogues was that of the odd waistcoat, in both single- and double-breasted models: "The contrasting colors of these articles varied from pale grey to buff to white, in cashmere and washable fabrics." Furthermore, this reporter's cameraman recorded many younger men wearing the new fold collar in place of the wing, the double-breasted jacket in place of the cutaway, and the bowler instead of the high silk hat. But for the tradition-bound reader who might regard these changes with some measure of alarm, he had this to say:

"Critics who contend that Fifth Avenue parades and other such events are not what they used to be, would probably be greatly disappointed if by a miracle we should suddenly be taken back to the standards and customs of living of a generation or more ago. They have lost sight of the progress and development that is constantly being made.

"We still have the same influential

classes, which set the fashions in customs, automobiles, and clothes, but their influence is greater and more quickly felt today than it was years ago. Modern methods of news dissemination tend to make the activities of the elite known to the populace immediately, hence this latter class is in a better position to be influenced" (*Men's Wear,* Apr. 25, 1928, p. 86).

And perhaps to salve the feelings of the reader who actually did feel the Easter parade was not what it used to be, the article contained a photograph of an elegant young man dressed in the height of formality: a cutaway, a light gray top hat, an ascot tie, a double-breasted white waistcoat, and a white boutonniere.

Yet even in the late twenties, to a stickler for tradition anything less than a frock coat or a black cutaway was still considered semiformal wear. From that vantage point, the following are four examples of semiformal day dress in 1928: a double-breasted black jacket worn with a single-breasted white Russian-cord waistcoat, black trousers with narrow white stripes, a primrose silk scarf, a black pearl pin, and black calf boots with buttoned tan cloth tops; a double-breasted black cutaway with a single-breasted white cloth waistcoat, silver-tone striped trousers, a white shirt and collar, a black-and-white tie, a gray top hat, black patent-leather boots, and white spats; a single-breasted cutaway and trousers of gray worsted worn with a double-breasted white linen waistcoat, a black tie, a pearl pin, a white shirt and collar, and black patent-leather boots with dull calf buttoned tops; and a single-breasted black jacket with a double-breasted waistcoat of the same material showing white facing, solid silver-tone trousers of gray cashmere, black shoes, a lavender shirt with a white collar and cuffs, a black-and-white tie, and a black homburg hat.

An example of formal day dress was a black frock coat worn with a double-breasted tan linen waistcoat, light gray self-striped trousers, patent-leather boots with buttoned tan cloth tops, a white shirt and collar, and a silver-tone figured tie. As an example of extremely formal day dress there was a black cutaway with lapels faced to edge with silk, a double-breasted white linen waistcoat, black cashmere trousers with white stripes, patent-leather boots with buttoned biscuit cloth tops, a silver-gray tie, and a jeweled pin.

Formal day neckwear in the twenties offered a man a rather wide variety of choice. Bow ties were now as correct as four-in-hands and ascots. And color was more prevalent than in previous decades, with stripings of gray and gold and figures of gray and lavender, along with the traditional black and white or silver gray.

An article in *Men's Wear* in 1928 covered formal and semiformal day dress in detail, beginning with the tailcoat, which was an elegant derivative of the classic frock coat:

"The extreme formal act in these garments is the one-button black coat made of vicuna or unfinished worsted in very plain weave. The lapels shown with peak are silk faced to edge, sleeves finished with put-on cuff and three buttons and all buttons of silk. The waistcoat should be double breasted in white of washable stuff, the collar rolling soft and the front lower edge slightly pointed at the center. Trousers of black with white or pastel colored stripes. Cut on the easy side but tapering at the foot.

"Boots and not shoes are a correct essential as accompaniment to this coat, and of patent leather with plain punched toe tips and either dull calf or light brown buttoned cloth tops. The uppers of the latter may have edges and seams finished with canary or brown leather and the buttons cut from white mother of pearl. If one is fastidious the use of black varnish on the lower parts gives an added elegance to the costume.

"Shirts of white, and never color, with this ceremonious coat is the exacting demand. Have them in broad pleats slightly stiffened or the plain starched bosom with white, single cuffs but faintly rounded at the points. In a choice of three collars: the plain band, poke or wing. One chooses what best becomes one and wears a full throwover scarf in plain or self marked black or pastel shade. The hat must positively be the high silk, which is happy with the wearer's face, though not astray from what fashion prescribes.

"Slightly less formal is the one or two-button black coat having plain or bound edges. The sleeves are finished as aforementioned, but the buttons may be either of bone or silk. Waistcoat of white or pastel linens cut double-breasted. Trousers from the striped blacks to silver effects in stripes or faint plaids to small shepherd's checks of black and white. The large effects in these checks are considered extremely bad taste. Boots, as described, collars, shirts and other accessories, the same. Neckties, either the full throwover or bow.

"For still less formal moments fashion gives us entire cutaway suits in medium shades of grey, dressed or undressed worsteds, which may be broken by a solid white, biscuit or pastel blue linen double-breasted waistcoat. The small things are the same here, except double collars with full flowing and four-in-hand ties and shirts of solid color with white collars and cuffs are acceptable. One may wear a cutaway of dark grey with trousers that blend, or if one likes this coat in its latest mode, play it double-breasted with a pearl top hat and the possible accessories given for semi-formal moments.

"Black jackets, single- and double-breasted, allow us to pass on to a stage of dress even less exacting. They may have braided or plain edges, silk or bone buttons and the waistcoat can vary—perchance matching the jacket with white facing or the double-breasted linen waistcoat of white or color. Regarding the trousers, one may select the dark effects or the brighter ones. Shoes are possible with these jackets, but never with the silk hat unless spats of tan or white cover them. Under no circumstances do well turned out men ever use grey spats or grey top boots. 'Tis a rigid law very closely observed for formal day dress.

"As to the cut of the cutaways, the waist still lingers at a line which will give a long leg aspect to the figure, with an increased trend to the swallow tail effect in the skirts. Narrow pleats in back with the skirts slightly fulled in at the waist seam on either side and the waistline rounding up over the hips. The waistline in these coats should be marked on the sides and at the front, with the back line from collar to end of skirt as flat as possible. Lapels are a whim, as is their cut, and the depth of collar in front to suit the long or round face. The jackets are form fitting with no vents, yet a bit longer than those for suitings. The number of buttons, one or two, like the shaping of lapels, is a personal whim. The fronts of single breasted can vary too, straight or cutaway with not too bold round. The sleeves finish one to four buttons or the put-on cuff and three buttons. We argue the wearing of the solid colored linen double-breasted waistcoats when an agreeable addition with any and all of this formal dress. We also decry figured scarfs, except they be of self color or in small checks. Last, but not least, it should be kept in mind that boots (high shoes) are the only correct footwear for formal day attire" (Mar. 7, 1928, p. 100).

1930–1940

After the twenties, a decade *Esquire* described as "easy and informal . . . when the average man felt disinclined to invest in morning clothes," the Depression thirties ushered in a period of greater formality, at least for the man still affluent enough to dress up. As an inducement, *Esquire*'s fashion staff in April, 1934, showed readers a slim-hipped and exceedingly debonair man in a one-button peaked-lapel cutaway jacket made of fine cashmere ("minus the braid which it used to carry as standard trim"). With this the model wore a double-breasted fawn-colored waistcoat, a deep blue shirt with starched white cuffs and collar, a

black-and-white shepherd's-check tie, and "if you're not afraid of advance fashions," black calf shoes with buttoned fawn tops. Readers were asked to note that the topcoat worn with such an elegant outfit need not be black or oxford gray: a navy blue coat would be equally correct. Alternate choices for waistcoat, tie, and shoes were a double-breasted white linen waistcoat, a blue-and-white polka-dotted ascot, and a pair of plain-toe black calf slip-ons. The copywriter added: "The dark red carnation is not essential but it adds a very smart finishing touch."

In 1934 *Apparel Arts* showed what it considered to be a complete wardrobe for spring. This included a formal day outfit consisting of a one-button peaked-lapel single-breasted cutaway coat, a pale yellow double-breasted flannel waistcoat, shepherd's-check cheviot trousers, a soft-bosom gray shirt with a starched white collar and cuffs, a blue foulard tie with white polka dots, a black top hat, a yellow carnation boutonniere, pale yellow chamois gloves, black polished shoes with buttoned cloth tops, and a malacca stick. The next year *Apparel Arts* reminded its readers that "Discrimination and scrupulous attention to detail are perhaps at their greatest premium in the selection of the proper clothing and accessories for the occasions of formal wear. . . .

"The single-breasted morning coat, without braid, may be in either the peak or notched lapel model; it may be made up in vicuna, cashmere, cheviot or unfinished worsted in plain or fancy weave. The short jacket of oxford grey, either single- or double-breasted, may be made up in similar fabrics. Trousers of worsted or cheviot

in lighter greys may be striped or carry herringbones, shepherd's check or Glen Urquhart patterns.

"Trousers worn with the short jacket may carry cuffs. White or solid colored shirts should be worn with wing collars or white stiff fold collars. Ascots, four-in-hands or bow ties are all accepted forms of neckwear. A pearl stick pin or gold animal figure stick pin may be worn in the four-in-hand or ascot. Single- or double-breasted fancy waistcoats may be in white, grey or buff. The silk top hat is the only correct hat with the morning coat, although the silk hat, black Homburg or derby may be worn with the black jacket. Black calf shoes with plain toe caps are correct, as are black shoes with cloth buttoned tops. Spats may be worn, if desired. Gloves should match the waistcoat, unless the waistcoat is black; in this case, grey gloves should be worn. Single- or double-breasted topcoats of navy blue or oxford grey are correct."

"For the first time in years, color is sanctioned in formal day dress," observed *Esquire* in April, 1935. Proof was exhibited in an outfit composed of a soft tan shirt worn with a widespread starched collar and a gray Spitalfields tie with a checkerboard stripe, fawn pigskin gloves, trousers in lightweight cheviot in a small black-and-white shepherd's-check pattern, and a double-breasted gray waistcoat. The next year the magazine in its April issue noted that color was creeping into semiformal dress too, "slowly but steadily, for some while back. The breakup of the monotony of black and white has been most noticeable in southern resort evening wear, but in semi-formal day dress, too, the encroachment of color has been just as

---

(opposite) In the 1930s men wore formal clothes for Easter Sunday. Across the top are an oxford-gray cutaway coat with a Spitalfields ascot, a wing collar, and a lavender or gray waistcoat; a cutaway coat and a matching waistcoat with a fold collar, a Spitalfields tie, a silk hat, cloth-top black shoes, and chamois gloves; and a black jacket with a blue shirt, a white fold collar, and a blue-and-white polka-dot bow tie. Across the bottom are a single-breasted jacket with a derby and striped trousers, a double-breasted jacket with a homburg and patterned trousers, and a two-button cutaway coat with a biscuit-color waistcoat and gray crash tweed trousers. From Esquire, *April 1938.*

steady if less spectacular." As a prime example the editors offered the new champagne color ("a jolt of bright-ness") in a soft shirt of fine zephyr broadcloth worn with a starched collar in the accepted widespread model. The reader was asked to appreciate the comparative gaiety of the gold animal-figure stickpin against the navy blue of the Spitalfields tie. The rest of this semiformal outfit consisted of a double-breasted oxford gray worsted jacket with a matching waist-coat, lightweight cheviot trousers in a fine glenurquhart plaid with a blue overcheck, yellow chamois gloves, a black homburg and shoes, and a blue cornflower boutonniere.

In the same issue *Esquire* showed what it considered to be "the nearest modern equivalent to the old time dress up costume known as the Sunday-going-to-meetin' suit." One outfit comprised a double-breasted unfinished-worsted jacket carrying only four buttons with the lapel rolled to the lower ones, cuffless trousers of glenurquhart cheviot, plain black shoes, a colored soft shirt with a stiff white collar and cuffs, and a dark Spitalfields tie with a fine white over-stripe. A second outfit, worn by a more mature man, consisted of a one-button peaked-lapel morning coat with a double-breasted waistcoat of fawn linen, a striped broadcloth shirt with a starched collar, and a gold animal stickpin in a Spitalfields tie.

The next year, 1937, *Esquire* was back with new Sunday-go-to-meeting clothes. This time fresh fashion news was to be found in a pair of sponge-bag trousers, so called after the small black-and-white shepherd's-check bags in which sponges were carried by Brit-ish army officers. Less obvious but im-portant, too, was the very narrow brim of the silk hat.

By the late thirties it was no longer news that the turndown collar and four-in-hand tie, except for weddings, had banished the wing collar and ascot tie. Yet morning clothes were rapidly becoming more important on this side of the ocean, *Esquire*'s fashion department decided in October, 1937,

pointing out that they were now being worn on Sunday afternoons and eve-nings as well as for fashionable wed-dings.

In April, 1938, *Esquire* showed what it called the "king-pin of Easter for-mality." The outfit consisted of a morning coat without braid, a match-ing waistcoat with a white piqué slip, white-striped black worsted trousers, a fine gray striped broadcloth shirt with a high starched turnover collar, a bronze Spitalfields tie, a silk top hat, black cloth-top shoes, and chamois gloves. A variation on this theme was an outfit consisting of a two-button notched-lapel jacket, with a double-breasted biscuit waistcoat, gray crash tweed trousers, and a gray-and-maroon tie. Other samples of Easter finery included on this fashion page were a lavender waistcoat, a pleated-bosom blue shirt with a stiff white collar, and a blue spotted bow tie. In April of the following year *Esquire* offered another Easter preview and included the correct boutonnieres: blue cornflower, white gardenia, and coral, yellow, or red carnation.

1940–1970

Esquire's preview for Easter, 1941, showed something new. In the fore-ground of the illustration was a gen-tleman in a cutaway coat, striped trousers, a pleated-bosom shirt, and a high silk hat. But in the background stood a man in what the caption writer called "a slightly less formal get-up." His outfit included an oxford gray jacket, striped gray trousers, a white shirt, a fold starched collar, a blue-and-gray four-in-hand tie, black straight-tip shoes, a black homburg, chamois gloves, and a white pocket handkerchief.

The bridegroom taking part in a formal day ceremony in 1941 had the satisfaction of knowing that he was dressed correctly if, like his father some twenty years earlier, he wore an oxford gray cutaway, gray striped worsted trousers, a white shirt, a wing collar, an ascot in silver gray and black silk, a plain pearl stickpin, a pale gray

unfinished-worsted waistcoat, gray mocha gloves, black silk socks, and black straight-tip shoes.

The bridegroom of 1971? *Esquire* moved in for a close-up in the June issue (after all, by then the formal wedding, official state functions, and the presidential inaugural ceremony were the only occasions that called for formal day wear) and decided that the groom of the peacock era expected formality with a little less fuss:

"Sometimes it would seem that the

An Easter morning outfit in 1940 consisted of a peaked-lapel black worsted cutaway coat with a red carnation in the lapel, small-check saxony cuffless trousers, a cream-color linen waistcoat with a collar and an almost square front, a tan broadcloth shirt with a starched collar, a checked tie with a stickpin, yellow chamois gloves, a high silk hat, and black shoes with tan tops. From Esquire, *April 1940.*

The accepted formal day attire in 1941 included a peaked-lapel cutaway, a pale gray waistcoat, boldly striped black-and-gray trousers, an allover-patterned ascot held with a pearl stickpin, a silk hat, gray gloves, and black shoes. From Esquire, *April 1941.*

formal look. This is not to suggest that we advocate the abolition of the cutaway and its accoutrements, but simply that, for the man who wants comfort at any cost, there should be an alternative. But now the problem of what to wear before six would seem to have been solved. The formal appearance of the bridegroom is not lessened by the comfort of his shaped six-button double-breasted oxford grey walking (or morning) coat, which has inset peaked lapels, deep flapped pockets, and a seventeen-inch center vent; traditional-looking oxford grey striped trousers also of Dacron and worsted; a wing collar shirt with French cuffs and a soft pique bosom; grey-and-white striped ascot; black patent leather shoes."

And so the "formality with a little less fuss" of the bridegroom's wardrobe in the early seventies had left traditional formal day wear relatively intact. The addition of comfort through new styling and the inclusion of man-made fabrics had been accomplished subtly and tastefully. On the other hand, formal day wear was dealt a severe blow by the inaugural ceremony of 1953, when President-elect Dwight D. Eisenhower chose to wear a homburg rather than the traditional high silk hat. And although John F. Kennedy did wear a high silk hat to his inauguration in 1961, that was perhaps the last time he wore a hat of any kind to an official state function.

By the last half of the century formal day wear, once an integral part of the fashionable American's lifestyle, had become restricted to fewer and fewer occasions. Conversely, formal evening wear flourished in the wake of the Peacock Revolution. Yet, considering the dynamics of the seventies and its nostalgic bent, it is not inconceivable that formal day wear may undergo a renaissance before this century is over. Certainly it is significant that many young grooms of this decade favor traditional formal wear. In the final analysis it may be the young American who will keep the tradition of formal day wear alive.

bonds of matrimony are rather less enduring than the cut of the clothes worn at a wedding. Now and then, of course, some flower child makes his mate an honest woman, and hippie culture dictates the attire at the ceremony. But most often, by and large, something a little more traditional is still in favor. And, since weddings are just about the last refuge left for traditional formal wear, we are all for it. Still and all, there is no denying that the customary cutaway coat, stiff collar, and starched dickey-bosom shirt for daytime ceremonies caused a certain discomfort. So the aim, then, was to incorporate a little more ease into wedding clothes without forfeiting the

Waistcoats and Cummerbunds

All waistcoats of the twentieth century descend from the original postboy waistcoat of nineteenth-century England. Worn by the postboy, or postilion, who rode as a guide on the near horse of a pair or of one of the pairs attached to a coach, it was intended mainly to be warm; so it was usually made of a woolen fabric front and back and was cut high under the armholes.

Styles of waistcoats in 1915 ranged from tattersall checks and double-breasted duck to U-shaped types in black or white for evening dress. [COURTESY OF BROOKS BROTHERS, NEW YORK]

Waistcoats for Day Wear

Clearly showing its descent from the postboy, the waistcoat of the first decade of the twentieth century was an essential part of the suit it matched. Usually single-breasted with a notched or shawl collar or with no collar at all, it was not only warm and decorative but utilitarian, since the wearer carried a heavy gold watch in one waistcoat pocket and his watch fob in another, a gold chain extending across the waistcoat to connect the two. Less popular was the double-breasted model with or without a collar.

As suits became softer and more comfortable in the second decade and younger men showed a marked preference for the new wristwatch, the waistcoat became less essential. More and more men now rated it strictly on its fashion appeal. In fact, as early as 1914 fancy waistcoats, advertised as "high-falutin vests," made their appearance. They were smartly fitted at the waist, and many of them had graceful rolling lapels. Cut high, they showed well above the opening of a suit jacket.

The British influence in suits, which became dominant in the late twenties, was characterized by a suit jacket that was broader at the shoulders and fashionably snug at the hips, with full sleeves and broad, curving lapels that rolled to the bottom button. The matching waistcoat, an essential part of this suit, carried six buttons and was cut high.

In 1928 the linen waistcoat in pastel shades of tan, gray, and blue had come into vogue to such an extent that *Men's Wear* decreed that it was "an important item in the wardrobe of almost every man who makes any pretense whatever at following the fashions. At the important polo games on Long Island, at seashore resorts such as Palm Beach and Newport, and at all

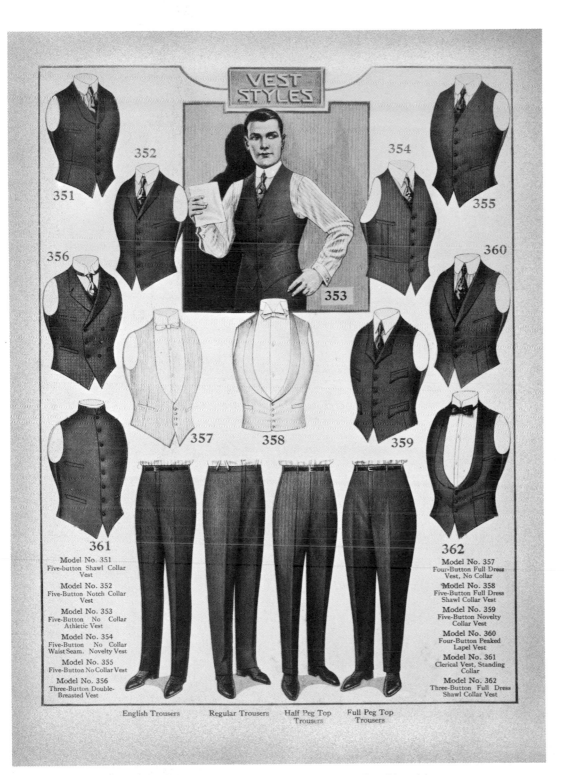

Waistcoats, generally called vests in 1920, came in single- or double-breasted models, with or without lapels or shawl collars, to match suits. Evening-dress vests in white or black came with or without collars. [FASHION INSTITUTE OF TECHNOLOGY]

postboy riding vest. In 1942, noting that "the new trend in semi-sports clothes is a hangover from hunting and riding togs," *Esquire* showed a "refreshing outfit which literally goes to town . . . may be worn inside the city limits providing you are en route to Connecticut on the afternoon train." This time the outfit was a gray glen plaid suit with a yellow flannel waistcoat.

Yet despite the not inconsiderable popularity of the odd waistcoat, the waistcoat per se was a waning fashion, and it was dealt a severe blow during

Suit waistcoats in a straight-cut double-breasted style with lapels (left) and a single-breasted style with flap pockets (right) were shown with pleated trousers in this national advertisement in 1928. [NEW YORK PUBLIC LIBRARY PICTURE COLLECTION]

The white piqué waistcoat with soft-roll lapels was worn in 1928 with a dinner jacket. [NEW YORK PUBLIC LIBRARY PICTURE COLLECTION]

sporting events where the smartest set gather, linen waistcoats have been a conspicuous item of dress for the past two years" (Apr. 25, 1928). By the mid-thirties another odd waistcoat, the single-breasted tattersall, was a popular part of a smart country weekend ensemble. The colors of these odd waistcoats were chosen to harmonize with the articles of apparel they were to accompany. Younger men, who had never before worn odd waistcoats, were cautioned to remember that the louder the color the quieter the style or cut should be. "For instance, the tattersall check," wrote a *Men's Wear*

editor, "is almost invariably seen in the single-breasted model, while the plainer, more conservative colors may be chosen in the double-breasted model."

By the early forties not only was a semisports outfit acceptable for town wear but, according to *Esquire,* it was "smart to be sporty." And to illustrate this contention, the editors chose in May, 1940, a three-button single-breasted gray cheviot tweed suit with a large red windowpane check. A distinguishing characteristic of this outfit was an odd waistcoat of gray box cloth carrying a step collar and cut like a

the war years, when War Production Board regulations decreed that no waistcoats could be made with double-breasted suits. And in September, 1955, in a guide to correct dress, *Esquire* noted that for business wear no waistcoat at all was "a trend favored by more and more men," although some men still felt more correct when they wore matching waistcoats with their natural-shoulder suits. For urban and suburban wear, however, the fashion department recommended a solid-color waistcoat like the jacket or a tattersall check or plaid. The odd waistcoat, often in a check, plaid, or very bright solid color, continued to be seen particularly on Ivy League campuses during the early sixties, but the waistcoat made to match a suit was seen less and less frequently.

When the Peacock Revolution ushered in the shaped suit, the suit lacked a waistcoat, although subsequently some shaped suits sported matching vests and *Esquire* photographed one in 1969: a three-button model of a natural-and-brown-striped crepe in a blend of silk and linen. But this was a rarity, and by the early seventies the conventional waistcoat had undergone some drastic changes in styling as it moved out from underneath the suit jacket to become a sportswear fashion in its own right. *Gentlemen's Quarterly* had sketched a "new wave" example as early as September, 1967: it consisted of a combination of vest and shorts made of sturdy canvas, with the vest carrying contrasting stitching and matching pockets as well as rawhide ties. The peacock was now a world away from the postboy.

Waistcoats for Formal Wear and Cummerbunds

The double-breasted white piqué or linen waistcoat with a deep roll collar dominated formal evening wear during the earliest years of this century, although some smart dressers preferred a single-breasted five-button model with short rounded points and a rolled collar. In 1923 a novelty evening waistcoat, a backless model, was introduced in London and brought home by visiting Americans, who won the envy of their peers. The backless waistcoat was usually single-breasted, since fashionable Londoners by this time had decided that the double-breasted white waistcoat had been overpopularized. Two of the most popular single-breasted evening waistcoats of the late twenties were a three-button model featuring double-breasted lapels with rounded corners and another three-button model with a V opening and angular lapels.

The dinner jacket was making great

The postboy waistcoat of 1938, a classic then as well as in earlier and later years, was made of flannel or box cloth in yellow or another color and had lapels and flaps on its pockets. Here it is worn with a tweed jacket and cavalry twill slacks. From Esquire, May *1938.*

The double-breasted linen waistcoat for formal day wear in 1934 had wide lapels and a horizontal line across the bottom. From Esquire, June 1934.

The white piqué formal evening waistcoat of 1934 had wide-angle lapels that complemented a big wing collar. From Esquire, November 1934.

headway, and one reporter covering the Palm Beach scene noted: "The popular waistcoat is black, and in most cases this garment is cut single-breasted with a 'V' opening. Three or four buttons are used. Silk is practically the only material used in the blacks, and in most instances it is a ribbed silk or grosgrain, to match the facings of the lapels. Fancy patterned silks are not worn by the best dressed men at Palm Beach.

"White piqué is also employed in this style of single-breasted waistcoat, but never white silk, and one of the touches that are favored by some of the smartest dressed men is a waistcoat with soft rolling collar. This is achieved by constructing the collar in such a manner that at the top of the garment it is buttoned down rather than sewed down. This permits the collar to be pressed out flat on the inner side and then, when worn, buttoned back into place.

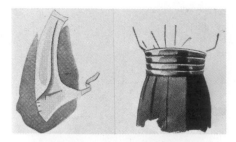

(left) The backless waistcoat with only a strap and buckle at the waistline was regarded as more comfortable than one with a back. (right) The pleated cummerbund in 1940 came in black, midnight blue, or maroon. In later years plaids and checks were adopted. From Esquire, November 1940.

"Another one of the dress accessories that has received slightly greater favor this year is the cummerbund, a black silk sash for wear instead of the waistcoat on warm evenings" (Men's Wear, Mar. 21, 1928).

A significant 18 percent of the best-dressed men attending the Princeton junior promenade in 1928 wore the

A blue, gold, and black patterned silk cummerbund with tie to match was worn with a gold-color silk shantung dinner jacket and dark blue dress trousers. From Esquire, February 1954.

evening tailcoat. The white waistcoat was of a white washable fabric, white silk no longer being considered the correct material in circles where dress traditions were observed. Those students who wore the dinner jacket favored the black single-breasted waistcoat of a material that matched the facing on the lapels of the jacket.

In 1933 the cummerbund came to the fore as an accessory for the white mess jacket, which looked much like a tailcoat cut off at the waistline. Quite narrow in width, some of the cummerbunds were in plain black silk, but many more were in bright red and dark blue. And while the mess jacket's popularity was short-lived, it did open the door to the white dinner jacket for summer formal wear and helped make Americans cummerbund-conscious.

By the mid-thirties the colored silk waistcoat had caught on despite, as Esquire observed in the November, 1935, issue, "the head shaking of the conservative element who felt that men would never depart from the traditional black and white for evening wear." With the new midnight-blue dinner jacket, many fashionable dressers wore a maroon silk waistcoat and a red silk breast-pocket handkerchief. "Color creeps into casual evening wear," noted Esquire, deciding that the new midnight-blue shade was correct for dinner parties at home, stag gatherings, and Southern resort wear— "all those not-quite-dress occasions." Warm-weather adaptations of the new formal waistcoats came in pale or vivid solid colors and in India madras plaid.

Hailed as important new formal-wear accessories were a double-breasted waistcoat and a wing collar with wider wings. This was scarcely headline news, but there was comparatively little variety in formal evening attire from season to season, and Apparel Arts observed in 1934 that it was "usually a period of ten or eleven years before any radical changes become noticeable." In 1937 Apparel Arts, commenting on the fact that the Depression had "stiffened the standards of formality in after-dark apparel," de-

cided that the new designs of waistcoats were of particular significance: "Most of them are single-breasted. Special favor has greeted single-breasted waistcoats with roll collars and very sharp points." And in 1938 Men's Wear, covering the first night of the London opera season, reported: "Waistcoats with points that were short yet not so wide spread, the garments having inverted pleats above the pocket so as to give more fullness to the chest, were the one outstanding new note in men's evening attire" (June 8, 1938. p. 30).

"Rules of formality are as strict as

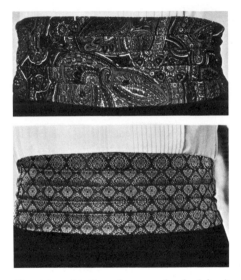

Two types of patterns in cummerbunds: (above) paisley in 100 percent cotton velvet; (below) snowflake pattern in 100 percent acetate (1971–1972). [AFTER SIX ACCESSORIES]

those governing a young ladies' finishing school with the possible exception of a curfew hour," Esquire noted in January, 1940, as a preface to a list of tips on correct formal attire. As for the waistcoat, the fashion pundits had this to say: "Today most vests are backless with adjustment buckle. Always wear the waistcoat snugly." Later that year Esquire presented still another feature on correct evening dress. This time it concentrated on the backless waistcoat first introduced in the twenties: "The backless waistcoat,

The pearl-gray backless waistcoat or cardigan for formal day wear is washable (*1971–1972*). [AFTER SIX ACCESSORIES]

Two backless vests are straight-cut across the bottom and finished with four satin buttons: (*left*) black mohair and worsted with satin trim; (*right*) paisley-pattern cotton velvet (*1971–1972*). [AFTER SIX ACCESSORIES]

tailored either in white piqué, black or midnight blue silk, has become an established fashion simply because the absence of extra fabric in back makes it much more comfortable than those with backs." It also stated that the waistcoat should be short enough to be concealed by the sides of the tailcoat. By this time the cummerbund was immensely popular, and *Esquire* observed: "The pleated cummerbund in black, midnight blue or maroon silk may be substituted for the black, midnight blue or white waistcoat with the evening jacket, either the midnight blue or white being acceptable for resort wear."

In 1948 *Esquire* launched the "bold look." For summer formal wear this was translated into a lightweight white worsted dinner jacket with wide, rolling, peaked lapels instead of a shawl collar, worn with a white rayon twill cummerbund, "a new high fashion which is in step with the new dinner jacket."

Formal wear in the latter half of the fifties exploded with color. "Parfait" colors, *Esquire* called them and, in February, 1955, devoted a double-page spread to these fashion-fresh concoctions: dinner jackets of silk and Orlon in strawberry, blueberry, and raspberry colors with matching ties and cummerbunds. As the decade drew to a close, the shorter, shapelier suit silhouette called the "Continental look" was adapted for evening clothes. The result was a dressier look with mohair dinner jackets with peak lapels and satin piping and braid, worn with matching bow ties and cummerbunds in jacquard, checkerboard, and honeycomb designs.

By the mid-sixties the Peacock Revolution had erupted in the United States, but it had little if any immediate impact on formal wear. By 1969, however, fashion journalists were writing in *Gentlemen's Quarterly,* "The peacock has replaced the penguin and once-sacrosanct traditional formal wear has been assailed by startling— but more elegant than ever—fabrics, designs and colors." Yet, despite the color wave black remained as elegant as ever, and so did the white piqué waistcoat. The outfit of white tie and tails and waistcoat was still the only correct one for the groom and guests at a formal evening wedding.

In fact, as the 1970s progressed, black-and-white formal wear became increasingly popular with younger men through the use of new and unusual fabrics and subtle refinements of the classic silhouette. The cummerbund, however, lost some standing because of the growing popularity of the six-button double-breasted Edwardian dinner jacket, so high-buttoned that a cummerbund was superfluous, and the advance of dress trousers with a traced waist. Yet for the semiformal summer evening wedding the colored cummerbund was still being worn with the white dinner jacket. And now that there was some variety at last in formal wear, the cummerbund, with a new look, might stage a comeback and be more popular than ever. For the safe and often-boring predictability of formal attire was no more. The Peacock Revolution had seen to that.

Dress Shirts

Mrs. Hannah Montague of Troy, New York, is credited with creating the detached collar, which, as Cluett Peabody & Co. has put it, was "to hold the world by the neck for one brief, shining century." Legend has it that one day in 1820, to reduce the drudgery of producing a fresh shirt every day for her blacksmith husband, Mrs. Montague simply snipped off the collar and washed it. Thus was born the first detachable collar.

1900–1910

By the turn of the twentieth century, years before the advent of mass

(left) Collars of many different styles became nationally popular as a result of Joseph Leyendecker's drawings of the Arrow collar man.

(below) The Arrow collar man of 1902 wore a high starched collar and a pleated-bosom shirt.

production, one plant with 6,000 employees was turning out 5,000 dozen collars a week. There were then approximately 400 distinctly different styles of collar, a fact that was to move *Esquire* to look back and decide: "Of all the absurd notions man has managed to hang himself with, the detached, starched collar stands as a singular monument to the extent of his foolishness" (May, 1969).

Not that soft shirts were not to be had in the first decade of this century. The Sears, Roebuck and Company catalog of 1900, for instance, listed "Men's Soft Negligee Shirts—made in the way that we think a shirt ought to be made to give perfect satisfaction. The material is a light colored madras cloth, spring weight with colors woven clear through (not printed). The length of the shirt is full 36 inches, not 30 or 32 inches, like most cheap shirts. This shirt has double yoke back, fine white pearl buttons, patent extension neck band, shaped sleeves and is cut full size, made in light plaid and fancy stripe patterns, fast color and will wash and wear beautifully. Sizes $14\frac{1}{2}$ to 17 only. A remarkably good shirt at a remarkably low price." That price was only 48 cents.

There were also soft shirts with attached soft collars in such fabrics as chambray, linen, percale, oxford, flannel, and cotton, as well as a fine twilled sateen for comfortable summer wear. But the well-dressed man at the turn of the century, anxious to be considered a man of property and propriety, ignored the soft shirt, regarding it as only a notch or two above a common work shirt. The stiff-bosom shirt with a detached starched collar indicated that the wearer was a white-collar gentleman who used brain power rather than muscle power.

In Cluett Peabody's Arrow line of 1900 there were twenty styles of starched collars of the poke type, a plain standing collar without tabs. These varied in their heights, front and back, ranging from a collar measuring $2\frac{3}{4}$ inches in front and $2\frac{3}{8}$ inches in back to one of $2\frac{3}{8}$ inches in front and 2 inches in back. There were also many wing collars, high standing collars folded back on both sides; some wings had small tabs and narrow openings, while others had broader tabs and wider openings. A collar button, of course, was essential to close any style of detached collar.

The array of shirt fabrics and colors was impressive. Bold stripes, in blue and white, red and white, lavender and white, and deep burgundy and white, were very popular. So were tiny polka dots and small, widely spaced patterns. Bosom-front shirts, plain or pleated, usually had detachable collars of linen, but cuffs, whether attached or separate, were most often of the same material as the shirt body.

By 1906 fashion emphasis had moved from standing collars in poke or wing styles to the turned-down, or fold, collar, and the figured shirt had gained in popularity. The "Arrow collar man" was celebrating his first birthday. Created by Joseph Leyendecker, the most famous fashion artist of the period, the Arrow collar man was considered to be "a hunk of male magnificence." Cluett Peabody surveyed his assets: "Languorous lid, the eyes piercing. The chin noble, the mouth innocent. Overall, an air of imponderable calm. Ah, but what power beat at that gate of purity!" The Arrow collar man became the recipient of fan mail, marriage proposals, and suicide notes and the subject of poems and songs. In the next dozen years he drove sales of Arrow's 400-odd collar styles to $32 million. His sex and sales appeal would remain unchallenged until the next decade, when the memory of a World War I uniform with its soft attached collar

The high-band stiff collar and the small-knot tie were popular around 1910 not only with men but also in women's fashions, as in this motoring scene. [CLUETT PEABODY & CO.]

would prompt the ex-doughboy to free himself from the starched detached collar once and for all.

1910–1920

A notched collar was introduced in 1911 as "the easiest collar to put on and take off. It is even easier to take a notch collar off than it is to put it on—all you do is to put a finger under an end and flip it off. It saves time, temper and money. It insures a close meeting collar. It prevents the ripped out buttonholes, the torn fingernails, the metal collar buttoner." Shirts with detached collars now usually had plain bosoms, although there were a variety of styles with piqué bosoms. Shirt bosoms measured from $13\frac{1}{2}$ by 8 inches to 16 by $9\frac{1}{2}$ inches, and Sears, Roebuck and Company, advocating a

Stiff white collars and boldly striped shirts were fashionable in 1912. [CLUETT PEABODY & CO.]

A new fashion at Palm Beach in 1939 was a beach shirt made of large cotton bandanna handkerchiefs. From Esquire, *June 1939.*

Three shirts popular in 1935, shown with various accessories: (left to right) a double-striped broadcloth with a pinned collar, a blue pleated-bosom shirt with a white collar and cuffs, and a soft pink shirt with a separate tab collar. From Esquire, *September 1935.*

(left) A casual shirt made of a lightweight wool plaid fabric shown in detail on the umbrella. This model also appeared in rayon. (right) A knitted cotton shirt with red-and-blue cross-stripes. From Esquire, *July 1944.*

Shirts

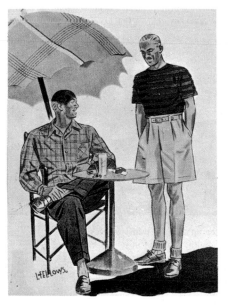

tions, with a low-set straight-front model the preferred shape. The attached collar worn by the Southern undergraduate had grown considerably shorter in 1928, with only 40 percent reaching a height of 3 inches or more. About 10 percent of the collars were worn pinned, and 5 percent buttoned down.

At the University of Southern California coarse weaves of oxford, cheviot, and basket-weave fabrics in white and blue were the favored shirtings, and green, which was declining in popularity in the East and Midwest, was still extremely popular there, both plain and with white stripes set an inch or so apart. The Barrymore shirt with long collar points and no neckband, named in honor of John Barrymore, was still being seen on this campus, with students registering a preference for 3-inch or longer points on their soft collars. At the Berkeley campus of the University of California, however, the Barrymore was rarely seen, the students there showing a partiality for collar points less than 3 inches long. A "milkman's shirt," a coarse cotton in equal narrow black and white stripes, was a campus favorite.

Although President-elect Herbert Hoover with his Berwick collar, a neck-confining $2\frac{1}{2}$ inches in front and 2 inches in back, raised the hopes of the collar business, the detached collar was all but gone by 1928.

A 1929 university style survey of shirts and collars (*Men's Wear*, Nov. 20, 1929, p. 20) covered the same territory as the 1928 survey. Illustrating this second survey was a photograph of a square-jawed Yale man wearing a blue-and-white–striped madras shirt with the newest collar seen on the Yale campus, one with short pinned points. The picture caption said that this combination was being worn by almost two out of three Yale men. The survey revealed that, as predicted the previous year, the number of shirts with button-down collars had jumped from 9 to 20 percent of the total at both Princeton and Yale during the intervening twelve months. "It comes

in oxford—the most popular shirting—and is being favored in white and solid colors." In fact, the percentage of oxford, which was rising in 1928, had almost doubled by the fall of 1929. The tab collar continued to be important at both universities and was being worn especially with clothes in the English cut (the fact that the visiting Prince of Wales had favored the tab collar was of no small significance). The newest collar, however, was a model with short rounded points worn with a pin, seen most often in fairly deep, fine stripes. Among the colored shirts, blue was still the most popular.

At New England universities all-white shirts had dropped in popularity, while blue-and-white shirts had advanced and green and green-and-white shirts had made a strong comeback. Along with the increase in colored shirts there had been a greater increase in oxford and madras fabrics. It was also significant that, though still in the minority, the button-down collar had risen in popularity and the tab collar was beginning to gain strong support, too. (In 1928, the button-down had been "almost entirely out of the picture.")

Important style developments in the Midwest during the fall of 1929 were

The pinned collar, favored from 1928 to the mid-thirties, was worn with pins that went through the collar and collar bars that snapped on the points.

The button-down collar with a soft roll and the points buttoned in place has been popular in varying degrees in every decade since 1920.

the increase of colored and fancy shirts, the gain of oxford fabrics, the acceptance of button-down collars, and the growing number of pinned collars, all of which could be interpreted as a compliment to the fashion impact of Princeton and Yale. The number of colored and fancy shirts had actually increased from 26 to 29 percent of the total, most of the gain being registered in blue, tan, and multicolor stripes. The share of oxford had jumped from 23 to 43 percent, whereas broadcloth was now favored by only one out of three college men.

An increase in fancy shirts and oxfords was also noted at Southern universities. At the University of Virginia, for example, cross-striped shirts with soft attached collars were very much in vogue, the stripes usually being spaced from $\frac{1}{2}$ to $\frac{3}{4}$ inch apart. The percentage of button-down collars was rising there, too, although at a slower pace than in the Midwest.

By 1929 students at the University of Southern California, who just the year before had still been wearing the Barrymore collar, had switched to collar-attached shirts with points less than 3 inches long. Green, still popular on the West Coast in 1928, had dropped, and blue and tan were now

The plain collar with medium-length points has been regarded as a basic fashion. It enjoyed its greatest popularity during the 1920s and 1930s.

The tab collar, with the points held in place by tabs under the knot of the tie, made fashion news in the late 1920s and the 1930s and was revived in the 1960s.

the undisputed leaders. Broadcloth, in third place at Princeton and Yale, was still the favorite fabric there, accounting for 55 percent of the shirts being worn. The pinned collar had attracted the greatest number of fashion converts, but the button-down collar, which was gaining in all other sections of the country, was just starting to be popular with California students.

In August, 1929, *Men's Wear* surveyed Wall Street and the shirt and collar fashions being worn in lower Manhattan, where, according to the writer of the report, men continued to maintain a high standard of sartorial perfection:

"Cool shirtings are to be seen on more than half of the fashionably dressed men," he observed. "Madras reigns supreme with 44 percent favoring it, while silk, also evidently chosen for comfort, is favored by seven percent. Broadcloth is worn by a quarter of the men as opposed to its heavier companion, oxford, which is only to be seen upon 14 percent of these perspiring mortals. Miscellaneous fabrics include linen and flannel.

"The most interesting developments in the matter of shirt colors, as contrasted with those prevalent among this class of men last winter, is the decrease of white and the increase of stripes. Almost a quarter of the shirts now are of the striped variety as contrasted with a fifth in 1927. The solid color shirt has also advanced in numbers with a corresponding decrease among the whites. White constitute 45 percent of the total now as contrasted with 54 percent then. Miscellaneous shades include gray, gray and white, tan and white, lavender, lavender and white, and various combinations of the colors already mentioned. The white pin or pencil stripe on a blue ground seems to stand quite high in popularity, while the blue stripe on white is also favored by a great many of the financiers. Cross stripes may be seen, but to a very limited degree, for they are worn by only one percent of the total.

"It is found that 52 percent of all the well-dressed brokers and bankers checked favored the starched or stiff collars. In comparison with the last analysis made during the winter months this total of starched collars shows a slight decrease (5 percent), which is to be expected with the thermometer registering 90 degrees in the shade. As a matter of fact, the predominance of starched collars indicates the style consciousness of these men during the torrid summer heat.

"A similar calculation reveals that 35 percent of the financiers favored various types of soft attached collars, including plain white, striped, and solid colored. Practically all these collars were of the 3-inch point variety with pins, and only a small number of men wore the buttondown collar. Note that six percent of the men showed a preference for a short point soft unattached collar, which style will gradually increase in popularity. The upward trend of this style is undoubtedly largely due to the influence of the Prince of Wales tab collar. Many of these short point collars were worn with a collar pin.

"Reports from different style sources in this country and abroad have previously emphasized the importance of the Prince of Wales type collar. The fact that this model, made in the correct, fine striped shirts, is available for the masses will tend to accelerate the national acceptance of it. Note that not one man was seen wearing this English collar in a solid colored shirting, every one being of the extremely neat striped fabric in one or two colors

The Barrymore collar with a low-set front and points 4¼ to 5 inches long was named for the actor John Barrymore, who wore it in the late 1920s. Its popularity lasted into the 1930s, especially with Hollywood stars and others in California.

on white. During the past six months a decline in solid color or striped starched collars to match shirts has been registered."

It would not require another six months to register a decline in the national economy; the stock market crash was only weeks away. Many fortunes would be wiped out before the end of this decade, and yet fashion would survive despite the Depression. In fact, the thirties would produce some of the most elegant men's fashions of the century.

1930–1940

In the depths of the Depression, when in retrospect we sometimes have a tendency to imagine a national chorus singing "Brother, Can You Spare a Dime," menswear buyers noted that despite the great amount of unemployment men were actually buying more clothes. Although it was unlikely that retailers all over the United States could paint such an optimistic picture in that dark period, there were still many men affluent and optimistic enough to continue investing in their wardrobes. There were, for example, those coteries of the very rich who still wintered in Palm Beach,

where their life-style continued to intrigue members of the fashion press, who, in turn, passed on their findings to menswear manufacturers and retailers.

A Palm Beach style survey conducted by *Men's Wear* in the winter of 1931 stressed the fact that a gentleman dressed in the Palm Beach mode possessed "that indefinable ability to wear clothes well," which, among other things, meant that "his neckwear was in good taste and his shirt blended with his outfit. Even a shirt can express a personality. If ill-fitting and slovenly worn, it denotes poor judgment and carelessness. A well-fitting shirt in tasteful color is expressive of efficiency and cosmopolitanism.

"Variety in colored shirts is the most interesting style news in this line from Palm Beach. About one-half of the men were wearing colored shirts of some kind. Blue and white has spurted from four percent last year to 15 percent, the leading position in the fancy field. A very high proportion of these are in narrow equal width stripes, which are becoming more important, not only in this color, but in practically all shades and white. A few were in very small checked effects, which are well liked by some of the best

turned out men. Blue came next with 12 percent, a decrease of 7 percent. While many of these were in medium and light shades, several were in very dark tones.

"Tan, tan and white, green, green and white and grey and white were favored by small percentages.

"Oxford is again the leading fabric with this class of men. Tied for second place are madras and broadcloth. The narrow equal width stripes were most frequently noted in oxford and madras shirts. End-and-end madras was favored by 10 percent, silk by seven percent and chambray and flannel proved to be minority styles.

"The most popular collar is the attached style with points measuring three to three-and-a-quarter inches long. Pinned points were worn by 45 percent of the men. The pins were plain gold collar pins or those showing golf clubs, polo mallets, riding crops or other sporting articles. There has been a decline in the wearing of plain attached collars. Only 17 percent of the men favored this type.

"White stiff collars were favored by one out of every ten men. These had short to medium length points. Buttondown collars were seen on shirts in plain white, solid colors or stripes. The

The California collar, with points 4½ to 5 inches long, was worn in the 1930s by Clark Gable and others throughout the country.

The tabless tab collar had points slightly longer than those of the tab collar and usually was worn with a pin. It was favored in the 1930s and 1960s.

The Windsor, or spread, collar was designed to accommodate the Windsor-knot tie, which was larger than the conventional four-in-hand tie of the 1930s.

short point pinned collar is another fashion in good standing" (Mar. 25, 1931, p. 77).

By 1934 *Men's Wear* was reporting that "issues for Fall in shirts as in politics are split. It may be said that one-half of the country is determined to dress well (which means appropriately), while the other half is bent on dressing up. In their shirt demands, the discriminating ask for materials to blend well with their tweed and cheviot suitings, and the colorings are strong. Those who buy shirts as they would order dessert at dinner are insisting upon a different type of garment—softer, lighter colors and more—well, formality isn't exactly the word, but it will have to do.

"The seductive use of color has lent itself admirably to treatment via the candy-stripe motif and these effects are to be seen in some quantity in the swatch books of the better producers. Two and two weaves, or constructions that look like them, are popular media for these stripes, which are frequently of two tones and often of three. The very last scream is a plain yet most clever window-pane design, with eighth and quarter inch stripes formed of dark cross lines against light grounds. British stripes, both in woven and printed fabrics, are still in the picture and indeed, the printed fabrics are so cunningly contrived in this day and age that from a distance of a few feet only the most practiced and discerning eye can distinguish between them and the woven goods.

"Checks are less in evidence even than last year, yet when they are seen it is noteworthy that they are very smart, made so by coloring as in the case of a green and tan gingham pin check.

"To leave the high style trend and to go the other way of the route, in the volume merchandise class there is just as much demand for what might be termed the 'dressy' shirt as there is for the more negligee article in the high style field. Demi-bosoms, a variety of pleats and hard collar models are to be the order of the day if merchants know what they are doing.

Both men in this illustration wore shirts with short-point collars, close-ups of which appeared at right. Also shown at right were a tattersall waistcoat and striped elastic suspenders. From Esquire, *February 1934.*

"Revival of interest is noted in demi-stiff bosom shirts, with stripes running either way and not infrequently with trick stud holes and center pleats. Sometimes the center pleat is omitted. The pleated bosom shirt is also well in the running and for those who command a novelty trade which can afford a good price, there is being shown a mushroom pleated demi-bosom. Cheviot shirtings, if you have the trade that can afford them, are sure to be a leader in the fall high style group. In stripes with grounds in deep tones, they are extremely smart and trim.

"It is being said here and there that a demand for silk and silk-and-something mixtures is noticed. In the high grade shirtings and in the custom and 'customized' lines nearly every one has a range of silks and this touch of silk is carried down into the volume trade in one or two outstanding instances. There has been no storming of the barriers for silk shirts, mind you. That is not the point. The fact is, though, that there is such a sufficiently substantial demand that volume houses with widespread trade have made it a point to have a very nice silk assortment.

A mid-thirties look: the striped lightweight oxford shirt in a very fine mesh. From Esquire, *July 1935.*

"As if to make sure, however, that the multiplicity of collar styles will not be merged into a smooth drabness of attached and laundered to match, there has appeared upon the scene a new type of button-down. This collar is cut away and spreads abruptly in the manner of the collar which has been so long favored by the Prince of Wales and is, of course, secured at the points by means of a buttonhole and button, giving a neat look" (Aug. 8, 1934, p. 16).

The British fashion influence was more dominant than ever during this decade, and *Esquire* recognized this fact in April, 1934, when it presented an all-English selection of fashion notes, "all items of London origin, although established in American acceptance, at least within that numerically small but fashionably important group of business and financial leaders who set the seal on this country's fashions." Among the fashion items were the dark striped shirt and the starched collar and demibosom shirt with horizontal stripes. The editors noted: "Starched collars are on the way back, there's no denying it, but the makers are offering a nice gesture of meeting the diehards halfway, by incorporating the eyelet holes for the collar pin, which are so popular in soft collars. This relieves the formality of the starched collar and has a practical advantage, too, in that it keeps the knot of the tie from slipping down." Another item that year that concerned the starched collar was a soft shirt made in a neckband style and worn with a starched collar.

Impressed by the undeniably elegant British look, *Esquire* in June of that year featured an oxblood-color shirt in oxford cloth with an attached round collar. It was, said the editors, very effective against a black-and-white herringbone suiting, especially when coupled with a black foulard tie with red-and-white spots.

Since the American man was finally getting a truly lightweight summer suit, it was time that he had a choice of diaphanous shirts to wear with it. By 1935 the choice extended from sheer fabrics looking like regular shirtings but much lighter to open effects, nets, and meshes. "There is hardly a shirtmaker who isn't showing a range of these wide-open materials," reported one fashion journalist.

"There are open weaves for different kinds of dress, business or sports. The former are usually both sheer and smooth. The drop-stitch broadcloths and lenos are especially prominent. In these it is possible to get a shirt that resembles a spring garment as far as pattern and appearance goes, but is infinitely cooler and lighter.

"Linen and cotton crashes to harmonize with clothing are being offered. Naturally, they are loosely woven and porous, and their absorptiveness is another quality that is expected to recommend them to public favor. The same slubs that crisscross the linen suitings are to be found in the shirtings. Cotton dealers have quickly offered linen replicas, some of which are being shown with high-colored slubs, such as grey on yellow.

"Chambrays and zephyrs, among the more conventional shirtings, are much as usual, but yarns are finely spun to achieve the considerably lighter weight.

"Color has entered the picture with vigor, all these fabrics being seen not only in white, but also soft and deep shades of blue, pale tan, brown, yellow and soft green.

"Collars are evoking a lot of attention—the majority being in the ordinary $2\frac{7}{8}$ inch point attached model. The buttonless collar, which did well in New York last summer, is being bought in mesh and open weaves. And the widespread collar worn by the Duke of Kent is being promoted this spring by some of the leading retail houses of the country.

"The fact that the shirtings for summer are divided into the business and the sportswear types has some bearing on merchandising plans. The public's attention should be called to this distinction" (*Men's Wear*, Apr. 10, 1935, p. 31).

Esquire proved that color had "entered the picture with vigor" in September, 1935, when it showed a red batiste shirt and a canary-yellow broadcloth on one page and, on the next, a vibrant blue houndstooth-check cotton with the Duke of Kent's widespread collar. Under the headline "The Man of Affairs Returns to Town" the magazine's fashion department presented appropriate accessories for executives, which included what the editors considered the outstanding fashion note: a wider-knotted wine-color tie on a blue pleated-bosom shirt with starched white collar and cuffs.

The Prince of Wales and his younger brother the Duke of Kent continued to dominate the news of men's fashions. In 1936, when the stiff white double linen collar was more popular than ever with Englishmen not only during business hours but also for leisure wear and at smart race meetings, it went without saying that the two royal personages had taken the lead in the revival. In fact, there was a collar known as "the Prince" (an exact copy of what they were both wearing at the time), cut with a small tie space but featuring a spread at the points of about 4 inches. For the man with a long neck who was knowledgeable enough to avoid a shallow collar, there was a stiff collar in which the points were not spread so far apart, the top did not meet, and the neckband was higher, giving the impression of a higher collar. Another collar that was especially smart with business clothes had an opening wide enough in front to allow the knot of the tie to sit high and a more conservative spread. The exact measurements of this collar were $1\frac{1}{2}$ inches at the back, $1\frac{3}{8}$ inches in front, and $1\frac{5}{8}$ inches for the spread in front when the collar was on the neck.

The smartest shirts seen in the spring of 1936 had heavy stripes on pale grounds, replacing the hitherto-prominent checks and plaids. *Men's Wear* viewed the situation thus: "Bold candy stripes alternating with fine hairlines get an exceptionally good rating. Deep and vivid stripes on pale-shade grounds signify a major trend. Front-rank in this category are

The short rounded collar of this pleated-bosom shirt was high fashion in the years 1935–1938. It was worn with a small-knot four-in-hand tie.

vari-colored lines done in tones adapted from Tyrolean costumes. The stripes are irregularly arranged and show up in different colors. One, for example, includes yellow, green, red, blue and grey.

"Color combinations exhibit the artistic touch. A pale straw shade is used to very good advantage in the backgrounds. It furthers the thought of getting away from the very dark colors that have become universally popular for spring and summer wear, and even from the dusty shades. Against the light straw-color ground, deep stripes look very well. New and smart are the dull red and green stripes used in this way. The browns are rich and dark for the most part, and blue and wine continue to be good.

"Satin stripes give depth to many of the shirtings. This construction feature of raised stripes in plain white or color is a potent style note. Most satin stripes are about $\frac{1}{8}$ inch wide. Such stripes are very much seen in the shirtings of English custom shops, not to mention the best-grade shirts here.

"Collar models are distinguished by extremes. On one hand is the long-point style with points that measure $3\frac{1}{2}$ inches. Set on a low-cut band, this type has a wide spread between the points. It is more than a style shown just to be different. Its feature is that the points of the collar extend under the waistcoat when worn—a feature that many men like. The same idea is carried out in a widespread model that has less length to the points and the same spread between them. This differs noticeably from the older Duke of Kent model.

"Then there is the short-point type, seen with both sharp and rounded points. Of late some of the leading stores have been experiencing a growing demand for the shorter points. In between these types are the more staple models, the plain 3-inch and the buttondown. The latter may be either low-cut with fairly long points or well-set-up with shorter points.

"Changes in the fabric situation are arresting. First of all, silk shirts are

The short-point button-down collar was popular in stripes and checks in the years 1936–1953 and in 1964. It was spaced for the small-knot tie.

being given more room on the sartorial stage. The reaction to some of the autumn offerings is so encouraging that some of the lines are stressing different kinds of silk. One is a heavy 24-mummy [momme] fabric that has all the earmarks of the custom cloths. Others are lighter. These are mainly in the off-white, cream shade. Spongy crepe is another cloth that is getting a play. Its rough texture, absorptive qualities and cool appearance commend it strongly. Even the staple fabrics are showing the effects of ingenious engineers. A twill broadcloth is one of the interesting innovations in this widely used material. Oxford, too, is being done in twills."

Summer shirts were prominent in the news again in 1936. The field, according to *Men's Wear,* was "virgin. There's no unwilling public to be conquered and wheedled and won over. Nobody *wants* to be uncomfortable." The fabric was the main point of discussion. There were "materials that have been subjected to the new style of finishing that rids them of lint, fuzz and loose fibers and increases their porosity without diminishing their tensile strength—the so-called 'air-conditioned' process. It is an ideal fabric for the man to whom comfort is the main consideration in warm

The eyelet collar, in rounded or angle style, had tiny holes with a stitched edging in which to insert a collar pin. It was worn in the 1930s and 1960s.

weather. This fabric is available in a full range of solid colors and makes up as good looking a shirt as the more closely woven fabrics.

"For the man who wants to be dressy as well as comfortable, a variety of chambrays is provided. They make up a dressy type of shirt with the plain or wide-spread collar, fused or not. The novelty slubs and nubs afford a wide choice of patterns for the man seeking variety. The lightweight ginghams, batistes, seersuckers, lightweight oxfords and meshes for the coming summer season are lighter and airier than ever.

"Drop-stitch zephyr broadcloths sound a stronger note than they did last year. Some of the shirts of this fabric have a screen-like appearance. Cord effects and an arrangement of the drop-stitches sometimes give the shirt the appearance of being self-striped. The drop-stitch has put windows in the shirt. The drop-stitch idea is a 'natural' in the trend toward ventilation in all items of summer wear.

"As far as color is concerned, deep tones are acknowledged to be safe promotions. The lightweight oxfords will predominate but a smaller quantity of sheer-weight fabrics will be seen in meshes and porous weaves. While deep blue or navy—the daddy of the deep

tones—is the No. 1 seller, a sharp rise has been noted in chocolate and the slightly lighter browns, and also in maroon or burgundy. Dark green will be more active this summer and will be seen in shirts worn with the lighter colored summer suits.

"Maize is again a sound favorite in the sheer fabrics, including the newer drop-stitch shirts. Light blue, tan, white and grey will follow in preference in the solid-colored lightweight shirts. Brown, green, red, blue, purple are featured in window-pane and district-check patterns.

"Collar models are varied. The widespread buttondown collar is a leader for summer, but a note is introduced from the West in the large Byronic roll, long-pointed, self-patterned batistes. While this is not new, its revival is good for the sake of variety. The fused collar will have its strong supporters, particularly among those men who want to retain a crisp appearance when the sun is boiling. The sophisticated tabless collar will be a dressy man's favorite even in warm weather. The widespread or Kent-model collar is being made up in varying heights and spreads between the points. One manufacturer is showing it with the collar 1½ inches in the back, and correspondingly low in front. He describes it as a Hollywood influence for extremely warm weather. It is the nearest thing to no collar at all that has been developed in the summer lines of collar-attached shirts. The fall-away widespread model is another favorite of the particular dresser. The larger, fuller model in the widespread collar of spring has given way to the lower and shorter-point model" (*Men's Wear*, Apr. 8, 1936).

The writer of this report concluded by offering the retailer "the scale idea—a time-tried but always effective attention-getter. Place a shirt on one scale and adjust to an even balance by placing feathers on the other. It suggests 'feather-weight' immediately." After all, he urged, "You can cash in on the new summer-shirt season if you've got what it takes—initiative, ability to dramatize porosity, coolness,

color and patterns, both subdued and bold. Go to it!"

Major developments in new shirtings for fall that year were more widely spaced stripes, horizontal stripes that crossed vertical ones to produce checks, and a merger of dark and light shades. A fashion journalist maintained: "This trend to wider-spaced stripings has a solid basis in authentic style. It comes after a natural fashion evolution, which began some years ago with the extremely fine and neat effect of the British stripings. This was followed by bolder and slightly wider motifs, and then ensued an era of checks and plaids, which rapidly soared to volume popularity. So popular did checks become that well-dressed men began to seek a new type of attractive and colorful design. Their choice has been these broader-spaced stripe effects, which now stand at the threshold of the volume market, quite new and thoroughly correct" (*Men's Wear*, Jan. 22, 1936).

The writer noted that, after the vividly colorful shirtings of recent seasons, "a touch of restraint is generally noticeable in these fall shirtings. Not only has style's fancy returned from the profound depths of coloration, but the extremely bold checks of yester-season have been toned down to smaller, more allover effects. This quieter shirt will blend better into the well-dressed ensemble than did its attention-getting predecessor."

It was not surprising, therefore, that the button-down collar was gaining momentum. What was surprising was that during this period of depression the demand for better-grade shirts was growing. In fact, a report stated that one firm was doing very well with extremely fine linen shirts, and silk shirts were seen more often in 1936 than they had been in many seasons. But more important from the point of view of high style was the growing popularity of the separate white collar. Here, as elsewhere, the widespread English influence was evident.

Men's Wear predicted that the stiff demibosom, pleated-bosom, and plain neckband shirts were all due for increases in sales, and added: "By no means remote is the possibility of the restoration to favor of the tab collar. Visiting Britishers, it is noted, are very fond of this style, and the number of its American wearers seems to be on the increase" (Jan. 30, 1937).

A preview of shirts for spring, 1937, said that the theme was color. "New spring shirts will pale the artist's palette," said *Men's Wear,* noting that one piece-goods mill had brought out authentic ice-cream colors: vanilla, strawberry, and pistachio. The silk shirt was gaining renewed popularity in solid colors and neat stripings despite strong promotion for rayon. "But on the whole," said this reporter, "men will need a lot of education before they will readily accept just anything in the way of a shirt frankly offered as rayon" (Jan. 30, 1937, p. 17).

Turning to the fashion-conscious university man, *Esquire* decided that when he packed his bags for the beginning of the fall-winter, 1937, semester, he would do well to include with his V-neck cardigan and military brush set a blue oxford collar-attached shirt and a striped starched demi-bosom shirt.

In February of that year *Esquire's* fashion department offered its readers a color guide, since colored shirts were becoming increasingly fashionable. Redheads were told to avoid brilliant colors: "Warm browns, medium greys and grey-greens are good." Fair-complexioned men were cautioned to avoid light shades of gray, tan, and yellow, and dark people ("provided the skin is not sallow") could wear rich colors to advantage. Men with gray or white hair were urged to avoid wearing pale tones "unless they prefer to be completely inconspicuous." The wise man clipped the color guide and kept it for reference, for color was indeed the dominant theme in shirts again in fall, 1938.

"The colors," said *Esquire* in its September issue, "do not run to the deep tones nor the pale pastels, but are in between. Many greens are present, taking the place of tans, which are few. Off shades are numerous and the idea of dubbing these shades with intriguing names has spread. Stripes, corded stripes, corded squares, squares and squares in combination with clipped figures, platinum stripes, all on colored grounds, are among the season's features. Iridescent grounds are seen in the lines. Many of the colors are softened by the use of grey. Herringbone and sharkskin patterns, borrowed from suitings and reduced in size to be appropriate in shirtings, are frequently seen, and satin stripes are more plentiful in the lines." As a footnote to this report, it was noted that the ensemble of shirt and slacks that had become popular around the country had also caught the fancy of shirt manufacturers, who in some instances were featuring slacks to match their shirts for fall wear.

In 1939 the sports influence was even more apparent in the shirts designed for spring. The negligee shirt, still the biggest item in men's furnishings departments throughout the country, clearly showed how creatively the dress shirt manufacturers were opposing the sports shirt that some men were beginning to wear to the business office.

"It is apparent," commented *Men's Wear,* "that leading shirt manufacturers have developed what might be termed a 'spectator sports' negligee shirt if that description is not too involved. Chief features of spring shirt lines are in the collars, the colors and the cloth constructions. No startlingly new collar idea is to be noted, but there is a decided trend to lower collars and longer points. Here the comfort feature of the sports shirt is noted. The spread for tie space continues liberal and in these low-band type collars there is just the suggestion of the old Barrymore and Byron. In the more daring measurements, these collar points have been noted as from $4\frac{1}{2}$ to 5 inches. Long points with round edges are in the lines, as are also tab collars and tabless tabs, and the buttondown collar, the doom of which has been frequently predicted, continues to survive in a slightly revised model.

"A very large proportion of collars continue to be shown in the fused variety. Old ideas in collar treatment with new variations are presented in the spring lines. In one line the celluloid stays are now placed in a pocket under the top fold, so stitched that this pocket is not discernible when the shirt is laundered. Airplane cloth in collars and cuffs has been a big hit. These have been produced only in white and solid colors. For Spring the idea has been expanded and is shown in a variety of 60 patterns and colors" (Jan. 11, 1939, p. 85).

This wealth of color was ironic in view of the fact that early in the next decade millions of American men would be wearing khaki and navy blue exclusively.

1940-1950

Cluett Peabody carried color coordination to the fullest extent when, in national advertising for Arrow shirts in 1940 and 1941, it presented harmonizing shirts, pocket handkerchiefs, ties, and shorts, with quintuple stripes predominating. Van Heusen's semistiff collar was still being sold with its "can't wilt or wrinkle, looks starched but isn't" advertising claims intact. By the mid-forties, the button-down collar worn with a bow tie assumed new fashion importance, and *Esquire* showed a chalk-striped rayon with a polka-dot bow and a pencil-striped oxford with a foulard bow. In general, however, with millions of men in uniform, there was little news in men's fashions.

Then, with World War II over and the ex-GI adjusting to civilian life, *Esquire* decided that it was time for him to dress up again. In the fall of 1948 *Esquire's* "bold look" was introduced, with the editors explaining in the November issue that "it wasn't just chance or coincidence that brought about this new concept of clothing design and merchandising. It came out because the American man who is being served today wants it that way—because he *demands* it that way.

"He's a new kind of man—this American of today. He's not the easy-

The command collar of the 1948 "bold look" had a wide spread between the points and a row of stitching set back ⅜ inch from the edge.

going, unconcerned chap that walked off to war a few years back. The war jerked him out of that complacency—made him realize for the first time that America's strength, America's leadership is *he*—the unit, the individual, the American man! And he intends never to forget that—and never to allow anyone else to forget it!

"He's the man who's responsible for the Bold Look. Dominant, dynamic, forceful—he wants his appearance to reflect those qualities, and to do so without any sacrifice of good taste. The Bold Look is his dish.

"It's his dish because the Bold Look does what no men's fashion program has ever done before: treats each piece of clothing and each accessory, not as a separate article, but as part of an interrelated ensemble; an ensemble in which each item 'goes-with' the others."

What kind of shirt would go with the broad-shouldered, wide-lapeled suit, the Windsor-knot tie, and the wider-brimmed hat of the bold look? *Esquire* said it was the widespread collar ("We call it the 'command collar'"), especially styled for wear with a Windsor knot. The fashion department gave the new bold look shirt a

full page in the November issue and the following description: "Its seam is a line of bold stitching set a half-inch in from the edge of the collar. The same bold treatment is given to the center pleat down the front; it's a good two inches wide with the stitching set a half-inch in on each side. The buttons are bigger and easy to finger. The French cuffs are longer (9½ inches around) and wider (2⅝ inches deep) and wear bigger links, such as the heavy gold discs shown." In October, 1949, with the bold look still forceful, *Esquire* promoted palladium-blue fashion tones in everything from shirts to suspenders and an iridescent hatband "with glints of Palladium tone."

In October, 1949, *Men's Wear* reported: "Manufacturers continue to be deluged with requests for nylon shirts, but at the present time it seems that those retailers who have failed to cover themselves at this time are going to be left out in the cold. According to the makers, all goods now in the market have been committed and there are no 'secret springs to tap' for either yarn or yardage." At the same time Cluett Peabody & Co. announced that no nylon shirts bearing the Arrow label would be on the market for the coming season. The story was reported in *Men's Wear* as follows:

"According to representatives of the firm, Cluett will withdraw from the nylon field for at least one season in order to check consumer reaction to their initial effort in shirts made of that synthetic. Executives of Cluett emphasized that they were not abandoning nylon and that experiments with the fabric are continuing. Market information is that the small offering that Arrow had in nylons for the current season was confined to the New York market 'to evaluate consumer reaction'" (October, 1949, p. 85).

In the same issue *Men's Wear* said: "Nylon talk continues to dominate the shirt market and major producers expect that deliveries for spring will continue to be made on an allotment basis. Rather than slacking off for the coming year, makers foresee increased interest in the synthetics despite some

complaints that the cloth is 'not a shirting fabric.'

"Some retailers feel that there will be a definite problem in counteracting unfavorable opinions formed by consumers who purchased 'parachute shirts' and those that were poorly made and sold at the prevailing prices."

1950–1960

Having successfully launched the bold look in 1948, *Esquire* started off the fifties by introducing what it termed "the most important fashion trend of the year—American Informal." The editors assured their readers that it was not a fashion slogan. Instead, it was "a much awaited clothing philosophy for men being built right into the new products. A quick look around town makes it easy to understand why the new move in fashion is a natural: Informality and ease have always been the choice but have not always been available to the typical American business man who runs the gamut from business-blue executive to full-dressed host in a single day. Now for the first time, he can feel the *part,* as comfortably as he has always wanted. Restrained, unexaggerated, the new fashions answer his demand

A pinpoint collar with angle points as guides for placement of the pin and adequate space for the smaller-knot tie of 1950.

for color, comfort, correctness and casualness—the Four C's that make it a real pleasure to wear the right clothes" (April, 1950, p. 80).

What style of shirt rated four C's? The new pinpoint collar, said *Esquire,* and for this issue it photographed two shirts to illustrate this collar style with and without tie and pin. The picture caption read: "Note the collar has straight sides to frame the smaller tie knot but the points are cut away toward the shoulders to lie flat and smooth on the chest. This collar must be worn with a two-inch pin inserted at the breakaway points. The pin should never pull the collar but simply hold it in place around the tie. The low slope of the collar makes it as comfortable as it is becoming . . . typical of all correct American Informal fashions."

In 1951 Van Heusen introduced the Van Chick shirt, which had "not a stitch showing on collar, cuffs and front." It was an attractive complement for "Mr. T," *Esquire*'s new narrow and restrained fashion silhouette, which was a very real expression of the conservative national climate of the early fifties. The following year, with Mr. T still a force to be reckoned with, *Esquire* reported in its August issue that

The widespread button-down collar became popular in 1953 with men who liked both the large Windsor-knot tie and the button-down collar.

"the big news in shirts for fall '52 centers around shorter point collars and a continuing trend to colored and patterned fabrics.

"The shorter point collars complement the lines of the natural silhouette suits while the colorful fabrics blend perfectly with the woolen fabrics that are enjoying a return to popularity.

"While the less padded jackets and nappy fabrics constitute the new trend in clothing, there will be, of course, many hard finished worsteds tailored in drape models sold. For these there are a bountiful selection of broadcloths, madrases, and other sleek shirting fabrics available and also a wide variety of vanishing band and bandless collars—many embodying constructural innovations.

"In many instances where the fancy checked, plaided, and patterned fabrics are combined with the casual collars, there is a very close relationship—almost a merging of sport and business shirts.

"Few seasons have seen a larger assortment of collar styles. In addition to the ever popular point models, there are buttondowns, widespreads, modified spreads, round points (to be worn pinned), short points, and, at the top level, a reawakening of interest in the old familiar British tabs.

"Buttondowns are appearing in many versions. Supplementing the standard types are short point versions, round point variations, and the unlined construction. Some firms have added an extreme roll buttondown wherein the cape flare is so pronounced that they must be shipped unbuttoned to prevent crushing."

The comfort and casualness that characterized the American informal look in 1950 was echoed in 1953 in the short-sleeved business shirt, which became an important factor in summer shirt sales that year. "Show them with ties that emphasize their dress-up status," *Men's Wear* urged retailers, reassuring them that the short-sleeved business shirt did not detract from sportswear sales and, in fact, meant added sales. "Use them for sales boosters" (Apr. 24, 1953).

The modified spread collar, with only a moderate spread between the points, appealed to men who, in 1953 and later years, avoided collars with extreme width between the points.

"The demand for business shirts is on the upswing again," *Men's Wear* stated in the same issue. "This trend has been credited to the new short collar styles and the increasing acceptance of colored and fancy shirtings. However, much of the new success of business shirts can be attributed to the styling of the collars and the fabric interpretations that make them even more comfortable than sports shirts for warm weather wear.

"Comfort starts at the collar in shirts and many of the current versions have been designed to give a maximum of breathing space at that point and at the same time provide neat and stylish lines at focal points of the outfit.

"This is accomplished by the vanishing band, bandless, low slope constructions of the collars combined with the use of lightweight, absorbent, and ventilated weaves in the fabrics.

"For those who prefer to retain the collar styles that they are accustomed to wear during the cool months, there are models made with round collars, buttondown collars, and the popular short point collars—also tailored of the cool fabrics and made with the increasingly popular short sleeves."

The rounded Continental collar, cut away sharply at the sides, was worn with a large-knot tie in the 1950s and 1960s.

The natural-shoulder and straight-hanging lines of Mr. T finally gave way to the Italian-inspired Continental look, which, in one way or another and in varying degrees, affected almost every item in the American man's wardrobe. Mr. T favored the pinpoint collar for his narrow tie, but the more elegant Continental look gave rise to a widespread collar that allowed ample space for a larger-size knot. Furthermore, the new shirts had softer tones and glamorous names: Tangier tan, Granada green, Bombay gray, Malacca yellow, and Persian melon. For the remainder of the decade there would be a struggle by the natural-shoulder Ivy League look and the shaped Continental look for fashion supremacy, with the result that the public would be presented with many refreshing new shirt designs reflecting the two schools of fashion.

By 1957 the Continental influence, coupled with the eventual relaxation of the conservative mood of the early fifties, resulted in a new freedom, a new assertiveness, in men's clothing that quickly became evident in more avant-garde shirtings. The university man who had tenaciously clung to chino pants and muted solid-color button-down shirts during the first half of the decade now blossomed out in the battalion-striped shirt and the rare-print shirt. The former featured contrasting dark and bright battalion stripes in a combination of gray, yellow, and red or gray, green, and blue. The rare-print shirt was a small-spaced print of the kind usually associated with neckties, cut in cotton and worn with solid-color ties, preferably knitted. The most popular colors were shades of tan, olive, and gray with hot-red accents.

For the more sophisticated man, *Apparel Arts* saw a new sophistication in its November, 1959, issue: "Muddy-colored flannels and tweeds will be supplanted by worsteds in clear tones of blue, brown and grey; brogans and droopy argyles will yield to pumps and lisles; the buttondown oxford shirt will succumb to the luster of fine broadcloth. Originality and creativity will emerge again as cardinal virtues in dress, finding expression in more inventive use of pattern, exotic materials and dramatic surface effects. Thus will the man about town clothe himself in elegance when autumn leaves again bedeck the boulevards." Photographs illustrating this new elegance in shirts showed a slate-blue shirt with a twilled bosom, a white piqué with white diamonds woven on its lustrous blue bosom, a white batiste with miniature pleats embroidered with scallops adorning the bosom, and a white broadcloth with blue huntsmen charging across it.

Noting that this look of elegance was still dominant, the fashion writer Stan Gellers wrote in *Men's Wear* in 1959: "Dress shirts approve of the hot-as-a-pistol Continental trend in clothing. Interesting fact is this: There appears to be collar and fabric to go with all the variations in the clothing picture. Ivy and otherwise. Some of the typical ideas range from Italian-inspired widespread collars (with longer points, higher bands) to new tab ideas (blunt and rounded ends, collars, etc.)."

1960–1970

"The white shirt that laughs at spots and stains," as the Manhattan Shirt Company put it, more or less summed up the easy-to-wear, easy-to-care-for shirt philosophy of the early sixties. The permanently pressed shirt made of a stay-neat blend of synthetic fiber and cotton was the fashion news in shirts until the Peacock Revolution. Then shirts appeared in flamboyant colors, shaped to the torso and having collars wide enough to accommodate the widest ties seen in many seasons, some puffing out to 5 inches.

President John F. Kennedy's predilection for the two-button suit prompted Brooks Brothers to introduce a natural-shoulder two-button model that, considering the firm's identification with three buttons, was almost revolutionary. Complementing this "JFK look" was a shirt with a new collar for the traditionalist, a modified spread permitting the use of a collar pin.

"Striped shirts are nothing new," wrote *Esquire* in April, 1963, noting the reappearance of stripes that spring. "Businessmen were wearing them at the turn of the century. 'The bolder the better,' they used to say. Then the stripes faded. Now they're back." To celebrate their return, the magazine's fashion department chose four shirts with stripes of varying intensity: a blue-and-white shirt with a wide stripe ("faintly reminiscent of an old-time favorite, the striped blazer"), a brass-toned sharp stripe ("narrower, but in a way even bolder") with a collar of moderate width, a blue-striped imported broadcloth with a spread collar and French cuffs, and a drip-dry all-cotton olive-striped shirt with a tab collar and two-way cuffs to button or link as the wearer saw fit. "In all, the word for businessmen is Striped Shirts," concluded *Esquire*.

Although *Esquire*'s fashion editors admitted in March, 1968, that there were some diehards who still retained the classic button-down collar, they assured their readers that the British were not among them and proved their point by printing an excerpt from the venerable British trade journal *Tailor and Cutter:* "The final banality of their buttondown shirts—with the buttons deliberately positioned to buckle the collar into simulated negligence." Noting that there was something of a vogue in the United States for the bloater, the very wide tie that looked best with a spread collar, *Esquire* devoted its fashion pages to a colorful spread of flamboyantly colorful widespread-collar shirts. Among them were an orange cotton broadcloth with yellow-and-green stripes and barrel cuffs, a green-and-black check of an end-and-end madras with French cuffs, a striped Beaujolais-red cotton chambray with French cuffs, a deep peach cotton broadcloth with barrel cuffs, a sheer cotton lawn in deep Beaujolais red with barrel cuffs, a yellow-ground cotton in a miniature tattersall check with a high spread collar and barrel cuffs, and a deep lavender Supima cotton with French cuffs.

The elegance that *Apparel Arts* had predicted a decade earlier flowered with the Peacock Revolution and the concomitant prominence of "name" menswear designers. For its March, 1969, issue *Esquire* gathered a group of the best-dressed men, equipped them with suits, shirts, and ties created by leading designers, and photographed the colorful results. By 1970 even the shirts in these photographs would seem tame.

Esquire considered that the new shirts of the seventies, with their tapered bodies, long-point collars, high neckbands, bold stripes, and brilliant prints, were going to be as functional as they were flamboyant. "Capable," said the fashion editor in August, 1970, "not only of moving a girl to the overwhelming emotion experienced by Daisy Buchanan upon seeing Gatsby's beautiful shirts, but also of fitting snugly beneath even the most severely shaped jacket. Thus, all excess fabric has been eliminated from the new shirts. Moreover, the collars have been designed to accommodate the large knots of Now." The solid-white shirt, said *Esquire*, had yielded place to a palette of rainbow hues, "even in once-stuffy Wall Street offices, even after dark on occasions of a certain small formality. It is part of man's liberation from the drab unimaginativeness of his apparel to the wearing of what is most becoming. In short, it has reached the point where there is no longer any clear-cut distinction between what is appropriate for the counting house and what for casual wear."

Allover geometric patterns, boldly striped silks, designs usually associated with wall tapestries—these were a few shirting examples of the "do-your-own-thing" fashion movement. The *New York Times Magazine* illustrated exactly how liberated, in sartorial terms, the American businessman had become by April 18, 1971, when it showed the following collection of "9-to-5 shirts": a geometric design printed on Italian voile; raised cotton and jacquard stripes alternating on a British cotton shirt; chickenwire-patterned panels separated by stripes on a Dacron-and-cotton shirt; fat and thin ice-cream–color stripes on a polyester-and-cotton shirt; a ribbon-and-pencil-striped cotton with French cuffs; and embroidered stripes on a puckered French-cuffed cotton.

Men's Wear in the spring of 1971 reported: "Dress shirts are ready to break for fall with a new set of ground rules to keep their star billing." The new rules were:

Stripes are growing. Pegged at 35 to 50 percent for fall, the white stripe suddenly looks right after several seasons of deep, dark colors. Both flat and textured stripes literally open up to show much more white, much more ground.

Textures add dimension. For stripes and solids, the talk is top beam [raised stripes] and tapestry textures usually at better prices in most lines.

Models are stabilized. Expect a minimum of change in the now-standard long point collar. Round ends, spreads and a few buttondowns are again reappearing in better lines where French cuffs are still a quarter of the business.

Young labels appear. Young-sounding labels bow in for the young executive with trim dimensions. These slim-cuts (to grow to at least 20 percent of the market) come through with faster cycling . . . interim offerings of fresh looks instead of reorder possibility.

Priced for volume. This time around, prices are realistically geared for volume with the greatest number of fashion looks at price points that mean business. With this, expect a dominance of polyester-cotton fashion fabrics that now reach up into higher price lines.

Solids get fancy. Still accounting for about 35 percent, solids will add percentage points with the addition of new "white-on-whites," but in color. Included: Clips, dobbies, satins, embroideries. Watch aubergine, ecru into orange, white.

Now neckwear names. For fall, a growing number of the makers are adding their names to dress shirts. Prices are on the medium to better side for this new round of fancy shirts that naturally come with coordinated ties.

New knits enter. Tricot shirts (up to five percent) will soon get a follow up with single and double knit dress shirts appearing for mid-fall selling.

The knit dress shirt came to the fore early in the seventies along with the knit suit, slacks, and jacket. A man in a polyester knit business suit might wear with it a shirt in an easy-to-wear, easy-care polyester-and-cotton blend, making his selection from a highly diversified collection of diamonds, squares, stripes, geometrics, and solid colors.

By the seventies a dress shirt was a real means of self-expression. In this fashion-wise decade one could learn a good deal about a man by looking at his shirt. For the peacock of the seventies, his shirt was his plumage.

The big, high-set collar with long points in the bold patterns of the 1970s was compatible with a high-knot tie 4½ to 5 inches wide.

Bold stripes and allover figures in a polyester-and-cotton blend were used for shirts in 1970. From Esquire, August 1970.

Three sheer styles worn in 1950: (top) an open-weave white shirt with a button-down collar; (center) an open-weave checked shirt with a spread collar; (bottom) a thin self-striped shirt with a low slope collar. From Esquire, July 1950.

The figured knitted shirt was an example of a trend toward allover designs in 1971. The 5-inch tie had figured stripes.

The collars of these four "bold look" shirts had stitching set back $\frac{1}{2}$ inch from the edge. From Esquire, July 1949.

Shirts

Shirts to make

Daisy Duchanan

shed a tear or two

With tapered bodies, long-point collars, high neckbands, bold stripes, and bold prints, these new shirts are as romantic as they are flamboyant—capable of moving a girl to the overwhelming emotion experienced by Daisy Buchanan upon seeing Gatsby's beautiful shirts—but also of fitting snugly beneath the most severely shaped jacket, for all excess fabric has been eliminated from the new shirts. Moreover, they have been designed to accommodate the big knots of Now. All these features are incorporated in the two woven-silk-and-cotton shirts in the illustration in the foreground, a Sero shirt and a Lanvin tie ($9); in the left, an Arrow shirt ($11) aided by a heavy-silk tie designed by Gant. In the three photographs at the right: a triple-weave cotton shirt ($20) and printed-jacquard tie both by Gant, and Lanvin's own shirt ($25) and printed silk tie. Center, a woven-geometric shirt ($16) and printed silk tie both by Amies, U.S.A., and a Dacron-and-Endel herringbone shirt and woven polyester tie by Pilgrim. Directly below: Ralph Lauren's cotton shirt ($12.50) and printed Qiana tie ($7), a voile shirt ($25) and printed silk tie both by Polo.

Bold Look, Command Collar. The wide spread favors the Windsor knot, the stitching is set back ½ inch from the edge. Shown in broadcloth, for business.

Command Collar, Round Points. Another new wide-spread collar style with a formal, sophisticated touch. The geometric pattern of the tie is bold without being noisy.

Forward Collar. This is the BOLD LOOK. Bold stitched low-sloped collar. The points are about 3½ inches long and they spread correctly toward the shoulders instead of pointing toward the ground.

Bold Look Button-Down. Old favorite, new casual smartness—Bold Look stitching, wider flare. Your Oxford button-down is best, of course, when sports and casual clothes are indicated.

Formal Shirts

During the stiff-necked, stiff-bosomed early decades of the twentieth
century, many comic cartoons depicted a man on his knees, collar
awry, hunting for a popped collar
button. Whether a man wore a poke
or a wing collar, two buttons were
needed to anchor it. The stiff poke
collar might measure $1\frac{1}{4}$ to 3 inches in
front and $1\frac{1}{4}$ to $2\frac{1}{4}$ inches in back.
The equally popular and equally re-
strictive wing style, a high standing
collar folded back on each side, was
considered proper for both daytime
and evening formal wear. The throw-
away celluloid collar was scorned by
fashionably dressed men but much
appreciated by waiters for its practicality.

The formal shirt of these early decades was stiff-bosomed and had
matching cuffs that might or might
not be attached. The bosom, usually

*Imaginative ideas in evening dress shirts of 1968: (top) a white
cotton shirt decorated with lace and ruffles; (lower left) a
black-and-gray–striped shirt with a matching bow tie; (lower right)
a blue cotton shirt with blue-green braided pleats. From*
Gentlemen's Quarterly, *November 1968.*

*This evening dress shirt, designed by Pierre
Cardin in 1965, had a corded piqué bosom
and collar to match, pleated ruching over a
slide fastener, and single cuffs. From* Esquire,
December 1965.

made of piqué, was set into the front
of the shirt by stitching at the shoulders and at the bottom and curved to
a rather imperfect oval. The bosom
ranged in size from a so-called regular
bosom measuring $7\frac{3}{4}$ by 15 inches to
a larger type of 9 by 15 inches; for the
shorter man there was a bosom that
measured merely $7\frac{1}{4}$ by $12\frac{1}{4}$ inches.
Most bosoms were plain, although
pleated models were available. A detachable bosom that could be slipped
over the body of the shirt, known as
a "dickey," became an essential part
of a waiter's uniform. Some evening
shirts had open fronts, which meant
that the two obligatory shirt-front
studs could be inserted before the shirt
was slipped on—a decided advantage
for the man who was not dexterous
when it came to shirt studs and collar
buttons.

By the 1920s, when "flaming youth"

was dictating so much of fashion for
both sexes, three shirt studs were as
acceptable as two, and the marcella,
a honeycomb weave, was vying with
the plain corded piqué or self-checked
piqué bosom. During this decade some
of the more affluent fashionable men
took to wearing matching bosoms,
waistcoats, and ties with their tailcoats. Such sets were custom-made
and expensive and thus had limited
popularity. Despite the tradition top-
pling of the Jazz Age, there were few
important changes in formal shirts.

It was not until the late 1930s that
the revolution in formal shirts began,
for this was the period when Ivy
League undergraduates began wearing their daytime button-down oxfords with their dinner jackets. Few
mature men followed their lead, but
the Ivy League man is generally credited with having paved the way for the

soft evening shirt. Meanwhile, the traditionalist of this period often preferred to wear with his evening shirt one of the new wing collars in which the line of the wing was practically horizontal.

The war years of the forties naturally curtailed the advance of new styling in formal shirts, but by the fifties, when the natural-shoulder daytime suit and button-down shirt prevailed, evening wear took on a more natural look too. A narrow-pleated soft-bosom shirt with a comfortable low-set collar was the perfect companion for a natural-shoulder dinner jacket with roll lapels. This was the decade of synthetic fibers, the so-called miracle fabrics, and the classic piqué evening shirt faced serious competition from the pleated or plain shirt of polyester and cotton.

By the latter half of the 1950s, when the ultraconservative "man in the gray flannel suit" made room for the man with the Continental look, evening shirts adopted an Edwardian air with tucks, pleats, frills, and eyelets. It was not unusual for the lacy cuff of one of these shirts to cascade for inches onto the knuckles of the man wearing it, but by November, 1959, *Gentlemen's Quarterly* conceded that while "elegance in evening shirts *does* mean fancy bosom treatments . . . the frilly feminine approach of recent years has been replaced by a bolder, more masculine look." To illustrate this new look, the magazine showed four evening shirts: one with buttons at the side and fine tucked pleats running horizontally across the bosom; a lattice-type–venetian-blind effect with two box-pleat panels having vertical black stitching; a scalloped, embroidered lace front with a blunt-point spread collar and small smoked-pearl buttons; and tucked pleats with a gray embroidered wave decoration down a fly front.

In December, 1965, *Esquire* predicted: "The days of the gaping shirt front are numbered." As proof it offered a full-page photograph of a revolutionary new dress shirt designed by Pierre Cardin. What made the

Ornate evening shirts were in fashion in 1969: (left) the jabot look achieved in white batiste with wide ruffles of eyelet embroidery and lace; (center) a cream-colored lustrous sheer cotton with a mandarin collar and horizontal tucked pleats; (right) a style decorated with embroidery and lace. From Esquire, *June 1969.*

difference, said *Esquire,* was the closure, a fine-tooth slide fastener extending from just beneath the neck opening; the slide itself was hidden by horizontally pleated ruching. The bosom, collar, and cuffs were made of a deep-corded cotton piqué, while the body and sleeves were made of a lighter-weight cotton broadcloth. The editors concluded by saying that they did not foresee the disappearance of the button—"just hard times." (This development brings to mind the fact that men had been grappling with gaping shirt fronts for generations; in 1900, for instance, Cluett Peabody & Co. advertised dress shirts with patent tabs to "prevent the bosom from bulging through the vest opening.")

Gentlemen's Quarterly asked this question in April, 1969: "So you think you're daring when you don those dinner shirts shaded in soft blues, yellows and pinks? Witness, then, these eye openers." The eye openers included: a terra-cotta voile with a fine-tucked front and a spread collar; a gold-color cotton with a mustard collar, cuffs, and braided, pleated bosom; a peach cotton, softly tucked at the bottom and black-embroidered on the placket and cuffs; a sky-blue Dacron, embroidery-emblazoned in front and on its back-zipped turtleneck; a white cotton with a scalloped

tucked front and a mandarin collar encircled by white lace that continued down the center of the ruffled placket; a large-collared cotton with bold black stripes on a silver-gray ground; and a bright blue cotton with blue-green braided front pleats.

By this time the turtleneck evening shirt had been introduced by Lord Snowdon, who commissioned the British shirtmaker Turnbull & Asser to create one for him in woven silk. His innovation was instantly copied in a white knit turtleneck pullover, and this combination of sportswear with a formal dinner jacket created fashion headlines for a couple of seasons before vanishing, leaving behind more durable evening shirts such as the natural-color silk with a tuck-pleat front, which in 1969 was one of the most photographed and expensive evening shirts. Not to be overlooked, however, were evening shirts of other light materials, such as voile and sheer cotton batiste, that were first seen at the Mexican resort of Acapulco.

Like everything else in men's apparel during the third quarter of the century, the formal shirt has acquired color, comfort, and fashion. Locked into a set look for generations, it is now an almost freewheeling fashion regarded as a kind of proving ground by innovative designers.

Sports Shirts

For almost three decades of the twentieth century only one sport, polo, could claim a specially designed shirt, a short-sleeved white wool jersey pullover with a turned-down collar. The golfer and the tennis player usually settled for a soft negligee shirt without a necktie and simply rolled up the sleeves. Then, in 1928, a knitted white tennis shirt came to the fore by way of the French Riviera, where it was introduced, and London, where it was adopted by such prominent sportsmen as the Marquis of Cholmondeley. The new shirt, which had a turned-down collar and opened in front for about 5 inches from the top

button, received a stamp of approval from the influential Palm Beach set when such well-turned-out men as Anthony J. Drexel Biddle were seen wearing it on the tennis courts of the Everglades Club.

1930–1940

The Depression compelled the fashion press to concentrate on the very rich for news, and this meant following them to their playgrounds. The French Riviera proved to be a gold mine for fashion journalists in the 1930s, and one of the most famous sportswear fashions that originated there was the so-called dishrag shirt. Constructed of a net weave and buttoned all the way down the front, the short-sleeved dishrag was usually in ecru or string color when it first appeared on the scene in 1933. By 1934 it was available in every conceivable color as well as in wild color mixtures, checks, overchecks, and ombré stripes. The most fashionable dishrag was the navy with an Eton collar and the sleeve and waist finished in a fringe; the front was open on the chest and was laced with a string of the same material.

Fashionable vacationers observed at Monte Carlo, Cannes, and Saint-Tropez in the mid-thirties were also partial to a navy blue cashmere pullover with the neck, puffed sleeves, and waist finished with Lastex yarn.

A report filed from the Riviera in 1934 commented on the status of the knitted polo shirt: "The ordinary solid-colored knitted polo shirt is still big, but only in the various shades of blue, nigger brown and wine red. The yellows, greens and other extreme shades have disappeared." The same reporter also noted the appearance of a new sports blouse that was a cross between the polo shirt and a pullover and was made from ecru twine or

The man in the background appeared in a loosely woven peasant linen shirt with a cord-laced front. From Esquire, *July 1935.*

macrame string. When his report is read today, it is difficult to believe that the fashionable world he wrote about was possible in the depths of a depression:

"Some of these sports blouses—I call them that deliberately because they are neither shirts nor jerseys—have most unusual collars and the fronts are always open on the chest, merely held together by a string with tassels or some fancy ending. The sleeves are generally puff, reaching just above the elbow, but I saw a few long ones, finished ribbed at the cuff with lastex yarn. Indeed lastex or rubber yarn is being much used as a finish for the necks, sleeves and waists of pullovers.

"Hunting yellow cashmere or cotton jerseys with a fisherman's neck and puff sleeves, worn with a black foulard muffler carrying a small white polka spot, and cream or white trousers, or again the yellow giving way to navy, and a scarlet handkerchief, formed an ensemble seen at some of the more exclusive villas, worn by yachting men. The whole Riviera drinks cocktails between 7 and 9:30 P.M. outside the Miramar Hotel at Cannes. I sat there on ten evenings and counted dozens of such ensembles favored by men who had come over from the surrounding villas in their yachts, motor boats or motor cars. An interesting feature was the introduction of initials cut from linen, cotton, kid or suede, about two inches deep, and stitched diagonally onto the left breast of jerseys and pullovers. Sometimes other motifs were used, perhaps a little flag, or two or three, forming a signal.

"Amongst the many new materials produced on the Riviera, I must make special mention of a very fine non-stretchable knitted fabric sometimes carrying a little tick or miniature curl. This the better class shops are cutting up by the yard for making into polo shirts that button the whole way

Two styles of sports shirts in 1938: (left) a multicolor plaid India madras; (right) a solid-color coarse cotton shirt worn with shorts having a wide waistband. From Esquire, January 1938.

down, coat fashion, having quarter sleeves finished with a turn-back of about two inches" (*Men's Wear,* Dec. 5, 1934).

By the mid-thirties the American man expected and was getting diaphanous shirts that lived up to the advertising claim "as cool as a zephyr." There were open weaves for different kinds of dress, business, and sports, and the sportswear group included some rougher textures, oxford being a particular favorite. However, patterned oxfords, though cool, had a tendency to disguise the ventilating system of the shirt. Also in the rough-looking sports shirt group were soft and porous cellular materials in honeycomb effects.

Esquire, noting in 1935 that the very rich were indeed the fashion leaders of the Depression years, headlined a page "On the Beach with the Sons of Riches" and included the perennial navy blue polo shirt worn with gray flannel slacks and a blue beret and a silk-and-wool beach shirt worn with a pair of blue sailcloth beach shorts. As the copywriter put it, "When the gilded playboys turn to bronze under the winter sun, that's when summer's beach fashions are born." Another pair of rich men's sons sketched at a fashionable resort in the summer of 1935 wore, respectively, a shirt of loosely woven peasant linen with a laced front and the "perennial" polo shirt, this time in chocolate brown.

In 1936 John Wanamaker in Philadelphia introduced a new sports shirt or jacket shirt that was called the Guayaberra, an authentic copy of the garment worn by sugar planters in Cuba. It was made of a fine-quality linen in a natural or beige color and also in dark blue, dark brown, and yellow. Its unlined collar was made to be worn buttoned or open, and its cuffs to be worn barrel or link fashion; among other styling features were side vents, a yoke, and a panel back. It was a substantial shirt for its $10 price tag, and soon Wanamaker was selling trousers made of the same material in matching or contrasting colors. The Guayaberra maintained its popularity and was seen in many different fabrics and patterns throughout the decade.

The most potent fashion influence of the twenties and thirties was the Prince of Wales. He had only to wear a simple dark blue linen sports shirt for it to become a leading fashion along the Riviera and in Palm Beach, which sportswear manufacturers and menswear retailers watched for trends. How important the moneyed and

fashion-conscious men of Palm Beach were considered is apparent in the following excerpt from a *Men's Wear* article:

"It is a little early for the sportswear picture to be completely clear and as usual much will depend upon what the arbiters of fashion see fit to wear at the better winter resorts here and abroad this month and next." Then the writer went on to illustrate the great variety to be found in sports shirts, which was especially noteworthy in view of the fact that the sports shirt per se was relatively new.

"Wherever men talk of shirt design there is also talk of jacket-shirts, single-breasted, double-breasted, with convertible collars, to be worn with or without neckties, tucked in or allowed to hang outside the pants. These shirts have shirred, pleated, tucked and norfolk backs, with and without belts. They are made in mesh and jersey fabrics, in twills and flannels, in cotton, wool and silk.

"They will not only push ahead the sport clothes idea for Summer, but they will have a powerful effect upon shirt design as a whole and undoubtedly will bring about a new era in shirt-making—regardless of the lukewarmness of public reception. No longer will a shirt be a collar, and a pair of cuffs more or less closely related to a bosom and back. The shirt is fast stepping up to the dignity of a major garment instead of walking humbly as an accessory" (Jan. 22, 1936).

By this time sportswear had been instrumental in effecting many innovations in the menswear field, not the least of which was the introduction of fabrics that in whole or in part were made of acetate or viscose yarns. The same *Men's Wear* article noted: "Both in the neckwear and in the shirting field there has been a decided tendency to 'style up' the acetates and the viscose materials. Deep, indeed downright dark, tones are conspicuous in the sport shirt collections, and here, particularly in the meshes and knitted fabrics, the viscose and acetate materials are being widely used for Spring. Producers of these yarns, in their en-

deavor to 'trade up' these fabrics in the menswear field as they have already done with a great deal of success in the women's wear trade, have adopted rigid standards of quality. One large organization that 'certifies' a fabric made with its yarn has the cloth checked in standard laboratories for tensile strength, abrasive quality, damp crocking, resistance to perspiration and color-fastness.

"In a season where prints are of great importance, the viscose and acetate constructions offer exceptional opportunities to the stylist. These fibres, when woven into cloth in the 'grey,' do not require a great deal of bleaching and show 'clean' whites. The result is that where printing is used the patterns against the white field are clearer and the tendency of the fabric to dye easily permits more brilliant harmonies and contrasts.

"Two of the outstanding fabrics in this class in the spring shirt collections are the 'brushed' acetates and the material with a suede-like finish that is being offered for double duty as a sport shirt and for street wear. There is no limit to the type of construction, however, and in the spring shirting lines there are taffetas, broadcloths, twills, tweedy ideas, oxfords, tussores and others produced by skillful intermingling of smooth and 'spun' yarns. Also there are all types of finish from dull 'matt' chalk effects to high-sheen fabrics."

In the first month of 1936 *Esquire* bypassed rich men's sons and turned the fashion spotlight on the more mature man who was affluent enough to vacation at a tropical winter resort. Acknowledging the influence of the French Riviera, the *Esquire* fashion writer said: "The past Riviera season affords the cue for the coming months at such places as Palm Beach, Miami and Palm Springs." He then predicted that fashionable men that winter season would be wearing the polo shirt of lightweight glove silk, the herringbone polo shirt of light wool, and the Egyptian cotton Romany-striped shirt in fine poplin. Equally popular that year, though it arrived from Nassau

The man in the foreground wears a cotton butcher shirt made of material like that used for the aprons worn by butchers in the south of France. From Esquire, February 1938.

(right) The splashy print shirt of silk or cotton made in Honolulu started a trend toward Hawaiian shirts in 1938. From Esquire, February 1938.

rather than the Riviera, was the shirt of fine poplin or sailcloth that was a faithful copy of the African bush shirt worn by explorers and British army officers in tropical climates. In the meantime, the most interesting sports shirt at Palm Beach was a double-breasted pullover in an oyster-shade mixture of linen and fine cotton.

By the last half of the decade almost everyone was in agreement with the *Men's Wear* reporter who observed in 1936: "Play has become a definite and most essential part of daily life, and play demands its own special apparel. The sport shirt is the big answer." The great majority of the new sports shirt styles ranged in price from $1 to $1.95

retail, although there was no lack of supply or demand for shirts selling at much higher prices.

A summary of sports shirt collections for 1936 maintained: "Probably the outstanding bet in the style-featuring lines is peasant linen and its derivatives. The natural shade, or those nearest to it, such as sand and oyster, are exceptionally good in this leader, and by far the most popular model is the so-called Prince of Wales style, with one button under the collar, which may be worn with a tie when buttoned or allowed to stay open and worn either with a handkerchief or plain. The 'gaucho' model with its loops and buttons is also well sold, and

these two models lead in all types of fabrics in the sports groups.

"Much attention has been given to fastenings, almost always at the neck, for the majority of these shirts, whatever the material, are pullovers. Heavy cords threaded through eyes, slide fasteners and various combinations of loops and buttons, and ordinary button holes give great diversity. In several of the new mesh models crew and V-necks are used, which is also true of terry cloth and ratiné. There is a draw-string at the neck in some of the mesh models.

"Fancy backs are being used extensively, particularly on those types intended to be worn outside the trousers.

Half belts, pleated arrangements, shoulder yoke with gathers—all the treatments made familiar in sport jackets—are used in modified forms suitable for shirtings. Raglan shoulders are a newish touch, dicky and guimpe models are many, along with big effects. Very notable is the increase of 'convertible' models which may be worn button-closed at the throat in conventional shirt-collar manner, or opened to form a V.

"Every type of cloth from the most open of open meshes to the heavy materials, basket weaves, and cloths similar to those mentioned above is used. In the acetate and rayon groups there are several with the appearance of wool jersey, many of these being particularly distinguished by their horizontal-stripe treatment, multi-striped and multi-colored variations of the Basque stripe.

"In general, colors tend to be very deep, blues and browns, wines and greens, with bright yellows strong favorites. Diagonal and herringbone patterns in the dishrag class give new and interesting effects, and a seasonal sensational in many ways is the use of printed knitted and jersey fabrics, principally in plaids, checks and strong colorings.

"Checks and plaids, by the way, are no less rife in sports models, (although tending to be bolder and more heavily color-contrasted) than they are in almost every other field of clothing and sports wear. There is no doubt that menswear is in for a chequered career" (*Men's Wear*, Feb. 5, 1936).

A tour of the Palm Beach golf courses in the late thirties revealed that most smart golfers were showing a preference for the half-sleeved coat shirt in natural linen with natural wooden or large pearl buttons, often with the wearer's monogram embroidered on the roomy breast pocket. This coat shirt became so popular that it eventually did double duty as a beach jacket. A new snug-fitting knitted shirt also popular on the links was a coarse-rib wool with a single chest strip in a contrasting color and a turned-down collar without buttons.

Most Palm Beachers wore their sports shirts outside their trousers, thus prompting manufacturers not to make their sports shirts too long.

Like practically everyone else during the Depression, the editors of *Esquire* seemed to be fascinated by the Riviera life-style, and in 1937 the magazine afforded its readers not only a glimpse of the latest fashions being worn there but also a little travel information about Saint-Tropez: "A tiny fishing village on the Cote d'Azur . . . an international harbor where yachtsmen gather to watch artists paint, to pick up unusual beach clothing and to patronize the numerous outdoor cafes along this waterfront street where hundreds of yachts are lined up daily during the season. There are no hotels in this village. The clothes worn here are both more colorful and more informal than those worn at any other Riviera resort." To illustrate this last point, *Esquire* showed a cotton basque shirt with a crew neck and horizontal stripes ("regulation in the French navy") and a plain blue silk-and-linen shirt worn with a knitted skullcap, "another item that owes its origin to St. Tropez, where the villagers knit them."

By the late thirties there was a growing demand for cowboy shirts, attributed to the new popularity of the dude ranch. As a *Men's Wear* writer saw it in 1937, "The shirts that cowboys and would-be cowboys pay $7 or more for have to be loud, trimmed with trick pockets, three pearl buttons on the cuffs, sometimes piped at the edges.

"The round-up shows advertise the cowboys' garb. Every time the rodeo comes to the big town the parade of colorfully clad cowboys draws a crowd. The silky shirts of bright orange, yellow, green, red or blue catch the eye more than do the wide-brimmed hats. Some of the bold striped ones are bizarre, yet never too bright for the hard-riding westerner. The clothes appear to be part of their act, but they are exactly the same as worn on the plains.

"The styles of shirts are several. The fabric may be silk, broadcloth, sateen or synthetic yarn. Solid colors in the most vivid shades are all being bought. Big squares are liked. Heavy stripings are in the distinguished class. The majority embody certain details in their mode. The collar is the conventional pointed, attached variety. The two chest pockets have buttondown flaps. The cuffs come together on the bias and have three close-set buttons.

"Such shirts are sold by specialists. In the big cities they may be had at sporting goods houses here and there. In the western part of the country retailers are stocking them more heavily, according to reports. One of the oddities of this business is that retailers in western towns of 3,000 to 5,000 population outdo the big-city stores."

Four photographs accompanied this feature, with a caption that read: "'Yippee,' scream these cowboy shirts, with all the do-dads the dude rancher seeks. The first is a gold-colored lustrous synthetic-yarn shirt with a black cord. Second is a yellow satin with black piping. The third, a broadcloth, has blue, red and white stripes and the fourth, also broadcloth, is yellow and dark blue. All these shirts have the novel three-button cuffs" (Jan. 20, 1937, p. 20).

Extremely popular during this decade was the Western shirt of wool gabardine, one of the earliest of the shaped shirts for men. Sometimes called a "gambler's shirt," it was seen primarily in solid colors, although it was popular also in plaids. Long-sleeved and having a crescent-shaped breast pocket, this shirt continued strong until World War II.

Also popular in solid colors and bright tartans of fuzzy wool was the long-sleeved wool gabardine shirt. It faded from the civilian scene during the war years but was revived in the postwar era and continued strong until finally, toward the end of the fifties, it settled into a niche of moderate popularity.

By 1937, the shirt suit, first seen in Monte Carlo, had reached fashionable American resorts. In its August issue *Esquire* showed a pair of suits, the one consisting of a cotton crash short-sleeved shirt with matching trousers and the other made of a cotton-and-linen mixture.

In view of the inordinate attention being paid to the Côte d'Azur and Palm Beach during this decade, it was refreshing when, in 1937, the writer Clyde E. Brown reported on the colorful sportswear being worn in Palm Springs, California, which, he said, appeared "to be undisturbed by Wall Street shocks as by earthquake trembles. There have been signs during recent seasons that a very definite type of apparel was taking form for desert wear, and this season more than ever reflects that trend. Easterners and Europeans coming here often exclaim with joy when they shift into the lightweight, brightly-colored sport costumes so popular here. The dry, hot sun, the cool night, the informal casualness of California life and the pioneering days of the old West, all show their influence on the clothes that mark this resort. Crashes, linens, peasant cloths, gabardines (both worsted and cotton) and denims are tops in the sartorial calendar there now. The matched or mixed ensemble of shirt or jacket and slacks in these materials is the outstanding highlight of the early sun worshippers' selections. The in-and-out shirt, both in the open front model and in the slip-on type, is so popular that it stands out as the leading item of the season thus far.

"For breakfast rides into the desert, for hiking, etc., the Western riding costume has taken the spotlight from almost everything else. To complete the Western costume, many choose the high-luster satin cowboy shirts, western boots and large western hats. The frontier pants, however, are also seen a great deal worn over the regulation style of English riding boots and with varied combinations of sport shirts" (*Men's Wear*, Dec. 8, 1937, p. 32).

Men's Wear, covering the sports shirt market in June, 1937, chose to illustrate the following models: a rayon bush shirt in a natural tone ("a little longer than last year's model") with nut buttons; a classic Guayaberra shirt in a noil silk that showed printed dark

The man in the center wears a colorful India madras shirt with a pair of khaki drill shorts having an extended waistband. From Esquire, *February 1939.*

red herringbones and stripes; a coat shirt in a natural-shade cotton ("resembling the Hawaiian pineapple cloth") with two patch pockets; a pale tan silk sports coat shirt with a roll collar ("a replica of a style popular along the Riviera"); a blue linen coat shirt with blue dome buttons, two

patch pockets, button flaps, and a deep collar; a three-button pullover in gray rayon; a fly-front one-button shirt in tan nubbed cotton with a deep low-band collar; a four-button short-sleeved shirt that could be worn as a sports shirt with slacks or with a tie and a summer suit; and a cotton gabardine showing brown-and-blue printed checks on a white ground.

In February, 1938, *Esquire,* commenting on the "colorful, unique and, above all, comfortable" sportswear seen on the island of Jamaica, proceeded to show two examples: a short-sleeved shirt of India madras worn with silk slacks and a very coarse cotton madras shirt worn with wide-waistband linen shorts. Also that year, the magazine's fashion department showed two important new fashions in beachwear under the headline "To Palm Beach via the French Riviera": a combination of a mocha-color linen-and-cotton beach shirt, made in the collarless style, worn with seaweed-color beach slacks; and a two-piece beach suit in Côte blue mixed linen ("the color worn by the French militia"), the shirt carrying a high-set collar, a four-button front, half sleeves, and two patch pockets.

Esquire in October, 1939, filled a color page with new beach accessories "seen first on the Riviera this past summer, and intended for sun sports at Southern resorts." Among them were a red cord mesh half-sleeved shirt, a natural-color half-sleeved mesh shirt with a contrasting boat neck, and a blue crew-neck open-front mesh sports shirt with half sleeves. The following *Esquire* issue showed one of the new native printed shirts of silk made in Honolulu. The model the artist had chosen to sketch looked lithe, tan, and prosperous, for the United States was in an optimistic mood as it moved from under the cloud of the Depression into what promised to be a more prosperous decade.

1940–1950

In February, 1940, *Esquire* observed that for beach apparel the rainbow was the limit and proceeded to show its readers a collection of "paint pot fashions guaranteed to enliven any Southern resort setting." Among these fashions were a clover-color half-sleeve polo shirt, a cabana-striped half-sleeve pullover shirt, a crew-neck half-sleeve mesh shirt in large block checks, an

Yellow was combined with gray in this bold overplaid shirt, which was worn with palladium-gray slacks in 1949. From Esquire, July 1949.

open-front three-quarter–sleeve boating shirt with vertical stripes, a lightweight yellow beach shirt with long sleeves and a crew neck, an India madras polo shirt, a cabana-striped cotton mesh beach shirt, and a knitted lisle shirt with brown-and-yellow stripes. It was all handsome proof that in 1940, with the Depression fading away, the sun would be, in the words of the magazine's fashion copywriter, "smiling down on miles of striped, checked, plaid and Paisley shore lines."

Since college girls and young wives had already discovered the attractions of men's button-down oxford shirts and fleecy sweaters, the ground for unisex fashions had been broken by this time. The next step was for sports shirts to be created in matching styles for men and women. *Esquire* showed a pair in February, 1942, reminding its readers that the outgrowth of femi-

nine borrowing seemed to be the increasingly popular custom of matching outfits for the two sexes. The fashion editor's example was a pair of Hawaiian printed silk shirts worn with washable slacks of harbor blue. To the right of the scene the fashion artist had sketched a matching pair of Scottish terriers that were "a bit bewildered by this new fashion trend." A more sophisticated pair would probably have taken it in stride, for by now the country was at war and a society of women without men meant a more masculine look for the female sex.

The military influence soon appeared in sportswear, and fashion pages during the war years were filled with references to the military, victory gardens, and ration stamps. An *Esquire* fashion page of 1944 showed an over-draft-age man dressed in tan cotton shorts ("an adaptation of the shorts worn by our Army in the tropics") and a cotton half-sleeve shirt striped in campaign colors ("inspired by the hues of American service ribbons, in this instance: Middle East Maroon and Atlantic Blue").

Esquire introduced the "bold look" in 1948, directing the ex-GI toward clothes which expressed the individuality that military conformity had stifled. The bold look dress shirt had a collar with a spread that was wider than ever, but the bold look sports shirt merely continued to be as bold and colorful as sports shirts had been for some time. Advertising copy, however, reflected the new emphasis, and menswear advertisements stressed virility. "Nothing bashful about these sport shirt colors!" announced the Wings Shirt Company, while another full-page advertisement in *Esquire* (October, 1949) shouted: "T-I-M-BERR! We call 'em 'Tall Timber Plaids' because they kind of reflect the *colors* of the Big Outdoors, and the men who live there—cowboys . . . forest rangers . . . Maine guides."

1950–1960

The emphasis was on color in the major sports shirt lines for 1950, fully washable new colors, nearly all vat-dyed and shrinkage-resistant. The styles included crew necks, gauchos, cardigan crews, pullovers, zipper models, and coat shirts, often with matching knitted caps. The consensus was that the vogue for pastels had reached its peak and that more strongly colored fabrics would be emphasized. This prediction was interesting in view of the fact that the early 1950s would be marked by a conservatism that would naturally be reflected in men's clothes, except for sportswear. Even the "man in the gray flannel suit" was a peacock when it came to sports clothes, particularly sports shirts. He apparently considered their bright colors and vivid designs an escape from humdrum everyday wear.

Sports shirts for the fall of 1952 ranged from heavyweight woolens and brushed cotton flannels to silk shantungs and nylon plissés. Included were cottons, synthetics, blends of synthetics, and jersey knits, marking the return of the original sports shirt fabric. There were collars with shorter points and new striped effects. But the big news was the washability, practicality, and comfort of the new man-made synthetics. These were widely publicized as luxury fabrics that could be laundered in a washing machine and come out with their luxury intact and their fit perfect. Furthermore, they needed little if any ironing.

There was good reason for the pride of menswear manufacturers in 1952, for the sports shirt had come a long way since the first polo shirt was introduced to the American public. An entire industry had grown around it. From a one-style summer item the sports shirt had become a major year-round article of apparel available in myriad styles and colors and involving completely new concepts in the styling of menswear. The following year there was even more reason for the manufacturers to rejoice, for golfers, gardeners, and city dwellers were by now regarded as potential customers for sports shirts. Of particular interest in the spring of 1953 were new textured weaves with rough, nubby surfaces

that were expected to blend well with articles of similar texture such as slacks, sports jackets, and leisure coats. The rough-surfaced fabrics were available in many types, among them seed cottons, rayons and blends, and luxurious pure silks. Native prints such as India madras and African prints, once considered novelties, by the early 1950s had become fashion staples as well suited to swim trunks, walking

shorts, and odd jackets as they were to sports shirts.

Esquire took a close look at knits in October, 1954, and decided that they added up to a "well-knit man." A fashion page was devoted to a display of knitted slacks, jackets, and shirts.

As had been predicted in 1950, the trend was toward stronger colors in sports shirts. *Esquire* called them "racing colors" and showed a bright

The Ivy look in shirts became increasingly popular in 1957: (1) A red, black, and white miniature tartan; (2) an irregularly striped multicolor jersey pullover shirt with a button-down collar; (3) a small-plaid cotton in maroon and gray; (4) a handwoven madras in club stripes with a button-down collar; (5) a striped gingham shirt; (6) a plaid polyester-and-cotton button-down shirt with an overplaid. From Apparel Arts, *May 1957.*

Ferrari red in a knitted cotton mesh, an Aintree brown checked shirt with an arched international-style collar, and a white-embroidered design on a ground of Santa Anita orange. One collection of short-sleeved shirts in blends of rayon, cotton, and silk was inspired by shirts being worn in Hong Kong and came in colors as dramatic and bold as a Hong Kong harbor sunset.

In May, 1956, *Esquire* said: "Mr. Kipling was never more wrong—not only have the twain met, but they're wearing twain fashions today. As vital as the bang in Bangkok, as subtle as the Sulu in a lull, these Far East fashions are but forerunners of a wave of such beauties to come. They combine a fine masculine dignity with a great variety of fresh and colorful patterns." Among the models shown were a collarless happi coat shirt and a two-tone cotton shirt with a standing collar.

The man in the gray flannel suit had emerged from his gray flannel cocoon by 1956 and was willing to experiment with the new, shapelier Continental suit silhouette as well as with other Italian-inspired fashion innovations that reached the United States. Arrow, in an advertisement appearing in *Esquire* in March, 1956, christened a new collection "Continental Stripes" in recognition of the fact that its stylists had found them in Italy, "where men's casual wear fashions so often begin." The fashion influence of England and France was also apparent. Full-dress regimental stripes, well-bred foulards, and aristocratic paisleys were enormously popular in sports shirts, and fashions seen at the resorts of the Côte d'Azur were reflected in knitted sports shirts with novel collar treatments and necklines.

The man of the late 1950s was obsessed with the idea of cool comfort, and manufacturers lost no time in responding to his wishes. Arrow advertised in *Esquire* in May, 1956: "When a shirt weighs less than five ounces—it just has to be cool! And here's less than five ounces of long-wearing gossamer cotton superbly tailored to ease you through the warmest summer days."

Esquire had taken note of the trend in August, 1955, when it showed a cotton overshirt that had several kinds of knit, "firm at the edges, loose elsewhere to let in the breeze."

In November, 1956, the Manhattan Shirt Company introduced a "new shape-it-yourself collar" in a full-page, full-color advertisement in *Esquire* that read: "Once upon a time, you bought a sport shirt. You could no more change the shape of its collar than you could the shape of the earth. The limitations presented by this type of shirt hampered and frustrated you." The new collar was said to be "so fantastically versatile" that a man could shape it to fit his mood, the occasion, or the tie knot he preferred.

The sports shirt picture toward the close of the decade forecast the fashion revolution that would soon change the American man's wardrobe. For just as the Ivy look struggled with the Continental look for supremacy in suits, a similar battle was being fought in sports shirts. While some men were attracted to brighter colors and bolder designs, the fashionably Ivy-clad group still preferred the small-figured sports shirt in softer colors, often made with a button-down collar.

1960–1970

In sports shirts, particularly knits, there was something to suit every man. A combination of interesting patterns and textures with casual appeal had brought knits to new heights of popularity. *Esquire* photographed several striking examples: a short-sleeved placket-front pullover, knitted in a cool open stitch, with a short knitted collar of the Continental type; a horizontally striped knit shirt jacket; a vertically striped model with a zipper front, a narrow stand-up collar, and three-quarter sleeves; a brass-buttoned crew-neck blue knit with white trim; a knitted cross-striped cotton shirt with a contrasting stripe at the chest; and a solid-color collarless pullover with piping at the edge of a three-button placket, a shirt of the British boat type that quickly became a campus favorite not only in solid colors but in checks and stripes as well.

The Continental influence of the late fifties was carried over into the early sixties. A handsome example was a black linen shirt with an Italian spread collar, vented sleeves, and a shirttail that could be worn in and out equally well. At the same time, the Ivy League devotee of the natural shoulder was being offered such fashion fare as a short-sleeved, open-weave oxford cloth shirt with a button-down collar. Still, a more outgoing look was apparent in Ivy sport shirts, which *Esquire* illustrated in June, 1964, with a full-page photograph of a bolder button-down, an extra large paisley of drip-dry cotton with a two-button placket. It was accompanied by the following text: "After several years of ultra-neat stripes, checks and restrained allover motifs bridling the appearance of 'Ivy' sport shirts, a more intrepid look now blossoms forth. These shirts, still a far cry from the gaudy-hued, Hawaiian-splashed prints of the Forties, maintain tradition in their buttondown collars, their predominantly dark tones and in the prints themselves, which employ respectable paisleys and madras-batik effects. There is a growing predilection in Club and Campus sport shirts for pullovers with plackets at the neckline rather than button-front coat styling."

For the avant-garde, *Esquire*'s fashion editor had brought back in 1960 a serape, or poncho, from South America and suggested that readers try it as an after-swim pullover. The Americanized adaptation was a terry-lined Aztec-inspired print with a concealed zipper pocket "for car keys and beer money." The more conventional man preferred a crushably soft velour pullover for both after-swim and general sportswear.

For its June, 1963, issue *Esquire* photographed a trio of men and their horses wading through a stream toward the cameraman to show the reader that denim was now being used to fashion what the editors called "beach Westerns." These sophisticated cowboys wore respectively a short faded-blue denim shirt jacket with angled cowboy-type pocket flaps and matching shorts, a short-sleeved blue chambray shirt and Levi's shorts with brass rivets, and a bright navy denim shirt jacket and matching shorts, the shirt double-stitched throughout in white, with a Western-style closure, a double front yoke, and a cigarette pocket on the left sleeve.

In contrast with the sophisticated folksiness of the beach Westerns were the ultrasophisticated sports shirts that were seen on the beaches of Bermuda. An *Esquire* photographer-writer team presented the following collection in January, 1965: a side-vented silk shirt jacket in a natural shade, carrying a large number of pearl buttons (five on the shirt front and others on the patch chest pockets and the cuffs); a sports shirt with a marine-life motif hand-screened in blue on tan, having roomy chest pockets, extra short sleeves, a small collar, and deep side vents; a short-sleeved silk pullover overprinted with luminous buccaneer stripes; and a silk twill long-sleeved shirt with bold circles generously splashed on newsprint.

By the mid-sixties the shirt jacket had become such a recurring fashion in men's sportswear that *Esquire* selected a trio that demonstrated that the 1964 edition was a little different from its predecessors: a Mexican-influenced pleated shirt with toggles and curved pockets, a seersucker bush jacket in light olive and white, and a two-textured white-and-tan shirt.

As a guide to what style-conscious fathers might welcome on Father's Day, *Esquire* suggested in June, 1965, a classic sports shirt of soft polished cotton, batik-printed in olive, rust, brown, and blue, with two upper pockets and pearl buttons; a wide-striped pullover of cotton broadcloth with a button-down collar, a deep front opening, and a buttoned flap pocket; a cotton bird's-eye knit with a rib-knit collar, cuffs, and waistband; and a short-sleeved knit with a fashioned collar, welt-edge cuffs, and a ribbed free-action underarm gusset for golfing comfort.

Shirt jackets in a variety of styles were popular in 1964: (left to right) a pleated short model with curved pockets; a striped seersucker bush shirt jacket with short sleeves; a two-textured white-and-tan shirt. From Esquire, *May 1964.*

Meanwhile, the young college man spending his Easter vacation in the South favored ultrabold stripes. Representative styles included a navy-and-white short-sleeved cotton knit, a black-and-white–striped nubby woven cotton shirt jacket with a Continental collar, and a turtleneck stretch nylon shirt in black, white, and royal blue, designed to be worn outside a pair of walking shorts. Once back on campus, the short-sleeved Henley-neck tapered shirt in solid colors, bold stripes, plaids, or checks was the favored shirt.

By 1966 the Peacock Revolution had struck, and even on already-liberated sportswear it had an impact.

On Carnaby Street in London, where the revolution began, military-inspired fashions were in vogue: sometimes the garment was an original taken from the attic and festooned with a few personal ornaments. The American youth soon followed this lead and bought his military look at the local Army-Navy store. Sportswear manufacturers took the hint, and soon CPO (chief petty officer) shirts were popular both summer and winter. These shirts were usually blue and had two flapped pockets in front. Two CPO shirts for warm-weather wear were a short-sleeved navy blue cotton with an anchor motif on the buttons and a short-sleeved medium blue cotton chambray set off with white stitching on the collar, front yoke, pockets, cuffs, and epaulets. "It is true that another name for CPO's is 'work shirts,'" wrote *Esquire* in June, 1966, "but in view of the style and the *esprit,* CPO sounds better." By the latter half of the decade bell-bottom trousers had become an important addition to the sporting man's wardrobe. Not every sports shirt was the ideal companion for bell bottoms; one that was, however, was a short-sleeved fisherman's knit jersey (another Army-Navy store fashion).

Gentlemen's Quarterly in April, 1967, advocated spending lazy days in king-sized paisleys such as an explosively shaded giant paisley pullover with a Continental collar, lower patch pockets, and side vents and a short-sleeved button-down in a red, blue, and gold paisley of pima batiste. The most striking example was a button-down shirt whose allover patchwork print in green, chili, gold, and tan combined paisley, foulard, and pop art.

By the early seventies the American flag would become a part of apparel for both sexes in the student age group, but as early as 1967 *Gentlemen's Quarterly* noted the appearance of knit shirts for men "rebelliously striped in flag-raising colors." When these were added to African prints and Aztec designs, it is evident that sports shirts had become uninhibited and imaginative.

"Shirts and swimwear—even sport coats—have now been engulfed by untamed, tempestuous patterns," remarked *Gentlemen's Quarterly*'s editor, in April, 1967, offering as proof the wild tropic-colored spirit of an acetate shirt topped by a stand-up collar with an attached ascot. Using a lush garden in Fort Lauderdale as a setting, the magazine's cameraman pictured two other examples of bold sports shirts: a high-spirited paisley on a handkerchief print shirt that was placket-fronted and had a stand-up collar; and a side-vented acetate shirt decorated with horizontals, zigzags, and sunbursts.

By 1969 tapestry prints and weaves, which hitherto had appeared solely in bell bottoms, were seen in sports shirts. In November, *Gentlemen's Quarterly* noted that such a sports shirt, with its heavier fabric and rich, vibrant design, was versatile enough to be "only a shirt or to replace a sport coat for touring the discotheque circuit." Illustrations included an extra long pullover with flared cuffless sleeves, a giant spread collar, an open placket, and an open-front vent, and a woven cotton in red, blue, and black on beige, creating a Persian effect in a pocketless spread-collared shirt with double-buttoned cuffs.

Art Deco made a brilliant comeback in the sportswear of the late sixties with a vivid mixture of patterns and polychromes. For its November, 1969, issue *Gentlemen's Quarterly* photographed a boldly chevron-striped long-sleeved shirt in a giant hopsacking weave with a very widespread collar and three-button cuffs; a long-sleeved, side-vented, gold-buttoned shirt in a variegated paisley pattern; and a shiny sateen shirt, printed in an orderly geometric design, with a long-pointed collar, a chest pocket, side vents, and a matching scarf.

The snug-fitting long-sleeved shirt came into its own with the introduction of the casual, or leisure, suit, an umbrella classification that included the vest suit, the tunic suit, and the shirt suit. The two parts could be made of the same fabric or of contrasting materials. A young man might choose to wear a pair of pleated cotton velveteen party pants with a polyester-and-cotton striped flocked shirt. The freewheeling casual suit, according to "GQ Facts" (June, 1970), was not a one-shot inspiration: "It's a highly adaptive type of styling, more so than the business suit, which it has already begun to supplant for casual occasions."

John Wanamaker's successful Guayaberra shirt of the 1930s, updated with the addition of front and back panels and buttoned patch pockets, was turned into a Dacron-and-cotton shirt jacket. In May, 1970, *Esquire* showed examples of the shirt suit that the editors thought would be fashionable that season: a cotton-and-Dacron model in a blue-and-natural reverse block print with jams-style slacks; a black-and-white printed silk; an orange cotton lisle knit shirt worn with cotton slacks in a black, white, and orange floral print; an intricately woven textured wool-and-cotton jacquard shirt, worn with dark velvet slacks; a wool crepe shirt with a zippered front and a leather belt, worn over flared slacks of a tweedy wool crepe; and a giant basket-weave print on a tissue silk tucked-front shirt, the print being repeated on wide-legged raw silk slacks.

Mare Moda '68, a widely publicized men's fashion show held on Capri, had shown the upper half of the apparently ageless tank suit worn as a sports shirt. By 1970 the tank top was being worn by members of the avant-garde who were narrow-hipped enough to combine it with hip-huggers or jean-styled slacks. In June, 1968, *Esquire* had previewed this fashion with two headless photographs of cotton knits, one striped and the other in a solid color, styled with a crab back, which had been designed in the mid-thirties to allow the maximum exposure of skin without breaking the law.

It was not surprising that the combination of a tank top and skinny pants became a unisex fashion. Men returned the compliment when they adopted the masculine counterpart of the transparent blouse: the see-through shirt acceptable in the late sixties and early seventies for both casual and business wear. For its January, 1969, issue *Gentlemen's Quarterly* photographed, for casual wear, an open mesh shirt of light blue cotton with a ringed white zipper and a stand-up collar; and for business, a mustard-color voile printed with lilac stripes and worn with a matching tie.

In its January, 1970, issue, *Esquire* remarked: "The really remarkable thing about resort wear this holiday season will be its range and diversity. In no season within memory have stylings touched so many different bases.

And this is all to the good, for no other kind of clothing should offer so many options, so much opportunity for personal preferences. This year, not even the quirkiest or most demanding man should have any problem finding something to his taste. And having found it, he can rest assured that no matter what it is, whether a Norfolk jacket or a shirt suit, a bikini or a tank top, it will be appropriate."

Despite the stiff competition, knits were the fashion leaders of the seventies. *Gentlemen's Quarterly*'s photographer went to Fort Lauderdale for its April, 1970, issue and took pictures of a ribbed white cotton pullover, trimmed in black at the waist and cuffs, with a mock turtle neckline, and a flat-knit wool pullover whose shoulder-linking cables and ribbed mock turtleneck were shaded in tones of blue.

With jeans (judged by *Men's Wear* to be "the high voltage category in men's and boys' wear to the tune of a billion dollars by 1970"), a knit shirt, particularly a skinny-rib knit shirt, was the ideal companion. There were the long-sleeved scoop-neck knit, the zip-front rib-knit, the sweater knit with a long placket, the canvas-trimmed knit pullover, the rib-knit golf shirt, the collarless short-sleeved tennis shirt of knitted polyester and cotton, and the knit polo shirt worn with a double-knit sports suit to produce a coordinated double-knit look. In short, there was a knit to fit every taste and every occasion. The Italian knits were outstanding for their imaginative designs.

In the spring, 1971, issue of the *New York Times Magazine*'s semiannual "Report on Men's Wear" five knits were shown: a rib-knit beige polyester pullover with lace-tied brass-toned grommets studding its placket, a shoestring-laced shirt blending natural-color cotton and linen in a nubby crochet knit, a diamond-de-

Three of the distinctive types of prints used for sports shirts in 1964: (left) an allover scenic print in silk; (center) a Persian pattern printed on thick-and-thin woven cotton; (right) a large allover geometric design printed on off-white cotton. From Esquire, *May 1964.*

signed string knit ivory-shaded cotton pullover in navy and red, a rope-woven cotton pullover with a boat neck and short sleeves, and a crocheted pullover of red-and-white cotton with a button-loop closure and side vents.

Sports shirts like these had become so expressive of the American life-style that it was difficult to realize that the sports shirt as a specific fashion category was only a few decades old. Certainly the new kind of casual clothes

being worn in the seventies owed much to the easygoing sports shirt. Long before the Peacock Revolution became a reality, the sports shirt had given the American man a touch of the peacock. By the seventies, when all masculine apparel had adopted the color and spirit the sports shirt had always had, the sports shirt itself was breaking new fashion ground with some of the most innovative designs in menswear.

Neckwear

For generations the necktie has been married to the shirt. Or, more correctly, it has been married to the shirt collar, since the space left there for the knot has naturally influenced the styling of the tie.

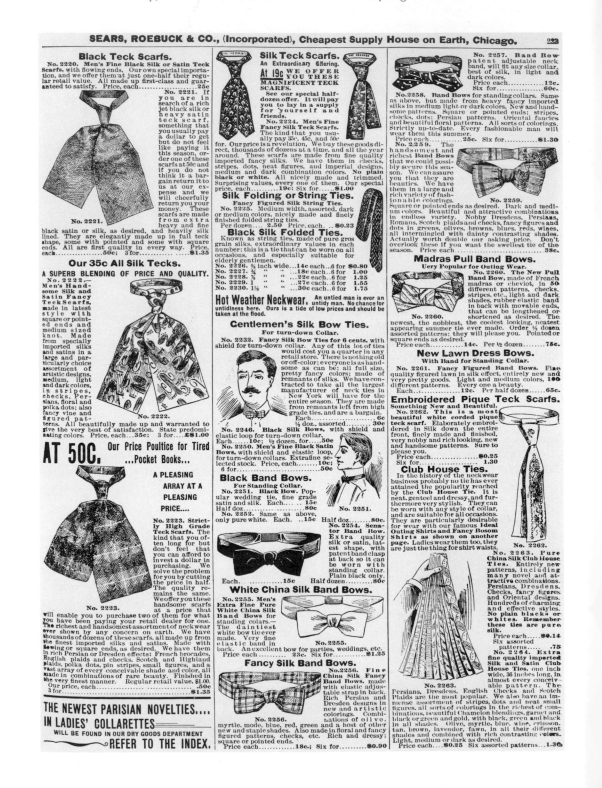

1900–1910

In the early 1900s (when the terms "necktie" and "scarf" were interchangeable), the popular wing collar called for a fairly large four-in-hand. The high starched collar, however, left a very small area for the knot and so was worn with a relatively narrow four-in-hand. Nevertheless most of the time little beyond the knot was on view, since suit jackets were of the high-button variety and were almost always worn with a waistcoat or vest. Yet there were some notable exceptions. The puff tie, for instance, required no tying at all because it was composed of two broad ends that crossed in front and were held together by a tiepin. Consequently, the puff tie managed to cover the area beneath the collar and above the vest.

The ready-tied scarf was also very popular, and two prominent styles were the Teck and the Joinville. The former was available with both straight

and flowing (pointed) ends; the latter was strictly a straight-end model. The 1900 Sears, Roebuck and Company catalog showed both styles, but described the Joinville as "the most popular and swellest gentleman's scarf ever produced. These scarfs are 6 inches wide and 34 inches long, and

1900

1914

Neckwear styles of two decades: (top) the four-in-hand worn with a high standing collar in 1900; (bottom) the dotted ascot for formal day wear, the butterfly bow tie, and the striped tie in a sailor's or four-in-hand knot, as worn in 1914. [NEW YORK LIBRARY PICTURE COLLECTION]

The size of the knot and the shape of the cravat worn in 1909 were influenced by the high starched collar, which was rounded in front to provide space for the cravat. [NEW YORK PUBLIC LIBRARY PICTURE COLLECTION]

(opposite) In 1897 the fashion in neckwear was to wear a big-shape Teck scarf in a figured pattern or a solid color. From the 1897 catalog of Sears, Roebuck and Company.

are made from purest woven silk specially imported by us. We have an immense assortment, comprising more than three hundred different designs: all light and medium colorings in nearly every color and shade ever thought of. They consist mostly of combination colors, just a few of which are blue, lavender, light green, cherry, strawberry, olive, myrtle, moss green, turquoise, opal, red, etc., all combined with light contrasting shades of cream, white, bright sunshiny yellow, pale blue and a host of other beautiful shades; handsome brocade patterns in Persian effects, Oriental effects, Dresden fancies, Chameleon grotesques, Roman novelties, Scotch and Highland checks, and an almost endless variety of artistic and fashionable designs. The De Joinville scarf is popular with fashionable gentlemen, because of its exclusiveness and because it can be tied into several different shapes." Among these shapes were the Prince of Wales knot and the puff, with a finger ring sometimes slipped just below the knot for added elegance.

"An untied man is ever an untidy man!" wrote the Sears Roebuck catalog copywriter, offering the reader a sumptuous collection of other neckwear fashions, which included silk Teck scarfs for 19 cents ("The kind that you usually pay 35¢, 45¢, and 50¢ for"); piqué Teck scarfs elaborately embroidered in silk down the entire front; white China-silk band bow ties for standing collars; fancy silk bow ties for the new turned-down, or fold, collars; the new pull-band bow ties of French madras or cheviot ("Very popular for outing wear"); and reversible four-in-hands in pure China silk ("alike on both sides and reversible . . . in very nobby patterns").

1910–1920

The high-band Belmont, a white starched collar, created a sensation when it first appeared and resulted in the introduction of the small-knot narrow tie whose knot appeared at the bottom of the collar. Equally popular at the same time, however, was the Henley shirt with a detachable collar that was worn with a wide, full-blown necktie that all but covered the shirt front. This shirt, with its wide openings and greater space between the points, attained fashion supremacy in this youth-oriented era. Naturally, such a shirt called for a wider tie with a larger knot.

Two entirely new forms of ties were also introduced during this dynamic decade: the butterfly bow and the long tie with the sailor's knot, both of which are still in vogue today.

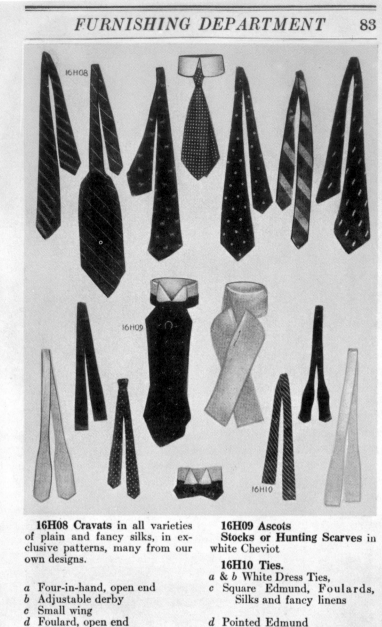

16H08 Cravats in all varieties of plain and fancy silks, in exclusive patterns, many from our own designs.

a Four-in-hand, open end
b Adjustable derby
c Small wing
d Foulard, open end
e Large wing
f Four-in-hand, Silk
Four-in-hand, Foulard
g Open end

16H09 Ascots
Stocks or Hunting Scarves in white Cheviot

16H10 Ties.
a & b White Dress Ties,
c Square Edmund, Foulards, Silks and fancy linens

d Pointed Edmund
e Square Edmund
f Black Foulard, Silk or Satin Edmund, plain or self-figured

Figured and striped silks for business wear, white and black dress ties, ascots, and stocks were among the styles of neckwear available in 1915. [COURTESY OF BROOKS BROTHERS, NEW YORK]

1920–1930

The start of the Jazz Age decade saw a most important invention for the neckwear industry: a resilient construction making use of a loose stitch and a bias-cut wool interlining that permitted the tie to spring back into shape after knotting. Prior to this time, flannel had been used for linings.

Young fashions dominated menswear now that the ex-doughboy was dictating what he wanted. Even the ultrasophisticated moneyed men of Palm Beach were, in 1924, showing a marked preference for regimental and club stripes in brilliant, youthful color combinations—colors, as one fashion reporter put it, "much more vivid and clashing in their contrasting combinations than heretofore." A brand-new necktie this reporter singled out for particular attention, however, was a washable linen four-in-hand, printed in vivid colors in "fantastic futuristic designs of unusually large bold patterns."

A survey taken at Princeton University the following year indicated that the best-dressed students on this enormously fashion-conscious campus leaned strongly toward colored shirts and figured foulards, black-and-white shepherd plaids, polka-dotted silks, and red-and-blue crocheted ties.

In 1926 a *Men's Wear* writer declared that colorful, exotic, and even weird neckwear ideas—"lightweight conceptions heavy with the atmosphere of the tropics"—were now standard summer fare from Maine to California. "Only a few years ago the gentleman's cravat was represented as something like the symbol hung on the door knob of the house of mourning. Gentlemen, we were told, did not sport the giddy scarf that blazes resplendently on the well dressed male bosom today" (Jan. 20, 1926). It was reported that rose, taupe, and beige were prominent in ties while black lost favor, and there were crepe ties in colors that, according to this writer, sounded like a report from the fashion salons of Paris. "The tendency in neckwear colors and fabrics," he concluded, "should suggest the sale of men's neckwear to women as well as men." Samples of the new look in ties were photographed and reproduced to illustrate this article: Japanese prints in faint pastel colors on white grounds; a crepe in two shades of blue with narrow maroon stripings and self-figures; a linen paisley motif with sand, white, gray, purple, and red figures on helio; and a foulard with black diamonds and red stripes on a white ground.

Yet, with all the diverting novelties, the broad knitted tie, a fashion staple, still found customers willing to pay $6 for it, particularly if the colors were bright. An analysis by *Men's Wear* of the types of neckwear worn by 300 of the best-dressed men in Wall Street that year also found that knit ties had increased in popularity with these men, who at the time were reputed to have a tremendous influence on the styles of younger men all over the

Silk crepe cravats in allover figures and stripes were advertised in 1926 by A. Sulka & Company. [NEW YORK PUBLIC LIBRARY PICTURE COLLECTION]

country. The following is a quotation from this report:

"The new notes in neckwear that should be carefully watched are the new silvers in heavy silk. Then comes the new gold neckwear. It is not yellow. It is gold and looks like gold. These silvers and golds are in figured ties with black or brown threads dominated by the silver or gold threads.

"The next important note is the increase in plain-colored patternless ties, in various shades of blue, grey, green and maroon. There are quite a number of greens. They are worn with the brown suits that are so popular with the best dressed men of New York right now."

Although the figured foulard tie had definitely declined in popularity with the Wall Street men by 1926, it still accounted for 25 percent of the ties worn, but the new figured and solid-color heavy silk was already in second place with 15 percent.

Bold allover prints were the vogue at Palm Beach in the late twenties. The fashionable business magnate en route to his winter quarters on Florida's Gold Coast might stop in at the second floor of Cartier's, New York, and buy a batch of these ties carrying the high-status Charvet label. But if he forgot in New York, there was no harm done; there was a Charvet shop in Palm Beach too.

Since no fashion roundup in this decade could be considered complete without delving into the Palm Beach scene, a 1928 *Men's Wear* survey noted: "The newest note in neckwear as worn by the best dressed men here is the variety of brighter colors that appears in the still popular small geometrical patterned foulards. Polka dots, which are included in these small patterns, were most popular in deep shades of blue or light shades of blue with white dots."

Men's Wear that spring looked in on a house party weekend at Princeton and reported an impressive number of animal-pattern ties. Few stripes were seen, for the good reason that crepe, then a leading spring-summer tie fabric, did not lend itself to striping. But the most popular tie seen that weekend was the Spitalfields, a high-grade silk featuring small geometric patterns, named in honor of the London district where the silk was woven.

A nationwide college survey taken in the autumn of 1928 began: "College men are extremely particular about their ties." Just any tie could not be sold to the collegian, "who insists on what he wants to the last ditch." And what the American college man was insisting on varied according to the geographical location of his seat of learning. At Princeton and Yale, for example, an increase in stripes was noted, with the general movement away from the old type of regimental stripes to more varied striped effects. A striped tie that it was felt had great possibilities among men in Ivy League colleges was the so-called Grecian stripe, which was a figured stripe spaced rather widely on a dark-tone background. An avant-garde minority at Yale, however, appeared at football games in satin ties. But the small-figured and solid-color neckwear con-

Unlined French moiré ties were featured in 1929 as crease-resistant neckwear. [NEW YORK PUBLIC LIBRARY PICTURE COLLECTION]

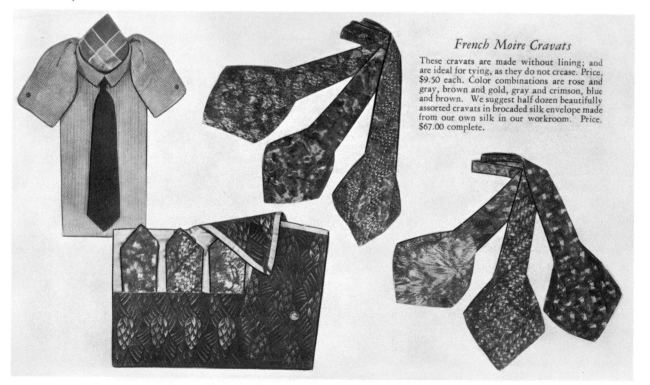

French Moire Cravats

These cravats are made without lining; and are ideal for tying, as they do not crease. Price, $9.50 each. Color combinations are rose and gray, brown and gold, gray and crimson, blue and brown. We suggest half dozen beautifully assorted cravats in brocaded silk envelope made from our own silk in our workroom. Price, $67.00 complete.

tinued in the lead, accounting for 57 percent of the ties worn that year on the two campuses.

At Midwestern universities it was discovered that rep neckwear had almost doubled its percentage in popularity and the Spitalfields type had shown a slight decrease. Also, 95 percent of the men surveyed favored the four-in-hand, with only 5 percent wearing bow ties. In the South crepes and heavy silks, along with foulards, accounted for nearly half the neckties worn by students, though reps still held first place largely because of the returning interest in stripes.

On the Pacific Coast the stripe that was so popular in the East was not at all active, with students preferring solid colors in lustrous silk. (A year later stripes would be second in popularity, with solid colors still in first place but this time in satin rather than silk—proof of the fashion influence exerted by the men at Princeton and Yale, whose innovations inevitably appeared a year later on campuses throughout the nation.)

The twenties were in fact such a dynamic period in menswear that in retrospect it might seem that the fashion press was mesmerized by the idea of polls and surveys. In 1928, for instance, even the denizens of Tin Pan Alley were polled as to what they were wearing, from hats to shoes. When it came to neckwear, it was reported: "The present mode is for patterns that are bold, to say the least. The traditional Christmas necktie has nothing on those favored by these young men." The chief note in striped ties was an interesting brightness in colors and a greater variety to the kinds of stripes. An extremely popular type was the "multiple striped," featuring variable stripes in different effects. All in all, it was concluded that "the bright—yes, verily, vivid—cravats adorning the necks of these sons of ragtime are so dazzling that even the rainbow is paled into insignificance."

In the late 1920s the silk-and-wool tie became prominent. The two fibers had previously been combined in poplin ties, but new interest arose in the ripple weave that gave these ties a three-dimensional effect. Although the shape was conventional and the colors conservative, these ties had exceptional shape-retaining qualities, and that plus their three-dimensional look made them popular throughout the country.

In November, 1929, one month after the stock market crash, Yale men started home for their Christmas holidays wearing ties with white stripes. The big questions: Would this white-striped college tie have the same success as the satin tie introduced the previous year at Yale? Many fashion experts thought it would. Why? Because, as one writer put it, "When Yale, Princeton or Harvard students are at home, they are the social 'king pins' in their home towns. To the younger generation of Americans, college men as a class comprise our American aristocracy." A sample of this new Ivy League tie had a 1-inch diagonal stripe of medium blue, below it a 1-inch stripe of maroon, then a 1-inch stripe of light blue, and then a 1-inch white stripe or one of very light gray. The Yale man not wearing this new striped tie was almost certain to be wearing an expensive, crunchy, hand-crocheted tie with spaced diagonal stripes. In any event, the stock market crash notwithstanding, the Ivy Leaguer was determined to look nonchalantly expensive.

1930–1940

Although silk was still by far the predominant neckwear fabric in all price ranges, by 1932 wool ties were being developed in such an amazing number of colors, effects, and designs that a trade journal used the following headline: "Will the New Wool Neckwear Repeat the Performance of Silk and Wool?" Stores from coast to coast were reporting outstanding sales in woolen ties in solid colors and pastel shades, in plaid patterns or foulard designs, stripes, small figures, and sports figures. Although they had been designed primarily for sports and country wear, these ties were also

(*above*) *Neckwear with small designs forming diagonal stripes became increasingly popular in 1934.* (*below*) *Rough-textured ties, which complemented cheviot suits, had bold patterns and the advantage of staying in place. From* Esquire, *January 1934.*

being seen in town with sack suits.

Autumn neckwear in 1934 echoed the trend toward rough fabrics in suits by the introduction of wide-wale twills, wide-wale reps, bouclés, wools (both cashmeres and homespuns), tweedlike silks, rabbit's hair mixtures, crocheted silks, and knitted wools. Argyle plaids, once seen only in socks and sweaters, were now turning up in ties of bouclé or a wide-wale twill silk outstanding for their rough texture and brilliant color. One neckwear firm went so far as to cooperate with a sock house, producing crochets that had backgrounds matching certain hosiery styles.

British fashion influence was enormously strong in the United States

Two types of sports neckwear popular in 1935: (foreground) a houndstooth-check lightweight wool throw-over; (center) an India madras bow tie. From Esquire, July 1935.

Two shapes of formal evening ties worn in 1935 were the straight club bow (left) and the satin butterfly bow with a long, narrow knot (right). From Esquire, November 1935.

during the Depression years. The fashion-conscious man of affluence, for instance, wore a short-warm coat, a double-breasted ulster, a double-breasted guards overcoat with a regimental striped muffler, or a double-breasted waistcoat—all English-inspired fashions. This pro-British trend dictated dressing for the occasion, and, according to *Esquire* in 1934, that meant a well-dressed business executive wearing a colored pleated shirt with a white starched collar and a four-in-hand Spitalfields tie and a college man wearing a solid-color crocheted tie or a striped rep.

The bow tie was more popular than ever by the mid-thirties, and *Esquire*

Patterns of various sizes in a random arrangement were used to create a large allover design in 1936. From Esquire, July 1936.

presented its readers with a batch of them: a pointed-end India madras (*elegant* with a natural-tan summer suit, white shirt, and brown leghorn hat); a foulard (*sporty* with a yellow cotton-flannel shirt, tweed jacket, and knickers); a plaid (the *last word* with a single-breasted gabardine suit, a brown-and-white candy-striped shirt, and a straw hat with a club-colored band); and a regimental stripe (*collegiate* with a Shetland sports jacket, gray flannels, and saddle shoes).

Polka dots were big news, and big dots by this time, and *Esquire* showed one example (a black foulard with white polka dots) as part of a British-inspired layout, gift-wrapping the en-

White piqué ties with slightly flared ends set the standard on formal evening occasions in 1938. From Esquire, *January 1938.*

The geometric design of this Spitalfields tie of 1938 was clearly defined in silver gray, light blue, and dark blue. From Esquire, *May 1938.*

tire presentation with the following fashion tribute to John Bull: "How do we get these fashions? We have observers, trained almost from birth, who practically commute to England where they haunt the very best places and ignore all but the very best people, slyly keeping statistics." Another very British-looking model sported a black cashmere tie with yellow polka dots, part of a horse-country outfit consisting of a bold-checked double-breasted suit, a tab-collared shirt, and a rough felt homburg hat. And equally British in spirit was the silk foulard or lightweight wool square or muffler seen at the country club or on the deck of a cruise ship; tied nonchalantly at the

neck, it obviated the necessity of collar and tie.

Apparel Arts in 1934 devoted a double-page spread to "The Evolution of a Hand Made Necktie," observing: "No way has yet been devised whereby a better product can be constructed by machine than by hand." A dozen photographs and terse captions told the story:

Lining cutting. Good lining, expertly cut, is the foundation of all good neckties. Good lining at its best is pure wool cut on the bias, determining not only the shape of the tie but its life.

Cutting. All really good neckwear is bias cut with a short knife against heavy cardboard patterns. The large and the small ends are cut one next to the other in re-

versed positions.

Hemming. Here occurs one of the few machine operations in hand made neckwear. The standard 24″ width goods requires a tie made of two pieces that are joined on the bias.

Piece pressing. The joint at the neck, or piecing, is pressed flat in this operation to insure that there will be no bulkiness to inconvenience the wearer at this portion of the neckband.

Laying in lining. A simple gauge of heavy cardboard is here used to place the lining in its proper relation to the tie itself so that the planned shape will be maintained at standard.

Pinning up. Here the unsewn tie is wrapped around the lining and pinned in place every few inches in preparation for the next operation—comparable to the basting operation in clothing.

Bouclé: The trend to rough weaves has made this almost chinchilla texture a new favorite. Bouclé is French for "buckled" which, in this case, applies to the manner of weaving.

Macclesfield: A rough, open weave which is a favorite texture for English school, club and regimental stripes. The name is derived from another English silk weaving locality.

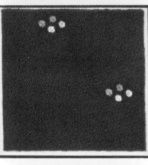

Ottoman: An appearance similar to corduroy gives this fabric both its individuality and its Turkish name. It belongs to the faille family, but has a wider, coarser rib which, in weaving, runs warp-wise.

Barathea: A fine texture best described as a broken twill. It is the most widely known of the weaves which are technically termed "armures."

Louisine: This weave, confined mostly to small checks and plaids, is in a fine basket texture barely visible to the eye. The origin of the name is so old as to have been lost in antiquity.

Regence: A soft, flat corded texture with a luxurious appearance. Also known by the name of the Parisian haberdasher who made it famous: Charvet.

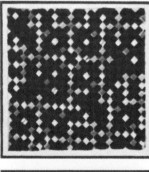

Natté: A basket weave of heavier construction, employing several colors to achieve a braided effect. The word is French and means "braided."

Rep: A corded fabric, particularly adapted to stripes, with the rib running across the fabric in weaving. The name may also be spelled with two "p's."

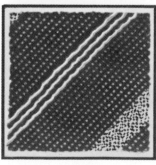

Spitalfields: This designates small all over designs, mosaic in appearance, that are produced in numerous weaves and textures. The name is derived from a famous English weaving district.

Grenadine: The most open weave of all neckwear. This luxurious gauze-like fabric was for years exclusively woven in Italy on hand looms.

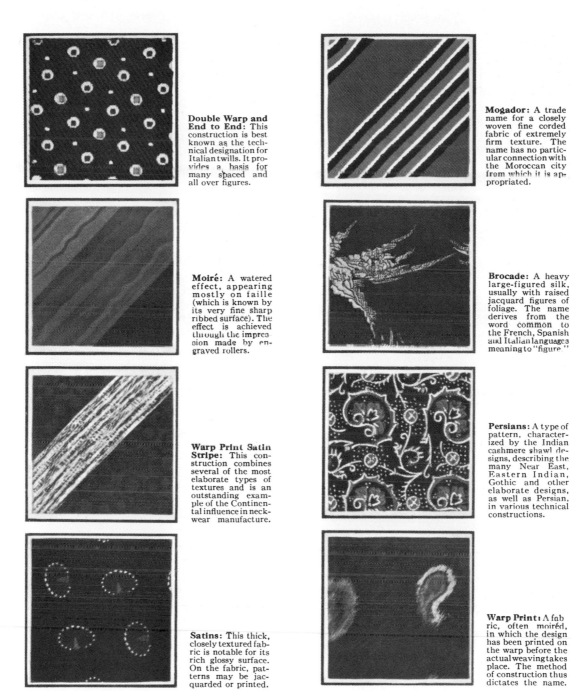

Double Warp and End to End: This construction is best known as the technical designation for Italian twills. It provides a basis for many spaced and all over figures.

Moiré: A watered effect, appearing mostly on faille (which is known by its very fine sharp ribbed surface). The effect is achieved through the impression made by engraved rollers.

Warp Print Satin Stripe: This construction combines several of the most elaborate types of textures and is an outstanding example of the Continental influence in neckwear manufacture.

Satins: This thick, closely textured fabric is notable for its rich glossy surface. On the fabric, patterns may be jacquarded or printed.

Mogador: A trade name for a closely woven fine corded fabric of extremely firm texture. The name has no particular connection with the Moroccan city from which it is appropriated.

Brocade: A heavy large-figured silk, usually with raised jacquard figures of foliage. The name derives from the word common to the French, Spanish and Italian languages meaning to "figure."

Persians: A type of pattern, characterized by the Indian cashmere shawl designs, describing the many Near East, Eastern Indian, Gothic and other elaborate designs, as well as Persian, in various technical constructions.

Warp Print: A fabric, often moiréd, in which the design has been printed on the warp before the actual weaving takes place. The method of construction thus dictates the name.

(opposite and above) A guide to silk neckwear fabrics published in Esquire, *showing eighteen important types.*

Slip-stitching. In this all-important operation the main seam which forms the tube of the tie is completed. Resilient construction is dependent upon loose, even stitches sewing lining to back.

Shaping ends. This operation may easily be eliminated—but only at the expense of the product. It entails the insertion of a cardboard form to maintain a standard shape at the ends.

Pressing. Without exception, this operation is done by hand for all fine neckties.

Neckwear, because of the lightness of the fabric, requires hand pressing to avoid a flat, dead look.

Labeling. Either by machine or hand, depending upon the requirement of the customer, this small but necessary opera-

In 1938 the club-shape midnight-blue satin tie had straight lines and a big knot. From Esquire, *July 1938.*

the crisp, cool-looking wash tie is right near the top of summer neckwear offerings." Or, in the words of still another writer, "Wash ties will travel in smart society." He added: "The neckwear mart abounds with interesting ideas in tub materials. There are striped cords and piques, striped and plaid seersuckers, printed twills, striped oxfords, silk ginghams, cotton boucles and crepes. Even the dishrag material has invaded the neckwear sanctum" (*Men's Wear,* Apr. 22, 1936).

A few years earlier wash ties had not been taken seriously, but now, in 1936, they had been improved in both design and construction. Wash neckwear, both four-in-hands and bows, was available in a twin-ply design, which gave added strength and wrinkle resistance. Spiral seams in the new wash neckwear also prevented ripping, produced resilience, and added to the life of the tie. Furthermore, designed in bias shapes, the ties guaranteed a perfect knot. Finally, hand bar tacking eliminated that old bane of a wash-tie wearer, loose stitching that unraveled after the tie was laundered.

The wash bow tie proved to be an especially big seller because of the popularity of the widespread collar, since a bow was considered a "natural" for this type of collar. And so, too, was the big-knot four-in-hand that eventually became known as the "Windsor knot"; through a series of loopings, it produced a triangular-shape knot. Although the Duke of Windsor publicly stated that he never tied his tie in this manner, the name Windsor knot became part of the fashion vocabulary. But not every man took a liking to the Windsor knot, and in 1939 *Esquire,* devoting a page to an "object lesson in restraint," showed a long, narrow bar tie of handwoven silk.

That same year *Esquire* ended the decade by offering its readers a guide to choosing ties based on hair color, complexion, and age. Among the neckwear included were a two-tone brown check; a solid-color rust knit; a green-and-yellow paisley; a black with spaced stripes of red and gold;

tion is accomplished—becoming the basis of a long-lived "advertisement."

Inspecting and trimming. This operation involves the elimination of unnecessary loose threads or ends by careful inspection and additional trimming of the loose threads by hand.

Packing. Because of its peculiar shape, neckwear requires exceptional care in packing. Banding, boxing and similar operations also play a part in adding the last finishing touches. (Vol. 5, no. 2, 1934)

The wash tie won plaudits in 1936. As a *Men's Wear* fashion report saw it, "The wash suit carried the cotton tie into fashion's festival last year. Now,

The narrow ribbon-shape bow tie in regimental stripes made fashion news in 1938. From Esquire, *August 1938.*

a blue-and-white geometric allover design; and a navy blue with gray-and-white geometric figures. The overall effect was conservative, muted, "an object lesson in restraint." With the military atmosphere of the months immediately preceding and following the outbreak of World War II in Europe already being felt in the United States, this understated neckwear clearly previewed the serious and cautious personality of the coming decade.

1940–1950

The popularity of the Windsor knot continued. *Esquire* in August, 1940, sketched a debonair gentleman wearing a two-button suit, a blue-and-gray striped shirt, and a red-ground foulard tie with blue-and-white figures "fastened with the popular Windsor knot, larger than the usual four-in-hand, to fill the space of the wide-spread collar."

By now the conservatism of the forties had taken hold, and in May, 1940, *Esquire* stated: "This ultra conservatism saddens us, and we find a perverse satisfaction in introducing the

most flamboyant colors that the Fashion Staff serves up to us." And what were they? A gray suit and a blue suit, though the copywriter hastened to add, "This is no ordinary grey, that is no ordinary blue. The grey is Granite Grey, and the blue—ah, the blue is Burgess Blue." What manner of shirt and tie did these "flamboyant colors" carry? The man in granite gray wore a broadcloth shirt with a separate white collar and a tie that was solid-colored except for a few stripes of blue, red, white, and black. The gentleman in burgess blue wore a blue-and-white striped broadcloth shirt and a blue, red, and white tie of white-warp heavy silk. And those ties were the liveliest items on the page.

Silk went to war in 1941, to be used in parachutes, and rayon became the top tie fabric. Recognizing the new status of rayon, *Esquire* showed a regimental tie of blue, silver, and red

A foulard tie with spaced blue-and-white figures on a red ground, tied in the popular Windsor knot. From Esquire, *August 1940.*

Large, splashy printed figures became widely popular not only in silk foulard but in rayon as well. From Esquire, *August 1943.*

stripes—"an example of the textile technician's skill," because it was a rayon with a dull finish ("so the silks from the Japs are not missed"). The wool tie maintained a strong position in smooth-finish materials done in stripes, checks, and plaids. Wool's appeal was its wrinkle resistance, and at least one manufacturer advertised it as "wrinkle-proof." In fact, a wool tie, button-down shirt, and single-breasted three-button suit constituted an extremely fashion-wise outfit during the early forties.

The panel, or center-stripe, tie gained a measure of popularity. This was a simple design featuring a vertical stripe of a solid color running down the center of the tie, or the center panel might be made up of herringbone, check, or some other type of weave.

Esquire in 1942 referred to "this new

Checks and figures were combined in the tie worn by the pipe smoker. A close-up of the tie is at right. From Esquire, *August 1944.*

wardrobe are accessories in the brave new colors inspired by American Service Ribbons," *Esquire* announced the same year. Neckties boasting these "campaign colors" cropped up in the magazine's pages with patriotic regularity, and among them were ties utilizing Middle East maroon, Far East green, Africa brown, Pacific blue, and Asiatic gold. And there were socks, suspenders, and garters that harmonized with these ties.

By 1944, with the war well in the Allies' hands, men's civilian clothes had assumed a more colorful, more aggressive personality. A case in point: *Esquire*'s sketch of a cigar-smoking father pouring beer for his young Marine officer son, wearing a boldly plaided double-breasted suit with broad shoulders and slight waist shaping, a widespread-collared shirt, and a wide tie featuring a zigzag pattern in victory red on a white ground, giving it the appearance of a bolt of lightning.

That year the rayon tie still reigned supreme, and *Esquire* showed a giant close-up of a checked figured tie of printed rayon, "favored by men who are among the first to take up a new idea." The next year, the magazine was showing a pale blue shirt as "an admirable example of the technical advancement in summer textiles. It is designed of rayon, made of one denier staple. It looks like silk, launders like cotton." With this shirt breakthrough the model wore a regimental-striped rayon rep tie.

During the war years, when the scarcity of materials could not fail to have an adverse effect on styling, the hand-painted necktie satisfied many men's yen for self-expression. It was seen in all sorts of patterns, everything from flowers to sailboats, and cost about $25. Such "art" demanded a larger-than-usual canvas, and most of these ties measured $4\frac{1}{2}$ inches in width, earning them the nicknames "belly-warmer" and "scrambled egg" ties. A wartime phenomenon, the hand-painted tie continued to be popular for a few years after the war and, in a certain sense, paved the way for

era of simple taste" and, as an example, sketched a handsome middle-aged couple (the man was clearly beyond the age of military conscription), with their elbows on a dining table ("an Emily Post-mortem attitude"). The most eye-catching part of this gentleman's outfit was his tie: of a heavy silk-and-rayon mixture, it was wide enough to fill the space of his shirt's extremely widespread collar.

In 1943 *Esquire* photographed a model at a showing of wartime posters in the Museum of Modern Art, New York, wearing a double-breasted suit of understated gray flannel. His printed foulard necktie in a geometric design showed plenty of spirit, however, and the caption writer suggested: "The psychiatrists might be able to tell you why there's been a trend from the conventional figures to angular patterns such as this."

"The newest things in the civilian

Printed rayon neckwear decorated with a large pattern and tied in a Windsor knot. From Esquire, *July 1945.*

the "bold look" neckwear introduced in the fall of 1948.

Esquire's bold look was heralded as the first truly new concept in men's clothes since pony express days—"a keen, direct, look-you-in-the-eye-and-take-your-measure look." This "dominant male" look accordingly demanded a shirt with a widespread "command" collar and a big-knot necktie with big dots, big checks, or strong stripes. It was a look that appealed to men of all ages, but in particular to younger men who, after suffering the conformity of khaki or navy blue, were ready to break out and show their colors.

The bold look continued to gather momentum in 1949, and in its April issue *Esquire* held forth on the subject of the bold shirt and tie: "You may think that your face is a permanent fixture—and that in the normal course of things, only age, a hangover, or a punch in the eye can change it—but the truth is that you can do awful things to it with the wrong tie and

shirt combination. A man who works over the stubble on his chin with all of the studied skill of a surgeon often picks his tie for the day as carelessly as he would pluck an apple out of a deep barrel. We don't mind, of course, if you prefer to wear a black knitted tie every day of your life, or go in for explosive effects suggesting a disaster in a hothouse or shingle factory. But you should have a fighting chance, we figure, at the color harmonics and collar styles that mark you as a man of good taste and pleasing individuality. Vary the colors you wear from day to day. Wear the style of shirt appropriate to the occasion. You might even experiment with a new kind of tie fabric than your usual—a lightweight wool, for example, will blend handsomely with your sports clothes, whereas with your business suit you might try a foulard with a small hand-blocked print effect characteristic of this fabric." The bold tie, *Esquire* reminded its readers, was bold without being noisy.

The hand-painted necktie was still on the scene and sold well during the holiday season of 1949. Earlier that year *Men's Wear*, casting a critical eye on neckwear in general and the hand-paints in particular, com-

In 1948 the wide-end satin butterfly bow tie complemented the piqué dress shirt with a wide placket, pleats, and collar. From Esquire, *December 1948.*

Tie sizes in 1949: (top) the pointed-end bow tie, which was 1¾ inches wide at the ends, ¾ inch wide where it crossed the bow, and 1 inch wide at the neckband; (center) the straight-end bow tie, 1¾ inches wide throughout, which tied in an easy, informal knot; (bottom) two narrower four-in-hands, the striped tie 4 inches wide at the bottom of the apron and the figured tie 4½ inches wide. From Esquire, *June 1949.*

mented: "Some people have no real appreciation of beauty. They see a herd of steers on the wide open plain and all they can visualize is a thick steak. We looked at the works of art in the neckwear lines and all we could see were sales checks" (July 22, 1949).

1950–1960

The hand-painted ties with their sporting motifs faded away as this decade ushered in a return of ultra-conservatism. Assessing the trends in 1950, *Esquire* decided in favor of lighter-weight apparel stressing ease and naturalness. "Restraint is the password," noted the fashion department, adding that the fashionable dresser must be "C-worthy." For "C" was the key "to the right clothes for the way we live today: C for Color, C for Correct, C for Casual, C for Comfort." That meant an oxford shirt and crocheted tie on campus and a broadcloth shirt with a graduated striped tie at the office.

The patterned wool tie with a Windsor knot was a favorite with country clothes. From Esquire, *February 1950.*

The smaller knot returned to favor along with the narrower brims and shoulders of 1950. From Esquire, *October 1950.*

The decade's policy of cautious understatement was not fully crystallized, however, until "Mr. T," *Esquire*'s symbol of the new trim look, strolled on the scene in September, 1950: "You're talking to an earthquake when you meet 'Mr. T'—the gent who symbolizes a tidal wave of top new fashions for men that has rolled back everything else in sight. This is not just another 'idea': This is the Big 'T'-formation that is sweeping the whole men's fashion field today. The 'T' is what men have been crying for, a top-to-toe formula based on smart and natural design principles that is stocking every major store in every community with a 'T'-Line of taller, trimmer, and more masculine clothes."

The "T look" meant tapered-crown hats, narrower shoulders, straight-hanging lines, tapered trousers, narrow brims, less bulky shoes, pinpoint collars, and smaller-knot ties. As the fashion writer put it, "Every detail in your new wardrobe boosts your height, trims you down." By 1952, influenced by Mr. T, ties had slimmed down to $3\frac{1}{2}$ inches in width, and even bow ties had narrowed down to where they had been in the late 1930s, when the skinny ribbon shape was news.

Men's Wear noted that the trend in ties for autumn, 1952, "has been earnestly represented by the manufacturers as tending to sparsely patterned grounds in rather neat effects. But conversely countless patterns and combinations of colors are produced each season and they all find takers. Just as there are those who steadfastly hew to the traditional line in their selection of neckwear, so are there those who shudder at the thought of wearing the staid staples and are constantly on the prowl for more and newer novelties or the more subtly styled smart stuff." But the really big news in neckwear during the first half of this decade had to do with the emergence of the new Dacron knits, which were being sold as washable, nonwrinkle, and no-stretch.

"*Esquire*'s Plan for a Man: RIGHT DRESS" was the title of a March, 1952, spread that spelled out for the reader the items that belonged in the wardrobe of any man who truly hankered to be considered well dressed. For

The tie with a small knot and a square end had a following in 1955. From Esquire, *November 1955.*

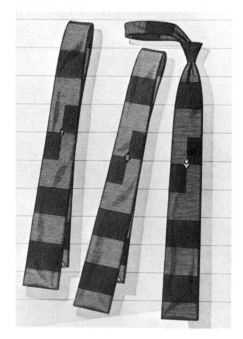

High-spirited bow ties: (left to right) a square-end silk tie with irregular stripes; a tie with black, gold, and white vertical stripes; a butterfly shape in textured silk with a pattern in metallic thread. From Apparel Arts, *March 1957.*

Three festive bow ties worn in 1957: (left to right) a tawny silk foulard printed in brown; a black ribbed silk evening tie with rounded ends; an Americana printed cotton. From Apparel Arts, *March 1957.*

business wear, the fashion department urged the reader to express his personality with "the four-in-hand or the bow, in stripes, figures, plaids, or solids. Wools, silks, knits—many kinds!" For urban and suburban wear, it was "the four-in-hand or the bow tie, either one. Your taste will find many in woven fabrics, knits, wools, stripes, repps, figures and foulards."

The next year the "feel of the fabric" was the headline news for spring. And the feel, said *Esquire,* should be rough, rugged, and breezy from head to foot—in short, the "nubby touch," through fabrics with soft, irregular textures. And ties of coarse silk and shantung automatically had nubby touch.

Woven goods dominated the neckwear market for autumn, 1953, and reps were again important. Fashion news was in the color trend too, with most colors generally lighter than those usually seen in fall neckwear. Blue was the favored color that season, even in Chicago, a city where red as a neckwear color had long been preferred. Meantime, the narrowing-down of tie shapes had more or less settled at about 3 inches, while some extra slims were as small as 2 inches.

By the mid-fifties the quest for new ideas in men's accessories had led many designers, editors, and manufacturers to tour world-famous shops abroad, where, according to *Esquire's* March, 1959, issue, "they are doing amazingly original things and yet at the same time these unconventional flights of fashion land by some creative miracle within the bounds of good taste." Outstanding neckwear from Paris, for example, included designs based on grapes, wine bottles, wineglasses, historic statues, town crests, and famous paintings, as well as cross-stripes, graduated stripes, and swirl designs. A typical innovation from France was a double-knot bow tie attached to the collarband—not especially startling except that both shirt and tie were in a checked design of varied hues of gay colors.

Neckwear from Italy, often featured in *Esquire,* most frequently appeared in black-and-gold combinations, complementing the black and gold that dominated in the popular shantung suits.

Neckwear from England included light-ground ties with dark stripes, as well as blends of silky fleece and angora mohair that were promoted as noncrush, no-wrinkle ties.

In short, the conservative years of the fifties were over, and a new, more colorful era had begun.

Wash-and-wear all-cotton neckwear was introduced in 1956. A special resin treatment enabled a natural fiber to assume its original shape and appearance after washing. That year *Esquire* devoted a full page to the cross-pleat shirt and the splite tie, considered an ideal team for formal business wear. This new splite tie, faintly reminiscent of the panel, or center stripe, of the previous decade, featured an inverted pleat to match the knot. The clip-on four-in-hand appeared in 1957. Hooking on the front of the shirt, it was held in place by two "arms" resting under the collar. It had a brief and unfashionable life.

Bow ties became fancier that year, and for its spring, 1957, issue *Apparel Arts* tied a selection of them around champagne glasses, brandy snifters, and goblets, with the comment: "New woven textures, new prints and a multitude of new surface decorations add spice to a lively variety of autumnal offerings." Among the fancier bows photographed were textured silk yarns handloomed in irregular stripes on square-end ties; a narrow cotton bow featuring black and bright gold stripes on a white ground; a butterfly of textured silk with the pattern in gold metallic thread; a tawny silk foulard with a printed design of brown demons; and an Americana print on striped cotton. Meantime the men on American campuses remained loyal to

1960–1970

The cross-stripe knitted tie, worn with a natural-shoulder Shetland suit. From Gentlemen's Quarterly, *October 1958.*

In 1966 there was a shift to wide ties, measuring 5 inches at the widest point. This dotted tie came from Turnbull & Asser, London. From Esquire, *February 1966.*

The British influence had by now shouldered the Continental look far out of the fashion spotlight, and the narrow-lapel suit with its straight-hanging lines looked handsomest with a button-down shirt and a tie of moderate proportions, generally in neat figures or regimental stripes. Imbued with the British spirit, *Gentlemen's Quarterly* noted in March, 1961: "The English have always drawn a definite line between what is right for town and what is correct for a country weekend. Now the London Line has helped influence Americans to adopt a special wardrobe for the country: the tweeds and heftier woolens, the Scottish plaids and district checks, the lovat and heather shades. All properly accessorized, of course, with sporting vests, oxford shirts and challis ties."

Neckwear took on a new dimension in 1964 as silk ascots were seen more and more in solid colors, printed figures, and allover patterns. They were invariably tucked inside the collar of the shirt, which was left unbuttoned at the collar level.

In February, 1966, *Esquire* daringly predicted the return of the wide tie: "Last seen in the late Forties, the broad-model tie made a hasty exit with the advent of narrow shoulders and overall slim styling. Thinner ties (two inches wide, as opposed to the old three-and-a-half or wider) were more in keeping with the new lines: narrow-brimmed hats, straight-hanging jackets, etc. But lately the trend has been to break up the straight lines with angles: the new shaped suit has wider shoulders, suppression at the waist, flair at the skirt. Hat brims are more pronounced. A resounding introduction of the wide tie was made in London's West End with a polka-dot . . . a king-size five inches at its widest point. Perhaps a four-incher would serve as well, but it is clear with the shape of men's clothes what it is today, only the wide tie is fit to be tied."

By 1968 this prophecy had come to pass, and *Esquire* was on hand with color photographs and pungent copy celebrating the fact. All the ties shown measured a hearty 3¾ inches in width and were called "bloaters": in London, said *Esquire,* they were always worn loosely knotted. From 1968 on, the wide tie was *the* tie. Or, as *Esquire* had put it in 1966, it was the only tie "fit to be tied." And in some instances it continued to grow, until it reached 5 inches at its widest point. Inevitably this supertie soon appeared in plush fabrics, and the combination resulted in a tie so opulent there was something almost challenging about it ("Are you secure enough to wear me?"). Now that the tie had the upper hand, it was the shirt that had to conform; and conform it did, spreading its collar wider and wider to accommodate the biggest knot that men had worn in twenty years. The tie of 1968 actually surpassed the bold look tie of 1948.

Now that a man's neckline was of prime importance again, silk neckerchiefs seemed a logical step forward in

the knitted tie, practically a collegiate staple by now and seen most often in a crochet style.

By 1957 fashion writers were referring to "the elegant air," expressed in coats and sports coats of opulent fabrics such as vicuña, cashmere, and llama fleece. Fabrics like those called for opulent neckties: a soft silk shantung featuring a Place Pigalle print in black and red on a pure white ground; heraldic stripes of deep brown, copper, and tan forming an underknot design on heavy, irregular silk in a coarse weave; and stylized black-and-white compasses parading across broad bands of clear red and blue on a straight-end tie. Furthermore, the elegant ties required protection from stains—and got it in 1959 when a finish that enabled stains to be washed out with plain cold water was introduced. One of the more widely advertised of these processes was called "Scotchgard."

244 | *Neckwear*

this era of the "peacock." Silk neckerchiefs, said *Esquire* in May, 1968, were the newest craze for the well-turned-out gentleman. Available in a dresserful of sizes, shapes, colors, patterns—ringed or ringless—"the hippiest, happiest thing about them is that they have no rules. How you choose to wear them is entirely up to you: ascot-style, Tom Mix-style, apache-style, sailor-style, whim-of-the-moment-style. Tied high, low, tightly, loosely, they add a dashing and elegant touch to casual and even more dressy attire." Illustrating these various points were a big, 3-foot gold-ground square, loosely knotted and worn over a turtleneck; a solid red sailor scarf, long and narrow, worn *à l'apache* with a sports shirt; a ringed paisley scarf worn to the side of an open-necked shirt; a 2-foot silk square of blue-and-green paisley worn ascot-style with a button-down shirt;

The big bow tie complemented the wide-brimmed hat in 1969: (top to bottom) a pretied India silk in a paisley pattern; a houndstooth-check silk; a blue silk with beige polka dots. From Gentlemen's Quarterly, *September 1969.*

a polka-dotted ringed scarf worn inside a Nehru shirt; and a long scarf-shaped silk, green on orange, tied low and loose.

"Doing your own thing" in fashion in the late sixties often meant reaching into the past for inspiration. A man might wear a plum-colored double-breasted velvet suit with a matching tie and a shirt of pastel stripings, or a lace-jabot shirt requiring no tie. Not that ties were in jeopardy—far from it—any more than hats were, a happy fact brought to the reader's attention in September, 1969, by the editors of *Gentlemen's Quarterly,* who headlined the feature "Big Bow and Big Brim." For in 1969 wide ties, wide brims, wide lapels, and square-toed shoes were saying that the "skinny look" was out and the "thirties look" in. To illustrate its feature, *Gentlemen's Quarterly* spread a collection of bow ties around the wide brim of a black wool felt hat. Among the bows were a pretied India silk in orange, green, and purple paisley; and two tie-it-yourself bows, one a gray-and-navy checked silk and the other a bright blue silk with beige polka dots. *Esquire* that year bowed to the bow, too, showing a blue foulard with white figures ("simple and sedate"); a small-figured foulard on a gold background ("tastefully muted"); and a plain bronze-colored bow ("a modified butterfly").

It had been ascots in 1964 and silk neckerchiefs in 1968; in 1969 it was the silk scarf that was being put, in the words of *Esquire,* to "protean uses": a 35-inch square or a 56-inch four-fold fringed silk rectangle worn as a neckerchief; a 35-inch Mondrian-inspired giant plaid tied like a four-in-hand; a 26-inch bold chevron print worn as an ascot; a 102- by 10½-inch crushed silk chiffon worn as a stock; a plum silk square, featuring green and black cheetahs, tied apache-style. It was, in other words, every man to his taste. Fashion was a means of vivid self-expression, and a man could choose to take a scarf 7 inches wide and 65 inches long and wear it as a sash without comment. It was a time of unisex fashions, and the versatile silk scarf fit

in nicely; how nicely *Esquire* demonstrated when it photographed designer Nino Cerruti and his favorite female model wearing identical shirts and scarves worn as ascots.

Fashion rules were for breaking if a "new wave" man was a true peacock; it was a case of mix-and-match or scramble when it came to shirts and ties. The shirts of 1970, for instance, had tapered bodies, long-point collars, and high neckbands, and came in an avalanche of bold stripes and brilliant prints. Neckties were equally uninhibited. A 3½-inch-wide printed-jacquard silk tie worn with a woven geometric cotton shirt? Why not? Or a plaid sports jacket and checked slacks worn with a figured tie? Of course. That was classic high style.

It was all part of man's liberation from the drab unimaginativeness of his apparel. In shirts and ties it had reached a point in the seventies where there was no longer any clear-cut distinction between what was appropriate for the boardroom and what for the discothèque. To make this point, *Esquire* photographed a clutch of "9-to-5 shirts" in a palette of rainbow hues, teaming them with equally

The big-knot four-in-hand tie and the big, long-point collar became dominant fashions in the seventies.

colorful big-knotted ties.

In fact, the necktie of the uninhibited seventies was designed not only to be seen but to be "heard" as well. A 1970 full-color advertisement of Liebert Cravats of New York in *Gentleman's Quarterly* summed up the new fashion philosophy with the following copy: "Next time you feel groovy, wear a tie that expresses all that. Sass out the world in a new five-incher. In opulent imported silks with that very, very affluent look." And nothing could be more opulent—or practical—than an Aztec tapestry design or a hieroglyphic stripe in Qiana nylon, whose wrinkles would simply smooth out by hand.

Neckwear has always been one of the most satisfying ways for a man to express his personality. And the king-size tie is as expressive of fashion's peacock as the spread of the tail is of the feathered peacock. Certainly in the present era of dedication to self-expression, or "your own thing," a man's necktie has become his most personal fashion statement.

Formal Daytime Neckwear

The classification "formal daytime" may seem an anachronism today, but in the early decades of this century it was extremely relevant. Then it designated not only Sunday church attire or what men of fashion wore to a before-6 P.M. wedding; many business executives wore formal day attire to their offices.

The English walking frock suit in black or oxford gray was supremely elegant, and even more formal was the black cutaway frock coat worn with striped trousers and a high silk hat. But whichever a man chose, his silk ascot or four-in-hand tie (often with a pearl or gold stickpin) added still another note of elegance. Certainly in that era nobody could ever mistake an executive for a clerk; the affluent businessman's clothes established his position on the corporate ladder.

In the second decade of the century the cutaway coat became more dominant, and the narrow bow tie, usually

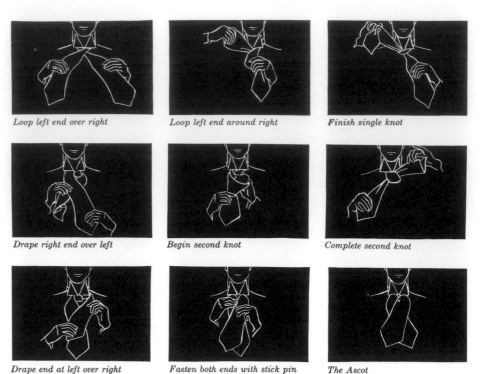

Loop left end over right   *Loop left end around right*   *Finish single knot*

Drape right end over left   *Begin second knot*   *Complete second knot*

Drape end at left over right   *Fasten both ends with stick pin*   *The Ascot*

How to tie an ascot. From Esquire, *June 1941.*

in solid gray or conservative black-and-white stripings, became as acceptable as the ascot and the four-in-hand. The basic outfit (oxford gray cutaway, striped gray worsted trousers, high silk hat, waistcoat, white shirt, and wing or poke collar worn with ascot, four-in-hand, or bow tie) remained the classic formal day outfit for decades to come.

During the 1920s, when the younger man back from World War I began to exert a powerful influence on fashion, ushering in an easy, more informal decade, there were some changes in formal day dress, but they were subtle and always in impeccable taste. The cutaway, for instance, often gave way to a single- or double-breasted dark gray jacket, and odd waistcoats in light gray or buff-colored woolens began to appear. And color began to appear even in the formal daytime shirt. Neckwear, however, remained constant as the following description of an Easter Sunday stroller on New York's Fifth Avenue shows: "Among the notables wearing good looking formal day clothes was William

Goadby Loew at St. Thomas' Church. His ensemble consisted of a high silk hat with a belled top, bold wing collar, black self patterned club bow tie, lavender and white pin-striped starched bosom shirt, fly-front black trousers with white stripes, and black shoes with tan uppers" (*Men's Wear,* Apr. 21, 1926).

Two years later, in 1928, a fashion journal showed a choice of neckwear considered appropriate for formal day wear. Among the four-in-hands were a black with self-stripes; one with fine stripes of gray and gold; one with fine stripes of black and white; and a silver-gray herringbone effect. Among the bow ties were a black striped in white; one with gray, gold, and black stripes; a gray with blue figures and stripes; a block weave in two shades of gray; and a black-and-white check. And the Fifth Avenue Easter parade that year saw many a younger man wearing a double-breasted oxford jacket, striped trousers, a black bowler, a bold wing collar, and a silver-gray puff tie.

In the Depression thirties, however,

when fashion impact returned to the very rich, there was an increased emphasis on formality. As *Esquire* viewed it in April, 1934, formal day wear was the accepted turnout for the Easter parade as well as for formal day weddings, "and for such Sundays as you do not spend on the golf course or in the country. If this doesn't add up into a sufficiently impressive total of possible occasions, you can always fall back upon the thought that a lot of men are taking to formal day clothes for smart cafe and hotel wear, now that drinks have come out of the low ceiling hideaways." Under the caption headline "For Easter or Wedding or Polite Drinking" the fashion editors presented a waxily moustached gentleman whose necktie was a black-and-white shepherd's check, worn with a deep blue shirt with white starched collar and cuffs. An alternate choice for this four-in-hand was a medium blue silk ascot with white polka dots.

By the late thirties the turned-down collar and four-in-hand tie had, except for weddings, succeeded in banishing the wing collar and ascot tie. The Easter paraders of this period wore the following neckties: bronze-colored Spitalfields; blue spotted bows; bar-shaped black satins with pearl stickpins; overall blue and white silk four-in hands; gray checks; maroon checks; and checks of brown, beige, and red.

Attire for the formal daytime wedding has changed only slightly over the decades. The fashionable groom of 1941, for example, invariably chose a silver-gray-and-black ascot held in place by a modest pearl stickpin, as acceptable in 1921 as it was in 1941 or 1971. Not that the groom had no choice of neckwear: instead of an ascot, he could wear perhaps a small-check tie. But that was about the range. As *Esquire* pointed out in 1970, "Weddings are just about the last refuge left for traditional formal wear."

Formal Evening Neckwear

Under the cover of night man has dared to tamper with the traditions of formal neckwear, although this was certainly not the case in the early 1900s. Formal evening dress meant but one thing: white tie and tails. The tailcoat was evening dress, and it tolerated only a white-bosomed shirt with a high standing collar and a moderately proportioned white bow tie in piqué, linen, or cotton. The tuxedo, although gaining some measure of acceptance, was considered semiformal evening dress. And while most men chose to wear a black tie with the tuxedo, many men preferred to dress it up with a white tie and white waistcoat. As late as 1920, however, the opening of the Metropolitan Opera season saw the truly well-dressed man bypassing the tuxedo for the tailcoat worn with starched shirt, wing collar, and bow tie in matching white piqué or linen.

Still, the tuxedo continued to gain ground and began to be identified as a dinner suit or dinner jacket and trousers. The twenties, dominated as they were by younger men, were a less formal era, and the tuxedo, so like a daytime suit, was more to their liking. Its accessories included a stiff-bosom shirt, a bold wing collar and black satin bow tie, studs, and cuff links. The long bow and butterfly ties were still the favorites, although some of the trend setters were showing a preference for the straight-cut, or pointed-end, bow by the late 1920s. But it was not so much in the cut of the tie that the change was found as in the length. Among the smart Palm Beach set, for example, bows were often elongated to such an extent that they protruded in some cases a full inch beyond both wings of the collar.

Meanwhile, the tailcoat was far from being extinct. At the annual junior promenade at Princeton University in 1928, for instance, most of the best-dressed undergraduates appeared in white tie and tails. But a substantial number of Princetonians wore dinner suits, black single-breasted waistcoats, fold collars, and straight-end bow ties. The more mature elegant dresser of the late twenties often preferred a dinner jacket with a silk shawl collar and cuffs of silk with a tie of the same silk. (It is interesting to note that, despite the independent spirit of the Jazz Age, the tuxedo, or dinner jacket, was still designated as semiformal or informal evening dress.)

The 1930s heralded a return to formality in evening dress. As a *Men's Wear* writer observed: "Men of culture and social standing have long maintained a tradition of elegance and correctness in dress by wearing the evening coat on any occasion where women are present, and their influence in sartorial matters has brought about a greater mass interest in the tail coat. The university student is also playing an important part in the furtherance of the formal evening coat fashion. Many undergraduates' wardrobes now contain a tail coat and a dinner jacket, with correct accessories for each. Cinema and stage stars, too, are doing much to spotlight formal evening attire" (Sept. 7, 1932).

The prevailing tie shapes in the early 1930s were the butterfly of moderate width, the straight club, and the pointed-end styles. For wear with the tailcoat the tie might match the shirt and waistcoat, while the tie accompanying the dinner jacket might be of the same cloth as the lapel facing or in a similar plain weave.

The mess jacket made of white linen or cotton gabardine achieved a relatively short-lived popularity in 1933. With this waist-length jacket (worn unbuttoned) a man wore black dress trousers, a single-breasted waistcoat to match (or a cummerbund in plain black, bright red, or dark blue), a stiff-bosom shirt, a wing collar, and a black bow tie.

The first signs of color in formal evening neckwear showed up in the mid-thirties with the advent of the midnight-blue dinner jacket popularized by the Prince of Wales. It was a subtle advance, however, since midnight blue tended to look blacker than black under artificial light. But now, with the midnight-blue dinner jacket and colored silk waistcoats and cummerbunds, a midnight-blue bow tie was rather to be expected, particularly

How to tie a four-in-hand, a Windsor knot, and a bow tie. From Esquire, *June 1943.*

with summer formal dress. In fact, in August, 1936, *Esquire* showed a sketch of a new green dress tie, "a believe-it-or-not item that has the loftiest sponsorship from London, and may or may not presage the further invasion of color into evening clothes, but may certainly be indulged for cruise wear,

with a silk dress shirt and a d.b. dinner jacket." And in Palm Beach that winter season dark red was the important note in bow ties, worn with matching cummerbunds and white dinner jackets.

A new wide wing collar made fashion news in the mid-thirties, and with

it the correct tie for formal evening wear was the white butterfly. Among the black-tie crowd the most popular dress bows were the pointed end, the long bat, and the butterfly.

The fold collar was by now challenging the supremacy of the wing, and its popularity signaled the revival of the old-fashioned club-shape bow tie, its large knot and blunt, rounded ends making it particularly well suited to this soft collar. When *Esquire* showed its revitalized club bow, it was part of an avant-garde outfit consisting of a midnight-blue dinner jacket with a blue-and-white polka-dotted handkerchief in the breast pocket. The tailcoat and white tie, however, were still adhering to tradition, permitting only the most subtle of changes: the absence of an outside breast pocket, for instance, and the extension of the broad wings of the wing collar beyond the ends of the modified butterfly tie.

The big-knot four-in-hand of the thirties, popularly known as the Windsor knot, inevitably inspired a Windsor-shape black satin tie for dress wear, although the semibutterfly bow was far more popular as men continued to prefer increasing formality in dinner clothes.

The more revolutionary changes continued to take place in summer formal wear, and *Esquire* in 1938 showed an especially smart summer formal outfit sketched against a gondola-dotted canal in Venice. The gentleman advancing up the steps of the Gritti Palace wore a double-breasted bone-color silk shantung dinner jacket, midnight-blue dress trousers, patent-leather shoes, a soft silk dress shirt, and a club-shape midnight-blue satin tie. Along with the club-shape bow, other popular shapes were the thistle and the ribbon, both very much on the narrow side. The white piqué tie, however, was now mostly seen in the butterfly shape with square ends.

By 1940 most fashion writers were no longer using the term "semi-formal." In fact, the following tradition-toppling outfit shown in the pages of *Esquire* that year was called "a formal outfit with flair": a midnight-blue double-breasted dinner jacket with gilt buttons, white tropical-weight dress trousers, and a soft white silk shirt. Only the jacket's satin lapels and the black satin bow tie actually followed tradition. In another issue that same year *Esquire*'s fashion staff decreed that white butterfly bow ties

were correctly worn in front of the collar wings with the tailcoat, and that the black or blue silk club-shape bow tie was gaining favor for wear with the dinner jacket.

Esquire introduced its aggressive bold look in the autumn of 1948, and suggested to its readers that "Evenings out are more likely to meet with success if you don the fresh, masculine essence of the BOLD LOOK, expressed in the rugged flare of the Bold Knot Bow"—a virile edition of the butterfly, with its lower ends having a longer, more rakish flare than the top ones. Accompanying this new-shape tie was the bold look dress shirt with the widespread command collar that had stitching three-eighths of an inch in on the collar plus a wide center pleat.

In 1950 the narrow shoulders of *Esquire*'s Mr. T replaced the broad-shouldered bold look. As the editors saw it, "Out on the town, Mr. T wears a dinner jacket that includes all of the natural, trim characteristics that dominate his daytime wardrobe." This meant a jacket with narrower shoulders and straight lines, worn with a narrow bow tie. Mr. T's bow, by the way, was very likely to be in a special twill fabric to eliminate droop.

By the mid-fifties, however, the conservative Mr. T had disappeared and men's apparel took on more color and shape. *Esquire* offered a stunning example of this new look: an iridescent gold-and-blue nubby silk shantung dinner jacket worn with a matching paisley silk cummerbund and bow tie. And since synthetic fibers were very much in the news, many dinner jackets were made of a combination of silk and synthetic, a mixture that matched the new parfait summer colors of the dinner jackets in smooth richness.

Ties and matching cummerbunds made fashion spreads in *Gentlemen's Quarterly* in 1959. Scattered across a Las Vegas roulette table were the following combinations: cummerbund and matching tie of black satin in dimensional honeycomb design; a dark gray design on silver silk brocade; champagne and black caviar silk with

an allover nailhead design; and black satin with a white jacquard-design center strip.

The 1960s brought in a new age of evening elegance. Accompanying the shaped Continental dinner jacket and fancy-bosom evening shirt was the crossover tie, with its two untied ends held in place in the center by studs. The clip-on bow was a fait accompli by the mid-sixties, and by then it was impossible to detect that it was pretied. It was particularly popular with the younger man who had neither the patience nor the skill to tie a correct bow. But pretied or not, by 1970 the dinner jacket's bow tie (now often in a plush velvet) had flared to anywhere from 3 to an exaggerated 5 inches in width—perhaps in retaliation for the evening turtleneck sweater and the lace-jabot shirt, both tieless.

Esquire summed up the new formal evening wear of the peacock seventies this way in October, 1970: "Permissiveness is one of its pleasantest and most persuasive points. It encourages brilliant colors, of course, but at the same time there is nowhere in its constitution, bylaws, or amendments any blasphemy against simple black and white." In fact, in the seventies the black dress tie was once again dominant. Many new wave men appeared to satisfy their craving for color by day, and by evening, when in a formal mood, much preferred traditional black and white. Nowhere was this steadfast loyalty to simple black and white practiced with more respect for tradition than in apparel for the formal evening wedding. The groom of the seventies *might* prefer a midnight-blue tailcoat to a black tailcoat, but he still wore the white piqué starched-bosom shirt, waistcoat, wing collar, and butterfly bow tie that his grandfather and great-grandfather had worn. And if his wedding was semiformal, his bow tie was always black and his shirt always white. A stylish formal wedding is still a black-and-white affair, even if the groom wears a plum-color jump suit as he and his bride motorcycle off to their honeymoon hideaway.

Mufflers

In the first two decades of this century mufflers were an essential part of a man's wardrobe, if not always for decorative effect then for comfort. Wool and cashmere were winter favorites, and for the more comfortable months there was silk. Sears, Roebuck and Company offered its catalog readers an interesting variety: dark-colored cashmeres in large-size plaid patterns; imported saxony wool mufflers in fancy stripe and check patterns; and pure silk in rich brocaded patterns, measuring 28 by 28 inches.

After World War I silk squares became prominent, in patterns as well as printed and woven designs. Oblong wool mufflers in stripes and plaids were also popular. And the more fashion-conscious young American was duly impressed by the panache of the young men at Eton, who wore their extralong (knee-length and beyond) knitted mufflers in the colors of that venerable school.

In 1928 *Men's Wear* made an analysis of the mufflers worn by 200 of the best-dressed New Yorkers, with the following results:

"There is a white muffler, which is worn only by the very best dressed men on the Exchange. The style element, so far as this item goes, is entirely in the color, as the material seems to make no difference. White woolen mufflers, flat knit, and with tassel fringed ends, are worn by some of these men. Others prefer the white silk muffler in the same cut, but usually with a monogram worked in one end. In the silks, the material may be knitted, crocheted, or woven into any one of the many different types that are produced from silk. Of course, most of the foulards and the crepes are cut in the square style, but such is not always the case, since these materials are also made up in the elongated mufflers with tasselled ends.

"Next smartest to the plain white

86   BROOKS BROTHERS

16H11-12-17 Knitted Silk Mufflers and Motor Scarfs

16H13 & 15 Square Silk Mufflers
Square Cashmere Mufflers

16H14 Black Silk Sash for wear with dinner jacket
16H16 Scarf Pins in plain gold and various designs
16H18 Sets of Studs; sleeve links; studs and sleeve links; and studs, sleeve links and waistcoat buttons for wear with tuxedo jacket or full evening dress, in boxes
16H20 Gold Safety Pins

16H19 Linen Handkerchiefs

Silk Handkerchiefs

16H21 Bandanna Handkerchiefs

Mufflers of knitted silk, striped woven silk, and squares were fashionable in 1915. Also featured were linen and silk handkerchiefs, collar pins, and dress jewelry.
[COURTESY OF BROOKS BROTHERS, NEW YORK]

comes the canary yellow, which, while worn by very few men, seems to be a coming shade for the man about town. In every case, the yellow muffler was worn with a blue double-breasted overcoat, and usually a black derby hat. The one spot of bright color adds considerably to an otherwise monotonous ensemble.

"Another important point about mufflers, as worn by these men of finance, is the fact the lightweight types are the only ones seen. Even the knitted wool mufflers are in a fine stitch and the brushed wool types are strictly town neckerchiefs, compact editions of the heavier, clumsier skating and sporting neckpiece.

"Only a small percentage of the men wear their chokers in an Ascot knot, but it is these men who are the smartest dressed. All the best dressed men show a generous amount of muffler above the coat collar and the muffler is folded always in such an apparently careless way that it appears to have blown up about the neck by the wind" (Jan. 11, 1928, p. 92).

A chart accompanying this report presented the following statistics: solid-color cashmere, 14 percent; figured foulards, 12 percent; figured heavy silks, 12 percent; knitted wools, 11 percent; plain-color twills, 10 percent; striped reps, 10 percent; striped knit silks, 9 percent; patterned cashmeres, 8 percent; solid-color knit silks, 6 percent; striped twills, 5 percent; and striped cashmeres, 3 percent.

That same year *Men's Wear* reviewed the mufflers being shown for the upcoming autumn and winter seasons,

concluding that the square shape was the leader. As to colors and designs, black-and-whites were very popular, with all-whites still important. In fabrics, twills, spun silks, crepe de chines, English jacquard twills, and gum twills were, as the reporter saw it, "on the front line." An interesting fashion

The very long flannel muffler in vivid colors, which had been established as a fashion in England in 1925, subsequently appeared in the United States.
[NEW YORK PUBLIC LIBRARY PICTURE COLLECTION]

The university man in the late thirties preferred the houndstooth-check wool muffler, shown on the figure in the center. From Esquire, *September 1936.*

decade and well into the next rayon mufflers, including acetates, were seen in plain white and were worn choker-fashion.

"Probably the most significant style development in mufflers," reported *Men's Wear* in 1933, "was the rather wide acceptance of the hacking scarf in some of the larger cities. Originally worn by the Prince of Wales in a spotted foulard, this muffler, measuring 72 inches in length and worn with the two ends placed together and slipped through the loop formed in the middle, sold well in both foulards and cashmere. The former were usually in blue or wine set off with white dots, while the latter ran to checks and plaids. One interesting development in this connection is the wool tie matching the hacking scarf. In most quarters, the hacking scarf is expected to be an outstanding feature for next Fall and Winter throughout the country" (Jan. 11, 1933, p. 60).

Americans in the 1920s and 1930s were growing increasingly sports-minded, and this in turn sparked a growing demand for more glowing and daring colorings in both summer and winter dress accessories. At fashionable Palm Beach, where the self-confident, ultrarich man favored brilliant colors for sports attire, it had become especially chic to tie on a terry cloth, flannel, or ratiné scarf in a dazzling color—a terry cloth scarf in a vivid blue, for example, picking up one of the colors in a tricolored beach robe. And when a wealthy sportsman went off to ski at St. Moritz, his ski outfit inevitably included a muffler of a brightly colored knit or cashmere, and it was the fashion to wear it twisted over the left shoulder, with one end hanging down the back and the other down the front.

By the mid-thirties the reefer-style muffler, usually measuring 52 by 13 inches, had become the favorite, having nudged out squares and hacking shapes. The woolen muffler for fall and winter was being seen on Ivy League campuses in very bold patterns and strong colors. In knitted wools, meanwhile, the trend was toward

note was the emergence of silver gray as the newest shade taken up "rather enthusiastically by the well dressed men as an evening muffler." Photographs accompanying this report showed an unusual design in a block-check-effect weave on a 36-inch English jacquard gum-twill square; a very neat design on a 36-inch English spun silk crepe de chine; and a block-check-effect weave on a 36-inch jacquard gum twill.

The popularity of the silk scarf during the twenties resulted in the appearance of artificial silk and other man-made fibers, and all during this

stripes in colors that matched the shades of the authentic English regimental colors; in some instances the stripes were used only at the border. And one of the very newest ideas was the all-white knitted wool scarf for evening wear. White, in fact, so popular in the late twenties, was still immensely popular in the mid-thirties. Other favorite colors were gray, maroon, navy, tan, and canary; canary was striking when worn with the dark-colored overcoat.

"Off to the land of the midnight oil" is the way *Esquire* introduced a page of back-to-the-campus fashions for fall, 1936. And along with two Irish tweed ties, a stitched tweed hat, a knit waistcoat, and a pair of argyle wool hose were two neatly patterned wool mufflers.

"The muffler business of 1936 shows gains ranging from 40 to 100 per cent over the business of 1935," reported a trade publication toward the end of that year, which in many ways was still showing the effects of the Depression. And the largest increase, it turned out, had been in sales of higher-priced merchandise. Furthermore, women had been the best muffler customers, and it was thought that perhaps this was the reason for the enlivening of colors and the broadening of the range of patterns. In fact, the fancier scarves were now running almost neck and neck with the staples, the plainer and more conservative mufflers. Muffler-and-glove and muffler-and-tie sets were gaining favor too. "The four-ounce scarf has proven to be the best weight for this country," the article concluded, adding the not surprising fact that in evening scarves whites were still setting the pace, with white knitted silks, woven silks, woven and knitted wools, and even cottons all finding acceptance.

About this time the debonair Fred Astaire had taken to inserting a silk tie through his belt loops instead of a belt, and *Esquire* went a step farther when it suggested that a fashionable gentleman sporting a pair of gabardine swim trunks might wear with

The golfer at left wears a plaid wool scarf in ratcatcher fashion with both ends slipped through the loop formed in the center. From Esquire, *April 1938.*

them a silk foulard paisley square instead of a conventional belt. In the same issue the fashion staff showed a lightweight wool polo shirt worn with a silk foulard muffler thrown over the neck ascot-fashion.

Nineteen thirty-eight marked the emergence of new fabrics, some containing blends of various fibers, introduced in winter mufflers. Worsted and kid angora were presented in woven and knitted cloths and featured with knitted gloves to match, and there were also silk-and-wool blends as well as rayon-and-silk in various effects—crepes, plain weaves, and jacquarded.

The white knitted or woven silk muffler with an embroidered monogram was invariably worn throw-over fashion (1940).

Rayon, meanwhile, remained popular, its versatility demonstrated by the variety of cloths brought out for mufflers: a new rayon velour, for instance, had a soft texture and was reversible, and a rayon challis was also prominent.

Patterns were important in 1938. Scottish tartans were being seen in many different colors, and paisleys ran the gamut from small allover patterns to huge effects. Both vertical and horizontal stripes were popular in many different arrangements as well as on scarf borders. Regimentals were also seen on the borders of many crocheted silk mufflers.

The late 1930s found *Esquire* extremely scarf-conscious, particularly of the neckerchief or neckertie worn with beach attire. Among the styles shown in full color were a figured linen beach neckerchief; an unusual lightweight neckertie in a marine design; an India-print neckertie worn with a Bermuda suit, wool anklets, and canvas shoes; and an India Choppa scarf worn as a neckerchief by a bare-chested young man in knitted swim trunks.

Esquire summed up this very Brit-

ish-conscious decade with a photograph of a colorful Fair Isle muffler worn in the English university tradition by a studious-looking Ivy Leaguer in a velvet cord suit and a fawn-color semisports hat. The effect was very British and very "high fashion."

The War Production Board's regulations regarding fashion during the 1940s played havoc with many articles of masculine apparel, but the muffler managed to hold its own. *Esquire* demonstrated how well it was doing through sketches of an Ivy League undergraduate in a gabardine storm coat and pincheck cap sporting a yellow plaid wool scarf that added a welcome note of color to the rather colorless garb. Chatting with the student was a nattily dressed alumnus whose yellow-and-red paisley scarf furnished a nice contrast to his rather conservative tweed overcoat.

Acrylic fibers resembling wools came to the fore in the 1950s in scarves that were usually of 52- by 12-inch proportions. In 1956 *Esquire*'s fashion editor decided that since a neckerchief (which by now was sometimes being simply called a "kerchief") did wonders in smartening-up the collar of a sports shirt, it was time every reader knew how to tie one. Using two photographs of a handsome silk square, whose design replicated the famous holes of Scottish golf courses, the editor prepared instructions that read as follows: "To ready it for this civilizing role, you prepare a neckerchief by successive folds of the opposite corners toward the center. This leaves you with a long scarf of several fold depths. This you then tie about your neck. One method is the simple ascot, with one end draped over the other. A double knot may also be used; it is more casual and holds tighter."

"College fashions in college colors—one of those naturals that should happen all the time and then doesn't," wrote *Esquire* in September, 1957. "But now sportswear has headed in where it belongs—on campus—and adopted the big name color combinations for the new items." Illustrating this feature were photographs of various

bearded busts of ancient intellectuals draped in mufflers of various colleges: the blue of Yale; the scarlet of Rutgers and Ohio State; the white of Bowdoin; the brown of Lehigh and Wyoming; the gold of Georgia Tech and Purdue; the orange of Princeton, Illinois, and Texas; the crimson of Harvard; and the green of Dartmouth and Baylor. The 6-foot-style muffler made a comeback at this time in college colors, and it remained popular with collegians throughout the sixties and into the seventies.

Although the white muffler was still the mode for formal evening wear, *Esquire*, in a display of formal accessories frankly chosen for richness, draped an elegant tasseled muffler of black broadtail fur with a red satin back across the hood of a Rolls-Royce. And *Gentlemen's Quarterly*, with an eye to the upcoming Christmas season, photographed a handsome wool-challis muffler in a yellow-and-red paisley design on a black background in its December, 1959, issue. No two ways about it, the emphasis in the late fifties was on luxurious fabrics, and very prominent was the combination muffler of cashmere on one side and

The soft wool tartan muffler is shown with a diagonal-weave overcoat and a homburg hat. From Esquire, *February 1944.*

silk on the other, usually in harmonizing shades of one color. In the early 1960s such lush combinations persisted, and *Gentlemen's Quarterly* showed a particularly handsome muffler reverse: burgundy cashmere to burgundy-and-black paisley on beige silk.

In 1963 *Esquire* described "the elegant man" and showed the various accessories that were the mark of elegance—a mark that, according to the fashion copywriter, "lies somewhere between the boundaries of impeccable taste and studied understatement." The elegant man in his formal attire, for instance, wore a white silk muffler that was large and rectangular and could be worn in fold-over style or in the throw-over ascot fashion. With a classic Burberry trench coat and soft green textured-felt hat, the elegant man wore a warm wool muffler with a broad plaid design on a canary-yellow background.

In 1964 *Esquire* in its annual roundup of Christmas gift suggestions included another classic, this one a wool-challis muffler. In 1966 the magazine's fashion department concentrated on paisley and attempted to analyze its legendary appeal: "One might well ask what it is about those swirling amoebic designs (which originated on Kashmiri shawls and were brought to the West via the mills at Paisley, Scotland) that has given them a place in fashion for more than a hundred and fifty years. Adaptability more than anything else. Any paisley, whether it be subdued or bright, can usually be worn with a variety of outfits, with the result that American men have taken to wearing it in ties, pocket handkerchiefs, belts, and scarves. All named after a town in Scotland which, incidentally, is also famous for its tobacco and marmalade."

But it was with the coming of the Peacock Revolution that the muffler really came into its own. When the maxi-greatcoat burst upon the scene in the late 1960s, a smart scarf was an essential, whether a paisley neatly worn ascot-fashion or a brightly colored wool tossed over the shoulder and hanging free.

In September, 1971, *Gentlemen's Quarterly,* in an issue celebrating "The Return of the Gentleman," showed scarves to be an important part of any number of outfits: a silk square tucked inside the collar of a suede safari suit; a paisley worn in a simple fold-over style with a banker's-gray maxi-length town coat; and a white silk scarf worn ascot-fashion by a gentleman in a black mohair evening suit and a silk print shirt. And the *New York Times,* in its fall, 1971, "Report on Men's Wear," showed a knotted silk scarf fluttering out of the collar of a chamois-suede shirt jacket, and a 6-foot triple-stripe crocheted muffler and matching stocking cap on a young skater.

The muffler is a durable staple with the kind of fashion cunning that permits it to change size and shape so that it never fails to complement the contemporary silhouette. Its versatility is

A paisley silk foulard muffler worn with a long belted tweed jacket having oversize patch pockets. From Gentlemen's Quarterly, *September 1969.*

nothing short of awesome, its style unquestionable, and its future assured. In this era of liberated fashions, the muffler with its chameleonlike personality is an integral part of the fashion scene.

Handkerchiefs and Squares

At the turn of the century the term "handkerchief" covered the silk square, which as a separate category did not come into being for several years. The 1900 Sears, Roebuck and Company catalog illustrated pure linen hemstitched handkerchiefs with white centers and "artistic fancy colored borders" in a variety of "perfectly fast colors." There were also cream-white Japanese handkerchiefs with a look and feel "almost the same as real Japanese silk." With a 1-inch hem and silk-embroidered initials, they sold for 15 cents each. For an additional 15 cents, one could order a pure white Japanese silk handkerchief with a hemstitched border and a silk-embroidered initial. A very heavy white Japanese silk initialed handkerchief measuring 21 inches cost 58 cents. There was a great variety of silk, both real and imitation. There were 22-inch plain black silks, 20-inch white silks with a 1-inch hemstitched border, and fancy brocaded silk handkerchiefs for ladies and gentlemen, most of them described as having "two or more colors beautifully shaded."

Fashionable Americans who could afford to frequent European winter resorts in the 1920s found new uses for the colored handkerchief. In a report from St. Moritz, *Men's Wear* noted that "brightly figured shantung and tussore, such as were reported as being popular at Oxford, were very much in evidence and were worn by the younger set not only to decorate the pockets and for general use, but as mufflers or twisted round the head pirate fashion" (Feb. 10, 1926, p. 70).

The twenties saw a sharp rise in handkerchiefs with decorative effects, seen mainly in the breast pocket. As worn by more stylish dressers, they harmonized with the wearer's tie but did not match it in fabric or color. In June, 1926, *Men's Wear* noted a tendency toward small designs and pat-

The colored sheer voile handkerchief with a wide border stripe was imported from France in 1923. [NEW YORK PUBLIC LIBRARY PICTURE COLLECTION]

terns, along with a penchant for futuristic designs, also in small effects. Satin bands on sheer linen were "highly regarded," some of the bands being worked in large self-checks that covered the entire handkerchief. The handkerchief preferred with the dinner jacket that year was black and white, and attractive border stripes in black were being seen in both linen and crepe silk handkerchiefs.

The vogue for fancy handkerchiefs gained momentum until, by 1928, it seemed that novelty was the element sustaining interest in both decorative and useful handkerchiefs. "Novelty," said *Men's Wear*, "has done for fine handkerchiefs and handkerchiefs not so fine what color and novelty have done for suspenders, garters, underwear and other merchandise" (Feb. 8, 1928). Colors were somewhat more subdued, and the colored and patterned centers so popular a few seasons earlier were seen less and less frequently, being replaced by more delicately decorated borders. The one exception was the white crepe handkerchief with a 2-inch border in such strong colors as green, maroon, wine, and navy. The fashion writer George Albemarle reported in *Men's Wear* (Nov. 21, 1928) on two of the newest designs in Irish linen handkerchiefs that year, one with a center of blue, with a wide white border patterned in a blue shamrock design, and the other having a white ground on which a green design had been printed. Both had rolled hems in the predominating color of the design.

"A cheerful little eyeful this spring will be the well known breast pocket handkerchief with blithe borders guaranteed to add just that touch of pleasing color needful to contrast with the plain grays, tans and blues that are scheduled favorites for spring suitings," observed *Men's Wear*, adding that "within the past few years handker-

The custom of wearing a figured silk handkerchief in the chest pocket was evident in 1934 and also was quite strong during the sixties. From Esquire, *September 1934.*

chiefs have become a significant style item and have emerged from the classification of a mere convenience article" (Nov. 21, 1928). Illustrating this feature were photographs of a fine linen in two tones of green on a white ground; a linen with burgundy-and-white satin border stripes; a blue-and-gray checked gingham on a white ground with a black-and-white satin border stripe; a white handkerchief featuring a ⅛-inch tan-and-blue stripe with checkered corners forming a border, plus a large allover check formed by narrow white stripes; and a black-and-blue check formed of hairline stripes with a navy-and-white border stripe.

During the thirties men more and more frequently chose a silk square related in color to the shirt and tie. The square was tucked into the pocket in a puff or casually with no points showing. Less fashionable was the nonsilk pocket handkerchief worn in the chest pocket with the points upward. With fashion dominated by the small number of still-affluent men, casual elegance was the keynote of the Depression decade. These well-dressed men looked to the well-dressed Britisher for fashion leadership and copied much of what he wore. In the mid-thirties, lawn bowling, an old English pastime, was taken up at a number of American country clubs, and in June, 1935, *Esquire*'s roving fashion artist sketched a dapper spectator sitting on a club veranda and wearing an India madras square around his neck and a silk puff poking up from the pocket of a brass-buttoned blazer. The next year, the magazine's fashion staff showed some resort wear for jaded town readers and included, along with a lightweight suit in the new hemp color and a coconut straw hat with puggaree band, a colorful printed silk handkerchief.

In the early 1940s some men were so fond of matching colors and patterns that shirt, tie, pocket handkerchief, and even boxer shorts all matched. This fad was excessive and did not last long. After the fashion doldrums imposed by World War II, *Esquire* introduced its "bold look" in 1948, and with it a wide-hemmed white handkerchief that was related to the new wide knot of the tie and the setback stitching of the command-collar shirt.

The late 1940s brought the TV-fold handkerchief, sometimes with initials embroidered at the border. This style, in which a white band about ½ inch wide was displayed above the jacket's chest pocket, was worn by many contemporary television personalities and then was adopted by the general public. It lasted about a decade.

"The elegant man about town puts pattern in his pocket," asserted *Apparel Arts* in an article in May, 1957, noting

Colored handkerchiefs were well accepted in 1935. The silk foulard (top) is blue with a red-and-yellow design, the cotton handkerchief (center) is tan with a maroon-and-brown border, and the figured linen handkerchief (bottom) has a green ground with red-and-yellow figures. From Esquire, *August 1935.*

Steps in folding a handkerchief for the chest pocket in 1949. (left) First step: unfold the handkerchief and hold it at the center, allowing the points to hang in an irregular manner. (center) Second step: fold the handkerchief in half so that the center falls just below the corners. (right) Third step: tuck the handkerchief into the pocket with the center point side toward the body, and let the points appear to be irregularly arranged, not flattened to look as though they were pressed with the pocket. From Esquire, *July 1949.*

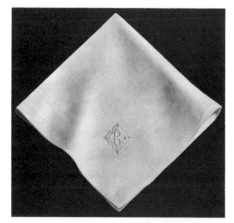

Renaissance initial embroidered on an Irish linen handkerchief with edge hand-rolled in Madeira. From Gentlemen's Quarterly, *September 1963.*

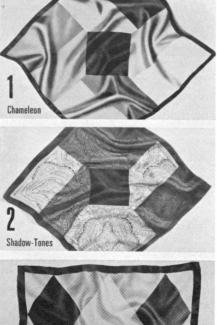

Three versions of silk pocket handkerchiefs. Each handkerchief is designed with nine hand-blocked colors. When the handkerchief is properly folded and tucked in the chest pocket, the desired coordinating color is revealed. From Gentlemen's Quarterly, *March 1964.*

Geometric figures and miniature paisleys are set off by the light-color grounds of these silk handkerchiefs. From Gentlemen's Quarterly, *summer, 1965.*

that "the pocket handkerchief is an index of fashion change. And the emergence of the elegant look in town wear is signaled by a puff of pattern in the breast pocket. Squares of silk and lustrous cotton are illumined with classic designs of paisleys, traditional foulard prints, geometrics. In the pocket, the high fashion form for these squares is that of the puff, with the center of the handkerchief showing above the pocket. The soft fold is also seen." Accompanying this article were photographs of four elegant pocket handkerchiefs: a silk square with a rich red ground and a blocked paisley print of green, black, blue, and gold; a soft combed cotton with paisley motifs forming a geometric pattern in red and black; a Sea Island cotton with a satin-weave border and gigantic checks forming four panels in different shades of gray; and a cotton handkerchief whose blue geometric print created a dimensional illusion.

To create various color effects in silk squares the segmented center was developed. This consisted of eight sections in different colors or shades fanning out from a black center about 3 inches in diameter. The wearer could relate his pocket handkerchief to the colors of his tie and shirt by showing only the segment of the desired color.

In October, 1962, *Esquire* observed that brown was back "but with a difference. The browns men are wearing, for instance, incorporate varying shades of gray and black, creating the tonal subtlety that was popular in olive; thus the brown is more subdued than before, and it provides a better background for different combinations of shirts and ties." The fashion department offered the reader a guide to the colors of accessories. Brown with red accessories, for instance, required a silk pocket square that matched a maroon silk twill necktie. Brown with blue accessories called for a silk square with blue printed figures against a golden background in coordination with a tie

of blue, gold, and gray broad stripings and a pale blue corded cotton shirt. Brown with gold should have a silk pocket square with golden tones that corresponded to a broadcloth shirt with stripings in four different shades of brown and a brown knit tie highlighted with a golden cast. Brown with green called for a silk pocket square with a pattern of eight colored segments, any one of which would harmonize with a striped twill tie that combined a multitude of colors including tan, wine, brown, black, gray, and green.

Lushly colored and opulently designed silk squares were seen in the early sixties, and *Gentlemen's Quarterly* focused its attention on three of them in December, 1962: a blue rose-window–effect medallion; a black-edged silk with dot squares of maize, gray, red, and light blue; and a Persian print in gray, black, and white. Perhaps the most outstanding square of all was not a silk but a cotton hand-screened with a horse-lore motif.

In 1963 *Gentlemen's Quarterly* suggested for Christmas gift giving a page of "furnishings with finesse," among them a tie and handkerchief set of black silk with blue dots and a silk pocket handkerchief with a stained-glass–window design in blue, gold, and green on a bright red ground. In March of that year *Esquire* turned its attention to "the elegant man." With a subtly pinstriped town suit, it suggested various accessories, which the fashion copywriter deemed all-important "because they can establish varied subtleties of mood. Wear a dark tie, dark handkerchief, white shirt, dark hat, and you create an ultra-serious impression, if that's what you want. Otherwise, you might take advantage of the accessories to introduce some color," which is what the fashion staff did. Among the colorful accessories was a regimental-striped silk square in navy blue and red worn in the puff style.

In 1964 Hickok introduced what it termed a "pocket practicality,"—a "spec kerchief" that looked like a furled pocket handkerchief and was actually a handy case for eyeglasses. It was fashioned of imported silk in neckwear foulards and solids and came in colors to match every tie and suit. That year the same firm also introduced a hand-rolled silk handkerchief carrying widely spaced lip prints in red on white or red on black, both bordered in red. "Tired of the prosaic?" asked the advertisement. "Add a romantic lift to your clothes . . . with 'Amore,' a distinctively new idea for every man of derring-do."

Esquire, noting in 1966 that the trend toward paisley was rising, filled a page of its August issue with paisley ties, belts, and handkerchiefs. The brightest paisley was a silk pocket square with a red background, a red border, and a design of blue, green, and yellow.

In the late sixties the silk square presented a problem: some "new wave" suit jackets dispensed with the chest pocket or featured one that was scarcely more than a token and had no space for a square. Fortunately, this was a fad that passed, and the silk square soon regained its former prominence. The colored woven handkerchief also returned to fashion. How strong a comeback it made might best be illustrated with the cover of the September, 1971, issue of *Gentlemen's Quarterly,* dedicated to "The Return of the Gentleman." A model wearing a double-knit suit and a fashionably broad-brimmed hat also sported a very assertive-looking pocket handkerchief with a woven border. It was an echo of the pronouncement made by *Apparel Arts* years earlier: "The pocket handkerchief is an index of fashion change." Now, in the seventies the costume party was over, and a more elegant look had returned. The nonchalantly worn pocket handkerchief signaled the return of the gentleman.

Jewelry

The well-dressed man of the first decade of the twentieth century wished to appear proper and prosperous, and the jewelry he wore heightened the impression of genteel well-being. With his heavily padded oversize business suit a vest was considered essential, and in one vest pocket he would carry his heavy gold watch and in another his watch fob, with a gold chain extending across the chest to connect the two. When worn, cuff links were conservative and most often were designed of metal.

For formal day wear, the fashionable American of this period wore a frock coat, a white shirt with a high-standing collar, a waistcoat, and a silk four-in-hand tie or ascot with a pearl

Jewelry worn by the frock-coated man of 1904 included a stickpin in his ascot, a watch fob, a key chain, and cuff links (not shown). [COURTESY OF CULVER PICTURES, INC., NEW YORK]

or gold stickpin. For formal evening wear, the tailcoat worn with a stiff-bosom shirt was correct; shirt studs were often large and mostly white (usually of pearl) and were worn with matching cuff links. Occasionally a particularly affluent man would wear a single stud of sapphire alone or combined with tiny diamonds, but this was scarcely commonplace. Some men, however, preferred the dinner jacket to the tailcoat, and these men invariably wore shirt studs of black or smoked pearl.

1910–1930

Shortly after World War I the younger man showed a fondness for the wristwatch, which had first appeared in 1914, and as men of all ages slowly but surely followed his lead, especially during the youth-dominated twenties, the heavy gold watch with its fob was marked for oblivion. "For the first time in history, men's jewelry is outselling women's," a fashion journalist noted in 1918 (quoted in the *Jewelers' Circular–Keystone,* June, 1969). And as more and more men shifted from the high starched collar to the soft shirt collar, a gold or gold-plated collar pin became part of a well-dressed man's jewelry wardrobe, while the collar button, essential to the stiff collar, faded from the scene. (In 1901, a leading jewelry manufacturer had reported sales of 1.5 million collar buttons in silver, gold plate, and gold.) The introduction of soft-collar grips in 1921 gave jewelers a new product. Grips held soft collars smoothly, without causing unsightly pinholes.

A recession in 1920 temporarily halted the postwar boom, but *Men's Wear* believed that jewelry prices were "not likely to share in the marked recession that is taking place in most articles of men's wear," for it was noted that despite the recession managers of the big New York hotels reported that reservations for social functions were exceeding those of the previous year, suggesting brisk business in formal evening apparel and the jewelry worn with it. Meanwhile, according to *Men's Wear*, tie clasps were "coming back strong after a quiescence that has prevailed since 1914," and "scarf pins as well have been rejuvenated after an indifferent popularity extending over a period of eight years" (Dec. 1, 1920).

By 1925 the recession was a memory, Americans were well into the so-called Jazz Age, and *Men's Wear* sent a reporter to the Ritz Carlton in New York to interview Rudolph Valentino, who as the most popular male lover of the silent films was an object of great curiosity. Valentino told the reporter that although he had none of the Latin love for loud colors, he had a passion for jewelry. And the reporter carefully noted that "his wrist was decorated by a gold linked slave chain bracelet, while a monstrous flexible key chain, hooked onto the waistband of his trousers, formed a huge festoon into his left hand pocket" (Nov. 18, 1925). The handsome actor said that he detested diamonds but liked sapphires and rubies. After listing the items in Valentino's wardrobe, the reporter came to the conclusion that "except for the idiosyncrasies in the way of jewelry," Rudolph Valentino was smartly dressed.

During the late twenties the shirt with a button-down collar, often worn pinned, was a leading casual style and the shirt with a plain collar, also worn pinned, was steadily gaining favor.

1930–1940

The tie clasp, which had started a comeback in 1920, was still in fashion in 1932, when, with the summer Olympic Games scheduled for Los Angeles and Americans more sports-minded than ever, tie clasps with sports motifs in black-and-white enamel became popular. As *Men's Wear* commented in 1934, "Take a tie clip and curlicue it to the limit and the cavalier will handle it regretfully and pass it over—at first. Change the decoration from roses, lilies and pansies to tennis racquets, dogs, guns and horses, and the gadget buyer will smile happily and purchase. It has been changed into sportswear by adding a golf club or a sail boat. The men who buy know nothing of horses, dogs, guns, boats and polo mallets. They may have a bowing acquaintance with tennis racquets and golf clubs, but they are not sportsmen in the accepted sense. They simply need an excuse for jewelry" (Sept. 5, 1934, p. 20).

There could be no doubt that men liked jewelry, *Men's Wear* continued, adding: "Given the chance and if fashion indicated, they would wear earrings or nose rings. Do you remember during the war, way back in '17 when the world was young and full of ideals about wars to end wars, that our stalwart soldiers seized upon the excuse of the silver identification tag and made it into a bangle? Some of these wristlets were pretty close to being real bracelets. That particular fashion is hanging on persistently, too. There are still plenty of silver dog tags attached to silver chains being sold and worn. It just goes to show how deeply rooted is the male desire to dress up and how foolishly shy and embarrassed the poor fellows are. Any excuse will do, but they have to have an excuse."

Meanwhile, it was noted that colors (reds, blues, and greens), which had been introduced in precious and semi-precious stones for evening wear in 1931 (the year the white evening jacket first created a stir in Palm Beach), were now prominent in dress sets. Colored stones were particularly in evidence in cuff links, and for men who could not afford real rubies, emeralds, and sapphires, there were substitutes from plain glass to the more expensive synthetic stones.

Reporting in 1935 from London (considered the fashion capital of the world by the most sophisticated Americans of the decade), an American fashion reporter observed: "One does not see the same amount of jewelry as in Victorian and Edwardian days, and it is sad that such is the case, for in my opinion even with dinner clothes, if a man wears a black waistcoat he does not seem really well dressed unless he adds a gold watch chain. Remember it should be one of the extremely thin ones." And this writer concluded his report with a word of warning: "Ostentation is never more marked than by a too lavish display of jewelry. It is better to wear little, and the younger the man, the simpler the jewels" (Men's Wear, Mar. 6, 1935, p. 38).

In the United States, Men's Wear was of the opinion that there was every indication that "something comparable to the 'costume jewelry' so dear to the hearts of the ladies is coming into vogue with men. Apparently it all started with the chain tie clip. First the chains were embellished, made fancier, then doodads were hung on them, now these loops have ceased to be chains in any but the broadest sense of the word and have become successions of objects strung together. The wilder they are the better the public seems to like them. The sky is the limit.

"Modernistic effects and combinations of white, green, red and yellow contribute to the feeling that costume jewelry for men is at least on its way if not present in the flesh. The feeling is even further and more completely strengthened by the action of one of the older firms which specializes to some degree in better priced dress sets. This firm, with its ear to the ground in the clothing world, is bringing out midnight blue dress sets in crystal. If that is not costume jewelry, there is no such animal" (Sept. 11, 1935, p. 21).

By the mid-thirties, despite the De-pression it was generally agreed that a man with pretensions to dress must have day jewelry and evening jewelry, jewelry for sports and jewelry for business and informal wear. The key chain attached to a pocket watch had taken on importance in evening jewelry when worn with the tailcoat in the twenties, and it became even more fashionable in the thirties, when, according to Men's Wear, it had become the uniform for both day and night. There was, it said, a chain for every purpose and for every hour. Particularly popular was the so-called "double snake" chain, which had two strands twisted together in a cable twist. The tie clip was by now a standard piece of men's dress jewelry, and from it all sorts of chain and clip arrangements had been derived. An important item was the chain tie holder, a tie clip with a chain attachment; the clip part was attached to the shirt, and the tie was slipped between the chain and the clip. The collar bar also emerged during the thirties. A direct descendant of the collar pin of the twenties, it had a clamp on each end to be attached to the collar points beneath the knot of the tie.

The white dinner jacket continued strong for summer evening wear in 1936, and consequently so did the colored-stone matched evening-wear sets that harmonized with the color of the tie and cummerbund. Especially popular were links and studs to match in ruby, garnet, sapphire, and topaz colors, in black and in white, in pearls and in moonstones.

"Clothing fashion, influenced by the sports trend, has brought into popularity an entirely new range of novelty jewelry," observed Men's Wear in an article published that year. "Combination sets for sportswear are many and it looks as if the scarf pin is coming back." Special attention was given to dog's heads ("authentic reproductions of pedigreed blue-ribbon holders") and horse's heads ("Man o' War's true portrait") in combinations of cuff links, tie clip, and scarf pin. As for the scarf pin, it was judged to be a great stimulant to the neck-wear business, setting off the tie and making it more important. "At the same time, the pin's continually piercing the tie makes it wear for far less time than the unpinned tie" (Feb. 19, 1936, p. 27).

"Painted and etched crystals constitute an almost perfect and a most flexible medium for expressing the sport idea in jewelry," stated Men's Wear in this article. "There is something clean, cool and clear—and yet colorful—about crystals that keeps the imagination of the real sportsman stimulated. And they are lovely to look at, from the cheap little fifty-centers up to the finest hand-cut and colored stones in the swankest jeweler on the Avenue."

In spite of the Depression many men still dressed up in tailcoats, prompting the journalist Lucius Beebe to write in the New York Herald Tribune in 1935: "A well-attired New York gentleman is worth $4,975 on the hoof after six in the evening" (quoted in Esquire, December, 1965). Listing the cost of each item in the man's wardrobe, Beebe estimated $1,500 for a diamond-and-platinum dress pocket watch and chain and $300 for a fouet, a gadget worn on the end of the watch chain and especially designed to eliminate carbonation from champagne.

"As more and more men turn out in full evening regalia, particularly midnight blue, the market for white and midnight blue evening jewelry expands," observed a fashion writer. "Plain white pearls are first and foremost. The flat type, edged with English gold finish and centered with a small cross resembling the thread of an ordinary button, also gold, has very good possibilities. Similarly, the white set with small gold globes in the center will find takers. Cut stones in white and midnight blue have the continental air about them. The screen-backed or mesh-effect dress set in white and midnight blue should register much better than it did last season. Shades of Cartier are evident in the plain pearls bordered with tiny brilliants. Crystal sets with small brilliants in the center also smack of the exclusive jeweler" (*Men's Wear*, Sept. 9, 1936, p. 25).

Cuff links were steadily gaining popularity, thereby increasing sales of French-cuff shirts. Simple colored stones edged with metal (preferably English gold) were among the most favored styles in both round and square antique shapes.

In October, 1937, *Esquire* sketched two debonair gentlemen in the back seat of a limousine. Beneath them were large sketches of their jewelry: a diamond racehorse stickpin with a colored-enamel jockey figure ("recently introduced by international sportsmen"); a heavy gold-link watch chain ("currently popular with Wall Street brokers for wear with town clothes"); and a cigarette box of plain gold ("coming into fashion"). Among the newer cuff-link ideas of 1938 were bold sports crystals. Described by one magazine as "almost as big as pigeon's eggs," they dealt a blow to the theory that links should harmonize with the color of a tie or shirt stripe. Different combinations were also seen in jewelry sets. In dress sets, both black and white pearl studs and links were winning favor, the idea being to outfit the wearer with jewelry appropriate for a tailcoat or a dinner jacket.

Watch chains during this decade were mainly of the key-chain variety. Some were single chains and some double chains, with a key ring on the end and a buckle to be attached to the trouser loop at the waistband and to a watch. The lapel chain was introduced in the mid-thirties; the first model was a leather cord, but soon styles in metal were developed. One end of the lapel chain went through the buttonhole, and the other was attached to the pocket watch, which was kept in the chest pocket.

1940–1950

Men's jewelry went through a blackout in World War II, although the military had a strong influence on jewelry during and after the war. The chunky-chained identification bracelet in a silver or gold finish became a

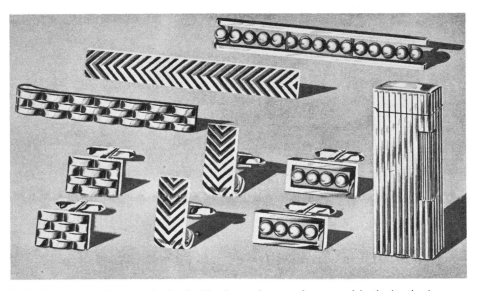

Palladium, a very pale gray color inspired by the precious metal, was used in the jewelry in this group: three tie holders across the top, matching cuff links below, and a cigarette lighter at right. From Esquire, *May 1949.*

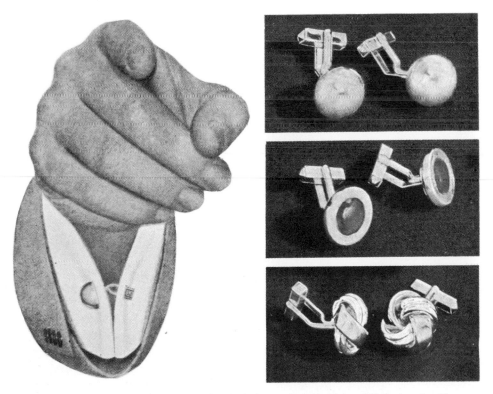

Angled cuff links made a neat appearance in 1948: (top to bottom) plain, slightly domed cuff links; links with colored stones; links in a knot design. From Esquire, *November 1948.*

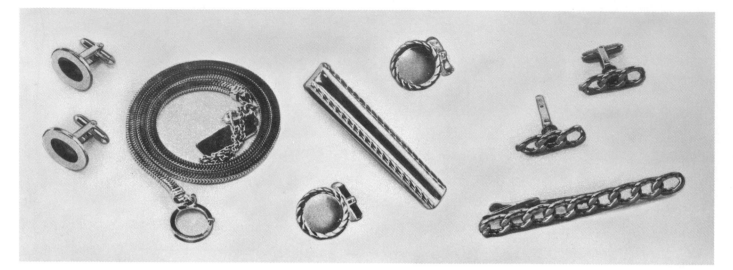

Hefty-looking "bold look" jewelry was designed to complement bold look accessories: (left) cuff links with oval colored stones and a rope chain; (center) cuff links of metal discs with a rope-pattern border and matching tie clasp; (right) loops of rope forming a pattern for cuff links and tie clasp. From Esquire, *November 1948.*

fashion for men not only in the service but in civilian life as well. So popular, in fact, did the ID bracelet become that it led to the rise of the big-link watch chain.

In March, 1948, *Esquire* showed the kind of jewelry worn by "men of affairs." The fashion artist sketched a lean six-footer carrying a briefcase as he alighted from a plane. The fashion copywriter added: "His offices touching on the two oceans, with branches midway between, our man has learned to fly thousands of miles as casually as he once travelled across town, and to keep his feet on the ground while reaching decisions with his head in the air. His role is modern, demanding; his appearance at the airport must be 100% perfect the minute they feather the props." Among the man's own props was a collection of "richly coordinated jewelry": a gold-ridged cigarette case, lighter, cuff links, tie holder, key chain, and gold-studded wallet.

In October, 1948, *Esquire* introduced the "Bold Look for the dominant male," the man of affairs with a handsomely coordinated wardrobe, from a broad-brimmed hat to hefty shoes. "It is, in short," explained *Esquire*, "the first actual expression—in the fabrics, the textures, the colors and

the cut of the clothes a man wears—of a predominant state of mind." The bold look shirt had a widespread collar ("we call it the 'command collar'") styled for wear with a Windsor knot. The French cuffs were longer (9½ inches around) and wider (2⅝ inches deep), and with such an assertive shirt a man wore bigger, chunkier cuff links, say, a ½-inch-square stone set in a wider gold base. His tie clasp, said *Esquire*'s fashion editor, should be a gold bar ½ inch wide "that holds its own" against the 3-inch stripes of his necktie.

The following year *Esquire* contin-

Coordinated jewelry: a ridged gold cigarette case, lighter, cuff links, and tie holder, a key chain, and a gold-studded wallet. From Esquire, *March 1948.*

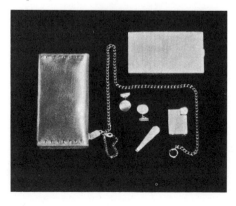

ued to promote the bold look, but now the jewelry featured a new color, palladium. Introducing it in the May, 1949, issue, the fashion editors said: "This is the first big color news for men since the war, inspired by the precious metal Palladium . . . snatched from industry's high-flying drawing boards and put into action as a luxurious masculine fashion." A collection of aggressive-looking cuff links and tie bars and a solitary but commanding cigarette lighter launched this new metallic color.

In May, 1950, the magazine announced that the new pinpoint shirt collar had inspired a new group of collar pins: "Here's a comeback for one of our favorite fashions—the pin collar. The wheel has come full circle again and pins are in. Leading the pin swing back into the public eye is the new pin point shirt. It has a revolutionary, new design for shirt collars—especially cut to take a two-inch pin and then break away toward the shoulders. The small knot tie is also back again with this type of collar. A long time favorite of pin wearers has been the short-rounded collar, but the tableless tab collar and regular collars are now being pinched by a pin, too.

"Still another innovation is the use

of the collar pin with the button-down collar. The return of the collar pin probably won't make much of a tremor on any scientist's seismograph; but for neatness and good grooming, it's hard to think of a more welcome accessory."

1950–1960

A conspicuous characteristic of men's clothes in the early fifties was their conservatism. Ties were extremely narrow, and tie bars became shorter as a result. Color was not missing from jewelry, however, and varicolored enamels, ceramics, and stones were seen in tie clasps, bars, and cuff links.

In 1952 *Esquire* conducted a kind of postgraduate course in the well-balanced wardrobe. "What's right to wear at the right time" was more or less the theme, and when it came to jewelry for formal evening wear, the fashion department decreed studs of pearls or precious stones for the bosom shirt, matching cuff links, a pocket watch, and "a good key chain." For semiformal evening wear it advocated

studs and cuff links of mother-of-pearl, enamel, gold, or colored stones, a pocket watch or a wristwatch, a key chain, and a lighter. Except for formal evening wear, the pocket watch had by this time lost its charm, and with it went the watch and key chains. The wristwatch had triumphed, and during this decade the elastic type of metal watchband captured the imagination of most men.

Esquire promoted the "nubby touch" in 1953, identifying it as a movement toward apparel made of fabrics with soft, irregular textures. A nubby touch sports outfit, said the fashion staff, would consist of a rough tweed jacket, an oxford shirt, and flannel slacks; nubby touch accessories would include a gold-finish set of tie holder and cuff links with horizontal-stripe stones. The next year, noting that "Americans enjoy leaving a shirt open at the throat," *Esquire* suggested in its June issue an innovation from Europe: a smart scarf with a touch of jewelry:

"The newest note in the neckerchief is the scarf with the ring on it. The ends of the scarf are slipped through

Modern designs in jewelry of 1957: (top) smooth walnut stripes on buffed gold in an ultramodern set of tie bar and cuff links; (center) cuff links of golden circles joined by a rope-mesh coil; (bottom) bright silver serpentine mesh used in cuff links and tie bar. From Apparel Arts, *April 1957.*

Collar pins were revived in 1950: (top, left to right) a 2-inch gold safety pin with a pinpoint collar, a bit pin with a rounded collar, and a hunter's-horn pin with a tabless tab collar; (bottom, left to right) a golf-club pin with a regular collar, a small pin with a button-down collar, and, in a group, a collar holder, a knob pin, a riding-crop design, a polo mallet, and a bit. From Esquire, *May 1950.*

the ring and the ring then slides toward the neck in order to obtain a secure closure.

"The ring itself is an interesting piece of jewelry which can take on many forms. Sportsmen will like the variety of horses and dogs framed in miniature under crystal. And lovers of antiques should appreciate the old-world design and finish of many other rings.

"The scarves themselves vary in fabric and in color, as well as in design."

By this time the Old World custom of the wedding band for men had been revived. Before World War II only a minority of weddings were performed

(top) Roman coin in antique silver decorating a key chain; *(center left)* a spiral design used in a set of cuff links and tie tack to minimize weight and size; *(center right)* interlocking silver squares framing a pearl in these trim cuff links; *(across bottom)* antique gold cuff links in a crown shape setting off synthetic rubies, a giant key with a St. Christopher medal to be used as a key ring, and Destino cuff links with Oriental jade centered in crossed gold bars. From Apparel Arts, *April 1957.*

in a double-ring ceremony, but by the fifties almost 90 percent of American husbands were wearing gold or platinum wedding bands.

In April, 1957, *Apparel Arts* devoted a double-page spread to Father's Day jewelry. Among the pieces shown were an ultramodern set of tie bar and cuff links featuring smooth walnut stripes on buffed gold; cuff links of golden circles joined with a rope-mesh coil and capped with high-finish nailheads; a set of cufflinks and tie bar in a bright silver serpentine mesh; a silvery set of links and tie tack featuring a lion on top of an imported onyx stone; a key chain utilizing a copy of an old Roman coin in antiqued silver; gold oystershell cuff links with a set-in pearl; small-size silver links and tie tack; crown-shaped antique gold links with a synthetic ruby; and Oriental jade centered in cuff links of crossed gold bars.

"Jewels In!" was an *Esquire* headline the next year. "Real jewelry regains its place in the best of men's apparel. Rings: a man-made sapphire glistens from Italian-finish metal; man-made ruby sparks another; the third is a horseshoe nail of gold. Antique excellence returns in lapel watches: more than a century old, with seal fob made in 347 A.D. Jewels stuff cuff links too—these are tiny sapphires. And good design links a modern watch to a simple identification bracelet."

In 1959 the fashion department emphasized cool blue as the foremost summer color and showed jewelry to match: cuff links with man-made star sapphires set in a sunburst of golden rays and an evening-dress set of studs and cuff links in a handsomely spun Florentine gold finish with stones of cool yacht blue.

1960–1970

Esquire celebrated the new elegance of men's high-fashion jewelry in June, 1961, with photographs of an extra trim small-link identification bracelet of 14-carat gold; a 14-carat gold money clip whose snap enclosure could be engraved with a photograph; a tapered cigar holder of 14-carat yellow gold; cuff links displaying 7½ cabochon emeralds set in 18-carat gold; an emerald stud set; a white-gold ring with a synthetic emerald set between two diamonds; and ("for the man who *really* has everything") a screwdriver set with 14-carat gold handles.

Although most wristwatches were square-shaped, there were exceptions. In the same article *Esquire* showed a few of these handsome exceptions, among them an egg-shaped watch of 18-carat gold; a cushion-shaped watch of 18-carat gold; a round evening

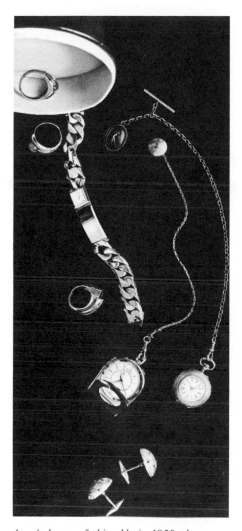

Close-up of cuffs to show such details as the proper exposure of linen, cuff links of deep red enamel, and a white-gold ring with a man-made star sapphire. From Esquire, *March 1964.*

Jewels became fashionable in 1958: three rings, consisting of a man-made sapphire set in Italian-finish metal, a man-made ruby, and a gold horseshoe nail; a watch set in an identification bracelet; a watch and chain with a fob seal; a watch with a flip-back stand alarm on a fob chain; cuff links set with tiny sapphires. From Esquire, *June 1958.*

Elegance in men's jewelry in 1961: (ascending from lower right) a gold small-link identification bracelet; a gold money clip; a 14-carat yellow-gold cigar holder; cuff links and studs with cabochon emeralds in an 18-carat gold setting; a white-gold ring with a synthetic emerald between two small diamonds; and a screwdriver set with 14-carat gold handles, consisting of one regular and one Phillips model. From Esquire, *June 1961.*

Revolution to turn men's closets inside out, and jewelry, like almost everything else that was wearable, was "liberated." Cuff links, advertised as "wild and wonderful," turned up in the shape of dragons, pythons, rams, turtles, and owls, each with jewellike eyes. Watchbands of leather and rugged chains grew wider and bolder, in keeping with the sumptuously buckled belts and opulent ties the "new wave" man now wore.

The turtleneck shirt and sweater and the collarless Nehru jacket became modish in turn, and soon men were draping massive pendants around their necks—the heavier and chunkier, the better. More avant-garde men

watch rimmed with diamonds; a sporty horseshoe-shaped watch; a white-gold octagonal dress watch; and a curved oblong watch with a gold-filled case and a shock-absorbing movement.

To be well dressed a man must be impeccable to his fingertips, maintained the fashion staff in 1964. Conservative jewelry was endorsed: a star sapphire ring in a simple white-gold mounting, and a pair of deep-red enamel cuff links.

In the late sixties came the Peacock

hung beads around their necks. All this may have seemed new and daring, but as *Gentlemen's Quarterly* noted in October, 1970:

"Necklaces have always gained ready acceptance in some form by men of all cultures in every era right down to the present. Whether in the shape of a relic- (or garlic-) filled amulet that warded off the devil and his ways, or a World War II dog-tag chain or the most recent pastel-colored beads, necklaces for men are O.K., Joe, and only the seriously uptight can condemn them as being unmasculine."

The uptight were more and more in a minority. For although the term "unisex" was rarely used in the seventies, its echo lingered on. The idea of a strict division into masculine and feminine categories no longer intimidated either of the sexes in the matter of emotions, manners, or fashions. Women wore pants and boots, and men wore their hair longer and their shirts and suits shaped without suffering any loss of gender.

True, the Peacock Revolution had bred some unfortunate fads, but by the early seventies fashion had settled down. In the words of the *New York Times* of April 18, 1971, "Clothes for the second summer of the seventies have cooled it." And they had done so without losing any of the color and

(right) The Italian Renaissance inspired the design of men's jewelry in 1965. From Gentlemen's Quarterly, *March 1965.*

(below) These convertible cuff links had detachable colored balls and a gold shank. The colors included green, opal, red, blue, brown, gold, and white. From Esquire, *May 1968.*

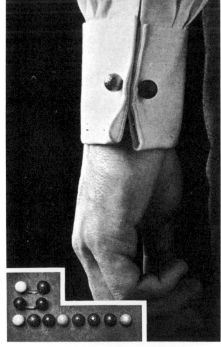

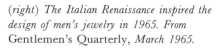

(right) Royal Copenhagen cuff links were sold by Swank in 1969. From Gentlemen's Quarterly, *September 1969.*

Designs in men's jewelry by Pierre Cardin in 1970 included knots, weaves, ropes, squares, geometrics, and colored stones. From Gentlemen's Quarterly, *April 1970.*

dash that were legacies of the revolution. Certainly jewelry was more imaginative than ever. This was particularly true of cuff links, of which the *Times* displayed a king-size collection: massive links of porcelain decorated with Nordic motifs, a tiger eye on frosted crystal, enameled Spanish tile, miniature mosaics in a beaded setting, and framed African malachite.

The tie clip, however, was a fashion casualty, its demise the direct result of the wider necktie, which was thrown off center when clipped. The tie tack, which was not affected by the wider tie, survived, although it lost substantial ground as more and more neckties were produced with a label loop specifically designed to hold the shorter end of a tie in its proper place.

By this time the conventional identification bracelet had been superseded by a bracelet that was frankly a bracelet. It could be made of gold, silver, or copper or of a massive band of leather that was sometimes studded with "hardware." Among the younger, more avant-garde dressers partial to the new kind of leisure wear it was sometimes worn on the upper arm. Bracelets for men may also have seemed new and daring, but as *Gentlemen's Quarterly* had pointed out in October, 1970, they were actually a form of jewelry that had never fallen out of favor, "primarily because man has always found a practical use for them— as guards against enemy swords, as amulets, as wristwatches, as identification bands. Historically, these orna-

ments have been so popular that artisans of the great civilizations— Egypt, Greece, Rome—applied their finest skill in making them.

"For years in the United States, however, only the chunky-chained identification bracelet was acceptable for men. Then came the introduction of the wide leather go-go watchband, replete with heavy masculine hardware."

The late sixties and early seventies saw a boom in handmade jewelry, as an offshoot of the hippie movement, but it was confined largely to a well-publicized minority of younger men who shopped in boutiques.

Esquire took a reflective look at the fashion scene in January, 1972, and came to this conclusion: "Once aroused, apparently, the peacock is not easily put down, and though the excesses of the recent revolution in male apparel have gradually disappeared, man is not yet entirely bereft of an urge to primp. Now this expresses itself in a growing vogue for medallions, dog tags, chains, bracelets, belt buckles, and rings that are considerably more discreet than those that garishly graced the pinkies of such as Frank Nitti in the Twenties. On the whole, it is a salutary trend, for done with taste and an accent on masculinity, it contributes a certain individuality." The Peacock Revolution sparked the imaginations of designers and artisans whose talents launched a renaissance of jewelry that very likely is still in its infancy. Certainly in no other category of fashion is the new freedom of the peacock on display as it is in the jewelry he wears.

In the meantime, the fondness of the conservative man of fashion for classic jewelry continues as strong as ever, for if the revolution has not prompted him to experiment with the more avant-garde designs, it certainly has made him more appreciative of the elegant cuff links, tie clips, and money clips that have always been an essential part of his jewelry wardrobe.

Belts and Braces

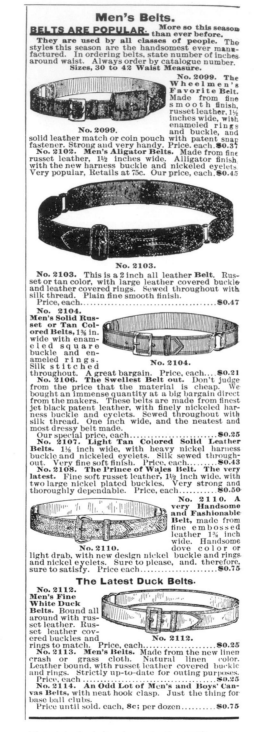

Materials for belts shown in the 1897 catalog of Sears, Roebuck and Company ranged from tan and russet leathers and alligator to fabrics.

During the first decade of the twentieth century trousers were made without belt loops, since braces were preferred for daytime wear and white braces were *de rigueur* for formal evening wear. And while many laboring men wore sturdy, plain leather belts with their work clothes, when it came time to dress up, they too reached for braces. A minority of affluent men had their suits custom-made with belt loops and sometimes wore belts, often along with braces, displaying handsome, importantly initialed belt buckles of silver or gold.

Although the words "braces" and "suspenders" were interchangeable, the Sears, Roebuck and Company catalog of 1897–1900 used "suspenders," reserving "braces" for the special braces designed to cure round shoulders. Among the suspenders displayed in the Sears catalog were nonelastic suspenders made from 1-inch webbing with seamless woven round plastic ends ("Very neat, dressy patterns, light or dark colors, with small polka dots, stripes or figures"); nonelastic suspenders made from imported silk and embossed with kid trimmings and ornamental gold sliding buckles; dress suspenders of close-woven imported white or black elastic webbing; jeweled suspenders ("a most attractive novelty") in light and medium colors embroidered in designs in contrasting colors, with embossed kid trimmings and each buckle set with a large imitation amethyst, emerald, or topaz; heavy elastic striped cross-back suspenders with heavy leather trimming and leather ends; extralong suspenders for very tall men; and imported elastic-webbing suspenders with embossed white kid trimmings, braided silk ends, and enameled Dresden-pattern buckles.

"The most economical and comfortable suspenders in the world," however, were made from a soft, plia-

220 **SEARS, ROEBUCK & CO., (Incorporated), Cheapest Supply House on Earth, Chicago.**

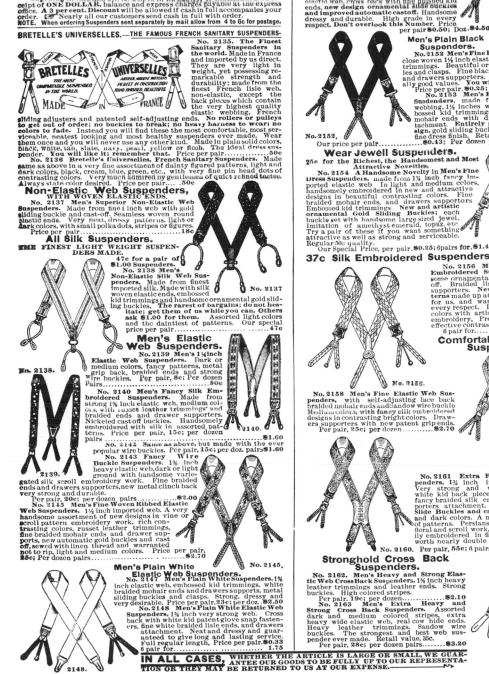

SUSPENDERS AND BRACES.

UNPRECEDENTED VALUES.

A MATCHLESS LINE OF MODERN SUSPENDERS AND SHOULDER BRACES made from best materials obtainable and possessing every new and modern improvement known to the best manufacturers of this class of goods. Every pair guaranteed absolutely perfect in every way and exactly as represented. All new, clean and fresh goods direct from the manufacture, at prices that discount all passible competitors.

Anything in this line will be sent C. O. D., subject to examination on receipt of **ONE DOLLAR**, balance and express charges payable at the express office. **A 3 per cent. Discount** will be allowed if cash in full accompanies your order. ☞ Nearly all our customers send cash in full with order.

NOTE. When ordering Suspenders sent separately by mail allow from 4 to 6c for postage.

BRETELLE'S UNIVERSELLES.—THE FAMOUS FRENCH SANITARY SUSPENDERS.

No. 2135. The Finest Sanitary Suspenders in the world. Made in France and imported by us direct. They are very light in weight, yet possessing remarkable strength and durability; made from the finest French lisle web. non-elastic, except the back pieces which contain the very highest quality elastic webbing, French sliding adjusters and patented self-adjusting ends. **No rollers or pulleys to get out of order; no buckles to break; no heavy harness to wear; no colors to fade.** Instead you will find these the most comfortable, most serviceable, neatest looking and most healthy suspenders ever made. Wear them once and you will never use any other kind. Made in plain solid colors, black, white, tan, slate, navy, pearl, yellow or flesh. The ideal dress suspender. **You will like it; remember that.** Price per pair..............50c

No. 2136 Bretelle's Universelles, French Sanitary Suspenders. Made same as above in a very fine assortment of dainty figured patterns, light and dark colors, black, cream, blue, green, etc., with very fine pin head dots of contrasting colors. Very much admired by gentlemen of quiet refined tastes. Always state color desired. Price per pair..... .50c

Non-Elastic Web Suspenders,

WITH WOVEN ELASTIC ENDS.

No. 2137 Men's Superior Non-Elastic Web Suspenders. Made from fine 1 inch web with gold sliding buckle and cast-off. Seamless woven round elastic ends. Very neat, dressy patterns, light or dark colors, with small polka dots, stripes or figures.
Price per pair..................................18c

No. 2137

All Silk Suspenders.

THE FINEST LIGHT WEIGHT SUSPENDERS MADE.

47c for a pair of $1.00 Suspenders.

No. 2138 Men's Non-Elastic Silk Web Suspenders. Made from finest imported silk. Made with silk woven elastic ends, embossed kid trimmings and handsome ornamental gold sliding buckles. **The rarest of bargains; do not hesitate; get them of us while you can. Others ask $1.00 for them.** Assorted light colors and the daintiest of patterns. Our special price per pair...............................47c

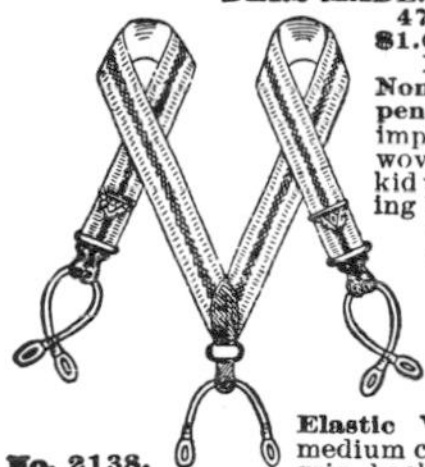

No. 2138.

Men's Elastic Web Suspenders.

No. 2139 Men's 1¼ inch Elastic Web Suspenders. Dark or medium colors, fancy patterns, metal grip back, braided ends and strong wire buckles. Per pair, 8c; Per dozen Pairs..................................80c

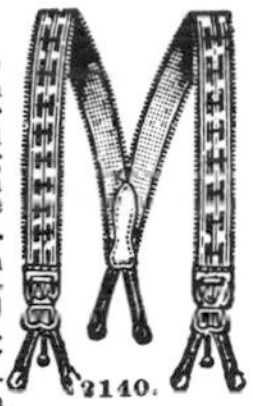

2140.

No. 2140 Men's Fancy Silk Embroidered Suspenders. Made from strong 1⅜ inch elastic web, medium colors, with russet leather trimmings and braided ends and drawer supporters. Nickeled cast off buckles. Handsomely embroidered with silk in assorted patterns. Price per pair, 15c; per dozen pairs $1.60

No. 2142 Same as above, but made with the ever popular wire buckles. Per pair, 15c; per doz. pairs $1.60

2139.

No. 2143 Fancy Wire Buckle Suspenders. 1⅜ inch heavy elastic web, dark or light ground with handsome variegated silk scroll embroidery work. Fine braided ends and drawers supporters, new metal clinch back very strong and durable.
Per pair, 20c; per dozen pairs..............$2.00

No. 2145 Men's Fine Woven Ribbed Elastic Web Suspenders. 1½ inch imported web. A very handsome assortment of new designs in vine or scroll pattern embroidery work, rich contrasting colors, russet leather trimmings, fine braided mohair ends and drawer supports, new automatic gold buckles and cast off, sewed with linen thread and warranted not to rip, light and medium colors. Price per pair, 25c; Per dozen pairs....................... ....$2.70

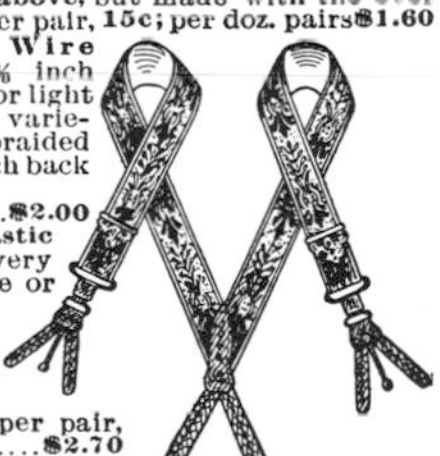

No. 2145.

Men's Plain White Elastic Web Suspenders.

No. 2147 Men's Plain White Suspenders, 1⅜ inch elastic web, embossed kid trimmings, white braided mohair ends and drawers supports, metal sliding buckles and clasps. Strong, dressy and very desirable. Price per pair, 23c; per doz..$2.50

No. 2148 Men's Plain White Elastic Web Suspenders, 1⅜ inch very strong web. Cross back with white kid patent glove snap fasteners, fine white braided lisle ends, and drawers attachment. Neat and dressy and guaranteed to give long and lasting service. Full regular length, Price per pair. $0.33
6 pair for............. .... 1.75

2148.

No. 2147 Men's Plain White Dress Suspenders, 1⅜ inch fine woven elastic web. Handsomely embossed kid trimmings, very close woven white mohair ends and drawers supporters. Fancy gold slide buckles, and **new automatic cast off.** Extra well made and finished. Retail value, 65c. Our price per pair..... ..$0.40; Per dozen $..... 4.30

Our 40c White Dress Suspenders.

No. 2149.

Rialto Dress Suspenders.

50c for 75c Suspenders.

No. 2150 The Rialto Fine Dress Suspenders, 1⅜ inch close woven imported white elastic web, cross back with fine finished kid ends, **new design ornamental slide buckles and improved automatic castoff.** Handsome dressy and durable. High grade in every respect. **Don't overlook this Number.** Price per pair $0.50; Doz. $4.50

Men's Plain Black Suspenders.

No. 2152 Men's Fine Plain Black Suspenders close woven 1½ inch elastic web. Embossed kid trimmings. Beautiful ornamental sliding buckles and clasps. Fine black braided mohair ends, and drawers supporters. One of our exceptionally good values. **You will like them.**
Price per pair. $0.25; Per dozen pairs. $2.70

No. 2153 Men's Fine Plain Black Dress Susdenders, made from imported elastic webbing. 1½ inches wide. Handsomely embossed kid trimmings. Fine braided black mohair ends with drawers supporters attachment. **Entirely new and beautiful design,** gold sliding buckles and clasps. Extra fine dress finish. Retail value 75c.

No. 2152.

Our price per pair................$0.43; Per dozen pairs............... $4.65

Wear Jewell Suspenders.

25c for the Richest, the Handsomest and Most Attractive Novelties.

No. 2154 A Handsome Novelty in Men's Fine Dress Suspenders, made from 1⅜ inch fancy imported elastic web In light and medium colors, handsomely embroidered in new and attractive designs in beautiful contrasting colors. Fine braided mohair ends, and drawers supportors Embossed kid trimmings. **New and artistic ornamental Gold Sliding Buckles;** each buckle set with handsome large sized jewel. Imitation of amethyst emerald, topaz, etc. Try a pair of these if you want something attractive as well as strong and serviceable. Regular 50c quality.
Our Special Price, per pair. $0.25; 6 pairs for. $1.40

No. 2154.

37c Silk Embroidered Suspenders.

No. 2156 Men's Extra Fine Silk Embroidered Suspenders, with handsome ornamental gold slides and cast off. Braided lisle ends and drawers supporters. **New and exclusive patterns** made up at the factory expressly for us, and warranted high grade in every respect. Light medium and dark colors with artistic and elaborate silk embroidery, Presenting charming and effective contrasts. Per pair $0.37
6 pair for......................... 2.10

No. 2156.

Comfortable Lace Back Suspenders.

No. 2158 Men's Fine Elastic Web Suspenders, with self-adjusting lace back braided mohair ends and Sandow wire buckle Medium colors, **with fancy silk embroidered** designs in contrasting bright colors. Drawers supporters with new patent grip ends.
Per pair, 25c; per dozen..........$2.70

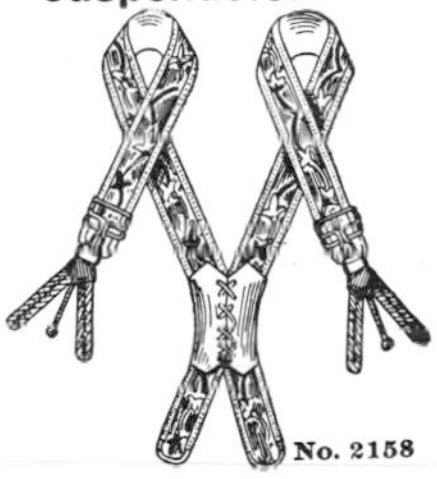

No. 2158

No. 2160.

No. 2161 Extra Fine Lace Back Suspenders, 1⅜ inch imported elastic web. Very strong and wear resisting. Fine white kid back piece. white kid trimmings fancy braided silk ends and drawers supporters attachment. **New Patented Gold Slide Buckles and cast off.** Medium, light and dark colors. A magnificent assortment of patterns. Persians, Orientals, Dresdens, floral and scroll work, beautifully and heavily embroidered in finest silk floss, actually worth nearly double our asking price.
Per pair, 55c; 6 pairs for..............$2.96

Stronghold Cross Back Suspenders.

No. 2162. Men's Heavy and Strong Elastic Web Cross Back Suspenders, 1⅜ inch heavy leather trimmings and leather ends. Strong buckles. High colored stripes.
Per pair. 19c; per dozen..............$2.10

No. 2163 Men's Extra Heavy and Strong Cross Back Suspenders. Assorted dark and medium colored stripes, extra heavy wide elastic web, real cow hide ends. Heavy leather trimmings. Sandow wire buckles. The strongest and best web suspender ever made. Retail value, 35c.
Per pair, 28c; per dozen pairs........$3.20

No. 2162.

IN ALL CASES, WHETHER THE ARTICLE IS LARGE OR SMALL, WE GUARANTEE OUR GOODS TO BE FULLY UP TO OUR REPRESENTATION OR THEY MAY BE RETURNED TO US AT OUR EXPENSE.

Suspenders in many patterns of elastic and nonelastic webbing were priced not only singly but by the dozen in the 1897 catalog of Sears, Roebuck and Company.

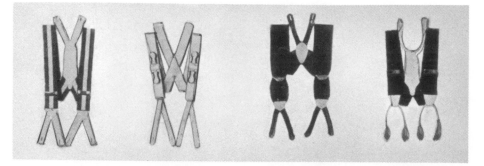

ble oak russet belt leather, according to the Sears catalog. It was claimed that they were more comfortable than elastic suspenders and wore more than twice as well. At 35 cents a pair, they cost almost four times the price of a pair of ordinary elastic-webbing suspenders, but 25 cents less than Dresden-buckle suspenders and less than half the price of embroidered satin suspenders that came in a glass-top case and sold for 98 cents. But, said Sears, the biggest news in suspenders was the "Bretelle's Universelles—the famous French sanitary suspenders. Made from finest French lisle web, non-elastic, except the back pieces which contain the very highest quality elastic webbing. French sliding adjusters and patented self-adjusting ends. No rollers or pulleys to get out of order; no buckles to break, no heavy harness to wear; no colors to fade. Instead you will find these the most comfortable, most serviceable, neatest looking and most healthy suspenders ever made. Made in plain solid colors— black, white, tan, slate, navy, pearl, yellow or flesh. The ideal dress suspender. *You will like it: remember that.* Price per pair . . . 50 cents." Featured more or less inconspicuously at the bottom of the page of suspenders and shoulder braces were men's elastic-webbing and silk-webbing garters in neat, fancy, and striped patterns.

1920–1930

The doughboy of World War I wore a coarse yarn belt with his khaki uni-form, and when he returned in 1919, he was decidedly belt-conscious. Braces, nevertheless, continued to dominate menswear throughout the twenties, since it was generally agreed that the high-rise, full-cut trousers with a pleated waistband draped best when held up by braces. Furthermore, manufacturers, who were keenly aware of the younger generation's interest in more colorful clothes, were now producing braces in livelier colors and more spirited designs. Yet by the late twenties belts were making inroads, particularly among younger men and especially during the summer months. The reason for this trend offers us an interesting view of the old-fashioned attitudes of many people during this Jazz Age era that is generally considered to have been so daring:

"Whatever the position of the contestants for the privilege of sustaining American trousers may be, as a summer factor belts lead suspenders by a wide stretch," commented *Men's Wear* in 1928, "because many American vests vanish under the persuasion of the hot summer sun. Regardless of their beauty or brilliancy, uncovered suspenders are embarrassing to men when exposed in mixed company. Consequently, when vests come off belts go on.

"The suspender industry has been going very strong because braces have been made ornate and colorful. This eye-catching feature has been of inestimable value in promoting suspender sales and it appears that this form of trousers support is in for a good long run of popularity, but not as a summer factor. Tradition has made the showing of suspenders disgraceful when exposed before ladies, but because they are one of the hidden beauties of masculine apparel has not dulled an appreciation of daring effects any more than it has a high regard for drawers done in stripings and figures whose colors rival an Italian sunset. At the same time drawers and suspenders are for private viewing, while belts now blossom out as the only visible means of support of American trousers.

"Why suspenders should not be shown by the wearer is one of the mysteries. Logically, if they are ornate and colorful, it would seem that these features are present to be seen. Much mechanical ingenuity has been expended on perfecting suspenders that they can be worn under the shirt to keep them out of sight. Why the sight of suspenders should shock esthetic feminine sensibilities is difficult to understand, but no strong minded woman will permit her husband to roam about the house wearing exposed suspenders. She would prefer to have the trousers held up as though by magic. The difference between exposed suspenders and belts is that subtle something which induces a man to be proud that he is a golfer and a little bit sheepish about being a bowler.

"For one thing, suspenders have begun to live down the imputation that they are for old men. Not so long ago the feeling was that a man took up suspenders when age had changed his figure and removed his waistline. When he donned suspenders it was an admission that he had arrived at a point in life's journey where he no longer could take interest in bathing beauties and when it was time he saw about making his will. The colorful ideas in suspenders not only made braces a style article, but they sharply brought to the attention of the world that club stripes in bright reds, yellows and blues were not merely for males on the verge of senile decay. These were for flaming youth, and business in suspenders for the last few years has boomed because the industry has uncovered a new market. Ornamentation and color that appeared in suspenders of a generation ago ran to embroidered forget-me-nots. Now the decorative features blaze out like a diagonal scarlet band across the white bosom of the dress shirt of a continental diplomat" (*Men's Wear–Chicago Apparel Gazette,* Apr. 11, 1928, p. 112).

Yet for all the popularity of stylish suspenders, the time had come for a well-dressed man to own also a wardrobe of belts. "It is ridiculous that a customer should be permitted to own only one belt as compared with several suits and dozens of neckties," said the *Men's Wear* fashion writer, urging retailers to follow the example of one manufacturer who was stressing the concept of different belts for different purposes or occasions. "He recommends a pin seal or a black calf belt for evening wear, braided belts for sports wear, something else for flannel trousers, and so on." And then the writer cast a jaundiced eye on what he termed "the apathetic retailer": "Some time ago a manufacturer brought out a genuine ostrich belt. Women had stopped wearing ostrich plumes and it did not pay the Australians to feed the birds. They were killed

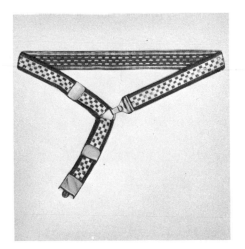

The narrow silk elastic garter in brown-and-white or black-and-white checks was a fashionable accessory in 1923. [NEW YORK PUBLIC LIBRARY PICTURE COLLECTION]

in large numbers and their skins tanned into leather that became very popular as handbags, and the like. Several belt manufacturers subsequently put out ostrich belts. While these had a good sale, because the retail price was high, merchants were timid about stocking them and selling them. Here was a distinct novelty with a genuine appeal, but apathetic merchants failed to grasp its significance" (Apr. 11, 1928, p. 113).

Meanwhile, among the best-selling belts in 1928 were braided belts of various widths and colors, snakeskin, alligator, zebra, walrus, and lizard belts, and leathers finished to resemble fabrics such as tweed. Buckles took on a more elegant, subdued look with enameled ornamentation.

Nevertheless, suspenders were far from fading out of the picture. "Suspender patterns and colors rival neckwear," headlined a trade journal in 1928, adding: "The spurt in suspender business is directly attributable to the striking patterns and colors that now are found in all priced classifications, from the exclusive imported article to the popular priced domestic merchandise. It is a fact that while no one would appear in exposed suspenders without a blush and an apology, the highly decorative article is the only kind of suspender that is moving out of retail stocks" (*Men's Wear–Chicago Apparel Gazette,* Apr. 25, 1928, p. 121). And while suspenders were still undercover accessories, in the late twenties they had become part of a man's total ensemble: some smart New York shops were displaying them in their windows with neckwear to match, and one manufacturer was showing swatches of suspender materials in the manner of a neckwear manufacturer. Furthermore, suspender prices had risen precipitously: whereas ten years earlier $1 was a decent price, suspenders were now selling for as much as $6. "Where there is a novel treatment, pretty nearly any price can be commanded. The charm of color is what has caught the popular fancy," noted the *Men's Wear* editor. There was, he commented, a marked contrast between

the old-fashioned suspenders and "the modern eye-catcher in strong stripes of reds and blues." He added: "'Comfort' once was the suspender slogan, and demonstrations of the human male stretching and bending into gymnastic positions to demonstrate how adjustable the braces were belong to the machine age. Authorities are affirming that now we are in an artistic age and for that reason the mechanical advantages of various suspenders are barely whispered, while the vivid dreams of the artist who designs these suspenders are exploited."

Wallach Brothers, a chain of New York men's furnishing shops, promoted the idea of matching end-and-end shirt fabrics with suspender webbing. And a new idea for formal dress was to wear suspenders with slides in gunmetal that harmonized with the wearer's smoked-pearl studs and links. Meanwhile, suspender patterns were growing more and more varied: narrow stripings on solid grounds; regimental stripes; checks in blue and white, red and blue, purple and white, and black and white; and basketweave webbing in solid white or black. As for the tabs that were attached to the trouser buttons, leather tabs were giving way to knitted tabs, which were considered to have a smarter, imported look.

Another boon to the belt during this decade was the great popularity of knickers and knickerbocker suits for sportswear. Knickers were seen on the links at elegant resorts and country clubs, in every fabric from flannel and tweed to gabardine and the new Palm Beach summer fabric of cotton and mohair. And by the mid-twenties vacationing American collegians had brought back from England the Oxford bags, voluminous trousers that measured 20 to 25 inches at the bottoms and were almost as wide at the knees. When John Wanamaker introduced Oxford bags in New York in 1925, the advertisement made the point that they "may be worn with braces" but were equipped with belt loops "as a concession to the American habit."

1930–1940

Men's Wear observed in 1931 that "Manufacturers of suspenders, braces or galluses are not unanimous in their approval of elastic webbing as suspender material," adding that one reason was that the elastic-webbing type limited design possibilities far more severely than the nonelastic type did. Illustrating this commentary was a pair of suspenders the webbing portion of which was covered with neckwear silk that was not elastic. Still, it was noted, "recently considerable development has occurred along the line of producing decorative webbing so that it now appears in good looking stripes and figures that approximate the results achieved in silk and in non-elastic webbing" (*Men's Wear–Chicago Apparel Gazette,* Feb. 11, 1931, p. 92). By 1933 there was a positive movement toward elastic webbing and away from nonelastic ribbon, and by the next year at least 75 percent of all suspenders had elastic webbing.

Garters, meanwhile, were showing more and more style. As the *Men's Wear* reporter saw it in 1931, "Few people today go about with the kind of garters that disgraced masculine calves a few years ago, and the improvement in wrinkleless sock maintenance is due to the pick-up in garter appearance and style." Two examples were a vertical-striped garter with a decorative horseshoe catch and a garter made of a narrow elastic with celluloid fittings and finished with cement, without stitching.

"Style and novelty have run riot in belts and suspenders for spring and summer," noted *Men's Wear*. "The producers of things to keep the pants up have done a lot to keep business up by borrowing ideas that are current and coming in the various divisions of men's wear and applying them to belts and suspenders" (Mar. 8, 1933, p. 47). Plaids and tartans, for example, prominent during this period in suits, shirts, ties, trousers, and socks, now turned up in belts and suspenders. One stylish suspender had tattersall-waistcoat checks and metalwork in the form of stirrups. The wool-tie idea had crept into suspender ribbon, and approximations of glenurquhart plaid, houndstooth checks, and other suiting fabric designs were seen in the newest belts and suspenders.

In the early thirties, inspired by the new summer wash suits, belt manufacturers developed a wash belt. There were also fashionable linen belts piped and backed with kid or calf, as well as silk belts for evening wear that somewhat resembled abbreviated cummerbunds.

Belts of this period also showed the influence of shoe fashions. Chamois and suede belts were popular in shades that matched or at least complemented the suede sports shoe that was a particular favorite of the Prince of Wales, at this time the undisputed fashion leader of the world. Whereas just a few years earlier the sports belt had shown the influence of neckwear and hatbands in the use of rep silk in club stripes as the facing of leather belts or in panels, the matching or harmonizing of shoes and belt was the new vogue.

One of the newest ideas being shown in 1933 was a suede-like fabric used primarily as a belt lining but also for suspender ends. "It adds a pleasant inside finish to the belt and absorbs perspiration," commented a trade writer. The following year a new development was a suspender made of fine corduroy; and a crocheted suspender, said to have been inspired by

Deep-colored garters with pads in brighter tones were still in fashion in 1935, but they would disappear from the scene as elastic-top socks became increasingly popular in subsequent decades. From Esquire, *July 1935.*

the popularity of the knitted necktie, gained favor. Such improvements in construction as a flexible leather cross-link in back led to suspenders that were guaranteed not to slip off the shoulders.

By the mid-thirties some men preferred to wear the belt buckle at the side rather than in the center, and for them there was a new buckle that was less a buckle than a flanged clip, the belt being pierced by a series of slots in which the clip gripped. The influence of shoe fashions on belts and suspenders proved short-lived, and once again neckwear was the dominant influence with regimental stripes, Spitalfields, and moirés predominant. Sports and jewelry also had an influence on suspenders. Motifs from polo, baseball, and fox hunting were woven into the elastic webbing, and the gut tabs were trimmed appropriately with leather and chamois.

"In the matter of trimming, there is a close relationship between the motif of the 'hardware' and the suspender itself," observed one fashion journalist. "Streamlined buckles are being executed in ways that suggest the most modern motor cars. Colored stones on buckles strike a new note. The alert retailer will seize this chance to promote suspenders as a component of the colored stone cuff-links-and-tie-clip ensemble" (*Men's Wear,* Sept. 5, 1934, p. 35). And as for tabs, white pig was being used with light-color webbing. Although white flat leather tabs were popular, natural pigskin was dominant because of its masculine associations and harmonizing adaptability. Chain tabs were being revived after an absence of several seasons. Among the new ideas in belt buckles was a box style with a double-prong back that was designed to divide the strain between two points.

The slacks of the thirties were loose and full-cut and were most popular in lightweight fabrics. With them the man of fashion wore sports belts of fabric, two-toned leather, perforated leather, rope, ribbon, and string. "The belt is stronger than it has ever been in its history, but it must be novel,"

A pigskin belt with a leather-covered buckle and braided silk-covered string suspenders. From Esquire, *October 1935.*

noted a *Men's Wear* writer from the French Riviera, the incubator of many sporty fashions, in 1934. Not only were there novelty belts but there were novelty buckles too, often featuring nautical motifs such as anchors and fish.

In 1935 shoe fashions were once again inspiring both belts and suspenders. The popularity of brown buck, for instance, led to a brown-buck set of belt, suspenders, and watch guard, and there was a Scotch-grain belt that matched the texture of shoes. Neckwear also continued to have an influence, and in 1937 *Esquire* showed lightweight suspenders and a silk belt, both featuring regimental stripes. Narrow belts were gaining popularity in the East, while braided leather belts in various widths were popular all over the country. The most fashionable belt leathers were alligator, pig, shrunken calf, Scotch grain, boarskin, long-grain seal, cape seal, and calfskin.

Seemingly more attention has been paid to the mechanics of the trouser uplift," commented *Men's Wear* in 1937, "and more study has been given to the human anatomy." It was agreed that this had resulted in better-constructed and more comfortable braces. "Lightness in weight is a universal characteristic. There are a number of styles from which to choose in the adjustable back variations, of the swivel construction. Suspenders follow body lines, bend as the body bends and move as the body moves. Their aim these days is to keep the trousers in one place. It is not as it used to be, when the pants were hooked onto heavy and unyielding harnesses which hiked the nether garments out

of place every time the victim bent over or stretched."

In belts this heightened awareness of human anatomy led to the development of the spring-buckle belt, which had a hidden spring attached to the end to allow for expansion at the waistline. Elastic webbing was still the leader in suspenders, but many substitutes were being offered. Among them were meshed and braided fabrics as well as leathers and knitted and loosely woven fabrics, some of them combined with short strips of elastic that often were concealed or unemphasized.

Comfort and color were the characteristics of belts and braces in 1938, and there was strong evidence that most men considered a narrow belt to be the most comfortable. "The assumption of comfort in narrow belts," said one trade paper, "is fostered by the fact that a smaller area of the waistline is covered by a narrow belt than by a wide belt. For a similar reason, the porosity of woven belts and the implied porosity of fabric belts carries the thought of ventilation.

"Another contributor to the narrow belt interest is the high rise trouser. Women stylists may shift the waistline anywhere in the area from knee to armpit and nothing happens because her dresses are suspended from the

In 1936 university men favored braces in authentic university colors. These were of a special type designed for easy action. From Esquire, *September 1936.*

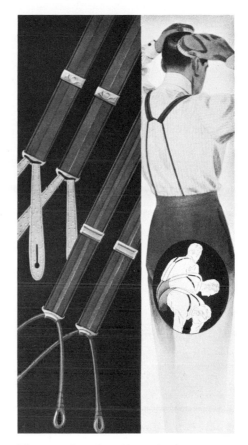

The coronation colors, blue and red, were featured in 1937 in braces made by Hickok with leather or elastic cord tips. From Esquire, *April 1937.*

shoulders. When the waistband of the trousers is moved up, nothing can be done about the anatomy of the hips. The narrow belt is liked by many high-rise trouser wearers because it is believed to follow more closely the waistline and is therefore more comfortable. The comfort angle appears again with the greater stress that is placed on flexible belts or belts that incorporate some method of permitting them to stretch" (*Men's Wear*, Feb. 9, 1938, pp. 45–47).

As examples of this vogue for narrow, flexible belts were photographs of a woven puggaree belt in blue, red, and white with a cinch buckle; a Bermuda-cloth belt in black, red, and yellow stripes with an enameled buckle; a black-and-white cord belt with grained-leather ends; a ribbon belt in red, orange, and white; a

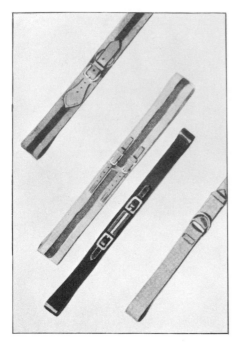

Belts created for country wear in 1938: (top to bottom) a wool web belt with a single-strap leather buckle; a colorful wool web belt with a double-strap buckle; a brown-dyed heavy leather belt with a double buckle and a striped band: a plain felt belt with a cinch buckle. From Esquire, *May 1938.*

blue-and-gray Lastex belt with pigskin ends; a tan elastic-cord belt; a plain white braided belt of five strands; a tan perforated leather with a light-tone buckle; and a gray Congo Cloth belt with a double-spring buckle, which permitted the belt to expand and contract in response to abdominal pressure.

Beach slacks and shirt and slacks ensembles with self-belts threatened to displace sports belts during the thirties. Belt manufacturers maintained that the self-belts were flimsily constructed, while the manufacturers of the slacks and shirt and slacks ensembles argued that the self-belts were more comfortable and neater-looking. Like beach slacks, walk shorts for sailing, fishing, and club wear were often beltless, having instead a waistband 4 inches wide.

Meanwhile, both belts and suspenders had become very narrow: belts had been reduced to a ¾-inch width and

braces to ½-inch width. The comfortable narrow braided-leather belts were immensely popular. They were extremely flexible and, as a *Men's Wear* writer put it in 1938, "porous as chicken wire."

For fall, 1938, rawhide was "the new, smart trick in belts and suspenders," aimed at winning the favor of the college man heading back to campus. It was not, pointed out *Men's Wear*, the raw, uncouth hide as it appeared before processing. "The job of complete tanning is held in suspense, but it retains the color and the slightly random mottled appearance of rawhide."

1940–1960

The first suspenders using "stretchable, adjustable" Vinylite material for ends were on the market in the early forties. Copy for a Paris advertisement in *Esquire* (October, 1941) read as follows: "Twin sets of button holes in the

Braces for evening wear in 1941 had boldly striped webbing. From Esquire, *August 1941.*

The "bold look" was apparent in bridle cowhide belts with saddle stitching and heavy-looking buckles. From Esquire, *November 1948.*

back tabs to assure correct and comfortable fit. You attach back tabs at lower button holes first, then adjust front buckles. If you wish to shorten suspenders you simply snip off the lower button holes in back and attach through those remaining." Guaranteed not to slide off the shoulders, these suspenders had limited appeal, although plastic turned up in belts, too, the copywriter noting, "This miracle plastic stretches gently, cleans easily."

World War II cut the production of belts and braces, but both were assisted by the launching of *Esquire's* "Bold Look for the dominant male." It was, said the magazine in July, 1949, "the first actual expression—in the fabrics, the textures, the colors and the cut of the clothes a man wears—of a predominant state of mind. And it is more than that. . . .

"It is a tremendous organized program on the part of a select group of outstanding American manufacturers and retailers to provide a service of preplanned and coordinated apparel design, color styling and ensemble selection for the *whole* man, from his hat to his heels—from his formal to his most casual clothing."

Bold look suspenders featured aggressive dots and double checks. "The doubloon dot," the fashion department called the pirate-size dot. "Big as a buccaneer's cartwheel," it was a full inch in diameter and was widely spaced on the strong, dark ground of woven elastic braces. As for the bold look belt, it was a hefty-looking leather

The checked borders of these webbing braces epitomized the geometric designs of the bold look. From Esquire, *May 1949.*

60). "Magic nylon" is the way one of these two manufacturers referred to the man-made fiber that had been introduced ten years earlier at the New York World's Fair. Its "silky texture and superb wearing qualities" were featured prominently in all advertisements for both suspenders and garters.

"Mr. T" was *Esquire*'s fashion promotion for 1950. Unlike the bold look with its husky, assertive personality, Mr. T was lean and conservative.

"The clocks in your socks, the new designs in neckwear, braces, mufflers, and even jewelry, all have the terraced, tall 'T' effect," commented the fashion department in October, 1950. And T braces with neat, vertical designs were coordinated with ties and socks.

The 1950s, or at least the first half of the decade, were conservative years, and fashion colors were obligingly muted. The "man in the gray flannel suit" preferred narrow dress belts of

"with free-and-easy, strong stitching along each edge—as supple as a saddle, and as virile!"

In 1949, while belt sales were climbing, suspender sales seriously declined. It was hoped that the introduction of all-nylon suspenders would turn the tide. "Though no one is quite sure of the assets of nylon suspenders, the two houses making them feel that the word itself will account for many sales," noted *Men's Wear* (July 22, 1949, p.

Reproductions of designer's creations in this 1955 advertisement featured (top to bottom) a double-ring buckle belt, a pigskin belt with a billet buckle, an elastic cord belt, and a charcoal-brown Continental belt with a clip buckle. From Esquire, *October 1955.*

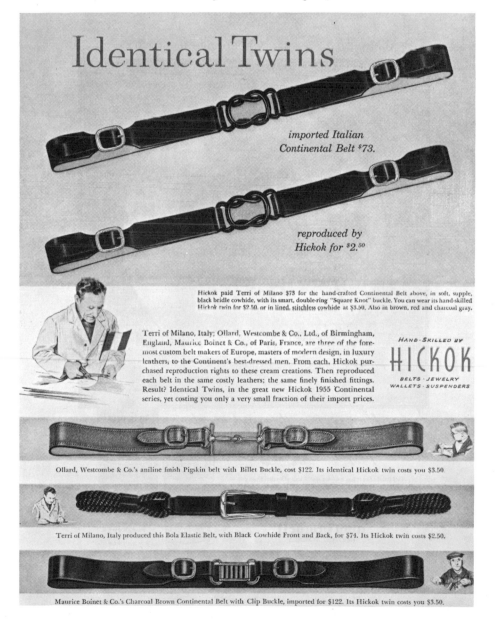

Identical Twins

imported Italian Continental Belt $73.

reproduced by Hickok for $2.50

Hickok paid Terri of Milano $73 for the hand-crafted Continental Belt above, in soft, supple, black bridle cowhide, with its smart, double-ring "Square Knot" buckle. You can wear its hand-skilled Hickok twin for $2.50, or in lined, stitchless cowhide at $3.50. Also in brown, red and charcoal gray.

Terri of Milano, Italy; Ollard, Westcombe & Co., Ltd., of Birmingham, England, Maurice Boinet & Co., of Paris, France, are three of the foremost custom belt makers of Europe, masters of modern design, in luxury leathers, to the Continent's best-dressed men. From each, Hickok purchased reproduction rights to these cream creations. Then reproduced each belt in the same costly leathers; the same finely finished fittings. Result? Identical Twins, in the great new Hickok 1955 Continental series, yet costing you only a very small fraction of their import prices.

HAND-SKILLED BY

HICKOK

BELTS · JEWELRY
WALLETS · SUSPENDERS

Ollard, Westcombe & Co.'s aniline finish Pigskin belt with Billet Buckle, cost $122. Its identical Hickok twin costs you $3.50.

Terri of Milano, Italy produced this Bola Elastic Belt, with Black Cowhide Front and Back, for $74. Its Hickok twin costs $2.50.

Maurice Boinet & Co.'s Charcoal Brown Continental Belt with Clip Buckle, imported for $122. Its Hickok twin costs you $3.50.

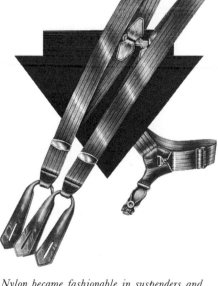

Nylon became fashionable in suspenders and garters in 1949. From Esquire, *October 1949.*

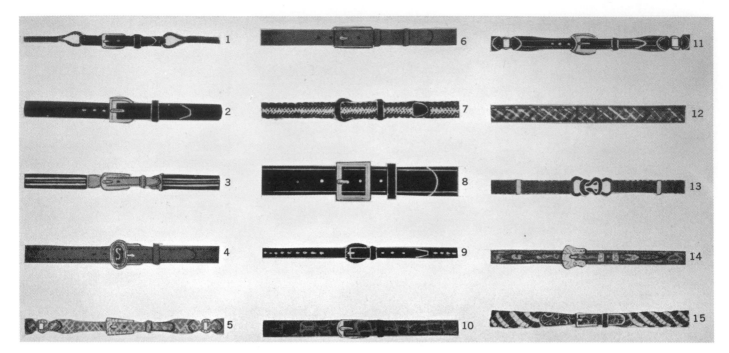

Fashionable belts of 1956 included (1) an elastic nylon cord belt with leather ends; (2) a calfskin belt with a short-tongue buckle; (3) a striped nonelastic belt; (4) a grained sealskin; (5) a reptile belt with hammered links and buckle; (6) a pigskin belt with a concealed spring attached to the buckle; (7) a striped elastic nylon cord belt; (8) a wide saddle-tan belt with a heavy brass buckle; (9) a narrow leather belt with heavy stitching; (10) a reptile or ostrich belt with a long-tongue buckle; (11) a three-piece belt with related links and buckle; (12) a diagonal fabric belt with concealed snap fasteners; (13) a woven straw belt; (14) a Western belt of tooled leather with an engraved silver buckle; (15) a braided elastic nylon cord belt in two colors. From Esquire, May 1956.

braided leather and elastic cords for sportswear. Suspenders were still being aggressively promoted, and *Men's Wear* on Feb. 20, 1953, opted for suspenders, asserting that trousers hang better when supported by suspenders. That same year *Esquire,* noting that one of the primary trends in men's apparel was the natural look, in its May issue showed a natural-shoulder gray flannel suit worn with blue mesh braces "which support trousers properly, comfortably." Still, the fashion staff played no favorites and included a narrow dark blue alligator belt. Meanwhile, the trade press strongly promoted belts, urging the menswear retailer to trim less colorful slacks with bright elastic belts in contrasting or harmonizing shades.

New slacks waistbands, some using self-belts and others designed to be worn without a belt, aroused controversy in the early fifties similar to that of the late thirties when shirt and slacks ensembles were being made with self-belts. One trade journal, noting that waistband fitting was now a selling feature of tremendous importance in slacks, attempted to describe the controversy:

PRO: Among the slack makers comment ranges from the flat prediction that in a few years most or all better grade slacks will be in self-belt or beltless models, to the contention that the new models are "extra" business, and as such do not hurt belt sales.

Producers using self-belts insist that the old complaint of flimsy construction does not apply to the present product. They add further, that the self-belts do not represent sales being "thrown away," but rather "plus" selling points for which a premium is charged on the wholesale price and regained in added markup.

CON: Aside from questioning the quality of self-belt construction, belt makers warn that retailers who go along with the new trend unnecessarily hurt a department that has consistently turned out a profit virtually unimpaired by the periodic mark-downs common to the business.

They argue that even though markup on slacks now being shown to be worn without regular belts may in some cases be as much as the combined markup on a pair of slacks and a separate belt, past experience has proven that this practice won't stand long in the face of competition . . . or a more difficult selling period. (*Men's Wear,* Feb. 8, 1952)

Italian fashion influence was potent in this decade. According to *Esquire* in May, 1956, "The renaissance in craftsmanship that began in Italy has refashioned more than just the shape of belts; it's changed their status in your closet. Heretofore, a man's belt has been more notable for versatility than variety. But the fashion-wise are currently having a field day, finding one for every pair of trousers—breeks to black mohairs—and guys on the lookout for convenience are up to the same thing, if only to avoid switching the same old suitcase strap from one pair of pants to the next. The variety of domestic buckles and belt ideas

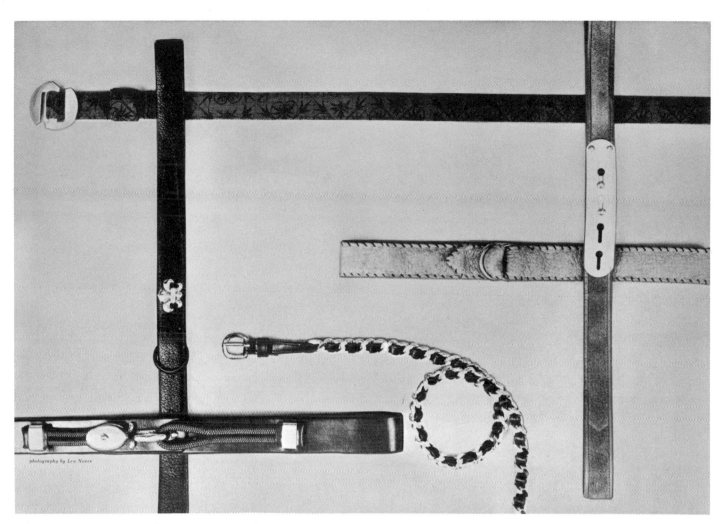

Distinctive belt buckles had selective appeal in 1957: (top) a novel buckle with a broken-O effect; (left) a fleur-de-lis closure on grained calfskin; (bottom left) a polished brass pulley with elastic cords; (right) a flat brass closure of the luggage type and a double-loop buckle on a soft pigskin belt with whipstitched edges; (looped below) a leather thong interwoven with a metal chain. From Apparel Arts, March 1957.

sparked by Continental handicrafts makes tempting bait for anyone who recognizes quality."

As a result, a man was encouraged to acquaint himself with the widths, leathers, and constructions of the various belts. *Esquire* offered to serve as a guide with sketches of fifteen belts and the accompanying copy:

1. The rope belt with leather ends is made of thick, elastic nylon cord, geared for active sports wear with plenty of give and take. This is only one of the many elastic fabrics employed for casual, high-fashion wear; most of them combine with leather.

2. Plain calfskin makes a classic belt for either sports or business. The short-tongue buckle makes this one especially masculine and rugged.

3. Fabrics in the non-elastic category include everything from felt (in brilliant colors) to silks. This one is a luxurious ribbon model of alternately high and dark shades, combined with leather ends and a sleek metal buckle.

4. Grained sealskin makes a more formal impression for business and professional wear; good accompaniment to grained leathers in urban shoes.

5. Surface interest grows more luxurious in reptile skins; this design is a natural for cruise and resort life, with its three-piece construction and hammered links and buckle.

6. Pigskin vies with cordovan (horse) as the all-time favorite. Both are extremely long wearing; cordovan is the most non-porous of conventional leathers, pigskin the most porous. This model employs a new theory of "give" for fast action: a steel spring is concealed under the buckle.

7. Striped nylon cord is typical of the new elastic webbings found here and on the continent.

8. Saddle leather is a sportsman's favorite, and here its extra sturdiness is reinforced by unusual width. Saddle tan with a heavy brass buckle.

9. Heavy stitching becomes decorative as well as functional in this simply designed, narrow leather belt.

10. Plain-cut reptile skins and, more recently, ostrich hide make distinguished daytime business wear. The long-tongue buckle on this alligator model gives it a sleek, well-tailored look.

11. Links and buckles become more

Novel shapes distinguished belt buckles in 1958: (left to right) a square-end triangular buckle on a calfskin belt; a gold-finish metal in a spiral design with a hook; an elliptical metal buckle on an ostrich belt. From Gentlemen's Quarterly, *spring, 1958.*

interesting; witness the design of this three-piece suede model for general day-time wear.

12. The diagonal-check fabric belt has concealed snap fasteners. You can find these in horizontal plaids, too, with or without buckles, made to match plaid sports shirts, and even watch bands.

13. Woven straw belts, inspired by Italian leisure shoes, make a fine change for vacation wear on the high seas or at home.

14. Picked up from the cowboys by the dudes: tooled leather migrates east to become high fashion with breeks or any kind of casual slacks. Engraved silver buckle is *de rigueur.*

15. Leather ends on braided nylon-elastic-tape belt in two high colors to keep your gray flannels jaunty and casual. (May, 1956, p. 102)

1960–1970

Belts continued to hold their own, and suspenders continued their decline during the early sixties. Then the Peacock Revolution exploded on the scene, and suddenly what counted was to have the biggest belt among your acquaintances. Big belts comple-

mented the new flared trousers, and as belts grew bolder, bigger, and brassier, belt loops on trousers and slacks had to be made longer to accommodate them.

By June, 1969, *Esquire* decided that it was time to illustrate just how bold, big, and brassy belts had become with a double-page spread entitled "A Bewitchery of Belts." Among the belts photographed on models wearing the newest jump suits and sweater suits were a sealskin with a brass buckle; twisted brass ropes joined by spaced brass and studded with colored stones; an antique harness leather with brass eyelets and domed nailheads; a saddle leather with a double-prong golden buckle; braided elastic and leather joined by a silvery link and covered buckle; stretch webbing with a safety-belt buckle; striped velvet with a golden snap-look buckle; glove leather and alligator; a satin-finish stainless-steel double-hole link chain; flexible hinged enamel sections on silver plate; a putty-colored hand-

crocheted belt with a covered buckle and change pocket; a black patent-leather evening belt with silver studs and oval; a contoured brown leather with an enamel-on-silver buckle; gold links with a white-gold buckle; a wide gold mesh with a lion's-head buckle; blocks of brown puma steerhide linked with gold; and an ostrich belt backed with saddle leather and buckled in satin-finish brass. Advertisements for this new kind of belt used muscular adjectives: strong, raw, tough, determined, spirited, honest, independent, rugged, giant. Colors were described as being everything from funky, wild, and out of sight to hot, suave, and smoldering.

The Peacock Revolution had made men body-conscious as never before, and their belts, like their shaped suits and new unstructured easy suits, proudly called attention to lean stomachs and flat hips. *Gentlemen's Quarterly* caught the spirit of the period when it hung a collection of wide belts over the nude torso of a black gladiator.

Novelty belts were more popular than ever, and those with patriotic and ecological motifs had a special appeal for younger men. The *New York Times,* in a 1971 "Report on Men's Wear," showed a white cowhide having a metal buckle with flag-colored stars and stripes, a perfect mate for sports apparel of a similar stars-and-stripes character. The demand for eye-catching belts had grown so great by the early seventies that some menswear retailers had opened a belt boutique or a separate belt shop-within-the-shop. The "touch" syndrome made the hanging-belt display essential to successful belt merchandising. "We've gone from boxed belts to 100 percent hanging belts," stated one buyer in a *Daily News Record* interview (Sept. 30, 1971). "You've got to sell belts near pants and have the belts hanging up so men can feel the leather and touch the buckle," advised the vice president of a menswear chain in the same article.

While belts became an integral part of the new look in men's apparel, braces remained static, maintaining

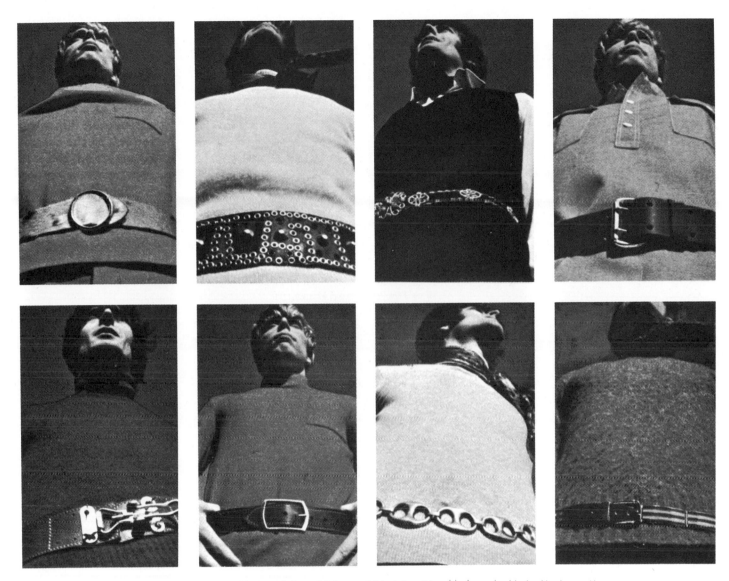

Belts became bolder, bigger, and brassier in 1969: (top, left to right) a sealskin belt with a big brass buckle by Cardin, antique harness leather with brass eyelets and domed nailheads, twisted brass ropes joined by spaced brass and studded with colored stones, and saddle leather with a double-prong buckle; (bottom, left to right) a wide bison belt with a buckle fashioned after a ski binding, husky stitched leather with a bronzy buckle, a satin-finish stainless-steel double-hole link-chain signature belt by Carlo Palazzi of Rome, and Gucci's belt with flexible hinged sections of enamel on silver plate. From Esquire, *June 1969.*

their fashion status only in formal wear. It seems, however, only a matter of time before interest will once again be focused on braces, which offer fertile ground for imaginative ornamentation. Just as many menswear fashions have begun in sportswear and been carried over into general wear, it is highly possible that braces will make a comeback through the new leisure wear designed for younger men. Long and abbreviated overalls with attached suspenders, for example, at-tracted attention in the early seventies, and Western-inspired leisure wear, which had already left its brand on town apparel, may revive interest in the colorful suspenders that were once as much a part of the frontier scene as boots and the ten-gallon hat. Perhaps the young will rediscover braces on a wave of nostalgia and take to wearing them along with their belts, in harmonizing or contrasting colors, leathers, and fabrics.

Late in 1971 trade publications were predicting a back-to-classics trend for belts, with the "neat look" the upcoming look: lighter leather and cleaner buckles. But, assertive or un-derstated, the belt of the early seven-ties had become a status symbol. By 1972 many suits were being manufac-tured with narrow belt loops in antici-pation of a return of skinny belts. Yet, whether wide or narrow, the belt of the seventies was firmly established as a distinctly sensuous article of masculine apparel.

Socks

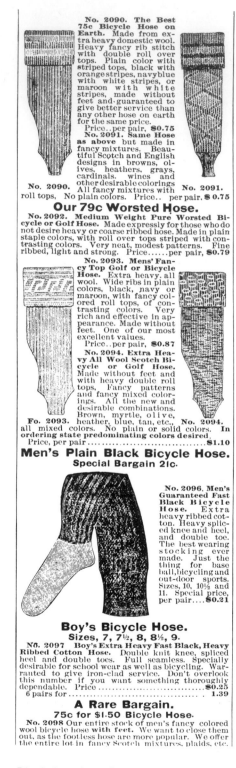

No. 2090. The Best 75c Bicycle Hose on Earth. Made from extra heavy domestic wool. Heavy fancy rib stitch with double roll over tops. Plain color with striped tops, black with orange stripes, navy blue with white stripes, or maroon with white stripes, made without feet and guaranteed to give better service than any other hose on earth for the same price. Price..per pair, $0.75

No. 2091. Same Hose as above but made in fancy mixtures. Beautiful Scotch and English designs in browns, olives, heathers, grays, cardinals, wines and other desirable colorings All fancy mixtures with roll tops, No plain colors. Price.. per pair. $0.75

Our 79c Worsted Hose.

No. 2092. Medium Weight Pure Worsted Bicycle or Golf Hose. Made expressly for those who do not desire heavy or coarse ribbed hose. Made in plain staple colors, with roll over tops striped with contrasting colors. Very neat, modest patterns. Fine ribbed, light and strong. Price......per pair, $0.79

No. 2093. Mens' Fancy Top Golf or Bicycle Hose. Extra heavy. all wool. Wide ribs in plain colors, black, navy or maroon, with fancy colored roll tops, of contrasting colors. Very rich and effective in appearance. Made without feet. One of our most excellent values. Price..per pair, $0.87

No. 2094. Extra Heavy All Wool Scotch Bicycle or Golf Hose. Made without feet and with heavy double roll tops, Fancy patterns and fancy mixed colorings. All the new and desirable combinations. Brown, myrtle, olive, heather, blue, tan, etc., all mixed colors. No plain or solid colors. In ordering state predominating colors desired. Price, per pair..................................$1.10

Men's Plain Black Bicycle Hose.
Special Bargain 21c.

No. 2096. Men's Guaranteed Fast Black Bicycle Hose. Extra heavy ribbed cotton. Heavy spliced knee and heel, and double toe. The best wearing stocking ever made. Just the thing for base ball,bicycling and out-door sports. Sizes, 10, 10½ and 11. Special price, per pair....$0.21

Boy's Bicycle Hose.
Sizes, 7, 7½, 8, 8½, 9.

No. 2097 Boy's Extra Heavy Fast Black, Heavy Ribbed Cotton Hose. Double knit knee, spliced heel and double toes. Full seamless. Specially desirable for school wear as well as bicycling. Warranted to give iron-clad service. Don't overlook this number if you want something thoroughly dependable. Price..............................$0.25
6 pairs for...................................... 1.39

A Rare Bargain.
75c for $1.50 Bicycle Hose.

No. 2098 Our entire stock of men's fancy colored wool bicycle hose with feet. We want to close them out, as the footless hose are more popular. We offer the entire lot in fancy Scotch mixtures, plaids, etc.

Bicycle hose, in wool or cotton and with plain or fancy tops, were important accessories for men in the 1897 catalog of Sears, Roebuck and Company.

There is probably no better way to demonstrate turn-of-the-century fashions in socks than to refer to the pages of the influential Sears, Roebuck and Company catalog of 1897–1900. "Progress is the watchword of the hour" is the way Sears headlined its hosiery section, noting that "Ours is the largest exclusive hosiery department in the world. We control the output of three of the largest and best hosiery and knitting mills in the world—two in America and one in Europe." What Sears offered its customers during the first decade of this century included seamless knit half hose in assorted gray, brown, and olive mixtures; cream-brown British seamless 40-gauge socks, with elastic ribbed tops and spliced heels and toes; fancy silk half hose, with embroidered stripes running down the front; black lisles, with fancy colored cross-stripes; black cotton half hose, with white heels and toes and white soles; and Sears' own special import—fine-gauge black seamless cashmere socks.

All men's hose during these early years were made with ribbed tops and were held up with elastic-webbing or silk-webbing garters. Wool was used for fall and winter, cotton lisle or silk for the rest of the year. In an era of oversize suits, high starched collars, and high-buttoned shoes, men's socks were neat and conservative. But after World War I, when suits shed their excess padding, stiff collars began to disappear, and high-buttoned shoes gave way to low, laced shoes, socks too began to reflect the heightened fashion consciousness of the American man. This was especially true in golf and sports hose.

1920–1930

In 1924 *Men's Wear* inspected some of the new, colorful golf hose imported from Sweden, Scotland, Norway, and Spain, concluding that "New arrivals

HOSIERY DEPARTMENT.

THE LARGEST STOCK OF HOSIERY EVER UNDER ONE ROOF.

PROGRESS IS THE WATCHWORD OF THE HOUR.

Ours is a progressive Hosiery Department. It is the largest exclusive hosiery department in the world. Our warerooms are full to overflowing and are full of good things, too. Never in the history of hosiery buying have we ever before been able to offer our customers such exceptionally good values as we hold out to them this season. We control the entire output of three of the largest and best hosiery and knitting mills in the world. Two in America and one in Europe. The products of these mills have attained a lasting reputation throughout two continents. We believe that the great majority of the people appreciate good hosiery and we are going to give them a chance to buy the best hosiery made at prices that will at once appeal to shrewd and economical buyers.

Men's Half Hose at Half Price.

Scale of Sizes.

Shoe size.5 6 7 8 9 10
Sock size.9 9¼ 10 10 10½ 11

Men's Cotton Half Hose.
No. 21050 Men's Full Seamless Knit Half Hose in assorted gray mixtures. Good weight; suitable for wear all the year around. Extra good value. Weight per dozen, 3 pounds.
Price, per dozen $0.55
No. 21051 Men's Very Strong Fine Knit Gray Mixed Cotton Socks. Full seamless foot; neat elastic ribbed top. The best light weight cotton socks ever offered for the money.
Price, per pair $0.08
Price, per dozen 0.90
No. 21052 The Nelson Knitting Co's Seamless Rockford Socks. Blue or brown mixed. Heavy double heel and toe and fine finished ribbed tops. Every pair warranted.
Price, per pair $0.08
Price, per dozen 0.90
No. 21054 Men's Extra Fine Full Seamless Half Hose in new and handsome brown and olive mixtures, also neat grey mixtures; extra fine quality, with finely finished foot and elastic ribbed tops. The equal of any 25c half hose in the market.
Price per pair.... .... $0.13
Per dozen 1.40
No. 21055 Men's Fine Gauge French Mixed Half Hose. Full seamless and knit from soft smooth cotton yarn; made with shaped feet and ribbed elastic tops; very neat grey and olive brown mixtures; easy on the feet and easy on the pocket book.
Price per pair ... $0.15 Four pairs for.... $0.50

Genuine British Socks.

No. 21056 Men's Genuine Cream Brown British Seamless Socks. Fine elastic ribbed tops, double heels and toes; knit to wear long and well and guaranteed to do so. Price per pair.. .... $0.15
Per dozen pairs 1.45
No. 21057 Men's Genuine Cream Brown British Socks. Same as above but finer in texture; very easy on the feet; extra durable.
Price, per pair $0.19
Per dozen pairs 2.14
No. 21058 Our Great 40 Gauge Genuine British Socks. Medium weight; full seamless, with elastic ribbed tops and spliced heels and toes; ecru or cream brown color; strong and dependable.
Price per pair.... $0.23 Per dozen..... $2.66

Men's Fancy Silk Embroidered Half Hose.

No. 21059 Men's Fast Black Seamless Cotton Half Hose. Very fine gauge, soft finish with fancy silk embroidered stripes running down the front. Handsome patterns and fast colors. Always sell for from 25c to 40c at retail.
Our price, per pair........ $0.18
Three pairs for .... .50

Fancy Lisle Socks.

No. 21060 Men's extra fine gauge, light weight, pure Lisle Thread Socks. Black, with fancy colored cross stripes. The handsomest striped half hose ever made. Full seamless and perfect fitting. Price, per pair 1.00
3 pairs for 1.00

No. 21061 Men's Fancy Silk Embroidered Socks. Full seamless, perfect fitting and very fine gauge. Assorted colors with neat fancy figures and dots embroidered in silk. All fast colors and strictly high grade goods. Sizes, 9 to 10½.
Price, per pair............. $0.35
Three pairs for............. 1.00

Men's Fine Balbriggan Socks.

No. 21062 Men's Extra Quality Fine Soft Finished Balbriggan Socks. Double heels and toes. Guaranteed real two-thread extra super stout color, ecru or cream brown color. Finely shaped foot and long elastic ribbed tops. Sizes 9 to 11. Price, per pair.............. $0.15
Four pairs for,.. $0.50
No. 21063 Men's Extra Fine Cream, Brown or Ecru Colored Balbriggan Socks. Our own special importation, made in neat fancy rib or drop stitch patterns, with seamless finely shaped foot, spliced heels and toes, and long elastic ribbed tops. Very fine gauge, close knit, firm and to be depended upon for hard service. Neat and dressy as well as good. Sizes 9 to 11. Price, per pair.... $0.19
Three pairs for...................... $0.50

Men's High Grade Half Hose.
SOOTHING SOCKS FOR TIRED FEET.
Black Cotton Socks.

No. 21064 Men's Fast Black Cotton Half Hose. Full seamless, made with spliced heels and toes. Fine elastic ribbed tops. Extra good value.
Price, per dozen.......... $0.09
Per dozen .... .98
No. 21065 Men's Fine Gauge, absolutely Fast Black Seamless Cotton Socks. Knit from fine combed Egyptian yarn, double heels and toes. Very soft and comfortable on the feet. Strong and full of good wearing qualities. Sizes 9 to 11.
Price, per pair............... $0.12
Per dozen pairs............... 1.30
No. 21066 Men's Solid Colored Fast Black Seamless Socks, with high spliced heels and toes. Medium weight and fine gauge. Fine elastic ribbed tops. High grade, soft finish. Sizes, 9 to 11.
Price per pair... $0.15
Four pairs for... .50
No. 21068 Men's Pure Domestic Lisle Half Hose, with three ply heels and toes and fine elastic ribbed tops. Strictly high grade in every respect. Regular retail value 25c. Sizes, 9 to 11. Plain fast black.
Price per pair.... $0.18
Per doz. pair.... 1.70
No. 21069 Men's Extra Fine Real Two-Thread Maco Cotton Socks. The very best made. Plain black, with double heels and toes and spliced soles. Long, elastic ribbed tops. Absolutely fast color. Sizes. 9 to 11. Price, per pair....... $0.25
Per dozen pairs...................... 2.70

Men's Fine Silk Half Hose.

No. 21070 Our Own Special Importation. Men's Extra Quality Plain Fast Black Silk Seamless Half Hose. Very fine soft high grade finish, light weight and thoroughly good; sizes 9 to 11.
Price per pair.............................$0.75
No. 21071 Men's Pure Silk Seamless Half Hose. Extra quality imported stock; absolutely fast black and stainless; sizes 9 to 11. Price per pair.....$0.98
Three pairs for 2.75

Black Hose With White Feet.

No. 21072 Men's Medium Weight Fast Black Cotton Half Hose, with white heels and toes and white soles; double heels and toes and fine ribbed elastic tops; made from extra fine real maco cotton; our own importation; sizes 9 to 11.
Price per pair $0.24
Per dozen.... 2.66
No. 21073 Men's Extra Quality Imported Cotton Half Hose. Warranted real Maco; soft fine finished, plain black with all white foot; full seamless with double heels and toes; sizes 9 to 11. Price per pair...$0.25
Per dozen pairs.... 2.70

Black Lisle Thread Socks.

No. 21074 Men's High Grade Pure Lisle Thread Socks. Our own special importation. Very fine and thin. Full regular made and seamless. It's downright refreshing to put on a pair of socks of this sort. Nothing finer for summer wear. Sizes, 9 to 11.
Price, per pair.............................$0.45

Men's Tan Colored Half Hose.
Sizes, 9 to 11.

No. 21075 Men's Fine Tan Colored Half Hose. Full seamless with spliced heels and toes and long elastic ribbed tops. Extra good value. Sizes, 9 to 11.
Price, per pair $0.09
Per dozen. .... .98
No. 21076 Fine Gauge Seamless Cotton Half Hose. Knit from fine combed Egyptian yarn. Made with double heels and toes. Soft and fine and very easy on the feet. Plain tans and browns
Price, per pair........ ....$0.12
Per dozen........... 1.30
No. 21077 Men's Extra Quality Seamless Cotton Half Hose, with double heels and toes, medium weight and fine gauge. Long elastic ribbed tops. High class finish. Made in light and dark tan colors. Price per pair.... . ..$0.15
Four pairs for..................... .50
No. 21078 Men's Fine Domestic Tan Color Lisle Half Hose. Medium weight with 3-ply heels and toes and elastic rib tops. High grade and fine gauge. Retail value, 25 cents.
Our special price, per pair.....................$0.18
Per dozen pairs............. .... 1.70

Something New Under the Sun.
Men's Ribbed Cotton Half Hose.

No. 21079 Men's Seamless Cotton Half Hose. Handsome shades of brown and tan. Spliced heels and toes. Fine elastic ribbed tops and full derby ribbed, close fitting legs. Fine gauge and thoroughly reliable. Sizes 9 to 11.
Price, per pair...............$0.15
Three pairs for 0.40

SAVE MONEY By Buying your —HOSIERY— in dozen lots.

No. 21080 Men's Plain Extra High-Grade Genuine Maco Cotton Half Hose. Handsome shades of tan and brown. Fine soft finish combed yarn with double heels and toes and long elastic ribbed tops, full seamless and fast color. Finely shaped foot and the most perfect fitting half hose made. Sizes, 9 to 11. Price, per pair.....................$0.25
3 pair for....................0.68

Men's Fine Merino Half Hose.

No. 21082 Men's Fine Soft Finished Merino Half Hose, tan and gray mixtures, medium weight suitable for wear all the year around. Seamless and perfect fitting. Sizes, 9 to 11.
Price, per pair, 15c; 2 pairs for $0.25
No. 21083 Men's Extra Fine Skin Soothing Merino Half Hose. Medium weight, fine close knit and made with double soles, high spliced heels and toes. Very strong and durable. Specially adapted to persons who cannot wear all wool hosiery. Handsome shades of mode and tan and reddish brown mixture. Sizes, 9 to 11. Full seamless.
Price, per pair, 24c; 3 pairs for $0.65

will tickle the tired business man—flaming youth will be pleased."

"'Who wears 'em?' the uninitiated might ask," continued the *Men's Wear* feature. "The answer is that many a dignified lawyer, doctor or professional man generally, the banker and perhaps even the pastor of the First Baptist Church, not to mention important business men and men of affairs. Just as the happy heir to somebody's estate will appear in melancholy black and exhibit a handkerchief hemmed deep with signs of grief for the funeral, so will the professional and business man dress the part for his commercial or scientific act. They deduce that it is good business to rig themselves out in dignified garb that suggests the opposite of gay and festive sporting attire. But give a lot of these fellows a chance to play with colors by removing the shackles of conventionality and they will run riot. They love them. The somber garb of many a man today is a living lie. Man has not dropped the fancy for the effect of tartans, slashed doublet and hose and the brilliant trappings of the age of romance. That was only yesterday. Only a little further back of that man was the savage, decking himself out in the plumage of wild birds or with leopard skins. He is still a savage. The urge to wear brilliant trappings demonstrates a throw-back into the centuries. It is hereditary and natural. Man needs only the encouragement of hardier spirits undaunted by the insincere mirth of the envious to eventually follow suit and preen himself in all the glory of the artificial plumage now worn mostly by the female, the courageous sex. *Who wears this vivid hose? They wear it who dare*" (Aug. 7, 1924, p. 65).

What the well-dressed golfer dared in the mid-1920s was woolen golf hose related in color and design to his strikingly handsome sweaters and plus-four knickers. There was, accordingly, a vast array of plain colors and heather mixtures as well as large and small diamond designs, cross and circular stripes, checks, and plaids. One fashion reporter noted that the patterns were "borrowed from lightning and other striking inspirations," and the color combinations from "the futuristic school of art."

All patterned socks were of necessity imports, since there was very little machinery in the United States at the time capable of producing them. In the 1930s, however, new machinery became available, making it possible for American firms to produce a plenitude of their own patterns. Spiral machinery, for example, made it possible to knit one color over another; wrap machinery produced stripes on top of the knitted fabric; and needle reverse plates enabled the creation of blended colors. Consequently, the growth in production of patterned socks in this country was closely related to the industry's progress in the use of more sophisticated machinery.

Although golf hose were exploding with uninhibited patterns and colors, socks worn off the links were still quite conservative. Work socks, for example, knit of medium-heavyweight cotton yarn with elastic ribbed tops, came in brown, blue, and black, usually with white or cream-color toes, heels, and soles. Socks for dress were often knit of rayon and cotton lisle yarns and were most often seen in medium gray, tan, dark brown, black, and navy blue. Fancy dress socks were also produced in diamond patterns or elaborate checks, and these gained popularity as more and more men switched to the new low shoes of the twenties. And, of course, a staple was the full-fashioned solid-color silk sock, although by virtue of price it necessarily had a limited public.

"The best dressed students attending universities in most sections of the country are showing a decided preference for lightweight wool hose in bright solid colors, with or without clocks," reported *Men's Wear* on November 21, 1928, "the only exception to this rule being the small figured effects and the Argyle pattern." The preferred solid colors were dark blue, light blue, maroon, bottle green, pearl gray, garnet shades, dark brown, oxford gray, heather mixtures, and blue gray. A conspicuous feature in the clocked hose was that the clocks were in brilliant hues, in decided contrast to the ground color. "The heavyweight wool hose have entirely disappeared from the wardrobe of the typically dressed student and these have been replaced by lightweight wool hose," continued the article, suggesting that the change was no doubt effected by the current tendency away from heavyweight shoes.

1930–1940

The fashionably dressed Britisher carried tremendous fashion clout during the 1930s; as a result, half hose in neat designs and quiet colors were conspicuous during this decade. "Today's half hose designs are entirely different from what we were familiar with a few years ago," cabled a *Men's Wear* reporter from London (Apr. 5, 1933, p. 23). "We have Glen Urquhart checks and plaids because of the great vogue for this type of pattern in suitings, neckwear, shirtings, in fact in male attire in general." An out-

Spaced figures and vertical group stripes were shown in socks for wear with business suits in 1934. From Esquire, *February 1934.*

White-ground argyle socks were especially popular in 1934. From Esquire, *March 1934.*

standing novelty at this time was a drop-stitch lisle sock with a cashmere foot and a lisle gusset at the instep, so that the woolen part did not appear above the top of the wearer's shoe.

All during the thirties *Esquire* continued to show the fashionable half hose on very British-looking models. "The old English pastime, bowling on the green, has been taken up at quite a number of American country clubs," the magazine noted in June, 1937, accompanying the comments with a sketch of a weekend spectator wearing a tweed jacket with brass buttons, pale yellow crash trousers, canvas shoes with crepe soles, and short white wool hose.

"Shorts are very much in order," wrote the fashion department's copywriter beneath a sketch of an elegantly bronzed gentleman wearing gray flannel shorts, a mesh half-sleeved sports shirt, a print neckertie, canvas shoes with rubber soles, and lightweight yellow wool anklets—"All very practical."

In 1934 heavier socks were deemed more suitable for winter wear; of wool or a mixture of other fibers, they went well with the cheviot, tweed, and Shetland suits and jackets being worn at leading universities. The British influence was turning up in almost every sock sold. There were argyles in a wide range of colors as well as diamond designs and small allover effects. In fact, argyle hosiery was so tremendously popular that, according to *Men's Wear,* it had started a "Scotch wave," and the argyle pattern was now available not only in wool but also in silk, artificial yarns, and cotton. Novelty weaves were rife, and prominent among them were crochet weaves, herringbone patterns, horizontal stripes, and bouclé effects.

The following year summer socks, most often ankle length, were making fashion news. It was, said one trade paper, only another indication that "the sportswear idea has taken complete hold of the men's wear designers. Tweed ankles for Summer may at first seem to be anomalous, but they are in tune with dishrag shirts, sailcloth pants and mixed tweed suits." There was even a sprinkling of argyles in the hot-weather lines.

"There is a decided spirit of adventure in the hosiery field," noted the same trade paper, remarking that even the most conservative silk houses were offering tastefully clocked silk socks in tomato red and an off-lavender shade. Summing up the 1935 summer line, the writer concluded that it fell into two major classes: "The highly colored and lacy and the boldly designed and rough. The one is for wear with white and tropical weight clothing in town and for 'dressed up' times, the other is for country, beach and leisure wear."

The year 1936 saw an increase in the demand for elastic-top socks. "The public's reaction, particularly down south and through the Middle West, has been so favorable to the half hose which are self-supporting that lines for this sort of merchandise have been broadened" (*Men's Wear,* Mar. 11, 1936). By 1938 a long elastic-top sock reaching to just below the knee was gaining popularity.

In 1936 *Men's Wear* presented the current hosiery story: "Circular stripes continue to set the tempo in the new hosiery for Fall. The neckwear motifs are important—deep tones, regimentals, polka dots. Tartans, led as ever by the Argyles, maintain their strength. Suiting modes are reflected in vertical stripes, some in two-color effects, and in windowpane checks. Clocks are losing caste. Colors generally are brighter and more varied. Materials include blends of cotton and wool, rayon and silk, silk and wool. Silk is in greater demand. That's the fall hosiery story in a nutshell" (June 24, 1936, p. 23).

In November, 1939, *Esquire* printed "Wardrobe Manners for Shoes and Socks," instructing its readers how to coordinate suits with shoes and shoes with socks:

For town. Blue hopsack unfinished-worsted suit was shown with a pair of black straight tip shoes and blue lisle hose with light blue fancy stripe pattern; brown pinhead unfinished worsted suit, brown calf straight tip shoes, and brown, fawn, and rust plaid design silk hose; grey sharkskin unfinished worsted suit, black calf

(center) Large plaids and miniature diamonds were combined in multicolor socks in 1935. From Esquire, *April 1935.*

The large single pale gray diamond on each side of this sock was set off by maroon and medium gray. From Esquire, *September 1937.*

half brogue shoes, and grey mixture lisle hose with black-and-white embroidered clock; blue unfinished worsted suit with colored stripes, brown calf quarter brogue shoes with perforated toe cap, 6 × 3 rib red and blue silk hose.

For semi-sports. Grey diagonal cheviot suit, black calf blucher shoes, maroon wool marl effect hose with bright red and light blue clock; blue flannel suit with white chalk stripe, black calf wing tip shoes, 6 × 3 rib blue lisle sock with red-and-blue clock; grey Glen Urquhart suit, brown calf monk front shoes, green mixture 6 × 3 fancy rib hose; brown herringbone cheviot suit, brown reverse calf shoes, brown and light blue fancy weave ribbed wool hose.

For country. Lovat Harris tweed suit, reverse calf ankle-high Chukka shoes with crepe soles, wide yellow brushed wool hose, grey flannel slacks, white buckskin shoes with red rubber soles and heels, blue short wool ribbed socks; velvet cord breeks worn with peasant type country shoes and broken herringbone wide rib wool hose; covert slacks, brown reverse calf blucher shoes with crepe soles and heels, white ground 6 × 3 rib green-and-yellow horizontal stripe hose; natural color summer weight suit, brown-and-white wing tip shoes, white lisle 6 × 3 rib hose with brown-and-tan horizontal stripe.

For formal evening wear. Dinner jacket, dress trousers, patent leather pumps, black flat silk hose with blue clock.

For formal evening wear. Midnight blue tailcoat, dress trousers, patent leather oxfords, flat black silk hose with self clock.

1940–1950

Esquire introduced its "bold look" in the fall of 1948—a complete color-coordinated fashion look "For the Dominant Male." It was, said the fashion department, "the most logical evolutionary development in the appearance of the male animal since the passing of the blue serge suit and the sunset of the celluloid collar." Bold look shoes were hefty, and socks were "as potent as a punch"—wool socks with patterns "as bold as the checks on a gambler's vest."

"Nylon They Want, Nylon They Get" was the headline of a 1949 *Men's Wear* story. (Nylon as a fiber had been introduced at the 1939 World's Fair in New York, but it was not until after World War II that it was used extensively in men's hosiery.) "History re-

Diagonally striped wool socks in red and gray (lower center) were keyed to sportswear, particularly golf clothes, in 1941. From Esquire, *July 1941.*

peats itself," started this feature. "Not so many years ago, nylon swept into the woman's hosiery field, bringing with it a wake of problems for the hosiery manufacturers. Some said it was a passing fancy, others thought it might last a few years, then women would go back to silk stockings. 'After all, there is no substitute for natural fibers,' are the words that were heard everywhere in the hosiery market. The nylons are still here. Now the same thing is happening in men's hosiery. Last spring nylons began to appear on retail counters, and consumers gobbled them up by the handfuls. Producers were skeptical; some still are. Again the market echoed, '. . . there is no substitute for natural fibers, nothing can take the place of wool, cotton, etc.'

"At first, hosiery manufacturers confined their nylon production to one or two styles—a flat knit and a spun nylon rib—playing the game cautiously. But the consumer set the pace, and nylon was the call at most men's hosiery counters.

"Next fall, nylon will dominate most lines, either in all-nylon hose or blended with other fibers. Nylon is also being widely used to reinforce toe and heel on cotton, rayon and wool hose.

"No longer is the retailer limited to just one or two numbers in nylon. If he shops the market he will find a large variety of styles made up in nylon.

"Supply of nylon is a limiting factor to nylon hosiery production. No one seems to be able to get enough of the

The "bold look" in socks in 1949 was interpreted (left to right) with geometric panels in red and white on blue, blue and white on red, and green and tan on brown. From Esquire, May 1949.

raw materials, and most manufacturers state that they expect their entire nylon production to be sold up for fall long before the cold weather sets in.

"At first, some manufacturers were concerned about nylon's absorbency, porosity, and clamminess in hot weather. If the nylon hose have any or all of these faults, the consumer does not appear to care. They are the best selling hose on the market today, and they are expected to be even bigger in the fall.

"The state of affairs in the hosiery market left much to be desired last spring, but the introduction of nylon seems to be the answer to the hosiery producer's dreams. It has given the market a powerful shot in the arm, and no one is complaining about nylon sales" (July 22, 1949, p. 130).

By the end of the 1940s fancy patterned socks accounted for 60 percent of all men's socks sold; 40 percent were in solid colors. The silk sock was virtually dead, the war having cut off the supply of silk from Japan, and, with the introduction of the soft man-made–fiber socks, few men missed it.

1950–1960

Esquire in 1950 introduced "Mr. T," an elongated fashion silhouette. "Take your eyes off Mr. T for a moment and look at the tallest building in town," urged the fashion copywriter. "See the terraced effect on top? It is a structural necessity that just naturally makes a tall building *look taller*. Transpose this same terraced idea to designs in men's accessories and you get the same effect—*altitude*. Therefore, a key pattern for Mr. T, modern as an architect's dream, is the *terraced treatment*. The clocks in your socks, the new designs in neckwear, braces, mufflers, and even jewelry, all have the terraced, tall 'T' effect." Three pairs of half hose were on display—two strictly for town wear, the third for sports—each with a vertical design that carried out the terraced idea. And since Mr. T was a man who *coordinated* his clothes, he also had a pair of "T" braces related to his socks.

The new decade saw the introduction of machinery that made possible the production of patterns whose color would not show through the back of the sock. And in a very real sense the early 1950s were ultraconservative, circumspect years symbolized by "the man in the gray flannel suit," who did his level best to remain anonymous—to hide his colors. The shoulders of his gray flannel suit were natural, lapels narrow, and trousers slim. This was a silhouette that called for lighter-weight shoes and neat, conservative

Angled-terrace designs appeared in different forms in anklet patterns for business (left, center) and sports (right). From Esquire, October 1950.

Argyle wool socks in brown and red with a yellow overplaid and wide-rib wool socks in a pale shade were intended for wear with tweed clothes. From Esquire, May 1945.

the
elegant
man
about
town
selects

The elegant man about town selected these socks in 1957: (left) a lisle sock with an intricate multicolor clock embroidered in silk; (upper right) a vertical-striped lisle sock with a geometric-design panel; (bottom right) a lisle sock with a double-diamond pattern spaced well apart. [APPAREL ARTS]

plain-toe bluchers; a 10 by 4 rib in pastel nylon, with suede and calf slip-ons; lisle hose with a brown-and-green clock on a tan ground, with English-last wing tips; a mercerized-cotton sock in a links-and-links pattern with a diamond panel, worn with pearl-type town shoes featuring a straight tip; a soft spun-cotton argyle in four colors, with a kiltie-tongued golf oxford; an all-wool argyle, with brogues; a 12 by 6 rib solid-color Dynel, with a trim blucher; a medium-weight wool diamond-patterned sock, with an imported suede gillie; and solid-color links-and-links cotton hose, with a crepe-soled moccasin.

In the spring of 1953 the all-cotton argyle in various diamond effects and a multitude of color combinations was still the staple in most men's socks

(top left) Spaced allover figures brighten a ribbed wool sock. (top right) Minute stitch designs and stripes lend interest to a nylon-and-polyester stretch sock. (bottom left) This silk sock has a clock formed by an open design. (bottom right) Ombré circular stripes distinguish this ribbed lisle sock. From Gentlemen's Quarterly, *spring, 1958.*

socks in small figures, stripes, or plain with clocks. During this era there was a strong feeling for proper things in proper places, and the more extroverted socks were reserved for spectator sportswear.

Ankle-length socks of crimped nylon fibers were introduced in 1951 in a one-size-fits-all format. The concept of one sock's stretching to fit every foot had great appeal, and as a result the short sock worn without garters became dominant.

Spring of 1952 brought an enlarged selection of socks made of the new synthetic fibers—nylon, Dynel, Dacron, Orlon, and Vicara—either 100 percent or in blends. Meanwhile, argyles and diamond-patterned hose remained as popular as ever.

Men's Wear paired the newest shoes with the newest socks and came up with photographs of the following combinations: a spun nylon sock in canary with a 6 by 3 rib, worn with

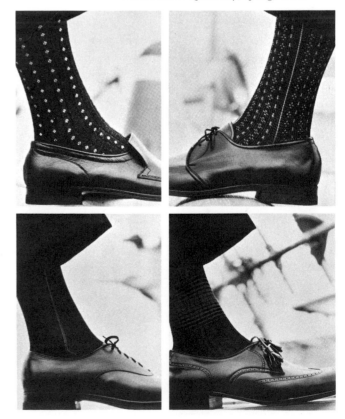

drawers. But the more conservative dresser preferred the new 6 by 3 rib lisles with an extra-wear feature, a raised, high-back heel.

Although the ultraconservative trend had diminished in men's suits, shirts, and ties by the last half of the decade, socks continued to be quiet, or, as *Apparel Arts* put it, played a "muted obbligato to the strong pattern interest of fall suitings. Classic clock and panel effects enliven fine lisles and smooth synthetics in ribbed constructions and in flat knits that enhance the silken luster of the yarns. The longer 'half hose' designed with elastic top or to be worn with garters are expected to stage a minor revival; we are coming to realize again that few parts of a man's anatomy are so improved by being covered as are his ankles and shins" (March, 1957, p. 66). Illustrating this feature were photographs of a fine lisle sock with an intricate multicolor clock pattern embroidered in silk; ribbed lisle featherstitched with vertical stripes and a geometric panel design; and lisle half hose featuring a widely spaced double-diamond pattern.

1960–1970

In the early 1960s socks fell very clearly into three categories. There were socks for business, socks for weekends, and socks for active sports. And any man with pretensions of being well dressed had a wardrobe of socks in crew (or anklet), mid-calf, and over-the-calf lengths. In the crew length, for instance, as many as seventy-five different shades were introduced in one year.

In 1963 *Gentlemen's Quarterly* printed a holiday gift suggestion page, and among the "furnishings with finesse" were four pairs of colorful crew-length hose: a stretch nylon Fisherman Knit in a two-tone effect; Orlon socks with an open-knit effect between double ribs; socks with rugby stripes in a blend of lamb's wool, Dacron, and stretch nylon; and cable-stripe socks of Dacron and cotton.

The Peacock Revolution, born in

England, struck these shores during the last half of the 1960s, and soon many hosiery advertisements were aggressively urging the American man to give fresh thought to his sock wardrobe. "Kick the dull sock habit!" was the theme of one hosiery firm's advertising campaign for its newly styled socks. "Are you a 'black with black,' 'brown with brown' designer?" asked the body copy. "Kick the dull sock habit!"

The flared trousers of the new shaped suits brought the eye down toward the foot, where one saw easy-care socks of man-made fibers in free-spirited patterns and uninhibited colors. This fresh, new look in socks complemented some of the most imaginative footwear seen in decades. Socks were fun because fashion was fun. One imaginative advertising man, reasoning that no one should part with an item of apparel that had been so

Subtle checks, designed to coordinate with twill weaves and modest-pattern suitings, appeared in wool-and-stretch-nylon socks in 1969. From Gentlemen's Quarterly, *winter, 1969.*

A deer design is set off in contrasting tones in a sock of 50 percent Orlon, 25 percent nylon, and 25 percent olefin (1970). [INTERWOVEN SOCKS DIVISION OF KAYSER-ROTH]

good to him ("weathered hundreds of washings and wearings"), made a list of things to do with old socks: turn them into turtleneck sweaters for dolls, cuffs for kids' jackets and snowsuits, zany bean bags, stuffing for toys, cover-ups for cans, cover-ups for cold feet, and puppets.

"Socks Join Fashion Boom" was a headline in *Men's Wear* on Jan. 7, 1970. "Socks in new patterns, colors and lengths have the look of status young people snap up. And they're the right mates for the new wave of stand-out shoes with bold toes, two tone leathers, hardware. New fiber blends in brawnier weights and textures work well with the look of more shoe. Added footnote is the fact that some of the newest spring socks match sleeveless sweaters and tank tops." Black hosiery, suggested the writer, would soon look as old hat as the tired tan raincoat. Illustrating this article were photographs of the following "new wave" socks: split-herringbone stripes in Orlon, nylon, and Creslan; midget diamonds in Orlon and nylon; a classic argyle in Orlon and nylon; a flame-stitch diamond in Orlon and nylon; a miniature heather glen plaid; a

Striking patterns were displayed in socks in 1970: (left to right) big diamonds in camel, black, and red Orlon and nylon; red-and-blue lattice-pattern socks in nylon and Orlon, designed by Bill Blass; brown-and-white king-size houndstooth checks in Orlon-and-nylon socks, designed by John Weitz; a paisley pattern in wool and nylon, an Italian import by Bonwit Teller. From Esquire, *October 1970.*

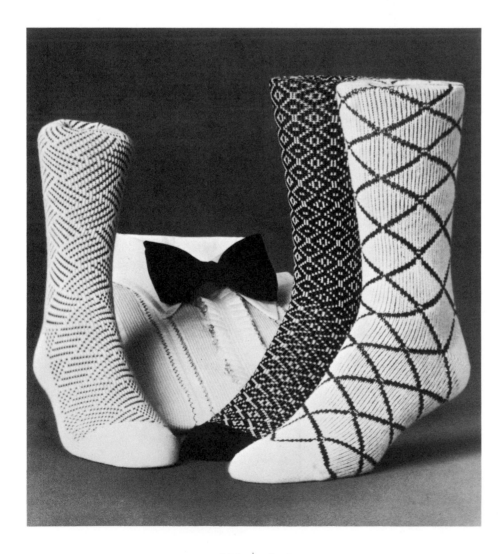

(above) A vertical-pattern ribbed sock in Orlon and nylon, designed by John Weitz, is worn with a linen-and-leather two-tone shoe. From Esquire, *April 1971.*

(left) Different blends of fibers are used to achieve knitting designs for socks in the seventies: (left) 50 percent Orlon, 25 percent nylon, and 25 percent olefin; (center) 55 percent nylon, 35 percent olefin, and 10 percent spandex; (right) 69 percent Orlon, 20 percent olefin, and 20 percent nylon. [INTERWOVEN SOCKS DIVISION OF KAYSER-ROTH]

two-tone split-diamond pattern in Orlon, Marvess, and stretch nylon; and an Art Deco patchwork of patterns in Orlon and nylon.

Antistatic socks made of a specially developed nylon yarn were introduced with strong advertising in all the media. "Eliminates trouser 'hang-ups.' You stand up, trousers slide down. Won't gather lint in washer-drier. It's great to be rid of static electricity!" wrote Carolyn Fiske about Esquire socks of Antron nylon.

An over-the-hip sock that climbed to the wearer's waist made its debut with considerable fanfare. A one-piece waist-to-toe tight with a fly front and ribbed socks from the calf down, it was much like the panty hose worn by the distaff side, although understandably enough men's hosiery manufacturers avoided any such association in their promotions. Accordingly, these warm waist-high socks were launched under such varied names as Warm Johns, Warmers, and Pant-He-Hose. Designed primarily as functional apparel to be worn by men who worked or played out-of-doors for long periods, they were also recommended for normal wear; one firm promoted its line as being essential under double-knit slacks "when the temperature drops and the wind-chill rises."

The *Daily News Record* in 1971 noted the rise of fancy and novelty socks, speculating whether they would soon counteract the "no-sock look" some of the younger men had adopted. Although the so-called dark basics were still commanding the largest number of hosiery sales throughout the country that year, fancy hosiery and patterns were making substantial gains, and there was, said the *Daily News Record*, "a growing story in the new fashion colors." In the meantime, it was reported that retailers who catered especially to the young trade were enjoying some degree of success with flag, ecology, and sex-symbol socks.

To be sure, there were still conservative men who wore black with black and brown with brown, but socks by the 1970s had leaped feet first into the fashion arena. In a decade of mix-and-match and pattern-on-pattern, men's hosiery had kicked up its heels, lost its inhibitions, and joined the revolution. "Sox appeal" was no longer just a pun; it was a reality. Socks in the seventies had become a status accessory, particularly with the younger man, and as such took their place as an essential part of the total fashion picture.

Footwear

The look of men's shoes bears a direct relation to the cut of the trousers being worn at the time. At the turn of the twentieth century men's shoes were high and usually were made in a pointed-toe style that perfectly complemented cuffless trousers tapering down to very narrow bottoms. This exaggerated trouser style was called "peg-top." Not until the appearance of deep trouser cuffs did the pointed toe give way to a so-called bulb toe (a bulb-shaped toe with sole extensions that were widest at the sides), which served to balance the new deeply cuffed trouser bottoms.

1900–1910

Whether pointed or bulb-toed, men's shoes in the first decade of the century were either laced or buttoned, and either style usually was equipped with a cloth tab at the back to aid in slipping the shoe on and off. Often the top half was made not of leather but of a closely woven cloth in buff or gray, which gave the shoe an especially dressy appearance. A sharp buttonhook was essential for buttoning and unbuttoning high-buttoned shoes. This sounds remarkably uncomfortable today, but the clothes-conscious man at the turn of the century did not demand or expect comfort from any item in his wardrobe. His shirt collars were high and starched, and his heavily padded suits were buttoned high. But since the laced shoe was somewhat less trouble than the high-buttoned shoe, by 1905 a substantial number of men were beginning to indicate a preference for the laced model finished on the upper part with four hooks on each side to expedite lacing up the shoe. Yet one trade paper noted that the button models were still "very popular among the city trade."

An issue of *Boot and Shoe Recorder* in 1905, the year cuffs first began to be worn on trousers, reported "a new last which is being brought out for the coming season, and which has been named as typical of high quality—

A high-buttoned dress shoe is shown in this illustration of formal evening attire in 1907. [NEW YORK PUBLIC LIBRARY PICTURE COLLECTION]

Marquis. It is a full toe, has a straight tread, with a fair amount of spring, and carries a regular heel. It is, in short, a good serviceable shape—one which will be in favor for more than a single season." Narrow toes still predominated, however, with black far outranking brown as the proper shoe color. Black glazed kids were being worn that year in all the different lasts and patterns, with both single and double soles. "Shiners" (patent kid, patent colt, and horsehide enamel) were popular in various combinations with dull leather tops.

Among the most desirable leathers in 1905 were box (boarded) calf, Eli calf, gunmetal and Black Diamond calf, French-process chrome calf, old-fashioned wax calf, black and colored cordovans, and willow calf. Storm leather in black and russet and French veal in black and color were being used in 10- and 12-inch bluchers. Two typical shoes in this storm line were a russet French veal 12-inch blucher on the whole-quarter pattern, made with a bellows tongue, having a full double sole to the heel, a half-Scotch edge, 18-square, and large eyelets to the top (this shoe was also shown in black leather); and a 10-inch seamless blucher made in black storm calf, with a double sole, a half-Scotch edge, and a small cable stitch. Recommended for the "snappy dresser" was a French-process chrome calf buttoned shoe with a pebble calf top, a perforated vamp, and a wing tip, made with a wasp toe (a name given to one of the six-odd most popular narrow toes), a double sole, and a military heel: "A very swell shoe for young men's wear."

A new "hygienic" shoe was introduced. Made with a felt innersole to absorb perspiration and ensure flexibility, it was said to be an improvement over the cushion sole in that it did not become hard and crack but remained soft and in place. The material for this innersole was identified as the best piano felting.

"Sidewalk" shoes were another footwear category, the name being chosen to help differentiate between dressier city styles and the storm boots or heavier footwear. Among them was a new last: a narrow toe with a good outside swing and a higher, military heel. Patent colt was the leading leather in sidewalk shoes, and button and blucher patterns were the favorites, the bal having lost some of its prominence in high-grade shoes. The "rivet shank" was a new feature in some sidewalk shoes and was publicized as furnishing an extra support to the arch of the foot.

By 1910 the oxford, or low shoe, was on the market and was being widely advertised. Most of the early oxfords were laced, although some had three buttons. Among the most popular leathers were patent, velour calf, and Australian glazed kangaroo. Heels varied from a broad low style to a medium heel and a semimilitary heel. The blucher tie predominated, a fancy perforated diamond or wing tip was very popular, and the bulb, or freak, toe was fashionable now that almost all trousers had deep cuffs. Although the oxford was a broader and much more comfortable shoe than earlier types, it was not to be accepted by the

The wing-tip shoe with a wide bow and a high heel was high fashion in 1909. [NEW YORK PUBLIC LIBRARY PICTURE COLLECTION]

general public for almost ten years. Like the high starched collar, the high shoe was to linger on despite the fact that as early as 1907 men's suits had begun to lose their overstuffed look and take on shapelier, more youthful lines. For the next several years, the oxford would be worn almost solely by the avant-garde dresser, who in this proper period was in the minority among American men.

1910–1920

By 1915 the oxford was being widely advertised. That year a full-page advertisement in the *Boot and Shoe Recorder* featured 3 of the 131 styles the Regal Shoe Company carried in stock: a russet calf oxford with a fawn cloth panel, a black calf blucher oxford, and a black calf with a black rubber sole

The high duck shoe in buff or white and the oxford in white or brown, both with navy rubber soles, were advertised as deck shoes in 1914. [UNIROYAL, INC.]

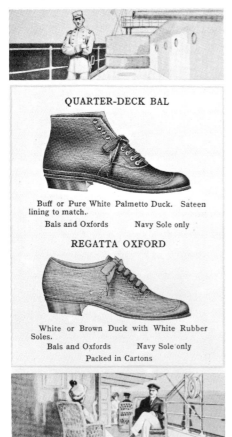

QUARTER-DECK BAL

Buff or Pure White Palmetto Duck. Sateen lining to match.

Bals and Oxfords   Navy Sole only

REGATTA OXFORD

White or Brown Duck with White Rubber Soles.

Bals and Oxfords   Navy Sole only

Packed in Cartons

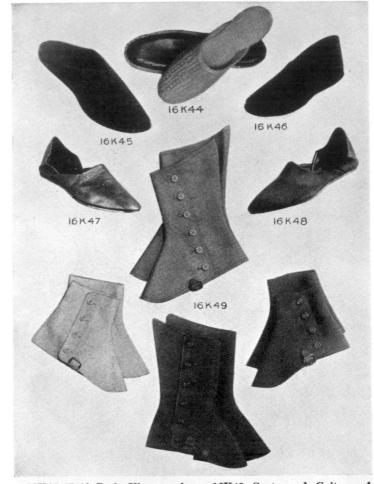

16K44-45-46 Bath Slippers of towelling and felt

16K47-48 House Slippers, domestic; and imported suède and morocco

16K49 Spats and Gaiters of linen, boxcloth and leather, four or six buttons, various shades

In 1915 slippers of toweling, felt, or suede or morocco leather appealed to men for indoor wear, while spats or gaiters met the outdoor requirements of fashion. [COURTESY OF BROOKS BROTHERS, NEW YORK]

and a black rubber heel. At this time both high and oxford shoes often featured new invisible eyelets for which "no metal tip" shoe laces had been designed. They were advertised as "guaranteed not to rust, pull off, fray out, look tinny, nor catch in the clothing. Always look new."

A 1918 survey of fashions seen at winter resorts in the South noted the increasing popularity of the oxford along with that of the knickerbocker suit. An especially fashionable outfit worn by one Palm Beach man con-

sisted of a knicker suit of rough herringbone silk and thin wool, a hat of soft leghorn, and white buckskin oxfords trimmed with brown calf. Reviewing this survey, a *Men's Wear* writer expressed a desire to see a gradual acknowledgment of the comfort of the various English lasts ("which our grandfathers wore"), which he judged to be far superior to "our modern, misshapen conception" (Mar. 6, 1918). These English lasts had strongly rounded tips and appeared in many forms, from medium-stout fancy

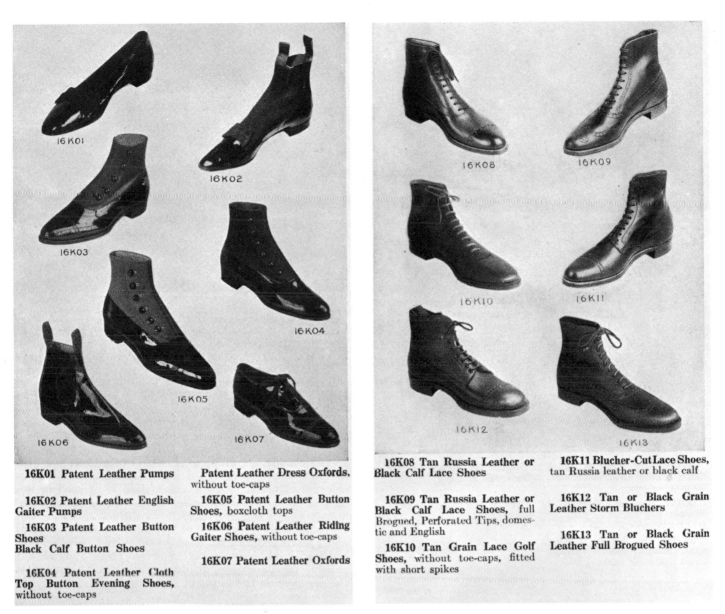

16K01 Patent Leather Pumps	**Patent Leather Dress Oxfords,** without toe-caps
16K02 Patent Leather English Gaiter Pumps	**16K05** Patent Leather Button Shoes, boxcloth tops
16K03 Patent Leather Button Shoes Black Calf Button Shoes	**16K06** Patent Leather Riding Gaiter Shoes, without toe-caps
16K04 Patent Leather Cloth Top Button Evening Shoes, without toe-caps	**16K07** Patent Leather Oxfords

Formal footwear in 1915 ranged from pumps and patent-leather gaiter shoes to high-buttoned shoes and patent leather oxfords
[COURTESY OF BROOKS BROTHERS, NEW YORK]

16K08 Tan Russia Leather or Black Calf Lace Shoes	**16K11 Blucher-Cut Lace Shoes,** tan Russia leather or black calf
16K09 Tan Russia Leather or Black Calf Lace Shoes, full Brogued, Perforated Tips, domestic and English	**16K12 Tan or Black Grain Leather Storm Bluchers**
16K10 Tan Grain Lace Golf Shoes, without toe-caps, fitted with short spikes	**16K13 Tan or Black Grain Leather Full Brogued Shoes**

High shoes with laces came in bal and blucher models in 1915.
[COURTESY OF BROOKS BROTHERS, NEW YORK]

country shoes to full brogues for all-around use.

The increasing popularity of the oxford was accelerated in 1919 by the serviceman returning from World War I, who much preferred it to the high shoe. The well-dressed man of the postwar period was comfort-conscious as well as clothes-conscious and, in the opinion of one fashion reporter, paid greater attention to the appropriate shape of boots and shoes for various occasions:

"Those for formal day or evening usually have a true formal look to them. They present a long, plain, severe appearance, with a narrower toe than made for informal use. The stouter, less ceremonious foot covering has a truly sensible appearance in its straight last and common sense width of toe and the various kinds for sporting use appear a study of comfort. Town shoes are, in the main, rather modest, with a plain tip across the toe, or maybe it is a bit newer to have this

toe punctured in some inconspicuous pattern. Full brogued shoes and those otherwise elaborately punched and recognized as belonging to country dress are often brown and white or black and white buckskins trimmed with brown or black calf. When the warm weather comes these lounge shoes will be equally popular in and out of town" (*Men's Wear*, Apr. 9, 1919).

Within the next few years, the college man (a fashion influence to be

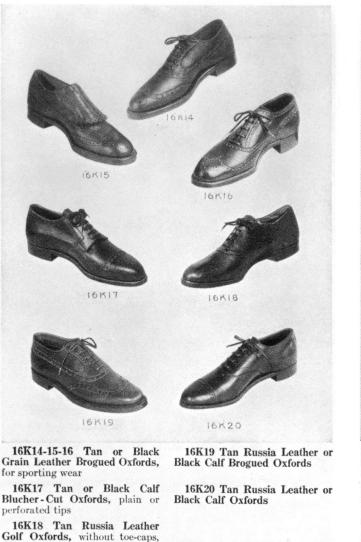

16K14-15-16 Tan or Black Grain Leather Brogued Oxfords, for sporting wear

16K17 Tan or Black Calf Blucher-Cut Oxfords, plain or perforated tips

16K18 Tan Russia Leather Golf Oxfords, without toe-caps, fitted with short spikes

16K19 Tan Russia Leather or Black Calf Brogued Oxfords

16K20 Tan Russia Leather or Black Calf Oxfords

Oxfords in black or brown were sought by the avant-garde in 1915. [COURTESY OF BROOKS BROTHERS, NEW YORK]

16K21 White Buckskin Oxfords, without toe-caps, rubber soles, without stitching

16K22 White Buckskin Oxfords, rubber soles
White Canvas Oxfords, rubber soles
Tan or Black Leather Oxfords, with rubber soles

16K23 Racquet Shoes, white buckskin trimmed with red goat, rubber soles

16K24-25 White Buckskin Oxfords, trimmed with leather, rubber soles

16K26 White Buckskin Oxfords, special corrugated rubber soles

16K27 White Buckskin Oxfords, perforated tips

16K28 White Buckskin Lace Shoes, with and without toe-caps, rubber soles

White buckskin and two-tone shoes were popular for resort wear in 1915. [COURTESY OF BROOKS BROTHERS, NEW YORK]

reckoned with in the era of "flaming youth") would turn to laced oxfords, and the high shoe would be gone except as worn by the diehard who also preferred a high starched collar.

1920–1930

By 1924 fashion scouts covering the Palm Beach winter season reported that white flannel trousers were replacing white linen knickers, white shirts were still being worn by more than 50 percent of the fashionable men, and white shoes were by far the favorite footwear. Most of the white shoes had heavy black and varnished rubber soles. "The white shoes with tan wing tips and straight tips are in high favor with the best dressed man. The soft leather or buckskin shoes are seen in a very small number" (*Men's Wear,* Mar. 19, 1924, p. 8). According to a survey of the shoe preferences of 300 of the best-dressed men vacationing at Palm Beach, the all-white shoe accounted for 20 percent of the shoes being worn; white with a tan wing-tip toe cap, for 19 percent; white with a tan straight-tip toe cap, for 14 percent; tan wing-tip, for 7 percent; white with a tan saddle strap, for 7 percent; tan straight-tip, for 7 percent; white with a tan toe cap and strap over the vamp, for 7 percent; and white with a black straight-tip toe cap, for 5 percent.

In late summer in 1925, fashion scouts covered the scene at Newport, Rhode Island, the most fashionable American summer resort. Blazers were being worn extensively, and with so many of the younger men wearing the new Oxford bags, the wide-bottomed trousers introduced in the United States that spring, many shoes not only featured a wide toe last but showed more extroverted styling as well. A reporter covering Newport for *Men's Wear* asked the following question:

"Supposing some shoe manufacturer came along and tried to sell you a white buckskin shoe with a bright red saddle strap and a loose, narrow, bright red ball strap across the toe of the shoe, what would you say to that manufacturer? You would say, 'Jazz!' wouldn't you?

"It all depends on who starts a style whether it is smart or 'jazz.' If someone of no reputation featured such a shoe you would still say it was 'jazz.' But supposing some store with a reputation for having only correct merchandise featured such a shoe, what would you say? 'Jazz'? Not on your life. You'd be all wrong! For if Brooks Brothers featured such a shoe it would be unquestionably a new and correct shoe.

"'How come?' you ask. Because if they featured such a radical shoe it would be sold to and worn by the men who make a new style correct.

"Well! They have featured such a shoe and I saw at least a half-dozen of the best dressed men at Newport wearing it. The artist has illustrated the shoe and if you think your shoe department is going to be up-to-the-minute next year on the new and correct shoes for men without this red idea in sport shoes, you've got another think coming to you. Next issue we will illustrate another new sport shoe coming to the front, the white buck shoe with the diminutive wing tip and side strap" (Sept. 9, 1925, p. 61).

Meanwhile, on the campus at Princeton University, generally considered the headquarters for the country's best-dressed students, undergraduates favored the tan shoe over the black shoe in all styles, in some cases by a ratio of 3 to 1.

An article in the *Boot and Shoe Recorder* on March 7, 1925, described several of the fashion trends that had

This rubber was advertised in 1920 as a light, high-cut, rain-protecting slipper. [UNIROYAL, INC.]

Trim appearance was stressed in 1921 in advertising this gaiter, or galosh, made of light jersey cloth with a black fleece lining. [UNIROYAL, INC.]

The tennis and yachting bal shoe of 1921 was a high canvas model with a ridged rubber sole. [UNIROYAL, INC.]

appeared or were about to appear in men's footwear:

"Styles for men do not center around any particular pattern. The vogue for broad-bottomed trousers insures the sale of broguey types to the younger men and shoe men are almost unanimous in their views that as long as the young men express their favor for loose-fitting trousers the place for the broad-toed and heavy-looking oxford is warranted.

"In sharp contrast to the clothing trend's relation to the shoe for younger men, the movement for lightweight, and in some cases featherweight styles, has gained more impetus than heretofore. It is a general opinion that the vogue for men's lightweight styles is one that must be brought about gradually. It is obvious that there are ever so many more manufacturers placing an extreme lightweight style before the retail shoe merchants this year than last. Almost without exception every shoe firm making men's footwear had samples made, which indicates a growing trend for this type of shoe when compared with the progress of a year ago. Last year there were few houses putting out a lightweight pattern and the development is a healthy indication.

"No doubt the history of the light tan movement for men, which was commenced a few years ago as a measure to increase per capita consumption, can be used as a parallel to the present lightweight shoe case. Light tan oxfords for spring and summer wear were not introduced overnight. It took a few seasons before they were worn to any marked degree by men, and perhaps we can use that knowledge as a guide for anticipating the rapidity of progress for the lightweight shoe. Men regarded the sharp change from the dark brown and reddish brown hues to the yellowish tan tones as too marked. But they gradually saw the 'light,' with the result that the light tan oxford is the ideal style for spring and summer. In fact, light tan shades are with us to stay. Likewise the contrast between those heavy-looking types, which have been men's style

In 1925 this plain-tip blucher shoe was recommended for golf because of its nonskid steel-studded leather sole and heel. [HANAN & SON]

The shoe favored by tennis champions in 1926 had a heavy bleached white duck upper and a thick outsole of vulcanized crepe rubber. [UNIROYAL, INC.]

leaders for some time, and the very light-appearing featherweight pattern, is also very marked. One manufacturer has made a wise move to overcome this feature by making a shoe that ranks just between the featherweight and heavier type, both in appearance and structure.

"There is every indication that marks the lightweight-shoe-for-man-movement as a healthy measure to bring about a greater per capita consumption which will consequently benefit the entire trade. There's no question but that it would be an ideal condition to have men buy a distinct shoe for spring and summer and regard it as solely a shoe for mild seasons, consequently resulting in the retail shoe merchant selling a heavier oxford or shoe for fall.

"The wider toe last has been used extensively in the manufacture of patterns for spring and summer wear, yet the styleful effect does not border too much on the broguey effect, due to the fact that the edges are closely trimmed. The wider extension employed on welts of shoes for the young men desiring the extreme brogue models, is missing in the new patterns. The effect is very good; it gives a broad and roomy shoe for a man, carrying plenty of style, which is brought about mostly by the skillful finishing of the closely-trimmed sole edges, rather than by broguey lines.

"Stitchings, mostly in double rows, are used in many styles. There seems

to be a tendency to break away from the practice of applying several rows of closely placed stitchings. Pinkings are very smart; finer designs being employed on many new styles. Pinkings extending along the vamp to the quarter are generously used. Tips are being perforated in lighter designs on shoes for street wear, but, of course, sport types call for heavy perforations."

The writer predicted that 1925 would be a big sports shoe year, expecting that the influence of the new biscuit-color flannel trousers for young men would have a favorable effect on sports shoes:

"One manufacturer, who always does a splendid trade on men's sports, has designed a shoe to match the biscuit trousers. It is a wide toe model with tan calf wing tip and elk vamp. The elk matches the biscuit shade very well. Black calf with elk is shown in many new sport models. The crepe sole is used very much, and is favored over any other type. White buck is also used in many sport types. It contrasts well with tan calf, which is used for tips, backstays, etc.

"The reception of the tie is a debatable question, but probably its place is in the classification for lightweight shoes. Some designers have taken a long step forward in trying to combine the most style possible in ties. A broad, almost square, toe tie is one of the latest developments in this tie. It's built over a brogue last."

Meanwhile, in some of the larger

The combination of tan and smoked elk and the cleated rubber sole were the salient points of these 1925 golf shoes. [NETTLETON]

American cities the young man who favored the newer, more extreme fashions was choosing the patent-leather oxford with side gores for street wear. The stylish but more conservative man who favored a highly polished appearance found it in an oxford of shiny leather.

Even with so many new ideas in styling and the fashion influence of the young, a national survey taken in 1925 revealed that the ratio of oxford sales to those for high shoes was 4 to 1. Unlike American women, who accepted fashion changes with alacrity, men sometimes ignored new fashions and clung to the old and familiar.

Chosen as a shoe for the 1925 man who wanted "a fair dash of style" was a tan oxford with a medium-round toe and fine pinkings. Yet despite the growing popularity of tan leathers, black oxfords continued to sell. Their sale was credited to the fact that the conspicuous tones of the light-colored shoes made them out of place in the evening for the man who wanted to be appropriately dressed.

A *Men's Wear* reporter noted in 1925 that, in his opinion, "the exacting workmanship necessary to manufacture high styles in women's footwear is just as much present in the patterns selling to men. Oxfords fit much better around the ankles than heretofore. Details, like finishing the heel, attaching the tongue to the lining beside the lace stay, are indications that steady development in style lines is being made. Development in comfortable-fitting qualities is evidenced by the prevailing types of wide, round and roomy-toed lasts.

"Blucher patterns are more attractive than ever before. Pattern makers have put considerable style into the lines. The presence of spring in the last allowing the toe and sole to swing slightly upward, adds much to the general appearance of the lines. It also serves to insure a better fit across the ball of the foot, off-setting creasing which very frequently develops when there is no toe spring."

A movement to increase men's per capita consumption of shoes took shape in New York in 1925 when committee members of the Joint Styles Conference recommended that retail shoe merchants and their salesmen put greater stress on the importance of "talking changing shoes more often" to their customers. Recommendations were as follows:

"Besides the importance of dressing for the occasion, it is of vital importance to shoe men who have their customers' interest conscientiously at heart, to see that they and their shoe fitters know the importance of changing shoes as often as one changes hose or underwear. It is a known fact that shoe linings absorb perspiration, the acid from the body, and retain the poisonous element more than hose or underwear and therefore must be left off to be ventilated and exposed to fresh air. Blisters and callouses and even infections are caused by wearing the same pair too often and for proper foot comfort and sanitation one should

The two-tone shoe with a strap stitched over the vamp was advertised in 1926 as suitable for golf. [FOOT-JOY BY FIELD & FLINT CO.]

have enough pairs of shoes to change frequently. This important health idea, plus the importance of wearing shoes for the occasion, if properly fostered by retail shoe merchants, will sell more pairs of shoes for them and work to the real advantage of the consuming public."

A *Men's Wear* fashion reporter, taking stock of what he judged to be some of the smartest men's footwear on the market in mid-decade, remarked: "All of these boots and shoes are void of that heavy or puffed effect at the toe. The rise is gradual from toe point to instep" (July 8, 1925). Among the styles he liked were an American custom-made shoe of white buck with brogue tips and facings of red mahogany brown calf; an American hand-made custom shoe of reddish tan Russia leather with a full brogue finish and a slight extension sole; an English handmade shoe, for summer town or country wear, of brown buck with tips and so on of russet Russia leather ("One of the best ready made shoes I've ever seen!"); an American custom-made gaiter boot of patent leather ("Today it is considered smart for winter evening dress"); an English handmade boot with lowers of patent leather and uppers of brown buckskin, having small bell-turned buttons of shaded mother-of-pearl ("This is a strictly dress boot for day wear that should never appear with informal day attire of any kind"); and an American custom-made boot with lowers of patent leather and uppers of heavy kid ("This is a model perfect in its shape, a pivot last around which varying fine fashions have fluctuated for more than a hundred years").

Paying a return visit to Palm Beach in 1926, *Men's Wear* reporters noted the popularity of the cocoa-brown buckskin shoe that had been worn by the Prince of Wales during his visit to the United States in 1923. Brown was an outstanding resort-wear color that year, and among the fashion sketches made was one that showed a particularly smart Palm Beach outfit: "A symphony in brown—brown leghorn hat, tobacco brown belted jacket, bis-

Spats were so fashionable in the late twenties that their appearance influenced the styling of this gaiter. [UNIROYAL, INC.]

cuit flannel trousers with a pair of Prince of Wales cocoa brown buck shoes."

In 1928 *Men's Wear* recommended that the retailer not ignore the element among the younger generation in his locality that "resembles to a large degree the Broadway type. They may spend the evenings in the drug stores and pool parlors, or else they may pass their spare hours in making a round of the homes of their fair young lady friends in rickety Fords or shining Packards. But still they have this desire to spice up their dress, and if you count upon their patronage to supply you with your daily bread and butter, it is necessary that you be progressive, and keep up with the latest styles worn by the lads along the Great White Way" (Dec. 5, 1928). A survey of the styles favored by the more affluent Broadwayites showed a great variety of shoes; among them the wing tip had risen in popularity from 8 to 14 percent. Whereas there had been little change in the relative number of broad-toe, or balloon, shoes as a class, there had been a distinct increase in the blucher model of this last. The margin of black shoes over tans continued to rise, but that year's 71 percent for black to 29 percent for tan was considered to be about the greatest spread that could be expected. The report concluded on this note: "An interesting thing to note in footwear is the number that wore spats. As you can see, it is a remarkably large num-

In 1928 three types of custom-made shoes were (left to right) the wing-tip shoe, the straight-tip shoe with a medallion design in the toe cap, and the straight-tip shoe in brown buckskin. [NEW YORK PUBLIC LIBRARY PICTURE COLLECTION]

ber—11 percent. Beige and medium light grey are the two prevailing colors."

A report on fashions worn at a Princeton University house party weekend in May of that year revealed that wing tips had risen slightly in popularity and that most Princetonians favored sports shoes of plain white, white with a black or tan saddle strap, and white with a black or tan wing tip.

Since progressive menswear shops in key American cities made it a rule to send their buyers to Palm Beach each winter to study the fashions being worn there, they were well aware in 1928 that the plain white buck shoe was preferred by the smartest men at exclusive clubs. As a *Men's Wear* reporter put it, "This shoe as worn by the majority has a heavy black rubber sole, or if the sole was originally of some other color, it is almost invariably varnished black, giving a neat and finished appearance to the footgear.

"Numerically, the wing tip shoe is far in the lead, if the various styles in this type are taken together, and one of the wing tip styles, as a single type, is in second place.

"The very latest style in footwear for men is the Deauville sandal of white leather with a design woven in a darker leather, but as yet this has not appeared to such an extent that it could be included in the survey."

By 1929 shoe manufacturers and retailers agreed that the way to sell more shoes was by "styleage" rather than "mileage." A speaker at the annual convention of the National Shoe Retailers Association in Chicago deplored the fact that the proprietor and the salesman in the shoe store were responsible for having taught the customer, when making a purchase, to think of how long it would wear instead of how it would improve his appearance or fit into his wardrobe. Almost simultaneous with this lament was the introduction of what the trade called "hot dogs": colored kid oxfords in blue, green, and red. Produced by a number of leading manufacturers, these eye-catching shoes were to be exhibited to shoe merchants throughout the country in order to promote lightweight footwear for summer.

The most newsworthy developments in 1929 were considered to be happening in the sportswear division. There were, for example, all-snakeskin shoes, although some critics expected that these, like alligator shoes, would prove to be too heavy and insufficiently porous for summer wear. There was certainly no question but that comfort was one of the chief factors in promoting satisfaction with shoes.

"Because of the continuous walking hither, thither and yon upon the campuses, the first requisite is that shoes be comfortable," said the preface to a survey in *Men's Wear* (Nov. 20, 1929) on shoes worn by college students in various sections of the country in the fall of 1929. At Princeton and Yale, considered to be the two most fashion-conscious universities, the popularity of the plain-toed all-white buckskin, especially the shoe with a black sole that had been so popular among fashionable men at Palm Beach in the winter of 1928, could not be overemphasized. Other survey findings showed that wing-tip shoes, especially in a deep mahogany color, were still in first place, the semipointed toe continued to be favored by the great majority of undergraduates, and the saddle-strap sports shoe retained its popularity in both black and white and brown and white. Among Mid-

western students wing-tip shoes had gained in popularity, and dark brown shoes were being worn in great numbers; of the sports shoes, the white shoe with a brown wing tip was preferred. At universities below the Mason and Dixon's line, the popularity of the wing-tip shoe had more than tripled in twelve months; heavy English-model blucher shoes also showed a marked increase. In the Far West, straight-tipped shoes in black were great favorites with students, and wing tips were being worn by about one out of six students. Black was the favorite shoe color, followed by tan in dark shades. A notable increase had been registered in wing-tip sports shoes, which were now worn by one of ten rather than one of fifty students; almost all these shoes were black and white. The heavy blucher (in reality, the army trench shoe with hobnails and steel caps) continued to be popular with upperclassmen at the University of California at Berkeley.

1930–1940

While during the Depression years many shoes were worn with holes in their soles, there were also well-groomed shoes in sufficient numbers to give the fashion press something to write about. Although the national economy was sagging, some fortunes remained intact, and it was to this well-shod minority that the fashion press turned its attention.

In 1931, for instance, a Palm Beach style survey found that "a higher percentage of men were seen at Palm Beach this season wearing well groomed, smart sports shoes than ever before. It is safe to say that practically every man at Palm Beach this season had at least two pairs of sports shoes. The influence of this class has done much to accelerate the mass acceptance of sports shoes and in turn put money in the shoe dealer's till" (*Men's Wear,* Mar. 25, 1931).

Getting down to specific preferences, the survey noted: "Although the two-color wing tip shoe is still the leading style, it has registered a decline of nine percent in the past year. Notice that four out of five men wearing this type of shoe preferred the brown trim as against the black.

"The all-white buckskin continues to step forward. The total of 27 percent, an increase of six percent over last year, is made up of 17 percent plain toe, six percent straight tip, and three percent wing tip. The rubber soles of these shoes are invariably finished with black enamel. Not a few have red rubber soles, but the sides are blackened.

"Two-toned shoes with straight tip trims are also more popular than they were a year ago, so an increase in the demand for this model can be anticipated during the next six months. Here again the brown trim is an overwhelming favorite. Practically nine out of ten men wearing this type of shoe preferred the tan or brown trimming and only a small minority had black strappings on their shoes.

"The grey jacket and tan flannel trouser combination has no doubt tended to increase the number of brown buckskin shoes worn this year. Many of the men favoring this ensemble choose brown bucks. Although

In 1931 the gaiter, or galosh, had a neat zipper closure, a snapped tab at the top, and a sturdy rubber sole. [UNIROYAL, INC.]

there has been a more widespread popularity of this style, it is believed that the movement of this style to mass acceptance will be gradual. Practically all the brown buckskin shoes had rubber soles with dark brown or black enamel on the sides. It is very significant that the majority of all two-toned shoes had brown trimmings."

A survey of men's clothing stores with shoe departments reported in *Men's Wear* on April 8, 1931, showed that $5 was the most widely carried price line, favored in 40.7 percent of the stores. The $10 shoe was in second place, accounting for 36.05 percent. (The prices in the stores surveyed ranged from $2 to $35.)

By the spring of 1932 the brown buckskin shoe favored by men of fashion was reportedly gaining public favor. Although it was intended originally for country wear, it was expected to be seen on city streets that summer. One trade writer described the rising popularity of this shoe with so many references to fashionable resorts that, to someone reading his report today, it hardly seems possible that it was written at the depth of the Great Depression:

"The brown buckskin shoe has been accepted to such an extent by well dressed men in England that no wardrobe is considered complete without at least one pair of these shoes. Men at Newport were wearing brown buckskin shoes last summer, while at Meadowbrook and Piping Rock they were favored so strongly last season by the polo crowd that it seemed that every man who really 'belonged' was wearing brown buckskin shoes. From Palm Beach came reports in February that the very smartest dressed men at the Seminole Club and other fashionable places were wearing brown bucks, not only for golf, but for general daytime wear. Wealthy members of the so-called horsey set that spends the season at Aiken showed a preference for this type of shoe in February and March" (*Men's Wear*, Apr. 20, 1932).

The writer concluded that both wing-tip and plain-tip styles of brown bucks were correct and could be worn

properly in town with tan, brown, olive, or gray gabardine jackets and odd trousers ("Many of the men attending hunt meets on Long Island are quite partial to the brown jacket and grey trousers combination with brown buckskin shoes").

In the meantime, although the vogue for white buckskins continued, it was anticipated that most sports shoe business that year would be done in the brown-and-white wing model and the all-white buckskin shoe. In two-tone wing-tip shoes the trend was moving away from the black-and-white combinations.

In 1934 *Apparel Arts*, as an incentive to shoe sales, published a photographic review of the correct shoe for the occasion, noting that "an important point is that additional sales may often be attributed to the intelligence of a salesman who is abreast of the fashion trends":

"A typical shoe for business wear is this conservative custom oxford with spade sole trim, in black or brown. Its simplicity and freedom from detail fit it for wear with any type of business clothes and are in keeping with office environment. Since the business shoe is not subjected to rough usage, it can be comparatively light in construction.

"This classic fully brogued oxford is characteristic of shoes which are classified as being for street wear. Note how both the sole and upper of this shoe are heavier than seen in the business shoe. In design, as well as in construction, it is in agreement with clothes of the tweed and rough worsted type with which it is usually worn.

"A plain toe blucher oxford of brown buckskin with thick crepe rubber soles—representative of shoes for country wear. Worn with country clothes, it is naturally sturdy in construction. Incidentally, this shoe may be worn in the plain blucher model and, in fact, is currently considered correct with the elimination of the extension tongue.

"To be classified among shoes for active sports wear is this full brogued golf oxford with heavy leather soles and steel spikes riveted through the

An early wearer of Norwegian moccasin slip-ons, or Weejuns, was sketched at left in a resort setting in 1936. The seated man wore two-tone moccasin shoes with laces. From Esquire, *July 1936.*

outer sole. Since it is intended for an active sport, it must be both comfortable and durable. Note the wide, comfortable toe and the adequate swing in the last, insuring an easy fit and avoiding crowding.

"The patent leather pump with light flexible sole—for formal evening wear. This is correct for any formal evening occasion where the tailcoat is worn. Its suitability to the occasion for which it is intended speaks for itself, and it might be mentioned that the pump, which has lost none of its dig-

nity through the years, is coming into wider vogue than ever.

"Suitable for formal day wear is this patent leather oxford with cap toe, worn with white linen spats and the correct clothes for daytime weddings, public ceremonies and other occasions of formal day wear. It is also correct for semi-formal evening wear. Its lighter construction and freedom from detail are in keeping with the purpose of the shoe" (vol. V, no. 1, 1934).

By the mid-thirties spats had all but disappeared from the fashion picture except for formal day wear. Derived from the heavy cloth gaiters worn by Britishers with knickerbockers in the country, spats came into vogue in the United States with the advent of the oxford and remained popular throughout the 1920s. For wear with business suits, spats were made of buff, gray, black, or dark brown box cloth with side buttons. They slipped over the wearer's shoe and were fastened with a buckle and strap underneath the shoe.

In April, 1934, *Esquire* featured the latest variation on the plain white buckskin shoe: a white buck with red rubber soles and heels, made without a lining. It was presented as a particularly stylish shoe for resort wear and spectator sports. In fact, red rubber soles reappeared in the fashion pages of *Esquire* in June, 1934, this time attached to a pair of white bucks with brown calf trim. In December of that year, a trade writer reported that the Prince of Wales had ordered from R. R. Bunting of London and Paris a pair of white buckskin shoes trimmed with brown, and the reader was informed of the following styling features: "The line of the Derby front is cut very straight, or to a point, with perfectly plain stitching, doubled around the cap and on the saddle."

In November, 1935, *Esquire* published photographs of what was almost a complete shoe wardrobe: "The virtual absence of black prevents our calling this a complete shoe wardrobe, particularly in view of the current fashion for black shoes with brown clothes, but here at least are the salient features in the season's best models: beaver velour type treated sheepskin slippers with heavy soles, Russian calf riding shoes, oil grain hiking and shooting shoes, calf polo or hacking boots, calf field boots, black hunt boots with mahogany colored tops, oil grain waterproof moccasins, calfskin brogues, long grain blucher calf shoes with imitation stitched tip, and brown reversed calf semi-brogues with square custom toe." To make this a complete shoe wardrobe the following should be added: "Evening pumps and one or two pairs of black shoes on a town last, plus a pair of patent leather dress oxfords."

By the mid-thirties, Norwegian-model shoes had been adopted by well-dressed Americans. Variations of the shoes made by hand by Norwegian fishermen during their off-season, they first became popular in London, where American tourists discovered them. Soon two variations were being seen at fashionable American winter resorts: a slip-on style with a moccasin front that was called "Weejuns" and a laced style with a moccasin front that was known as the Norwegian-front shoe. The July, 1936, issue of *Esquire* showed Weejuns of brown polished calf and a pair of brown-and-white Norwegian shoes.

During the last half of the decade increasing emphasis was placed on lightweight summer clothing, and soon shoe manufacturers adopted the concept of seasonal changes, particularly in summer footwear. Shoe men remembered that textiles often make satisfactory substitutes for hides, and

This drawing of the original Norwegian peasant shoe, which became known as Weejuns, shows the strap over the instep with a cutout diamond pattern and a moccasin tip. From Esquire, *July 1936.*

by 1936 huaraches and espadrilles were vying for attention at American summer resorts. Inspired by Mexican peasant footwear, huaraches had woven straps of leather over the top and only a single strap toward the rear. Brought from the Basque country, the espadrille was a casual slip-on with a top of canvas or other fabric and a rope sole (or a sole of rubber or other material made to resemble rope).

"Comfort is the big watchword of the new summer shoes," wrote a trade writer in 1936, when many summer shoes were not only lightweight but also perforated to make them cool. The perforated shoe was already an established fashion in the South and West by the early 1930s, and by 1936 men in the East and North were also wearing these air-cooled shoes with their lightweight summer suits. Giving a more detailed account of these shoes, the writer said: "They are cut to the minimum in serviceable weight; they are made with plaited leathers or with fabric for the sake of comfort, freedom and ventilation. Their soles will be flexible leather or rubber. Many are being made with 'stuck-on' soles to eliminate surplus weight. Indians, mountaineers, North and South, have been consulted for ideas to add utility and comfort, and perhaps a fresh style note" (*Men's Wear,* Mar. 11, 1936).

Although all-white shoes, with or without perforations, continued to be the favorite summer shoes, many perforated shoes gave their wearer not only cool comfort but a splash of "hot" color as well. A prime example was a yellow chamois blucher with a red sole.

"Wash and wear clothing will be of great importance and will call for lighter colors or combinations in shoes," continued this 1936 article. "The new ideas in fabric shoes (footwear styled in Palm Beach or other summer-suiting fabrics to match clothing) fit well into the town-style picture." Among stylish examples of the fabric footwear of the thirties were a white sailcloth oxford trimmed with white calf and a beige sailcloth

trimmed with brown calf. Both shoes had leather soles. Handsome shoes fashioned of Palm Beach cloth included one finished with brown leather piping at the toe cap and around the top edge and another finished with brown patent leather.

By the mid-thirties sandal styles ranged from beach types to near oxfords; they came in many leathers, including smooth and reversed calf, in trimmed models and in combinations such as brown calf on white reversed calf or buck. In 1936 *Men's Wear* published a photograph of the film director Mervyn LeRoy wearing brown sandals with a tweed suit, although the reader was advised that, when correctly worn, sandals were "strictly a beachwear style. On the Riviera the well dressed men wear them with a pair of sailcloth or linen slacks and a knitted sports shirt, always at the seashore and never with lounge suits in town. This is a point the merchant cannot overstress in selling sandals to the customer. Correctly sold and worn, sandals mean extra sales. If this job is incorrectly done, there lies a danger of sandals competing with sports shoes." Three years later *Men's Wear* reported: "The growth of sandal business is enormous. Men are not satisfied with one pair, and these shoes are being retailed at very reasonable prices, thus making them very popular."

Moccasins were more important than ever, and the retailer with a customer who normally refused to consider novelty footwear was assured that he could make a lifelong convert by selling him a well-made moccasin. As a *Men's Wear* journalist said, "There has evolved a real man's shoe for a man's purposes in every conceivable situation and for every need."

By the spring and summer of 1938 toes were more rounded, ventilated shoes were registering greater gains, and the status of the all-white shoe was being questioned by some buyers, who considered it inappropriate for wear with lightweight suits in the new synthetic yarns and washable fabrics. Meanwhile, all-gray, trimmed gray, and two-tone gray oxfords were selling

The first pair in the upper row of shoes in this display is in the monk-front style with a strap and buckle over the instep. Next to it are moccasin-pattern bluchers. Across the second row are (left to right) black wing-tip shoes, brown ankle-high turf boots, reversed-calf quarter brogues, and black blucher shoes with medallion toe caps. Appropriate socks include (left to right) two lisles, a wide-rib wool, a big-diamond pattern, a camel's hair wide-rib, a 6 by 3 lisle, and a wool mixture. From Esquire, *March 1939.*

well in the Central West and South, although their sale in the East was extremely limited.

Molière boots became popular for spectator sports or simply for a country squire look. Slightly more than ankle-high, these boots, usually in reversed calf, were often featured in the fashion pages of *Esquire* in the late thirties. Pigskin, a new leather for men's shoes, was first used in the United States in the Molière model. By the end of the decade, however, the Molière had been supplanted by the chukka, or desert boot, a sports blucher, usually with two eyelets, that covered the ankle.

A double-page spread in *Esquire* in 1938 demonstrated the enormous variety of shoe styles from which the American man could choose. For beachwear there were red espadrilles and yellow goatskin sandals; for resort wear, reversed-calf monk-front shoes, blue canvas shoes with rubber soles, and brown-and-white shoes with crepe soles and heels; and for the beach club, brown-and-white Norwegian moccasins.

That year there was a trend toward shorter vamps in the new spring shoes. A *Men's Wear* writer observed that it was now possible to make a man's foot look smaller by proper shoe proportioning, based chiefly on the principle of the shorter tip and shorter vamp. The tip was shortened in both straight and wing designs. The broader toe, an established style that had been dominant in men's shoes for several seasons, also helped give a short effect. Bluchers also had a new look that was a compromise between the rounded "raglan" models and the square cut of earlier seasons.

Esquire in November, 1939, featured a shoe and socks wardrobe. Prominently displayed were bluchers, half brogues, monk-front shoes, Norwegian shoes, and chukka boots. Their fashion importance was enhanced by the fact that trousers were now narrow in cut and were worn short.

1940–1950

"University undergraduates dress like normal people, only more so," observed *Esquire* in September, 1940. To prove this contention the editors showed Ivy Leaguers in Shetland sports jackets, covert slacks, Harris Tweed topcoats, and such shoes as brown calfskins with red rubber soles and fringed tongues, white-and-brown or white-and-black saddle-strap slip-ons, chukka boots in the monk-front style with a strap and buckle over the instep, and brown reversed calf with a moccasin tip and a thick crepe sole. Thick soles on sports shoes were becoming commonplace both on and off campus not only in the chukka boot but also in plain-toe bluchers and laced moccasins. Many shoe advertisements in 1940 and 1941 promoted "double-soled protection" or "overweight sole." Shoes were described as "smooth and suave to see, plenty husky underneath."

In November, 1943, during World War II, when fashion was restricted by the reality of ration coupons, *Esquire* attracted its fashion-conscious readers with a spread of shoes that included this "patriotic" model: "a simulated wing tip that conserves material by dispensing with the usual extra layer of leather for the perforations." War Production Board restrictions on wearing apparel affected shoes, and composition soles were being used to conserve leather.

After the privations of the war, men were in a mood to dress up and express themselves. In the spring of 1948 *Esquire* launched the "bold look," an appearance of husky self-confidence that affected every item in the American man's wardrobe. Hefty, thick-soled bluchers, wing-tip moccasins, and brogues were perfect complements for broad-shouldered, aggressively patterned suits, widespread shirt collars, and ties with Windsor knots.

After a temporary dip in popularity the white shoe made a strong comeback with the introduction of the slip-on white moccasin in 1948. Christening the shoe the "Cat-Cay" after Cat Cay in the Bahamas, *Esquire* recognized it as embodying the bold look

for resort sportsmen and in its November issue featured it in white reversed calf with a strap over the instep and a red rubber sole that could be black-enameled: "Not only obviously good-looking but the deep soles are ridged to give you the firm and soft footing you normally get from specially built sports shoes." The Cat-Cay enjoyed a popularity that continued well into the next decade.

1950–1960

Just as the bold look had reflected the hearty optimism of 1948 and 1949, so did *Esquire*'s new trim look, called "Mr. T," reflect the cautious conservatism of the early fifties. Mr. T was neat and trim from head to toe, from the narrower brim of his hat down to the narrower, trimmed sole extension of his shoes. "One of the many good things about the T-formation is *comfort*," observed *Esquire* in October, 1950, and illustrated the point with a thong-moccasin loafer and a brushed-leather blucher. That year *Esquire* coined the name "American informal" for the new conservative mood in men's apparel, noting that it was a sign that fashion was now reflecting, among other things, the American man's insistence on comfort. Meanwhile, the traditionally comfort-conscious college man preferred white bucks with red rubber soles and plain toes, brown wing tips, Scotch-grain plain-toe shoes with leather soles, and dark cordovan moccasins with crepe rubber soles.

By 1953 the trend toward lighter, trimmer shoes became even more pronounced as the slimmer, more natural lines of men's lightweight suits demanded lighter-weight shoes styled with more restrained detailing. The tasseled slip-on was an ideal style in a wide assortment of leathers that included calf, calf combined with suede, grains, suedes, and reptile prints. Equally popular was the gored slip-on moccasin with a cool nylon mesh vamp. All these shoes had single soles of moderate to light weight.

That year even beach sandals be-

Footwear fashions for summer, 1940: (left) "gummies," reversed-calf shoes with thick crepe rubber soles; (center) cotton espadrilles; (right) Norwegian peasant moccasins. From Esquire, *February 1940.*

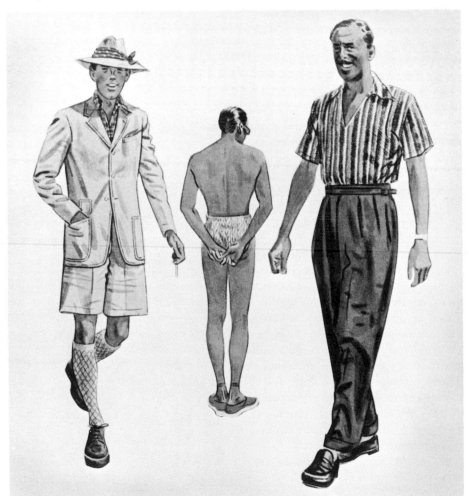

Three 1950 styles of casual shoes on comfortable lasts: (left to right) a brushed-calf and grained-leather tassel moccasin; a brushed-leather blucher; a short laced moccasin with a crepe rubber sole. From Esquire, *October 1950.*

Shoes for wear after dark in 1950: (top) opera slipper with a leather sole, for at-home wear; (left) a two-eyelet patent-leather evening shoe; (right) a patent-leather pump for wear with a tailcoat or dinner jacket. From Esquire, *October 1950.*

came lighter. Among the lightest were a pair of open-weave fiber beach shoes with rope soles, which *Esquire* photographed on a Bermuda weekend, and a slip-on beach boot with a natural-shade fabric top and a sole combining thin crepe rubber and felt.

In the mid-fifties the shorter, shape-

Trim-looking shoes were compatible with natural-shoulder clothes in 1950: (top) a straight-tip shoe with neat perforations at the seams; (bottom) a wing-tip shoe with a slightly extended lightweight sole. From Esquire, *October 1950.*

lier Continental suit silhouette came to the United States from Italy. Almost simultaneously shoes took on a leaner, longer Latin look, with the uppers cut lower than ever before, the soles sliced slimmer, and the heels often somewhat raised. In October, 1955, *Esquire* showed two samples of this basic Latin design: a brown plain-tip shoe with a black sole and a pointed tip and a black wing-tip version with a curved vamp border. United States shoe manufacturers soon were advertising American slip-ons featuring these new low lines.

With his suits becoming increasingly comfortable thanks to the new "miracle" fabrics, the American man expected and got more comfort from his shoes through soft air-cushion innersoles. "When your foot sinks into this cushion you'll think you're walking on air! Nothing is more comfortable," stated an advertisement of the Mason Shoe Manufacturing Company. "An invisible cushion of soft rubber eases every step you take!" said another. There was no question but that a foamy air cushion inside a shoe made of "softie leather" or "kitten-soft, cashmere leather" promised to deliver unprecedented foot comfort.

By mid-decade, walking shorts were being worn not only at resorts but often on city streets. The low cut of

Italian-inspired slip-ons was judged "right in key with shorts," and in May, 1956, *Esquire* showed a handsome featherweight pair with a buckskin strip around the bottom. Other models deemed correct with shorts were a Continental blucher of woven straw with a casual heel and the tropical leather moccasin.

In 1956 the open-toed shoe for men was introduced. *Esquire* devoted an entire page to a shrunken-calf exam-

The Australian bush boot, introduced at Esquire's *Fashion Forum in 1956, was made of sturdy olive-brown leather with elastic insets at the sides. From* Esquire, *November 1956.*

ple, slipping a fireman-red wooden "foot" inside it to emphasize the shoe's seminude look. Besides the open toe, styling features included two straps and a buckle closure over the instep. "Shoemen have uncorked some corking new designs," said *Esquire*'s fashion department in May, 1956, reminding its readers that that year also had seen the emergence of the Australian bush boot, an above-the-ankle tip boot that lacked laces but had elastic insets at the sides. Rugged yet pliable, the bush boot has often been credited with starting the boot boom of the next decade.

1960–1970

In 1960 slip-ons took on even more style, and in its March issue *Esquire* made certain that its readers were aware of the fact by offering them glossy close-ups of the following models: a black brushed leather with a calfskin buckled strap angled over a side opening; a flexible, cool shoe composed of strips of brown leather in a basket-weave pattern; a moccasin-tip slip-on circled with woven leather; and a center-seam slip-on of black calf decorated with a leather tab and metal spiral. That month *Gentlemen's Quarterly* showed its own collection of slip-ons, among them a square-toed model in a smooth antiqued brown leather, kiltie-fringed and buckled and strapped in leather, and a slip-on in grained brown leather with a ring and strap in front.

With white slacks growing in popularity and improved tannage methods creating white leathers that were either washable or easier to clean, white shoes were important in summer sports wardrobes. It was the white slip-on that was seen most often. Particularly stylish were these models: a slip-on that was all white except for its narrow black strap and black leather sole, a two-eyelet slip-on with a perfectly plain toe, and an all-white slip-on with stitching around the edge of the tip and a black border and sole.

The Australian bush boot of the late fifties had made men boot-conscious,

and it was not surprising when, in 1962, the fashion writer William J. Ullmann reported in *Men's Wear*: "Boots and the boot look are marching across the national fashion scene for the fall selling season. Teen men and some young adults have been wearing the high-cuts right through the summer months. Choices vary from high-heeled Flamenco-types, through rubber-soled Wellington-types, to campus-oriented chukkas. Even the suave sophisticates and the devotees of weighty brogues can find acceptable boot-types for wear with both slick sharkskins, tweedy country suits and, of course, sport jackets and slacks." The boot look even appeared in oxfords with squared and rounded toes. In 1964 Ullmann took another look at boots and decided that, having been successfully merchandised by leading retailers for more than two years, boots and shoes with the look of boots would be sold in volume with the arrival of autumn. "Style stimuli for the high-risers are seen as emanating from two sources," he wrote. "1. Trim trousers worn well above the 'break point.' 2. The look of 'more shoe,' indicating a movement away from 'dainty' styling rather than a return to heavyweight multi-soled brogans" (*Men's Wear,* Sept. 25, 1964).

The year 1963 saw the comeback of the Scottish gillie (ghillie). In its April issue *Esquire* began its editorial discussion with the question "And what's a ghillie?" There was good reason for this approach, since the shoe had been out of fashion for years. Popularized in the 1920s by the Prince of Wales, the gillie reappeared now with certain refinements.

"A ghillie is a shoe that has leather loops instead of eyelets, a motif derived from the heavy old Scottish ghillie shoes," wrote *Esquire*. "The new models are lightweight and have only one or two pairs of loops rather than six or seven. This creates a streamlined shoe; casual, simple and just that much easier to lace." Plain or stitched, the new gillies all showed a definite economy of line. Among the new models accompanying this feature

The newmarket boot of the 1960s, which had long been a traditional fashion, combined linen or canvas and tanned leather. [COURTESY OF H. KAUFFMAN & SONS SADDLERY CO., NEW YORK]

were a plain-toe shoe in calfskin, with an elastic fabric instep for close fit and easy slipping on and off; a rugged grain leather with low moccasin-line stitching around the tip and laces with tassels; a double-eyelet model in plain black leather with a moccasin-design toe; and a two-tone model in matte-finish leather and smooth calf, with a wide blucher-style throat and leather soles.

The sixties were notable fashion years for several reasons, among them the shoe industry's ability to produce the softest shoes men had ever worn. In April, 1964, *Esquire* filled a page with them: a brushed-leather tasseled moccasin with a square-cut tongue; a boldly stitched brushed-leather blucher with crepe rubber soles; a brushed-leather slip-on with a tapered panel design, perforations, and pinking; a water-repellent, soil-resistant blucher with a brushed-pigskin upper; and a wild-honey suede boot with an unusual collar line and a big brass buckle.

A decade after the introduction of man-made suiting fabrics, shoes also had a man-made material, Corfam. Introduced in 1963 by E. I. du Pont de Nemours & Co., Inc., this micro-porous, permeable leather substitute

In 1968 Cardin boots combined a square tip and a flexible leather buckle with border-panel seams extending to the top. An inside zipper facilitated a snug fit and easy entry and exit. From Esquire, *January 1968.*

was said to "breathe, wipe clean, resist weather and need no breaking in." For its February, 1964, issue *Esquire* photographed four shoes ("four portents of future footwear") whose visible parts were made of Corfam: a blucher moccasin, a plain slip-on with distinctive side lacing, a low-set moccasin style with a three-eyelet tie and a vamp set in with stitching, and a plain slip-on with hefty perforations. All had leather soles.

By 1966 the Italian designer Gucci had educated many well-dressed American men and women to prefer footwear embellished on the instep with metal trim. Clever Italian shoe designers continued to attract attention during this decade, and according to *Esquire* fashion editors, one of the most creative developments in footwear abroad was the convertible shoe found chiefly in Italy. As demonstrated in the magazine in July, 1966, it could be a slip-on of moccasin design in polished antelope that, with a change of straps, was converted from a buckled-strap to a snap closure, or a reversed-calf shoe that, with a slight

variation in the way it was tied, could be changed from a moccasin loafer to something resembling a boot.

Esquire turned its attention to the boot in January, 1968, and predicted that the "almost fanatical interest in men's boots should ensure the success of the handsome blunt-toed Cardin creation that will go perfectly with the strong, masculine fabrics of this season's suits and slacks—tweed, cavalry twill, husky flannel, saxony, and wide-ribbed corduroy." The Cardin boot was a square-toe model with a flexible leather buckle forming part of a raised panel that extended all the way to the top. An inside zipper assured a snug fit and easy entry and exit. *Esquire*'s prediction proved correct, and boots, both buckled and nonbuckled, became an important fashion.

The slip-on shoe, which, in the form of the grosgrain-bowed patent-leather pump, had been accepted as proper for formal wear long before it gained approval for daytime wear in town, was now suitable for all occasions. In March, 1968, *Esquire* showed a collection of slip-ons with samples of the most appropriate suit or slack materials. For instance, a high-front wing-tip slip-on called for a wool whipcord suit; a calf monk-style wing-tip, for a double-breasted worsted shaped suit; a slip-on featuring a monk strap high over the instep, for a Dacron-and-worsted double-breasted suit; an instep-strap slip-on with horizontal tucks, for a single-breasted worsted suit; a slip-on with a Gucci-like metal instep trim, for wool tweed slacks; a hand-sewn Weejuns grained-leather monk-style slip-on, for Dacron-and-worsted Bermuda shorts; a gold suede low-cut slip-on with an instep strap through a tunnel loop, for Dacron-and-worsted slacks; and a monk-style slip-on with a velvet-covered buckle, for a tropical worsted dinner jacket.

In 1969 slip-ons were given a "wet look" finish as well as color. Most models had a square or blunt toe and an instep trimmed with a leather or metal strap or a Pilgrim-like buckle. Glistening greens, reds, blues, and

blacks predominated. In suede and smooth leathers, colors ranged from canary yellow through violet, rose, and russet, but these flamboyant colors were only moderately popular.

With the arrival of the Peacock Revolution in the United States, footwear was embellished with buckles, straps, chains, and studs. In June, 1969, *Gentlemen's Quarterly* photographed some of the new shoes and boots on everything from feet to silk Persian rugs and Barcelona chairs. Among the styles shown were a slip-on in lustrous antiqued brown-black patent leather with brass studs on the strap of its bellows-tongued moccasin front; a wet look shoe in antiqued gray-tan patent leather, double-strapped and buckled at the instep; a shoe in burnished tan leather with three buckled perforated straps and a quarter of wing design; an ultra-blunt-toed slip-on in honey-colored grained leather with a brass-studded strap; a moccasin-front slip-on in shiny brown leather with a studded leather buckle inset with brass; a burnished brown smooth-leather slip-on with narrow buckled straps criss-crossed on the front; a side-buckled simulated tortoiseshell slip-on with a squared-off heel; a two-tone shoe in gold-and-brown leather featuring a blunt toe, perforation, and a bold buckle and strap; and a gold-green antiqued patent-leather slip-on with an impressive metal buckle.

The mod influence of the Peacock

The Regency look in footwear of 1969 was typified by the squarish-tip boot with a strap, at left, and the moccasin-design slip-on with a strap over the instep, at right.

Revolution startled many traditionally dressed Americans, and *Gentlemen's Quarterly*'s 1969 discussion, titled "'Good Taste'—A Concept in Flux," was well timed. The following is an excerpt from that article:

"Taste is, of course, a very personal thing. One man's idea of 'good taste' is another man's concept of poisonous excess. Every man, no matter how wild or gregarious his clothes, will tell you, 'Sure, I like to wear something different, but always in good taste.'

"Nevertheless, there was, until recent years, some consensus among the educated about how a *gentleman* should dress. It was always part Brooks Brothers, part Savile Row. The emphasis was on understatement. A man's face, not his clothes, was what friends or passersby should be aware of. This was a dictum forged by our New England Puritanical heritage—and gentlemanly conduct in this country was, let us face it, set by Boston Brahmins.

"But the young are changing all that. The leaders among the young, the spokesmen—the tastemakers are likely to hurl four-letter words into the face of the establishment and its ideas of propriety. What Dad wore at Yale is a big bore. Being 'cool' doesn't mean being sedate; it means 'doing your own thing' and not worrying about what father or professor or boss thinks.

"When young men, often the brightest young men, often the in-group leaders, decide on a new course, tastes change. A new generation has overturned the rules, and taste is always but a reflection of what the educated, best men in the community are doing. In the eighteenth century it may have been the sons of the landed gentry. In the latter 1960's it is the rebellious offspring of the middle class. Like it or not, bewail the fact or suffer it in contemptuous agony, standards do alter.

"And how do you react to those honey-colored shoes young men have been wearing with any suit they feel like—whether brown or blue or gray or black? All wrong? Or terribly sophisticated? Before you answer, don't forget that Fred Astaire has always worn brown suede shoes with a blue suit, a custom he picked up in England.

"Speaking of footwear, remember only a few years ago when slip-ons seemed too casual to wear with a suit? It sounds ridiculous today, when laced shoes are practically vestigial. Young men wear boots to the office now, and when you consider the total effect, it works" (September, 1969, p. 171).

Insofar as boots were concerned, *Gentlemen's Quarterly* editors asked in October, 1969: "Will they continue to enjoy their high popularity?" They answered: "You can bet your buckled boots they will!" The boots they showed were persuasive arguments for their contention: a side-zipped leather boot with a leather buckle strapped to the front; a side-pocketed boot in glove leather with an ornate buckle and a perforated strap; a buckle-strapped boot in navy suede, 11 inches high, with a concealed side zipper; an antiqued leather boot, double ankle-strapped and buckled; a Pilgrim-buckled burnished brown-olive leather boot; and a plain-front demiboot in grained brown leather, side-buckled and strapped. That such high-fashion boots as these were being worn in many business offices by the late sixties illustrates the freewheeling atmosphere of what, in fashion terms, was the most explosive period of the century.

It was expected, therefore, that after several seasons of frenetic change, men's fashions at the start of the next decade would pass through a cooling-off period. However, this did not mean a colorless look. Men's apparel continued to be colorful and imaginative, but fashion appeared to have outgrown its growing pains and showed a more purposeful sense of direction, a trend that *Footwear News* claimed was due to the influence of the footwear industry:

"While the apparel fashion makers were still doing psychedelic shirts and slacks, jump suits in freaked-out designs and cartoon sweaters and coats, the footwear industry was fast at work taking the radicalism out of fashion,"

Patent-leather shoes, traditional for formal evening wear, livened the casual-wear scene in 1969: (top, left to right) a brown patent-leather square-toe slip-on with a monk strap and a darker-brown blunt-toe loafer with an instep strap; (bottom, left to right) a blue-green patent-leather slip-on with a metal mesh band, a black patent-leather evening pump with a high-front blunt toe, and a pump of dull-finish patent leather with a colonial-style buckle. From Esquire, June 1969.

wrote Don Fullington. He called this trend "down-to-earth"; acknowledging that there seemed to be confusion in the industry about its meaning, he proceeded to define it as follows:

"It is a concept rather than a single look. The concept is simply to take the freak out of fashion without losing zest and freshness. It is not limited to one type of footwear, but rather pertains to everything from high-style boots and shoes to jeans footwear. Likewise, leathers are not just limited to oily harness types, but include kids, suedes and calves as well.

"What has been removed are the garish colors, the ugly-extreme patterns and the wild looks. As a result, fashion comes down-to-earth. It goes back to the old belief that good taste must prevail.

"Within the good taste boundaries, there is plenty of room to create fresh new looks and have fun with fashion. Already footwear manufacturers are proving this with their new designs.

(top row, left to right) Crepe-soled red canvas sports shoe, worn with cabana-brown beach slacks and yellow 6 by 3 rib lightweight wool hose; natural-color ribbed cotton and argyle anklets; Norwegian slipper, worn with cabana-green beach slacks; brogue shoe, worn with navy silk hose and a sharkskin suit (alternate hose: French-type garnet lisle and gray chevron stripes); blucher town shoe, worn with ribbed silk hose and a blue-gray worsted suit (alternate hose: blue silk-and-wool and blue 2 by 3 rib lisle). (second row, left to right) Rubber beach sandal, worn with a terry cloth robe; yellow mesh anklet and green mesh anklet with a white top and foot; brown-and-white resort shoe, worn with ribbed white lisle hose in horizontal stripes and a hemp-color lightweight wash suit; Norwegian shoe, worn with wide-rib hose and a tweed suit (alternate hose: blue wool with a plaid motif and antique argyle wool); wing-tip brogue, worn with cable-pattern hose and a cheviot suit (alternate hose: camel-color wool and Scotch-plaid wool). (third row, left to right) Town shoe, worn with fancy ribbed lisle hose and a worsted suit (alternate hose: French-type lisle and clocked garnet silk); patent-leather oxford, worn with silk dress hose and a midnight-blue tailcoat (alternate hose: black silk and silk with a clock); yellow pile slipper, worn with a heavy wool ski sock and gabardine downhill ski trousers (alternate hose: two colorful wools); black ski boot, worn with natural-color wool hose and an anklet with a blue-and-white border. (bottom row, left to right) Monk-front shoe, worn with 6 by 3 rib wool hose and a glenurquhart suit (alternate hose: herringbone wool and a diagonal pattern); Norwegian shoes, worn with argyle wool hose and a Shetland tweed suit (alternate hose: Scotch plaid and herringbone-rib wool); a sheepskin-lined slide-fastener après-ski boot, worn with red hand-knitted ski hose and blue gabardine ski trousers; peasant-type shoe, worn heavy wool hose and velvet cord breeks (alternate hose: a wool peasant pattern and a wool diamond pattern). From Esquire, November 1939.

A footwear wardrobe of 1935: (clockwise from upper left) beaver velour treated sheepskin slippers, on blanket; Russia calf laced riding shoes; oil-grain hiking and shooting shoes; calf polo or hacking boots; calf field boots; black hunting boots with mahogany-color tops; oil-grain waterproof moccasins; calfskin brogues; long-grain blucher shoes with stitched straight-tip seams; and brown reversed-calf semibrogues with square custom toes. From Esquire, November 1935.

Shoe fashions of 1963: (top to bottom) a fleece-lined après-ski boot with a small elasticized inset in front, a pull tab in back, and a soft composition sole; a close-trimmed moccasin slip-on; a two-eyelet high-rise boot in a moccasin design; a brown thong-fastened boot with a crepe rubber sole; a four-eyelet shoe with a perforated medallion design and no seams on top; a Scotch-grain long-wing-tip blucher. From Esquire, October 1963.

(from upper left) Laced antique-finish kidskin with a blunt cap toe, from Italy; a jodhpur-type antiqued side-gored boot with a wraparound buckle strap, from Spain; an Italian shoe with a shield cap toe, bold perforations, and a brass buckle; an Italian-made laced glove-tanned kidskin with a toe cap; a brass-buckled leather-and-Belgian-linen shoe; a patent slip-on made in Portugal; a laced glove-tanned goatskin shoe with a cap toe, from Italy; a blunt-toed white shoe with a perforated brown leather overlay and a brass buckle; and an antiqued-brown slip-on with a brass buckle and a black cap toe and strap.

Footwear

Cruise and Southern Resort

Fall-Winter

Ski and Northern Resort

Fall-Winter

**New footwear—
the styles,
the shades,
the skins**

Fancy footwear with a higher heel: (left to right) a dressy suede shoe with a harness strap and ring and a squarish toe; a leather boot with double seaming, a side zipper, and pleated self-trim on the instep; a Western-style slip-on of canvas and suede; a crinkled patent-leather model with an overlay front and a side zipper; a leather boot with multicolor panels and a knob toe; a leather boot with mock speed lacing, a side zipper, and a squarish toe; a suede platform boot with self-lacing.

And the youth of the country (he appears to be the best testing-ground for most new fashions today) is accepting them" (Apr. 1, 1971, p. 23).

Sturdy sandals with metallic ornamentation were in keeping with the trends of 1971. From Gentlemen's Quarterly, *May 1971.*

Maintaining that rugged, down-to-earth looks were dominating men's leather and man-made shoes, *Footwear News* showed what it considered the brightest examples: a bold monk strap with a double-layer buckle in a goat-grain Porvair (a poromeric material) that was deeply antiqued to emphasize the grain; an over-the-ankle side-gored boot in burnt-chestnut calf; an ankle boot in a deep-print calf with a turned-up toe, tied with four eyelets; an ankle-high jeans shoe in an oily natural leather with a bumper toe and a strap across the vamp; and a calf-high glazed-kidskin speed-lace boot in saddle tan and navy.

The fashion pages of *Esquire* and *Gentlemen's Quarterly* in the early seventies offered further proof that footwear could be eye-catching without being freakish. Flared trousers by that time were the rule rather than the oddity, and to complement them a shorter tapered last with a blunt or squared toe had evolved. Fashion reached into the past and, among other things, revived the leather-and-fabric combination shoe that had been popular in the

thirties and now featured the blunt toe that, as *Men's Wear* observed, "literally booted the domestic shoe market into a lively business that's playing to the same young customers who made jeans, belts, vests and funky knits today's status items" (Feb. 26, 1971, p. 82).

Boots, demiboots, and shoes were designed in great style and good taste with two tones, blunt toes, and often artfully positioned straps and buckles. *Gentlemen's Quarterly* welcomed the "new look in casual footwear" and for its April, 1970, issue photographed a soft demiboot in burnished leather with a buckled strap set high over hidden side gores, a multistrap slip-on in brown leather with a beveled toe, a blunt-toed golden-brown leather slip-on with a lighter shade forming a modified spat effect, and a burnished slip-on in two-tone leather featuring a wing tip, a blunt toe, and a buckled strap. To prove that, despite the overwhelming popularity of the slip-on, the laced shoe was a perennial, the magazine included a brown blunted square-toed shoe with laces.

The elegance of other eras influenced the styling of shoes in the seventies. In the top row are (left to right) a four-eyelet laced shoe in smooth and suede leather, a five-eyelet toe-cap shoe with contrasting stitching, and a high-rise shoe with side gores. In the next row are a three-eyelet ankle shoe with a cap and a squared heel, an updated strap-and-buckle shoe with a high front, and a six-eyelet bubble-toe shoe of suede and leather. In the third row are a five-eyelet mock-laced slip-on in blue and white, a three-eyelet scalloped tie shoe with satin laces, and a blue-and-white saddle-strap shoe with a crepe sole. In the bottom row are a one-eyelet goat-leather ankle shoe and a shoe of suede and smooth leather in the strap-and-buckle style with an inside zipper. From Esquire, *January 1972.*

Esquire offered further proof that the laced shoe was far from gone by photographing a six-eyelet shoe, a combination of golden-tan grained patent leather with soft suede; a six-eyelet cobbler kid in brown and golden tan with a 1½-inch heel; a stained tan calfskin five-eyelet shoe with a slightly perforated cap; a six-eyelet model in palomino calf whose single inverted seam created a curved cap toe; a brown-and-tan stained-calf three-eyelet shoe with perforated trim, a squarish toe, and leather lacing; a black-and-tan cap-toe shoe with brass ring eyelets; a three-eyelet cap-toe in red, white, and blue calf; an updated laced Italian spectator brogue in brown-and-black textured leather; a sturdy laced kidskin with a boxy cap toe; a seven-eyelet shoe of glove-tanned goatskin with a cap toe; a three-eyelet model in antique-finish kidskin with a blunt cap toe; and a four-eyelet brown patent-leather wing-tip shoe with white grain-calf trim.

Far from being extinct, the laced shoe was a dominant fashion in the early seventies. One fashion writer predicted: "If it's not at least a five or six eyelet tie, it just won't do . . . and if laces match the uppers, it's an over-30 shoe."

In 1970 and 1971 there was a boom in boot sales. There seemed to be a boot style for every type of man and, in a few instances, a style that appealed to his entire family. A lug-soled demiboot was a case in point, and Abercrombie and Fitch advertised their five-eyelet denim version in the *New York Times* in 1971 as a "lightweight, tough little boot for the whole family . . . a gem for hiking, walking, working and playing. The thick rubber heel/sole is deeply treaded and really flexible. Tops of mini-checkered denim are bulk free and pliable; removable inside pad helps keep it cool. A terrific 'work horse' of a shoe for the money!"

The National Association of Men's Sportswear Buyers provided an analysis by customer type of what was selling in footwear in 1970 and 1971 as well as what was expected to sell in the near future:

The high fashion man. Customer of the avant-garde shop or boutique. Over-the-calf boots, often lace-ups, designed to be worn with knickers or with pants tucked in. This customer insists on the shaped "Cuban" heel, and is starting to look for the same heel in dress shoes. This heel is the footwear complement to flare pants bottoms that slope down toward the heel.

In shoes, the avant-garde man is going for bold two tone ideas, lace-ups with colorful laces, and is expected to be the customer for bubble or bump toes and high walls, which are now coming into the market. He also should be the prize customer for the closed front sandal, a projected new style for summer '71.

The youth customer. The teen in jeans is complementing his work clothes and military surplus outfit with work boots. Since many of them are looking for the real thing, much of this business is being lost to the Army-Navy store. However, men's stores and shoe stores are selling some work boot styles manufactured by their regular suppliers. The teen man is also into fun shoes in a big way. These include rubber soled shoes, round-toed models, stitchouts, brushed suedes, cartoon color combinations, sneaker styled saddle shoes, etc., mostly in the $6 to $18 retail range. The big new trend for this customer in 1971 is expected to be lined shoes for the sockless look.

The dressed up mature man. Formerly the

basic shoe customer, is now buying demi-boots (six to nine inches), conservative two-tones (brown and dark brown, black and burgundy, etc.), and is moving into buckle styles. He is currently firmly entrenched in the squared off broad toe. Among the casual styles now being shown, (including cruise lines, at about $20) he prefers soft leather slip-ons in colors that match his sportswear, such as white, blue and beige. Also, crepe sole suedes in white, blue, red and beige. Beige is expected to be important in two-tone dress shoes for spring.

Knowledgeable shoe people are also predicting a movement to updated classics . . . two-tone wing-tip spectator shoes in lace-up models with high wall styling. This would be aimed at suit-oriented high fashion customers.

All the above trends, as noted, are governed by customer types. The key type omitted is the basic brogues man, who is part of a diminishing market that belongs to the last remaining basic shoe specialists and the popular priced shoe chains. (However, even this man may be a good "second shoe" customer for the men's store . . . casual shoes for weekend, vacation, etc. The men's store has a valuable clue to his second shoe identity in the kind of sportswear he buys.) (*Footwear*, 1971, p. 5)

Suede became an all-season item, moving from winter into summer and back into fall lines. Shoe men alert to the popularity of youth's frontier-inspired fringed suede jackets translated this penchant into Western and Indian fringed boots. Two-tone suedes and suede-and-leather combinations were being seen in everything from knee-high knicker boots to dress monk-strap slip-ons.

Sales of sandals were growing in the early seventies because of their suitability for the new leisure suits and shirt and slacks outfits. *Esquire* photographed this casual look in a belted navy waistcoat suit of triple-knit polyester worn with a puckered cotton shirt and brass-ringed harness-leather sandals. In 1971 the National Shoe Retailers Association noted a trend toward larger, shaped sandal soles, with square-toed soles becoming important. There was also a trend toward patterns that covered more of the foot and gave the sandal a better fit and greater holding power. The spaghetti-strap design (a network of cross straps) was cited as an example.

On March 17, 1971, E. I. du Pont de Nemours & Co., Inc., which had introduced Corfam in 1963 with a multimillion-dollar sales promotion campaign, announced its decision to stop producing the poromeric shoe material. The *New York Times* was the first to carry the story that the manufacture and sale of Corfam would be discontinued within twelve months. At the time of this announcement, a Du Pont spokesman estimated that between 75 million and 100 million pairs of shoes with Corfam uppers were "currently walking the streets." A Du Pont press release stated: "Corfam has been widely recognized as an excellent upper material for footwear in which ease of care, shape retention, durability and water repellency are essential features. However, the product's relatively high cost compared with that of the inexpensive 'non-breathable man-mades' has been a major barrier to volume sales in the price-sensitive footwear market."

The following day the *Daily News Record* used the headline "Du Pont's Decision on Corfam Cheers Rival Material Makers" and stated that B. F. Goodrich Company had no plans to drop its poromeric material, Aztran, although it had been learned that General Tire had decided against pilot production of a poromeric shoe upper because of manufacturing problems and costs. The *Daily News Record* observed: "The death of Corfam will undoubtedly leave some legacies with the shoe industry, one of which would be the word *poromeric*—now part of the industry jargon."

The spring-summer, 1971, men's footwear forecast of the National Shoe Retailers Association offered some insight into the cautious buying habits of the period and their effect on the footwear industry:

As we progress from Fall through Winter and into Spring/Summer 1971, money will remain tight and consumers will retain uptight spending habits until some measure of confidence is restored within the U.S. economy.

This means that the intelligent and discerning buyer will apply tight editing and control of inventory to make certain

he is covered, but not over-extended to meet wardrobe needs of all customer types and age groups for business, dress-up leisure, and casual leisure. ("Life Style" is becoming a much-used expression, meaning that marketing executives must consider the living habits of consumers and, in particular, their private or leisure lives where they are not bound by codes of conformity apparent in business dress.)

It would seem, therefore, that most retailers will find it essential to think in terms of these basic footwear groups:

Conservative and classic footwear. For the man who replaces depleted wardrobes with the same or very similar styling . . . even coloring.

Fashion footwear. Tested and accepted styling, contemporary color and shape . . . but all in good taste. This is for the man who wants to be in mid-stream, not too conservative or far out.

Forward fashion. For those who want the latest, most daring, and have no wish to melt into the crowd or to be subtle.

Item footwear. Most often falling into the leisure-casual category, but also affecting street dress. One of a kind, played in right sizes and colors, will most usually suffice . . . may be a fringe boot, clog, or "work shoe," etc.

The association went on to remind the retailer: "To merchandise any product in the 70's, retailers will find themselves involved in more trends than just lasts, leathers and hardware. It's a market time of 'total environment' sale techniques . . . geared to social and economic trends, as well.

"In order to describe the combination of apparel and footwear, it is necessary to discuss FASHION & ACCESSORIES, remembering that shoes, like it or not, *are* only accessories: man does not start with his feet and work upward in his dressing habits.

"Fortunately.

"In Spring/Summer 1971, men's 'accessories' will provide the punch, the individualism in street and business dress.

"Among men's business dress suits, the various styles in the shaped silhouettes (waist definition without repression, shaped and wider lapels) have reached satisfying perfection and good volume acceptance. Men now feel and look more securely distinctive and confidently comfortable in the new garments. If the look is bold by comparison with the era of its natural-shoulder Ivy predecessor—it is elegant and wearable boldness, in good taste.

"As styling has become more stabilized in suits, the accessory field provides the greatest area of freedom to express one's individuality. Even a casual observer can immediately recognize that accessories—shirts . . . ties . . . and shoes—are the impact areas in dressing for town and business. But, each suit requires the right assortment of shirts for completeness. Shirts also demand that tie be selected with shirt in mind, rather than picked up casually with hope of final coordination.

"Footwear coordination takes the same thoughtful consideration. Not every suit—or look—will take the same footwear styling direction. The variety of suit models summons up a new balance of toning from light-to-medium-to-dark in each color family, with more emphasis on patterning and weaves (stripes, checks, herringbones, random herringbones, natural linen, and homespun weaves). Thus, no *one* shoe look (or color) can fill all needs for business-street-dress footwear.

"Acceptance of present direction in footwear convinces us that men now feel confident and secure in updated, fashionable shoes. The variety . . . the balance . . . the bold but elegant trend in business dressing would indicate fashion in footwear will demand greater care in handling, detailing, and presentation."

Of particular significance in the seventies was the entry of "name" designers into the footwear field. Having successfully established themselves in the men's apparel field, designers like Bill Blass presented collections of boots and shoes specifically designed to complement their high-style clothes. By the seventies footwear had become as appealing to the eye and as subject to fashion change as every other item in a man's wardrobe. The day was gone when a black or brown oxford well polished and freshly soled and heeled was practically all that was expected of a well-shod man. A look at the shoe wardrobe of a fashionable man would reveal a range of styles so varied that it could not have been

collected a decade earlier: a square-toe slip-on, a slip-on with Gucci-type hardware, demiboots, boots, a brogue style for foul-weather wear, white patent-leather sports shoes, a brushed-leather oxford with a strap and buckle, and patent-leather evening pumps and boots. If this man happened to be a golfer, he would have a saddle-strap wing-tip shoe; a skier, specially styled ski boots; or a horseman, jodhpur boots and high riding boots. Moreover, he would be continually adding to his collection, for as *Esquire* concluded long ago, "Of all items in the male wardrobe, shoes unquestionably express a man's vanity at its most indulgent."

The peacock was easily the most elegantly shod man in history, and sometimes he appeared to be the tallest, as heels grew increasingly higher in the early seventies until many a blunt-toed shoe boasted a heel measuring 2, 2½, or even 3 inches.

Evening Shoes

In reviewing the evening footwear of this century, one cannot fail to be impressed by the fashion durability of patent leather. In a sense it is a legacy passed down to us by the turn-of-the-century fashion plate, who favored patent leather in such styles as the high shoe with an upper of plain black cloth, the low plain-toe evening shoe, and the pump. All three of these styles were popular, and all were likely to have sharply pointed toes. They remained dominant nationally through the 1920s, although a fashion reporter covering the opening night of the Metropolitan Opera Company for *Men's Wear* (Dec. 1, 1920) noted that the best-turned-out gentlemen wore low laced evening shoes of patent leather.

Patent leather still dominated evening footwear in 1924. The tuxedo, or dinner jacket, was gaining wider acceptance, and many well-dressed men that year wore double-breasted black shawl-collar dinner jackets, dress trousers with one broad satin stripe on each leg, and patent-leather pumps

with long vamps and square toes. Two years later an analysis of evening clothes worn by 200 of the best-dressed men in Palm Beach revealed that 89 percent of them favored the low plain-front patent-leather evening shoe, the same style that the well-shod opera-goers had preferred in December, 1920.

By 1928 the high shoe was outmoded for day and evening, but patent leather was as popular as ever. *Men's Wear* that year observed that the two most fashionable evening shoes were the plain-front patent-leather laced shoe with a fairly pointed toe and the long-vamp patent-leather pump. In the early 1930s, however, patent leather was challenged temporarily by highly polished black Russia calf. A preference for black Russia evening shoes or pumps was considered "one of the significant footwear developments in fashionable circles. These shoes, when properly groomed, have such a luster that they are hardly distinguishable from patent leather, and, of course, are comfortable and do not crack" (*Men's Wear,* Sept. 7, 1932).

The slip-on moccasin was introduced in the thirties. Soon thereafter the patent-leather evening slip-on appeared, paving the way for other adaptations of sports shoe styles to evening footwear. One of the best-known and most successful of these adaptations was the patent-leather monk-front shoe. Introduced in 1937, it was a plain-toe model with a strap and buckle that hitherto had been seen mainly at sporting events. Fashionable Englishmen vacationing in the West Indies were the first to wear the patent-leather monk-front shoe with formal evening dress, often with the midnight-blue dinner jacket popularized by the Prince of Wales. Yet this decade was characterized by increasing formality in dress clothes, and despite such innovations as the monk-front shoe, traditional patent-leather pumps and oxfords were worn most often with both the tailcoat and the dinner jacket. Nevertheless, even the most tradition-bound man could be a secret maverick: black patent-leather evening pumps were available with a red lining.

All through the forties patent leather continued to be synonymous with evening footwear in all seasons. In January, 1940, for instance, *Esquire* showed what it called "a formal outfit with flair, consisting of white tropical weight dress trousers with midnight blue double-breasted dinner jacket of the same lightweight fabric. The gilt buttons, nautical but nice, are a pleasant surprise." Patent-leather pumps were included among the "easy-going accessories."

In 1948 *Esquire* introduced the "bold look," which for evening wear meant a more virile edition of the butterfly bow, a widespread-collared dress shirt, a satin-lapeled dinner jacket, and black suede pumps. Later, however, the magazine's fashion staff once again advocated the low-cut patent-leather shoe and the long-vamp patent-leather pump as the correct footwear for either formal or semiformal evening wear.

The 1950s saw the rise of the more shapely dinner jacket and the plain-toe slip-on shoe, which was popular both in patent leather and in highly polished calfskin. Before the decade was over, two- and three-eyelet patent-leather bluchers had been admitted to the ranks of correct evening footwear.

In the sixties, with the Peacock Revolution, the slip-on boot with elastic insets at the sides and the slip-on shoe with a squared-off toe and a metal buckle or chain ornamenting the instep were innovations in evening shoes, in an era noted for such innovations as the six-button velvet Edwardian dinner jacket, the fancy-bosom dress shirt, and the outsize black velvet bow tie.

All popular evening footwear styles, from the laced bal-front shoe with a plain toe to the boot, were available in poromeric material, but the most revolutionary innovation was the introduction of color in formal shoes as a by-product of the colored dinner jackets *Esquire* had previewed as early as February, 1956, under the headline "Peacock Tones Have Arrived." Din-

ner jackets in gold, cognac, claret, and citron stimulated the creation of patent-leather evening shoes in shades of blue, brown, and burgundy.

Meanwhile, shoes for the formal or semiformal evening wedding remained traditional even in the "do your own thing" seventies. Patent-leather low evening shoes or patent-leather pumps were still recommended, and only the informal day or evening wedding gave the groom more leeway, with *Esquire* merely advocating black shoes.

Slippers

The slippers of the early 1900s were plush and ornate, much like contemporary clothes and home furnishings. The Sears, Roebuck and Company 1900 catalog, for instance, showed embroidered slippers in silk plush chenille or velvet as well as a high-style high slip-on softly constructed of Dongola kid with elastic insets at the side, an adaptation of the gaiter of the 1880s and an early forerunner of the dressy slip-on the fashionable man of the 1950s wore to his office. Less opulent and considerably less expensive but enormously popular was the carpet slipper with a leather sole and heel and an upper of carpeting material.

The classic opera slipper of the first decade, in which front and back met over the shank at the level of the innersole, retained enormous popularity for years. In 1925 a pair of mahogany leather opera slippers were judged "perfection in slippers," not only for their good looks but for the fact that they had been designed to slip on easily and stay on. The opera slipper in tan or red kid or patent leather was a best seller in 1928, and *Esquire* showed a pair of red morocco opera slippers with a paisley dressing gown in 1938. A more abbreviated style, the leather mule, was recommended by *Esquire*'s fashion department in June, 1939, as an ideal Father's Day gift.

A decade later, on November 25, 1949, *Men's Wear* observed: "No longer are slippers drab and uninteresting as they were during and immediately following the war years. Top quality

has returned and with it are the bright and colorful leathers that won't be put to shame by the Christmas tree." After all, the article continued, "Slippers and holiday gift giving are almost synonymous." Several models were shown to illustrate the fact that comfort, style, and novelty were combined in slippers: an opera slipper, a moccasin, and a Robin Hood style (a high-front shoe with elastic at the sides). At the bottom of the page was this postscript: "The era of the carpet slipper has passed."

In 1952 *Men's Wear* noted: "The advent of the TV or parlor pajama indicates that if men are going to wear their boudoir gear about the house they will want style as well as comfort in their slippers." Among the best slippers that year were the striped-vamp opera ("a perennial favorite"), the hard-soled opera in light palomino leather, the soft-soled opera in supple calf, and the moccasin with a soft sole.

By 1969 the shopper had a very wide choice of slippers. Popular models were slip-ons in wide-wale corduroy and tapestry and in crochet knit with a generous turnback cuff. Then came the seventies, and slipper styles came full circle, with the ornate look of the early 1900s dominant once again. In August, 1970, *Esquire* devoted a full page to "slippers for at-home evenings or après-anything" and said: "Now, with more attention being paid at-home attire, a number of slipper styles are being produced." Among the styles photographed were a black velvet leather-soled shoe, piped in leather, with a gold silk–embroidered crest; a black satin slipper with black patent piping and a narrow instep strap; a multicolor needlepoint slipper on a black ground, a hard-soled carpet slipper for the seventies; a black-on-brown leopard-print furry calf with a soft sole; a natural python over-the-top design combined with black glove leather and a soft sole; and a dapple-print calf in beige, tan, and brown, combined with brown glove leather and a suede sole.

In sum, when the peacock was in a mood to relax, he dressed up. Al-

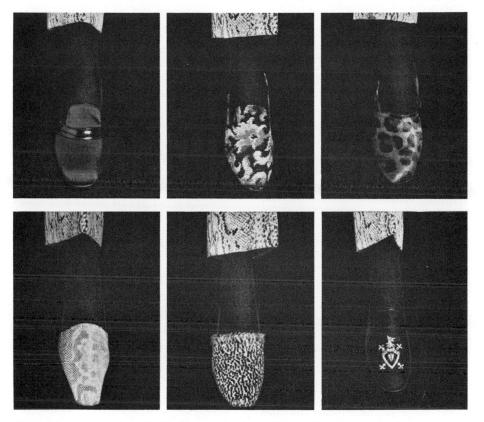

Slippers became more decorative in the seventies: (top, left to right) a black satin slipper with patent-leather trim, a multicolor needlepoint on a black background, and a black-on-brown leopard-print furry calf slipper with a soft sole; (bottom, left to right) a natural python over-the-top design combined with black glove leather, a beige, tan, and brown dapple-print calf combined with black glove leather and a suede sole, and a black velvet slipper with a gold silk-embroidered crest and a leather sole. Photographed by Fred Smith. From Esquire, *August 1970.*

though he would not dream of wearing the stuffed, heavily padded suit of the turn of the century, he had the fashion sense to adopt one of the most comfortable and attractive legacies of that dressy era, the slipper that in those days had often been the handiwork of an artisan.

Tennis Shoes

With riding one of the most tradition-bound sports, tennis for a long time would not tolerate fashion changes of any kind. The all-white costume was the only proper costume, but oddly enough this rule did not include the player's footwear. So the contestants in the first Davis Cup competition in 1900 might wear white duck oxfords with rubber soles or high shoes in black cotton sateen, provided everything else they wore was white.

When, in 1910, A. G. Spalding & Bros. introduced new rubber-soled shoes with "little suction cups placed about ¼-inch apart on the bottoms of the soles," they were available in kangaroo and tan or smoked horse leather as well as in the traditional white canvas. For tennis in inclement weather, the stylish player of the period wore black oxfords with leather uppers and spiked leather soles.

By the 1920s the high tennis shoe was clearly dominant. A 1920–1921 catalog of the United States Rubber Company showing a selection of rubber-soled fabric shoes featured a twelve-eyelet model, in which six eyelets were laced and six fastened with hooks. It also showed what was probably the most popular tennis oxford of the day: a five-eyelet brown canvas shoe with gray or red rubber soles for those who disliked black. Although the high tennis shoe remained popular throughout the twenties, a trend toward the oxford was noted among the champions. The most favored oxford was a five-eyelet model with an upper of heavy bleached white duck and a thick crepe outsole.

By the mid-thirties the leather tennis oxford was outmoded, and black and brown tennis shoes had almost disappeared. In August, 1934, *Esquire,* noting that "many tournament officials still stick to the traditional rule against any deviations from plain white in the attire of contestants," showed a young player wearing a white polo shirt, white flannel trousers, and plain white sneakers. (However, the fashion editor thought that the new Cuban jai alai shoe, a blucher with a leather upper and a rubber sole, was smarter-looking.) In August, 1935, *Esquire* showed the new white duck tennis shorts and "the new blue canvas sneakers that have been taken up by many well known professionals."

In 1939 the tennis champion Fred Perry designed a tennis shoe called the Fred Perry Pro, which had a durable duck upper, a crepe rubber outsole, white eyelets, white tubular laces, and an arch-support insole with an arch and heel sponge cushion. It was available in white, blue, and green.

The washable blue or white crepe-soled oxford was the leading style in the early 1940s. In fact, blue was fast becoming a second color on the tennis court, serving as a border stripe on a white short-sleeved shirt or as a side stripe on white gabardine or duck shorts. Complementing such a tennis outfit was a blue canvas oxford with a white crepe sole and white eyelets.

In the 1950s the American man became extremely conscious of comfort in his summer wardrobe, and tennis shoe manufacturers advertised "side ventilating eyelets" and "full breathing uppers" made of a porous fabric.

The Wimbledon lace-to-toe tennis shoe was introduced in 1959–1960. It featured not only a snugly fitting arch, a cushioned insole, and a crepe rubber outsole but a protective rubber toe cap as well.

By 1963 the oxford favored by most of the leading players was a washable lace-to-toe style with a circular vamp, a molded sole, and such features as a shockproof arch cushion, an extra heel cushion, a fully cushioned insole, a scientific foot last, a reinforced toe cap, and ventilating eyelets.

Esquire, observing in August, 1965, that "any change from the traditional is met with pooh-poohs from the crusty bastions of the game," offered a "few modest proposals," which, however, did not extend to footwear. The five models photographed were all wearing spotlessly white tennis sneakers. Again, in July, 1968, *Esquire* decided that "in time quickly to come, colored clothing will become commonplace on the courts." To illustrate this point, a pair of well-dressed players were posed in outfits of blue and yellow respectively, but their tennis sneakers were white.

The Tennis Ace, introduced as a completely new tennis shoe in 1969, was described as an extremely lightweight shoe made of an open mesh fabric that was said to be much cooler than army duck yet twice as strong. It had a deeply cut zigzag outsole for sure traction.

By this time tennis sneakers—in fact, rubber-soled canvas footwear in general—were being worn by younger men as knockabout shoes in suburb and city. Although they were most often all white, in a few years youth's infatuation with the fashion possibilities of the American flag would see canvas knockabouts in red, white, and blue.

The 1970s brought some truly avant-garde tennis clothes: short-sleeved, short-legged zip-front jump suits of cotton mesh knit, two-piece nylon warm-up suits in a rainbow range of colors, and thigh-length jackets of wide-wale corduroy lined with a navy, white, and red floral print.

Most often worn with these tradition-breaking costumes was the all-white tennis shoe. Color and innovative designs, first seen decades earlier in tennis footwear, had now spread to the rest of the player's apparel, and, for the moment at least, his shoes were the most traditional part of his outfit. Yet, by 1971 many teen-age players were showing a penchant for the high tennis shoe, this time with bright racing stripes. Influenced by the fashion boldness of the younger player and the fashion leadership of the tournament player, the tennis shoe, once the player's only badge of individuality, was certain to be seen in exciting new styles in the last quarter of the century.

Golf Shoes

Golf clothes in the first decade of this century had a decidedly Scottish character. Along with knickers and a tweed suit jacket, the fashionable golfer wore sturdy, thick-soled shoes. A plain brown blucher style, sometimes with a spiked sole to give the wearer a more solid stance, was the most popular model.

In the latter half of the second decade men's fashions became more youthful and comfortable, and golf clothes in general followed suit. Golf shoes were the exception, however, and it was not until the 1920s, with the rise to prominence of famous golfers, that golf shoes began to look like golf shoes instead of modified street shoes. Two of the most popular of the new golf styles were the blucher with a nonskid steel-studded leather sole and heel and the oxford of tan and smoked elk with a cleated rubber sole that, according to the copywriter, would "grip and hold to the turf."

By the late twenties golf had become such a popular sport, particularly with younger men, that it was taught in college, and this helped make golf apparel even more youthful. The natural-shoulder sports jacket became the vogue, and the same ease was apparent in slacks and knickers. Shoes, whatever their fashion, had wide toes in contrast to those of more formal

footwear. White canvas shoes with red-brown trimmings, brown-gray self-strapped and -tipped buck shoes, full-brogue brown shoes with slashed tongues, and brown saddle-strap shoes were representative of the new, more fashionable golf shoe.

Golf Illustrated noted in April, 1926: "Perhaps no men are so closely watched today as professional golfers. The fact that practically every one of them now wear spiked shoes while playing is bound to create a demand for this type of shoe." A *Men's Wear* reporter covering the National Amateur Championship matches in 1928 observed: "Hardly any of the shoes carried rubber soles, the prevailing mode being spiked leather soles" (Oct. 10, 1928). He also noted that the outstanding footwear fashion seen on the links was the moccasin shoe in two-color or plain tan leather. In the two-color effects, black-and-white shoes were more popular than tan-and-white ones.

A journalist covering the National Open Championship that year observed: "Every smartly groomed golfer has a careful carelessness about his dress and is not conscious of his attire" (*Men's Wear,* July 11, 1928). In shoes, the trend setters showed a marked preference for the black-and-white or tan-and-white wing-tip sports shoe, the two-tone Scotch-tip shoe, and the brown-and-white, black-and-white, or plain brown moccasin. "That rubber soles are not looked upon with great favor by the golfers is shown by the fact that 99 per cent of the men wore leather soles with spikes."

A 1932 golf survey showed that the two-color wing-tip style had declined in popularity, while the plain white buckskin had gained. That year a fashion spread devoted to "The Complete Shoe Wardrobe" included the all-brown saddle-strap golf shoe and the moccasin-type golf shoe in either white-and-brown or white-and-black combinations (*Men's Wear,* July 20, 1932). In 1934 *Esquire* showed the golfing outfit worn by the Prince of Wales, which included black-and-white moccasins. A year later, *Esquire* again focused on the fashionable English golfer, this time showing the new British rubber with a strap and soft hobnails.

Like almost everything else in the American man's wardrobe, golf shoes showed little innovation during World War II. In the 1950s, however, golf shorts revolutionized golf apparel, and the slip-on shoes often worn with these shorts became lighter in weight.

The boar-nose golf shoe was welcomed by *Esquire* in 1956 as a spectacular new shape, "smart and masculine as you can ask, a man's shoe if there ever was one. The big step forward is, of course, the strongly accented square toe. Notice how the sole is molded to the shoe at tip and throughout." The particular shoe featured in *Esquire* was in a grained leather of the llama type.

In the 1960s golf apparel became steadily more colorful, and so did the golfer's shoes. Noting that a golfer usually walks about 4 miles during an average eighteen-hole game, *Esquire*'s fashion editor decided that what he needed was a shoe as sturdy as it was fashionable. The reader was offered a choice of four: a pair of black-and-red wing tips; a soft green brushed-leather shoe with smooth-leather trim and a kiltie tongue; a brushed-leather shoe in denim blue with a fringed tongue and a spiked, cushioned rubber sole; and a copper-color brushed-leather pigskin.

The seventies saw the introduction of a golf shoe with spikes that, owing to a special spike plate construction, were guaranteed not to wear out or fall out during the normal life of the shoe. It was eminently utilitarian, but the big news was the uninhibited styling of the "new wave" golf shoes that, according to *Esquire* in April, 1970, owed much to the "proliferating rash of new materials, more colorful and less expensive than the orthodox ones of yesteryear." Although the shoes *Esquire* showed had an elegant gaudiness about them, the copywriter assured the reader that they were "some of the more sedate shoddings for this season." Included were a kiltie-tongued wing-

Fashions in footwear for golf in the seventies became more varied: (clockwise from the top) a white poromeric shoe with black crocodile-grained material; a white poromeric shoe with a blue grained tip and kiltie tongue; a brown wing-tip shoe with a strap and buckle; an all-white poromeric wing-tip shoe with a kiltie tongue; a strap-and-buckle model with blue patent-leather trim on plaid fabric; a black-and-white poromeric shoe with a buckled strap and a blunt tip; a two-tone leather shoe with a straight tip; a white-grained poromeric shoe with brown lizard-grained trim; a white strap-and-buckle slip-on with black grained-leather trim. From Esquire, *April 1970.*

tip saddle blucher in white-grained Aztran; a rounded-toe monk-strap model in a combination of blue patent leather and plaid fabric; and a kiltie-tongued wing-tip shoe of brown lizard-grained and white-grained Corfam.

By the seventies the golfer had rid himself of the vestiges of so-called traditional clothing, and no other article of links apparel was as uninhibited as his footwear. The stolid Scottish flavor that had once dominated the American golfer's outfit had been thoroughly diluted, and what remained, especially in footwear, was colorful, brash, and uniquely American.

Ski Boots

Skiing achieved national prominence in the 1930s, when the press looked to the very rich for fashion news. Since skiing was obligatory for the mobile fashionable men of the day, ski clothes with their distinctly European flavor began to appear in newspapers and magazines. By January, 1937, *Esquire* was showing the latest ski clothes being worn at Sun Valley and noted: "Clothes like these would have stopped a clock a few years back. But the enormous growth in the popularity of winter sports during the past three seasons has made the sight of fashionable winter sportswear a commonplace virtually everywhere in the northern half of the United States."

The following excerpt from the 1936 guide to buying ski boots issued by the Winter Sports Committee of Massachusetts offers an excellent picture of the footgear then being used for skiing:

"Ski boots should be strong, well made and able to 'take it,' and should have steel shanks to prevent buckling. This is absolutely essential. Otherwise the tremendous strain of the heel strap will buckle the boots in a few weekends. They should be all-leather construction. Rubber permits ice to form under the feet and will not stand the stress. They should have straight sides, to eliminate side-play in bindings, should fit snug at the ankle over the customary socks for skiing, preferably should have a box toe, especially if toe strap is used, with a good groove for the heel strap. It is desirable that they should be low cut at front of ankle, to prevent chafing and give free movement. They should have sole protectors to prevent wear and buckling.

"Strapped models in ski boots are getting much attention. Since the American Olympic team wore these while competing in Germany last winter, sportsmen have become aware of the advantages of this sort of footwear. Even at some of the winter sports centers over here many of the experts favored them. Now makers offer a variety of styles. One house, for example, is showing an exact replica of the boot which the Olympic team wore. It is made from tanned American veal and is lined with leather. It laces to the toe, a feature which enables the wearer to adjust the boot over the ball of the foot. A strip of hard material is built into the sole at each side near the top to protect the sole from wear against the binding. Like most ski boots, it has a steel shank in the sole.

"Another model has a double strap, one going over the instep and the other around the top of the boot. The advantage claimed for it is the support the straps give to the foot. The toe strap has the added virtue of keeping the snow out of the boot. A third model is the blucher style with a strap and buckle at the instep. This is patterned after the conventional model, but, of course, has the addition of the strap.

"In the plain models many of the boots slope toward the front, which adds considerably to their comfort and minimizes the friction of the boot against the shin. All leather are treated with oil or waterproofing compounds so that water and snow do not penetrate them.

"Little details are by no means overlooked. One firm is using a specially constructed fabric lace, which is treated, making it several times stronger than rawhide and not apt to become untied easily. Even the hexagon-shaped metal eyelets, which were so prevalent on imported boots, appear on some of the domestic boots. The strength of the box toe is being stressed, too. With certain bindings having a strap over the tip becoming so popular, the need for a stiff box toe is great. Felt edgings around the top of the boot tend to keep the snow out. The variety of brass protectors is great. Some are in two pieces, others in one, but all are designed to fit snugly against the binding, allow no play and prevent the leather of the sole from being pressed out of shape. Even the welts are points of interest. In the less expensive boots, the regular welt is used. But in the better grades, the reverse welt is pretty general."

The cross-country skier wore a pair of wool ski knickers and, for added warmth, usually a canvas gaiter that was wrapped around the top of his ski boot and held snugly in place by a strap that went under the boot.

The late thirties saw many novelties come and go. The sealskin boot introduced by the Norwegians, for instance, had a certain popularity but offered no real competition to the more conventional black leather ski boot, which was often enlivened with red lacings. Neither did the two-tone Norwegian ski boot nor the double-laced boot.

In the latter half of the fifties, when the American man seemed determined that his apparel for both business and sports should be lightweight and comfortable, nylon and the new synthetic fabrics gave him what he wanted in ski jackets and trousers, and the ski boot became more streamlined, too. In January, 1956, *Esquire* showed a boot in black grained leather with a foam-fitted inner boot and a sole that had corrugated rubber and metal at the tip and heel. Far less bulky than its predecessors, this boot seemed the perfect companion for the new slimmer-looking, lighter-weight ski clothes.

The calibrated ski boot was the big news of the sixties. *Esquire* examined this block-shaped boot in December, 1966, and decided: "There hasn't been anything quite like it on the ski slopes before: a fiberglass ski boot that has a swinging door, five settings for different forward stiffness, a movable cuff that can be angled inward or outward, according to the wearer's stance and leg-bone curvature, and adjustable inside padding. This near-custom-tailored boot weighs less than most other boots on the market, and it fits all of the popular bindings. With all these advantages, plus clean-flowing lines and a smooth block shape, the boot surely qualifies as one of the most popular innovations available to skiers."

The red ski boot with plastic buckles attracted some attention in the early seventies, but the most interesting new item of skiing gear was the anatomically fitted boot, made possible by drying plastic foam around the foot while it was encased in a shell lined with soft vinyl. *Gentlemen's Quarterly* published photographs showing exactly how an anatomically fitted boot was made by the Lange Injection Boot process, observing: "The only hard part is standing still in it for the 15 minutes it takes to harden. Another 12 hours are needed for 'curing'—without you, of course."

Since the ski boot is the most utilitarian part of the skier's costume, fashion innovation has come and will certainly continue to come through technological developments. The increasingly lighter-weight, less bulky-looking boot will be an engineering feat, to which the fashion designer will add color and novelty.

Après-ski footwear. Since skiing is one of the most social sports, the *après-ski* outfit is almost as important as the skiing outfit itself. In the late thirties and early forties, for example, yellow pile slippers, slide-fastened sheepskin foot muffs, and slide-fastened bootlets of brown buckskin were the vogue. In the fifties knitted *après-ski* socks with soft leather soles became popular. A decade later *Esquire* photographed the newest type of *après-ski* boot, made of Danish bear hide with a black crepe sole, a small elasticized V inset at the front, and a pull tab at the back. By 1971 a rubber boot with bright racing stripes and a navy blue shaft was being seen in fashionable ski lodges.

Riding Boots

Like the gentlemen of England, the gentlemen of North America have more or less dutifully preserved all the intricate conventions proper to the hunt. In fact, the American horseman has proved himself to be as tradition-bound as his British cousin. The type of riding dictates the proper apparel, and only since the Peacock Revolution of the 1960s has there been even the slightest sign of deviation from the norm:

Formal hacking. Black or brown long boots and cloth gaiters or stone, fawn, or tan jodhpurs with jodhpur boots.

Informal hacking. The canvas-sided boot known as the newmarket, jodhpur boots worn with jodhpurs, or stout ordinary shoes.

Town or park riding. Patent-leather gaiter boots, although the traditional kit consisting of a black cutaway coat, a white flannel shirt with a wing or fold collar, a puff tie, and a tattersall waistcoat is no longer compulsory.

Field or dress. Black leather boots with patent-leather tops.

Semiformal dress. Plain black calf boots with patent-leather tops or without tops.

Hunting. For members, black calf boots with pink or mahogany tops; for nonmembers, boots without tops.

Show ring. Whether formal or informal attire is required, boots must always be highly polished. Spurs, which are optional, should be of the short-neck variety, worn high on the counter. The setting and time of the show determine attire. For the morning or

The riding boot of the seventies has a shaped calf, a low heel, and finely turned leather uppers. [COURTESY OF H. KAUFFMAN & SONS SADDLERY CO., NEW YORK]

afternoon formal show, the evening formal show, and the formal country show, black shoes are worn; for the informal country show, dark brown or black shoes.

Even the spectator should adhere to certain rules: for spectator wear at horse shows and hunt races, canvas leggings and high-cut shoes; at country hunt races, newmarket boots.

Although riding clothes are as much a tradition in the United States as in England, the period after World War II, in which riding was taken up by the middle class, witnessed a gentle but definite change in riding apparel. The popularity of the dude ranch, for instance, led to ranch-style riding clothes and fancy Western boots. By 1970 these boots ran the gamut from 14-inch-high leather-lined cowhides with blunt toes to authentic Western classic boots in black with inlaid designs in gold, white, and blue. Yet, despite the fashion liberation generated by the Peacock Revolution, it is unlikely that the classic lines of the riding boot will change drastically. How stolidly tradition still rules may best be illustrated by the fact that the left hunting boot must still be pulled on first. In this aristocratic sport, tradition is fashion and fashion is tradition.

Rubbers

In the first decade of the century, a man seeking rubber footwear to protect his shoes from snow and rain had many styles from which to choose. Among the most popular were the conventional black rubber with a high front and a wool lining and a low-cut style, the clog, which some men did not consider practical for anything heavier than a drizzle. Whether high-front, low-cut, or very low-cut, the black rubber could be had in four basic shapes: the regular broad toe; the London, or rounded, toe; the opera style, more pointed than the London; and the needle, or extremely pointed, toe.

Even more impractical than the clog in the opinion of some men (highly stylish in that of others) was the slip-on with a sole that covered only the front half of the shoe and a band around the back to hold it on. Here, too, a man had a choice of styles: the regular broad toe; and the Piccadilly, or pointed, toe.

Winters in the early decades of the century were severe in many sections of the country, and the arctic boot (by the 1920s known also as the gaiter or galosh) was the best protection a shoe could have. Most often made with a rubberized cloth top, a rubber outersole, and a fleece lining, the arctic was fastened with one to four buckles and therefore could stop at the ankle or extend up the calf. Some arctics had a bellows fold as additional insurance against the invasion of snow and water.

By 1915 red rubbers enjoyed a limited popularity. Still, the Apsley Rubber Company of Hudson, Massachusetts, advised retailers "not to buy a big stock of these red rubbers. Thoughtful people will buy black rubbers. Occasionally you will find a faddish person who will call for a red or white rubber, just as you will occasionally see a red or white automobile or wagon; but the substantial person, the people of good judgment, steer clear of these fancy things." He was correct, of course. When rubber footwear took on added style, it did so by design rather than with color.

By the mid-twenties the zipper had been introduced as an alternative closure to the buckle. Before another decade came and went, it had all but replaced the buckle, which had been an inconvenience for men who were not dexterous. A popular and aptly named short boot featuring the zipper in 1931 was the men's spat gaiter. Usually gray on the top half and black on the lower, it was snug-fitting and had a cleverly concealed zipper. Meanwhile, rubber footwear continued to be available in three basic styles: the high-front storm boot, the circular-cut rubber, and the still-popular low-cut clog.

By the late thirties, finish had become a fashion factor. Two types were the general bright finish and a leather finish with the appearance of pin seal. In the early forties there were many unlined rubbers in black or saddle brown with the look of a man's shoe. There were slip-ons, molded rubbers with wing tips outlined with perforations at the vamp, border, and foxing, and even models featuring reproductions of laces.

Stormy-day best sellers in 1949 included the fleece-lined blizzard boot with a zipper closing and tab and the suburban boot with a strap-and-buckle fastening, designed to be worn over the trouser leg. In addition to these heavyweights there were the new featherweight models and, returning for the first time since the end of World War II, dressy styles in black or brown with molded wing-tip and moccasin patterns.

Soft, flexible roll-up unlined rubbers originating in South America had a strong impact in the late fifties. The ease with which they could be put on and taken off, plus their lightweight, streamlined look, made them very popular. In the 1960s this combination of fashion and utility was evident in the unlined slip-on gum rubber boot designed to cover the bottom of the trouser leg as well as protect the shoe. Without a closure of any kind, boots of this type could be folded over neatly to a fraction of their size and fitted into a pocket-size tote bag.

Certainly fashion and utility will continue to produce innovations in rubber footwear for men, as they have in rainwear. For there is something about inclement weather that induces a style-conscious man to meet the challenge head on and look not only comfortable despite it but fashionable because of it.

Headwear

Changes in styles of headwear in the twentieth century have been as far-reaching as those in any other item of men's apparel.

1900–1910

The first decade of the century was a formal period, and men's clothes

were a status symbol. Only a man very low on the social ladder would appear in public hatless. The variety of hats a man could choose from was extraordinarily large, and each style had its own personality. Although men's suits were heavily padded and loose-fitting, their hats were handsome and shapely.

The hat pages of the 1897–1900 Sears, Roebuck and Company catalog suggested that there was a hat not only for every man but for every mood of every man. Prominent among the dress hats was the derby in black or brown, which was available in three dominant styles. There was the Dunlap, described as "The Prince of all derby hats . . . a strictly high grade stiff fur hat. Silk ribbon band and binding, extra fine hand finish. Finest goat leather sweat band." There was the young men's derby, which had a higher, less full crown with a very sharp dip to the front and back of the brim and a wide curve at the bound edge of the brim. And last but not least there was the flat-topped derby favored by the financier J. P. Morgan.

Almost as popular as the derby was the fedora hat, a soft felt named in honor of the drama *Fédora* by Victorien Sardou, which had a full-crown shape, a turned-up brim, and binding at the edge of the brim. Besides showing a line of felt fedoras in black, brown, and gray, the Sears, Roebuck catalog devoted considerable space to nutria fedoras, prefacing the display with the following copy:

"The finest hats in the world are made in America, and the finest American hats are made from clear nutria fur." The catalog proceeded to

(*above*) *Among summer hat styles shown in 1909 were the stiff sennit at left and the soft-body straw with a striped band at right. (below) Two prominent headwear fashions in 1909 were the full-crown derby with a rolled brim at left and the center-creased soft felt hat with indentations in the crown and a sharply rolled brim at right.* [NEW YORK PUBLIC LIBRARY PICTURE COLLECTION]

describe the fur: "Nutria comes from a small South American animal, greatly resembling the beaver, but much more plentiful. The skins of these animals are imported into this country in immense quantities by manufacturers of fine hats. The fur is thoroughly cleaned, combed and pounced, being finally transformed into felt, out of which the finest hats are made. Nutria fur is particularly desirable for this purpose, as it is very fine, soft and silky, and when prepared into felt contains no lumps, impurities or other objectionable matter. A clear nutria fur hat is as soft and smooth as a piece of silk, will retain its shape and color and will outwear any other kind of hat made."

Although a man could spend as much as $2.25 for a nutria fur fedora, Sears offered what it called a 98-cent wonder, a year-round nutria in black or brown with a wide silk ribbon band

(*opposite*) *Derbies, mostly in black but also in brown, predominated among the hats shown in the 1897 catalog of Sears, Roebuck and Company.*

and binding and a heavy satin lining. Nutria, of course, appeared in styles other than the fedora, such as Stetson's tower hat, which had a 6-inch crown and a 3-inch brim, with a narrow silk ribbon band and a raw edge, and what Sears, Roebuck called the bike hat, an "entirely new young men's hat" with a medium-low crown, a curled brim, and a silk ribbon band and binding.

Winters in the early 1900s were severe in many sections of the country, and Prussian-style beaver hats were much in demand. These hats were so soft that they could be rolled up and tucked inside a pocket, a selling point that earned them the name "pocket hats."

For summertime wear, linen crash hats were, according to the Sears, Roebuck catalog, "the coolest, lightest and most comfortable summer hats in the world." These hats were available in both fedora and derby styles, with ventilated crowns. They were extremely light in weight and, at 50 cents for the fedora and 79 cents for the derby, light in price, too. Summer straws were, of course, much in demand for both country and rural wear. Urban straws had flat brims and wide ribbon bands. The more picturesque country or resort straws had round ventilated crowns and wide rolled brims. The latter, which were promoted as "very desirable for fishing and rusticating," closely resembled many of the big straws seen today at fashionable beach resorts.

The Western part of the nation was still frontier country, and the Sears, Roebuck catalog contained a full supply of Western-style hats, dominated by the cowboy sombrero of nutria fur

Headwear in the well-dressed man's wardrobe in 1915 ranged from high silk and collapsible formal hats to derbies and rolled-brim soft felt hats. [COURTESY OF BROOKS BROTHERS, NEW YORK]

Soft felt hats with bands of various heights and creased crowns were shown together with wool fabric hats in 1915. [COURTESY OF BROOKS BROTHERS, NEW YORK]

16J01 Opera Hats. Imported and Domestic
Ribbed Silk
Best quality Cashmere

16J02 Silk Hats. Imported
Lock & Co.'s
Herbert Johnson's
Domestic make

16J03-04 Derbies. Imported
Lock & Co.'s
Herbert Johnson's, Black, Brown and Grey
Domestic

16J05-06 Imported and Domestic Alpines. In rough and smooth felts

16J07-08 Soft Hats in rough and smooth felts

16J09-10 Imported and Domestic Crush Hats, all shades from white to black

16J11-12 Tweed Hats

Men's Prince Charlie English Fatigue Caps

English Raider Hats, Khaki with silk puggaree bands

created by Stetson in the 1870s. The military also influenced hat styles during this period. The Governor, a popular hat of this type, was described as "a clear fur hat with full shape 6-inch crown and 3½-inch brim. Fine silk ribbon band, raw edge, fine finish." It bore a marked resemblance to the hat worn in the U.S. Cavalry, with one exception: the brim had a slight roll, whereas the regulation Cavalry hat had a flat-set brim.

Caps were an important part of the headwear picture in the early 1900s. There were woolen outing caps with eartabs that could be worn down over the ears or folded over the top of the crown and tied together. Short-peaked caps in corduroy and tweed were designated for steamer and automobile travel as well as for golf and general outing wear.

1910–1920

A look at the pages of the 1915 Brooks Brothers catalog illustrates the vast variety of hats then available. Many of the Brooks hats were British-made, since this store was the exclusive agent in New York for Messrs. Herbert Johnson & Co., of New Bond Street, and J. & G. Lock, of St. James's Street, London. Among the styles in the catalog were the high silk hat (still the only correct hat for both day and evening formal occasions); soft hats in rough and smooth felts; imported and domestic crush hats in all shades from white to black; Prince Charlie English fatigue caps; Austrian velour hats; sombreros; Italian panamas (later known as leghorns), Japanese panamas, South American panamas, and Milan straws;

Sennit straw hats, traditional by 1915, were shown with other straws and with ranch and velour felt hats. [COURTESY OF BROOKS BROTHERS, NEW YORK]

Among the summer hats shown in 1915 were optimo and telescope shapes in Italian panamas (leghorns), milans, and panamas. [COURTESY OF BROOKS BROTHERS, NEW YORK]

16J13 Austrian Velour Hats.
All shades
Feathers for same

16J14 Ranchero Sombrero

16J15-16 Straw Hats
Imported
Domestic

16J17-18 Mackinaws

16J19-20 Italian Panamas

16J21 Milan Straw

Beach Panama

16J22-23 South American Panamas

Japanese Panamas

The rolled-brim fedora with a dented crown was worn in 1918 with a narrow-shoulder jacket, a high starched collar, and a striped tie with a stickpin.

caps; leather sou'westers; English fishing helmets and tropical helmets; hunting silk hats and caps of silk velvet; English cork-lined polo caps and English pith polo helmets; and boys' panamas, straw hats, and derbies.

"Shall we ever return to the magnificent fashions of other days?" asked the writer of a 1919 *Men's Wear* fashion feature. He did not think so, and his pessimistic attitude might have been the result of his unsuccessful attempts to find a "real Homburg hat" in New York. "There are shops which carry a so-called Homburg," he wrote, "but it has neither the conical crown nor the brim which holds the curl. And as for these hats in smart colors, beyond the pearl shade, they do not seem to have a vestige of an idea of present vogue" (May 7, 1919, p. 113). As far as he was concerned, the homburg was "the real thing in soft hats," and he expected that it would be for many seasons to come. And he was absolutely correct. The elegant homburg with its distinctly tapering crown and moderately narrow, rolled brim remained one of the most popular hats for several decades.

The same *Men's Wear* article drew the reader's attention to the pedigree of the homburg:

"Though the Homburg hat is of Tyrolean origin, it derives its name from the town of Homburg, in the province of Hesse-Nassau in southern Germany, where this style was made famous by the late King Edward who, as the then Prince of Wales, frequently visited Homburg as a recreation and health resort.

"King Edward always wore this hat with a small, brightly colored feather stuck in the side bow, a fad that followed the hat from its Tyrolean source.

"Here in America, as well as in England, this style of hat has been a favorite with fashionable men of the extremely well-dressed class for the past several years, but it was not until the current season that this particular style was more generally adopted by other men.

"When worn by a man to whose features this shape is becoming, it is one of the smartest hats to be had today, and because of the fact that it has now come to be looked upon as of the more formal type, it makes its best appearance in the darker shades.

"In solid black, the Homburg shape is now the favorite hat with fashionable men for wear with the informal evening jacket. Its correctness and authority is established by that court of last resort from which there is no appeal—the cultured, smartly turned out men of the world who have social position, inherent good taste and the means with which to satisfy it."

1920–1930

The soft felt hat replaced the stiff hat as the best seller in this decade, although the still-popular derby certainly did not lack publicity. The brown derby practically became synonymous with the Democratic party in the person of Alfred E. Smith, Governor of New York and his party's nominee for the Presidency of the United States in 1928. Soon there was even a Hollywood restaurant called the Brown Derby. Perhaps it was this kind of fanfare that helped dampen some fashionable men's enthusiasm for

the derby and turned them toward the fedora style. In the meantime, although the homburg was not flattering to every man, it too became popular.

An analysis by *Men's Wear* (Mar. 19, 1924, p. 48) of apparel worn by 300 of the best-dressed men at Palm Beach revealed that a three-button medium gray sports jacket and white flannel trousers worn with a medium-brim sennit straw formed the most popular outfit. Yet the wealthy Palm Beach man had many favorite hats, with the panama running a close second to the sennit and the leghorn (formerly known as the Italian panama) not far behind in third place. A lightweight gray felt was the fourth choice.

During the 1920s the dapper and youthful Prince of Wales was the most powerful fashion influence in the world. He set the fashion for the blue chinchilla British guards overcoat, the

Mayor James J. Walker, photographed at a sports event in the 1920s, wore his distinctive hat, snapped down on one side, a fur-collared coat, gloves, and spats. [NEW YORK PUBLIC LIBRARY PICTURE COLLECTION]

glenurquhart suit, and the shepherd's-check four-in-hand tie (some called it the Prince of Wales check) as well as the newest soft hats:

"The weekly newsreels and the Sunday newspapers' illustrated sections are the average man's guide to the fact that the snap brim still remains the favorite headgear for men in the public eye, for town and country comfort. But it will be noticed that the brim is considerably wider and that the higher crown tapers more to a point when worn with single center crease than the average hat. This is still another minor but new and correct change in the detail of men's wear sponsored and introduced by the Prince of Wales" (*Men's Wear*, Oct. 8, 1924, p. 47).

British influence was not restricted to the Prince. The English team playing in the international tennis matches held in Newport in 1925, for instance, introduced (among other things) a new color in the snap-brim soft felts the Prince had popularized. It was a cocoa brown, and *Men's Wear* (Sept. 9, 1925) published a sketch of one of the members of the Oxford-Cambridge team wearing it with a tight-fitting double-breasted jacket and the new Oxford bag trousers. Among other hats seen at Newport that summer were a panama with a square crown and an unusually wide, flattish wavy brim, a lightweight gray felt, and a brown leghorn with a square crown and a brim turned down all around.

The winter playground of Palm Beach was always being examined for fashion trends, since what the moneyed men of fashion wore there in the winter very often became nationally famous by summer. A fashion scout covering the scene in 1926 reported: "I will start right in with hats. While at this writing the analysis of the various articles of men's apparel at Palm Beach has not been completed, I think we will find a marked increase in the popularity of leghorn hats.

"The new thing in hats is the Milan straw hat. This is the hat that better class men's wear stores throughout the

CLOTHES APPEARANCE IS important to your success—don't slight it—be judged by your clothes taste, Kuppenheimer good clothes.
You'll not only buy the best made clothes, but you'll buy the best clothes appearance. You never go wrong, any way, selecting Kuppenheimer clothes.

Open-weave straw hats topped shapely suits in this 1920 advertisement. [NEW YORK PUBLIC LIBRARY PICTURE COLLECTION]

United States must stock and introduce this summer as the new and correct summer wear hat, along with Panama hats and the brown and natural leghorn hats.

"The crown of the Milan straw hat is rather high and is telescoped. The brim is wide and is rather flat set. It is invariably worn with the brim turned down all around, as are the Panamas and leghorns. Like the leghorns, these Milan straws in white, grey and the natural leghorn color are worn by the better dressed men here at Palm Beach, with rather wide crepe silk white or brown puggree bands.

"The very best dressed men at Palm Beach who wear Panama hats naturally wear what appear to be the most expensive Panamas. These have the square-top crown—very square—and the wide, flattish set brims.

"Also it is most noticeable that the sennit is not only worn with a black

The Vogue in Men's
Bond Street De Luxe
$4.95
93K6315—Medium gray with black band.
93K6317—Black.
93K6318—Sand tan.
93K6319—Dark gray with black band.
Sizes, 6¾ to 7½. State size. Shipping weight, 2¾ lbs.
Bond Street De Luxe Hats are correctly styled. Highest quality and lowest price guaranteed. An extremely beautiful and popular shape made of extra fine fur felt in the season's newest shades. Lined with super quality silk hat lining. The crown is about 5¾ inches high. Bound curled brim, about 2¾ inches wide.
Silk Lined
Our Sombrero
$1.98
93K6275
Nutria tan.
Sizes, 6¾ to 7¾. State size. Shipping wt., 3¼ lbs.
Men's Good Quality Wool Felt Sombrero Work Hat. The crown is about 4¾ inches high. Bound brim, about 3½ inches wide. A durable work hat at a low price.
Our Crusher
98c
93K6184—Black.
93K6185—Steel gray.
Sizes, 6¾ to 7¾. State size. Shipping weight, 4 ounces.
An inexpensive lightweight wool felt crusher style hat that is very comfortable and will give excellent service. The crown is about 5½ inches high. Raw edge curled brim, about 2½ inches wide.
Our Big Boy
Measure Your Head Before Ordering See Chart on Opposite Page
Bond Street De Luxe
$4.95
93K6287—Black.
93K6288—Brown.
93K6289—Nutria tan.
Sizes, 6¾ to 7¾. State size. Shipping weight, 3¾ pounds.
You will be pleased with this Extra Fine Quality Bond Street De Luxe Fur Felt Hat. A larger shape with an extra wide brim that has lots of swagger to make it most popular. The crown is about 7½ inches high. Bound curled brim, about 4½ inches wide. For those desiring a hat of this character, we recommend Our Big Boy as it is the best value offered at our low price.
The Norge
$3.45
93K6135—Medium gray.
93K6136—Dark gray.
93K6137—Sand tan.
93K6138—Black.
Sizes, 6¾ to 7½. State size. Shipping weight, 2¾ pounds.
A Smart and Rakish Bound Brim Fancy Band Hat. Attractively styled and correctly dimensioned. Made of a good quality fur felt. The crown is about 5⅝ inches high. Bound snap brim, about 2⅝ inches wide. A becoming style adaptable to either young or old. A very desirable hat at our low price.
The Beach
$3.95
93K6179—Dark gray with black band.
93K6180—Medium gray with black band.
93K6182—Black.
93K6183—Sand tan.
Sizes, 6¾ to 7½. State size. Shipping weight, 2¾ lbs.
An unusually smart and fashionable Fedora Style Hat. A dressy model correctly styled and detailed. Made of Fine Quality Fur Felt. The crown is about 5¾ inches high. Latest curled bound brim, about 2¾ inches wide. A quality rarely equalled at our price.
Hats of This Quality Usually Sell for $12.00 to $15.00 Elsewhere
Silk Lined
$7.95
93K6380—Medium gray with black band.
93K6381—Dark gray with black band.
93K6382—Nutria tan with brown band.
Sizes, 6¾ to 7½. State size. Shipping weight, 2¾ pounds.
One of the season's newest styles smartly fashioned of Fine Clear Beaver Fur Felt, by one of the country's best known manufacturers of quality hats. Super quality silk lining. A hat that appeals to the particular man who wants the best. The crown is about 5¾ inches high. Bound curled brim, about 2¾ inches wide.
Silk Lined
$7.95
93K6370
Medium gray with black band.
93K6371—Dark gray.
93K6372—Nutria tan with brown band.
Sizes, 6¾ to 7½. State size. Shipping weight, 2¾ pounds.
A style and quality endorsed by the most discriminating dressers, is this newest welt edge brim style hat. Made of a Fine Quality Clear Beaver Fur Felt, by a manufacturer of the highest grade hats. Lined with the finest super quality silk lining. The crown is about 5½ inches high. Welt edge brim, about 2⅝ inches wide.
Fur Felt Crusher
$2.48
93K6176—Black.
93K6177—Gray.
93K6178—Brown.
Sizes, 6¾ to 7¾. State size. Shipping weight, 4 ounces.
Men's Lightweight Crusher Style Hat. Made of a good quality fur felt. The crown is about 5½ inches high. Raw edge curled brim, about 2⅝ inches wide. A durable hat that will give good service.
Our Columbia
$3.39
93K6145—Black.
93K6146—Nutria tan.
Sizes, 6¾ to 7¾. State size. Shipping weight, 2¾ pounds.
A very popular staple style of exceptional merit is this Men's Columbia Style Hat. Made of good quality fur felt. The crown is about 5⅝ inches high. Raw edge curled brim, about 3 inches wide.
410₂
SEARS, ROEBUCK AND CO. WLS The World's Largest Store

band, but its popularity is mainly with the more conservative man of middle age. There is no doubt whatsoever that the young man and the athletically inclined even of middle age are favoring the body hat to a marked degree. The younger men at Palm Beach consist entirely of wealthy young business men" (*Men's Wear,* Feb. 24, 1926, p. 60).

Illustrating this report was a photograph of a well-known New York financier in a pale gray-blue summer suit, a blue shirt with a detachable blue collar, a yellow crepe tie, white buckskin shoes, and an alpine-crease panama hat.

Golf was the leading sport at Palm Beach, and the fashionable golfer might turn up on the links wearing anything from a white duck hat with a green underbrim to a gray felt with a pinched crown or a panama with the brim turned down all around. And after a hotly contested game of tennis, a player might put on a sennit straw hat and wrap an absorbent terry scarf around his neck. For evening wear with dinner suits the best-dressed Palm Beach men preferred the sennit straw with a black band.

The *Men's Wear* fashion observer noted that the sennit straw with a medium brim and crown continued to lead all other styles in 1926, although some men favored the panama hat with a medium brim and a squarish crown. Felt hats of the lightweight type had increased in popularity, particularly with younger men, who favored their felts in light or medium gray with a narrow brim, a raw edge, and a tapered crown, worn with the brim dipped down in front and turned up back or with the crown creased down the center and the front pinched. Tan was the second favorite color, dark or cocoa brown the third,

The pinched-crown felt hat with a slightly upturned brim was in fashion in 1928.

and olive green the fourth.

The writer of the report also noted: "Second to the Panama among the body hats is the natural leghorn with a puggree band to harmonize with the color of the hat. For the much older man, a wide flattish brim hat with a square crown is accepted by the very best dressed men at Palm Beach.

"Hat bands on the sennit straw are black, although there will be a very light demand for the striped band. Puggree bands are accepted for wear with the leghorn, the oatmeal straw, the Milan. For the Panama hat, the band will also be of plain black silk.

"The cocoanut straw is a hat that will be generally worn this coming summer, except at the most informal occasions in the country, where there is little demand for a dressier hat. This cocoanut straw is similar to the leghorn, but of a coarser weave. Woven from dried strands of the cocoanut palm, it is heavier than the average straw, but being loose in weave, it offers protection from a hot sun and at the same time adequate ventilation. The fact that the straw when dried takes on various shades of brown makes it a colorful sports hat, and this is enhanced by the brightly colored puggree band that is worn with it. The band is broad, extending almost to the top of the hat."

Little hat news was gleaned by *Men's Wear* during a house party weekend at Princeton in the spring of 1928. Few of the college fashion leaders were

wearing hats, but those who did favored the snap-brim felt and the homburg. Attention was directed to the manner in which many of these fashionable young men were denting the crowns of their hats. Instead of adopting the center crease and pinched front, they tended merely to dent the top of the hat and pinch the front.

A national college survey in the autumn of 1929 noted: "The significant change in hat styles this fall has been a great increase in browns, especially the darker shades. With the coming popularity of blue-grey as a suit color, there will be more grey hats worn next spring. For this winter, the Homburg should be a more popular hat than ever before. Together with the Homburg, the small shape derby should also be a very good type of headwear" (*Men's Wear,* Nov. 20, 1929, p. 44).

It was unfortunate that a financial forecast was not included with these fashion predictions, for the stock market crash was only a week or two in the offing. One might have expected the resulting Depression to sweep fashion away, but it had the opposite effect. Despite the Depression, or rather because of it, the next decade proved to be one of the most casually elegant periods in twentieth-century men's apparel.

1930–1940

The Great Depression naturally decreased the number of men who could afford to dress fashionably. As a result, the socially elite with their fortunes still intact were more than ever the focal point for the fashion press. And since Palm Beach was their habitat each winter, reporters and photographers followed hard on their heels. Communiqués from the resort filed during this period offer today's reader not only a fashion picture but insight into the life-style of the very rich, who not only survived but flourished during this troubled period. As a *Men's Wear* writer put it, "Persons who have always had money still have big bank accounts and are entertain-

(opposite) Descriptions of hats illustrated in the 1927 catalog of Sears, Roebuck and Company included dimensions of crowns and brims. The colors were black, gray, brown, and tan.

ing very elaborately. One retired banker maintains his place, as in former seasons, with a skeleton force of 34 servants and an additional crew for big luncheons and dinner parties. There are many others in a similar position. It will take more than fluctuations in security prices to interfere with the pleasures of the real set, which has been escaping the snow and slush of northern winters and basking in the tropical sun for years" (Mar. 25, 1931, p. 67).

The same issue of *Men's Wear* included this fashion report:

"Old Sol and the sombreros were playing a game of hide-and-seek much of the time at Palm Beach this season. When Helios had a chance to shoot her healthy rays down on the frolickers in the Florida east coast's Garden of Eden, most men put their hats into hiding. Life seemed to revolve on whether the sun would be out on the next day or not. Apparently many persons at Palm Beach did not want to have to sit under an artificial light to get their epidermis darkened in order to prove that they had been south for the season. As this much worshiped heavenly body went into seclusion under the eclipse of endless clouds, hats came forth from their hiding places and adorned the craniums of the elite.

"It is claimed that a smart summer sports ensemble is not complete without a head covering of some kind. Yet, there are many men, who, being the possessors of many hats, did not wear any. These same men would never think of going about in town without a hat. Although there were sufficient numbers of hats seen to compile a survey of what is in fashion, it must be kept in mind that this is an analysis only of the hats observed.

"The Panama is again the leading straw hat style. This was true last year, but since then there has been an increase of four percent in the popularity of this hat. The bulk of these hats had narrow bands in solid colors. Striped bands were worn by only a small number. Hardly any of the hats had turned-up brims, the majority being snapped down all around and some having the brim flopped down on the side. The regulation optimo shape is the thing and narrow, medium and wide brims are in favor, with special interest shown in the last mentioned. A few of the hats were of the flat top crown variety reminiscent of the telescope shape. Panamas can again be counted on to sell in a big way next summer.

"The trend toward lightweight felt hats for summer, which was so noticeable last season, is even stronger this year . . . jumping from a popularity of 35 percent to 41 percent. Greys are again the leaders and browns and tans follow. Many of the brown hats were in very dark shades, which, in some instances, gave a striking contrast to the ensemble. Mr. E. F. Hutton, for example, wore a very dark brown snap brim hat with a white flannel double-breasted jacket suit and colorful accessories. Green was also used as a blending or contrasting color and should be a smart summer hat color. Green hats were worn with greyish green jackets or with dark brown jackets. One man wearing the grey jacket and biscuit trouser combination topped it off with a green hat. Quite an individual ensemble it was!

"The snap brim is the favorite. Brims continue to be fairly narrow and bands match or contrast in shade with the color of the hat. A few telescope crown hats were seen.

"There are still many men who believe that there is no better looking summer hat than the sennit straw. Hats of this type seen at Palm Beach were of medium proportions, having crowns of moderate height and medium width brims. It is especially interesting to notice that two-thirds of the men wearing sennits preferred club striped bands. Not only were the colors of the Bath and Tennis, Seminole and other Palm Beach clubs to be seen, but many men disported the stripings of New York clubs. Practically all the bands were of the regulation width, a few being of the 17 ligne width. Colored bands increased eight percent since a year ago.

"Leghorns and Milans were worn by five percent of the men, which is a little less than their popularity twelve months ago. Some of the leghorns were in optimo shape, which is indicative of the Panama trend. Most of the Milan straws were in the telescope shape. These hats were also worn with the brim flopped down all around, and usually had puggree bands" (Mar. 25, 1931, p. 74).

A popular outfit seen on many younger men at Palm Beach in the winter of 1931 included a gabardine jacket, white flannel trousers, a pink-and-white shirt, a blue tie, black-and-white shoes, and a sennit straw hat. But the ultimate in sophistication was the English ensemble of a reddish brown tweed jacket and contrasting gray flannel trousers, a crepe tie, white buckskin shoes, and a panama hat.

The fashion reporters in attendance at the Yale-Harvard crew races in 1934 decided that headwear honors were divided among lightweight felts, panamas, and sennits: "Felts were mostly grey, with dark brown a close second. The feature of the Panamas was the large shapes and the fact that more and more men were wearing the brim turned up. Sennit hats ran to pretty much the same proportions as heretofore and showed the usual club or organization colors in the bands. A new model in regular weight felt, a tapered crown hat with a moderately wide saucer brim, was seen on well dressed men. Watch this hat in the Fall! This differs from the semi-homburg hat in that the brim is not higher at the sides than front or back. When snapped in front and on both sides part way back, the brim has a rolled dip" (*Men's Wear*, July 11, 1934).

That autumn, a look at the fashionable men attending the United Hunts Meet at Belmont Park, Long Island, showed that the homburg was more prominent than at any meet during the past few years. One version had a welt edge and a matching hatband with a colorful feather tucked in the rear of the band, indicating the strong Tyrolean influence that was being seen more and more in sportswear. The leading homburg, however, was a more conventional gray with a black band and gray silk binding.

By 1934 "porkpie" had been added to the American fashion vocabulary as the name of a low-crowned hat of the telescope type. First seen in England, the porkpie hat moved to the United States, where it was worn by well-dressed men at polo games and race meets before being accepted for business and casual wear as well. Many retailers promoted the hat as being strictly British, and the trade considered it the first major change in men's hats in years. One well-known New York retailer who took an active part in styling his line reportedly ordered a porkpie variation inspired by the manner in which he had observed some Yale men wearing their hats: denting them deeply in back and wearing them on the back of the head, thus giving a backward-sloping line to the crown when seen from the side. They also snapped the brim sharply down in front and gave the crown a front pinch. The hat made to be worn in this manner, said a fashion reporter, "has an egg-shaped contour to its tip looking at it from above, and the crown is sloped down in back. It is therefore broad at the rear and narrow in front. The rear of the hat is telescoped when it is worn and the narrow crown in front allows the pinch to be most effective. It is said that the block on which this hat is shaped has actually been dimpled where the front pinch comes so that these dents will be deep and regular. The brim, of course, snaps" (Men's Wear, Nov. 21, 1934).

The porkpie having established itself in felt, the stage was set for the introduction of porkpie straws. Such models were soon available in panamas, leghorns, bangkoks, and other straws. Ventilation in male attire during this period moved from foot to head, and the popular perforated summer shoe was joined by the summer hat with a perforated body, brim, band, and head leather.

The Tyrolean hat rose to fame in the mid-thirties when the Prince of Wales arrived in Vienna wearing a green Tyrolean hat complete with brush. During his visit the Prince purchased several more hats in shades of rust and brown as well as plain black. It was reported in Men's Wear (Mar. 20, 1935) that he made his selections "with great care, taking pains with the models and the styles, frequently expressing his fondness for Austrian hats and haberdashery for country wear." These hats were characterized by a deep roll in back of the brim, a tapered crown, and the inevitable feather mount pinned into the corded band.

The Tyrolean hat was a flattering style for many men, and it retained its popularity throughout the thirties, being featured repeatedly in the fashion pages of Esquire. A full-page feature in October, 1936, titled "A Complete Hat Wardrobe for Fall and Winter," included it with the porkpie and six other hats, with the promise that this collection should suit a man for every occasion with "the exception of his favorite sports, which may include additional and specialized headgear." Fashion copy read as follows: "Only one snap brim hat is necessary and one type of country hat. However, every other hat on this page should be included in the wardrobe of those men who wish to be dressed correctly for every occasion." The eight hats were:

The English-type snap-brim, suited to men with long, lean faces and correctly worn for every fall in town and weekend wear.
The modern college-type snap-brim hat with lower crown and wide brim with stitched welt edge suitable for most young men and most worn at the universities.
The bowler with full crown and narrow straightish brim, to be worn in town with business clothes, topcoats and overcoats. In the right proportions the derby can be worn by anyone.
The midnight-blue homburg, suitable for men of all ages but for an oval face the crown should not be too high and should have a definite taper and a brim fairly wide with a well-defined roll, for town wear.
The brown porkpie hat, meant only for country wear and for men who have small faces.
The authentic Tyrolean hat with cord band and plumage. Adapted to men with small

or square faces. To be avoided by men with full faces. Green cannot be worn by those who have pallid complexions. This is meant only for country wear, football games, etc.
The correct cap with a one-piece top, suitable to most men for very informal country usage, golf and other active sports wear.
The midnight-blue silk opera hat in the new shape with $5\frac{3}{8}$-inch crown. This model is made especially for the younger man with small face and is correct with dinner coat and tail coat.

In April, 1937, *Esquire* included a brown-mixture Tyrolean hat with a green cord band and a silk edge as part of the "foibles and fancies of a country squire." In September, 1938, it showed four Tyrolean hats among other "heterogeneous semi-luxuries to

Two classic styles of summer hats in 1937 were (left) the boater with a vertically striped university band and (right) the optimo panama with a striped band. From Esquire, *June 1937.*

which the undergraduate might blow himself ere his impending return to school." The next month both a pair of semi-Tyroleans and a full-fledged Tyrolean were included in a collection of new hats and shoes that the caption writer, on second thought, decided would probably be more correctly dubbed "current" rather than new, since "men's fashions march to a slow tempo of change so gradual as to be almost imperceptible." One semi-Tyrolean hat was black with a self-finish band, and the other a fawn color in pebble-grain felt. The full-fledged Tyrolean was in green complete with cord and brush.

Suggested hats for spring bearing the *Esquire* seal of approval in March, 1938, included the following:

Dune color corduroy cap, introduced last season in England and widely accepted by American sportsmen for country and travel wear.
A black Lord's hat, so-named because it has been seen on practically every well dressed peer in London, correct with all types of town clothing. It is more informal than the popular Homburg, inasmuch as the crown is worn pinched and the roll brim carries a raw edge.
Lightweight Cavalier hat worn by the best dressed men in England and America for town and semi-sports wear.
Green rough finish semi-sports hat for informal country occasions.

While straw hats were popular during this decade, to many fashion experts they simply were not popular enough. "Sportswear is taking its toll of straw hats," said an *Esquire* writer in August, 1939. "A felt is indubitably the thing to wear with a mixed ensemble. A stiff sailor is out of place on the golf course. (It is almost perfect with whites and it is ideal for evening wear with white dinner jacket.) Colored straws have been timorously promoted when they have been promoted at all," he concluded, reasoning that the time had come for designers, advertising experts, and sellers to agree on a program that would put the straw hat over. But, he cautioned, there was one thing they had to recognize and be prepared to combat:

"The reason why men, young men particularly, like the felt hat is because

it is practical. It will take a lot of beating without being ruined. On a hot day a man can take it off and toss it on the floor of the car, and it is not a donkey's breakfast when he reaches the country club."

Meanwhile, the hats that, the writer hoped, would give straw added appeal were in the natural tints, such as a tannish gray that was almost an oyster shade, in a smooth braid with ventilation in the sailor form. It was expected that these natural shades would combine well with the natural tone of the new wash-and-wear summer suits: "It does certainly look as though the makers of wash suits and the straw hat men had a great deal in common and that they might profitably form some sort of mutual aid society. The wash suit was introduced as a comfort feature, but it never really took hold until a couple of seasons ago when it became a style item in a big way. There is food for thought in that idea. Everybody knows straw hats are comfortable. Is it not possible to dramatize their fashion significance?"

One of the most stylish straws was the large jipajapa hat, although it was restricted to resort and beach wear. In white or natural and bearing a wide, colorful, and sometimes pleated band, it was first seen at Caribbean resorts and soon afterward at smart resorts in the United States. Originally it was the hat worn on sugar plantations, and so it became known as a planter's-style hat. Casual and dashing, the jipajapa has never lost its popularity.

Caps continued to gain favor during this sports-minded decade. In October, 1939, *Esquire* spotlighted the checkered cap at one point, admitting: "Devotees of the checkered cap have been rankling over a crack we made about it some months back, in the course of one of our learned disquisitions on the whats and hows of evening clothes. ['But don't, under any circumstances, wear a derby with a dinner jacket. Better go bare headed or wear a checked cap or an immigrant's shawl!'] The checkered cap, like limburger cheese, has a very definite but restricted place in the lives of men. For

golf and motoring, it is perfectly suitable, with certain reservations as to its cut and pattern. As to the former, it should be a one-piece, and as for the latter, the houndstooth pattern is preferable to the monotonous regularity of the simple square check." Illustrating this page was a sketch showing a British-looking gentleman entering a champagne-colored roadster, dressed in a double-breasted gray flannel suit, brown wing-tip shoes, and a one-piece checkered cap.

Among other caps featured in *Esquire* during the late thirties were a rough tweed worn with a lightweight two-piece rain suit, an outfit intended for shooting, fishing, and spectator country wear; a corduroy cap in the then-popular dune color, worn by a spectator at an informal race meeting whose outfit also included a tweed jacket, narrowly tapered khaki drill trousers, and a silk hunting shirt with a cotton stock; and a tweed cap with a flat one-piece top worn by a gentleman at a country dog show.

Although many college men during the late thirties wore the small-shape bowler with a flat-set crown for weekends in town, the derby was declining in popularity.

Since the still-rich American held the reigns of fashion firmly in his hands during this decade, it behooved anyone seriously interested in clothes to follow him to the sporting events and resorts he frequented. *Esquire's* fashion editor did just that, noting that the very appearance of these men at outdoor sports events exerted a perceptible influence on the fashion trends of the country. "These fashion-setting sportsmen constitute a small group, numerically," *Esquire* granted, "but of large importance socially and financially. Their whim of today is next month's law in designers' workrooms."

At the races in Saratoga, for example, among those photographed for the June, 1934, issue were two rather mature men of fashion. The somewhat younger man wore a double-breasted suit of blue tropical worsted, a white rounded-corner starched collar, a blue foulard bow tie with white spots, and a sennit straw with a club-color band. The older man's suit was a three-button gray glen plaid, worn with a fawn-colored linen waistcoat, a white shirt with a white stiff collar and a colorful striped tie, and a homburg hat.

Covering the Yale-Harvard regatta for the same issue, *Esquire* photographed a spectator in a light tan jacket of gabardine, light gray flannel slacks, white buckskin shoes, and a brown leghorn hat with a white shantung puggaree band: "You may not go for the brown leghorn hat, and if you don't it's all right, because you can always substitute a sennit straw or a Panama, but if you do happen to like it you may wear it with the satisfaction of knowing that it is no longer considered an old man's style, as it was for some years."

At a polo match, *Esquire*'s roving fashion editor took copious notes on the attire of one distinguished spectator, prefacing his report in the September, 1934, issue as follows: "This is a spectator sports outfit that is typical of those front runners of fashion whom you see at the horsey gatherings on Long Island. These fellows stick with a fashion only until the mob catches up, and then they drop it cold. This outfit has not yet traveled far west of Westchester." The outfit, still beyond the reach of "the mob," consisted of a three-button single-breasted tweed suit of lovat green; a cream-color oxford-cloth shirt; a striped rep tie; a tattersall waistcoat of cream flannel; brown buckskin shoes; and a hat of rough scratch felt.

Covering Newport, Rhode Island, during the invitation tennis tournament, *Esquire* commented (July, 1937, p. 152) that the conservative wealthy men at this resort were so bound up in tradition that there was really nothing new to report. A case in point was a young man wearing a single-breasted natural-shoulder Shetland jacket ("very very Newport—in fact it has been for about twenty years, never altering a jot in either model or fabric"), white flannel trousers ("typical,

too, of the traditional Newport manner—rather short and narrow, with natural turn-up at the bottom"), and a button-down collar-attached tan oxford shirt ("which hasn't changed appreciably since the war"). All in all, it was decided: "By contrast, the India madras four-in-hand tie and the cocoanut straw hat seem almost daring innovations."

After strolling over the greens of an exclusive country club and noting that the old English pastime of lawn bowling had lately been taken up at quite a number of American country clubs, an *Esquire* fashion artist sat down and sketched for the June, 1934, issue a tanned member sitting on the patio and looking casually elegant in a double-breasted natural-color silk suit and a coconut straw hat with a light blue puggaree band. In Nassau, where, as *Esquire* reminded its readers in October, 1938, the braid of the coconut straw hat was woven, a staff photographer snapped a well-dressed vacationer wearing one with the brim turned up all around as he tossed coins into the water for boys to dive for.

As this style-conscious decade drew to a close, *Esquire* offered its readers a refresher course on the proper hat for the occasion. The hats in this feature (October, 1939, pp. 116–117) included:

The rough-finish yeoman-style bowler, correct for town or spectator wear but not with a dinner jacket.

The gray felt hat with a welt edge and an upturned brim, correct with town clothing.

The black lord's hat with an upturned raw-edge brim and a pinched crown, correct for business and semiformal day and evening wear.

The black homburg with a silk-bound edge, correct for semiformal evening and day wear.

The brown snap-brim hat with a tapered crown and a medium-wide raw-edge brim, correct for town and semisports occasions.

The lightweight brown cavalier hat worn in a casual manner, correct for town, semisports, and travel.

The rough-finish Tyrolean hat with

a white cord band, correct for spectator sports, travel, and country.

The rough-finish semisports hat with a low crown, a medium-wide brim, and a narrow silk band, correct for semisports and country.

The green rough-finish porkpie hat with a narrow club-striped band striking a new note, correct for semisports and country.

The plaid tweed cap with a flat one piece top, correct for country, motoring, and active sports.

The collapsible silk grosgrain opera hat for wear with a dinner jacket or full dress, correct for the theater or a nightclub.

The silk top hat for wear with formal day and evening clothes, correct for weddings, balls, and state and other strictly formal occasions.

With this feature *Esquire*'s fashion department offered an illustrated guide, "Care of Hats." During the next decade, however, millions of men were, of necessity, going to be more concerned with the care of their military headgear.

1940–1950

With war clouds on the horizon, men, particularly younger men, showed a penchant for the military colors of khaki, blue, and green. The cliché "any color that's blue" was no longer a conservative's dirge, for blue was now high fashion. And in July, 1940, *Esquire* demonstrated how potent these military colors had become. A man "definitely in season, judging from his plumage," wore a glenurquhart plaid jacket of blue and white, flannel slacks with a tinge of blue that echoed the color cast of the jacket, and a hat that was "an offspring of various parentage. The pork pie shape is derived from that of a felt hat, while the shade follows that of the khaki headgear which men at the smart universities adopted as their favorite. Of very soft fibre, the hat conforms readily to the contours of the head. A colorful plaid cotton band enlivens its appearance. At first sight a resort type of headwear, the hat has recently been

Hats for winter, 1940. From Esquire, *October 1940.*

a gray lightweight felt with a trishade silk puggaree band and a wide, supple brim was recommended for semisports and country.

There was an air of studied casualness about the hats of the early forties, which Stetson expressed in a hat whose crown blocked higher on one side than the other. In its advertising, the makers claimed that this slope-crown hat had "nonchalance blocked in."

In July, 1941, *Esquire* took a long look at straws and came to the conclusion that there was almost as much variety in soft straws as in neckwear: "From the sporty Jippi Jappas and cocoanut palms to the staple Panamas and sennit is a wide zone of fashion." Exactly how wide varied according to the type of fiber, shape, and trimmings, a fact *Esquire* demonstrated with a collection of eighteen hats that included a wide-brimmed Montego hat for resort wear, a brown panama with a colorful native band, a two-tone coconut palm with an Americana silk puggaree, an optimo panama, a

adopted for business wear as well."

In the same issue, the fashion staff showed a model in a greenish hemp hat with a blue puggaree band. "Originally a campus fashion, this hat has since been taken up by men of all ages and popularized far beyond the confines of the campus. It is exceptionally soft and open in weave." Furthermore, the new fashion color of that year was sandune, which bore a strik-

ing resemblance to the suntan color of an army officer's uniform. Even the bucket cloth hat, a porkpie of processed cotton, was most popular in khaki. Featuring a floppy snap-brim and side air vents, the bucket hat was first worn on the golf course but was soon taken up for country and campus wear.

Felt hats took on greater dimensions early in the decade, with brim widths expanding despite the fact that the favorite hat of the well-dressed Britisher was narrow-brimmed. *Esquire,* still a stickler for propriety, in May, 1940, again displayed a collection of hats and noted the occasions for which they were appropriate. There was, for instance, the rough-finish derby with a flat-set brim; hardly a very popular model any longer, it was judged correct for business or travel for the man who still had to have a derby in his hat wardrobe. Then there was a blue turned-down-brim felt with a single center crease, considered an all-around hat for town, country, and semisports. A green allover-stitched felt with a narrow dark felt band and a lighter felt brim binding, worn shaped and dented, was correct for both campus and town. A khaki felt with a lighter silk band and brim binding was also correct for campus and town. Finally,

Summer hats worn by commuters in 1945: (left to right) a high porkpie hat in a mesh panama; a pinched-crown panama with a broad brim; a panama with a horizontal-ridge effect; a coconut palm hat with a printed puggaree. From Esquire, *June 1945.*

A lightweight felt hat with a narrow band was worn with sports clothes in 1942. From Esquire, *May 1942.*

The bold look "executive hat," worn with a double-breasted jacket with long-roll lapels and related accessories. At right is a side view of the hat. From Esquire, *April 1949.*

slope-crown panama, a featherweight baku with a Javanese puggaree, a coconut palm with a bright gingham puggaree, an open-weave panama, a brown lightweight felt, a sennit straw, an open-weave coconut palm with a white silk puggaree, a watersilk palm with an Americana striped band, a cocoa baku with a sandune puggaree, a ventilated-crown brown panama, a dark palm with a green puggaree, a porkpie jipajapa with a green puggaree, a broad-brimmed hanoki with a maroon crepe puggaree, and a tan cotton porkpie for golf.

Making certain that the reader got the point, the copywriter added a few lines of doggerel: "Though Grandpop wore the selfsame skimmer/When snow would fall or sun would simmer/Variety, to coin a phrase/Is quite the spice of life these days."

During World War II *Esquire*'s fashion pages managed to show the latest civilian fashions while saluting the men in uniform. For example, a collection of military hats was shown with the observation that their regulation design made lily gilding superfluous; civilians, on the other hand, said *Esquire*, kept changing their hats as often as their minds. So it gave its readers a chance to catch up with hats as of July, 1943, by a display of the following models: a panama that was really a porkpie, with an extra tapered crown and a narrow, colorful band; a buff-color mesh panama whose crown followed the shape of the conventional snap-brim felt ("The brim is quite wide, conforming with the current trend and shading the eyes from the sun at one fell swoop"); and a lighter natural-tone panama, also in the snap-brim felt shape, carrying a plain blue puggaree band.

Another fashion page in the same issue showed a handsome ensign and a dazzling Wave with a trio of mature gentlemen. Here the copywriter noted that there had been a pronounced trend toward green in headwear, spotlighting a green felt with a matching ribbon. The other civilian hats were a formal homburg that was unusually lightweight and, despite its formal tone, had an easygoing brim that could be rolled into any shape; and an African-brown felt with a welt-edge brim and a crown creased in the center only—"a token of restraint that usually indicates the wearer thereof has become resigned to dressing his age."

In October, 1944, *Esquire* showed four hats said to be "brimful of comfort," an important consideration since, in addition to possessing good proportions and color, "a hat has to be comfortable." This quartet included a gray homburg with a good curl to the brim and a tapered crown; a brown snap-brim with a welt edge to help it keep its shape; a ruddy brown with the brim turned up all around; and a green soft-finish felt that was definitely a sports type for wear with odd tweed jackets and slacks. Among the "brand new lids" for spring that year were a pinched-crown gray felt with a welt-edge brim of moderate proportions; a green stitched felt of roughish texture in a semiporkpie shape with indentations at the sides; and a soft brown felt with a quite narrow raw-edge brim, worn with a center crease and no side indentations.

Men's apparel in the postwar years grew increasingly lighter in weight, and hats were no exception. In September, 1945, *Esquire* observed that "socially conscious manufacturers" had begun making after-Labor Day felts of lightweight fabric. Even the more or less formal homburg was lighter and easier to wear now. And in the meantime there was a definite trend toward narrower brims—that is, until 1948, when *Esquire* presented its "bold look" and brims expanded once again.

The bold look "executive hat" featured a tapered crown with a bound edge showing $\frac{1}{8}$ inch on the upper side of the broad brim and $\frac{3}{8}$ inch on the underside. It was typical of the bold concept of a good-size brim and crown worn in coordination with a widespread collar, a big-knot tie, bulky shoes, and a suit with broad shoulders and wide lapels. The bold look also affected straw hat styling; a prime example was the light-as-a-zephyr big alpine straw homburg with a tapered crown, a brim flat at the sides and front but strongly curled in back, and a wide double-pleated puggaree. All in all, a bold look hat was a lot of hat.

The alpine straw homburg of 1949 had a center-creased crown and a brim that was flat at the sides and front but had a pencil curl in back. From Esquire, *June 1949.*

But a lot of hat was not the kind of hat "Mr. T" wanted in 1950. *Esquire*'s symbol of the new decade's new trim look, Mr. T looked taller and trimmer in suits with straight-hanging lines and narrow snap-brims with tapered pinch crowns. About Mr. T *Esquire* had this to say in October, 1950, "Mr. T is tall. Of course, the real payoff is for grey matter, but most men still want to look taller. That's where the notched lapels and the slim 'up' lines of the new T formula come in. And this idea of loft is carried to its most logical conclusion in the design of the new *Tremont* hat. The crown is tapered—instead of full—giving you a real air of altitude. Brims are narrower, too, and the colors are picked to make you the man on top. And, perhaps most important is the versatility of the Tremont. With the *brim up* and a center crease only, Mr. T has that necessary touch of formality that readies him for the most important engagement in town. With the *brim down* and a center crease only, the

Three lightweight hats: (top) a soft leghorn with a paisley-pattern puggaree; (center) a tapered-crown baku with a big-figured rayon puggaree; (bottom) a toast milan with a corded puggaree band. From Esquire, *July 1950.*

The tapered-crown hat of 1950 was worn with a center crease only and a turned-up brim (top) or a snapped brim (center) or with a pinched crown and a snapped brim (bottom). From Esquire, *October 1950.*

Tremont is more casual. And again the same hat, with a *pinch crown* and snapped brim, offers still more casualness and informality."

As lightweight summer suits became even more popular with the advent of man-made fabrics, many of which were washable, straw hats took on even greater importance. "The only hat worthy of your head this summer is the one that lets the breeze through," *Men's Wear* advised the style-conscious and comfort-conscious American of 1952. The journal observed that although the trend to narrower brims continued in sections where narrow brims were worn, "in areas where big shapes are wanted the $2\frac{3}{4}$ inch, $2\frac{7}{8}$ inch, and 3-inch brims show no signs of diminishing in size of acceptance.

"In the big cities of the East as well as in a few other isolated spots $2\frac{1}{4}$ inch, $2\frac{3}{8}$ inch, and $2\frac{1}{2}$ inch brims sell in many of the smart shops. Nevertheless, the tradition that straw hats are worn in slightly larger dimensions than felts still influences many men even in those spots.

"One of the outstanding features of the new lines are the puggrees used to trim the straws. The shantung silks that were so well accepted last season are being repeated in a greatly enlarged assortment of colors. India madras and Indian prints, some employing gold metallic decoration, tie silk reps in conservative as well as colorful stripings, and an almost limitless selection of cottons, rayons and blends will brighten up the 1953 straws.

"A successful bandanna trim cocoanut with bandanna to match of last season is being followed up this year by a promotion of pork pie Milans available in three shades and trimmed with pocket kerchief with kerchief to match.

"While Panamas show no sign of losing their niche as the prime favorite of the American market, Milans and leghorns are tabbed as the top fashion hats with cocoanuts maintaining their position of popularity in the larger metropolitan sections.

"Balibuntals, for the first time shown in a wide variety of colors, are said to be gaining due to the shortage of Bakus—the production of which is stymied by the chaotic condition of the Chinese market.

"Umbria palm and Bari braid are new starters to retail at $5 and bear a very close resemblance to Milan.

"Sennits continue to sell to their comparatively small coterie of fans and this year they can be had in all of their many types including flatfoots, pineapples, china splits, and yeddos.

"The center crease Belmont model has made fair progress in the big cities and is expected to show further gains in '53" (Aug. 22, 1952, p. 104).

Accompanying this report were photographs of a coconut sports cap with a long visor and a half-bandanna trim in front, a typical cowboy-style panama with a "Texas-style" pre-blocked crown and a wide brim, a

Shapes, textures, and trims of hats in 1954: (top left) an average small-shape hat with proportions shown; (top right) a concealed-visor cap, epitomizing the trend toward smaller shapes; (center left) a back bow in keeping with the smaller brim; (center right) a low-crown porkpie with a wool band for wear with tweeds; (bottom left) a Tyrolean shaggy felt suburban hat; (bottom right) a small-shape homburg. From Esquire, *November 1954*

balibuntal in one of the new darker shades with a silk puggaree, a reed hat of the pith-helmet type for beach and spectator sports wear, an African-print sports cap in a lightweight cotton, a Western-style straw with a fancy ventilated-weave crown, and a coconut palm hat in the Tyrolean style.

A swing to rugged wool and tweed suits and topcoats gave rise to hats with unusual finishes such as suedes, scratches, and pebbles, and Tyrolean and semi-Tyrolean models enjoyed a revival of popularity. In general, new hats for autumn, 1952, featured nar-

rower brims and lower, more tapered crowns. Caps were enjoying a strong comeback for sports and suburban wear, and three of the most popular shapes were a full English type, a new oval model, and a small shape that was preferred by college men.

The homburg in the smaller proportions of 1953 was given strong encouragement when President-elect Dwight D. Eisenhower eschewed the traditional high silk hat in favor of a homburg for his inaugural ceremony. "Rarely has a man's hat received as much good publicity and public interest as has Ike's Homburg," wrote one trade reporter, reminding retailers that the new President had provided them with ammunition for early spring business. The homburg, he maintained, was not only the smartest hat for Easter but was also "the distinguishing mark of the up and coming business and professional man" (*Men's Wear,* Feb. 20, 1953, p. 95).

By November, 1954, the conservative trend was declining, and *Esquire,* observing that men's hats were already reflecting this change, reminded its readers in a "Head Man" feature: "A hat is truly your badge of personality. Johnny Appleseed chose to wear for a hat a saucepan with a long handle (for tipping) as he strode across Ohio and Indiana sowing the orchards that weight the green hills today. The bishop has his mitre, the admiral his scrambled eggs, the umpire his blue beanie, and the butcher his battered straw to keep his scalp warm when he goes into the icebox. A man at an outdoor dog show, foolishly without headgear, recently wore a paper plate on his head, generously donated by the makers of a famous dog food.

"We mention this rather wide-flung company by way of suggesting that the hat is a humble and useful object which is worthy of attention, the more today because the headpiece itself is now in a phase of personality which offers many interesting variants.

"There are new textures, for instance, which you may not have stopped to observe—rough and nubby surfaces, as well as the conventional smooth felts. There are new bindings on the edges, sometimes contrasting with the color of the crown. There are new bands, narrow or wide or pleated. But probably the newest and most marked fashion of the moment is in the small-shape hat, which has come out of London. Its popularity is already well-established in Eastern metropolitan areas, where it has become the mark of the smartly turned-out executive type of man.

"We don't suggest that you take a tape measure into your favorite hat store, but the details are interesting: a hat that runs $5\frac{3}{8}$ inches or $5\frac{1}{2}$ inches in height now has a brim only about $2\frac{1}{4}$ inches wide. Some even come down to $2\frac{1}{8}$ inches or even a flat two. This is running through all styles of hats, and is a trend you might as well recognize. You needn't consider yourself to be over-conscious of fashion if you note these things, either. If you've looked at any old photographs recently, you will have observed that men of a generation or so ago actually wore their hats high on the head and down in front. Any crowd at a boxing match, for example, pictured in the old days, favored this downslope by the thousands. You wouldn't do it on a bet today, but they were the guys

The suede hat trimmed with pile fabric was an example of the popular fur look of 1957. The earflaps were retractable. From Esquire, *September 1957.*

who wouldn't do anything else on a bet. So it goes.

"Other hat tips: the pork-pie, surviving its remarkable name, continues as a great favorite, especially in company with tweeds and flannel get-ups. The midnight-blue Homburg is still the best bet with your midnight-blue evening clothes. A fine and elegant new fashion is the soft felt in midnight blue with silk or twill facing on the underside of the brim—very man-about-town. The casual type of soft felt with the brim turned up all around is very popular these days, in midnight blue or black. Gay blades in London dip the brim on one side, a la Jimmy Walker, but you've got to have quite an air (or be an heir) to get away with this.

"The cap, of course, is making a terrific comeback. The last time it was seen around was when Wally Reid wore his with the peak backwards to show how fast he was driving. After that, a couple of thugs were shot in caps in G-man pictures, and a gangster wouldn't be found dead (and frequently *was* found dead) in anything but a felt hat.

"But the sports car, the links, and other sportive backgrounds have capped the climax now and you can get them in every kind of fine tartan and, in some cases, with the brim built into a sort of beret effect which has shape to it without being a wind-catcher.

"If you keep your head, and most

A small-shape cap in striped tweed that was popular with university men in 1956. From Esquire, *September 1956.*

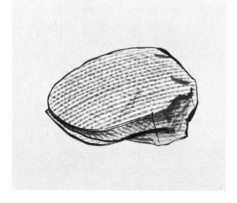

The low-crown porkpie hat with a matching felt band had a following on campuses. From Esquire, *September 1956.*

of us plan to, you might as well do something with it, we say."

Illustrating this feature were sketches of an average small-shape hat, a Tyrolean hat with a tapered crown, a shaggy felt, a low-crown porkpie with a wool band, a small-shape homburg, and a concealed-visor cap that also epitomized the swing to smaller shapes.

Since a hat really is a badge of personality, there were some significant departures from conventional shapes. Prominent was the hat carrying the flat top of a Spanish hat or, as some more nationalistic fashion writers called it, the flat top of an aircraft carrier. Whatever the top was likened to, it was flat, and the hat was finished with a very wide band that covered three-quarters of the crown. In the late fifties novelty headwear was popular, too, with hats of pile fabric and fur as well as suede leather and pile fabric combinations. An especially popular model was a suede hat, trimmed with a high-pile furry fabric, with attached earflaps that were concealed within the crown when not in use. The caption for a photograph of this hat in *Esquire* (December, 1959) rather bluntly stated: "Genus: fur fad."

1960–1970

Early in the dynamic sixties the British took over the fashion scene. The "British look" suit had lightly padded shoulders, definite waist suppression, a moderate cutaway front, slanting pockets, and pronounced side vents. Characteristic of the British look in hats were a deep roll of the brim in back and a tapered crown. This basic concept turned up in various finishes of felts and in hats with raw edges, welt edges, and narrow silk-bound edges.

In February, 1962, *Esquire* paid tribute to the longtime fashion influence of Great Britain. At the time it would have been difficult to imagine that the well-dressed Britisher, with his steadfast concern for tradition, would soon be superseded on the fashion scene by teen-agers and the uproar they caused

The British-shape hat of 1960 had a tapered crown and a rolled brim with a forward-sloping line.

that was eventually called the Peacock Revolution.

"When you walk down Bond Street in London you see a score of elegantly dressed men. At first they look quite uniform—the dark suit, the bowler hat worn absolutely straight and low on the forehead, the shiny, starched white collar and, always, the (rarely opened) hand-pressed umbrella. But there are subtle differences. They have not all gone to the same tailor or shirtmaker. Some tailors have exclusive patterns, too. And there is the effect of great assurance—elegance even in their attitude. The result is an *easy look*, which, I suspect, is as studied as Charles Laughton's quiet, strong diction."

Insofar as hats were concerned, *Esquire*'s fashion department favored James Lock & Company, Ltd., hatters on St. James's Street, London, where the passing of the years was observed with placidity. "Asked, for instance, about the admiral's hat in the window they explain: 'We're not quite sure of its history, sir, but we believe it *might* at one time have belonged to Lord Nelson.'"

The Peacock Revolution was still in the future when, in 1963, the fashion writer George Frazier commented in *Esquire*: "What is so nice about men's

clothes is that their obsolescence is never obligatory. That is the reassuring thing—they do not go out of style very swiftly. It is not that they never change, but, rather, that they change so gradually, so almost imperceptibly, that only in retrospect does one realize that there has been change."

The spring of 1963 prompted a color display of straw hats in the April issue of *Esquire*: a triangular-creased coconut palm, a generously broad-brimmed hat that resembled a Jamaica planter, a light natural raffia with a feather band, and a classic

British-influenced hats of 1961: (top to bottom) a tapered-crown model with a deep-rolled brim; a narrow-banded snap-brim; an olive felt having a brim with a deep roll in back and at the sides but only a slight turnup in front; a pinched tapered-crown hat with contrasting binding on the turned-up brim. From Esquire, *November 1961.*

panama in the modernized optimo shape with a center crease.

In July, 1963, *Esquire* titled a double-page headwear feature "A Hierarchy of Summer Straws" and prefaced it with the following copy:

"The admirably dressed man never goes hatless. There is a correct hat, no matter what the weather, what the occasion. Summer headwear offers scope and variety enough to afford a full wardrobe for the punctilious male. But beyond correctness, straw hats are especially appealing. There is actually more variety in straws than in felts, colors are lighter on the whole, the various textures of different fibers give each straw a distinctive character, bands are much more colorful. There is, in short, greater fashion choice, a wider opportunity, to exercise one's individual taste. And all of today's straw hats are lightweight, effortless to wear. The major fashion trend the past few years, in all hats, has been, of course, the trimming down of the silhouette—brims are narrower, crowns lower, in keeping with the slimmer proportions in all men's clothing today. More specifically, recent seasons' fresh contributions have been the rise of the bizarre straw—imaginative, even zany concoctions for golf course and beach; the comeback of those two pioneering straw styles, the boater and optimo; and the introduction, this year, of geometrically shaped crowns."

Illustrating these fashion points were these hats:

Center crease. Of Milan, or any other soft fiber, these hats are usually preblocked, sometimes with pinch fronts. Colors range from medium to dark in greys, blues, black; bands are usually striped. This popular model can be worn by—and looks fine on—almost any man. It coordinates well with most summer suits—from washwear blends to silks—and dressier sport coats.

Oval telescope crown. This hat comes in a wide range of shades (tans, blues, greys, olives), and is most favored in the more textured fibers, like cocoanut and raffia. Its more casual look calls for sportier bands (madras, batik and polka dots); choice of band, in fact, may tone the hat up or down, for wear with a suit or a sport coat.

Geometric crown. The geometric-shaped hat was introduced just this past spring, which means this summer will be the first time it has been available in straw. Radical innovations in hat design, these are business models in softly defined and unique silhouettes. The crown is slightly convex on top and tapered at the sides, and the snap brim is upswept in back.

Homburg. The center-creased straw Homburg with curled brim is usually of Panama (but may be found in baku or Milan) and most frequently natural shaded (although darker shades are available). The usual band is black. Narrow-faced men should be careful to choose a tapered crown and one of the models available today is in a narrow- to moderate-width brim. Most often worn by the mature executive, the Homburg is a more formal hat, and is perfectly correct with a summer dinner jacket.

Optimo. The classic optimo-shaped off-white Panama hat features a crown which is ridged and slightly tapered, and a narrow ribbon band. The optimo may also be worn with sport clothes of a dressier character. It, too, is generally the choice of the more mature man, and its balanced proportions should go well with any facial type.

Boater. This hat—known variously as a sennit, skimmer, sailor—is made from sennit straw (which, incidentally, is also used for other hat shapes). It is always in the natural shade, most often sporting a striped band. Worn correctly with either suit or sport jacket, its jaunty good looks are flattering to almost every type of face. A truly classic style, its popularity has resurged in recent years with the advent of natural-shoulder clothing, whose youthful enthusiasts have championed it; but many older executives have also welcomed its return. Adorned with a black band, it may be worn with a dinner jacket.

Sport hats. A summer weekend and vacation wardrobe is likely to include at least one slightly wild sport hat. Perfect for golf, driving, relaxing—everywhere from the mountains to the beach—it is probably the only hat which seems right with walk shorts. In textured, open weaves, most are telescope and Tyrolean types, and anything goes on the bands and decoration. Biggest boosters of bizarre hats have been younger men, but there is really no age limit for these lighthearted straws.

"Yo Ho The Boater!" was the headline of an *Esquire* fashion department article in April, 1964, in praise of a summer straw said to be "really a hybrid, offspring of an inspired cross-pollination between two classics. On the paternal side is the traditional boater hat; on the maternal (we presume) is the Haitian cocoanut palm that used to go into softer hats. Result: the soft Sun Tan shade of cocoanut, the well-balanced shape." The boater was a fine accompaniment for nearly any summer suit, including the classic white suit that in the early sixties was suddenly as popular as it had been in the early forties.

Cloth hats were also much in demand. According to one fashion writer, the reason for their popularity was the development, with the help of modern technology, of town-type hats in summer fabrics. "While these compete with straw hats to some degree, they also appeal to many young men who would never buy a staple straw. These hold-outs enjoy headwear as much as any African chief, but naturally they fear formality. They don't wear the same clothes as Poppa did, and don't respond to the same old hats. The cloth hat, with its modern connotation and its ability to coordinate with every new fashion fabric and color, speaks their language" (*Men's Wear*, Sept. 25, 1964, p. 142).

Continuing his analysis, the writer thought another factor encouraging the summer cloth hat was "the decline of the gimmicky play straws. For several years, gentlemen and bums have been capering under cheap straw hats trimmed with bottles, fish, shells and dancing dolls. Inevitably, these reached the drug store tables, and, while play straws are still in the picture, they are in the better grades and exclude the mass market. But the fun hat mood still operates, and the hat mood still operates, and the fabric people seem to have found the answer—colorful cloth hats, light, comfortable and crushable, and tuned to specifics like golf, fishing, boating or beaching."

The new cloth hats were designed to be lighter, airier, and more crushable. Nylon mesh was used for ventilation in complete sides and in decorative inserts as well as for weightless tennis hats. There were dress hats in raw silk, nubby tussah cotton, and Italian Bemberg. As the *Men's Wear* reporter said, "Name the young man's town dress or sport jacket, and there's a hat to go with it."

In holiday hats, multicolored patch fabrics proved popular and were seen in seersucker, madras, and batik. There were many two-tone hats, with the crown in one color or fabric and the brim in another. Rain hats, once considered simply utility items, became fashionable thanks to the cloth hat trend. They were available in tattersall, seersucker, stripes, and two-tone fabrics, muted by an oiled silk which many men admired even in fair weather. Summer cloth caps and sports hats were more popular than ever. The round or bold-front golf crown, once called a baseball cap, was suddenly a best seller, and the flat-topped bucket-shaped sports hat in seersucker was practically an indispensable hat for a well-dressed sportsman's wardrobe.

The shaped suit was fashionable in 1964, and with it came the tapered hat. Tapered and pinched-crown hats with highly contoured brims were considered perfect accessories for the shaped jacket, whose object was to break up the long-popular straight lines. A sculptured hat, it was thought, achieved the same end.

By 1965 the Peacock Revolution

This Cardin hat of 1967 had a full crown and a wide, tightly furled brim in back.

was under way, and hats grew increasingly stylish. There was, for example, a new Tyrolean. Its peak had a small dent, the front sloped more gradually, and the back was slightly upturned. The particular model shown by *Esquire* (April, 1965) was made of a rough felt in a dark green heather mixture and carried a four-cord band and feather.

In September, 1966, *Esquire* predicted that "the movement which inspired first the wide-shouldered, wide-lapeled jacket, then the wide tie and recently the wide shirt collar will culminate with the return of the wide-brimmed hat." Although wide-brimmed hats had not been seen since the bold look period almost twenty years earlier, *Esquire* decided that their revival was only a matter of time: "Men's fashions change according to the domino theory, and overall fashion profiles come into focus gradually. With the Big Hat, the picture will be complete and well-balanced. The brim of this hat is about two-and-a-half inches wide, the fullness of the crown is proportionately scaled. The brim has only a slight upward curve so that it may be turned up all the way around, or snapped in front." The British never really gave up the Big Hat, concluded the writer, but "for several years Americans have been wearing the tapered, narrow-brimmed model, which, fairly soon, will be rather old hat."

In the mid-sixties fur headwear became popular as men in the northern part of the country adopted fur and fur-trimmed coats. The trim cossack style of hat, in caracul, otter, mink, sheepskin, and other furs as well as in pile fabric, added a new dimension to the headwear scene.

In 1966 Pierre Cardin, the French couturier who had already become known for his men's apparel, turned his attention to headwear, and the results inspired *Esquire*'s fashion department, in the October issue, to label him "a hatter not so mad." Cardin, said *Esquire*, was "one of the few men of all seasonings—on the one hand, a haut couturier who adds the dash of spiciness to women's wear,

The large-shape hat with a broad brim was in keeping with the wide lapels, big collars, and wide ties of the seventies.

and, on the other, a designer of such men's apparel as beatified the Beatles in the eyes of many a beholder. It is a measure of this man that when he enters into something, he does so whole hog for he knows, better than most designers, that it is the ensemble, and not the individual items, that appeals or affronts. So, since there is the Cardin suit, there is also Cardin headgear—nor is it without some influence, either. The original Cardin hat prodded a whole industry into reappraising the conventional models most men wore simply because there were no alternatives. Now hatters everywhere are responding to this influence. They realize, for example, that the shaped look in suits should be complemented by the styling of hats. Now hats have slightly higher crowns and brims which are wider and more tightly furled in the back. And the width gradually tapers to the front, which is never, not ever, sharply snapped."

In 1968 *Esquire* predicted success for another new item: the three-way hat. This new hat was a soft, pliable felt that, as the name suggested, could be worn three ways, with the brim snapped only over the narrow width in front, or the brim dipped fore and

(clockwise from upper left) A black homburg with a silk-bound edge, worn with a striped business suit, a blue shirt, a starched white collar, and a gray checked tie; a silk top hat, worn with a tailcoat, a wing collar, and a white tie; a brown snapbrim hat with a tapered crown and a medium-width raw-edge brim, worn with a cheviot suit, an ivory-color shirt, and a striped tie; a gray felt hat with a welt edge and an upturned brim, worn with a lovat-color suit, a striped gray broadcloth shirt, a starched white collar, and a Macclesfield tie; a rough-finish semisports hat with a low crown, a medium-width brim, and a narrow silk band, worn with a glen tweed suit, a gray checked shirt, and a wool tie; a collapsible silk grosgrain opera hat, worn with a blue double-breasted overcoat and a white silk muffler; a plaid tweed cap with a flat one-piece top, worn with a checked tweed sports jacket, a flannel shirt with a soft lounge collar, and a foulard tie; a black lord's hat with an upturned raw-edge brim and a pinched crown, worn with a sharkskin suit, a striped shirt, and a foulard tie; a green rough-finish porkpie hat with a narrow club-striped band, worn with a brown sports jacket, a plaid shirt, and a striped tie; a green rough-finish Tyrolean hat with a white cord band worn with a Shetland tweed suit, an Eton-blue shirt, and a crochet tie. From Esquire, *October 1939.*

The stiff collar with a rounded opening for a larger tie knot was a new fashion just before World War I. It was worn with a pinched-crown felt hat. [CLUETT PEABODY & CO.]

Headwear fashions in 1949: (counterclockwise from the bottom) a gray homburg; a welt-edge ruddy-brown snap-brim; a hat with a pinched crown and an upturned brim; and a green rough-felt hat for sportswear. From Esquire, *September 1949.*

Summer hats of 1944: (top to bottom) a coconut palm with a blue-and-yellow puggaree; a mesh panama in a natural shade; a loosely woven wide-brimmed porkpie panama. From Esquire, *June 1944.*

Headwear

aft to give a high roll to the side, or, in the strictly American style, the brim simply snapped down across the front.

Preshaped, extremely lightweight summer straws made news in the summer of 1968, but before the fall had begun, there was bigger news with hats that were once again assertive. "The brasher the better," wrote a fashion columnist in *Gentlemen's Quarterly* in March, 1970, no doubt echoing the sentiments of the new youthful elite. Among the new broad-brimmed models were giant Western-style straws with braided leather bands; felts of gold fur, biscuit wool, red wool, and teal fur; soft brown leather cowboy hats; and colorful velours that were especially well suited to the big shape with floppy brims. Many young men took to these hats with enthusiasm.

Yet the hair-consciousness of the young led them to adopt an increasingly casual attitude toward hats in general. If a particular style appealed to them, they wore it, but often they chose to go hatless. Unlike their fathers, they did not regard the hat as an essential part of an outfit. And, too, with youth exerting such a dynamic influence on fashion, many more mature men also began to go hatless. This unpredictable attitude presented hatmakers with a challenge that they met with exciting new hat styles, in shapes ranging from subtle to bold and dashing. It was too soon to predict the future of the hat, but with manufacturers determined to create hats that would fit into the fashion formula of contemporary living and men, particularly young men, always eager for the new and different, it seemed inevitable that the hat would make fashion headlines again.

Gloves

Probably the oldest glove known to man turned up in the 1920s when the tomb of Tutankhamen was opened and a glove of linen cloth was discovered. Gloves of the working variety were the first to be made in quantity. They date back to around 330 B.C., when slaves who kneaded pastry at the court of Alexander the Great were ordered to wear gloves.

The first sporting gloves of record date to the Middle Ages. They were worn by ladies and gentlemen who enjoyed the sport of hawking and required gloves that would protect their hands from the sharp claws of the bird that perched there. Centuries later, the English dandy Beau Brummell would further the wearing of gloves when he decreed that "a perfect gentleman" changed his gloves six times a day.

By the twentieth century gloves were a staple item in every man's wardrobe, and in the early decades his social status more or less dictated their fabric and styling. The Sears, Roebuck and Company catalog of 1897 offered an impressive variety of gloves and mittens. As the copywriter worded it: "We have everything from the cheapest oil tanned working gloves to the finest imported kid gloves." There were, for instance, muleskin gloves ("not very pretty, perhaps, but full of real goodness and wearing qualities. Tough and strong yet not stiff or clumsy"); heavy yellow oil-tanned unlined gloves of grained leather with cord fasteners; imported hogskin gloves, heavyweight and unlined ("with a world wide reputation for durability"); medium-weight cape goat driving gloves, with silk-stitched welted backs, patent snap buttons, and cut seams, silk-sewn throughout; cordovan horsehide gloves with stitched backs and banded wrists ("the best fireproof gloves in the world"); fleece-lined kid gloves and mittens; lined leather gloves with a fancy elastic wrist; heavy all-wool mittens; fine kid dress gloves, silk-sewn throughout and fastened with patent buttons; and richly embroidered buckskin gauntlets with heavily silk-stitched backs. In short, there was a glove for every man and every occasion. It was not until the twenties, however, that fashion became a truly strong factor in glove selection.

In 1924 *Men's Wear* noted: "The old description, 'It fits like a glove,' will need revision in view of the current tendency to wear gloves that are loose fitting. With those who give consideration to style, gloves are no longer the snug fitting article of yesterday, but instead a proper glove is one that follows the tendency in clothing. It subscribes to the comfort idea and is now being worn in larger sizes, in harmony with the more loosely fitting clothing that is in the mode.

"The man who formerly wore an 8, now wears an $8\frac{1}{4}$ or sometimes an $8\frac{1}{2}$. The wanted glove no longer fits snugly across the knuckles, for the hands demand a greater freedom. The glove that is wanted by the style customer is not so much the smooth surfaced, dark colored affair that has been standard for a number of years, for sports and the rough-and-ready, free-and-easy sentiment seems to have left its mark on glove preferences.

"The 'pock-marked' pigskin glove, for example, is the antithesis of the kind of glove that would be worn with the snug fitting suit of a few years ago but is in harmony with the sports influence on men's apparel.

"Probably the outstanding feature of the glove field is the progress that

---

(opposite) Gloves of kid, hogskin, and buckskin were strongly featured in the 1897 catalog of Sears, Roebuck and Company.

GLOVES AND MITTENS.

We Guarantee Satisfaction in Gloves and Mittens.

In this department we have a complete line for men women and children. We have everything from the cheapest oil tanned working gloves to the finest imported kid gloves.

We buy these goods direct from the manufacturers in immense quantities, and by contracting for the entire output of a factory on a spot cash basis, which we often do, we get the very lowest possible figures at which they can be sold. We are thus enabled to offer them to you at prices heretofore unheard of. We guarantee every pair of gloves or mittens to be just as they are represented in the quotation. **Your money back** if you are not satisfied.

Men's Domestic Kid Gloves.

Sizes, 8 to 10½ Only.

No. 2401.

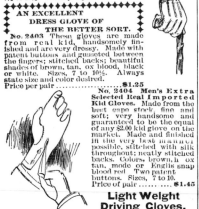

No. 2400 Men's standard quality unlined domestic kid gloves. Smooth carefully selected stock, stitched backs and patent buttons, sizes 8 to 10½ only, dark brown colors only.
Price, per pair.. ....**$0.48**

Special Men's Stock Domestic Kid Glove.

No. 2401

One button with soft dress finish, stitched backs. Good weight and very durable. Black or brown, sizes 8½ to 10½ only.
Price per pair **$0.75**

Men's Fine Kid Dress Gloves.

Sizes 7¼ to 10½.

No. 2402 Men's Imported Stock Kid Gloves, fine dress finish, medium weight with new welt stitched backs and patent buttons. Silk sewed throughout. **All the new shades,** browns, tans and English reds. Sizes. 7½ to 10½. Price per pair........**$0.95**

AN EXCELLENT DRESS GLOVE OF THE BETTER SORT.

No. 2403 These gloves are made from real kid, handsomely finished and are very dressy. Made with patent buttons and gusseted between the fingers; stitched backs; beautiful shades of brown, tan, ox blood, black or white. Sizes, 7 to 10½. Always state size and color desired.
Price per pair **$1.25**

No. 2404

No. 2404 Men's Extra Selected Real Imported Kid Gloves. Made from the best cape stock, fine and soft; very handsome and guaranteed to be the equal of any $2.00 kid glove on the market. Made and finished in the very best manner possible, stitched with silk throughout; neatly stitched backs. Colors, brown, h ox tan, mode or Englis snap blood red. Two patent buttons. Sizes, 7 to 10.
Price of pair **$1.45**

Light Weight Driving Gloves.

No. 2405 Men's Mocha Driving Gloves similar to **castor** buck but softer and smoother. Made with **one** button and out seams. Sizes 7½ to 10½. Browns **and** tans only. **Warranted genuine Mocha.**
Price per pair **$0.95**

No. 2406 Finest Quality Velvet Finish Genuine Mocha Driving Gloves; unlined, with two patent snap buttons; silk sewed throughout and silk covered seams on backs. These gloves are noted particularly for their excellent wearing qualities and soft fine finish. They have long been **the most popular Driving Glove on the market.** They are light weight and fit as perfectly as the finest kid glove. Made in browns and tans only. Sizes 7½ to 10½.
Price per pair..............................**$1.25**

White Cotton Military Gloves.

No. 2407 Men's regular made, set in thumb, White Cotton Military Gloves. Good weight, very durable and neat fitting. Price per Pair.......**$0.12**
Per dozen pairs.............................. **1.35**

Black Berlin Gloves.

No. 2408 Men's Black Berlin Cotton Gloves. Good weight; neat and very durable; elastic adjustable wrists. Price per pair..................**$0.08**
Price per dozen pairs.............. .... **0.85**

Men's Unlined Leather Gloves.

We undersell all competition on this class of goods. We will sell you better made and better wearing gloves for less money than any concern on earth. Our prices are shining marks showing the true road to economy in glove buying.

Mule Skin Gloves.

Here's value for you that will open your eyes. Your pocket book too, if you're wise.

No. 2420 Men's genuine unlined Mule Skin Gloves. Not very pretty, perhaps, but full of real goodness and wearing qualities. Tough and strong yet not stiff or clumsy. Warranted to wear long and wear well. Made with string fastener.
Price per pair ....**$0.23** Per dozen pairs.**$2.45**

No. 2421 Mens' Yellow, Oil Tanned, Heavy, Unlined, Grained Leather Gloves, with cord fasteners. Full size and excellent value. Price, per pair.**$0.25**
Per dozen pairs.............................. **2.70**

Mens' White Napa Goat Gloves.

No. 2422 Mens' Genuine Unlined White Napa Tanned Goat Skin Gloves, light weight, soft and pliable and very tough. Price, per pair........**$0.25**
Per dozen pairs.............................. **2.70**

No. 2423 Mens' Extra Selected White Unlined Napa Tanned Goat Skin Gloves, extra well made and sewed, cord backs and patent string fasteners. Soft and pliable, wide band tops. Price, per pair......................**$0.35**
Per dozen pairs.............................. **3.90**

Olive Napa Tanned Goat Gloves.

No. 2424 The Real Thing. Men's Medium Heavy, Olive Color, Genuine Napa Tanned Goat Skin Gloves. Unlined, made with stitched backs, wide band tops and patent cord fasteners. Soft and pliable and fire proof.
Price, per pair..............**$0.48**

No. 2425 Men's Heavy Unlined Oil Tanned Yellow Grain Leather Gloves, full size with cord stitched backs and band wrists; extra well made and sewed. Patent back string fastener. Clear stock and warranted to wear. Price per pair..........................**$0.39**

No. 2426 Men's Extra Selected Stock Yellow Oil Tanned Unlined Grain Leather Gloves. Heavy weight, strong and dependable. Overstitched welt backs, and broad band wrists. Patent back string fasteners. Price, per pair.........................**$0.45**

No. 2427 An Exceptional bargain. Men's Heavy Oil Tanned Grain Leather Gloves, with patent button fastener, stitched backs, extra well made and sewed. Price per pair..................**$0.50**

Genuine Calfskin Gloves.

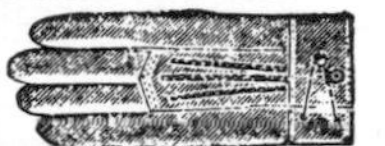

No. 2429 Men's Genuine Oil Tanned Heavy Weight Calfskin Gloves. The sort that have never failed to give real satisfaction. Extra well made and sewed. Patent string fasteners, stitched backs and band wrists. Warranted genuine calfskin. Unlined and clear stock. Price per pair.......**$0.69**

Matamora Hogskin Gloves, 70c.

No. 2430 These Gloves are made from genuine imported Matamora hogskin. Heavy weight and unlined, with patent string fasteners. They are extra well sewed and finely finished and have attained a world wide reputation for durability. They are rapidly taking the place of genuine buckskin. We recommend them very highly.
Price per pair........................ ....**$0.70**

Genuine Peccary Hogskin Gloves.

They Never Wear Out.

No. 2431 Genuine Imported Peccary Hogskin Gloves. The toughest, best wearing and most thoroughly satisfactory gloves made. Made with patent back snap buttons and stitched wrists. Heavy weight and unlined. Actually worth half a dozen pairs of ordinary gloves. Price per pair.....................**$0.98**

Real Unlined Calfskin Gloves.

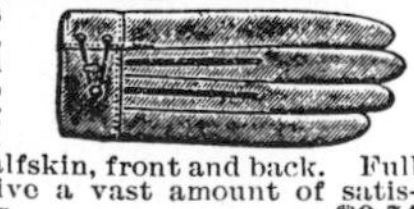

No. 2432 Men's Real Calfskin Gloves. Heavy weight, unlined and oil tanned. Made with patent back string fastener and out seams. Guaranteed all solid calfskin, front and back. Full of goodness and will give a vast amount of satisfaction. Price per pair.........................**$0.74**

Men's Super Stout Driving Gloves.

A line of driving gloves unequalled anywhere on earth. Every pair is made from first quality prime leather and our guarantee stands back of them. You will make no mistake in selecting any of the following numbers. They are positively the best driving gloves made.

No. 2433 Men's Genuine Medium Weight Cape Goat Driving Gloves, with silk stitched welted backs, patent snap buttons, cut seams and silk sewed throughout. Sizes, 8 to 10½. Tan color. Price per pair..... **$0.50**

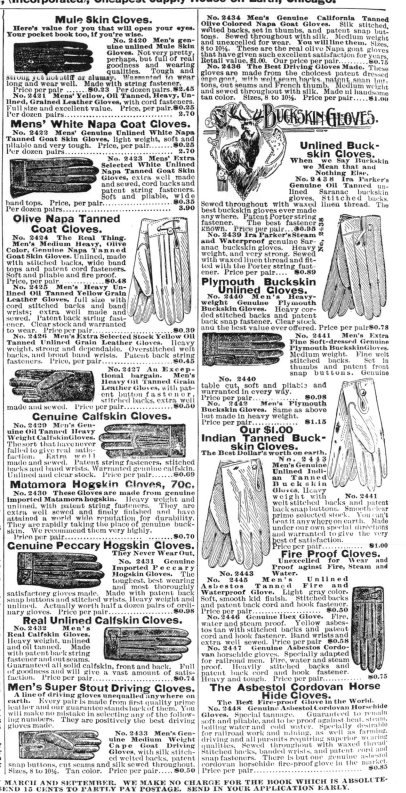

No. 2434 Men's Genuine California Tanned Olive Colored Napa Goat Gloves. Silk stitched, welted backs, set in thumbs, and patent snap buttons. Sewed throughout with silk. Medium weight and unexcelled for wear. **You will line them.** Sizes, 8 to 10½. These are the real olive Napa goat gloves that have given such excellent satisfaction for years, Retail value, $1.00. Our price per pair..........**$0.75**

No. 2436 The Best Driving Gloves Made. These gloves are made from the choicest patent dressed cape goat, with welt seam backs, patent snap buttons, out seams and French thumb. Medium weight and sewed throughout with silk. Made ni handsome tan color. Sizes, 8 to 10½. Price per pair.....**$1.00**

Unlined Buckskin Gloves.

When we Say Buckskin we Mean that and Nothing Else.

No. 2438 Ira Parker's Genuine Oil Tanned unlined Saranac buckskin gloves, Stitched backs. Sewed throughout with waxed linen thread. The best buckskin gloves ever made anywhere. Patent Porter string fastener. The best fastener known. Price per pair...**$0.95**

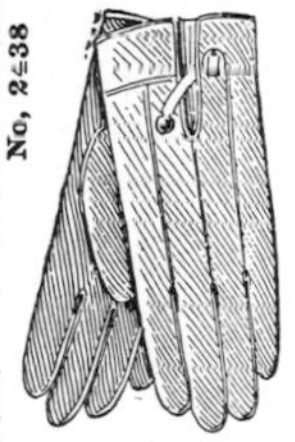

No. 2438

No. 2439 Ira Parker's Steam and Waterproof genuine Saranac buckskin gloves. Heavy weight, and very strong. Sewed with waxed linen thread and fitted with the Porter string fastener. Price per pair.... **$0.89**

Plymouth Buckskin Unlined Gloves.

No. 2440 Men's Heavyweight Genuine Plymouth Buckskin Gloves. Heavy corded stitched backs and patent back snap fastener. Clear stock and the best value ever offered. Price per pair**$0.78**

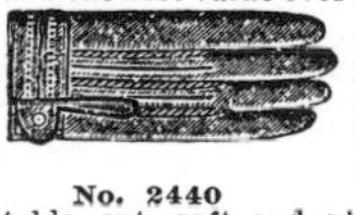

No. 2440

No. 2441 Men's Extra Fine Soft-dressed Genuine Plymouth Buckskin Gloves. Medium weight. Fine welt stitched backs. Set in thumbs and patent front snap buttons. Genuine table cut, soft and pliable and warranted in every way.
Price per pair.............. **$0.98**

No. 2441

No. 2442 Men's Plymouth Buckskin Gloves. Same as above but made in heavy weight.
Price per pair.............. **$1.15**

Our $1.00 Indian Tanned Buckskin Gloves.

The Best Dollar's worth on earth.

No. 2443

No. 2443 Men's Genuine Unlined Indian Tanned Buckskin Gloves. Heavy weight with welt stitched backs and patent back snap buttons. Smooth clear prime selected stock. You can't beat it anywhere on earth. Made under our own special directions and warranted to give the very best of satisfaction.
Price per pair.............. **$1.00**

Fire Proof Gloves.

Unexcelled for Wear and Proof aginst Fire, Steam and Water.

No. 2445 Men's Unlined Asbestos Tanned Fire and Waterproof Glove. Light gray color. Soft, smooth kid finish. Stitched backs and patent back cord and hook fastener.
Price per pair...................... **$0.50**

No. 2446 Genuine Ibex Glove. Fire, water and steam proof. Yellow asbestos tan with stitched backs and patent cord and hook fastener. Band wrists and extra well sewed. Price per pair **$0.58**

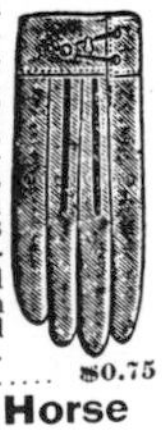

No. 2447 Genuine Asbestos Cordovan horsehide gloves. Specially adapted for railroad men. Fire, water and steam proof. Heavily stitched backs and patent back cord and hook fastener. Heavy and tough. Price per pair............ **$0.75**

The Asbestol Cordovan Horse Hide Gloves.

The Best Fire-proof Glove in the World.

No. 2448 Genuine Asbestol Cordovan Horsehide Gloves. Special tannage. Guaranteed to remain soft and pliable, and to be proof against heat, steam, boiling water and cold water. Specially desirable for railroad work and mining, as well as farming, driving and all pursuits requiring superior wearing qualities. Sewed throughout with waxed thread. Stitched backs, banded wrists, and patent cord and snap fasteners. There is but one genuine asbestol cordovan horsehide fire-proof glove in the market.
Price per pair.............................. **$0.85**

OUR CATALOGUE IS ISSUED REGULARLY IN MARCH AND SEPTEMBER. WE MAKE NO CHARGE FOR THE BOOK WHICH IS ABSOLUTELY FREE. WE REQUEST YOU TO SEND 15 CENTS TO PARTLY PAY POSTAGE. SEND IN YOUR APPLICATION EARLY.

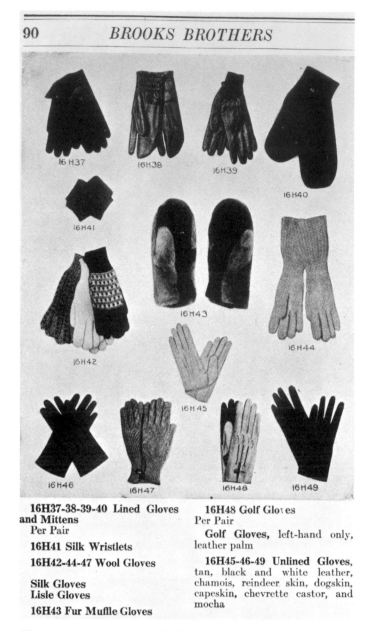

**16H37-38-39-40 Lined Gloves
and Mittens**
Per Pair

16H41 Silk Wristlets

16H42-44-47 Wool Gloves

**Silk Gloves
Lisle Gloves**

16H43 Fur Muffle Gloves

16H48 Golf Gloves
Per Pair

Golf Gloves, left-hand only,
leather palm

16H45-46-49 Unlined Gloves,
tan, black and white leather,
chamois, reindeer skin, dogskin,
capeskin, chevrette castor, and
mocha

*Gloves for dress and sports in 1915 ranged from lined and unlined
leathers to knits and fur.* [COURTESY OF BROOKS BROTHERS, NEW
YORK]

In the thirties, when casual elegance was favored, style-conscious Americans took up the new washable goatskin glove in a pearl shade that was already considered correct in England for wear at weddings and on other formal occasions.

The still-affluent American of the Depression decade, member of a small minority, was an enthusiastic sportsman, and gloves for sportswear assumed importance. Noteworthy were the glove with a tan cape palm and net back that was especially designed for summer motoring and golf and the easy-fitting sports glove, usually of chamois or light kid, that was designed

Glove fashions highlighted accessories in 1937: (top) giraffe palm and reindeer back with whipstitch edges; (down right side) Russian rough-finish bearskin, reindeer gauntlet gloves, and self-lined pigskin gauntlet. From Esquire, *October 1937.*

is being made in the popularizing of buck. Years ago buck was mostly viewed by the consumer as a work proposition, but in recent seasons as a glove for street wear it is making friends rapidly. It is soft and at the same time has the somewhat rough finish in keeping with the sports influence and in contrast with the more formal cape of other seasons" (Feb. 20, 1924, p. 54).

Four years later, darker glove shades

were preferred for fall, and pigskins were enormously popular, buckskin, mocha, and capeskin gloves having declined in popularity. Ultrafashionable was the pigskin glove that looked like a cross between ostrich and chamois, an effect achieved by a process that brushed off the surface of the skin. The side-vented glove was in vogue, and the oversize model with stubby fingers was still being promoted successfully.

The flannel-suited man of 1939 wore natural chamois slip-on gloves of the gauntlet type. From Esquire, *May 1939.*

for hot climates, featuring ventilated holes in the back and sometimes also between the fingers. Skiing was a favorite sport of fashionable men of this period, and finger gloves and mittens with Scandinavian designs were seen at winter resorts both in the United States and in Europe.

In the mid-thirties glove shades were greatly influenced by the shades of men's shoes and hats, and as a result black and very dark brown attained great popularity. Meanwhile, knitted gloves, often worn with a matching muffler, were making significant gains, and the appearance of a new gazelle type of leather was considered one of the "big glove developments in recent years" (*Men's Wear,* Sept. 19, 1934).

"Coarse grain leathers give a fillip to the new array of gloves for Fall," observed *Men's Wear* on Apr. 22, 1936, paying special attention to a pair with a crinkled surface that was said to be mildly suggestive of the walrus traveling bag. "Dolled up with a brass button or in an unusual model, it seems to be one of the answers to the question,

'What's new in gloves?' The soft brown and grey tones of this rugged leather go well with the fleece and tweed overcoats. It has a heft that many men like."

In the upper-price brackets, the chamois glove held sway in a natural shade for dress daytime wear and in plain white for evening wear. Meanwhile, the chamois-lined capeskin glove was finding favor as a warm glove without bulk. Knits continued to gain strength, and both cotton and wool string knits were seen in a range of colors and in many different novelty stitches, wine tones being particularly popular in the novelty stitches. In sports gloves there were checks with small figures, and for the spectator sportsman who preferred a less bulky glove of finer texture there were the softer wools, including cashmere and knitted wools with a bouclé effect.

During the latter half of the thirties glove shades continued to grow paler and paler and, in a sense, more impractical. Fawn, pearl gray, lemon yellow, and London tan were as popular in the United States as they were in England.

Many Americans were "ski-crazy" by the late thirties, and winter sports apparel grew increasingly important. While controversy raged over the suitability of ski pants versus knickers, there was a tremendous variety in hand coverings for winter sports. Though most men preferred gloves with buckskin palms and thumbs, knit wrists, and canvas backs, there were also knitted wool gloves with leather-laced backs and wool shaker-knit mittens, as well as beaver gloves with a lining of baby lamb's wool for general cold-weather wear.

Pigskin continued strong throughout the decade, especially in a new shade described as oatmeal, which was somewhat lighter than the familiar natural color. "Excepting, perhaps, pigskin, there is no national favorite in men's gloves," commented *Men's Wear,* adding: "The situation is quite different from that in the women's field, where the style and color favored in New York circle across the country

and find favor everywhere. In men's gloves, slip-ons are liked in one spot, buttons in another, and snap-fasteners at a third" (Mar. 23, 1938, p. 44).

The British look in men's apparel, with the British blade suit silhouette and the stiff white collar popularized by the new king George VI, had by 1937 swept the United States. In its October issue, *Esquire* paid homage to the British fashion influence, and, along with a suit, a raincoat in English tan, and a homburg with a raw-edge brim, the fashion department showed four pairs of stylish gloves designed to complement this look of casual elegance: a pair with a giraffe palm and reindeer back; a Russian rough-finish bearskin; a reindeer gauntlet in fawn color; and a self-lined pigskin gauntlet.

In April, 1941, noting that "of late more and more men are adopting town clothes and accessories with a definite dress-up connotation" and calling this trend "the return of simple elegance, "*Esquire* sketched an incomparably dapper gentleman in a tri-striped oxford worsted suit and a black homburg, carrying a pair of chamois slip-on gloves.

Men's Wear in 1952 displayed the following selection of glove and muffler combinations:

. . . Wool muffler in natural with yellow and brown check. Pigskin whipstitch slip-ons.

. . . Italian grey silk scarf with red,

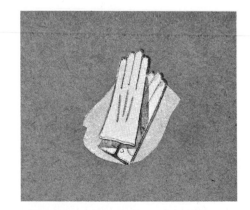

White gloves were obligatory for formal and semiformal evening wear in 1940. Either white kid or mocha was acceptable with the tailcoat; white mocha, in good taste with the dinner jacket. From Esquire, *November 1940.*

Glove fashions of 1956: (across top) a slip-on gauntlet with acrylic lining, a deerskin thong glove (one pull opens, one closes), a snug golf glove with perforated fingers, a hand-stitched mocha glove, and a mocha glove with a chamois lining; (across bottom) a knitted wool-and-angora glove with a leather palm, a capeskin glove with knitted sidewalls, and a leather fishing glove with open fingers and a knitted wristband. Photographed by Rouben Samberg. From Esquire, November 1956.

opens"); and a slip-on gauntlet with an Orlon lining.

Apparel Arts, noting in its May, 1957, issue that "combinations of leather with knit and fur head up the news in glove fashions for fall" and that "leathers are generally softer, more supple, more varied in texture," illustrated these points with photographs of a buttery buckskin glove for dress wear, featuring an elasticized tuck at the wrist, a pinked top, and a stitched rail effect on the back; a blend of raccoon fur, wool, and nylon in natural camel gray knit in a cable pattern for the back and a palm of Dutch goatskin; and a glove of Orlon-Dynel "fur" with a supple goatskin palm.

By the time the sixties arrived, the "hardy perennials" were still as popular as ever. And *Esquire*'s Christmas Gift Guide for 1964 proved it by choosing a pair of gloves in antelope and wool knit. That year *Gentlemen's Quarterly* showed a collection of gloves as noteworthy for their utilitarian appeal as for their undeniable style.

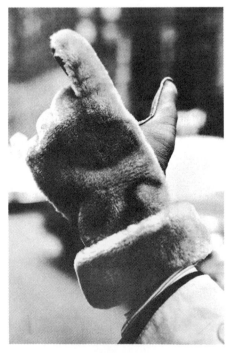

The fur look was achieved in 1957 with an acrylic pile fabric back and turned-back cuff combined with a soft goatskin palm. From Esquire's Apparel Arts, May 1957.

white, and black paisley design. Unlined goatskin cork-colored slip-on, with whipstitch.

. . . Wool challis square in red with orange and black paisley motif. Oatmeal-colored pigskin in swagger stitch.

. . . Lightweight wool muffler with vertical stripes in tan and green. Wool back and fourchettes, pig palm.

. . . Sporty maroon wool set off with white plaid design. Hand-drawn, capeskin back; hand-sewn, tan fourchettes.

. . . Reversible wool and silk in maroon and light blue combinations. Cape lined with 70-denier nylon, raw-edge stitch.

. . . Imported woolen muffler from Scotland in grey and white. Contrasting maroon and blue border. Two-in-one item: nylon shell, wool inside.

In November, 1956, *Esquire* observed: "There's a signally wide choice of new gloves you can tune into the occasion," and proved it with a full-page display: a snug golf glove with perforated fingers and an elasticized palm; a traditional stitched mocha for either daytime or evening dress; a mocha dress glove with a chamois lining; a leather fishing glove with open fingers and a knitted wrist; a goatskin with a Chromspun lining; capeskin slip-ons with knitted sidewalls; a driving glove backed with wool and angora on a leather palm; a soft deerskin thong glove ("one pull closes, one

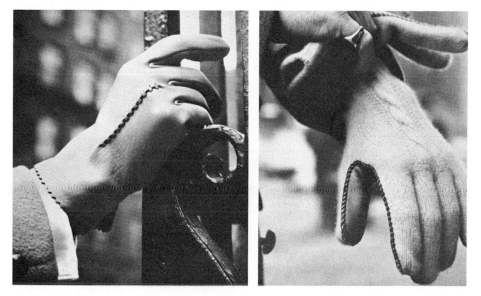

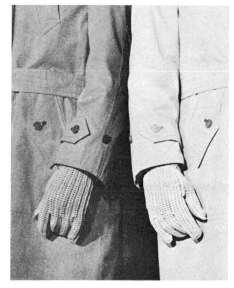

(*left*) *A soft buckskin glove of 1957 had a pinked top and a stitched rail-effect back.* (*right*) *Cable-stitch pattern on the back of a glove of knitted raccoon fur and nylon with a goatskin palm. From* Esquire's Apparel Arts, *May 1957.*

Close-ups of open-stitch knitted gloves with leather palms (1960). Photographed by Emma Gene Hall. From Gentlemen's Quarterly, *April 1960.*

"Hand-in-glove with Winter" was the headline of this feature, for which the editors selected the following:

For fishermen. A pair of tough water-resistant boarskin gloves with rubber strips on the palm and fingers for a nonslip grip and stretch nylon finger sidewalls.

For golfers. Strong, thin cabretta leather elasticized at the wrists, side-walled in stretch nylon and back-lined in wool.

For hunters. A pair of sturdy boar-skin, the palms and fingers of which were reinforced with tough deerskin strips; sidewalls of stretch nylon.

For skiers. A quintet of fur-backed gloves each with soft calfskin palms, permitting a firm grip on the ski poles: black Persian lamb with rabbit lining; beaver, lined in lambskin; leopard, lined in rabbit; natural muskrat, lined in rabbit; and black hair seal, lined in lambskin.

"The ultimate winter sports glove," stated a 1971 Whitehouse and Hardy advertisement in *Gentlemen's Quarterly* for an imported mitten for which mitten warmth and glove mobility were claimed. The copy read: "So different, it's patented. Mitten portion flips back for complete finger freedom; first joint of trigger finger is bared. Inner hands and fingertips chamois-trimmed for firm grip. Lofty wool knit—ideal for hunting, driving, ski-ing, skating, ice fishing, stadium."

By then the Peacock Revolution was a matter of fashion history. Despite the changes it had brought about in menswear in general, however, it had had little effect on the appearance of men's gloves, for the very good reason that for decades gloves had been con-sistently showing a good deal of style. And so the Peacock Revolution not-withstanding, the staples still domi-nated the fashion scene: the knits of wool and cashmere; the glove lined with nylon, fur, or cashmere; and the elegant glove of chamois, pigskin, mocha, or leather.

In September, 1971, *Gentlemen's Quarterly* observed: "In the wake of the frenzy and fury of the fashion revolu-tion ignited on Carnaby Street in the mid-Sixties, all signs point to a wel-come and promising new era in men's fashion during which the individual will stand supreme and his inherent taste, selectivity, independence and sense of dignity will be asserted." It was a movement that the editors heralded as "the return of the gentle-man," and it should go without saying that he wore superb gloves.

Knits

The principles of knitting date back to prehistoric times, the making of fishnets being a basic form of knitting used by almost all primitive peoples. During the time of William the Conqueror, in the eleventh century, hand-knitted garments were popular in England. The first modern knitting machine, however, came into being in 1589, when the Reverend William Lee, of St. John's College, Cambridge, invented and constructed a machine that would knit stockings, and his invention remained in use substantially as he designed it for almost 200 years. In the 1800s improvements in machine knitting came rapidly; by 1863 William Cotton, another Britisher, had perfected a power-driven knitting machine that would shape the fabric as it was knitted, and this was the basis of our modern full-fashioned machines.

1900–1910

In men's apparel in this decade, knits played a restricted role, confined to sweaters, underwear, and swimwear.

Sweaters were worn mostly by the workingman, who chose on the basis of warmth and utility, and a feature common to all sweaters was the knitted wristband. Some sweaters during this period were referred to as jerseys because sailors of the Isle of Jersey wore a heavy knitted type.

The following sweater copy is taken from a Sears, Roebuck and Company catalog of this period:

Men's and Boys' Sweaters

Open the pores. Nothing will open them quite so well as a SWEATER. No garment in the whole world has ever attained such universal popularity as the sweater of today. All sorts and conditions of mankind are numbered among its devotees. And our sweaters have more special features and are made from finer yarns than any other line of sweaters known.

Among the sweaters sketched in the Sears catalog were heavyweight knit cardigan jacket sweaters in both single- and double-breasted models, the latter with satin-faced lapels and both featuring ribbed elastic wrists; extra heavy knit, all-wool turtlenecks, with or without contrasting stripes on the collar; large sailor-collared sweaters of heavy wool with two contrasting

The extra-long pullover with a double-V pattern across the chest was worn in 1902 by Malcolm D. Whitman, ex-singles tennis champion of the United States. [COURTESY OF CULVER PICTURES, INC., NEW YORK]

The high-neck sweater with a double-rolling collar, forerunner of the modern turtleneck style, the V-neck sweater, and the jersey coat sweater were the knitwear styles shown in this 1909 advertisement of R. H. Macy & Co., New York. [NEW YORK PUBLIC LIBRARY PICTURE COLLECTION]

stripes on the collar; medium-weight cottons with turtlenecks; and a "new 'Bike' sweater" of heavy wool, heavy ribbed and full-fashioned with what was described as "the new style shirt collar." In solid colors with white stripes on collar, cuffs, and skirt, this, according to the catalog copywriter, was a sweater "preferred by all the leading wheelmen."

The most popular sweater colors were black, maroon, and navy, although knitted cottons for spring wear were often in shades of tan, cream, and ecru.

Insofar as underwear was concerned, lightweight ribbed-cotton union suits were heartily recommended for year-round wear. Knit of good-grade cotton yarn with smooth, flat-locked seams throughout, this cream-colored underwear with long or short sleeves was a bargain at 72 cents. And for only 45 cents a man could order from the Sears, Roebuck catalog a ribbed, form-fitting undershirt of fine combed Egyptian cotton with pearl buttons and finished seams, "knit to fit the form perfectly and not show a wrinkle." A matching pair of drawers cost another 45 cents.

In this decade, when a man liberated himself from the discomfort of a summer suit made of a heavy fabric

SPORTING DEPARTMENT 39

16C34 Sweaters, plain and mixed wool

16C35-36 Wool Half-Hose and Stockings, in plain and fancy mixtures, for general country wear

16C37 Scotch Wool Garters for golf hose

16C38 Golf Grip Mittens, Scotch wool

Wool Cuffs or Wristlets

16C39 Scarfs and Mufflers of Shetland and Angora Wool, plain and fancy

16C40 Norwegian Skiing Hose, suitable also for tobogganing and other winter sports

16C41 Canadian Wool Caps and Helmets, in various designs of plain and fancy Shetland and Angora Wool

16C42-43 Shetland and Angora Sweaters and Waistcoats.
Light Shetlands
Heavy Shetlands
Angora

like flannel or alpaca and took to the beach, he wore an often riotously striped knee-length jersey swimsuit, a modified version of which was to make its appearance many decades later, thus proving that fashion need not necessarily be functional.

1910–1920

During World War I the khaki-colored sweater was an important item in the wardrobe of the doughboy. In addition, many a mother, wife, and sweetheart posted her fighting man a sweater she had knitted with loving care. When the war was finally over, the long-sleeved and sleeveless wool sweaters carried over to young America's postwar wardrobe, now in a range of popular colors that were a welcome relief after the drabness of khaki.

As a result of his rigorous training, the former serviceman was in top physical condition and ready to engage in outdoor sports. Golf attracted him, and unlike the older man who often wore a sports jacket on the links, this younger golfer preferred pullovers and coat sweaters. Meanwhile, the most affluent Americans were discovering the joys of skiing at fashionable European winter resorts, where sweaters were often ablaze with color. During the next decade the American passion for active sports would catapult the once primarily utilitarian knits into the world of fashion.

1920–1930

By the early twenties golf and golf apparel had come of age. The leading professional golfers were wearing knickers of tweed, linen, or flannel with knitted cardigan jackets. These

Highlights of knitwear in 1915 included pullover and coat sweaters, and waistcoats in Shetland and angora wool. Also shown were knitted mufflers, socks, and headwear. [COURTESY OF BROOKS BROTHERS, NEW YORK]

men served as fashion leaders for the weekend golfers.

In 1923 a member of the American golf team, playing on English links for the Amateur Championship, set a new fashion by wearing a pair of silk waterproof knickers topped by a wool sweater whose neckline was knitted in a thick ribbed stitch. An analysis of golf apparel worn by 200 well-dressed men on fashionable metropolitan links, made by *Men's Wear* the following year, revealed that brown sweaters accounted for 48 percent of the sweaters seen, with the white sweater noted on another 20 percent.

"Novelties in imported knit goods a riot of color" was the headline of a fashion article in *Men's Wear* (May 7, 1924). "New arrivals will tickle the tired Business Man—Flaming Youth will be pleased," promised the subheadline. "Color effects that might stop traffic if worn on the busy streets of cities but quite all right on the fairway are a feature of imported lines of sweaters and golf hose," observed the writer. And as if bright colors were not enough, the designs were startling as well, many inspired by what the writer termed "the futuristic school of art." Furthermore, no longer were golf clothes emanating principally from the British Isles; now Norway and Spain were also contributing to colorful golf hose.

Illustrating this article were photographs of sweaters featuring three-fourths-inch checks and of others with cross-stripes in a zigzag pattern. Matching designs in hose and sweater were not uncommon at this time, and particularly popular was a diamond pattern—perhaps a sweater with a blue diamond pattern on a mauve ground, worn with hose of black and gray diamonds on a gray ground.

"Novelty is still the object of most producers of knitwear," wrote a fashion writer in 1926, also noting that smaller and more intricate patterns in restrained colors were the rule in sweaters and golf hose that year. Illustrative of this trend to smaller patterns was a Scotch cashmere sweater with an allover design in brown and tan. At the same time everything from animals and maps to historic buildings were forming the designs in woven mufflers, one of which showed the spires of Westminster Abbey in two shades of purple.

The V-neck pullover with sleeves greatly outnumbered all other sweater styles in the late twenties, although the V-neck sleeveless had its devotees, too, particularly since the Prince of Wales, the greatest fashion leader of the era, favored it for wear on the links.

The tremendous fashion influence of the smartly dressed professional golfer was not fully recognized. As a reporter for *Men's Wear* observed, "If Walter Hagen wears plain black golf hose in the National Open Golf Championship, there are going to be a lot of professional and amateur golfers all over these large United States who will want plain black golf hose" (June 24, 1925). Hagen, possibly the most dudish of all players, was sketched while resting on the green, wearing a blue pullover, gray knickers, black-and-white vertical-zigzag hose, and white buckskin shoes.

To one fashion reporter it seemed that the paucity of sweater patterns had brought into vogue the most brilliant shades of blue, green, and other colors. In the forefront were Prussian blue, royal blue, copen blue, pale green, apple green, and bottle green. Some idea of the popularity of the solid colors was reflected by the fact that 83 percent of the most noted golfers were wearing patternless sweaters. In golf hose, too, the passion for solid color began to express itself, with blue and green the most popular colors; the avant-garde dresser moved toward new shades such as red, maroon, garnet, oxblood, and burgundy.

"College men cannot be expected to be dressed up in their 'Sunday best' at all times," wrote a fashion journalist in *Men's Wear* (Nov. 21, 1928), reasoning that the informal life of the campus called for more informal wear. "So it is little wonder that they are outfitted a good deal of the time," he noted, "even in the dead of the winter season, as if they were about to venture forth upon the golf course. Sweaters and golf hose are two items that he must have in his list of clothing." Taking a turn around the more fashion-conscious campuses of the nation, this writer observed that the best-dressed men at Princeton and Yale in 1928 were wearing solid-color, patternless pullovers with crew necks. "Tans, greys, bluish greys, rust-browns, canary-yellow, blues, and some greens are meeting with great favor at New Haven and Princeton. One of the new features of the crew-neck pullovers is that the back of the opening is cut lower than formerly. Not a few of them are finished with a 'rope edge,' which insures long wear and adds to the smartness of the style. Soft brushed cashmeres and brushed angoras are most popular and the heavy shaker-knit sweaters are less in evidence than formerly. Of course, the wearers of varsity letters wear nothing but the heavy shaker-knit style. A few of the men favor loosely knit sweaters in the shell-stitch pattern."

"The golf hose favored by these men," he went on to say, "continues to be of the solid colored variety, and the increase in popularity of pastel tones has brought about a decline of plain black hose. Yellowish beige, bluish-grey, blue, blue-brown, dark brown, and various shades of grey are the outstanding colors. A small number of men are to be seen wearing large patterned Argyle hose."

The crew-neck sweater was by far the favorite on the New England campuses, with most undergraduates favoring it in the chain-knit models. Golf hose, meantime, was divided between large patterns and solid colors. On the campuses of the Middle West, bright solid colors in sweaters and golf hose dominated. Light blue, tan, bluish gray, gray, rich brown, rust, and deep red were the leaders. At the Southern colleges, the heavy black or dark blue shaker-knit crew neck was still important, although lighter-weight pullovers, in round or crew-neck styles, were standard.

Novelties in knit goods continued strong throughout the remainder of this decade. Throw-over mufflers that matched sweaters and often knitted caps as well were being sold at exclusive shops for winter sports, and they were especially popular with the wealthy Americans who frequented St. Moritz each winter.

A fashion report filed from St. Moritz had this to say: "Never before has there been such a riot of color at the Swiss winter resorts as is notable at the present moment. I am writing from St. Moritz, and before arriving here I visited Mürren, Davos and Caux and without hesitation I can say that not only Englishmen, who, here at St. Moritz, are certainly in the minority, but visitors from all over the world, more particularly America, are calmly wearing patterns and colors that a few years ago would have caused exclamation. No doubt this tendency has arisen from the Fair Isle vogue. Here 80 per cent of the men are wearing Fair Isle jerseys, the most popular being those having a ground color of tan, brown, grey, the new blue, or white. Where jerseys are concerned there is but one kind—the pull on over the head.

"The importance of knitted wear cannot be over-emphasized. Another new development this season is the popularity of the knitted cap in what is termed a fisherman or jelly-bag shape, worn flopping over the side of the head and finished with a tassel. The American contingent here is very large; it is the biggest supporter of the bright caps and stockings and hence there is little doubt that these very caps will eventually make their appearance on the playgrounds of the United States. Mufflers are also varied in color, while knitted gloves are to be seen having the gauntlets finished in the most absurd colors and patterns imaginable" (*Men's Wear*, Feb. 6, 1924).

Covering St. Moritz, *Men's Wear* photographed Captain Duff-Taylor, one of England's ice-skating experts, wearing a Fair Isle sweater in a cream, pale blue, and yellow design, along with a matching cap (Feb. 10, 1926). And still another skater was photographed in a beige Fair Isle jersey that carried a design of chocolate, yellow, and purple, his cap in the same colors and design. Skiing socks, meanwhile, were most often seen in brilliant scarlet or lemon yellow. And just about everybody at St. Moritz wore brightly colored knitted mufflers, with one end hanging down the back and the other down the front.

Tennis was growing increasingly popular during this decade, and the much-photographed professional and amateur players had considerable fashion impact. Coming to and from the court, the more stylish player often wore over his white shirt and flannel slacks a heavy white cable-stitch sweater, usually with club colors set in around the neck and waist.

The late 1920s also saw the debut of a new tennis shirt, a white knit with turned-down collar and half-length sleeves, that arrived on the scene in fashionable Palm Beach after success on the French Riviera. "The characteristics of the shirt," wrote a fashion reporter, "are that it is pure white, knitted—sometimes of cashmere and sometimes of silk and wool—with a soft, close texture, and with the very desirable absorbent features; it has a turned down collar, which may be buttoned at the neck or left open, this front opening extending down the front about five inches from the top button, and usually closing with two buttons" (*Men's Wear*, Feb. 22, 1928). In short, this new tennis shirt was not unlike the shirt used for polo in the United States and in England, and when such fashion notables as Anthony J. Drexel Biddle, Jr., and Prince Chlodwig von Hohenlohe-Schillingsfürst were photographed wearing it on the tennis courts of the Everglades Club at Palm Beach, its future was assured. Within a year American mills were turning it out in a range of solid colors as well as the original white, and not only for tennis but for golf, too, as well as for out-of-door sports in general.

During the twenties the knit tie gained popularity among fashion-conscious men of all ages. A fashion survey taken at Princeton University in 1925, for example, revealed that the best-dressed students on this very stylish campus leaned strongly toward colored shirts and red-and-blue crocheted ties. As late as 1929, Yale men were showing a preference for an expensive, crunchy, hand-crocheted tie with spaced diagonal stripes. In 1926 a fashion reporter noted that, despite a growing tendency toward colorful, exotic, even weird neckwear, customers were still willing to pay $6 for the broad knitted tie, a fashion staple, particularly if the colors were bright.

In swimwear, meanwhile, men were attracted by vivid colors as well as scantier suits. The two-piece bathing suit appeared on the more fashionable beaches, and screen star Ramon Navarro was photographed in a horizontal-striped knit bathing shirt with separate blue flannel trunks. Far scantier was a new one-piece suit that stopped high on the thigh, and it was in this model that the more brilliant colors were displayed. The entire suit might be solid purple, or pale blue, or even yellow or scarlet; sometimes the top and trunks were of contrasting colors, orange and black being a favorite combination. But the skimpiest bathing suit of them all was a new "legless" model that gave the bather the appearance of not wearing trunks but merely a somewhat longer than customary top. Yet, despite the new brevity, one note carried over from the swimsuit of earlier decades: stripes. The striped bathing suit—often bold prison stripes—was more popular than ever during the late 1920s.

Sears, Roebuck continued to promote sweaters aggressively and, in 1927, featured a heavy single-breasted coat style with a large shawl collar and the shaker knit with knit-in pockets, as well as pullovers in plaid patterns or jacquard designs for wear on the golf course. Toward the end of this decade, however, the leather blouse for sports-

---

(*opposite*) *Patterns were featured in the pullover and coat-style sweaters offered in the 1927 catalog of Sears, Roebuck and Company.*

Rich-Colorful-Handsome
Unusual Values

A $4.98 EACH

B $3.98 EACH

C $3.39 EACH

See Opposite Page for Descriptions

F $2.19 EACH

G $1.89 EACH

D $2.35

Quality Mufflers

H $3.98

J $2.98

E $7.95 EACH

K $1.45

L $1.25

M $1.79 EACH

wear was giving the sweater some competition. Yet, as a *Men's Wear* fashion writer saw it, the leather blouse had a style limitation that operated against it: "The uniformity of countless suede jackets that all look just about alike handicaps its style favor in a sport where the general dress is colorful and varied. Golfers now know that the suede jacket, while it serves admirably for certain purposes, by no means completes all requirements. The leather jacket cannot be styled with lines that can be put into a fabric sports jacket, for when that is done, the freedom of motion is curtailed. The suede jacket requires a flannel shirt or a sweater under it, otherwise perspiration cannot escape and cold is the result. For these reasons the sweater is returning to its former favor."

"A factor that is holding back sweater business," he continued, "is the vogue of plain colors and modest effects. The customer is not intrigued with much that appeals to the eye in these plain numbers. In the sweater lines for men, small patterns continue to be the feature. The model wanted usually will depend upon the type and age of the man. Young men want the full sleeved pullover sweater with crew neck for general wear. Slightly older men favor the buttoned jacket or cardigan. Many of the latter are coming through in the sleeveless variety."

As this writer viewed the situation, the high colors and conspicuous patterns of the sweaters of a few years earlier would be a welcome relief from the conservative sweaters most men were wearing in the late 1920s. "Novelty is missing from the average showing of sweaters for next spring," observed another writer in the winter of 1928; he also noted that matched sets of golf hose and sweater were popular. And it was here in the matched set that he thought one would find the reason for the general toning-down of sweater patterns: "Loud stockings have not been highly regarded of late excepting in certain plaids which are almost standard. With plainer stockings, the matched idea calls for plainer effects in sweaters."

Despite its conservative air, however, the sweater had bested the suede blouse, and as golf and tennis were to become even more popular during the next decade, a sweater wardrobe would be essential to any man who hoped to be thought of as a stylish sportsman.

1930–1940

A fashion journalist reporting from Scotland in *Men's Wear* on November 9, 1932, made the following predictions: "Novelties in knitted wear that will make history by 1933, comprising pastel shades; new weaves, created on new frames or machinery; entirely new models embodying two different stitches, for instance the top in a basket, mesh or one of the new open-work effects, the lower part ribbed, and changes in the shoulders."

Then, concentrating on the present, this writer went on to report: "One leading manufacturer is about to launch for next spring a 'floating stitch' on golf hose. This is a new idea, a closely knitted ground on top of which appear individual stitches in a bright marl. Here also did I see the pattern of the stocking extending lower down on the heel so that the self or mixture part of the foot does not show above the shoe. Another development is splicing at the heel so as to give extra strength.

"Reviewing what one or two of the leading Scottish knitted manufacturers are producing for American and English high grade firms, I would comment upon a fisherman's jersey in which, as often as not, the shoulders and yoke are of a tight basket stitch, contrasting with the lower part of the garment, which is generally ribbed, the neck welted with an elastic stitch.

"A new slipover made of reversible three and one rib, then a space, of three reverse stitches, I am illustrating, but I wish I could show the actual garment. And there's a new slipover for tennis with a semi-open neck, that will capture the business because of its individual touch.

"A real novelty pullover consists of

The turtleneck sweater was recommended with knickers, a belted jacket, and a beret for skating. From Esquire, *January 1934.*

the old chain stitch thrown on a gauze ground which has the suggestion of being transparent. Rather a thick ply or strand of wool is used for the chain, producing a beautifully soft handle, yet light in weight, and evolved from excellent pastel shades, both self and in shot effects, the chain sometimes in marl mixtures.

"Then I saw an eyelet stitch worked out on a ground of light pastel tone with a marl of darker shade running over it, bringing out mixtures of colour combinations that I have never seen before.

"Scottish hosiery manufacturers are certainly anticipating a revival in trade next year. I often accuse them of lethargy, but in this case I must praise their activity."

In 1934 *Esquire* showed the golfing outfit then being worn by the Prince of Wales: maroon-and-white hounds-tooth knitted shirt, dark gray tweed knickers, solid-color wool hose of wine red, and black-and-white moccasins. (The fashion department pointed out that the hose carried plain white tops, "another idea of English origin," and then went on to advise the reader that "it is better not to match up the golf hose and the polo shirt in both patterns and color—they may well match in one or the other, but not in both.") By this time the Prince of Wales had become such a fashion barometer on both sides of the Atlantic that *Esquire* in this decade grew almost self-conscious regarding the frequency with which his name appeared in its fashion pages (e.g., ". . . being worn by the Prince of Wales—in case you care").

That same year, 1934, the editors took a long look at what the golfers in Palm Beach were wearing and decided it was worthy of a full-color, full-page sketch. The copy read: "If any sports kit could be said to have approached the status of a uniform at Palm Beach last winter, it was this combination of navy blue polo shirt and tan slacks. This was out in front and off by itself, in the favor of well dressed men of all ages. It was one of those races where there just wasn't any second."

By 1935 golf clothes for the Florida season had, in the opinion of some fashion writers, become pretty much standardized. "A knitted shirt, a pair of slacks, sturdy shoes, woolen half hose, a cap or hat, and a pullover on chilly days comprise the most popular ensemble. The knitted sports shirt is an odds-on favorite. It's a wool jersey, solid color or white, [and] has short sleeves and a buttoned collar.

"On cool days solid color cashmere, Shetland and shell-stitch alpaca pullovers are much worn. Tan, yellow, light blue and white are the prevailing colors. White cable stitch pullovers in sleeveless models have been taken up by fashionably dressed golfers. Heavy border stripes at the bottom and V-neck opening introduce accent colors" (*Men's Wear*, Mar. 20, 1935).

Autumn neckwear in 1934 reflected the trend toward rough crocheted silk and knitted wools. Argyle plaids, heretofore seen only in socks and sweaters, were now turning up in ties of bouclé or a wide-wale twill silk outstanding for rough texture and brilliant color. One neckwear firm cooperated with a sock house to introduce crochets that had backgrounds matching certain hosiery styles.

About this time *Esquire* also took a look at the plenitude of knit goods available and decided to feature a whole page just for "the knit goods addict." Among the styles shown were

The Fair Isle sweater, which had been made fashionable by the Prince of Wales in the 1920s, was revived for golf wear in 1935. From Esquire, *March 1935.*

Four distinctive knitwear fashions: (diagonally from upper right to lower left) a red cord mesh half-sleeve pullover; a natural-shade mesh shirt with a blue-bordered boat neck; a blue mesh shirt with a white-bordered boat neck; and a plaid cotton mesh shirt with a buttoned front.

The versatility of knits in 1956 is shown here in a varied sampling of styles, colors, and textures.

(left to right) The herringbone polo shirt of lightweight wool was worn with gray slacks for golf in 1936. From Esquire, *January 1936. The turtleneck cashmere dickey was suggested for wear under a tweed jacket for riding and golf. From* Esquire, *April 1935. The multiple patterns of the Fair Isle sweater appealed to the golfer in 1935. From* Esquire, *March 1935. The horizontal-striped cotton basque shirt with a crew neck and three-quarter-length sleeves was popular on the Riviera. From* Esquire, *July 1937.*

Knits

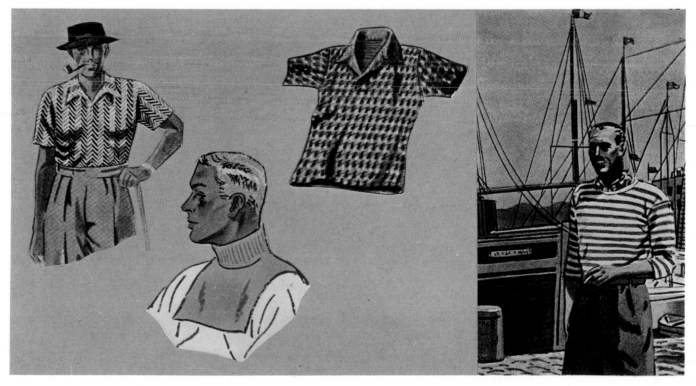

A gray turtleneck pullover with a deep roll was worn by a country gentleman with his glen plaid cheviot suit. From Esquire, *March 1936.*

"not meant, as the picture might wrongly suggest, to match the houndstooth check golf hose."

The next year *Esquire*'s fashion staff focused on the early-season sailor, suggesting for small-sailboat wear an outfit consisting of a heavy-knit crewneck sweater, gray flannel slacks, and white jai alai shoes. Another fashion publication that same year showed a solid-color knit shirt worn with gray flannel slacks as a comfortable and popular ensemble for deck sports; and a white knitted cotton slip-on shirt worn with linen or cotton gabardine shorts, touted as "another active sports combination, good for hot days."

In 1936 *Men's Wear,* reporting on the sweater schedule for the fall, commented: "From the style point of view, the coat types are outselling the pullovers, and on the former, slide fasteners outsell the buttoned models. Sport backs are absent in the top ranges but predominate in the lower brackets. Fancy stitches are helping to create mounting sales. Various rib effects are strong. There are inklings here and there of patterns coming back into the realm of brisk-moving style. Blends of alpaca or mohair with worsted are present, and camel's hair is the latest entry for style honors in the better grades." Yet, pullovers were not without their style vagaries. *Men's Wear* noted, "The conventional V-neck with fairly narrow opening is the best selling style in the better grades. In the intermediate and the lower levels, the crew-neck or round-neck styles are the leaders. The pullover with the 'gaucho' neck and collar is generally shown. The sport-back rage has been so strong that pullovers are also being livened with a half belt, possibly a yoke and lots of pleats and shirring. Turtlenecks are present, sometimes just for tone: one firm is stressing a low turtleneck for horseback riding and skiing."

By 1937 the cardigan was firmly entrenched as a smart fashion, and *Esquire* trained its camera on a particularly handsome example, a cashmere cardigan with chamois front. The pale shades and the general paucity of pat-

a new short sleeveless cardigan with a close-knitted sports belt; a polo shirt sporting contrasting collars and cuffs; a yellow knitted waistcoat; a silk-and-wool shirt for golf and country, with striped broadcloth collar; a solid-color silk-and-wool polo shirt and three crocheted ties; a pair of hand-knit polka-dot wool hose; a light gray short sleeveless sweater of India cashmere with contrasting trim; and a lightweight sweater, in small checks,

terns that had characterized sweaters for several seasons came to an end in 1938, when new sweaters showed plenty of bright color and novel textures for spring and summer. Bright blues and brownish reds came to the fore, and oxblood red was an important dark shade. One reporter summed up the trend as follows:

"Many innovations in textures reveal a strong sportswear character. A principal type is the tweed effect. This is knitted worsted, showing a wide wale or herringbone that may or may not be marked with a large oversquare. Another is the hand-knit effect which appears in different versions of all-over self patterns. Self panel stripes, produced by variations of ribs, have excellent possibilities. Honeycomb is another means of reflecting this tendency.

"Sweaters made of two different fabrics are big features. The variety of fabrics used for the fronts of sweaters is great indeed, yet classifications show some degree of concentration as to finish and texture. Prominent is the use of summer suitings. There is a big range of sweaters that have woven rayon fronts and knitted sleeves and backs. Another capitalizes [on] the publicity given to loden cloth by showing sweaters fronted with this fabric, which incidentally is light in weight. Woven tweeds and lightweight worsted are shown in solid colors, checks and plaids."

Leather and knit, once rivals, had by now made peace and were turning up in bi-fabric styles. Men were also growing increasingly aware of the fact that certain sweater fabrics had a more pleasing touch than others, with the result that the mohair and zephyr yarns were in demand for their softness, and camel's hair was making a formidable comeback. Luxurious alpacas from Austria and soft cashmeres were also enormously popular.

Shaker knits were making a strong comeback, too, sporting various chest and shoulder stripes as well as school initials and insignia. Closely allied with the heavy shakers were the genuine cable effects. Worn by such tennis

The collarless cardigan of 1938 (right) was a knitted wool in a tweed effect, with patch pockets, a four-button front, and single buttons at the cuffs. The other man in the illustration wore a classic cable-stitch sweater. From Esquire, *September 1938.*

luminaries as Bill Tilden in white with deep-color border stripes, the new versions were being seen in a range of ground colors. But the jacket sweater was king, often with four patch pockets and slide fastener and some-

times with a belt. And a very new style, first seen along the Riviera, was collarless with a three-button front and plain back. Pullovers continued to be most popular in the crew-neck style, and a combination of a sleeveless pullover worn with a jacket was still very much in vogue. The color range in sweaters was more extensive than it had been for several seasons, with the green sweater leading in shades from dark Dartmouth green to lovats. Red was also gaining favor, especially in cross-stripings of shakers.

An American expert scanning English knitwear for 1939 reported that it was more colorful and unusual than in past seasons. And, in his opinion, the biggest news of all was "the revival of the Fair Isle in a new guise." As an illustration, he showed a sweater from the West End men's furnishing shop that supplied the King and other members of the royal family. Cut like a waistcoat with sleeves, it had a white ground and a design in blue and a subdued red. Still another sweater cited as "an outstanding example of progress" was a beach sweat smock created to fill two wants: covering and a towel. Made of an absorbent cotton, it had elastic ribbing at the waist, cuffs, and neck, boasted a very wide armhole, and came in such colors as scarlet, royal blue, navy, yellow, white, and ecru.

Another new style was the "pig's whisker," made of a rough-handling wool. This was developed in a pullover with lumberjack checks, in navy and brick, black and brick, royal and black, and tan and light green—all on a cream ground. A beautifully shaped sweater, it boasted a shawl collar and was shown with matching stockings that had a Lastex top for support.

Meantime, as *Esquire* noted in 1939, there was no longer anything very daring about the degree of undress seen at the nation's beaches. Among examples it showed were a pair of very brief knitted swimming trunks in a herringbone pattern; lightweight knitted alpaca trunks; and another knitted pair in a smart peppermint-stick pattern. Coarse-textured materials in knitted trunks, resembling hand-knit effects, were also very much in the mode, and on the West Coast the younger men were wearing them in extremely abbreviated styles with low waistlines.

1940–1950

Just as knitwear was gathering new momentum through a plethora of fresh colors and patterns, the advent of World War II halted further innovations. But not until *Esquire* had noted that color had finally splashed over into tennis clothes: "If there were any phase of men's attire that time could not wither, you'd think it would be the good old tennis outfit—white shirt, white flannels, white socks and sneakers, and there you are. But no you aren't. The world does move and the outfit does change. The wielder sketched here wears a white knitted cotton shirt with blue border stripes, side-striped white cotton gabardine shorts, plain white belt, plain socks and blue canvas shoes with white rubber soles. The sweater is a white cable-stitch type, and the white tennis cap has a green under-visor."

Before the fashion blackout, *Esquire* also had time to cast an admiring glance in the direction of the *après-ski* clothes that had become increasingly important. The fashion staff selected a colorful crew-neck, long-sleeved sweater in a red, white, and blue diamond pattern with ribbed shoulders, topped off with a blue silk

The "bold look" keystone pullover accented the chesty effect with a broad bar across the front. From Esquire, *May 1949.*

polka-dot muffler, worn with matching full-length hose; a coarse-yarn ski sweater, worn with a tartan wool shirt, tooled Western belt with sterling silver buckle, and yellow knitted socks with soft-leather soles; an after-ski jacket of dark blue whipcord, worn with matching trousers, a yellow turtleneck jersey, and fleece-lined moccasins; and a reindeer-design sweater, worn with a tartan flannel shirt, bluish-gray gabardine trousers, and fleece-lined, slide-fastened bootlets of brown buckskin.

Thereafter, the magazine's fashion pages were practically bereft of knits until the end of the war and the introduction of its fashion-coordinated "bold look" and the new bold look sweater with a keystone neck. "It's as new as a fin-tailed Cadillac—as different as modern design," wrote the caption writer. "Its opening is keystone-shaped, cut low and wide in the front to make your shirt look smarter—your collar and tie neater. If you want a sweater that gives you a broad-shouldered, deep-chested look, a sweater that does things for your face as well as your figure—this is it!" Illustrating this article was "the arête," a suitably bold sweater of ribbed wool, "as rugged-looking as the Rockies." Not surprisingly, bold look sweaters turned up both with sleeves and sleeveless.

1950–1960

The early 1950s marked one of the most conservative fashion periods of this century—everywhere, that is, except in sportswear. Here the "man in the gray flannel suit" remained colorfully extroverted and, more than ever, partial to those sweaters that had the feel of luxury. The sleeveless V-neck cashmere pullover, for example, was not only warm and good-looking but soft to the touch. *Esquire* showed one that was the color of country butter, and along with it a pair of matching argyle socks.

Men's Wear in 1952 noted that the trend in neckwear leaned toward sparsely patterned grounds in rather neat effects, but the really big news in neckwear during this conservative period was the emergence of the new Dacron knits, which were being advertised as washable, nonwrinkle, and no-stretch. Later in this decade, when men began to dress again with more personality, the knitted tie, usually a crochet style, was still the most popular tie on American college campuses.

By 1952 there was no doubt that sweaters were even more popular than they had been before the war. Coat styles were still leaders and were now dressier than ever through chest stripes and panels that until now had been seen almost exclusively on ski sweaters and other pullover types. In 1955 *Esquire* conducted a sweater survey and printed a full-page report of its findings:

Cashmere is wool from beneath the hair of Himalayan, Kashmir or Tibetan goat, and is probably the softest, most elegant substance in a man's wardrobe. Lamb's Wool, on the other hand, comes from the lamb, and while some of the wooliest of these are grazing away in the Hebrides, a good lamb's-wool sweater can come from almost any place in the world.

Alpaca wool has joined the luxury class more recently in sweaters, and is quite a favorite in international sports circles. Man-made fibers such as Orlon, Dacron, Nylon, Acrilan, Vicara and Dynel—all of them warm and exceptionally long wearing—are softer and more richly textured than ever before; they have the additional advantage of retaining their shape through innumerable washings and long wear.

The V-neck classic is a steady favorite still for tie and collar; in plain colors, and sans sleeves, it is an attractive alternate for your waistcoat under casual suits. In bright patterns, it serves as a wind-breaking companion to open-necked sports shirts. The crew-neck pullover is an indispensable item in the undergraduate's wardrobe. This year the cardigan coat sweater emerges from the sports world with a new, low opening that keeps it unseen under a buttoned suit jacket, and allows it to act as a decorative vest when the jacket hangs open. Another low-cut style that doubles as a vest is the European pullover surplice that also appears with low batwing sleeves for active sportswear. News on turtlenecks this year is that some of them can be rolled one way for one color and reversed for another color. And the rolled-shawl-collar pullover that came

for the well-knit man

Styles for the well-knit man: (left) white group stripes running lengthwise on the sleeves of a navy blue pullover of lightweight wool; (above) a blue-and-white cross-stripe with blue inset and sleeves; (center) a blue-and-red diagonal-jacquard jacket with cuffed three-quarter sleeves; (below) a sleeveless pullover with Fair Isle trim at the neck and waist. From Esquire, March 1954.

to us from Scotland a few years back is now firmly established in the sportsman's and vacationer's wardrobe, worn buttoned at the throat or open like a sports shirt.

Since we are in the midst of a high-color era, almost anything goes: bright reds, blues and even pinks turn up in all these styles, along with softer shades of grey, green, gold, beige and ruddy brown. For any kind of casual wear, you have your choice of subtle stripes, bold Argyles, space figures, checks and allover patterns. For business, plain hues of muted grey, green, blue or brown, keyed to your suit color, are pleasantly conservative.

A word about knits: There are four basic stitchings, and they have a great deal to do with the weight of your sweater. Flat-knit sweaters are the lightest—that is

treated like jersey. Shaker knits and rib stitches are considerably heavier (among rib-knit sweaters you can now find horizontal patterns—interesting to look at, with the same, spring resilience as the vertical rib). Shell-stitch models have a lacy effect that is especially handsome in more formal, alpaca sweaters.

The shell-stitch alpaca had become the leading golf sweater. Professional players wore it on the links, and when the TV camera moved in for a close-up, the man watching at home could admire the smart cardigan styling with button front and the easy, bell-shaped sleeves.

The knitted golf shirt was still an-

Fashionable knits of 1956: (upper left) a miniature-checked sports shirt with a short collar; (upper right) a tan sleeveless cashmere sweater with a blue intarsia design; (center) a striped knit sports jacket with a tweedlike pattern; (lower right) a reversible pullover. From Esquire, *March 1956.*

coarse-weave sweaters that were porous and wonderfully full and easy to wear. As examples the fashion department showed one in a ribbed coat style; another with cross-stripes; a Scandinavian sweater with novel collar and yoke treatment; and, finally, a cardigan featuring a two-color double-shawl collar, flat metal buttons, and a ribbed trim that repeated the collar colors.

That same year, *Esquire* also showed a pure wool pullover with triangle insets, calling it a "border design sweater," and predicted that popular usage was bound to establish this in the permanent language of college fashion. "With the exception of the triangles that comprise the border," wrote the caption writer, "the sweater should remain unadorned in order to support the impact of these brilliantly contrasting colors."

Just as the coat sweater had already picked up some of the stripes and panels of the ski sweater, by 1957 hefty yarns were moving off the ski slopes and into towns and campuses across the country, their bulk more apparent than real because coarse stitches kept them soft, light, and easy to wear. Early in the year, *Esquire* sketched a trio: a red-and-black checkerboard knit with a shawl collar that could be worn rolled or high; a red-and-black cardigan; and a fireman-red convertible-collar model that worked with buttons and loops.

The border design sweater elicited further attention later that same year, this time from the editors of *Apparel Arts:* "The snowballing trend toward stronger, bolder patterns in knitwear is presaged by these high fashion border designs. Small in themselves, they call dramatic attention to their presence by the simple method of contrast with a plain ground." To illustrate this feature they used a starkly simple woolen sweater, the color of vintage port, with a boat neck, and a waist trim of wool mesh triangles in an assortment of colors, including blue, green, chartreuse, and white.

Gentlemen's Quarterly, which first appeared in the summer of 1957, took

other dominant style, and the undisputed leader at this time was the short-sleeved Lacoste shirt, a cotton knit distinguished by a cuff on the sleeve and a tail longer in back than in front. Introduced in white in 1953, the Lacoste was soon seen in a full range of colors.

In 1956 Munsingwear advertised that it had asked 240 of America's top golf professionals what they wanted in a golf shirt, and based on their replies had created a golf shirt with patented free-swing action—"and everything else you want." Knitted of a porous cotton lisle and with a shirttail that was 2½ inches longer than on ordinary shirts, Munsingwear's "grand slam" golf shirt was machine-washable and guaranteed not to shrink.

Esquire proclaimed 1956 as the year of the big stitch, emphasizing bulky

a small band of models off to Rome and then Norway, and came back with some striking photographs. For casual strolling in a Roman piazza, the magazine showed a suede sweater with knitted wool sleeves and back, and a bold neckline that combined black, white, and beige. Then, on the ski slopes of Norway, *Gentlemen's Quarterly* photographed a young Viking in the act of hurling a snowball, wearing a rib-knitted sweater in blue and white, its cuffs and double half-neck designed for maximum protection from icy winds and its vertical stripes presenting a sharper contrast in the front and back yokes. Brilliant, flamboyant red—"hot red"—was prominent in ski sweaters that year, and *Gentlemen's Quarterly* showed one on a model leaning against a carved wall in Norway—a bright red turtleneck patterned in black and white, with the rugged turtleneck red on the outside and white on the inside.

As the 1950s drew to a close, however, the big news in skiwear was the stretch fabrics developed in Austria that, in the next decade, would banish less-than-sleek ski trousers from the slopes forever.

In 1959, swimwear showed a vast variety of lengths. There were new "highs" and "lows" in knitted one-piece suits and a range from a low-rise bikini to a Bermuda length, dubbed the "swim-walker."

1960–1970

This proved to be the decade of the knits. By the end of the 1960s knits had infiltrated practically every single category of menswear.

"Time was when 'knitwear' meant sweaters," observed *Esquire* in 1960, "but knitting machines have learned many a trick since then. They create knit jackets, trousers, outercoats—and accessories." Regarding accessories, the editors showed the expanding sphere of knits in three handsome country-look ties, two of them crocheted and the third knitted; a wool-knit sports hat sporting an Icelandic sweater pattern; olive capeskin gloves with wool-knit back; a two-yards-long brushed-wool knit muffler; and a black-and-olive plaid wool-jersey vest with brass buttons.

Varying shades of grape made fashion news that year, and *Gentlemen's Quarterly* photographed satirist Mort Sahl, whose sweaters had become a trademark, in a wool blazer cardigan boldly striped in chianti and Concord, with stabilizing black at every third stripe and around the border; and in a horizontally striped bulky-knit pullover employing deep-tone mountain grape and Piedmont blue to brighten light and charcoal grays.

"The rugged, husky look of a knit is ideal for outercoats for sports occasions," commented *Gentlemen's Quarterly* that same year, adding that most often wool knit was combined with some other material. For example, a soft brushed-leather coat in a subtle green-brown featured bulky-knit sleeves and collar. The virile appearance of the coat was further underscored by a stitched-yoke effect and leather loop and button closures as well as by its alpaca pile lining.

In 1960, said *Esquire,* the well-dressed golfer wore a cotton yarn shirt in canyon gold, the magazine's favorite summer color, the body of which was a cool mesh knit. On both the golf links and the tennis court, the fashion-aware sportsman preferred knitwear. And no longer was tennis an all-white affair; many a man sported a yellow or blue ventilated knit, often with collar, cuff, and bottom in contrasting stripes.

In sports shirts there was something for everyone, particularly in knits. *Esquire* photographed several striking examples: a short-sleeved, placket-front pullover knitted in an open, cool stitch, with Continental-type short knitted collar; a horizontally striped knit shirt jacket; a vertically striped model with zipper front and narrow stand-up collar and three-quarter-length sleeve; a brass-buttoned, crew-neck blue knit with white trim; a knitted cross-stripe cotton shirt with a

A crossover-effect surplice-front sweater of Shetland wool was accented by border stripes. From Gentlemen's Quarterly, *October 1959.*

Solid-color sweaters in cable stitch (left) and wide rib-knit (right) were compatible coordinates with tartan slacks. From Esquire, *August 1966.*

Après-ski *sweater (left) has a novel horizontal-stitched design and raglan shoulders. The next man wears a blue mock turtleneck pullover with a gold neckband and panel stripe in front. From* Esquire, *December 1966.*

contrasting colored stripe at the chest; and a solid-color, no-collar pullover with piping at the edge of a three-button placket—a British boat-shirt style that quickly became a campus favorite, not only in solid colors but in checks and stripes as well.

Hot-red sportswear continued to be popular, and in 1963, using red no-seam paper and laminated red stools, *Esquire* photographed a group of models in the following knits: an imported English knit vest of 100 percent wool; a red wool jacket with black knit banding that looked something like a West Point jacket; a red nylon zippered jacket with black cotton rib-knit cuffs and collar; and a red-and-gray Acrilan knit shirt with rib-knit cuffs and waistband.

That same year, *Gentlemen's Quarterly* sent a crew to Hong Kong, where it photographed sweaters that carried the "tweed look," a revival of interest in tweed that also carried over into sports shirts. Among the tweed-look sweaters were a silver-gray ribbed turtleneck wool pullover that gained tweed status by being nubbed in burgundy and blue; and a pullover of brown, gray, and tan wool yarns, the entire sweater in the tweed-texture manner except for its rounded V-neck border stripes, which were, again, in brown, gray, and tan.

Leather and wool, those former foes, were very much together again in 1964, with a *Men's Wear* reporter noting, "Hardly a sweater maker hasn't hopped onto the leather bandwagon for fall. Result is a new breed of sweater that merges the best features of knits and lightweight outerwear." Illustrating this virtue were a classic cardigan with a suede front on a wool body and a cross-over suede-front cardigan. *Esquire* decided that 1964 was "the time of the turtle," in that the turtleneck sweater had moved out from undergraduate circles to reach a new level of elegance. The "layered look" surfaced that year too, in V-neck sweaters equipped with their own turtleneck, crew neck, or "fake" shirt collars. There were also the heavier-weight sweaters that perpetuated the ski look at home or on the campus.

Skiing in the sixties was more popular than ever, what with special ski trains and budget-priced package weekends making it possible for many people to indulge in this sport, which at one time had been almost the exclusive province of the rich. *Esquire* held to the opinion that, for some, the most important aspect of the ski weekend might very well be what takes place in the ski lodge after a day on the slopes. Accordingly, it displayed a selection of what it called "fireside togs" for after-ski wear, noting that the classic favorites had always been warm sweaters, ski pants or wool slacks, and after-ski boots. "This year is no exception," wrote the feature writer, "but there will be a number of original designs in sweaters." Proving this point were a white V-neck wool sweater in a novel horizontal-pattern knit, with raglan sleeves; a mock turtleneck pullover with a contrasting neckband, front panel, and horizontal panel just above the waistband; and a Himalaya bulky-knit cardigan with cable panels in front. "In sum," he concluded, "the trend is to luxurious sweaters of original design."

That same year *Esquire* predicted new ideas in knitted shirts: "The contemporary short-sleeved knit shirt is derived from two sources: the polo shirt, a simple pullover with a button placket and turndown collar; and the Henley boating shirt, with no collar." The fashion department therefore showed a shirt that was a combination of both, with these new features: wide ribs, slanted lines, a mock turtleneck, and a Henley-polo (collarless) look.

"The cycle is coming back to heavy sweaters," noted *Esquire* late in 1966. "Thick, bulky, masculine pullovers."

To illustrate this, the fashion department photographed an oyster-white extra-heavy wool with a fisherman's knit, high crew neck, and full bell sleeves. Burly weaves were turning up in sports shirts, too. "The textured sport shirt, achieved with bold patterns and hefty weaves, will be a strong favorite on the college scene," predicted *Esquire*. "With sharp patterns leading to a three-dimensional effect, and coarse yarns providing surface interest, the shirts will take on a vibrant sportiness."

Swimwear in 1966 was often inspired by basketball trunks, just as boxing had been a previous source of inspiration. To illustrate this smooth transition from court to water, *Esquire* showed a pair of navy stretch trunks of acetate, cotton, and spandex, edged and striped with white; maroon stretch trunks of acetate, cotton, and Lycra, with navy binding; and navy trunks that were a blend of Dacron, cotton, and Lycra, trimmed in beige. The style was moderately trim-fitting with side vents.

The year 1967 saw golf apparel gain even more color. "No sport permits its participants the freedom of imagination, the choice of colors and styles, and the opportunity to dress tastefully yet uniquely that golf does," said *Esquire*, adding that nowadays the greens were ablaze with the brilliant plumage of the players. Even the clothes the golfer donned for wet-weather action on the links came in happy, extroverted colors. "Swinging in the rain" is how *Esquire* saw the man who braved the soggy links in an orange Dacron-and-cotton permanent-press knit shirt paired with plaid slacks and a poplin Tyrol golf hat.

Because of the steadily increasing popularity of the turtleneck sweater from "the time of the turtle," in 1967 *Esquire* fashion writer George Frazier offered the magazine's readers "An Intellectual History of the Turtleneck Takeover":

Now, in a time when there are no golden boys anymore, no Hobey Bakers to make wonderlands of all our winters; when the bright college years have become blighted, when being tapped for Bones no longer seems the grail it did when Dick Stover was all sand and whipcord—now, in a mutinous time when unscrubbed undergraduate insurrectionists, and not fleet seabacks, not even football captains, are the lions among the ladies, and when the word 'students' summons up an image, not of ivied college quadrangles and dark-paneled common rooms, not of the Whiffenpoofs singing plaintively at Mory's on warm evenings in the springtime or of stadiums made madhouses in the gathering dusk of Saturdays in November, but of terribly bright, awfully smug little punks making their own bombs or painting placards or illegally occupying the premises of others—now, in a time like this, when so much grace and gallantry has gone from the campus, there is a welcome and unwonted air of innocence to something as totally lacking in strife and sociological significance as the prevalence of turtlenecks at the colleges this season. About it there is an echo of New Haven in the courtly time when grown men stood up and took off their hats in homage to the likes of Ted Coy. It has a sense of style—and God knows it was needed. But quite apart from the gladsome touch of the dégagé that it contributes to semesters besieged by protests, the turtleneck takeover proves that this classic sweater affords far more play to a man's clothes sense than one would suspect strolling along Madison Avenue on a fine Saturday afternoon, when every other man, or so it seems, is in a white turtleneck and a double-breasted navy-blue blazer, the lot of them looking, as somebody said, like a reunion of U-boat commanders.

And the turtleneck, unlike such campus crazes of other years as yellow slickers, white bucks, and bell-bottom trousers, offered enough variety in pattern, style, and material to lend genuine individuality to a man's appearance. To illustrate this, the fashion department photographed a dozen or so undergraduates in their turtlenecks, with no two alike. Among them were a cable-stitch wool; a giant herringbone design in all-wool; an open-stitch turtleneck; an all-wool of thick and thin yarns; and a blue-striped wool-and-Dacron.

The next year, *Gentlemen's Quarterly* flew a crew to Portugal and entered Lisbon "turtlenecked. Last fall's runaway favorite shows no sign of slowing up. Rather, it has moved away from solids to take on intriguing textures and a panoply of patterns." Whether outside an ancient church, beneath a picturesque windmill, or down at the beach hobnobbing with the granite-

University men are shown wearing the popular turtleneck pullovers in a variety of patterns and stitches. From Esquire, *September 1968.*

Photographed by Steinbicker/Houghton

faced fishermen, it was the turtleneck sweater that dominated the fashion picture. Among those photographed were a bulky-knit wool pullover with ribbed turtleneck, raglan shoulders, and ribbed-knit cuffs and waist; an easygoing waffle-knit Orlon pullover in camel and orange, with orange ribbed crew neck, sleeves, and waistband; a ribbed turtle-topped pullover emboldened with a cabled, striped front; and a bulky wool pullover, black-cross-divided into supersize squares of red and white.

Leather and knit were also dramatically paired in turtlenecks, as evidenced by a jerkin-style mustard suede—saddle-stitch-trimmed and angle-pocketed—fronting a knitted wool pullover topped by a ribbed turtleneck striped in cream, yellow, and gold. A year later, the *Gentlemen's Quarterly* cameraman turned up in Iran and, with a mosaic mosque as a backdrop, photographed another striking combination of leather and knit—this time a body-shaped sweater jacket of a flat-knitted blue wool, with gold leather both for its stand-up collar and as trim to conceal the full-length ring-pull zipper.

But, of course, knits were rampant in more than sweaters. *Esquire* showed ribbed double-knit slacks; stretch-knit swim trunks; a black cotton-knit terry cloth beach kimono; a double-knit sports coat; and a shaped white ottoman suit with vertical slashed pockets. In still another issue, the magazine's fashion department discussed knits: "There is much, much to be said for knits, which will soon be seen in sport jackets, slacks, business suits, and even formal evening wear. For one thing, they are relatively inexpensive. For another, they are extremely comfortable, being both porous and elastic. And, for a third, they can have the look of twill, hopsack, Bedford cord, or nailhead fabrics." Illustrating this feature were a red-and-white-striped double-breasted blazer; a shirt suit in camel-color double-knit wool; a one-piece jump suit of knit polyester; a dinner suit of Crimplene polyester with a satin shawl

A double-breasted knitted blazer in red-and-white stripes was worn by Yannis Tseklenis, the Athens designer. From Esquire, *April 1969.*

collar and an almost indiscernible jacquard pattern; and a brown shadow-check town suit also of knit Crimplene.

To illustrate that knits could indeed have the look of other fabrics, *Esquire* showed that they could even simulate the lustrous look of silk: "The elegant sheen identified with silk has been captured by a number of other fabrics as well and just in time for a new interest in it for tailored clothes and sportswear." Proving this point were a silk coat-style sweater in a tweed knit, a silk-knit turtleneck shirt, and a crushed-knit velour pullover.

By 1968 the Peacock Revolution had rolled across the nation's tennis courts and touched off an explosion of color. *Esquire* gave its readers a preview of the outfits chosen for the Davis Cup team of the United States Lawn Tennis Association, "that notorious bastion of tradition." Not surprisingly, knits were prominent: a yellow ensemble, trimmed in blue and white, that included a nylon zippered jacket with

knit collar, cuffs, and waistband, a cotton mesh V-neck shirt, and cotton-twill shorts with a soil-release finish; and a blue outfit, trimmed in white and yellow, that included an all-wool cable-knit pullover, a Dacron-and-cotton knit shirt, and durable-press Dacron-and-cotton shorts.

Often new tennis fashions were as revolutionary for their avant-garde design as for their use of color. Two of the most provocative new knit tennis fashions were a designed-for-action short-sleeved, short-legged, zip-front jump suit of washable polyester-and-cotton mesh knit; and a two-piece outfit consisting of a long-sleeved white jacket with stand-up collar and shorts made of a stretchy polyester knit. And certainly among the more significant double-knit fashion breakthroughs in tennis clothes were a white ten-button blazer and a brass-buttoned, sleeveless double-breasted vest-jacket.

In 1969 *Esquire* detected what it thought to be a move toward a little more discretion and a lot more coordination in golf clothes: "There will always be a brilliance of color, of course, but where once it was a positive riot, now it will be employed with that certain restraint that constitutes taste." The next year, the fashion department was complaining that what was wrong with golf clothes was that they were a lot more colorful than comfortable. Then, acting out of what it termed "functional, not idle curiosity," the magazine petitioned some of the most resourceful men's designers to create an authentically new look for the links. Most of them naturally enough chose to work in knit, which, being durable, practically wrinkle-resistant, and allowing great freedom of movement, was already a favorite with golfers. So it was actually no idle boast when one prominent knit manufacturer advertised: "Golfpeople are Knitpeople, too. Knitsweaters, knitslacks, knitshirts, socks, jackets, you name it."

In the second half of the 1960s, swimwear evidenced more than just a touch of the thirties, and *Esquire* sketched four echoes of the two-piece bathing suit, "which, on the bashful beaches of those years was more functional than fashionable, since male bathers were not permitted to appear topless." The new-look suits included a stretch-nylon tank top with stretch shorts of acetate, cotton, and Lycra; a cotton-knit top with matching beach or surfing pants of cotton, rubber, and Lycra; and a Roman-striped cotton-knit basque-type shirt with matching mid-thigh-length white-belted trunks of stretch nylon.

In 1969 *Esquire* considered that "the unclothed male torso may be a rarity among the avant-garde at fashionable watering places" that year. What proved more popular than the bikini were jump and tank suits, such as a short, raglan-sleeved, zip-front jump suit of royal blue stretch-knit Orlon and Lycra; a navy-and-white-striped tank suit of stretch nylon; and stretch-nylon belted trunks with a contrasting horizontal-striped knit tank top.

Since fashions reflect the times and knits were the big fashion news of the early 1970s, it was natural that they appear in campus clothes that were clearly less tradition-minded than ever before; for example, a skinny sweater, a ribbed-knit pullover that when slipped on hugged the body. The one *Gentlemen's Quarterly* chose to show was of brown-and-green-nubbed off-white wool, with buttoned leather patches placed at the side of its mock turtle-neck and along the cuffs.

Esquire paid still another tribute to knits as "*The functional made fashionable.* If one thing more than any other characterizes clothes in these times, it is the astonishing increase in comfort. The creativity of chemistry has wrought wonder fabrics undreamed of in all the eras of elegance that have gone before. And eventually, in the case of each new fabric, the bugs were eliminated, and what originally might have looked a little slovenly became quite stylish. We have been mentioning knits for quite a few issues now and it hardly seems necessary to add much about their incomparable practicality.

They resist not merely wrinkles, but almost everything else as well. Even staid Brooks Brothers, an establishment not given to overstatement, grows lyrical in its endorsement. And small wonder, for now that knits are no longer novelties, they are accepted as an integral part of one's wardrobe. Their flexibility is a designer's delight." Illustrations accompanying this full-hearted tribute to knits included a double-knit Dacron sports coat in a black-and-white jacquard pattern; a Dacron double-knit blazer suit; and a three-button belted double-knit suit of Fortrel.

The incomparable practicality and comfort of knitted suits, jackets, and slacks inevitably led to the knitted overcoat of the early seventies. Both flat knits and fuzzy, lofty knits of wool and wool-and-polyester blends were used in both single- and double-breasted styles. Advertising a weather coat of double-knit fabric, one manufacturer said it would follow the wearer's every move "as easily as a shadow" and then slip back into the perfect lines of its tailoring. "Too much cannot be said for the comfort of knitwear as it has been improved by the alchemy of contemporary laboratories," wrote *Esquire*. "No fabric's more flexible, none as ideal for formal wear or for the easy living of *après-swim*." And knits for *après-swim* and easy living included two shirt suits photographed by the fashion staff in Mexico City: a cotton-knit shirt with four-button placket and matching pants; and a cotton double-knit shirt suit in giant houndstooth and geometric print.

"Double-knits have reversed the course of the clothing industry," the *Daily News Record* stated in the summer of 1971. "For the past several years the industry was hard hit: The sluggish state of the economy forced the average suit customer to put off his purchases; retailers sharply cut back the size of their clothing orders, and model confusion prevailed. The mood of the market has now switched from frowns to smiles—thanks mainly to double-knits. Clothing executives, bubbling

over spring business prospects, are once again talking about sales increases. In some instances, clothing firms have already withdrawn some spring knit styles because of a sold up position. Most clothing companies project that knits will represent more than half of their spring business. A handful of firms do upwards of 90 percent of their volume with double-knits. Some companies are being formed to specialize in knits; while others are setting up separate divisions with the accent on knits. Partially sharing the spotlight with knits are the newly developed textured wovens—stretch fabrics which have many of the characteristics of knits. In fact, many firms are merchandising knits and textured wovens as part of action fabric programs for spring."

Meanwhile the young, many of whom had gravitated to the avant-garde boutiques for their apparel, had discovered that the flexible knits were ideal for the easy or unstructured suits

The belted cardigan of 1970 had a round neck, narrow rib-knit to the waistline, and coarse rib-knit below.

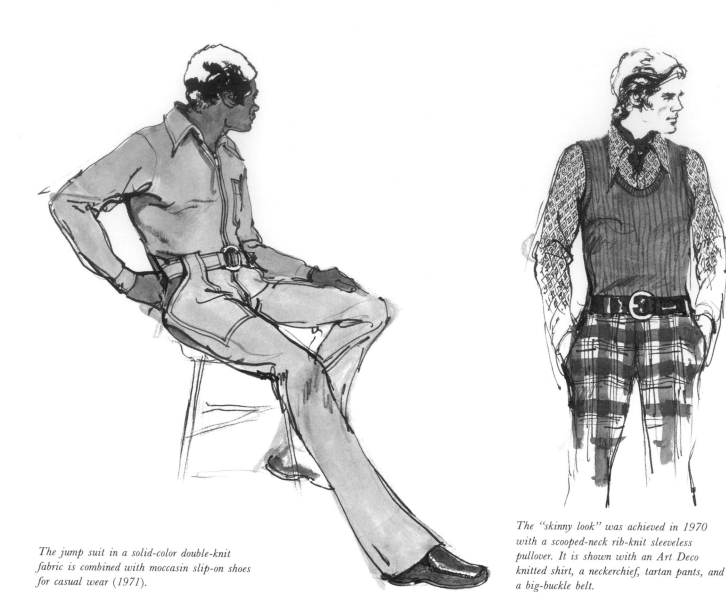

The jump suit in a solid-color double-knit fabric is combined with moccasin slip-on shoes for casual wear (1971).

The "skinny look" was achieved in 1970 with a scooped-neck rib-knit sleeveless pullover. It is shown with an Art Deco knitted shirt, a neckerchief, tartan pants, and a big-buckle belt.

that in so many cases were not really suits at all; for example, a boutique sweater suit that was bought as separates, consisting of a nylon knit top and pleated cotton velvet jeans. When commenting on the under-twenty-five boutique shopper, one fashion writer noted in *Men's Wear:* "For this type of customer it can be as simple as mixing any knit pant with a pullover—or as hard as a pant-vest-pullover-shirt-tunic-midi cardigan combination, which switched within its own ingredients, comes up with an entire knit wardrobe of sweater suits. There are manufacturers catering to both boutique customers. Some are showing tweedy skinny knit sweaters that echo the dusty or crayon box colorations of

a completely separate line of tiny jacquard knit pants; others are 'doing their own thing' and allowing whatever combinations that do come up to be entirely the choice of the wearer. The only consistency is in a skin-fitting line: Tight-ribbed sweaters worn in or belted out of flared knit pants." And under those knit pants were briefs and mini briefs (sometimes with matching athletic shirt tops) of lightweight, body-molding knit.

With jeans, judged to be "the high voltage category in men's and boys' wear to the tune of a billion dollars by 1970," a knit shirt was the ideal fashion companion: the long-sleeved scoop-neck knit; the zip-front rib-knit; the sweater knit with long placket; the

canvas-trimmed knit pullover; the ribbed-knit golf shirt; the collarless short-sleeved tennis shirt of knitted polyester and cotton; and the knit polo shirt worn with a double-knit sports shirt—the ultimate—the coordinated "double-knit look." In short, a knit to fit every taste, every occasion. And as the seventies picked up steam, knits were being worn by the more mature man, too. As a fashion writer put it, "Comfort sells knits"; and what man did not want comfort as well as style from his clothes? One knit manufacturer reported: "Our customer is any swinging man from 20 to 65."

Perhaps none of the "new wave" innovations took to knits with the dash of the jump suit, whose success *Esquire*

Knits invaded all areas of men's fashions. In 1971 they were found in such outercoats as this polyester-and-wool midi coat in a belted wrap style with big lapels and collar.

predicted as early as 1968, noting at the time that some of Europe's most avant-garde menswear designers predicted it would be a replacement for dressing gown and pajamas. Illustrating this 1968 feature story was the photograph of a model wearing a jump suit in a royal blue-and-red lightweight-wool knit with button front. Throughout the remainder of this decade and well into the seventies, *Esquire*'s fashion staff continued to promote the bravura of the knit and double-knit jump suit. In 1969, for example, a photograph appeared of a particularly handsome one worn aboard a yacht in the Mediterranean: a one-piece knitted white jump suit of washable Acrilan with front zipper

and mock turtleneck and trimmed in double stripes of royal blue.

Gentlemen's Quarterly took up the cause, too, and sketched any number of new jump suits including a lanky model of stretch denim with body tracings in back, contrast railroad stitching, and long-point fashion collar; a double-knit polyester with flare collar, flare leg, epaulet shoulder, leather-covered buttons and buckle, and three cargo pockets; an all-wool double-knit with zippers galore—on sleeves, front, and all four of its patch pockets; and what was called a "uni suit," of 100 percent polyester double-knit—a precisely tailored jump suit that gave the appearance of a two-piece suit through body tracings and a satin-finish brass buckle. By the early 1970s the knit jump suit had not only invaded the bedroom but the golf links as well. An outstanding golf model was an action-styled uni suit of rib-knit with easy raglan shoulders, two-way zipper, elasticized waistband, and handsome metal buckle.

In the late 1960s allover geometric patterns, bold stripes, and tapestry designs had made the headlines in dress shirts. But in the 1970s fabric made the headlines and the knit shirt was the star attraction. (By the late 1960s the knit shirt for formal evening wear had already made its debut. After Lord Snowdon had popularized the turtleneck evening shirt of woven silk, his innovation was instantly copied on both sides of the Atlantic in a white turtleneck pullover that had a spectacular though brief vogue.) Merchants throughout the country enumerated the strong points of the knit dress shirt as follows: It could be easily worn for dress or sportswear; it was comfortable; it was washable; and it held its shape exceptionally well under the worst possible conditions. There were many who felt that the knit dress shirt could become an integral part of the knit's dominance throughout menswear classifications.

In shirts and ties, men's liberation from unimaginative and/or constricted apparel reached a point in the early 1970s where there was no longer

any clear-cut distinction between what was appropriate for an executive board meeting and what for casual weekend wear. There were knit shirts in vibrant colors and eye-catching patterns teamed with big-knotted ties, like the awning-striped double-knit polyester featured in the fall "Report on Men's Wear" published by the *New York Times*.

In the July–August, 1971, edition of the newsletter published by the National Association of Men's Sportswear Buyers, knit clothing was covered in depth. "In America there is massive consumer demand, seemingly spontaneous for knit clothing," began the article. "Some attribute it to the American woman, who has become a great advocate of knits in the past few years. Others say it's because the groundwork has been laid by the great mail order chains, who were among the first into knits. Whatever the explanation, the demand does exist."

In recognition of this demand, the editions of the 1971 "Report on Men's Wear," published semiannually by the *New York Times Magazine,* were rife with knits. The spring–summer edition, for example, declared: "In tailored clothing the big news is knits—lightweight and agreeably easy to move around in." As proof, it printed a double-page spread of knits for town that included photographs of a jacquard-woven double-knit suit of polyester and wool, with across-the-chest yoke and vertical welting, sewn-down back belt, waist-high side vents, and side-welted pants; a two-buttoned polyester suit in a miniature geometric design, with scalloped-flap pockets, center vent, and traditional trousers; a herringbone-striped suit of double-knit Dacron and wool; an overplaided houndstooth check of double-knit Dacron; and an all-white double-knit sports suit of polyester and pure Irish linen.

In the same issue there were also knitted golf slacks—a pair of corded rib-striped polyester knit, with angled front pockets and button-tab waist; and another of knitted polyester in a Greek-key design. Attention was paid to double-knit sports jackets, too, such as a random-striped linen-and-cotton with even a lining in a stretch fabric; and a jacquard-patterned jacket of double-knit polyester, with wide, notched lapels, buttoned scalloped-flap pockets, and center vent.

In the fall-winter edition, the cover showed a pair of knit suits: one a honeycomb-patterned polyester, two-buttoned, patch-pocketed, back-belted, and side-vented; and the other a two-buttoned chevron-striped double-knit polyester featuring flapped pockets, center vent, and slightly flared trousers. Inside, on the introductory page, was the following editorial tribute to the power of knits:

This season the big news is knits, which turn up in everything from tailored clothing to shirts and neckties. The new knitted clothing—lightweight, comfortable, body-conforming, wrinkle-resistant and easily packable—has eliminated most of its initial problems and those men who have worn them have mostly praise for knitted suits, jackets and slacks. Some kinks remain—snagging, alteration difficulties, a tendency to be warm in hot weather and too porous for wintry blasts—but, judging by their increasing acceptance, the pluses appear to outweigh the minuses.

In suits, both knitted and woven, the favorite is the two-buttoned, single-breasted model—waist-shaped, shoulder-expressed and flaunting those 1930's movie star lapels some men were scoffing at not so long ago. In the fall of 1971 they look fresh and sophisticated. The necessary with-it touch: flared trousers topped by a wide, unique-looking belt.

For winter sports a bevy of sweaters were shown, many of them reflecting the Art Deco influence sparked by the success of the Broadway revival of the 1925 hit musical *No, No, Nanette,* which abounded with Art Deco-designed pullovers. In 1971, too, printed knits were moving into the sweater field, and the *Daily News Record* sketched a close-fitting zippered turtleneck angora-and-wool sweater in a leaf print. "Knits are everybody's fashion bag," maintained fashion writer Stan Gellers. To prove his contention he created eight pages of knitwear keyed to specific customer types:

Middle American knits. The all-weather coat doubling as a topcoat and/or rain-coat; casual slacks in moderate dimensional patterns for golf and spectator sports; the blazer suit of twill textured double-knit with leather trimmed flap pockets; geometric patterned double-knits that become the base for three four-piece put-togethers with trousers, matching safari jackets, tunics, blazers.

Metropolitan knits. The wool double-knit jump suit that splits into three parts with sleeveless one-piecer, turtleneck and a zip-up battle jacket; the double-knit checkered sport coat and slack with a Western yoke and front welted seams; dress up jeans of Fortrel double-knit; the double-knit safari jacket worn with matching or patterned slacks.

Knits for youth. The jeans suit of double-knit Fortrel-Zefran featuring a Western personality via authentic detailing and stitching on a denim look; the shirt suit; knit jeans; and the sport suit with a totally unstructured easy jacket in a double-knit, worn with matching or contrasting jeans.

Boutique knits. Chic jeans with jacquard tweed effects, herringbones come together in a pattern-on-pattern multi-knit layered look; knit knickers put together with fashionably skimpy knit shirt or sweater; water repellent knit outerwear—like a pile-lined cotton knit coat; the slim, shaped knit safari suit, in a belted, bomber length or midi coat suit style.

And into whichever category a man might fit, he would find a knit for his sleepwear. There were colorful and comfortable pajamas of nylon tricot that coordinated with machine-washable soft plush robes of brushed Arnel and nylon.

Suckling's, a retailer in Hollidays-burg, Pennsylvania, adopted in 1971 a policy of providing information about knits, both to educate its customers and to forestall complaints from people who did not take proper care of their knit garments. "Knits make the news in men's clothing," its ad read, "but they are not the ultimate, perfect fabric. They have many advantages, but also a few disadvantages. We wear them and like them; but we believe customers should have all the facts."

Under the heading "Advantages" the store listed:

. . . Wearing qualities are excellent.
. . . Shape retention is exceptional.
. . . Price, a bit higher than wovens.
. . . Alterations are no problem for an experienced tailor.

. . . Elasticity makes them very comfortable.

Cited under "Disadvantages" were:

. . . Knits snag easily and cannot be rewoven.
. . . To correct a snag, thread a needle and pull it through at the snag. It will pull through with the thread to the reverse side. Do NOT clip it off.
. . . Hot ashes from a pipe or cigarette will burn a hole very quickly. It will not flame, but will char through. It cannot be repaired.
. . . Dry clean for best results and NEVER use a hot iron on knit fabrics.
. . . Knits must be tailored by an expert with stretch thread.

On the subject "How To Sell Knits," *Men's Wear* decided that the sales technique of the Detroit department store J. L. Hudson Company, in a program created to educate both their salesmen and their customers, displayed a high level of professionalism. The program, said *Men's Wear,* followed this pattern:

Several of the largest manufacturers in the knit industry were invited to come to Detroit and tell all the menswear sales personnel about the qualities of knits in general and the properties of knits in their particular fashions.

Salesmen were allowed to purchase knit merchandise at cost. (The store's merchandise manager said "The best way to familiarize a salesman with knits, is to have him wear them.")

Once the sales personnel were knowledgeable the next step was to introduce the knit concept to the public. Hudson's chose to do so with a special promotion. "The Knit Week." All newspaper ads during the week carried knit messages, the word knit was given full prominence in the menswear departments and the salesmen walked around with "Ask Me About Knits" buttons. The customers apparently asked and bought.

Customers who asked were told that knits travel well, do not crease, retain their shape, are lightweight, are easy to take care of and are more comfortable than wovens.

All the menswear rear windows and interior displays showed only knits.

By the early 1970s several leading rainwear producers were moving strongly into the knit all-weather coat picture. The switch to knits posed no problem, said one outerwear maker, but more work and detailing went into a topcoatlike knit raincoat than into a woven raincoat. Seen most often were knee-length all-weather coats of all-acrylic, acrylic-and worsted blends, or all-worsted, in double-breasted models with wide lapels and generous Napoleonic collars, and in single-breasted models with raglan sleeves and convertible collars.

A staple in the wardrobe of every well-turned-out woman, knits in the 1970s were indispensable to the wardrobe of every well-turned-out man. In 1971 *Esquire* demonstrated their faith in this proposition by photographing four models whose outfits, except for foot- and headwear, consisted entirely of knits, which the fashion department called variously "The now thing," "The latest miracle of modern chemistry," and "The fabric of the Seventies." The models wore, for example, four knit overcoats: a single-button double-breasted midi of wool and Trevira; a corduroy-looking Fortrel and wool, also in midi-length; a tweedy midi with a pile-finished lining and strap-and-buckle closures in simulated reptile; and a trench coat of Trevira and wool.

The knit-aware man of the seventies was also infinitely more fashion-aware because of the sophistication and daring generated by the Peacock Revolution. From the knit he wanted a look, a fashion statement. And so fashion, and not merely fashion construction, became the *raison d'être* of the knits, which added a new, fluid dimension to menswear, reflecting a whole new way of life.

Underwear

Underwear in the first two decades of this century was exactly what the name suggested: apparel worn underneath outer garments the sole purpose of which was to protect the wearer from the elements. For the winter months there were many different weights of knitted wool underwear, and a man chose his according to the section of the country in which he lived and the severity of its winter. As warmer weather approached, he changed to knitted balbriggan underwear that was light in weight and cool; yet it too had the long sleeves and long legs of his winter underwear. A page from the Sears, Roebuck and Company 1900 catalog advertised balbriggan summer underwear as follows:

Men's Fine Gauge French Balbriggan Undershirts: Fancy collarette neck, pearl buttons, and ribbed close fitting cuffs; fine soft silky finish; actually worth double our asking price of 39 cents.

Drawers to match above, made with fine sateen band and pearl buttons. 39 cents.

Extra heavy winter-weight underwear was often made of Australian lamb's wool; it was considered a bargain at 98 cents for the shirt and 98 cents for the matching drawers. While ecru and camel's hair were the more or less standard colors for summer underwear, this extra heavy underwear usually came in olive brown and dark tan. These styles continued through the second decade, although there were scattered reports from the front during World War I that indicated a growing interest in silk underwear, not so much from an aesthetic point of view as for reasons of practicality: silk dried more quickly than wool.

The twenties saw the arrival of the one-piece union suit, a more athletic type of underwear with long or short sleeves. Sears, Roebuck and Company advertised its union suit for year-round wear and assured the catalog

"Pa's Got His New B.V.D.s On"

HE had old-fashioned notions about Underwear, until the Boys went out, bought B.V.D. and made him put it on. Look at him! Now, Pa joins right in the young folks' fun, because he's cool.

Loose fitting, light woven B.V.D. Underwear starts with the best possible fabrics (specially woven and tested), continues with the best possible workmanship (carefully inspected and re-inspected), and ends with complete comfort (fullness of cut, balance of drape, correctness of fit, durability in wash and wear).

If it *hasn't*
This Red
Woven Label

MADE FOR THE
B.V.D.
BEST RETAIL TRADE

It *isn't*
B. V. D.
Underwear

(Trade Mark Reg. U. S. Pat. Of. and Foreign Countries)

B.V.D. Closed Crotch Union Suits (Pat. U.S.A.) $1.00 and upward the Suit.

B.V.D. Coat Cut Undershirts and Knee Length Drawers, 50c. and upward the Garment.

The B.V.D. Company,
New York.

London Selling Agency: 66, Aldermanbury, E. C.

A union suit and two-piece underwear for summer were featured in this advertisement of May 1916. [NEW YORK PUBLIC LIBRARY PICTURE COLLECTION]

The formfitting union suit was featured in this national advertisement in 1923. [NEW YORK PUBLIC LIBRARY PICTURE COLLECTION]

reader: "These suits will fit you no matter how you're built. Knit of long staple combed cotton yarn . . . strongly sewed with smooth flat locked seams throughout. Fine elastic ribbed. The tall, slim man will find comfort in the specially designed long body suit which eliminates all feeling of tightness in the crotch. The short, stout suit is made by a manufacturer who makes a speciality of correctly tailoring suits to fit short stout men."

The nainsook suit, made of a lightweight cloth of strong basket-weave construction, was a sort of super-athletic union suit in that it had short legs and was sleeveless. One of the more stylish union suits was a short model with buttons on the shoulder, perhaps one of the earliest indications that underwear could have some point of difference. Meanwhile, flat-knit balbriggan shirts and drawers were still sold as late as 1927.

Just as the returning doughboy had insisted on more comfort and more natural styling in his suits, so he wanted his underwear to be more comfortable. By the later years of this decade he got what he wanted in "athletic underwear," which was cut very brief and came in a variety of staple and fancy woven cloths. Its "trouser seat" was designed so that when it opened it was entirely free from the body, and its usually sleeveless shirt (some models had quarter sleeves) had deep armholes. Two-piece garments were also very popular, with shorts designed to prevent binding in the seat and over the hips and side tabs spaced to allow the wearer to adjust the size of the waistline.

By 1928 the rayon union suit had become important enough to warrant a full-page article in *Men's Wear,* which stated that "a protagonist of this product, among other advantages, asserts that the wearer of a rayon union suit could stand under the shower in it, soap it well and wash it then and there while it was on his body. He could then rinse it out, hang it up, and by the time he had dried himself the union suit itself would be dry enough to wear. This is because the rayon garment would absorb a much smaller percentage of water than would a similar suit of wool, wool mixture or of cotton. Whether this water resisting property of rayon can be counted an underwear virtue or a disadvantage may be a question, but regardless of that, rayon, when used as a mixture or for decorative effect, has an eye appeal that aids sales over the counter" (Apr. 11, 1928, p. 131).

The all-rayon gym-type undershirt was very popular. Indeed, the combination of gym shirt and shorts had gained ground at the expense of both the nainsook union suit and the rib-knitted union suit.

Athletic shirts and shorts were the favored combination in the 1930s, with shirts in gaily colored knits and shorts in colored stripes. Advertisements extolled their smart appearance, comfort, and freedom of action. French-back shorts in woven fabrics with adjustable tabs at the waistband in back became important fashion items ("Puts you in locker-room style"). Later, the boxer shorts worn by prizefighters served as prototypes for underwear.

The sleeveless athletic shirt of the thirties was adapted from the top half of the tank swimsuit worn by American men in the early years of this century. Although extremely popular, the athletic shirt was supplanted in the forties by the T-shirt with short sleeves worn by the servicemen of World War II, who continued to wear it under their postwar apparel too. By the fifties the T-shirt was actually doubling as sportswear, as many of the very young men aped movie idols like James Dean and Marlon Brando, who wore T-shirts in lieu of sports shirts with their blue jeans.

Less popular during the thirties was a ribbed-knit pullover undershirt. Collarless and border-striped, with small pearl buttons running halfway down the front, it was favored mostly by mature men, and, in fact, ultimately became known as "the Wallace Beery shirt" because that rubber-faced character actor was so often shown wearing one on screen. Ironically, although this undershirt was not taken up by the younger men, its style was eventually adapted to sports shirts and went on to become a best-selling sportswear look for young men for many years.

"There's something new in a woman's article of apparel almost every hour of the day," noted a trade publication in 1934, "but the sensational news of a new kind of garment that men can wear occurs only once in a long, long time." The "new kind of garment" was the jock-type shorts inspired by the extremely brief bathing trunks first seen on the French Riviera in 1932. It was claimed that the new shorts (sometimes referred to as "bathing suit" or "supporter" underwear) would fit the male figure everywhere: "No-gap opening with gentle support, elastic fabric, no buttons, no bulk, no binding." With the shorts a man wore a matching shirt that eliminated superfluous material at the bottom with a swallowtail effect. The "sensational news," however, did not quite offset the blow dealt the undershirt when, in the Academy Award–winning film *It Happened One Night,* Clark Gable took off his shirt to reveal a bare torso. In an era

The Y-front construction of this knitted underwear patented by Jockey was advertised in 1946 as "scientifically perfected for correct masculine support."

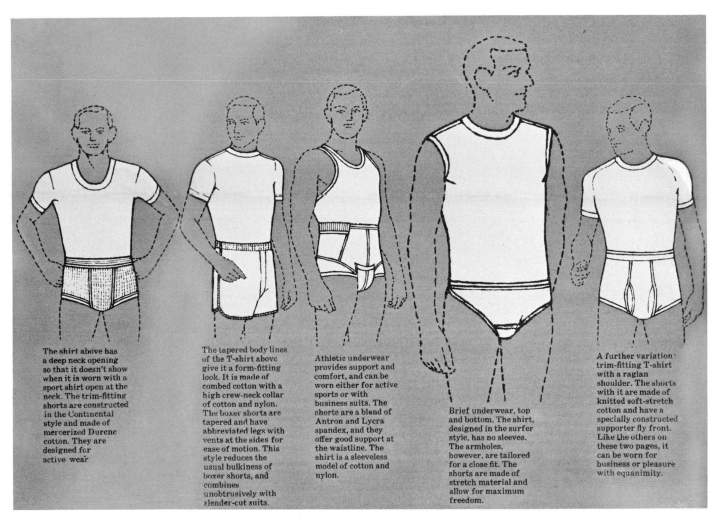

The shirt above has a deep neck opening so that it doesn't show when it is worn with a sport shirt open at the neck. The trim-fitting shorts are constructed in the Continental style and made of mercerized Durene cotton. They are designed for active wear

The tapered body lines of the T-shirt above give it a form-fitting look. It is made of combed cotton with a high crew-neck collar of cotton and nylon. The boxer shorts are tapered and have abbreviated legs with vents at the sides for ease of motion. This style reduces the usual bulkiness of boxer shorts, and combines unobtrusively with slender-cut suits.

Athletic underwear provides support and comfort, and can be worn either for active sports or with business suits. The shorts are a blend of Antron and Lycra spandex, and they offer good support at the waistline. The shirt is a sleeveless model of cotton and nylon.

Brief underwear, top and bottom. The shirt, designed in the surfer style, has no sleeves. The armholes, however, are tailored for a close fit. The shorts are made of stretch material and allow for maximum freedom.

A further variation: trim-fitting T-shirt with a raglan shoulder. The shorts with it are made of knitted soft-stretch cotton and have a specially constructed supporter fly front. Like the others on these two pages, it can be worn for business or pleasure with equanimity.

Various types of shirts and shorts worn in 1966. From Esquire, *March 1966.*

when motion-picture stars had great fashion influence, Gable's brief appearance on screen without an undershirt had an adverse effect on sales for some years to come.

Men's Wear summed up what it thought men's underwear should be: "Underwear should have the grace of Apollo, the romance of Byron, the distinction of Lord Chesterfield and the ease, coolness and comfort of Mahatma Gandhi" (Apr. 10, 1935, p. 14). By that time it appeared that manufacturers of men's underwear were at last offering truly comfortable garments. The new "short scants" were available in three variations: a jock type with matching shirt, a fine-quality swiss ribbed cotton with a buttonless fly, and a G-string in the form

of an elongated apron of acetate that owed more than a little to the dhoti of Mahatma Gandhi. Although the cut had changed very little, the shorts now came in meshes and drop-stitch fabrics with novelty knitted constructions.

The latest thing in knit goods in 1935 was specially styled underwear for skiing and the other winter sports that were fast gaining popularity. One suit in a shade of hunting yellow was made of double-thickness knitted cloth, with wool on the outside and cotton underneath. The shirt was a slip-on with a round neck and long sleeves, thus looking more like a sporty pullover than an undershirt. The bottoms, in a three-quarter length, had two diagonal openings running from

the crotch to the waistband, guaranteeing maximum comfort for the active sportsman.

Meanwhile, the man who preferred the summer jock-type or supporter shorts could now buy a winter version that had short legs. The main style feature in woven shorts in the mid-thirties was the use of shirting patterns and materials, with checks and extremely bold tartans in the lead.

In 1936 airy, lightweight summer underwear made news. Fabrics ran to open-weave and netlike effects, and porosity was developed to an unprecedented degree in lightweight knits, meshes, batistes, acetates, voiles, sheer broadcloths, crashes, and seersuckers. Color was rampant.

Among new types of supporter

Vivid colors and bold patterns appeared in men's underwear in 1971. This nylon tricot athletic shirt and boxer shorts are in a paisley pattern with a deep background. [JOCKEY MENSWEAR]

The boxer shorts of 1971 retained the traditional waistband, but the little side vents of track and basketball shorts had been added. Both T-shirt and shorts are of cotton. [JOCKEY MENSWEAR]

shorts were shorts attached to a solid-color knitted shirt, making a one-piece cotton sportswear garment; a knitted version of cotton and silk with a broad elastic-mesh band that served as a supporter for the abdomen; and shorts of gaily printed knitted cotton. One prominent underwear manufacturer concentrated on flat-knit rayon shorts in high colors with leg openings edged with elastic strips to assure a close fit. The most avant-garde styling was seen in a flared-leg one-piece suit inspired by the bathing suit. It had two buttons at the side of the right leg for adjustment, and the wearer put it on by stepping through the neck opening.

Boxer shorts, some of them made with grippers, continued to gain popularity during the early 1940s, but after World War II the ex-GI, who had grown accustomed to the absorbent

quality of the T-shirt, favored knitted underwear. By the last half of this decade, various types of knitted shorts, ranging from knee-length models to trim-cut briefs, were big sellers.

The 1950s were the decade of the so-called miracle fabrics. Soon nylon underwear was in vogue, and after that polyester and cotton blends. Color was still news, and so were novelty shorts featuring red ants or turn-of-the-century muscle men, although in a much more limited way.

With the explosion of the Peacock Revolution and the body awareness that accompanied it, men's underwear took on even more color and style. Underwear was now fashion underwear; shirts and shorts were color-coordinated and matched in a myriad of colors, patterns, fabrics, and even silhouettes. Indicative of the new trend

were bikini and mini-bikini briefs in black, gold, red, and royal blue and body suits of washable nylon in similarly extroverted colors.

Gentlemen's Quarterly in 1971 ran a "Brief Encounter" feature and showed a cotton-mesh raglan-sleeved top and matching bikini; a geometric-patterned cotton brief in cream, beige, and white with a seamed fly pouch; and a pair of wine nylon lace briefs. Even the long, cover-up underwear for winter sportswear was fashionable; splashed with fancy colors and styled with crew or boat necks in a skinny rib with knit cuffs, it had the casual, easy good looks of sportswear.

Back in 1900, Sears, Roebuck and Company had headlined the men's underwear page of its catalog: "Astonishing temptations for all mankind." Despite the wording, it was referring simply to price. In the 1970s, in contrast, when the Spruce men's underwear firm headlined an advertisement "Why our underwear feels sexier than lingerie" (*Men's Wear,* Apr. 3, 1971), it had nothing to do with price. At last the male of the species knew the psychic lift that came from feeling well dressed from the skin out.

Sleepwear

In the early 1900s a little boy had his Dr. Dentons, a kind of turn-of-the-century jump suit with feet. They were warm, and in an era of long, blustery winters and drafty rooms that was important. As for the man of the house, he wore the classic nightshirt of muslin, a collarless pullover with long sleeves and side vents to make pulling it over the head that much easier. The nightshirt extended below the calf and usually had three buttons in front and a chest pocket. It, too, was noted for its warmth. Less popular was the pajama with a coat top, probably for the reason that a two-piece garment did not ensure the warmth of the one-piece nightshirt.

1920–1930

Not until the 1920s did sleepwear take on any noticeable style, but then it did so with a vengeance as if to make up for lost time. By 1925, with central heating taken for granted, pajamas had replaced nightshirts except for old-timers who clung to the familiar and resisted the new. Even the large, stout man who formerly had favored nightshirts was changing to pajamas. And why not? For that was where the most attractive fabrics and liveliest colors were appearing.

Men's Wear observed: "Nothing seems to be too extreme in the color treatment to obviate its use as a pajama feature. Big checks, startling stripes, spots and vivid designs will make the slumbering male a thing of beauty. Flannel or flannelette pajamas still find a place, but the evidence is that these things are yielding to style influences that are at work.

"For example, the college boy who brings from his home several suits of flannelette pajamas is soon 'kidded' out of them by his college associates. Collegiate pajamas must be light weight and in step with what the rest of the boys are wearing. Better heated homes have made frigid nights scarce, even in the far places, so that bundling up for the night has passed out.

"Husbands and sons of women who attend the movies have learned that the smart night wear is expressed in pajama suits that blend with the

Figured silk in conventional-style pajamas (left) and plain silk in longer lounge pajamas (right) provided the theme for this advertisement in 1925. [NEW YORK PUBLIC LIBRARY PICTURE COLLECTION]

CORRECT is style, comfortable in fit, pleasing in design, Ernest Simons New Pajama Line for 1926 is most outstanding. The wide awake dealer, quick to appreciate customer demand, will not hesitate to stock up with these irresistable garments.

No pleasing color combination has been overlooked, every detail has been carefully inspected—and most important—they have been priced to allow generous dealer profits.

NIGHT *SIMONS IDEAL* WEAR
"The Rest is Easy"

We have been manufacturers of Fruit of the Loom Pajamas and Night Shirts bearing the registered Fruit of the Loom label since the idea originated with us many years ago

Beginning January 1st, 1926 the registered label will be confined to us and only one other manufacturer for use on Men's and Boys' Night Wear.

FIGURED SILK PAJAMAS
to retail at $15

TRUHU SILK LOUNGE PAJAMAS in 9 colors with contrast trim—to retail at $25

ESTABLISHED 1876
Ernest Simons
Manufacturing Company
PORT CHESTER, N.Y.
NEW YORK SALES ROOM
25 MADISON AVE.
At 25th Street

well-furnished apartment. People sit up now listening to the radio while clad in garments that are tastefully tuned in with modern life.

"For this reason it seems that a long coat, 35 inches to be specific, is the wanted idea in the pajamas that garb the form of the man who is notably well dressed, so far as his outer apparel is concerned.

"The slipover idea in pajamas is another feature that is gaining with each season. Possibly it is not generally known, but many people are now wearing the coat section of the pajamas tucked into the trousers and this no doubt has fostered the popularity of the slipover pajama shirt.

"All sorts of collars are being worn, but from the style standpoint the English type of collar, and perhaps also the convertible collar, which is an English type collar that may be turned back, is the most progressive idea.

"Hip pockets have appeared in pajamas. Why they are necessary is difficult to imagine when the coat has a breast pocket; but still it is a fact that pajama suits with side pockets, breast pocket, and a hip pocket for the trouser companion piece are wanted and worn.

"In materials the foulard sleeping and lounging suit carries a distinctive air, although its price may be out of reach of the populace. Broadcloths in stripes, jacquarded broadcloths, fine cotton fabrics and a variety of materials contribute to the attractive appearance of the modern pajama. It seems that broadcloth in plain white is not as well received as it once was. The urge is for color in the better grades of pajamas" (Aug. 5, 1925, p. 70).

Illustrating this article were three pairs of colorful pajamas: cerise and black on a white ground with a cerise collar and cuffs; white polka dots on an orange ground serving as a back-

Patterned pajamas with a sash to give a trim-waisted look were advertised to the trade in 1923 as one of a group of special designs. [NEW YORK PUBLIC LIBRARY PICTURE COLLECTION]

ground for ornate white silk frogs; and two tones of purple and white with a purple collar, cuffs, and pocket trim.

These vivid colors and designs were not for every man, and the 1927 Sears, Roebuck and Company catalog catered to the more conservative element, offering the classic white muslin nightshirt, now trimmed with fancy braid, as well as cotton pajamas in both the coat style and the newer slipover or middy top in white, blue, and tan. The coat might be trimmed with rayon frog loops and have pearl buttons, making a quite stylish garment that sold for as little as $1.39. The most elegant pajamas Sears offered in 1927 were made of genuine broadcloth, the jacket having rayon frog loops and pearl buttons, at a price of $2.25.

While the newer middy-style pajama top was very popular (and practical, too, since it had no buttons to be lost), the coat style remained the favorite with most men, particularly after the introduction of the English collar that buttoned to the neck and turned down like the collar of a shirt. It had the tailored good looks a style-conscious man admired. Give him a pair of pajamas like that in, say, a bold stripe, let him insert a handkerchief in the chest pocket, and his mirror told him he had dash.

Not that a man had to settle for striped pajamas. As one fashion writer observed, "There are more models and more variety in pajamas than can be found in shirts, suits, hats and shoes. Man is going to bed all dressed up. New wealth since the war has given large numbers of men an appreciation of refinement that approach even the effeministic with regard to their personal belongings and apparel. It is a long stretch in progress from the days when mother, pedalling her foot-power sewing machine, turned out nightgowns for the whole family from bleached and unbleached muslin, unadorned by any ornamentation save, perhaps, a pocket for the handkerchief. Within one generation, we have adopted the most exotic ideas in sleepwear.

"What happened to the modest, retiring nightgown is nobody's business but that of the pajama manufacturing trade and the retailers who are now selling many thousands of dollars' worth of fancy pajamas in comparison with hundreds of dollars' worth of unadorned nightgowns. It is reported on fair authority that in a few remote spots, probably where wild Indians still range, the nightgown can be worn without occasioning a guffaw from a sophisticated, modern person who expects to see the nightgown topped with a tasseled night cap, otherwise the ensemble is upset. There are obese persons and independent individuals who wear nightgowns to bed. These have vents on either side of the skirt to permit a liberal stride when putting out the cat and blowing out various lamps and candles, but the modern gentleman who reads in bed by the aid of a soft boudoir light while reclining on tinted sheets, is horrified at the mere thought of a nightgown unless, of course, it is silk and even then it must adorn the form of some fair feminine creature.

"What has happened to the pajama business is that pajamas are no longer strictly sleeping garments. They are now lounge suits. Summer and winter gay and festive pajamas are the uniform of the new domesticity which includes protracted hours in front of the loud speaker, and vigorous evening exercise with three-quart cocktail shakers. The nightgown was an early retiring garment, while the modern pajama is a forward moving bit of apparel that goes to bed rather late.

"To illustrate, one of the brilliant sleeping and lounging suits recently viewed employs a background of black in order to show groups of overlapping polka dots in the brightest red, orange, green and all shades thrown by the spectrum. The space here is too limited to attempt even a partial description of what is on the fire for Merry Christmas and beyond, but the reader can visualize high solid colors piped with sharply contrasting binding. For instance, a green will have tan piping, peach will have black, then there is canary and black, white and green, tan and blue, green and yellow, and a list of most noticeable shades and contrasts. In patterned ideas almost every conceivable motif is used. All-over patterns that include paisley ideas, peacock tail effects, modernistic conceptions, and an unlimited range of designs are present. Oxblood, claret, maize and every imaginable masculine and feminine shade, tint and hue is in the showrooms. While it is true that blue is the favorite among colors, it has no strong plurality, because of the extended assortment available. Of all the ideas that shatter tradition, the one that imposes clean looking colors as preferable in bedroom and bathroom appears to have bent double, for the black and white combination in checks and in stripes has been one of the big sellers in pajamas.

"There is some effort to differentiate between seasons, according to pajama manufacturers. The dance of the seasons is interpreted by one manufacturer in the foliage reproduced in his designs. Fall designs are replete with autumn leaves. While autumnal conceptions glow with the bright hues of expiring vegetation, spring is expressed in bursting blossoms. Darker grounds and heavier effects are for fall and winter, light grounds and more widely spaced patterns in pastels form the spring motifs" (*Men's Wear,* Aug. 8, 1928, p. 88).

As the twenties neared their close, broadcloth vied with sateen for first place in sleepwear fabrics, while among pajama collars the high English collar remained the favorite, followed by the shawl collar, the middy, and, for a dogged minority, the military collar, which was a holdover from the heyday of the flannel pajama. Before the stock market crash of 1929 there was a flurry of new designs. Notable among them was the so-called cossack model, which had a jacket buttoning on the right side and a neck with a military look. As *Men's Wear* saw it, "The Cossack suits now being featured carry the impression of a mad dash across the steppes on galloping steeds accompanied by salvos of musketry rather than snores" (Apr. 10, 1929). It probably goes without saying that the cossack pajama was not suitable for every man.

By 1929 there was no question that style was important in men's sleepwear, to the extent that many men preferred a sash on the jacket of their pajamas despite the fact that it presented laundering problems and sometimes twisted about like a snake during the night. But the sash had panache and made a pair of pajamas look more expensive, and so it survived despite its obvious drawbacks.

1930–1950

By the mid-thirties the Russian influence had reached new heights of popularity. "Communism may satisfy the Muscovites of Moscow," wrote a *Men's Wear* fashion reporter, "but Americans going Russian to bed demand that their pajamas be Imperialistic. So a large percentage of the new fall sleeping suits button on the shoulder and at the side of the chest. They have military collars and double eagles are embroidered on the top pockets, not to mention sashes, fringed and plain. Next to being presented at court, going to bed will be the Winter's most regally dressed occasion. However, there is always the contingent of snorers who find buttons anathema. For these there have been developed numerous 'middy neck' pajama models. One style house has turned out a 'sport' model, the feature of which is a collar and neck opening like the current sport shirts, with a long pointed turnover collar and a group of small buttons at the neck" (July 24, 1935, p. 34).

Despite the strong Russian influence, many men preferred pajamas with stripes: blazer stripes, awning stripes, multiple stripes, and ombré stripes. And for men who placed a premium on ease and comfort, there were special models with "full but toned" pants and bellows pleats under the armholes. Also prominent were silk pajamas in jacquarded patterns with designs from such sports as whippet races, golf, tennis, and swimming. Others showed Chinese scenes or illustrated other romantic ideas.

Variety was the spice of life in sleepwear, and so there were swashbuckling military styles too. Nearly every sleepwear line had a model called "Grenadier" or "Musketeer." All this prompted *Men's Wear* to ask: "Will little timid fellows with bald heads buy these sleeping garments, or will they be purchased by great brawny athletic types?" (July 24, 1935, p. 36).

The popular summer pajamas were sheer and short. It was "a lot better

Pajamas in the pullover middy style with a collar, the coat style, and the high-necked cossack style were shown in 1932 in Club and Campus, *a syndicated retail catalog published by interests that brought out the first issue of* Esquire *in the fall of 1933.* [NEW YORK PUBLIC LIBRARY PICTURE COLLECTION]

to blush than to blister. Better too, to be cool and vile in voile than vilely boil in flannel" (*Men's Wear,* Apr. 10, 1935, p. 20). Voile was the leader; though sheer, it was strong enough to resist laundering wear. A selling point in the mid-thirties was the claim that a summer pajama cloth was "as light as a handkerchief." Linen and cotton crashes were added to summer sleepwear fabrics in models that featured

extension waistbands and pleats for added comfort. These pajamas were now categorized as lounge pajamas and were promoted for at-home leisure wear as well as for sleepwear.

In 1936 the vogue for lightweight sleepwear was heightened, and the "air-conditioned" cloths—the voiles, zephyr broadcloths, and batistes—were the biggest sellers in a range of solid colors. Important too was crisp,

cool seersucker, whose crinkled pattern produced tiny air pockets; especially attractive was a two-tone seersucker pajama top in a sports-shirt model worn with harmonizing solid-color trousers. Almost as much in demand were sheer rayons and extremely thin ginghams.

"The diversity of colors and patterns is so great," commented *Men's Wear*, "that no tastes have been overlooked. The solid tones include not only the light blues, yellows, tans and greens, but also the deep-shade shirting ideas—navy, wine, chocolate, black. A lot has been done in combining both lights and darks. One is used to accent the other in the body or trimming of the suit. Flowers, ocean waves, Grecian motifs, cathedral windows and paisleys are all printed in the sheer cloths to achieve something bizarre and eye-filling. In some instances the entire ground is covered with the pattern. In others the large figures are spaced well apart on dark-color grounds.

"Tartans are present no matter

(*above*) *In the center front of this 1936 layout is a silk pajama suit in maroon with white piping. From* Esquire, *January 1936.*

(*below*) *The Cat Cay pajamas of 1949 showed the influence of the sports shirt. At right is a pair with a blue top and yellow trim, with the colors reversed in the trousers. From* Esquire, *August 1949.*

where one goes in the pajama market, and their presence is justified, for right now the public is well-sold on tartan designs in accessories of all kinds. The summer selling season follows so soon after the spring offerings that this preference for tartans will not vanish. Tartans in no end of bright color combinations are being used—for complete suits, for the tops over solid trousers or the reverse, or for the trimming. Less conspicuous squares are also being liberally used.

"Small figures borrowed from neckwear make up an important group. Polka dots are easily the most important. White or light-color dots on dark backgrounds appear in almost every conceivable color combination but the leading trio is blue, wine and brown, each showing white dots. A lot of reversing is being done in giving the summer night suit a bright touch. The white of the dots becomes the background for the colored spots in the trimming. Other small figures are used to good advantage. Here too the trim is carefully worked out. An example is a red and black figure on white ground for the top, while the trousers are black and the red stripe down the sides matches the color in the figures.

"There are also novelties which are more interesting than the three big sellers the coat style with convertible English collar, the pullover with notched collar and the collarless middy. Sport-shirt styles have their place in this group—one in particular, the pullover with a single knot and loop to fasten it at the throat, is worthy of special attention. The knitted top with woven fabric trousers or shorts is still in the limelight. Suits with shorts and shirts of abbreviated cut are shown everywhere. While this is regarded as the practical summer suit, so far it accounts for a minor part of the business. The coat style with square neck is one of the innovations in sleeping wear this season.

"Of all the different branches of the summer-furnishings field, none is more undeveloped or offers greater possibilities to the retailer than pajamas" (Apr. 8, 1936, pp. 27–28).

In 1936 the development of metallic printing was regarded as a major change in the pajama field. For years fabric technicians had been considering the idea of a process that would print fabrics with metal to meet requirements for laundering and wear, and before the year was out one firm beat its competition when it was the first to offer a range of metallic prints. Colored buttons were now often seen instead of white pearl buttons, and sometimes pajama coats featured the knots and look of a mandarin jacket in place of buttons and buttonholes.

1950–1970

"Sell comfort when you sell pajamas," advised *Men's Wear*. "If at all possible unpin and iron at least ten of your leading numbers and hang them on a fixture or rack near the pajama counter. This will facilitate easy handling by salesmen and browsing customers. Comfort features such as fullness of sleeves, fullness of trouser legs, and type of waist closure can easily be viewed and examined. This method saves time and shows off the garment to its best advantage.

"Washability is your next big sales point, especially with women. Make sure you know the facts.

"Lounge numbers are your chance for that extra sale, especially during the holidays. Concentrate on style, color, and pattern in your sales talk" (Aug. 8, 1952, p. 123).

Accompanying this feature were photographs of a silk pongee pajama with a standard coat-style jacket trimmed in maroon; a gray broadcloth middy style with maroon collar trim and monogram; a fancy knit top with slack trousers; and a contrasting jacket and trousers in blue-and-white rayon with a stylized motif.

The big, bold stripes so popular in the thirties were back in the late fifties. *Gentlemen's Quarterly* sketched a pair in its September, 1957, issue, and with it ran the following dictionary-type copy: "*Blaz'er stripe pa-ja'ma:* An afterhours version of your daytime sports blazer and slacks; of lightweight cotton; dis-

Pajamas for Mr. T in 1950 combined color and comfort in a blue top patterned after a blazer and gray trousers with an elastic inset at the waistband. From Esquire, November 1950.

tinguished from other pajamas by a three-button front, tailored lapels and patch pockets. *Blazer* connotes especially bold color, e.g., red, blue. *Stripe* implies well-dressed man, awake or unconscious."

By this time the popular combination of knit top and broadcloth trousers was a well-established style in both contrasting and harmonizing colors, and it maintained its popularity through the sixties and into the seventies. By 1963 men's pajamas were combining the best of sportswear and dress shirts. Prime examples were short-legged models in batiste, featuring the Henley neckline, a classic crew neck with a three- or four-button placket in the center; chambray pants worn with a knit seersucker shave coat or sleepcoat, a button-front collarless version of the traditional nightshirt updated to a belted knee length; and simple cardigan pajamas in a bold British stripe.

By the early seventies sleepwear had acquired even more of a sporty leisure-wear character. And since the

The patterned sleepwear of the thirties was updated in the sixties in nightshirts that could be worn by women as well as by men. The models with horizontal stripes and bull's-eye dots are of 50 percent cotton and 50 percent polyester. The big multicolored prints are of 100 percent Orlon. From Esquire, *June 1968.*

384 | *Sleepwear*

Leather-lined slippers of brocade tapestry brighten this lounge suit (1971).

and sometimes in contrasting fabrics. Typical of the contemporary sleepwear look were sleep shorts of striped cotton seersucker combined with a matching belted button-front toga. These could be worn together or separately for sleeping, shaving, or lounging. Not all pajamas were short-legged. Important, too, were long-legged solid-color pajama pants in a synthetic or blended knit combined with a long-sleeved top in a sports shirt style or a toga style top with three-quarter sleeves and a sash. The nightshirt made an impressive comeback, now in a knee-length model with long or half sleeves, often in a printed or barber-pole–striped knit. The designer Pierre Cardin offered a floral-striped model with a full collar and side vents. A flannel in fireman red was a Christmas highlight.

"Unjamas" one house called its two-piece knit sleepwear, emphasizing its lounge suitability over its sleepwear appeal. Another coined the name "Kimojamas" for its sleepwear and lounging fashions. "It is often difficult to differentiate between what is being offered as loungewear and what is being carried in the sportswear department," noted Peggy Menaker in the *Daily News Record* (June 1, 1971, p. 6), describing a group of loungewear models featuring tank-top jump suits, two-piece shirt and pants sets, and hot pants or short shorts worn with a short samurai robe. By this time whatever proved popular in sportswear had been adapted in sleepwear (denim, for example, important in sportswear, had become equally important in sleepwear), prompting *Gentlemen's Quarterly* to ask, tongue-in-cheek fashion, "Whatever happened to pajamas?" (October, 1970, p. 94).

A serious reply to that question must be that today's peacock wants to be stylishly turned out at all times, awake or asleep. The Peacock Revolu-

This polyester-and-cotton pajama suit has a top with a shirting pattern on a white ground and solid-color trousers. The slippers are soft-sole moccasins (1971).

"new wave" man wore his robe (often a one-size-fits-all kimono) around the house to lounge, more and more lounge items were being designed to wear with the robe. Consequently, never before had pajamas and robes been more strikingly coordinated. Many sleepwear manufacturers were putting together mix-match coordinate packages, sometimes in one fabric

tion liberated every item in the masculine wardrobe, but perhaps no area reflects the new freedom with as much imagination and wit as sleepwear. The earliest and the latest hours of a man's twenty-four-hour day are now spent in apparel that is the ultimate in self-expression. And despite the progress that has already been made, the evolution of sleepwear has merely begun.

Robes

In the earliest years of the twentieth century robes, like many other articles of apparel, were first and foremost utilitarian; central heating was far from commonplace, and a warm robe was a necessity. Long robes of the wool blanket and cotton blanket variety were most often worn in solid colors and plaids, and it was not until the post-World War I period that fashion became a significant factor. By the mid-twenties, however, a fashion-conscious man was almost as thoughtful in choosing his robe as in choosing his overcoat.

1920–1930

The most stylish robe of the twenties was long, extending almost to the ankles. In 1926 the New York firm of A. Sulka & Company offered a particularly handsome robe in a lightweight French flannel with exceptionally broad horizontal stripings and a heavily fringed tie sash. Also popular was the heavy silk brocade with abstract or representational designs depicting everything from bullfights to Spanish dancers and Oriental pastoral scenes in shades of gold, wine, purple, or blue.

Just how far men's robes had evolved from the cotton and wool blanket days was graphically illustrated in *Men's Wear* (Dec. 5, 1928, p. 69), which showed photographs of four Hollywood film stars modeling their own dressing gowns. The British leading man John Loder wore a brilliantly colored dressing gown with a black Oriental pattern on an orange ground and collar, cuffs, and belt in black; Ralph Forbes had a gray-and-black brocaded silk gown with a wide shawl collar and cuffs of black; Conrad Nagel struck a debonair pose wearing a shawl-collared silk robe with a pattern of broken stripes in black on a tan ground; and Edmund Lowe appeared in a silk robe whose pattern of large, brilliantly colored squares covered both collar and cuffs.

FURNISHING DEPARTMENT 89

16H30 & 32 Bath Robes, English, French and domestic eiderdown, flannel, towelling, etc.

16H31-33-35 House Coats and Breakfast Jackets, silk, velveteen, and wool

16H34 & 36 Dressing Gowns and Room Suits in silks or vicuna wool, with or without quilted lining and quilted silk trimmings

Robes in flannel, silk, vicuña, or toweling and housecoats in silk, velveteen, or wool were fashionable in 1915. [COURTESY OF BROOKS BROTHERS, NEW YORK]

For the man whose income was not of motion-picture star proportions, the 1927 Sears, Roebuck and Company catalog offered less opulent robes costing from $3.98 to $10.98. For $3.98 a man could order a bathrobe made of "good quality cotton blanket cloth" in a double ombré pattern with two large pockets and a cord girdle. The sum of $7.50 could buy a bathrobe and slipper set of a fine-quality cotton bordered blanket, the robe featuring a large notched collar with cord trimmings that were repeated on the pockets, cuffs, and front, a rayon girdle, and pearl buttons. For $10.98 a lighter-weight robe of brocaded rayon could be purchased. It was significant that this robe was referred to as a lounging robe, while the bathrobe identification tag was reserved for the less costly and heavier cottons.

In 1928 *Men's Wear* speculated that men might become "coolie coat conscious," noting that thousands of stylish women had taken up the Japanese coolie coat for lounging and beach wear. "Because the feminine notion ran to coolie coats last summer, it is believed something similar may have possibilities in the men's field. For several winters fashion reporters and photographers have published and illustrated the style news that Palm Beach, Florida, and points abroad to a limited extent have approved the kimono sleeves on beach robes and that a dragon scampering across the back supplies just the right note in robe decoration" (Nov. 21, 1928, p. 83).

Japanese and Chinese robes were reportedly selling well in a number of the smarter shops for both men and women, and in the same issue *Men's Wear* offered its readers a primer on the coolie coat, pointing out that while it had been intended primarily as a laborer's coat, there were enough variations and elaborations of this garment to appeal to the American man whose

heaviest official labor might be the lifting of a fountain pen: "Coolie coats are usually low price cotton garments in black, printed with border and other designs in red. Blue with red figures is a popular conception. A variation of the coolie coat recently seen was in wool with narrow stripings in the brightest shades. These coats are excellent as house coats or beach coats if the wearer is inclined to like bizarre effects and their presence on the beach

The flannel robe, or dressing gown (as it was known in England), was in vogue in 1925, especially in strong patterns and vivid colors. [NEW YORK PUBLIC LIBRARY PICTURE COLLECTION]

Attractive Robes
Make Ideal Gifts

$10.98

33K1938 Blue and navy blue two-tone.
33K1939 Wine and blue two-tone.
Sizes, 34 to 48 in. chest measure. State size. Shipping weight, 2 pounds.
Men's Part Rayon Brocaded Lounging Robe made in a very neat pattern. The pocket trimming, collar, cuffs and underfacings are made of Skinners' satin. Rayon cord girdle. This robe would retail for a much higher price elsewhere and is a remarkable value at our price. Makes an appropriate gift for men.

33K1940 Navajo gray.
33K1941 Navy blue.
33K1942—Light brown. **$7.98**
Sizes, 34 to 48 in. chest measure. State size. Shipping weight, 3½ pounds.
Men's Cord Trimmed Cotton Beacon Blanket Cloth Bathrobe in a new Indian pattern. This robe is offered in three popular ground colors with the typical Indian patterns of beautifully blended colorings. Has shawl collar and three pockets. Good quality cord girdle. All seams are reinforced.

$7.50
33K1920—Blue.
33K1921—Gray.
33K1922—Brown.
Sizes, 34 to 48 inches chest measure. State size. Shpg. wt., 4 lbs.
Men's Bathrobe and Slipper Set. Made of a fine quality cotton bordered blanket in a popular ombre or shaded pattern. Has large notch collar that can be worn two ways, as illustrated. Cord trimmings on collar, pockets, cuffs and front of robe. Rayon girdle and pearl buttons.

$5.79
33K1932—Blue.
33K1934—Brown.
Sizes, 34 to 48 inches chest measure. State size. Shipping weight, 3½ pounds.
A very low price for a Cotton Bordered Blanket Bathrobe. Made with large shawl collar and three pockets. Excellent quality Rayon cord girdle. A large and roomy garment, finely tailored. All seams are reinforced to prevent fraying.

$9.98
33K1950—Brown and tan double ombre.
33K1951—Blue and tan double ombre.
Sizes, 34 to 48 inches chest measure. State size. Shipping weight, 3¾ pounds.
Our Finest Shawl Collar Blanket Robe. Made of a heavyweight genuine Beacon double ombre cotton bordered blanket. The beautiful deep shaded pattern of well blended colors, cord trimming and fine Rayon cable and cord girdle make this a very rich looking robe. Finely tailored with all seams reinforced. Three pockets and pearl buttons. A high grade robe with plenty of warmth.

$3.98
33K1928—Blue and gray ombre.
33K1929—Brown and blue ombre.
Sizes, 34 to 48 inches chest measure. State size. Shipping weight, 3¼ pounds.
Men's Bathrobe made of good quality cotton blanket cloth in a very attractive new double ombre or shaded pattern. Has two large pockets and cord girdle. All seams reinforced. We believe this garment to be superior to any low priced robe on the market, as it is cut as large and tailored as well as the higher priced robes.

Do Your Christmas Shopping From This Catalog

445

Cotton blanket and rayon robes in 1927 were of generous length, boldly patterned, and worn with cords.
From the 1927 catalog of Sears, Roebuck and Company.

adds color to the scene. They keep the sun off nicely and roll up into small compass when packed for traveling."

Yet, despite its undeniable glamour, the coolie coat won only limited favor, never becoming nearly as popular with the American man as it was with the American woman.

1930–1940

Meanwhile, beach robes were becoming more and more commonplace in the United States, gathering fashion momentum like many other new styles after having received the approval of the habitués of Palm Beach, the smartest American winter resort. A style survey in 1931 revealed that beach robes were worn by a higher percentage of bathers at Palm Beach that season than ever before, and this, observed *Men's Wear,* clearly suggested that the beach robe was in style, since what was worn at Palm Beach in February was certain to be worn the following summer at fashion-aware Northern resorts. The survey taker also noted:

"Solid color flannel is the top choice in robes with the men at this southern spa. This type has increased from 26 per cent last year to 38 per cent this season. Coming in both single- and double-breasted styles, the colors include yellow, blue, green, brown, tan, maroon and white. Many are finished plain, but contrasting piping at the edges is preferred. While solid color flannels have shown a steady gain, striped flannel robes have witnessed a decline from 26 per cent last year to 12 per cent this season. This comparison emphasizes the superiority of the solid color robe over the striped robe in the minds of style-influencing consumers.

"After the solid color flannel and terry cloth robes, the most important note is the popularity of figures. These are in linen, cotton and woolen fabrics. The all-over design washable fabrics in gay colors are still being worn by some of the best dressed bathers. However, small shepherd checks, as well as small all-over patterns, are extremely important in flannel and washable goods.

"A small number of the men seen at the beaches favored solid color ratiné robes. In addition to the smartness of this robe, practicality recommends it. Blue is the most popular color in this style of robe, although yellow, tan and green are also effective. A few of the men had scarfs to match" (*Men's Wear,* Mar. 25, 1931, p. 81).

The brocaded dressing gown in a double-breasted style dominates this 1930 page from the Observer, *a syndicated catalog for retailers published by the antecedents of* Esquire *magazine.* [NEW YORK PUBLIC LIBRARY PICTURE COLLECTION]

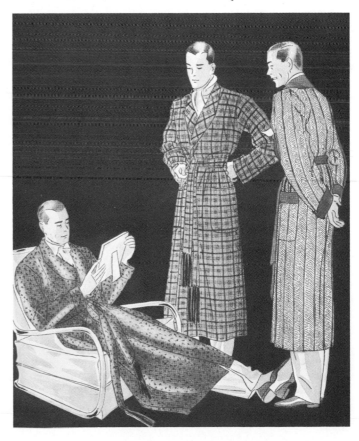

In 1932 figured silk, glen plaid, and striped flannel robes of generous length were in fashion, as shown in this retail advertisement. [NEW YORK PUBLIC LIBRARY PICTURE COLLECTION]

A mandarin-style robe of white silk with a self-jacquard design was displayed by Howard Wilson, who appeared in the film Success Story *in 1934. The black-and-gold dragon design embroidered on the back was repeated in smaller proportions on the pockets in front.* [COURTESY OF CULVER PICTURES, INC., NEW YORK]

Men's Wear, taking a look at the robes being prepared for fall, 1934, concluded that they preserved the "tradition of dignity and luxury" and predicted that it would be difficult for a man to buy a robe that was anything less than rich, smart, and colorful.

"Outstanding among the fabrics are the soft, very fine woven woolens, many of which are imports from Scotland and bear a strong Scottish influence. In these fabrics, checked and plaid designs, such as have been used so effectively in sports coats this Spring and Summer, are to be seen, but exaggerated and glorified—grounds of lemon-yellow, or lime-green, or burnt orange, with cross hatching in reds and green and blue and browns. The effects are gorgeous and, generally speaking, these robes are not for everybody. The price precludes that. Such a robe must come into the market to sell at $20 and over. Some of the vicuna and other luxury woolens will sell as high as $75 at retail.

"The balmacaan overcoat, which cut such a swath last Winter and proved its comfort and utility, has been plagiarized by the robe makers and a balmacaan model is to be seen in several lines. Another sport idea in clothing design which has been adapted to the lounge and bathrobe needs is the belted back and the pleated 'swing' back in its several manifestations and ramifications. Nearly all of the robes that are being shown for Fall are of two types. First, the double-breasted, six-button model, and then the wrap-around. Perhaps the wrap-around is gaining in popularity, inasmuch as the wrap-around robe is more easily adjusted to the needs of the individual figure and men dislike more buttons than they need. Shawl collars are to be seen in many of the silk and fine woolen robes, particularly where contrasting colors or tone on tone trimming is used. Some Cossack collars and some which are convertible are being shown. Wine tones are very popular and there is an increasing demand for black, particularly when piped in white or in gold" (Aug. 22, 1934, p. 22).

Yet a few robes of traditional types were still breaking sales records. Plain-color flannel robes, for example, were proving enormously popular in a number of models and in every conceivable color, often with a monogram or an emblem decorating the breast pocket. And the sturdy, long-wearing blanket robe had taken on a new lease on life; the old-fashioned allover wallpaper patterns and wallpaper colors were being replaced by neat checks and plain colors.

By the mid-thirties a campaign was under way to "beautify" the American male in his natural habitat, his home. The so-called average citizen's taste in at-home attire had irked many fashion writers, who now openly lamented the fact that while Americans were "probably the undisputed best dressed men in the world . . . once the kindly screen of his own front door obscures him from the comment of his neighbors, the ordinary Yank goes native." As these arbiters of fashion viewed the situation, the solution was to promote the handsome robe as a year-round item and not simply as a holiday gift item. But first they sounded this note of caution: "Men want color and even romance in house garments, but they do not necessarily demand to be made ridiculous. In fact, they would prefer to become irresistibly attractive. There never was any excuse for the Arabian Nights type of garment" (*Men's Wear,* Aug. 7, 1935, p. 12).

Meanwhile, flannels were becoming richer and more colorful. *Men's Wear* in August, 1935, sketched a double-breasted flannel robe in orange-and-brown ombré stripes and another in an oversize gingham design.

By the mid-thirties the fancy velvet smoking jacket had begun to lose popularity. In its place emerged a new and colorful cocktail or lounge jacket designed, as one fashion editor put it, for "evenings at home before the fire . . . or if friends drop in for bridge . . . or that awkward Sunday period before it is time to go to church. For the very sophisticated, undoubtedly the cocktail jacket is useful wear at cocktail time, but for the majority of plain mortals it has its principal appeal as a good looking and comfortable house coat, which harmonizes with the modern apartment or penthouse" (*Men's Wear,* Aug. 7, 1935, p. 12).

By 1936 men had abandoned the bathing shirt and were being seen bare-chested on the beach, a fact that, in the opinion of most fashion authorities, made the beach robe "as necessary to bathing trunks as bread is essential to a filling in a sandwich" (*Men's Wear,* Feb. 5, 1936, p. 19). Yet it was noted that "too many house gowns" were being pressed into service on the beach. It was reasoned, therefore, that what were needed were robes so obviously and handsomely designed for the beach and only for the beach that the man who made his bathrobe do double duty would look gauche. As

Fashions in loungewear were depicted in this 1934 layout: (upper left) a lightweight silk foulard robe in a paisley pattern; (upper right) a solid-color velveteen jacket styled like a suit jacket, for entertaining at home; (center) a wrap-style cocktail jacket of three-quarter length, in brown velvet with wine-color silk trim; (bottom) a blue flannel double-breasted jacket and a tan flannel robe with brown trim. From Esquire, *February 1934.*

a *Men's Wear* fashion reporter argued, "The age of specialization in clothing is here and apparently here to stay. That means that robes and pajamas or lounge suits intended for beach wear should be so obviously only for the beach that the wearer would feel some hesitation in using them elsewhere. At the same time these garments would have to have such a strong 'pull' and allure and should be so priced that the buyer will not feel that their purchase is a hopeless extravagance." Cotton, it was felt, had merit, and so did some of the new waffle weaves, the heavy-appearing basket weaves, the monk's cloths, seersuckers, and peasant weaves, all of which were judged to be not only good-looking and rugged ("truly he-man styles") but nearly ideal for absorbing water and "remaining presentable under the exacting conditions of the beach" (Feb. 5, 1936, p. 19).

As for at-home wear in 1936, *Men's Wear* was certain that the American male was going to be more luxuriously robed than ever before: "Since it is estimated that 95 per cent of the robes are bought by women, it is no small wonder that designers have sought to outdo their achievements of the past. They first endeavored to make robes that would please the woman customer who might envision her husband or friend clad as a romantic cinema lover. This, of course, encompasses a broad field. Next, the adept craftsman gave much consideration to the male recipient" (Aug. 5, 1936, p. 14).

What resulted were such fashions as a two-tone blue plaid flannel robe with solid-color trimming, double-breasted lapels, and slash pockets; a wrap model in a large dark-red-and-white plaid zephyr twill; a solid-color flannel with a two-initial monogram on the chest pocket, worn with the collar turned down, the top button unfastened, and the lapels rolling to the middle button; a solid-color jacquarded silk with satin trimming; a roomy mandarin model of crepe printed with red-and-yellow figures on a black ground; a solid-color chiffon velvet robe with satin trimming and lining; a brown velvet robe with a yellow embroidered basket-weave effect in a plaid design; a flannel cocktail jacket with the chalk stripes of the then-popular gray flannel suit; an orange-and-tan crepe cocktail jacket with black silk facings on the lapels and cuffs; a cocktail jacket of blue crushed velvet trimmed with blue satin; an overchecked flannel robe in brown, orange, and tan, embodying the raglan shoulders and military collar of the balmacaan topcoat; and a yellow flannel robe styled like the classic polo coat.

The trend in 1938 was toward a greater use of tailoring in men's robes, and, said a *Men's Wear* fashion writer, in a few instances a robe would be so impeccably tailored that it might almost be worn on the streets as a topcoat. The street-wear influence affected not only the tailoring of the robe but also the appearance of its fabric, which was now often tweed, herringbone, or a suiting stripe. "Patch pockets and pockets with flaps intensify the outdoors look, while slightly padded shoulders, yokes and a topcoat finish generally heighten the street wear effect" (Aug. 10, 1938, p. 35).

A trend was also noted toward flannel, challis, and wool robes, all of which were more functional than fancy. There was a marked restraint in the use of color. Noteworthy was the introduction of gabardine as a fabric for robes in a range of shades; it was being made up along severely plain lines without piping, contrasting trim, or other embellishment. Simplicity was the overall theme for robes during these Depression years.

By 1938 rayon had become established as an important robe fabric, and makers were getting into the habit of labeling each robe with a rayon ticket. Meanwhile, at the New York World's Fair the Man of Tomorrow, looking ahead to the approach of the new home entertainment medium of television, was fashionably robed. Buttons on robes were losing popularity as more and more men showed a prefer-ence for the freedom of the looser buttonless wrap style. "Past experience demonstrates," concluded *Men's Wear*, "that the average man doesn't want to bother with buttons, but prefers to wrap the robe and tie the sash" (Aug. 10, 1938, p. 35). By 1938 a robe with a slide fastener was also being promoted.

1940–1960

World War II put a freeze on innovations in robes, as it did on many other articles of men's apparel, but beginning in 1948, with the introduction of *Esquire*'s "bold look," a coordinated fashion concept, a new look emerged in robes, exemplified by a double-breasted model along the lines

The "bold look" was apparent in a double-breasted flannel robe in a blue-and-gray check with solid-blue trim patterned after the polo coat. From Esquire, *November 1948.*

of the popular polo coat or, as the caption writer phrased it in the April, 1949, issue, "the *lusty* lines of a polo coat rather than the soft shape of the robe you've been wearing." The new bold look robe was "*double*-chested," and instead of a shawl collar it had wide, flaring peaked lapels that added breadth and stature to the chest and shoulders, plus a belt stitched on in the back, which was pleated for fullness and comfort. And so buttons on robes had not been discarded after all. In fact, the bold look called for outsize buttons. By the late 1940s most people were television-conscious, and *Esquire's* fashion department compared the tall, broad-shouldered, high-powered look of a lounging robe with high-peaked lapels to a television tower.

In 1950 the bold look gave way to *Esquire's* "Mr. T," a slimmer, trimmer look. For Mr. T the fashion department chose a solid-color flannel robe with much narrower lapels and a notched collar that could be closed at the throat.

Now that the summer suit had finally achieved a maximum of cool comfort, the man of the fifties expected the same comfort in everything else he wore, which prompted *Esquire* to note in August, 1950, that the biggest news in summer comfort was the thin fabric that made living easy: "Even more important than a cool shower and plenty of ice in your drink are the cooling abilities of underclothes, pajamas, and robes you wear when your main objective is summer comfort." A prime example of the cool-as-a-zephyr robe was a fine-dotted thin cotton in blue and white.

By 1953 man-made fibers had found a permanent use in both robes and pajamas, often being blended with natural fibers to create fabrics with special advantages. Judged ideal for vacationers and travelers were the seersuckers and wrinkle-resistant oxford shirtings then being used in robes. "The lightweights have sure-fire sales appeal" is the way a *Men's Wear* reporter summed it up.

Men's Wear, reflecting in 1953 on the national trend toward lightweight

This wrap-type maroon flannel robe with raglan shoulders and slanting pockets qualified as a Mr. T fashion in 1950. From Esquire, *November 1950.*

clothing, noted that as a result a new year-round use in robes had been found for cotton, ranging from utilitarian terry cloths through luxurious fancies to exotic Indian madrases. Illustrating this "cotton comeback" feature were photographs of an above-the-knee robe of terry cloth trimmed with plaid at the belt, collar, and cuffs ("a welcome addition to any beach outfit"); a coin-dotted robe high-

lighted by solid-color trim on the pockets, cuffs, sash, and shawl collar; and a crinkled seersucker robe.

Attempting to analyze the robe-buying habits of the American man of the early 1950s, *Men's Wear* admitted: "There's no accounting for which fellow will want the elaborate jobs and which will want the severely conservative models. It seems that the wearer's choice of business and sports attire has no relation to the type of robe which he prefers to wear for relaxing, or in which he scuffs to and from his daily ablutions. So, here is at least one instance when the salesman can't size up his customer's taste by casting an appraising eye over the clothes he is wearing.

"The conservative businessman turned out in a mouse-grey suit, black shoes, and non-obtrusive accessories to match, is just as apt to be a prospect for a chartreuse and black modern robe as his more flamboyant brothers.

"By the same token, a zoot-suited sharpy may find his heart's desire in a solid colored job" (Feb. 22, 1952, p. 33).

Many of the popular robe prints in the mid-fifties were inspired by English sporting motifs with rod, reel, and fly or horses and jockeys screen-printed on light, rich-looking pure silks. Actually the customs, arts, and sports of many lands were depicted in these robe prints, but England was by far the most frequently represented.

1960–1970

Now that the American man had discovered the greater freedom of a lightweight robe, the heavier fabrics suffered a decline. Even in the very early sixties, before the outbreak of the Peacock Revolution, the American college man had cast his vote for lightweight knee-length kimono-styled robes and short-sleeved collarless shave togas in such fabrics as cotton terry velour and basket-weave wool. By the mid-sixties the knee length was the popular length, and beneath this short robe the liberated peacock more often

(left to right) A patterned polished-cotton shave coat with matching pajamas (slightly visible); a kimono robe in miniature-checked wool; and a three-piece set consisting of polka-dot cotton short pajamas and a shave toga (over the shoulder). From Esquire, *May 1966.*

than not wore a pair of matching short pajamas.

In the 1930s robes had evidenced a tailored street-wear influence, and in the early 1970s there was a marked movement toward sporty leisure-wear clothes that many fashion authorities thought could easily be worn on the street. One trade reporter commented on the difficulty of differentiating between so-called lounge wear and what was being carried in the sportswear department. In short, robes had taken on new dimensions and under the broad umbrella of "lounge wear" were easing their way into sportswear.

Making this "new wave" leisure wear ultracomfortable were soft, supple terry cloths, velours, triacetate jerseys, and the widely acclaimed knit and double-knit fabrics. "Most agree that the bathrobe is not the utilitarian item it was once and no longer is used primarily for keeping warm," wrote the *Daily News Record* in 1971, adding that "a man wears a bathrobe around the house to lounge." To illustrate this point, the *Daily News Record* sketched a 100 percent bonded Acrilan robe with wide lapels, a tie belt, and four pleated patch pockets; a notched-collar model of 100 percent cotton terry cloth in a nubby textured popcorn pattern; and an acetate one-size-fits-all kimono robe that in 1971 was the best-selling item in sleepwear departments. Soon the kimono robe was being given the more exotic name "Kabuki robe" and was being shown in dazzlingly hot, bright colors. Often a family was dressed in look-alike kimonos accented with monograms.

(left) Kimono-type wrap robe, or "Kabuki robe," with three-quarter sleeves, striped in red, yellow, and blue, worn with slightly grained leather moccasin slippers. (right) Maroon velour wrap-style robe with a monogram on the chest pocket, worn with suede sheep's-hair slippers (1971).

Although the wrap model was by far the leader, the buttoned robe was not gone. The robe resembling an overcoat, made in a knit or double-knit triacetate with a napoleon collar, wide lapels, and patch pockets, had assertive-looking buttons. Despite the overwhelming acceptance of the short robe, there were avant-garde men of fashion in the early seventies who favored the floor-length caftan-inspired robe. Often made in wide-track stripes with three-quarter sleeves and a deeply scooped neckline, it could also serve as a beach robe over the contemporary abbreviated swimwear. The sporting motifs of the robes of the fifties were revived in the seventies, with hunting dogs and game birds enlivening many lightweight cotton one-size-fits-all kimonos.

It was "do your own thing" in robes just as it was in suits, shirts, ties, and every other item of male apparel, for the Peacock Revolution abolished the timeworn bathrobe that once hung on the back of the bathroom door. In its place is a wardrobe of robes, because the new wave man is as conscious of his appearance when he is alone as he is when he is on display. Pride being part of the peacock's personality, his at-home lounge wear reflects this pride. No woman of fashion ever selected a negligee with more fastidious care than today's man of fashion selects a robe, which has become one of the most provocative items of apparel in his wardrobe.

Canes and Umbrellas

No man of quality out for a Sunday stroll at the turn of the twentieth century would have been seen without a cane any more than he would without his hat or stickpin. And the man who could afford it had a wardrobe of canes. Malacca, rosewood, and bamboo canes were in the dressy category for town wear, while the blackthorn, a natural native thorn cane, dominated the sporty category as the first choice of well-attired men rusticating at fashionable country places. An important contribution to the world of canes came from Great Britain early in the century: the shooting-stick cane, which when unfolded became a seat for the spectator, who carried it not only at shooting events but eventually at golf matches, horse races, and other sporting events.

The types and shapes of cane handles varied, the silver handle on a black ebony cane being preferred for formal evening wear. Shapes ranged from straight to crooked, and still other canes featured the knob type of handle.

The introduction of the motorcar signaled the eventual demise of the cane as an important fashion accessory, but its popularity waned gradually. As late as 1926 a reporter noted 248 canes hanging from the hat shelf at one fashionable resort. He took the occasion to comment that the cane was indeed a "benefactor" of fashion: "The reason is clear. The man who decides to carry a stick automatically decides that he will not wear a battered old hat, down-at-the-heel shoes, a questionable suit or overcoat, badly soiled or worn gloves, or the kind of furnishings favored in the five-and-ten-cent stores" (*Men's Wear*, Mar. 10, 1926).

Although a smart malacca stick with a crooked handle could be had for $5 in 1926, the pride of any serious cane collector was a full-bark malacca, a stick made from wood in which no joint appeared, which cost $50 or

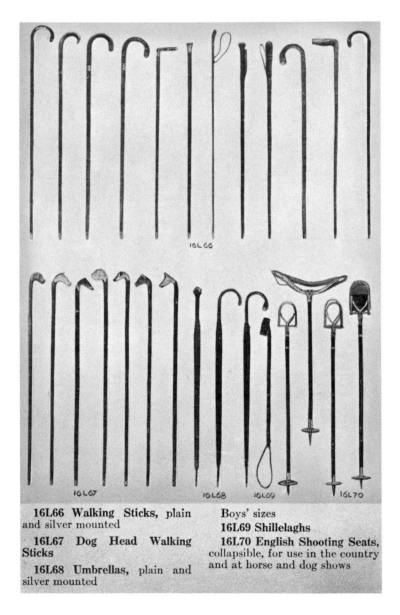

16L66 Walking Sticks, plain and silver mounted

16L67 Dog Head Walking Sticks

16L68 Umbrellas, plain and silver mounted

Boys' sizes
16L69 Shillelaghs

16L70 English Shooting Seats, collapsible, for use in the country and at horse and dog shows

The custom of carrying canes was so firmly established in 1915 that available types included not only ebony, malacca, ash, and other canes but shooting sticks for sports events. Umbrellas had either plain or silver-mounted handles. [COURTESY OF BROOKS BROTHERS, NEW YORK]

more. A *Men's Wear* writer observed: "Just as the pipe collector will commit arson to gain possession of a straight grain briar bowl, although the straight grain improves the smoking qualities not a whit, the man who knows canes yearns for the full bark specimen just because of its rarity. From the natives who cut it in the jungle down to the final cane-wise customer this isolated specimen is eagerly sought, and there is where the chief difference in price occurs. At a few feet distance even the man who knows canes could not tell the difference. Failing of achieving the full bark, the next desirable stick is that which contains the longest stretch of wood without a joint" (Feb. 10, 1926, p. 104). Meanwhile, there were such novelties as an alligator-covered handle on a malacca stick; a snake-wood stick with a composition-amber handle and a plain silver band; and a lizard-skin–covered, straight-handled malacca stick with a silver band.

"In spite of the vogue of color in clothing, color in sticks, excepting for handles, has not met with wild enthusiasm," this *Men's Wear* article noted. "The pimento stick and even the ebony has lost ground. The straight handled ebony stick frequently mentioned as the correct stick for evening wear is not as fast a seller as its frequent mention by fashion writers might lead to believe.

"Sticks with gold bands, the bands employed with restraint and decorated usually with engine turned design are in favor, and the highly ornate gold headed presentation cane has gone the way of chin whiskers. Rather than a lavish exhibition of the jeweler's art, walking stick decoration has taken the form of composition, horn or hide handles. In recent years there have developed crook and straight handles made of substances which in appearance resemble amber. Some of these

have given trouble in that they were brittle and when carelessly dropped or knocked involved a trip back for expensive repairs.

"Pigskin, sharkskin, lizard and a number of conceptions are staples and novelties that some shops find little

The shooting stick with a folding seat, held by the man in the foreground, has been part of the fashion scene since the beginning of the century, and still is in the seventies. From Esquire, *March 1939.*

difficulty in selling and one of the newer ideas is a handle in a composition in color resembling jade. Ebony and other sticks with inlaid domino designs in ivory are distinctly different designs that do not sell well. One of the appreciated designs in the stick itself is the mottled effect in Malacca sticks made by the secretions of jungle insects which, it is said, for some unknown reason will swarm over one stick, patterning it in a salable fresco and totally ignoring neighboring sticks."

This writer concluded his report on an optimistic note: "It is a safe assertion that cane carrying can be fostered through the intelligent and consistent efforts of men's wear merchants who will feature the article. Styles in clothes that are here and predicted as on the way will encourage the keeping of hands out of pockets. With no pockets to hide them, these hands will be well gloved and well employed when carrying sticks."

And canes did manage to maintain a certain measure of popularity throughout the Depression thirties, owing to the fact that a small group of very wealthy Americans then dominated fashion. These were men who shopped Savile Row in London and were very much under British influence. They favored elegant, softly constructed lounge suits with double-breasted waistcoats, bowler hats, and homburgs and, as *Esquire* observed in June, 1934, showed a penchant for the black bamboo cane for town wear.

The magazine's fashion editor followed these gentlemen ("a small group, numerically, but of large importance socially and financially") to the races at Belmont Park and Saratoga and reported what they wore. Casual elegance was the characteristic of their outfits no matter where they happened to be, and at the races, with a pair of binoculars slipped over his shoulder, the man of fashion might wear a single-breasted glen plaid suit, a double-breasted fawn-colored linen waistcoat, a striped tie, and a homburg hat and carry "one of those bamboo sticks which have a gold pencil

inserted at the turn of the handle." When such a man indulged in the hobby of farming or breeding show dogs or horses, he would carry a rough wood stick 52 to 57 inches long with a V-shaped cut at the top that earned it the name "thumb stick."

In October, 1945, *Esquire*'s fashion department devoted a full page to canes, headlining the feature "Canes Come Back" and explaining why: "Outlets for self-expression in male dress are somewhat limited, but you can let go with canes. Of real functional value in the country for hiking over rough terrain, many canes also come to town just because men 'like the looks of them' or like the feel in their hands as they swing along smooth paving." Illustrations accompanying the article showed canes and clothes that teamed with them: a rugged blackthorn with an overplaid tweed suit, a rosewood with a double-breasted pencil-striped business suit, a malacca cane (straight or crooked) for semiformal dress, and a natural ash with a plaid jacket and flannel slacks.

Yet, despite its undeniable style, the cane continued to slip further into obscurity. In Great Britain, where tradition still counts for something, the cane has survived in a limited way, but in the United States the cane had become an almost historic item by the early 1970s. The Museum of the City of New York, in fact, took pride in its collection of some 275 models.

The cane nonetheless has not completely disappeared, and the 1970 catalog of the Uncle Sam Umbrella Shop in New York contains several canes ("practical canes and canes for conversation"). Among them are a pocket folding cane of aluminum ebony that opens to 36 inches and collapses to 10 inches; a black ebony evening cane

with a buffalo horn handle; a heavy-duty lucite ("See-Through Cane"); and a "5-flask cane," a freewheeling copy of a cane that enjoyed some popularity during the prohibition era.

Umbrellas

Umbrellas are first and foremost utilitarian, but anything that serves a man of fashion never fails to pick up style, and umbrellas have not been an exception. The fashion-conscious American man has often been strongly influenced by his British counterpart, for whom the umbrella is practically an instrument of survival. The thin, furled silk umbrella was in style both in England and in the United States during the first decades of this century, although the less affluent carried cotton umbrellas. The umbrella has always been regarded with respect by Americans, but the British have regarded it with a little less than reverence, as the following excerpt from a turn-of-the-century magazine article indicates:

"Oh, what a good friend to a man is an umbrella in rain time, and likewise at many other times. Moreover, who doubts that you are a respectable character provided you have an umbrella? The respectable sees that you have an umbrella and concludes that you do not intend to rob him, and with justice, for robbers never carry umbrellas. Oh, a tent, a shield, a lance and a voucher for character is an umbrella. Amongst the very best of friends of man must be reckoned an umbrella" (George Borrow, quoted in *A History of the Umbrella*).

The very nature of the umbrella has prevented any drastic changes in styling. The umbrella handle, however, has managed to display considerable

The classic umbrella with a pigskin handle and a pencil in a slot, popular in 1934, has endured through the years.

mon with umbrellas. There was, for example, an umbrella-cane set of malacca, the umbrella having a malacca shank as well as a malacca handle. Cane and umbrella were matched both as to wood and as to their engine-turned silver bands. When not in use, the set was held together by two black straps.

In March, 1939, *Esquire* showed a lightweight overall rain suit ("for shooting, fishing and spectator country wear during wet weather"). With it the model carried a boldly striped large golf umbrella.

The silk umbrella was the leader until the development of nylon in the 1940s, but since then this sturdy fiber has dominated the field for both men and women.

The colorful big golf umbrella, shown here in a 1937 version, has retained its fashion status. From Esquire, *May 1937.*

This wooden-shanked umbrella, a traditional British type, has a natural malacca handle. From Esquire, *September 1938.*

variety: handles have been fashioned of rosewood, malacca, furze, bamboo, silver, gold, various kinds of horn, and plastic. The so-called crooked handle has been dominant through the years, but some men have shown a preference for the straight handle set at a right angle to the shaft of the um- brella, while others have favored a short handle with a knob. A staple feature has been an ornamental metal stud, usually set at the base of the handle.

Canes were still rather important fashion accessories in the mid-twenties, and they often had features in com-

A telescopic folding umbrella with a black leatherette handle and zipper case (1971). [POLAN, KATZ & CO. INC.]

(below) The motion-picture actor Michael York carries a red, white, and blue umbrella coordinated with his red-striped blue alpaca-and-wool cardigan, white polyester slacks, and poromeric shoes. From Esquire, April 1971.

(above) Julie Christie and Alan Bates cope with the rain in Norfolk, England. Bates carries a small-patterned umbrella by Louis Vuitton to protect their belted raincoats. From Esquire, February 1971.

This automatic self-opening umbrella has a nylon cover (1971). [POLAN, KATZ & CO. INC.]

400 | Canes and Umbrellas

Along with the slimmer Continental suit styling of the late 1950s came the Continental-styled umbrella with a lightweight frame and covering that enabled it to be rolled almost pencil-slim. The handle of this umbrella was usually either of black leather covered with stitched sides or of polished wood. The push-button, or self-opening, umbrella that popped open at a touch entered the wet-weather picture in the fifties, and early in the next decade came the small folding umbrella based on a German pattern; it telescoped to 15 to 18 inches and slipped into a leather or plastic case that could be carried in a raincoat pocket or an attaché case.

In the early 1970s the push-button style was introduced in a walking-stick model and advertised as "big, brawny and definitely impressive—a conversation piece you'll be proud to carry. This true collector's item has a 10 ribbed umbrella nestled inside its handsome cylinder. It's almost three feet long from its smart leatherette handle to its golden tip. All-plated steel mechanism opens to a wide 42" to keep you dry." And although the black umbrella was still the leader in men's umbrellas, this new push-button model was also popular in a rich shade of brown. The folding umbrella in the seventies was widely advertised in print and on television as a travel umbrella and a "tote-type" umbrella. It was described as small when it was hiding and big in the rain.

As men's clothes increasingly became a means of self-expression in the wake of the Peacock Revolution, it was inevitable that the large, often-flamboyant golf umbrella would be seen in town as well as in the country. Although the multicolored sixteen-rib golf umbrella did not become a national fad but instead was confined to a minority of men in the larger cities, perhaps it can be said to have encouraged more uninhibited novelty umbrella designs. In October, 1970, GQ Facts, a fashion apparel current-trends service compiled by *Gentlemen's Quarterly,* showed a collection of nylon umbrellas designed "to complement leather boots, belts and jackets." They featured knob handles topped with four different leather straps: an Indian braid trim with a fringed bottom, a studded strap with a fringed bottom, a peace symbol, and a fringed strap. All were in brown and came with simulated suede cases that were coordinated with their straps. Equally avant-garde was the sports seat umbrella, although its ancestry could be traced to the shooting-stick cane that had doubled as a seat for the spectator sportsman.

Unlike the cane, the umbrella remains in wide use today. And if it sometimes does not seem to reflect the "new wave" attitude toward self-expression in fashion, perhaps that is because it so well expresses man's no-nonsense attitude toward inclement weather.

Golf Clothes

American golf links have long served as a bucolic setting for business transactions. From the outset golf carried with it a certain status; practically every United States President of this century has been an avid golfer. And in the first decade of the century, when the country was in the process of building its industrial power, golf, then considered a rich man's sport, was already popular with enterprising businessmen.

Since golf had originated in Scotland, the more fashion-conscious American golfer at the turn of the century took care that his garb had a Scottish character. Knickers, which evolved from the knee breeches of English court dress, were worn, along with a tweed suit jacket (often with a matching waistcoat), a business shirt with a starched collar, a bow or four-in-hand tie, long stockings, sturdy shoes, and a tweedy cap or a woolly felt hat. This combination made a rather impressive-looking though not very practical golfing outfit. But since formality was the order of the day, the well-dressed golfer who took pride in being correct did not balk at apparel that today's golfer would regard as a serious impediment to his game.

Still, not every golfer paid so much attention to his attire on the links, and the ordinary golfer could take heart at the publication of a photograph of President William H. Taft swinging a golf club while dressed in shirt sleeves,

Simplicity characterized the apparel of early amateur golf champions. (left) Charles B. MacDonald, the first champion, in 1895, favored an all-white outfit. (center) H. J. Whigham, the champion in 1896 and 1897, wore close-fitting knickers. (right) Findlay S. Douglas appeared in a jacket with turned-back sleeves and trousers with deep cuffs.
[COURTESY OF CULVER PICTURES, INC., NEW YORK]

trousers from an old suit, and a straw skimmer. Only when golf began to attain a measure of mass popularity would the more affluent golfer begin to pay serious attention to his apparel, then using his more expensive and varied wardrobe as a means of separating himself from the Johnny-come latelies who had just discovered the game.

1910–1920

The vitality and prosperity of the post-World War I era had many happy effects on men's clothes. The ex-serviceman, who had come to enjoy the facile lines of his military uniform, returned home determined to look and feel just as comfortable in his civilian clothes. He was in no mood to accept uncomfortable apparel simply because it was considered proper. He insisted on more natural styling, and so the heavily padded suits of the previous decade gave way to suits of trimmer cut and softer tailoring. Oxfords replaced high-button shoes, the high starched shirt collar gave way to the soft collar, and the new wristwatch made the heavy gold watch and fob seem antique. Furthermore, the returning soldier was in much better physical condition than his father had been at his age. Full of energy and very sports-minded, he developed an interest in golf. And at about the time he was learning to swing a club, the wealthier American golfer grew increasingly clothes-conscious. In fact, one visiting Britisher found his American hosts so nattily dressed when they approached the links that he was inspired to write a fashion report for *Men's Wear:*

"This host of mine was down early to breakfast with me and before nine we were out in the air. He was sort of a picture in his idea of golf dress of various shades of brown—a dark brown, plain, vicuna jacket, lighter

Golf's big triumvirate: (left to right) J. H. Taylor, James Braid, and Harry Vardon, portrayed in a painting of 1913. Vardon's jacket was easy-fitting, his knickers were close-fitting, and his stockings had turned-back tops. [THE BETTMANN ARCHIVE, INC.]

brown wool waistcoat, white cheviot shirt and collar, green and taupe knitted tie, tan cord knicker breeches, two-tone brown stockings, stout, brown golf shoes and a greenish woolly felt hat.

"Everything was right. I mean in the way of appropriateness. The jacket looked smart, and yet as though he could get a proper swing in it without its hitching up in the neck. There was plenty of room in the shoulders and skirts and bully, big pockets. The breeches had the necessary length and no semblance of a screw. Most of the men wore this fashion of jacket and the knicker breeches for golf" (Nov. 15, 1919, p. 108).

There were many smartly dressed golfers as well as spectators, however, who preferred the norfolk jacket, which had been inspired by the jacket of the Duke of Norfolk's hunting suit in the early eighteenth century. Its distinguishing features were two box pleats down each side in front and two down each side in back. The first American copies of the norfolk carried a belted back, and soon all-around belts also appeared. Fashioned of Harris or Donegal tweed and worn with knickers, heavy woolen knee hose, and a tweed cap, it made for a handsome golf costume. Often the norfolk jacket was the top half of a country suit and therefore was doing double duty when it was worn with knickers for golf or with white flannel trousers for resort wear.

In 1919 the sportswriter Grantland Rice wrote a magazine article on the psychological effect a golfer's clothes had on his game. It was titled "Dressing to Beat Par":

A man, to be in a decent frame of mind for play, doesn't have to be 3 up on Beau Brummell, of course. We are not referring here to any select or overpowering styles, imported or home made. We are referring in the main to a feeling of neatness and respectability. If the golfer knows that he presents a decent appearance on the course, he is that much better off in his own frame of mind—and mental attitude has more than a trifle to do with Scotia's ancient game.

Some time ago we noticed two golfers starting on a certain course from the first tee. Both wore shoes that looked as if they might have been salvaged from rear area after a big attack.

Neither had shaved that day. The weather was not particularly sultry, yet neither had on a collar. Their trousers had known more than one hard campaign. One had on an old hat and the other a badly stained and badly disjointed cap.

"Who are they?" we asked the club professional standing nearby. "The two worst duffers in the world," he answered. "Neither ever broke 120 in his life and both of them are crabs."

Their costumes had already answered the bulk of the query. Their clothes were merely running true to form. As neither took any particular pride in his clothes, so neither took any pride in his game. Both completely forgot—or didn't care—that they owed something at least to the other club members.

It is worthy of note that practically none of the leading golfers, amateur or professional, are ever untidily arrayed for battle. The golfer owes neatness in dress to his gallery. If he carries no gallery he owes it to his other club members. If there are no club members around he owes it to himself. It will not help him in any physical way, but it will undoubtedly help a lot in the way of increased morale. And there are times when morale is badly needed following the entrance into a yawning bunker or the depressed feeling that comes after missing a two-foot putt.

And it is well enough that a badly dressed or rather an untidily dressed golfer, even if he is pretty good, will always be taken for a duffer of purest ray serene by those who see him on the course. In this way the apparel will very often proclaim his score. (*Men's Wear,* July 9, 1919, p. 97)

1920–1930

The widespread interest in golf that became apparent soon after World War I developed into a boom in the early twenties. As a fashion writer noted in *Men's Wear,* "Every town or city of any size in America today has one or more golf links, and new clubs are springing up overnight everywhere. Every summer sees hundreds of thousands of American men taking up golf for the first time. Most stores sell golf clothes and the dress accessories that go with golf clothes" (July 9, 1924, p. 37). American golf and golf apparel came of age in this era of "flaming youth."

In 1921 the leading professional golfers preferred knickers of tweed, linen, or flannel. A knitted cardigan jacket and adaptations of the norfolk jacket were considered fit companions for knickers, though actually some of the adaptations had little in common with the British original and often any jacket with vertical box pleats was referred to as a norfolk.

The National Open Championship matches in 1923 brought out the fash-

ion press, who noted the predominance of plus fours (knickers that extended 4 inches below regular knickers), plaid diamond and check golf hose, and white shirts. The following year an analysis in *Men's Wear* of golf apparel worn by 200 well-dressed men on fashionable metropolitan links revealed that knickers were predominant, with plain linen plus fours, light brown plus fours, tweed mixtures, gray plus fours, brown medium knickers, and gray medium knickers vying for favor in that order. White flannel trousers occupied seventh place, and gray flannel trousers tenth. Brown sweaters accounted for 48 percent of the sweaters seen, and white sweaters for 20 percent. Medium brown golf hose were the most popular, with gray a close second. The tan wing-tip shoe was the leading golf shoe, but the tan saddle-strap low shoe was almost as popular, with the tan moccasin in third place.

Hot-weather golf attire during this period had, according to a *Men's Wear* reporter, "less 'dress-up' in it than the things men wear on the golf links in early spring. In other words, the men of wealth who play on such exclusive links as those of the Piping Rock Club on Long Island, or Shinnecock Hills at Southampton, and around Newport, R.I., seem to have changed their ideas in regard to two things this year.

"In hot weather they make no pretensions to 'dolling up' on the links as much as they did last year. They wear button-down collar shirts (many open at the neck and without ties). They wear light colored golf hose, with the largest percentage (34 per cent) wearing white linen knickers.

"It is also worthy of note to see, as indicated by the analysis made at Palm Beach last winter, that an increasing number of men playing golf are wearing white buck shoes trimmed with both tan and black leather. Most of these shoes have long wing tips. You will recall that the first golfer of note to wear white buck shoes with leather trim was Gene Sarazen on his return from winning the British National Open Championship two years ago.

"Also note that the increasing demand for comfort on the links is increasing the popularity of the white duck hat with the green underbrim and the white linen cap. These are articles without any degree of style, it is true, but with a large degree of comfort" (Aug. 20, 1924, p. 61).

Since golf was born in Scotland, dedicated and affluent American golfers had more than idle curiosity about what was being worn on, say, the links at St. Andrews, then as now the most famous of all golf courses. A fashion writer played there and filed a report in *Men's Wear* (Oct. 22, 1924, p. 70) to the effect that the knicker was now truly a plus four. ("So baggy and so long that it might be the grandmother of those we see in the south.") Jackets were not so highly shaped but were more workmanlike and straight. ("Loose, easy, and show little attempt at style and yet they convey the impression that they are worn by men who know how to dress.") There was a great variety of materials, but they were never loud. ("Peculiar heather browns in a rich red shade or russet, or again chocolate and paler shades, are very popular.") Knitted jackets in quiet heather, herringbone, or self-color effects were also popular. Stockings were being worn in a new shade that was rather like fern "when it turned in the autumn before it dies—an ideal shade for a plus four suit." Crushed and powder blue, heather and biscuit, powdered grays, blues, browns, and greens were seen everywhere, but none of the stockings had a turndown top. ("The best dressed men are wearing the stocking quite plain, drawn up inside the knicker, thus eliminating the turndown top.") Baggy, soft caps with full tops and generous peaks outnumbered soft felts, although the writer noted that in England there was a falling away of the cap's popularity. Shirts were interesting because men were wearing soft woolen materials of the silk-and-wool, taffeta, or fine flannel types. ("The collars always match and are made double shape, the outer fold never extending over the inner. I would say

that they are in height an inch to an inch and a half, and they are held closed because of the interlining or tiny tabs that button on to the collar stud.")

In 1925 another analysis was made of summer golf apparel, this time of the clothes worn by 156 professional and amateur golfers participating in the Metropolitan Open Championship held in Bronxville, New York. A writer reporting on the results in *Men's Wear* (June 10, 1925) said that he had never seen "so many 'dude' golfers before in all my study of men's apparel. Talk about style in golf apparel. These men were the acme of style." Apparently these men, unlike the golfers in the 1924 analysis, had decided to ignore the humidity and dress up. "Not one man finished at the 18th hole without his necktie in proper place." Like Grantland Rice, who had considered the positive effect smart golf attire could have on a man's score, this writer also came to the conclusion that "dress or style consciousness must help a man's golf game."

Among these golfers, plus fours in white linen were the first choice, with linen and flannel plus fours in medium gray and light gray the second and third choices. Black leather and striped silk belts were immensely popular; most belts carried harness buckles, but almost one-third were in the silver- or gold-color box buckle style that had no prong but simply slipped through the buckle. These well-dressed sportsmen made a point of wearing golf hose that were coordinated with their knickers, so that there was a vast array of plain colors and heather mixtures, as well as large and small diamond designs, cross and circular stripes, checks, and plaids. White linen and panama hats each accounted for 20 percent of the headgear worn, with caps of light brown, light gray, and blue gray adding up to 31 percent. Some 80 percent of the men wore white shirts (86 percent had worn white shirts in the 1924 analysis), and 5 percent wore blue, the second color choice, which had accounted for 8 percent in 1924. Figured foulards were

The well-groomed golfer of the 1920s turned out in a pair of full-cut tweed plus fours, small-patterned golf hose, two-tone moccasin shoes, a white shirt, and a four-in-hand tie. [COURTESY OF CULVER PICTURES, INC., NEW YORK]

the leading necktie choice, with the striped rep in second place and the striped knit a rather weak third. The plain attached soft collar was worn by 37 percent of the golfers, with 23 percent preferring the button-down attached soft collar, 21 percent the plain attached soft collar with pinned points, and 16 percent the semisoft collar.

The fashion influence of the smartly dressed professional golfer was just beginning to be recognized, and in 1925 one reporter observed: "If Walter Hagen wears plain black golf hose in the National Open Golf Championship, there are going to be a lot of professional and amateur golfers all over these large United States who will want plain black golf hose. Eighteen percent of the 200 topnotch golfers of the country that met out at the Lido Club, at Long Beach, Long Island, wore the same identical shoe that Walter Hagen introduced to the golfing fraternity of America two years

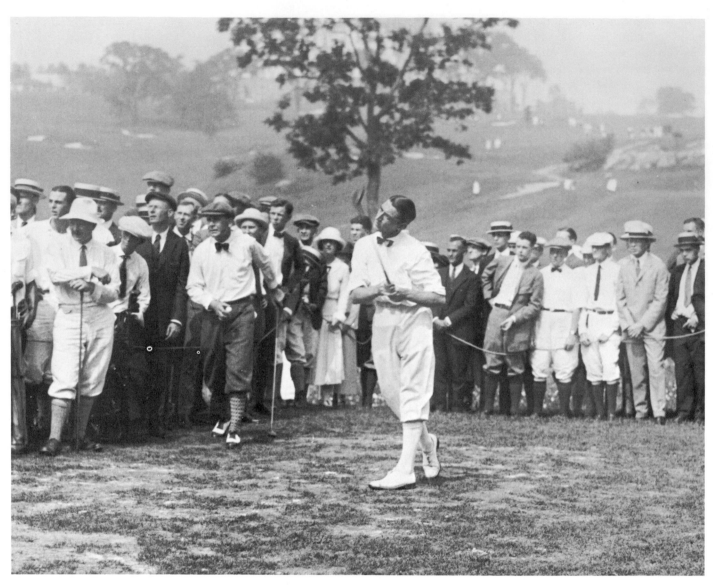

Tommy Armour, teeing off at the Westchester Biltmore Country Club in 1923, wore white knickers with side creases, hose with rolled-back cuffs, white shoes, a white shirt with rolled-up sleeves, and a bow tie. Most of the spectators wore knickers.
[COURTESY OF CULVER PICTURES, INC., NEW YORK]

ago—and the shoe he still is wearing" (*Men's Wear,* June 10, 1925, p. 47). At the Lido, Hagen was sketched while resting on the green and being admired by a group of caddies. He wore a blue pullover, gray knickers, a white shirt, a blue-and-gray striped tie, black-and-white vertical-zigzag hose, and white buckskin shoes trimmed with black leather. Bobby Jones, taking a swing at the ball, was dressed in a blue foulard bow tie, a white shirt, and white flannel knickers with a tan-and-black plaid.

Pullovers were as popular as ever,

with the V-neck style prevailing. The solid-color pullover was preferred, but all sorts of patterns were seen. Tan, pale blue, blue-brown, blue-gray, and tan-gray were some of the favored color combinations. Photographs tended to substantiate the writer's contention that the best-dressed professional golfers wore knickers without creases in the front. ("The absence of the crease gives the correct informal, nonchalant, country sport effect.") The best-dressed professionals also showed a decided preference for the white buckskin shoe trimmed with a

tan or black wing tip, the sole being made of leather with small steel spikes or studs. Nevertheless, the reader was reminded that the tan shoe with a tan saddle strap was as popular as ever. One of the new notes in golf hose styles observed at the qualifying tourney was plain-color pale blue hose. ("Pastel shades are the thing just now.")

In 1925 sleeveless pullovers permitting free arm action began to be seen on California golfers. It was reported that the white sleeveless pullover with a colored V neck was the most popular style at the picturesque Pebble Beach course in Del Monte. Blazer jackets and vertically striped sweaters were also seen occasionally, and it was of more than passing interest that several pairs of solid black stockings like those worn the previous spring in the East by Hagen and Sarazen were also being worn.

That year, golfers at the Los Angeles Country Club adopted knee-length khaki shorts of the kind worn by British army officers stationed in India, and a goodly number topped the shorts with the new sleeveless sweaters. A group photograph of some of these prominent golfers, among them the singer Al Jolson, shows that despite the warm California climate and the cool shorts, practically all the men wore ties.

The champion golfer was becoming more and more of a fashion plate, and in October, 1926, *Men's Wear* devoted a page to the golf wardrobe of Bobby Jones. Among the outfits photographed were plus fours with a checked plaid pattern, worn with vertical-stripe hose, a white shirt, a bow tie, and all-brown golf moccasins; and a solid-color pullover with pockets, white flannel knickers, wide-ribbed hose, and white-and-brown shoes.

Although men of fashion wintering in Palm Beach in the season of 1928 still favored plain white linen knickers and a white linen cap, many tweed and woolen knickers were being worn with matching caps, since Palm Beach mornings that year were often unexpectedly cool. According to *Men's Wear* (Mar. 21, 1928, p. 78), 43 percent of the Palm Beach golfers wore the sleeveless pullover sweater, while 41 percent remained true to the pullover with sleeves; the remaining 16 percent had adopted the coat sweater with sleeves. The two sweater styles outstanding for stitch and material that year were the lightweight shell-stitch sweater and an angora wool with the surface brushed up so that the stitch could not be distinguished.

The color-coordinated hose-and-sweater combinations considered so fashionable only a few seasons before were frowned upon by the well-dressed men of Palm Beach in 1928. The tan leather shoe with a saddle strap of the same material, a lightweight leather sole, and short spikes led all other shoe styles, as it had the previous year. The plain white buck was steadily gaining popularity, however, possibly because it was now being seen more and more for general wear as well.

The most important fashion news originating in Palm Beach in 1928 was the appearance of long flannel trousers or slacks on the links of the Palm Beach Country Club and the Everglades Club. The growing acceptance of slacks for golf had a practical basis: many of the style leaders were going directly from luncheon to the links, and instead of changing to golf clothes, they simply removed jacket and vest, waiting to change to fresh clothes for tea after the round of golf. Still, in 1928 no one yet suggested that knickers might soon be unfashionable, particularly when the Prince of Wales was still wearing them.

Once again, in the summer of 1928, the fashion press equated smart clothes with low golf scores, pointing out that the golfers who turned in the best scores in the National Open Championship that year were the best-dressed men entered in the tournament. It was hardly necessary, wrote one reporter, to reiterate the importance of the influence exerted on national golf apparel styles by the men competing in this championship match. "During the past few years these professionals and amateurs have led the way in various fashions, which have become popular with the masses of golfers and multitudes of non-golfing, sports-apparel-wearing men throughout the country" (*Men's Wear,* July 11, 1928, p. 65). A partial list of the styles launched by the golf champions of the 1920s would include solid-color golf hose in high pastel shades, plain black golf hose, solid-color pullovers in brilliant hues, white Shetland knickers, white linen knickers, and two-tone golf shoes.

Walter Hagen, who was generally regarded as the golfer exerting the greatest individual influence on golf apparel styles in this period, chose on the first day of the National Open of 1928 to wear a gray-and-red foulard tie, a white silk shirt, a braided belt, white Shetland knickers, pale gray hose, and black-and-white shoes. His outfit on the third day of competition, considered by the fashion press to be "the acme of dress excellence," consisted of a brown-and-white polka-dot foulard tie, a white shirt with attached collar, a brown shell-stitch pullover with a V neck, reddish brown tweed knickers, cocoa-brown golf hose, and tan-and-white wing-tip shoes.

Johnny Farrell, who won the championship and $1,500 in prize money, accepted congratulations in a gray-and-black pullover sweater, a brown-and-white checked tie, a white oxford shirt, white Shetland knickers, blue hose, and black-and-white shoes. Farrell had already earned a reputation as a fashion innovator the previous year, when he appeared wearing green hose; the next season at Palm Beach green was the preferred color for golf hose.

An analysis in *Men's Wear* (Aug. 22, 1928, p. 68) of summer golf apparel worn by 300 of the best-dressed men on the links of fashionable country clubs showed the white duck hat, white linen cap, gray cap, and brown cap to be the favorite hats, in that order; the white shirt accounted for 86 percent of the shirts worn by these golfers, with blue, the second choice, adding up to merely 8 percent. Some 58 percent of the neckties worn were foulards, with striped, regimental, or club ties in second place, accounting for 23 percent; blue was by far the favorite foulard color. White linen plus fours were worn by 22 percent; white linen medium knickers, by 12 percent; brown and gray plus fours, by 11 percent each; gray flannel trousers, by 9 percent; and white flannel trousers, by 8 percent. Light brown golf hose accounted for 29 percent; medium brown, 28; gray, 17; and blue, 11. Tan saddle-strap shoes were worn by 28 percent; tan wing-tip, by 18; tan blucher plain-front and tan straight-tip, by 9 each; white buck trimmed with tan leather, by 8; white buck trimmed with black leather, by 7; and white shoes and tan moccasins, by 6 each.

1930–1940

In 1933 the 148 contestants and more than 10,000 spectators at the Thirty-seventh Annual National Open Tournament, held in Glenview, Illinois, were generally thought to have set a record for the number of new lightweight summer ensembles at a golfing event. For the third successive year the Open had been staged during a severe heat wave, and the players again had experimented with various types of apparel in an effort to keep cool. A combination that appeared particularly refreshing was a gray broadcloth shirt worn with either

In the rawness of early spring weather, this golfer wore a heavy cable-stitch sweater with a silk square thrown over at the throat in ascot fashion and a flannel shirt underneath it, a checked wool cap, flannel slacks, and brown buckskin shoes with rubber soles and heels. From Esquire, *April 1935.*

gray cotton or flannel slacks or knickers. About two-thirds of the golfers preferred slacks to knickers, and the knickers that were worn appeared to be cut less full than previously. Flannel took first place in both slacks and knickers, and it accounted for more than 12 percent of the cap fabrics, too. Because of the intense heat few players wore neckties, although the better-known professionals such as Hagen, Sarazen, and Farrell preferred to wear silk ties, chiefly in crepe, foulard, shantung, and rep. Only one bow tie was reported in the tournament.

In an attempt to analyze the decline in the popularity of knickers, a fashion writer for *Men's Wear* (June 21, 1933, p. 16) wondered if it might not be due in part to a lack of new designs in golf hose, noting that an overwhelming number of the golf hose seen were in plain solid colors. It was considered significant that Walter Hagen preferred slacks on the first and third days and donned knickers on the second day. In any event, whether in slacks or in knickers, the best-dressed golfers preferred them in solid colors, solid gray being especially popular, principally in flannel. Practically all the slacks had two side straps, and bottoms generally measured about 19 or 20 inches. A keen-eyed manufacturer might have noticed that a large number of the players turned up the cuffs of their slacks, and one leading professional explained that this was being done to reduce the amount of flapping and give the player more assurance in his stance. Consequently, more than one fashion journalist complained that slacks were not yet being made properly for the golfer.

There was a huge preference for the linen cap; 76 percent of headgear worn consisted of caps, and linens accounted for almost 55 percent. More than 85 percent of the caps worn were of eight-piece construction. During the three hot days of the tournament almost half of the hats seen were panamas with ventilated perforations around the lower part of the crown. The wing-tip oxford in single or combination leathers was the style of shoe

seen most often on the links, although one-third of the players still preferred the moccasin. Less than 10 percent wore plain-tip oxfords.

In March, 1934, *Esquire* sketched the golfing outfit currently worn by the Prince of Wales: a maroon-and-white houndstooth knitted shirt, dark gray tweed knickers, solid-color wool hose of wine red, and black-and-white moccasin shoes. Yet despite his still considerable fashion influence, American golfers were abandoning knickers. In the same issue and recommended for the golfer who played in any weather were an oilskin blouse and three-quarter-length trousers of the same fabric, the trousers being long enough to cover a pair of knickers.

By 1935, in the opinion of some fashion writers, golf clothes for the Florida season had become pretty well standardized. In the words of one journalist:

A knitted shirt, a pair of slacks, sturdy shoes, woolen half hose, a cap or hat, and a pullover on chilly days comprise the most popular ensemble. The knitted sports shirt is an odds-on favorite. It's a wool jersey, solid color or white, has short sleeves and a buttoned collar. Solid blue, white, wine red, yellow and copen-colored sports shirts are plentiful on the golf courses. Here and there a vividly colored cross-stripe sports shirt brightens the landscape. These are in fine lisle. In woven materials, meshes, in white or solid color, are best liked.

The well dressed golfers like flannel slacks better than any other kind. Grey in medium to dark tones is easily the best color. Gabardine slacks are becoming more popular. Both grey and tan are seen to a considerable extent. White is worn not only in flannel and gabardine but in wash materials as well. Small checked trousers, particularly in bluish green, though observed only occasionally, are extremely smart looking. All trousers are made high-waisted and have pleats at the waistband. The knicker situation is about the same—few are seen.

On cool days solid color cashmere, shetland and shell-stitch alpaca pullovers are much worn. Tan, yellow, light blue and white are the prevailing colors. White cable-stitch pullovers in sleeveless models have been taken up by fashionably dressed golfers. Heavy border stripes at the bottom and V-neck opening introduce accent colors.

The man in the center made fashion points with (1) a green lightweight-silk poplin windbreaker, (2) brown-and-white houndstooth-check knickers, (3) a plaid wool muffler, (4) bottle-green 6 by 3 wool hose, and (5) brown wing-tip shoes with fringed tongues. The man at left scored with a heavy-ribbed tight-fitting sweater in cocoa brown, a flat-top tweed cap, and moccasin-pattern golf shoes. From Esquire, September 1936.

The plus-four suit, out of fashion for a number of years, staged a comeback in 1937. The man at left wore a typical outfit in lovat cheviot with a rust double overplaid. The other man's outfit consisted of a blue turtleneck sweater, a tan processed-fabric jacket with raglan shoulders and a zipper front, gray flannel slacks, a rough felt hat, and brown moccasin shoes. From Esquire, March 1937.

Yet at the British Open Championship matches in England that year knickers were worn by 70 per cent of the players and spectators, often with a jacket to match. And in March, 1936, *Esquire,* perhaps encouraged by this show of British tenacity, ventured to predict a "homecoming for the prodigal knicker": "The knicker got into bad company some years back and had itself banished by the best dressed golfers as a result. It was really the white knicker with its leering suggestion of absent-mindedness on the part of the hurried dresser, which got the whole blooming family into Fashion's dog house. But Fashion is both fickle and short of memory and here comes the knicker back with a bang and a British accent in the way of a cord that wraps once around the leg and then tucks in under itself, in place of the old time buckle at the cuff." But despite British tenacity and *Esquire* optimism, knickers did not stage a comeback, although the magazine did its best by showing a model whose new-style knickers were worn with a porkpie hat, a two-button sports jacket with wide lapels, flap pockets on a slant, and side vents, solid-color hose, and Norwegian-model golf shoes.

In 1936 even the British were beginning to favor trousers over plus fours. At the British Open Championship at Hoylake, Cheshire, plain gray flannels and flannels with white chalk or ground stripes were popular. Plus fours, it was noted, were worn by several of the American players, including Gene Sarazen, but even among the spectators, several of whom wore loudly checked sports jackets, there was a predominance of flannel trousers.

That summer, in its June issue, *Esquire* showed what it considered a very practical sports outfit, consisting of overplaid glen flannel trousers, a rough-finish natural-color silk shirt, a porkpie hat, and Norwegian golf shoes. A more avant-garde dresser shown on the same page wore what the editors said was typical of outfits seen at Nassau the past season: gabardine shorts of khaki color in the regular British style, with a khaki shirt of fine broadcloth made in a military style with half sleeves. The model's cuffless golf hose were of medium-weight wool in a light camel's hair color, worn with brown buckskin golf shoes. The reader was asked to note the silk foulard polka-dot handkerchief peeking out of the right-hand pants pocket. This was, concluded the editors, an outfit that was also suitable for boating, fishing, and general country wear in hot weather.

Three months later, *Esquire* was again promoting knickers for golf wear and decreeing that gray flannel slacks had passed the point of interesting fashion, since nine out of ten men competing in the National Open Championship that summer had worn slacks. By March, 1937, *Esquire* was actively advocating the plus fours suit, which had been out of fashion for a long time, stating that "its comeback began last year and gives added promise, by all advance reports, of increasing this season. Aside from being ideal for early and late season golf it is a useful knockabout outfit and has a definite place in the wardrobe."

In the middle of the controversy between slacks and knickers, shorts appeared and gained a solid foothold, much as feminine hot pants (short shorts) did in 1971 during the controversy between miniskirts and maxiskirts. *Esquire* took notice and in July, 1937, showed a pair of "the new fashionable white shorts," which, the editors admitted, had much the same resemblance to underwear generally blamed for the early demise of white linen knickers. Still, these rather longish shorts were being seen in steadily

increasing numbers in smart suburban centers around New York, and so the editors sketched a pair worn with a lightweight wool sports shirt, plaid-patterned golf hose, and reversed-calf shoes. It was also noted that George VI and the Duke of Windsor had popularized shorts. In June, 1938, *Esquire* was still showing shorts, this time a pair of lightweight cotton corduroy shorts supported by a colorful striped belt and worn with wool hose without cuffs, brown-and-white Norwegian-model shoes, and a crew-neck half-sleeve shirt of cotton mesh. A second model on the page was evidence of just how much variety had crept into golf apparel: he wore dark gray flannel trousers. The cardigan was firmly entrenched that year as a smart fashion, and in October *Esquire* showed a particularly handsome example: a cashmere cardigan with a chamois front. On the same page was an assortment of other golfing fashions: striped tweed ties, solid-color golf hose, a tweed cap, and a brown suede-finish belt.

Rain suits came into prominence during this decade, and in April, 1938, *Esquire* displayed an especially dashing foul-weather outfit: a lightweight waterproof golf jacket with a slide fastener, matching trousers, wing-tip brogue shoes, a semisports hat, a striped oxford shirt, and a plain-color knitted tie. There was a decided military air to the outfit, and since World War II was less than six months in the offing, that was perfectly understandable.

1940–1950

One of the wartime influences on golf was the appearance of the battle jacket, also known as the Eisenhower jacket, whose roomy shoulders allowed for a healthy swing. Waist-length, with set-in sleeves, two box-pleated chest pockets with flaps, and a waistband attachment for a snug fit, the battle jacket was usually made of processed cotton. Tan was the preferred shade, just as shades of tan and brown were popular in sports jackets and slacks

The golf umbrella with segments of red, yellow, green, and blue added color to the fairways in the thirties. Its carrier wore a water-repellent cotton jacket with raglan shoulders, saxony slacks in a glenurquhart pattern, a wool muffler, a green felt hat, and brown shoes with crepe-rubber soles. His opponent wore a knitted pullover in sweat shirt style with knitted elastics at the cuffs and around the bottom, chalk-stripe flannel slacks, and brown smooth and reversed-calf combination shoes with crepe-rubber soles. From Esquire, *April 1940.*

during the war years. Invariably the man wearing the battle jacket on the links topped it off with a pinch-crown hat of processed cotton. Patterned slacks were becoming increasingly popular at the time, and a pair of shepherd's-check slacks was a stylish companion for the battle jacket.

Shorts were so popular by the end of the decade that *Mens' Wear* was moved to use the headline "Shorts Are Sensational!" (Sept. 9, 1949). There was no doubt that they had become a major item in sportswear.

1950–1960

The chief fashion news early in the fifties was the debut of the new "miracle" fabrics, the synthetics *Apparel Arts*

The golfer in the foreground wore a tan, brown, and maroon checked processed-cotton jacket with a zipper front, a tan cotton hat processed to be water-repellent, an oxford shirt, a wool tie, and covert slacks. His pipe-smoking opponent wore a blue cashmere pullover, a glen plaid oxford shirt, a dotted foulard tie, a lightweight felt hat, gray flannel slacks, and brown-and-white moccasin-pattern shoes. From Esquire, *April 1941.*

called "fabulous new fabrics, created entirely through scientific methods, without the use of natural fibers." With permanent-press, wash-and-wear, and miracle fabrics, the American golfer had no excuse not to look colorful, comfortable, and casual on the putting green. In fact, the increasing use of synthetics allowed the golfer to look fresh from the first to the eighteenth tee.

Off the links, the American man of the early fifties was "the man in the gray flannel suit," a neat, circumspect, conservative man who carried an attaché case and regarded a pink button-down shirt as his one sartorial fling, that is, until he exchanged his attaché case for a golf club; on the links he became a peacock. Consequently, golf clothes in the fifties were ablaze with color. The Peacock Revolution was a decade in the future, but

in retrospect it can be seen that the golf apparel of the fifties broadly hinted at the American man's growing attraction to attention-getting color.

The shell-stitch alpaca became the leading golf sweater. Professionals wore it on the links, and when the television cameras zoomed in for close-ups, the viewer at home could admire the cardigan styling with a button front and the easy bell-shaped sleeves. Color television was not yet available to do justice to the wide range of colors of the sweaters.

The knitted golf shirt was another dominant style, and in 1953 the short-sleeved Lacoste shirt, a cotton knit distinguished by a cuff on the sleeve and a tail longer in back than in front, made its appearance. Introduced in white and instantly popular, the Lacoste was soon being manufactured in every conceivable color as well.

The tapered slack that originated in Rome came to the United States in the early fifties and quickly became popular. Cuffless, it usually tapered sharply to $17\frac{1}{2}$ inches at the bottom, and models with adjustable waistbands were considered ideal for golf. Knitted slacks were introduced in the mid-fifties and were worn by some golfers, but shape retention was still a problem to be solved, and they had to wait until the 1970s to realize their potential as a major fashion.

Shorts were more popular and more colorful than ever. In 1954 *Esquire* ran an extensive article on shorts and gave them the highest rating both for wear on the links and for *après-golf* relaxation. Then, in 1956, it published a second "shorts story," one that "was longer than ever before, in terms of style and fabrics." Accompanying color photographs showed shorts in everything from candy-striped seersucker to India madras and cotton glen plaid.

With the summer suit epitomizing comfort and smooth good looks and with modern air conditioning commonplace, it was only natural that golf clothes should become cooler and more comfortable, too. By 1957 the

popular natural-tan shorts were being worn shorter, and many related golf clothes were becoming lighter in weight. Caps were lightweight, and knitted cotton shirts were zephyr-cool. Even the slip-on shoes often worn with golf shorts were lighter in weight. About the only item of golf apparel that had not lost ounces was the golfer's high-rise socks, still regarded as a requirement for wear with shorts.

1960–1970

By the time the Peacock Revolution arrived in a burst of color in the early sixties, golf apparel was already there, for in the otherwise-understated fifties, sportswear had been an oasis of color. Inhibitions had been discarded when the man in the gray flannel suit stepped outdoors and played his way toward the eighteenth hole. As *Esquire* put it, "In a time when the male of the species is proudly displaying his plumage, even tennis is no longer an all-white affair, stiff and starchy. But no sport permits its participants the freedom of imagination, the choice of colors and styles, and the opportunity to dress tastefully yet uniquely that golf does." The well-dressed golfer appearing on a full-color page in the May, 1960, issue of *Esquire* wore a cotton yarn shirt in canyon gold, the magazine's favorite summer color, the body of which was a cool mesh knit. His tapered slacks, of wash-and-wear lime-green Dacron and cotton, had a detachable hip pocket for golf balls, a strap for tees, and another for a towel. His cap was brilliant India madras.

By the mid-sixties even shorts were tapered and often were boldly plaided. Knickers finally did manage a comeback on the links, but this time they were plus twos, and only their lush colors kept them from seeming almost self-effacing. Still the plus twos were regarded as a noticeable fashion trend, although tapered slacks and shorts clearly dominated sportswear. Bluegrass was the sportswear color for spring, 1966, appearing in everything from plus twos to a nylon jacket with a zipper front, zippered pockets, and

Swinging in the rain in 1968. The man at far left wore a green nylon zipper jacket with a concealed hood, plaid shorts of polyester and cotton, and green brushed shoes with black saddle straps. The man next to him wore an orange polyester-and-cotton jacket, a blue polyester-and-cotton permanent-press knitted shirt, plaid slacks of polyester and cotton, a poplin Tyrolean hat, and brown-and-white wing-tip shoes with saddle straps. The third man had on an orange, brown, and white polyester-and-cotton jacket with a soil-release finish, matching slacks, an orange knitted Ban-Lon shirt, a nylon pouch hat, and tan brushed-leather shoes with brown saddle straps. The fourth man wore a putty-color nylon pullover with a mock turtleneck and a zipper pocket, plaid polyester-and-cotton slacks, a stitched nylon hat, and wing-tip kiltie-tongued white-and-black poromeric shoes. From Esquire, *April 1968.*

a hood concealed in a short standing collar. The pleatless front of most golf slacks now had low angled pockets, and some of the younger golfers favored the new hip-riding, low-rise models.

In 1967 golf apparel became even more colorful. Noteworthy for color and styling was a pair of tapered copper-color check slacks of Dacron and cotton that just above the knee had a large golf ball pocket with a Velcro-closure flap. A terry cloth towel backed with the slacks fabric buttoned onto the back of the slacks and was used for wiping off golf balls. Golf shoes that year offered the fashion-conscious golfer great variety. Noting

that in an average eighteen-hole game a golfer walks about 4 miles, *Esquire* lined up on a practice putting green four candidates for attention: black-and-red wing tips, a soft green brushed leather with smooth leather trim and a kiltie tongue, brushed leather in denim blue with a fringed tongue and spiked, cushioned rubber soles, and copper-color brushed pigskin.

In the latter half of the decade more and more attention was paid to fashions for the golfer who braved the links in inclement weather. Among the more notable rainy-day fashions were a nylon zipper jacket with a concealed hood, a Dacron-and-cotton poplin drizzle jacket with a zipper closure

concealed by a fly front, and a poplin Tyrolean golf hat.

In April, 1968, *Esquire* observed that the game of golf, once something of a stately ritual, had become rather a romp and noted that "now only Gene Sarazen still wears plus fours." In a roundup of golf fashions, the magazine's fashion department showed not one pair of knickers, focusing attention instead on shorts and slacks worn with short-sleeved shirts, cardigans, pullovers, peaked caps, and porkpie hats in a dazzling array of colors. The headline was "The Bright Look of the Links."

"Among great golfers in our time, only the South African, Gary Player, is conspicuous for the severity of his attire. Dressed all in black, he is like a Paladin of the links. For in these colorful days, the greens are ablaze with the brilliant plumage of the players—and what is so odd, incidentally, is that by and large the male of the species is more flamboyant than the female, his tastes running to vivid blues, flaming greens, chrome yellows, at times even in his shoes."

In its April, 1969, issue *Esquire* wondered if perhaps golf clothes had not become too colorful. "Of all gamesmen, golfers are the most daring dressers," wrote the editors, "—and sometimes the damndest, too. Nor is the duffer inspired to become more conservative by the sight of what is so often on the backs of his betters. Sitting before his television set on a summer's Sunday afternoon, a man is emboldened by the plumage on view to go out and do likewise. As a result, the links have become populated with peacocks. This year, however, golf fashions betray a distinct disposition toward a little more discretion and a lot more coordination than at any time since the skills of the pros became one of the treats of color television. There will always be a brilliance of color, of course, but where once it was a positive riot, now it will be employed with that certain restraint that constitutes taste." As evidence that good taste need not be dull, an accompanying fashion picture showed a red and-white diamond-pattern mock T-neck shirt worn with red-and-white–striped slacks of rayon and Dacron in a Western cut.

In 1970, while some of the leading golf professionals were serving as stylists for golf apparel and being photographed for advertisements selling their name labels, *Esquire* campaigned for greater style in golf clothes. "The trouble with golf clothes is that they are a lot more colorful than comfortable," maintained the editors in the April issue. "In their concentration on flamboyance, designers would seem to have overlooked the fact that, over all the years since plus fours went the way of tennis trousers, nothing really in-

novative has happened to the *styling* of golf wear." Motivated by what it termed "functional, not idle, curiosity," *Esquire* asked a few of the more resourceful men's designers to create an authentically new look for the links. It was not surprising that most of the designers chose to work in knit, which, being durable and practically wrinkle-resistant and allowing great freedom of movement, was already a great favorite with golfers.

The designer Allen Case created a one-piece T-neck golf suit of polyester double knit with a zippered front and half-moon lower pockets. Case's suit had a saddle-shoulder construction, a box-pleated action back, and a brass-buckled belt. The slacks were narrow and cuffless.

Larry Kane designed what he termed "a second skin for golf." Using a double knit of polyester and wool in a broken-zigzag pattern, he devised a loose-fitting short-sleeved shirt and high-rise, large-cuffed, pleated knee-length slacks, both trimmed with the underside of the fabric. The socks and underwear resembled a one-piece half body stocking.

Franklin Bober designed a cotton corduroy suit consisting of plain-front belted knicker slacks with a wide extension band and a hip-length jacket with a rounded neck, a button front, cuffed sleeves, a leather belt, and two roomy flapped patch pockets. With it his model wore knee-high socks of cotton argyle.

John Weitz, whose design philosophy is apparel ease, created a slightly shaped free-falling jacket and slacks of a light windproof fabric. The jacket had an oversize collar, two diagonally zippered chest pockets, side vents, snaps down the front, and loose cuffed sleeves that could easily be rolled up.

Oleg Cassini designed a knit golf suit, a shirt-and-slacks ensemble in seersucker knit. The semifitted open-collar shirt had a placket front, and the straight-cut slacks were self-belted and cuffless and had horizontal pockets. Ideal for the fairways, it could, with the addition of a double-breasted blazer and a silk scarf under

The patterned jacquard brown-and-tan wool knit sweater and matching knickers make a distinctive golf outfit. The placketed pullover top has an inset shawl collar in a solid rib-knit. The glove is white with yellow trim. From Esquire, *April 1971.*

the shirt collar, be converted to *après-golf* wear appropriate in the most correct clubhouse.

Golf clothes, perhaps more than any other category of sportswear, have undergone the most dynamic changes in the twentieth century, in no small measure because of the fashion influence of the great golfers, who have always used clothes to express their individuality on the links. The tournament players of today, bona fide television personalities, are fashion catalysts who have taught millions of American men to dress up for golfing. The importance of golf as a television sporting event, combined with the fashion flair and magnetism of the great players, guarantees that golfing apparel will continue to be a leader of fashion innovation for the remainder of the century.

Glen plaid slacks and tan gabardine shorts were two choices for the golfer in 1936. From Esquire, *June 1936.*

The golfer at left combined a link-stitch green alpaca-and-worsted cardigan with a blue mock-turtleneck knitted pullover, twill-weave polyester-and-cotton slacks, black-and-white short-wing-tip shoes, and an adjustable yellow cap. The putter wore a wide-ribbed knit alpaca pullover with a deep V opening, a polyester-and-cotton shirt, silk slacks, and monk-front shoes. Drawn by Ken Dallison. From Esquire, *April 1968.*

On the eighteenth green at Dorado, Michael York wore a U-neck wool knit sweater over a Dacron-and-cotton knit shirt, Orlon knit slacks with an elasticized waistband that were seamed front and back to give the effect of permanent creasing, Corfam monk-strap toe-cap shoes, and a fabric hat with a floppy brim. From Esquire, *April 1971.*

For wear on the courts in 1935: (left) Washable white tennis shorts with blue side stripes, worn with a round-neck pullover shirt, white socks, and blue canvas sneakers. (right) The more traditional combination of slacks, cable-stitch sweater, and polo shirt. From Esquire, *August 1935.*

The championship look in tennis apparel depends on good design: a raglan-sleeved shirt with a permanent stand collar, a wool cardigan with low-set pockets, and shorts with an adjustable waist and mesh pockets (1971). [ABERCROMBIE & FITCH]

Golf Clothes

Tennis Clothes

Tennis Clothes

Often referred to as "the most genteel of sports," tennis in the early decades of the twentieth century was a status sport. So was golf, but the man on the links wore sturdy tweeds and broad, sensible shoes; the tennis player, in contrast, wore a white oxford or broadcloth shirt with the sleeves rolled up, white or cream-color trousers of flannel or cricket cloth, white socks, and shoes with pliable rubber soles. Going to and from the court he might wear a heavy white cable-stitch sweater, often with club colors set in around the neck and waist. Some players preferred a white or cream-color blazer instead of a sweater, and a minority wore the roomy, loose-fitting, and opulent-looking tennis overcoat of camel's hair or camel pile.

Only a man of means could afford to indulge in a country club sport that carried with it such a large laundry and dry-cleaning bill. And the tradition-bound sportsman apparently enjoyed the snobbism inherent in his basically all-white outfit; so when, in 1928, an American player turned up at Wimbledon wearing white trousers with stripes, he was responsible for a minor *cause célèbre*. In fact, as late as 1934 many tennis tournaments in both the United States and England were still ruling against any deviation from plain white in the attire of contestants.

In the first two decades of the century about the only part of the tennis costume that allowed for variation was the tennis shoe. It could be a high shoe extending above the ankle or a low-cut oxford style, made of black sateen, kangaroo, or tan smoked leather as well as of the more traditional white canvas, and equipped with a rubber sole or with sports spikes. Except for his shoes, the tennis player of this period adhered closely to the all-white rule, but occasionally a professional player of uncommon presence might

A. F. Wilding.

Norman E. Brookes

Champions from over the Seas.

Early tennis fashions: A. F. Wilding wore a striped blazer with white slacks and shoes, and Norman E. Brookes had on a double-breasted "wait" coat with his tennis outfit. [COURTESY OF CULVER PICTURES, INC., NEW YORK]

The contestants for the doubles tennis championship in 1916 at Forest Hills, New York—Maurice E. McLoughlin, Ward Dawson, William M. Johnston, and Clarence J. Griffin—wore white shirts with rolled-up sleeves, high-cut white trousers, and black leather shoes with spikes. Johnston and Griffin were the winners. [COURTESY OF CULVER PICTURES, INC., NEW YORK]

wear a black trouser belt instead of the conventional white.

Not until 1928 did the tennis outfit undergo a significant change, with the introduction of a short-sleeved, closely knit all-white shirt. First seen on the French Riviera some two years earlier and then taken up by the more fashion-conscious British tennis players, it was given the stamp of approval in the United States by the smart set that frequented the courts at Palm Beach. Sometimes of cashmere and sometimes of silk and wool, the new tennis shirt had a turned-down collar that could be buttoned at the neck or left open. In some models the sleeves were mod-

erately loose, while in others they fit more tightly at the elbow. The shirt resembled the polo shirt that had been seen in the United States and England for many years, and it was destined to be called a "polo shirt" for decades to come. By the summer of 1928 many American stores were offering a variation of this shirt that had a rib-knit bottom and was advertised as a "cool sweater shirt." In all white, it was definitely a tennis shirt, with or without the rib-knit bottom, but solid-color styles, often with long sleeves, were recommended for golf and outdoor sports generally. (Six years later, *Esquire,* exhibiting the diehard person-

In 1934 the court costume consisted of a knitted shirt, white flannel slacks, and white sneakers. A deviation was the colored silk square tied as a belt, but the border-piped blazer was traditional. From Esquire, *August 1934.*

ality of the true tennis buff, would refer to the white oxford button-down shirt as "the best tennis shirt there is, next to a mesh shirt that is made especially for tennis.")

Also in 1928, the very full pleated tennis trousers became popular, in no small measure because of the fashion influence of William Tilden, who topped his pleated trousers with a new tennis shirt with a shawl collar.

In 1932 Bunny Austin, the top-ranking player in England, created a sensation when he turned up for the Men's National Tennis Championship at Forest Hills, Long Island, wearing white flannel shorts cut well above the knee. Though the shorts were cool and

comfortable, in the view of a writer for *Men's Wear* their cut could have been greatly improved: "They were made in such a way that the belt was an extension of the main part of the shorts, reaching over a distance of about eight inches in front. When the belt buckle is fastened, all the excess fullness across the hips is pulled to the front. There were no pleats in front or back and no side straps to provide fullness at these points. While this extension belt idea is very practical, it should be supplemented with pleats in front and side straps, in the opinion of this observer."

Actually shorts for tennis were not a radically new development in 1932, but the prominence of the player wearing them and the event itself brought them to public attention. Pictures of Austin were carried in newspapers throughout the United States with such captions as "Long on Shorts," "Sawed-off Pants," "Air-cooled Trousers," and "Ventilated Pants." Brooks Brothers, however, had already advertised tennis shorts featuring belt loops and side straps and reported it had done quite well with them, recommending them for wear on both tennis and squash courts.

By the mid-thirties white tennis shorts had been accepted, although *Esquire* said in 1935 that "without the famous little Englishman's sponsorship, it is doubtful that the fashion would have gone very far." The August issue that year showed a pair in white duck featuring a navy blue side stripe that, the fashion editor assured readers, could be worn without a qualm for its correctness in this usually tradition-bound sport. With these shorts the model wore a short-sleeved, collarless all-white shirt originally developed for squash, white socks, and blue canvas sneakers, which at that time were being seen on many well-known professional players. Over the model's arm was a blue flannel blazer, which *Esquire* said could be worn at the courts and, with white or gray flannels, for general country usage. Next to this trend setter stood a young man in the more typical tennis

costume of a white lightweight-wool polo shirt with short sleeves, white flannel trousers, white sneakers, and a heavy white cable-stitch sweater. The sweater was cited as "a recent revival," since many of the younger tennis players were at this time showing a preference for a lighter-weight sleeveless sweater.

Yet, despite the appearance of tennis shorts, *Esquire* had recently shown a more traditional outfit as what it considered the "court costume for the season of 1934": "Except for the silk foulard handkerchief worn as a sash in place of the more prosaic belt, this outfit is unreservedly recommended for tennis players of every rank," began the picture caption. "The reservation regarding the colored waist-handkerchief is not made as a matter of taste, since this item is as smart as all get out; simply in recognition of the fact that many tournament officials still stick to the letter of the traditional rule against any deviations from plain white in the attire of contestants. So, if you are a tournament player you'd better have a white belt handy, if only for the actual playing time spent in organized competition. The Polo shirt is of white, lightweight wool, with half sleeves; the trousers are of white flannel, or that finish which goes by the name of cricket cloth; the shoes are plain white canvas sneakers (although the new Cuban Jai Alai shoes [a blucher style with a leather upper and a rubber sole] are equally suitable, and smarter in appearance). The breast insignia is a small monogram."

But while white still ruled the courts, to and from the game even the most proper player now often carried or wore a solid-color blazer with piping of a contrasting color running from the lapels down the front and around the bottom as well as across the tops of the pockets. And in 1939 the socially impeccable tennis professional Fred Perry introduced a new tennis shoe available in white, blue, or green. Called the Fred Perry Pro, it had a durable duck upper, a crepe outsole, white eyelets, white tubular laces, and an arch-support insole with

Blue was used to accent tennis clothes in 1940. It appeared at the border of the white knitted cotton shirt, in piping at the sides of the cotton gabardine shorts, and as the tops of the rubber-soled canvas shoes. From Esquire, August 1940.

arch and heel sponge cushions.

By August, 1940, *Esquire* was pointing out further changes in tennis clothes: "If there were any phase of men's attire that time could not wither, you'd think it would be the good old tennis outfit—white shirt, white flannels, white socks and sneakers, and there you are. But no you aren't. The world does move and the outfit does change. The wielder sketched here wears a white knitted cotton shirt with blue border stripes, side-striped white cotton gabardine shorts, plain white belt, plain socks and blue canvas shoes with white rubber soles. The sweater is a white cable

stitch type, and the white tennis cap has a green under-visor."

Even the costume of the spectator had changed. In 1935 white flannels were still most obviously appropriate, but now in 1940 *Esquire* sketched a gentleman in slacks the shade of sand, and a foulard necktie had replaced the traditional regimental stripes.

The 1950s saw the birth of the spectacular synthetic fibers, and almost immediately wash-and-wear and drip-dry fabrics were being used for every item in the tennis wardrobe. How well they sustained their popularity can be judged by the following tennis fashions shown by *Esquire* in June, 1965, more than a decade after the man-made fibers had come into prominence (it was significant that even in the liberated sixties *Esquire* was still mindful of the traditions that made even relatively slight changes in tennis clothes newsworthy.

"Every once in a while someone comes along and suggests a wholesale revision of tennis fashions. Sometimes these would-be innovators are in it just for kicks, other times they have logical arguments for their suggestions. But whatever the purpose, any change from the traditional is met with pooh-poohs from the crusty bastions of the game. What's needed is a moderator, and that's where we come in." To prove its qualifications, *Esquire* offered photographs of a collection of new tennis clothes that were "patterned with due respect after the traditional design": a white cotton twill zipper jacket with a crew neck and navy piping down one side and burgundy piping down the other, worn with a knit shirt of Kodel and cotton and cotton shorts; a terry knit cotton shirt with a front zipper, striped in navy blue and deep red, worn with Dacron-and-cotton shorts; a long-sleeved sweater of virgin wool with the classic color combinations reversed in favor of burgundy-and-white stripings on a navy ground, worn with white Arnel and Avron slacks; a white open-mesh knit shirt with a V neck and red, white, and blue bands on the ribbing at neck and cuffs, worn with white

cotton shorts and striped socks; and a crew-neck cardigan made of two-ply cotton lisle striped in red and blue, worn with shorts of Dacron and cotton. All the models wore tennis oxfords of polyester and cotton with rubber outsoles, rubber having moved crepe from first place for the good reason that it provided better traction.

By July, 1968, the Peacock Revolution had reached the tennis courts and touched off an explosion of color, prompting *Esquire* to title a feature "A Court of Many Colors": "In tennis there is never any end to the imaginativeness of the players' apparel, and always it is the elite who are the innovators—from the short, swirling ballet skirt of Suzanne Lenglen to the incomparable chic of Baron Gottfried

The player at left wore the border-striped clothes popular in 1965. His crew-neck white cotton twill jacket with a zipper closure had blue piping down one side and burgundy down the other. The man at right wore a terry knit zipper-front shirt with red-and-blue border stripes. Both players favored white shorts, socks, and sneakers. Photographed by Robert Freson.

Two players posed in apparel selected for the Davis Cup team by the United States Lawn Tennis Association in 1968. The ensemble at left consisted of a yellow nylon zippered jacket with a striped knitted collar, a yellow pullover with blue-and-white border stripes, and extension-waistband shorts. Blue was predominant in the ensemble at right, a cable-stitch pullover with yellow-and-white border stripes worn with Dacron-and-cotton knit shirt and durable-press shorts. Photographed by Terry Stevenson. From Esquire, *January 1968.*

von Cramm, from Helen Wills Moody's eyeshade to Gussie Moran's lace panties; down the cavalcade of the courts from Ellsworth Vine's cap to Lacoste's *le crocodile* shirt, from Big Bill Tilden's baggy white flannels to the spruce shorts introduced to tournament tennis by Bunny Austin in the Thirties. And, as is the way of fashion, everything at first *outré* eventually becomes old hat, with the slightly scandalous of today the stylish of tomorrow. So there is reason to believe that, in time quickly to come, colored clothing will become commonplace on the courts."

Esquire proceeded to give the reader a preview with two of the outfits chosen that year for the Davis Cup team of the United States Lawn Tennis Association, "that notorious bastion of tradition": a yellow ensemble trimmed in blue and white that included a nylon zippered jacket with knit collar, cuffs, and waistband, a cotton mesh V-neck shirt, and cotton twill shorts with a soil-release finish; and a blue outfit trimmed in white and yellow that included an all-wool cable-knit pullover, a Dacron-and-cotton knit shirt, and Dacron-and-cotton durable-press shorts. It is interesting to note that innovation had moved from the tennis shoes to the rest of the outfit: both the colorfully garbed models wore all-white tennis sneakers.

In 1969, the Tennis Ace, described as a completely new tennis shoe, was introduced. A lightweight shoe in an open-mesh fabric, it was said to be much cooler than army duck yet twice as strong, and it also had deep-cut zigzag outsoles for sure traction.

Esquire returned to the subject of colored clothes for tennis in 1970, observing that when it had broached the subject two years earlier, color was "almost unthinkable." Now, however, "the courts have come to accept color." Illustrating how far this acceptance reached were new fashions that in many instances were as revolutionary for their avant-garde design as for their use of color. They included a two-piece warm-up suit in nylon that came in a rainbow range of shades. The front-zippered jacket had raglan sleeves, circular-yoke construction, and knitted cuffs and neck, while the tapered trousers had an elastic strap under the instep and ankle-to-calf zippers. A two-piece knit suit in Dacron had a jacket with a zippered front, cuffs, and pockets and trousers with all the features of those of the nylon suit. White nylon warm-up pants were worn with a cotton-and-polyester shirt and a wool cardigan, all three being piped in navy and red. Long white polyester trousers were shown with a rib-knit polyester shirt and a thigh-length jacket of wide-wale corduroy lined with a navy, white, and red floral print. Again, save for the model in the nylon warm-up suit, who had shoes with soft leather uppers, the models wore white tennis oxfords.

In the early seventies the heavy cable-stitch tennis sweater shared honors with the wool bouclé sweater, seen in both classic V-neck and zippered cardigan styles. Knits, which were now being used in many types of menswear, also had an impact on and off the tennis courts. Two of the most interesting new knit tennis fashions were a short-sleeved, short-legged, zippered-front jump suit of washable polyester-and-cotton mesh knit, available in white with a navy belt and trim or in navy with white; and a two-piece outfit consisting of a long-sleeved white jacket with a stand-up collar and shorts of stretchy polyester knit.

Esquire showed more knits for tennis in June, 1971, when it published photographs of Arthur Ashe and the Columbia University tennis team coach Butch Seewager. Ashe modeled two costumes; polyester knit shorts, a Dacron-and-cotton crew-neck shirt, and a rib-knit Orlon cardigan piped in blue and red; and a stretch-nylon knit warm-up suit consisting of pants with an elasticized drawstring waistband and a jacket with a rib-knit collar, cuffs, and waistband. Seewager wore horizontal-rib–knit Dacron shorts, a cotton-and-Dacron shirt, and an acrylic-and-nylon knit cardigan. Among the more significant new double-knit tennis clothes to be shown were a white ten-button blazer and a brass-buttoned, double-breasted, sleeveless vest jacket.

The *New York Times Magazine* also focused on tennis knits in 1971, when its issue of April 18 featured a long-sleeved pullover of knitted white Dacron with red-and-navy stripes on the collar and oversize lower patch pockets, a collarless short-sleeved white shirt of knitted polyester and cotton with navy-and-red stripes at the neck and cuffs, and a Dacron-and-cotton mesh pullover with a four-button placket and black trim and chest insignia, worn with rib-knit polyester shorts.

In the meantime, the tennis shoe also was changing. The high shoe, which in the 1920s had been the popular tennis shoe and then had almost disappeared, was seen again in the early seventies as the younger player favored the high canvas shoe with bold racing stripes. Undoubtedly it is with the younger player that further innovations in tennis clothes will originate. These innovations may mean new uses for color one year and a nostalgic return to white the next year. For the world of tennis, with the exception of riding the most tradition-bound active sport, is enjoying its sartorial freedom, and today's tennis clothes express this joy. Menswear can only gain from this state of affairs. It is highly likely that, in this era of casual clothes, fashions starting on the tennis court may be seen in the business office in the space of a single season.

Beachwear

The turn-of-the-century American did not expect, much less demand, comfort from his clothes. The man who sweltered through the summer months encased in a high starched collar and a flannel suit stepped out onto the beach encased in a woolen tank suit that more or less defied the sun to reach him. Women were equally inhibited by their clothes, what with choker collars and bustles, even in summer, and knee-length bathing suits and long stockings at the seashore.

The tank suit of this period came down to just above the wearer's knee-cap, and its sleeves came midway between his shoulder and elbow. Still, a man's bathing suit was more colorful than a woman's, which was usually of a solid color and very often black; a man's tank suit most often had bold horizontal stripes. But striped or not, a man's bathing suit during the first two decades of this century was first and foremost cumbersome. It was not until the 1920s that he was liberated, through the arrival of a one-piece suit with short skirt and deep armholes, as well as of the new two-piece suit—both sporting vivid colors and lively stripings of various widths.

1920–1930

In 1925 *Men's Wear* took a fashion survey of California beaches starting

The tank suit was regulation for members of the 1907 swimming team at Princeton University. [COURTESY OF CULVER PICTURES, INC., NEW YORK]

with the exclusive beach of the Santa Monica Swimming Club. The following prologue to their findings illustrates the new freedom of this "flaming youth" decade:

Tanned young men and women are on the sand beneath gaudy parasols. A few venturesome persons experiment, first cautiously, then boldly, in the thrilling surf. Most lie contentedly basking in the hot sun, or chat lazily propped against back-supports. One looks in vain for pale faces and puny limbs. Golden brown skins stand out in sharp and comfortable relief against raw, concentrated, screaming color. And oddly, little of it seems in bad taste, or unduly conspicuous. This is not the South Seas, but color is being handled with vestiges of skill. The effects are gorgeous, rather than jarring, as the whole picture is pitched in a high key.

From Santa Barbara to Coronado, including the crowded stretches of Santa Monica's ocean front, the beaches are alive with color and chest stripes in the prison-stripe effects. Manufacturers in California seem to have intelligently grasped the situation. One advertises stripes in club colors; another has brought out swimming shirts in Fair Isle patterns; a third reports a run on bright purple, over the standard navy blue line.

Not only are colors vivid this season, but they are more diversified than ever before. Multi-hued and vari-shaded, even subdued combinations are in odd tones not usually associated with beach outfits. Film actor Tom Moore wears carefully matched striped shirt and trunks in brown and cream. The trunks, while full cut, appear to be knitted rather than of flannel. Full cut flannel trunks are seen in blue, grey, and white, or occasionally of black mohair; many have contrasting side stripes or edging. Mr. Craig Biddle, of Philadelphia, wealthy society man and amateur athlete of great distinction, whose clothes are always interesting combining as they do smartness with practicability, trots waveward in a black one-piece suit marked by fine, almost invisible, chest stripes.

It is in the one-piece suit with short skirt and deep armholes, often with narrow straps to keep the front and back from gaping, that the more brilliant colors are displayed. Sometimes the entire suit is solid purple, or pale blue, or even of yellow or scarlet; another fancy is to have the

The one-piece knitted wool racing suit was worn in 1925 by the champion, Johnny Weissmuller. [JANTZEN, INC.]

skirt and trunks of a contrasting color. Both these ideas are frequently modified by the addition of every variety and shade of striped effects. Orange and black is a favorite combination.

White jacket sweaters, occasionally in conjunction with white duck trousers, are most generally worn while lounging about the beach or veranda of the clubhouse. However, we have so far counted three turtleneck jerseys pulled on over bathing suits. Due to climatic reasons, this is not a practical garment for Southern California wear. If it goes over on a large scale, it will be solely the result of the strong style appeal carried. One or two men are wearing flannel blazers, while others have donned knitted pinch-back single-collared jackets.

Flannel beach robes in gay stripes, and robes of terry cloth in bright colors, have by no means been neglected. Both appear in considerable numbers. Many of the former are extremely light in weight, while the stripes run to pastel shades. Figured cotton and linen garments, lined with terry cloth, have been noted in strictly limited numbers, but on particular men. Still another notion noted on the beaches here is a rubber gown lined with terry cloth.

Endorsed by William Bachrach, coach of champion swimmers, in 1926, this swimsuit had an unbreakable button at the shoulder, a shaped body, and patented trunks with a nonrip crotch. [JANTZEN, INC.]

Already the Deauville sandal, of woven strips of leather, may be noted on a scattering few. For headcovering, the aristocratic Panama in negligee shapes is far in the lead, while the brown leghorn with high crown and wide band appears to be making its debut under favorable auspices. The lowly and humble Japanese Toyo hat, for the most informal sort of wear, has attained a respectable following, both on the beach and golf course. It does not stand up well, but its price is insignificant, and its light, cool pliability makes for comfort during these midsummer days. (*Men's Wear,* July 8, 1925, pp. 58–59)

The next year bathing togs in southern California were the subject of still another fashion survey (*Men's Wear,* Jan. 20, 1926, pp. 62–63), illustrated with a photograph of film star Ramon Navarro wearing a horizontally striped bathing shirt and a pair of blue flannel trunks. But as far as the survey reporter was concerned, a new note in swimming suits that he felt would be seen along the beaches the following summer was the "omnipresent blazer stripe as seen in a one-piece swimsuit worn on the exclusive beach at Santa Barbara." He continued:

So far, this craze for vertical stripes has affected only the younger generation, in so far as swimming suits are concerned. Some of the combinations are wild beyond description, four or five of the most violent contrasting colors being used in alternating stripes.

One more word about the preference of California boys. They seem to like suits cut along the scantiest possible lines still compatible with prevailing beach regulations. Armholes extend to the waistline with narrow strips of fabric that hold the front and back snug against the body to prevent unseemly gaping. Backs are low and narrow, while the width of front and length of skirt often fail to function in accord with our national conception of masculine modesty. Were it not for the legal bans, the silk tank suit with its slight weight and water-resistance would undoubtedly be more widely worn. As it is, several of the more expert swimmers at Coronado wore these silk one-piece suits—with the skirts, however, which are generally omitted from the actual racing garment.

For the rest, horizontal chest stripes dominate the field. Wide single stripes, series of narrow stripes, and stripes of graduated width appear in one-piece suits and on separate shirts.

Unless the separate trunks be of knitted fabric, they are generally cut loose and long of flannel in shades of blue, grey, or white. Very full trunks of black mohair or alpaca appeared on occasion, worn by extremely smart men. The tendency in this direction, here, is quite as noticeable as is the opposite among the youthful wearers of one-piece coverings.

Among the fashions most photographed at the Los Angeles Spring Apparel Exhibition in 1926 were a diagonally striped bathing suit with knitted trunks matching the dark stripe on the skirt; an athletic one-piece swimsuit with double straps under the arms to keep the front and back from gaping; and a bathing suit in Fair Isle pattern with knitted trunks to harmonize with the colors in the shirt.

No fashion survey of the 1920s could afford to ignore Palm Beach, described by one fashion writer as "the garden spot of the world." A *Men's Wear* report (Mar. 10, 1926, pp. 66–70) noted that the European vogue of the bathing robe, about which many fashionable American men had shown some hesitancy, had hit Palm Beach "with a bang! This means that we will see every year from now on more and more robes at bathing resorts all over the country. Men who have never even had a lightweight robe at home will be buying them for the beach and you will see that these robes will express man's natural liking for colorful articles of apparel. Now that a well known group of men have had the temerity to sport in public a robe of many colors in such a place as Palm Beach, other men all over the country will start wearing them. Personally, if two years ago anyone had told me that regular two-fisted he-men would loll around on the beach in one of those 'Charvet' linen robes with big wallpaper-like figures two feet in diameter adorning them, I would have said, 'Crazy.' But they are doing it; 10 per cent of the men wearing beach robes have the nerve to do it. Of course, the largest number are wearing the awning striped flannel robes."

As to bathing suits, 23 percent of the fashionable vacationers at Palm Beach

At the Olympic games, all 26 men on the U.S. swimming team preferred Jantzens. And so did many of the swimmers on competing teams . . . England, Germany, Canada, Hungary, Denmark! While at famous beaches everywhere . . . Newport, Palm Beach, Brighton, Deauville . . . you find Jantzens worn. Striking evidence this, that Jantzen, the ideal swimming suit, is the choice of both active and fashionable swimmers throughout the world.

Pictured here you see two popular Jantzen models for men . . . the *Twosome* and the *Speed-suit*. Conveniently buttonless, in sizes to 42; larger sizes with unbreakable rubber button. Like all Jantzens, they are tightly-knitted from the strongest long-fibred wool. And the perfection of Jantzen-stitch assures you perfect fit, long service and lasting satisfaction. See these colorful, color-fast models at leading stores here and abroad. Your weight is your size. Jantzen Knitting Mills, Portland, Oregon; Vancouver, Canada; Sydney, Australia.

*From personal interviews at Amsterdam by Jantzen representatives.

Jantzen
The suit that changed bathing to swimming
JANTZEN KNITTING MILLS, Dept. 50, PORTLAND, OREGON
Send me free Jantzen Color Harmony Guide showing new Jantzen styles and colors.

This is the Jantzen Speed-suit for men. Neck, armholes, and trunks cut away to give utmost freedom. Arm-straps part of suit. Conveniently buttonless in all sizes—trim—comfortable —smart.

Every one of the 26 men on the U.S. Olympic swimming team wears a Jantzen. And so do many of the swimmers on foreign teams . . . England, Germany, Canada, Australia, Hungary, Denmark. These swimmers chose Jantzen in preference to all other swimming suits.

You, too, can have the same suit that champions wear. These trim-fitting, freedom-giving suits are on display at leading stores in the United States and 49 foreign countries. Tightly knitted from the strongest long-fibred wool, the perfection of Jantzen stitch assures you perfect fit, long service and lasting satisfaction. Your weight is your size. Jantzen Knitting Mills, Portland, Oregon; Vancouver, Canada; Sydney, Australia.

*From personal interviews at Amsterdam by Jantzen representatives.

Jantzen
The suit that changed bathing to swimming
Address Jantzen Knitting Mills, Dept. 56, Portland, Oregon, for free Jantzen Color Harmony Guide.

The speed suits of 1929 had the neck and armholes cut away to give the swimmer maximum freedom. The two-piece outfit at the left consisted of a cross-stripe shirt and solid-color trunks. [JANTZEN, INC.]

preferred the solid-color one-piece model, while 24 percent held to the cross-striped shirt with trunks. In third place, with 14 percent, was the solid-color one-piece swimsuit with colored borders; and in fourth place, with 12 percent, was the solid-color shirt with trunks. The white shirt with trunks was a very close fifth, with 11 percent of the men of wealth preferring this combination. "The newest

thing in bathing suits," observed the survey writer, "was a white shirt [and] green two-tone plaid flannel trunks with a single breasted flannel beach robe of the same material."

The rotogravure pages of the newspapers in the winter of 1926–1927 reflected the profusion of striped bathing suits and striped beach robes at the most fashionable beaches. The prevailing fashion among devotees of

the cross-striped bathing suit in the mid-1920s was to wear the shirt outside the trunks. By 1928 men's bathing suits had become progressively more revealing. There was, for instance, a new "legless" suit, a one-piece skirted suit with legs so short that it gave the impression that the bather was wearing only a shirt. Commenting on this growing urge for novelty, *Men's Wear* noted (Feb. 8, 1928, p. 98): "While staples in bathing suits still are what keep the wheels in motion, each succeeding season finds more customers swinging over to more startling designs and color effects, and it may not be many years before the navy or the black will be worn only by aged gentlemen who seldom swim." Summing up the urge for change, the writer decided that a more rapid and radical revolution was taking place in bathing suit styles and shades than in hats.

Still another fashion journalist taking a look at the new bathing suit styles for men observed: "The stylish bathing suit is in solid color, the shirt of one color and the flannel trunks of another. The shades employed are tans, blues, reds, and the run of traditional bathing suit shades, and also pastel shades. For instance, a light oxford grey shirt, solid color, will be assembled with blue flannel shorts. A tan shirt will have a darker tan accompaniment in trunks." He added, "There is a tendency to expose more of the male figure to the sun and this is promoting deep cut armholes which usually are equipped with bands" (*Men's Wear*, Feb. 8, 1928, p. 99). A Palm Beach fashion report of 1928 noted that, to be appropriately attired at the various sports and social functions he attends, a man at Palm Beach must have at least five different types of apparel.

Color was rampant in bathing suits, with cross-stripes still predominating: two equal stripes in contrasting colors were in the lead. One of the outstanding developments was the variety of the solid-color shirt worn with trunks of a different color. Bright shades of blue, light shades of brown and tan, and also greens were seen in these, as well as black and white, and the same range of colors was used in the trunks. Summing up this trend, the writer noted that next to the dark blue or black trunks the light gray flannel trunks led the others, and these were worn with either a white shirt or a colored shirt of tan or blue.

Striped robes were still the vogue, especially in flannel, but the solid-color terry robe was gaining in importance.

"Some of the smartest dressed men at the beaches wore this robe, and it was in most cases cut double breasted, in the manner of an overcoat, with large patch pockets with flaps. The popular color was light blue-grey, with medium blue of secondary importance. Some of the very smartest dressed men, however, were observed wearing figured linen robes with terry lining, shawl collar and sash" (*Men's Wear*, Mar. 7, 1928, p. 84).

Two of America's most popular summer resorts—Atlantic City, New Jersey, and Long Beach, Long Island—both annually visited by persons from all parts of the country, were subjects of fashion surveys in 1928. At Atlantic City it was noted that all the colors of the rainbow appeared in cross-stripes, vertical stripes, diagonal stripes, small patterns, and large patterns, and in many other ways. One-piece bathing suits in solid colors predominated, however, with dark blue and black the most common. Of the two-piece suits, the most popular combination seen at Atlantic City was the white jersey with dark blue or black trunks. Blue flannel trunks were the most widely used with all combinations. A few novelty belts were worn with these two-piece suits, the regular white web being the most popular.

The colors and styles of bathing suits worn by men at Long Beach were more varied. "Perhaps the most outstanding style note was that of the solid colored shirt in blues, red, greens, tans, or other colors, with dark blue flannel trunks, which fashion is undoubtedly an echo from Palm Beach. This latter fountainhead of men's fashions was the first place at which was observed this custom of wearing a certain colored shirt one day, another color the next, and still a different color on the third day" (*Men's Wear*, July 25, 1928, p. 65). And although the plain white belt was still the style worn by most men at Long Beach, there was a growing interest in colorfully striped and checked bathing belts.

A much wider variety of beach robe styles was observed at Long Beach

than at Atlantic City. Men at the former resort wore robes of striped and figured terry cloth, solid-color flannel, brilliantly striped broadcloth, bold patterned flannel, striped madras, and solid-color shantung and heavy silk. But by far the most popular style was the striped cotton crepe robe in the single-breasted shawl-collar model.

1930–1940

By 1931, "The most important note in bathing suits is that they are getting scantier and scantier. There is so little left of the present popular bathing shirt, that if any more trimming away is done, it will no longer be a shirt. It is the fashion to get a good coat of tan, hence more and more of the surface of the body is exposed to the sun's rays. Most of these low-cut bathing suits are in solid colors, and are to be seen in one- and two-piece styles. In the latter type the ensemble idea is always evident." An accompanying illustration of a bright yellow silk shirt worn with brown shorts trimmed with yellow piping demonstrated this point. In the two-piece suits, solid-color shirts had increased in popularity from 23 to 32 percent during the preceding year.

Said *Men's Wear*: "Developments in the bathing suit field within the last six or seven years have changed the entire complexion of a business that had become prosaic from the style angle. In the last decade bathing suits became swimming suits. The water garments that were worn to conceal nakedness have been redesigned to admit of the utmost freedom of movement and within the last two seasons they are more revealing than concealing. The change came about by devoting thought and effort to the improvement of the construction of bathing suits, followed by intelligent and successful efforts to demonstrate these improvements to the ultimate customers. . . . Shortened summer working hours, daylight saving and an increasing interest in outdoor activities aided by the widespread distribution of motor cars contributed thousands of visitors to bathing beaches where only hundreds were interested before. Bathing or swimming suit business has grown to a sizable industry as the result" (Feb. 11, 1931, p. 89).

Cross-stripes were still enormously popular, and the widths that stood out most prominently were the 1¼-inch equal-width stripes. Stripes appeared, for the most part, in two-color effects, and three color stripes were also seen in fair numbers. The most popular colors were yellow and brown, yellow and blue, gray and blue, red and tan, black and gold, blue and white, and green and gray.

Many men were reported wearing beach shoes in colors that harmonized with their bathing suits. Brightly striped canvas espadrille beach shoes with rope soles were a favorite, and so was a high canvas shoe with zippered front.

A good heavy silk knitted bathing shirt sold that year for $7.50 and was a great favorite. It had elasticity, shed water quickly, and was mothproof. Most men preferred to wear it with flannel trunks.

By 1934 men's bathing suits had become so streamlined that a *Men's Wear* fashion reporter referred to them as "glorified supporters." Tennis star Fred Perry, photographed chatting with Marlene Dietrich during a Hollywood visit, wore a knit pair that fit snugly at the waist and leg bottoms but loosely around the hips and seat. A growing demand was also reported for the brief blue flannel trunks with laced fronts, for extremely abbreviated gabardine shorts with a low waistline, and for a flat knit with a simulated fly and flannel top.

Beach slacks, a major fashion along the Riviera for several seasons, finally became popular in the United States during the mid-1930s. Sailcloth was a popular material, in blue as well as white, its practicability neatly balanced by a snob appeal earned by its association with the big racing yachts. Knitted slacks, mostly all white, were also popular.

As to belts for bathing shorts, the heavy white cotton belt with metal buckles was the most popular, although rope belts with anchor fasteners were being seen in colors.

In 1935 *Esquire* observed: "It is in bathing suits and their various concomitants that there have been more innovations in the past few seasons than in any other branch of the tradition-bound masculine wardrobe. Men will indulge in fancies of color and cut at the seashore that would make them rear up on their hind legs in dismay anywhere else. And yet, despite the general truth of the foregoing, we must record the fact that blue is still the most popular single color." To illustrate this point, the fashion department chose to show a pair of white ribbed swim trunks with a blue belt on one model; and on another, an entire outfit in a wide range of blues, from a houndstooth polo shirt to washable beach slacks and canvas sneakers. Regarding the footwear, the

Swimwear in 1931 included net and deeply cut athletic tops and shorts of knitted and woven fabrics. [NEW YORK PUBLIC LIBRARY PICTURE COLLECTION]

Streamlined trunks of 1935 were of solid-color knitted wool with a white belt and neat side stripes. [JANTZEN, INC.]

The light-color athletic shirt and dark trunks of this suit are joined by a zipper so that the shirt may be removed easily. [JANTZEN, INC.]

caption writer assured the reader they were "new and very good." Tucked into a corner of the picture frame was a terry cloth beach robe in yellow, the second-ranking beachwear color that year.

"Bathing suits are getting less and less. Robes are getting more and more," said *Men's Wear* in 1936. "Shirts are diaphanous in weave—yet it is almost a crime to appear upon the beach without some sort of fancy covering, like slacks and shirt, or robe." The writer also commented that the trend in beachwear was comfortable and gay: "Statistics would seem to show that the male half of the bathing-swimming public will more than ever tend to rise out of their bathing suits like Aphrodite arising from the waves. Feminine bathing suits have long since taken all the mystery out of human anatomy, men seem to have discarded shirts entirely and the low-rise bathing trunk is fast coming along."

Accompanying this article were fashion sketches showing one man wearing a dark blue knit "gaucho"

shirt, natural-color linen shorts, and red-and-blue–striped espadrilles; a second in a blue, gray, and white cotton beach robe worn with a light blue terry cloth scarf; and a third whose ensemble consisted of a blue, yellow, and white cotton shirt, natural linen slacks, and brown-and-beige huaraches.

"Starring the pirate stripe beach shirt" was the lead of an *Esquire* fashion feature that same year. "The comet-like fashion career of the pirate stripe beach shirt is said to have begun one day on the Riviera when a couple of high grade Greeks found themselves fresh out of beach shirts and wore the tops of their loudly striped silk pajamas instead. That's how fashions are born. In its subsequent peregrinations, with prolonged stop-overs at Nassau and Palm Beach, the original fabric seems to have undergone a sea-change from silk to linen, but the stripes are still there." Grouped around a red-and-white pirate stripe shirt were a pair of gabardine swim trunks worn with a silk foulard paisley square instead of a belt; black-and-white twine Trinidad beach sandals with leather soles and heels; a pair of beach slacks of yellow sailcloth and another of blue mohair crash; and yellow raffia beach sandals.

In 1938 *Esquire* filled still another fashion page with beach finery: a lightweight washable beach suit whose shirt was cut similarly to a jacket but with a snug waistband and subtle blouse effect; Hawaiian cotton swim trunks in native coloring and pattern; an unusual lightweight neckertie in a marine design; and a pair of goatskin sandals, new and recently successful at the fashionable Southern resorts. "Give the fashion staff enough rope and they'll corral all the latest beach fashions for your delectation," *Esquire* boasted, this time concentrating on fashions a man could lounge about in with a certain degree of resplendence. These included a figured linen beach neckerchief; a striped terry cloth beach robe; a narrow red cord belt with double chromium clasp; a beach shirt in brown, tan, and yellow Hawaiian de-

sign; fancy knitted swim trunks in blue, red, and gold vertical stripes; red canvas beach sandals with crepe rubber soles; a blue-and-white loose-knit skullcap; a boat-neck beach shirt in a horizontal woven stripe design; and full-cut swim trunks in a diagonal pattern.

In 1939 *Esquire*'s fashion staff expanded its coverage of beachwear. Featured in January, for example, were a Mexican poncho (originally worn at Saint-Tropez) made of lightweight terry cloth and other toweling fabrics in the new reed color that, according to the caption writer, would probably supplant the beach robe; and, for wear to and from the cabana or beach club, a silk net shirt in Algerian brown, with half sleeves and open front, worn with light gray shorts and brown-and-white Norwegian slippers. Another popular outfit (seen at Eden Roc and Cannes) was the Algerian-brown cabana coat with carnelian shorts (sporting cuffs like regulation trousers), worn with sandals whose soles were rectangular leather blocks. In February, *Esquire* sketched a beach costume seen at Paradise Beach, Nassau, consisting of a cabana-red string mesh pullover ("fresh from the Riviera") worn with moss-green trunks.

"Beach fashions have been going native for several years now," said *Esquire* (July, 1939, p. 134), "but this season they aren't merely going—they're already gone native and with a mild bang. The handwriting on the wall was especially bold and colorful in the aboriginal beach costumes observed last winter at such fashion centers as Palm Beach, the West Indies and West Coast resorts. The newest comer among the native-inspired accoutrements is the bandanna beach shirt in an almost paper weight cotton, made in the open front style with short sleeves and sport collar. Its decorative qualities speak for themselves, but it is also a handy gadget for nullifying nature's sunray toasting process, and it composes well with colorful slacks or shorts to make up a smart all-around beach outfit." To illustrate this, the fashion staff chose a beach shirt devised of three large hand-blocked cotton bandanna handkerchiefs in a paisley pattern of yellow, black, and white. With it, for swimming, was a pair of lightweight gabardine trunks in plain white. And on the model's head sat a floppy jipajapa hat with a puggaree band.

Esquire also chose to show "Palm Beach highlights" in June, 1939: a pastel mesh shirt with white collar and cuffs; the reversed-calf chukka shoe, in nutmeg, with crepe soles; knitted swimming trunks in the popular herringbone pattern; and a cotton bandanna beach shirt, this one made of two large cotton bandanna handkerchiefs. Still another fashion page (February, 1939) showed two models in swimming trunks—one wearing a pair of paisley cut-and-sewn shorts ("better adapted to a generously proportioned torso than the knitted type") and a pair of hand-sewn goatskin sandals; and the other in a pair of lightweight knitted alpaca swimming trunks ("of a variety originally introduced at Palm Beach").

"Shirts are very much in order,"

declared the magazine's fashion editor, "for those holiday-bound for the West Indies or South America." He chose to show a colorful native madras shirt worn with khaki drill shorts and red canvas rope-soled shoes; and a lightweight hemp-color jacket with nickel buttons and patch pockets, worn with gray flannel shorts, a mesh half-sleeved

sports shirt, an India print neckertie, lightweight wool anklets, and blue canvas rubber-soled shoes. A layout headed "Beachcomber, 1939 version" showed two models dressed in typical Bahamian manner: one wore a Nassau coconut hat with a wide, colorful puggaree band and knitted swimming trunks in a peppermint-stick pattern;

Plaid India madras swim shorts, first seen in 1936, were accepted even though the colors were not fast. From Esquire, *July 1937.*

the other wore an open-front mesh sports shirt in a large plaid design with gray flannel trunks (June, 1939, p. 128).

1940–1950

Esquire began the 1940s by showing a man in an outfit that, if he but doffed his hat and coat, would be appropriate for a round of golf or for sailing (February, 1940, p. 106). As it was, however, he looked perfectly correct lounging on the patio of a beach club. His outfit consisted of a single-breasted blue flannel blazer with brass buttons and patch pockets, tan gabardine shorts, a coconut straw hat with a yellow puggaree band, yellow wool anklets, brown polished Norwegian slippers, and a yellow silk scarf. Talking to this splendidly turned-out gentleman was a Johnny Weissmuller type wearing swim trunks of ribbed wool, cut very short, with a double stripe at the side that harmonized with his brightly colored canvas espadrilles.

In August, 1940, the magazine's fashion copywriter recommended the following beach fashions: coral beach slacks of a honeycomb design in the new Bahamian coral shade, worn with a gray knitted lisle pullover; a pair of coarse-ribbed knitted shorts with a belt of red webbing, worn with crepe-soled blue-and-white cotton mesh sandals and a copper-colored knitted cotton pullover; a multicolored striped cotton robe, worn over a pair of shorts in a blue-and-white pincheck; and a pair of pale tan rayon shorts with pockets and contrasting green belt, judged to be as suitable for land sports as for bathing.

Esquire struck a near-nudist note when it showed a pair of brief white swim trunks, worn with blue rope-soled espadrilles and a blue hat of featherweight waterproof gabardine. On the same page the fashion staff included the "Bermuda suit," which, according to the caption writer, originated when some wise vacationer told his tailor to cut off the trousers of his lightweight suit above the knee because he liked shorts. The reader was especially asked to note the neat wool

socks worn by the model—calf covers complete with elastic tops—as well as the inch-thick gum-soled reversed-calf "gummies" and the wide-brimmed native straw jipajapa hat with a tied handkerchief band.

In 1941 *Esquire* sketched a young man on a Florida beach wearing a dark blue knitted pullover of fine cotton yarns with a short nap to the surface. With it he wore a pair of coarsely knitted wool trunks that showed the military influence so prevalent then through red-and-white chevron stripes down the sides. In the same frame sat a less athletic type sporting a flattish brimmed Montego hat decorated with colorful raffia, a knitted lisle pullover with bar stripes in copper and rust shades, a pair of natural-color slacks, and brown reversed-calf shoes.

In 1945 the magazine exhibited a pair of swim shorts of a pinchecked rayon-and-worsted blend that provided the wearer with extra freedom in swimming through the pleats on either side. And when he stepped out of the pool, he topped his shorts with a cross-striped knitted pullover.

1950–1960

The 1950s brought in the so-called miracle fibers noted for their fast-drying property as well as for their resistance to wrinkles. The tailored trunk continued to increase in importance during the first years of this decade; the snug-fitting, tailored idea in swimwear was finding special acceptance among high school and college students on the West Coast. Styled for a trim appearance, most of the tailored trunks had extended waistbands and zipper flies; some carried a side zipper and others had pleats that made the trunks strongly resemble walking shorts. Still, it was the medium-length boxer short that was the biggest seller, with the elasticized trunk gaining in popularity. Many swimwear firms offered cabana shirts styled like sports shirts to coordinate with trunks.

By the end of this decade there was a swimsuit length to suit any man,

from the low-rise bikini to the Jamaica and Bermuda lengths that were named swim-walkers. *Men's Wear* (Oct. 23, 1957, p. 88) showed a collection of suits in various lengths: Jamaica-length trunks in Lastex, with a contrasting waistband, worn with a cotton boat-neck shirt with a deep V insert; Bermuda-length shorts in a striped elasticized knit; short-legged Lastex trunks with a partial self-belt, worn with a terry cardigan; and Hawaiian-cut cotton gabardine trunks with a fly front and a curved slit on each leg outlined in contrasting colors, worn with a cotton mesh pullover with a crossover boat neck.

By the early 1960s Acapulco had joined the ranks of those fashionable resorts on which anyone interested in fashion trends would do well to keep an eye. Here, in 1963, jacket shirts (or shirt jackets) with ventilated paneling were being worn on the street with slacks or walk shorts; on the beach with swim trunks; and in the evening, everywhere, and by everyone. Fashion writer Jack Hyde reported in *Men's Wear* that a new, longer, hip-length jacket shirt in a dressy, pleated-front style with contrasting cording was a favorite for evening wear. For the mature man, a more practical concept was the jacket shirt made in a longer length, with some clothing details.

Snug-fitting swim trunks or shorts in handwoven Mexican cottons in shorter or mid-calf length were Acapulco favorites. Many had double-stitching detail, adding what Hyde felt to be a rugged look in keeping with the handwoven fabric.

1960–1970

Swimsuits were briefer than ever in 1960. "The male bikini is no mere theory—we saw it last summer on the West Coast," reported *Esquire*. "The bikini is not for every man—it is not for the old man or the fat man, nor for the conservative or timid man. It is for the lean young man who likes the least attire to gain the most sun." For this ideal man the fashion staff suggested a cotton wraparound bikini in a tropically inspired red-and-white print, elasticized at the waist and legs; and a snug-fitting wool knit in an allover pattern of white-and-gold diamonds. For the less than ideal physique there were still the slightly longer Jamaica trunks.

No matter what the length of a man's bathing suit, *Esquire*'s itinerant fashion editor suggested a sarape or poncho as an after-swim pullover. The one he chose to photograph boasted an Aztec-inspired print, side buttons, and a concealed zipper pocket. Furthermore, it reversed to its terry lining and made a fine beach towel.

Under the title "Swim Short Story" *Esquire* showed the latest trends in swim trunks as of 1963—looser-fitting, slightly longer models. Examples included a pair made of patchwork corduroy; blue-and-olive–striped trunks in a quick-drying Dacron and poplin, boasting adjustable side tabs and a rear flap pocket; a pair of blue-and-red cotton twill trunks cut with slightly wider legs of medium length and side leg vents—the colors split half-and-half, harlequin style; and Bermuda shorts–length trunks in red-and-white checks in a blend of Dacron and cotton, with a brass-buckle closure and zipper fly front.

Denim for beachwear, carrying a strong Western look, came to the fore during the early 1960s; for example, a set composed of a denim shirt jacket and walk shorts in bright navy, double-stitched throughout in white. The shirt had a Western snap closure with a double-front yoke and a cigarette pocket on the left sleeve. The shorts had quarter-top front pockets, a patch hip pocket, and tunnel belt loops.

By 1966 bold, vividly colored swim trunks were making the beach scene again, just as they had some forty years earlier. Some were called jams because the legs were loose-fitting and the waist had a pajama drawstring. *Esquire* showed three pairs: trunks in a red, white, and blue abstract floral print; jams in black, yellow, green, and pink; and a pair in a brown-and-tan batik print. Equally popular was the surfer trunk, and an avant-garde

pair sported an Art Nouveau print.

"Terry cloth, a light porous fabric, has always been very big in towels and bathrobes, but only occasionally used for other things," wrote *Esquire* the same year. "Its time has come, apparently, and in the form of extremely sensible fashions." Among these sensible fashions were a beach sports shirt in vivid shades of gold, yellow, and orange, worn with blue Corbin swim trunks; a kimono robe in brilliant shades of royal blue, red, and bronze, with a blue binding and tie belt; a dark green terry cloth jacket worn with a pair of Dacron-and-cotton–poplin stretch swim trunks; a scoop crew-neck pullover in light blue terry cloth with a single shallow kangaroo pocket and side vents; a white terry cloth bush jacket, worn with fire engine-red swim shorts; and a bold black-and-yellow plaid short-wrap kimono made from two terry cloth towels.

Swim shorts showed the strong influence of surfer styles, and *Esquire* featured a one-piece suit styled exactly like the surfer's rubber wet suit. The fashion editor's choice for 1966 was a pair in navy blue industrial-weight nylon with a red chest stripe and a zipper down the front.

"Once again, the new design in swim trunks has been adapted from another sport," noted *Esquire* that year. This time the sport was basketball, its influence seen in a moderately trim-fitting style whose trademark was side vents and contrasting piping. Examples shown included white cotton shorts with navy binding down the sides and around the legs; navy trunks of a blend of Dacron, cotton, and Lycra, trimmed in beige; navy stretch trunks of acetate, cotton, and spandex, edged and striped with white; and maroon stretch trunks of acetate, cotton, and Lycra, with navy binding.

Paper fashions gained instant popularity with both sexes in the late 1960s, and *Esquire* proceeded to show a paper caftan; a tweedy-looking paper knit shirt with a stand-up funnel neck; and pajama-style pants with a drawstring waist.

"Deck-doters and beachophiles alike have understood the appeal of trim three-quarter-length clam-diggers—or deck pants," wrote *Esquire*, pointing up a pair that was quad-striped (four stripes to a grouping) in gray on smooth white cotton and was worn with a double-rope belt. With his clamdiggers, the model wore a black linen shirt with an Italian spread collar and vented sleeves, its shirttail going in or out with equal aplomb.

Andy Warhol and pop art were captivating the avant-garde, and by 1968 there were pop art trunks of brass-eyelet–waisted cotton in electric light bright colors. Other "fun" trunks included magnified zebra-striped

The male bikini appeared on the beach scene in 1960. Shown here is a pair of knitted wool in a gold-and-white pattern with a solid-color waistband.

These bold-pattern swim shorts of 1966 were known as jams because they were loose-fitting like pajamas and had a concealed cord at the waist.

trunks of stretch cotton and acetate and stretch nylon bikinis striped in several color combinations.

Gentlemen's Quarterly sent a crew to the Greek islands in 1968, which, starting on Mykonos, photographed a model wearing a pure silk shirt with brilliant bands of color running diagonally across its fly front and chest pocket, worn with a pair of coordinated swim trunks of corduroy; a mustard-colored cotton terry bush jacket–style beach coat with four metal-buttoned patch pockets; and a white-plaided light blue corded cotton beach coat, worn with side-vented co-ordinated trunks. On the shores of the walled city of Rhodes, the cameraman snapped a model in surfer trunks of stretch nylon striped in orange, green, blue, and white, worn with a cinch-buckled white webbed belt. Then, on Crete, the camera was trained on a model wearing a pair of above-the-knee stretch-knit trunks striped in red, green, and white, belt-looped and belted with white webbing. Finally, an arresting beach set of printed cotton hopsack was photographed; it was horizontally group-striped in myriad colors and had a zip-front jacket with a lay-down collar, chest pocket, and elasticized tucks at the sides.

During the last years of the 1960s swimwear showed more than just a touch of the 1930s. That fashion-elegant, money-depressed era was echoed in such swimsuits as a stretch nylon tank top worn with stretch shorts of acetate, cotton, and Lycra, with a wide belt through tunnel loops; a cotton knit top worn with surfing pants of cotton, rubber, and Lycra; and a pair of mid-thigh, white-belted trunks of stretch nylon, worn with a matching cotton knit basque-type shirt. In 1969, as men's clothes—from suits to shirts to underwear—became more figure-hugging, the unclothed male torso became more and more of a rarity at the more fashionable watering places.

"Fashion is forever appropriating from the past and, on the whole, this is all to the good," *Esquire* decided. "But sometimes such trends take odd turns, creating styles that are, at once, both *avant-garde* and *anachronistic*. This is certainly true of the influence of the early Thirties on men's swimwear in the Summer of 1969. Now, in an era when the stage, and, somewhat less flashily, the screen, seem positively teeming with performers in their birthday suits, the man on the beach is suddenly eschewing the exposure—the toplessness that he fought so hard to make legal in those summers when the naked torso was deemed indecent."

Jump and tank suits were *le dernier cri*, said *Esquire*. Illustrations included a short, raglan-sleeved zip-front jump suit of royal blue stretch-knit Orlon and Lycra; a one-piece navy stretch denim walking short with fly front and buckle shoulder straps; a stretch-knit white tank suit of nylon; a navy-and-white–striped tank suit of stretch nylon; and a stretch nylon tank suit striped in navy, red, and yellow.

The 1970s

Still considering tank suits in 1970, *Esquire* concluded: "There is really no great sense in encasing the torso in a tank suit. For one thing, it shields from the sun (which is not precisely the purpose of going to the beach), and, for another, it constricts the swimmer. But herein is posed a question, to wit, 'Since when has fashion felt obligated to be functional?'" Yet, for the man who still preferred a bikini, the fashion staff offered not only hope but a nylon stretch-knit bikini. It would appear, in 1970, that any suit—from tank to bikini—was correct so long as it was a knit.

The second-skin tank trunks were the natural evolution for the young, trim man. There were, said *Men's Wear*, ". . . few-if-any restrictions in cut with stretch action and comfort built right in, nylon tricot that dries in a flash and a flash of colors generally reserved for swim teams. Credit the Olympic swimmers with this one."

The only rules are no rules, said *Esquire* in 1971; it proceeded to illustrate the new sartorial freedom that extended to beachwear through such disparate styles as Lastex swim trunks worn with a cotton terry cloth shirt; plaid trunks worn with a relatively long, sleeveless beach coat; striped trunks with a tank top; polyester knit swim trunks with a waist-length shirt; stretch nylon trunks with a matching crew-neck cotton shirt; and stretch terry cloth trunks.

While some men exposed lots of flesh, others covered up. And *Gentlemen's Quarterly* in 1971 covered both conceptions in an issue devoted to beachwear that underscored *Esquire*'s contention that "the only rules are no rules." Among *Gentlemen's Quarterly*'s fashion coups were bib-style shorts with buttoned suspender straps and turned-up cuffs; one pair of cotton jams with a collage of film star faces forming the pattern and another with a comic-book-character motif; a navy nylon swim outfit including short boxer-style trunks and a two-tone paneled top featuring an elasticized waist and zippered front; a speckled beige ribbed cotton lace-up top; a pair of very brief red, white, and blue nylon swim trunks; a rope-belted, widely striped caftan-inspired cotton robe with three-quarter-length sleeves and a deep scoop neckline; a cream-colored cotton mesh and canvas vest, worn with short tie-dye denims; striped cotton terry overalls; a pink safari shirt worn with rose-colored knit shorts with cuffs; a blue cotton pullover with a red collar, short gold sleeves, and a white four-button placket front, worn with banana-colored corduroy jeans; a beige-and-brown speckled cotton knit sleeveless suit; and black-and-white–striped nylon cord swimsuit in a 1920s style.

The same issue also showed "frankly masculine bikinis," such as a red-and-white–checked bikini that zipped up both sides. Far more avant-garde swimwear was shown, including an animal print on a nylon "jungle suit" with one shoulder strap; a deep-sea blue body stocking in rib knit with a full-length double-slide zipper; and white snap-fly shorts with cuffs and front yoke design, worn with a vertically striped tank top of double-knit nylon. Summer overalls of white stretch denim and a chalk-colored summer jump suit in two-way stretch poplin were among the after-swim outfits illustrated.

The *New York Times*'s "Report on Men's Wear" in 1971 deemed terry cloth "a shore thing" and proceeded

The belted tank suit of the seventies with low-cut armholes is an updated version of the two-piece suit of the thirties.

to illustrate this with a page of terry cloth fashions: a club-striped jacket of plush cotton velour, two-buttoned, chest-pocketed, and vented; a stretch terry short-length jump suit of a cotton-and-nylon blend; a multistriped cotton terry beach coat with a zip front, snap-flapped pockets, and a drawstring waist; and a terry beach cap.

Other beach or poolside fashions in the same issue included a cotton duck beach shirt, stitch-edged, brass-snapped, and chest-pocketed; two pairs of stretch swim trunks, one with laced vinyl-paneled sides and the other

boldly anchored; a rib-striped, lace-placketed linen-and-acrylic beach shirt, accompanying swim trunks with a drawstring waist; a pool suit of cotton, linen, and rayon, with the shirt zip-fronted and the pants flared and angle-pocketed; cotton denim overalls, fitted, shaped, and flare-bottomed; an Arnel-and-nylon cabana set striped in red, white, and blue; a navy-and-white–striped beach set of cotton sailcloth, with the jacket zip-fronted and the slacks flared; and a pair of generously flared, jean-styled slacks of blue-and-white cotton in an Early American tapestry weave.

Beachwear for 1972 moved toward an athletic look suggesting that the era of body awareness, rather than fading out, was just beginning to gain momentum. "Hot pants," an immediate success on the distaff side, showed up in beachwear for men, who, after years of having their shirts, sweaters, and jeans "borrowed" by their women, were at long last doing a little fashion thievery of their own. Masculine hot pants, first seen in 1971, gained strength in 1972; they were embellished with all kinds of details, including studs, industrial zippers, and elaborate pocket treatments. Après-swimwear took on an easy, loose-fitting look that year, in all-cotton woven fabrics, knits, and terry cloth, in robed, shirted, and pullover models.

The 1970s marked an end to conventional masculine and feminine role-playing. A man's hair could be and often was longer than his date's, and she might wear thigh-high boots while he wore demiboots. But *they* knew who was HE and who was SHE, and, not surprisingly, this unflappable sense of identity found some of its most stylish expression in beachwear. For not since the 1920s had the American man showed such a healthy awareness of and respect for his body, and beachwear, vividly colorful and unabashedly sensual, said it all.

The man at left wore rib-knit wool shorts with a white belt, a cross-stripe lisle pullover, and raffia sandals. From Esquire, *August 1935.*

Swimwear fashions in 1940: (upper right) coarse rib-knit shorts, emulating a hand-knitted texture, worn with close-fitting mesh sandals with crepe rubber soles; (lower right) multicolor striped cotton robe, worn over lightweight pincheck woven worsted shorts; (lower left) pale tan rayon shorts with pockets. From Esquire, *August 1940.*

The beach set worn by the man at right consisted of a printed cotton jacket and swim shorts in a design of the India madras type. The jacket was trimmed and lined in terry cloth. The boxer shorts were respectively of black nylon and a Grecian-key print. The clogs were of springy cork. From Esquire, *July 1949.*

A sleek blue ski outfit, worn with a yellow helmet and goggles.

A bright yellow two-piece ski suit accented with red pockets and green straps.

Beachwear

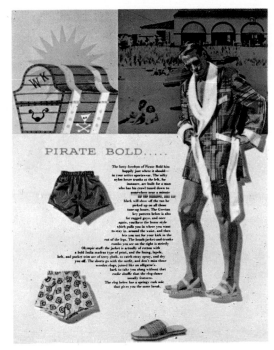

PIRATE BOLD.....

Skiwear

Skiwear

The Norwegians "invented" skiing not so much as a sport but as a practical and pleasurable means of locomotion. Americans adopted it as a sport after World War I and then, in typical fashion, took to the slopes with a burst of energy. Since the earliest and most serious American skiers were the socially elite, the skiwear they wore at the important European winter resorts had considerable news value.

1920–1930

The following excerpts have been taken from a fashion report covering the 1924 season in St. Moritz:

"Never before has there been such a riot of color at the Swiss winter resorts as is notable at the present moment. I am writing from St. Moritz and before arriving here I visited Mürren, Davos and Caux and without hesitation I can say that not only Englishmen, who, here at St. Moritz, are certainly in the minority, but visitors from all over the world, more particularly America, are calmly wearing patterns and colors that a few years ago would have caused exclamation. No doubt this tendency has arisen from the Fair Isle vogue. Here 80 per cent of the men are wearing Fair Isle jerseys, the most popular being those having a ground color of tan, brown, grey, the new blue, or white. Where jerseys are concerned there is but one kind—the pull on over the head."

Getting down to details, the report noted: "The importance of knitted wear cannot be over-emphasized. Another new development this season is the popularity of the knitted cap in what is termed a fisherman or jelly-bag shape, worn flopping over the side of the head and finished with a tassel. The American contingent here is very large; it is the biggest supporter of the bright caps and stockings and hence there is little doubt that these very caps will eventually make their appearance on the playgrounds of the United States. Mufflers are also varied in color, while knitted gloves are to be seen having the gauntlets finished in the most absurd colors and patterns imaginable.

"Leather or suede belts were very

The skier of 1919 wore a knitted cap, a turtleneck pullover, knitted gloves, pants with straps over boots, and strapped ski bindings.
[COURTESY OF CULVER PICTURES, INC., NEW YORK]

This skier at Lake Placid, New York, in 1926 wore baggy Norwegian-style knickers for a cross-country race as spectators in long ski pants looked on. [COURTESY OF CULVER PICTURES, INC., NEW YORK]

nearly as popular as Fair Isles. Every man wore one of these around his waist and from experience I can say they are excellent, for they keep the body warm and prevent the wind from getting in underneath. All colors were to be seen, but the most fashionable were the new shades of brown, tan and champagne."

The rest of the St. Moritz ski outfit that season usually consisted of a single- or double-breasted jacket of a lightweight waterproof material and long baggy pants of a similar material or knickers worn with stockings and square-toed boots. Though the fisher-

man knitted cap was an eye-catcher, many Americans wore a Norwegian-style woolen cap with turned-down flaps for the ears.

The *après-ski* fashion picture was quickly sketched in by the writer of the report: "Men come in from skiing and discard their outer jackets, exchange their heavy boots for a light brown shoe, and dance in plus fours, riding breeches, or jodhpurs and colored jerseys. The scene can well be imagined and, indeed, it is hard for the fair sex to outrival the color schemes created by many men" (*Chicago Apparel Gazette–Men's Wear* (Feb. 26, 1924).

In fact, women appropriated many articles of men's apparel for winter sports at St. Moritz in 1926. Nonetheless, men still dominated the scene with such skiwear as self-colored jerseys with turtlenecks and a new close-fitting cap shaped to the head so as not to impede progress when skimming down a slope. Such bright colors as scarlet, yellow, jade, orange, and chili still prevailed, but some of the most fashionable skiers of both sexes were beginning to show a preference for beige. "This sounds unlikely," wrote one fashion reporter, "for it is not a shade that makes a contrast against the snow, yet it is successful, more particularly when the brilliant colored skiing socks are donned." The younger set started a fad that year for brightly colored, brightly figured handkerchiefs of shantung and tussah, using them not only to decorate pockets but as mufflers or twisted around their heads in pirate fashion. The more sophisticated skiers, however, preferred mufflers of knit or cashmere, and the fashion in 1926 was to wear the muffler twisted over the left shoulder with one end hanging down the back and the other in front.

Although a few purists did not consider plus fours suitable for skiing, many men continued to wear them on the slopes. Riding breeches, on the other hand, were thoroughly acceptable, and one stylish young Britisher vacationing in St. Moritz was photographed in an outfit consisting of a white cable-stitch sweater, riding breeches of lemon corduroy, matching puttees, white ski socks, and boots.

1930–1940

By the 1930s skiing had become so popular that the Olympic Games added it to their schedule of competitive sports. One writer commented: "The northern universities, especially those in hilly country like Dartmouth, Cornell and Michigan, are turning out thousands of ski-minded graduates each year. Discussions of 'form' and learned dissertations on the 'telemark turn' or the 'herringbone' are almost

as common in athletic circles in this country as they are abroad." Special ski trains charging comparatively low fares were carrying thousands of Americans to ski resorts every weekend, and skiwear was a part or about to become a part of many a man's wardrobe. Needless to say, the skier needed fashion guidance at this stage, and so did many of the retailers eager to sell him these special clothes.

Apparel Arts in its winter, 1936, issue covered contemporary skiwear from top to bottom:

Caps. Of the three types of ski caps worthy of consideration, the Norwegian type of navy blue Melton, serge or gabardine has a perfectly round flat top with

A fashionable and practical ski outfit of 1936 included a double-breasted lightweight windproof jacket, dark wool knickers, a dark turtleneck sweater, cable-stitch hose, canvas gaiters, boots, wool gloves, and goggles. From Esquire, *January 1936.*

a long, squarish peak and ear-flaps that fold inside the cap when not in use. The flaps are equipped with strings that tie under the chin. The Swiss type cap is shaped to follow the contour of the skull, carrying a more rounded peak and a double extension flap which, when not in use, folds on the outside of the cap and is fastened in front with a small lace. This double extension flap can be dropped down to serve as protection for the ears, back of the head and neck, in which case the bow is tied across—not under the chin but above or below the mouth. The Swiss type cap is preferable for wear in stormy conditions, since the Norwegian cap offers less protection and might require the use of a parka hood. A third type of cap is one of a more sporting character which, although not following the authentic lines of the other two, also has ear-flaps. It might be described as a jockey or hunting type cap and to some extent is favored over the other two in this country. Although the preferred color is navy blue, these ski caps are also made in white or light neutral shades to match jackets of lighter colors.

Headbands. Many skiers prefer a headband for all-around skiing, although these do not offer adequate protection for extremely low temperatures or stormy conditions. They are satisfactory for ordinary weather, however, provided they are so constructed as to completely protect the forehead and ears. Headbands of knitted wool become damp in a fall and therefore defeat their purpose; consequently, they should be made of the same material as the ski caps. The headbands carry an elastic adjustment in the back and crossbands that go over the head, preventing the headband from slipping over the face. They come in various colors, with black and white the favored combination.

Snow goggles. The primary purpose of the snow goggle is to protect the eyes from the wind, although they also provide protection against sun and snow glare if they are colored, the most effective color being a lavender tint. Snow shields which are kept in place with elastic and which may be worn with a cap or headband serve the same purpose as the goggles and are gradually displacing them, due to the inherent disadvantage of goggles in frequently steaming up.

Gloves and mittens. Any serviceable type of wool knitted glove or mitten is acceptable for skiing, although the preference is for those carrying Telemarken patterns. While wool mittens provide adequate warmth, they do not protect against wind or moisture and consequently an outer mitten of windproof and water-repellent material, such as poplin, should be worn.

Ski boots. Cheap ski boots are a bane to

Skiwear popular in 1936: (top, left to right) a double-breasted Austrian wool jacket for wear with knickers for cross-country skiing, a Norwegian skiing cap, and a heavy sleeveless sweater; (center) a pigskin belt and sandwich case; (bottom, left to right) heavy Tyrolean hose, Norwegian wool gloves, leather mittens with a sealskin back, and a cotton shirt with a colored kerchief. From Esquire, *January 1936.*

in natural, neutral shades or in navy blue, although there is no objection to colors.

Ski trousers. The full cut knicker is rapidly becoming the preferred type of ski trouser, since it allows more freedom in action. The Swiss trouser is also an acceptable type of garment, possessing the advantage of tucking into the boot and thereby protecting the legs from snow and water. The Norwegian style, however, which is tight to the leg, is only used for jumping and is not a requirement for the average skier.

From all this the American winter sportsman made his choice, and in the mid-thirties this choice most often was an outfit consisting of a blue gabardine ski suit with semi-balloon-cut trousers, a dark blue faille shirt, a round-crowned ski cap, and plain knit gloves.

For cross-country skiing, *Esquire* suggested in January, 1936, a double-breasted lightweight windproof jacket, dark wool knickers, heavy cable-stitch hose, a dark turtleneck sweater, canvas gaiters, wool gloves, heavy ski boots, and snow goggles. According to the fashion department, the following skating outfit could, with the jacket left off, also be worn for cross-country skiing: a single-breasted houndstooth-check jacket with matching knickers, a navy blue turtleneck sweater, navy blue wool hose, and black-and-white Norwegian mittens.

With the popularity of skiing rising rapidly, the manufacturers of skiwear accessories kept pace with changing tastes. There was, for example, a tremendous variety of gloves and mittens from which to select: leather mittens with sealskin backs, cut-and-sewn coarse knitted wool with contrasting edging, knitted wool with a knobbed back, and yellow wool shaker-knit mittens with red pattern work.

Despite the increasing popularity of United States ski resorts, European winter resorts still held glamour for the more affluent, status-conscious Americans. Kitzbühel in the Austrian Tyrol, for example, added to its glittering reputation when the Prince of Wales, traveling incognito, visited it. For skiing the Prince wore most of the time a navy wind jacket, trousers of buff

the skier, since professionals agree that, if anything, the boot is of more importance than the ski itself. Aside from highly specialized forms of skiing, such as langlaufing, a practical boot covering all normal requirements is one having a high, roomy, square-shaped toe-box, stiff instep which is usually reinforced with steel. The lacing portion should not fit too closely, allowing sufficient room for take-up when the boot gets wet and stretches. An instep strap is preferred on ski boots, providing a means of holding the boot in place so that the foot does not slide forward in the boot away from the heel. It is important that the upper leather be soft, pliant and water-repellent. Sole protectors of brass or steel are used on the outer sole of the boot and inner soles are used to absorb perspiration. Boot grease should be applied to boots immediately after wearing. This boot grease is made of fish oils and alone is correct for the purpose. No other oils should be used with the exception of saddle soap on boots of Russian tanned calf.

It is also advisable to tree boots when not in use.

Stockings and socks. The type of stockings selected depends on the choice of ski trousers. A heavy ribbed wool stocking should be worn with knickers, together with a short outer boot sock which turns down over the top of the boot. With Swiss style trousers, the shorter woolen stocking is preferred. Some professional skiers recommend wearing either silk or lisle hose next to the skin. In any event, care should be taken to insure that the boot provides adequate room even with the use of heavy and bulky stockings.

Ski jackets. A popular type of jacket is the double-breasted short jacket which has been taken up in the Tyrol. Another type is the Austrian waistcoat style which has one button, crossed in front and ties at the side. There are also various gathered-back types, single-breasted, which close with a slide fastener. Parkas are also popular, many of them being made with removable hoods. All of these garments are preferred

This double-breasted gabardine jacket drew attention on fashionable slopes in 1938. The matching tapered trousers were tucked inside the heavy boots. The outfit was completed by a plaid cotton flannel shirt, a wool tie, a black Tyrolean hat, and wool mittens. From Esquire, *January 1938.*

corduroy velvet, and a scarlet scarf. In February, 1936, *Esquire* dubbed Kitzbühel the fount of winter sports fashions ("perhaps due to the Walesian visitation"), and the fashion editor showed what he judged to be the pre-

vailing Kitzbühel mode: a ski suit consisting of a single-breasted, lightly woven windproof ski jacket with matching knickerbockers, worn with a gingham plaid shirt and a yellow Salzburg tie, yellow anklets, yellow

wool gloves, blue wool hose, a blue knitted headband, and regulation ski boots.

In 1936 Dick Bowler, former Dartmouth College intercollegiate ski champion and now a consultant on ski sportswear, gave advice on what to wear for skiing. He stated that ski suits must be styled for exercise, with both jackets and trousers cut with plenty of freedom and swing by means of bi-wing backs, shoulder darts, and easy armhole construction. Noting that the skier gets very warm while in action, Bowler said that ski fabrics should be light in weight, windproof, and waterproof. For the amateur skier, he thought the best choice was a colorfast 100 percent wool fabric of 24-ounce weight that would shed snow, repel water, and resist wind. In his opinion it was also an excellent choice for the well-dressed spectator.

In January, 1934, *Esquire* had focused on the spectator, too: "Since the spectators, in most instances, get an even worse break from the weather man than the participants, warm windproof garments are a necessity even if the only event in which you compete is the standing broad grin." So the fashion department assembled a spectator outfit which "almost yodels in its Swiss accent":

"The jackets are best when belted and may be either of heavy tweed or of the lightweight twill fabric which is both windproof and snowproof. Under these jackets a heavy sweater, a dark flannel shirt and a corduroy or heavy flannel waistcoat should be worn. The knicker breeches can be made of either of the jacket fabrics, but needn't—and some go so far as to say shouldn't—match in color. Keeping your feet warm is more than half of the battle against the elements, and it is folly to attempt it with one pair of socks. It is equally foolish, however, to try to wear two pair, unless the footwear is built to accommodate that second thickness. Your feet will get colder, if pinched and cramped, with two pairs of socks, than they will with one pair. A pair of heavy wool hose, of three quarter length, teamed up with a pair of wool ankle socks, makes the proper combination, encased in stout well-oiled ski boots—but the latter must fit or you'll be wretched. Knitted woolen gloves, a muffler (in which item bright colorings are to be encouraged) and a close fitting cap, either knitted or of fur, complete the kit."

In 1938 *Men's Wear* declared: "The ski ensemble is becoming more and more standardized. A blouse or jacket of lightweight cotton in light shade and a pair of instructor's style trousers or knickers of dark blue gabardine suffice. The too-too-ultra ideas and the tricky designs find no place in the ski scheme of things.

"Jacket models come down to three basic types. The style with off-center slide-fastener is No. 1. This has gained the approval of so many of the well dressed and expert skiers that it should rank as the top seller. It may be closed all the way up to the side of the collar or only part way, with the lapel rolled back. The slide fastener on the pocket as well gives adequate closure and the protection against the snow and wind. Next is the double-breasted with buttons. Third is the single-breasted with slide fastener" (July 20, 1938).

As an example of this functional look, the article featured a photograph of the polo player Thomas Hitchcock, taken at North Conway, New Hampshire. He wore a blue knitted headband, a natural-shade cotton jacket, and blue gabardine trousers.

Color was still popular in ski accessories, and colorful shirts headed the list. *Men's Wear* described them in the same issue: "The brilliant tartans seem to have greater intensity and depth of color this year than they did last. They are wool flannel, and bright red is particularly prominent, in combination with other colors. Solid color shirts, coming in a range, are either gabardine or flannel. More and more men seem to be taking to the coat-style shirt as against the pullover model.

"Homespun effects in wool neck-wear have the stamp of approval of well-turned-out skiers. Many are in tartans for wear with solid color shirts,

and others showing more modest designs or no pattern at all are suggested for wear with the bright plaid shirts.

"Harmony of hue and fabric characterizes the headwear. The newest style cap really reverts to the original Norwegian model with telescope-shape crown."

Meanwhile, *Esquire* continued to fill its pages with accessories for the ski-conscious outdoorsman. The large collection shown in January, 1936, included a black Tyrolean hat, a reversible wind jacket with flap pockets, Norwegian mittens, Austrian ski hose, a heavy white sleeveless sweater, a blue ski cap of "ever-popular gabardine," peasant slippers for after skiing, a double-breasted lightweight windproof jacket with a Norwegian peasant muffler, and canvas gaiters.

Although the fashionable American winter resort was now firmly established, the skiwear seen there still had a distinctly European flavor. To illustrate this point, in January, 1937, *Esquire* showed a model dressed in a short double-breasted white jacket made with a blouse effect at the waist, a medium-weight turtleneck sweater, wool knickers, heavy cable-stitch hose, anklets, and ski boots. As a footnote the caption writer added: "Wool knickers are practical for all types of skiing except for ski-jumping, which calls for a pair of the regulation long ski trousers."

Among other European inspired outfits shown in January and February, 1938, were a single-breasted gray gabardine ski suit with plus fours and a convertible collar, Tyrolean hose, and a gray Tyrolean hat ("for skiing on low slopes and wear after skiing"); a single-breasted loden jacket with a standing military collar and blue gabardine downhill trousers and headband; a crew-neck wind jacket of the sweat shirt type with a contrasting border at the neck and wrists, opening easily by means of a slide fastener, worn with a knitted headband and gray ski trousers; a blue single-breasted wind jacket and blue plus fours, short slalom gaiters, and a white

gabardine cap with earlaps; a blue gabardine ski suit with a scarlet string tie, a white felt Tyrolean hat with a narrow brim, black ski boots with red lacings, and peasant mittens (another jaunty outfit designed for skiing on low slopes and for after skiing); and a gabardine ski suit with a double-breasted coat cut a little shorter than the jacket of a regulation suit and with lapels cut so that they could be buttoned closely about the neck, trousers cut full but tapering quite a bit at the bottom and tucked inside Norwegian-model ski boots, a cotton flannel plaid shirt, a wool tie with Tyrolean figures, a black Tyrolean hat with a green cord and band, and wool mittens (again the caption writer added a cautionary footnote: "This suit is ideal for after skiing; in high slopes of course, a wind jacket or parka would probably prove to be more practical"). The last of these outfits demonstrated the fact that by 1938 the baggy balloon pants had begun to shed some of their bulk as skiers showed a marked preference for more tapered pants that narrowed more sharply to the boot top.

Skiing enjoyed such a boom during the 1930s that by the end of the decade the season had been extended through March and into April, thus necessitating the development of lighter outfits for the spring ski season. In March, 1938, *Esquire* sketched some of the stylish results: a single-breasted wind jacket of lightweight cotton with a slide-fastener front and pockets, worn with trousers of lightweight windproof green cotton, a lightweight silk scarf, an authentic Tyrolean hat, and two-toned Norwegian ski boots; and a lightweight poplin jacket with a slide-fastener opening and a vertical–slide-fastener pocket, worn with marine blue gabardine ski trousers. An even more springlike outfit consisted of a half-sleeved Tyrolean checked cotton shirt, blue gabardine ski knickers, light wool hose, white slalom gaiters, black ski boots, and a gabardine ski cap with invisible earlaps.

The "ever-popular gabardine," as *Esquire* called it (others referred to gabardine as the most practical ski material), was especially well adapted to the extended ski season. An example was a single-breasted ski suit in dark green gabardine with a convertible military collar, four outside pockets with flaps, and considerable fullness at the shoulder blades.

1940–1960

Après-ski clothes became increasingly stylish in the early 1940s, and in its January, 1941, issue *Esquire* showed a group of fashions for wear with a glass in the hand and a roaring fireplace at the feet. Among them were a colorful crew-neck long-sleeved sweater in a diamond pattern of red, white, and blue with ribbed shoulders, topped off with a blue silk polka-dot muffler and worn with matching full-length wool hose, blue knickers of windproof gabardine, and slide-fastened sheepskin foot muffs; a

Ski apparel for cross-country wear and the end of the trail in 1940 included a heavy wool sweater with red, gray, and blue diamonds topped off with a blue polka-dot muffler. The hose matched the sweater, the knickers were blue gabardine, and the zipper boots were of sheepskin. From Esquire, *February 1940.*

(above) Both fashion and practicality were guides to skiwear in 1941. The hip-length tan cotton jacket on the man at left had a drawstring at the waist to keep out snow and cold air. On the inside, beneath the collar, was a hood that formed a yoke. The knitted wool headband kept the ears warm. The other man wore a waist-length blue cotton wrap-style jacket with a convertible collar. Both men wore downhill ski pants. From Esquire, *January 1941.*

(right) Clothes for après-ski *fireside wear were varied in 1945. The man holding a mug wore a gabardine shirt, a knitted tie, tapered gabardine ski pants, wool socks, and Weejuns. The pipe smoker had on a colorful tartan wool shirt, dark blue tapered downhill pants, and fleece-lined ankle-high boots. From* Esquire, *March 1945.*

(above) The man at left wore a heavy wool native-design sweater tucked inside gray worsted gabardine tapered trousers, a knitted wool headband, a yellow foulard scarf, a gabardine shirt, leather-palmed cotton mitts, and brown boots laced fore and aft. The second skier's outfit comprised a processed cotton jacket tucked inside blue gabardine trousers, a white cotton cap, a tartan flannel shirt, a homespun wool tie, leather mitts, a Western belt, and dark brown blucher ski boots. From Esquire, *January 1942.*

(top to bottom) A pullover ski jacket of blue nylon with black trim; a black grained-leather boot with a foam-fitted inner boot; tapered downhill-style trousers of sheen gabardine, 55 percent Dacron and 45 percent worsted, with a silicone finish; a white wool parka with red-and-blue toggles and a navy blue quilted lining, as worn by members of the United States Olympic team at Cortina d'Ampezzo, Italy; a processed nylon mitt. From Esquire, January 1956.

coarse-yarn ski sweater, worn with a tartan wool shirt, a tooled Western belt with a sterling silver buckle, and yellow knitted socks with soft-leather soles; an after-ski jacket of dark blue whipcord, worn with matching trousers, a yellow turtleneck jersey, and fleece-lined moccasins; and a reindeer-design sweater, worn with a tartan flannel shirt, bluish gray gabardine trousers, and fleece-lined, slide-fastened bootlets of brown buckskin.

Except for this flurry of activity early in the decade, skiwear fashions were in eclipse during World War II. During the postwar fifties skiing gained even greater popularity among a new generation of sports-minded Americans, while at the same time the new man-made fabrics proved to be eminently practical for skiwear.

Meanwhile, ski trousers continued to lose their baggy look as more and more skiers adopted tapered downhill-style trousers. In 1956 Esquire showed a pair made of 55 percent Dacron and 45 percent worsted with a silicone finish. On the same page and coordinated with them were an outer coat of white wool fleece with red-and-blue toggles and fasteners and a navy blue quilted lining (the kind of coat worn by the United States Olympic team that year), windproof processed-nylon mitts, an authentic Norwegian-design sweater, a pullover ski jacket of blue processed nylon with a slide-fastener closure and black trim, and black grained-leather ski boots with foam-fitted inner boots. An immensely popular sweater of the fifties was a heavy cable-stitch model with bold chest stripes, a particular favorite of ski instructors, who were exerting a tremendous influence on skiwear. As the decade drew to a close, the big news in skiwear was the stretch fabrics developed in Austria that in the next decade would banish from the slopes ski trousers that were less than sleek.

1960–1970

Skiing became even more popular in the sixties than it had been in the fifties, creating a fresh demand for exciting ski fashions.

"What to wear at Squaw Valley this year—this is, if you intend to do some skiing of your own?" asked Esquire in January, 1960. Answering this question, the fashion staff started from basics—mesh or thermal insulating underwear—and moved outward to a cotton or lightweight wool shirt, buttoned to the neck or worn with a silk scarf, or a turtleneck knit pullover, and over that a sweater or a nylon parka ("or, if it's really cold, the sweater and the parka over it"). The staff also recommended "stretch ski pants, tapered, close-hugging. Boots rigid at soles and sides, but cushioned and comfortable inside. A cap or hood; mittens or gloves; goggles." To wear on the lift to the cold mountaintop it suggested "a 'lift' or 'tram coat'—a heavier parka, a cape, or a fur or pile fabric coat." As an example of something luxurious to wear on this ride to the mountaintop, the fashion editor chose a pile parka in brilliant red with a quilted lining, trimming of silver fox tails on the hood, and a woven border design at the bottom and cuffs. A relaxed outfit for an evening at the fireside included a bright blue loden cloth jacket with knitted wool binding at the edges, pockets, and cuffs and a silver button and chain at the demishawl collar. This particular jacket, said the caption writer, was resilient enough to serve on the slopes as well.

Whether for skiing or for after skiing, the new tapered ski fashions were bursting with color. In sharp contrast to the dark blues, browns, and blacks

This ski outfit consisted of a royal blue all-wool boat-neck sweater with a shoulder zipper, wool-and-nylon gabardine stretch pants, a leather crash helmet, poplin ski mitts, and goggles large enough to be worn over glasses. From Esquire, January 1960.

This knitted zipper ski jacket in an allover Icelandic pattern was lined with quilted nylon. From Esquire, *July 1963.*

parkas. For instance, leather might cap a shoulder, edge a zipper, or outline a sleeve. There were also real fur parkas for the skier who wanted to be outstanding. Only sweaters remained constant: there did not seem to be anything more attractive or cheerier than the Tyrolean cardigan or the Scandinavian boat-neck sweater.

College students swarmed over the slopes in Vermont and New Hampshire during their Easter holidays, enjoying bright sun and spring temperatures along with their skiing. Ever the innovators, they introduced to skiing such spring and summer sportswear as solid-color and striped walk shorts, Western-style dungarees (some even cut down), and chinos. With these they wore such diversified items as regular ski parkas, single-layer nylon pullovers, sports shirts, and button-down dress shirts. The only true winter holdover was the cotton knit turtleneck.

Patterned parkas made their appearance, and the length of parkas in general fluctuated. Some skiers preferred the longer, seat-covering parka as being more practical and comfortable, while others contended that the shorter parka had a sleeker race look and was more versatile, since it looked stylish enough to wear on campus as well as on the slopes. Meanwhile, the tow coat had lost inches, and most young skiers preferred theirs in the above-knee length.

"*Sleek* is the byword for this season," said *Esquire* in January, 1964, observing that even quilts now had only a fraction of their former bulk. Water-repellent and breathable fabrics were favored for parkas, and color was everywhere. "Black is merely for utility," declared this writer, noting, "Burgundy is a fresh idea; so is a soft yellow; and a richer ski blue." Stretch wear, already popular, received an official accolade when the 150 men and women athletes representing the United States in the Ninth Olympic Winter Games paraded in stretch wear at opening-day ceremonies in Innsbruck, Austria. Even for travel and *après-ski* wear the United States team

of former years were such outfits as a nylon parka and tapered stretch pants of brilliant orange and a boat-neck sweater, gabardine stretch pants, and leather crash helmet all in royal blue (an ideal outfit for downhill racing).

In the mid-sixties skintight stretch ski pants began to show boldly striped sides, and knickers began to reappear

on the slopes. The thigh-length lift or tow coat was now a fashion staple, often being made with a drawstring or snaps at the bottom to shorten the length for active skiing. Quilt parkas reversing to quilts were gaining favor, and corduroy was a favorite parka shell. Important, too, was the use of leather trim on quilted and plain

wore stretch clothing; a stretch Dacron-and-worsted blazer was part of the official travel wardrobe.

The real or synthetic fur parka was a new fad in parkas, and in January, 1965, *Gentlemen's Quarterly* featured one of Orlon pile "fur" dyed blue except for a white V that framed a lighter blue chevron in front. It had an attached hood, a full front zipper, zippered slash side pockets, and rib-knit cuffs, and it reversed to a navy blue filament-nylon side. Such colorful ski and after-ski clothes, said *Gentlemen's Quarterly,* would be seen not only on slopes and in ski lodges but also in stadiums and on campuses and suburban lanes. To illustrate the versatility of this new skiwear ("as warmly welcome on a suburban Sunday as after a swoop down the slopes"), *Gentlemen's Quarterly* showed a bulky fingertip sweater coat with a Mayan design in orange, black, white, and gray emblazoned across the chest and sleeves and a hefty shawl-collared furlike outercoat of light beige with leather buttons and brown suede-cloth piping. An "after-ski natural," according to the magazine, was a rugged outercoat in a blend of brushed wool and cotton. Of a pale oatmeal color, it had a stitched-down yoke effect at the shoulders, oversize stitched frame pockets, an attached hood, a cotton poplin lining, and an all-around belt.

The calibrated ski boot made news in 1966. In its December issue *Esquire* declared this glass fiber boot to be one of the most original innovations available to skiers. The boot had a swinging door, five settings for different forward stiffnesses, a movable cuff that could be angled inward or outward according to the wearer's stance and leg bone curvature, and adjustable inside padding. It was a lightweight, near-custom-tailored boot that also had clean-flowing lines and a smooth block shape. *Esquire* summed its advantages up when it wrote: "There hasn't been anything quite like it on the ski slopes before."

Skiwear took on still another look in the late sixties with the appearance of Western-style outfits. A particularly

Fashions for the ski slopes in 1963: (left) medium-wale corduroy knickers, patterned wool hose, and strapped boots, worn with a dark red heavy-knit wool sweater; (center) a blue-and-gray harlequin-design sweater, a blue cotton T-neck sweater, and wool-and-nylon stretch pants; (right) a royal blue outfit of top and pants in worsted and Helanca nylon stretch fabric with a water repellent finish. From Esquire, November 1963.

handsome example consisted of jacket and trousers of a tan stretch denim. The jacket featured a stand-up funnel-style collar, a deep front and back yoke, upper flap pockets, and lower zippered pockets. The trousers were hip huggers designed to carry a wide belt and had straight bottoms so that they could be worn over ski boots.

In the late sixties, warm-up pants were being worn as ski pants by many ski enthusiasts. Made of wool, wool and polyester, or polyester and cotton with or without an acrylic lining, warm-up pants, as well as other articles of ski apparel, were being worn for snowmobiling, too.

Knickers had been revived, although they did not regain their former great popularity. Some of them, made in a fabric of 30 percent polyester and 70 percent cotton, had a leather look. Worn with a zippered-front jacket of the same fabric, they produced a ruggedly masculine effect.

In the late sixties, the ski train had competition in the form of the low-fare charter flight, which carried middle-income skiers to European winter resorts that in earlier years had been the exclusive playground of the very rich.

Skiing in the Seventies

Gentlemen's Quarterly representatives in the French Alps in January, 1970, decided: "The slopes are going to have a different look this year. Tradition has had it!" Exhibit A was "the ski suit of ski suits," a fireman-red crinkled patent-leather jump suit with a zipper running from the hood to the pants bottom. Exhibit B was a Moroccan-look tapestry-print jacket trimmed and lined in pile. There were no closures in front, and the jacket was reversible. It was not for skiing but was considered ideal for after-ski wear or for spectatoring." Still many European ski enthusiasts wanted nothing so much as a parka with a Western feeling, and *Gentlemen's Quarterly* photographed one with Mont Blanc as a background: a nylon parka with a front zipper closure, two front flap pockets with buckle-through closures, a red lining for warmth, and black quilted shoulder patches.

"There are sweaters and there are sweaters," declared *Gentlemen's Quarterly* in its winter, 1970–1971, issue, noting that there were, for instance, "scoopy-doopy necks and hippy-dippy types, but one idea most of them present is the tapered or 'shrunken' fit. An après-ski possibility is a bold houndstooth patterned style in navy-and-red, with a scoopneck. The cuffs and bottom are tightly ribbed, conforming to the prevailing fit for a Seventies sweater."

"Even the greenest novice looks like dynamite with the glossy ski gear available now," said *Gentlemen's Quarterly* by way of introducing its readers to the new anatomically fitted boot, which was made possible by drying plastic foam around the foot while it was encased in a shell lined with soft vinyl. "The only hard part is standing still in it for the 15 minutes it takes to harden," advised the feature writer. Still, it was not the very newest type of ski boot, for *Esquire* recorded the arrival of a "new and authentically ingenious boot" that was in reality two boots in one, being both ski and *après-ski:* a glass fiber shell encased an all-leather *après-ski* boot, snapping firmly into place by means of four buckles. The shell opened in half and could be removed expeditiously.

"Skiing seems the most stylishly garbed of all sports," said *Esquire* in November, 1970, taking a panoramic look at the "new wave" skiwear. "Infinitely more tasteful than golf, for example, and a lot less inhibited than, say, tennis." In fact, the streamlined sleekness of the ski fashions of the early seventies had a look of adventure and exploration that was both casual and chic. *Esquire* collected some samples and posed them in front of the mock-up lunar module in the NBC News Space Center in Rockefeller

This nylon warm-up jacket and pants have stretch inserts to break sliding in the event of a fall. The gloves are roomy, and the goggles and helmet are constructed for safety. The boots have big buckles for easy entry and exit as well as good control of skis. From Esquire, *December 1971.*

Center: a hooded *après-ski* parka of natural yak with lynx sleeves, worn with matching wool stretch pants and huge boots of unclipped mouton with natural-leather thong crisscross ties; a short, hooded tangerine-color nylon ski-lift jumper with a zippered visor and matching over-the-boot wool pants, buckled ski boots, and black cowhide gloves with web wrists and padded knuckles; and an Italian-oriented *après-ski* outfit consisting of a Gucci calf jacket worn with leather-trimmed linen-and-polyester slacks with an enameled buckle and tan buckled jodhpur boots.

As long ago as the twenties women had begun to appropriate men's skiwear. Now, in the early seventies, there were such eye-catching unisex fashions as an Aztec-inspired poncho with an oversize collar and white pile trim for him and a matching pile-trimmed vest for her.

Zippers were used extensively in ski jackets, thus prompting *Gentlemen's Quarterly* to declare in its winter, 1970–1971, issue: "Skiing is a many-zippered thing." Proof was offered in the guise of such stylish jackets as a black ciré nylon with a two-way zippered front and two zippered patch pockets and a nylon hip-length navy jacket with a stand-up collar having a two-way front zipper and a big zippered side pocket.

Although the ski slopes of the United States were still ablaze with color, smart black skiwear was not lacking, as *Esquire* proved in November, 1970, when it showed a nylon black-and-white belted pullover wind shirt, worn with black over-the-boot racer pants of wool, nylon, and Lycra, a black-and-white wool knit cap, and pile-lined black capeskin gloves. Still, color was dominant, as *Esquire* demonstrated with a three-quarter vinyl lift coat of sou'wester yellow; a one-piece featherweight stretch-nylon jump suit in royal blue with allover stitched pleating, zippered vertical chest pockets, and a cinch belt, topped with an orange visored helmet; and a snap-front red nylon vest that reversed to shearling, worn with brown-and-beige glen plaid over-the-boot warm-up pants.

So, in a relatively short time skiwear evolved from a function-oriented industry to one in which fashion and practicality joined to produce high fashion both for the slopes and for the *après-ski* hours, which some persons thought were the best part of a skiing expedition. In the seventies, the handsome, sun-tanned ski instructor found that, when it came to fashion influence, he had a strong rival in the handsome, sun-tanned Olympic champion, who in this decade emerged as a genuine celebrity.

This man wears a russet nylon ski-lift jumper with a double zipper closure, matching over-the-boot pants, buckled black boots, and black leather gloves with padded knuckles (1972).

Riding Clothes

A modern British guide to correct dress for all riding occasions maintains that the horse invented sports clothes and bases this contention on the fact that it was the early-eighteenth-century British sportsman's passion for horses that dictated special clothes for wear in the hunting field. The concept of special clothes for active sports evolved from this equestrian, who sat in his saddle wearing a simple cloth coat cut at the fronts for freedom and comfort, a pair of breeches, long leather boots, and a high-crowned hat. It does not demand great imagination to see how much the riding clothes of the twentieth century owe to this stylish and eminently practical outfit or how much it eventually influenced the tailoring of suits worn in town.

This fox hunter photographed in Leesburg, Virginia, in 1909 wore the correct pink riding coat with metal buttons, round-crowned black velvet cap, white stock, and black boots. [THE BETTMANN ARCHIVE, INC.]

Types of Clothes

Riding clothes are basically English in both design and material and, until the second half of the twentieth century, remained substantially unchanged generation after generation. Then the development of man-made fabrics and, finally, the sartorial freedom generated by the Peacock Revolution affected even riding clothes. Yet no other sport continues to dictate such rigid fashion rules as riding. For every fashion revolutionary who dares to flaunt one of these rules, there are many men who regard them as something akin to the Ten Commandments. For these purists, the important consideration in the selection of proper apparel and appointments is the type of riding for which they are intended.

Hacking. The term "hacking" is traced to the hack, or hackney, the saddle horse chosen for ordinary riding as opposed to the horse used for hunting or jumping. The most widely worn riding clothes are in the hacking style, and the choice of individual items of apparel for hacking or country riding depends on the quality of the ride. The hacking jacket, for example, has certain general styling features, but a more informal ride dictates that its material be tweed rather than the more formal melton or cavalry twill.

Regardless of its material, the hacking jacket usually has a three- or four-button front, leather buttons, high-fronted, short lapels, a throat tab, a long center vent, an ample skirt that is tail-lined with waterproof material, two side pockets, a ticket pocket, and an outside breast pocket with flaps, and a large inside hare, or poacher's, pocket. The pockets are larger than the normal size and sometimes are cut on a slant. The jacket cuffs are sometimes fitted with wind-resisting wrist lining, and the back of the jacket is usually lined with a checked wool material.

For the more formal style of hacking, the jacket can be in black, dark gray, tan, dark brown, or a neat tweed design. A hard bowler hat (a man's riding bowler) is worn; it weighs between 6 and 8 ounces, and the crown is loaded with shellac and reinforced with a shellac gossamer tip. A riding shirt, usually of an absorbent material such as flannel or wool, has a soft collar and is worn with a solid-color tie. (The shirt should have a detachable collar so that it may also be used for wear with a stock for hunting.)

In place of a tie, the rider may prefer a colored stock fastened with a plain gold pin. A classic stock (sometimes referred to as a "ratcatcher stock," a term going back to the days when a horseman preparing for a country ride often had to contend with rats that infested the hayloft in his stable) has a front buttonhole, a slot in the back, and a loop for the back stud or button at the back of the shirtband. Today ready-made stocks are also available. Stocks may be made of piqué or linen or of pure silk, which is the correct material for hacking. A hunting scarf of silk with a polka-dot design is acceptable in place of a stock.

For more informal hacking, a soft felt hat or cap is worn in place of the hard bowler, along with a collar-attached shirt and tie or a knitted turtleneck pullover. As noted, a hacking jacket of tweed is correct with this outfit.

For either formal or informal country riding, breeches and high boots or jodhpurs and jodhpur boots are correct. The newmarket boot most often seen with breeches is quite light in weight and is usually made with canvas legs lined with leather. The jodhpur, originally a cotton trouser from the Indian city of Jodhpur, was introduced into England as a riding garment during the last decade of the nineteenth century. Its upper part is much the same as breeches, tapering down to a close-fitting knee, calf, and ankle. Jodhpurs may be cuffed or cuffless, and some have straps to slip under the jodhpur boot. This ankle-high boot evolved from the polo boot and became popular in the 1920s. It is available in a strap model or in one with an elastic side. In lieu of jodhpur boots, stout ordinary shoes may be worn with jodhpur gaiters to hide the gap between the bottom of the jodhpurs and the top of the shoes. Breeches and jodhpurs are acceptable only in stone, fawn, or tan color; footwear may be either black or brown.

Town or park riding. The traditional kit, used much less by 1970, consists of a black cutaway coat in a two- or three-button model, a white flannel shirt with a white wing or fold collar, a puff tie, a tattersall or plain waistcoat, dark blue saddle trousers with heavy black braid on the sides and straps under the feet, patent-leather gaiter boots and box spurs, a silk hat with a guard, and white buckskin gloves. A white stock may be used instead of the puff tie, and in either case a sporting pin is used.

Field or dress. The ensemble consists of a black or dark gray cutaway coat, a matching primrose or tattersall waistcoat, white moleskin or cord breeches, a white stock, black leather boots with patent-leather tops, white gloves, and a silk hat.

Semiformal dress. The silk hat gives way to the derby, and the cutaway is supplanted by a three-button riding jacket in black, gray, or dark brown. Colored breeches may be substituted for white breeches, and plain black calf boots without tops are worn in place of patent-leather–top boots.

Hunting. The well-dressed sportsman wears the "pink," or scarlet, coat, which has an interesting history. Ac-

16C18 Hunting Full Dress 16C20 Hunting Frock Coats
Coats
16C19 Hunting Swallowtail 16C21 Beagling Coats
Coats

All of the above are made to order only from the regulation
materials, with the buttons, facings and collars of the various Hunt
Clubs.
An extra charge is made for cutting dies for initials on buttons.

16C22 Polo Waistcoats, made
to order, reversible, two colors

16C23 Polo Belts, red, white,
blue, black, or green

16C24 Jockeys' Blouses in racing colors, to order only

16C25 Breeches Trees, London
make

16C26 Jockeys' Caps to order
only

16C27 Single-breasted Kennel
Coats of linen duck

16C28 Single-breasted Flannel
Blazers, for tennis, cricketing,
etc.; for wear with white or fancy
flannel trousers

Odd Trousers, plain white or
striped flannel or serge; or fancy
flannel in light or dark colors, for
Golf, Tennis, etc.
Youths' sizes

16C29 Polo Ulsters, in white,
tan, grey, lovat, or brown blanket
material

*In 1915 formal hunting clothes included the traditional pink with
the buttons, facings, and collars of hunt clubs.* [COURTESY OF
BROOKS BROTHERS, NEW YORK]

*Apparel for sportsmen in 1915 included polo waistcoats, polo belts,
polo ulsters, and blazers.* [COURTESY OF BROOKS BROTHERS, NEW
YORK]

cording to Sydney D. Barney in *Clothes
and the Horse* (Hutchinson Publishing
Group, Ltd.), "Professionals and Hunt
servants refer only to scarlet coats.
Some say that only non-hunting lay-
men use 'pink.' Others say it is an
accepted term to cover the elderly field
coats which have lost their brilliance
and bloom through frequent cleaning
and washing. One old saying runs,
'Fight in scarlet—hunt in red—dance
in pink.'

"Nevertheless, there is evidence that
the word 'pink' was in common use
early in the nineteenth century. Perhaps it was an early slang term. In an
article in an Oxford sports magazine,
1826, one reads 'even in the strictest
college, "pink" could walk unmolested
across the court.' In 1834 Disraeli—in
a letter to his sister—wrote ' . . . in
pink, the best mounted men in the
field. . . .' Since it cannot be wrong to
say Hunting Scarlet perhaps it would

be more diplomatic not to mention
'pink' in mixed company."

Whether the hunting coat is called
pink or scarlet, it is a three- or four-
button cutaway model, a four- or
five-button frock coat, or a six-button
shadbelly swallowtail coat. If the
wearer is a member of the hunt, the
club colors are shown at the collar; if
not, the collar matches the coat. Brass
buttons on club members' coats carry
the club insignia, and those of non-

members are plain. The odd waistcoat, in a postboy or a plain long style, may be in white, hunting yellow, or tattersall check in the colors of the club. A white stock with a sports pin is the correct neck dress with this outfit, and the breeches may be in white moleskin or a heavy cord material. Boots are in black calf with pink or mahogany-color tops, and boot garters are in plain white to go with the breeches. Nonmembers of the hunt should wear boots without tops. The hunting silk hat is usually about $5/8$ inch lower in the crown than the formal silk hat. The crown and brim are constructed of laminated twill and calico impregnated with shellac, each layer being ironed on individually, making for an extraordinarily strong hat. The body is then covered with silk. Finally the brim is shaped, and the hat is ready for trimming with a wide leather band and a drawcord that must be adjusted so that the head will be cushioned inside the hat in the event of a fall. The tall silk hat is worn by everyone except the master of foxhounds, secretary, and servants, who wear black velvet caps.

A clipping from the *St. James's Gazette* of London, dated January 16, 1797, indicates that the first top hat worn in public had a traumatic effect. The wearer "was arraigned before the Lord Mayor on a charge of breach of the peace and inciting a riot . . . he appeared on the public highway wearing what he called a silk hat—a tall structure, having a shiny lustre calculated to frighten timid people. . . ."

Show ring. Whether formal or informal attire is required, the following rules must be observed:

1. A show cane is carried in place of a whip.

2. Boots are highly polished, and spurs (optional) should be of the short-neck variety and worn high on the counter. Chains should never be worn under the feet.

3. Garter straps should be about $1/2$ inch wide and buckle on the inside of the breeches buttons with the end pointing outward.

The setting and time of the show determine attire:

Morning or afternoon formal show. A gray top hat, a black oxford gray or dark lounge suit, black shoes, light hogskin gloves, and a gray or fawn plain knee rug with a strap to buckle at the back.

Evening formal show. A black silk hat and full evening dress; or a dark lounge suit or black jacket with striped trousers, a bowler hat, black shoes, gloves, and a rug.

Formal country show. A black bowler, a dark lounge suit, black shoes, gloves, and a rug.

Informal country show. A black bowler hat, a subdued tweed jacket and trousers, dark brown or black shoes, gloves, and a rug.

Polo. The game of polo originated in Persia more than 2,000 years ago. Brought to India about 1860, it was introduced into England by officers of 10th Hussars about 1870. The proper clothes for the game are a white polo cap or helmet, a white woolen shirt with an open neck and half sleeves (most teams normally have their own shirts colored to a registered design), white cotton breeches with self-strappings, brown polo boots, brown leather garters (polo spurs if required), polo or leather gloves (usually a left-hand glove only), a polo belt of wide canvas ribbed with whalebone to give support to the body muscles, and a cashmere or camel's hair coat to wear between chukkers.

The polo whip is longer than a riding whip. Polo sticks are made from rattan or malacca and vary in length to suit the player and the size of his pony. Spurs worn at polo must be blunted.

Rainwear. The earliest examples of equestrian rainwear are said to have been large squares of woven fabric treated with latex taken from the rubber tree. In 1823 Charles Macintosh of Glasgow produced a waterproof fabric by cementing two pieces of cloth together with a solution of naphtha and crude rubber. He used his fabric to create a waterproof garment called the "mackintosh." The waterproof

riding mackintosh of today is distinguished by taped and sealed seams; a long back vent, at the top of which is a fan of the same material to cover the saddle and allow plenty of skirt when seated; and knee flaps to protect the knees or a strap to keep the coat in position in windy weather. A covert cloth coat, though not waterproof, is showerproof, and a thigh-length style is used mostly for lightweight coats for riders.

Riding raincoats are generally of two basic types: an extra strong, translucent plastic; and a three-quarter-length style of fine cotton poplin laminated with rubber, with pommel and cantle flaps to keep out the rain, leg straps, wind sleeves, and underarm ventilation. A ventilated vinyl rain suit that slips over riding clothes is suggested for showing and hunting. The jacket has snaps and elastic at wrists, and the pants have elastic at the waist and stirrups to prevent slipping. A rain suit expressly designed for exercising horses is made of waterproof nylon coated inside and out, with a corduroy collar for warmth, elasticized wrists and ankles, snap buttons, and a protective gusset.

Tradition and Change

Fashion photographs and sketches reveal how very little riding clothes changed during the first five decades of the twentieth century. Sketches from 1928, for instance, show outfits for both formal and informal hacking. The formal outfit includes a black derby, a dark brown jacket, a white waistcoat with an overplaid of black and red, tan cord breeches, soft leg boots in mahogany brown, a cream-color flannel shirt, a very dark brown tie with a sports pin, and white buckskin gloves. For the informal style the sketch depicts a cap of soft cashmere in a light biscuit color, a medium brown tweed jacket with a belted back, breeches of mottled check of a brown slightly darker than the jacket with strappings of light brown, and mahogany-brown blucher boots.

In 1932, when despite the Depression more and more men in all parts of the country were reportedly taking up horseback riding as an active sport, the most popular style of hacking jacket was the three-button model. The jacket length was approximately 1½ inches longer than a suit jacket, and the sleeves were finished with a vent and four buttons that buttoned through. The most popular fabric that year was Harris Tweed in plain and checked effects, although Shetlands were making a substantial gain. A *Men's Wear* reporter noted: "The waistcoat either matches the coat or is a checked tattersall flannel. A plain white or colored flannel shirt with attached collar and a striped or figured tie comprise the most popular neckdress. A very few men prefer the white stock. Biscuit color or brown cord breeches should have ample length in front between the crotch and knee and considerable length in back as well" (Aug. 10, 1932).

Jodhpurs and jodhpur boots were rapidly gaining popularity in the early thirties. Riding gloves in chamois or buff-color leather were considered essential, and sports pins were a customary decoration for the collar points and tie.

For its November, 1934, issue *Esquire* sketched a hunt member wearing a pink coat in the favorite three-button cutaway model, a yellow postboy waistcoat, a heavy silk-and-wool hunting shirt, a riding stock of handwoven white silk fastened with a heavy gold safety pin, breeches of heavy Bedford cord, regulation hunting boots of black calf with brown tops and heavily patterned spurs, yellow buckskin gloves, and a silk hat with a guard. Two years later, in November, 1936, *Esquire* filled a color page with hunting apparel that included, along with a fox doorstop, "the correct pink coat to be worn by the master of the hunt, shown here with a hunting stock of white pique, carrying a hunting horn stick pin. Thrust between the coat's two top buttons is a hunting horn. A velvet hunting cap is shown with white string rain gloves,

and a pair of hunting boots with mahogany tops."

For country hacking and warm-weather wear, *Esquire* recommended in 1935 a riding kit consisting of a single-breasted tan linen riding sack with 12-inch side vents and slanting flapped pockets. The editors informed the reader that under this smart jacket was a lightweight yellow silk-and-wool hunting shirt with a foulard polka-dotted riding stock. Because of the warm weather, breeches were discarded in favor of jodhpurs of lightweight tweed in a gun-club check, and brown blucher riding shoes replaced riding boots. A jaunty cap of glenurquhart plaid almost, but not quite, matched the pattern of the jodhpurs, the editors pointing out that the use of matching patterns for these two items was to be avoided: "With a checked pattern in the jodhpurs a plaid pattern is called for in the cap. If a plaid pattern were selected for the nether garment, then a small check would be called for as the pattern for the cap." In any event, this sun-tanned equestrian was impeccably turned out, and his outfit was judged to be equally in style for spectator wear at country race meetings. Had he decided to top his blucher riding shoes with buttoned cloth puttees featuring leather cuffs, his outfit would still have won high approval.

With the numbers of well-dressed men depleted by the sagging economy of the thirties, the fashion press focused on the relatively small but powerful group of men still rich enough to dress up, and writers and photographers followed them to their stables and noted their riding attire. For the November, 1937, issue, for instance, *Esquire* sketched a young man dressed in an informal hacking outfit consisting of a tweed riding sack, jodhpurs, jodhpur boots, a turtleneck sweater, and an old felt hat. Another smart-looking equestrian was shown ready for country riding and exercising in a black-and-white shepherd's-check riding sack cut on very informal lines, a turtleneck sweater, breeches, and a felt hat old enough to qualify as a kind

of status symbol. For the rider venturing out in colder weather that year, *Esquire* suggested a postboy waistcoat of heavy flannel with a convertible collar.

Apparel Arts, is a series on active sports apparel in 1936, observed that although "the average man earning $35 a week will seldom spend more than that amount for a suit of clothes, he will usually spend several times that much on equipment for riding, shooting, fishing or whatever his hobby may be." As a result, the periodical referred to riding clothes as "an avenue of extra profit" for men's stores handling this type of merchandise. Illustrating this feature were sketches of the following merchandise:

1. Well-cut riding breeches with a split-fall front, for country or park riding.
2. A blue porkpie hat, for country hacking.
3. Correct riding underwear with long legs and waist support.
4. A turtleneck sweater for country hacking and exercising.
5. Reinforced pigskin riding gloves.
6. Jodhpurs with a split-fall front, for country hacking and exercising.
7. A blucher-front calf riding shoe, to be worn with leggings of canvas or box cloth and also permissible with jodhpurs.
8. A correct tweed riding sack with slanting pockets, a tattersall postboy waistcoat, and a foulard riding stock with a gold safety pin, for country hacking or park riding.

In October, 1938, *Esquire* devoted a page to what it referred to as "rainwear." For country hacking it showed twill jodhpurs, a velvet cord hacking jacket with saddle pockets and side slits, a lightweight wool jersey turtleneck sweater, and a porkpie hat. For country hacking or spectator wear at horse shows and hunt races, a tweed riding jacket, matching breeches, canvas leggings, high-cut shoes, a semi-sports hat, and a colored stock were recommended. For spectator wear at country hunt races and for country hacking, a tweed jacket, twill breeches, newmarket boots, a fingertip-length covert coat with side slits, and a tweed cap were depicted. In a corner of the page was a sketch of a new postboy waistcoat of chamois with a red knitted wool back. Like all riding waistcoats, it featured four pockets with outside flaps designed to keep the contents intact during riding.

Toward the end of the decade, *Esquire* did a fashion roundup that once again demonstrated how little riding clothes were affected by change: it featured a single-breasted shadbelly pink coat ("as worn at famous hunts in England"), a yellow waistcoat, white twill breeches, mahogany-top hunting boots, a white hunting stock with a gold pin, a hunting top hat, string gloves, and a proper hunting crop

World War II brought War Production Board restrictions that sliced men's suits and also cut the extra length and flare from riding coats. In the opinion of some fashion editors, this compromise with quantity was not unsuccessful, and to illustrate the point *Esquire* showed in October, 1942, a tweed jacket patterned after the Western frontier coat with a convertible collar and slanting pockets. The rest of the outfit was judged to be "regulation—tan flannel shirt, red ground figured foulard tie, red, black and white checked tattersall waistcoat, brown lightweight felt hat and tan jodhpurs." The same issue noted that the triple-strapped boots then being worn by cavalry officers were almost certain to become a postwar boon for tired equestrians: "They take the backache out of boot-pulling and still retain that slick silhouette about the calf."

Before the war was over, *Esquire* showed these boots again and again, calling them "a future staple at stables." One particularly stylish equestrian wore these military-inspired boots with a side-vented riding jacket of brown plaid with a green overplaid, a tan oxford shirt, a green-and-red foulard tie, a lovat-color sweater, yellowish Bedford cord breeches, string knit gloves, and a green felt hat.

The postwar era of national prosperity saw riding become the vogue of the middle class, a phenomenon that, in the eyes of some born-to-the-saddle Americans, was certain to result in a general laxity and deterioration in appearance. In any event, by the 1950s millions had turned to riding for pure athletic activity, and in the next decade they had a youthful President who shared their enthusiasm. John F. Kennedy maintained a home in Middleburg, Virginia, in the heart of the hunt country, and when his wife gave him an informal riding habit for hacking, sketches of the outfit were sent by the wire services to newspapers throughout the country. The hacking kit was described as follows: "A natural, handwoven shetland hacking jacket; Austrian cavalry twill jodhpurs with a convertible cuff featuring a hidden zipper at the bottom; tan jersey turtleneck; English brown calfskin laced riding shoes."

Man-made fibers, with their crease resistant, shape-retaining properties, were adopted for riding apparel in the 1950s. Then, in the 1960s, the shapelier apparel of the Peacock Revolution influenced riding clothes, and combinations of stretch nylon and sturdy rayon gave the "new wave" equestrian formfitting machine-washable breeches and jodhpurs.

The popularity of the dude ranch and the impact of Western-style clothes, which was felt strongly in the sixties and seventies, led to ranch-style riding clothes that found an immediate following among the young. A classic riding outfit evolved that consisted of blue denim pants, a jeans jacket with patch pockets, a patterned or solid-color work shirt in a faded blue cotton or wool, a wide-brimmed hat, and fancy Western boots. The jeans jacket with metal buttons and bold stitching was often in blue denim to complement the blue denim jeans and was sometimes blanket-lined for cold weather. Leather vests and fringed frontier coats of suede were other important fashions of the early seventies, and on the dude ranch the traditional waistcoat gave way to a capeskin vest and the stock and sports

pin to a narrow Western tie. Western boots in 1970 varied from 14-inch-high leather-lined cowhides with blunt toes to an authentic classic Western style in black with an inlaid design in gold, white, and blue. Rainwear on the dude ranch most often took the form of a durable yellow oilskin slicker made with inverted flaps to cover the saddle.

Riding suits in the early seventies had many of the styling features of regular suits, including medium-wide lapels and modified bell-bottom trousers. A black or midnight-blue tuxedo saddle suit for formal evening events, for instance, might be a one-button model with a silk satin shawl collar, side pleats, and a full flare; accompanying jodhpurs with a stripe of silk satin to match the jacket's collar facing flared gracefully over the shoes.

The classic string and buckskin riding gloves were now only two in a long list of riding gloves made of pigskin, calfskin, deerskin, and capeskin. Horse-head or fox-head blazer buttons were added to the riding coat, sports jacket, or blazer and praised as "doing more for your jackets than your tailor did."

More protective headgear was devised in a helmet-type riding cap made of rugged Cycolac, the material used in astronauts' helmets, with a Styrofoam inner lining, a complete retaining harness to keep the cap in place, and a collapsible brim made of Ensolite (a material used by the Ford Motor Company in dashboards), which holds its shape until impact and then folds to protect the face against injury.

In a dynamic society with rapidly shifting values, riding clothes have retained their status despite certain peripheral changes. Their pure, elegantly simple lines continue to be a joy to the eye and a boon to the men who wear them. Riding is still the sport of kings, steeped in tradition, and its still largely rigid rules for apparel will no doubt continue to be honored by horsemen who regard proper attire as an essential part of this thoroughbred sport.

Western Wear

The classic American Western look remains unchallenged as the epitome of virility in men's clothing. Derived from the cowboy's work clothes, it is part of the national heritage and as such has made its way through twentieth-century men's fashions.

Western wear gained enormous popularity in the thirties with the discovery that a visit to a dude ranch

(*above*) *This Eastern visitor to a ranch adopted real Western gear: a ten-gallon felt hat, a plaid wool shirt, a bandanna, a husky belt, blue denim pants, and black boots with patterned uppers. From* Esquire, *July 1935.*

(*right*) *Western clothes were fashioned for the high country or for lower-level ranches. The standing man wore a patterned shirt of checked cotton, a neckerchief, blue denim Levi's, black boots, and a black felt hat. The man in the saddle favored a laced-front shirt and tan gabardine pants. From* Esquire, *August 1937.*

Black sombrero with telescope crown and white cord band

Hand-forged silver steel spur

Light tan sombrero with fancy silver trim

Cowboy shirt in broadcloth with contrasting piping

Open neck lace front shirt of fade-proof broadcloth

Western cattle brands on a heavyweight pure silk muffler, silver slip-ring

Brown leather belt with fancy silver trim

Cowboy boot of lightweight French calf

Robert Goodman

Going west, young man?

The annual trek to the dude ranches, by now at the head of many a vacation list, continues at a merry clip, with the Eastern dude adopting all the colorfulness and the zest of the old Western cowpuncher's dress. Three practical and widely favored Dude Ranch outfits are shown above, left to right: Tan sombrero, yellow shirt, brown frontier trousers and brown boots. . . . Black telescope crown sombrero, grey shirt with black trim, blue dungarees, black calf boots. . . . White cowboy hat, cherry color shirt, leather chaps, brown boots.

(For answers to all dress queries, send stamped self-addressed envelope to Esquire Fashion Staff, 366 Madison Ave., N. Y.)

The zest of the Western cowpuncher's dress has had a continuing influence throughout the United States and in many other countries. From Esquire, August 1939.

Varied Western apparel: (left) a suede jacket with leather fringe; (center) a plaid shirt and blue denim pants; (right) a gabardine shirt with a checked yoke and cuffs and checked pants. Drawn by A. J. Pimsler. From Esquire, *June 1947.*

offered a splendid summer vacation. For its July, 1935, issue *Esquire* sketched an urbane gentleman rolling a cigarette while perched on a fence. How well he fared with the cigarette is not known, but his outfit was a complete success: a lumberman-model plaid wool shirt, blue dungaree trousers with a wide silver-buckled leather belt, high-heeled black boots, a sombrero with a pinched crown, and a red bandanna worn as a neckerchief.

In 1937 *Esquire* visited dude ranches again. In its August issue it depicted a pair of dudes whose outfits typified "the workmanlike accoutrements that are essential to this type of vacation." One man wore a colorful checked cotton shirt with a silk neckerchief, Levi's of blue denim, and black calf boots 12 inches high with underslung heels and plain round toes. The second man, astride a pinto, wore a tan ten-gallon hat, a satin shirt with horseshoes on the collar and a laced front

opening, tan cotton gabardine trousers, and low brown calfskin boots.

"The old home range never has been the same since the dudes took over the West," commented *Esquire* in July, 1938, though the fashion department admitted that the dudes had retained much of the true Western flavor in their clothes: "The bright blue sateen shirt and blue denim jeans worn by the man at the left are real cowboy stuff, and so are the black leather sleeveless waistcoat and black sombrero with white binding. The boots are gen-u-wine, and cost plenty. The other dude has on his Sunday-go-to-meetin' clothes, consisting of bright red sateen shirt, frontier trousers of sturdy tan twill, heavy calf belt, sombrero with telescope crown, and lightweight silk scarf held in place under the collar by a decorative steer's head. Under the trousers are worn black boots with brown tops."

The number of Americans visiting

dude ranches continued to multiply in 1939, particularly now that the Depression was nearing its end, and in July *Esquire*'s fashion editor showed three widely favored dude ranch outfits: a tan sombrero, a yellow shirt, brown frontier trousers, and brown boots; a black telescope-crown sombrero, a gray shirt with black trim, blue dungarees, and black calf boots; and a white cowboy hat, a cherry-color shirt, leather chaps, and brown boots.

"For that vacation West," *Esquire* had concrete suggestions to offer in July, 1947, noting first: "Dude clothes, praise be, are a cinch to select. All you need worry about are four items—shirts, trousers, hats and boots. Shirts are gaudy, with absolutely no color inhibitions, and come in gabardine, bright wool tartans or what you will. Trousers are tight about the hips, low at the waist and can run the gamut from denim dungarees to checked riding models. Hats come in three types: flat crown, broad brim; conical shape, broad brim; broad brim, center-creased crown and narrow band. Finally, no cowboy boot qualifies without high heels."

In the 1950s stockman's clothes, a dressier type of Western wear, became increasingly popular not only for men but for women and children too. Typical of the fashions preferred in the early fifties were dress-model stockman's pure worsted suits with wide peaked lapels and buttoned jacket pockets and washable rayon gabardine shirts with ornate embroidery and sueded felt appliqués.

Gentlemen's Quarterly observed in July, 1961, that although the once wild West now preferred nothing more perilous than the click of revolving roulette wheels, opportunities to wear the indigenous mode of dress endured. As proof it showed an outfit consisting of a white Western-style shirt of cotton and Cupioni rayon, embroidered on both sides of pearl-covered snaps and equipped with crescent-shaped chest pockets; black wool gabardine riding trousers with such Western details as tapered lines, sturdy belt loops, and slant pockets; a tooled belt with a large metal buckle; ornate square-tipped leather boots; and a stiff white felt Stetson hat.

In July, 1962, *Gentlemen's Quarterly* again showed Western-inspired clothes, this time noting that the Western look was moving into new country, "the dude country of suburbia, where it will be a hot-as-a-pistol fashion influence." To a man eager to be "West-dressed in the country," the editors recommended a fingertip-length coat in cotton that had pointed stitched yokes in front and back, sturdy stitching all around the edges, large pointed-flap buttoned patch pockets, a knitted wool collar, and brown buttons set in leather frames; and a brown satin-lined pinwale corduroy coat, also of fingertip length, featuring a fancy pointed stitched yoke design crossing both front and back, leather-trimmed sleeves, angled pockets, and three bone buttons.

Before the 1960s were over, the Western look had won acceptance not only throughout the United States but in Europe as well. In the United States the Peacock Revolution with its accent on youth had arrived, and a large segment of American young people turned their backs on so-called establishment clothes in favor of the sturdy jeans and work shirts of the cowboy. As the young adopted a back-to-the-soil, back-to-the-roots philosophy of life, makers of Western wear prospered.

In 1971 the *Daily News Record* observed: "The Western influence is penetrating practically all areas of men's wear. But rather than carving a separate niche for itself, Western fashion is becoming an integral part of the total men's wear picture" (May 26, 1971, p. 4). It was felt that by this time the Western influence had become so well accepted that it was a part of fashion rather than a distinct way of dressing. Jeans were used to illustrate the point: with their wide appeal and acceptance, jeans had all but lost their Western flavor. In short, Western wear had entered the mainstream of American fashion. Men, par-

This outfit was right for the dude as well as the real rancher in 1961, and it has continued to hold a place among Western wearables. The embroidered shirt is closed with pearl-covered snap fasteners and has crescent-shaped chest pockets. The black gabardine riding pants are tapered, and the tooled leather belt has a Texas-size metal buckle. The hat is a stiff white felt, and the boots are square-tipped. From Gentlemen's Quarterly, *July 1961.*

ticularly young men, liked its rugged, casual look.

The so-called Western shirt, long limited to the Southwest, was by 1971 moving in all directions. It was, said the fashion editor Richard Greene, "a perfect put together with its Western fashion predecessor, jeans. It has the fit of today . . . often has hardware touches and, in some models, a touch of the hand-crafted through use of embroidery." Just how artfully the manufacturers of true Western wear were adapting their clothes to the national demand for clothes with a Western look was demonstrated in *Daily News Record* sketches of a classic Western shirt in a bold, allover blanket plaid of 100 percent wool, a durable-

press shirt with a button closure and buttoned pockets, and a corduroy shirt featuring canvas for the pocket trim and snaps for the closure.

By the seventies men who had never ridden a horse and never intended to were wearing clothes with the Western look, although often they did not consciously recognize it as such. As the *Daily News Record* had observed, the fashion impact of Western wear was by then so great that it was not a Western image but a rugged, casual image they were seeking in their Western-influenced denim suits, boots, tight slacks, and wide belts. Western wear had left the category of special clothing and put its brand on almost every item in the American man's wardrobe.

Riding clothes and accessories regarded as classic fashions: (across the top) a postboy waistcoat of chamois with a red knitted wool back and a pigskin-covered riding cane; a tweed jacket, twill breeches, newmarket boots, a fingertip covert coat with side slits, and a tweed cap; a whipcord riding coat and trousers, black riding shoes, a bowler, and a silk stock; a single-breasted pink coat, a yellow waistcoat, white twill breeches, mahogany hunting boots, a white hunting stock with a gold pin, a hunting top hat, string gloves, and a crop; (across the bottom) a brown corduroy hacking jacket, twill jodhpurs, a wool turtleneck sweater, and a porkpie hat; a modified forward saddle and washable brown goatskin gloves with reinforced string fingers; and a tweed riding jacket, matching breeches, canvas leggings, high-cut shoes, a semisports hat, and a colored stock. From Esquire, *October 1938.*

Two 1941 riding outfits that have survived as traditional apparel: (left) a greenish-brown tweed riding coat with slanting pockets and a center vent, a soft felt hat, a yellow flannel shirt, a fox-pattern printed wool tie, a tattersall waistcoat, cavalry twill jodhpurs, and brown jodhpur boots; (right) a brown plaid riding coat with side vents, a green felt hat, a green-and-red foulard tie, a tan oxford shirt, a lovat-color sweater, string knit gloves, yellow Bedford breeches, and brown field boots. From Esquire, *April 1941.*

Favorites in 1941: (left) a duck shooter wearing a cotton twill parka with a pile fabric lining and a lined hood, lined trousers to match, a wool hat, hip rubber boots, and mitts made with an opening for the trigger finger; (right) an upland hunter of pheasant and quail, wearing a red-collared norfolk jacket of processed cotton twill with roomy pockets, breeches to match, a red felt hat, a flannel shirt, a wool tie, red-top gray wool stockings, and laced boots with rubber soles. From Esquire, *November 1941.*

The outfit for a hunter in 1971 included a polyester-and-cotton hat with a Curon lining, an alpaca-lined polyester-and-cotton coat with large pockets and wristlets, and hunting trousers to match with a Curon lining. The cotton vest with an alpaca lining and plaid wool shirt shown at lower left gave added warmth. [ABERCROMBIE & FITCH]

Riding Clothes

Shooting Clothes

Shooting Clothes

Turkey hunting was the first American sport born of necessity. After the early settler days, however, man's innate hunting instinct had less and less to do with survival and more and more to do with pleasure. No longer faced with the alternative of score or go hungry, the hunter became increasingly aware of his attire.

By the late 1920s Americans had grown tremendously sports-minded

The hunting coat shirt of 1924, made of 30-ounce all-wool felted cloth in a red-and-black plaid, was of double thickness over the shoulders and halfway down the front and had large game pockets that buttoned at the sides. [WOOLRICH WOOLEN MILLS]

16C10 Shooting Coats of Khaki Twillette, etc., with cartridge belts, game pockets, shoulder pads and pivot sleeves

16C11 Corduroy Shooting Coats

16C12 Light - weight Belted Shooting and Fishing Coats of Josette, etc., with game pockets

16C13 Single-breasted Mackinaws with belt

and fashion-conscious—a combination of qualities that, among other things, produced a market for an all-wool hunting suit which, according to an advertisement of the Woolrich Woolen Mills in 1929, possessed the distinct advantage of being "noiseless." The suit was said to be warm and comfortable without being bulky and to be well tailored, with all the seams double-stitched and bound for long wear. It was further claimed to be "as nearly waterproof as possible" by virtue of a fulling process that "closes the pores yet retains softness and beauty." The

(left) Shooting coats in cotton twills, corduroy, and coarse weaves were shown in 1915 with generous pockets. [COURTESY OF BROOKS BROTHERS, NEW YORK]

suit had deep pockets, plus a double game pocket running from seam to seam across the back with openings on both sides, inside waistbands, a five-button fly front, and adjustable tabs on the sleeves.

Wealthy sportsmen of the British Isles had been stalking the Scottish moors for years in pursuit of grouse, partridge, and pheasant, but it was not until the early 1930s that wealthy Americans joined their ranks in impressive numbers. In November, 1934, *Esquire*, taking note of this fact, paid homage to the shooting season that begins in Scotland each August. Some splendidly togged sportsmen and their kilted host were sketched amid damp

At a shooting party held at Coombe Alley, the Warwickshire estate of the Earl and Countess of Craven in the early part of the century, Bradley Martin (right) wore a tweed suit with an overplaid, leather puttees, gaiters, and sturdy shoes. [THE BETTMANN ARCHIVE, INC.]

kit affected by well-dressed sportsmen on the Scottish moors for grouse and partridge shooting. It consists of a single-breasted, notched lapel tweed jacket and knicker breeches in a bold Scotch plaid, worn with a heavy green sweater, checked flannel shirt, knitted tie, heavy wool hose, stout brogue shoes, leather anklets and a checked one-piece top cap." For bigger game, such as moose and deer, a recommended outfit for cold weather should, said the editors, consist of "matching Mackinaw jacket and breeches, made of heavy, all-wool material that is processed to be water-repellent. A heavy turtleneck sweater, and under that a heavy flannel shirt, and under that our own vote goes to the good old wool underwear in that delicate shade known as Fireman's Red. Heavy wool lumberman's socks, smoked elk moccasin boots and the usual peaked red hunting cap."

Apparel Arts in the fall of 1935 devoted an article to skeet shooting, a year-round sport. It not only described

A skeet-shooting jacket of 1931 was made of navy blue wool with sateen sleeves. The pockets were reinforced with leather inside and out, and there was a leather recoil pad at the shoulder. [WOOLRICH WOOLEN MILLS]

what the fashionable skeet shooter wore but offered its readers a history of what the editors called "the most difficult—and yet the most fascinating—form of claybird shooting ever devised. And almost as interesting as the game itself are the clothes that go with it." As for those clothes, the editors said:

"The skeet shooter dresses in a Norfolk type jacket of woolen material, usually in woodland colors, brown being preferred. This type of jacket has the Norfolk straps, buttoned down on the two patch pockets to keep them from sagging and ripping under the weight of shells. The sleeves are of waterproof silk material and the right shoulder has a large recoil patch of chamois. The arm pits are full cut and roomy and the lapels are fashioned to button over in coolish weather.

"Another skeet jacket is the windbreaker type of chamois leather, reinforced at the shoulder with self-recoil patch. Sometimes these garments are lined with lamb skin; the sleeves, however, are unlined and full cut and may or may not have knitted wristlets.

"Skeet trousers are the usual slack type, with tweeds predominating, particularly Lovats and soft woodland browns. Brown snap brim hats are the

The hunting outfit of 1929 consisted of a maroon-and-black plaid coat, pants, and cap, which reversed to bright red. The fabric was made as nearly waterproof as possible by a special fulling process. The sleeves had inside wrist warmers, and the large game pocket in back opened on both sides. [WOOLRICH WOOLEN MILLS]

grass and heather, and the caption writer reminded the reader: "In a real siege of wet weather, short rubberized jackets are worn over the tweed shooting jackets, also an extra pair of outer trousers, made of the same waterproofed material and cut off at the calf. Heavy outercoats are never worn, being supplanted by heavy cashmere or Shetland sweaters."

In the same issue the fashion department showed outfits suitable for bird shooting and for bigger game. The outfit recommended for all types of upland shooting was "typical of the

The stag shirt of 1930 had a double front and back. It was made of 28-ounce plaid wool in red-and-black, brown-and-green, and navy blue overplaid. [WOOLRICH WOOLEN MILLS]

customary headwear [some men preferred a Tyrolean-type hat or a round-crown visored cap], and glasses must always be worn by all skeet shooters to protect them from paper wads and bits of the incoming clay birds.

"Shoes are generally ankle high, although the oxford is also worn. These may be the Norwegian calf brogue or the various heavy suedes and should have leather soles studded with soft hob-nails to prevent slipping. Hose are of wool, while the shirt may be either the flannel woodman's shirt or the button-down collar oxford shirt, preferably in solid colors. Club colored neckwear or knitted striped ties are to the fore."

In November, 1936, *Esquire*'s fashion department offered a selection of clothes for hunting and shooting neatly spread across a full fashion page:

For deer shooting. A practical ensemble includes shirt, coat and breeches of a

A skeet jacket of 1935 (left) with neither collar nor lapels. The pockets were designed to hold a full quota of extra shells, and there was a leather recoil pad on the shoulder. The back had gusset pleats at the shoulders. With the jacket were worn shepherd's-check tweed trousers. From Esquire, *March 1935.*

heavy Mackinaw cloth, moccasin boots and two pairs of wool socks. The bright red cap is a favorite of men who shoot in the big woods.

For field trials. The majority of men at field trials wear tweed knicker suits and dress similarly to the men who shoot in Scotland. Note the canvas anklets, the tweed grouse helmet, heavy brogues.

For upland shooting. Many men wear the white duck shooting coat with khaki breeches, high boots, flannel shirt and a felt hat.

For duck shooting. Demands warm, waterproof garments since one spends many hours motionless in the blind. Heavy flannel shirts and chamois underwear are recommended. [Duck-shooting parkas are immensely practical. Made of closely woven cotton, they feature alpaca lining and interlining between two layers of a coated nylon to make the coat absolutely waterproof.]

By 1938 enough sports-minded Americans had rediscovered the wild turkey's attraction as a game bird to prompt *Esquire* to focus attention in its March issue on a man's need to hunt it in style. This, said the fashion staff, meant wearing one of these outfits:

1. An English kit consisting of a lightweight jacket with an all-around belt and large bellows pockets, with breeches to match, made of a cloth that was windproof and thornproof; a red flannel shirt; 16-inch elk-hide moccasin boots; high gray wool socks with red tops; and an authentic Tyrolean hat with a cord band and brush.

2. A light shooting coat of very coarse white or khaki cotton with large game and cartridge pockets and cotton drill trousers.

In November, 1939, the *Esquire* fashion pages depicted a pair of handsomely turned-out sportsmen dressed for upland shooting. The crinkle-eyed Nordic type on the left wore a norfolk-model cotton windproof shooting jacket with large shell pockets and detachable inside game pockets, an authentic Tyrolean hat, a flannel shirt in a glen pattern, a red wool tie, trousers of tan waterproof cotton with horsehide reinforcements in front of the legs, and high waterproof boots with moccasin fronts. His pipe-smoking companion was dressed in a checked Harris Tweed jacket with

This practical wool coat of 1936 was designed for skeet shooting in the fall. It had a shoulder pad and bellows-pleat pockets held in place with panel pieces of fabric. With it were worn Shetland trousers and brogue shoes. From Esquire, *November 1936.*

knicker breeches to match, a flannel shirt and sweater, a blue silk scarf with white spots, a tweed shooting helmet, heavy wool hose, ankle-high blucher brogues, and leather anklets.

In November, 1940, *Esquire* filled a page with shooting apparel and in the accompanying copy gave the reader a kind of primer course on what a sportsman should wear:

"The idea of shooters shooting one another, instead of game, is a fantastic one. But it happens only too frequently, even though that is presumably the element which gives the pheas-

One of the classic hunting jackets, the belted safari style of the mid-thirties and also of the seventies, shown at left, has an all-around belt and box-pleated bellows pockets. Of cotton twill, it is worn with matching breeches, a red flannel shirt, gray wool socks with red tops, and elkhide moccasin boots 16 inches high. From Esquire, *March 1938.*

ants and grouse their true sporting chance. The red felt hat, of course, is smart not so much in the fashion as in the life-preserving sense. Other shooters are supposed to realize, however reluctantly, that you're not fair game if you're wearing a red hat. The red cloth collar on the jacket is an additional stop sign. In addition to the law of self-preservation, some states have laws that call for an even greater display of red, in which case a scarlet-colored vest-like appendage can be worn conveniently over the shoulders.

"The rest of the outfit is pretty much camouflage, designed to blend in with the thicket. We don't know enough about the subject to explain why the man with the gun will look at the hat and collar and the game will gaze only at the jacket and trousers, but that's what is evidently expected of them. The tan cotton coat is a workmanlike job, its double thickness of processed fabric affording ample protection against wind and rain. There is plenty of pocket space, including a huge game pocket which crosses the lower part of the coat in back. The wool flannel shirt is an authentic Tartan, and the solid-colored dark-red coarse homespun wool tie is compatible. The tan trousers are of the same fabric as the jacket and have knitted wool bands at the bottom to hold them closely around the ankles. A brown leather belt with harness buckle holds them up.

"Upland shooters may be divided into two groups—those who think only softies wear gloves and those who are sensible enough to keep the digits warm with a pair of soft deerskin gloves with ridged palms like the ones shown here. Heavy grey wool socks with red tops come under the heading of standard footwarmers, while more and more men are turning to twelve-inch boots of moccasin pattern with rubber soles and leather thong laces. Other items: cowhide-covered chaps to ward off brambles, a bird strap for loop-knotting your hits, double-barreled gun and leather case with compartments."

When World War II was over and the American man was once again using a gun strictly for sport, *Esquire* celebrated the fact with a full-color double-page fashion spread in November, 1949, titled, "It's an Open Season on Outdoor Garb." It was, noted the feature writer, "time now to check your guns and gear and look into Esky's ideas on what nimrods need in the way of wardrobes." Two men in a rowboat about to inveigle some unsuspecting mallards were comfortably turned out for duck shooting. One wore a tan processed-cotton jacket of alpaca pile with matching trousers. His companion was encased in a hooded processed-fabric coat with an all-around belt. A hunter who had just bagged a deer wore a bright red flannel jac shirt with chest and lower pockets providing storage space for his rifle rounds, heavy wool flannel trousers, a bright red hunting cap, boots, and red stockings. A pair of men with a pair of dogs and a day set aside for upland bird shooting were dressed as follows: the man on the left wore brown heavy wool flannel trousers, a bright red heavy flannel shirt, and a tan processed-cotton jacket with ample pocket space. His partner was similarly dressed in processed cotton. A solitary hunter patiently stalking a moose wore an outfit of red-and-black heavy wool plaid consisting of jacket, cap, and breeches all in the same fabric. Back at the lodge a pair of sportsmen swapping tales wore, respectively, a heavy wool shirt in a tartan of bright red and black with flaps and two buttons and a corduroy-type jacket ("a big hit with many outdoorsmen").

In the 1970s, while hunting clothes do not carry on a tradition in the manner of, say, riding apparel, they nevertheless remain fairly inflexible because the rigors of the sport, plus the climatic conditions (and often early hours) in which the sportsman finds himself pursuing his pleasure, impose certain restrictions on fabrics and styling. Consequently, what the well-dressed hunter of today wears is not very unlike what his predecessor wore twenty or even thirty years ago. Colorful and rugged, hunting clothes have always had an undeniable appeal for the American man, and this is especially true today, when their no-nonsense good looks and sturdy character are symbols of stability in an otherwise unpredictable world.

Fishing Clothes

According to legend, the American fisherman is a determined optimist prone to telling tall tales of the big one that got away. But there is no exaggeration in the clothes he wears while pursuing his sport; they are good-looking and practical.

In the Depression year 1935, for instance, *Apparel Arts* displayed the following garb for the fisherman: a four-button norfolk-model fishing jacket of waterproof tan twill, featuring large bellows pockets lined with oiled silk and a convertible collar; and a stitched gabardine fishing hat with a self-band in a sturdy, lightweight water-repellent construction. The same year, in its April issue, *Esquire* stated that brown was the new color for trout-fishing boots, "the notion being that they are much less readily discernible to the fish." Along with brown hip boots, the nattily turned-out model wore a tweed hat stuck with flies, an odd jacket of deep lovat tweed, a gray flannel lumberman's shirt and trousers, and a crochet tie. Comparing notes with this fisherman was another sportsman in an outfit that, according to the caption writer, was "as British as the name Con-

The angler of 1930 wore a cotton jacket, rubber waders, canvas-top shoes, a plaid cotton shirt, and a felt hat. [UNIROYAL, INC.]

In 1931 the angler's jacket was of heavy black wool and had two front patch pockets for fly hooks, two top front pockets, a fishing rod–holder tab, two sleeve pockets for fly oil and hooks, and snaps at the side and cuffs. [WOOLRICH WOOLEN MILLS]

No. 585
Woolrich Angler's Jacket

This Jacket is one of our latest productions and is just the thing for anyone who wishes to wade or for upland shooting. It is made of 22 ounce storm proof fabric and has ten pockets, and is just the coat for waders, as it is not long enough to bother your hips or legs in walking. This coat has a full double back pocket for carrying lunch, game or any small package, two front patch pockets for fly books, two top front pockets, one fishing rod holder tab, two sleeve pockets for fly oil and hooks with side snaps and button over cuffs. We are positive that you would be more than pleased if you should purchase one of these jackets. Grey and Black Plaid only. Sizes 36 to 44.

naught": a close-fitting tweed hat with a semistiffened brim, English waders of thin rubberized material extending from the toes to high above the waistline ("about like a pair of overalls with feet in them"), wool socks worn over the feet of the waders, lightweight canvas wading shoes with thick, hobnailed leather soles, a cashmere muffler, and a checked tweed jacket.

Clothes and accouterments for deep-sea fishing also came under the scrutiny of *Esquire*'s fashion department, in August, 1934: "Using the leather harness as well as the rod-socket of the fishing chair is like wearing suspenders and a belt—undoubtedly the safest thing to do. As for the hip length boots, they are useful only in very dirty weather—but very nice to have them. The long visored sword-fish cap is an essential and so is the kerchief if you don't want the back of your neck broiled. You need the canvas gloves when a 6-0 reel begins to scream. Fishing with heavy tackle is hardly a dress-up affair, which is why we show and recommend the outfit consisting of a gray flannel shirt, a pair of blue dungaree trousers, white wool hose and sneakers."

In July, 1937, *Esquire*'s fashion artist sketched a pair of anglers who had beached their canoe in the North woods and were about to fry their day's catch. The angler in charge of the frying pan was wearing a heavy plaid wool lumberjack shirt with wool trousers of forestry green, stout canvas braces, heavy wool hose, and soled Indian moccasins. His companion, carrying a rod and reel and a brace of fish, had a heavy gray flannel shirt, breeches of a very tough English drill that had a smooth, suedelike finish (waterproofed to shed rain), moccasin hunting boots of black waterproof chrome leather, and regulation wool lumberman's socks. An *Esquire* feature that August, headlined "When You

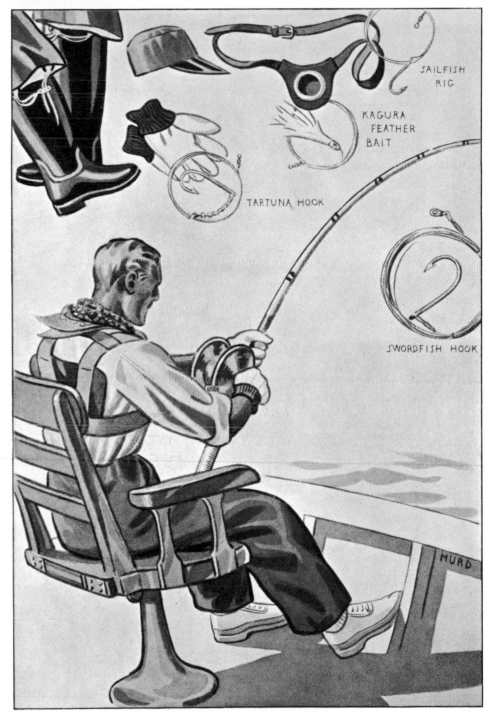

Apparel for the deep-sea fisherman in 1934 included hip-length boots for dirty weather, a long-visored cap, a kerchief, cotton gloves, a flannel shirt, blue dungaree trousers, white wool socks, and sneakers. From Esquire, *August 1934.*

The fishing outfit in 1938 consisted of a short processed-canvas jacket with big pockets, a wool shirt, a soft tweed hat, and rubberized-cotton waders. From Esquire, *April 1938.*

magazine's fashion staff no longer restricted itself and, along with a trout rod, a creel with a harness, and a fly book with flies, showed its readers the following fishing paraphernalia: a lightweight Scotch-plaid shirt, soft leather hobnailed boots, wading trousers, and a shockproof and waterproof wristwatch with radium figures.

In April, 1956, *Esquire* photographed a collection of special-occasion gloves, among them a leather fishing glove with open fingers and a knitted wrist. And in 1960 the fashion staff suggested that a fisherman who braved the wintry winds should wear a pair of tough, water-resistant boar-skin gloves with rubber strips on the palms and fingers for a nonslip grip and stretch-nylon finger sidewalls.

"Ever-hopeful, our All-American Sportsman is multifariously pocketed," observed *Esquire* in August, 1961, displaying a processed-cotton fishing vest that boasted a patch for flies, a rod holder, a back bellows pocket, and a screened creel. With it, the fisherman wore matching plain-front trousers. His rubber hip boots had deeply corrugated soles and inside snap straps.

The processed-cotton fishing vest of the seventies was even more lavishly pocketed, with a nylon screen pocket to hold the trout conveniently, fly box pockets on each side, and inside pockets for glasses and a knife or scissors. Back interest included a bag for lunch or an apple, plus a ring between the shoulder blades to hold the net.

Like shooting clothes, apparel worn for fishing is not subject to the dynamic changes that have affected much of the American man's wardrobe since the Peacock Revolution of the sixties. Weather conditions and the obvious need for clothes with easy mobility dictate that, first and foremost, fishing clothes be sturdy and practical. That they also manage to look ruggedly stylish is a tribute to the makers as well as to the determination of the sportsman who insists on looking his best, even when he does not expect to see an eye any more critical than that of a fish.

Go Down to the Sea and Fish," included an oilskin coat and canvas gloves with reinforced leather fingers.

The beginning of the trout season inspired a full-page feature in April, 1938, this time showing a pipe-smoking sportsman wearing rib-high rubberized English waders that were held up by braces, a pair of heavy wool rag socks, canvas-and-leather wading boots, and a very short waterproof and windproof fishing jacket with roomy pockets to accommodate books of flies, a knife, and other requisites of the sport. In April, 1939, with the cloud of the Depression lifting, the

A trout fisherman wearing a white cotton jacket, a checked flannel shirt, a green felt hat, rubberized waders, and studded boots. From Esquire, *May 1940.*

(left) *A casual cotton bush shirt of 1937, resembling the safari jacket of the 1970s, worn with gabardine shorts and moccasin slip-ons. The man carried a jipajapa hat.* (right) *A lightweight wool crew-neck pullover, worn with blue linen pants and blue canvas shoes with yellow rubber soles. Under the man's arm was a white duck cap with a green underbrim. From* Esquire, *February 1937.*

Yachting fashions in 1934: (upper left) *an outfit for a guest, consisting of a flannel jacket, white flannel trousers, rubber-soled buck shoes, a soft shirt, and a light sweater;* (top center) *sailing clothes consisting of a blue jersey sweater, sailcloth or duck trousers, and white canvas sneakers and hat;* (upper right) *a yacht owner's evening outfit of blue dinner jacket and cape;* (center) *evening dress for a club member or owner, consisting of a navy blue straight-front dinner jacket with braid-trimmed sleeves and a club tie;* (lower left) *a serge or duck jacket with gilt buttons and matching trousers, worn with white buck shoes with red rubber soles and a white shirt and starched collar;* (lower right) *a correct costume for a yacht club member. From* Esquire, *June 1934.*

The standing sailor wore a blue processed cotton jacket with a zipper, matching pants, a cross-stripe knitted lisle shirt, and blue canvas shoes with cut herringbone soles to give him a solid footing. From Esquire, *September 1941.*

Fishing Clothes

Yachting and Sailing Clothes

a hopsacking type of fabric, with metal or black buttons and patch pockets. Trousers may be of gray or white flannel. Headgear may be the traditional white-top yachting cap or a more casual cap of wool with a fairly long visor. Again, a white shirt and a conservative tie complete the outfit.

On extremely cold days the yachtsman may substitute one of the following: a CPO shirt of navy blue melton cloth with a tailored collar and large pockets; a double-breasted navy melton pea coat with slash pockets and anchor buttons; or a zippered Windbreaker of melton cloth of the same weight (32 ounces) as the pea coat, featuring two large slash pockets, a zippered breast pocket, and cuffs, elbows, and pockets trimmed in horsehide leather.

The third classification contains the apparel the seafaring man wears for foul weather, and here it is practicality that counts. Clothes include the oilskin slicker or coat-and-trousers combination, under which may be worn a pair of flannel trousers and a wool sports shirt, along with heavy wool hose and canvas shoes with rope soles (or, depending on the weather, hip-length rubber boots); and a nylon jacket with a zipper closure and cord attachment and double-seat pants, both processed to be waterproof. Most recently, a jump suit made of a waterproof stretch fabric or of layers of polyurethane has become a foul-weather favorite. And, almost as a defiant gesture as well as for visibility in fog or mist, these foul-weather outfits are most often made in cheerful shades of blue, orange, and yellow.

Sailing clothes are more rugged and functional, for the sailor must be active. Yet here, too, much of what is worn today was in vogue in the 1930s. In August, 1934, for instance, *Esquire* showed two men aboard a dinghy and said:

"You are going to get wet as a matter of course, so the only sane thing to do is dress accordingly, with the obvious advantage of looking no funnier wet than dry. This rigid specification is met by both the outfits sketched

and both are recommended. One consists of just two pieces (unless you wouldn't dream of doing without underwear), a heavy navy blue crew neck shaker with long sleeves and a pair of white duck trousers. The other rig, somewhat more imposing, consists of a pair of khaki trousers (or even shorts) into which is tucked a navy blue polo shirt, worn with a floppy white hat with black visor and, at your option, a pair of sneakers or Jai Alai shoes. You won't be a dinghy racer worthy of the name unless you have spilled a few times, so wear nothing to which salt air and water are inimical. The only exception is winter dinghy racing, when the recommended garb is a moth eaten raccoon coat of the early jazz age vintage."

In May, 1937, the magazine's fashion artist sketched a young man wearing the uniform "of those who own and sail small boats": a heavy-rib crew-neck sweater with rolled-up long

The cap-wearing skipper had on a knitted blue polo shirt, cotton gabardine shorts, and moccasins with crepe rubber soles. The man at right wore a white cotton hat, a knitted wool sweater, faded-blue denim slacks, yellow wool socks, and blue canvas shoes with rubber soles. From Esquire, *June 1940.*

sleeves, cotton gabardine trousers, a white sailing cap, and canvas shoes with rope soles. In July of that year *Esquire* featured two outfits, both of which it said had won general acceptance for sailors of small boats at fashionable West Indies resorts during the past season:

"The man in the foreground is wearing a double-breasted blue homespun tweed blazer with black plain buttons and patch pockets. The shorts are of flannel in a cream off-white shade. Beneath the blazer is a lightweight lisle shirt with half sleeves, worn with a colorful silk or cotton scarf. The shoes are blue canvas with rubber soles and heels. The same outfit could be worn with white or grey flannel slacks. For actual sailing on larger boats, shirt and tie as well as regulation shoes would be in order. The man in the background is wearing one of the new denim dinghy suits in the shade known as Bimini Blue. It consists of a sailor's type jumper with three-quarter length sleeves and a small collar, worn outside the trousers. Wine color espadrilles with rope soles and heels. Suitable for sailing, fishing and beach club wear."

In July, 1938, the fashion editor described an ideal outfit for informal sailing or knocking about a boatyard: a crew-neck, heavyweight long-sleeved sweater, lightweight denim cotton slacks or dungarees, blue canvas shoes with rubber or crepe soles and heels, and a white sailing hat.

Any of these outfits of the thirties would be acceptable today, and some, like the sailor's type of jumper, appear to have foreshadowed some of the seagoing apparel of the seventies. Nevertheless, although the Peacock Revolution scarcely changed a seam of the equestrian's jacket, it did have an effect on cruising clothes, as evidenced by the "new wave" garb *Esquire* showed in 1968 with the following copy:

"Humphrey Bogart, a man who was wont to go down to the sea in his ship, once observed that he wouldn't trust a man in a yachting cap. He would have been pleased that we seem to be

Three 1971 styles of water-repellent sailing gear in sueded denim, which had the heft of sailcloth and the softness of leather: (left) a 30-inch jacket with slanting pockets; (center) a jacket with big pockets and a T-bar–pull zipper; (right) a jacket with four pockets and snap fasteners. [MIGHTY-MAC]

achieving an end of such nonsense and that hardly anyone tries to look like Sir Thomas Lipton anymore. On this page are three cruising costumes that combine color and comfort—and not a single damn yachting cap in view. At the left, a cotton crepe shirt, striped in coral, sand, yellow and purple, is worn with textured white cotton pants that rather resemble a paisley-pattern brocade. Center, Himalaya's open knit crew neck of string color Durene cotton and all-wool shadow-plaid slacks. Right, stark, white cotton terry knit pullover with navy pin stripes and a zipper closure on the left shoulder, worn with Fortrel and cotton white ducks with side stripes of navy grosgrain."

Far more avant-garde were the cruising clothes photographed by *Gentlemen's Quarterly* three years later. These January, 1971, fashions were designed to "rock the boat of the old flannels-and-blazer brigade." Among them were a beige-and-brown speckled cotton knit sleeveless suit worn with a wide leather belt; a double-knit shirt suit with a white patent leather belt; a nylon sailing suit with buttoned-flap chest pockets; pirate-style suede pants with 6-inch cuffs worn with a lace-up top; a white cotton sailing suit with a zippered-front jacket, flap pockets, and a nylon hood; striped cotton terry overalls; and a pink safari shirt worn with rose-color knit shorts with cuffs.

In the same tradition-toppling vein were the clothes the *New York Times Magazine* photographed on the deck of a yacht sailing off San Juan for the April, 1971, issue of the "Report on Men's Wear": a rope-belted, zipper-front boating jacket with angled zippered pockets and ship's-wheel buttons at the neck; an awning-striped cotton canvas jacket, boldly zipper-fronted; a hooded yellow nylon boating pullover with a kangaroo pocket, a zippered placket, and a drawstring waist; and a fireman's-red boating bush coat with two buttoned-flap patch pockets, worn with matching zipper-pocketed pants.

The new wave yachting and sailing clothes are in lively colors and, though comfortable, are decidedly figure-conscious. And as more and more young men take to boats (the Kennedys sailing off Hyannis heightened interest in the sport during the 1960s), the clothes they wear will continue to reflect the new sartorial freedom.

Toiletries

The change in the American man's attitude toward good grooming aids since the early 1960s has been enormous. Men who once used nothing but a splash of witch hazel, a pat of talcum powder, and a deodorant now indulge in everything from colognes and skin conditioners to hair colorings and skin bronzers. Today no area of the male body need go untended.

There are those who explain this revolutionary change by suggesting that the male animal is only obeying a primeval instinct. They point out that the male in almost every species has brighter plumage, better fur, and a louder mating call than the female.

The designs and shapes of bottles for toiletries have undergone many changes over the years. This collection is from Yardley.

Man is therefore heeding nature when he enhances his masculinity. Furthermore, those who hold this view have the scrolls, parchments, and ledger books of history to prove that toiletries have a colorful past.

The Egyptians were making beautiful jars and vases for men's toiletries thousands of years before Christ. The Bible speaks of frankincense and myrrh, perfumes popular with the pharaohs. And when the tomb of King Tutankhamen was opened in the 1920s, a large number of cosmetic jars were discovered, their fragrances still potent after more than three millennia. Even George Washington used perfume as well as other toiletries. His personal accounts are filled with such entries as "Perfume—22 shillings, 6 pence" and "Contingent expenses paid for Hair Powder, Pomatum [hair grease], etc." (quoted in *Good Grooming Guide*, 1966, p. 14).

But a stern Puritan ethic soon dominated the new nation and carried with it a mistrust of the "fancy," and toiletries, especially the use of a fragrance by men, were closely identified with European foppery. Still, a newspaper article written in 1912 recognized man's wish to smell good and feel attractive, and his barber shop as the one place where he could indulge this instinct without embarrassment:

"To begin with men like to smell sweet. Being ashamed to purchase perfume, they buy hair tonic. The shelf in front of every barber's chair looks like the buffet of a fancy drink fiend. After a man has been shaved and massaged, has had his hair cut and has been shampooed, he is ready for the finishing touches. All that has gone before is just a groundwork on which what is to follow is built.

"Suppose a man lacks color, his cheeks are white and have not the healthy peach bloom of the simple life. The barber rubs his cheeks with rouge or a liquid preparation and colors them in this fashion.

"Suppose that the lips are not red enough or the skin on the lips is not soft, the barber rubs them with a lipstick or treats them with various softening and healing preparations.

"Suppose there are not eyebrows enough or those that are there are not dark enough. The barber either paints in new eyebrows or colors up the old colorless ones.

"Suppose the moustache is not quite brilliant enough or stiff enough. It is long enough, perhaps, but it drops and has not that jaunty, bristling, cock's-comb appearance that is admired in men's moustaches. The barber rubs it with a liquid preparation which makes it brilliant, stiff, bristly, and beautiful.

"Suppose any part of the facial geography is too red. The nose may be flowering like the scarlet geranium or the ears may be too encarmined. The barber treats the offending parts with a preparation which takes the color out of the skin.

"There are many other little processes, such as removing pimples and so on, that the man orders before the barber is through with his face. When all the small details have been attended to he usually has a rub with some sort of scented toilet water, and then the barber returns to the hair which was left tied in the towel after the shampoo.

"The towel is taken from the head, and the hair is found nearly dry. It may be necessary to curl the hair in front. This is done with a curling iron,

just as the ladies' hair is curled. Any little fancy waves the customer wants are put in and the hair is parted. The man is now released from the chair.

"Having had his head and face beautified one would think that the

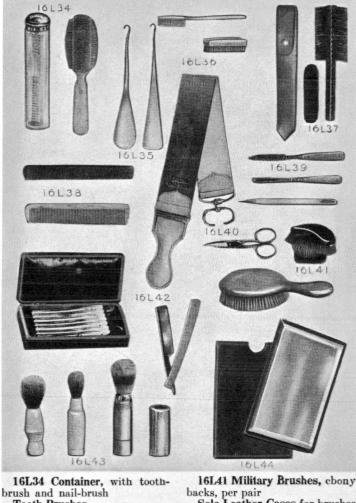

16L34 **Container**, with tooth-brush and nail-brush
Tooth Brushes
Nail Brushes
16L35 **Combination Shoe Horn and Button Hooks**
16L36 **Razor Strops**
16L37 **Folding Hat Brush and Buffer**, in leather case
16L38 **Combs**
16L39 **Nail Files**
Tweezers
Nail Cleaners
Nail Cutters
16L40 **Scissors**

16L41 **Military Brushes**, ebony backs, per pair
Sole Leather Cases for brushes

Brushes with regulation handles, singly and in pairs
16L42 **Razors.** Singly
In sets of seven, engraved with days of week
Razor Cases
16L43 **Shaving Brushes**, with bone or silver handles
Curling Lamps
16L44 **Shaving Mirrors**, in various designs

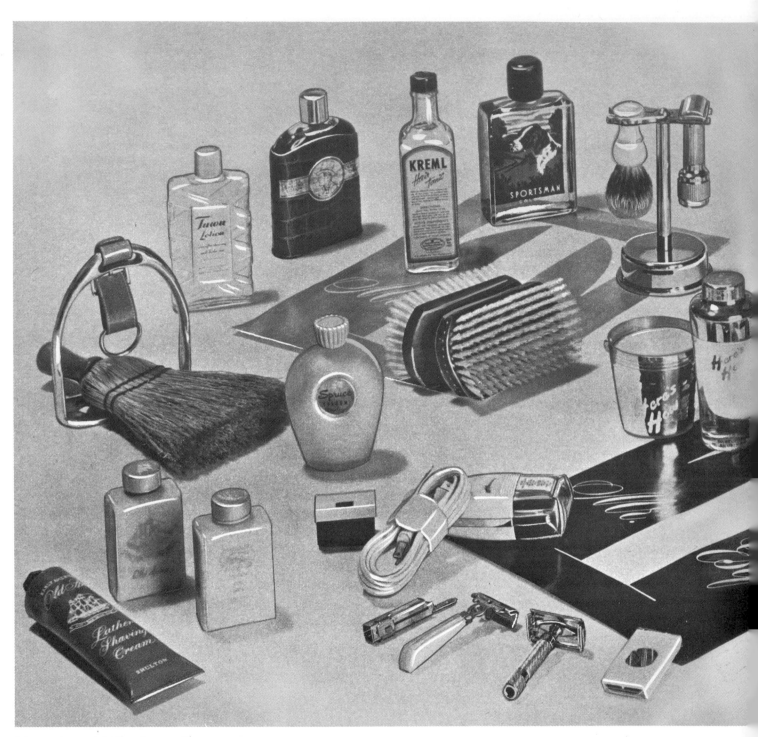

(*above and opposite*) *Grooming to a T was a part of the Mr. T fashion platform in 1950. Shown here is an assortment of aids for better grooming. From* Esquire, *October 1950.*

man would be satisfied—satisfied, at least, that he had been made as pretty as the barber shop could make him. But not so. The modern barber shop has a manicure girl—many of them—

and the modern man must have his fingers prettified before he trusts himself on the street alone. . ." (quoted in Richard Corson, *Fashions in Hair,* Hastings House, New York, 1965).

After World War I men's clothes became trimmer and more colorful, and many a younger man broke precedent by wearing a dash of women's

perfume under his jacket lapel. Others followed the lead of the motion-picture actor Rudolph Valentino and wore a cologne that reportedly charged the air with a cool, citrusy scent.

In 1920 the *Barber's Journal* carried a news item from Cleveland: "It's here at last—the eyebrow plucking parlor

for men. James Macaluse, proprietor of a barber shop at East 11th Street and Superior Avenue, announced his intention of conducting a plucking establishment in connection with his regular tonsorial work. 'I've had a number of men come in recently and ask where they could get their lashes drooped or their brows wecded out

and run into nice curves,' he said. 'I'll practice on the first one, and then after a time I'll get the knack of pulling 'em out gently'" (Corson, op. cit.).

These signs of change were scattered and insignificant; not until after World War II, for instance, were after-shave lotions used in any quantity. And it was not until the mid-1950s

that there was a really dynamic change in the attitude toward toiletries; then, not surprisingly, it came through the younger man, who was free of the old prejudices and feelings of embarrassment. Yet, as early as 1950 *Esquire* noted the way the wind was blowing and offered advice on good grooming to its readers:

"What about good grooming? The facts are that it has always been a source of satisfaction to men, but only in recent years has it come out of a rather suspicious area into its completely masculine position of today. Cleanliness and sophisticated grooming are closely integrated now with business and social success. But there was a time when a bottle of Bay Rum was the only sweet-smelling concoction in the medicine chest. Anything else was *verboten*. After World War I, when taboos in general were taking a lacing, the definition of masculine began to change. Cigarettes and wrist watches were no longer considered 'sissy.' Sports champions—men who were tough enough to get away with it—began to use scented mixtures and make others follow after. The rest of the male population became interested. Perfume specialists, knowing a good thing when they smelled it, were soon turning out attractively packaged, he-man shave lotions and colognes that sold like Prohibition whiskey. Of course, there wasn't any mass smashing of Bay Rum bottles, but today you'd have to do a lot of looking to find a man still using the stuff. Grooming is as important as correct apparel."

Along with a page of deodorants, colognes, lotions, and talcs, the editors included a travel manicuring set, brushes, and other equipment "that give a man a real lift."

Life magazine, reporting on August 13, 1965, on the "Big Boom in Men's Beauty Aids," traced the start of the new era to American college men on holiday in Europe who began buying "a chic French cologne called Canoe (pronounced Can-Oh-ay). Citrusy and sweet-smelling, Canoe was widely used by Frenchmen as an all-day-long scent. Soon it became a fad in U.S. colleges for a guy and his gal both to slap it on." According to a fashion executive quoted in the article, "when the boys came home wearing Canoe, the old man got adventuresome and tried a little too."

By this time many barbers were calling themselves hair stylists and

The custom of using toiletries in the morning leads to better grooming. From Esquire, *May 1966.*

offering their customers razor cutting, tinting, and permanent waving along with facials and pedicures. A profusion of grooming aids in all price ranges saturated the market. In addition to using the more prosaic colognes and after-shave lotions, men began to pamper their faces with creams and cleansers, spray their hair with sweet-smelling preparations, lacquer their nails, and in general use cosmetics to the point where the business began to resemble the women's beauty products industry. Men's grooming bars were opened in leading department stores. At an *Esquire* fashion seminar in the fall of 1963, one executive quipped: "Man does not live by soap alone."

The editors of *Esquire* published an illustrated handbook, titled *Esquire Fashions for Men*, in which they included data on the six basic sources of fragrances designed to make a man "smell good" (1966 ed.):

From all the brands of after-shave lotions, colognes and toilet waters, there are, once you get down to it, only six basic aromas from which the scents are derived: wood, citrus, flowers, leather, spices, and tobacco.

The fresh, pungent smell of citrus was the earliest fragrance used in making men's cologne. Citrus is still heavily used but other aromas used alone or in combination are now readily available. Long-lasting floral scents are especially strong and, as cologne grows in popularity, more and more colognes will have floral aromas.

Almost all the colognes now marketed derive from the natural oils of flowers, leaves, wood, roots, seeds and fruit. Synthetic scents are important too since they can re-create certain smells of natural objects like gardenias—that do not yield essential oils.

Woody fragrances are often derived from aromatic chemicals, but there are natural sources like cedar, linaloe and sandalwood as well as gums like myrrh, balsam, storax and tolu. Sandalwood and rosewood are often combined with earthy oak moss and ferns to create "foresty" scents. Citrus oils for cologne are extracted from lemon, lime, orange and bergamot trees and fruits. Tobacco, an aroma never used as a main theme, is introduced into other essences as a minor note to add a masculine overtone. Floral scented colognes are either fragrances that are made solely from the blossoms of a single flower or blends of different flowers that are held together with heavier substances like ambergris, musk and vetiver. The oils most frequently used are of the bitter orange flower, jasmine, lavender and rose. Leather is a scent largely derived from chemical combinations. Spicy colognes as cinnamon, clove and ginger are often combined with similar pungent floral essences.

For the connoisseur, there is a vocabulary of smell comparable to the language of the wine-taster. A cologne like Arden's Sandalwood, for example, is described as "woodsy with an underlying base of lavender, a green leaf topnote." Topnotes are the first fragrances detected by the sense of smell. The base is a fixative that holds the scent elements together. In between the base and the topnotes is the body; this gives the fragrance its main theme or essential character.

But why choose one theme over another? The only test for the customer is comparative sniffing. No words are able to give anybody a complete idea of what to expect. If the aura of the cologne itself can somehow be made to include the aura

(opposite) "Tons and Tons of Toiletries" was the title of this illustration, which showed almost all the men's toiletries available in 1970. From Esquire, *April 1970.*

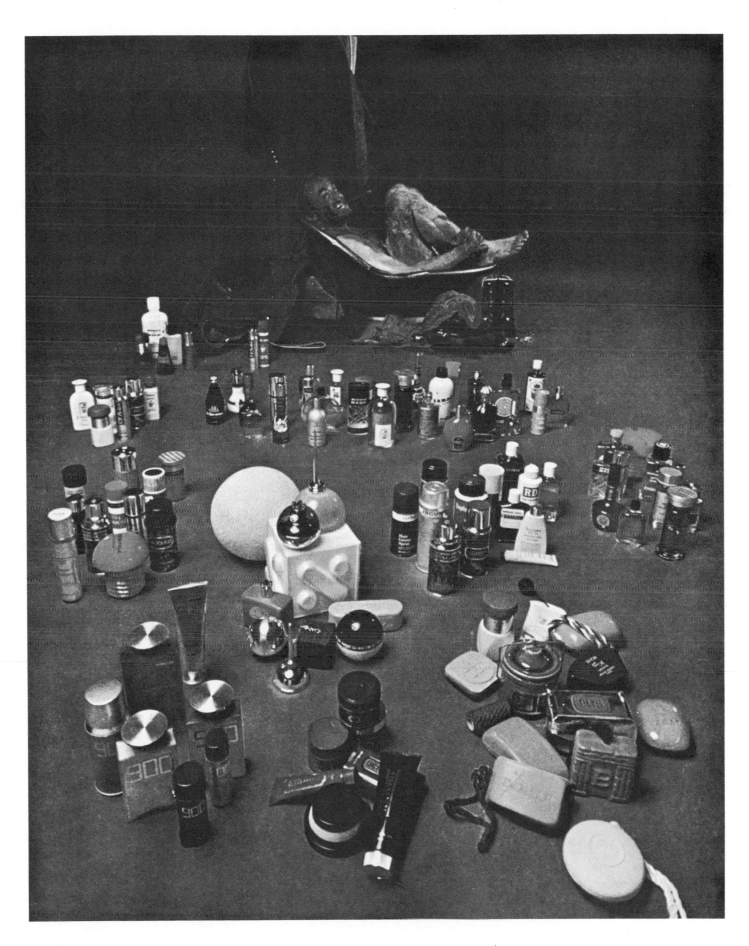

of what it can do for you (as an aphrodisiac, for example), then so much the better.

One of the classic cases of enhancement by reputation is the hundred-sixty-year-old Jean Marie Farina brand of cologne. Legend has it that it was the favorite of Napoleon who used ten cases of six bottles each every month.

There are other uses for colognes besides the obvious slosh-it-on-the-face one. First, it can be used as a body rub. After a shower, men apply it liberally to the chest and arms and under the arms; the alcohol evaporates, leaving them feeling dry, refreshed and pleasantly scented. (There are also men's after-shower lotions with slightly less perfume content than in cologne.) Many men like to keep a bottle of cologne in the office; they will wash their face before a business or social date, especially at the end of the work day, and then apply cologne for an uplifting refresher. (And some men use facial talc at that time of day, too, to cover "five-o'clock shadow.") There are men who dab a bit of cologne on their pocket handkerchief or on the shoulders of their shirt, to create a faint scent that will be pleasing to themselves and the lady they are dancing with.

In 1966 the *Daily News Record* interviewed the manager of the women's cosmetics department in a large Southern specialty department store, who said she felt there was a definite market for skin conditioners and lotions, scented cream hair dressings, hair sprays, and tints to cover gray, all produced especially for men: "We already have a few of these," she said, "and they sell very well. We hear from wives that their husbands are dipping into their various skin creams and hair cosmetics, experimenting with this and that . . . so they might as well have their own."

That year, women's magazine beauty editors reminded their readers that the man of the house could now buy his own cosmetics necessities. They also considered what this new preoccupation with looks and sex appeal revealed about the American man. Did it, for instance, mean that he was becoming sissified? The consensus was that he was not. Women readers were reminded that long ago cosmetics were solely the property of men and women were not allowed to beautify themselves. Now, in the new era of good grooming and youth consciousness, a man could smell as fresh and clean as his woman. The beauty editors unanimously concluded that the American woman should be happy to share her beauty secrets with her man if they would make him feel and look as wonderful as they made her feel and look.

Good Grooming for Men, published by *Esquire* in 1967, listed the product categories that reflected this "new wave" in men's toiletries:

When the West was wild and woolly and a frontiersman got the urge to comb his hair, he reached for the nearest jar of bear grease. In the early 1900's, it was Vaseline [petroleum jelly]. Today, as a by-product of chemical advances in other fields, we find men's toiletries taking on new and exotic nuances. While it would be obviously absurd to compare these with chemical contributions to medicine, for example, they do bring a measure of comfort and pleasure to millions of men. And, in an era of strain and anxiety, who can say this is without meaning? Take, for instance, deodorants. . . .

1. Deodorants: It is not difficult to understand why unpleasant body odors can be a problem when you consider that the human body contains about 2 million sweat glands discharging as much as several quarts of fluid every day, during warm weather. This fluid is about 99 per cent water, but it also contains urea, sodium chloride and other salts. When these reach the surface of the skin and come in contact with bacteria there they decompose rapidly and give off odors.

Every drug store today carries an extensive line of deodorants, most of them quite effective. Some, in cream form, contain petrolatum which absorbs the odor. Other creams and powders, known as anti-perspirants, contain aluminum chloride which stops perspiration for a while. There are also liquid deodorizers using formaldehyde or vinegar, and others based on chlorophyll. An essential ingredient of all these products is some type of pleasant perfume which disguises any lingering trace of sweaty odor, as well as the basic ingredient of the deodorant itself.

People sometimes wonder if an anti-perspirant will injure their health by shutting off perspiration. The answer is "no." Checking perspiration under the arms or on other parts of the body where it is plentiful will not interfere with the normal functioning of the body. There are plenty of outlets for the perspiration, in those millions of sweat glands discussed before.

Deodorants come in varying guises. There are sprays, which are usually anti-perspirant, and have the advantage of drying almost immediately instead of obliging the user to stand around and wave his arms for a couple of minutes. These sprays should be capped tightly and kept closed between uses in order to avoid evaporation. There are also special sprays containing deodorant talc for the entire body.

Roll-on anti-perspirants take a little longer to apply and dry. They are recommended for men with heavier underarm hair growth which the spray cannot penetrate. A deodorant stick, having both anti-perspirant and deodorant qualities, dries immediately, and is quite popular. However, the spray-ons seem to be chalk-

ing up the heaviest sales, perhaps because of their convenience.

If the number and variety of oils, creams, ointments and soaps for men continue to increase, they will soon rival those made for women. Already, one sees eye pads, "an antidote for smoke-filled rooms, fine print or late nights." Men have begun to buy these pads that use an eye-soothing formula; they are also using a silicone cream ten-minute facial that tones up the skin, and covering cream that conceals blemishes and razor nicks. Even men who say they don't use anything but soap, water and shaving cream, usually find, on thinking it over, that they are better customers for the toiletries industry than they realized. The number of men who do not use some kind of after-shave lotion, hair shampoo and hair stay is growing smaller all the time. Millions have succumbed to the lure of products like these:

2. Colognes: (Some brands claim they are based on aphrodisiac roots, or at the very least are highly pleasing to the opposite sex. There are no statistics available on this yet.)

3. Special bath soaps: They leave "an invisible protective glove" on the skin that keeps dirt from entering the pores.

4. Friction lotions: These contain capsicum, a peppery skin stimulant, and menthol, and are for after-shower use.

5. Shampoo on a rope: This bar can't get lost, attached as it is to a short rope that can be slipped over your arm—or on a hook in the shower. Saves that crawling around after the shampoo container.

6. Water soluble hair stays: These can be revived many hours later with just a damp comb or brush. Non-greasy.

7. Hair sprays: Guaranteed to conquer the wildest cowlick without giving you a slicked-down look.

8. Pre-shave astringent: Cleanses the skin and prepares it for a better shave. Soap and water dissolves water soluble dirt. This takes off some non-water soluble oils, makes better sitting for the razor.

9. Hand creams: For dry, rough or chapped hands, in any kind of weather.

Men used to sneak their wives' creams—a bit abashedly. Now they can buy a non-scented brand all their own.

Meanwhile, the advertisers of colognes did their best to eliminate any remaining vestiges of male resistance. Brand names were aggressively masculine, and there were advertising slogans such as "For the man who gives a woman a sporting chance," "How to light a new fire under an old flame," and "If you have any doubts about yourself, try something else."

In 1967, at *Esquire*'s Second Men's Fashion Toiletries Marketing Conference, Amelia Bassin, speaking on the importance of provocative packaging ("seen first . . . communicates first"), quoted from a report on the packaging of Brut by Fabergé:

"First we open a box made of cardboard at least three or four times as thick as the kind ordinarily used, immediately conveying the message to our fingers that this product is expensive, fragile and imported. We must unwind a string to open it, a little ritual reminiscent of the fastenings on important folios and secret documents—and the very antithesis of modern efficiency. Finally, we withdraw the bottle, grasping it by its long, thin neck—and, at this moment, it is difficult to resist the idea that the bottle itself is a piece of phallic symbolism. It is the very essence of masculine virility."

A trade publication noted: "The vague self-consciousness which marked the beginning of the cologne boom has given way to a mass acceptance of the product as unassailably masculine. Enough so that the main question now

is not *should* you use it but how many should you use. Our suggestion is five or six."

Pursuing this line of thought, the writer Raoul Demont observed: "One day it may be a lime-based cologne, the next day a leather. The result is that men who only five or six years ago used no cologne at all now use several. Colognes have begun performing the same function in men's grooming as individual items in a clothing wardrobe. The feeling is that just as one would not want to wear the same suit two days in a row, the same cologne would not do either. Which cologne one wears at any given time may be only a matter of whim (this kind of choice is totally subjective), but some colognes actually strike their users as seasonal or evocative of certain degrees of dressiness, and thus they are worn for specific reasons" (*Good Grooming for Men*, 1967).

Another writer, noting that a woman was as susceptible once she was within scent distance of a well-groomed man as he traditionally was supposed to be to her perfume, advised men as follows: "By all means use scents, colognes or the pungent after-shave lotions. There isn't the slightest suspicion of effeminacy connected with them any longer and without one on, you're not quite, well, *de rigueur*" (*Good Grooming Guide*, 1966).

Writing on the subject "The Smell of Love," Drs. Eberhard W. and Phyllis C. Kronhausen, psychiatrists, had this to say: "In the arsenal of love and lovemaking, one of man's most potent weapons can be, of all things, his smell—not his sense of smell, but

his personal body odor." They concluded their article by reminding the reader of the line in Charles Darwin which reads: "The most odoriferous males [in the animal world] are the most successful in winning the females." They then added this final word of caution: "If a man's odor is to fulfill its romantic purpose, it must stimulate pleasant fantasies by whispering to her unconscious mind in a code that eludes the censorship of the conscious. There must be only a trace, a mere allusion—all carefully subdued—to the sexual. Otherwise, the odor will be considered vulgar if not downright repulsive and the whole effect will be lost. In short, be discreet, be sparing, be artful" (*Good Grooming Guide*, 1966).

In October, 1969, *Gentlemen's Quarterly* examined the booming toiletries business and said: "Nobody is sure why men's cosmetics have exploded into a big business practically overnight. One reason may be that there are few things as valued in the U.S. as a healthy and youthful appearance. There's nothing the American male wouldn't do to avoid leading the kind of life that would naturally lead to such a look. If it can be packaged and sold, men will flock to buy it. It can, and they do.

"Part of the cosmetics explosion among the skin conditioners, face-firmers and sauna splashes, are makeup preparations. Admittedly, few companies put out actual camouflaging makeup preparations comparable to pancake makeup for women. But almost all manufacturers of men's cosmetics include tanners or bronzers in their lines. Hair coloring is also attracting more interest as Youth becomes more cherished in industry and business.

"Taking the subject of makeup from a logical point of reasoning, a man has more need for makeup cover than a woman. He is growing a beard twenty-four hours a day, and about five hours after his morning shave, new growth becomes evident. Also, he is more susceptible to skin blemishes, pimples and razor burns as a consequence of daily shaving."

Gentlemen's Quarterly then proceeded to call attention to a pancake powder that was, it said, the answer to five-o'clock shadow. It came in an anonymous-looking compact case and was applied to the face with a sponge applicator. On hair coloring the magazine had this to say: "Gray at the temples, which was once cultivated as a mark of distinguished achievement, as well as that of a great lover, has become something that men are trying to hide. Almost all hair stylists for men offer hair coloring as part of their regular bill-of-fare. The man who doesn't like to admit that he's darkening his gray by showing up suddenly with duotoned hair can do it himself gradually."

In April, 1970, *Esquire* reported on what it termed "Tons and Tons of Toiletries":

"As far as the well-turned-out man of the Seventies is concerned, the Age of Aquarius was meant to be anointed and aromatic, for it is an age dedicated to the pursuit of physical perfection—to looking one's very best. Nor are the means to achieve this aim in short supply, for practically everything except frankincense and myrrh is available these days. What is so admirable about this is that it represents a new sophistication, a hitherto uncommon sense, for it was not so very long ago that most men regarded the use of toiletries, especially colognes, as a little effeminate. A drop or two of Lilac Vegetal at the barber's perhaps—possibly a touch of talcum powder and, if one had a walk on the wild side in mind, maybe a mud pack. But now such mild ministrations, once so devilish, so dudish, are ancient and unenlightened history, part of the shy, naive years when *Esquire* was a periodical men pored over only in the stag surroundings of the barbershop. Now men are being sensible, openly availing themselves of the cornucopia of conveniences and cosmetics for sale even in small-town drugstores. The range is all but infinite, for now, in addition to the shaving creams, colognes, and skin balms that have been around for a while (but are now in more functional forms—sticks, gels, creams, cakes, etc.), there are controls, colorings, oils, and sprays for the hair; hand soaps, grit soaps, and shower soaps on ropes; aerosols and sauna splashes; deodorants for every purpose, for every part of the body, not excluding the genitals; bronzers and blemish concealers; and almost endlessly on and on." It was, said the feature writer, "a panacea for all the poxes that plague a man's aspirations for his appearance."

George Mazzei, writing in *Gentlemen's Quarterly* in May, 1970, took a long view of the development of men's

grooming products, "from the first bottle of bay rum to the present sweet disarray of sophisticated toiletries," and traced its stages as follows:

1. The bay rum stage, later refined into the old spice stage: The era of the all purpose lotion, since the only time a man was permitted to use a fragrance was right after shaving.
2. The shower-soap-on-a-rope stage: It was silly and had a high potential for self-strangulation, but was better than getting a tie for Christmas.
3. The after-shave/cologne stage, later separated into two bottles, which was questionable, since you still couldn't use a fragrance, unless you had just shaved.
4. The 1966 stage—actually a three-year period—when bath oils, bronzers, moisturizers, hand creams, face creams, sauna sprays, genital sprays, men's deodorants and all-purpose splash-ons forced department stores to create separate men's cosmetics counters.

This last stage was, and is, the most important. Although during this period most toiletries were introduced as sidelines by women's cosmetics manufacturers, this fact was played down. Names like Aramis (from Estee Lauder), Braggi (Revlon) and Brut (Faberge) gained a distinct status as men spent more and more on personal grooming aids (reportedly over $620 million during the last fiscal year). What

previously had been a cosmetic link between the sexes became a parallel, coinciding only at the end result—sexual attractiveness.

It's now been about four years since the newspapers printed the first aghast, giggly articles (usually in the women's section) about how perfumes and cosmetics for men were (Wow!) turning into big business and men were (snicker) getting as vain as the girls!!!

As you may have suspected, all the foregoing is leading up to something. That something is the new dimension in men's cosmetics, the Problem-solving stage—and I think they'd better come up with a new word, since neither "toiletries" nor "cosmetics" applies.

The products evolving from the problem-solving stage were, said Mazzei, "not meant to groom and polish in the traditional sense, but to actually treat problems connected with the hair, the face, the body and shaving." The approach, he said, was clinical.

"The key to this upsurge in preventive maintenance is its emphasis: where once these products were only stressing better looks via their use," said Mazzei, "now they're changing the texture of skin and hair. The point

is to actually make you more attractive, rather than just *looking* better through camouflage."

Gentlemen's Quarterly in March, 1971, noted: "These days, there's even such a thing as a perfect shave," listing the new advances that made this possible: hot lather, shave creams containing healing agents, and gels with lubricating agents that protect the face against cuts.

It was the combination of toiletries and fashion in the 1960s that produced the consummate peacock, splendidly garbed and looking, feeling, and smelling like a healthy male animal. Furthermore, the peacock had no intention of ever being anything less. With the endless parade of new products being created in the men's fashion toiletries field, there was no reason why he should. As Jerry Jontry of Esquire, Inc., said in a speech before the all-female Fashion Group on February 11, 1965: "Scientific progress is extending our lives but just because men are going to live to be a hundred, doesn't mean we have to *look* that old!" It was obvious that the toiletries industry could only continue to grow.

Styling and Care

After being in eclipse for nearly two centuries, the beard came back in the 1850s and flourished for the next half century. By 1901, however, it was on its way out of fashion again, prompting Edith Sessions Tupper, a reporter for the Chicago *Chronicle*, to write: "If the twentieth century should remove whiskers from the face of mankind, it will be glory enough for one hundred years." It is interesting to quote further from her article, since it undoubtedly reflected the attitude of many turn-of-the-century women on the wearing of beards:

"Moustaches are not so bad as whiskers. They give a man a soldierly air which is not unpleasant. If a man must wear hair on the face, let it be in this shape. A moustache often covers ugly teeth and lips, thereby proving a boon to mankind. . . . Heroes of novels by women as a rule sport long, blonde silky moustaches, which they are constantly curling and stroking.

"Lately, however, the Richard Harding Davis and Charles Dana Gibson men have set a new vogue, that of the smooth-shaven, stern-faced, dogged-chin chap. It has proved immensely popular and all classes of men have followed this fashion. So that nowadays it is difficult to tell coachmen from their masters or actors from clergymen.

"It is a cleanly fashion and one to be commended to all men with reasonably good features. There is a certain distinction about the clean-shaven man which the wearer of whiskers can never possess. Moreover, a smooth face is a stimulant to high thoughts. For behind walls and hedges and brambles of hair mean, low, cunning thoughts can conceal their traces, but they are blazoned forth on the open of a smooth cheek" (quoted in Richard Corson, *Fashions in Hair*, Hastings House, New York, 1965).

Another woman journalist, C. E. Humphry, writing in the London magazine *Etiquette for Every Day*, observed: "Regarded from merely the ornamental point of view a beard of any kind is a mistake when a man possesses a well-cut chin" (quoted in Corson, op. cit.). A chin, for instance, like that of the famous Arrow collar man, a clean-shaven model whose noble chin and piercing eyes had, according to Cluett Peabody & Co., earned him the accolade "nature's glowing gift to enamoured womanhood."

Although some older men clung tenaciously to their whiskers, more and more men were shaving theirs off during the first decade of the twentieth century. And the reference to a clean-shaven face as "a cleanly fashion" was not to be taken lightly, as an article the following year in *Harper's Weekly* indicated:

"To be perfectly frank, at the risk of being somewhat disgusting, we must own that the full beard collects dandruff, which plentifully bestrews the neckcloth and the waistcoat; but it is not filthier in other respects than the moustache, which sops itself full of soup and gravy and coffee . . . and is absurd besides.

"The gain of manly beauty through the fashion of clean-shaving has not as yet, it must be confessed, been very great. Those who had not grown beards, of course, remained as they were, in their native plainness; but it is in the case of those who had worn beards that the revelations are sometimes frightful: retreating chins, blubber lips, silly mouths, brutal jaws, fat and flabby necks, which had lurked unsuspected in their hairy coverts now appear and shake the beholder with surprise and consternation. 'Good heavens!' he asks himself, 'is that the way Jones *always* looked?' Jones, in the meanwhile, is not seriously troubled.

The man of 1905 wore his hair with a part on the right side, a curled effect on top, and sideburns. [COURTESY OF CULVER PICTURES, INC., NEW YORK]

# of Hair

He is pleased with the novelty of his aspect; he thinks upon the whole thing that it was a pity to have kept so much loveliness out of sight for so long. As he passes his hand over the shapeless expanses, with the satisfaction which nothing but the smoothness of a freshly shaven face can give, he cannot resist the belief that people are admiring him. At any rate, he has that air" (quoted in Corson, op. cit.).

The article went on to point out that half a century earlier defenders of the beard had argued in favor of its comeback on the ground that whiskers contributed to a man's health by keeping his throat warm and filtering the air entering his lungs.

In 1907 in another *Harper's Weekly* article, titled "The Revolt against Whiskers," William Inglis noted: "Perhaps no greater evidence can be found of the sure and rapid growth of the aesthetic sense of the American people than the present revolt against whiskers." That year, a Democratic assemblyman from Essex County, New Jersey, introduced in the Legislature a bill to tax whiskers, asserting that he had made many inquiries and collected much valuable data on whiskers and the majority of men he queried had said that they "wore beards as a matter of economy, to save both barbers' fees and the cost of neckties." The English magazine *Punch* thought a tax on whiskers a splendid idea: "It ought to be introduced in England at the earliest opportunity, but the taxes are not heavy enough. If men insist upon going about as if they were blots on the landscape I don't see why they should not pay a high price for the privilege. There is no reason why moustaches should not be taxed also" (quoted in Corson, op. cit.).

The moustache, however, had its staunch allies, and many mature men took special pride in the kind of bristling moustache worn by the Kaiser.

To keep the tips pointing upward in the true Kaiser style, a moustache binder, a gadget of German origin, was often used. Constructed of silk gauze, two little leather straps, and two pieces of elastic webbing, it was pressed close to the face, covering the moustache, and was fastened behind the head.

While the majority of men were willing to sacrifice facial hair to the razor, they were much concerned about maintaining the hair on their heads, which was worn short, neatly trimmed, and parted, usually on the side. Baldness, then as now, was the chief fear.

1910–1940

During the second decade of the century the beard was passé, although some elderly men still wore full whiskers. World War I had made the Kaiser-style moustache unpopular, and it had been replaced by the so-called toothbrush, or Charlie Chaplin, style. The war had also had a noticeable effect on hair styles, ushering in the military haircut, in which the head was clipped close all around, leaving the hairline at approximately eyebrow level. An unfortunate style, it did not become popular to any great extent except in small towns and rural areas.

For the man who was bald or balding, a wig shop was the answer. And if he disliked the gray hairs that came with middle age, he could have them dyed at his barber shop, and the brush might be applied to his eyebrows and moustache, too. If the barber was *au courant,* he made certain that he had an impressive selection of shampoos available: egg shampoo, tar shampoo, patent preparation shampoo, and so on. As one writer for the *Barber's Journal* noted in 1912, "The shelf in front of every barber's chair looks like the buffet of a fancy drink fiend."

The pompadour or the crew cut has been in favor through much of the twentieth century. This man of the early 1900s preferred a bushy top and closely trimmed sides and back. In the 1950s the short version of the crew cut was known as the butch cut. [COURTESY OF CULVER PICTURES, INC., NEW YORK]

By 1921 the *Barber's Journal* reported, no doubt with relief: "That once furiously popular military haircut, in which the clipper moved the neckline up as near the crown as possible, is as good as dead . . . partly because it became moribund in the east and the boys who went east and noted its condition came back and turned thumbs down in the west. Its waning is also part of the general tendency among so many men who went to war to get away from military things as much as possible" (quoted in Corson, op.cit.). (Although this skinned look disappeared in most cities, it lingered on as late as the 1960s in certain rural areas.)

The *Barber's Journal* also noted that men's hair styles in the early 1920s showed little variety: "About the only choice a customer has is between having it cut long or having it cut short. As between these two styles, the 'long' group is leading. . . . The style in which the hair is left long on top and brushed straight back or parted is gaining in popularity all over the country, especially in big cities" (quoted in Corson, op. cit.).

The brushlike Chaplinesque moustache was replaced in the late twenties by a pencil-line moustache, the kind worn by the motion-picture actor John Gilbert, whose studio publicized him as "the great lover." Meanwhile, pomade had made men's hair increasingly shiny. The ultimate was the patent-leather look popularized by the actor Rudolph Valentino, who also began something of a vogue for long sideburns, although they were a little too Latin for most American men and never really became fashionable. What was fashionable was to have a pencil-line moustache, its tips smartly waxed, and moderately pomaded hair parted in the center.

The 1930s were noted for the casual elegance of the remaining rich, which was in sharp contrast to the Depression that was gripping the nation. Although the British-inspired clothes worn by this minority of rich Americans were out of the reach of most men, any man could wear his hair in the approved style: short and natural and parted on the side. Wavy hair was popular, especially with younger men, and the plastered-down look of the twenties was definitely dated. Proper cutting and an aptitude with comb and water helped some men approximate the waved hair of such youthful motion-picture actors as Buddy Rogers and Charles Farrell. Conservative moustaches were still being worn by older men of a certain sophistication, and even here the British influence was so strong that the moustaches were usually copied from those worn by the British military.

1940–1960

During the forties, which were marked by World War II, the moustache was seen less often. Edith Effron, writing in the *New York Times Magazine* in 1944, suggested that it had too many unfortunate connotations for most American men, from French affectation and Sicilian villainy to Chaplin pathetic and Hitler psychopathic, and was thus scarcely appealing in a wartime period of overwhelming patriotism. Miss Effron quoted from a psychoanalyst: "America is a young country. We are young in many ways and we don't like to assume the burdens of age. The moustache is a symbol of maturity, and the American who doesn't care to grow older shaves it off. That's why the ideal of this nation is a clear-cut, clean-shaven youth. In general, it is a sign of bad adjustment if you do not follow the style of your country. The waxed moustache—or the moustache shaved in an artificial pattern—is an affectation in America."

The first zoot suit of record was ordered in 1939 from a store in Georgia. This rather grotesque garment, with its exaggerated shoulders, extra long jacket, and absurdly high-rise trousers, had a short and florid career and along the way inspired a duck-tailed pompadour hair style that, like the zoot suit, had a limited and short popularity. Yet one might see in both fads a postwar generation's first attempts to look radically different. They were, in a sense, a rather freakish preview of the antiestablishment long hair and "mod" clothes that were to come in the 1960s.

By the 1950s some of the more avant-garde barbers were calling themselves hair stylists, and a few of the more expensive shops were offering hair coloring and permanent waves. The New York advertising man David Ogilvy created a classic campaign when he photographed a middle-aged moustached model in a Hathaway shirt and an eye patch. Inevitably, other advertising agencies began to use moustache-wearing models, all of which prompted the *New York Times Magazine* in 1954 to ask the question: "Is this evidence that the moustache is also returning to the common lip?" The following year, the editors of *Look* magazine pointed out that more and more young men were wearing beards.

During the 1950s men of all ages were becoming increasingly hair-conscious, and wigs were more commonplace; the so-called average man was being encouraged to consider one because at least two or three of his favor-

In 1956 this style of hair was described as not too long and not too short. From Esquire, *March 1956.*

ite television performers admitted to wearing them. In 1958, *Time* magazine reported that Sears, Roebuck and Company was sending out 30,000 catalogs advertising "career-winning toupees." The catalogs were slipped into "discreetly unmarked white envelopes," and the toupees sold for $109.95 to $224.95.

There was also a wider variety of hair styles to be seen during the fifties than in any preceding decade of the century, ranging from the crew cut, reminiscent of the military cut of the twenties though not so extreme, to the long Elvis Presley style. As it developed, the trends noted in this decade were merely faint indications of the future: it took the 1960s with the Peacock Revolution to reveal the trends in toto. A new era, marked by man's new awareness of his physical self, was at hand. And although many an impeccably garbed urbane individual might not care to acknowledge kinship with the long-haired, bearded, and beaded hippie, it was this cultural dropout who was responsible for starting the movement toward more hair.

Wearing the hair brushed back with a part on the left side was in style in 1966. From Esquire, *October 1966.*

1960–1970

"When a man reaches 40 or 50 these days," said Charles Revson of Revlon, Inc., who had recently begun to produce men's grooming aids as well as cosmetics, "he simply doesn't want to be old. He wants to swing a little. He wants all his clothes shapely, tailored, fitted in the figure. This man is also open to something for his face. He's open to something for his hair. He's open to something for his body. That's what's happening" (*Life,* August, 1965). When it came to "something for his hair," *Gentlemen's Quarterly* decided that he wanted hair styling, often hair coloring, "and, failing those possibilities, a hairpiece."

By 1966 it was no longer smart for a man to leave the barber's chair looking as if he had just had a haircut. In all the new hair styles the bare neck was taboo. The new men's hair-styling parlors, said *Gentlemen's Quarterly,* were not always in the heart of a great city

and, in February, 1966, proved this statement with a photographic tour of suburban towns having Gay Nineties barber shops with gold-plated washbasins and waiting rooms decorated with elk and buffalo horn.

The big news, however, was the return of the beard. As early as 1963, Kent had introduced, for the first time in decades, a moustache and beard good-grooming brush that measured $5\frac{1}{2}$ inches in length. And the man who wanted hair on his face also wanted a full head of hair on his head. As a result, baldness was an even greater cause of concern, and gray hair, no matter how premature, was considered a telltale sign of age. "Modern science has devised ingenious methods of camouflaging grayness and/or baldness. Whether you select a rinse, a dye or a toupee, don't worry. They all work. Only *you* will know," said *Good Grooming Guide* in 1966. Under the heading "Styling the Hair," the reporter Ralph Bass had this to say:

"In many large cities, a new type of 'hair stylist' has sprung up to guide your hair along the lines that do most for you. These people think of themselves as specialists, not just general practitioners. They have thrown away their clippers and most of their scissors as well, although they usually retain a curved variety for working the hairline over your ears. Working mostly with razors to taper and shape your hair more efficiently, they get from $5 to $10 for about an hour's treatment, which usually includes shampooing and 'setting.' For some men with thin hair they may recommend what amounts to a permanent wave to create 'body' and fullness. After overcoming the initial trauma of seeing themselves in a hair net, and possibly in clips, many men find it hard to go back to the old-fashioned dollar barber shop. If their wives can spend ten bucks in a beauty parlor, why not they? Formerly, these fancy establishments were patronized largely by the-

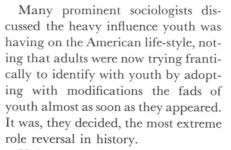

(*above and right*) *Sideburns, moustaches, and beards give a man an entirely different appearance. Shown in this group are stick-on styles of hair for the face. From* Gentlemen's Quarterly, *September 1968.*

atrical types (in Hollywood one genius gets $30 per haircut), but the number of solid citizens taking the full treatment grows all the time.

"As a result, during the past few years men's hair styles have been transformed. Perhaps because of the Beatles and similar groups, the younger element have swished, switched, that is, to longer hairdos. The hair stylists have not discouraged this trend; if anything they favor it because it affords them greater scope for the employment of their art. The crewcut, of course, is definitely out."

The *New York Times* agreed. The reporter Marilyn Bender observed: "Such traditional squares as stockbrokers, physicians and corporation executives are relinquishing the crewcuts to which they have clung since they returned from service in World War II." According to Miss Bender, European travel, the surge of masculine interest in fashion, and nagging, stylish wives were responsible. And so, too, was the influence of youth. The impact of youth was evident everywhere.

Many prominent sociologists discussed the heavy influence youth was having on the American life-style, noting that adults were now trying frantically to identify with youth by adopting with modifications the fads of youth almost as soon as they appeared. It was, they decided, the most extreme role reversal in history.

Hair was vitally important, therefore, because hair was young. And there was much more to choosing a hair style than, say, the shape of one's face, as the California hair stylist Jay Sebring made clear in a 1968 article in *Good Grooming Guide:*

"What's your status in life, your profession, your age? Do you live in a split-level, a pool apartment, a colonial mansion or a communal pad? Are you large for the Longines Symphonette or the Jefferson Airplane? What's the shape of your face—round, oval, long or square? Do you ski, golf, scuba, bowl? Is your car a Cadillac, Falcon, Lamborghini, VW, or '61 Rambler? Are you outgoing or introverted? Does your taste run to Franz Kafka, Ernest Hemingway, Gore Vidal, Thomas

Wolfe, Ian Fleming or Truman Capote? Is your bag Chess, or Five-Card Stud? Does your hairline recede, your cowlick behave? Will you change your tie with a change in mood? Do you order a Boilermaker or a triple sec Martini?

"All these considerations can affect my determination of a suitable hair design for you. After all, you are and should *look* like what you do, feel, think, prefer and aspire to."

What most men aspired to was hair—the more, the better. "Long hair is here to stay, at least for a while," commented *Men's Wear* (Oct. 23, 1970, p. 122), "and as long as it does, men will buy wigs." Even young men with no problem of baldness often invested in a wig for a different look. As the writer Robert J. Lukey noted, "A draftee or IBM man who has to cut his hair will wear a long haired wig on weekends. The bald man wears his wig for one reason—he wants hair. Unlike the young man, his is not a passing fad phase. He wants to have hair and he wants to have it permanently."

Wigs were now so popular that when Macy's announced the opening of its wig boutique in advertisements in the *New York Times,* it sold $10,000 worth of wigs in the first four days. And it was reported in 1968 that his and her "togetherness wigs" for teenage steady daters were on sale for about $70 at more than 1,000 department stores throughout the United States. But the newest development, said *Men's Wear,* was men's stretch wigs, with stores with wig departments and wig boutiques reporting phenomenal business:

"The stretch wig is usually made of synthetic fiber, but there are some human hair wigs. The fibers most commonly used are the Japanese Kanegafuji Company's Kanekalon and Union Carbide's Dynel D-50. These look like human hair but are lighter, easier to work with, easier to take care of and inexpensive. Unlike human hair, they are also non-flammable although they melt when exposed to excessive heat. A fiber wig can be swished in lukewarm sudsy water and it comes out clean and ready to wear; human hair wigs have to be cleaned by professionals.

"The wigs (both human hair and synthetic) are usually machine made. They are sewn onto a stretch lace cap (skull cap) which ideally fits all heads. Some companies also have hand-knotted versions which are slightly more expensive but give a more natural look, are lighter and better ventilated. The wigs retail at anything from $35—$50 and up, representing a 100 to 200 percent mark-up for retailers. All wigs come in different styles and a range of shades" (Sept. 25, 1970, p. 90).

The article ended on this practical note: "The lighter the wig, the less likely it is to cause discomfort. Wig weights vary tremendously—from 1½ ounces to 3 ounces and heavier." (One of the most fashionable New York hair stylists, Jerry at Bergdorf Goodman, when introducing "an entirely new line of hairpieces," referred to them as "whisper-weight.")

A hairpiece was not the only recourse open to the bald or balding man. *Gentlemen's Quarterly* informed its readers of some of the other alternatives: "There's been a lot of hocus-pocus and charlatanry attendant on the treatment of baldness, but there's been a lot of serious work, too. Fortunately, in the Seventies, you have the option of being bald one day (which isn't really unattractive once the stigma is removed), hairy the next, straight the next and a freak over the weekend. And it's all done with hair" (April, 1971, p. 82). Then the writer got down to details:

The weavers. Hairweaving is basically

"Semismooth shag" is the name the stylist Elton Pamplin gave to this style. Photographed by Donald Palmer. From the Men's Hairstylist and Barber's Journal, 1971.

The conventional businessman's cut, styled by Siro Paglia, is neither overly long nor too short. From the Men's Hairstylist and Barber's Journal, 1971.

The "layer-pick" cut, created by the stylist Steve Zaita. Photographed by Richard Thater. From the Men's Hairstylist and Barber's Journal.

The casual trim, as executed by Steve Landes, covers a good part of the forehead From the Men's Hairstylist and Barber's Journal.

just that: the weaving of foreign hair to what's left of your own. There was a brief hairweaving fad across the country about two years ago when everybody and her sister was doing it in their beauty salons. A lot of people went for it; and a lot of people got disgusted with it and had the weaves snipped off.

The process begins when a couple of strands of braided nylon thread are stretched across the bald or balding part of your scalp, then crocheted onto the hairs at the beginning of your remaining denser growth. This forms a foundation onto which new hair is attached. Then the newly-woven hair is styled. It's permanently attached to your head, but as your own hair grows, the foundations must be tightened.

The advantages: you can comb it, swim in it, live in it just as if it were your own real hair. The disadvantages: it costs $25 to have it tightened—and you *must* have it tightened every six weeks or so—or it flops all over. And it needs to be replaced every two or three years as the hair wears out. Some people have contracted irritations from the friction of the foundation

and the inability to properly clean the scalp beneath it. Also, artificially attached hair is just plain uncomfortable for a lot of people.

Hair implantation. Hair implantation is, among other things, a misnomer. No hair is planted anywhere. Basically it's another process to permanently attach a hairpiece to your head—this time surgically.

In the implantation process, plastic- or Teflon-coated wires are sutured into your scalp by a surgeon. Sections of these implants are left exposed on your head to serve as anchors onto which a hairpiece is attached.

The hair is custom-fitted and matched to your existing hair, but is no more natural in appearance than the individual operator is able to make it. If he can make a natural-looking piece, you're in luck. If not. . . .

The disadvantage of an implant is simply that if you're not happy with it after it's done, you're sort of stuck with it. Even if you had the anchor wires removed following a change of mind, you'd still have the scars on your scalp.

Hair implanters generally make very very sure that this is what their clients really want.

Hair transplants. Hair transplanting is a surgical method of hair restoring conceived about 10 years ago by a New York dermatologist. Since then other doctors have learned to do it and their names are available to interested persons either from the American Medical Association or local county medical groups. Doctors don't advertise and transplants are most definitely within a doctor's frame of reference.

The process is not recommended for the squeamish—it's painful and bloody. Small plugs of hair-growing skin are moved from the "fringe" area encircling the head with a special surgical punch. A corresponding piece of skin is removed from the bald area and replaced with the hair-growing "plug."

Enough transplants are made over the bald area to produce a reasonably dense hair-growth. The scab formed by the dried blood acts as the anchor that holds the plug of hair in place until it heals. During the healing process, the transplanted hair breaks off. However, when the healing is completed, the hair re-emerges and continues growing.

This process is based on the fact that most men don't lose their fringe hair, even though they may go bald on top. So, the transplanted hair will continue growing only as long as the fringe hair does. Besides being messy, uncomfortable and expensive, transplants are also extremely popular, mainly because they produce real hair growing out of a previously bald scalp. The growth is even and generally full enough to please anyone.

When a man finally had the hair and the hair style he wanted, there was an abundance of hair care products and grooming aids on the market to help him maintain them. As *Gentlemen's Quarterly* put it, in November, 1971, "A few short years ago the man desirous of maintaining his hair style at home had to furtively use products possessed by some distaff member of the family. That's no longer the case, as several manufacturers have come to his aid." Among the special aids available were a hot comb for teasing and straight combing (a hot comb, or electric drying comb, was actually a *styling comb* that also served as a hair dryer; thus a man could comb his hair into place while drying it), an ultraviolet comb to massage and stimulate circulation, herbal shampoos and conditioners, a two-speed dual-voltage hair dryer, and scented and unscented hair sprays. (In order to eliminate any hint of the effeminate, manufacturers of hair sprays employed broad-shouldered athletes of the caliber of Yogi Berra to advertise their wares on television.)

No matter which way the trends of the future lead, to long hair or short, a clean-shaven face or one smartly bearded, we can be certain that men are following because they want to and because they will not remain trapped in any one look for fear of change. The preoccupation with hair, which began as an antiestablishment symbol and then absorbed men of all ages and on all rungs of the socioeconomic ladder, freed them from their inhibitions.

Glasses
and
Sunglasses

Glasses at the turn of the twentieth century complemented the rather formal, sometimes ostentatious clothes of the period. Pince-nez glasses were in style, and Theodore Roosevelt wore his on a courtly black ribbon. An equally impressive-looking eyeglass was the oxford, finely wrought in solid gold with gadroon-engraved rims.

Little innovation took place in glasses during the early decades of the century. A catalog of the early 1920s included round nickel frames with 10- and 14-carat gold ornaments, lorgnettes with 14-carat gold ornaments. and rimless frames with a metal bridge piece and metal temples and ends attached to the lens. The overall effect of these glasses was one of conservative and fragile good looks. An imitation-shell frame made of a plastic that was basically cellulose nitrate was introduced during the decade. A major innovation was the full-view endpiece, which raised the attachment for the temples from the center line of the lens to a point high on the frame.

The first real hints of fashion in men's eyeglasses did not appear until the 1930s, when there was a trend toward a heavier, more authoritative-looking frame. Fiorello La Guardia, the volatile mayor of New York, wore these new frames and often slipped them off and used them to punctuate his staccato statements.

World War II brought another addition to the style picture: the metal aviator goggle. Although it was used primarily as sunglasses (for this purpose it was known as pilot's glasses), it was accepted as a basic masculine style and became something of a classic.

The postwar era saw the advance of the lighter-weight frame, the soft-square eye, and decoration in such forms as little leather-type plaques on the endpieces and temples. About this time the combination frame, with plastic on top and metal on the bottom, was introduced. Millions of glasses of this type were sold, and it has remained a staple of the eyeglass industry.

In the mid-forties the half eyeglass was accepted by men as a genuine style item; this new version of half spectacles featured a thin metal wire across the top, thus eliminating a barrier to vision. Light in weight and very compact, the style became popular with women and soon was part of their eyeglass wardrobe, too.

"The eyes have it," observed *Esquire* in 1956. "In this country where almost half the male population wears glasses, fashion has finally come to roost on the bridge of your nose. To wear one pair for all occasions is not only false economy, but it is also inappropriate

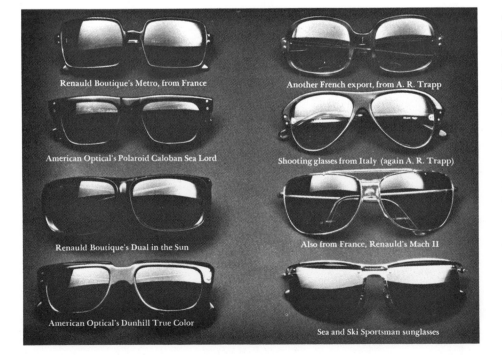

Renauld Boutique's Metro, from France

Another French export, from A. R. Trapp

American Optical's Polaroid Caloban Sea Lord

Shooting glasses from Italy (again A. R. Trapp)

Renauld Boutique's Dual in the Sun

Also from France, Renauld's Mach II

American Optical's Dunhill True Color

Sea and Ski Sportsman sunglasses

Sunglasses were available in a variety of frames in 1968.

today to make one pair stretch among evening, business, sports and casual occasions" (March, 1956, p. 102). The editors reasoned that there was a style and color to match a man's mood and the time of day. There were frames with heavy hinges, blinkers, and interchangeable colored lenses that went with heavy tweeds and sports clothes ("very posh"). It was plain that "Your cheaters that used to be a handicap are now an asset—and high styling has made the difference."

The fashion department offered visual proof with sketches of appropriate glasses. It suggested semirimless semiformal glasses for everyday business wear: "The brow line comes in black, brown, grey or pin-stripe; plastic accents make them suitable for daytime wear; gold-filled bridge and temples add a touch of extra dignity that qualifies them for semi-formal occasions."

For formal business and evening occasions there was a streamlined version of the classic gold-filled frame: "It comes in gold or with rhodium plating—metal is always your most distinctive rim for evening wear, only slightly less formal than rimless models. This one is equally good for the conference room."

Also shown was a pinstripe equivalent of horn-rims that, according to the caption writer, would go anywhere you would wear horn-rims and were "tough enough for lots of on-and-off treatment while you gesticulate. The pin-stripe pattern is a little livelier than the standard tortoise shell, with the advantage of a color range that has something for everyone: brown, grey, flesh, demi-amber and demi-blond. Whichever looks best with your coloring is fine for sports or casual business."

A pair of mock-tortoiseshell sunglasses was sketched. To get full value of sunglasses, *Esquire* recommended

Unbreakable lenses and frames.

Squared lenses, narrow gold frames.

Thin frames set off circular lenses.

Heavy frames, slightly curved lenses.

Frameless lenses joined by double bar.

Bottle-green lenses and metallic trim.

Shades and shapes made fashions in glasses in 1969. From Esquire, *May 1969.*

that a man know his lenses. "Sage green is for average glare conditions, good everyday protection. Gradient density lenses are for extra-tough overhead glare or light reflected from water, snow or highway. (The trick with these is metallic coating which increases in thickness from center to top, or to both top and bottom on the 'double gradient' models.) Neutral grey lenses give a really true color view in brilliant sunlight and, for this reason, have become standard for the U.S. Armed Forces. Beyond that, you can find special yellow glass for sharp vision on hazy days; red and orange lenses for special snow conditions, and so on."

Sports or skeet glasses for shooting, fishing, or sports in general had large, deep-curve lenses to protect vision

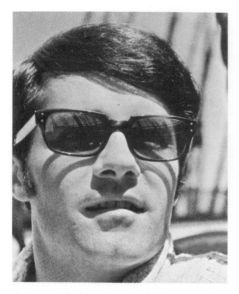

Amber sunglasses were styled with angular detailing in 1971. [AMERICAN OPTICAL CORPORATION]

from all angles and a special lens-hardening treatment that made them impact-resistant. Brow bars, said the caption writer, served "a double function in holding the glasses dependably still while you take aim, plus guarding against perspiration from your forehead on hot days."

In 1968 *Gentlemen's Quarterly* commented that now that eyeglasses had become fashionable, men with bad eyes could finally be proud of them. Glasses, the writer Tom Ferrell said, were now so stylish that "a very well-turned out young executive might show up at the office in a different pair every day of the week." Furthermore, there were special-purpose glasses: a wire-rimmed pair for contact sports; and golf bifocals, with a tiny short-focus spot just big enough to read the scorecard with, leaving the rest of the visual field clear.

This *Gentlemen's Quarterly* feature also gave its approval to rimless glasses— "very chic among European students, especially French, and reasonably becoming with longer men's hair styles." Perfectly round tortoiseshells, with low bridges and thin rims, were rated "fine for withdrawing from the world and looking smart." Lenses tinted for purely cosmetic purposes were most often seen in neutral gray, although "outlandish tones—bottle-blue or garnet red" were available for extroverted men. Lenses tinted in yellow were deemed "particularly chic, since they are actually shooting glasses, and they call up visions of hunt country and boxes in Scotland to the susceptible."

For its May, 1969, issue *Esquire* photographed a collection of sunglasses that clearly showed the fashion influence of the Peacock Revolution: squared lenses with narrow gold frames, frameless lenses joined by a double bar, heavy frames with slightly curved lenses, circular lenses set off by thin frames; and pilot's glasses with the coated portion of the lens preventing glare while the lower part allowed a clear view.

What kind of sunglasses should a man select? In *Your Sunglasses and Your Eyes* the Better Vision Institute asked this question and answered: "It is important to wear sunglasses with precisely ground and polished lenses of flawless ophthalmic quality. The glass or plastic used must be as fine as that used for everyday corrective spectacles, but with extra properties of light-filtering or light-softening added."

In the early seventies, a major advance in sunglass fashions was made through the development of a polarized lens that, although nearly a clear true-color gray indoors, grew progressively darker when worn outdoors, how much darker depending on the brightness of the sun. The peacock of the seventies took a fresh view of the world, and it was appropriate that the glasses he looked through should express his new viewpoint.

Luggage

No. 21647 Grain Leather Gladstone. This bag is made from the very best full stock grain leather, double strong frame, nickel corner protectors, large nickel lock, with combination handle, heavy English snap catches, grain leather straps, full leather lined.
Brown and Orange.

14 inch.	Each.....$3.75	20 inch.	Each.....$4.88
16 inch.	Each..... 4.12	22 inch.	Each..... 5.25
18 inch.	Each..... 4.50		

No. 21650 Leather Gladstone. Very fine pebble leather, grain leather straps all around, double flange frame, large nickel flat key lock, heavy nickel catches, double stitched leather handle, heavy rings, linen lined.
Brown.

14 inch.	Each.....$1.55	20 inch.	Each.....$2.45
16 inch.	Each..... 1.75	22 inch.	Each..... 2.65
18 inch.	Each..... 1.95		

No. 21652 Alligator Leather Gladstone. Made of selected goatskin leather, heavy double flange frame, nickel double hasp lock and side catches, heavy English handle, with ring attachment, cloth lined, portfolio. Tan and chestnut.

14 inch.	Each.....$1.70	20 inch.	Each.....$2.30
16 inch.	Each..... 1.90	22 inch.	Each..... 2.50
18 inch.	Each..... 2.10		

Canvas Gladstone.
Strong, Serviceable and Popular.

No. 21655 This is an exceptionally **Fine Gladstone Bag.** Made from extra heavy canvas with morocco leather corners, grain leather straps all around and large handsomely nickel-plated lock. Finely japanned frame and heavy stitched grain leather handle. Full linen lined. **One of our specially good values.**

14 inch............ $1.37	20 inch............ $1.90
16 inch............ 1.50	22 inch............ 2.25
18 inch............ 1.67	

Canvas Cabin Bag.
The Handsomest Bag ever Made.

No. 21657 The **Famous Canvas Cabin Bag.** Made from extra strong heavy weight canvas. Opens at top with spring clasps.

14 in., price.. $0.74	18 in., price.. .98
16 in., price.. .85	20 in., price.. 1.05
22 in., price..... $1.25	

Canvas Telescope Cases.

No. 21658. Riveted leather corner and bottom tips, heavy stitched handle; two straps.

14 inch.	Each......$0.35	20 inch.	Each.....$0.65
16 inch.	Each...... 0.45	22 inch.	Each..... 0.75
18 inch.	Each...... 0.55	24 inch.	Each..... 0.85

No. 21659 Heavy canvas, leather bound, hand sewed, heavy leather tips, grain leather straps all around.

16 inch.	Each.....$1.10	22 inch.	Each.....$1.75
18 inch.	Each..... 1.25	24 inch.	Each..... 1.98
20 inch.	Each..... 1.50	26 inch.	Each..... 2.23

With patent lock strap, 50 cents extra.

No. 21660 Extra Heavy Canvas; edges bound all around with wide leather; very heavy corner protectors; two and three sole leather straps; best handle made.

16 in., each ...$2.00	
18 in., each ... 2.50	
20 in., each..........$2.85	22 in., each..........3.25
24 in., each......... 3.60	

Since men's clothes in the first decade of the twentieth century consisted of heavily padded, oversize suits, shirts with high, starched collars, and high-buttoned shoes, the man of fashion required luggage ample enough to accommodate such a wardrobe. A trip abroad, for example, called for a steamer or stateroom trunk (it would return home "decorated" with the labels of the best foreign hotels). The pages of the 1900 Sears, Roebuck and Company catalog advertised such formidable, almost fortresslike trunks, and the descriptive copy listed the following selling features: "Sole leather straps, canvas covered, heavy Japanned steel clamps and corners. A *large box* covered with heavy canvas, painted, wide iron bound, heavy hardwood slats full length of trunk, body and end slats, heavy bumpers and steel clamps, rollers, etc. and *brassed Excelsior lock,* with heavy bolts, iron bound, all protected with *two heavy sole leather straps,* high set-up tray with hat box, and slide compartments all separately covered and cloth faced."

The twentieth century ushered in the automotive era, and with it came many changes in luggage. Individual hand wardrobe cases gained in popularity over the family trunk. Hand luggage in canvas, for instance, came to the fore, and the term "valise" was rather loosely applied to many different types of hand luggage. The gladstone bag proved immensely popular with men and was soon the largest-selling type of luggage. A forerunner of the modern suiter bag, it had two

The grain-leather gladstone bag was a leader at the turn of the century, as featured in the catalog of Sears, Roebuck and Company.

16L01 Trunks, flat top, canvas covered, with trays, 38 inches

Same for boys, 34 inches
16L02 Black-enamel Duck Continental Steamer Trunks, 36 inches
38 inches
16L03 Wardrobe Regulation Trunks in various grades, to hold 6 to 10 suits, 40 to 45 inches

16L04 Auto Boxes, black enamel, dust-proof, with tray and heavy pigskin trimmings and brass lever lock, 26 to 30 inches

16L05 Steamer Trunks, 34 to 44 inches
16L06 Oval Top Trunks, brown, canvas covered, two trays and accommodation for silk hat, 36 inches

16L07 Suburban Cases
Other Suburban and Week-end Cases
16L08 Small Week-end Trunks, 26 inches
16L09 English Portmanteaux or Coat Cases, 27 inches
30 inches
16L10 English Golf Kit Bags Tan grain leather
Grain Carpet

Sole Leather Fishing-rod and Umbrella Case, 46 inches
16L11 English Sole Leather Trunks
Wood Fibre Orient Trunks, with tray
16L12 English Kit Bags, heavy sole leather, with straps sewn on side
Smaller Collapsible Bags, 16 to 20 inches
Pigskin Grips

(left) Wardrobe trunks, steamer trunks, and automobile boxes were in demand in 1915 by long journey travelers. (right) Spacious portmanteaus, along with trunks and golf kit bags, were the choice of seasoned voyagers that year. [COURTESY OF BROOKS BROTHERS, NEW YORK]

sides of equal depth, one for jackets and trousers and the other for accessories. The gladstone opened flat like a book, and its two parts were joined at the bottom by special hinges attached to the vertical frame sections.

A flat steel crossbar was riveted to the bottom of the bag. Gladstones were made either rigid or soft, and the Sears catalog showed both kinds in every material from selected grain leather, alligator leather, and heavy sheepskin

16L13 Cabin Bags for soiled linen

16L14 Leather Travelling Pillows

16L15 Steamer Rugs in great variety

16L16-18 English Grips, 18 to 24 inches

Gladstone Bags

16L17 English Sole-leather Suit Cases

Special light-weight Suit Cases. Double lock

Suit Cases in various sizes

Coat Case. Double lock, leather lined, 26 inches

Black-enamel Cases

Leather-lined Suit Cases

16L19 Shawl Straps in various sizes

Umbrella Straps

Bag & Trunk Tags

16L20 Holdalls of waterproof canvas

16L21 English Kit Bags, 26 inches

16L22 English Hat Boxes, oval shape, Single

Double

Treble

16L23 Black-enamel Hand-bags, club shape, 17 to 23 inches

Stanley shape, 17 to 21 inches

16L24 Tan Grain Leather Handbags, 17 to 23 inches

Stanley shape, 17 to 21 inches

16L25 Square English Hat Boxes, to hold three or more hats 18 inches

16L26 Square Single Hat Boxes, sateen lining

Leather lining

Square Hat Boxes, to hold three or more hats, 18 inches

(left) The gladstone and English kit bags were outstanding in the array of articles for the traveler presented in the 1915 Brooks Brothers catalog. (right) Leather luggage for headwear appealed to the properly dressed man in 1915. [COURTESY OF BROOKS BROTHERS, NEW YORK]

to canvas. They were available in sizes ranging from 18 to 28 inches, the 24- and 26-inch sizes being the most popular.

Almost as popular as the gladstone, but today almost obsolete, was the kit bag made in 22-, 24-, and 26-inch sizes, with a few in a 28-inch or even a 30-inch size for European travel. The kit bag was usually in a rectangular box shape (some models were V-shaped), with a "square mouth" frame that opened to the full width. Two straps usually went all around the bag. All in all, the kit bag's massive size, thoroughly masculine styling, and roominess made it a great favorite.

Also popular but not generally considered stylish was the telescope case, which was inexpensively made and therefore quite common. Designed in two separate sections, one of which fitted inside the other, it resembled a gift box and lid. The 1900 Sears catalog advertised telescope cases made of heavy canvas with riveted leather corner and bottom tips and grain-leather straps all around. A 26-inch size cost $2.23, and with a patent lock strap, $2.73.

1920–1930

After World War I and all during the following period of affluence, the American man was increasingly fashion-conscious, and this attitude quite naturally influenced the luggage he chose for travel. "If the Pullman porter's eye glistens when he spots the smart-looking bag, others, too, are apt to estimate the man by his luggage," observed *Men's Wear*. "Cheap and battered bags draw porters only after the smart luggage disappears. Porters are self-trained to detect the best tip possibilities and the man with smart luggage looks like ready money" (May 23, 1923, p. 82).

In the same issue, *Men's Wear* reported as follows: "Many men are buying traveling bags with an eye to their picturesque effect, just as women buy ornamental dogs to sit with the chauffeur or gowns that will be in harmony with the tapestry of the parlor furniture. When buying a traveling bag it is not only a question of whether it will safely transport a maximum of luggage for its size, but the question develops along the line of whether it is the smart thing to be seen with as well.

"Right now the English type of kit bag is the proper thing to be seen with. Each season brings an increasing call for kit bags and a commensurate lessening of interest in the suitcase, not that the suitcase is not still the best selling article of luggage, but rather that the smart dressers find the kit bag an aid to the *tout ensemble* they desire to create. The suitcase is just a trifle too democratic, too plebian, for the kind of customer who was among the first to wear a madder foulard scarf, and those who followed him with respect to the scarf likewise have been leaning to the kit bag. The call now is the big stuff in the way of luggage. Big kit bags, bags that are the size of trunks, extra size suitcases, and, in fact, everything that is wanted, seems to be wanted in large sizes."

The reporter conceded that a big kit bag was an awkward travel companion aboard a pullman sleeper. Nevertheless, he said, "customers are buying kit bags because they like their looks."

By the 1920s the gladstone had declined somewhat in popularity, but it showed signs of making a comeback, "to a limited extent, probably because it is old enough to be new to a lot of customers." It had advantages and disadvantages, however, and a *Men's Wear* writer noted both:

"The traveler can open it up and select desired articles from one side of it without disturbing the contents of the other side. But it has the disadvantage of being too small to contain a suit of clothes in anything like the pristine freshness with which it was first packed. None but the most expert may pack a suit in this container and hope to remove it unwrinkled. In addition, its width does not permit it to get into places that will comfortably accommodate a suitcase. However, there is more interest exhibited in Gladstone bags than has been the case in a long time" (Apr. 25, 1928, p. 98).

The coat case, a kind of glorified gladstone, was an attempt to eliminate one of these disadvantages. By virtue of its larger size, usually 28 or 26 inches by 12 inches, it could accommodate a nicely folded suit.

Light-colored leather became popular in luggage during the twenties but only to a limited extent, since the new shades of London cream and light

Brown leather luggage in various shapes and a briefcase were among the requirements of the traveling executive in 1934. From Esquire, *February 1934.*

A big green trunk (lower left) and various types of cases were a part of the scene at customs in 1939. From Esquire, *July 1939.*

walrus bag was often the incentive chosen. But now, as it faded from the scene, the man of fashion discovered that the bag of whale hide was just as tough and serviceable but had the added advantage of being light in weight.

In 1928 a *Men's Wear* writer, while noting that Americans were doing more traveling both in the United States and abroad, deplored the fact that luggage was suffering what he called a "serious affliction." To wit: "A considerable part of the business in traveling equipment in the United States is done by pawn shops." Certainly, he continued, the logical shop for a man to buy his luggage was not "an establishment where unfortunates have deposited the family watch, but rather the place where smart grooming and the care of clothing is the life-blood of the business." As far as he was concerned, the merchant indifferent to the advantages of a luggage department was missing "one of the tricks in modern business." The writer also urged luggage manufacturers to be alert and ingenious in developing styles and models, "because this is such a fiercely contested market that only those in step with mechanical progress may survive.

"Years ago, a trunk was just a box whose chief merit was its ability to resist the savage energy of baggage handlers. Today the trunk is a traveling wardrobe. The customer of today has so many dress requirements that were absent in the preceding generation and he travels so much more frequently that his traveling equipment must match his manner of living. The wardrobe trunk was a development of this and it permitted men to go about with their suits nicely hung on hangers, trousers neatly pressed, shoes and hats safely accommodated, jewelry in place, and, in fact, a man can now live in his trunk.

"The latest development is to add the features of the wardrobe trunk to the traveling bag. A container that is selling today in large numbers is practically an enlarged suitcase, as to form, but its interior equipment is much like

chestnut were generally thought to soil easily and, most important, sometimes the tanning and matching of the different parts of a piece of luggage were not well done and the parts turned out in different shades. As a result, the more dependable color russet was the masculine favorite. Meanwhile, the college man was beginning

to show a penchant for trunks with stripes in college or fraternity colors.

The twenties saw the demise of the walrus bag and the advance of the bag made of whale hide. The walrus bag had been tremendously popular during the first two decades of the century; when a firm wanted to offer a prize to its salesmen, for example, a

that of the wardrobe trunk. One of these, which is 29 inches long, can fit under a Pullman berth. Its clothes hangers will carry five suits of clothes and there is a compartment for shoes and a haberdashery tray. This also comes with a cover for automobile travel" (*Men's Wear,* Apr. 25, 1928, p. 98).

By the late twenties 85 percent of all traveling bags came in color. This writer reported that these wardrobe trunks were made in six colors, often to match the colors of the various makes of popular cars. "A particularly well received color is grey, picked out in a red stripe. Women, however, are the better customers for the colored cases, while men prefer them in brown."

In hand luggage, meanwhile, the gladstone continued to gain in favor. It was especially popular with undergraduates in walrus-grain seal, which was lighter and therefore more acceptable than the now-defunct walrus bag.

The attaché case of tan cowhide with a red leather lining accommodated papers and a change of linen. From Esquire, *March 1949.*

1930–1940

The thirties were a decade of casual elegance in men's clothes, and lightweight, stylish-looking luggage was considered essential. Consequently, leather was, as a *Men's Wear* reporter put it, "slipping from the luggage throne. A solid leather bag of good stout cowhide was once and still is to some extent the king of the trade. But it is wobbling. The men have seen some of the things that are being made for the ladies and they like them. Weight is a consideration all along the line. The traveller by autobus or automobile cannot depend upon porters and red caps at convenient points—that is, points convenient for the traveller. After hefting a solid leather suitcase, a kit bag and a Gladstone in and out of the rumble seat of a car half a dozen times, the man who travels begins to look around for something that will give as much service and will weigh a lot less.

"He also wants looks. He wants color too, if he can get it. He has a new and gleaming car, the chances are, or at least he keeps it gleaming if he has any pride (and he probably has, being a traveller); therefore his luggage must also be new and gleaming. If modern man travels by train he requires that the train be aircooled, or heated according to the season, and he demands the last word in fittings and convenience. He wants to wash, to dine, to listen to the radio, and his luggage must be in tune with the luxury note. A shabby suitcase,

The rigid suitcase with detailing like that of a trunk had a strong appeal for the voyager. From Esquire, *August 1939.*

sticking its corner out from under his section seat or in shoddy evidence in his compartment, simply will not do.

"Hence the new ideas in leather and in fabrics which are going into men's luggage. Not so long ago the colorful canvas was the lady's prerogative. [Canvas coverings for hand luggage and hard wardrobe luggage were first introduced in 1925. Hitherto, the most common covering had been cowhide.] Now the sterner sex, finding canvas light, durable and colorful, has taken to it and the sale of canvas to men is increasing. Rawhide is an innovation in men's luggage and an extremely sensible one. The leather is light in weight and it takes a fine, smooth and durable finish. It is virtually indestructible at its best and it is smart looking. It may be that rawhide luggage will be the first challenger of importance to pigskin, which has long been the leather *de luxe* for luxury luggage. Pigskin, it might be said, is the high style item of men's luggage.

"A new finish for luggage which will be featured by one of the smart Fifth Avenue shops in New York is the football grain. That round, smallish, pebbly-grained leather which has distinguished footballs for so many years makes an ideal covering for luggage, too. It is rough and tough and will stand the gaff. Football leather likes the boys to play rough and is prepared to take it.

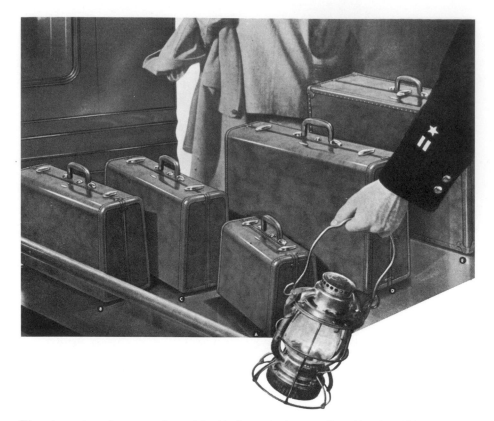

necessary. But the ultimate solution lay in the synthetic materials that soon influenced both luggage design and construction, with fixtures of aluminum and Duralumin and hangers in plastic, vinyl and other plastic films, and plastic laminates. (Plastic luggage was first developed for the Army Air Force during World War II in the form of Fiberglas cut in the shape of a suitcase.)

World War II curtailed civilian travel and naturally had a dampening effect on the luggage industry, but one of the positive effects of the war years was the popularization of the zipper closure in hand luggage through its use in the cloth hand luggage carried by army officers. From then on the metal zipper continued to be used increasingly in all kinds of luggage (in the late sixties, the lightweight nylon zipper, heretofore used primarily in clothing, began to appear in luggage, too).

By 1949 *Men's Wear,* while commenting that "nobody expects a boom in luggage," conceded that many manufacturers hoped to be out of the

The color cordovan brown was featured in this Samsonite luggage. From Esquire, *February 1949.*

"Another smart finish in men's luggage leather for the fall and winter season is the English long grain, an old favorite with those who know and love good leather. This has divided popularity with pigskin in the upper reaches in some places. Buffalo, baby walrus and shark finishes are also being asked for.

"Luggage is distinctly becoming a style item" (*Men's Wear,* Sept. 5, 1934).

Fashion (even moustaches) showed the British influence that dominated this decade, and in May, 1934, *Esquire* devoted a page that, it said, was "all very much in the English manner, from the somewhat surprising combination of bowler hat and pullover sweater to the shape and proportions of the shirt collar." The model alighting from a train, carrying a pencil-slim umbrella under his arm and a polo coat over it, was accompanied by a porter who carried his golf bag and his weekend travel bag, a box-shaped kit bag featuring one wide white and one

wide blue stripe running vertically down the center of the bag on both sides. In 1936 *Esquire* devoted a full-color page to packing a suitcase, a feature that included a blueprint, suggesting that the greatest saving in both time and temper would be accomplished "by having an allotted place for everything and having everything in its allotted place."

1940–1960

With the expansion in air travel during the next decade there was an even greater emphasis on lighter-weight luggage, since airlines limited the amount of luggage that might be carried without payment of extra charges to 40 pounds on travel within the United States and 55 pounds on intercontinental travel. The first "airplane" luggage used the same basswood, plywood, veneers, and canvases employed in the making of airplanes, where lightweight construction was

The trunk with reinforcements at edges and corners, drawers, and hangers was among the luggage featured in 1954. From Esquire, *February 1954.*

doldrums in 1950. In the meantime, more and more young Americans were becoming ski enthusiasts, and the winter vacation was giving the luggage retailer a vigorous second selling period.

In 1954 *Esquire* gave its readers a kind of preview of the shoulder tote bag that would be in vogue more than a decade later. The fashion staff christened the bag the "side-kick" and explained that it was engineered "so that front may be extended forward to allow easy access to cigarettes, lighter, passport, pencil, etc." It was made of rugged leather, shaped like a trout fisherman's creel, and would, said *Esquire,* take "those lumps out of your pockets by taking over hand-sized necessities every guy wants to have nearby, but not necessarily stashed away on his person."

In April of that year, *Esquire,* in an editorial salute to the innate beauty, durability, and utility of leather ("leather naturally expresses the masculine character"), showed some of the types of merchandise in which leather was arousing fresh fashion interest. Along with footwear, jackets, vests, gloves, and belts, it displayed bags in soft-side carryall, two-suiter, and small zippered styles as well as in a frame construction. "In luggage and small leather goods . . . leather is the fashion leader," was the conclusion.

This was the decade of the "man in the gray flannel suit," a conservative man who invariably carried his business papers in an attaché case. The smallest-size suitcase, the attaché case became extremely popular with businessmen and remained popular throughout the sixties and, to a somewhat less degree, into the seventies. A shallow case made in sizes ranging from 14 to 20 inches, it derived its name from its original use by British attachés in the diplomatic service to carry important documents. The model imported from England was frequently leather-lined, with no interior pockets, and of steel-frame construction. The American-made version was made more often than not over a wood frame, was fabric-lined, and

came either with one pocket in the lid or with a nest of staggered pockets.

1960–1970

In 1966 *Esquire* published a book, *Esquire Fashions for Men,* in which it devoted a chapter to travel tips (pp. 182ff.), noting: "Wherever you are going, and for whatever the time you are going to spend, there is a suitcase somewhere that is just the right size and shape for you. It is hardly any problem to find it. Nowadays it's pretty easy to come by lightweight suitcases, because synthetic materials have made it possible to produce them. And furthermore, they are as rugged, if not more so, as the old heavy models of a few years ago.

"The new vinyl coatings and synthetics simulating good leather are looked on with favor because of their durability. And the new expandable, soft-sided suitcases of vinyl or leather

are especially popular because, as one traveling executive said, 'You can stuff them like a pregnant cow.'"

Running down the list of preferred luggage, the writer described the following styles:

The one-suiter. Definitely a trend. This small suitcase is most commonly seen with "soft" sides and a zippered closure. It is just small enough in over-all size to rate as a "carry-on" suitcase. In other words, you can take it right on the jet with you and put it under your seat. Aside from the obvious benefit of saving time at the airport, this case is an efficient means of getting yourself about on a short business trip.

The suit frame. Since one-suiters are pretty low on space, if you do not take particular precautions while packing you may wrinkle your suit. Enter the Suit Frame. This little gimmick enables you to pack your suit neatly and make sure that it doesn't get mashed into a corner in transit. Basically it consists of a square metal frame that folds in half. A hanger is attached to one side and rod goes across the middle. You start out by folding your

This carry-on luggage of 1971 featured four elements: a hanging suit bag, a briefcase, and a shaving kit in one soft-sided bag. It came in black or tan vinyl. [SAMSONITE LUGGAGE]

A carry-on one-suiter of 1971, weighing 7 pounds, with a removable suit rack. The covering is made of vinyl. [AMERICAN TOURISTER]

trousers separately and placing them in the bottom of the case (you don't need any frame for them). Then the jacket is placed on the hanger with the center rod in front and the lower rod behind. The sleeves are folded around the sides of the jacket, and then the frame is folded over itself twice. It makes quite a neat package, and it will stay that way until you unpack it many miles away.

Expanded one-suiter. This new model combines suitcase and briefcase. In the service of "economy" one could hardly ask for a more efficient use of space.

The two-suiter. Let us say you are going on a longer trip. The one-suiter isn't big enough, so you'll have to use a two-suiter (and, of course, you'll have to check it at the gate when you board the plane). One

of the tricky things about it is, again, packing the suits properly. If you aren't going to use the frame, try folding them this way. Lay the trousers in the case. Place the jacket on top of it with the sleeves folded in front. Then fold in the bottoms of the trousers and, over them, the ends of the jacket. This makes a secure, interlocking bundle that stays put.

The stand-up bag. A brand new unique item, on rollers, this model has engendered quite a good deal of interest. It is a kind of portable closet which stands about a yard tall and resembles the canvas fold-over wardrobe bags, except that it can't be folded. A capacious item, it can be made to contain even more by using two ingenious triangular plastic packs. These fit right above each shoulder and hold small things like socks, handkerchiefs, jewelry.

During the sixties luggage shapes and types changed very little. Even the traveling garment bag was basically one of the features of the original dress trunk and resembled the conventional suitcase when folded for carrying. In March, 1969, however, *Esquire* went out on a limb and predicted shaped luggage: "Now, at mercifully long last, an end to all the knocked knees, all the bruised bodies, suffered as one tried to carry his bags through Kennedy or Grand Central in time of contumelious congestion." The answer, said the fashion department, was new Italian-designed contoured luggage that permitted a man to cradle a suitcase to his body or leg. The samples photographed in color were made of hand-stained antiqued leather and had Florentine-finish brass snap locks, buckled straps, hand-tooled edges and trim, and contoured handles. Yet, although shaped luggage was as attractive as it was utilitarian, it did not catch on.

The Peacock Revolution could not help but have an effect on luggage, since by this time luggage had become a full-fledged fashion accessory for both sexes. And since Americans by now were using so many different modes of travel, their luggage had to be adaptable, that is, light in weight, easy to handle, and as sturdy as possible. The fashionable man of the seventies, as a result, had a wider selection than ever to choose from. New luggage

This group of bags combines the casual appearance of corduroy, popular in apparel, with sturdiness (1971). [BAGAVOND BY ATLANTIC]

Blue Denim by Bill Blass

(above) Blue denim, a classic fabric in many categories of apparel, was utilized in 1971 by Bill Blass in designing this group of bags and cases. [WINGS BY UNITED LUGGAGE CO., INC.]

(right) Christian Dior luggage for men and women, designed in 1971 by Marc Dior, the chief designer of the firm, features covering that is a vinyl interpretation of the Dior signature tapestry and sculptured handles. [MANUFACTURED BY THE BALTIMORE LUGGAGE COMPANY]

included a calf-trimmed flight bag of water-repellent cotton that was so compactly sized it could slip under an airline seat and yet, complete with hangers and rack, serve as a week-ender, briefcase, grooming kit, and overnighter all in one; a jaunty fabric

Fashions in vinyl luggage of various types, ranging from a mini car bag and an attaché case to a two-suiter and an eight-suit garment carrier (1971). [AMERICAN TOURISTER]

suitcase with leather trim and a detachable shoulder strap; and a folding suitcase of cotton and rayon with vinyl trim and an outside zippered pocket.

Meanwhile, there was still a need for trunks, and the larger, medium-sized, and small wardrobe trunks in which garments could be hung as in a closet were in demand for long trips by ship. But unlike the trunks of the early decades of the century, the new wardrobe trunks were much lighter in weight and were available in smaller sizes and styles suited even for briefer trips.

Vinyl was as popular as ever in this era when men traveled by every conveyance from jet airplanes to motor bicycles. Not only was it stain-, tear-, and scuff-resistant and cleanable with soap and water, but it was now made to look like suede. The shoulder tote bag with its roomy interiors and zipper pockets, in soft vinyl or supple leather, was an important part of the luggage of the seventies. Noteworthy, too, were leather bags with such markings as scratches and brands still on them. Whether styled as a suitcase or as a shoulder tote, these rugged leather bags were the epitome of globe-circling sophistication.

A lot has happened to luggage since the days when it was first made to hold a Stone Age ax. Man has progressed from foot to horseback, from carriages to ships, from railroads to automobiles, and from propeller planes to jets. Spaceships are no longer futuristic curiosities but an actual mode of transportation, and before this century is over they may well become a form of civilian transportation. And as man's clothes adapt to space travel, so will his luggage, for in this century luggage has become a fashion accessory as well as a travel necessity and consequently the real revolution in luggage is still ahead of us.

Leather Goods

The innate beauty, durability, and utility of leather impart a lasting quality that has significant appeal for men. Luxurious in hand, varied in color, supple and adaptable to many different design interpretations and end uses, leather naturally expresses the masculine character." This excerpt is taken from an *Esquire* feature published in April, 1954, but had the magazine been in existence in the first decade of this century, it might well have said the same thing. For leather has been a fashion leader for generations.

The extent to which leather goods contributed to the distinctiveness of a fashionable man's wardrobe and toilet in the second decade of this century can be gauged by leafing through the Brooks Brothers catalog of 1915. Under the heading "Leather Goods & Sundries" we find the following: travel clocks in leather cases; leather jewel cases; leather cravat cases, silk-lined; shirt cases; novelty coat hangers in small leather cases; scissors cases; fitted English dressing cases; English sole-leather boot kits; shoe trunks with heavy pigskin trimmings and brass lever locks; razor strops; a folding hat brush and buffer in a leather case; sole-leather cases for brushes; English golf kit bags of tan grain leather; a sole-leather fishing-rod and umbrella case; and flasks covered in wicker and leather. There were also leather luggage, leather riding canes, walking sticks and umbrellas with leather handles, and collapsible shooting seats of leather for use in the country and at horse and dog shows.

16L27 Unfitted Suit Cases

16L28 Same Cases with solid silver fittings
Fitted Carriage Bag, 18 to 20 inches
16L29 Unfitted Dressing Rolls, with adjustable straps
16L30 Scissors Cases

16L31 Fitted English Dressing Cases

16L32 "Bonsa" Tool Companions
Pocket Knives
16L33 English Sole-leather Boot Kits
English Fibre Boot Kits, 30 inches, with one tray
With two trays
Shoe Trunks, black-enamel duck, tray, heavy pigskin trimmings, brass lever lock, 15 x 21 in. x 12 in. deep

Leather goods continued to gain popularity during the affluent twenties, and *Men's Wear* noted: "Leather goods are today playing such an important part in the wardrobe of the well dressed man that any development or introduction of new ideas is well worthy of consideration by the live retailer" (Jan. 20, 1926, p. 70).

The writer added: "The development of sport has necessitated an equivalent development in traveling gear and equipment," illustrating this point with photographs of a golf bag made from natural pigskin, fitted with "the new lightning fastening and the lock fast hood to protect the club heads"; and a novelty tennis kit case, featuring

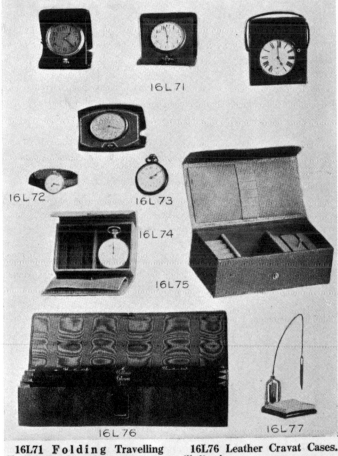

16L71 Folding Travelling Clocks, run thirty hours

Eight-Day Clocks
Radium Clocks
16L72 Wrist Watches

Radium Wrist Watches

16L73 Alarm Watches
Radium Alarm Watches
16L74 Stop Watches
16L75 Leather Jewel Cases

16L76 Leather Cravat Cases. silk lined
Sole-leather Collar Boxes and collar bags
Leather Watch Alberts

Silver Key Chains
Shirt Cases
16L77 Handy Pencils
With pads attached
Silver and Gold Pencils

Novelty Coat Hangers, in small leather cases

16L78, 80 Wallets, Card Cases, and Bill Folds, unlined and with leather or silk lining

16L79 Leather Photograph Cases

16L81-82 Leather-covered Notebooks and Diaries

16L83 Leather Writing Cases

16L84 Motor and Aeroplane Records

16L85 Tuck Purses and Coin Cases

16L86 Leather Letter Racks

16L87 Key Cases
16L88 Document Cases

Pigskin Brief Cases
Poker Patience Sets
Bridge Sets
Leather-covered Clips
Despatch Boxes

Everything necessary for perfect grooming was to be found in the fitted case of red-lined black cowhide at lower right. From Esquire, *January 1938.*

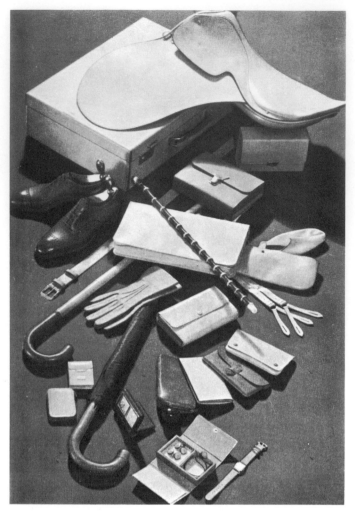

Pigskin in a variety of uses: (top to bottom) a pigskin saddle, a suitcase, a bottle case, a traveling utility case, a fitted case, town shoes, a whangee and pigskin riding cane, a belt, a malacca cane with a pigskin handle, pullman slippers, braces, a trout fly book, gloves, a silk umbrella with a pigskin handle, a cigarette case, a wallet, a jewelry box, a traveling clock, pigskin cuff links and watch guard, and a wristwatch with a pigskin strap. From Esquire, *April 1938.*

a special compartment of soft leather fitted to the outside of an ordinary attaché case large enough to hold a change of flannels.

Novelty goods in the 1930s were, as one writer put it, "one of the big present-day influences, making everyone more conscious of the niceties and amenities of life. All men like nice things and all men fall for shiny toys, for that is what they are in the final analysis—toys for grown-ups" (*Men's Wear,* Sept. 11, 1935, p. 78). Among these luxury "toys" were a roulette wheel and chips handsomely enclosed in a pigskin traveling case; a combination checkers, chess, dice, and domino set in a black calf case; a police dog–pattern clothes brush of leather; and a leather cigar humidor with a chromium lid.

In the same issue *Men's Wear* noted: "What with streamlining and air conditioning, travelling has become not only a pleasure, but a dream of luxury. Accessories for the man who lives in trunks and suitcases, or for that other traveller who travels to see things and for pleasure, have been styled to suit their ultra-modern surroundings. Everything that may be made compact and readily accessible has been cased in a special fitting of its own and the interior of a Gladstone bag no longer looks like the Sunday newspa-

per after the pup has been at it. The toilet cases, those necessities among the luxury fittings, have gone modern. One of the leathers that is being featured is 'hazel pig' which is somewhat darker than natural pig and stands the gaff better. In this leather, with fittings in dull, black, modern design, toilet and brush sets are the last word.

"There are also billfolds, some of them big enough for money, travellers' checks, letter of credit and passport—almost attache cases. There are neckwear and shirt boxes. Black, with color, with chromium, or with both, is used. One of the best selling items of the whole list, however, is just a case without anything in it. It is made about the size of a large toilet kit, is in stiffened leather and is lined inside with oiled silk. Men like them for their own assortments of toiletries" (Sept. 11, 1935, p. 16).

Accompanying this article were photographs of a tan calf toilet set, a brown-and-yellow composition cigarette box, a hazel pigskin case with black-and-white brushes, a pigskin collar and stud case, a traveling clock in a brown leather case, a pigskin case with a complete toilet set, a toilet set in a pigskin case with an oiled-silk bag, and a hazel pigskin wallet.

"Christmas is not really Christmas without the faint aroma of tanned leather," commented a *Men's Wear* writer in 1936. "Someone in the family is bound to receive a toilet set, billfold, wallet, tobacco pouch, utility case, necktie and handkerchief case, a manicure set or some other article in leather. For this year the showings are quite comprehensive and lean heavily to the luxury side. The dull glow of fine hazel pigskin sets off the chrome or satinwood fixtures of the toilet sets. Even gold plating adorns the fixtures of some. The saddle stitching on stout cowhide has its stylish air. The combination overnight case and toilet set has its practical features. Wallets and billfolds range all the way from jacquarded black silk for evening to the hazel pigskin and antelope leathers. Fitted tobacco pouches appear in sharkskin and other strong leathers. Manicure sets for men are perking up.

"The leathers used are satisfactory to the most discriminating buyer, who seeks fine quality, utility and style in toilet sets. Hazel pigskin is in the platinum class. Its dull glow, which grows duller with use, appeals to men and women alike. Cowhide is not only stout and practical, but has a sporty touch in the saddle-stitched edges. It is seen not only in the fitted cases, but also in the utility case, sans fittings, but with oiled silk lining. Alligator, walrus, buffalo and sealskin are pres-

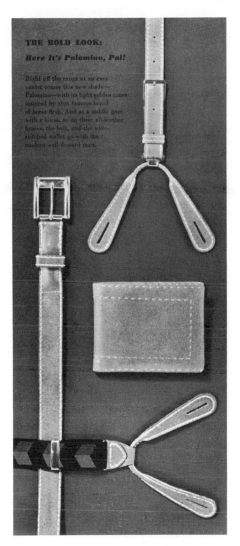

A light palomino shade was used for these "bold look" leather accessories: braces, belt, and wallet. From Esquire, *May 1949.*

ent in the showings.

"Leather cases for furnishings items are most popular if they are in the same leathers as the toilet cases. Tie cases, collar boxes with jewelry compartments and handkerchief cases are all to be had in these leathers. A novel touch is the combination of pigskin with two-tone morocco.

"Tobacco pouches, both fitted and plain, are offered in different leathers. Hazel pigskin, sharkskin and fine suede are in the better grade brackets" (Sept. 9, 1936, p. 22).

Photographs of the following leather goods accompanied this article: a saddle-stitched cowhide tie case

and rack; an alligator billfold with space for a passport book and a concealed compartment for bills; a hazel pigskin toilet set with sandalwood fittings; a combination wallet and key case in black leather; an ostrich-skin wallet; a fitted tobacco pouch in sharkskin; a black antelope hip-pocket case for cigarettes; a tan calf utility case with saddle stitching, an oiled-silk lining, and a slide-fastener top; a toilet set with nonbreakable composition fittings in a cowhide case; a pigskin case with a military brush set, comb, and file; a pigskin clothes brush with a sliding handle; a soft antelope tobacco pouch; and a crocodile and gold wallet and key holder.

In April, 1938, *Esquire* paid homage to the infinite variety of pigskin. It was "a handsome leather to begin with and its attraction is further enhanced by the fact that it grows old so gracefully. In accessories for men it comes made up in all manner of things." A full-color page included pictures of a pigskin saddle, a pigskin suitcase, a pigskin bottle case, a pigskin traveling utility case, a pigskin fitted case, a whangee and pigskin riding cane, pigskin town shoes, a pigskin belt, a malacca cane with a pigskin handle, pigskin pullman slippers, pigskin braces, a pigskin fly book for trout fishing, pigskin gloves for town or country, a silk umbrella with a pigskin handle, a pigskin cigarette case, a pigskin key case, a pigskin pipe and tobacco pouch, a pigskin wallet, a pigskin jewelry box with pigskin cuff links and watch guard, a wristwatch with a pigskin strap, and a traveling clock covered in pigskin. All this prompted the caption writer to conclude: "As a man's gift, pigskin strikes the common denominator of masculinity and still allows ample leeway for individuality."

In November of that year, the fashion department gave alligator a similar full-page display, showing articles "all made out of various percentages of alligator leather." Among them were an ashtray with minute cross wires over the top of tray, a stud box, shoes, a collar box, a bridge set, mili-

1. To carry those surplus "musts," a colorful cotton carry-all in authentic Tartan cotton, trimmed with leather.

2. Fitted toiletry case in rich brown leather with slide fastener closure contains the essential toiletry articles including brushes and containers for lotions.

3. The Toiletry Threesome are in a saddle stitched leather case. A set of hair brushes and a narrow clothes brush and comb fit compactly into a grain leather case.

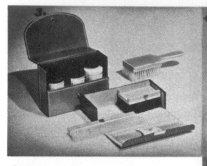

4. Pigskin back clothes brush with strapped leather shoe horn; saddle stitched pigskin jewelry case with suede lining.

5. Fitted manicure set with slide fastener closure. The flat large envelope style pigskin toiletry case is a boon to travelers.

6. Rust colored "scuffs" of brushed leather are easily packed in matching leather case.

7. Pigskin tie case holds your prizes on a rack at the top and prevents them from becoming wrinkled en route.

8. An unfitted leather toiletry case with water-proof lining and a terry cloth toiletry case with huge pockets that may also be used as an apron.

9. Sturdy leather case with Tartan fabric top holds a bottle of spirits, held tightly in place with a strap that may be locked.

10. New type of camera which enables traveler to get a complete picture —just one minute-and-a-half after it is taken. Leather case for protection.

Hide brown was a fashionable color for men's leather articles in 1949. From Esquire, *August 1949.*

tary brushes in an alligator container, a cigarette box, an alligator-covered metal humidor, an automobile map case, a fitted dress case, suspenders, a cigarette case with a clock, a pocket cigarette case, a passport case, a wallet, an envelope cigarette case, a tobacco pouch, a clock-barometer-thermometer combination, a weekend bag, a belt, and a wristwatch.

In the post-World War II period and all through the fifties among the most popular gifts for men were the leather wallet (ostrich was one of the choicest leathers), leather desk and table lighters for home or office use, the miniature tool kit in a leather case, the manicure set in a gold-initialed leather case, leather pullman slippers in a matching case, and the leather home shoeshine kit, the spit-and-polish appearance demanded of military shoes having made the American man extremely conscious of the appearance of his civilian shoes. In 1954 *Esquire* observed that in luggage and small leather goods such as wallets, briefcases, and toiletry kits leather was the fashion leader.

"In wallets, it's exotic leathers," *Apparel Arts* noted in its winter, 1957, issue. "When the waiter proffers the tab on a silver salver, reaching for one's wallet can be more pleasant than might be imagined. For the newest creations in billfolds are wrought of exotic specialty leathers that appeal to the hand as well as to the eye." Outstanding among these exotic and sen-

One of the first leather bags for men had a shoulder strap and was known as the "sidekick." The interior, shown below, contained compartments for cigarettes, lighter, passport, etc. From Esquire, June 1954.

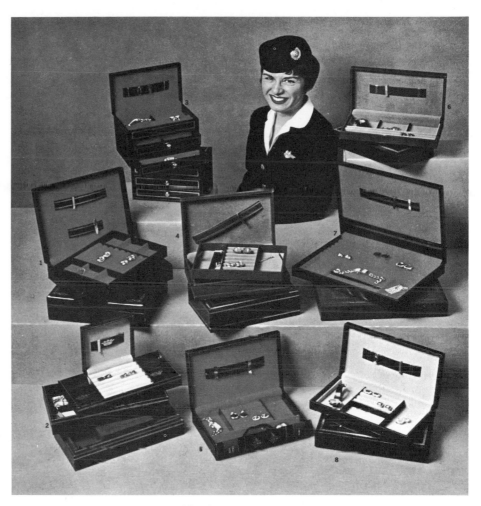

Gold-tooled jewel boxes and valets with velvet linings were designed to keep jewelry in a fine array. From Gentlemen's Quarterly, September 1964.

Distinctive leathers used for wallets in 1957 included (top) Persian velour (reversed calf) lined with French calf, (left) elephant hide, and (right) brown-and-white pony skin. From Apparel Arts, March 1957.

suous leathers were Persian velour, elephant hide, alligator, and pony skin.

The Peacock Revolution of the sixties liberated men's fashions, and one of the most stunning innovations in leather was the shoulder bag or handbag for men. With a shaped suit a man had little room for a wallet, key case, cigarette case, credit cards, and so on. Most important of all, he did not want to spoil the looks of his suit with unsightly bulges. The shoulder bag or handbag was a practical solution to the problem of the bulging pocket.

The shoulder bag had carryall convenience, said Chip Tolbert, Esquire's fashion director, in November, 1970. "Some of the newest models are miracles of convenience," he contended,

This deep duffle bag of olive-brown leather lined with plaid had a free-swinging compartment for toiletries. Gentlemen's Quarterly, March 1965.

Bags for men became important fashion news in 1970: (left to right) a squashy brown leather bag with outside file compartments; a steerhide camera-style bag; a brown antiqued-leather bag with a brass lock; a bag of rough canvas and leather with envelope-flap closures. From Esquire's European Fashion Trends Report, *November 1970.*

Billfolds and pocket cases of pin seal and soft calf in various styles had a luxurious look in 1971. [BUXTON]

"compartmented in such a way as to make them essentially portable desks and file folders as well." Samples collected by the fashion staff included a soft brown leather shoulder bag with outside file compartments; a caramel steerhide camera-style bag with a shoulder strap; a brown antiqued-leather handbag with a brass lock; and a rough canvas and leather handbag with envelope-flap closures.

"The U.S. male is in bags," commented Amy Teplin of *Men's Wear* in 1971. "Just a decade or two ago it became hip at Harvard to lug over-the-shoulder green laundry bags filled with books, pencils and other collegiate paraphernalia. Now those 'hip' curiosity pieces have hit Fifth Avenue. The rest of malekind is soon to come.

"Handbags for men may still be the butt of bad jokes, yet they're certainly no more funny looking than a sophisticated swinger in a slim, shaped suit with pockets bulging at hips and rear. Or how about the ultimate in travel chic—carrying a plastic Lufthansa flight bag for overnight sprees?

"What IS funny is that no one's ever questioned the masculinity (or taste-lessness) of that style. It has an airline's name on it, which seems to provide the wearer with protection from strange looks. That alone has made it an okay item in any man's wardrobe.

"For first-time bag toters who may still have cold feet over the new fashion, equally acceptable disguises are being produced in leather, suede, pig-skin and canvas.

"Mark Cross, one of the 'status' stores doing big business in men's bags, is offering a line-for-line reproduction of the map case Italian officers carried during the war. Fashioned in brown pigskin, it has two outside pockets and swings flat and close to the body on a shoulder strap. It is the chic boutique's best-seller too, along with leather envelopes that resemble miniature attache cases.

"For the truly cautious, there are 'camera case' styles; for the nostalgic, 'school bags.' Studs, fringe and painted appliqué are being hand-fashioned for the far out, while canvas carry-alls and soft leather pouches are finding their way onto airplanes. Frank Sinatra's been spotted toting his. Even Bing Crosby is into bags other than golf.

"It's as old as the Crusaders carrying money pouches, and as progressive as pocketless pants. If women can wear the latter for comfort, it's high time men returned the fashion compliment and started carrying their own weight in bags" (Apr. 23, 1971, p. 122).

That is precisely what the more avant-garde male did. In the early seventies the demand for the adjustable shoulder bag far exceeded the demand for the handbag. "The man's shoulder bag that's all man," is the way Horn Luggage and Leather Goods advertised its bag in December, 1971, while another manufacturer gave all his bags for men the tag "manbag," predicting that their acceptance would grow with changes in clothing fashions. Slacks had fewer pockets, and clothing in general was more form-fitting.

On April 23, 1971, the *Daily News Record* showed domestic shoulder bags of llama, one of which had a novel and useful feature: a removable passport case held in the back of the bag with a snap fastening.

In the meantime, while the masculine bag was garnering the greatest publicity, other classic leather goods were enjoying wide popularity. The smartest catalogs for Christmas, 1971, showed skinny billfolds and wallets of calf kid; eyeglass cases of black pigskin; a moustache comb with trimming scissors and mirror in a cowhide case; a black pin-seal credit-card case; a brown calf jewel roll with a suede lining and a snap closing; a leather-lined leather briefcase; a bridge set consisting of two packs of playing cards, a scorepad, and a pencil in a zippered black calf case; a black calf pill case; a set of black calf luggage

The fashion of white billfolds and cases was associated with yachting in 1971. [BUXTON]

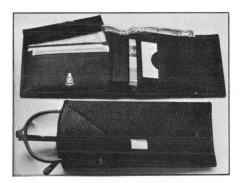

(top) A skinny billfold in matte calf with two bill pockets, four card pockets, and two double-pocketed transparent holders for eight cards; (bottom) a double eyeglass case in black pigskin (1971). [MARK CROSS]

tags; a black pin-seal pocket case containing a silver-mounted tortoiseshell comb and nail file; picture frames of stenciled pony skin; a miniature travel clock with a dime-size dial and a seventeen-jewel alarm, carried in a black leather case; and, of course, the omnipresent shoulder bag in leather or can-

vas with leather trim, sometimes presented as a "his and her" fashion accessory.

As the younger man of the seventies continued to view fashion as a means of self-expression, leather appeared even in jewelry, with wide leather bracelets and neckbands, often studded with metal. And just as no woman of fashion would be content with one handbag, no matter how luxurious, her masculine counterpart now tended to acquire a wardrobe of thin wallets in a variety of leathers and colors. The modern trend was toward soft, natural-looking leathers, casually made. Leather, "luxurious in hand . . . supple and adaptable to many different design interpretations," was still a very real expression of the masculine character. With the Peacock Revolution that character had changed, becoming gentler, more sensitive, and more sophisticated, and the new leather goods of the seventies expressed that change perfectly.

Evolution of Apparel

The manufacture of wearing apparel is one of the oldest and most durable of all modern industries. From the time primitive man wore animal skins to the middle of the nineteenth century, the making of apparel was exclusively a handicraft: clothing was made either by the women of a family or by what today might be described as custom tailors. Except for a change in the type of needle used, the production of apparel remained much the same. To underscore this absence of technological progress one need only note that the inch tape measure was not invented until the early 1800s. A half century later two events combined to usher into being the industrialization of apparel manufacturing in the United States: the invention of the sewing machine by Elias Howe in 1846 and the outbreak of the Civil War in 1861. But it is significant that the evolution of the apparel industry, from a handicraft to the machine-based mass production industry of modern times, actually required about 125 years.

The sewing machine was the catalyst that launched the apparel industry into a century and a quarter of progress. The first practical sewing machine, invented by Howe, used one thread from a needle and another from a bobbin to form a locked stitch. Eleven years later, in 1857, James Gibbs created a machine employing only one thread that formed a chain of stitches. The changes that followed may be divided into spans of twenty-five years:

Job specialization, 1850–1875
Mechanization, 1875–1900
Organization, 1900–1925
Systemization and professionalization, 1925–1950
Industrial sophistication, 1950–1970

Naturally, developments often overlapped, and each of them contributed to further advances. The story of the American apparel industry and the route it traveled in its struggle to arrive at its present industrialized state is a fascinating one, and the end has yet to be written. The industry directly employs approximately 1,400,000 persons, or about 0.7 percent of the population. Of the total, approximately 1,250,000 persons are production workers. By 1970 the wholesale value of their output had reached $24 billion. If this rate of progress continues and automation becomes a reality in the industry by the end of the century, it seems likely that a mere fraction of the present number of workers will be able to clothe the nation.

Early model of a sewing machine [COURTESY SINGER COMPANY]

Era of Job Specialization, 1850–1875

The introduction of sewing machines was firmly resisted by the tailors

Manufacturing

of 1850, who were deeply concerned by the possibility that the new machines would eliminate their jobs. It required the Civil War to override resistance and even longer to overcome objections. The war provided two circumstances that combined irresistibly to usher in the era of mass production. First, the sudden explosion of demand for army uniforms overwhelmed suppliers and quickly exhausted the numbers of available craftsmen. Second, the need to order huge quantities of highly standardized uniforms de-emphasized individual talent and creative skills in favor of physical capability to perform repetitive and routine functions. Clothing manufacturers seized upon the opportunities inherent in these developments to introduce sewing machines into their factories.

It cannot be claimed that an organized revolutionary plan was formulated for the use of the sewing machine; what ensued was merely an opportunistic attempt to free the tailor from the portion of his work that could safely be executed by apprentices, who were available in larger numbers. To a small degree this procedure had been employed before the sewing machine was invented. Now, however, the apprentice was taught on a machine instead of by hand. Whether by accident or by design, the effect of this change was electric and far-reaching.

In order to accelerate the learning process and minimize errors, learners first were assigned to make a small part of the product. As they became experienced, their skills were traded up and more difficult operations were undertaken, each step being facilitated by the highly standardized nature of the product and by fabric uniformity. The combination of these conditions provided the basis for a totally unexpected and considerable increase in overall productivity, thus ensuring the continuation of job specialization and the permanent retention of the sewing machine as an essential tool of the trade.

The success of job specialization in assembling products encouraged a similar treatment of cutting operations, in which garments were cut from fabric and prepared for assembly. According to traditional practice, a master tailor designed the style, created the patterns, inscribed (marked) their outline upon the fabric, laid up (spread) the material, hand-cut the fabric according to the marker outline, and then supervised the construction of the product. By the theory of specialization these functions were separated into (1) pattern development and marker making, (2) fabric spreading, and (3) cutting.

Once the job specialization princi-

The Wheeler and Wilson sewing machine employs the rotary hook and stationary bobbin and the four motion feed invented by Allen B Wilson in 1851 and 1854.

ple had become firmly entrenched in cutting operations, it began to influence operating procedures. The Civil War continued to contribute to these developments by supplying larger orders. The marker-making function changed from the loose interlocking of the parts of one garment to the relating of the parts of multiple units, with valuable reductions in consumption of material per unit. The advantage required the use of longer tables upon which to spread the fabric. In addition, the piling (spreading) of plies of fabric improved because of the longer runs available.

The value of these lessons was not lost upon the apparel industry. Through the experience gained during the Civil War the industry had learned how to produce standardized products of good quality at a reasonable cost. It was only logical that in the postwar years the large industrial capacity that had been created would be directed toward the production and sale of ready-to-wear garments. Consumer response was quite favorable. The burgeoning population added to the opportunity, and the modern concept of mass production began to evolve. Custom tailoring continued to attract patrons, but on an ever-decreasing proportional scale.

Era of Mechanization, 1875–1900

As the apparel industry grew in size and importance, it drew the interest of machinery manufacturers. The direction they followed was influenced by the fact that job specialization was intensified. As specialization continued, machine operators became increasingly capable of executing complicated tasks that had previously been performed by hand. In response, builders of machinery began to design specialized machines of a more sophisticated nature and to increase operating speeds.

Patent records confirm that an automatic buttonhole machine was invented in 1862. In 1875 a button sewer was patented, and in 1886 a bar-tack machine was invented. This group of automatically operated machines was complemented by the development of more sophisticated special machines. Noteworthy were two-needle machines that produced parallel rows of stitching simultaneously, blind-stitch machines that pricked fabrics instead of sewing through them, and overedgers that wrapped thread around the fabric edge to produce a finished appearance.

The industry also began to develop special attachments for sewing machines. These devices enabled an operator to join several parts in a single seaming instead of sewing them separately in sequence. Complementing such developments were mechanical devices for the turning of parts. Each new device propelled the industry toward the continued specialization of jobs and the further reduction of the handicraft content of the product.

The proliferation of sewing machinery and attachments naturally drew attention to the means by which they were driven. The original sewing machine was started by spinning a handwheel. The initial momentum was transferred to a treadle, which was pumped in a rocker motion by the feet of the operator. To stop the machine the operator palmed the handwheel. Generally a bank of individual sewing-machine stations was arranged side by side, with the rows of operators and machines facing in one direction.

When electric power was introduced in the late 1800s, a considerable change took place. Since the first electric motors were both large and expensive, it was considered practical to employ one large motor to drive twenty to twenty-four sewing machines. However, each machine occupied 3 feet of length, and a row of machines therefore required 60 to 72 feet of drive shaft. The difficulty of maintaining a perfect motor and shaft alignment, coupled with space restrictions, necessitated a change. Instead of machines in single rows facing in one direction, two rows of machines were placed face-to-face. The large motor was located at the end of the bank of machines so that the drive shaft, which was coupled to the motor, could be centered between the two facing rows. The transfer of power from the center shaft to the sewing machines required a pulley locked onto the main shaft drive. The pulley was aligned with an idler that was part of a clutch mechanism attached beneath the machine table. The clutch mechanism consisted of two flat discs that when pressed together engaged a third wheel at its end. The third wheel was in a direct line with the handwheel of the sewing machine above. Round leather belts, which encircled the central shaft pulley and idler and the clutch drive and handwheel, enabled power to be transferred from the drive shaft to the idler and thence to the machine. When the operator pressed upon a foot treadle, which was connected to the idler in a forward-down motion, the idler was forced against the clutch face, thereby engaging the wheel, which transferred the drive to the machine. When the operator wished to stop the machine, he engaged a simple braking device by bringing pressure upon the rear of the treadle.

Late in 1889 a patent was granted on a fractional-horsepower clutch motor that was to make a considerable change in apparel-manufacturing methodology. However, the full effect of this development was not felt for about a quarter of a century. Whereas continuous-running fractional-horsepower motors were employed to operate the automatic machines of the period, the clutch type achieved a much slower rate of application.

The various mechanical developments combined to encourage continued job specialization. To accommodate this trend, virtually every aspect of manufacturing operations had to be altered. The division of the work into small segments meant that the work had to be moved on from one job to another until the product was completed. The work unit employed was a stack of uniform parts produced by cutting out multiple layered plies in the cutting department. The block thus created was termed a "bundle," from which the name "bundle system" was derived.

In its earliest form the bundle system required that as each operator completed a bundle of a given operation, he returned it to an inventory storeroom. There the bundle was checked in for work credit, and a new supply of work was obtained. Later, to reduce the time spent in walking to and from the inventory room, the operator was allowed to deposit completed work in a bin provided for its accumulation. Ultimately service workers were used to supply work. To facilitate this method of processing the work, the system usually arranged for the placement of operators and equipment in rows, each of which represented a step in the process of completing the product.

The bundle system established the need for a change in management organization. During the transformation from the custom-tailoring era of the early 1800s to the industrialization of apparel manufacturing by 1900, management had retained its tailor character. The plant manager continued to be primarily and almost exclusively a master craftsman. To qualify for his position he was required to know the product from design to completion. Ability to organize, direct, control, and manage operations was entirely subordinate to practical experience and knowledge. When a company became too large for a single manager to be able to direct operations, men who possessed exactly the same qualifications as the plant manager would be selected from among the tailors in the factory. Sections of the plant were assigned to these foremen, as they were titled. In modern terminology, there evolved a completely line-type organization in which each management element was all things to all employees.

The end of the nineteenth century may best be described as having completed the transformation of the industry from the customized concept of apparel manufacturing by hand to the mass production of apparel by machines. By modern standards of manufacturing the level of achievement was elementary and slow, but as every thinking person is aware, breaking with tradition is exceedingly more difficult and time-consuming than the progress that inevitably follows once the basic change has taken place. The fact is that all the developments and procedures that were to follow, whether correctly or incorrectly formed, grew out of the trial-and-error experimentation of the nineteenth century. Students of the history of apparel manufacturing should note that from its inception the industry did not produce its improvements on an elective or planned basis. Every achievement of the nineteenth century was born out of external influences. That pattern continued to characterize the apparel industry in the twentieth century.

Era of Organization, 1900–1925

The quarter century from 1900 to 1925 was a period of consolidating and organizing earlier achievements. Many developments continued to emerge. Some were new; others simply represented refinements and improvements of established procedures. When one realizes that the population had increased from 5,297,000 in 1800 to 74,000,000 in 1900, it is easy to comprehend the preoccupation of the apparel industry simply with growing up.

At the turn of the twentieth century, the apparel industry was located either close to the New England textile mill centers or in large cities. This placement had been encouraged by the dependence of the industry upon railroad transportation for the receipt of raw materials and for the delivery of finished products. New York became the unquestioned center for apparel manufacturing, not alone for its excellent geographical position but for the immigrants who settled there. Although immigrants from Eastern Europe could not speak English and generally lacked education and training, such handicaps were not liabilities in learning how to sew apparel, and the newcomers found ready acceptance as apprentices in the garment factories. Because of their urgent need for income, they accepted wages, work hours, output standards, and working conditions (the garment factories were known as sweatshops) that contributed to the low cost of apparel products.

The availability of cheap, productive labor, the growing market, and the ease with which one could enter the apparel-manufacturing business were an irresistible combination for the more enterprising immigrants. Establishing a business required only a small, low-rent loft, a cutting table erected from used lumber, and a bank of powered machine tables. As a condition of employment, the workers were required to provide their own sewing machines. In fact, a very familiar sight of the lower East Side of Manhattan was the itinerant tailor who carried his machine on his back as he sought employment in one factory or another.

Those who managed to scrape together a little capital or credit purchased fabric, which they paid for in cash, cut and made samples, and then set about obtaining an order, which was rushed into production. Those who owned their own production plants became manufacturers. Those who lacked capital or credit were not to be deterred and became what were known as contractors. They set up their small plants and sold their labor service to another class of manufacturers. The latter group preferred not to invest their capital in equipping factories. Reserving for themselves the function of cutting fabrics, they sent the work to contractors for assembly.

The manufacturer-contractor relationship proved to be enduring in the field of ladies' ready-to-wear, in which the uncertainty of sales tended to discourage investment in wholly owned manufacturing facilities. Producers of staple products generally operated their own production plants. Thousands of such businesses were formed. Competition was intensified, and ever-better products were offered at extremely low prices, thus adding im-

Sewing plant about 1900. [BROWN BROTHERS, NEW YORK]

petus to the expanding ready-to-wear market.

Meanwhile, progress in equipment continued unabated. Cutting, sewing, and finishing operations were all beneficiaries of improved machinery. Undoubtedly, the most significant contribution stemmed from the development of efficient electrical equipment. Producers of electric motors were able to refine their products so that size was reduced, efficiency increased, and cost lowered. These advantages combined to encourage diverse and widespread applications.

One of the most significant applications of powerful small motors was in the cutting department. An individually powered portable cutting knife was invented. The first such knife, which was available by 1900, drove a round rotary blade. A powered vertical knife followed by 1920. Both knives could slice through layers of fabric, and with the vertical blade fabric could be piled as high as 10 inches. The ease with which the machines could be maneuvered, their extreme accuracy, and their great efficiency signaled the end of scissors and short-bladed hand knives, which had been the traditional cutting tools. Thus, another manual craft disappeared, and with it the high cost of hand-cutting a few layers of fabric at a time.

Another useful new cutting department tool was the cloth-spreading machine. This unit consisted of a four-wheeled vehicle that was guided by a track affixed to one edge of a cutting table. The bulky fabric was mounted onto the machine, thus enabling the operator to push the unit ahead, aligning the edges of the fabric with one hand as the machine moved forward. Not long after, the spreading machine, too, became motor-driven.

The small electric motor continued to play a significant role in the evolution of the sewing department. The first application substituted a direct drive for the centrally located power shaft. A small motor was placed in a housing directly beneath the row of sewing machines. One leather belt was thus eliminated, and power was transferred directly from motor to transmitter. The effectiveness of both operating and braking was significantly

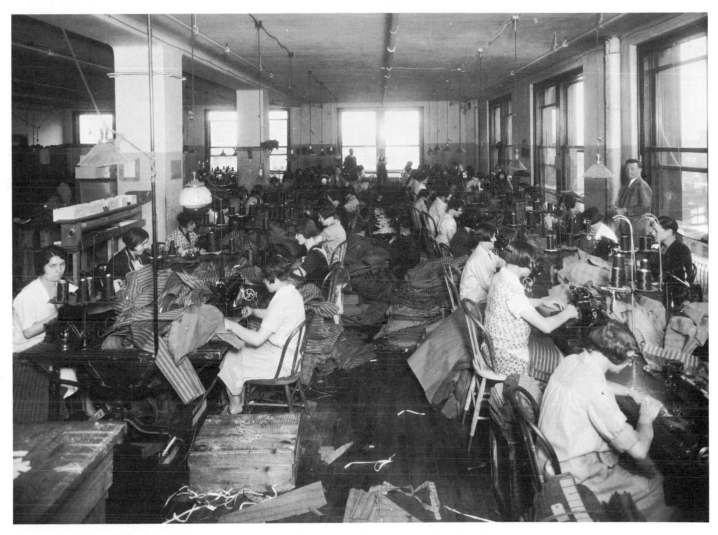

Sewing plant in the 1920s. [BROWN BROTHERS, NEW YORK]

improved, thereby contributing to the operator's control. This development was known as the safety table. Because of its modest cost in comparison with the individual clutch-type motor, it retarded widespread acceptance of the latter. In some instances the common face-to-face, side-by-side machine arrangement was retained, but the new motor also permitted a single-line arrangement with all operators facing in one direction. Instead of two face-to-face operators having to share a common shallow trough into which completed work could be fed, each station could be fitted with a hopper to accommodate larger quantities of work in process.

There were parallel advances in pressing. In earlier years an iron weighing 12 to 14 pounds, heated first by coal and then by gas, was applied to a wet cloth to steam and press the product. Now irons and pressing machines were built that fed live steam directly to the equipment. With pressing machines, which first became available in 1905, the head could be closed under considerable pressure to press the fabric. Special types were designed to provide the shape and form required for the product.

In an effort to consolidate and use the advantages obtained through the mechanical innovations, the industry sought a means of measuring output. When the tailor had produced a complete product, counting his output was a simple matter. When many operators shared in the product, the work contributed by each to the finished product was difficult to ascertain. The solution to the problem was elementary but effective. As each operator completed a section of work, the finished work was carried to an inventory room, where it was checked in by a clerk and credited to the individual operator. In time the output data thus collected began to identify the differences in quantities produced by individual employees and the amounts that appeared to be average.

At first such information was employed to cost the work produced, and this in turn became a tool for measuring individual performance. It was then just a short step to divide the output into the established wage in order to fix a cost per piece. With that information at hand, what was more logical than to relate that cost per piece to productivity? When output was linked to take-home pay, the employee applied greater effort and the piecework incentive system came into general usage. This development was to have a far-reaching effect. As workers produced more and more output and their earnings exceeded the standard prevailing wage, employers arbitrarily reduced piece rates. The practice of rate cutting created a field of antagonism between employer and employee that was to divide the two groups permanently. Abuses were so widespread that the system proved to be an important catalyst in encouraging workers to accept membership in the clothing unions of the following decade.

By 1925 the character of apparel manufacturing under industrialized concepts had been definitely formed. The industry had required about seventy-five years to be transformed from a handmade custom-tailor form to a machine-made mass production structure. Characteristically, the progress that had been achieved was stimulated involuntarily. This responsive attitude continued to influence future conduct, as was shown by the following quarter century with its mounting rate of unionization, higher wages, intensified competition, and depression.

Era of Systemization and Professionalization, 1925–1950

The simple solution to the problems of the apparel manufacturer was to move from the large urban areas of concentration to the rural sections of the country, and the movement was begun by the producers of textiles, who turned southward. The exodus from New England to Southern areas was encouraged by large reservoirs of low-wage labor, proximity to cotton sources, and extensive community support (land grants, training subsidies, tax abatement, and low-interest long-term loans provided by the sale

of bonds). What started as a trickle in the late 1920s developed into a torrent during the 1930s, and apparel manufacturers soon followed.

At first the apparel producers were wary of relocating too far from the industrial centers. For the most part apparel businesses were sole proprietorships, and there was a natural reluctance to enter into absentee management. At first, therefore, caution limited transfers to small towns not too far from urban centers. New York manufacturers sought locations in New Jersey, Pennsylvania, and Maryland, a pattern that manufacturers in other large cities followed. However, encouraged perhaps by success and also courted by Southern towns, the movement was accelerated until the apparel industry had located itself throughout the country. The only producers who did not relocate were men's clothing and women's wear producers, who remained in the large cities. For one thing, the skills of the urban workers were deemed to be too difficult to replace. Moreover, the unions exercised contractual control over these manufacturers. The transfers that did take place were accompanied by a number of changes in operating conditions, and the 1930s marked the beginning of the modern manufacturing establishment.

Business owners required considerable courage and conviction to relocate in rural areas and to accept problems attendant on training unskilled employees as well as substantial financial risks. It was, therefore, not surprising that industrialists of such a type would want to introduce as much improvement as possible into their new establishments, and their intent was fortified by the availability of low-cost financing, anticipated reductions in operating costs, and the considerably lower cost of available labor.

The first decision was to create a one-story building, which because of low construction costs permitted the elimination of the crowded conditions characteristic of earlier industrial establishments. Whereas 25 to 30 square feet per work station had previously

been utilized, twice as much space was now provided. Freed of the restrictions imposed by existing buildings, the manufacturer could locate each department and function in a logical progression that facilitated the movement of products through the factory's multiple processes.

By 1930 producers of electric motors had succeeded in creating efficient low-cost fractional-horsepower units. These motors offered several important advantages. First, they could be mounted on individual tables so that they could be placed in preferred locations. Second, their speed enabled them to exploit the more advanced equipment provided by the manufacturers of sewing machines. Third, the flexibility of the individual motor drive and workstand made possible a revolutionary change in the system of manufacturing. The effect produced by the system's changes was so pronounced and widespread that it is necessary to retrace their evolution.

The first change in production systems began when the master tailor employed an apprentice to assist him. The advent of the sewing machine encouraged further job specialization, which was confined initially to making whole parts of a product but later evolved into producing a single operation. Over the years job specialization required the development of the bundle system to manage work in process.

The bundle system suffered from a number of deficiencies. First, service personnel were required to collect completed work and provide a new supply. Second, the servicer had to provide work for a large number of operators and therefore was not always available when needed, so that there was a certain amount of waiting time, which was a loss to both operator and manufacturer. Third, each time an operator received a bundle, he had to untie the cord that bound the unit together before he could sew the material. Fourth, having completed the sewing, he was required to draw back the series of pieces that had been sewn together and cut them apart with a scissors, thus re-creating the bundle, which had to be tied for the next transfer. Fifth, because of the practice of accumulating work between operations, in-process inventories frequently became quite large, thus adding to inventory investment and delaying production of the finished garment.

The defects of the bundle system came under attack by industrial engineers in the early 1930s. The solution they found was to place successive operations in close physical proximity and connect them by a gravity chute. As each operator completed his part of the work, it proceeded directly to the succeeding operator. The receiving operator was required to detach the nearest unit from the chain of pieces and perform the next operation. By this arrangement each operator was compelled to supply the succeeding operator, with very little in-process inventory between them, until the product was completed. This manufacturing concept, which was labeled the "straight-line system," sent a sharp wave through the industry. Its influence was to affect productivity standards, process time, space utilization, management organization, quality control, incentive systems, and production insurance.

Productivity increased to totally unanticipated levels. The sources of this radical improvement were the direct savings in time formerly devoted to the opening and closing of bundles, the elimination of the cutting and stacking of work, the response to the direct supply of work, and the demands of succeeding operations. In most installations a group-incentive system was employed, thus inducing the response of individuals to the demands and discipline of the entire group.

The time required to process the product also became radically altered. Under the bundle system each operator was supplied with an inventory of work both at the station and in the inventory bins. In the straight-line system one bundle generally provided the work supply for a group of twenty to thirty operators. As each operator received a part, it was completed immediately and dispatched to the succeeding operation. Instead of the three or four weeks that normally had been required to process a garment, one day usually sufficed.

Now more space was required per work station. Formerly, it had been possible to group work stations into banks of machines with the in-process inventory of work located in bins that required little floor space. The individual motors and stands employed in the straight-line system and the chutes connecting them increased space per station to between 60 and 70 square feet.

The impact upon management organization was equally dramatic. First, the personnel normally required to service and supply operators was eliminated. Second, without in-process inventory reserves to fall back upon in case of emergency, management had to become highly responsive to operating conditions. Trouble at one operation immediately became subject to the domino effect. Lest the balance be upset by an inefficient producer, specialized attention had to be paid to operator training. While it was true that the straight-line system was essentially self-operating through its direct interoperator supply procedure, it placed great pressure upon management to ensure that the finely tuned balance and flow were maintained.

The operation of the system also forced management to employ a corps of reserve operators termed "utility" operators. Usually selected from among the most experienced personnel in the plant, they could handle several types of operation efficiently. When absenteeism occurred (in what by then had become a female-oriented industry), the absent member was instantly replaced by a utility operator to ensure the continuity of production.

Notwithstanding the accelerated pace and high rate of productivity, the straight-line system produced a quality product. When an error was committed, it reached and affected the succeeding operation immediately. Because of convenient proximity the faulty construction was returned immediately to the operator who had created it. The burden imposed upon coworkers and the awareness that a faulty part would be returned promptly combined to produce a discipline that management itself had been unable to generate. Worthy of note, too, is the fact that because the product remained either on the worktable or in the chute it did not become dirty.

Not every manufacturer embraced the straight-line system. The major reason was the fact that only highly uniform products could be produced under this system. To many manufacturers the sensitivity of the system was deemed to be so hazardous that the risk factor prevailed over the advantages. But even those who did not embrace the straight-line system were influenced by its conduct and results. Production standards were reexamined and generally raised. Process duration came under study, and alternative systems were evolved to reduce process time. Time-and-motion–study engineers were employed to refine methods, improve work-station development, and measure output potential scientifically. The practice of employing utility operators was widely adopted. Quality control procedures were formally developed and installed.

The introspective and more scientific approach to production management eventually produced a system of manufacturing, called the "progressive bundle system," that found general acceptance in the industry. The new system took various forms but essentially involved the placement of the individual operator at right angles to the flow line. The operator was flanked to the left by an inventory station from which work was obtained, and upon completion of the work he was able to dispose of the completed material in a very convenient manner.

The operations that were required to produce the complete product were so located that the work could progress from one station to another until the product was completed. By proper management of in-process inventory, process duration, depending upon the product, was stabilized at about one or two weeks. This system could handle a considerable variety of styles and products with minimum interference. By a slight overloading of capacity and a reliance upon a moderate amount of inventory in process, absenteeism or other interrupting factors could generally be overcome.

The period between 1925 and 1940 may thus be marked as one that released the industry from the last of its ties to the past and opened the door to the era of scientific management. It had relocated, broken with traditional systems of manufacturing, and upgraded standards of productivity, quality, and cost. And, to cope with these matters constructively, the industry introduced into its organizations the industrial engineer, a change that provided the impetus for the advances in industrial technology that were to follow.

Under the direction of the industrial engineer, the teachings of men such as Frederick Taylor and Frank Gilbreth, who fathered the science of management, exerted a dominating and continuing influence. The industrial engineer concentrated upon development of the management organization, scientific work measurement, refinement of incentive systems, and formalization of operating procedures and controls.

In analyzing the traditional management structure of the industrial plant, the industrial engineer took issue with the generalized theory of management. He recognized that it was virtually impossible for one individual to provide all the service to the working staff to the extent and at the time that it was needed. He observed that the demands upon the manager's time occurred with such frequency that the manager could not resolve one problem effectively before another demanded his attention. It was also noted that the extraordinary variety of functions which the manager was required to perform virtually precluded the development of any single skill. The engineer therefore concluded that the manager was primarily responsive and was totally incapable of devoting

himself to preventive practice. The obvious solution was to specialize management, dividing it into highly restricted and concentrated areas. Following that logic, five specialized functional areas were identified:

1. Management and service, concerned with directing, coordinating, and generally servicing personnel

2. Quality supervision, involving the determination of quality standards, instruction, and monitoring of quality performance

3. Job training, providing for the proper training of learners, the retraining of experienced personnel, and the maintenance of formal standard operating procedures

4. Production control, embracing planning, scheduling, work loading, operation balancing, routing, and control

5. Efficiency, maintenance, and control, obtained by monitoring time achievements and performance and alerting management elements to observed deficiencies

By assigning the management-service function to one individual and arranging that he report directly to the plant management, the integrity of the existing line-type organization was preserved. The individual in charge of the management-service area was relieved of all other management duties and could therefore be expected to be more effective in controlling and managing a larger number of operators.

It was hoped that the other four positions which were created would satisfy all the other needs of the manufacturing plant. The individuals involved would be able to concentrate within their specialized areas and thus have sufficient time to attend to each need and to develop a higher level of proficiency in a particular skill. While the specialists would deal directly with their functional areas, they also would provide essential intelligence and information upon which the management-service element could act. The group would therefore function as staff members and in effect complete the "line-staff" organization form.

The line-staff organization structure

enjoyed several other important advantages. First, the staff members could become candidates for promotion to the position of manager, thus providing for succession. Second, by concentration in a limited area the quality of performance could be substantially improved. Finally, it became possible to introduce a specific measurement of performance (accountability).

The evolution from the line type of organization to the line-staff form had been very gradual. Where it was employed, its advantages and superiority were clearly defined. Plants that adopted this type of structure generally produced at a level of efficiency more than 15 percent above that of the line type of organization. Today it is generally accepted, although not quite universally applied, that management must become highly professional and devote itself more to how things are done than to their simple doing.

Among the most troublesome tasks of plant management was work measurement. As noted above, with the introduction of the piecework system of payment injudicious rate cutting by an uninformed management had laid a foundation of suspicion that was never removed. In fact, the procedure for developing the piece-rate value of an operation had evolved into bargaining sessions in which the two sides guessed at the true value, offered more or less than they expected to accept, and eventually reached a compromise. Since discussions concerning piece-rate development involved money, the negotiations were invariably emotional.

The practice of formal time study to measure work was one of the first efforts by management to evaluate the work content of an operation intelligently. It was certainly a marked improvement over the pure guesswork that had previously been employed. When practiced by professionals, time study proved to be a fairly practical technique, although it suffered from some inaccuracy because the time-study observer had to measure (level) the performance of an operator in order to obtain a standard time value. But because time study separated the total job into separate elements, it was possible to improve the quality of such judgments. Once the work standard had been established, it was divided into the wages which the operator was expected to earn and which produced the piece-rate value to be employed. The results were frequently subject to question and modification, but time study gradually became an accepted basis for the negotiations that ultimately ensued.

It was inevitable that the time-study procedure should be refined. Several industrial engineers undertook comprehensive and exhaustive studies of all motions possible for human beings in an effort to establish predetermined values for these motions. Electronic equipment and motion pictures were employed in the measuring process. When the final data were assembled, the result was identified as "methods-time-measurement (MTM)." The accuracy of the values expressed was beyond question, but it did depend upon a thorough definition of the motions to be performed.

The availability of both time- and work-measurement procedures eliminated much of the guesswork and in well-managed plants provided satisfaction to both employee and employer. In such plants it was routinely recognized that an alteration in the work content would be accompanied by a modification in the time measurement; thus a considerable amount of emotionalism was removed from this sensitive area. Notwithstanding these developments, however, the largest part of the apparel industry continued to employ "guesstimate" and argument as the final work-measurement tools.

A corollary to the improvement in the technique of work measurement was the introduction of an alternative incentive system. Industrial engineers held that if productivity could be separated from compensation, a more constructive attitude would prevail. They therefore undertook to employ time measurement as the basis for determining how much work should be produced in a given operation. Either time study or MTM was employed to obtain this information. When the time was developed, it was offered to the employees for consideration. By studying the source data, both the engineer and the operator could evaluate objectively the time elements employed in developing the standard. It was even possible to arrange a test of the time value under actual operating conditions. Generally, agreement could be reached without the tension that normally accompanied the setting of piece rates.

To transpose the time value to a monetary value, it was necessary to negotiate wages. Although such discussions were usually of a personal nature, they nonetheless could be negotiated as an independent matter. The method under which these two pieces of information became an incentive system may be readily described. If the time value of an operation had been agreed upon at one minute, a normal operator was expected to produce sixty pieces per hour, in which event credit for sixty "earned" minutes was given. Since it was entirely possible that the time allowance of one minute per piece could be improved upon, an operator could earn more than sixty minutes of credit. If the negotiated wage was $2.40 per hour, or 4 cents per minute, then the earned minutes multiplied by the value of 4 cents per minute represented the incentive wages earned. Example: 70 minutes earned × 4 cents = $2.80.

This form of incentive system, which was called the "standard allowed minute system (SAM)," offered a number of advantages. Most important, it separated time measurement from money measurement, and bargaining discussions therefore were conducted more objectively. From the employee's standpoint, SAM offered protection because a change in job content automatically invoked a change in time value. From management's standpoint, it presented an advantage in that the employee would relate production to time and therefore could pace his efforts. For employer and employee, the system provided a reliable means of negotiation in an area critical to both.

Much time and attention were dedicated to the formalization of operating procedures and control. The majority of these procedures were necessary to the function of the staff members of the organization. The production controller required formal procedures for scheduling, work loading, routing, and balancing. Quality controllers required inspection procedures, measurement evaluations, and statistical procedures. The job trainer needed to employ standard operating procedures, formal operator training procedures, and related controls. The efficiency controller employed audit control procedures and production studies.

These are but a few of the many formal procedures that were developed for the use of management. They were important in that they represented the developed techniques for performing each function in the factory. The procedures were in fact the tools that helped to form the knowledge which would ultimately lead to the professionalization of the management organization. The 1940s may thus be marked as the time when the dominance of practical management ended and the era of professional management emerged.

Era of Industrial Sophistication, 1950–1970

From 1950 on the apparel industry undertook to improve the utilization of plant facilities by every means available, including new machinery, automation, computers, the Tex-O-Graph method of marker making, and manufacturing systems. The goals it sought to achieve were the further reduction of human labor, the decrease of process time, and the improvement of quality. A great deal was accomplished, but much remains to be done.

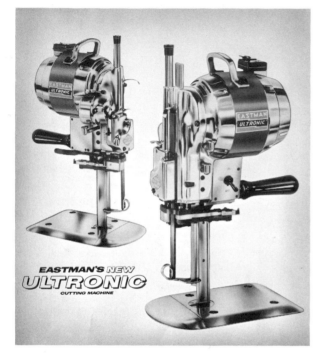

(above) Powered vertical cutting machine.
[EASTMAN MACHINE CO.]

(upper right) Electric spreading machine.
[CUTTING ROOM APPLIANCES]

(lower right) Operation employing the mobile
transport system. [COURTESY S. J. CAPELIN
ASSOCIATES, INC.]

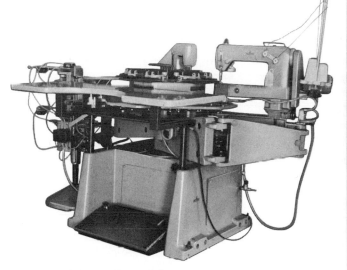

(above) Suits are cut by a computerized device employing a laser beam. [HUGHES AIRCRAFT COMPANY]

(upper left) Contour seaming machine. [COURTESY COMPO INDUSTRIES, INC., REECE ADLER DIVISION, WOBURN, MASS.]

(lower left) A computer directs a pattern generator to produce a complete range of sizes from an original pattern. [COURTESY IBM CORPORATION]

To evaluate the accomplishments properly one must realize that only 12.5 percent of the average time required for an operation was occupied by pure machine-sewing time. The remainder was employed to deliver work to the machine, manipulate it during processing, and remove it upon completion. To improve efficiency industrial engineers therefore elected to invade the 87.5 percent time block.

Early efforts were directed toward the automatic separation of threads derived from the repetitive sewing of similar pieces, and a variety of devices were developed. Some acted as guillotines; others, in a scissors fashion. The most sophisticated device trimmed the threads at the point where the seam was completed, both above and below the sewn part, after the needle had been extracted automatically from the sewn material. The second achievement naturally followed the first. Once the pieces had been separated, their mechanical removal from the work area was invited. This was accomplished by reciprocal and rotating stacking devices that withdrew the work from the machine after it had been sewn and piled it neatly behind the machine. The third attempt to eliminate manual action involved the use of photoelectric light, microswitches, and solenoids to start a machine, stop it as required, and either raise or lower the feeding parts for the rapid insertion and removal of work.

These are but a few of the mechanical developments that took place in the 1950s. One success followed another, and each of them invaded the 87.5 percent time block, reduced operating fatigue, and added appreciably to the operating time of equipment. Such improvements became almost a daily occurrence in the apparel industry and subsequently were accepted as standard equipment in the modern plant. It is significant that each of these mechanical inventions forged a link in the chain of development that presaged full automation. Several steps were later taken in that direction.

The first step concerned sequential automatic processing. Developments in automatic needle positioning and thread trimming, stackers, and other mechanical devices suggested that a series of operations might be linked together and executed automatically. Two problems were encountered: sewing curves and the mechanical transfer of the cut part, which was porous and nonuniform in construction. A solution to the curve problem did not present itself. The transfer problem between operations could be solved in part by available mechanical means. Since cam- and gear-operated machines had already been successfully produced, their availability was exploited.

The developers chose a man's shirt as their vehicle because of its uniformity and stable characteristics. The first device to emerge was a unit that positioned a pocket and folded, formed, and automatically placed it on the front of the shirt, ready for attachment. The machine then sewed around the perimeter of the pocket and trimmed the threads; finally the shirt was removed from the machine. This development was paralleled by the linking of a series of operations that treated the edges of the front of a shirt, following which the shirt was transferred to machines where buttons and buttonholes were automatically applied.

Meanwhile, equipment designers continued their efforts to automate sewing operations. The cuffs of sleeves of knit shirts, for instance, have been completely and automatically produced. Contour seamers, which sew around the periphery of a part such as a collar, pocket flap, or cuff have become available. These parts are automatically turned out and pressformed, ready for further processing. Efforts are being made to execute programmed seams, with parts being placed automatically in a machine where they are guided through the seaming operations until they are finally discharged to a stack.

While such attention was being concentrated upon the sewing machine, similar developments were in process in cutting. For example, the cutting department benefited by the introduction of electric-powered spreading machines that guide the edges of fabric by electronic controls. Another important development uses a miniaturized pattern for the marker-making process. This system employs a pantograph that reduces patterns to a twenty-fifth of their size, measures their surface area, and enables their placement on a proportionately scaled marking table. This system, developed by the Tex-O-Graph Corporation, reduces the skill level required, provides for the most efficient use of materials, and offers an excellent control over their efficient employment.

Two further developments are equally dramatic. The first is the use of a laser beam for the cutting of cloth to patterns. The laser cutting system consists mainly of four components: a computer programmed with cutting instructions, a positioning device, the laser, and a conveyor. The cutting operation is performed as follows. A single layer of material is unrolled from a bolt and moved along the conveyor until it is directly under the positioning device. Turned on by the computer, the laser's beam (but not the laser itself, which is stationary) is directed automatically by mirrors and maneuvered intricately above the cloth. The beam cuts each garment to programmed instructions that include directions to accommodate such matters as size and style. The conveyor then moves the cut material to a location where the pieces are removed, and another section of material moves into the cutting area. The laser beam actually burns rather than cuts, "vaporizing" the fabric with high-intensity heat and light (the light of the beam has been described by scientists as "brighter than the center of the sun"), but the resulting incision is knifelike. Among the benefits expected from the use of the laser beam are lower industry costs, a quicker response to fashion changes, sharp reduction of large and risky inventories, and an important advantage for the domestic product over competing foreign imports since no one can fill orders as fast or as accurately as the American manufacturer. (The accompanying photograph shows the laser beam cutting men's suiting in the computer-controlled machine developed by the Hughes Aircraft Company for L. Greif & Bro. of Fredericksburg, Virginia, a division of Genesco, Inc.)

The second development occurred in the use of computers for pattern making, grading, and fabric utilization. IBM developed a program that interprets measurement data and expresses the resulting patterns in perfect graphic detail, scaled proportionately according to grade. Another program selects the preferred assortment of sizes of garments to be employed in a given fabric width.

Late in the 1960s a major step was taken in the field of manufacturing systems. This development attempted to present the work to be done by the operator vertically rather than horizontally. As the basis for the system, an overhead trolley rail was employed; suspended from the rail was a transport vehicle from which hung the individual pieces of a work bundle. The loaded transport trolley was moved along the rail until, by means of a switch, it was brought directly to the side of the operator. The suspended unit was located conveniently for efficient selection and transfer of the part to the needle area. Upon completion of the operating cycle, gravity conveyed the finished unit to a receiving trolley. When the entire segment had been finished, the trolley was conveniently conveyed to the next work center. This system enjoyed several unique advantages. It improved supply service, reduced fatigue, facilitated work handling, reduced preparation time, eliminated disposal elements, foreshortened process time, and improved quality by maintaining the product in its unwrinkled original state.

It is possible that this system may become the means for the continued improvement of efficiency in apparel factories. It is reasonable to assume that automated sewing equipment will complement the mobile transport system by enabling a machine loader (not an operator) to place work in a series of machines. By the introduction of power-driven systems that are already in use, the transport of work in process from one station to another is most likely to occur. In this fashion a semi-automated concept may be developed, providing a link with full automation.

The consideration of such developments must entertain the further engagement of computers. Since 1950 the emphasis for the use of computers has been placed upon sales analysis, inventory management, and financial operations, including the complete automation of payrolls. Computers have yet to invade the manufacturing area, where the need is equally great if not greater. Illustrating the potential requires reference to the mobile rail system just described. Since the time value in each work center may be precalculated, there is little doubt that an electric signal may be engaged to register the output at each work center by remote control into a computer. The continuous signaling of such information would provide the basis for all balancing functions, measurement of efficiency performance, and eventual interpretation into payroll and cost records. It is also readily conceivable that the entire routing process and control of production operations may be conducted intelligently by remote control.

Developments of this nature provide a fairly accurate indication of the trends that may be expected in the future. Major efforts undoubtedly will be concentrated upon the deskilling of operations, probably through the use of automatic equipment. Attempts will be made to extend automatic serialized sequences, although it is more likely that the mobile rail system will provide an interim stage. The effect will be to continue the process of reducing the labor minutes required to produce articles of apparel.

Eventually, manual labor for the manufacture of garments may become virtually extinct. This trend is well on its way, for one operator is capable of producing $100,000 worth of whole-sale product value per year. In 1940, $10,000 was considered normal; by 1969 the figure had advanced to $20,000. The substitution of machinery for manpower may be expected to alter completely the character of the apparel industry. For one thing, the management organization will change. The factory of the future will require its management to include computer-oriented specialists, electronic and mechanical engineers, chemists, and professionally educated managers. For another, an investment of only $2,500 is needed to house and equip an individual operator today, and a modern factory employing 200 direct-labor employees may be assembled with an investment of $500,000. Under the changes envisioned, the sum could increase tenfold, to $5 million. At that point, the apparel industry will have completed the transition from its tailor, labor-dense character to an automated, capital-intensified entity.

There is considerable speculation that future apparel products may be molded, and this is a distinct possibility for some of them. It is more likely that plasticized materials with "breathing" capability that may be seam-bonded will be developed. Undoubtedly, the largest proportion of all apparel will fall into these categories. Such a conclusion need not alarm apparel producers. As in the beginnings of garment manufacturing, there will always be individuals who desire and can afford custom-styled and -fitted products.

The apparel industry may therefore be expected to separate into two segments. One will continue to supply the personalized market. Its plants will be small, offering part-time, convenient employment to local people. The other will be of the automated, mass-producing type. With the continued progress that may be expected, in all probability the labor force is unlikely to grow notwithstanding the exploding population that is anticipated. For a nation oriented toward an ever-higher standard of living, that is a course to be encouraged.

Developments in Closures

No item in the apparel field can surpass the button for longevity. Prehistoric buttons of pottery and stone unearthed in Egypt are generally believed to have been worn on cords or chains despite the fact that they had shanklike apertures.

Buttons

In the early decades of the twentieth century the basic four-hole ring-style button was the leading type. For men's suits and coats it was made either of horn or of bone. The pearl variety, which was used on men's shirts, was both functional and modestly decorative.

The development of plastics during World War II gave rise to the plastic button, which revolutionized the button industry and gave the fashion industry a man-made button that was more durable and cost much less than the pearl button and could look just as ornamental. At first the cards on which buttons were displayed listed the names of the various plastics used—odd-sounding tongue twisters that at the time must have had an almost otherworldly ring: cellulose, acrylic resin, phenolic, urea, styrene, casein, methyl methacrylate. Soon, however, the public stopped trying to differentiate between plastics, and button manufacturers decided it was enough simply to identify the new button material as plastic insofar as consumer advertising and promotion were concerned. The plastic buttons either matched the suit and coat colors or were dyed in a complementary shade. Moreover, an electroplating process made it possible to produce plastic buttons that could simulate the metal buttons worn on blazer jackets, which had become classic jackets for men of all ages.

It was the growing fashion importance of the blazer during the 1930s that influenced the development of varied styles of metal buttons and, later, of metal-looking plastic buttons. As the blazer, which originally had been confined more or less to the tennis court for after-the-game wear, gained fashion acceptance off the court, it helped make the style-conscious man button-conscious as well. There were blazers with flat buttons of polished brass (frequently described as "gilt"), dome-shaped buttons often bearing naval insignia or the crest or emblem of a club, and ridged buttons in gold- and silver-color metal. Finally, in the 1960s the combination of the Peacock Revolution and an affluent society saw a rise in popularity of solid gold buttons, with sets costing $100 or more. By this time the blazer had affected the styles of buttons on both suit jackets and sports jackets, as shown by the growing popularity of the bone or plastic button with a metal rim.

The development of the polyester button coincided with the more decorative look in men's dress and sports shirts. Hitherto polyester had been used in men's suits and, later, in blends for shirts and slacks. As a button material, it proved to be extraordinarily versatile, lending itself to any number of unusual carvings and looks compatible with the "new wave" fashions for men. Furthermore, it could be dyed to match any of the fashionable new colors for menswear. Of major importance was the discovery that polyester could be reformulated with resin-base chemicals to obtain striking effects simulating the look of natural wood, marbleized granite, and unusual textures as well as that of rare stones, until then approximated only in costume jewelry.

Other innovative button materials also emerged in the sixties, among them opaques and laminates. In the early seventies there were several new

Under the name C-curity, the first slide fastener was offered to the public in 1905.

developments that promised fresh interest in buttons: (1) a method whereby the button might snap onto the garment by means of a permanently attached shank, (2) a research-oriented project designed to fuse the button to the garment by means of a small shaft, (3) a method by which one button could blend with ten to twenty shadings on a single garment, and (4) a research project for the creation of unusual materials for buttons.

Zippers

The zipper, prized today for its invisibility, originated as a highly visible device called a "clasp locker" that was attached to the flaps on a pair of men's shoes. A patent for this first version of the zipper was issued on August 29, 1893, at which time it was described as a "clasp locker or unlocker for automatically engaging and disengaging an entire series of clasps by a single continuous movement." The mechanism was provided with "a movable guide," the counterpart of the slider in the modern zipper. An improved version was used as a fastener on some twenty mail pouches, but it took another two decades to perfect the machinery for producing slide closures, and it was not until the 1930s that the fastener with two sides that came completely apart was used on the flies of men's trousers. Even then the acceptance of the zipper was slow. The reasons were given in *A Romance of Achievement*, published by Talon, Inc., in 1963 to mark the fiftieth anniversary of the company:

"He [S. M. Kinney, a marketing executive] began with an appeal to men. First of all, he had to cope with the psychology of modesty and with some of its curious inhibitions. Successful application of the fastener to work clothes without the precipitation of any kind of moral crisis had helped

to reassure some defenders of decorum. But such evidence weighed little with custom tailors who still held that the zipper could have no place in a gentleman's wardrobe. When T. F. Soles [legal adviser to the company and later chairman of the board of directors] asked his tailor to sew one into a new suit, that great artist flatly refused.

"And there was, worst of all, the matter of price. Two cents would buy the buttons for a pair of trousers. To a depression-time suit, designed to retail for $35 with two pairs of trousers, one dollar had to be added to the price if fasteners were used. It seemed absurd to talk of adding significantly to the expense of producing such a garment."

Still, two Chicago manufacturers were persuaded to use the fastener. Hart Schaffner & Marx placed a small order, and B. Kuppenheimer & Company followed suit. Meanwhile, engineering experts were working to improve both the fastener and the means of applying it to trousers. Finally, a fastener was produced that, in the terminology of the trade, could be "plastered" whole into the trousers. But this was only the first stage: "The process of introducing the fastener into trousers was complicated by the traditional resistance of certain types of workers to any departure from routine practice. Unions at no time actively opposed the use of the fastener, but leaders created issues about training for the new tasks, about piecework rates and other matters."

The company decided that what was needed was an entirely new way of making trousers, and so it helped manufacturers to develop a new method of assembly that facilitated the application of the fastener. Convinced that the time had come to advertise the zipper aggressively, it allocated $800,000 for a spring, 1937,

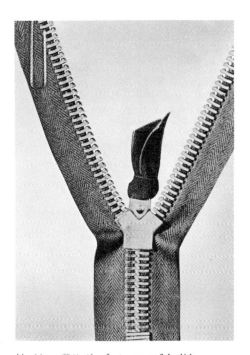

Hookless #2, the first successful slide fastener, was marketed in 1913.

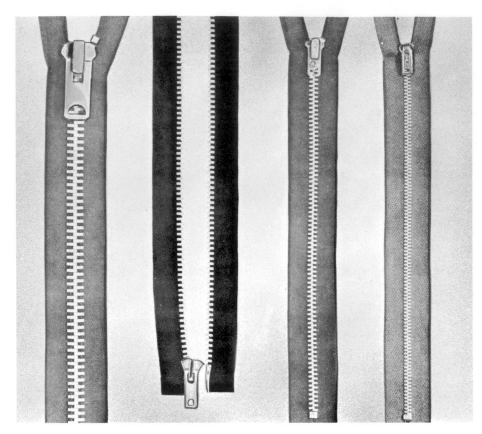

(left to right) The Big-Zip, a heavyweight jacket fastener; a regular-weight jacket fastener; a zipper with a memory lock, for work clothes; Little-Zip, for men's trousers (1963).
[TALON, INC.]

1923 Goodrich registered the word as a trademark, and the name "Zipper" first appeared in a Goodrich ad. Subsequently the word became a general term for a slide fastener.

Today there are few items in a man's wardrobe that do not carry zippers, some of which are so thin they can be used in a nylon dress shirt, while others are as rugged as the work clothes to which they belong. Zipper closures are used extensively in luggage and leather goods. Moreover, many new fashions have been launched successfully, and the styling and designing of existing fashions revolutionized, by the inclusion of a slide fastener. The topcoat with a removable liner, for example, had been available for more than a quarter of a century before it achieved wide acceptance with the addition of a slide fastener. The uses of the zipper are still increasing.

Other Fasteners

In 1936, just as the zipper was finally being accepted in menswear, the first advertisement appeared for a new closure for underwear that was, in essence, a forebear of the snap fastener and was in fact called the "Flat-Snap." By the end of 1940 shorts with snap fasteners accounted for more than 76 percent of the retail volume, and fasteners had replaced buttons on many work clothes, shirts, and pajamas. Although the elastic waistband eventually displaced the snap fastener

Two mating strips of tape make up the Velcro brand of hook-and-loop fastener. The male section is covered with stiff little hooks, and the female section with tiny soft loops. When pressed together, the hooks and loops engage.
[PATENT 1955 TO 1970 BY VELCRO CORPORATION]

campaign in the *Saturday Evening Post, Collier's,* the *New Yorker,* and *Esquire.*

"The result of this campaign was a zigzag upward sales curve. It was curiously difficult to persuade manufacturers to forsake the old ways entirely. They would put out part of their line equipped with zipper and part with buttons. Pressure was exercised on one of the first and most enthusiastic customers for two years before he could be persuaded to use only zippers.

"Then quite suddenly on a day in August, 1937, Meadville was inundated with letters, phone calls and telegrams, all from customers who wanted to put the zipper into men's clothing. A special staff was needed to cope with these communications. And manufacturers and retailers the country over began to advertise on their own, that their garments contained zippers."

The word "zipper" itself was a name created by the B. F. Goodrich Company in 1922 for its slide closure, which had been developed in cooperation with the man who invented the original clasp locker in 1893 and who by now had formed the Hookless Fastener Company, which in 1937 would change its name to Talon, Inc. The Goodrich slide closure had been put into rubber galoshes called the "Mystik Boot." Advertisements referred to "the patented Hookless Fastener," which opened "with a pull" and closed "with a pull." Goodrich salesmen did not like the name "Mystik Boot," which in their opinion did not convey the character of a highly practical article. At a sales meeting the company president remarked, "What we need is an action word . . . something that will dramatize the way the thing zips," and the name "Zipper Boot" was adopted. In

in the underwear field, fasteners went on to replace the button at the top of the zipper on men's trousers, and later novelty snap fasteners with pearl and plastic tops became popular in the sports shirt field. Next dress shirt manufacturers adopted the snap fastener, using it particularly on the cuffs and at the collar.

The hook-and-loop tape fastener was patented in 1955 and is now used by scores of industries. In the men's apparel field it has been employed principally in casual outerwear, specialized sports outfits, sturdy footwear, and military clothing. The principle behind its construction is based on the tenacious tiny hooks of the clinging burdock burr found in country fields. The hook section of the fastener is covered with stiff little hooks; the loop section, with tiny soft loops. When the two sections are pressed together, they become embedded and cling to each other with astonishing strength until the wearer "peels" them apart. Snag-proof, jamproof, washable, and dry-cleanable, the tapes can be attached to almost all materials, including metal.

Fibers

Textile fibers may be classified into the natural fibers, such as cotton and wool, and the man-made or synthetic fibers such as rayon and nylon.

Natural Fibers

The natural fibers include cotton, the bast fibers, wool, silk, and the specialty fibers.

Cotton. Cotton continues to be the world's major textile fiber. In the United States it accounts for slightly more than 40 percent of total fiber consumption. The title King Cotton, first used because of the former overwhelming importance of the cotton crop to the Southern economy, is still applicable.

History. Precisely when the use of cotton as a textile fiber was discovered is open to conjecture, but students of prehistory know that cotton fabrics were being woven in India at least 5,000 years ago. And cotton appeared in China at least 2,300 years before Christ but at first was grown only as a decorative plant. As early as 500 B.C., the Indians of the Paracas Peninsula in Peru had mastered the art of weaving cotton textiles; many of their brilliantly embroidered cottons still exist, their colors as bright as ever. The Egyptians knew cotton and prized cotton fabrics long before the birth of Christ, women of noble birth clothing themselves in sheer cotton sheaths and their servant girls in sheaths of hand-painted cotton.

Phoenician merchants introduced cotton to Greece, and the Romans imported cotton from Arab traders, who brought the cloth from India. In the wake of Alexander the Great's invasions of the Near and Middle East, the cultivation of cotton spread. Alexander's empire reached as far as Ethiopia, where cotton clothing was found to be cool and comfortable. Meanwhile, in the Far East artisans had already perfected dark cottons with colorful embroidery for tribal costumes, designs that would influence fabric and fashion designers of a twentieth-century Occidental world.

Cotton was introduced into Spain by Moorish invaders, and by the fourteenth century a flourishing cotton industry had been established in Granada. But it was the Crusaders returning from the Holy Land who introduced the wonders of this Eastern fabric to the rest of Europe.

Early explorers of the New World found a highly developed culture among the Aztec and Mayan Indians of Mexico, where cotton was so highly prized that cotton fabrics were often used for money. In Columbus's journal of October 12, 1492, he wrote of the natives of Watling's Island: "They came swimming toward us and brought us parrots, and balls of cotton thread and many other things which they exchanged with us for other things which we gave them such as strings of beads and little bells."

The East India Company popularized the cottons of the Orient in England, where imported cottons were status symbols during the Restoration period. The eighteenth century saw the invention of the spinning machine and the power loom in Great Britain spark the Industrial Revolution, which in turn led to less expensive mass-produced cotton fabrics. But the heart of fashion was located in France, or more precisely at the court of Louis XV in Versailles, and it was Mme. de Pompadour who persuaded the King to lift restrictions on imports of cotton from India so that she could add cotton garden dresses to her wardrobe.

Planting of cotton for commercial purposes first took place in the New World in Virginia early in the seventeenth century, with seed brought from the West Indies. The South, with its huge plantations, gave birth to the cotton industry, and by the middle of the nineteenth century the industry was booming.

At the turn of the twentieth century, cotton was serving the needs of Americans of all classes. For men there were cotton shirts, dusters for wear when driving the new automobiles, white cotton duck trousers for smart week-end wear, and nightshirts and robes of comfortable cotton flannel. World War I found men donning khaki-colored cotton cord and poplin uniforms.

Cotton continued to gain popularity during the Jazz Age of the 1920s; cotton cord, poplin, duck, oxford, and broadcloth were all represented in the wardrobe of the increasingly fashion-conscious young American man. Cotton played an even more important part in the menswear scene of the 1930s, with suits of seersucker, corduroy slacks, cotton knit shirts, and the then-new slack suits. And when the dapper dresser of this period took to wearing beach robes (a fashion first seen on the French Riviera), the robes were of cotton flannel and terry cloth.

World War II put cotton to work in the military again, but in the postwar 1950s it established itself once more in men's civilian garb via chino slacks, Bermuda walking shorts in multi-colored cotton, and poplin jackets and cotton corduroy car coats for leisure wear. In the 1960s cotton turned up in the more colorful shirts, wider ties, new shaped suits, and the jeans that had become the uniform of the young of both sexes. As formal and semi-formal evening wear took on a fresh personality, there were dinner jackets of cotton seersucker, madras, and velvet. Corduroy was used more than ever before in men's apparel, playing a dominant part in tailored clothing and in resort wear and skiwear. The back-to-grass-roots movement of the late 1960s gathered momentum in the early 1970s, and cotton denim became the Americana fabric.

Production. The United States is the world's largest individual producer of cotton, producing about 10 million bales a year. The bulk of American production takes place in the South, since cotton is best cultivated in a warm, humid climate.

The U.S.S.R. is the second largest producer of cotton in the world. In North America, Mexico is second to the United States. China is the largest producer in Asia and the third largest producer in the world, and India is the fourth largest producer. Brazil is the leader in South America, and Egypt is first in Africa.

Cotton is graded by fiber length, or staple, by fineness, and by geographic location. There are five basic groupings in the first of these grading systems:

1. Very short: Not more than $\frac{3}{4}$ inch in length and coarse in texture. Cotton in this staple class is used chiefly as batting and wadding.

2. Short staple: Between $\frac{13}{16}$ and $\frac{15}{16}$ inch. This cotton is used in the cheaper fabrics.

3. Medium staple: Between $\frac{15}{16}$ and $1\frac{1}{8}$ inches. Most of the cotton produced in the United States falls in this category.

4. Ordinary long staple: Between $1\frac{1}{8}$ and $1\frac{3}{8}$ inches. (The name of pima cotton, an American-Egyptian variety that has an extralong-staple fiber, is often used in the trade as a term for any long-staple cotton.)

5. Extralong staple: From $1\frac{3}{8}$ to $2\frac{1}{2}$ inches long.

In the second, or fineness, grading system, there are nine basic divisions: middling fair, strict good middling, good middling, strict middling, middling, strict low middling, low middling, strict good ordinary, and good ordinary.

Cotton is picked either by hand or

(top left) Flax pulling by machinery. (top center) Flax after scutching, in which the woody portions are removed by rollers. (right) A hackling machine combing fibers to prepare the flax for spinning. (bottom left) A spinning frame preparing fibers for weaving under controlled warm, moist atmospheric conditions. [THE IRISH LINEN GUILD]

by mechanical means. A picker can gather about 15 pounds by hand in an hour, whereas a spindle-type mechanical picker can harvest up to 650 pounds in an hour. However, mechanical harvesting has one decided disadvantage: it picks up much waste matter along with the lint.

After picking, the cotton must be cleaned in preparation for spinning. This cleaning process, which is known as ginning, is still based in principle on the mechanical cotton gin invented by Eli Whitney in 1793. The seed cotton, as the newly picked cotton is called, is fed into the gin stand. A series of circular saws projecting through steel ribs separates the lint or fiber from the seeds. The fiber is then carried to the baling press, which compresses it to a density of about 28 pounds per cubic foot. The bales of cotton, each weighing about 479 pounds, are wrapped in jute and sent to the spinner for processing.

Processing. Cotton moves through six stages in the process of being changed from a raw cotton fiber into finished yarn.

1. Picking: At the mill the cotton bales are opened and fed into a blender, which arranges the fibers for uniformity. The fibers are then processed through the picker, which picks out the heavier impurities such as seed and dirt. It then forms the lint into laps resembling rolls of absorbent cotton, each lap measuring approximately 45 inches in width and 18 inches in diameter.

2. Carding: From the picker the lap goes to the carding machine, which straightens the fibers and lays them in parallel rows by drawing them over a revolving cylinder with teeth. They emerge from the carding machine as a thin, wide web that still resembles absorbent cotton. This web is gathered together into a rope known as a sliver.

3. Combing: If a higher quality of cotton fabric is wanted, the fiber goes

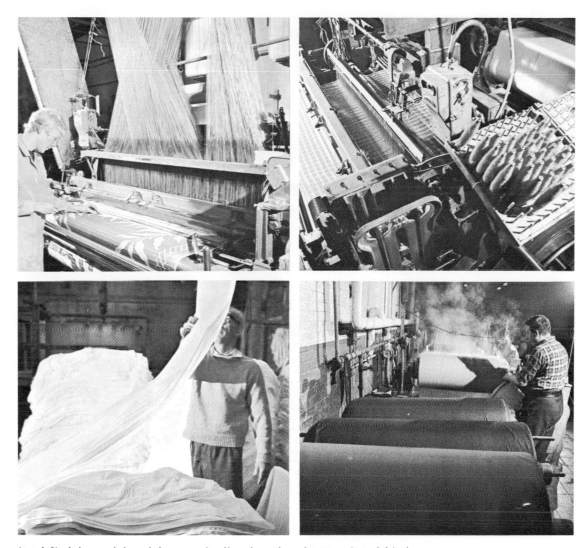

(top left) A jacquard damask loom weaving linen in a planned pattern. (top right) An automatic box-loom. (bottom left) Linen immediately after it has been bleached pure white. (bottom right) A vat-dyeing jig. [THE IRISH LINEN GUILD]

from the carding machine to the combing machine, where it is straightened by fine-tooth combing until all the short lengths have been removed. The fiber is then formed into comber slivers.

4. Drawing: From the carding or combing machine the slivers pass through a drawing operation in which several slivers are combined and drawn out or pulled into thinner strands. These fibers remain parallel.

5. Roving: This operation is basically a twisting process. The sliver may move through several slubbing frames, depending on the fineness of yarn wanted. The first stage is known as the slubber; the sliver is drawn out into a thinner strand and given a few twists. At this point the cotton is known as a roving.

6. Spinning: The spinning frame takes the roving, and the process of drawing out and twisting continues until the finished yarn emerges and is wound on bobbins. Warp, or lengthwise, yarns require more twisting than filling yarns because they are subjected to greater tension in the weaving process.

Having gone through these stages, the resulting yarn is classified by thickness. The basic unit of measurement is the hank: a hank 840 yards long and weighing 1 pound is classed as 1s. A finer yarn classed as 2s takes twice the yardage to make 1 pound. A 30s count, then, means that there are 25,200 yards of yarn in each 1-pound hank.

Weaving and knitting. Weaving cotton yarn consists of interlacing the lengthwise warp yarns with the crosswise filling yarns. This is basically the same way in which the yarns of other fibers are woven, but in the case of cotton the warp yarns may first be coated with starch or sizing to prevent breaking, since these yarns are subjected to great tension.

Cotton yarn is knitted on automatic

(*top*) *The finishing range.* (*bottom*) *Final processing of printed linen.*

machines of either the circular or the flat type, including warp, tricot, and raschel equipment. In the circular machine the yarn travels round and round, producing a continuous tube of cloth. As the machine revolves, the needles, which are arranged in a circle on a rotating cylinder, knit the rows of loops and the cloth emerges as a circular tube. In the flat machine the needles are arranged in a straight line in a flat plate, or bed. The yarn travels alternately back and forth to make the cloth, which can be shaped or varied in width during the knitting process. It is estimated that knitting machines generally can make cloth two to five times as fast as weaving looms.

Finishing. Fabrics can be finished in many different ways, depending on the texture and feel desired. Among the processes used in finishing cotton are the following.

1. Beetling: The cloth is beaten by metal or wooden hammers that force the fibers together, flattening the yarns and producing a lustrous, linenlike effect.

2. Bleaching: Bleaching agents turn the cloth from its natural off-white color to a pure white.

3. Boiling: The cloth is boiled in large tanks called kiers to remove sizing, specks, waxes, and other impurities.

4. Calendering: This process re- moves wrinkles and gives the cloth a smooth, ironed appearance. Pressure, moisture, and heat are applied with a series of heavy rollers. Depending on the type of fabric desired, the calen- dering may be light or heavy. In addi- tion, steel rollers with a raised surface pattern may be used to give texture to the cloth.

5. Compressive shrinking: This is accomplished by applying water, steam, and heat while compressing the fabric in the warp direction. "San- forized" is the patented name for the best-known compressive shrinking process.

6. Crease-resistant finishes: A resin is applied to the cloth in a water solu- tion and baked into the fibers, then neutralized and rinsed. A cotton fabric thus treated is crease- or wrinkle- resistant.

7. Dyeing: Cotton can be dyed at any one of three stages in its prepara- tion: as fiber, as yarn, and as woven cloth.

8. Mercerizing: A 25 to 30 percent solution of caustic soda is applied to the fabric, swelling and straightening the fibers permanently to give them a smooth, silklike luster.

9. Napping: Rollers inset with wires are revolved rapidly as the cloth is drawn against them over a drum. A nap is raised on the cloth, giving it a soft, fluffy surface.

10. Permanent glazing of chintz: To produce a finish that will not be affected adversely by washing and dry cleaning, heat and pressure are used in conjunction with special resins. The resins also tend to stabilize the fabric so that it will not shrink excessively when it is washed.

11. Printing: Colors are printed on cotton cloth by the use of pastes con- taining starch and resin that carry the dye. The actual printing is accom- plished by several methods, the most popular being roller and screen print- ing.

12. Singeing: Hot plates or gas flames are used to burn off lint and loose threads.

13. Shearing: To produce an evenly napped surface, rotating blades are

used to cut off any surface irregularities.

14. Tentering: While the cloth is still damp, it is stretched to uniform dimensions on a tenter frame that grasps the cloth in clips at the selvage. The cloth is passed over a continuous belt as it is dried and set in its dimensions.

15. Waterproofing and water repellency: For waterproofing, the fabric is coated with rubber, linseed oil, neoprene, or a comparable substance. Water-repellent finishes are based on resins, plastics, waxes, or emulsions that impregnate the cloth. They may be cured or heat-set to make them more durable.

16. Special finishes: Many different finishes may be applied to give cloth resistance against such conditions as mildew, stains, and perspiration.

Cotton apparel. While more than 25 percent of the cotton consumed in the United States is applied to industrial uses, about 40 percent is used for apparel. Cotton's low cost, durability, high absorbency, and easy care make it suitable for men's shirts, slacks, suits, jackets, coats, knitwear, hosiery, underwear, work clothes, sleepwear, beachwear, caps, hats, belts, rainwear, and neckwear. Among the most popular cottons for menswear are broadcloth, batiste, chambray, chino, corduroy, denim, flannelette, duck, gabardine, jean, oxford, piqué, madras, lisle, pongee, poplin, rib-knit, sailcloth, seersucker, cotton shantung, terry cloth, twill, and whipcord.

A major factor contributing to the popularity of cotton is its washability; it is actually stronger wet than dry. It can be boiled without damage, resists shrinking, has excellent colorfastness, and can be ironed safely at temperatures as high as 425°F. Despite the rise of the many man-made fibers, cotton has retained its position as the world's major textile fiber.

Bast fibers. There are a great number of bast fibers, which are obtained from the fibrous mass situated between the outer covering and the inner core of the stem of certain plants. Seven have achieved special importance in the making of textiles: jute, flax, hemp, sunn, ramie, kenaf, and urena. Of them, jute is first in terms of quantity, although flax, generally considered to be the most ancient of all textile fibers, is the best known since it is the only fiber that can be used legally in the manufacture of linen goods. The three bast fibers that, in varying degrees, are used in today's fashions are described below.

Jute. This fiber is obtained from the stalks of the jute plant *Corchorus*, a herbaceous annual that grows to 12 feet or more in height with a stalk diameter of $\frac{1}{4}$ inch to 1 inch. The word *jute* comes from the Hindi and Bengali name for this plant. The yield of fiber from the jute plant is two to five times as great as that from the flax stalk.

Commercial jute varies in color from yellow to brown to a dirty gray. Though reasonably strong, the fiber has poor elasticity. While this is certainly a drawback in the fashion field, it makes jute remarkably well suited to its primary use as a bagging cloth. The United States imports more than 700 million pounds a year, and although jute is employed far more extensively in industry than in fashion, it is used in sportswear fabrics for both men and women.

Flax. This is the fiber surrounding the woody core of the flax plant *Linum usitatissimum*, which is used in making linen. A prehistoric textile fiber (fragments of linen cloth have been found in remains of Stone Age lake villages in Switzerland), flax lays claim to the title of the most ancient of bast fibers. Flax possesses most of the qualities of cotton but is stronger and more absorbent. Long the world's most important textile fiber, it was eventually replaced by cotton, which is easier and cheaper to raise. The U.S.S.R. is the world's largest producer of flax fiber and consumes most of its flax production domestically.

The flax fiber is a long, smooth cylindrical tube ranging in color from creamy white to light tan and punctuated by bamboolike joints. The stalk from which the fibers come is composed of two parts, a cell wall and an outer bark, which are held together by a gum that is dissolved as the fibers are processed. Flax is composed mostly of cellulose, and after boiling, bleaching, and drying it is almost pure cellulose. The following steps are involved in converting the flax fiber into finished fabric.

1. Retting: This process involves soaking the flax stalks in warm water to rot away the woody core and dissolve the gums so that the fibers can be loosened and pulled away. In the United States retting is done in man-made tanks in which the water is heated to between 80 and 90°F. In some other parts of the world retting is still done in natural waters; in Belgium, for instance, the water of the Lys River is used in the production of the well-known Courtrai flax. In any event, the water must always be clean, soft, and free from impurities that would discolor the flax. The retting process may take anywhere from four days to three weeks, depending on the methods used.

2. Scutching: The retted and dried flax is sent to the mill, where scutching rollers break up and separate the woody portions of the stalk from the usable fiber.

3. Hackling: This process involves cleaning and straightening the fibers with combs. It is basically the same as the carding and combing process in cotton manufacture.

4. Carding, drawing, roving, spinning, and weaving: These are the same processes as those used in preparing cotton yarn for the weaving operation. They involve additional cleaning, drawing out, and doubling the fibers into strong yarn for warps and filling.

5. Finishing: Linen requires little finishing. Boiling and bleaching are basically the same as in the cotton process. Some linens are also subjected to beetling, in which the cloth is pounded with large wooden blocks to give it a permanent sheen.

Linen is a cool, absorbent fabric. Its natural lack of wrinkle-resistance is corrected by a process which impregnates the fabric with a synthetic resin that penetrates the fiber. After being exposed to the resin solution, the linen is stretched back to its original width on mechanical frames and run through a curing chamber to settle the resin in the fiber and thus make its resistance to creasing permanent. This process may be followed by any desired type of finish.

Because of limited production, linen is one of the more expensive fashion fabrics, but its durability and crisp looks have made it extremely popular for suits, sports jackets, slacks, shirts, ties, and shoes.

Hemp. The true hemp plant grows from 7 to 10 feet high and has a stalk about ½ inch in diameter. (There are at least fifty other fibers, of different botanical species, also known as hemp.) Like flax, hemp is a prehistoric fiber reportedly first used in Asia. In fact, it was the first textile fiber developed by the Japanese. Hemp is retted and processed much like flax, and the yellowish brown fiber looks very much like the flax fiber. Hemp, too, consists predominantly of cellulose.

The U.S.S.R., Italy, and Yugoslavia are the largest producers of hemp. The chief use of hemp is in the manufacture of cordage, although linen-type woven fabrics are being made of fine Italian hemp.

Wool.

History. Wool's history begins in Central Asia 10,000 years ago, when men discovered that sheep could furnish them with two essentials: soft, warm covering and food. At first men used the sheep's fleece as a kind of tunic. It was not until 3500 B.C. that men discovered how to spin wool.

Between 3000 and 1000 B.C. domestic sheep and wool spread to Europe via ancient Greece, and during succeeding millennia they were brought into North Africa and Western Europe. When the Romans conquered and occupied Britain beginning in 55 B.C., they brought with them the craft of wool textile manufacture. (The craft became an art from which the British Empire grew.) By A.D. 50 the Roman conquerors had set up a woolen manufactory in Winchester. Through-out the Middle Ages England and Spain were prime rivals in the world wool trade; the voyages of the early Spanish explorers were financed from the wool trade. By 1660 wool textile exports comprised two-thirds of England's foreign commerce.

Wool manufacturing machinery was developed in England, and the demand for wool cloth grew so rapidly that new sources of raw wool were needed. The supply was found in South Africa and Australia, where climates as warm as that of Spain favored the development of sheep flocks.

Sheep came to the New World with the first explorers and settlers, just as they had accompanied other adventurers in earlier times. When Columbus made his second voyage in 1493, sheep were among the livestock he brought to Cuba and Santo Domingo. On the mainland, the first sheep were introduced into Mexico in 1519 by Spanish troops under Hernán Cortés. Herds spread eventually through California and New Mexico. The importance of wool at this time is illustrated by the fact that a law was passed in 1664 by the General Court of Massachusetts that required youths to learn to spin and weave.

The British tried to discourage the woolen industry in the American colonies, and the resentment of the colonists at the restrictions placed on sheep raising and wool manufacturing was one of the causes of the Revolutionary War. Immediately after the Revolution, the new nation's leaders became acutely aware of the lack of the best grades of apparel wool. George Washington (he had been inaugurated in a suit of American wool), long a sheep breeder at Mount Vernon, imported merino rams from Spain to improve his sheep and required his people to spin and weave at least a yard of cloth each day on their handlooms. Meanwhile, weavers and other wool craftsmen from Europe were offered immediate citizenship in the United States, and a newer, bigger industry began to be built.

Throughout the nineteenth century, as men moved across the fertile river valleys of the United States, the sheep population moved with them. By the middle of the century, millions of sheep were grazing on the lands of the Spanish in the Southwest. Today sheep are grown in every state of the Union, the largest producers being Texas, Wyoming, California, Colorado, Montana, South Dakota, Utah, New Mexico, Iowa, and Idaho. They number about 20 million. Woolen mills engaged in the conversion of wool into wool products account for goods with an annual retail value of about $5 billion.

The United States is the sixth largest wool producer in the world, following Australia, the U.S.S.R., New Zealand, Argentina, and South Africa. The total sheep population of the world is estimated at more than 1 billion, and the annual raw-wool yield is about 6 billion pounds in the greasy state, or about 3.3 billion pounds after the wool has been cleaned. Of this total, about three-fourths goes into the manufacture of clothing and household and industrial textiles; the rest, into carpets.

Sheep breeds. Important to wool production are the breeds of sheep that yield the various types and qualities of wool. There are approximately 200 breeds, of which the following are the most important: Cheviot ram, Columbia ewe, Corriedale ram, Cotswold ram, Dorset ram, Hampshire ram, Rambouillet ram, Romney marsh ewe, Southdown ram, Targhee ram, Tunis ram, and West Highland ewe.

The variety of breeds is infinite. A merino crossed with a pure breed like the long-wool sheep is called a half blood. The offspring of a long-wool and a half-blood sheep is a quarter blood. Breed names are applied to the wools as well as to the animals themselves.

In general, merino sheep produce the best wool. The merino is a kind of poodle sheep, with only its snout and its feet free from wool. The fibers are only 2 to 4 inches long, but they have more sawteeth to the inch than any other wool and so make the finest fabric.

The next best are the long-wool sheep. They are of English origin and have a coarse, lustrous wool with fibers sometimes as long as 12 inches. Long wools such as Leicester, Lincoln, Cotswold, and Romney marsh were often crossed with merinos to produce crossbreeds.

The Shropshire breed is easy to care for and has fair wool and good mutton. Southdowns, Suffolks, Hampshires, Oxfords, and Dorsets give good mutton but are short on wool. Scotch Cheviots make fine tweeds; Shetlands are best for hosiery and knit underwear. Leicesters crossed with an Irish breed produced the Roscommons.

Shearing. In general, wool is shorn in the spring of the year. Where the climate permits, many producers prefer to shear before lambing time. Shearing is done with a powered handpiece similar to a barber's clippers but much larger. Good shearers are highly skilled, and most can shear 125 head of sheep per day. The very expert can shear a sheep in less than five minutes.

The fleece is rolled off with long, smooth strokes, then rolled up and tied, identified, and packed in bags holding thirty-five fleeces each and weighing 200 to 400 pounds. Once sacked, the wool is identified with a number and sent to the warehouse or mill for processing. Processing the wool fiber into yarn or fabric may require any or all of the following procedures, the number depending on the type of fabric desired.

Grading and/or sorting. Wool is classified according to the average diameter and length of the fibers in the fleece. The end use of the product determines the grade of wool required.

The oldest of the grading systems is the blood system, originally derived from the fine-wool merino and Rambouillet sheep. Their wool was called fine. If a sheep was one-half Rambouillet or merino and one-half another breed, usually an English mutton-type breed, the fibers were almost always coarser or larger in cross-section diameter than those of the pureblood sheep. These wools were called one-half blood. The same prin-

ciple applied to the terms three-eighths blood and quarter blood, which designate the amount of fine-wool breeding behind the particular sheep that produced the wool.

The numerical count system is a more technical classification of wool in terms of fiber diameter. The count refers to the number of hanks of yarn, each 560 yards long, that can be spun from 1 pound of wool top. Thus, a 64s wool would yield 35,840 yards (560 yards $\times$ 64), or 107,520 feet, of yarn. In other words, 20.4 miles of yarn could be spun from 1 pound of 64s top.

The micron count system is a substantially more technical and accurate measurement of the average diameter of wool fiber in a given lot of wool. The micron ($\frac{1}{25,000}$ inch) is used as the average diameter measurement. An 80s wool that averages 18.1 microns is less than half the average diameter of a common and braid 36s that has an average diameter of 39.7 microns. There is a growing effort to institute the use of the micron system in the technical description of wools for tariff classification. Eventually this system may become the standard for describing wools in the United States.

Washing and scouring. The wool is washed thoroughly in troughs containing a soap or detergent and water solution at temperatures up to 140°F. When the natural grease (lanolin), suint, and dirt are removed, the wool loses 30 to 70 percent of its weight. After being rinsed in cold water, the wool is passed through a squeeze roller and dried at the correct temperature to permit ease of handling. The purified lanolin is a by-product used in the manufacture of face creams, soaps, and ointments.

Blending. Wool yarn is ordinarily spun from several different lots of wool in order to obtain various color mixes and to maintain uniformity and quality. The blending is achieved by putting together several lots of wool of different colors in desired proportions and mixing them technically. If the bulk wool is dyed, the different colors of the separate lots merge at this stage.

Dyeing. Dyeing may be done at any of several points during processing. If bulk wool is dyed immediately after washing, it is said to be stock-dyed. Dyeing the wool after it has been spun into yarn is called yarn dyeing. Wool may also be dyed after it is made into fabric (piece-dyed). Wool absorbs and holds color so well that dyeing at any stage is equally effective.

Carding. Carding is the process of opening and separating the wool fibers, causing them to lie in the same direction. The wool passes through a system of rollers that vary in diameter and move at different speeds. The rollers are covered with wire teeth that draw the fibers straight and interlace them in a thin web. In the woolen system, the web is divided into narrow strips or slivers, which when gently rubbed together form roving. From the roving the yarns for woolen fabrics such as tweeds and fleece fabrics are made. The roving still contains some short wool fibers that lie in several directions, a circumstance that makes woolen fabrics relatively dense and their surfaces somewhat fuzzy. The next two steps, combing and drawing, are omitted for woolen yarns.

Combing. In making worsted yarn for crisp smooth-surfaced fabrics such as gabardines and crepes, the carded slivers are combed. Combing further straightens the fibers, lays them parallel to one another, and removes any short fibers. The resulting strand is condensed into a thinner rope of fibers called a sliver, which is wound into a ball called top. The short fibers removed at this stage are called noils; they are used in the woolen system.

Drawing. Wool for worsted yarn is next drawn through a series of machines that gradually reduce the top to a thin, slightly twisted strand called roving. The roving is placed on large spools ready for spinning.

Spinning. Yarns for both woolens and worsteds go through spinning processes. After the spools are in place on the spinning frame, the ends of the roving are drawn through small rollers that draw the fibers out still further. They are then wound onto revolving bobbins that apply a twist to the roving and create finished yarn of a specified size.

Weaving and knitting. Weaving is the production of cloth by the interlacing of two sets of yarn at right angles. The threads running lengthwise in the loom are known as the warp, and those running crosswise as the filling or weft. As each warp thread passes through the loom, it is raised and lowered by a wire eyelet through which it is threaded. Warp threads are alternately opened and closed as the threads are raised and lowered by the loom. At each shift a filling thread is shot through the opening created in the warp, thereby forming a woven fabric.

The knitting operation is accomplished on machines that simulate hand knitting. In knitting, the fabric is formed by interlocking series of loops of one or more yarns.

Finishing. All the processes to which the wool fabric is subjected after leaving the loom are called finishing processes. Some of the differences in the surface appearance of wool fabrics are due to special finishing processes, and much of the beauty of woolen fabrics is developed at this stage.

Woolens are often brushed to raise the ends of the wool fibers above the surface of the cloth in a soft, fuzzy nap. Naps range from the lightly brushed surface of flannel to the deep-pile effect of fleecy coatings. The nap may be cropped and carefully brushed in one direction, as with wool broadcloth. It may be pressed flat to form the glossy, lustrous surface of a zibeline. It may be sheared to an even, velvety smoothness as in a wool plush.

Worsteds go through less radical changes in finishing, although the characteristic crisp, firm appearance of worsted fabric is sometimes enhanced by special treatment. Occasionally, worsteds are lightly napped to give them a woolenlike face. This process produces a fabric with the softness of a woolen and the firmness of a worsted.

Before the fabric is subjected to any finishing, it is thoroughly examined for imperfections or blemishes, which are then removed. The construction of the fabric is perfected, sometimes by reweaving spots by hand. When the cloth is perfect, it is ready for wet-finishing operations, which are required for some types of fabric and finishes. The fabric may be dyed at this point if it has not been dyed previously. It is then washed again to remove dirt before being subjected to the fulling process.

1. Fulling: Fulling is the important finishing process that gives a wool fabric body by tightening the weave. It shrinks the fabric in both length and width under carefully controlled conditions. The fabric is thoroughly dampened, pressed through rollers, and then washed to remove oil and other impurities. The greater the shrinkage in fulling, the stronger the fabric. Fabrics like meltons and doeskins are fulled to the extent that the weaves are completely obscured.

2. Decating (decatizing): The stability of a fabric is enhanced by winding it under tension on a perforated cylinder through which steam is passed.

3. Crabbing: Crabbing sets the cloth and yarn twist by rotating the fabric over cylinders through baths of first hot and then cold water. The fabric is held firmly and tightly to prevent wrinkling. Repetition of the treatment with increased pressure sets the fabric and the finish.

4. Sponging: Wool fabric may be preshrunk by dampening it with a sponge, rolling it in moist muslin, or steaming. Sponging is applied to woolens and worsteds before cutting to prevent contraction of the fabric in the finished garment as a result of stresses created in manufacturing. A popular sponging treatment is the London-shrunk process, in which definite shrinkage percentages are obtained under controlled conditions and guaranteed by the manufacturer. The fabric is refinished after this treatment.

5. Other special finishes: Additional rainproofing and spotproofing may be applied to reinforce the natural water repellency of wool. Wool fabrics are also treated chemically for permanent mothproofing, machine-washability, and machine drying.

6. Dry finishing: Woolens and worsteds may go through additional dry-finishing operations. Napping is the process used to raise the fibers on the face of the goods, creating a soft, smooth texture. The nap may then be sheared to a level surface, either high or close to the weave. A closely sheared surface nap is seen on melton, jersey, and beaver cloth.

In singeing, the cloth is passed over a series of gas jets that burn off protruding or stray fibers and produce a smooth, uniform surface. This process helps give the characteristic hard finish to many worsted fabrics.

"Unfinished" is a term applied to worsteds the face of which has been given a napping treatment. In unfinished worsteds the weave is difficult to distinguish beneath the nap, giving them an appearance quite different from that of standard worsteds, which have a clear finish or, simply, no finish.

Final operations. After the appropriate finish has been applied to each piece of goods, the fabrics are pressed and ready for final inspection. The goods are then measured for bolt lengths of 50 to 100 yards. Tags giving essential information are attached to each piece or bolt, and the fabrics are given a final check. Then the goods are wrapped for shipment to the consignee.

Wool apparel. Apparel consumes by far the largest single portion of the world wool supply. In menswear wool is used for overcoats, topcoats, hats, caps, suits, shirts, sweaters, jackets, hosiery, underwear, robes, neckwear, belts, scarves, gloves, slippers, and interlinings.

Specialty fibers. While not officially designated as wool, this group of fibers has many of its characteristics. The specialty fibers are also noted for the creation of special effects or for the addition of special qualities to fabric.

Alpaca. Alpaca is the long, smooth hair obtained from the animal known as the alpaca, a member of the same genus as the llama, found at altitudes of 14,000 feet in the Andes Mountains. The fiber is lustrous, strong, and soft to the touch; the fleece, which is usually taken after a two-year growth, is rich and silky and usually weighs about 10 pounds. In color, the fibers vary from white to brown to black. There are three varieties of fiber: fine alpaca, which is $4\frac{1}{2}$ to 8 inches long; medium alpaca, $5\frac{1}{2}$ to 9 inches long; and coarse alpaca, 7 to 11 inches long. Coat and suit fabrics and sweaters are made from alpaca, mostly in combination with wool.

Mohair. Mohair is the long, fine fiber clipped from the angora goat, which originated in the province of Angora (Ankara), Turkey, and is also raised in the southwestern part of the United States. It is so smooth and soft that it must be combined with other fibers in weaving. After cleaning to remove impurities, scoured mohair appears smooth and white; it is particularly lustrous and resilient, with much tensile strength. Mohair is particularly popular in formal evening clothes.

Camel's hair. This hair is taken from the fine, woollike undercoat of the two-humped Bactrian camel found in Central Asia. The fibers are collected by shearing and gathering the hair that falls off in clumps during the spring molting period. Lustrous and almost incredibly soft, camel's hair varies in color from light tan to a brownish black. It is woven or blended with fine wool to produce overcoats, topcoats, sportswear, and hosiery. The camel's hair polo coat is a fashion classic dating back to the 1920s, when Ivy League undergraduates popularized it after having seen the coat worn by members of a visiting British polo team.

Cashmere. This fiber is obtained from the soft undercoat of the Kashmir goat. Only a few ounces are taken from each goat. More like wool than any other fiber, cashmere is soft and downy to the touch and brownish in color. It is used in expensive overcoats, sports jackets, and sweaters.

Guanaco. A member of the same genus as the llama and a native of South America, the guanaco produces a soft honey-colored fleece that is used in its entirety.

Llama. A member of the camel family, the llama, a beast of burden weighing approximately 250 pounds, is raised successfully in the mountains of Bolivia, Peru, southern Ecuador, and northwestern Argentina. Its outer coat is coarse, but the fleece next to the body is extremely fine and much like that of its relative, the alpaca. The fleece, which is shorn every two years, is used in woolens and hair-fiber materials that are light, warm, and lustrous.

The llama and the alpaca freely interbreed and produce two hybrids: the huarizo, born of a llama father and an alpaca mother; and the paco llama, or misti, born of an alpaca father and a llama mother. Both hybrids produce fleece that can be used in fine fabrics.

Vicuña. The smallest and wildest member of the genus *Lama*, the 3-foot-high vicuña lives in almost inaccessible heights of the Andes Mountains of Peru, northern Bolivia, and southern Ecuador. Vicuña is the aristocrat of fibers. Less than 0.002 inch in diameter, or little more than half the diameter of the finest sheep's wool (2,500 strands side by side would not measure 1 inch), vicuña fiber has strength and resilience and may be employed in its natural reddish brown state or dyed. The soft, silklike fleece is used in the manufacture of the softest and most expensive overcoats in the world.

Silk. Silk fiber is a continuous protein filament produced by the silkworm in order to form its cocoon. The principal species used in commercial production is the mulberry silkworm, which is the larva of the silk moth, *Bombyx mori.*

History. The story of silk may be traced to the China of 4,000 years ago. Ancient Chinese literature credits the empress Si-ling, wife of the legendary emperor Huang-ti (third millennium B.C.), with raising silkworms and inventing the silk loom. Silken fabrics, in fact, were used by the aristocracy of ancient China as a medium of exchange. China prospered with its silk trade to such an extent that the threat of death hung over the head of anyone who spread the secret of the craft beyond the borders imposed by imperial decree.

Eventually, however, knowledge of the silkworm and its product passed beyond the boundaries of China. About A.D. 300, legend has it, four Chinese concubines were smuggled into Japan through Korea to instruct the Japanese court and nobility in weaving silk. Another Chinese legend says that the eggs of a silk moth and a seed of the mulberry tree were taken to India in the headdress of a Chinese princess. (A major silk industry did not develop in India, however, until after the Mogul conquest of the sixteenth century.)

The path of silk led next to Persia and Central Asia and eventually to Europe, where bits of silk brought back from the wars were regarded as treasure by women fortunate enough to receive them. Since the cultivation and manufacture of silk were highly profitable, they were encouraged by the rulers of such cities as Florence, Milan, Genoa, and Venice. In 1480 the French king Louis XI started the first silk mill at Tours, and some 200 years later France was so enthusiastic about its silk industry that it offered premiums for the planting of mulberry trees.

Silk making was encouraged in England in the sixteenth and seventeenth centuries, when skilled silk workers from Flanders and France settled there. A guild of French silk workers was set up in Spitalfields in 1629. King James I endeavored to introduce the silkworm into the British segment of the New World, bolstering the incipient industry in Virginia by means of bounties and rewards, and laws were passed to stimulate its development. At the time of the American Revolution, Benjamin Franklin was in the midst of trying to establish a silk mill in Philadelphia. After the new nation was formed, Connecticut tried by means of the bounty system to encourage home silk raising, and practically every state in the Union emulated its lead and continued doing so until as late as 1872.

From the mid-nineteenth century until the present day, Japan has dominated the international silk market. China, the U.S.S.R., India, and South Korea are the next largest producers of silk.

Silk textiles reached the peak of their popularity here in the United States in the period just after World War I. A time of affluence, it saw factory workers wearing $25 silk shirts to their jobs.

Production. The following account, printed originally in *Apparel Arts* magazine in 1932, describes the production of silk from the silkworm egg to the silk fabric.

What goes into a piece of silk? The silkworm, or Bombyx Mori, to use his biological name, is raised for the most part in a domesticated state by farmers in the rural districts of China, Japan and Italy, and to a limited extent, in certain near eastern countries. There is also to be found in China a species of wild silkworm feeding on the oak tree in preference to the mulberry tree of the white cultivated silkworm. An energetic worker, the silkworm is as fussy about his working conditions as any prima donna, or since this is a story of masculine control of silk, as any operatic tenor. From the time the egg is placed on a bit of paper and carefully examined for traces of any disease (pebrine affects seriously the quality of the silk thread) to the time when the worm begins to spin his cocoon, the little worker changes his coat four times, a boon to any tailor. After dieting for a month on the succulent leaves of the mulberry tree, he seeks a twig which the silkworm farmer conveniently places near him, and immediately winds himself up into a knot by spinning a thread of a substance exuded from two little glands in his head. These figure eight loops of thread about his body (there are about 300,000 of them in all) make the silk cocoon.

Silk from the wild worm is called *Tussah* and is woven into the pongee family of cloth—pongee, honan, shantung. Silk from the cultivated worm is that generally found in silk fabrics, while the cocoon from which the moth has emerged is made into spun silk, a short staple yarn going into radium, shirtings, tub silk and sport weaves.

Carefully removed from the twig, the cocoon is sent to the filature, or factory, where the reeling is done. A few cocoons are retained for breeding purposes and from these emerge the silk moths. In the filature are long rows of reeling-girls; each sits before a basin of water attached to a machine for winding the silk onto a large reel. The cocoons are placed in the water, usually very hot. This softens the natural gum with which the silk thread is coated, and makes it possible to unwind the cocoon as one continuous thread. This thread may run 1000 yards in length. But one cocoon is too fine a thread to put into fabrics. The reeling-girl takes four and five cocoons and joins their filaments by unraveling them together. The soft gum solidifies the several threads which then find their way as a single strand to the slowly revolving reel above. Much skill is needed. If a filament from one of those four or five cocoons should suddenly break, the reeling must be stopped at once lest the size of the thread be thinner for that length. Failure to repair a break results in an uneven appearance in the finished silk; so-called "rings" in a silk sock are an instance. As in all handmade products, perfection is, of course, impossible, but the demands of silk wearers compel producers and weavers of raw silk to make a constant effort to maintain evenness of size in reeling the silk. In the silk trade, it is customary for buyers of raw material to specify that there shall be no more than a certain percentage of unevenness in the silk, and hundreds of bales of silk are rejected yearly when deliveries fail to come up to requirements. The more responsible the manufacturer, the more care is taken to protect the finished product.

Reeled skeins are twisted into hanks, packed into what are known as "books." Bundles of about 30 skeins are baled, burlapped and shipped to this country by fast steamers. Due to its high value, and resultant high interest and insurance charges, the silk starts immediately for New York from the Pacific Coast. From New York it is shipped to outlying mills.

Before it can be woven, the silk must be "thrown"—an adaptation of an old Anglo-Saxon word meaning to "twist"—and that is really what the process is. Several raw silk threads, which singly are about the thickness of a human hair, are twisted together. The number of threads and the number of times they are twisted per inch of length depends upon the type of fabric. Radiums, taffetas, and tub silks have a small amount of twist. Crepes, such as crepe de chine, canton crepe, faille crepe are tightly twisted to achieve the characteristic crinkle. Crepe is derived from the Latin word "crispus," meaning to crinkle, and that's what the twisted yarn does when it is in the cloth. At the time it is thrown or twisted, the number of twists per inch runs from 40 to 80. It is wound immediately on spools and woven into fabric before it is dyed. Otherwise, it would snarl. In the case of the more lightly twisted yarns, such as those used for weaving taffeta, tie silks, or hat bands, the yarn is dyed before weaving. Happily, in the case of tie silks and hat bands, the color demand is not as changeable as in dress fabrics. A beautifully woven piece of real tie silk is always in good taste. There is a difference between tie silks and those used in ties. At one time, all men's neckwear was made from tie silks. In recent years, dress fabrics have been added to the list.

It is a common fallacy that silk does not wear as well as other fabrics, and substitution of other fibers has developed widely during the past decade. As a matter of fact, silk is the strongest fiber known to man. When well woven in a plain weave, and by that is meant a fabric in which the crosswise threads run alternately over and under each lengthwise thread, and when properly laundered, silk will not only give the satisfaction demanded of it, but will also give greater comfort. Excellent non-conductor of heat, it preserves the body heat in cold.

A bath was one of its earliest experiences as we have seen when the thread was immersed in boiling water to reel it. Later too, in the throwing process, it got a thorough soaking in water and a neutral soap. Still later, in the dyeing process, there was plenty of hot water applied. Colors, therefore, need not trouble anyone. The very process of dyeing means that the color was boiled in the fabric under temperatures never approximated by the average laundry conditions. A good washing with moderately warm water and plenty of soap suds refreshes any silk, and that washing should be frequent especially in the case of those who perspire heavily.

Not all silk is thrown, however; some silk is spun on the cotton system. Unlike reeled silk, which is a continuous filament, this silk has a short fiber like cotton and is therefore spun into yarn by the same methods. The fiber comes from cocoons that have been pierced by the emerging silk moth, from the inferior beginnings and ends of the cocoon filament, and from silk waste produced at various stages of processing. Before spun silk can be processed, the gum must be removed by boiling off the waste silk in soapy water. The fibers are then washed in clear water, dried, and processed like cotton lint.

Yarn size or count. There are three methods of determining the size or count of silk yarn: the ounce system, the denier system, and the dram system.

1. Ounce system: This system is an English method that is used not for general silk measurement but in insulating and in the knit goods trade. It is based on the number of yards of silk yarn by ounce of weight. There are about 20,000 yards of yarn in 1 ounce of silk.

2. Denier system: The most widely used of the three methods, the denier system is employed for raw silk and thrown silk on the Continent. The weight of the denier, a small coin derived from the Roman denarius, was established in the sixteenth century by the French king Francis I as the standard measurement of the budding silk industry. Today the denier is the unit of a numerical system used to describe the fineness of yarn. The higher the denier, the thicker the yarn. Silk with a fineness of 1 denier has a weight of 50 milligrams, or 0.05 gram, for 450 meters.

3. Dram system: This system is based on the weight in drams of a hank of silk 1,000 yards long. (In avoirdupois weight there are 16 drams to 1 ounce.)

Silk characteristics. Known as nature's luxury fabric, silk has physical characteristics that have made it a favorite for apparel. It is lighter in weight than wool, cotton, linen, or rayon, and it is extremely strong (a filament of silk is stronger than an equivalent filament of steel). Silk is absorbent, being capable of soaking up 30 percent of its weight in moisture, and it will stretch as much as 20 percent of its length without breaking, although it will not spring back if it is stretched more than 2 percent. It is not injured by temperatures as high as 284°F. Silk has a special luster because the smooth, translucent filament of raw silk, when processed, becomes a smooth, lustrous, luxurious fabric that can be dyed in brilliant colors and has excellent wrinkle recovery.

Uses. Among the types of silk used in menswear are tub silks, or radiums, once widely employed in underwear.

For neckwear there are brocades and more conservatively figured silks that retain their depth of color and general appearance after being tied many times. Crepe de chine in a close weave and plain colors is used in shirts, while crepe de chine, pongee, and striped silks in a plain weave are highly satisfactory for pajamas. Shantung, a rough plain-woven fabric made from tussah silk, makes a dressy summer-weight suit.

Man–made Fibers

The man-made or synthetic fibers include the cellulosic fibers such as rayon and acetate and the noncellulosic fibers such as the acrylics, polyesters, and nylon.

Rayon. Rayon is the oldest and least expensive of the man-made fibers. The first fiber was created in France in 1884, after some seven years of work, by Count Hilaire de Chardonnet, who used the extract of mulberry leaves. This process of manufacture was known as the nitrocellulose method, and cloth from this yarn was first shown to the public in a fabric exhibit at the Paris Exposition in 1889. Rayon was first made in the United States in 1910 by the American Viscose Company. Then known as "artificial silk" (or simply as viscose), it was given the name "rayon" in 1924, at the suggestion of Kenneth Lord of Galey & Lord. The new name was derived from "ray," to suggest the sheen of the fiber, and "on" from cotton, to designate a textile fiber. Today the United States is the leading producer of rayon, followed by the U.S.S.R. and Japan.

Rayon is classified as a cellulosic fiber since its raw material is a cellulose obtained either from cotton linters, the short brown fibers left on cottonseed after the first ginning, or from wood pulp. Wood pulp for rayon comes from spruce, pine, or hemlock chips. Very simply, the production of rayon follows this formula: a solid (cellulose) is dissolved to a liquid and then hardened back into a solid (textile fiber). In detail, the process is as follows: purified cellulose is converted chemically into a honeylike solution.

This liquid is forced through the holes of a spinneret, a disc that resembles a very fine shower nozzle. The hairlike filaments that come from the spinneret are solidified as they emerge and are twisted together to form a rayon yarn of any desired size, or denier. Viscose, cuprammonium, and saponified rayon are the three chief types produced today. Each type is the product of a different type of cellulose used in conjunction with different chemicals and different manufacturing techniques.

Viscose rayon. Most rayon is made by the viscose process. The fibers and yarns of viscose rayon range from thick and bulky to fine, thin, or thick-and-thin. They may be also dull or lustrous. Uniform, lasting color is assured by solution dyeing, in which the dye is added to the cellulose while the fibers are being formed so that it becomes a basic part of the fibers.

In brief, the viscose process of rayon manufacture involves converting purified cellulose to cellulose xanthate, dissolving the xanthate in dilute caustic soda, and then regenerating the cellulose from the product as it emerges from the spinneret. Step by step, the process is as follows.

1. White sheets of bleached cellulose sulfate pulp are steeped in a solution of caustic soda to form an alkali cellulose.

2. After steeping, the sheets are shredded into fine crumbs by the revolving blades of a shredding machine. The crumbs are then stored in bins to undergo aging.

3. After the crumbs have aged, they are chuted to tumbling barrels, where carbon disulfide is added. The crumbs turn a bright orange and at this point are known as xanthate crumb. This step is known as the xanthation process.

4. The crumbs are fed into viscose dissolvers, where they are mixed with weak caustic soda to form a viscose solution, a thick honey-colored liquid.

5. The viscose solution is filtered.

6. The solution is pumped to a spinneret, extruded through the spinneret's holes into a sulfuric acid bath, withdrawn, dried, and skeined.

Continuous filament rayon is available in a variety of deniers and is used in many different fabric constructions. Shown here is American Viscose rayon filament. [FMC CORPORATION, AMERICAN VISCOSE DIVISION]

HOW RAYON FILAMENT IS MADE

The manufacture of rayon involves the processing of cellulose, derived from wood pulp or cotton linters, with the action of chemicals. Solid cellulose sheets are converted into a solution and hardened back into a solid in the form of a fiber, the process being achieved with a minimum of chemical and molecular degradation. The steps in the production of rayon filament are shown in the photographs and chart below. [FMC CORPORATION, AMERICAN VISCOSE DIVISION]

1. The cellulose is steeped in alkali: *Cellulose pulp is shipped to the plant in the form of white sheets resembling blotting paper. The sheets are placed in a hydraulic ram and steeped in a solution of caustic soda. The resulting product is known as alkali cellulose.*

2. The alkali pulp is shredded: *After steeping, the soft, damp sheets are dropped into a shredding machine, where revolving blades break them up into alkali cellulose crumbs. These flakes are stored in aging tanks, where the caustic soda continues its chemical action.*

3. The crumbs are treated with carbon disulfide: *After aging, the crumbs are placed in mechanical churns, where a measured amount of carbon disulfide is gradually added. Known as xanthate crumb, the crumbs are now orange in color and are ready to be dissolved in a dilute caustic soda solution.*

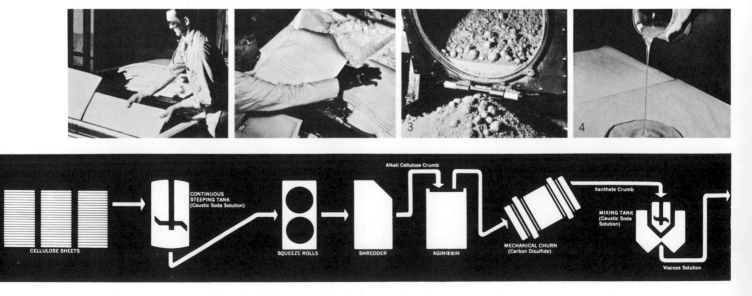

4. A viscose solution is formed: *When the xanthate crumb is dissolved in caustic soda, a viscose solution resembling honey in appearance and consistency is formed.*

5. The solution is aged: *The viscose solution is aged in large storage tanks and filtered to remove any foreign matter. It is then pumped into spinning tanks and delivered automatically to the spinning machines.*

6. Viscose is spun into an acid bath: *The spinneret shown (top) is made of platinum and rhodium. (Spinnerets are manufactured with holes ranging from .002 inch to .005 inch in diameter.) The alkaline viscose solution is pumped through the holes of the spinneret. As it is extruded, it is coagulated in a sulfuric acid spinning bath. Each of the holes in the spinneret forms a filament, as shown in the laboratory demonstration (bottom). The filaments are then combined to form rayon yarn.*

7. The yarn is collected: *The actual spinning operation is shown here. The spinnerets are immersed in the acid bath at the bottom of the tank. Thousands of filaments are extruded and hardened simultaneously and are then guided by godet wheels to a spinning box, where the yarn is collected.*

8. The finished yarn is wound: *Continuous filament yarn comes from the spinning machines in the form of cylindrical cakes. After chemical processing and drying, the cakes are then wound into cones. These are one of the forms in which rayon is shipped to American Viscose customers.*

Viscose rayon that has been modified to give greater dimensional stability in washing is known as high wet modulus rayon.

Cuprammonium rayon. Generally referred to as Bemberg rayon, cuprammonium rayon is made by the Bemberg stretch-spinning process, which involves the following steps.

1. The raw material, either cotton linters or wood pulp, is bleached a pure white in the washing machine. This is the only bleaching required of this type of rayon.

2. In a solution mixer the bleached cotton or wood pulp is dissolved into a cellulose solution by the addition of cuprammonium liquid.

3. Impurities are filtered out in a solution filter, leaving behind a pure, clean, dark blue spinning solution.

4. The solution is placed in storage tanks and allowed to age before being moved to the spinning machine.

5. After spinning, the filaments are passed through the twisting machine to give the yarn the desired twist. The size of Bemberg rayon filaments is not limited by the size of the spinneret holes but achieves fineness through the stretch-spinning device.

6. The finished yarn is wound on reels in skein form and, while being revolved, is lowered in racks into a washing bath.

Saponified rayon. This type of rayon is produced when extruded filaments of cellulose acetate are reconverted to cellulose. It therefore dyes like rayon rather than acetate.

Rayon characteristics. Rayon fibers are strong and extremely absorbent. This absorbency gives rayon fabrics a high affinity for dyes and special finishes and permits the use of cross-dyed and two-tone effects. Because of its ability to soak up moisture, rayon dries more slowly than some other man-made fibers. A tendency to shrink, which is shared by all absorbent fibers, can be controlled in the production of the fiber and in the finishing of the final fabric. Rayon is mothproof, is not affected by ordinary household bleaches and chemicals, and drapes well.

Uses. Rayon is used for suits, coats, rainwear, sports shirts, jackets, slacks, linings, work clothes, and ties.

Care of rayon fabrics. Fabrics of rayon fiber are either washable or dry-cleanable. The washable fabrics may be hand- or machine-washed, but a sheer rayon is best washed by hand in warm water with a mild soap and rinsed carefully.

Acetate. A cellulosic derivative, acetate was first produced commercially in the United States in 1924 by the Celanese Corporation. Like practically

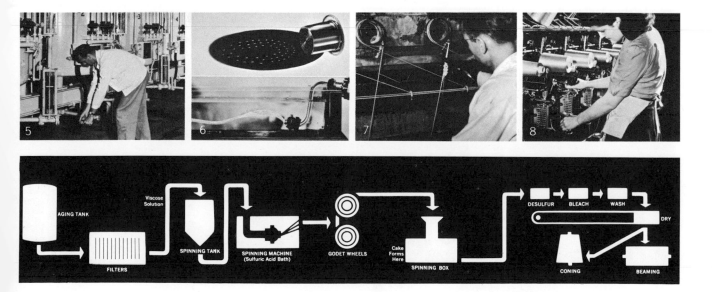

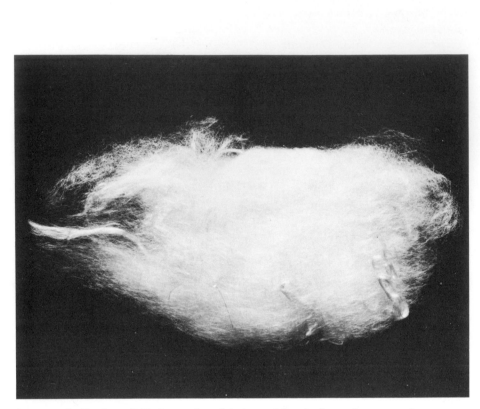

Rayon staple fiber is available in a variety of deniers and lengths for use in woven and knitted fabrics. The rayon staple shown here is ready to be spun. [FMC CORPORATION, AMERICAN VISCOSE DIVISION]

HOW RAYON STAPLE IS MADE

The manufacture of rayon staple, like that of rayon filament yarn, is dependent upon cellulose as the raw material, to which certain chemicals are applied. The processing sequences, from the shredding of the cellulose through the dissolving of the crumbs into a viscose solution, are similar. [FMC CORPORATION, AMERICAN VISCOSE DIVISION]

1. The cellulose is steeped in alkali: *Cellulose pulp is shipped to the plant in the form of white sheets resembling blotting paper. The sheets are placed in a hydraulic ram and steeped in a solution of caustic soda. The resulting product is known as alkali cellulose.*

2. The alkali pulp is shredded: *After steeping, the soft, damp sheets are dropped into a shredding machine, where revolving blades break them up into alkali cellulose crumbs. These flakes are stored in aging tanks, where the caustic soda continues its chemical action.*

3. The crumbs are treated with carbon disulfide: *After aging, the crumbs are placed in mechanical churns, where a measured amount of carbon disulfide is gradually added. Known as xanthate crumb, the crumbs are now orange in color and are ready to be dissolved in a dilute caustic soda solution.*

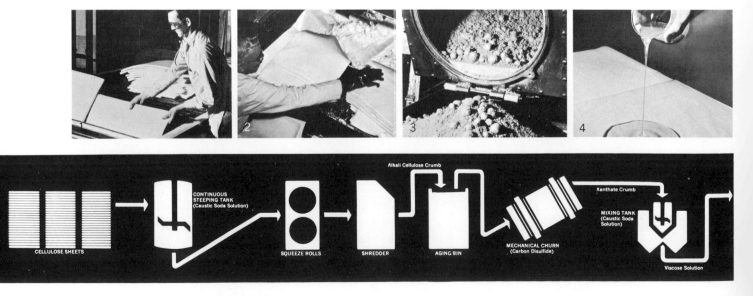

4. A viscose solution is formed: *When the xanthate crumb is dissolved in caustic soda, a viscose solution resembling honey in appearance and consistency is formed.*

5. The solution is aged: *The viscose solution is aged in large storage tanks and filtered to remove any foreign matter. It is then pumped into spinning tanks and delivered automatically to the spinning machines.*

6. Large jets are used for staple: *The large jet at left, with 3,000 holes, is used for spinning rayon staple. (By contrast, the smaller platinum jet at right, with 350 holes, is one of the types used for spinning continuous filament yarn.) The viscose solution is pumped through the holes. As it is extruded, it is coagulated in a sulfuric acid spinning bath. Each of the thousands of holes in the jet thus forms an individual filament.*

7. The tow is collected: *Thousands of the individual filaments are guided by godet wheels down into a tow wheel, where they are collected in strands known as tow.*

8. The fiber length is controlled: *The tow is fed downward into cutting blades, which cut the filaments into precisely controlled lengths, producing rayon staple.*

all man-made fibers, acetate fibers are formed when a solid substance is changed to a liquid and then reconverted to a solid form. More specifically, the following steps are involved.

1. The raw material, either purified wood pulp or cotton linters, is mixed with a solution of acetic acid to form an entirely new substance, cellulose acetate. This substance is hydrolyzed (or ripened) in storage containers before being moved to the next step.

2. The cellulose acetate solution is plunged into cold water, precipitating into solid particles that are then washed in clear water until they are free of acid. The flakes are next dissolved in acetone, which produces a clear, very thick solution ready to be spun into yarn.

3. Emerging from the tiny holes of the spinneret, the cellulose acetate solution falls in fine streams that, when exposed to the warm air, form a long hairlike filament that is almost pure cellulose acetate.

The shape and appearance of the acetate filament can be controlled to meet different end uses. For textured fabrics, the filament can be made curly and kinky. For smooth-surfaced fabrics, it can be twisted together to form long, smooth strands. It can be thick, thin, or thick-and-thin, bright or dull, round and smooth or flat and ribbon-like with a sparkle.

Acetate may be dyed by the solution-dying process, in which dye is added to the solution before the acetate filaments are formed. Thus the color becomes a basic part of the fiber and retains its character for the life of the fabric no matter how often the fabric is washed or dry-cleaned.

Acetate characteristics. Unlike rayon, acetate does not absorb moisture readily and therefore is relatively fast-drying. Acetate fibers and yarns are economical, supple, and resilient. Thus acetate fabrics have a soft hand, drape well, and are sensibly priced. Acetate's thermoplastic quality makes it possible to heat-set durable pleats into acetate fabrics and imprint patterns and decorations on the surface, and a light pressing with a low-heat iron is sufficient to keep fabrics fresh-looking. Shrinkage-resistant acetates have a built-in resistance to moths, perspiration, mildew, and mold. Although acetate does not accept the dyes used for rayon or natural fibers but takes only its own dyes, this selectivity is an advantage, since special color or striking two-tone effects can be achieved by combining acetate and other fibers in a fabric.

Uses. Acetate is used for shirts, slacks, sportswear, and lining fabrics.

Care of acetate fabrics. Acetate fabrics dry-clean beautifully. Many fabrics containing acetate are also machine-

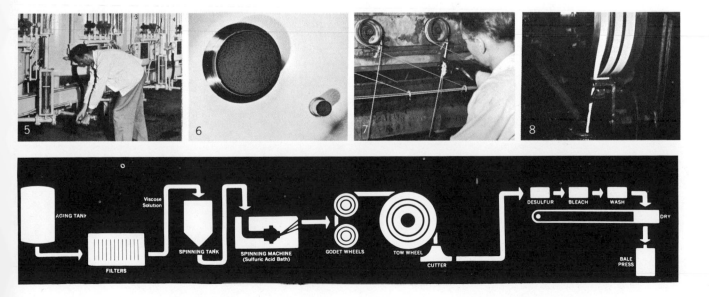

Acetate continuous filament is available in various deniers and is used for knitted and woven fabrics. Acetate adds softness to satins, taffetas, and other fabrics. [FMC CORPORATION, AMERICAN VISCOSE DIVISION]

HOW ACETATE FILAMENT IS MADE

The manufacture of acetate filament involves the chemical conversion of cellulose, derived from wood pulp, into a liquid solution and then into solid textile fibers. Unlike the regenerated-cellulose process employed to produce rayon filament and staple, this process results in a completely transformed chemical compound, cellulose acetate. [FMC CORPORATION, AMERICAN VISCOSE DIVISION]

1. The pulp is shredded: *Rolls of cellulose pulp resembling blotting paper are shipped to the plant and shredded into fine particles.*

2. The pulp is acetylated: *The shredded pulp is treated with acetic acid and a catalyst to prepare it for the reaction. The treated pulp is acetylated by reaction with acetic anhydride in a heavy-duty mixer to produce cellulose triacetate.*

3. Secondary cellulose acetate is formed: *The resulting clear solution of cellulose triacetate in acetic acid is extremely viscous. After some water has been added, the triacetate is hydrolyzed in solution to secondary cellulose acetate in another mixer.*

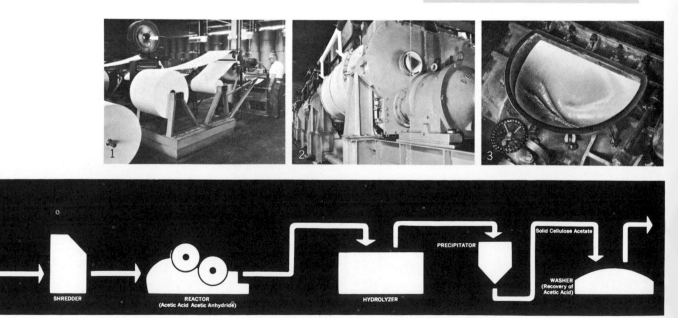

4. The cellulose acetate is washed: *The viscous acid solution is precipitated in very dilute acetic acid to produce solid particles of cellulose acetate, which are then washed free of acid and dried.*

5. The spinning dope is prepared: *The cellulose acetate particles are blended and dissolved in acetone, which produces a very viscous solution for spinning. The solution is then thoroughly filtered and delivered to the spinning operation.*

6. The acetate is spun in warm air: *In the spinning machine the filtered solution is extruded downward through the small holes of the spinneret. Fine filaments of acetate fiber form and are dried in a stream of heated air in the spinning tube. These filaments are gathered together to form a single strand of yarn.*

7. The spun yarn is wound on bobbins: *The yarn strands coming from the spinning machine are wound on bobbins. Subsequently the yarn is transferred from the bobbins to beams, cones, or tubes for shipment to American Viscose customers.*

washable, but when specific care instructions are not given by the manufacturer, hand laundering is recommended:

1. Use warm, not hot water.
2. Gently squeeze water through the fabric. Do not soak colored fabrics or wash with white articles.
3. Rinse in lukewarm water. Do not wring or twist.
4. Iron on the wrong side of the fabric while it is still damp, using a warm temperature (rayon setting). The garment should then be hung on a nonrust hanger to complete the drying.

Since acetone and alcohol dissolve acetate fibers, nail polish remover and perfume should be used with care around acetate fabrics.

Triacetate. Triacetate was first produced commercially in the United States in 1954 by the Celanese Corporation. It is formed by combining cellulose with acetate from acetic acid and acetate anhydride. The cellulose acetate solution is dissolved in a mixture of methylene chloride and menthanol. As the filaments stream out through the holes of the spinneret, they harden on exposure to the warm air, and, as in the case of acetate, fibers

of almost pure cellulose acetate are produced. Triacetate fibers contain a higher ratio of acetate to cellulose than acetate fibers do.

Triacetate characteristics. Because of the heat treatment that is a part of their normal finishing, fabrics made from triacetate have an extremely high heat resistance, and garments made from them can be safely ironed at temperatures up to 450°F and dry extremely fast. Like acetate, triacetate is resistant to wrinkles, shrinking, mold, and mildew. Although triacetate is dyed with acetate dyes, the heat treatment given it in finishing increases immeasurably its colorfastness. A thermoplastic fiber, triacetate gives its fabrics superior crease retention.

Uses. Triacetate is used for sportswear.

Care of triacetate fabrics. A high temperature setting is safe when ironing, and little ironing or special care is necessary because of the fiber's built-in resistance to high temperatures. While most garments containing triacetate are machine-washable, pleated garments should be hand-laundered.

Acrylic. Acrylic was first produced commercially in the United States in 1950 by E. I. du Pont de Nemours &

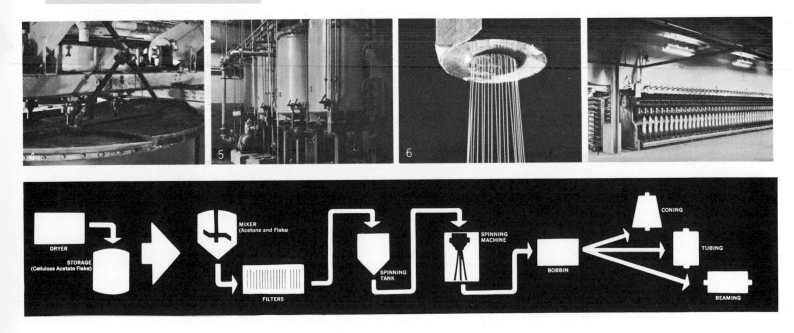

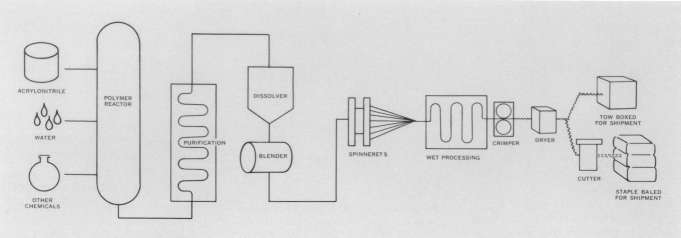

chemical area

fiber area

HOW ACRYLIC FIBER IS MADE

Acrylonitrile and other ingredient chemicals are stored in large tanks near the chemical area of the plant. These materials are metered into a reactor, which produces the basic polymers. After several purification stages the polymers are dissolved, forming a special spinning solution. Fiber is formed by extruding the spinning solution through spinnerets into a chemical bath, which coagulates the liquid streams into the solid fibers. Extreme precision is required to maintain the physical and chemical integrity of the resulting fiber. From the spinning bath the fiber passes through a series of treatments that contribute to its strength, extensibility, and other properties. The last of these treatments is crimping, which imparts the degree of crimp necessary for textile processing. After crimping, the tow is either boxed for shipment as tow or cut into staple for delivery to the textile trade.

[AMERICAN CYANAMID COMPANY]

Co., Inc. Acrylic fibers may be fine or heavy. They are produced from acrylonitrile, a chemical compound derived from chemicals found in coal, water, air, petroleum, and limestone. The following steps are involved:

1. Acrylonitrile and other ingredient materials are metered into a reactor, which produces the basic long-chain molecules called polymers, which, after several purification stages, are dissolved, thus forming a special spinning solution.

2. The solution is extruded through the spinneret disc. The long, slim filaments that stream out are coagulated into solid fibers in a chemical bath, dried, and stretched.

Acrylic characteristics. Lightweight and resilient, acrylic fibers have a soft, fluffy quality that holds up through long use, since they are very strong and resistant to sunlight, smoke, moths, mildew, and chemicals. Like acetate and triacetate fibers, they are thermoplastic, and durable pleats and creases may therefore be heat-set in fabrics containing them. Since these fibers do not absorb moisture readily, they dry quickly. Acrylics are easy to dye, and dyes may be applied at the fiber stage, yarn stage, or fabric stage as well as at the solution stage. They blend successfully with both man-made and natural fibers.

Uses. Acrylics are used for suits, slacks, sweaters, socks, ski suits, swimsuits, and sports and work clothing.

Care of acrylic fabrics. Whether a garment made from acrylic fiber is washable depends not only on the fiber but on the construction of the fabric and the way it is dyed and finished. If the garment is sturdy and is washable, either machine or hand laundering is acceptable. If a washing machine is used, the spin cycle should be used. The garment should be removed from the dryer as soon as the tumbling cycle has stopped. Sweaters should be washed by hand and dried flat. When ironing is required, a moderately warm but never hot iron should be used.

Modacrylic. Modacrylic was first produced commercially in the United States in 1949 by the Union Carbide Corporation. Modacrylic fibers are made from resins that are combinations of acrylonitrile and materials derived from elements found in natural gas, air, coal, salt, and water. The following steps are involved:

1. Acrylonitrile and certain modifiers are combined into polymers.

2. A suitable solvent and the polymers are placed in a tank and stirred together until the polymers have dissolved and the mixture has a consistency similar to molasses.

3. This mixture, the spinning solution, is forced through the tiny holes of the spinneret and emerges in the shape of thin continuous strands of solution. The solvent is removed, leaving the polymers.

4. The strands of filaments are cut into short lengths called staple fiber.

Modacrylic characteristics. Bulky and crush-resistant, modacrylic fibers are easy to dye and are resistant to abrasion, acids, and alkalies. Fabrics made from them dry quickly and keep their shape well. When used in blends, modacrylics provide increased flame resistance.

Uses. Modacrylics are used for simulated fur, pile fabric coats, deep-pile trims and linings, hairpieces, and wigs.

Care of modacrylic fabrics. Some modacrylic garments may be machine-washable. Warm water is recommended, and a fabric softener should be used for the final rinsing cycle. If a dryer is used, a low setting is recommended, and the garment should be removed as soon as the tumbling cycle has stopped. If touch-up ironing is desired, use the lowest temperature setting. For deep-pile garments, dry cleaning or fur cleaning is suggested.

Nylon. Nylon, the first of the completely man-made fibers and as such a major breakthrough in fabric technology, was first produced commercially in the United States in 1939 by E. I. du Pont de Nemours & Co., Inc., and introduced to the public at the Golden Gate International Exposition in San Francisco in the guise of nylon stockings.

Nylon is a polyamide fiber. Its manufacture is extremely complex.

1. Two chemicals, hexamethylene diamine and adipic acid, are made by high-pressure synthesis in a series of steps. They are combined, and nylon salt is formed. Dissolved in water, the salt is shipped to plants for manufacturing.

2. To make a yarn, some of the water must first be evaporated from the salt. The salt is then placed in an autoclave, a piece of equipment that resembles a giant pressure cooker. The heat of the autoclave combines the molecules of the two chemicals (hexamethylene diamine and adipic acid) into giant molecules called linear superpolymers. It is this process that

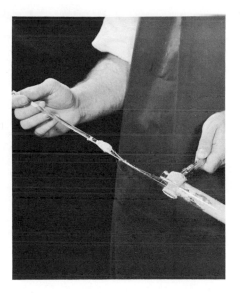

The fiber-forming possibilities of nylon in a research chemist's test tube gave birth to a man-made fiber. [DU PONT]

A forerunner of nylon fiber surprised Du Pont scientists by its stretching characteristics. When drawn and stretched, the material became "fixed," and with the molecules thus drawn into line the fiber was remarkably tough. [DU PONT]

HOW NYLON IS MADE

The production of nylon fibers begins with hard white fragments called nylon polymer chips. The chips are melted, and the fluid is pumped to a spinneret, where it is extruded and solidified to form continuous monofilaments. Assembled continuous monofilaments are taken up on a bobbin, which is transported to an area where the nylon is stretched. The stretching allows the molecules within the continuous monofilaments to be arranged in a more orderly pattern. The assembled continuous monofilaments are then twisted into yarn, which is wound onto bobbins. The yarn is now ready for shipment. [MAN-MADE FIBER PRODUCERS ASSOCIATION]

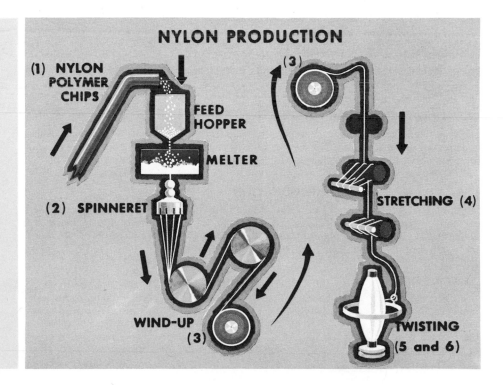

NYLON PRODUCTION

(1) NYLON POLYMER CHIPS
FEED HOPPER
MELTER
(2) SPINNERET
(3)
STRETCHING (4)
WIND-UP (3)
TWISTING (5 and 6)

The first step in making nylon yarn is taken in an evaporator where the moisture content of the nylon salt solution, which has been received at the plant in tank cars, is reduced. [DU PONT]

Storage hoppers containing nylon flake to be transformed into yarn ensure adequate mixing and a uniform product. [DU PONT]

gives nylon a molecular structure similar to that of materials like wood and silk. It is also the source of nylon's strength and elasticity.

3. Removed from the autoclave, the nylon is cooled, hardened, and ground into little chips.

4. The chips are spun by melting them over heating grids and pumping the melt through the tiny holes of a spinneret.

5. The thin strands that emerge through the holes of the spinneret can be stretched. After cooling, they can be stretched to three and even four

---

(*left*) In a nylon plant the chemical process known as polymerization takes place in receptacles called autoclaves. The small molecules join together to make large ones, creating the nylon polymers. [DU PONT]

times their original length, adding immeasurably to their strength and elasticity.

These nylon filaments can be handled in any one of three ways: (1) A single solid strand may be used to make a fine yarn, called a monofilament yarn, that is used in sheer garments for women. (2) A number of tiny, very long strands may be twisted together to form a yarn. The size of the yarn depends on the size and number of strands and the amount of twist used. The resulting yarn, called a multifilament yarn, is the most widely used type. (3) The filaments may also be cut into short, wavy strands from 1 to 5 inches long. Known as nylon staple, such strands are spun into soft, springy yarns that are used in sweaters and socks.

Nylon characteristics. Nylon is extraordinarily strong, pliable, and resilient, and fabrics made of this fiber return readily to their original shape after being stretched or crushed. They are resistant to perspiration, abrasion, and moths as well as to damage from oil and many chemicals. Fabrics of nylon are easy to wash, and since their

Yarn beaming at a manufacturing plant involves transferring the yarn from individual pirns to a big beam so that the fabric maker can handle the yarn efficiently. [DU PONT]

Molten nylon is forced through the tiny holes in a spinneret, a metal disc about twice the size of a half dollar, and is cooled by airflow to form gossamer nylon fibers. [DU PONT]

smooth fibers do not absorb moisture easily, they dry quickly. At one time nylon resisted some dyes, but dye producers have developed a full range of new dyes especially created for this fiber, and today it can be dyed in a wide range of colors.

Uses. Nylon is used for suits, rainwear, shirts, underwear, Windbreakers, ski apparel, swimsuits, and lightweight knits.

Care of nylon fabrics. Most garments made of nylon are machine-washable; warm water should be used, and a fabric softener added to the final rinse cycle. The dryer should be set at a low temperature, and the garment removed as soon as the tumbling cycle has stopped. If ironing is required, a moderately warm but never hot iron should be used. Most nylon garments require less pressing if they are dripdried, and knitted nylon fabrics re-

quire no ironing after tumble drying. Oil or grease stains should be spotcleaned with a dry-cleaning solution before washing. Nylon garments are noted for their easy care, and if they are put away clean and smoothly folded, they can be stored indefinitely in a cool, dark place without deteriorating.

Olefin. Olefin, first produced commercially in the United States in 1961 by Hercules, Inc., is a product of the petroleum industry. It is derived from propylene and ethylene gases combined with chlorine extracted from salt water by electrolysis. The chlorine and gases combine to form a simple molecule called trichloroethane, which is polymerized into the basic vinylidene chloride resin and then melted, extruded, and stretched into filaments.

Olefin characteristics. Olefin fibers have the lowest specific gravity of all

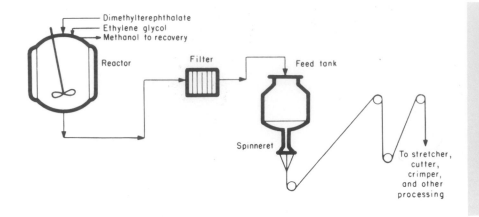

fibers and thus are extremely light although very strong. Fabrics made of these fibers are very comfortable because they draw body moisture away from the skin and through the fabric interstices to the outer surface. Since olefin fibers do not absorb moisture, they are naturally quick-drying. They are also resistant to weather, water-based stains, mildew, rot, perspiration, abrasion, and deterioration from chemicals and are very sensitive to heat.

Uses. Olefins are used for sportswear, ties, socks, sports shirts, sweaters, pile fabrics, and knitwear.

Care of olefin fabrics. Machine-wash garments in lukewarm water and add a fabric softener to the final rinse cycle. Use a very low setting for the dryer, and remove garments as soon as the tumbling cycle has stopped.

Since olefin fibers are very sensitive to heat, gas-fired dryers of the laundromat type should be avoided. If ironing is required, use the lowest temperature setting. Never iron garments made of 100 percent olefin.

Polyester. Polyester was first produced commercially in the United States in 1953 by E. I. du Pont de Nemours & Co., Inc. The basic chemicals from which the polyester fiber is made come from coal, air, water, and petroleum, and the manufacturing process is very similar to that of nylon. The basic chemicals are put in a vacuum at an extremely high temperature until they combine to form a hard, porcelainlike substance. This substance is melted down to a honeylike liquid that goes through the spinneret machine. As the molten liquid streams from the tiny holes of the disc, it solidifies into longer hairlike filaments, which are stretched to many times their original length.

Polyester fibers are used in both filament and staple fiber forms to produce yarns from which fabrics are knitted or woven. The size and number of filaments used, as well as the amount of twist, determine the size and appearance of the yarn. The staple fibers, which are cut into short, uniform lengths, are spun into the softer, bulkier yarns used in fabrics with gently textured surfaces.

Polyester characteristics. Polyester is a strong, lightweight, and very resilient fiber that, wet or dry, springs back to its original shape no matter how often

it is twisted or stretched. Polyesters are smooth and crisp, and fabrics made of all-polyester fibers retain their looks and feel even in damp, muggy weather. Since polyester is a thermoplastic fiber, heat-set pleats and creases remain through countless washings, and the fabric is therefore also resistant to shrinking and sagging. Furthermore, polyesters are easy to dye and are resistant to weather, sunlight, moths, mildew, abrasion, and most chemicals. They blend well with cottons and rayons for use in durable-press garments, and they are credited with opening the door to the production of these garments.

Uses. Polyesters are used for suits, shirts, slacks, underwear, and durable-press apparel. They are employed in a wide range of blended fabrics, usually comprising at least 50

Polyester staple, of which an example is shown here, imparts resilience and strength to fabrics of many different kinds in the men's apparel field. [FMC CORPORATION, AMERICAN VISCOSE DIVISION]

The polyester continuous filament, of which an example is shown here, lends abrasion resistance to woven or knitted fabrics. [FMC CORPORATION, AMERICAN VISCOSE DIVISION]

Moving diagonally from the upper right, polyester fiber in ropelike form is rushed into the drawing machine (not shown), where the fibers will be stretched to give them the proper strength. [DU PONT]

After being extruded through the spinerets, the polyester filaments are guided into the roving cans and then to the stretcher. [HOECHT FIBERS, INCORPORATED]

In a final inspection of polyester fiber, an inspector checks for uniform size, damage, and any signs of defective yarn. After the inspection has been made, the cake of yarn is wrapped in cellophane for protection. [DU PONT]

percent of the finished garment. When first introduced, the polyester fiber was considered suited only for spring and summer apparel, but today it is an all-year fiber. It is the major fiber in menswear knits.

Care of polyester fabrics. Most garments made from polyester are machine-washable. Warm water is used, and a fabric softener should be added to the final rinse cycle. Garments should be machine-dried at a low temperature and removed from the dryer as soon as the tumbling cycle is completed. If ironing is required, use a moderately warm but never hot iron. No ironing of permanent-press or double knits is needed if they are tumble-dried at the low temperature of 160°F. Some garments of polyester blends can be washed, while others must be dry-cleaned. If label instructions are not perfectly clear, dry cleaning is recommended.

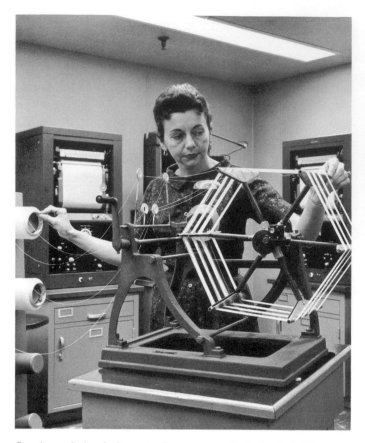

Running a denier check on spandex yarn in a plant, this technician performs one of the many tests necessary to maintain a standard of quality. [DU PONT]

The spandex yarn is put through a creeling operation as part of a testing procedure to make certain that the yarn will run satisfactorily on the equipment used by manufacturers in the trade. [DU PONT]

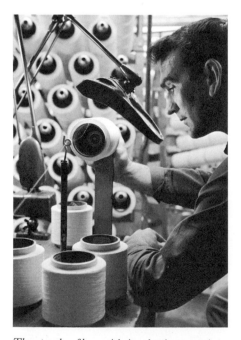

The spandex fiber, with its elastic properties, is checked visually on the thread line by an operator. [DU PONT]

Rubber. Rubber was first commercially produced in the United States in 1930 by the United States Rubber Company. According to the Federal Trade Commission definition, rubber is "a manufactured fiber in which the fiber-forming substance is comprised of natural or synthetic rubber, including the following categories:

"1. A manufactured fiber in which the fiber-forming substance is a hydrocarbon such as natural rubber, polyisoprene, polybutadiene, copolymers of dienes and hydrocarbons, or amorphous (non-crystalline) polyolefins.

"2. A manufactured fiber in which the fiber-forming substance is a copolymer of acrylonitrile and a diene (such as butadiene) composed of not more than 50% but at least 10% by weight of acrylonitrile units. The term 'lastrile' may be used as a generic description for fibers falling within this category.

"3. A manufactured fiber in which the fiber-forming substance is a polychloroprene or a copolymer of chloroprene in which at least 35% by weight of the fiber-forming substance is composed of chloroprene units. . . ."

Natural rubber fibers are made from the concentrated sap of certain trees; synthetic rubber fibers are made from a synthetic polymer derived from petroleum products. The softened rubber is extruded as a monofilament.

Rubber characteristics. One of the ways to make a cloth elastic is to use a thread of rubber as a core around which yarns of natural or synthetic fibers are wrapped. Any fabric with a rubberized coating on one or both sides is considered a rubberized fabric.

Uses. Rubber is used for surgical supports and elastic webbing.

Spandex. Spandex was first commercially produced in the United States in 1959 by E. I. du Pont de Nemours & Co., Inc. The fiber-forming substance of spandex is a long-chain synthetic polymer composed of at least 85 percent of a segmented polyurethane. Spandex is extruded as a monofilament or in a multiplicity of fine filaments that coalesce instantly to form a monofilament.

Spandex characteristics. This soft, smooth fiber is stronger and more durable than rubber, having stretch and holding power. Lightweight, supple, and resilient, spandex can be stretched repeatedly and always recovers its original length without breaking. In fact, it can be stretched more than 500 percent without breaking. It is resistant to damage from body oils, perspiration, lotions, and detergents and to abrasion.

Uses. Spandex is used for support and surgical hose, ski pants, swimwear, golf jackets, football pants, waistbands for slacks, and underwear.

Care of spandex fabrics. Spandex fabrics may be machine-washed and dried at low temperatures, but fragile garments should be hand-laundered. Whites should be washed separately. If ironing is required, a low temperature should be used. The pressing should be done rapidly, and the iron should not be left in one position for long. A chlorine bleach should never be used on any fabric containing spandex; only an oxygen or sodium perborate type of bleach is recommended.

Processes of Fabric

Processes for the manufacture of textile fabrics from the raw product include the cotton, woolen, and worsted systems and knitting.

Cotton System

Cotton yarn is produced by means of the cotton system, whose process

The cotton plant at harvest time yields bolls with fiber and seed. [COTTON INCORPORATED]

This stripper-type mechanical cotton harvester removes the bolls and transports the crop. [COTTON INCORPORATED]

Masses of cotton bolls are ready for ginning. [COTTON INCORPORATED]

Tieing on of cotton at the gin. [COTTON INCORPORATED]

Manufacture

involves the following steps.

Picking. Cotton is sent from the gin to the mill in bales of 478 pounds, wrapped in jute. Upon arrival at the mill the bales are opened and fed into a blender, in which the cotton fibers are arranged for uniformity. After blending, the raw cotton is processed

Ginning removes burrs, sticks, leaf matter, and other foreign material from the cotton. [COTTON INCORPORATED]

The cotton is formed into a lap about 45 inches wide and rolled on a cylinder. It is now ready for carding. [COTTON INCORPORATED]

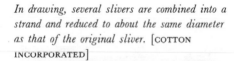

In carding, the tangled cotton fibers are straightened, shaped into a thin web, and formed into a ropelike sliver. [COTTON INCORPORATED]

In drawing, several slivers are combined into a strand and reduced to about the same diameter as that of the original sliver. [COTTON INCORPORATED]

Slivers are fed into a roving frame, where the cotton is twisted slightly and drawn into a smaller strand. [COTTON INCORPORATED]

Several hundred warp yarns are rewound from cones into large section beams, ready for loom beams and weaving. [COTTON INCORPORATED]

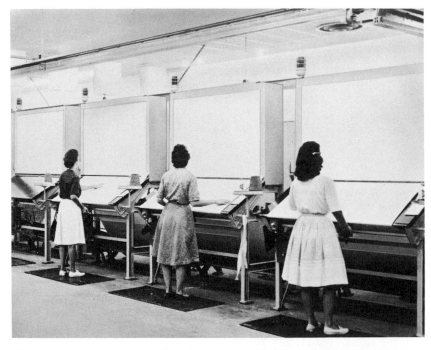

As the cotton cloth is inspected, imperfections are checked. [COTTON INCORPORATED]

Roving is fed to the spinning frame, where it is drawn out to final size, twisted into yarn, and wound on bobbins. [COTTON INCORPORATED]

through the picker machine, which pulls the cotton apart, picking out seed, dirt, and other debris. The machine then shapes the cotton lint into rolls, or laps, which resemble absorb- ent cotton and measure about 45 inches in width and 18 inches in diameter.

Carding. The laps move on to the carding machine, which untangles and straightens the fibers and then, by drawing them over a revolving cylinder with teeth, lays them in parallel rows that emerge from the machine as a wide, thin web. The web is drawn into a ropelike strand called a sliver.

Combing. The higher grades of cotton move on from the carder to the combing machine, a steel-toothed device that further straightens the fibers, removes most of the foreign matter left after the carding operation, and separates the shorter fibers.

Drawing. When the slivers arrive at this point after the carding or combing operation, they are combined several at a time and pulled lengthwise into slimmer strands.

Roving. This step begins the twisting process, during which the drawn-out slivers are given a few twists and pulled or drawn still further into a smaller strand on a roving frame or on several roving frames, depending on the fineness of the yarn desired. The cotton strands resulting from this operation are known as a roving.

Spinning. At this point the roving is transferred to the spinning frame, in which it continues to be drawn out and twisted. The finished yarn is then wound on a round device known as a bobbin. Warp yarns must be made stronger than filling yarns since they must withstand greater tension. This is usually done by twisting two or more warp yarns together and then winding them on spools.

Woolen System

The numerous steps required to transform raw wool into a finished fabric are known as the woolen system.

1. Since there are several different grades of wool fiber, after the fleece has been sheared from the sheep's back, it is hand-sorted by a skilled sorter. The best grade is usually obtained from the back and sides of the sheep near the head.

2. Once the wool has been sorted, it is scoured by being immersed in a solution of soap and soda, which removes the dirt and yolk (natural oil).

3. The wool is dried and may then be dyed. If it is dyed at this stage, it is said to be stock-dyed.

4. Wool tops are inspected to determine the quality of the wool before beginning the spinning operation.

5. Since the natural oil of the fleece was removed during scouring, the fibers are now lubricated with an oil emulsion as they move into the mixing picker.

6. The wool is opened up and blended into fiber masses by the revolving wheels of the mixing picker.

7. The scoured and blended wool is loaded into a hopper, which controls the weight of the batches that are to be fed into the carding machine.

8. The roving is mounted in large spools on the spinning frames, where it is twisted and drawn out in a continuous strand known as yarn, which is then wound on a bobbin. If the wool has not been stock-dyed, it may now be yarn-dyed.

9. Prior to weaving, all kinks are removed from the yarn by steam pressure.

10. The bobbins of yarn are mounted on a warping creel for winding on the warp beam of the loom.

11. In the warping process (as winding the warp yarn on the warp beam is called), the yarns from the creel are threaded through the condenser reed (a comblike device that moves the warp yarns as desired) and wound on the loom beam.

12. Each warp thread is drawn in through the eyelet of a fine steel wire called a heddle and through a dent of the reed. It is this drawing in that controls the pattern of the fabric.

13. The yarn is woven by interlacing the lengthwise yarns (the warp) with the crosswise yarns (the filling) at right angles, thus forming the fundamental structure of the fabric. Woolens dyed at this stage are called piece-dyed fabrics.

14. The woven cloth is now submitted to the burling process, in which knots, lumps, and loose threads are removed by hand with tweezers called burling irons.

15. The cloth is milled, or fulled, in a process that combines heat, moisture, friction, and pressure to shrink the cloth and thus give it added strength and thickness.

This dobby woolen loom is capable of weaving four-color fabrics of many varied patterns. It accommodates all the popular woolen and woolen-blend sizes of yarn now in use. [CROMPTON & KNOWLES CORPORATION]

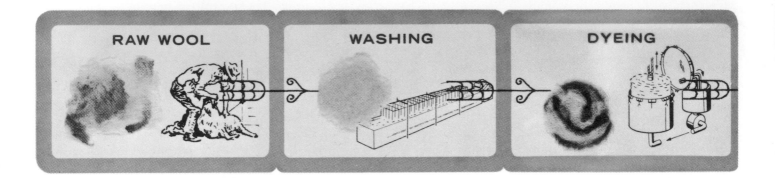

RAW WOOL WASHING DYEING

(above and opposite) Steps in the woolen and worsted systems. Combing and drawing are worsted steps only. [THE AMERICAN WOOL COUNCIL AND THE WOOL BUREAU, INC., WOOL EDUCATION CENTER]

16. The milled cloth is washed and rinsed to remove all dirt and impurities and is then dried and straightened on heated rollers.

17. The weave and yarn twist are set permanently by the crabbing process, in which the cloth is immersed in alternate baths of hot and cold water while it is held under tension.

18. Impurities such as burrs and seeds are removed from the wool by carbonizing, a chemical process in which the wool is immersed in a dilute solution of sulfuric acid and is then dried and baked, thus reducing the vegetable matter to carbon, which can be dusted from the cloth.

19. The cloth is sheared on a machine whose revolving blades trim off irregularities and give the fabric a uniformly even nap.

20. After being moistened on a dewing machine, the cloth is pressed and passed between a pressure plate and a steam-heated cylinder.

Worsted System

There is a marked similarity between this system and the woolen system, but in the worsted system the short fibers are removed, thus creating a smoother, more tightly twisted yarn. The basic steps are as follows.

1. The raw wool is sorted by hand.

2. The wool is scoured in a solution of soap and soda. Stock-dyeing may take place at this point.

3. Wool tops are inspected to determine their quality before spinning.

4. The wool is carded by machine, which opens the fibers, makes a homogeneous mix, and rolls it through rubbing aprons to produce an end product called a roving.

5. The wool is combed by running a steel-toothed device through the fibers, straightening them, removing foreign matter and noils, and placing the fibers parallel to each other in a uniform staple length. Uniform length is of paramount importance in order to give the fibers the twist characteristic of worsted fabric.

6. Next the wool is wound on perforated tubes through which dyes are forced at enormous pressure, which serves to set the colors evenly on the yarn.

7. After the tops have been dyed, they are washed to remove any impurities picked up in the process thus far.

From this point on the yarn is treated exactly as it is in the woolen system. The finished worsted is washed, dried, sheared, and pressed. The resulting fabric is harder and smoother than woolen fabric, with a minimum of fuzziness and nap.

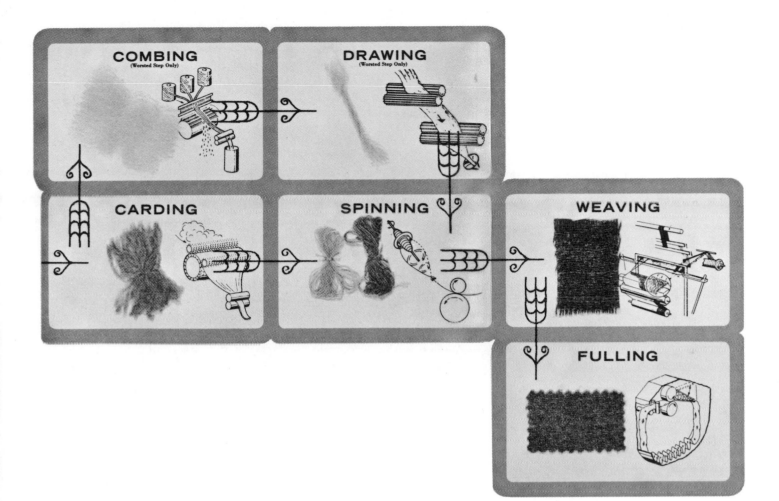

Knitting

There are two basic types of knitted fabric, a weft knit in which the yarns run crosswise and a warp knit in which the yarns run lengthwise. Most knitted fabrics are weft knits; they can be made on either flat or circular knitting machines, of which there are a number of varieties. Like the loom, the flat knitting machine produces a flat fabric. The needles are set in a straight line, and the yarn moves alternately back and forth to knit the fabric. The circular knitting machine has needles set in a circle on a rotating cylinder and is a faster machine than the flat type. It produces a circular cloth. Two basic types of needles are used: latch, for heavier or coarser knit fabrics of low gauge; and spring, for finer knit fabrics of high gauge. Knitting gauge is the standard measure of the texture

of a knit fabric. The higher the gauge, the finer the needles and the finer the texture of the knitted cloth.

Fabrics made by the weft method use three basic stitches, plain, purl, and rib. The plain stitch produces a smooth fabric with lengthwise wales showing on the face and crosswise courses on the back. The purl stitch, also known as links-and-links, requires special needles with a hook and latch at each end. This stitch draws alternate courses of knitting to the other side of the cloth to present an identical crosswise-rib look on both sides. The resulting fabric has great lengthwise stretch. The rib stitch, a combination of the plain and purl stitches, requires two sets of needles that form alternating loops on both sides of the fabric, producing a vertically ribbed cloth with great horizontal stretch.

In the production of warp-knit fab-

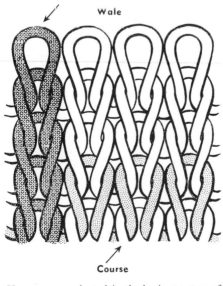

How yarns are looped in the basic structure of knitted cloth. From Knitting Times.

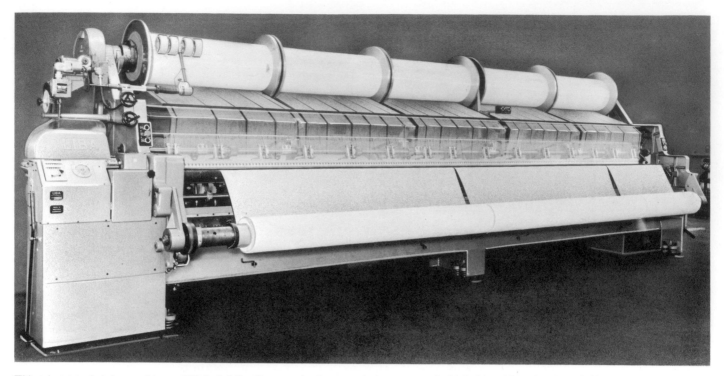

This tricot-type knitting machine, a 210-inch Liba Copentra, is shown producing two panels 60 inches wide and one panel 30 inches wide of shirting in a spun cotton-and-polyester blend. [CROMPTON & KNOWLES CORPORATION]

rics, parallel lines of yarn are arranged like the warp in a woven fabric. Each yarn is controlled by a separate needle that loops it onto itself; the yarns are connected to the next vertical row by being moved back and forth from side to side, directed by metal guides. Tricot, a run-resistant type of warp knit, is the best known; it is produced with either single or double sets of yarn. It has fine vertical wales on the face and pronounced crosswise ribs on the back.

The double knit has become so important in menswear that *Knitting Times* deemed it wise to explore the fabric in depth so that the fashion trades would have a clear understanding of the term "double knit." The article, written by the editor, Charles Reichman, follows.*

Toward a Clearer Definition of Double Knits

From the inception of the vogue in the

*Reprinted from *Knitting Times,* Nov. 9, 1970, pp. 47–49.

early 50's there has been far from trade-wide unanimity, at least among knitting technologists here and abroad, as to the meaning of the term, "double knit."

A double knit fabric may be a certain kind of fine gauge rib cloth to one knitter, an interlock fabric of a somewhat lesser degree of fineness to another, and a special type of warp knit fabric to still a third knitter.

Are all three correct? To formulate an answer to this question, it is first necessary to establish what makes a fabric a double knit and thus sets it apart from all the other fabric types in the vast hierarchy of weft and warp knitted materials.

Does the answer rest in the type of machine on which the fabric has been knitted? Is it the gauge (fineness or coarseness) of the fabric structure? Or is it the way in which the fabric is actually knitted that determines whether it is or is not a double knit?

First machine type. Although virtually all double knit fabrics being marketed today are produced on circular yardgoods machines equipped with cylinder and dial needle housings, these units are not the sole media for turning out such fabrics. Overlooking gauge for the moment, double knit fabrics can also be knitted on V-bed flat latch needle machines and on circular sweater-strip machines. Thus, the type of machine on which the cloth is knitted is not necessarily a governing

guidepost for denoting the fabric.

Of what importance is fabric gauge in determining whether a cloth is a double knit or not? The overwhelming proportion of double knit cloth presently on the market is of 18-cut construction. However, some cloth is finer. There is 20-cut goods available and, more recently, yardgoods knitters have introduced 22- and 24-cut double knit fabric. But many mills have produced and many cutters have fabricated into garments double knit cloth precisely similar in appearance to the 18- to 24-cut materials but of 12-, 14- and 16-cut in fineness, some even knitted on V-bed flat latch needle machines and others on circular interlock sweater-strip machines. Are these fabrics any less qualified as double knits than an 18-cut or finer material? Clearly not.

Obviously then, it is the way in which the cloth is knitted that determines whether it is a double knit. What is this special technique? There are two ways in which this question can be answered:

1. The needle action that is common to the construction of all double knit cloth.

2. The number of sets of needles necessary to produce double knit fabrics.

Manifestly, there can be no one program of needle action that would cover all double knit fabrics. If this were so, then there would be none of the vast variety of double knit fabric types that is now found on the market. The answer then rests in the number of sets of needles required. It is this, more than any other consideration, that enables a knitter to distinguish double knit cloth generically from what is known as single knit cloth.

The latter category comprises all knitted fabrics requiring only a single set of needles for their construction. The needles may be arranged in rotary fashion in slots in a cylinder or horizontally in a slotted or leaded needle bar. How yarn is fed to this single set of needles—in a filling-wise direction, one end of yarn at a time to the assemblage of needles, or in a warp direction, one end of yarn to each individual needle in the set-out—will establish whether the fabric is a warp or weft knit. But this will not alter its single knit designation.

By the same line of reasoning, a double knit fabric is any knitted material, the production of which requires two sets rather than one set of needles. Apart from the way in which the yarn is fed to these two sets of needles—in a fillingwise or warp direction—whether the double knit cloth is a weft or warp knit also hinges on the manner in which the two sets of needles are arrayed in relation to each other.

If the two sets of needles are disposed horizontally, back to back, the fabric produced on them would be a warp double knit. If, on the other hand, the fabric is produced with the two sets of needles set out at right angles to each other, it would be a weft double knit.

On this basis the term double knit is seen as being more readily descriptive of a broad generic class of knitted fabrics rather than of specific knitted fabric types. To refer to a weft knitted fabric produced with two opposed sets of needles as a double knit without recognizing that warp knit fabrics can also be of two needlebed construction, clearly makes the term, double knit, a misnomer.

If the term, double knit, from the technical point of view has a less restrictive and far broader meaning than it is generally understood to have in the market, how then are fabrics commonly bearing that designation to be characterized?

There are various ways in which this can be done. But perhaps the most logical approach is within the overall compartmentalization of knitted fabrics as either weft or warp knits sub-divided in turn into single or double knits.

Under the weft double knit classification thus would fall all those plain or non-jacquard and patterned or designed fabrics produced on knitting machines equipped with two sets of needles. No reference to the gauge of the machine or the construction of the machine—circular yardgoods, circular sweater-strip or V-bed flat—need be made on the technical

This circular double-knit machine, with two sets of needles arranged in a circle, produces fabric in tubular form. Yarns are worked horizontally, and the fabric is stretchable both lengthwise and crosswise. From Knitting Times.

premise that as long as the fabric is produced with two sets of needles arrayed at right angles to each other, it is a double knit.

However, a clear distinction nevertheless must be drawn between one type of weft double knit fabric and another. The range of fabrics producible on machines with two opposed sets of needles is obviously quite extensive and any classification system requires that all possible varieties or sub-types of weft double knit fabrics be provided for.

Accordingly, it is suggested that fabrics be categorized somewhat more specifically than has been the case up to now, distinguishing more clearly between one type of plain weft double knit fabric and another. To this end the category of weft double knit fabrics—what the knitting technologist heretofore has always loosely classified as rib fabrics—would consist of the following two generic groups based on the type of machine in which the fabrics are produced.

Rib structures
Interlock structures

Both categories would be sub-divided into those fabric types most common to these two groupings. The classification of rib structures would comprise the following kinds of fabrics:

Narrow and broad ribs
Tuck ribs
Welt ribs
Intermediate rib jacquards
Full rib jacquards

The interlock category would sub-divide into all those structures produced on interlock machines—units with alternate short and long needles in the opposed cylinder and dial needle housings—as distinguished from rib machines and including the following, in addition to standard interlock:

Patterned interlock
Eightlock

Knit and miss and knit and tuck structures knitted on an interlock rather than a rib basis

By narrow and broad ribs are meant all those fabric structures marked by distinctive vertical rib effects. This class ranges from the simplest 1×1 and 2×2 rib formations to such broader rib combinations as, say, 6×3 but not necessarily limited to this combination of ribs. Included in this category, naturally, would fall those rib structures that bear the so-called skinny rib designation. The needle set-out for the most basic 2×2 rib structure is shown below:

The tuck rib grouping encompasses all those rib structures involving some form of loop accumulation. Included in this range are the various bulky sweater type rib fabrics as well as the considerably finer cut rib structures used in stitch-shaped underwear. Perhaps the best examples of tuck ribs are the full and half cardigan structures that today form the basis of many types of bulky knit and semi-bulky knit sweater-dresses and pants suits. The full cardigan structure as illustrated below is produced on a two-feed basis by tucking all dial needles and knitting all cylinder needles at the first feed and knitting all dial needles and tucking all cylinder needles at the second feed.

Although the half cardigan structure is also produced on a two-feed basis, tucking only occurs on the dial needles at the second feed while all the cylinder needles knit. At the first feed all dial and cylinder needles knit as in the following rendition of the needle action:

The category of welt knit structures covers all those fabrics produced on a knit and miss basis. It is within this sub-classi-

fication that virtually all of the fabrics generally defined or referred to in the market as non-jacquard double knits are produced. It is this type of structure that is the basis of such popular fabric types as Swiss and French pique, Milano rib and blister stitches. The typical knit and miss needle action involved in knitting a Swiss pique is as follows:

Intermediate rib-jacquards represent those patterned or designed fabrics in which the pattern area is limited to one machine revolution. Fabrics of this type are generally limited to small checks and geometric effects. In the production of these fabrics no mechanical or other type of needle selecting mechanism for actuating selected cylinder needles is employed.

Full rib-jacquard structures, as their name implies, comprise those fabrics embodying a much larger pattern area than that of the intermediate-jacquard fabric structures. Technically, in this group the pattern field extends beyond a single machine revolution and the design requires the use of a mechanical, electrical, electro-magnetic or electronic mechanism to select cylinder needles to knit or miss in accordance with the design being produced, while the dial needles are programmed to knit either collectively or alternately at each of the machine's knitting feeds.

In the knitting of a full rib-jacquard structure the face side of the pattern is produced by the cylinder needles and the reverse side by the dial needles.

Interlock fabric is closely related to the basic knit and miss structures and bears a slightly remote kinship to the class of basic narrow and broad rib fabrics. Inherently, interlock fabric is two interknitted or interlocked 1×1 rib fabrics. Apart from the unique needle set-out required, as previously noted, the needles in the dial are positioned directly above those in the cylinder. This is known as interlock gating and contrasts with rib gating, the way the dial and cylinder needles are set up in relation to each other on rib as differentiated from interlock machines. In rib gating each dial needle is centered between two opposed cylinder needles. The manner in which plain interlock cloth is knitted is depicted below:

Although most interlock cloth is marketed as plain solid-color material, it is possible to knit it in patterns comprising combinations of vertical and horizontal designs and in check and similar designs. This is done by rearranging the needles in the dial in other than the normal long and short set-up and by introducing, by appropriate creeling, yarns in two, three or four different colors to accentuate the pattern.

A variant of the standard 1×1 interlock formation is eightlock, a fabric structure—it's the needle action drawn below—which requires that the standard interlock needle arrangement in dial and cylinder alternate two long and two short in the former and two short and two long in the latter. Here too patterning can be created by a rearrangement of the orthodox way in which the long and short needles are disposed in their dial and cylinder slots.

Offshoots from the basic 1×1 interlock structure are a series of knit and miss and knit, tuck and miss fabrics utilizing the basic interlock instead of the rib needle gating. Typical of the knit and miss structures is the Ponte di Roma fabric structure below. The needles, of course, unlike depicted are set out alternately long and short in the dial and the reverse in the cylinder.

Another example of the knit and miss interlock-base structure is piquette produced on a six-feed basis.

In the group of knit, tuck and miss interlock-base fabrics are a rather extensive range of different types, including but not necessarily restricted to the following:

Ever Monte
Texi-pique
Royal interlock
Pin tuck interlock
Interlock pique
Super Roma

Ever-Monte and Super Roma, which is a form of tuck bourrelet, are both knitted on an eight-feed basis. Construction of pin tuck interlock, texi-pique and interlock pique involves a six-feed knitting cycle. Only royal interlock of the group can be knitted on a four-feed arrangement.

Conclusion. The weft double knit reclassification, as suggested above, it is recognized, leaves much to be desired, if not in technical terms, at least from the point of view of those engaged in the merchandising and marketing of knitted fabrics. The latter always tend to favor definitions and descriptions of knitted fabric structures that are less precise and more subject to liberal interpretation for obvious sales purposes. The less exact a fabric term, the easier it is to [palm] it off as something which, from a purely technical point of view, it is not, and the simpler the job of promoting it as a substitute for the "real thing."

The knitting technologist is naturally differently motivated. His approach tends to be more objective; more consciously scientific and less blatantly sales oriented. But a re-classification in keeping with the suggestions outlined above is not without a number of technical stumbling blocks. Among these are:

1. At what point does a conventional rib structure become a narrow rib and a

broad rib?

2. Is a fabric knitted on a circular or flat links (purl) basis with the distinctive double headed latch needle a weft double knit? Should such a fabric be separately classified?

3. What is the difference between knit and miss fabric knitted on an interlock and on a rib basis?

Weaves

Weaving is the process that creates a fabric on a loom by interlacing yarns at right angles to each other. All woven fabrics are derived from variations of three basic weaves: plain weave, twill weave, and satin weave.

Plain Weave

This is the simplest and most common of all weaves. Plain weave is an over-and-under pattern formed by the alternate interlacing of the warp (vertical) and filling (horizontal) yarns. Since the threads are interlaced the tightest, this is also the strongest weave and is used in about 80 percent of all woven fabrics.

Plain-weave materials include batiste, broadcloth, cambric, chambray, dimity, flannel, lawn, muslin, nainsook, organdy, poplin, and voile from cotton; albatross, balmacaan, broadcloth, challis, flannel, and homespun from woolens and worsteds; crash, dress linen, handkerchief linen, and butcher's linen from linen; and broadcloth, chiffon, China silk, habutai, mogador, moiré, ninon, radium, shantung, taffeta, and some plaids and novelties from silk, rayon, acetate, and other man-made fibers.

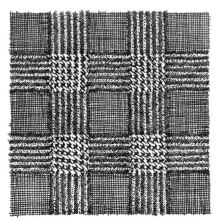

Glenurquhart (glen plaid).

Twill Weave

Twill weave is created by interlacing the warp and filling threads so that the fabric shows a pronounced diagonal rib. The weave may be a right-hand twill, going from lower left to upper right, or a left-hand twill, going from upper left to lower right. Twills may be predominantly warp ends or filling picks on the face of the fabric or may be what is known as an even-sided twill, with warp and filling given equal importance. It is estimated that approximately 85 percent of twill-woven fabrics are made with a right-hand twill effect. When the direction of the diagonal rib is changed, weave variations such as herringbone, drill, and chevron are created. Twill weave accounts for about 12 percent of all woven fabrics.

Twill-weave materials include some doeskin, drill, twill cloth, some gabardine, denim, and lining fabric (right-hand twills) from cotton; cassimere, cavalry twill, cheviot, covert, doeskin, elastique, flannel, gabardine, gun-club checks, Shetland, serge, tweed, tricotine, and whipcord (right-hand twills) from woolens and worsteds; some bird's-eye and ticking (right-hand twills) from linen; and foulard, gabardine, silk serge, surah, plain cloth, and tartan silk (right-hand twills) from silk and man-made fibers.

Satin Weave

Satin weave is the weakest of the three basic weaves because its threads are more widely spaced than those of plain and twill weaves. It consists of threads which skip over or under a definite number of other threads that run in the opposite direction. There are a warp-faced satin weave, in which warp ends predominate on the face of the fabric, and a filling-faced satin weave in which filling picks predominate on the face.

Satin-weave materials include brocade, brocatelle, cape or cloak fabric, cotton-back sateen, damask, jacquard fabrics of many types, sports fabrics, and tie fabrics from silk, rayon, and other man-made fibers.

Variations

There are innumerable variations of the three basic weaves. The following types are simply a few of the most popular seen in menswear.

Basket weave. This type uses two or more yarns going both ways instead of one yarn, as in plain weave. Hopsacking, used for suits and sports jackets, is a softly woven two- or three-ply basket weave. Oxford shirting is a basket weave with slight variations in the thickness of the warp and filling yarns.

Herringbone. This is a broken-twill weave formed by a rib effect running to the right and then to the left for an equal number of threads, thus creating an inverted-V design resembling the vertebrae of a herring. Herringbone is used predominantly for suits, sports jackets, topcoats, and overcoats.

Pile weaves. These weaves are created by loops formed on the surface of the fabric by means of extra warps or extra fillings. Corduroy and velveteen are filling pile fabrics, and velvet is a warp pile fabric.

Piqué weave. This weave creates a crosswise raised cord effect by means of filling yarns that skip over and under definite warp threads, thus forming a rib.

Rep (repp). This is a weave with a ribbed effect produced by distinct crosswise ribs. It is seen most often in neckwear.

Waffle weave. This weave is created by warp and filling yarns that skip or float at fixed intervals, producing a square or oblong box formation that appears on both the face and the back of the fabric.

Designs

Jacquard. Name given to fancy figured fabric designs woven on the jacquard loom, which is actually a special mechanism situated over a hand or power loom. The advantage of the jacquard loom is in its ability to govern individual warp threads in each repeat of a pattern, thus giving the designer greater freedom to create the fancy figured effects seen in neckwear, shirts, and handkerchiefs.

Dobby designs. Dots, small geometrics, floral patterns, and other designs woven on a dobby loom. They are usually seen in cotton, rayon, and silk shirts.

Plaid. Rectilinear pattern produced by the crossing of lines in a fabric woven of yarn-dyed fibers.

Check. Small pattern, usually of white combined with colors, woven in or printed on a fabric.

Chalk stripe.

Herringbone pattern.

Shepherd's check.

Gun-club check.

Fabric Finishes

A finish is what is done to a fabric after it has been woven, and it can dramatically change the fabric's appearance. There are more than 500 finishes on the market, but each of them can be put under the umbrella of one of three general categories: basic finishes, texturizing finishes, and functional finishes.

Basic Finishes

Calendering. This finishing process is applied by a calender machine, which is basically an ironing machine with two to seven heavy heated steel rollers through which the cloth passes at a pressure of up to 2,000 pounds per square inch. The type of calender roll determines the effect on the cloth.

Steam-heated rollers covered with a papermaker's felt give the cloth a smooth finish; known as Palmer calendering, this process is usually applied to satins, taffetas, and twills. A series of extremely fine lines or ridges is created by the use of a roller on which such lines or ridges have been engraved; the result is a cloth with a rather muted luster. Embossed effects are achieved by engraving a design on one roller and using padded rollers in the rest of the calender machine. Watermarking (moiré) effects are attained in the same way on cotton, silk, acetate, and rayon fabrics. A glazed finish is achieved by a combination of cloth-covered and steel rollers that produces a friction calender. The friction pull occurs when the steel rollers pick up speed and literally tug the fabric from the slower-moving cloth-covered rollers.

Beetling. A thready finish with a high sheen is produced by beating the cloth with steel or wooden hammers, which flatten it and fill the spaces between the warp and the filling. Beetling is used primarily with cottons and linens.

Boiling. This process involves boiling cottons, linens, and silks to remove the natural gums. The large tank in which cottons are boiled is called a kier, and the boiling process for cottons therefore is known as kier boiling; it is always combined with the bleaching process.

Bleaching. Unfinished cloth taken from the loom is a light cream color, and if the fabric is to be printed or sold as white, this natural color must be removed chemically. Furthermore, bleaching increases the ability of the fabric to absorb dye uniformly. Chemicals such as chlorine and peroxide, which release oxygen, are most often used, along with such reducing agents as sulfites and oxalic acid.

Singeing. A fabric is given a smooth hand by literally singeing the cloth and thereby burning off the fuzz of protruding fibers. This is done by passing the cloth over hot metal plates or gas jets. Immediately after the cloth has been singed, it is immersed in water, which often contains dilute sulfuric acid to dissolve starch and other sizing matter. Singeing is a process used on cotton, silk, rayon, linen, and wool.

Shearing. Like singeing, shearing reduces the nap on cloth, but instead of using heat, it uses a shearing machine with one to six blades that, in the manner of a lawn mower, trims off any irregularities. Fabrics that can be singed can be sheared, and the shearing machine is also used to even the nap on pile fabrics.

Decating. The purpose of decating is to improve the look and luster of a cloth and give it a smooth, wrinkle-free finish. It can be either a dry or a wet process. In the dry process the cloth is wound on a perforated drum equipped with a vacuum or steam system; this is used on wool, rayon, cotton, and silk. In the wet process the cloth is wound on a roller and treated in a hot-water or steam boiler that also has a vacuum system; this is ordinarily used only on wool.

Sizing. Sizing is done to give fabrics more body and strength. The cloth is filled with starch by means of a size bath or rollers that resemble the mangle on a washing machine. The starch can be washed out.

Tentering. During some finishing processes the cloth gets out of shape and must be straightened and stretched back to its original dimensions. This is accomplished with a tentering machine to which the cloth is hooked by nails called tenterhooks or tenter clips. The clips grasp the cloth at the selvages and stretch it back to its original dimensions. The moist cloth is then carried via a chain over gas flames or through hot-air drying chambers, thus setting the weave to its original width. All types of fabric respond to this process.

Shrinkage control. To control the amount of shrinkage in the final garment, the fabric is subjected to various processes that establish limits of shrinkage. Cotton, rayon, and wool are preshrunk by a number of finishing processes each of which bears a trademark or brand name.

Cotton, for instance, is subjected to constant stretching throughout its manufacture. The process by which cotton is preshrunk at the mill level, which is done under various trademarks, is called comprehensive shrinking. The damp cloth is brought into firm contact with a thick, endless blanket that has been stretched over a roller; the blanket contracts, and the cloth contracts with it and later is set by heat.

Rayon is generally preshrunk by impregnating the fibers with a solution of caustic soda, which swells the fibers permanently and fixes the yarns in the weave formation.

When washed, wool fibers relax and shrink. Furthermore, they have a nat-

ural tendency to felt, and this also causes shrinkage. There are many different processes for controlling wool shrinkage. Some use a resin or rubber derivative as a kind of additive, impregnating or coating the fibers. Another popular process uses a wet-chlorination technique to blunt the ends of the fibers and thus prevent them from felting.

Special wool finishes. Wool is a living fiber, and in addition to finishes that may be applied to many other fibers, it is given finishes used for wool alone. The seven key finishes are as follows:

1. Fulling: This is the process by which wool fibers are pounded and twisted in warm, soapy water to make them interlock and mat. Immediately thereafter the wool is rinsed in cold water.

2. Carbonizing: The wool is immersed in a dilute solution of sulfuric acid to carbonize out impurities. It is then dried and baked, reducing the vegetable matter to carbon, which can be dusted from the cloth.

3. Scouring: This is the washing process by which wool fabric is scoured thoroughly with soaps and alkalies or chemical solvents to remove natural oil (yolk), dirt, and other impurities.

4. Burling: This process removes knots, lumps, and loose threads with tweezers called burling irons.

5. Crabbing: The weave and yarn twist of the wool are set permanently by immersing the cloth in alternate baths of hot and cold water while it is held under tension.

6. Specking: This is the same process as burling, except that the tweezers are used to remove burrs, specks, and motes.

7. Pressing: In the final processing step the wool cloth is pressed by passing it through hot calender rolls.

Mercerizing. Mercerizing, named for John Mercer, an English calico printer and highly respected chemist who made important contributions to the development of cotton fabric finishes, is the process by which cotton achieves a permanent luster. The cotton fabric is treated under tension with a solution of caustic soda, which causes the crinkly cotton fiber to lose much of its natural twist and become round, taking on more of the appearance of the silk fiber. Mercerization does more than impart surface sheen: it adds to cotton's strength and cylindrical diameter as well as its affinity for dyestuffs. There are many degrees of mercerization, and the process can be adapted to give the finished garment a high, medium, or subdued luster.

Texturizing Finishes

These are the finishes that change the texture of a cloth after it leaves the loom. They can be divided into two classes: traditional textures such as brushing, puckering, and calendering; and texture treatments using synthetic resins.

Traditional textures.

Napping. One or both sides of a fabric may be napped. The process raises a soft fuzz by running the cloth through a series of rollers covered with wire brushes or teasels. The operation creates cotton flannel, brushed rayon, and sueded fabrics. This process is also known as gigging, raising, sueding, and brushing.

Flocking. Flocking is the spraying or electrostatic depositing of extremely short fibers on fabric to achieve a plush or velvet effect. Flocking may be applied to any type of fabric.

Synthetic resin textures. The first synthetic resins for finishing were introduced in the late 1930s. Since then there have been scores of new synthetic resin finishes, some of which qualify as texturizing finishes while others extend the function of the cloth and are therefore functional finishes. The resins are applied to the fabric hydraulically. When the cloth has dried, it is ready for the texturizing process, which is done by the heavy heated rollers of the calender machines. Calendering applies the new texture,

which is made permanent by polymerization, a reaction that results from curing the fabric with heat and a catalyst, thus locking in the resins that have impregnated the fiber. The synthetic resin treatment not only creates an almost limitless number of textural effects but also adds to the fabric's crispness, dimensional stability, and wrinkle and stain resistance.

Functional Finishes

Functional finishes are chemical treatments that extend the function of the natural fabric. Most of these finishes are fairly new, having been developed primarily for the natural fibers, which in some instances have experienced serious competition from the newer man-made fibers.

Water-repellent finishes. The purpose of these finishes is to make fabric shed water. They are among the oldest, if not the oldest, functional finishes. There are two basic types of water-repellent finishes, permanent and renewable.

Impregnating the fibers of the fabric with a resin or other thermoplastic chemical produces a permanent water-repellent finish. Since the interstices of the fabric are not coated with the chemical, the cloth is able to breathe and the garment is comfortable to wear. There are scores of trademarked processes that can impart such a finish to fabric.

Renewable finishes, as the name suggests, must be reprocessed with each washing or dry cleaning. These finishes are wax applications, either vegetable or mineral.

When a fabric has a water-repellent finish, either permanent or renewable, it also has the ability to resist water-borne spots and stains. However, even permanent water-repellent finishes can be destroyed by soap, and it is important that all soap be thoroughly washed out of any garment that boasts one of these finishes.

Crease-resistant finishes. The function of these finishes is not so much to resist creasing as it is to slow down wrinkling and, when wrinkling occurs, to help

the garment more quickly to recover its smooth appearance. The majority of crease-resistant finishes are produced by applying a synthetic resin to the cloth, baking it, and then neutralizing the resin. The molecules of the resin are cross-linked permanently with the molecules of the fiber. The cross-links resist distortion, thereby helping the fabric to resist wrinkling. When wrinkling does occur, they pull back after the stress that caused the wrinkles has been removed and so help the cloth to recover from the creases and wrinkles. Fabric impregnated with synthetic resins also enjoys other benefits, such as quicker, easier washing and faster drying with less leftover odor.

Waterproof finishes. Fabrics are made waterproof by coating the fibers with synthetic resins or drying oils and waxes. Since such finishes coat the interstices of the fabrics, garments made from them are nonporous. While water cannot pass through them, neither can air.

Starchless finishes. Originally developed for organdy, these finishes are now applied to a wide variety of fabrics including muslins, voiles, and lawns. Permanent starchless finishes seal down the fibers in the yarn, thus keeping the fabric smooth and strong for its lifetime without additional starching.

Flameproof or fire-retardant finishes. As in the case of water-repellent finishes, these are two types of flameproof finishes, permanent and renewable. Since these finishes are costly, their use in wearing apparel has generally been limited to work clothes, in which the effect is most often achieved with a coating of polyvinyl chloride.

Mildew-resistant finishes. These finishes are achieved by treating the fabric with toxic compounds, such as compounds of copper, chromium, and mercury. (Chlorinated phenol followed by metallic soap is also effective.) Exposure to an excessively hot, moist atmosphere or the soaps and sizings used in processing may cause mildew, mold, and fungus to form on a fabric. A waterproof finish will usually render a fabric mildewproof as well.

Insulated finishes. The purpose of these finishes is to keep the fabric from losing its natural heat. The fabric fibers are processed with an aluminum derivative that adds heat-reflecting scales to the fibers, causing internal heat rays to rebound to the body and external heat rays to bob off the surface.

Hygienic finishes. Created to inhibit the growth of bacteria in fabric and thereby to prevent odors and combat mildew and mold, these finishes are achieved by treating cloth with hygienic additives. Their use in wearing apparel has been confined mostly to underwear and coat and suit linings.

Wash-and-wear finish. This finish involves the process of impregnating the fiber with a synthetic resin, baking it, and then neutralizing the resin. This is the same treatment as that used for crease resistance, except that here it is applied to synthetic or man-made fibers or to natural fibers that have been blended with these fibers. The result is a crease-resistant fabric that can be washed, drip-dried or machine-dried, and then worn with little or no ironing.

Fibers for wash-and-wear fabrics can be put into one of two categories, hydrophobic and hydrophilic. Hydrophobic fibers are synthetic fibers whose molecular structure resists moisture, allowing only an absolute minimum to penetrate the surface. Consequently, the very nature of hydrophobic fibers gives them wash-and-wear qualities. Nylon, the first synthetic fiber to achieve prominence, belongs in this category. Fibers in the hydrophilic category readily absorb moisture, and to qualify as wash-and-wear they must either be blended with compatible hydrophobic fibers or be given the wash-and-wear resin finish. Wool, rayon, silk, acetate, and cotton are the major fibers in this category. Since all resin finishes weaken fiber strength to a certain extent, the quality of the cloth and resin largely determines the extent to which a garment will maintain its good looks with little or no ironing.

Color and Color

"Any selection of colors should never be too orthodox. Good expression calls for taste and feeling rather than an impersonal adherence to fixed conventions." This is an excerpt from *Color,* by H. E. Martin (Bridgman Publishers, Pelham, N. Y., 1928), and what it says is as true today as it was when the book was written more than forty years ago. Furthermore, the book was not referring to color as used in apparel but to color as used by the portrait painter. All this proves two salient points: creativity is essential to all forms of artistic self-expression (and dressing well is one of them), and the effective use of color in one's clothes calls for both taste and feeling.

Two basic concepts guide a man in choosing what colors to wear: harmony and contrast. The question is how to achieve the first without its becoming monotonous and the second without having the colors fight each other. Some men seem to be born with an intuitive sense of color, which other men have to acquire. But certainly no man with the hope of being considered well dressed can earn that reputation without knowing how to make color work for him.

1900–1920

The well-dressed man of the first decade of this century was for the most part a conservative dresser who used color judiciously. A sack suit of dark blue, dark gray, or black was a staple in his wardrobe, and against such an ultraconservative background color was called for in shirts and neckwear. Shirts with high starched collars came in an impressive array of fabrics and colors. Bold stripes in blue and white, red and white, lavender and white, and deep burgundy and white were very popular. Almost as popular were colorful tiny polka dots. Neckwear consisted mostly of narrow and conservative four-in-hands, although there were colorful ready-tied scarves, usually made of pure woven silk in a combination of colors such as blue, lavender, light green, cherry, and opal with light contrasting shades of cream, white, and bright yellow.

Early in the next decade the nation became increasingly youth-conscious, and so did men's clothes. The fall of 1912, for instance, saw a radical change in color, with purple becoming the most advertised color for suits. This was a short-lived fad, but after a decade of conservatism it proved to be a forecast of the fashion freedom that would come later in the decade when a natural-shoulder suit silhouette would become the vogue and almost everything in a man's wardrobe would become more youthful. It was this emphasis on dressing young, plus post-World War I economic prosperity, which led to a silk shirt boom between 1918 and 1921 that saw factory workers punching time clocks while wearing candy-striped silk shirts.

1920–1930

By the mid-twenties the fashionable man was showing an increasing fondness for colored shirts. A reporter writing in 1924 noted that while many well-dressed men were still "evident slaves to white shirts and soft white collars," their numbers were dwindling fast and predicted that "colored shirts will not be a fancy of a season or two, but, instead, a staple part of lounge dress for a long time to come" (*Men's Wear,* Feb. 20, 1924). Neckwear kept pace as youthful fashions continued to dominate menswear. In 1924 even the sophisticated men of Palm Beach, the wealthiest American resort, were showing a preference for brilliant color combinations in their ties—colors, as this reporter put it, "much more vivid and clashing in their contrasting com-

Combinations

binations than heretofore" (*Men's Wear*, Feb. 7, 1924).

In 1926 another fashion writer observed: "Only a few years ago the gentleman's cravat was represented as something like the symbol hung on the door knob of the house of mourning. Gentlemen, we were told, did not sport the giddy scarf that blazes resplendently on the well dressed male bosom today." An accompanying fashion report showed that rose, taupe, and beige were the most prominent colors in ties that year, while black had lost favor. Furthermore, there were crepe ties in colors that, according to this writer, resembled those in reports from the fashion salons of Paris.

Since this was a youth-oriented decade, what the college man chose to wear had considerable fashion impact. In the mid-twenties green was his favorite shirt color, and his ties were boldly striped and patterned. In 1927 Ivy Leaguers introduced a new "ice-cream suit" in pale shades such as tan, gray, blue gray, and gray blue. What made the impractical ice-cream suit even more newsworthy was the fact that it was usually made in a husky diagonal tweed fabric, which produced an incongruous but strikingly smart-looking effect.

With color in fashion and not every man wholly confident he could handle it, articles offering color guidance began to appear in the press. One such article in 1924 offered "a synopsis of the choice of colors for differing complexions," concluding with the following advice: "Not more than three [colors] should be used at one time and two are recommended, two colors of varying shades that create harmony and dignity" (*Men's Wear*, Feb. 7, 1924). When it came to beachwear, however, most men with a flair for fashion were uninhibited as to color. A *Men's Wear* survey of California beaches during this "flaming youth"

decade made the following comment:

"Golden brown skins stand out in sharp and comfortable relief against raw, concentrated, screaming color. And oddly, little of it seems in bad taste, or unduly conspicuous. This is not the South Seas, but color is being handled with vestiges of skill. The effects are gorgeous, rather than jarring, as the whole picture is pitched in a high key.

"It is in the one-piece swim suit that the more brilliant colors are displayed. Sometimes the entire suit is solid purple, or pale blue, or even of yellow or scarlet; another fancy is to have the shirt and trunks of a contrasting color. Both these ideas are frequently modified by the addition of every variety and shade of striped effects. Orange and black is a favorite combination" (July 3, 1925).

A Palm Beach fashion report filed in *Men's Wear* in 1928 noted that color was rampant in beachwear there, too, though more subtle than on the West Coast. An outstanding development was the variety of plain-colored shirts worn with trunks of different colors. Bright shades of blue, light shades of brown and tan, and greens, as well as black and white, were seen in shirts and trunks. Summing up this trend, the writer observed that, next to dark blue or black trunks, light gray flannel trunks led the others, and these were worn with either a white shirt or a colored shirt of tan or blue.

The late twenties saw Palm Beach men adopting the European vogue of the bathing robe. "Now that a well known group of men have had the temerity to sport in public a robe of many colors in such a place as Palm Beach, other men all over the country will start wearing them" rightly predicted a fashion journalist, adding that the largest number seen were of awning-striped flannel (*Men's Wear*, Mar. 10, 1926).

1930–1940

The Depression of 1929 returned fashion to the hands of the relatively few men who could still afford to dress well, men whose inborn feeling of security gave them the daring to improvise and break fashion rules. Consequently, the decade of the thirties was one of the most elegant sartorial periods of this century. The suit look was decidedly British, emphasizing the English drape silhouette with its broader shoulders, nipped-in waist, and high-waisted, full-cut, double-pleated trousers. Immediately popular in solid colors, the English drape was soon seen in stripes of all widths as well as in plaids. Blue, medium gray, gray blue, and greenish shades were the leading suit colors.

The British fashion influence extended beyond suits to a total look. Representative color combinations in the fashion pages of *Esquire* showed the good taste and savoir faire of the well-dressed man of this decade. "Clothes for a weekend in the country," said the magazine's fashion department in April, 1934, could come back to town "without feeling that you ought to take to the dark alleys," if one wore a suit of a soft gray lovat tweed, a waistcoat of cream-color flannel doeskin, a bold red-checked flannel shirt, a bottle-green tie, and a brown snap-brim hat. Throughout the decade there was a strong emphasis on gray suits in intermediate tones, and garnet, a deep shade of red, was often the dominant shade in accessories including shirts, neckwear, hosiery, and braces.

As we have noted, the fashionable dresser dared to improvise and break fashion rules, wearing, for example, black shoes and hat with a brown suit. *Esquire* in October, 1935, showed such a combination, noting that it was new, smart, and worn by the best people. The elegant model wore a brown sharkskin suit, a topcoat of a mixture of black-and-brown soft Shetland fabric, a black wool tie with red polka dots, a gray-checked broadcloth shirt, black oxfords, a black bowler, and a pair of fawn hogskin gloves.

The blazer jacket, previously more or less confined to tennis courts for after-game wear, became a genuine fashion item. Originally most popular in classic navy blue and worn with intermediate or dark gray slacks, it now turned up in other colors such as brown, green, maroon, gold, yellow, and camel's hair tan, and with these colors were combined slacks in solid colors or patterns of harmonizing or contrasting hues.

The truly lightweight summer suit finally made its debut in this decade, launching what soon became known as the third season in the men's clothing field. The classic Palm Beach suit, a blend of cotton and mohair, was enormously popular in both its original shade of oatmeal tan and in white as well as in biscuit and shades of gray. Gabardine also became one of the most admired summer fabrics despite its heavier weight, and both college men and their fathers adopted single- and double-breasted suits of gabardine in shades of tan, gray, blue, navy, and brown. Linen, long a preferred summer fabric despite its weight, also enjoyed a new surge of popularity in fresh shades of blue and brown. Lightweight pinwale corduroy was promoted as a summer corduroy and achieved a measure of acceptance in slacks and sports jackets of navy, brown, and blue gray, particularly among preparatory school students and university undergraduates.

With white or light-colored suits, diaphanous deep-toned shirts came into prominence and served as a contrasting background for white or light-colored neckwear. In 1936, for instance, *Men's Wear,* while noting that deep blue or navy was the best seller in sheer shirting fabrics, observed that there was a sharp rise in shades of chocolate, dark green, and maroon. Blue-and-white accessories for summer were strong for both daytime in town and formal evening wear. In July, 1935, *Esquire* devoted a page to them: a dark blue pinstriped tropical worsted suit with a medium blue shirt, a blue polka-dot tie on a white ground, and a natural straw hat with a blue-and-white band; the popular new white double-breasted dinner jacket worn with midnight-blue trousers, a white shirt, and a midnight-blue silk bow tie; a medium blue checkered sports jacket with a white button-down shirt, a navy blue tie, and a lightweight blue porkpie hat; and a scattering of other blue accessories including a linen handkerchief with white satin stripes, a blue-and-white braided string belt, and blue dress jewelry.

The elegant man of the thirties, being the trend setter he was, introduced some startling innovations into even the traditional field of formal evening attire. Early in the decade, for example, he took to the white mess jacket in linen or cotton gabardine. It looked very much like a tailcoat cut off at the waistline, and *Esquire* called it a "ridiculous craze" in January, 1935. And although it proved to have a very short-lived popularity, it did open the door to the white dinner jacket for formal evening wear. By 1936, in fact, summer white and cream-color dinner jackets were competing with black and midnight blue for fashion leadership, thus paving the way for more color in summer formal wear, with plum, dark green, wine, bright blue, light navy, and gray giving a refreshing fillip to moonlit country club patios.

Color coordination was the next logical development. Dark red was the important note in bow ties and cummerbunds, and black hose often had red clocks. Red and cornflower-blue boutonnieres lent a final dash of color.

All during the thirties brown was the most important color in suits and sports jackets, and related accessories included tan as a harmonizing shade and gold, green, or yellow as contrasting tones. In November, 1939, *Esquire* presented what it called a "thoughtful study in charcoal brown," introducing an outfit that it judged almost perfect "when it comes to maintaining a due degree of formality for definite in-town occasions." The single-breasted suit was in "the important new charcoal brown shade. This color can be worn by men of any complexion and combines perfectly with black or brown accessories. The shirt is a white ground broadcloth with spaced brown cluster stripes, worn with white starched collar and black satin tie with diamond sporting stickpin." Also shown were a black coat with a brown fur lining and collar, yellow chamois gloves, a black bowler hat, and a white linen pocket handkerchief.

Slate brown was another popular brown that in May, 1935, *Esquire* endorsed for spring, in a brown double-breasted flannel suit, advising any man who protested that he could not wear brown that his phobia did not apply to slate brown, "a blend of brown and grey that, by the simple subtraction of all red and yellow tones, becomes flattering to any complexion." Accessories included a sand-colored shirt in a half-tone shade and a patterned bar-shaped tie with maroon as its dominant color.

Color was the principal theme in shirts in the late thirties. Off shades were numerous, with the deep tones and pale pastels very much in the minority. Shirt and slacks ensembles had captured the fancy of some shirt manufacturers, who in some instances were featuring slacks to match their shirts for fall.

Since the Depression compelled the fashion press to concentrate almost solely on the very rich for news, this meant following them to their playgrounds. The French Riviera, for instance, proved to be a gold mine for fashion journalists, and one of the most famous sportswear fashions originating there during this decade was the so-called dishrag shirt, a short-sleeved sports shirt constructed of a net-type weave and buttoned down the front. When it first appeared in 1933, it was usually in ecru or string color, but by the next year it had blossomed out in every conceivable color as well as in wild color mixtures, checks, overchecks, and ombré stripes. However, by far the most fashionable dishrag shirt was navy blue with an Eton collar.

A fashion report filed from the Riviera in *Esquire* in August, 1936, commenting on the status of the knitted polo shirt, noted: "The ordinary solid-colored knitted polo shirt is still big, but only in the various shades of blue, nigger brown and wine red. The yellows, greens and other extreme shades have disappeared." The following year the "perennial" polo shirt was most popular in chocolate brown. In June, 1936, *Esquire,* noting that the very rich were indeed the fashion leaders of the thirties, headlined a page, "On the Beach with the Sons of Riches," and included the navy blue polo shirt worn with gray flannel slacks and a blue beret and a silk-and-wool beach shirt worn with blue sailcloth beach shorts. As the magazine's fashion copywriter put it, "When the gilded playboys turn to bronze under the winter sun, that's when summer's beach fashions are born."

That same year, John Wanamaker's men's store in Philadelphia introduced a new sports shirt or jacket shirt it called the Guayaberra, an authentic copy of the garment worn by sugar planters in Cuba. It was made of a fine-quality linen in a natural or beige color and also in dark blue, dark brown, and yellow. Its unlined collar was made to be worn buttoned or open, its cuffs to be worn in barrel or link fashion; other styling features included side vents, a yoke, and a panel back. Soon Wanamaker's was selling trousers made of the same material in either matching or contrasting colors. The Guayaberra maintained its popularity and was seen in many different fabrics and patterns for the rest of the decade.

By the late thirties there was a growing demand for cowboy shirts, attributed to the new popularity of the dude ranch. As one fashion writer saw it, "The shirts that cowboys and would-be cowboys pay $7 or more for have to be loud, trimmed with trick pockets, three pearl buttons on the cuffs, sometimes piped at the edges.

"The styles of the shirts are several. The fabric may be silk, broadcloth, sateen or synthetic yarn. Solid colors in the most vivid shades are all being bought" (*Men's Wear,* Jan. 20, 1937).

Esquire wrote in July, 1938: "The old home range never has been the same since the dudes took over the West," although the fashion department admitted that the dudes had done a pretty good job of retaining the Old West flavor in their clothes. The reader's attention was called to the bright blue and red sateen shirts worn by the models shown in the feature.

Along with the lightweight suits and diaphanous summer shirts of the thirties came lightweight summer shoes, some of which were perforated for additional coolness. Although the all-white shoe so popular in the twenties continued to be the favorite summer shoe with or without perforations, many perforated shoes of the thirties gave the wearer not only cool comfort but a splash of "hot" color too. A prime example was a yellow chamois blucher with a red sole.

Reviewing beachwear worn at the smartest American resorts, *Esquire* reported in July, 1935: "Men will indulge in fancies of color and cut at the seashore that would make them rear up on their hind legs in dismay anywhere else. And yet, despite the general truth of the foregoing, we must record the fact that blue is still the most popular single color." Illustrating this point, the fashion department chose to show on one bronzed model a pair of white ribbed swim trunks with a blue belt and on another a rhapsody of blue from a houndstooth polo shirt to washable beach slacks and canvas sneakers. In February, 1940, *Esquire* observed that as far as beach apparel was concerned, the rainbow was the limit and proceeded to show readers a collection of "paint pot fashions guaranteed to enliven any Southern resort setting."

1940–1960

The military climate of the early forties had its effect on men's clothes, particularly on college campus fashions, in which the so-called Americana color theme of red, white, and blue

The Bahamian coral shade of the slacks worn by the man in the foreground was neutralized by the natural tan shade of his metal-buttoned linen jacket. From Esquire, *January 1942.*

Contrasting colors are used to create an effect in this outfit. The blue, white, and red of the checked jacket interplay with the shirt and tie, while the burgundy slacks, the brushed-leather shoes, and the band of the panama hat offer additional contrasts.

A blue shirt served as a bridge between tie and multicolored tweed sports jacket. From Esquire, *August 1966.*

Three examples of color in golf apparel: (left) an ensemble in green and brown; (center) an outfit in which green predominates; (right) an ensemble combining two shades of blue with green. From Esquire, *April 1969.*

Color
and
Color Combinations

appeared in suits, sportswear, and related accessories. Air blue, inspired by the U.S. Army Air Force color, was seen in faint chalk-striped worsted both on and off campus. And khaki-color suits in worsted, a civilian adaptation of cavalry twill, had a military air, especially in shades of tan and olive brown. Gabardine suits, particularly in "red-back" gabardine with its faintly reddish glints, were also popular both on and off campus. A khaki porkpie hat often completed the patriotism-inspired outfit of the Ivy Leaguer.

Air blue also appeared in the wardrobe of the more mature man. "Air Blue . . . Ace Color" headlined an *Esquire* feature of April, 1941, that showed three versions of this patriotic blue in men's clothes: a chalk-striped flannel business suit of this color, worn with an ivory-color shirt and a blue striped rep silk tie; a Shetland sports jacket marked with a plaid of this hue, combined with sky-gray flannel slacks, a blue-and-white striped shirt, and a red figured tie; and an air-blue cheviot suit suitable for town or country, worn with a solid blue shirt, a blue plaid tie, and a brown hat with a blue ribbon in close harmony with the rest of the outfit.

Star gray and sandune were two other colors that reflected the American man's desire to dress down during the war years in colors that were closely related to those worn by the military. Star gray, a leading color in men's apparel for spring, 1942, was a mixture of blue and gray that looked like gray when compared with navy blue. Against a pure gray, however, it had a distinct bluish cast, and *Esquire* considered it a complimentary color for all men. Sandune had first appeared during the Southern resort season and had then traveled north. One of the main features of this neutral shade was its affinity for practically any color. A pair of sandune slacks, for instance, would go well with an odd jacket in blue, brown, gray, green, or tan. Many men mixed sandune with star gray. For its August, 1940, issue *Esquire* sketched such a man

wearing a glenurquhart plaid jacket, star-gray flannel slacks, a sandune shirt with blue stripes, a red-ground foulard tie, and a khaki porkpie hat.

In October, 1944, *Esquire* showed its readers what it called the "ABC of Colors." Figure A showed a grayish-haired gentleman wearing a blue suit ("basic in the wardrobe") with a red-and-blue tie and a white collar-attached shirt. Next to this sketch were fabric swatches offering an alternate combination: bluish worsted suiting, blue-and-white striped broadcloth shirting, and red, black, and white checked rayon for the tie. Figure B presented a chocolate-brown suit worn by a dark-haired man with a tan shirt and a red-and-yellow figured foulard tie. Sample swatches for an alternate combination included grayish brown worsted suiting in a striped two-tone effect, tan broadcloth shirting, and a copper-color foulard tie. Figure C showed a blond man in a gray suit, a pale blue shirt, and a blue-and-red figured tie. Swatches next to this sketch consisted of striped gray unfinished worsted for the suit, striped blue-ground broadcloth shirting, and a red-ground foulard tie fabric.

The military influence soon expressed itself in beachwear and sportswear too. An *Esquire* fashion page in March, 1941, showed a lithe man in coarsely knitted wool trunks with red-and-white chevron stripes down the sides. A fashion feature in 1944 showed an over-draft-age man in tan cotton shorts ("an adaptation of the shorts worn by our Army in the tropics") and a cotton half-sleeved shirt with stripes in campaign colors ("inspired by the hues of American service ribbons, in this instance: Middle East Maroon and Atlantic Blue").

The "man in the gray flannel suit" typified the conservatism of the first half of the 1950s. His suit was invariably a charcoal gray, darker than oxford, and it was often worn with a pink shirt and black tie. Yet even he was a veritable peacock when it came to sports clothes and, in particular, to sports shirts. He apparently looked upon their bright colors and vivid

designs as an escape from his rather humdrum everyday wear. Native prints such as India madras and African prints, once considered a novelty, had become fashion staples as common in swim trunks, walking shorts, and odd jackets as they were in sports shirts.

As predicted in 1950, the next few years saw a swing toward stronger colors in sports shirts. *Esquire* called them "racing colors" and in June, 1956, showed a bright Ferrari red in knitted cotton mesh and a white-embroidered design set off on a ground of Santa Anita orange. But town wear during the summer months continued to be conservative, and a white piqué tie combined with a cool blue shirt was considered a newsworthy fashion in 1953, particularly when combined with a gray, bluish gray, or blue town suit. And when the fashion-conscious man reverted to dark city colors in the fall, he chose one of the new lighter-weight suits in the new black burgundy. "Dark lightening" is what in October, 1950, *Esquire* called this trend toward the lighter-weight suit in dark city colors.

Almost as popular as gray during the early fifties was olive, its successor in the affections of the Ivy League man, who first popularized it, next of the young business executive, and then of men of all ages throughout the country. Olive tones appeared in suits of chalk stripes and pinstripes, glenurquhart plaids, and other patterns. Related accessories were strongly influenced by the basic suit tones, and, as a result, not only olive but gold tones were included in shirts, neckwear, socks, and headwear. Even leather used for footwear changed from brown to olive casts of brown. Olive, in fact, became so strong during this period that brown practically disappeared as a suit color and with it related accessory tones.

But as the decade progressed, the political climate became less gray and so did men's clothes. As Americans regained some of their innate optimism, color once again became apparent in men's wardrobes. Two or even three colors—multiple or compound colors—were introduced in the otherwise staid grays, browns, and blues of nubby suiting fabrics, such fabrics being popularized by the late-fifties vogue for silk shantung suits in black, beige, brown, blue, elephant gray, and gold.

All through the fifties, even in the ultraconservative first years, the man in the gray flannel suit, as we have noted, satisfied his longing for color in sports clothes. This was especially true of the costumes he wore on the golf links. Walking shorts were more popular than ever with the golfer, and *Esquire* showed them in everything from candy-striped seersucker to India madras and cotton glen plaid. The shell-stitch alpaca was the leading golf sweater, and it came in a variety of luscious colors. So by the time the Peacock Revolution exploded in a burst of color in the sixties, golf apparel was already liberated. As *Esquire* saw it in June, 1960, "No sport permits its participants the freedom of imagination, the choice of colors and styles, and the opportunity to dress tastefully yet uniquely that golf does."

Although the early sixties gave little indication of the revolution that would soon revamp menswear, a fashion tour of the European capitals in 1958 convinced *Esquire* fashion director O. E. Schoeffler that fashion excitement was on its way. "Europe is brimming with fashion excitement," he reported in the *Esquire International Sketch Book* (December, 1958). "There's news in tailored clothing from Savile Row. Leading London tailors have turned from the tapered concept to a new flare in clothing. There are new colors from Scandinavia and the Mediterranean—blue in a dozen shades, peach, lime, reds and greens. Colors will be light and bright in sportswear. Blue from light to bright and dark shades. Peche (soft peach shade) significant in South of France resorts. Limenado (lime shades) new accent color. New reds take an orange cast. Influence of soft green noted quite generally." And since Schoeffler found knits "the most versatile fashion idea" he saw in Europe, he illustrated his report with many knits: lightweight knits, bulky knits, knits by themselves and knits in combination with other knits, porous knits, printed knits. Sketches accompanying his report included a long-sleeved cardigan and a solid-color pullover combination of bright scarlet with a white accent; a graduated-rib cardigan with varied widths of dark blue stitching against a background shot with red; and a wide rollneck pullover with neck interest emphasized by the use of red-and-white stripes against a body of blue-and-white stripes.

1960–1970

Golf clothes in the early sixties grew increasingly colorful, hinting at the peacock soon to emerge. The well-dressed golfer appearing on a full-color page in the May, 1960, issue of *Esquire* wore a cotton yarn shirt in canyon gold, the magazine's favorite summer color. The model's tapered slacks were lime green, and he topped his costume with a cap of a brilliant India madras. Canyon gold also turned up that year in terry cloth beach blazers and after-swim cotton knit sweat shirts. A more muted shade of canyon gold was used in sports jackets, shirts, and ties.

Off the golf course, however, men in the earliest years of this decade were wearing more subtle colors. "Vineyard" colors were promoted by *Esquire* as ideal for warm-weather wear in everything: dress shirts and ties, sports shirts, sports coats and sweaters, rainwear, and silk dressing gowns. These colors included three tones of grape, claret, sunny champagne, sparkling port, sauterne, and Altos blue. Grape, said *Esquire* in October, 1965, provided a subtle flavoring, adding royal richness to fine worsteds, and demonstrated this with a predominantly black suit having a faint grape fleck threaded through the weave. Even shoes showed a little grape color with vintage brown, a new rich brown with a slight undertone of dark red chianti.

Then came the Peacock Revolution, and color was in fashion as never before. For, in the words of John Stephen, generally acknowledged to be its founding father through his closet-size shop in Carnaby Street, London, it began with "a crusade to brighten men's clothes. When one is young and one feels everything is grey and drab, you *know* they want something new and exciting. It wasn't a matter of being in the right place at the right time. I made it happen. When I started I had to fight to sell our clothes. People laughed at pink and red slacks. Frilly shirts. They said they were clothes for women and were effeminate. Word of mouth really made us. Some boy would buy a colorful shirt or tie and some friends would see it and ask, 'Where'd you get it?'" (*Gentlemen's Quarterly*, February, 1966).

Esquire's Color Forecast for Fall and Winter, 1967, reported that tailored apparel was making a dramatic breakaway from the dark, deep tones of seasons past and that the fashion accent was now being placed on "a spirited about face in the direction of brighter, lighter, Black-and-White-plus color combinations." As for sports clothes, vibrant shades of blue, green, and orange promised to monopolize apparel headlines, particularly in sweaters, knitted shirts, and sports socks. The fashion department's Color Forecast for Spring and Summer, 1968, promised a new range of color gradations in the metallic-looking shades for tailored apparel, "a logical outgrowth of last year's Copper and Bronze hues." Lighter and clearer in tone, the new shades, said *Esquire,* would have a natural affinity for blue, both in interwoven combinations and patterned ideas.

For sportswear and leisure wear, the magazine's color forecast introduced "fairway" colors in blue and green. "Pure clarity of tone identifies these two new shades: one is a strong, concentrated lime, the other a vibrant, blazing blue. Used alone, they're brilliant strokes of color against a background of beach or bunker, boat or backyard. Combined with white, black or grey, they'll add a vigorous accent to every kind of casual apparel.

An interesting innovation this season is the inter-knitting of Fairway Blue and Green to produce a vibrant iridescence."

Even formal-wear shirts took on dashing new colors, prompting *Gentlemen's Quarterly* to comment in November, 1969: "So you think you're daring when you don those dinner shirts shaded in soft blues, yellow and pinks? Witness, then, these eye openers." Among the eye-openers were a gold-color cotton spiced with a mustard collar and cuffs; a peach cotton, black-embroidered on placket and cuffs; and a bright blue cotton with blue-green braided front pleats. Liberated by the Peacock Revolution after having been locked into a set look for generations, the formal shirt had by 1970 become a proving ground for innovative menswear designers.

Golf clothes became increasingly colorful until the greens were ablaze with every conceivable color in every conceivable shade, prompting *Esquire* to comment in April, 1969: "Of all gamesmen, golfers are the most daring dressers, and sometimes the damnedest, too." The Peacock Revolution even swept across the tennis courts, touching off an explosion of color in what *Esquire* called "that notorious bastion of tradition." In June, 1968, the fashion staff gave its readers a preview of two of the outfits chosen for the 1968 Davis Cup team of the United States Lawn Tennis Association: a yellow outfit trimmed in blue and white and a blue outfit trimmed in white and yellow. Soon even the white tennis shoe was starting to feature bold racing stripes.

While traditionally colorful beachwear and sportswear grew still more colorful, even the apparel a man wore to bed became a form of self-expression. A man could choose sleepwear in the form of sleep shorts, togas, kimonos, nightshirts, tank-top jump suits, and hot pants, in everything from fireman-red flannel to barber-pole–striped knits.

New patterns and lively new colors in socks gave relevance to the old expression "sox appeal." And casual outercoats had linings of such colors as fireman red and billiard green that matched the swagger of the new coats. Finally, reflecting the body awareness characteristic of the Peacock Revolution, men's underwear became fashion underwear with shirts and shorts color-coordinated and matched in a myriad of colors, patterns, and fabrics. Exactly how liberated the Peacock Revolution had made the once dark-suited and white-shirted American businessman was illustrated in April, 1969, with an *Esquire* page of nine-to-five shirts in rainbow hues, coupled with uninhibited big-knotted ties in opulent fabrics.

Footwear, too, took on new colors, and it was generally agreed that no one shoe look or color could fill all needs for business, street, and dress footwear. And in October, 1971, *Gentlemen's Quarterly* filled a double-page spread with a collection of shoes, boots, and demiboots in tones and often two-tone combinations of aubergine, wine, deep burgundy, and bronze. The peacock was certainly the most colorfully shod man of the century.

In August, 1971, the *Daily News Record* predicted that colors for fall, 1971, fashions would be "brighter, clearer and cleaner as menswear returns to a more traditional look." And *Gentlemen's Quarterly,* heralding "the return of the gentleman" in November, 1971, predicted that "Men's fashions will never be dull again," that clothes with spirit, flair, and color were here to stay. For the peacock would not have it any other way. And as for color, what is a peacock without it?

Influences on Fashion

Most often a designer would be hard-pressed to explain exactly how he arrived at a certain fashion formulation. Like most successful creative people, the topflight designer seems blessed with a sixth sense, the sensitivity of a tuning fork, and is enough of a visionary to be able to anticipate what people will look for in their fashions the *next* season. Still, there are many concrete factors that influence the creator of menswear, and these are what will be specifically dealt with here. Broadly, these areas can be classified as follows: sports; the military; art and artifacts; heraldry and historical design; and news events.

Sports

Americans are a sports-loving people, and the various sports interesting them have had a strong influence on their apparel; very often a fashion specially created for active or spectator sportswear has been adapted for urban wear. Necessity—in the form of the specific requirements of the particular sport—is generally the catalyst for a sportswear fashion, and once the new fashion satisfies these basic requirements, it inevitably takes on added style and color.

A classic case history is that of the polo shirt, the first bona fide sports shirt, created early in this century for men who played the aristocratic and vigorous game of polo. The short-sleeved white pullover made of knitted wool and featuring a turned-down collar permitted all the freedom of action and comfort the polo player demanded. Having met the basic requirements of the sport for which it was created, the polo shirt served as the pattern for the tennis shirt of the late 1920s. Exactly how much the design of this new shirt owed to the polo shirt, and how much more style

had been added, can be seen from the following description written by a fashion reporter covering Palm Beach, where fashionable players were sporting the first tennis shirts:

It is pure white, knitted—sometimes of cashmere and sometimes of silk and wool—with a soft, close texture, and with the very desirable absorbent features; it has a turned down collar, which may be buttoned at the neck or left open, this front opening extending down the front about five inches from the top button, and usually closing with two buttons. There is a little variety in the style or finish of the sleeves and collar. On some of these shirts the sleeves are moderately loose, on others they fit tighter at the elbow. The shirt is not greatly unlike the polo shirt which, of course, has been used for polo in this country and in England for a great many years. (*Men's Wear,* Feb. 22, 1928)

By 1934 the knitted polo shirt was popular off the polo fields and tennis courts, being seen in various shades of blue, brown, and red. A new sports blouse—a cross between the polo shirt and a pullover—made from ecru twine or macrame string was being worn by some of the best-dressed men on the French Riviera, many of whom had never sat a horse, let alone swung a polo mallet. *Men's Wear* gave American men a preview of this sports blouse, and again it was evident how a fashion classic—in this case a knit originally designed for active sportswear—could influence the design of a new fashion created for more sedentary wear.

That same year the original polo shirt was evolving new styling features of its own. The finest shops on the Riviera, for example, were turning out polo shirts in a nonstretchable knitted fabric sometimes carrying a little tick or miniature curl, and these new-style polo shirts buttoned the whole way down, coat fashion, and had quarter sleeves finished with a turn-back cuff of about 2 inches. The all-white polo shirt originally designed for the polo player had by the 1930s become a fashion classic and, in every imaginable color, was being worn on the golf links, on the beach, and for lounging. And from it had come the inspiration for any number of other sports shirts.

There are, of course, many other sports whose gear has influenced fashion, but polo has had a special impact for several reasons, not the least of which is that it is a status sport and one that, so far at least, has been played only by men. The wide belts worn by polo players have inspired adaptations for general wear—wider-than-usual belts in heavy canvas with double buckles and straps. And the tan polo coat, one of the most popular outercoats ever worn by the American man, came to the fore by way of the polo field.

No coat in the 1920s or 1930s had the fashion impact of the camel's hair polo coat. Although it had not been expressly designed for the polo player, it had nevertheless been introduced to the United States by members of the English polo team who came to these shores to play in the international polo matches on Long Island and who casually tossed these sporty coats around their shoulders while relaxing during plays. Undergraduates at Princeton and Yale took up the fashion in 1926, and soon the double-breasted camel's hair polo coat with a half belt was being worn on the leading Eastern and Midwestern university campuses. Newspapers and magazines were full of photographs of men in polo coats attending the United States–Argentina polo matches in 1928, and although the six-button double-breasted model with a half belt was the classic, other variations were seen: a single-breasted box coat; a four-button model with raglan shoulders and an all-around belt; and a wraparound style with no buttons and a tied belt.

Men's Wear was doing its best to impress upon retailers the relevance of polo coats and polo games to their business success: "What difference does it make to you that Mr. So-and-So, noted member of eastern society, wore a camel's hair coat at the recent International polo matches on Long Island? None at all, in so far as your interest in Mr. So-and-So goes, but a great deal in that he is a member of the set which sets the styles for the rest of the American people. If he were the only one who wore a polo coat there would be no need mentioning it, but the fact that a number follow him in favoring this garment means that this imitation will be carried on, and that it should be a big factor in stocking your goods for the future. That this process is continually taking place and that the fashionable members of society who attend these great polo games influence the sartorial trends throughout the United States has been proved time and time again, and the very repetition of it, combined with the additional proofs that are being given, should be enough for you to notice and to prepare yourself for future demand" (Apr. 10, 1929).

The following autumn camel's hair polo coats outnumbered raccoons at the Yale-Princeton football game, and so once again a fashion born of one sport moved into another sports area and, as in the case of the tan polo coat, became an acceptable fashion in town as well.

Knickers, of course, were originally designed for the golfer. They originated in the British Isles, where golf had long been a leading sport, but it was not until after World War I that the golf boom began in the United States and the well-dressed American golfer was seen wearing knickers. Here, once again, the requirements of the sport dictated the styling of the fashion; golf demanded something comfortable that would permit an energetic stride through the rough. Knickers, a baggier version of the knee breeches of English court dress, combined with sturdy woolen stockings were the answer.

During the early 1920s college men vacationing in England made two discoveries: plus fours, knickers that hung 4 inches below the knee; and Oxford bags, the voluminous trousers the Oxford undergraduate wore to camouflage the knickers he was not permitted to wear to class. The Ivy Leaguer brought both fashions back to the United States, where each proceeded to flourish, independent of the other. Knickers, in fact, proceeded to grow longer and baggier by the year, until, in addition to plus fours, there were plus sixes and plus eights. And when the Prince of Wales wore knickers while touring the cattle ranches of South America in the late 1920s, their popularity skyrocketed. Knickers were now being worn on and off the golf course, and besides the tweedy ones there were knickers in every imaginable fabric from linen and flannel to gabardine, whipcord, and the then-new Palm Beach summer fabric of cotton and mohair.

Inevitably, manufacturers in America and Europe introduced the knicker suit to the general public, and in the United States it was often a four-piece suit of tweed or cheviot, consisting of a jacket, vest, and matching trousers. By the late 1920s the college man, who had started the vogue for knickers off the golf course, was wearing his knicker suit in so-called ice-cream shades.

A decade later, however, slacks began to supplant knickers both on and off the golf course, and the knicker started to go into total eclipse. In the early 1970s the knicker suit made a comeback, this time not on the golf course but on city streets, where it was worn by the avant-garde youth of both sexes. Very few fashions originally created for a specific sport have had as varied and mercurial a career as the knicker.

By the 1920s, as one writer of the period noted, "Every town or city of any size in America has one or more golf links, and new clubs are springing up overnight everywhere. Every summer sees hundreds of thousands of American men taking up golf for the first time." And designers of sweaters proved they were tuned in to the demands of the sport when they created the bell-sleeved sweater in shell stitch or similar open knit.

More recently, basketball and track have influenced sportswear. The side-vented shorts worn on the basketball court, for example, have been successfully adapted to swim shorts, and the three diagonal stripes seen on each side of the instep of the track shoe have been adapted to casual footwear.

The year 1971 saw a major change occur in footwear as the result of a sport's popularity—in this instance bicycling, which created the need for a bicycle sneaker, which, in turn, sparked the comeback of the sneaker per se. As the sneaker boom gathered momentum (many fashion savants seeing it as the latest progression of the jeans generation), the new styles bore scant resemblance to the original basic white canvas sneaker that, some years before, had composed the bulk of the men's sneaker business. All of this prompted *Footwear News* writer Don Fullington to observe: "What is a sneaker? If you ask retailers, manufacturers and importers, most likely you'll get a variety of answers. The variations in definitions go on and on. That there is such a great variation in thinking is interesting. But even more so is the fact that almost no one includes the basic white canvas sneaker in the definition anymore." In other words, the bicycle sneaker—a bulb-toed, high-heeled blucher specially designed for a new generation of cyclists—is a definitive example of a sport not only spawning a new fashion but, in the process, revitalizing an industry.

Big-game hunting has had a limited but noticeable effect on menswear, with the bush, or safari, jacket inspiring many designers. This rather long jacket with four patch pockets in front and an all-around belt has been adapted for general jacket styling. In the early 1970s it was copied for beachwear, leisure wear, and even sleepwear.

Boating, too, had a decided influence on men's fashions of the early 1970s. The *Daily News Record* commented: "Nautical motifs are building up as one of the major themes for summer of '72. Boats, anchors, flags—all contribute to the look. Not only is the nautical look big in sportswear, but in swimwear, sleepwear, neckwear . . . just about every category of menswear."

The Military

The years immediately preceding a war invariably have a decided effect on men's fashions. It's as though the nation girding itself for a war in which youth must serve tries to "youthify" all its men through trimmer, slimmer clothes. Early in the second decade of this century, as the world was moving toward the brink of World War I, men's suits had already begun to shed their oversize proportions. Where the barrel-chested physique with massive arms and Herculean thighs had been the ideal of the previous decade, the ideal of this second decade was the youthfully lanky; and so suits were made to emphasize this look where it existed, and to create the illusion where it did not. By 1912, in fact, shoulders of suit jackets had become more natural, and many a retail advertisement proudly trumpeted the news that its new suits had no padding. Sleeves were narrow and boasted a new feature: four buttons set well up from the edge of the cuff.

Trousers were cut narrower at the waist and were not only cuffed but also creased front and back. By 1914 the natural-shoulder suit dominated, and a full-page advertisement in the *Saturday Evening Post* the following year reflected the effect World War I had already had on men's clothing when it noted the "shaped body with military high-waist effect." This slim, high-waisted look continued to be in vogue for years after the conclusion of the war, reaching its peak with the introduction of a waist-seam coat cut extremely sharp and high under the arms.

Overcoats of this period also reflected the growing influence of the military climate on menswear. A New York fashion article written in 1912 noted a double-breasted hussar's coat of dark blue melton cloth, with military frogs and a Persian lamb lining and trim on the collar, deep cuffs, and peaked lapels; and a double-breasted chinchilla army coat, with a narrow belt at a short waistline giving it a decided waist effect.

In the spring of 1941, only months before the entrance of the United States into World War II, the military influence on men's clothing was evident. Khaki-colored suits in worsted, a civilian adaptation of the cavalry twill used in army uniforms, were immensely popular with college men. (Even porkpie hats came in khaki color.) Also popular on the campus was the covert cloth suit in shades of tan and olive brown. Furthermore, patriotic themes of red, white, and blue had begun to appear in suits, sportswear, and related accessories. It is interesting to note the comeback of chino, the light tan or khaki-cast shade, for men's slacks in 1971, a year marked by the nation's increasing preoccupation with its involvement in Vietnam.

One of the few benefits of military service appears to be the comfort of the uniforms. World War I, as a result, sounded the death knell for the high starched collar, and World War II led the way to zephyr-light summer suits, since after having grown accustomed to the comfort of the tropical worsteds the United States government had given him, the ex-serviceman was determined to have the same degree of comfort in his civilian garb.

In other, more direct ways the military also influences fashion. Designers have traditionally taken inspiration from the trim, slim lines of uniforms, as seen, for example, in the trench coat, a rainwear classic. In response to a need for an all-weather coat that would provide foul-weather protection

Model No. G.10

Model No. G.9

The Famous "Aquascutum" Storm Coats

THE centre illustration above (No. G.9) depicts our world famous Storm coat. This was originally designed for the rigorous conditions created by trench warfare, and is one of the most successful weatherproof coats yet designed. It is, however, equally suitable for either civil or military conditions where absolute security against torrential rain is desired. It is made of the finest quality Egyptian cotton, lined with self material and a special waterproof interlining, it has raglan sleeves, deep storm collar, large throat tab, strap cuffs, large D.B. lapels, a yoke back, and inside leg straps for riding. The shoulder straps are detachable. Ready-to-wear or made to measure.

A classic example of the military influence on civilian fashion was the switch of the trench coat from the army officer (left and center) to the business executive (right). [AQUASCUTUM, LTD., LONDON]

for the World War I soldier fighting in the trenches, Thomas Burberry, an Englishman, created a trench coat of a fine-twill cotton gabardine, a yarn-dyed fabric chemically processed to repel rain. Since this processing did not in any way affect the porous quality of the fabric, the trench coat also allowed for ventilation. In short, it was a water-repellent coat and as such very quickly became the official coat of the Allied fighting men. A fantastic success as a military coat, it was carried over into civilian life to become, as already noted, a rainwear classic.

The so-called guards coat is still another example of a fashion borrowed from the military, in this instance the uniform coat worn by members of the British Grenadier Guards. For years smartly dressed Britishers had been wearing it in a dark blue, and admiring American fashion editors had been encouraging American men to follow their example. Finally, in the 1930s, when British fashion influence was stronger than ever, the double-breasted guards coat came into vogue in the United States. For winter it was made of dark blue chinchilla, and for spring of dark blue cheviot. But regardless of season the fashion features remained constant: wide lapels rolling to the middle button of the three pairs, with the upper buttons spaced slightly apart; in back, an inverted pleat running almost all the way up to the collar instead of stopping at the conventional spot between the shoulder blades; and a stitched-on half belt loose enough to accommodate deep folds on either side of the inverted pleat—in short, a military coat with the casually elegant look prized by the fashionable man of the 1930s.

Even the neckwear worn by the Grenadier Guards inspired civilian fashion. The dark red and blue of their neckwear was adapted for ties worn by the man in mufti, and this led to the production of many other neckwear color combinations borrowed from the colors worn by other regiments both in England and the United States.

More recently, in the late 1960s, the high-waisted maxi- and midi-length coats showed a strong military influence. *Esquire* at the time showed several that appeared to have sprung from the Napoleonic Wars replete with wide collars, military buttons, and deep inverted back pleats and shaped to a bold flare.

The British officers' warmer, often called the English short-warm coat, or British warm, also became popular in the thirties; understandably enough, it enjoyed a resurgence of popularity in 1941 and went on to become something of a fashion staple from the early 1960s on. Ending just above the knee, it has the snappy military air and easy leg movement many men prefer.

Of equal importance are the original blazer jacket, first worn aboard the H.M.S. *Blazer,* a sailing vessel of the 1860s; the famed Eisenhower jacket of World War II, which subsequently served as a prototype for postwar civilian sportswear; the pea coat of the U.S. Navy with a similar history; and the walking shorts worn for the first time on American golf links in the 1920s, which were direct copies of the khaki shorts favored by British military men stationed in the tropics.

The leather jackets of wartime pilots have inspired various styles of leather jackets designed for casual wear. *Esquire* in 1968 observed that of all materials used in clothing, leather had the most personality and, in fact, was "the most masculine of all materials." According to the editors, it suggested the fliers of World War I: "The very word reminds you of somebody like Buddy Rogers or Richard Arlen or Gary Cooper as he gets into the cockpit, a lady's white silk scarf around his neck, and always he is wearing that leather jacket as he pulls the goggles down over his eyes and gives that gallant little wave. And of course leather was the uniform of Hitler's S.S. and Montgomery's Desert Rats."

Despite the disenchantment of much of today's youth with the military, in the early 1970s it still had a potent influence on their clothes, which, ironically, sometimes seemed to be worn as a kind of antiestablishment statement. Many a rich man's son walked around a campus wearing army boots and a sheepskin-lined leather jacket picked up at an Army-Navy surplus store. Camouflage-print fabrics were in vogue with the young of both sexes, and other details of the military uniform were picked up and used independently of the uniform. The epaulet, for example, was seen on everything from shirts and outercoats to pajamas.

Art and Artifacts

The early 1970s found the nation awash with nostalgia for earlier periods that, at least in retrospect, seemed much happier and more carefree. The revival of *No, No, Nanette,* a 1925 musical comedy, became one of the biggest hits of the 1971–1972 Broadway season, filling the stage with lively young dancers and singers in Art Deco–designed pullovers. In record time, sweaters and socks featuring Art Deco designs were selling in stores from coast to coast—a case of the jeans generation responding to a 1920s art form that was a magnificent blend of Art Nouveau, cubism, the Russian ballet, American Indian art, and the Bauhaus.

Meanwhile, many men of the post-

Primitive art and designs were utilized in developing a theme called "New Primitives" for men's sportswear and accessories. From Esquire's First International Fashion Forum, 1954.

Two adaptations of designs originated by the Indians of Central and South America. From Esquire's First International Fashion Forum, *1954.*

jeans generation were showing an increasing fondness for extravagantly designed ties in opulent fabrics, and to this trend ancient cultures were contributing fashion ideas, such as Aztec-inspired designs and stripes adapted from Egyptian hieroglyphics, both expressions of modern man's preoccupation with the past. Roman statues, columns, and pillars, long the basis of designs in neckwear, robes, and pajamas, also enjoyed a new surge of popularity.

Heraldry and Historical Design

Heraldic designs turned up in neckwear and fancy buttons. Although most Americans had scanty knowledge of the history of heraldry, they

The patterns of these ties were inspired by (left to right) grapes, wine bottles, and glasses; historic statues; town crests; and famous paintings. From Esquire, April 1953.

admired the ties and buttons that featured lions, ancient shields of arms, crosses, and other sturdy mementos of the Age of Chivalry. By the end of 1971 this trend was gaining momentum, as can be seen in the announcement by a fabric house of a new line of parchment prints in durable-press fabrics: "Hear ye! Hear ye! Age-old elegance comes to the menswear revolution."

News Events

One of the major accomplishments of the Peacock Revolution was to encourage men to regard their clothes as a form of self-expression. A fashion, in other words, made a statement about the man who wore it, and in the rebellious, assertive 1970s any thinking man had a lot to say. For one thing, he had discovered ecology. According to Webster, ecology deals with the interrelationships between organisms and their environment. Therefore, besides pressing for the preservation of some threatened species of wildlife and for the purification of the environment, the man who considered himself a dedicated ecologist sometimes liked to wear something that reflected this

The Japanese kimono was the inspiration for the styling of this lounge suit in 1954. From Esquire's First International Fashion Forum, *1954.*

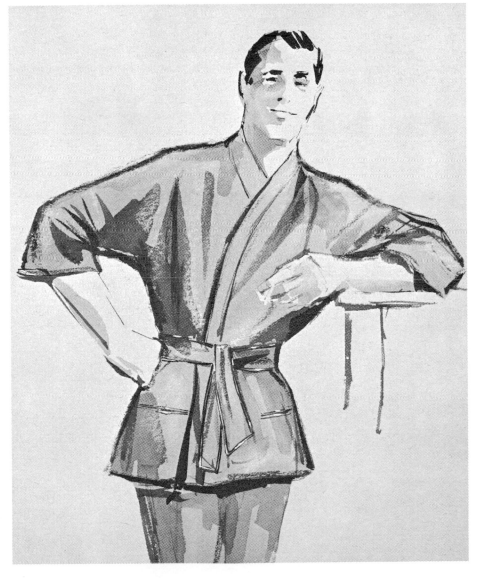

dedication. Furthermore, he had an ample range of clothes to choose from: sports shirts, slacks, ties, and swim shorts, all with flora and fauna artfully splattered against earth-tone backgrounds. And if he felt strongly about his country's involvement in Vietnam, there was also apparel carrying the peace symbol in its design, as well as fashions and fashion patches featuring the Stars and Stripes.

The 1960s had seen the country grow painfully aware of the black man's fight for equality, and by the early 1970s the nation's increasing awareness of minority-group problems had brought the plight of the American Indian into sharp focus. While the sympathetic young white man could comb his hair Afro style and adopt some of the colorful new boutique fashions that had a strong Harlem flavor, he could go several steps further, sartorially speaking, if he wanted to *wear* his concern for his Indian brothers. This led one prominent fashion reporter to decide that the American Indian look of the 1970s sprang from "forces quite different from those which brought forth the headbands, moccasins and home-made Indian inspired shirts of its last incarnation." This time an honest appreciation of authentic Indian costumes and jewelry was being shown. Designers, he decided, had obviously researched Indian clothing through actual specimens, books, and pictures, with the result that "styles inspired by what Zane Grey termed 'The Vanishing American' have turned out to be anything but vanquished fashions for spring '72." To many another fashion writer, the Indian look shirts, belts, and fringed jackets were the logical extension of cowboy wear that in the 1960s represented the under-twenty-five generation's yearning for a simpler way of life. Then, too, the young had eschewed the colorful satin shirts and other glamorous Western garb admired by the dude ranchers of the 1930s and were insisting upon authenticity—sturdy jeans and work shirts, the *functional* clothes of the cowboy.

Although man's first trip to the moon brought on an avalanche of fanciful fashion sketches of futuristic apparel, it had little actual influence on menswear. A news event with less drama but more fashion clout was President Richard Nixon's announcement in 1971 of his forthcoming visit to the People's Republic of China. This promptly led to prints in what the *Daily News Record* called "The Oriental Mood," seen most frequently in sports shirts reflecting the color and detail for which Oriental prints have been famous over the centuries. Brightly colored parasols, pagodas, trees, ponds, and bridges decorated long-sleeved sports shirts of nylon and nylon blends.

Although the speed with which today's fashions evolve has been accelerated to a point that, a decade ago, would have been unthinkable (as late as 1963 the fashion writer George Frazier of *Esquire* observed that what was so nice about men's clothes was that they changed "so gradually, so almost imperceptibly, that only in retrospect does one realize that there has been change"), the major influences that help shape these new fashions can still be traced to the same five major catalysts that have provided inspiration for so many generations.

Fashion Cycles

Some years ago, a group of fashion analysts worked out a rule-of-thumb formula that gauged the life-span of a single fashion to be a seven-year period from conception to a peak of popularity and then through decline to final disappearance. A valiant attempt to chart the course of fashion, it was, of course, unsuccessful since no two fashions ever move at exactly the same rate of speed or last the same length of time. Like love, fashion is almost totally unpredictable, as a review of some of the major fashion cycles of the twentieth century proves.

Outercoats

The history of the chesterfield overcoat reflects a varied degree of acceptance through the early decades of the century. From 1900 to 1941, for instance, the chesterfield was a very important part of the fashion scene, though not without significant changes in its appearance. Before 1915 the popular model reached well below the knees and on occasion dipped almost to the ankles. At this time the chesterfield was associated mainly with the mature businessman. Then, during the 1920s, it was taken up by the Ivy League undergraduate and emerged as a shorter coat, usually about 46 inches long and predominantly single-breasted with a fly front, that was acceptable for both daytime business wear and formal evening wear. During the forties and fifties the chesterfield's popularity declined. While it rose again in the sixties, the coat had clearly passed its heyday.

The raccoon, or coonskin, coat cycle moved to quite another rhythm. The coat came in during the twenties and, along with the Charleston and the Stutz Bearcat car, became an integral part of the "flaming youth" era. Priced from a low of about $350 to $1,000, it obviously was limited to the more affluent American. The stock market crash of 1929 put the raccoon coat into eclipse, and it did not regain favor until the 1960s, when fur coats for men came into vogue and the under-twenty-five set began rummaging through the family attic or the nearest secondhand store in search of "authentic" raccoon coats of the 1920s.

Like the coonskin coat, the tan polo coat started off on the top rung of the social ladder, coming into the limelight during the international polo matches in 1924. Although it was most popular in camel's hair, it was also seen in luxurious cashmere, and it turned up not only in the classic double-breasted style but also in single-breasted styles in dark blue-gray and black. The polo coat fashion cycle lasted through the 1930s. The coat varied in popularity thereafter, but it never completely disappeared and today has achieved the status of a fashion classic.

Coat lengths have always been strongly influenced by changes in life-styles. The convertible car of the 1930s and 1940s, for instance, helped put over the fingertip-length coat. And the more flamboyant clothes inspired by the Peacock Revolution called for more extravagantly designed outercoats, which, with their napoleon collars and generous lapels, demanded longer lengths.

Suits

The heavyweight suits of the early 1900s started a cycle that lasted almost fifteen years. During this period there was only one truly major variation in style: the long flared jacket worn with peg-top trousers finished with deep cuffs. This fashion innovation started in 1908–1909 and lasted for approximately five years.

Men's suits began to lose their over-stuffed proportions shortly before

World War I. By 1914 the natural-shoulder suit dominated the wardrobes of the best-dressed men, and by the end of the war it had spawned a number of variations, which in turn started other, short-lived cycles. Most noteworthy was the postwar "jazz suit," a pinched and exaggerated version of the natural-shoulder silhouette that was related to the jazz craze of the period. Its cycle extended from 1919 through 1923.

The natural-shoulder suit silhouette won new adherents during the twenties, when Ivy Leaguers took it up and virtually made it their own; custom tailors in New Haven adapted this style with their own signature of round notched lapels. The suit became a symbol of understated elegance and good breeding, and it went on to enjoy varying degrees of popularity in the thirties and forties. In a shade of charcoal gray, the natural-shoulder suit became the "uniform" of the well-dressed man of the conservative fifties and so enjoyed a fashion cycle that extended over more than forty years.

The English look, with its broader shoulders and high-waisted pleated trousers, came in during the early twenties but did not gain real strength until the Depression decade of the thirties, when the British blade or English drape, a lounge suit, caught the fancy of the affluent men who then dominated the fashion scene. This silhouette lasted until the forties, by which time it had departed from the original concept of fullness over the chest and shoulder blades.

Esquire's "bold look," introduced in 1948, brought the broad-shouldered, wide-lapel suit jacket back into the limelight, although the spirit of the look actually depended more on accessories than on the suit itself. This frankly aggressive look enjoyed a two-year cycle, which was followed by the magazine's "Mr. T" silhou-

(top to bottom) The long-point collar, first worn in the late twenties and the thirties, became popular again in the late sixties and the seventies. Pleated trousers were worn in the twenties and thirties, then gave way to plain tops, and were revived in the seventies. Small-knot ties peaked in the early sixties and then disappeared, while narrow lapels lasted a few years in the mid-sixties. The action-back jacket of the twenties and the thirties returned in the late sixties and the seventies.

ette, a trim look characterized by natural shoulders, narrow lapels, and straight-hanging lines. The resurgence of the natural-shoulder trend lasted through the entire decade of the fifties and continued into the early sixties.

Less durable was the Continental style of suit, with its shorter jacket, shapely body lines, short side vents, and tapered trousers. A modification of an Italian design, it was less flattering to the American man's larger-boned physique, and despite much fanfare its cycle lasted only about three years.

The sixties ushered in an updated version of the British look, which involved a suit jacket with shaping starting at the armholes, side vents, and trim trousers. Lapels continued to widen, and soon even single-breasted suit jackets had double-breasted or almost double-breasted lapels. Next came fancy-back jackets reminiscent of the thirties, patch or regular pockets with arched flaps, and trousers with a flare at the bottoms. And almost, if not entirely, as important as the new shaped suit silhouette was the debut of the knit suit. Flexible and wrinkle-resistant, with all problems finally eliminated, the knit suit was at last a fashion reality.

Sports Jackets

The cycles in the sports jacket category are invariably of relatively long duration. The first sports jacket, the dark blue double-breasted suit jacket worn with a pair of white slacks, took hold in the early 1900s and retained its popularity until the early twenties. Actually it was not until 1923 that the best-dressed men at such fashionable resorts as Palm Beach began to wear a specially designed odd jacket that could honestly claim to be a sports jacket.

The next major cycle got its start in the mid-twenties with the introduction of the fancy-back sports jacket, which had a belt stitched across the waistline in back, with four pleats above and below it. At first this fashion was confined almost totally to gabardine, but as it grew in popularity, it included other fabrics such as Shetland, linen, and tweed. The fancy-back cycle carried over into the thirties, but it petered out in the last half of the decade and was out of fashion by the forties.

Just as the fancy-back jacket was reaching its peak of popularity, the blazer jacket, a plain-back model, was becoming prominent. The blazer had started in England as a tennis and club jacket, in a dark blue single- or double-breasted style with metal buttons. In the thirties it began to be seen in solid colors, sometimes with piping at the edges, and the boldly striped blazer in a lightweight fabric was a summer favorite. The blazer has never gone out of fashion, and in the sixties, when it became a favorite with many of highly publicized designers, it was firmly established as a fashion classic.

The decline of the fancy-back jacket and the growing dominance of the blazer started the cycle of the plain-back sports jacket. In fact, by 1938 the plain-back jacket had replaced the fancy-back jacket as the leading style and appeared in a great variety of patterns and fabrics. In its September issue *Esquire* took a look at the back-to-school wardrobes of the well-dressed college men of 1938 and noted: "Almost everything is three-button, with a plain back."

Sports jackets more or less disappeared during World War II, but in the postwar period they came back in patterns that were stronger than ever. The new patterns were perhaps best typified by the colorful India madras, which grew so popular during the late forties and the fifties that American mills made cottons and blends of cottons in patterns and colorings typical of the authentic madras.

Fashion cycles in suits have always influenced sports jacket styles. The natural-shoulder concept, for example, applied not only to suits but to sports jackets as well, especially in the fifties. The Continental styling of suits similarly affected the sports jackets of the late fifties and early sixties. With the shift to wider lapels in the mid- and late sixties, lapels on sports jackets grew wider too. And when the fancy- or action-back suit jacket began to stage a comeback in the last half of this decade, the action-back sports jacket also appeared. Similarly, the debut of the knit suit opened the door to the knit sports jacket in solid colors, geometric designs, and a wide assortment of plaids and stripes.

Slacks

White slacks have enjoyed one of the most enduring fashion cycles in the history of menswear, having been worn in varying degrees in every decade of this century. White slacks dominated the 1920s, and although they gave way to colored and patterned slacks during the 1930s, they never vanished from the scene. They continued to hold their own during the 1940s, lost ground in the 1950s with the emergence of walking shorts, and then made a comeback in the 1960s, when there was a resurgence of white in many different fabrics. Despite these changes, the white slacks cycle shows a certain consistency.

So, too, does the cycle of the pleated slack. This style came in during the mid-1920s with the high waist, and it remained a factor through the 1930s, 1940s, and early 1950s, years when natural-shoulder clothing more or less dictated plain, unpleated trousers for both business and leisure wear. The pleatless slack maintained a dominant position throughout the 1950s and 1960s, but in the early 1970s the pleated slack began a modest comeback in the wake of a revival of the 1930s look.

A cycle of shorter duration was that of the Oxford bags of the twenties, voluminous slacks with a pleated waistline, baggy knees, and bottoms measuring from 22 to 25 inches. In the space of a year they swept the country, and within another year the cycle had started to decline; but as an aftermath they left most style-conscious young Americans in favor of a widely cut slack. As a result, the next cycle swung in the direction of slacks measuring

18½ to 20 inches around the bottoms, and these slacks remained in vogue for several years.

Special styles in slacks have had cycles of varying duration. During the twenties, for instance, regatta or block stripes (stripes of equal width alternating a color and white) started a new trend. The cycle of slacks in many different arrangements of stripes lasted about nine years.

In 1933 covert cloth slacks appeared on Eastern college campuses and started a trend of a special nature. At first topcoating fabrics were used, but these soon proved too heavy for slacks. However, the look and general character were so pleasing that mills turned out covert cloth especially for slacks, and these slacks retained their popularity for about eight years.

Glenurquhart slacks gained acceptance in the early thirties, making an emphatic change in the appearance of slacks. They looked especially attractive when worn with a solid-color sports jacket, and their cycle lasted ten years.

In May, 1954, *Esquire* focused its attention on the new tapered slacks that were then being seen in Rome. The fashion department dubbed them "very handsome in their smooth fit, narrow cut and tapered legs. The effect is a Continental version of that long-legged look that cowboy pants give our native croupiers." The cycle of the trim slack extended over two decades.

Denim slacks and jeans provide the longest fashion cycle of all. Jeans, a particularly durable slice of Americana, are described in the *Dictionary of American Slang* as "a pair of stiff, tight-fitting, tapered denim cowboy work pants, usu. blue with heavily reinforced seams and slash pockets." The first pair was cut in 1850 by Levi Strauss, who used the same canvas material he sold to Western miners for tents and wagon covers. Shortly afterward, Strauss turned from canvas to a tough cotton fabric that came to be known as denim, and the specially cut denim jeans became basic equipment for ranchers and cowboys. For the next

(top to bottom) Big-knot ties were important in the late sixties and the seventies. The natural-shoulder cycle peaked in the twenties, thirties, and fifties. The porkpie hat was most popular in the thirties and forties. The India madras shirt was favored in the thirties and fifties and again in the seventies. The chukka boot, worn in the thirties and forties, became very popular in the sixties.

100 years jeans were worn around dude ranches and farms and enjoyed varying degrees of popularity with high school and college students of both sexes. The fashion of blue jeans spread around the globe, and in 1970 jeans sales, growing at more than three times the rate of slacks sales, were accounting for just under half of the $3 billion pants market and American manufacturers were selling blue jeans in forty countries throughout the world.

An increasing number of novel styles followed blue jeans from 1966 on. Young people appeared determined to express their individuality in everything wearable, and certainly this included slacks, which were made in awning stripes, bold stripes, big checks, and patterns of every conceivable size, color, and color combination. There were tight-fitting slacks, flared slacks, bell bottoms, and cuffed and cuffless models in an astonishing assortment of fabrics.

Knit was the magic word in the fashion vocabulary of the early seventies, although knit slacks in solid colors were causing excitement as early as the late sixties. By 1971 patterns were plentiful, and the new knit jeans were gaining headlines. And so the knit cycle started, and it promised to be one of the most newsworthy and durable of all cycles.

Shirts

Some of the fashion cycles in men's shirts are broad in scope and of great length. Most of the shirts worn in 1900, for example, were of the neckband variety, which stayed in fashion until 1918, when the downward slope of this cycle commenced. The decline was rather gradual, lasting until 1930, by which time neckband shirts had become a rarity. The reverse of this cycle was that of the collar-attached shirt, which took hold during World War I and promptly began to ascend the fashion scale, becoming the dominant fashion in the thirties not only for business shirts but for sports shirts as well. It has retained this position, and so its cycle has lasted well over half a century.

As the collar-attached shirt ascended the fashion scale, variations in its style had their own cycles. The button-down collar, on the scene by 1917, became increasingly popular during the twenties, when Ivy League undergraduates adopted this style. There were ups and downs in its vogue in subsequent decades, but it never completely disappeared.

Two diametrically opposed fashion concepts in collars were present at the same time and enjoyed different cycles, since each appealed to different types of men. One was the tab collar, so called because it had two tiny tabs on the inside of the points that fastened to the collar button. This style was given some impetus during the twenties, after the Prince of Wales had worn it during his visit to the United States, and it remained in fashion until the early thirties, when it began to be replaced by the similar-appearing tabless tab collar. The tab collar made a brief comeback during the fifties, but its cycle declined before the decade was over.

The opposite style was the long-point Barrymore collar. Unlike the tab collar, which set high on the neck, the Barrymore collar set low, so low that there was scarcely any space for a neckband. Points were about 4½ inches long and had an easy-flowing appearance. The Barrymore remained in fashion for several years and was adopted by many men in the California motion-picture colony. Its cycle lasted throughout the thirties.

During this Depression decade British fashion influence was especially strong, and when the Duke of Windsor and his younger brother the Duke of Kent were photographed wearing spread collars, this style was taken up by most of the best-dressed men in the United States, many of whom chose to wear it with a collar-attached shirt. The spread collar was the ideal companion for the larger Windsor-knot tie, and this cycle lasted for at least fifteen years.

The bold look introduced in 1948 featured a variation of the spread collar with longer points and stitching set back ½ inch. Hard on the heels of the bold look's two-year cycle came *Esquire*'s Mr. T, a trim natural-shoulder look with collars of smaller proportions. It was at this time that the button-down collar made its strongest advance.

The shaped Continental suit of the fifties gave rise to a widespread collar that allowed space for a larger knot. The Continental concept in shirt collars made a strong impression that lasted into the sixties. Although its popularity declined from 1962 to 1965, it rose again as the Peacock Revolution dictated wider lapels and wider ties.

Neckwear

The cycle of regimental stripes in neckwear got off to a good start in the 1920s. Ivy Leaguers liked the stripes, and the visiting Prince of Wales, who wore the red-and-blue striped tie of the Grenadier Guards, gave them a giant boost. Regimentals remained as ties widened, narrowed, and widened again; they have never really disappeared from the fashion picture, although their popularity has been more robust in some periods than in others.

The crochet tie was a particular campus favorite all through the twenties and into the thirties, but toward the end of the thirties other types of neckwear superseded it. The wool-tie cycle proved more durable. The wool tie made its appearance in the last half of the twenties and grew in popularity in the next decade. There were various kinds of wool ties: the loosely woven tweedy type of homespun wool; wool worsted, which was more closely woven and smooth-surfaced; and wool challis, usually seen in neatly intricate patterns. Wrinkle resistance was one of the chief virtues of the wool tie, and by 1932 such ties were being made in an amazing number of colors and designs.

The big-knot tie came into prominence during the thirties, mainly because the Duke of Windsor preferred it with a spread collar. The triangular knot called the Windsor knot was achieved with a series of loopings. Although the Duke said that he had never tied his tie in this manner, the name stuck and became part of the fashion vocabulary. The Windsor knot continued to be popular, being worn by many men well into the fifties and sixties, when it slipped into oblivion with the advent of the wide tie, which by 1970 in some instances had billowed to a full 5 inches.

The big tie with a wild pattern had a spirited though relatively short cycle that began in the last year of World War II, when with the war well in the Allies' hands men's civilian clothes assumed a more colorful and aggressive personality. Its vogue was enhanced by the scarcity of many other articles of apparel. A widespread-collared shirt and a wide tie featuring a zigzag pattern in, say, victory red on a white ground produced a fashionably bold look. Tie designs were big and colorful and were sometimes described as "ham 'n egg" patterns. This desire for unusual patterns was carried over into the cycle of the hand-painted necktie, which was seen in patterns ranging from flowers to sailboats and often carried a price tag of $25. Many hand-painted ties were 4½ inches wide, a width that earned them the name "belly warmers." A wartime phenomenon, the hand-painted tie continued its popular run for a few postwar years and, in a sense, paved the way for the bold look neckwear introduced by *Esquire* in the fall of 1948. The fashion department took pains, however, to point out that its bold tie was bold without being noisy.

The predictable reaction to the bold fashion concept was the shift back to natural-shoulder suits and Mr. T accessories. Hat brims narrowed, shoes became trimmer, and neckwear grew narrower and took on more sedate patterns. The emergence of the Continental-style suit brought the widespread collar and wider neckwear for some men, but in general the narrow, more conservative tie trend lasted through this decade, and in 1963, when narrow suit lapels and related neckwear were at the peak of their popularity, ties ranged from 2 to $2\frac{1}{2}$ inches in width.

The narrow-tie cycle finally ended in 1966, when a leading accessories firm in the West End of London brought out a wide tie called the kipper. It measured a then-astonishing 5 inches at its widest point of apron and served to start a major fashion cycle that was in perfect harmony with the wide lapels and big-collared shirts of the Peacock Revolution. The wide-tie cycle continued to rise throughout the latter half of the sixties and by 1971 was at its peak.

The bow tie has had a long and spotty history. The butterfly bow was introduced during the second decade of this century, but the bow tie per se did not begin to rise in favor until the 1920s, and it did not reach its peak until the mid-thirties, when *Esquire* served its readers a batch of them: an elegant pointed-end India madras, a sporty foulard, a spirited plaid, and a classic regimental stripe. The cycle started to dip in the forties, but in the late fifties the bow came back fancier than ever in new woven textures and prints. Yet the revival was a minor one, and not until the mid-sixties did the bow tie really make news, with *Gentlemen's Quarterly* headlining a fea-

(top to bottom) The shirt with a Windsor collar was popular in the thirties, forties, and fifties along with the Windsor-knot tie, which has never really been out of fashion since then. The white dinner jacket was worn in the thirties and forties. Argyle socks attained their greatest popularity in the twenties and thirties and again in the late sixties. The moccasin slip-on has been favored since the thirties.

ture of July, 1964, "Big Bow & Big Brim." By 1969 wide ties, wide brims, wide lapels, square-toed shoes, and wide, flared bow ties combined to show that the thirties look was in fashion. *Esquire* bowed to the bow tie that year, too, in July, 1964, showing a collection noted for a more simple and sedate look. "Look at it this way," said the caption writer, "bow ties are neat and brisk-looking, they are eminently acceptable and adaptable, and you cannot slop them in your soup." And so the bow tie had made an honest comeback, but despite the national nostalgia for the thirties, when the bow had enjoyed its greatest popularity, the wide four-in-hand was the genuine front-runner of the seventies and the bow tie, no matter how wide and flared, only an also-ran.

Hats

Cycles of fashion in men's hats often cover long spans of time. The stiff derby, for instance, which came in many different shapes, was prominent from 1900 to 1920 and only began to decline in the post-World War I period, when there was a greater spirit of casualness and ease in men's apparel. During the same period the soft felt fedora hat, a style with a lengthwise crease in the crown, rose in popularity from the early part of the century to the mid-twenties. The snap-brim felt cycle got started in the mid-twenties (this was yet another fashion given impetus by the Prince of Wales) and has remained a basic style in various shapes and types ever since.

The panama hat first attracted national attention when Theodore Roosevelt was photographed wearing one at the construction site of the Panama Canal. (Although Roosevelt had gotten his hat in Panama, it had actually been made of jipijapa fiber in Ecuador.) The panama enjoyed some fashion status for many years, and the optimo shape (a full-crown shape with a lengthwise ridge down the center) remained popular through the twenties and thirties. A fashion reporter noted: "The very best dressed men at Palm Beach who wear Panama hats naturally wear what appear to be the most expensive Panamas. These have square-top crowns . . . very square . . . and the wide, flattish set brims" (*Men's Wear,* Mar. 25, 1935). In the late forties the panama was seen in the optimo shape as well as in center-crease

styles, but in the fifties it finally was replaced by other summer hats.

The homburg, with its tapered, creased crown and rolled brim, came into the limelight about 1920, although the previous year *Men's Wear* had already maintained that the homburg was "the real thing in soft hats" and expected that it would be for many seasons to come (May 7, 1919). This prediction proved absolutely correct, as the elegant homburg went on to become one of the most popular hats for several decades. In 1928, for example, few of the fashion leaders at Princeton University were wearing hats but those who did favored the homburg. Also, in black and midnight blue it was appropriate for wear with evening clothes. The homburg remained in the vanguard of fashion throughout the thirties and forties and well into the fifties. Prime Minister Anthony Eden favored this style of hat, and Dwight D. Eisenhower bypassed the top hat in favor of the homburg for his inauguration in 1953. In all, the homburg cycle lasted some three decades.

The porkpie, a low-crowned hat of the telescope type, came into prominence in the mid-thirties. First seen in England, it moved on to the United States, where it was worn by well-dressed men at polo games and race meetings before being accepted for business and casual wear as well. Many retailers promoted the porkpie as strictly British and referred to it as "the first new hat block idea in years." Having established itself in felt, the porkpie next turned up in panama, leghorn, bangkok, and other straws. This cycle peaked in the late thirties and declined in the mid- and late forties.

The so-called executive hat, with a wide brim and a full crown, was part of *Esquire's* bold look in 1948. It was carried over until the natural-shoulder clothing and trim lines of 1950 called for a narrower-brimmed hat with a tapered crown, a style that lasted into the sixties.

The shaped hat with a tapered rolling brim accompanied the shaped suit

silhouette of the British look of 1959. In 1965 the Cardin hat, designed by the French couturier Pierre Cardin, appeared. A tapered-crown hat with a brim turned up sharply in back close to the crown and snapped down in front, it had a short-lived career, but its concept exerted an influence on hat fashions for a few years.

The year 1968 marked the beginning of the big-hat cycle. "The brasher the better," wrote a nationally syndicated fashion columnist of the broad-brimmed models that were ideally suited to the new wider lapels, wide ties, and large-collared shirts.

Footwear

The high-shoe cycle, which was strong in 1900, maintained its strength until about 1920. In the high-shoe category were laced shoes, high-buttoned shoes, and congress gaiters with elastic insets at the sides. Tips were sharply pointed, a style that was a perfect complement to the cuffless, peg-top trousers that tapered to very narrow bottoms. In 1905 cuffs began to be worn on trousers, signaling the ascendancy of a bulb-shaped toe, which, in effect, served to balance the new, deeply cuffed trouser bottoms.

Although the oxford or low shoe was on the market and was widely advertised as early as 1910, it was not accepted by the general public for almost another ten years, in the interim being the more or less exclusive property of the avant-garde dresser. By 1919 the oxford was given a tremendous boost by the returning serviceman, who much preferred it to the high shoe (the previous year, a *Men's Wear* survey of fashions seen at winter resorts in the South had noted the increasing popularity of the oxford, along with the knickerbocker suit). And by 1920 the cycle of the high-top shoe had come to an end and the cycle of the low shoe had begun to climb. The low-shoe cycle continued through four decades, and not until the very late fifties and early sixties was there a recurrence of the high shoe, and then it appeared in the form of the boot.

During the ascendancy of the low shoe, it was associated with two types of leather, Scotch grain and cordovan. Cordovan had been used extensively for military puttees and boots during World War I, and the ex-serviceman continued to show a partiality for its high polish.

Another important footwear cycle was that of the sports shoe, a cycle that ascended rapidly, paralleling the American man's growing interest in active sports. Dominant were the all-white buckskin shoe with a plain tip and usually a red or black rubber sole and the white shoe with a brown or black wing-tip trim; the latter was to retain its popularity for twenty years. Also part of the sports shoe cycle of the twenties and thirties was the brown buckskin, which achieved a fairly dazzling amount of publicity when it was worn by the Prince of Wales during his visit to the United States in 1923. Yet while it became very popular and, in the thirties, began to be worn on city streets in the summer, the brown buckskin never achieved the classic sports shoe status of the all-white shoe. The sports shoe cycle continued to climb throughout the thirties. In 1931, for instance, a Palm Beach style survey found that "a higher percentage of men seen at Palm Beach this season had at least two pairs of sport shoes. The influence of this class has done much to accelerate the mass acceptance of sport shoes" (*Men's Wear,* Mar. 25, 1931).

Spinning off from the sports shoe cycle was the boot cycle, which began with the appearance in the mid-twenties of an ankle-high laced chukka boot. In brown reversed-calf buckskin or brown smooth calf, the chukka remained popular until 1956, when it shared honors with the Australian bush boot. Thus the boot cycle maintained a slow but steady climb until the sixties, when, as fashion writer William J. Ullmann observed in *Men's Wear,* "Boots and the boot look are marching across the national fashion scene . . .

teen men and some young adults have been wearing the high-cuts right through the summer months." The "boot look" even appeared in oxfords with squared and rounded toes. And in 1964 *Esquire* noted "the almost fanatical interest in men's boots." By the late sixties the cycle suddenly rose to a high point as the vogue for all types of boots caught on. "Will they continue to enjoy their high popularity?" *Gentlemen's Quarterly* asked in September, 1969, and promptly answered its own question with "You can bet your buckled boots they will!" This prediction proved to be accurate as the boot moved into the seventies and a higher, chunky heel, decorative lacing, and functional side zippers helped place it still more firmly in the category of high fashion.

The slip-on shoe cycle started in the mid-thirties with the appearance of a slip-on style with a moccasin front, a variation of the shoes made by hand by Norwegian fishermen during their off-season. These Norwegian shoes achieved their first success in London, where American tourists discovered them, and soon they were being worn at fashionable American winter resorts. Thus began a cycle that lasted for the next thirty-five years.

In 1948 hefty thick-soled footwear was keyed to the bold look, *Esquire*'s coordinated fashion look that added weight to practically every item in the American man's wardrobe. The bold look reflected the hearty optimism of the postwar years 1948 and 1949, and when this optimism was replaced in 1950 by a mood of cautious conservatism, the masculine silhouette assumed the trim new Mr. T look, with narrower lines from head to toe, from the narrower brim of the hat to the natural shoulders of the suit and down to lighter, trimmer shoes.

In the mid-fifties the shorter, shapelier Continental suit silhouette came to the United States from Italy, and with it a Latin look in shoes: leaner, longer-looking, with uppers cut lower

than ever before, soles sliced slimmer, and often even somewhat raised heels. Soon American shoe manufacturers were advertising slip-on versions of the new low lines.

Both the cycle of the trim type of shoe and that of the low-cut Continental shoe lasted well into the sixties. Meanwhile, in 1960, the blunt- or squared-toe shoe had evolved to complement the new shaped suit. This footwear cycle moved upward and then dipped during the decade, only to revive and move upward again in the early seventies, when flared trousers became the rule rather than an oddity.

Hair Styles

The crew cut, like the sports shoe, came into vogue in the twenties as the American man pursued sports with new vigor. It was a practical, easy-to-care-for hair style for every sportsman. And although the motion-picture stars of the twenties and thirties, who had a certain fashion influence, rarely had crew cuts (most cameramen contended that a great deal of hair on the head tended to give the face better proportions for the camera), the crew cut nevertheless lasted for some men well into the sixties.

Long hair, however, took over in that decade, and the title of the anti-establishment Broadway musical *Hair* pinpointed the role that long hair, sometimes of shoulder length, played in youth's determination to achieve visual as well as audible self-expression. In the early seventies, the frizzed Afro cut of the black man was sometimes copied by white youths as a sign of brotherhood. Sideburns continued to grow long, and beards and moustaches flourished for the first time since the earliest decades of the century. Occasional shaved heads (in London they were dubbed skinheads) appeared on teen-age boys, but the long-hair cycle showed no signs of abating.

Fads and Foibles

A fad, according to *Webster's Third New International Dictionary,* is "a pursuit or interest" followed for a time "with exaggerated zeal. . . ." One of the differences between a fad and a fashion is that the former stresses caprice in both acceptance and abandonment. *Webster's* defines a foible as "a minor flaw or shortcoming. . . ." One might regard a foible as a fad whose prime reason for being is to

The peg-top pants of 1907, cut wide over the hips with deep cuffs, remained in fashion for the next several years. [NEW YORK PUBLIC LIBRARY PICTURE COLLECTION]

draw attention to the individual wearing it. It is not surprising, therefore, that fashion's fads appeal to extroverted personalities, and its foibles to a smaller segment with an even more compelling urge to be noticed.

Peg-top pants. In this century there have been numerous fads that affected a relatively small portion of the male population but often received a tremendous amount of publicity; they have varied greatly in duration. One of the earliest fads of the twentieth century and one that came close to becoming an outright fashion was peg-top pants. This exaggerated trouser style had pleats at the waist and much fullness about the hips and thighs, tapering to exceedingly narrow bottoms. The suit jacket was longer than normal, and to accommodate the peg-top pants it had a definite flare at the bottom. By 1911, however, even semipeg trousers were losing favor as men began to move toward trimmer suits with narrower cuffed trousers creased front and back.

Jazz clothing. Although the natural-shoulder suit dominated the fashion scene during and after World War I, the fad of so-called jazz clothing began in 1919, unquestionably as an expression of the new passion for jazz music that was to earn the next decade the name "Jazz Age." Here the natural-shoulder line was nipped away for a tight, pinched look. The jacket, with three closely spaced buttons, was extremely tight-waisted, and the center vent of its long skirt measured 12 inches. The trousers were either stove-pipe-skinny with bell bottoms or peg-top with trim lines down the legs. In its own way, the exaggerated jazz suit was as much a freak suit as the outsize suit of the previous decade; yet it was carried over into the twenties mainly through its acceptance by sharp dressers in the theatrical profession, who even copied this extreme silhouette for their tuxedo suits. Always anxious to be noticed and eager to take up the latest fad, the vaudevillians who congregated outside the Palace Theater in New York, which was considered the home of two-a-day vaudeville, were especially partial to the latest jazz innovation: a seam running around the jacket from front to back, a postwar influence of the military. The jazz-clothing fad petered out in 1923, when there appeared cheaper and poorly made versions resembling caricatures of a caricature, but not before a jazz overcoat had been created to complement the jazz suit.

Oxford bags. The next trouser fad had a more distinguished origin, starting with Ivy League students vacationing abroad, who, like their fashion-conscious fathers, were susceptible to British fashion influence. In 1924 they noticed the widely cut trousers called Oxford bags, then worn by undergraduates at Oxford, and picked up the style for themselves. The bags were the Oxford students' solution to a problem: knickers had been banned from the classrooms. Bags, since they measured about 25 inches around the knees and 22 inches around the bottoms, could act as camouflage, slipping easily over the forbidden knickers. The Ivy Leaguers brought bags back with them, and soon New Haven tailors were making natural-shoulder suits with trousers measuring from $18\frac{1}{2}$ to 22 inches around the bottoms and billowing over the wearer's Scotch-grain shoes.

In the spring of 1925 John Wanamaker in New York introduced Oxford bags to the general public with a full-page newspaper advertisement (quoted in *Men's Wear*, Sept. 23, 1925). At $20 a pair, the bags were available in a selection of solid-color flannels: biscuit, silver gray, fawn, lovat, blue gray, and pearl gray. In featuring their Oxford bags, which

The jazz suits of the post-World War I era had narrow shoulders, shaped body lines with or without waist seams, and tapered trousers.
[HART, SCHAFFNER & MARX]

had been made within a stone's throw of Oxford University, Wanamaker's dressed up several salesmen in them and directed them to stroll about the Redleaf-London Shop, a department that specialized in British clothing and furnishing ideas. Since British fashion influence was at its peak and Ivy Leaguers were the fashion leaders among American youth, the Oxford bags scored a great success and affected the suit silhouette of many young men. By the autumn of 1925 the fashion press reported that the bags had caught on among city dwellers as well as collegians, and a story

Oxford bags, very wide pants measuring 25 inches at the knees and 22 inches around the bottoms, were a fad with young men in the mid-twenties. [COURTESY JAYMAR-RUBY, INC.]

headlined "Oxford Bags Arrive on Coast" went on to report that while "women may giggle hysterically ... men stop in their tracks to swear harsh and lusty western oaths, the Oxford Bags have arrived—and are doing very nicely indeed, thank you—in San Francisco and on the University of California campus.

"It was more than half expected, by even the most dubious members of the trade, that the college extremists would pounce with joyful cries upon the bags. And why not? Their 25-inch width is scarcely more radical than the 22-inch flannel and corduroy slacks so widely worn at present. Thirty-five inches is a different matter but only one of degree; although the writer cannot vouch for the statement personally, it has been reported that even the latter measurement has been recorded by Berkeley observers. This to the distress of city stores, who fear such extremes will kill the style around town" (*Men's Wear*, Sept. 23, 1925).

In a decade dominated by "flaming youth," the bags proved to be very durable. The cartoonist John Held, Jr., sketched them on his ukelele-strumming sheikhs, and the popular cartoon character Harold Teen wore them as he vaulted into the front seat of his tin lizzie. Eventually, as with all fads, the enthusiasm died down, but while they were in vogue, the bags, a fad that had started at the top of the social ladder, enjoyed a much wider and longer acceptance than, say, jazz clothing, which had begun on a lower rung.

Zoot suit. Fads sometimes have a way of playing return engagements. The zoot suit of the early 1940s had a silhouette not unlike that of the roomy suit with peg-top trousers worn by the dandy of the early 1900s. The zoot had a very long jacket, flared at the bottom, and exaggeratedly padded shoulders; and trousers with pleats at the waistline, cut very wide over the hips and tapering down to such narrow bottoms that men with big feet had trouble slipping the trousers on. The pattern of the zoot suit was invariably of an eye-popping stripe in a zigzag arrangement. Accessories were equally flamboyant. Extra long key chains were fastened to the belt loop of the trousers and draped into the trouser pocket. Cuff links were enormous, shoes extremely pointed, and hat brims very wide.

Good fashion standards were upheld when the War Production Board (WPB) banished the zoot suit as a glaring example of wasteful manufacture. Nor was it a complete surprise when teen-agers throughout the country registered their outrage, for the zoot suit, in the opinion of some psychologists, was more than a fad. It was a sign of the rebellion of the young men of a less fortunate class against the everyday environment. The first zoot suit of record had been ordered in February, 1939, from a store in Gainesville, Georgia, whose owner was so startled by the purchase that he had the suit photographed. The purchaser, a busboy, paid $33.50 for a suit that two years later would be referred to as the badge of the hoodlums. Credit or blame for inspiring the zoot suit

Such exaggerated features as an overly long jacket, peg-top pants, and a long key chain characterized the zoot suit of 1940.

generally goes to the cartoonist Al Capp, whose Lil' Abner traded in his too-small, too-tight suit for one cut full and roomy because to him the excess cloth was a sign of affluence.

The psychological implications of the doomed zoot suit were explored in the wake of the WPB ban. It was thought that the boys who adopted the zoot suit wanted, first of all, to express themselves. The zoot suit was a perfect medium for self-expression, since it was undeniably different. It was considered unfortunate that the suit became a sign of disorder in the eyes of some, inasmuch as it showed the concern of the young men for clothes and fashion and also indicated the possibility of developing native and sectional fashions in the United States.

Although the zoot suit had an abrupt and farcical demise, it entered fashion history as the first concentrated attempt by less affluent young people to create a fashion of their own, and one that was in every respect at odds with the current mode of dress.

Teddy boys and the Edwardian look. As the zoot suit died in the United States, the "Teddy boys" in London came to the fore with a fashion of their own: an exaggerated version of the elegant Edwardian look. Lower-class boys who had obviously been impressed by their American counterparts' ability to launch the zoot suit, the Teddy boys bastardized the Edwardian silhouette and thus made it their own. Their version had a fairly long-waisted jacket with a moderate flare and deep side vents and close-fitting stovepipe trousers. This fad was confined to the Teddy boys and other youths in their socioeconomic bracket, and although it did spread to other parts of the world, it

The English Teddy boys' outfit included a jacket of generous length with sloping shoulders, a narrow chest, slanting pockets, and sleeve cuffs, narrow stovepipe trousers, and thick-soled shoes. The young man shown here was elected the Brummell of the Teddy boys in 1955. [NEW YORK PUBLIC LIBRARY PICTURE COLLECTION]

had only a limited and brief influence.

In the late sixties more traditionally inspired Edwardian suits and jackets enjoyed a fresh run of popularity in the United States among men who had recently been liberated by the Peacock Revolution. Distinguished by long multibuttoned double-breasted jackets with waist suppression and deep center vents, this Edwardian styling, in opulent fabrics such as brocade and velvet, had a theatrical flair that appealed especially to many younger men. Naturally, a brocade or velvet Edwardian jacket with a great-coat collar required something more romantic than a conventional shirt and tie, and shirts with lace jabots and lacy cuffs spilling over the wrists became a vogue.

Edwardian suits for spring and summer daytime wear featured six or eight highly placed and closely spaced buttons, angled flap pockets, and tapered trousers. With or without a greatcoat collar, the Edwardian daytime suit in a cotton twill or in one of the man-made fiber blends was too avant-garde for a man with a less than perfect figure. Consequently, the Edwardian look had a short but colorful career.

Mod fashions. The brief notoriety of the Teddy boys and their flamboyant clothes paved the way for the mod fashions fad launched by British teen-agers in the late fifties. Mod fashions were born in 1957 on Carnaby Street, an alley-narrow side street 125 yards long in a corner of unfashionable Soho. John Stephen, who is generally recognized as the founding father of mod fashions, described the birth of this fad in *Gentlemen's Quarterly* (February, 1966) as "a crusade to brighten men's clothes. When one is young and one feels everything is gray and drab, you *know* they want something new and exciting. It wasn't a matter of being in the right place at the right time. I made it happen. When I started I had to fight to sell our clothes. People laughed at pink and red slacks. Frilly shirts. They said they were clothes for women and were effeminate. Word of mouth really

The Edwardian fashion of the fifties and sixties was characterized by a long jacket and trim trousers. This outfit of velvet (including the waistcoat) was worn with a stock (1969). [NEW YORK PUBLIC LIBRARY PICTURE COLLECTION]

made us. Some boy would buy a colorful shirt or tie and some friends would see it and ask, 'Where'd you get it?'"

The youngsters who wore the colorful Carnaby Street clothes were, in the main, members of a motor scooter group called the Mods. And the Mods were "mod," short for "modern." Beginning with shirts and ties, Stephen proceeded to design and manufacture entire wardrobes for his mod clientele, and a Carnaby Street look evolved: low-rise tapered trousers; fitted jackets, four-buttoned and vented to the waist; and Chelsea boots. British youth of all classes began dressing mod, John Stephen became a millionaire, and Carnaby Street became a tourist attraction. For the first time fashion was truly starting at the bottom of the social ladder and working upward

One of the most noticeable fads of the sixties was mod, which emanated from Carnaby Street in London and moved rapidly to many other centers. Here the singing group called The Lovin Spoonful wear various interpretations of the mod look: (left to right) a six-button double-breasted jacket with a high closure; a waist-length cowhide jacket, a floral print shirt, and checked flared pants; a chalk-striped wool blazer, blue pants, and white boots; a high-front dinner jacket worn with a ruffled shirt with a high collar. From Esquire, June 1966.

rather than the reverse. All the more extraordinary was the fact that this was happening in class-structured Britain.

American tourists visiting London brought mod clothes home with them, and by 1965 Carnaby Street had come to Main Street. By the end of 1966, however, an avalanche of unattractive merchandise advertised as "Carnaby Street–inspired" had appeared in retail stores and failed to move, and soon retailers across the country became disenchanted with mod fashions. By 1967 the mod craze had dissipated, but not before its break with tradition had sparked the Peacock Revolution that was to liberate the wardrobes of American men of all ages.

Nehru suit and jacket. The Nehru fad caught on late in 1966 and died out less than two years later. One fashion reporter, looking back on the fashions of the dynamic sixties, concluded that it was a time when clothes for both sexes often became costumes and costumes became acceptable as clothes. And perhaps that best explains the meteoric rise of Nehru styling in men's suits and jackets. The Nehru suit, worn for many years by men in India and glamorized for American and European taste by the handsome appearance of Prime Minister Jawaharlal Nehru, first appeared on the international scene when salesmen in Adam, the Paris shop of the designer Pierre Cardin, took to wear-

ing gray flannel Nehrus soon after a trip Cardin made to India. The jacket, an exact copy of the Indian original, was close-fitting with a shaped back, a buttoned front, and a $1\frac{1}{2}$-inch standing collar. The trousers were slim and tapered. Soon afterward, the Nehru suit or simply the jacket was being seen in London and then in New York and other American cities. Versatile, it lent itself to a variety of fabrics. It was styled for business in flannel and twill woven worsted in gray, dark blue, brown, and tan. For summer, the jacket looked handsome in such lightweight fabrics as cotton, linen, and man-made blends, most often in tan and white. For evening wear, a Nehru jacket of a sumptuous acetate brocade or velvet was worn with dark formal trousers. There were also Nehru evening suits of colorfully brocaded silk.

A photograph of Lord Snowdon wearing a black Nehru dinner jacket with a white satin turtleneck sweater appeared in almost every major newspaper in the United States, and many leading magazines published fashion spreads on the Nehru as worn by men in all walks of life. Johnny Carson appeared on television in a businessman's Nehru jacket with a turtleneck sweater, and within twenty-four hours retailers throughout the country reported a phenomenal increase in Nehru suit and jacket sales. Soon Nehru styling was adapted for knitted

The Nehru jacket with its standing collar fitting closely at the neck, four buttons, and square front flashed on the scene in 1966 and disappeared less than two years later.

zipper-front sweaters and sports shirts, and by 1968 some fur coats designed for men featured the Nehru collar. The Nehru inspired a new kind of men's jewelry, linked chains carrying large metallic pendants worn about the neck; and some younger men took to wearing beaded necklaces with their Nehru jackets.

As suddenly as the Nehru had come into prominence, it began to pall, and the man in the gray flannel Nehru suit began to wonder how he could convert the jacket to another style. But the distinctive look that had first attracted him to it made conversion impossible, and the Nehru in his closet became a fashion antique.

Beads. A legacy left by the Nehru was a fad for beads. Although it was relatively short-lived and was never really accepted by a large number of men, it opened the door to at least a new concept of jewelry for men. This, in turn, led to the bracelets, necklaces, and more avant-garde masculine jewelry that became so popular in the seventies.

Turtleneck pullover. Closely linked with the Nehru fad was the turtleneck pullover, which, however, created a fad of its own independent of its status as a favored accessory for wear with the Nehru dinner jacket and the Nehru business suit. During the late sixties there was a sales boom of knitted sweaters with turtlenecks, and in many cities the turtleneck sweater alternated with the shirt and tie and, among very young men, often displaced the shirt and tie. As an accessory for formal evening clothes, the turtleneck clearly violated all traditional canons of dress. Despite sensational publicity, it had a career of short duration and in this context qualified as a fad and nothing more. But for casual wear and spectator sportswear with jeans, slacks, and unstructured suits, the turtleneck proved so durable that by the early seventies it occupied a unique position halfway between fad and fashion. Whether it declines to the status of a fad or remains in vogue long enough to qualify as a fashion remains to be seen.

The combination of a white turtleneck pullover with a dinner jacket, first worn by Lord Snowdon, was a revolutionary idea that drew international attention. The knitted pullover shown here with a black seersucker dinner jacket had French cuffs. From Esquire, *December 1967.*

Costumey look. With the youth take-over of the sixties continuing into the seventies, the fad of costumey clothing was born, and from it evolved an antiestablishment look that was widespread among members of both sexes under twenty-five. A salient feature of the costumey look was its pretentious unpretentiousness. It was a classless look that sometimes almost bridged the gap between a laboring man's weekend and work wardrobes. It got its start with streaky-looking bleached denim slacks, which were soon combined with work clothes and military gear bought at Army and Navy stores. As this fad caught fire, "new wave" boutiques offered so-

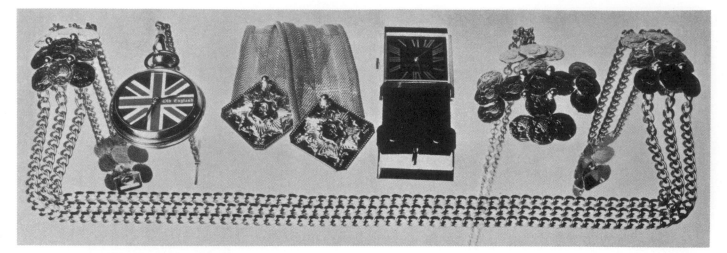

Oddities in jewelry created a fresh fad in 1968: (around the sides and bottom) a triple-chain belt with a buckle of Roman coins; (left to right) a watch with the Union Jack on the face and a fob chain, a metal mesh crossover tie that could be worn either as a tie or pinned at the watch pocket as a fob, an oversize wristwatch with gold numerals and a black suede slip-through band, and a Maltese cross made up of Roman coins with a chain. From Esquire, *June 1968.*

called funky versions of these basic clothes by means of embroidery, fringed edges, plush textures, and the like. As a result, this faddish look was divided into two distinct types, the outright secondhand-store look and the boutique look.

Other youth fads. Spinning off from the boutiques and their trendy customers came a number of new fads during the early seventies. Still anti-establishment, they were much less militantly so; in fact, their youthful designs often had a kind of little-boy personality. Prominent were knickers, now revived in many different styles,

overalls (still reflecting youth's continued preoccupation with work clothes, clothes that *function*), and hot pants (short shorts), all often worn with skinny knitted pullover athletic shirts. And although the term "unisex" was no longer in fashionable use, many of these faddish clothes were being worn by teen-agers of both sexes.

Ever since the Peacock Revolution liberated men's clothes and, in doing so, destroyed the traditional start-at-the-top concept of fashion, the often-thin line separating fad from foible has seemed to blur. Frequently it is the wearer's attitude that determines

whether what he wears is a fad or a foible. A smart over-thirty Britisher who often wears costumey outfits not only has appeared regularly on the international best-dressed list but in 1971 was voted "forever elegant" by its compilers.

So in this age of dedicated self-expression today's foibles may become tomorrow's fad and, if blessed with the proper amount of charisma, take hold and become a genuine fashion. The only safe prediction that one can make about men's clothes in the last quarter of the twentieth century is their unpredictability.

Designers

Walter Albini

Walter Albini was born on May 9, 1941, in Busto Arsizio, Varese Province, Italy, and attended the Liceo Classico in Milan, later completing his studies at the Istituto di Belle Arti in Turin. He worked as an apprentice in Paris for three years before returning to Milan, where in 1965 he established his own design studio. Among the manufacturers for whom Albini has designed are Montedoro, Krizia, Billy Ballo, Glans, Paola Signorini, Cadette, and Mr. Fox. His plans encompass the design and production of ready-to-wear clothing for men, women, and children, to be marketed throughout the world under his own Walter Albini label. In addition, he is branching out into theatrical design and is producing the costumes for the new version of the film *The Blue Angel*.

Albini admits to having been greatly attracted to the thirties throughout his career and says that his ready-to-wear designs have always been inspired by the elegance of that decade. He is also a collector of houses and owns three: one in Milan, one in Venice, and one in Sidi-bou-Saïd, Tunisia. Albini is inspired by the sea and, like many of his compatriots, is devoted to dogs. He is a voracious reader in his leisure time. ∎

Hardy Amies

Hardy Amies was born in London on July 17, 1909. After completing his education at Brentwood, he was sent abroad to learn French and German. When he returned to England, he joined the weighing-machine firm of W. & T. Avery. This career was interrupted in 1934 by an offer to design for the leading women's tailoring house of Lachasse. Amies's first big success came through the promotions resulting from the coronation of King George VI in 1937, when American buyers flocked to England.

At the outbreak of World War II in 1939, Amies joined the Army as a private, subsequently obtaining a commission in the Intelligence Corps. He eventually earned the rank of lieutenant colonel and headed the Special Forces mission to Belgium, for which he was made an Officier de l'Ordre de la Couronne in 1946.

Even during the war Amies was able to continue designing and was twice given special leave to design export collections for the house of Worth (London) Ltd. After the war, in 1946, he opened his own establishment at 14 Savile Row, London. The firm soon became recognized as a couture house of international standing. Amies's early training at Lachasse plus his natural inclinations produced impeccably tailored clothing that was im-

W. ALBINI

H. AMIES

ation that became H. A. Ready-to-Wear.

Since 1957 he has been vice president of the Clothing Institute, and since 1964 he has served as senior lecturer at the Royal College of Art. He is also a design consultant to various British and overseas manufacturers. He was named chairman of the Incorporated Society of London Fashion Designers in 1959–1960 and was elected to the Faculty of Royal Designers for Industry. Amies received Caswell-Massey Awards in 1962, 1964, and 1968. He published his autobiography, *Just So Far*, in 1954 and *ABC of Men's Fashions* in 1964. ■

Remo Argenti

Remo Argenti was born in Rome on June 16, 1936, the scion of three generations of master hatmakers: Argenti hats have been produced in Rome since 1850. After completing his regular studies, he devoted himself to the arts—painting, ceramics, and architecture; he still frequents studios and galleries where the works of the best contemporary artists are to be found.

At twenty-seven Argenti opened a boutique for men on the Via del Corso in Rome and began designing avant-garde hats for high-fashion designer collections like those of Valentino, Palazzi, Datti, and Antonelli, as well as collaborating with the Accademia dei Sarti d'Italia. His hats are now shown in the most important collections in Italy and are exported all over the world. In 1967 he was admitted to the Camera Nazionale della Moda Italiana, and in 1970 he opened a second boutique in Spoleto. Among the official recognitions he has received are the Diploma della Accademia dei Sarti d'Italia in 1968, the Premio Moda Mare Cefalù in 1969, and the Premio Centenario Roma in 1970.

Argenti believes that fashion, as an

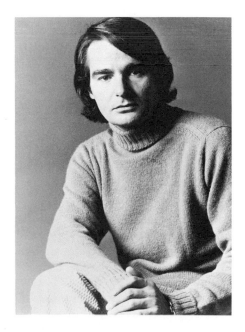

mediately successful, especially with Americans. He dressed the most influential women in society including Queen Elizabeth, who granted him the royal warrant in 1955. Meanwhile, in 1950, he opened a boutique to sell ready-to-wear clothing, which was expanded to include a wholesale oper-

art, is the expression of contemporary man and that the function of a fashion creator is to bear witness and to express, with his own sensibilities and intelligence, the needs of the society in which he lives. He is convinced that fashion for men in the seventies will see the triumph of accessories: hats, shirts, shoes, belts, and the like. Basic clothing will continue to have a narrow silhouette, strongly characteristic in fabric and style, Argenti thinks, but accessories, made of new and unusual materials, will provide the fun and the capriciousness that make fashion. ■

Pierre Balmain

Pierre Balmain was born on May 18, 1914, in Saint-Jean-de-Maurienne, in Savoy, France. After graduating from the Lycée National of Chambéry, he went to Paris in 1933 to prepare for the entrance examinations of the architecture section of the École des Beaux-Arts. These preparations were interrupted in 1934, when he joined the house of Molyneux as a designer. Balmain remained with Molyneux for five years, continuing his work even during his military service in the French Air Force. Then, in 1939, he accepted a position of greater responsibility with the house of Lucien Lelong. Recalled to active duty in

Savoy after the outbreak of World War II, he met Gertrude Stein.

When Lelong reopened his establishment in 1941, Balmain was persuaded to return to Paris, where for four years he shared with Christian Dior the responsibility for the Lelong collections. In 1945 he decided to open his own *maison de couture*. The first collection, shown on October 12 of that year, brought Balmain prompt recognition from the Paris fashion world. The next year he made a lecture tour of the United States under the sponsorship of Gertrude Stein. This was the first of many trips that have taken him all over the world. Meanwhile, he formed new departments and subsidiary companies for perfume, ready-to-wear clothes, scarves and ties, knitwear, stockings, eyeglasses, handbags and luggage, and cuff links. He also began to make ready-to-wear clothes for men. According to Balmain, a man of fashion is one whose clothes are so nearly perfect that he can serve as an example without description.

Balmain's clothes are worn by many celebrated actresses as well as by the Queen of Thailand and members of other royal families. He has been honored by Denmark and Italy and holds the cross of the French Legion of Honor. ■

P. BALMAIN

Geoffrey Beene

Geoffrey Beene was born in Haynesville, Louisiana, on August 30, 1927, and spent three years at Tulane University in premedical studies before turning to fashion. He also attended the Traphagen School of Art in New York before enrolling at the University of Southern California in Los Angeles, where he worked nights in the display department of I. Magnin. Some of Magnin's executives saw Beene's sketches and recommended that he study in Paris.

He did so, attending the École de la Chambre de la Syndicale and simultaneously learning tailoring as an apprentice with the house of Molyneux. After returning to the United States, he worked for the couture organization of Mildred O'Quinn and on Seventh Avenue in New York with Samuel Winston, Harmay, Sylvan Rich of Martini, and Teal Traina, where he gained experience in design and contributed substantially to the success of the collections produced by these manufacturers.

In 1962 Beene opened his own Seventh Avenue operation for the design of women's clothes, which was subsequently expanded to include furs, bathing suits, jewelry, scarves, handbags, and, in 1968, men's ready-to-

wear clothing, which is manufactured by Eagle Clothes. The original line is now called Geoffrey Beene Deluxe, covering the more expensive clothing, and the Geoffrey Beene label is being used for a newly established and less expensive collection geared to the younger, less affluent man.

Beene has received two Coty Awards, two Cotton Council Awards, and the Neiman Marcus Award. It is his basic philosophy that men's clothes, like women's, should be simple, pure, and beautifully cut from fabrics with unusual textures, designs, and colors. His clothes are marked by an easy, casual elegance with a built-in drama suitable to today's life-style.

Beene is a devotee of the theater and film and collects contemporary art. He loves animals and flowers and is a dedicated gardener. ■

Stanley Blacker

Stanley Blacker was born on May 9, 1922; he attended George Washington High School in New York and was graduated from New York University with a degree in business and finance. While at NYU, he was one of the ranking intercollegiate tennis players in the eastern United States. After graduation he was associated with his father for fifteen years in the clothing firm Blacker Bros. Then, in 1954, he formed Stanley Blacker, Inc., to design and produce tailored sports coats, slacks, and other tailored clothing as well as general sportswear and men's apparel of leather and suede. In 1956

S. BLACKER

the company employed 50 people; by 1972 it employed 1,100.

Blacker has been credited with revitalizing the sports coat industry, which had been in the doldrums for many years, and he could be called a pioneer in the development of separates. He believes that five distinct collections per year can best serve the retailer and the consumer, and his ambition is to develop color-coordinated sportswear, sports jackets, slacks, sweaters, and vests. His company designs its own fabrics in special colors and patterns, and Blacker is considered a brilliant fabric stylist. He has won Caswell-Massey Awards for his sports jackets and slacks.

Married to an interior decorator and the father of three children, Blacker continues to count tennis as his principal off-duty interest. ■

Bill Blass

Bill Blass was born in Fort Wayne, Indiana, on June 22, 1922. After graduating from Fort Wayne High School, he enrolled at the Parsons School of Design in New York. He then became a sketch artist for the sportswear firm of David Crystal but resigned to enlist in the United States Army during World War II. Discharged as a ser-

geant, he became a designer for Anna Miller & Co., which in 1958 was merged with Maurice Rentner Ltd. He designed his first collection for Rentner in 1959, becoming a vice president of the firm two years later and a full partner in 1962. He is now sole owner of the company, known today as Bill Blass Ltd.

Blass's first menswear collection was designed for the Philadelphia-based manufacturer Pincus Brothers–Maxwell. Subsequent collections earned him a special Coty Award in 1968. His custom collections for women received the Coty American Fashion Critics' Award in 1961, 1963, and 1970, the third award elevating him to the Fashion Hall of Fame; in 1971 he received a special Coty citation for overall excellence in many fields of fashion.

In addition to Bill Blass Couture (for women) and Blass for P.B.M. (men's fashions), he has designed rainwear for Bond Street, men's shirts and sweaters for Fred Gates, neckties for Seidler-Fuerman, furs for Revillon, luggage for United Luggage, and sheets and towels for Springmaid. He

has created for Revlon a line of men's grooming products that bears his name. In 1970 he introduced a four-season collection of ready-to-wear sports clothes for women called Blass-port.

The crisp elegance of Blass's designs is inspired primarily by superb fabrics and guided by his flair for color, line, and style. The resulting fashions bear the Blass trademark of utter simplicity. For relaxation, Blass swims, paints, and collects antiques. ■

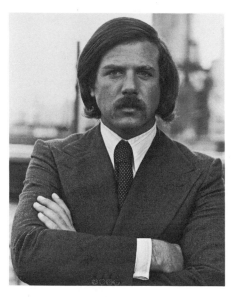

Franklin Bober

Franklin Bober was born on March 25, 1945, in New York, where he attended George Washington High School and Hunter College. One of the youngest clothing designers, he thinks that the young men who follow fashion should have a designer with whom they can identify, one who is nearly their own age or at least of their generation. Bober established himself as a designer with the firm of Clinton Swan Clothes from 1966 until 1970, when he founded his own firm, Berhen & Company, in New York. The business of the new firm doubled, increasing from $1 million to $2 million, in its first two years. Bober has been represented in design collections for the Raeford Company, a division of

Burlington Industries, and his designs have also achieved wide exposure to television audiences on the "Mike Douglas Show," "Joan Rivers Show," and "Tonight Show." He won the Creative Menswear Award and placed first in the 1970 Foam Fashion Forum Awards.

Bober believes that clothing is an extension of a man's way of life, and he tries to design apparel that is both exciting to wear and individually styled. Today's young men are looking for new things to wear, and Bober feels that it is his obligation as a designer to set trends that will coincide with the fast pace of the modern world. Too many designers, he says, create simply to be different, without regard to the taste level. The subtle exposure to ideas, on the other hand, is what causes invalid "trends" that appear on the scene to vanish as quickly as they appeared, and Bober tries to give his designs a lasting quality. Married to the actress Julie Allen and the father of three daughters, he enjoys horseback riding and is a tennis player. ■

Margit and Erik Brandt

Margit and Erik Brandt, who form a husband-and-wife design team, were both born in Copenhagen, he in 1943 and she two years later. They were married in 1966. Margit Brandt was trained in the Margretheskolen, Copenhagen, a textile and fashion school where she studied for three years before earning her diploma, afterward becoming apprenticed to one

M./E. BRANDT

of the oldest tailoring firms in the city. She subsequently went to Paris and became a model, first with Pierre Balmain and later with Louis Féraud; she also studied in both designers' ateliers, learning to cut and sew. After a year in Paris, she returned to Copenhagen, where she began to design rainwear and coats. Erik Brandt, whose father owned a coat and suit factory, attended a commercial school in Copenhagen; at the age of eighteen he was sent to Amsterdam to learn production, spent a second year studying fabric buying, and a third in Paris, where he was apprenticed in the ready-to-wear divisions of Patou and Castillo.

When Erik Brandt returned to Copenhagen, he and Margit opened their own business, which now utilizes six factories in Denmark as well as others in Great Britain, the United States, Yugoslavia, Hong Kong, and Sweden. Their yearly turnover is $15 million, and they are consolidating their offices, showrooms, and shops in a new building in Copenhagen. They have no present intention of expanding their ready-to-wear lines, which encompass menswear (including suits, coats, and furs), children's wear, women's dresses, coats, and suits, leather and suede clothing, rainwear, shoes, and underwear, since they feel that they might lose the tight control they now have over their operation. However, they do plan to expand in other areas of design such as silver, kitchenware, and perfume.

The primary emphasis in their lines is on sportswear or on a sporty look, whatever the garment. In their men's designs they prefer a classic look in good taste, using fine tweeds, gray flannel, and other traditional fabrics. The Brandts enjoy tennis, horseback riding, and skiing. They are avid ballet fans and also collect antiques. ■

Gaetano Savini Brioni

Gaetano Savini Brioni was born on September 10, 1909, in Terni, in southern Umbria, Italy, and was educated locally. His early love for Pirandello led him to the theater, where he began his career as a scene and costume designer, gaining experience both in Rome's tailoring shops and in its theatrical ateliers between 1930 and 1940. During that time he also acquired the expertise to collaborate with the textile industry as a consultant, knowledge that was to prove useful when he opened his own establishment with two partners in 1944. At that time, as World War II was drawing to a close, high-quality clothing and accessories were extremely difficult

to find, but within the next six years the rehabilitated fabric mills and manufacturers began to work closely with Brioni, and Italy's postwar fashion reputation became worldwide.

In 1950 Marchese G. B. Giorgini decided to present a collection from the best Italian women's tailoring shops in Florence to buyers returning from the Paris couture collections. Brioni persuaded him to include twenty-five to thirty men's fashions. Brioni's practical lightweight silk shantung evening suit was the hit of the Florence show, which provided much of the impetus for the men's fashion revolution that slowly began to take shape. The list of awards Brioni subsequently received is almost endless. It includes six Caswell-Massey Awards and special awards from *Esquire* and *Gentlemen's Quarterly,* the city of Winnipeg, Mexico City for his participation in the 1969 International Fashion Week, and São Paolo for his contribution to men's fashion in Brazil. In addition, he was awarded almost every silver and gold medal presented by Italy in recognition of the leadership he had given Italian fashions for men.

Brioni's philosophy of fashion is grounded in a continuous evolutionary esthetic involving not only clothing but parallel trends in art, archi-

tecture, decoration, music, drawing, and design. Married, he has a married daughter and three grandchildren. ∎

cessory boutiques, Adam for men and Eve for women.

As the first couturier for women to enter the menswear field, Cardin introduced his revolutionary cylindrical silhouette in 1962; it was accepted enthusiastically throughout the world. The rapid growth of his designs for men dictated the transfer of his menswear operation to its own building in 1966. Since then boutiques selling Cardin merchandise exclusively have been opened in Athens, Beirut, Brussels, Caracas, Geneva, Hong Kong, Manila, Montreal, Barcelona, and Tokyo, and there are more than 200 other outlets for Cardin's men's fashions.

Cardin's creativity is not limited to couture and ready-to-wear apparel. Some 225 products, ranging from linens to furniture and flatware, from the packaging of chocolates to the interior design of American Motors' Javelin cars, bear the distinctive Cardin look. Of his designing, Cardin says, "Every day brings satisfaction to me. I am happy with what I create. Though no one should be smug about

his art, I do find great joy in projecting into the future. I find that what I design today will be worn on the street five years from now. There is joy in development, whether it is developing the suit for the man or the linens for the bed."

Cardin's many interests include L'Espace Pierre Cardin, a cultural center in Paris housing two theaters, a gallery, a restaurant, and conference rooms. ∎

Pierre Cardin

Pierre Cardin was born in Venice, Italy, of French parents and was educated in central France. Originally he was attracted to architecture, but when he moved to Paris in 1945, he became friendly with Jean Cocteau and Christian Bérard, through whose influence he began to design costumes. Turning to high fashion, he worked in the ateliers of Paquin and Schiaparelli and then joined the house of Dior, where he headed the coat and suit division when Dior's "new look" was introduced. In 1950 he opened his own couture house; by 1953 he was so firmly entrenched as a leader of fashion that he was able to establish himself in the Faubourg Saint-Honoré, simultaneously inaugurating two ac-

P. CARDIN

Allen Case

Allen Case was born in Dallas, Texas, and grew up in the fashion business— in the tailoring shop and on the selling floor of his father's menswear store. His early ambition was to be a doctor, but while he was taking a premedical course at Southern Methodist University, his singing voice earned him appearances with the Dallas Civic Theater, changing his goals completely. He appeared on Arthur Godfrey's morning radio show and soon was a Broadway star, singing in such musicals as *Damn Yankees, Once upon a Mattress,* and *Hallelujah Baby.* His role in *Damn Yankees* led to a contract with Universal Studios, where he costarred with Henry Fonda in the series "The Deputy" and as Frank James in *The Legend of Jesse James.*

A. CASE

During his theatrical career Case designed his own clothes, and as the menswear market emerged and changed, he thought the time was ripe to express his own ideas. He entered the fashion industry with a line of designer fur coats for men in 1968, meeting with extraordinary acceptance from the press and retailers alike. Today's manufacturer, according to Case, cannot be everything to everybody. Neither can a designer be true to himself if he tries to appeal to every group in society. In an age of specialization Case concentrates on the forgotten "middle American." Caught up in the fast-moving menswear revolution, this man is thoroughly confused and should be provided with specific ideas that relate logically to his business, social, family, sports, and leisure activities. ∎

Emmett Cash

Emmett Cash was born on April 25, 1942, in Oakland, California, and educated at Pasadena City College and Howard University, where he majored in drama with a music minor. He entered the menswear industry with the backing of Du Pont and Bancroft Marketing, for which he created a suit collection of Dacron double-knit fabrics and a complementary line of knit dress shirts in Ban-Lon. Cash now owns his own fashion house,

E. CASH

with offices in Los Angeles, California, and Como, Italy. His menswear line includes toiletries, fun furs, outerwear, casual slacks, formal wear, neckwear, and scarves.

The smooth, flowing lines of Cash's designs are the hallmark of the personal and professional wardrobes of many celebrities, including Johnny Mathis, Tom Jones, Barbra Streisand, and Raquel Welch. He also designed a 7-foot silk body scarf for Leslie Caron to wear in a motion picture. "I create for the man who wants to appear casually elegant, and when I design an ensemble, the look I strive for is a seemingly effortless, natural style," Cash

says, adding: "During the 70s, one of the most necessary objectives in fashion will be to massproduce a garment without abusing the individuality of the wearer. Individuality will be the signature of the successful man during the 70s." ∎

Oleg Cassini

Oleg Cassini was born in Paris, France, on April 11, 1918. His parents, Count and Countess Loiewski-Cassini, had planned a diplomatic career for their first-born son, but the Revolution of 1917 sent the family into exile. Cassini's father had been attached to the Imperial Russian Embassy in Denmark. After settling in Paris, the family moved to Florence, Italy, where Cassini and his younger brother Igor grew up and he attended the Accademia di Belle Arti and graduated in law from the University of Florence.

His mother supplemented the family's small income by opening a couture salon in Rome, and Cassini launched his career in fashion by sketching for her salon. After a year as a sketch artist for Patou in Paris, he returned to Rome in 1935 and opened his own salon. Cassini then emigrated to the United States, where he worked as a cartoonist for the Washington *Times-Herald* in 1938. By

O. CASSINI

1939 he had started a new career as a designer for Paramount Studios in Hollywood. During World War II he served for four years in the United States Army. After the war he was head of wardrobe at Eagle-Lion Studios and special design consultant to Twentieth Century–Fox.

In 1950 he opened Oleg Cassini, Inc., on Seventh Avenue in New York. The firm became a dominant force in women's and men's fashion as well as a sought-after label for retail licensees. By 1972 it did an annual business of $15 million. Cassini has won a number of Caswell-Massey Awards, the Gold Coast Fashion Award, and the Golden Accolade of the International Fashion Festival in Las Vegas. His name was made famous throughout the country with his appointment as official couturier to Mrs. John F. Kennedy.

Cassini believes in total freedom from regimentation and characterizes his designs as having luxurious simplicity and barbaric splendor. Divorced from the actress Gene Tierney, he is the father of two children. ■

Ernesto Celli

Ernesto Celli was born in Milan, Italy, on February 26, 1931. After receiving his basic education in Milan, he earned a degree in accountancy and, in 1952, joined his father's firm, P. Celli & Figlio, the Milan manufacturer of knitwear. A period of training and specialization in business, organizational, and manufacturing techniques followed, and he served as an administrator in the company until 1962. At that time he began to design for Celli, specializing in men's fashions, and he has conceived and created all subsequent collections. He later expanded his interests to include the women's high-fashion field and

E. CELLI

opened a boutique in Milan that features the designs of the Paris couturier André Courrèges.

Celli believes that it is possible to be up to date in one's wardrobe even with classic styling, which he thinks has enduring chic and is always suitable for a fashionable man. Well-chosen colors, especially in jacquards, with a classic cut or accurate full-fashion styling, make classic knitwear smart enough to stand on its own despite transitory oddities in fashion. Celli looks at fashion as the means whereby a man can express himself and his feelings in a continuous reaction to the rapid changes in modern society. His collections are always newsworthy, and he has received a number of fashion awards for the high quality and styling of Celli products, which are bought by fine boutiques all over the world.

The father of a daughter, Celli is a sportsman who plays golf and tennis and skis. His hobbies include photography and the collection of stamps. ■

Michael Cifarelli

Michael Cifarelli was born on December 14, 1904, in Pomarico, Matera Province, Italy, where he attended local schools. After emigrating to the

M. CIFARELLI

United States, he worked as a custom tailor for such New York establishments as Stadler & Stadler and Brooks Brothers, where he received the training that was to be of inestimable help to him when he turned to designing ready-to-wear for Monroe Clothes, also in New York. He subsequently designed for Pincus Brothers–Maxwell in Philadelphia and for Norman Hilton Clothes; his long association with the latter firm established Cifarelli's reputation as a designer of fine natural-shoulder-styled clothing. He is now chief designer for Botany 500, one of the country's largest and most prestigious manufacturers.

Cifarelli has always advocated elegant and graceful lines for tailored clothing, along with comfort, which he feels is required by the American man. He thinks that the so-called Peacock Revolution is at an end and that fashion will return to fine clothes and elegance. Cifarelli is married and has a married daughter, Yolanda; he is an ardent golfer. ■

Gordon S. Cohen

Gordon S. Cohen was born in Philadelphia on January 10, 1922. Although born into the tradition of fine clothing for men (his father, Perce Cohen, was chief designer for Tip Top Tailors, Ltd., in Toronto), he chose to

major in textile chemistry and engineering at the Philadelphia College of Textiles and Science, from which he was graduated in 1942. After he served in the United States Army during World War II, his ambitions changed direction, and he apprenticed himself to Tip Top Tailors under his father's tutelage. On his father's retirement in 1956, he became chief designer for the tailoring establishment, a position he held for the following decade. In 1966 he joined the men's clothing manufacturer Michaels Stern & Co., Inc., of Rochester, New York, and later became vice president in charge of design for the firm.

The first staff designer for a major manufacturer to present his own designer collection in the United States, Cohen believes that fashion represents the interaction of three major factors: the creative expression of the designer, the scientific production techniques of the manufacturer, and the degree of acceptance by the consumer. He feels that clothes should be designed to be in harmony with people's needs, surroundings, activities, and personalities. The creative designer can make a style, but only the three factors can make fashion.

Cohen served as president of both the Toronto and the Rochester clothing designers' clubs and of the International Association of Clothing Designers, and he received the Design Award of the May Company of Los Angeles. He lives with his wife Dorothy and their two children in Rochester. ■

G. COHEN

Massimo Datti

Massimo Datti is the heir of a long tradition of cutting and tailoring, handed down from father to son. Each generation inherited from the previous one a natural inclination toward sartorial perfection, culminating in the

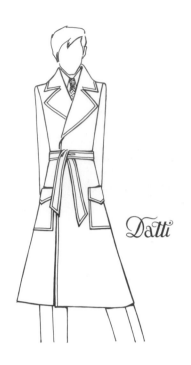

Datti

refinement of technique and taste exhibited by the current representative of the family.

The best pupil of his father, Arcole Datti, the younger Datti became one of the Big Four designers and stylists who brought Italian couture for men worldwide recognition after World War II. He rapidly established a solid reputation for the originality and functionalism of his designs, for which he won a number of prizes; his lines have been particularly well received in the United States.

Datti has participated in every official presentation of the Alta Moda Maschile of Italy since its inception. In a recent showing of the International Fashion Council he won first, second, and third prizes for the wearability, practicality, and style of his fashions as well as the harmony between fabric and cut exhibited by his designs. ∎

7th Baron De Freyne

Francis Arthur John French was born in Dublin on September 3, 1927. On the death of his father in 1935 he succeeded to the title of 7th Baron, the Lord De Freyne of Coolavin in County Sligo, Ireland. When he reached his majority, he took his seat

in the House of Lords and continued to manage the family estate, Frenchpark, in County Roscommon. In 1953 he turned Frenchpark House and, the rest of the estate over to the Irish government and entered the world of commerce as a director of companies in Ireland and other countries. He now lives in County Wicklow with his wife and three children.

In association with Comdr. Harold Y. D. Bonsole, he founded De Freyne Designs Ltd., to design and produce men's sportswear in 1968. It had been an area of great interest to him for many years, probably, he says, "a result of my personal revolt against the unimaginative clothing produced in my native Ireland," in spite of the

DE FREYNE

excellence and worldwide acceptance of Irish fabrics. "It seemed that everybody else was able to use these unique and interesting fabrics except ourselves," he comments. De Freyne resigned himself to designing clothing whose concept would never be accepted on the local market, but the problems attendant on creating an Irish look acceptable throughout the world were almost insurmountable. Later, however, there was a growing awareness of the possibilities of Ireland not only as a source of materials but as a place where intelligent styling was possible, and De Freyne became more actively engaged in the design of menswear, particularly sports jackets. His first efforts were directed toward the American market, and the resulting designs were a compromise that was neither Irish nor American. He therefore resolved to create his own Irish conception of fashion, remaining true to his ideal of what a gentleman should look like: a combination of style, comfort, and originality. ∎

Oscar de la Renta

Oscar de la Renta was born on July 22, 1932, in Santo Domingo, where he completed his early studies at the Escuela Normal in 1950, subsequently enrolling in the National School of Art. Soon afterward he went to Madrid, where he studied art and painted abstracts before becoming interested in fashion. Some of his designs caught the eye of Mrs. John Lodge, wife of the American Ambassador to Spain, who commissioned him to design a gown for her to wear at her daughter's debut. Both the dress and its wearer appeared on the cover of *Life* magazine; encouraged by this early recognition, De la Renta abandoned painting and apprenticed himself to the Madrid house of Balenciaga. In 1961 he joined Lanvin-Castillo in Paris as assistant to Antonio Castillo, specializing in tailoring. Two years later, De la Renta moved to New York to design semiannual custom and ready-to-wear collections for Elizabeth Arden. In 1965 he bought into the firm of Jane Derby, Inc., as a partner and designer. Not long afterward Miss Derby retired, and the company became De la Renta's, although his name did not appear on the label until several years later.

In 1966, recognizing that not every woman could or would pay couture prices but still wanted well-designed designer-label clothing, De la Renta established a boutique, or ready-to-wear, line. In 1969 his entire operation was acquired by Richton International. Under the Richton aegis a new division of De la Renta designs for men manufactured by the Philadelphia-based firm After Six was established.

In addition to several Coty Awards, De la Renta received the Neiman-Marcus Award and the Italian Tiberio d'Oro, and President Joaquín Balaguer of the Dominican Republic made him a knight of the Order of Juan Pablo Duarte. De la Renta is married to the former Françoise de Langlade, once editor in chief of the French edition of *Vogue*. ■

Xavier de la Torre y Haro

Xavier de la Torre y Haro was born on July 31, 1934, in Guadalajara,

Mexico. As a child he sketched, but despite his interest in art his parents decided that he should become a priest and enrolled him in a seminary at the age of fifteen. Within a few months, having violated seminary rules, he was returned to his parents; as punishment they sent him to Hollywood, California, to live with an uncle who enrolled him in a business school. He spent more time in sketching than in studying, however, and finally left this school to pursue a full-time career in design. De la Torre attended the Chouinard School of Design and the California School of Design. He then returned to Mexico, where he attended the Instituto de la Moda and La Esmeralda Instituto de Diseño.

Before opening his own boutique in Puerto Vallarta in 1962, De la Torre was associated with the interior designer Alex MacDonald and employed as a special designer for I. Miller Salons. His first year in business was difficult, but his beach and sports clothes for men and women began to sell, and by the third year he was showing a small profit. Today his fashions are in demand in Los Angeles, San Francisco, Denver, New York, and Miami Beach. Among the firms for which he has designed are Dudley Geiger/Propinquity, I. Miller Salons, Maya de México, Textiles Victoria,

X. DE LA TORRE Y HARO

Hollywood Needlecraft, and Little Country Girl of California. He received the Design Award in Popular Arts of the Los Angeles County Museum and awards from the Amsterdam fashion magazine *Sir* and the Mexico City *El y Ella*.

De la Torre's designs are created to enhance the personalities and physical endowments of individuals. Twice married and the father of two children, he enjoys riding and water-skiing and sculpts, engraves, and paints. ■

Giuliana di Camerino

Giuliana di Camerino was born in Venice, Italy, on December 8, 1920. She was educated in Italian schools and matriculated in classical studies. Racial persecution during the Mussolini regime forced the Camerinos to take refuge in Lugano, Switzerland; it was there, primarily as a hobby, that Giuliana di Camerino first began to design handbags. Because of their originality they proved successful, and the firm Roberta, named after her daughter, was established.

In 1945 she returned to Venice and reestablished Roberta with the help of one worker. By 1972 Roberta di Camerino employed more than 200 people and utilized the services of more than 3,000 master craftsmen who

P. DIMITRI

worked autonomously but were supervised and guided in every detail by Giuliana di Camerino. She has described the international status of her growing business as satisfactory and has bought at auction a small Venetian island called Polveriera delle Vignole, where she presents her collections to friends, buyers, and the press.

Among the items in the Roberta collections that have found favor throughout the world are her handbags (especially the bags for men, which are more accurately described as portable desks, carefully compartmented for business papers and supplies), suitcases, scarves, umbrellas, neckties, and sweaters; she specializes in individual and original prints that make Roberta products easily recognizable. Her designs have won many awards, including the Neiman-Marcus Award in 1956 and the Tiberio d'Oro in 1968. Her fashion philosophy is grounded in the esthetics of what she is doing; during the process of creation her mind is completely occupied by the image and the colors of the accessories she envisions.

A widow with two grown sons, Giuliana di Camerino is the proud grandmother of three little girls. She enjoys motorboating on the canals and waterways of Venice and is fond of dogs. ∎

Pietro Dimitri

Pietro Dimitri was born in Palermo, Sicily, on July 1, 1933. He disliked school, and when he was twelve, his father got him a job as a tailor's apprentice. His formal design training was received at the Sartotecnica school in Milan, after which he worked with some of Italy's most gifted designers. One of his masters at the Sartotecnica subsequently advised him to take his talent and tailoring skill to the United States, where he found a job with a dress house on Seventh Avenue in New York. After a year, in 1968, he left this firm to form his own establishment, Dimitri of Italy. Upon becoming an American citizen in 1971, he dropped "of Italy" from the firm name.

The identifying characteristic of Dimitri's designs is his classic interpretation of the look of the thirties, coupled with an awareness of and enthusiasm for forward-thinking fashion, both implemented by a superb sense of tailoring. The man for whom he designs is not necessarily either young or old but is definitely a man of today: an activist, a thinker, a doer. This ideal customer has a classic sense of style and flair and is not afraid of the Dimitri blend of revolutionary new fabrics and classic cut: he believes, as does Dimitri, that the truest fashion is

one that withstands the test of time.

The demand for Dimitri's clothes far exceeded the production possible in his custom workrooms, and in 1972 he decided to manufacture a line of ready-to-wear clothing. He also plans a licensing program for shirts, ties, jewelry, cosmetics, watches, leather goods, and related accessories. He is the first American designer to whom the Italian fashion magazine *Petronio* devoted an issue. A former soccer player, he would like to have time to play the game and to ride with his four children. ∎

Ernst Engel

Ernst Engel was born on June 4, 1910, in Vienna, Austria, where he studied at the Academy of Commerce. He became known as a versatile amateur athlete: a member of the all-star Austrian hockey team and an internationally famous skier as well as a keen competitor in soccer, tennis, track, and swimming. After the Nazi take-over of Austria, Engel went to the United States and became a citizen. He was head ski coach at Cornell University from 1938 through 1942 and helped pioneer skiing in America. It was during this time, in 1938, that he began to design sportswear for the Ken Wel Manufacturing Co., in Utica, New

York. While on active service in the Aleutians during World War II, he received a severe knee injury that terminated his career as a professional athlete, but he continued to ski for fun.

Engel's entry into the design field was accidental. While in London with the Austrian hockey team, he bought a few yards of "balloon silk," actually a tightly woven combed cotton poplin used for rainwear, and had it made up in an unlined zip-front jacket, the first modern ski parka. Soon Engel found himself in the skiwear business. He used gabardines for ski pants and the tightly woven poplin for parkas in place of the bulky melton and loden cloth of contemporary ski clothes, and he still works with manufacturers to develop better fabrics for sportswear. Engel was the first to use nylon for parkas, and in the 1950s he introduced stretch fabrics to American skiers. He also produces tennis, golf, and sailing clothes.

Among the honors Engel has won are the American Wool Fashion Award, the first Lincoln-Mercury Sports Fashion Award, the first Creative Menswear Award (1969), the Coty Award, and seven Caswell-Massey

Awards. He sums up his fashion philosophy succinctly: to combine function and fashion. Married and the father of two daughters, he is still a dedicated sportsman. ■

Jacques Esterel

Jacques Esterel (original name, Charles Martin) was born on June 5, 1927, in Bourg-Argental, Department of the Loire, France, and attended the École Nationale des Arts et Métiers. Meanwhile, at the age of sixteen, he began his career as a newspaper cartoonist. After graduation from school he became a manufacturer of machine tools; he has had forty-two inventions patented.

In 1955, in his own words "a self-made man in the world of high fashion," he established his own firm in Paris, which now licenses Esterel designs for men, women, and children to 107 manufacturers in twenty-four countries throughout the world; articles of clothing bearing his label are sold through 1,500 retailers, with a turnover of $30 million at the manufacturers' level. He is the owner, president, and general manager of Jacques Esterel, S.A., in Paris. There are two Jacques Esterel shops in the United States: a large one in Locust Valley, Long Island, where he has pioneered the concept of custom design whereby

J. ESTEREL

the selection of model and style and the client's measurements are made in New York and telexed to Paris to be executed; and a small boutique on the upper East Side in New York. In 1968 he won a gold medal for French ready-to-wear fashion, and his unisex total look in jersey has received international recognition.

In Esterel's opinion, high fashion opens the doors to what's possible, while ready-to-wear opens the doors to what's probable. The two areas of fashion act as a system of checks and balances. Esterel believes in exploiting ready-to-wear fashion for one season only, while his high-fashion designs explore new ground. Married and the father of a daughter, Jacqueline, Esterel is a playwright and composer of repute: he has written seventy-two songs, three plays, and a musical; eight of his songs have been recorded. ■

Gilbert Feruch

Gilbert Feruch was present at the inception of the Paris menswear movement. He made suits for Pierre Cardin before Cardin entered the menswear field, and the long, lean close-to-the-body cut that ultimately triumphed under the Cardin label is said to have originated in Feruch's atelier. Feruch is a man's tailor, not a couturier who turned to men's fashion, and he ap-

concepts, beginning with the introduction of the Nehru collar and followed by innovations like the jump suit, the knicker walking suit, and the full-cut A-shaped coat with a full back for ease and freedom. In fact, *l'aisance* (ease) is his byword, and he aims at an elegant silhouette combined with the rational comfort of sportswear in all his designs. In the United States, Delton Ltd. is fulfilling Feruch's desire to have his custom-tailored clothing made available to the general public. He has made several trips to make sure that the manufacturing plant is cutting the clothes exactly the way he wants them cut. ■

women's store and its public relations director, and in September of that year he opened his own high-fashion shop for men in Rome.

With Brioni, Datti, and Litrico, Franzoni founded the Italian Menswear Stylist Group in 1962; the Big Four, as these designers came to be known, focused world attention on fashions from Italy. As an ambassador for Italian fashion, Franzoni presented his designs in Africa, Asia, Europe, North and South America, and Australia. He was named the outstanding Italian stylist by the International Festival of Men's Fashion in San Remo in 1965 and again in 1967. In 1968 he closed his business in Rome and emigrated to the United States, where he joined the International Fashion Guild of Hart Schaffner & Marx, for which he now designs exclusively.

Franzoni's fashion credo is based on sophisticated simplicity. He believes in pure anatomical lines, with an accent of elegance and individuality. A man of taste and culture, he is deeply interested in musicology, art, modern literature, and social studies of ethnic minorities. He is the father of a thirteen-year-old son. ■

G. FERUCH

proached ready-to-wear clothing only after years of having established a firm reputation as a custom tailor to such clients as the designers Yves Saint-Laurent, Givenchy, Marc Bohan, and Philippe Venet as well as Cardin, Picasso, and several members of the Rothschild family.

Feruch believes that he has liberated men from the drab cocoon of the conventional suit with his uninhibited

Luciano Franzoni

Luciano Franzoni was born on March 23, 1926, in Bergamo, Italy. He studied industrial sciences at the University of Parma, law at the University of Rome, languages at the Pro Deo University, and social work at the Guido Calogero School in Rome. Despite his formal education, which led to a position with UNESCO (1948–1950), Franzoni decided that fashion was the career he wished to follow. In 1951 he became the men's store director and stylist of the Roman firm of Son & Man, and in 1954 he joined Palermi in the same capacity. In 1958 he became the director of Luciani's

Fred Freund

Fred Freund was born on August 26, 1911, in Aschaffenburg, Germany. He attended the Fashion Academy in Berlin and gained a thorough knowledge of fashion, serving an apprenticeship with Elsbach & Frank in Hannover. Subsequently he went to Paris, where he studied at the Ateliers Canard; during the next five years he gained experience in design and merchandising. It was in Paris that he developed and marketed Loisir, the first leisure suit. Arriving in New York in 1939, he designed clothes for Oldin-Dennis and S. Dennis, Inc. In 1951 he established Fredwin Creations for the design and manufacture of shirts and sportswear; it was soon recognized as a style leader.

In Germany, France, and the United States, Freund patented con-

struction and design innovations; in New York he was involved in the development of pile fabrics and their first use as outerwear linings and trims, and he designed the first fake fur coat, using a deep pile as the outer shell rather than in its customary role of lining. He was also responsible for combining shirt and vest in a one-piece garment that produced a layered look.

In 1957 Freund sold the successful Fredwin company to the Puritan Sportswear Corporation, of which he became design and merchandising director. He started the Fred Freund Company, a consulting service for men's and boys' sportswear, in 1963. Among the manufacturers for whom he has designed are Bronzini Ltd., Lucien Piccard Sportswear Ltd., Revere Knitting Mills, Miller Brothers Industries, and DiFini Originals. He has received awards from the Knitted Fabrics Institute and the Men's Fashion Guild.

Freund believes that a good designer must lead in the right direction at the right time, sometimes by revolutionary ideas and sometimes by evolutionary designs. A father and a grandfather, he relaxes as a weekend gardener and painter. ∎

Michael Gee

Michael Gee inherited his flair for fashion from his father, Cecil Gee, a

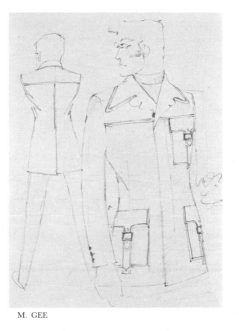

M. GEE

master retailer for more than forty years; the son now controls the family group of fifteen menswear stores throughout the United Kingdom. Discontinuing the free advice service his father had been providing to international menswear manufacturers, he launched the Cecil Gee Design Consultancy, which became a major company in its own right within the group of family enterprises. Among the consultancy's international clients is the Cooperative Wholesale Society of Great Britain. Gee is also a founder-member of the Clothing Export Council of Great Britain; in this capacity he has led a number of overseas

trade missions. He visits the United States regularly four times a year and travels about the Continent in much the same manner as he travels about the British Isles. He is married and the father of two children.

A designer himself, Gee supports his father's yearly award to the best student in the menswear field at the Royal College of Art. His own philosophy of fashion has its roots in his training as a chartered accountant and in retailing: in his directives to the Gee team of designers, he is often heard to say: "Give me a handful of uninhibited design, but give me two handsful of merchandise we can sell!" ∎

Tom Gilbey

Tom Gilbey was born on May 19, 1939, in London, England. After leaving school at fifteen, he apprenticed himself to a bespoke tailor, then to an established firm of West End tailors, and went on to cutting patterns for women's clothes. At eighteen he went into the Coldstream Guards; during his military service he designed posters at the War Office and represented the Army on swimming and water polo teams, as a champion cross country runner, and as a fencing instructor. In the same period he studied dress design at the Shrewsbury Art College and received a design diploma in men's and women's wear.

The next few years were spent on the Continent. While at a women's couture house in Lausanne, he was invited by one of the major British tailoring groups, John Temple/ Neville Reed, to work on a Continental collection. This led to a design consultancy business with John Michael; in 1966 Gilbey opened his own organization. In 1968, deciding that he was neither sufficiently distinct from other designers nor building the kind of reputation he wanted, he founded his own couture house in London.

"Fashion," Gilbey says, "is never a whole statement; fashion is always a way of life—a reflection of the times or a rejection of the times. It can contradict itself, whereas architecture, computers, cars—everything we live with—do mold and become part of our establishment. The more we get into the seventies, the more clothes will have a chance to reflect the world of architecture and what's happening in the scientific world." ∎

T. GLAZIER

Timothy Glazier

Timothy Glazier was born on January 20, 1934, in Surrey, England, and was educated at private schools. At twenty he joined Herbert Johnson Ltd., the world-famed London firm manufacturing and selling hats, of which his grandfather had been one of the founding partners. During his stay with the company, he developed his designs to meet its needs and helped reestablish the firm name in the forefront of headwear design. He was instrumental in producing the big hat pioneered by Herbert Johnson, and he introduced rich fabrics such as silk and velvet; in addition, he was responsible for a functional "bog" hat of Donegal tweed, a new look in cotton summer hats, and a wide-brimmed straw.

Glazier subsequently designed the youth-oriented Take Cover line for the Associated British Hat Manufacturers Ltd. In 1970 he formed an independent establishment, Timothy Gla-

zier Designs, to distribute headwear and accessories in Great Britain and other countries. Besides the hats he designs for his collection and on private commission, his studio in London features ties in unusual fabrics. His belts have buckles made of hand-beaten copper, reproductions of seventeenth-century seals, and glazed ceramics, and his cuff links are often scaled-down replicas of the belt buckles.

Glazier believes that the low ebb of the men's hat industry is due to manufacturers who do not pay attention to the wishes of potential wearers. The middle-aged man has either given up wearing hats or opts for something inconspicuous for wear on special occasions. Attempts to cater to the young have been a failure. Glazier says, "I believe that men enjoy wearing hats, but that the headwear for *today* has not yet been designed. I aim to do it."

Married and the father of two children, Glazier is interested in the visual arts and in economic and political issues. ∎

John Paul Goebel

John Paul Goebel was born on April 17, 1929, in New York; he was graduated from the Fashion Institute of Technology with a degree in scientific management in 1949. During the next ten years, before opening his own business as a design trend consultant and designer for the fiber, textile, and men's sportswear industries in 1960, Goebel worked as a designer and merchandiser for various women's, children's, boys', and men's clothing man-

ufacturers. Among his clients since establishing John Paul Goebel Inc. are Jantzen, Inc. (men's outerwear); Shipton Sportswear (boys' and men's outerwear); Du Pont (men's and women's wear); Borg Fabrics (pile fabrics); Crompton-Richmond Company (corduroy and velveteen); Travis Fabrics, Guilford Mills, and Russell Mills (tricot and woven fabrics); Alamac Knitting Mills (pile fabrics); Scott Paper

J. GOEBEL

Company (laminated fabrics); and Talon, Inc. (menswear). His firm serves as a consultant to a maximum of ten clients on a yearly retainer, and he now has prospective clients waiting for openings.

Throughout his career, Goebel says, he has tried to bring timely and fashionable design concepts in fabrics and ready-to-wear clothing to greater numbers of the population. His primary concern when creating a new concept is the consumer, followed by the needs of the retailer, the manufacturer, and the mill. He believes that if a concept has advantages for all concerned, it has been successful. Goebel has won the Mortimer C. Ritter Award of the Fashion Institute of Technology, the Leather Industries of America Design Award for menswear, the Hess Brothers Design Award for children's wear, and the Knit Fabrics Award.

Married and the father of two boys and two girls, Goebel has homes in Ramsey, New Jersey, Vale do Lobo in Algarve Province, Portugal, and Saint-Martin in the French West Indies. He enjoys swimming and skiing and is an ardent gardener and painter. ■

Peter Golding

Peter Golding was born in London in 1940 and attended the City of London

P. GOLDING

School. At twenty he was managing Rael Brook U.K., a shirtmaking factory with 350 employees, but left it to attend art schools in Paris. Opening his own business in London in 1965, he rapidly achieved international recognition: he was the first menswear designer to be elected to the Master Society of Industrial Artists and Designers, and he was selected by the International Wool Secretariat as Great Britain's representative for Project Adam, its investigation into clothes for man in the twenty-first century. He also established the first professional design consultancy in Britain.

Golding is inspired by the colors and fabrics of India, Nepal, and Tibet; he spent three months in India looking, sketching, and costing the fabrics that are frequently used in his collections. The underground youth scene is the other great influence on his designs. He believes that there are two extremes in England: the bowler-hatted symbol of Britannia, which he thinks is on its way out; and the new Britain whose birth was presided over by the Beatles. The mass in between are the ones who really need color in their lives, in Golding's opinion, and he tries to give it to them.

For all his advanced ideas, Golding is esteemed by such establishment organizations as the International Institute for Cotton, for which he designed

a line of clothes manufactured in thirteen countries. He revamped the Aertex Company for Viyella International and has produced special collections for Phillips–Van Heusen in the United States and L. & P. Widengren in Sweden. He has received awards from the Menswear Association of Great Britain and the International Fashion Council, as well as several consecutive Caswell-Massey Awards. Married to a French designer of children's wear, he enjoys sailing, music, and the visual arts. ■

Karen Hellemaa

Karen Hellemaa was born in Finland. As a small child she accompanied her parents to Argentina, where her father, a scientist, worked on a research project. After attending schools in Buenos Aires, she spent a year studying art in New York and later pursued her art studies both in Spain and at the University of Helsinki. Married to a Finnish industrialist, she is the mother of two children.

Mrs. Hellemaa began to design leather clothes for her children in the early sixties. Extending her range, she subsequently became the chief designer of the Friitala-Finland leather factory. Her designs enjoyed increasing popularity and were well received at the Semaine de Cuir (Leather Week) showings in Paris. Although her designs are avant-garde, she maintains that fashion should serve man, and not the reverse. Clothes should be wearable for many seasons. Mrs. Hellemaa considers her designs for men a sideline of her overall creative career. ■

Sighsten Herrgård

Sighsten Herrgård was born on January 8, 1943, in Helsinki, Finland. He started his design career at fifteen, working before, during, and after school; he received a bachelor's degree in Latin in Stockholm in 1963, after which he spent a year in military service at Boden. After his discharge he attended other schools, including Croquis, the Academy of Couture, and the Anders Beckman School of Fashion in Stockholm and the Academy of Couture in Copenhagen.

Recognized as a designer by the age of seventeen, Herrgård has continued to expand his operations, with collections and designs shown in nearly every exhibition scheduled in major fashion capitals. He has left his American management company and is working as a free-lance designer. He has opened new offices in Stockholm and London and a shop in Stockholm, called "16," to be the first of a chain of Swedish shops featuring Sighsten designs for boys and girls from six

through sixteen. He has also licensed manufacturers in Japan and Canada to produce apparel under the Sighsten label, and his ready-to-wear clothing is available in England, Sweden, and Finland.

Herrgård has received recognition for the originality of his designs from the earliest days of his career, including awards from Courtauld's in England, Peek & Cloppenburg in the Netherlands, the Concours d'Élégance Gold Medal in France, the Instituto Mexicana de la Moda, and Creative Menswear Awards (1968 and 1969) in the United States. He thinks of himself as a constructor of basic clothes in basic colors. He works from fiber to fabric, pattern, and production on three different levels: ready-to-wear clothes for boutiques and for department stores and couture. Herrgård hates the pigeon-holing of age groups and dislikes interlined and padded clothes. He wants to design for today and tomorrow, not yesterday and not the twenty-first century. ■

Jon Jolcin

Jon Jolcin was born on March 11, 1935, in Tel Aviv. From 1950 to 1953 he studied industrial and fashion design at the Sydney Technical College in Sydney, Australia, where he also was apprenticed to David Jones, the high-fashion retail establishment. In

1958 he emigrated to the United States, settling first in California and then in New York, where he became president of Jon Jolcin, Inc., an international designing and merchandising organization. Among the manufacturers who have produced his designs are Spencer Industries, Alden's, McGregor-Doniger, Inc., Robert Lewis, and Aspen Ski Wear. He has also served as a fashion consultant to the Israeli Export Institute.

Jolcin believes that fashion is a great art based on two principles, beauty and utility; in the contemporary sense, it is the art of designing beauty into useful things. In our time, he says, the

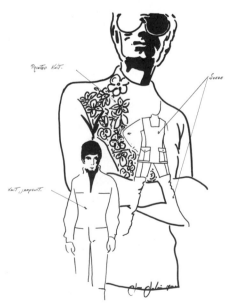

industrial fashion designer has proved that mass-produced consumer products can be attractive as well as useful, thus affording millions of people an enjoyment once reserved to the wealthy.

He won the Caswell-Massey Award for outerwear in 1968 and was named Designer of the Year for his 1972 collection for the International Fashion Council; his 1972 Cotton Council of America collection won a first prize. Jolcin enjoys swimming and horseback riding. ■

Larry Kane

Larry Kane was born on January 24, 1930, in New York, where he began a career in the theater at the age of ten. He was a leading juvenile actor on the stage and in radio from 1940 through 1947, meanwhile studying at the Lodge Professional School. He also attended New York and Columbia Universities in New York and George Pepperdine College in Los Angeles. From 1948 to 1952 he was an agent and manager of theatrical talent. Then, in 1953, he embarked on a new career, apprenticing himself to Stanley Blacker, Inc., the tailored sportswear manufacturers. He stayed with Blacker, learning every phase of the design and manufacturing of fashion,

L. KANE

until 1969, when he established Larry Kane for Raffles Wear, Inc., a division of Kayser-Roth Corporation.

"The unstructured, nonplastic form of fashion appeals most to my senses," Kane says. "I allow myself the flexibility of working with an unlocked mind, keeping it loose, fluid, and available for any and all outside influences to inspire design. Atmosphere, music, economic conditions, the tone of the times, youth values, sports, native country dress—all of them suggest design and style to me." Raffles Wear, he thinks, is representative of the new breed of manufacturer, giving the retailer the opportunity to buy less but more frequently, the opportunity to buy closer to the delivery point, and the desire to buy "items" rather than just merchandise and a theme to go with them. Kane has received the Coty Award and four Caswell-Massey Awards, and he is the first United States president of the International Fashion Council.

Married and the father of a daughter and a son, Kane is an avid tennis and handball player. He enjoys the beach and collects shells that he fashions into images. ■

Peter A. Knize

Peter A. Knize was born on June 16, 1924, in Vienna, Austria, where he

attended the Academy of Maria Theresa. He subsequently studied in Paris and at Outershaw College in England, arriving in New York with his family in 1941 shortly before the United States entered World War II. He served in the United States Army during the war and then attended New York University while completing his apprenticeship in custom tailoring, which he had begun under the tutelage of his father, Frederick Knize, in Paris. In 1949, after his father's death, Knize took over the family business. In addition to maintaining its international headquarters in midtown Man-

P. KNIZE

hattan, he opened a new shop in the General Motors Plaza on Fifth Avenue in 1969.

To Knize, fashion is more than a philosophy or a way of life. "It's a religion," he says, "a living thing that mirrors the mores of the period in which it is created. The heritage of Knize tailoring goes back 112 years, yet our patrons are among the most 'venturesome conservatives' in the world. They neither move with nor counter to the fashion pendulum but, rather, let us innovate for them within the framework of tasteful standards of fit and appearance.

"Our fashion expressions begin with comfort, without which function cannot be fulfilled—and without function, few fashions get beyond the 'fad' stage. We believe in change, but not just for change's sake! Fashion must reflect its time and its environment."

Knize's wife Lili is an art teacher, and the couple live with their three children in New Canaan, Connecticut, where Knize pursues his avocations of linguistics, photography, and chess. ∎

Nancy Knox

Nancy Knox (original name, Therese Holland) was born in North Hollywood, California, on April 16, 1923. She was graduated from St. Xavier's Academy in Providence, Rhode Island, in 1941, and also attended Regis College in Weston, Massachusetts, and Bryant College in Providence. She married James W. Knox in 1946 and entered the shoe business in 1953 as assistant fashion director of I. Miller in the company's New York headquarters. As cofounder of Jags Unlimited, Inc., she began to design men's shoes in 1956. In 1963, with Peter Barton and Genesco, the fashion conglomerate, she cofounded another men's shoe business, Renegades, of which she is now president and designer.

Among her design innovations was the introduction of the Australian bush boot, the first fashion boot accepted by the American public. Her designs for Jags Unlimited won Caswell-Massey Awards in 1961, 1962, and 1963; after the establishment of Renegades, she won five additional Caswell-Massey Awards. In 1969, as a designer for Renegades, Mrs. Knox also received the Creative Menswear Award (the only footwear company to achieve such recognition), and in 1971 she was given a special Coty Award for bringing variety, change, and elegance to men's shoes.

Mrs. Knox believes that today men's fashion is men's life: a life of business (formal or informal), leisure (winter or summer), and sports (active or spectator). Fashion, she feels, mirrors the American life-style; when that life-style changes, so does fashion, and shoes are integral accessories for men's varying wardrobes.

A dedicated sportswoman, Mrs. Knox enjoys bicycling, horseback riding, and golf. She spends much of her spare time restoring and decorating old houses. ∎

Michael A. Kramer

Michael A. Kramer was born on April 2, 1940, in Lyon, France. He was graduated from the Lycée Ampère in Lyon in 1960 and from the Textile School in Krefeld, Germany, as a textile technician in 1961. He gained experience in weaving with Dumas Textiles in Lyon before being called to military duty.

At the request of Herbert Bergheim, he went to the United States in 1963 as an assistant designer for Yapre Neckwear. The following year Kramer joined Wembley, Inc., as the head stylist for the Helen Liebert Designer Neckwear Division of the company. In 1966 he resigned to join Handcraft Inc., Walter Handley Associates, for which he designed collections of scarves, pocket squares, mufflers, and neckwear; he became vice president of Handcraft in 1968 and an associate with Walter Handley in 1970. Subsequently he formed Pedigree Men's Fashions, a division of the A. Ruderman Co.

Kramer created and registered the Turtle Neck Ascot in 1968 and created the Sailor Scarf and Sailor Square, registered for Handcraft, in 1969. Among his other innovations are the use of scarves as belts, the introduction of hand-printed Indian silks for men's scarves, a 250-centimeter-long muffler to be worn with the maxi coat, and a collection of squares signed "Michael K."

Kramer predicts that within ten years the workweek will be reduced to four days, giving men three days of leisure. He feels, therefore, that the greatest designing efforts will be directed toward the creation of the leisure look in men's fashion, and he is involved in creating a sportswear look in the neckwear accessory field, in which he believes the future of the neckwear industry lies.

Married and the father of two children, Kramer lives in Rye, New York. He collects and refinishes antiques and is an avid skier on both snow and water. ∎

Ralph Lauren

Ralph Lauren was born on October 14, 1939, in New York, where he completed courses at the City College of New York at night while working days, first at Brooks Brothers and later as assistant buyer for Allied Stores' New York buying office. In 1967 he

established the Polo division of the Beau Brummell neckwear company, through which he reintroduced the wide tie, fomenting a revolution in men's neckwear. The following year, in partnership with Norman Hilton, Lauren founded Polo Fashions, Inc., as a separate clothing company. Its interests were soon broadened from ties to a total look, encompassing clothing, shirts, sportswear, knitwear, outercoats, shoes, and luggage, all designed by Lauren. In 1971 the Ralph Lauren label was established as a new division of high-priced ready-to-wear clothing for women, including shirts, sportswear, outerwear, and leisure apparel.

Lauren's philosophy is to lead fashion, to sense what his customers want before they know it themselves. He believes that the success his fashions have achieved is due to their appropriateness for the time and place where they are worn. He has an eye for the authentic details that make the kind of clothes he wants to wear or wants his wife to wear but is unable to find anywhere else. He won the Coty Award for menswear in 1970, and he was one of the first recipients of the Tommy Award of the American Printed Fabrics Council.

Married and the father of two sons, Lauren bicycles, swims, and plays basketball. ∎

Sid Lawson

Sid Lawson began his career as a singer and actor in the legitimate theater in New York, appearing in such productions as *Call Me Mister, Miss Liberty, Lend an Ear, Diamond Lil,* and *Call Me Madam.* Following up his serious interest in creative design, he apprenticed himself to a leading fashion house in 1956, becoming a full partner in the firm three years later. Despite the discouraging climate for creativity in the menswear industry at the time, he received recognition from the fashion press and enjoyed several major successes. Among these were a toggle jacket for Skaggerac Sportswear; a bush jacket for the McTague Manufacturing Company; the first imitation fur coat for men, which was shown at the National Outerwear and Sportswear Association fashion show in 1966; and a see-through vinyl raincoat for women for the United States Rubber Company. In 1963 he became president of Lawson Designs, specializing in original fashion design, sales promotion, and merchandising. ∎

Angelo Litrico

Angelo Litrico was born on August 15, 1927, in Catania, Sicily. As the eldest in a large family (an eventual twenty-four brothers, of whom twelve are still living), he left school at an early age and apprenticed himself to a tailor. His creativity was evident from his earliest years, but it was not until he went to Rome in 1952 that his real fashion career began. He began working for his own clients in 1953.

He opened his first shop on the Via Sicilia, where his headquarters still remains. It was here that he inaugurated the first fashion shows for menswear and that he made his first foreign sales. Gradually, he became one of the best-known designers in Europe,

Litrico says that he does not wish to become too sophisticated or too big. He wants to remain a good designer in his shop, like one of the Italian artists of the Renaissance. He wants to make a good suit for a client, to cut it and follow the fittings to an ultimate elegance. But he also wants every man to have at least one good suit, and to that end he has given his designs to factories all over the world. He has received hundreds of awards, including every important award in his native Italy, at least ten Caswell-Massey Awards, the award of the International Fashion Council, and awards from Brazil, Argentina, Germany, Australia, and Japan. ∎

counting among his clients President John F. Kennedy and Premier Nikita S. Khrushchev, Prime Minister Levi Eshkol of Israel and President Gamal Abdel Nasser of Egypt. Litrico's designs are also produced under license by Toyorayon and Sogo in Japan, Herren Globus in Switzerland, Rex Trueform in South Africa, Ducal in Brazil, Modart in Argentina, and C. & A., the initials under which the largest chain of fashion stores in Europe, Brenninkmeyer's, does business in Germany, the Netherlands, Belgium, France, and England (in the United States under the name of Ohrbach's).

Don Loper

Don Loper was born on August 29, 1907, in Toledo, Ohio, where he attended the public schools. He subsequently studied at the Fagan School of Design in London, England, but his original career was as a professional dancer, beginning at the age of fourteen. Among the Broadway hits in which he appeared were *One for the Money, Very Warm for May,* and *All in Fun.* His career in design began in 1938, when he recostumed his dancing partner, Maxine Barrett. The team

played a two-year engagement at the Copacabana in New York, and Loper went on to produce, direct, and design all the Copa shows for the next three years. He made his film debut as Ginger Rogers's dancing partner in *Lady in the Dark;* MGM then gave him a multifaceted contract as dancer, choreographer, costume and set designer, actor, director, and producer.

In 1946 Loper and Col. Charles C. Northrup opened a couture salon on the Sunset Strip in Hollywood. The salon was moved in 1951 to its current Beverly Hills location, where it functions as a total design center, producing not only couture clothes for men and women but uniforms for such companies as TWA, Pan American, Eastern Airlines, Hertz Rent-A-Car, and Security First National Bank of California. Companies for which Loper has designed include Duke of Hollywood, Ram Knitting Mills, Superba Cravats, Keeper's Hosiery, Dante, Cinco, Inc., Handkerchief Craft, and Sidron. He won Caswell-Massey Awards in 1964 and 1968.

Loper's battle cry was "Sanity in Fashion." Good taste, he believed, is the key to being well dressed; clothes must be a background for the personality and must never overshadow the wearer. He designed simple, understated clothes to be worn by gentlemen who look like gentlemen.

He died in November, 1972. ∎

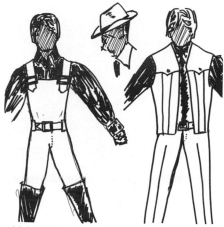

M. MANDEL

Rupert Lycett Green

Rupert Lycett Green was born in London on October 24, 1938, the son of Comdr. D. C. Lycett Green, who founded one of Britain's largest engineering complexes. He was educated at Eton College, received training for a business career, and subsequently became a second lieutenant in the 9th Queen's Royal Lancers.

In 1962 he opened in London his now-famous establishment Blades, to fill the needs of what he considered a neglected section of the public: the fashion-conscious man who was interested not only in a well-made suit but also in cut, color, and design. The growth of Blades necessitated a move from Dover Street to larger quarters in Burlington Gardens, and Lycett Green became recognized as one of the most creative and successful designers working in menswear. He has proved himself a leader in the design revolution, and the look projected by Blades clothes has made its mark in every aspect of men's fashion. Lycett Green tries to design and make clothes that will brighten the life and spirit of the wearer. He pioneered the long, lean line in British tailoring by redesigning the traditional Savile Row suit, and he believes that men's clothes should be elegant, colorful, but, above all, simple.

Lycett Green has also designed for Alfred Dunhill of London, Inc.'s New York shop and for Deisho Keori of Tokyo. He won the British Tailor and Cutter Exhibition's silver medal in 1967 and first prize and Dormeuil Trophy in 1970. In addition, he received *Playboy*'s Fashion Award of the Year in 1968 and 1969 and the Creative Menswear International Award.

In 1963 he married Candida, the daughter of Sir John Betjeman, the Poet Laureate, and they have three daughters. He is an international skier and bobsledder, rides his own horses in point-to-point races, and plays tennis and squash. ■

Mannie Mandel

Mannie Mandel was born in Budapest, Hungary, on June 30, 1920, and went to the United States in 1937. He studied at the School of Business Administration of the City College of New York, and his career in fashion has encompassed sales, manufacturing, merchandising, styling, and design. He considers himself to be self-educated within the apparel industry, in which he has worked since 1941.

In 1961 Mandel was prescient enough to foresee the coming fashion revolution in men's clothing and opened his own business as a style and marketing consultant, specializing in ideas that could be translated into volume operations. Among his clients are the Puritan Sportswear Corporation, Thane Knitting, Cresco Leathers, Darwood-Triton, Carter-Ringer, the Manhattan Shirt Co., Chief Apparel and American Male, the Modern Coat Company, Target Sportswear (Manhandlers), and Polaris. The services of his consulting company are in full demand.

Mandel believes that if we see through the eyes of youth, a new look and a new fashion language can be found in every generation. To create a fashion concept, he says, you must begin with free expression and end with self-discipline. You must accept change and travel the world for fresh, new viewpoints.

Married and the father of a boy and a girl, Mandel is a devotee of tennis and enjoys snowmobiling in winter and boating in warm weather. ■

Leslie Marshall

Leslie Marshall was born in New York and attended Erasmus Hall High School before entering Union College in Schenectady, from which he earned a B.S. degree. He was associated with the New York stage and the motion-picture industry for several years in varying capacities and still holds an Actors Equity card.

Marshall entered the fashion field as a member of the sales force of the Van

L. MARSHALL

for his designs. Among his clients in this area are the York Luggage Company and the Sardis Luggage Company.

In his role as a consultant Marshall has created complete wardrobe concepts in men's apparel, encompassing design, fabrication, and color coordination. He thinks that the swift changes of the sixties have resulted in the fashion emancipation of the American male. However, the full impact of the fashion revolution will be realized only in the seventies, when a middle road between extremes will be found and men will seek comfort as much as eye appeal. Marshall believes that simplicity and understatement are the essence of good taste and that true fashion is what looks good on the individual man.

Married and the father of two sons, Marshall is a golfer and spends much time as a fund raiser for the cancer research projects of the Columbia Presbyterian Hospital. ■

Bill Miller

Bill Miller was born on July 25, 1918, in New York, where he attended local schools and earned a B.S. degree *cum laude* from the City College of New York in 1938. After service during World War II in the United States Air

Raalte Company, after which he formed his own firm to design and manufacture women's sleepwear. In this capacity he was responsible for the introduction of pajamas with matching slippers and mandarin styling in women's pajamas. In 1956 he became a fashion consultant with clients in such widely diversified fields as men's and women's fashions and children's sleepwear. Later, he became interested in the design of luggage. He created a new concept for soft-sided luggage, incorporating new fabrications and trims, and had several patents issued

Force, in which he attained the rank of captain as a navigator and meteorologist, he taught industrial arts in New York City high schools and earned a master's degree in vocational education from New York University. From 1948 to 1950 he was a counselor at the Veterans Administration.

Beginning in 1950, Miller worked with his father in the Angora Knitting Mills in New York. Then, in 1956, he opened The Village Squire in Greenwich Village. One of the first avant-garde men's shops, it featured Miller's original designs. By the 1970s there were two Village Squire boutiques. In addition, Miller operates a flourishing mail-order business and, on a freelance basis, designs for M. & D. Simon Co. and Host Pajamas, Inc., collections sold under the label "Village Squire by Bill Miller."

Miller arrived on the fashion scene when the Ivy League look was in the ascendancy. He believes that his lack of experience was an advantage since he was not inhibited by convention: he questioned the traditional and got the answers in his own laboratory, his boutique. There, he arrived at a total tapered look, from underwear to sports and dress shirts and to tapered trousers, low-rise slacks, bells, and flared-bottom pants. Other innovations followed, including furs for men, vest suits, knitted suits, tank tops, and tank suits.

Miller is the only menswear designer to have received eight consecutive Caswell-Massey Awards; in 1968 he was given the Caswell-Massey Hall of Fame Award. He enjoys horseback riding and swimming and lists carpentry and electrical work among his avocations. ∎

Jean-Claude Morin

Jean-Claude Morin was born on April 24, 1936, in La Roche-sur-Yon, Department of the Vendée, France. After receiving his baccalaureate degree, he embarked in 1958 on a fashion career as an assistant stylist, first with Maggy Rouff and then with Jacques Heim. He subsequently became a stylist for Christian Dior, spending seven years with the salon as a specialist in underwear, knitwear, and handbags. He also designed men's and women's rainwear and arranged prestige fashion shows for Boussac, the French fabric house.

In 1969 Morin opened his own business as a free-lance designer and produced women's ready-to-wear collections for Modelia, Inc., handbags for Coblentz, and men's furs for Biegeleisen & Schour, all New York manufacturers. He created a new line,

J.C. Morin 70

called 106 Paris, in double-knit Fortrel polyester for Catalina Martin of California in 1970; included in this line were casual jersey sportswear with a Western look, tunics and pants for outerwear, polyester crepe evening wear, and bouclé sweaters with matching pants. In Europe he designed a line of jersey garments comprising pants, tunics, cardigans, and coats for men and women for Bruestle of Munich, women's jerseys for Avagolf of Milan, and underwear and beachwear for Armonia of Como and Rosy in France.

Morin believes in the use of double knits and stretch fabrics with a traditional look. He hates fancy dress and clothing that is overly detailed and thinks that fashion must be attuned to men who move about. The future lies midway between high fashion and volume business, in his opinion. Moreover, men's fashions must please women, since few men will buy without their advice or consent.

Morin enjoys horseback riding and water-skiing and likes cooking, entertaining, dancing, gardening, and cars. He travels approximately 200,000 miles a year, preferably to New York, California, or Italy. ∎

Stuart C. Nelson

Stuart C. Nelson was born in Lynn, Massachusetts, on October 31, 1933.

He attended Tilden Preparatory School and was graduated from the University of Vermont in 1956 with a B.A. degree. He began his career in 1957 as a salesman for Himalaya Knitwear. Joining Cortefiel de Espana in New York in 1960, he soon discovered that he had great talent for designing and styling sportswear. For the firm of Robert Lewis, with which he next became associated, he created the exciting Skua Bird, which embodied the new coordinated concept in men's sportswear. First attracted to California during a promotional trip for the Skua Bird, he had the opportunity to settle there when he joined Martin of

S. NELSON

California in 1964. Since he found the state's environment and life-style ideal for a sportswear designer, he remained in California when he founded his own firm a couple of years later. "From the studios of Stuart C. Nelson," as the firm is called, is located in its own building in Beverly Hills.

A sportsman himself, he became known for his high-styled and fashionable sportswear. His use of canvas and leather, detailed stitching, and heavy hardware produced the distinctive Stuart Nelson look. Nelson believes in knowing the man for whom he designs clothes. That man is between twenty-five and forty-five, travels widely, has taste, and appreciates clothes that are individual and not faddish.

Besides his studio and shop in Beverly Hills, Nelson has a shop in Las Vegas and departments in a number of large stores, among them J. L. Hudson in Detroit, Halle Brothers in Cleveland, and Bullock's-Wilshire. He also designs and serves as a consultant for several companies. He is married to the television actress Myrna Ross. ■

T. NUTTER

old, the family moved to Edgware, Middlesex, where his father worked in the aircraft industry and where he attended secondary school before entering Willesden Technical College to study design and architecture. At eighteen he went to London to work as a draftsman in a building firm and then became a clerk at the Ministry of Works.

Nutter's interest in men's clothes was whetted to the point that he went to work as an errand boy for G. Ward, the Savile Row firm of tailors. Encouraged by his new employers, he began to learn tailoring in their workrooms and subsequently studied at the Tailor and Cutter Academy. He then began to learn the mechanics of running a tailoring establishment and became involved in the management side, where he dealt with customers, advising them, assisting at fittings, and thinking in terms of design.

In 1969 Nutter opened his own bespoke tailoring shop in a new building on the site that had been occupied by G. Ward. He subsequently expanded his custom operation into Nutter's Shirts, Ltd., because he wanted "to create full wardrobes with a complete look and style for our patrons." The new shop included Liberty silk shirts, Nutter-designed scarves, ties, kimono-style dressing gowns, and hand-knitted sweaters.

The object of Nutter's operation is to serve his clients with the high standards of Savile Row while offering a fresh approach to classic tailoring. He believes that fashion adds something to a person's life by changing his look constantly, by giving him clothes that are different and new. Shapes should change gradually, and natural fabrics like flannels, tweeds, gabardines, and wools still suit the body best; mixed together, they give a look that is completely original but still maintain a classic image. ■

Carlo Palazzi

Carlo Palazzi was born on March 5, 1928, in Urbino, Italy. After completing his education at the University of Urbino, he taught school in a small village. Shortly thereafter he moved to Rome, where after trying several unsatisfactory lines of work, he joined the staff of Battistoni, the men's shop on the Via Condotti, in 1950. As an apprentice he studied every aspect of fashion for men, from the weaving and cutting of fine fabrics to the meticulous finish of buttons and the design of accessories, and he eventually directed the operations of the establishment.

In 1964 Palazzi opened his own fashion house on the Via Borgognona, which quickly became noted for its excellence. His 1968 collection at the

Tommy Nutter

Tommy Nutter was born of English parentage in Barmouth, Wales, on April 19, 1943. When he was a year

C. PALAZZI

Bruno Piattelli

Bruno Piattelli was born on August 2, 1927, in Rome, Italy, where he received his secondary education and a degree in law from the University of Rome. In 1944, while he was still in school, he joined his father's firm, which operated retail outlets for men's and women's clothing. Increasing contact with manufacturers and clients widened his knowledge of the field, and in the course of setting up manufacturing facilities for the production of clothing Piattelli became well known as a stylist in Italy and other countries.

This experience gave him a firm belief in the possibility of educating men to adopt a style of dress that

B. PIATTELLI

Mare Moda showings on Capri was a stunning success that brought him worldwide recognition. That year he went to New York to present for the Monsanto Company a collection featuring its fabrics. This successful undertaking led to an invitation to show his designs in *Playboy* magazine's Creative Menswear Collection in New York. He subsequently became a member of the Camera Nazionale della Moda Italiana, in whose seasonal collections his designs are shown.

In 1970 Palazzi signed a contract with Jaeger of America, which established "Carlo Palazzi for Jaeger" boutiques in the United States and Europe to distribute his designs. Distribution is handled directly by his own house to other shops throughout the world; he now has three shops in Rome. Like many other designers, he has separated his custom and ready-to-wear operations.

Palazzi tries to combine classic and modern ideas in what he calls "a subtle romanticism which avoids the 'costume' look while providing a new freedom of expression within the bounds of true elegance, good taste and practicality." He devotes much of his leisure time to gardening at his house in Rome and enjoys piloting his glider.

■

incorporates the rules of elegance; to that end, he opened an atelier dedicated to men's fashion. Among his first clients were luminaries of the Italian theater and film industry. He designed the uniforms worn by the male employees of Alitalia Airlines. His rainwear designs are manufactured by Burberrys Ltd., his shoe designs carry the label of the Fratelli Rossetti, and his knitwear is produced by Gianni Erba. Internationally known manufacturers and retail shops that stock Piattelli designs include D'urban of

Tokyo, Barney's in New York, the Executive's Shop of Johannesburg, Hoechst of Germany, Personality of Milan (ties), Wearover of Arona (rainwear), and Lady Pamela of Rome (household linens).

Piattelli believes that fashion is an expression of the life-style of a man during a particular period in history and must reflect the environment in which he lives as well as his outlook and activities. Among the awards he has won for his quietly elegant fashions are the Italian Fashion Oscar in 1968, the Silver Mask International Fashion Oscar in 1968, the Mexican Fashion Award in 1971, and the Tiberio d'Oro Award in 1972. Piattelli is married and the father of two children.

■

Emilio Pucci

Marchese Emilio Pucci di Barsento was born on November 20, 1914, in Naples, Italy. He studied at the Liceo Galileo in Florence and the University of Milan and in 1935 went to the United States, where he received a master's degree in social sciences in 1937 from Reed College. He was awarded a doctorate in political and social science from the University of Florence in 1941. Pucci's original in-

E. PUCCI

B. REED

ace, built for his ancestors nearly 1,000 years ago.

Pucci's expertise and taste have been called upon by such diversified companies as Rose Marie Reid (swimwear), Formfit-Rogers (lingerie), Tootals (linen textiles), Rosenthal and Ginori (porcelains), Perugina of Italy (chocolates), and Braniff International (stewardess uniforms). In 1969 he launched his first collection for men, reflecting his fashion philosophy of a return to the classic without losing the best of the new ideas which have been introduced into men's fashion. His work is marked by simplicity, color, style, and movement. Pucci has received two Neiman-Marcus Awards (1959 and 1965), the *Sports Illustrated* Designer's Award (1961), the International Designers Award (1968), and the Tiberio d'Oro.

Married and the father of two children, he enjoys sports and plays bridge and chess. Since 1963 he has been a deputy in the Italian Parliament. ■

tention was to follow a diplomatic career, but during his obligatory service as a pilot in the Italian Air Force World War II broke out and he became a career officer instead.

His career in design began by chance. In 1948 he was photographed at Zermatt in a ski outfit he had designed himself. This led to a small collection of women's skiwear that was featured in *Harper's Bazaar* and sold in the United States. Two years later he designed a holiday wardrobe for a friend, and its success led to the establishment of a small atelier in Florence. By 1950 his collections were so widely acclaimed that he enlarged his workrooms. His studio is in the Pucci Pal-

Barry Reed

Barry St. George Austin Reed was born into the men's fashion and retailing business. His grandfather was the founder of Austin Reed of Regent Street in London, his father is chairman of the company, and he himself

now serves as its managing director. During the Korean war he joined the Middlesex Regiment and was awarded the Military Cross. After demobilization he gained experience in the manufacturing and retailing of clothing in the Netherlands, Denmark, Sweden, Canada, and the United States before joining the family firm in 1955; he was appointed managing director eleven years later.

Determined to maintain the original concept of service to the customer at the forefront of the company philosophy, Reed has steered the firm into catering to well-dressed men of all ages. In the early sixties he introduced the shaped suit he called "British Classic," an advanced idea because of its slim-waisted silhouette, raised seaming, and wide choice of fabrics at a time when ready-to-wear suits were considered second-rate. Another innovation was the introduction of a line of combination knit and tweed tops with matching trousers. In 1965, foreseeing the impact of the men's fashion revolution, he opened a series of Cue Shops, catering to the young men's market, throughout the chain of Austin Reed stores. Reed believes that it is neither possible nor wise to be dictatorial about the "right look" or, on the other hand, to attempt to be all things to all men. His aim is to reflect the best in wearable men's fashion.

Reed has been president of the Menswear Association of Britain and was chairman of the Retail Alliance from its inception in 1967 until 1970. Married and the father of two children, he is a dedicated sailor. ■

Paul Ressler

Paul Ressler was born on October 7, 1917, in New York, where he was graduated from Erasmus Hall High School. After attending the City College of New York, he entered the United States Army, in which he served during World War II. Since 1946 he has been the owner of the family apparel business, Paul Ressler, Ltd., in New York. He began to design women's apparel and men's and women's skiwear in 1950 and established the manufacturing end of the business in 1966.

Ressler recognized early in his design career that the young people of America admired and would wear the less formal fashion ideas embodied in Western-style apparel, adaptations of the military look, and work clothes. This insight led to a complete line of moderately priced young men's trousers for wide distribution. Ressler's ideas included snugly contoured low-rise trousers with shaped knees and hems, wider waistbands with a double

P. RESSLER

closure, and 2-inch belt loops to accommodate a garrison belt. He was able to inspire several leading fabric mills to explore the possibilities of less expensive fabrics with properties of surface, comfort, and service that could be used to produce well-designed garments at prices young people would pay.

Ressler's aim is to produce an affordable seasonal wardrobe collection of compact, lightweight sportswear geared to today's active life-style. To achieve this aim he wants to utilize every technological advance, combining the inspiration of classic designs with the courage to use contemporary ideas. He has received three Caswell-Massey Awards, one in 1959 and two in 1968. Married and the father of two sons who have joined the firm in executive capacities, Ressler relaxes by collecting and refinishing antiques and engaging in boating, fishing, and tennis. ■

Ruth Rogers

Ruth Rogers was born in Vienna, Austria, where she completed her education at the Kunst Gewerbe Schule, graduating in 1938 with highest honors in art and fashion. She began her fashion career as a stylist with Herzmansky, Vienna's largest department store. Attracted by the vitality of the American fashion industry, she

moved to New York and established a consulting designer firm. Her first account was Mavest, Inc., the men's sportswear manufacturer; it was followed by Bloomingdale's, where she launched the store's first skiwear center for men, women, and children and its first fashion fabric center.

In 1951 she established Ruth Rogers Enterprises (RRE), a management consulting service for apparel manufacturers, specializing in design and styling. Among her clients have been the Burlington Madison Yarn Company; Helen Harper, a division of Charlie's Girls, Inc.; the White Stag Manufacturing Company; the Williamson-Dickie Manufacturing Company; Koret of California; Bernhard Altmann A. G., Vienna; Deering Milliken, Inc.; and Pendleton Woolen Mills.

Mrs. Rogers originally established RRE as a men's and women's sportswear design firm. Today it is involved in consulting, colorcasting, and coordination, designing and developing new products from the concept stage through yarn and fabric selection to finished apparel. Mrs. Rogers's fashion philosophy stresses seasonless cosmopolitan colors and fashions, reflecting the contemporary mobile life-style and the need for adaptability. She believes that the consumer's demand for self-expression and convenience must be met with variety, esthetic appeal, tactile feel, and function.

Married and the mother of two daughters, she enjoys skiing, tennis, and swimming. She collects art and paints, and she has served as a special consultant to the Costume Institute of the Metropolitan Museum of Art. ■

Jack Romm

Jack Romm was born in New York on September 4, 1913. At the age of sixteen he went to work in the display department of Saks Fifth Avenue, helping to design and set up the store's menswear windows, and subsequently worked in the same capacity for F. R. Tripler & Co. During these years he received a thorough grounding in color coordination and the planning of a man's wardrobe.

When he was twenty-two, he opened his own retail business in midtown Manhattan. Called the Clyde Shop, it was a forerunner of today's men's sportswear boutique and was soon a center for well-dressed men. Among Romm's creative innovations carried exclusively by the shop were shirts made of authentic batik, with matching swim shorts and kimonos; and shirts, vests, bell-bottom slacks, and kimonos in mattress ticking, denim, and corduroy, which had previously been considered industrial or work

fabrics unsuitable for high fashion and which have only recently come completely into their own. Clyde's also designed especially for such celebrities as the Duke of Windsor, for whom it made a wardrobe of pale blue corduroy, including the now-classic corduroy robe and the six-pocket shirt. Romm was also responsible for the buttonless crossover shirt on permanent exhibition at the Museum of Modern Art in New York.

The manufacturing end of Clyde's was expanded to handle wholesale orders from stores all over the country. Meanwhile, Romm became a consultant to Mark Cross, for which he established the first men's and women's apparel departments. For the Mark Cross men's shop he created the knitted crossover vest and the turtleneck dickey, developed the use of tussah silk for sport jackets, and formed the Brinj T-shirt.

Romm is now a vice president of the sportswear division of Bronzini, Ltd. He is married and has two sons. He has won numerous awards for his photographs. ■

Renzo Rossetti

Renzo Rossetti was born on July 29, 1925, in Verona, Italy. He began his

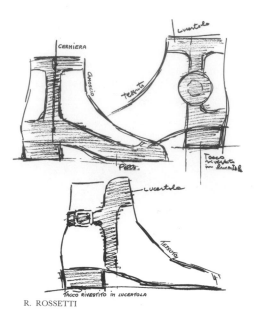

R. ROSSETTI

working life very early and changed jobs often before he found the right one for him. Among his early experiences was an attempt at industrial design, which was not successful but which proved useful when he established his men's shoe factory, Calzaturificio Fratelli Rossetti, with his brother Renato. Meanwhile, he attended evening classes at the Academy of Fine Arts of the Brera in Milan and lived in an attic with his painting gear until, at nineteen, he decided that he would rather be a good shoemaker than a mediocre artist. He transferred his taste for form and color to footwear and created his first pairs of shoes in a back room.

Of his fashion philosophy Rossetti says, "I don't like dressing in a sophisticated way myself; I am a bit casual, and lazy, too, about buying things for myself. That is why my success in the fashion world often amazes me. I think my flair is due basically to a sense of esthetics which guides me to the proper lines, plus a good dose of perfectionism which makes me keep a close watch on the product in all its stages and eliminate any defects meticulously. My shoes must meet the requirements of contemporary living; in my view, the up-to-date shoe is one that takes into account the various conditions of modern life and fits inevitably into the environment of the wearer, his way of living and, of course, of dressing."

Rossetti's shoe designs are in demand throughout the world and have won many prizes. Married and the father of three sons, he enjoys relaxing in the countryside. ■

Sergio Salfa

Sergio Salfa was born in Viterbo, Italy, on February 16, 1922. He attended the University of Naples until 1942, when he was called up for military service. In 1945 he joined the film company formed by Vittorio De Sica and Giuseppe Amato, and the following year he branched out into journalism, writing film criticism and other articles. Toward the end of 1946 he began designing shirts and other clothing for himself, primarily as a hobby. He was the first to repudiate the traditional shirt, converting the shirt into an article of primary fashion importance with a pioneering close-to-the-body cut. His interest in this new form of dressing developed into a serious productive activity, culminating in the formation of Samo of Rome, a firm whose name combined his own with that of his friend and partner, Vittorio Mori.

Salfa subsequently began to explore the entire field of men's fashion design,

S. SALFA

including coordinates; he is credited with originating the concept of the shirt suit. Among other innovations from the Samo collections are the lace shirt, brighter colors for evening and leisure wear, and the high rounded collar that came to be known inaccurately as the Mao collar. Today the models created by Salfa have achieved worldwide acceptance, especially among young men who appreciate their carefree comfort and functionalism as well as their taste and elegance. Among the awards Salfa has received are the Mercurio d'Oro in 1965, the Fashion Oscar in 1966, and the Samia Prize in 1968.

To Salfa fashion is a means of self-expression, a personal interpretation of the time in which one lives. He believes that man must shake off preconceived ideas and that finding new solutions gives fashion its *raison d'être* and contributes to a freer and fuller life-style. He is married and has two daughters. ■

Robert Schafer

Robert Schafer was born in New York and was educated at New York University and the Fashion Institute of Technology. He began his career in the 1950s by designing custom cloth-

ing for show-business personalities, with the expectation of going eventually into design for the theater. In the meantime, he held various positions in the textile industry and in women's wear. By 1954, however, he had begun to realize the need for design talent in menswear and started to design sportswear for Damon Creations. At the end of 1955 he joined the established neckwear firm of Burma-Bibas Inc., for which he designed the first sportswear collection. In 1960 Schafer became a vice president, and several years later a full partner, of Burma-Bibas. He won the Caswell-Massey Award in 1965 for his Italian knit shirt designs; in 1967 the firm garnered two more awards, including one for having reintroduced the wide tie into men's fashion.

R. SCHAFER

Schafer believes that well-designed clothes become timeless and that they should be easily convertible for wear on more than one type of occasion. Highly imaginative clothing should be reserved for leisure hours, he says, whereas business clothes should express the status and personality of the wearer. A bachelor, Schafer divides his time between an apartment in New York, a winter weekend house in Connecticut, and a summer weekend house at the beach. He is an avid tennis player and lists bridge, the study of foreign languages, painting, and sculpture among his interests. He spends three months each year in Europe on business. ∎

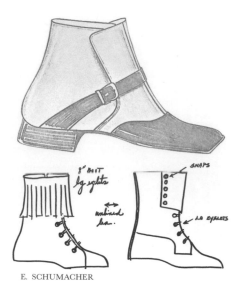

E. SCHUMACHER

Edward H. Schumacher

Edward H. Schumacher was born on August 18, 1928, in Janesville, Wisconsin, and was graduated from high school there in 1946. He served in the Army during the Korean war, reaching the rank of sergeant and completing several extension courses from the University of Wisconsin. Prior to the war, in 1949, he had begun his career with the Freeman Shoe Co. of Beloit, Wisconsin, and he returned there after his Army service. Starting as a truck driver, he worked his way up through sales correspondence, sales and service, tabulating, and, finally, total manufacturing. He joined Freeman's style and design department in 1956, was promoted to stylist in 1957, and became vice president in charge of product development in 1968. Schumacher was instrumental in developing Freeman's Famous Free Flex Construction and Freeman's Contour Cushion. He won the Men's Designer of the Year Award from the Leather Industries of America in 1965 and 1972.

He believes that men's fashion footwear is now well established and that shoes can no longer be regarded as mere foot covering. Footwear has become one of the most important parts of a man's wardrobe. Schumacher wants to give the footwear-fashion–conscious man a new selection of looks four times a year instead of the traditional two times, to help him differentiate between dress and casual shoes, and to induce him to wear an appropriate pair with each part of his wardrobe and so achieve a total look. Married and the father of a boy and a girl, Schumacher hunts and fishes for relaxation and is an avid fan of football, basketball, and baseball. ∎

Alexander Shields

Alexander Shields was born in San Francisco, California, into a family of shipowners. His background enabled him to travel around the world in his youth, becoming fluent in many languages and observing how people dressed in colorful ports and islands. It was this enthusiasm and appreciation for comfort, color, and unusual fabrics that eventually led to his career in design. Meanwhile, Shields attended the Menlo School in Menlo Park, California, and the California Institute of Technology, where he specialized in civil engineering and Italian. He subsequently attended the Foreign Service School of Georgetown University in Washington, D.C.

He spent his World War II service as a navigation officer on armed ships of the merchant marine, emerging as a commander. After the war he moved to New York and married another ex-

A. SHIELDS

Californian, his wife Sandy. It was at this time that Shields decided to do something about what he regarded as the dreary state of affairs in men's clothing, to try to get men out of uncomfortable, uncolorful, and unimaginative dress, and to design what he calls "getaway" clothes. In 1947 he opened Alexander Shields, Inc., to design and manufacture menswear on a wholesale and retail basis.

Shields believes that, as in architecture, in fashion "less is more" and uses the principles of engineering to simplify manufacture and design. He thinks that clothes should be comfortable and easy to wear as well as colorful. He also believes that a man should not expect his clothes to cover figure faults but should stand straight and tall to look his best.

In 1970 he won the Woolknit Design Award for his use of double-knit jerseys for jackets and trousers, and in 1972 he received the Coty Award. He and his wife have one daughter, Zia, and he is a dedicated tennis player. ■

Ken Smith

Ken Smith was born on March 5, 1923, in Kansas City, Missouri, where the artistic ability he showed at an early age was encouraged in local schools. He attended the University of Kansas City and the Kansas City Art Institute and School of Design before enrolling in the Parsons School of Design in New York, from which he was graduated. He also attended classes at the Art Students League and the Fashion Institute of Technology in New York.

During World War II he spent three years in the Army Air Force, mostly in the South Pacific. He began his design career in junior suits and coats, then turned to misses' sportswear, and continued in women's fashion until 1961, when he joined Jantzen, Inc., as a designer of men's swimwear, sportswear, and knit shirts. Among the manufacturers for whom he designed before joining Jantzen were S. Augstein & Company (Sacony) and Forest City Manufacturing. During his tenure with Jantzen Smith has won three Caswell-Massey Awards and placed second in the Monsanto Designers Competition in 1971.

Smith believes that the greatest influence on men's fashion today is increased leisure and that clothes should therefore be nonrestrictive: they should move with the body and be comfortable for leisure, travel, work, and sports. His creative ideal is tastefully styled masculine merchandise that appeals to a broad spectrum of the population. A man's wardrobe should give him a well-dressed appearance that is not offensively stylish but is easy to wear and casual.

Smith spends his weekends at his 200-year-old house in Bucks County, Pennsylvania, which he has restored authentically and furnished with carefully collected antiques, including early American redware. He is a tennis player and swimmer, enjoys horseback riding, and paints in oils. ■

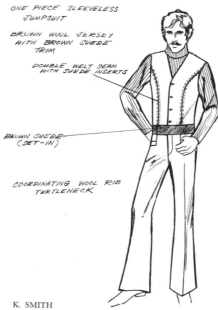

ONE PIECE SLEEVELESS JUMPSUIT

BROWN WOOL JERSEY WITH BROWN SUEDE TRIM

DOUBLE WELT SEAM WITH SUEDE INSERTS

BROWN SUEDE (SET-IN)

COORDINATING WOOL RIB TURTLENECK

K. SMITH

Richard Smith

Richard Smith was born in Kent, England, on July 26, 1942, and was educated at St. Olave's and St. Saviour's School in London. He began his career in advertising, serving as art director of J. Walter Thompson Co. Ltd. from 1960 to 1966.

Smith began to design shoes largely because he did not like the shoes in the shops. He had his designs made up by a cobbler, and this was the beginning of today's Chelsea Cobbler shops.

With two partners Smith began designing and producing boots and shoes, operating out of his London studio. By the spring of 1967 it had become evident that the Chelsea Cobbler was a commercial proposition, and the partners opened a shop in Chelsea, offering handmade made-to-measure boots and shoes in a wide variety of designs and a choice of leathers. At first they relied entirely on outside workers, but by August 1967 they had opened their own small factory, employing four cobblers.

The Chelsea Cobbler opened a second shop in Mayfair in 1969 and a shop in New York, which is as close as possible to the English shops in atmosphere, in 1970. Smith has designed the interiors for all the Chelsea Cobbler shops, maintaining a corporate image in each of them. There are Chelsea Cobbler shops in France, Switzerland, Germany, and Ireland, and Smith has also designed shoes for Devorá Shoes of Alicante, Mamar Shoes of Naples, and several smaller Spanish and Italian companies.

Smith believes that a designer, in addition to having original ideas on shape and form, must be aware of the continuing changes in the world, which affect people's life-styles. He himself finds these observations inspiring, keeping him from becoming inward-thinking about his creative work. Smith enjoys travel, reading, television, music, and the cinema. ∎

Louis Stanbury

Louis Stanbury was born in Botpalad, Hungary, on October 10, 1908. At thirteen, after attending the Protestant College of Botpalad, he was apprenticed to Kaldor of Budapest, where he learned the basic skills of tailoring and making coats. At eighteen he emigrated to London and worked first for Peacock & Company, then with Leslie & Roberts, where he acquired his expertise in cutting and pattern control. In 1932 he opened his own tailoring business in Paris.

At the outbreak of World War II in 1939, Stanbury volunteered for the

L. STANBURY

French Army, which in 1940 awarded him the Croix de Guerre. Captured by the German Army, he escaped and was recaptured. Escaping again, he made his way to Paris, where he joined the underground movement and survived to take part in the liberation of the city. After the war Stanbury returned to London, joining Kilgour, French & Stanbury, Ltd., the tailoring establishment of which his brother Frederick was managing director. He himself is now deputy chairman of the firm.

Since his return to England, he has been very active in fashion trade organizations, including holding the chairmanship of the Men's Fashion Council. He is vice chairman of the International Federation of Master Tailors, and in 1960 he was elected Tailor of the Year in the *Tailor and Cutter*'s annual competition, which awarded him the Gold (Dandy) Trophy. Stanbury also received medals from the World Federation of Master Tailors and the German Federation of Master Tailors.

Stanbury's philosophy about custom tailoring is, in his words, "very simple." He wants to make clothes to suit the personality of the client. He believes that while materials will become lighter and more colorful, design will continue to be based, with minor variations, on the classic concept. Married and the father of three children, Stanbury enjoys playing the violin, painting, sculpting, and making abstract collages. ∎

Richard Steinweg

Richard Steinweg was born on October 8, 1905, in New York. He was graduated from Allegany County High School in Cumberland, Maryland, and attended Columbia University. During World War II, from 1940 through 1945, he was supervisor of process engineering for General Motors (Eastern Aircraft Division). Sixty days after the war, as an executive of Cohen, Hall, Marx's woolen division, he was in England, Ireland,

R. STEINWEG

R. TORRES

Steinweg's philosophy of fashion is simple: Anything that is decorative should be functional. Married and the father of three married children, he is a football fan, enjoys swimming and driving a sports car, and gardens at his country home. ∎

and Scotland to survey the supply of available wool. He subsequently worked as general manager and stylist for Eastland Yarn Mills, vice president in charge of styling and production for Barclay Knitting Mills, director of styling for McGregor Sportswear, and director of styling for the sportswear and knit divisions of Phillips Jones–Van Heusen, where he was instrumental in adding cabana wear, beachwear, walk shorts, and slacks to the company's established lines.

In 1957 Steinweg established his own studios and became a consultant designer in the textile field, working with only one account of a kind in a particular industry. The studios have often gone beyond styling and designing, working closely with merchandising and sales and providing style influence to keep production flowing smoothly. Among his clients have been Fox-Knapp Manufacturing Co. (outerwear), Hanes Corporation (knit shirts), Glen Raven Mills and Collins & Aikman Corporation (knit fabrics to the trade), Fieldcrest Mills (linen and domestics, toweling), Bernard's of Mexico City (knitwear for infants, children, and men), Regent Knitting Mills of Montreal (men's and women's knitwear), Cresco Manufacturing Co. (men's and women's leather sportswear), and Sears, Roebuck and Company (knitwear styling for several of its subsidiaries).

Ruben Torres

Ruben Javier Torres was born on May 28, 1930, on his family's Texas ranch, where he grew up. He was graduated from Southern Methodist University in Dallas and served with the armed forces in the Far East from 1953 to 1955. Torres gained valuable experience in American ready-to-wear operations as a designer for Justin McCarty in Dallas and with Loomtogs and White Stag in New York before leaving for Paris and the couture. He was apprenticed to Nina Ricci for a year and was a couturier for the same house from 1960 through 1964.

Torres then began to feel that his work was no longer timely and that the couture was not in touch with contemporary life. He decided to set up his own organization to combine high creativity and industry, and in 1967 he presented his first collection of clothing for men and women under the Ruben Torres label. Now the

group of Torres offices and boutiques in Paris, plus licensed operations in other countries, permits him to design his own fabrics, clothing, and accessories, priced within the reach of his chosen customers: young men and women. The clothes are designed for the automobile age and jet travel and are uncluttered and contemporary.

The French government selected Torres to design the wardrobes for the French men's and women's teams at the 1968 Winter Olympics in Grenoble, and he also served as clothing adviser to the Mexican Olympic Committee for the 1968 summer games in Mexico City, for which he received a gold medal. He received the Creative Menswear International Award in 1969 and 1970.

An experienced horseman, Torres breeds Santa Gertrudis cattle on his ranches in Texas and Mexico. He collects prerevolutionary paintings from Russia, and his fashion library is one of the largest private collections in Europe. ∎

Frank Toscani

Francis D. (Frank) Toscani was born on January 2, 1915, in Philadelphia, Pennsylvania, where he attended high school and vocational school, spending many hours in shopwork. During his service in the United States Army

F. TOSCANI

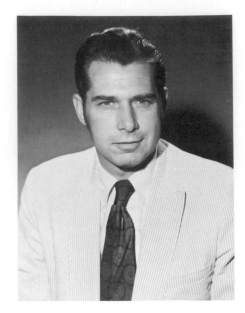

H. Daroff & Sons, the last-named from 1959 to 1969. That year he formed Frank Toscani Enterprises, serving the industry in free-lance design, consultation, quality control, and general troubleshooting. Among his clients are the Shelby Clothing Co., V-Line, After Six, Lawrence Clothes (K-R), Asher Sportswear, and Trinity Textiles Ltd. He has won Caswell-Massey and Creative Menswear Awards and has served as president of the Philadelphia Club of Clothing Designers, general chairman of the International Association of Clothing Designers' conventions and trade shows in 1963 and 1968, and president of the IACD in 1965.

Toscani believes that a man's life must be rational. Since rationality is what makes a man superior to other creatures, he says, reason must transcend man's every action and express his inner self. He believes that his finger is on the pulse of man's inner self and its expression, and that is what he designs for.

An ardent sportsman, Toscani swims, plays golf and pocket billiards, and was a record weight lifter. Married and the father of six children, he enjoys painting, sketching, and fashion illustration. He also has served on the faculty of the Philadelphia College of Textiles and Science. ■

Tibor E. Toth

Tibor E. Toth was employed originally as an apprentice shoe-pattern maker by the International Shoe Company in 1948, and he has remained with various divisions of the company ever since. He served as manager of the pattern department for eleven years and as a stylist for the Winthrop Division for twelve years. He is now director of style (men's shoes) for the entire company. Toth won the Leather Industries of America Award in 1962, and he is past and present chairman for men's dress shoes of the National Shoe Retailers Association Style Committee. He is the father of three children.

Toth believes that the application of

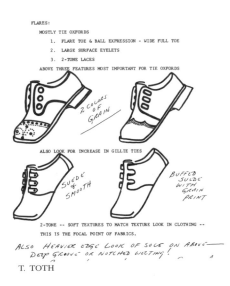

T. TOTH

fashion to shoe styling requires many approaches: keeping in touch with clothing, leather, and last manufacturers to determine the silhouette of tomorrow's clothing; finding out what is being introduced in the factories (not the retail outlets) on the European continent; and ascertaining whether a new fashion is being accepted gradually or whether there is a sudden change in the making. Men's shoe fashions are constantly changing, according to Toth. He believes that shoe fashion involves the creation and popularization of design to make high fashion, good fashion, and quality available to the mass market. ■

he studied radio operating and mechanics and radar mechanics. While still in school, from 1925 through 1932, he worked with his coatmaker father. He learned drafting, grading, and cutting from Tillio Di Giovanni and advanced ready-to-wear production from such Philadelphia tailors as Frank Barbieri, Michelangelo Petrizzi, and Achille Mongelli. In 1932 he established himself in a custom-tailoring business in Philadelphia.

Manufacturers for whom Toscani subsequently worked include Ruby Jacobs, Middishade, Max Udell, and

Yannis Tseklenis

Yannis Tseklenis was born on November 6, 1937, in Athens, Greece, where he was graduated from the Greek American College. Member of a family that owned a famous fabric house, he took an early interest in the business. His principal interest was in art, however, and he won prizes for his paintings while still in college. In 1962 he decided to combine his talents and put them to commercial use; he established his own advertising agency, Publica, which soon became a thriving business.

Tseklenis inherited the family busi-

Y. TSEKLENIS

ness in 1965 and began to design prints for its fabrics. The same year he participated successfully in the Mediterranean Fashion Festival, which led to a fabric collection that was purchased by Elizabeth Arden. He subsequently designed for the Puritan Fashions Corporation and David Crystal Inc. In 1967, in collaboration with Berketex in the United Kingdom, he produced the Attikon collection of fabrics; the following year he converted the Athens shop into a boutique and began to create styles using his own prints. At the same time he opened a second boutique in Salonika and three others aboard cruise liners.

Tseklenis entered the field of menswear in 1969, and his "total look" for both men and women was complete. He reached an agreement with Frank Usher in London for the production and distribution of the Tseklenis collections throughout Europe and the British Commonwealth. In 1969 he was awarded the Gold Medal of the Hellenic Fashion Institute. His business now supplies thirty countries and eleven boutiques throughout the Greek islands.

Tseklenis believes that fashion should make people carefree. His fashions must be fresh and new, in tune with today. His print themes have been inspired by English and Byzantine heraldry, impressionist paintings, and ancient Greek vases.

Tseklenis enjoys water sports. He is separated from his wife and has a nine-year-old son. ∎

Valentin

Valentin spent much of his early life traveling throughout the United States with his family, which was involved in various business and civic projects. He was graduated from Howard University, where he was class president for two years and simultaneously pursued a successful modeling career. His love of fashion found its first expression in the clothes he designed for himself. This led in turn to designing for friends, especially in the entertainment world.

VALENTIN

The House of Valentin was incorporated in 1969. Valentin has designed men's and women's sportswear in real and simulated furs as well as leather outerwear for Animal World, robes, wash-and-wear shirts, and swimwear for Dal Industries, and a shoe and boot line for the Global Shoe Company. In 1970 he received a certificate of recognition from the Los Angeles Recreation Corporation for teaching grooming and fashion in the ghettos and barrios, and the city of Los Angeles appointed him fashion production designer and coordinator for the all-city Black Festival.

Valentin believes that fashion is always moving and that a designer must consistently observe, explore, and experiment, taking into consideration the many new fibers, fabrics, and other innovations. In his opinion a garment, besides being geared to today's world, should be comfortable and practical. ∎

Philippe Venet

Philippe Venet was born in 1930 in Lyon, France, where he received his education and was apprenticed for six years to the city's best men's custom tailoring house. He then moved to Paris and was fortunate to obtain a position with the couture house of Schiaparelli, where he met Hubert de Givenchy. When the latter left Schiaparelli to establish his own couture house, Venet accompanied him as head of the Givenchy workroom.

Nine years later, in 1961, he established his own business on the Rue François Premier, where it took him less than four years to make his mark in the world of fashion; by the 1970s his couture operation employed more than sixty people. In addition, Venet ready-to-wear boutiques were opened on the Avenue Georges V in Paris in 1968, at Bullock's-Wilshire, Los Angeles, and in Geneva in 1969, and in Gstaad in 1970. Perfumes, ties, shoes, and accessories are manufactured under license in the various European countries.

The least flamboyant of Paris couturiers, Venet owes his success to his knowledge of cutting and to an infallible sense of color and fabric. He has expanded his interests to include men's fashion, and Monsieur, as his men's line is called, incorporates traditional concepts as well as supple, unconstructed clothing without interlinings, collars, or lapels. The result is what Venet terms "the new classicism," an unpretentious elegance that reflects the organized mind and the realism that are his outstanding characteristics. He likes comfortable, sporty-looking town suits made of checks and plaids that are elegant and without gimmickry.

Whenever he can get away from Paris, Venet goes to his country house near Versailles, where he enjoys horseback riding. ∎

John Warden

John Warden was born on December 28, 1939, in Niagara Falls, Canada. After completing his education in Canadian schools, he studied at the Parsons School of Design in New York, where he won several awards. Following graduation he joined the Parsons European summer session and toured the fashion centers of France, England, Italy, and Germany. On his

return to New York he worked for the couture establishment of Bob Bugnand as an assistant designer. He then went to Seventh Avenue, where he designed for Sylvia de Gay, Jonny Herbert, and Arthur Jablow. While working for Robert Sloan, he met Auckie Sanft, a Montreal coat and suit manufacturer, who persuaded him to return to Canada and design a special collection for Sanft's house. While designing for Sanft, Warden won two Canadian Cotton Council Awards and a Union Label Award.

In 1965 he left Sanft to open his own boutique. At the same time, he began work on a free-lance basis with such manufacturers as the Hudson Cloak Co. (for which he won four awards), the Croydon Manufacturing Co., the Pierre Marquez of Canada and Les Tricots Dubonnet divisions of MacDonald Stewart Textiles, Alvin Duskin, and Dune Deck Swimsuits.

Warden opened a boutique for men in 1967 and combined the two boutiques into one in 1970; the store carries both his own boutique collection and his manufactured designs. He serves as fashion consultant to Rose Knitting Mills, and he is under contract to design women's coats and suits for Beverini, Inc., and a young men's collection for Bagatelle. He was responsible for the uniforms worn by the Canadian team at the 1972 Summer Olympics.

Warden believes in clean, clear fashion and thinks men should look young, classic, and masculine. Divorced and the father of a child, he enjoys water sports, painting, traveling, and cooking. ∎

H. WARMFLASH

Howard S. Warmflash

Howard S. Warmflash was literally born into the fashion business on January 21, 1929, in Newark, New Jersey; his father, Louis Warmflash, was one of the foremost designers at the time. After graduating from William Penn High School in Harrisburg, Pennsylvania, he enrolled in Lock Haven State Teachers College. He left college to join the United States Army in 1945 and served in Japan. His first job after leaving the Army was with McGregor-Doniger, Inc., in which he was advanced to the position of assistant designer in 1947. During the next ten years he designed sportswear, outerwear, and children's apparel for several manufacturers. Then, in 1958, he joined his father at Louis Warmflash Associates, Inc., and is now president of the company.

Warmflash is a member of the International Association of Clothing Designers. The diversified apparel and fabric houses for which he has designed include Robert Lewis Co., Inc., DeLong Sportswear, M. Rubin & Sons, Stanley Blacker, Eastland Woolen Mills, Windbreaker, and Midwest Outerwear Manufacturing Co. Among his design accomplishments are a walking suit, a 36-inch coat with matching slacks; a five-in-one coat, consisting of a fully lined raincoat that had, instead of a zip-in lining, a zip-in reversible ski jacket with a detachable hood; and the first complete line of fur-look pile fabric coats for men (1958). He won Caswell-Massey Awards in 1966 and 1968.

Warmflash says fashion "should be created with an eye to the masses of people, rather than exclusively for a narrow segment of the population," adding that it should therefore not only be functional, comfortable, and appealing but should be capable of being produced easily and relatively economically. Married and the father of two children, he enjoys golf, swimming, and tennis as well as working with youth groups. ∎

John Weitz

John Weitz was born on May 25, 1923, in Berlin, Germany. After the accession of Hitler, he moved with his family to England, where he was educated at the Hall School and St. Paul's School in London. He studied for five months at Oxford before deciding to apprentice himself to the couture on the Continent with, among others, the Paris designer Molyneux. Weitz served in the OSS during World War II. In 1946 he opened in New York a design house that was incorporated in 1954.

Weitz was the first "name" designer of menswear to be presented by such leading retailers as Lord & Taylor in New York, Austin Reed Ltd. in London, and Daimaru of Japan. His de-

J. WEITZ

signs are now under license to eighteen United States manufacturers including the Palm Beach Co., the Majer Co., Harbor Master Ltd., McGregor-Doniger, Towne & King, Inc., and State O'Maine. In 1972 he entered the Latin American market with a new business in Mexico.

The worldwide distribution of Weitz's fashions for men reflects the fact that the man for whom he designs has no national identification. Weitz says, "The modern male must never look as if he is of any *specific* nationality. The jet plane has wiped away all those differences. Modern clothes must be featherweight, easy to pack, wrinkleproof. They must *contour* themselves to the body without heavy interlining or darting of stiff fabrics."

Weitz has won almost every honor bestowed on designers, including the Hess Brothers Award, the Tommy Award of the American Printed Fabrics Council, and four Caswell-Massey Awards. A dedicated sportsman, he raced sports cars from 1954 to 1959. He shoots, water-skis, and sails. In 1970 he published a novel, *The Value of Nothing*. He is married to the actress Susan Kohner and has four children. ■

Kjell G. Wikestam

Kjell G. Wikestam was born on August 8, 1941, in Borgholm, Sweden, where he got his start in the fashion industry at the age of fifteen as an apprentice in his father's chain of clothing stores. This early taste of fashion convinced him of the desirabil-

ity of enrolling in the Swedish Institute of Apparel Design, from which he was graduated first in his class in 1963, winning, in addition, a scholarship for continued study abroad. Part of this study was undertaken in the United States, and it was as a member of the training staff at Filene's in Boston that he first recognized the possibilities of introducing Scandinavian fashion to the American market.

Wikestam returned to Sweden, where he established contact with the major producers of men's fashion. In 1966 he designed his first collection of men's suede and leather coats for Ericson of Sweden. The next year he formed the Swedish Fashion Group Ltd. in New York, representing Ericson and Tiger of Sweden, for both of

K. WIKESTAM

whom he designs, and Pingvin of Scandinavia. The group has grown steadily and is rated as one of the important quality fashion importers, especially in suedes and leathers that combine Continental styling with the right amount of flair for the American market.

Wikestam believes that fashion is a way of expressing one's personality and good taste—a way of living, often inspired by different moods. Although it is hard to change the average American male's conservative view of fashion, Wikestam thinks that fashion has become very important for the menswear industry.

Wikestam is married and is a tennis player and skier. For relaxation he paints. ■

Glossary

A

Aberdeen socks Coarse wool socks manufactured in Scotland in solid colors and mixtures for sportswear.

abrasion tester Mechanical device used to measure or evaluate a fabric's ability to withstand friction or surface wear.

abstract design Pattern that has certain parts of an original theme which provide the basis or inspiration for the completion of a design.

Acala Type of cotton native to Mexico; also grown in Texas, Oklahoma, and Arkansas.

accordion pleat One of a series of folds in material that resemble the folds in an accordion, used in shirts and other articles. The width of the pleat ranges from ⅛ inch upward.

Acele Brand name of Du Pont acetate.

acetate Fiber made from cellulose (obtained from wood pulp or cotton linters), acetic acid, and other chemicals.

acetate, color-sealed *See* COLOR-SEALED ACETATE.

acid dye Type of dye used for animal fibers.

Acrilan Brand name of an acrylic fiber manufactured by the Monsanto Company.

acrylic Pertaining to fiber made from acrylonitrile.

acrylonitrile Polymer resulting from the reaction of ethylene oxide and hydrocyanic acid. Brand names: Acrilan, Creslan, Orlon.

admiralty cloth Melton woolen cloth used for U.S. Navy uniforms.

African print Allover pattern printed on cotton in exotic colors of types favored by natives in various parts of Africa; adapted for sportswear and beachwear in the United States.

Agilon Trademark of a stretch nylon yarn manufactured by Deering Milliken, Inc.

aiguillette Braid or cord, sometimes in a gold color, used as a decoration on military uniforms.

air conditioning Chemical process that seals small fibers into yarn.

airing Hanging woolen clothes outdoors in order to revitalize the fibers and thereby improve wearing qualities.

air permeability Porosity of a fabric, which determines its warmth or coolness. Air permeability is therefore a gauge of the wind resistance of a given material.

airplane cloth Cotton fabric, styled for shirts and sportswear, that is derived from the fabric used on airplane wings in early aeronautical days.

ajiji Muslin type of cotton made in India, often in colorful stripes.

albert cloth Dressy overcoating of the double-cloth type, suitable for a heavyweight chesterfield.

alligator Skin of a water reptile with a squarish pattern on its surface; used for shoes, bags, luggage, etc. In 1970 the sale of alligator skins was made illegal in New York.

all-wool Term applied to any fabric made completely of wool of any kind, including reworked or reprocessed wool.

alpaca Fiber from an animal resembling a llama, used in pile fabrics for insulated coats and knitted into shell-stitch sweaters. In the 1920s and 1930s alpaca was blended with cotton for summer suitings and linings.

alpargata Slip-on footwear with a rope or hemp sole and a cloth or strap upper.

American-Egyptian cotton Type of cotton developed in Arizona and California as a result of an exchange of seeds by cotton growers in the United States and Egypt.

Anavor Filament polyester made and registered by the Dow Badische Co.

angora Fiber of the angora goat, made into a knitted or woven fabric alone or in a blend with other fibers. The name is derived from Angora (Ankara) Province, Turkey, where goats thrived.

Anguilla cotton Cotton grown on the island of Anguilla in the eighteenth century; the source of Sea Island cotton.

aniline dye General term for any synthetic organic dye.

aniline leather Leather impregnated with aniline dye, which tends to make the pattern of the grain more visible.

animal fiber Any fiber derived from animals for weaving, knitting, or felting. Examples: alpaca, angora goat, camel's hair, cashmere, coney, fur, llama, mohair, silk, vicuña, wool.

antelope Skin of an antelope, ordinarily suede-textured, used for belts, leather goods, shoes, and apparel.

anticrease finish *See* CREASE-RESISTANT FINISH.

antiquing Process of applying stain, wax, or oil to leather, allowing it to be absorbed or set, and then rubbing the leather with a cloth or brushing it. Subsequently, a light wax is applied and polished. The result is similar to a rich glow known as the bootmaker finish.

Antron Registered brand name for nylon

alpargata

that has a trilobal shape at cross section. It is manufactured by Du Pont.

apache Casual; applied to the manner of wearing an article of apparel, such as a casually tied neckerchief.

appliqué Ornamentation stitched, embroidered, or pasted to fabric.

apron Wide end of a four-in-hand tie.

Aralac Synthetic fiber derived from casein.

arctic Overshoe, extending above the ankle, with a cloth and rubber upper and a rubber sole, fastened with buckles or a zipper.

argyle Generally multicolored, knitted diamond pattern with an overplaid; used for socks, sweaters, and other articles.

Argyll Branch of the Campbell clan and the tartan representing it. The word is sometimes used interchangeably with "argyle."

Aridex Finish, made by Du Pont, that covers fibers with an invisible film and renders the treated fabric water-repellent.

Arkwright, Sir Richard Inventor of machine processes for the spinning, drawing, and carding of cotton. His plans for a mill involved the mechanical method of production and helped initiate the Industrial Revolution.

armscye (scye) Lower side of the armhole to which the sleeve of a jacket or coat is sewn. If this area fits closely, it is known as a high armscye. If it is placed low to a large armhole opening, it is called a low armscye.

armure Fabric of miniature weave with an embossed effect.

Arnel Trademark of a triacetate fiber made by the Celanese Corporation.

Art Deco Type of geometrical design in sweaters and other articles of apparel. Art Deco is an assertively modern style of art inspired and influenced by Art Nouveau, cubism, American Indian art, Russian ballet, and Bauhaus (the angular). Designs are symmetrical or rectilinear, never asymmetrical or curvilinear. The term "Art Deco" is also used to mean a revival of the 1930s.

artificial silk Early name for man-made fibers resembling silk. Silkworms extruding their filaments influenced the creation of rayon and acetate. When these man-made fibers were first extruded from the spinneret, they were known as artificial or art silk. The term was dropped after further development, and by 1935 the fibers were merchandized on their own merits and by their names.

ascot Double-knotted tie with one end draped over the other and held in place with a stickpin for formal day wear; also a single-knot scarf for casual wear. It derives its name from Ascot Heath, the English racetrack where the tie was first worn.

assili cotton Long-staple Egyptian cotton with a high tensile strength. The word *assili* means "thoroughbred."

astrakhan Fur obtained from a breed of karakul lamb; also a deep-pile fabric with curled loops that resembles it.

asymmetric Having more on one side than on the other; one-sided; off balance. Example: a shirt with button closure on the side.

athletic shirt Pullover knitted undershirt of cotton, cotton and polyester, rayon, or other fibers, with deep armholes and a low neck.

attire Clothes; a complete outfit.

aubergine *See* EGGPLANT.

Australian bush boot *See* BUSH BOOT, AUSTRALIAN.

Australian merino Breed of sheep, descended from the original Spanish breed, whose fleece is dense and uniformly high in quality.

automatic wash-and-wear Designation descriptive of a garment that may be run through the washing and spin cycles of an automatic washer, dried in an automatic dryer, and worn again with little or no pressing.

Avisco Brand name of rayon fibers made by the FMC Corporation, American Viscose Division.

Avril Brand name of rayon fibers made by the FMC Corporation, American Viscose Division.

awning stripes Bold stripes used in thick fabrics for awnings; also stripes for sportswear.

Aztran Brand name of poromeric material formerly made by the B. F. Goodrich Co.

B

baby shaker sweater *See* SHAKER SWEATER.

backed cloth Cloth with an extra weft or warp, woven or knitted on the back to obtain increased thickness, different color effects, or both.

backless waistcoat Waistcoat, usually for formal evening wear, made without a back and held in place by means of bands, fastened with a buckle or button, across the back at the waistline.

ascot

argyle

which the dye is not fast and comes out when wet.

blending Combining two or more distinctive types of fibers of different lengths to produce yarn and fabric of uniformity. Different colors brought together achieve a controlled mixture as a result of blending.

blind stitch Stitch hidden from view.

bloater Necktie with wide, flared ends, shaped somewhat like a fat herring that has been cured by salting, smoking, and drying.

block pattern Enormous square printed or woven pattern.

block printing Printing fabrics by hand with wooden blocks that have patterns of carved wood or metal.

blood Basis for standardization of the qualities of wool. The full-blooded merino sheep, the result of full-blooded merino parentage, is at the top of the scale. Other grades are quarter blood, half blood, and three-quarter blood. They now merely indicate fineness, not the parentage of the sheep. The blood system has generally been replaced by the numerical or count system.

blouse Loose-fitting shirt worn inside or outside trousers.

blouson suit Suit with a blouse type of shirt or top.

blucher Originally a military boot with an open laced front over the instep, named after General Gebhard Leberecht von Blücher, who led the Prussian Army opposing Napoleon; later a low shoe with a similar open-throat front.

blue, copenhagen *See* COPENHAGEN BLUE.

blue, Côte *See* CÔTE BLUE.

blue, ensign *See* ENSIGN BLUE.

boarding Making a false grain on leather by folding the grain in and pulling the skin back and forth under the pressure of a cork board. A box grain is thereby achieved.

boardy Descriptive of a fabric that is hard and stiff to the touch.

boater *See* SENNIT.

boat neck Horizontal opening at the top of a knitted pullover.

bobbin (spool) Cylinder of wood or other material to hold yarn during spinning or weaving.

boiled shirt Inelegant term for a stiff-bosomed dress shirt.

bold look Appearance of a complete outfit worn in 1948 and afterward. The look included neckwear with big dots, broad stripes, or strong checks, a shirt with a spread collar and seams set back ⅜ inch, massive jewelry, a hat with wide binding at the edge of the brim, positive-design socks, and bulky shoes.

boll weevil Insect that punctures and lays larvae in the bolls of cotton, doing great damage in cotton-growing areas.

bolo tie Tie of heavy braided cord fastened with a slide device.

bolt Length of fabric folded on a cardboard from which smaller lengths may be cut.

bombast Padding of cotton or other fibers used to increase the thickness of an article or to provide insulation.

bomber jacket Waist-length jacket worn by U.S. Air Force pilots, adapted for civilian purposes in leather with a sheepskin lining or in fabric with a pile fabric lining.

bonding (laminating) Causing two pieces of fabric to adhere and form a single piece by means of an adhesive or by the insertion of a layer of foam for insulation. For example, a lining may be bonded to another shell for sports outerwear. The term "bonding" also denotes a method of pressing fibers together with an adhesive to produce a nonwoven fabric.

book Thirty skeins of silk. There are thirty books to a bale.

boot Any high shoe, as distinguished from a low shoe, oxford, slipper, or pump. Depending on the height, it may have a laced or a zipper closure or no closure. Leather, poromeric materials, fabric and leather combinations, rubber, or other materials may be used.

boot, carpetbagger *See* CARPETBAGGER BOOT.

boot, cavalier *See* CAVALIER BOOT.

boot, Chelsea *See* CHELSEA BOOT.

boot, cowboy *See* COWBOY BOOT.

boot, Hessian *See* HESSIAN BOOT.

boot, hunting *See* HUNTING BOOT.

boot, jodhpur *See* JODHPUR BOOT.

boot, napoleon *See* NAPOLEON BOOT.

boot, riding *See* RIDING BOOT.

boot, ski *See* SKI BOOT.

boot, Wellington *See* WELLINGTON BOOT.

bootjack Wooden frame with a V- or U-shaped opening to hold the heel of a riding boot while it is being removed from the foot.

bootmaker Person who makes boots or shoes.

boot tree Wooden or metal form to be put inside a boot in order to keep it in shape when it is not being worn.

Borgana Trade name, registered by Borg Fabrics, of a pile fabric of 100 percent acrylic fibers for coats and liners.

bosom Part of a dress shirt that covers the chest.

bosom, pleated *See* PLEATED BOSOM.

bosom, starched (stiff) *See* STARCHED BOSOM.

botany Wool designation derived from Botany Bay, New South Wales, which had been named by Joseph Banks, botanist on Captain Cook's expedition, for the wide range of plants that grew there. Merino wool, later grown in this area of Australia, was given the name "botany" to denote the source and the excellence of its quality. Botany is also a brand name registered by Bernhard Ulmann Co.

bottle green Deep shade of green like that of certain glass bottles.

bouclé Yarn made with loose loops; also a textured fabric made from bouclé yarn (a French word, *bouclé* means "curly"). Wool, cotton, rayon, polyester, acrylic, silk, or linen fibers may be used.

boutique Small shop in which the stock consists mainly of accessories.

boutonniere Carnation, cornflower, or other flower worn on the lapel of a jacket or outercoat. Feather or other artificial flowers are also classed as boutonnieres.

bow Two or more loops of fabric or cord

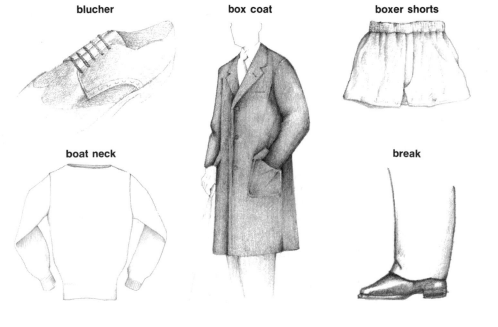

blucher

box coat

boxer shorts

boat neck

break

knotted together or fastened with a clip.

bowler *See* DERBY.

bow tie Woven fabric tie knotted with two looped ends and two straight ends.

bow tie, clip-on *See* CLIP-ON BOW TIE.

bow tie, club *See* CLUB BOW TIE.

bow tie, one-end (single-end) *See* ONE-END BOW TIE.

bow tie, thistle-shaped *See* THISTLE-SHAPED BOW TIE.

box cloth Melton type of coating woolen, usually in a heavy weight. A lighter-weight box cloth was used for spats.

box coat Straight-hanging overcoat, top-coat, or jacket with set-in sleeves. Outer-coats may have a fly or a button-through front.

boxer shorts Underwear or swim shorts with an elastic waistband, patterned after the shorts worn by prizefighters.

boxford collar Attached shirt collar in a widespread, button-down style with seams set well back from the edges.

boxing Reinforcement of leather or other material used in the tip of a shoe to hold its shape.

box-loom Loom with several shuttles used to weave fabric with more than one type of filling yarn or with a regular filling pattern.

box pleat Pleat with the folded edges facing in opposite directions, used on the pockets of shirts, jackets, and coats or in other ways.

braces *See* SUSPENDERS.

Bradford spinning English process of spinning wool into worsted yarn. Before the wool is combed, oil is applied so that the yarn will be smooth.

braid Woven, knitted, or plaited material used for a trimming or binding.

break Crease or fold across the vamp of a shoe, caused by wear; also the crease in trousers above the instep.

breeches Knee-length trousers.

breech wool *See* BRITCH WOOL.

breeks Colloquialism for breeches; also a term for trousers, implying trim lines.

briefs Knitted undershorts of minimum proportions.

bright wool Wool from sheep grown east of the Mississippi River, which is quite clean in comparison with the fleece of sheep from the Western ranges.

brilliantine Fabric in a twill or plain weave with a cotton warp and wool or mohair filling; type of lining for apparel.

brim Rim of a hat extending outward from the bottom of the crown.

britch (breech) wool Coarse wool from the hindquarters of a sheep, woven into fabrics for mackinaws and other outerwear.

British blade *See* BLADE.

British warm Double-breasted outercoat of military origin, in knee or above-knee length, with shaped body lines and a flare toward the bottom and often with epaulets. It is usually of fleece or melton cloth.

broadcloth Closely woven fabric with the rib running weftwise, made of lustrous all-cotton, polyester and cotton, all-polyester, or other fibers. It is used for shirts, undershorts, and sportswear. Wool broadcloth is a twill-back fabric with a smooth, slightly napped face.

brocade Luxurious-appearing fabric of silk, polyester, or blends, in a jacquard weave, usually with floral or other raised designs.

brogan Work shoe of ankle height with heavy pegged or nailed soles. It is not to be confused with a brogue.

brogue Historically a rough, heavy shoe of untanned leather with a thong closure, worn in the Scottish Highlands and Ire-land; more recently a wing-tip oxford shoe with perforations on the tip and border seams.

brolly British term for an umbrella.

Brummell, George Bryan, known as Beau Brummell (1778–1840) Dandy in early-nineteenth-century England; a close friend of the Prince of Wales (later George IV).

brushing (napping) Raising nap on a knitted or woven fabric by running the material through a machine with a series of wire brushes. These pull the fiber ends up to form a fuzzy surface. Gigging is a similar process.

buck Short for buckskin; also a young dandy.

bucket hat Telescope-crown hat for active and spectator sportswear, made of a cotton or blend fabric processed for water repellency.

buckle Fastener, of rectangular or other shape, that is attached to one end of a strap or belt. It has a single tooth that is slipped through a hole on the opposite end.

buckle, cinch-ring *See* CINCH-RING BUCKLE.

buckle, ring *See* RING BUCKLE.

Bucko Trade name for reversed calf.

buckram Hard-finish coarse-weave cotton, linen, or hemp used for interlining coats, other apparel, footwear, and leather goods.

buckskin (1) Soft-napped leather of deer or elk, used for gloves, shoes, and other garments; (2) a cotton fabric with a smooth surface and a napped back; (3) a heavy woolen fabric with a cropped-nap surface, used for riding breeches and overcoats.

buckthorn Tree or shrub with thorny branches that are used to make canes.

buffalo check Design of big squares or blocks, usually red and black, in fairly heavy fabrics of wool or other fibers, used for shirts or outerwear.

buffalo leather Rough-textured leather from the hide of the water or domesticated land buffalo. It is used in shoes, luggage, and miscellaneous items.

bulb toe High, rounded tip of a man's shoe.

bumbershoot Inelegant term for an umbrella.

bumpkin Awkward person; a provincial dude.

bump toe High, rounded tip of generous proportions of a shoe or boot.

buntal (buri) Fine white fiber from the leaves of the talipot palm, used for weaving into men's summer hats.

bunting Lightweight, close-woven wool or cotton fabric used for flags, banners, and sports shirts.

burgundy Deep, rich red shade suggestive of burgundy wine.

buri *See* BUNTAL.

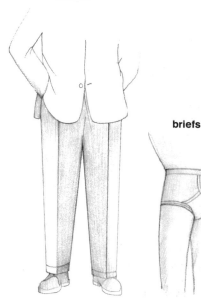

breeks

briefs

British warm

brolly

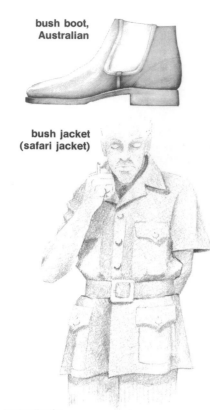

bush boot,
Australian

bush jacket
(safari jacket)

butterfly tie

button-down collar

cable stitch

caftan (kaftan)

burlap Coarse-woven, textured jute or hemp fabric used for bags and occasionally for sportswear.

burling Removing loops, knots, and vegetable matter from fabric in the finishing section of a woolen or worsted mill.

burnish To polish metal with a coarse or smooth cloth. Fabrics in colors that have a sheen like that of polished metal are said to be burnished.

burnous (burnoose) Woolen capelike cloak with a cowl, as worn by Arabs and by Moors in Africa.

burnsides Whiskers at the sides of the face, as worn originally by General Ambrose E. Burnside.

busby Tall fur cap, with or without a plume.

bush boot, Australian Above-ankle slip-on boot with a plain tip and elastic insets at the sides.

busheling Repairing or altering suits, jackets, slacks, or outercoats.

bushelman Tailor who repairs or alters apparel.

bush jacket (safari jacket) Belted, single-breasted shirt jacket with four patch pockets and flaps.

butcher linen Plain-weave crash fabric with an irregular texture, used mainly for sportswear.

butterfly tie Bow tie with flared ends, designed for a small knot. It is used primarily for formal evening wear but also for day and casual dress in a variety of fabrics.

button Flat or knoblike device of bone, horn, wood, plastic, or other material attached to one part of an article of apparel, which it fastens to another part by being slipped through a buttonhole.

button-down collar Attached shirt collar the points of which are held in place by buttoning them to the shirt.

button glove Leather or fabric glove extending to the wrist and fastened with a button and buttonhole.

buttonhole Slit through which a button may be passed to fasten a garment.

button-through Designating the closure of an outercoat or jacket in which buttons are fastened in buttonholes cut completely through the fabric and not covered with a fly.

Byrd Cloth Twill-weave cotton for rainwear and sportswear, named for Adm. Richard E. Byrd. The name is a registered trademark of Reeves Brothers, Inc.

Byron collar Flowing, long-point, low-set collar similar to one Lord Byron is supposed to have worn.

C

cabana Small individual cabin or one of an attached group at a beach. The term "cabana clothes" is used to denote casual apparel for wear at the beach.

cable stitch Overlapping knitting stitch, made by machine or by hand, that resembles a cable. It is used in sweaters and socks.

cabretta Soft leather from a sheep that has hair instead of wool; used for outerwear and footwear. Sources: South America, Africa, and India.

cadet Type of short-finger glove.

cadet cloth Official heavyweight woolen fabric of the U.S. Military Academy at West Point.

caftan (kaftan) Arab and Turkish garment with long sleeves and a sash, worn as an undercoat. In the 1970s it was adapted as a beach and patio garment for women and men.

calendering Mechanical finishing process that produces a hard, shiny fabric, sometimes with an embossed pattern.

calf, French *See* FRENCH CALF.

calf, reversed *See* REVERSED CALF.

calf, shrunken *See* SHRUNKEN CALF.

calf, wax *See* WAX CALF.

calfskin Durable, soft skin of a calf tanned and processed for use in footwear and other leather goods.

calico Plain-weave cotton cloth; also an inexpensive figured cotton.

California collar *See* BARRYMORE COLLAR.

cambric Tightly woven cotton material calendered on one side to resemble linen; also a linen fabric with a sheen, used for shirts, underwear, pajamas, handkerchiefs, and other accessories.

camel's hair Fiber from a camel, ranging in color from natural tan to brown. Used alone or blended with wool, it is made into woven or knitted material for outercoats, suits, sweaters, hose, and sportswear.

candy stripes Equal-width stripes of a color and white on fabrics used for shirts and sportswear.

cane Stem of bamboo, reed, or other plants; in men's fashion, a walking stick or staff made of such a plant or of other material.

cane, malacca *See* MALACCA CANE.

canton flannel Cotton twill with a long nap on one side; used for work gloves.

canvas Coarsely woven fabric of heavy cotton or linen used for outerwear, slacks, and other apparel.

canvas shoe Shoe with a canvas upper and, usually, a rubber sole.

cap Visored fabric headpiece with a rounded crown, cut in either eight-piece–top or one-piece–top style.

cap, Eton *See* ETON CAP.

cap, hunting *See* HUNTING CAP.

cap, one-piece–top *See* ONE-PIECE–TOP CAP.

cap, short-visor *See* SHORT-VISOR CAP.

cap, ski *See* SKI CAP.

cap, toboggan *See* TOBOGGAN CAP.

cap, yachting *See* YACHTING CAP.

cape Outer garment without sleeves but with slits at the sides for the arms.

capeskin Leather of fine grain from haired sheep, used for gloves and other articles. It derives its name from the original source, the Cape of Good Hope area.

capote Hooded coat or cloak; a military overcoat.

Caprolan Brand of nylon 6 fiber made by the Allied Chemical Corporation.

caracul Fur from the karakul lamb, characterized by its short, curly, yet flat appearance.

carat (karat) Unit of weight of precious stones; also $\frac{1}{24}$ fineness in gold.

cardigan Kind of knitting stitch; also a knitted sweater or jacket without a collar or lapels, made with or without sleeves. The cardigan was named for the 7th Earl of Cardigan, who led the charge of the Light Brigade in the Crimean War.

carding Process of preparing wool fibers for spinning. The fibers are placed automatically in proper alignment, and impurities are removed.

Carnaby Street Two-block street parallel to Regent Street, London, where many shops introduced "mod" clothing and, later, such styles as flared slacks, figured shirts, and adaptations of American Western clothes.

Carothers, Wallace H. American chemist who, with a team of Du Pont scientists, did research in chain polymers between 1928 and 1937 that resulted in the synthesis of the polyamide later named nylon. This step led to a widening world of synthetic fibers.

carpetbagger boot Boot with a leather upper and a top of tapestry design resembling carpet.

carpincho Skin of the capybara processed for use in gloves and leather goods. It has elastic qualities and is similar to pigskin.

carroting Applying a solution of mercury and nitric acid to fur fibers for felting into hat bodies.

casein Fiber derived from milk. It is blended with wool, cotton, rayon, or mohair for weaving or knitting into fabrics.

cashmere (kashmir) Fine wool from the undercoat of the long-haired Kashmir goat, which is woven or knitted into soft fabrics that are luxurious to the touch. The fabrics are used for coats, suits, sweaters, and many other articles of apparel.

cassimere Clear-faced woolen fabric in a twill weave. The diagonal effect may be combined with vertical stripes for suits, jackets, or trousers.

castor Woolen fabric for outercoats. Lighter in weight than beaver cloth, it has a heavy milled finish.

cavalier boot Ankle-high slipper with a turned-back cuff, made of soft, pliable leather.

cavalier hat Men's soft felt hat with a sharply pinched crown and a casual, floppy brim turned up all around.

cavalry twill (tricotine) Sturdy diagonal-cord fabric made of wool, worsted, cotton, rayon, or blends of fibers; used for suits, jackets, slacks, outercoats, and riding apparel.

Celanese Registered brand name for textiles and other products manufactured by the Celanese Corporation.

Celaperm Brand name, registered by the Celanese Corporation, for acetate yarn with the color sealed in the fiber.

Celcos Brand name of a combination of acetate and viscose rayon in a single fiber, controlled by the Celanese Corporation.

cellulose Substance derived from wood or cotton linters treated with chemicals to produce rayon or acetate fibers.

cellulosic Pertaining to the man-made fibers rayon and acetate, both derived from cellulose.

cement, dye-fixing *See* DYE-FIXING CEMENT.

center vent Slit in the center of the lower part of the back of a jacket or coat.

chain loom Knitting machine that turns out flat-knit fabric. The yarns are placed on needles next to each other.

chalk stripes Stripes in men's suit fabric resembling chalk lines.

challis Slightly napped fabric of lightweight worsted, spun rayon, or blends. It usually has printed figures such as a small allover design or paisley.

chambray Woven cotton, polyester, or rayon material with a colored warp and white filling; used for shirts, sportswear, and other apparel.

chamois Tanned skin from the European goat of that name or from a sheep or lamb. With the grain removed it has a suede or velvetlike surface on both sides. Mostly in yellow, it is used for gloves, jackets, or sportswear accessories.

chamois cloth Woven or knitted yellow cotton fabric with a napped surface that resembles chamois; used for gloves and sportswear.

change pocket Small pocket, with or without a flap, above the right-hand lower pocket of a jacket or coat.

chaps Leather leggings, open in back, worn by cowboys as protection against brush and thorns. The word is short for the Mexican Spanish chaparajos, or chaparejos.

Chardonnet, Count Hilaire de French chemist and physicist who studied the natural process whereby silkworms extrude filaments and in 1884 made the first nitrocellulose yarn, known as artificial silk. Progress was made thereafter

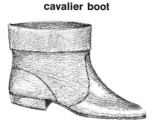
cavalier boot

chesterfield

until by 1924 artificial silk was outselling genuine silk.

Charvet (Régence) Silk fabric of the reverse rep type with a double-ridge ribbed surface, featured by Charvet et Fils; used for neckwear squares and mufflers.

check Square, either printed or woven, in white or a light shade combined with an alternating square in another color or shade. Types of checks include buffalo, district, gun-club, harlequin, houndstooth, pajama, and shepherd's.

cheese Tube of spun yarn to be put on a warp beam for weaving.

Chelsea boot Boot, extending well above the ankle, with elastic insets at the sides or a zipper closure on the inside and a higher-than-normal heel.

chesterfield Plain-back, slightly shaped overcoat, in either a single-breasted fly-front or a double-breasted style. In dark gray, blue, or black, it may have a velvet or a self-collar. The coat is named for a nineteenth-century Earl of Chesterfield.

cheviot Originally a woolen fabric of coarse texture woven of fibers from a breed of sheep grown in the Cheviot Hills, on the border of Scotland and England; now a rough fabric of wool or blends of fibers in a herringbone or twill

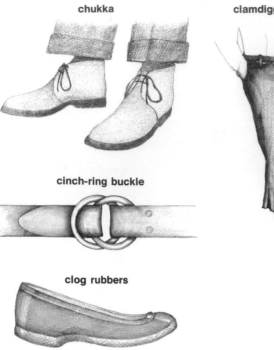

chukka

cinch-ring buckle

clog rubbers

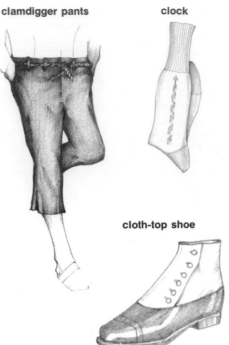

clamdigger pants

clock

cloth-top shoe

weave, used for suits, outercoats, and sportswear.

chevron weave Up-and-down–zigzag broken twill resembling a herringbone; used in suits, sportswear, and topcoats.

chinchilla cloth Long-napped tufted or nubbed fabric of wool or a blend of fibers; used for outercoats.

chin clout Term for a muffler.

chino cloth All-cotton twill used in military uniforms; also a blend of polyester and cotton used for slacks and sportswear.

chiton Short sleeveless tunic worn by the ancient Greeks, forerunner of the present shirt.

chlorinated wool Wool that has been treated chemically to minimize shrinkage and enhance penetration of dyes.

choker Muffler worn tied in a single knot, with one end draped over the other.

Chromspun Brand name, registered by Eastman Chemical Products, Inc., for acetate yarn and staple fiber for which the dyes are added to the solution before the fiber is extruded from the spinneret.

chukka Boot that extends above the ankle and fastens with a lace through two eyelets. It may be in smooth calfskin or suede with a rubber or a leather sole. The name is derived from the chukka, or chukker, a playing period in polo.

chukker shirt Open-necked knitted pullover shirt with a collar and short sleeves, worn originally by polo players.

cinch-ring buckle Double-ring fastener for a belt, similar to that used on gear for horses.

circular-knit (seamless-knit) fabric Fabric made on a hand-knit frame or knitting machine in tubular form; used for socks, sportswear, underwear, neckwear, and sweaters.

ciré Term applied to nylon, silk, and other fabrics treated with wax, heat, and pressure to give them a glossy appearance. The word means "waxed" in French.

clamdigger pants Tapered pants, in cotton, linen, or blend fabric, extending to mid-calf or halfway between knee and floor. They have 1-inch vents at the sides of the bottoms and are held up with a rope or other belt.

Clarino Poromeric material made in Japan and distributed by Marubeni-Iida, a Japanese company with New York offices.

classic Something of enduring value and interest, as in literature or apparel. In apparel a classic is characterized by simple lines or design maintained year after year.

claw hammer Name for the tailcoat.

clay worsted Worsted fabric in a weave of three-up and three-down right-hand twill; named for J. T. Clay of Rastrick, Yorkshire.

cleaning *See* DRY CLEANING; WET CLEANING.

clear-face worsted Closely woven fabric of twisted worsted yarns, with the nap removed and thoroughly scoured so that the weave is clearly visible; used for suits and outercoats.

clip-on bow tie Ready-made bow tie attached to a metal clip with side arms that snap on the sides of the collar.

clipped figures Small embroidered figures on fabric from which the floats between the figures have been clipped.

clock Knitted or embroidered vertical design on the side of a sock.

clog Slip-on shoe with a heavy sole, often of wood or cork.

clog rubbers Rubber footwear with low-cut uppers and molded design soles for good traction.

cloth *See* ADMIRALTY CLOTH; AIRPLANE CLOTH; ALBERT CLOTH; BACKED CLOTH; BALANCED CLOTH; BALLOON CLOTH; BANDOLIER CLOTH; BARK CLOTH; BEAVER CLOTH; BILLIARD CLOTH; BOX CLOTH; BYRD CLOTH; CADET CLOTH; CHAMOIS CLOTH; CHINCHILLA CLOTH; CHINO CLOTH; CONGO CLOTH; FACED CLOTH; GRANITE CLOTH; GRASS CLOTH; GRENFELL CLOTH; HARVARD CLOTH; ITALIAN CLOTH; MONK'S CLOTH; PALM BEACH CLOTH; OXFORD; POLO CLOTH; SUEDE CLOTH; UNION CLOTH; VENETIAN CLOTH; WAFFLE CLOTH; YACHT CLOTH.

clothier Retailer or, sometimes, a manufacturer of men's suits and outercoats.

cloth-top shoe High buttoned or laced shoe with black plain or patent leather on the lower part and box cloth, usually gray, on the upper part. The style was used for formal day wear in the 1920s and 1930s.

cloverleaf lapel Jacket lapel having a notch with a rounded corner that is shaped like a cloverleaf.

club bow tie Straight formal evening bow tie of medium width, with straight-cut, square, pointed, or rounded ends, so that when it is tied the knot is of generous proportions. It comes in black, midnight blue, or dark brown silk or satin for wear with a dinner jacket and white piqué for a tailcoat.

coat Outer garment with sleeves, worn for warmth. Style, fabric, and length vary with fashion.

coated fabric Material coated, impregnated, or laminated with a film-forming composition adding at least 35 percent to the weight.

coat shirt Shirt open all the way in front and slipped on like a coat.

coat sweater Knitted garment opening in front and fastened with buttons or a zipper.

coconut straw Fiber of palm fronds plaited into the body of a hat. A coconut straw hat may be of porkpie or center-crease style with a fairly broad brim.

collar Separate or attached band worn around the neck; also a narrow piece of leather stitched around the upper edge of a shoe for decorative detail.

collar-attached shirt Shirt with any style of collar, interlined, fused, or concealed-stay, sewn to the neckband.

collar button Device to fasten the collar of a man's shirt.

collar rise Vertical dimension of a collar.

collar stand Vertical dimension of a collarband in front.

color Quality of absorbing, reflecting, or transmitting light rays of red, yellow, blue, or mixtures.

Coloray Brand name of Courtaulds North America, Inc., for viscose rayon colored before the fiber is formed.

color coordination Proper relation between the colors of accessories and the basic color of a suit; in sportswear a similar association of jacket, slacks, and accessories. The colors may harmonize or contrast.

color-sealed acetate General term for acetate yarn dyed in solution by Du Pont.

combing Process of arranging fibers in parallel alignment and removing any fibers that are shorter than a determined length. The result is a smooth yarn for spinning and weaving.

Compo Brand name of a process of cementing the sole of a shoe to the upper.

cone Bobbin on which the yarn is wound before weaving.

coney See RABBIT.

Congo Cloth Brand name of an all-spun-rayon fabric registered by Brand and Oppenheimer, Inc.

congress gaiter Slip-on ankle-high shoe with elastic insets or gores at each side of the leather or cloth upper.

conquistadores Leaders of the Spanish conquest in Mexico and South America, where they encountered a cotton industry. High-quality fabrics were being woven by skilled natives in cotton and in blends of cotton and llama fibers. Sheep ranches were founded by Cortés,

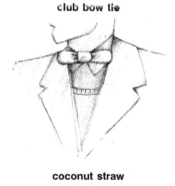

club bow tie

coconut straw

and in 1541 a flock of 5,000 sheep was taken north to the American plains.

construction Formula for making a fabric; namely, the number of warp and filling threads per square inch and the weight of the yarns.

Continental look Appearance of a suit with a short, shapely side-vented jacket and tapered cuffless trousers.

Continental system (French system) Basic method of spinning worsted yarn in which the fibers measure less than $2\frac{1}{2}$ inches and no oil is used.

contrapuntal pattern Combination of two or more patterns in a single fabric. Example: plaid design with diamond patterns in the open areas.

contrasting stitching See STITCHING, CONTRASTING.

converter Middleman who finishes, or converts, basic gray goods according to customers' orders or his own estimation of future demand.

convertible collar Collar that may be worn closed and fastened or unbuttoned and open.

coonskin Skin of a raccoon.

coordination See COLOR COORDINATION; HARMONY.

copenhagen blue (copen) Soft medium shade of grayish blue.

coral Branchlike underwater growth of various shades of pink, from light to dark. The word is used to describe colors of apparel and accessories.

cord Fabric with a raised rib effect, produced by twisting two or more yarns together.

cord, Bedford See BEDFORD CORD.

cord, Russian See RUSSIAN CORD.

cordovan Leather for footwear and other articles, made from split horsehide or from the inner hide of the horse's rump. Tanned with vegetable materials, it is nonporous. The leather is named for Córdoba, Spain, where it was first made.

corduroy Plain- or twill-weave fabric of cotton, rayon, polyester, or blends with a cut-pile surface of wide or narrow wales; used for sportswear, jackets, slacks, outercoats, and boys' apparel.

core-spun yarn Yarn with an inner fiber around which other fibers are wrapped. For example, high-stretch spandex fiber serves as the core around which acrylic fibers are spun to produce a stretch yarn for stretch fabrics.

Corfam Poromeric material originated by Du Pont. The rights now belong to Polmax-Cekop for marketing in all parts of the world except North America and Japan.

corkscrew twill Clear-face worsted of a spiral twill weave in which the filling is concealed.

Cor-Val Brand name of Courtaulds North America, Inc., for a cross-linked cellu-

losic fiber with special chemical modifications.

cossack Term applied in men's fashions to a hat, coat, boot, blouse, or other article showing the influence of clothing worn by the Russian cossack troops. It is also applied to a pajama top with a high band at the neck and a side closure.

costume Complete outfit typical of the clothes of a country or period, as worn to a costume ball.

Côte blue (Côte d'Azur blue) Light bright blue associated with sportswear worn in the south of France, on the Mediterranean coast.

cotton Soft fluffy white fibers from the seedpods of the cotton plant (*Gossypium*). The fibers are spun into yarns for weaving or knitting to produce many different kinds of fabrics. The principal sources are the United States and the U.S.S.R.

cotton, American-Egyptian See AMERICAN-EGYPTIAN COTTON.

cotton, assili See ASSILI COTTON.

cotton, Egyptian See EGYPTIAN COTTON.

cotton, long-staple See LONG-STAPLE COTTON.

cotton, mercerized See MERCERIZED COTTON.

cotton, polished See POLISHED COTTON.

cotton, upland See UPLAND COTTON.

cotton-back fabric Fabric with a wool, silk, or other face and cotton on the reverse side.

cotton covert Fabric made of single yarns with a mock twist, half white and half black or blue, to resemble wool covert; used for slacks and shirts.

cotton gin Machine that separates cottonseeds from cotton.

cotton quality The value of cotton is based partly on the length of the fibers, and the longer fibers are found in the best qualities. Among the leading long-staple types are Sea Island, Egyptian sakel, and pima.

cotton system Sequence of steps in producing cotton yarns: picking, carding, drawing, roving, and spinning.

count Number of warp and filling threads per square inch of a woven fabric; also a measure of the size and weight of yarn.

counter Piece of stiffening material or leather inserted around the back of a shoe to support the outer leather.

count system See NUMERICAL OR COUNT SYSTEM.

course One of the horizontal rows of loops in a knitted fabric or a sweater. Courses are similar to filling in a woven fabric.

court dress Formal dress consisting of a velvet tailcoat, velvet knee breeches, black silk stockings, buckled low shoes, white gloves, a cocked hat, and a small dress sword.

court tie Low men's shoe, usually of black

patent leather with a silk tie, prescribed for ceremonial court dress in England.

couturier Man who designs apparel; the head of a dressmaking establishment.

coverall One-piece garment worn by aircraft workers among others.

covert Tightly woven woolen twill fabric made with two yarns in different shades in the warp and a single color in the filling, resulting in a mixture effect; used for topcoats, sportswear, and suits. It may also be made of fibers such as polyester or spun rayon with wool or cotton. The material was first worn by hunters, and the name is derived from the word "covert" for a hiding place for game.

covert, cotton *See* COTTON COVERT.

covert, venetian *See* VENETIAN COVERT.

cowboy boot High leather boot with a high, tapered heel and, usually, an ornate upper. The high heel is designed to keep the boot from slipping in the stirrup.

cowboy hat (ten-gallon hat; Western hat) Large, wide-brimmed hat with a deep curl at the sides and a dented crown, worn by cowboys, ranchers, and others.

Cowes coat Name for a dinner jacket.

CPO shirt Civilian adaptation of a chief petty officer's shirt. Made of wool, cotton, or blended fabrics, it has an attached plain collar and chest pockets with flaps.

crash Rough-textured fabric produced by combining thick and uneven yarns in weaving. It may be of wool, cotton, rayon, polyester, linen, or blends of fibers.

cravat Term for necktie, derived from the French *cravate*. In the seventeenth century, Croatian mercenary soldiers employed by the French government wore linen scarves around their necks. Frenchwomen took up this kind of neckwear, occasionally adding lace. Men then adopted the idea, which spread to England, where the scarf was called a cravat. It was the origin of the modern necktie.

Cravenette Trademark, controlled by the Cravenette Co., U.S.A., for a water-repellent process for fabrics and articles of apparel.

crease-resistant (anticrease) finish Finish obtained by applying synthetic resin to a fabric or a finished garment and heat-setting it to make the material wrinkle-resistant.

crenellated design Design with an indented edge based on the outline of a battlement.

crepe Fabric with a crinkled surface, made of cotton, silk, polyester, wool, rayon, or blends; used in neckwear, robes, sports shirts, slacks, and other articles. The crinkled effect is obtained by using yarns twisted alternately right and left in the filling.

crepe rubber Crinkled resilient sheets of natural or man-made rubber for footwear soles and heels.

crepe stitch Irregular or crepe effect in hosiery or other knitwear achieved by the mechanical crimping of the yarn before knitting.

crepon Heavily constructed crepe-weave material.

Creslan Brand name of an acrylic fiber manufactured by the American Cyanamid Company.

cress-faced Term applied to woolen material with a slightly napped surface.

crew neck Straight collarless opening at the top of a knitted or woven pullover sweater or shirt.

crew socks Ankle-high sports or casual socks with coarse ribbing running lengthwise.

crimp Crinkled characteristic of wool fiber, the finest qualities possessing the greatest crimp; also a similar effect in man-made fibers.

Crimplene Modified high-bulk yarn of the polyester Terylene, made and registered by Imperial Chemical Industries, Ltd. A stable yarn with low stretchability, it is used in knitted fabrics.

crinoline Stiffened material used as an interlining and as a support at the edge of a hem.

crochet Material handmade or machine-knit with hooks. Of silk, polyester, nylon, wool, or blends, it is used in neckwear, sweaters, and sportswear. The word "crochet" is derived from French, in which it means "hook."

crocking Excess dye that rubs off an article of apparel in leather, material with a napped or pile surface, or other types of materials. Crocking occurs because of improper dyeing or the use of a wrong formula for a specific type of material.

crofting Soaking linen in an alkaline solution and putting the fabric in the sun to whiten it.

Crompton, Samuel English inventor of the mule frame (1779), which was based on existing spinning equipment created by Hargreaves and Arkwright.

crop Short riding or hunting whip.

crossbred wool Wool from a sheep that is the result of crossing two breeds.

cross-dyeing Process of coloring a fabric made up of two kinds of fibers, one of which takes the dye and the other resists it or is not colored by it.

crotch Part of trousers, shorts, or knickers where the legs are joined.

crushed leather Leather that shows its natural grain or has an artificial grain embossed by the boarding process.

crusher Soft, lightweight felt hat that may be rolled up or stuffed in a bag.

Cubaverra Brand name of a shirt jacket registered by Mall Marshall, Miami, Fla. Originally the style was patterned after the Guayaberra shirt jacket favored by sugar-plantation owners in pre-Castro Cuba.

cuff Band at the end of a shirt sleeve, with a button and buttonhole or with two buttonholes for cuff links, in a single or French type; also the turnup at the bottom of a trouser leg.

cuff, barrel *See* BARREL CUFF.

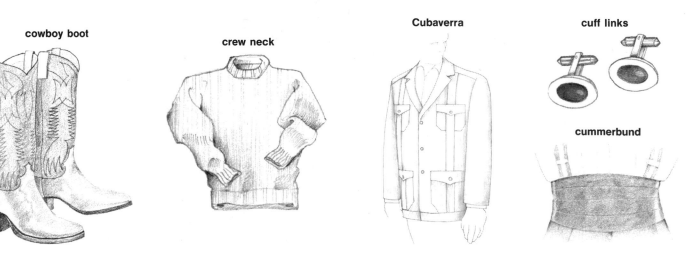

cowboy boot

crew neck

Cubaverra

cuff links

cummerbund

cuff, French (double) *See* FRENCH CUFF.

cuff, puff *See* PUFF CUFF.

cuff, single *See* SINGLE CUFF.

cuff box Receptacle for separate starched cuffs, often of leather.

cuff links Jewelry for fastening buttonless shirt cuffs.

cummerbund Waistband of solid-color or patterned silk, polyester, rayon, cotton, or other fabric made with or without pleats for wear with a dinner jacket. Originally a sash worn in India (Hindi *kamarband*), it was brought to the West by the British.

cummervest Type of cummerbund, cut with points and resembling a waistcoat, for wear with a dinner jacket.

cuprammonium process Process for making rayon from regenerated cellulose in a solution of ammoniacal copper oxide. It makes the production of fine-denier yarns possible.

curing Setting the finish of fabrics to which resins or chemicals have been added to make them resist wrinkling.

curvilinear Deviating from a straight line, as in a fabric woven on a curved line to form an arc for a specially constructed collar.

cushion-foot socks Hosiery with feet of fleece, short-pile fabric, or looped knit, made usually in styles for golf, tennis, and other sports for the comfort of the wearer.

custom-made Term applied to shoes or apparel made to conform to the measurements of an individual customer's feet or body.

cut-and-sewn Term applied to apparel cut from woven or knitted fabric and sewn to size by hand or machine.

cutaway In formal daywear, a coat having tails extending to the break of the knees in back and a one-button, single-breasted front with notched or peaked lapels. The coat is cut away on a slanting line from the waist in front to the rear. It may be black or oxford gray worsted, cheviot, or cashmere and have braided or plain edges and is worn with a matching pale gray, white, or buff waistcoat. A suit jacket or sports jacket the lower part of which is cut sharply in front also may be called a cutaway.

cut staple Any filament cut to specified and uniform lengths.

cut velvet Short-pile or looped fabric that has been cut with an allover design.

D

Dacron Brand name of polyester fibers manufactured by Du Pont. They are woven or knitted into fabrics, either alone or with other fibers, and made into a wide range of men's apparel.

Dancool Registered brand of Dan River Mills, Inc., for a permanent-press fabric of 50 percent cotton and 50 percent polyester, made in checks and plaids for sportswear.

Danel Brand name of a yarn-dyed durable-press fabric of 50 percent cotton and 50 percent polyester, registered by Dan River Mills, Inc.

Dantwill Registered trademark of Dan River Mills, Inc., for piece-dyed durable-press fabrics of 50 percent cotton and 50 percent polyester.

dart Tuck, usually at the waist of a jacket or coat, taken in to fit the garment to the body.

Dartmoor Sturdy breed of sheep grown in the Devonshire moorlands.

Darvan Trademark of a man-made fiber registered by the Celanese Corporation.

decating (decatizing) Process of finishing fabric by sponging or steaming it on rollers to set the width and length as well as to achieve smoothness.

deerskin Skin of a female deer or antelope, usually in white or natural shades but sometimes in colors.

deerstalker Hat, made of woolen tweed or other cloth, with a visor in front and in back and, usually, with earflaps outside and tied on top.

degumming Eliminating a gluelike substance, sericin, from silk with a solution of soap. The greater the amount of sericin removed, the higher the quality of the silk.

Delaine Breed of sheep, grown in Ohio, Pennsylvania, and Midwestern states, that produces high-grade wool regarded as the best in the United States for worsted fabrics. Originated in 1819 in New Harmony, Indiana, it derived its name from the French words for "of wool."

demibosom Short, starched plain or pleated bosom of a shirt. Designed primarily for formal and semiformal day wear, the demibosom shirt may also be worn with a business suit.

denier Measurement unit of silk, rayon, polyester, nylon, or acrylic yarn based on the fineness of yarn weighing 0.05 gram per 450 meters. The smaller the denier, the finer the yarn.

denim Sturdy twill-weave fabric, in cotton or a blend of fibers, with a solid-colored warp and a white filling. It may be blue, brown, red, or another color with white. The surface is smooth or brushed to achieve a suedelike finish. Denim was first made about 200 years ago in Nîmes, France, and its name is a corruption of "de Nîmes."

dents *See* REED.

derby (bowler) Hard-finish felt hat with a rounded crown and a stiff, curled-edge brim.

It derives its name from the Derby, a

deerstalker

demibosom

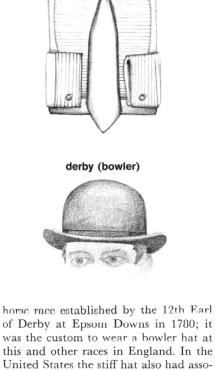

derby (bowler)

horse race established by the 12th Earl of Derby at Epsom Downs in 1780; it was the custom to wear a bowler hat at this and other races in England. In the United States the stiff hat also had associations with horse races, particularly the Kentucky Derby.

developed dyeing Method of dyeing to make a fabric more resistant to sunlight and washing or, with direct dye, to change the shade of a color.

diagonal weave Steep twill weave with noticeable lines that appears in many fabrics, such as woolen tweed, worsted, rayon, polyester, cotton, and blends.

diamond Design with four sides of equal width and two obtuse and two acute angles on opposite corners.

dickey Detached shirt front, sometimes with an attached collar.

dimensional stability Shape-retaining quality of material in a garment that is worn and washed in a normal manner.

dinner jacket Evening jacket for semiformal or formal occasions. It may be single- or double-breasted, in black, white, or colored fabric, with lustrous facing on peaked lapels or a shawl collar. The jacket is worn with matching or black dress trousers.

dip-dyeing Method of dyeing socks, sweaters, or other articles after they have been knitted.

direct dye Dye for coloring a fiber or fabric without a fixing agent. Coal-tar colors are usually direct dyes.

discharge printing Imprinting a pattern on a previously dyed fabric with bleaching chemicals. The chemicals remove the dye, thus creating the pattern.

dishrag shirt Pullover shirt, for sports and beach wear, in a coarse-yarn cotton of open weave similar to a dishrag.

district check Pattern for woolen and other fabrics created by crossing vertical and horizontal stripes in colors and arrangements originally associated with various districts in Scotland. Clothes made of such fabrics were worn by foresters, gamekeepers, and others employed around a manor house.

djellaba See JELLABA.

dobby loom Loom with special attachments that make it possible to weave small allover designs, dots, and stripes in raised woven or self-color effects. It is possible to weave thirty different shapes of designs, including bird's-eye worsted.

doeskin Suede side of the skin of a doe, lamb, or sheep, used for gloves and other leather goods; also a closely woven woolen worsted fabric with a slightly napped surface, used for slacks and sportswear, and a similar fabric in other fibers.

doffer Textile worker who removes bobbins by machine or by hand.

doffing Removing fibers from a cotton carding machine by means of a cylinder or bar with teeth.

dolman sleeve Full-cut sleeve with great width at the armhole.

Donegal tweed Woolen tweed originally woven by crofters in County Donegal, Ireland. Characteristic of the fabrics are colorful nubs. Now machine-made as well, Donegal tweed is used for suits, sportswear, and outercoats.

Dongola process Process of tanning goatskin, calfskin, or sheepskin to resemble kid. It is named for a region of the Sudan.

dope dyeing See SOLUTION DYEING.

dotted swiss Sheer cotton fabric with woven dots made by a lappet attachment.

double-breasted Term applied to a jacket, waistcoat, or outercoat in which the fabric overlaps by a few inches in front. There are two vertical rows of buttons and a single row of buttonholes with, usually, a single button on the underside

to secure the fabric on other side.

double cloth Overcoat material composed of two fabrics joined together with a binder yarn. One side may be plaid, and the other a solid-color diagonal weave. Either side may be used as the face.

double cuff See FRENCH CUFF.

double knit Double-faced material firmly knitted with a solid color on both sides or a special pattern on one side. All-wool, polyester, cotton, or acrylic fibers or blends of fibers may be utilized.

double-soled Term applied to a shoe or boot with extra thickness in the sole.

doublet Close-fitting garment resembling a jacket.

doubling Combining two or more rope-like cotton slivers into one after they have been fed into a machine; also combining an S-twist yarn with a Z-twist yarn to produce a double yarn with torque eliminated.

drafting See DRAWING.

drape Manner in which the fabric of a garment hangs from the shoulders or waistline. The word is derived from the French *drap*, meaning "cloth." In England a draper originally was a maker of cloth; now he is one who sells fabrics and other goods.

drape, English See ENGLISH DRAPE.

Draper, Ira American inventor of the loom temple and improved fly-shuttle handloom, in 1816.

drawers Undergarment, in a woven or knitted material, designed like trousers or shorts.

drawing (drafting) Combining several ropes or slivers of textile fibers into one, following carding or combing.

drawn grain Finish of leather the grain of which is shrunken or noticeably wrinkled.

drawstring Cord of braided material drawn through the hem at the waistline of pajama pants or other trousers or of golf or ski parkas for adjustment to a desired fit.

dressing gown See ROBE.

dress shirt Neckband shirt with a plain or starched piqué bosom and single or double cuffs for wear with formal day or evening clothes; also a collar-attached shirt for wear with business clothes or with a dinner jacket. The shirt worn with a dinner jacket may have a pleated bosom with or without embroidered details.

dress shoe Originally, a shoe appropriate for wear with formal clothes; more recently, a shoe for daily business wear as distinguished from a sports, casual, or work shoe.

drill Material with a twill weave extending upward toward the left selvage, made of all-cotton, cotton and polyester

or rayon, or all man-made fibers.

drip-dry Term applied to a fabric from which water or moisture will dry quickly without wringing, spinning, or squeezing the garment.

drop stitch Open design in a knitted fabric, created by omitting a needle and thereby dropping a stitch as the machine rotates.

dry cleaning Process of cleaning materials or garments that may not be laundered. To take out spots and dirt, the articles are placed in an organic solution such as carbon tetrachloride.

dry goods (soft goods) Fabric offered to the consumer by the yard through retail channels formerly known as dry goods stores; generally, textile products as distinguished from hardware and the like.

duck Plain, closely woven fabric resembling lightweight canvas, used for slacks, sportswear, and work clothes. Duck is usually made of cotton, but blends of cotton and polyester or rayon may also be employed.

duckbill Term describing the squared tip of a shoe.

duffle coat Three-quarter–length loose-fitting coat with a hood, fastened with

dinner jacket

duckbill

dolman sleeve

duffle coat

loops and toggles of wood or horn. This style, in a heavy woolen fabric and known as a convoy coat, was worn by British sailors in World War II.

Duke of Kent collar Separate starched or soft attached collar having medium-length points with a moderate spread between them, as worn by the Duke of Kent in the 1930s.

dummy Display fixture for draping suits, coats, jackets, and accessories; also a form of wood and fabric shaped like the upper portion of the human body.

dungaree Coarse twill cotton, originally made in Bombay and taken up for wear aboard ship by sailors in the eighteenth century. The word "dungarees" now refers to a pair of work slacks or jeans in blue denim.

dupion Double silk fiber from two cocoons nested together. Irregular and thick, it is used in shantung-type fabrics for which coarse, nubby yarns are desired.

durable-press (permanent-press) Term applied to a fabric or garment processed and heat-set so that a well-pressed appearance remains after washing, making ironing unnecessary for the retention of pleats.

Durene Brand name of combed cotton plied and mercerized according to standards defined by the Durene Association of America.

duster Lightweight outercoat worn in the early days of the automobile.

dye See ACID DYE; ANILINE DYE; BASIC DYE; DIRECT DYE; FLUORESCENT DYE; UNION DYE; VAT DYE.

dyed-in-the-wool (wool-dyed) Dyed in the fiber stage, when chemical solutions can penetrate the wool completely.

dye-fixing cement Chemical that reacts with dye and fibers to minimize the effect of water or washing on colorfastness.

dyeing Applying chemicals to fibers or fabrics to color them in a controlled or desired manner.

dyeing, dip- See DIP-DYEING.

dyeing, dope See SOLUTION DYEING.

dyeing, resist- See RESIST-DYEING.

dyeing, skein See SKEIN DYEING.

dyeing, solution See SOLUTION DYEING.

dyeing, tie See TIE-AND-DYE.

Dynacurl Fabric with an appearance similar to Persian lamb, developed by the Dynel Division of the Union Carbide Corporation and the Multiplex Products Corporation.

Dynel Registered brand name of fiber manufactured by the Union Carbide Corporation. It is derived from acrylonitrile and vinyl chloride.

E

earmuff One of a pair of coverings for the ears, attached to either end of a metal spring or band, to keep the ears warm in cold weather.

Eastman 50 acetate fiber Acetate fiber made by Eastman Chemical Products, Inc., in Chromspun and Estron.

easy suit Suit of casual appearance, consisting of a straight-hanging jacket with little or no inner construction and matching trousers.

ebon (ebony) Black, like the color of ebony wood.

ecru Beige or pale tan shade of unbleached silk or linen.

Edwardian Descriptive of fashions favored by King Edward VII (r. 1901–1910); also of subsequent fashions based on the originals, such as long jackets and drainpipe pants.

eggplant (aubergine) Purple shade of the vegetable.

eggshell Off-white shade of an eggshell, used to describe this tone in accessories.

Egyptian cotton Cotton grown in Egypt, a designation that implies long staple and high quality. Since many varieties of cotton are grown in Egypt, however, there are many different qualities of Egyptian fiber.

Eisenhower jacket Waist-length jacket of olive-drab wool worn by Gen. Dwight D. Eisenhower and others in military service in World War II. Later, various versions of this style were adapted for civilian wear.

elastic cord belt See BELT.

elasticity See RESILIENCE.

elastique See WHIPCORD.

elastomeric Term applied to a fiber the elasticity of which depends entirely on its molecular construction. Rubber, natural and synthetic, is elastomeric.

elk Soft, chrome-tanned calfskin smoked to resemble real elk.

ell Unit of measure for cloth formerly used, equal to 45 inches.

elysian Overcoat material in which the nap is laid on diagonal lines in a wavy effect.

embossed leather Leather treated with heat and pressure in a hydraulic press to give it a grained look.

embroidery Art of ornamentation with needlework on fabric, leather, or other material.

embroidery, schiffli See SCHIFFLI EMBROIDERY.

end See WARP.

end, head See HEAD END.

end, mill See MILL END.

end-and-end (end-to-end) Term applied to a weave of alternating white and colored warp yarns that form a minuscule check effect; used in chambray, broadcloth, and oxfords for shirts, pajamas, underwear, and sportswear.

English drape (English lounge) Style of men's single- or double-breasted jackets and outercoats with fullness across the chest to form vertical wrinkles and extra fullness over the shoulder blades.

Enka Brand name for viscose rayon made by the American Enka Corporation.

ensemble Total costume or outfit composed of articles related in color, design, and fabric.

ensign blue Dark navy blue, associated with the color of an ensign's uniform.

epaulet Strap or ornament stitched to or buttoned on the shoulder of a garment, used originally on military uniforms and later on rainwear, jackets, and sports shirts.

epicene fashion Fashion favored by both men and women.

espadrille Sandal with a canvas upper and a rope sole for beachwear. It was originally worn by dockworkers in France and Spain.

Estron Brand name for acetate yarn and staple fiber made by Eastman Chemical Products, Inc.

elastic cord belt

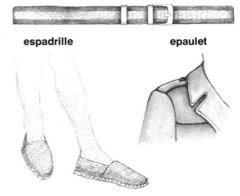

espadrille   **epaulet**

etamine Loosely woven cotton material of lightweight yet coarse texture.

étoile Star-shaped design. The word means "star" in French.

Eton cap Short-visored, close-fitting cap originally worn by boys at Eton College.

Eton jacket Waist-length jacket with lapels, used mainly for boys' clothing.

everett Men's slipper, high in front and low in back, for wear at home.

executive hat Soft felt hat with a full crown and a wide brim, finished with binding showing $\frac{1}{8}$ inch on the upper side of the brim and $\frac{3}{8}$ inch on the underside. Its appearance is allied with the bold look.

extrusion process Producing synthetic fibers by forcing a syruplike liquid through the tiny holes of a spinneret. The continuous hairlike filaments are then hardened by passing them through a chemical solution.

eyelet Small hole or perforation made to receive a lace or tape, as in a shoe or in certain styles of sportswear.

F

fabric Any textile material, whether woven, knitted, crocheted, or felted.

fabric, bareface *See* BAREFACE FABRIC.

fabric, circular-knit *See* CIRCULAR-KNIT FABRIC.

fabric, coated *See* COATED FABRIC.

fabric, cotton-back *See* COTTON-BACK FABRIC.

fabric, flat-knit *See* FLAT-KNIT FABRIC.

fabric, high-count *See* HIGH-COUNT FABRIC.

fabric, imported *See* IMPORTED FABRIC.

fabric, impregnated *See* IMPREGNATED FABRIC.

fabric, knitted pile *See* KNITTED PILE FABRIC.

fabric, multiple *See* MULTIPLE FABRIC.

fabric, processed *See* PROCESSED FABRIC.

fabric, rubberized *See* RUBBERIZED FABRIC.

fabric, Sanitized *See* SANITIZED FABRIC.

fabric, seamless-knit *See* CIRCULAR-KNIT FABRIC.

fabric, stretch woven *See* STRETCH WOVEN FABRIC.

fabric, tubular *See* TUBULAR FABRIC.

fabric care Since dust is destructive to fabrics, clothes should be brushed regularly. Food stains and perspiration weaken fabrics, and apparel should therefore be dry-cleaned or washed frequently. When not in use, garments should be stored in plastic bags.

fabric weight Number of ounces per square yard of a fabric. Summer suiting, for example, weighs 9 ounces per square yard; tweed for a sports jacket, 14 ounces; material for a coat, 19 to 22 ounces.

face Better-looking side of a fabric, usually the one on the outside of a garment.

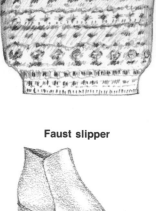

Fair Isle sweater

Faust slipper

faced cloth Fabric woven with the warp or filling on the back side of the material.

facing Lining or covering at the edge or other part of a garment. Example: covering of the lapel of a dinner jacket.

fad Custom, craze, or short-lived fashion.

faille Rib-weave fabric with a cord effect, achieved by using heavier yarns in the filling than in the warp. Of silk, cotton, polyester, or rayon, it is used for lapel facings on formal evening clothes, other trimmings, and neckwear.

Fair Isle sweater Sweater of allover colorful design, originally hand-knitted on Fair Isle, off the coast of Scotland. Crofters on the island knitted scarfs, socks, and sweaters in multicolor allover and cross patterns.

fake fur Woven or knitted pile fabric that simulates the fur of an animal; used for outercoats, jackets, and sportswear. It may be dry-cleaned.

false twist (memory twist) Method of imparting stretch characteristics to specific synthetic yarns. The yarns are wound under heat, and the twist is removed in a continuous operation. The tendency of the yarns is to retain the twist, and fabrics woven from them have elasticity.

fancy-back Term descriptive of material the back of which is distinctly different from the face, as in a plaid-back overcoating; also of a jacket having a stitched-on belt in back with or without a gusset or inverted pleats.

fashion Pattern, color, shape, or model of clothes and accessories in use at a specific time.

fashioned Shaped, made, or created for wear.

Fashion Institute of Technology Public institution under the State University of New York and the Board of Education of the City of New York. It offers courses in apparel, interior, and textile design and fashion illustration as well as two-year courses in advertising display, illustration and photography, and textile and apparel marketing.

fashion marks Small indentations around the collar and shoulders of a garment, showing that it was knitted in one piece and then stitched; also the marks showing where stitches have been added in full-fashioned hosiery and other knitted articles.

fast Term applied to a color that retains its original shade after exposure to sunlight, water, bleaching, pressing, heat, etc.

fastener Metal or plastic device that holds two parts together, such as a slide fastener or a snap fastener.

Faust slipper Soft-soled house shoe of the boot type, with adjustable openings at the sides.

fearnought Cheviot type of heavyweight overcoat fabric with a shaggy finish, utilizing reworked fibers.

fedora Men's soft felt hat with a center crease and a rolled brim. It takes its name from the drama *Fédora* (1882), by Victorien Sardou.

felt Material produced by matting moistened and steamed fibers with heat and pressure. Shellac is added for certain hat felts and other stiff felts. Rabbit or coney fur, wool, hair, cotton, or blends of fibers may be used.

fez Cone-shaped cap without a brim, as worn in the Middle East.

fiber Single strand or filament, either natural or man-made, used in combination with others for matting or bonding into a nonwoven material or for spinning into yarn, which is then woven or knitted into materials.

fiber, animal *See* ANIMAL FIBER.

fiber, hair *See* SPECIALTY FIBER.

fiber, polyamide *See* POLYAMIDE FIBER.

fiber, protein *See* PROTEIN FIBER.

fiber, soybean *See* SOYBEAN FIBER.

fiber, specialty *See* SPECIALTY FIBER.

fiber, vegetable *See* VEGETABLE FIBER.

fiber, zein *See* ZEIN FIBER.

Fiberglas Trademark of glass textile fibers, used in making yarn for weaving into strong fireproof fabrics.

fiber length For wool or cotton, fibers of greatest length produce strong, smooth, clear-finish fabrics. Short fibers result in fuzzy-surface fabrics of less strength.

Fibro Registered name of a viscose rayon

fiber manufactured by Courtaulds North America, Inc.

Fibro, matt *See* MATT FIBRO.

figures, clipped *See* CLIPPED FIGURES.

filament Continuous rayon, acetate, nylon, or polyester fiber produced by the extrusion process. The silk fiber is formed of two similar filaments, but other natural fibers such as cotton and wool are of limited length.

filling (pick; weft; woof) In weaving, the yarn running at right angles to the lengthwise, or warp, yarn. The word "filling" is also used to designate chemicals added to fill in the spaces between yarns in order to increase the weight of a fabric.

findings General term for articles needed in the manufacture, trimming, or care of shoes, including arch supports, heel plates, insoles, buckles, and laces.

fine Term applied to grades of wool such as 64s, 70s, and 80s.

fingertip length Length of a coat that extends to the tips of the fingers, or midway between the hips and the knees.

finish *See* HARD FINISH; MAT FINISH; MILL FINISH; POSTCURE FINISH; PRECURE FINISH; RESIN FINISH.

finishing Treating a fabric by covering the surface to improve its appearance or by bleaching, dyeing, printing, or waterproofing it.

fireproofing Processing a fabric to make it resistant to fire. In one method, the cloth is steeped in a heated solution of sulphate of ammonia, boric acid, borax, starch, and water, then squeezed and dried.

Fisherman knit Trade name registered by Camp & McInnes, Inc.

fishnet Wide open mesh in cotton or blends of fibers, resembling a net used by fishermen.

fixing Making a color permanent by applying heat, steam, or chemicals to a fabric.

flameproof Term applied to a fabric that has been processed to be resistant to fire and not sustain combustion.

flannel Loosely woven fabric with a napped surface to conceal the weave, made mainly of wool in men's apparel but also in blends of wool with polyester, rayon, cotton, or other fibers. The word is probably derived from the Welsh *gwlanen*.

flannel, canton *See* CANTON FLANNEL.

flannel, outing *See* OUTING FLANNEL.

flap, gun *See* GUN FLAP.

flared slacks *See* SLACKS, FLARED.

flat-knit fabric Fabric made on a flat knitting machine rather than a circular knitting machine. It has vertical rows on the face and a crosswise effect on the back.

flax Plant that yields fibers from the stem by retting; the source of linen.

flight jacket

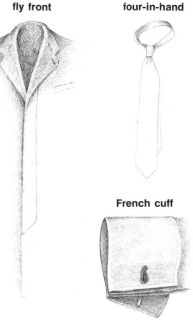

fly front **four-in-hand**

French cuff

fleck Mark or dot in a fabric, placed regularly or irregularly.

fleece (1) Lamb's wool clipped when lamb is eight months old; (2) hide tanned with the wool on it; (3) all the wool sheared at one time from an adult sheep; (4) woolen material with a napped fuzzy surface, used mainly in outercoats.

flight jacket Waist-length jacket of leather or other material with a sheepskin lining and trimming, fastened with a slide fastener or with buttons.

float stitch Knitting stitch in which a needle in a weft position passes a carrier of yarn without forming a loop. The yarn therefore floats in tension across the back of the material.

flocking Design or surface finish created by spraying short fibers so that they adhere electrostatically to a fabric, leather, or other material.

floss, silk *See* SILK FLOSS.

fluorescent dye Dye that intensifies colors and adds to the brilliance of a fabric because it reflects more light than a conventional dye.

fly front Closure in which a placket or a piece of fabric covers the buttons or zipper; used in outercoats, sportswear, and trousers.

fob Chain or ribbon hanging from a pocket watch, connecting it with an ornament.

fold collar Attached or separate double collar worn turned down.

footwear Outer covering for the feet, such as shoes, boots, galoshes, rubbers, and slippers.

formal Term applied to clothes and accessories for wear on full-dress occasions: tailcoat or dinner jacket for evening; cutaway coat or oxford jacket with striped trousers for daytime ceremonies.

Fortisan Registered brand name of cellulose acetate made by the Celanese Corporation.

Fortrel Trade name of a polyester fiber manufactured by the Celanese Corporation.

forward collar Low-set collar attached to the shirt with stitching $\frac{1}{2}$ inch from the edge.

foulard Lightweight silk or rayon twill fabric with small printed designs; used for neckwear, robes, squares, and mufflers.

four-in-hand Neckwear knot, tied by wrapping the apron, or wider end, of a tie around the other end, drawing it under and then through the loop formed, and tightening and sliding it into place. The name is derived indirectly from the four-in-hand coach. The driver of a coach drawn by four horses, in two teams in tandem, held the lines of all four horses in one hand. Such a driver wore a slipknot tie, which became known as the four-in-hand.

foxing Leather used in the lower part of the quarter, or back portion, of the upper of a shoe.

French-back serge Double-faced material with a twill weave on the front and a satin weave on the back; used for suits.

French calf Firm calf leather waxed to give it a smooth, dull gloss, used in shoes of fine quality.

French cuff Turned-back or double cuff of a shirt, fastened with cuff links, for wear with a dinner jacket or for business.

French-felled seam Seam made by stitching edges together on the right side, trimming close to the stitching, then turning to the wrong side, and stitching

frog

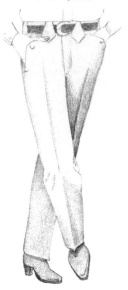

frontier pants

again to conceal the edges.

French system *See* CONTINENTAL SYSTEM.

French tip Finish of the end of a necktie in which the fabric is turned over to form a point on the right side and a pocket on the opposite side.

friar's cloth *See* MONK'S CLOTH.

frieze Heavy, fuzzy woolen overcoating weighing from 22 to 30 ounces per yard. A double cloth of twill weave, it is also made in blends of fibers.

frock coat Double- or single-breasted coat extending to the knees, usually of black or dark gray worsted. It has plain peaked lapels, often partially or entirely covered with silk facing.

frock suit *See* WALKING FROCK SUIT.

frog Looped braid fastening used on pajamas and other garments.

frontier pants Close-fitting pants cut along tapered lines, as worn by Western ranchmen and cowboys.

fugitive Term applied to a color that runs or fades readily.

fuji Smooth fabric with a lustrous finish made in viscose and acetate yarns.

full-fashioned Term applied to a flat-knit process in which the number of stitches is increased or decreased so that the desired shape may be achieved when the fabric is sewn into a garment. The process is used for sweaters, underwear, socks, sports shirts, and other sportswear.

fulling Finishing woolen material by dampening the fabric, then beating it under heat to make the weave less visible.

fur Hairy coat of certain animals, consisting of leather, soft underfur, and longer outer fur, cured and tanned for use in garments.

fur, fake *See* FAKE FUR.

fused collar Collar stiffened to hold its shape and minimize wrinkles by the insertion of an interlining containing acetate threads, which enable the outer fabrics to be laminated by heat and pressure.

fustian Fabric of cotton and linen.

G

gabardine Steep twill fabric of wool, polyester, rayon, cotton, or blends of fibers, closely woven of single- or two-ply yarn. It is made in solid or iridescent colors for suits, jackets, slacks. outercoats, and sportswear.

gaberdine Long garment or smock worn in medieval times.

gaiter Fabric covering for the ankle and lower leg with a button closure on the outer side and a strap and buckle beneath the shank of the shoe; also an overshoe with a rubber sole and a buckle or zipper closure.

gaiter, congress *See* CONGRESS GAITER.

Galashiels Burgh in Scotland where many of the tweeds of this name are woven.

galatea Husky cotton twill fabric in solid colors or prints; used for sportswear, beachwear, and uniforms.

galluses Name formerly applied to suspenders.

galosh Overshoe of rubber or rubberized fabric with a rubber sole, closed in front by a zipper or buckles.

garment Any article of apparel worn to cover the body or any piece of clothing designed to be becoming to the wearer.

garnetting Method of getting fibers from hard-twisted wastes and rags for reuse.

gassing *See* SINGEING.

gaucho hat High-crowned, broad-brimmed hat, as worn by the gauchos of South America.

gaucho shirt Pullover sports shirt in a knitted or woven fabric with a closure of four loops and buttons and an attached collar. It was popular in the 1930s.

gauge Unit of measurement of knitted fabric, referring to the number of knitting needles in $1\frac{1}{2}$ inches of the knitting bar of certain types of machines. Gauge determines the thickness or fineness of knitted fabric.

gauntlet Long glove flared from the wrist to a point in the forearm.

gear Apparel or clothing.

geometric design Pattern based on such shapes as triangles, hexagons, rectangles, and circles.

ghillie *See* GILLIE.

gigging Producing a nap on a fabric by passing it across rollers equipped with teasels. Brushing is a similar process.

gillie (ghillie) Shoe without a tongue, laced across the instep; also a servant or guide in Scotland.

gimp Strip of twisted threads of silk, wool, cotton, or other materials augmented with a cord or wire, used as a trim; also a stomacher or a neckerchief.

gin *See* COTTON GIN.

gingham Plain-weave cotton material in checked or striped patterns or plain colors. Blends of cotton and polyester or other fibers may also be used. The word is derived from the Malayan *genggang,* which became the French *guingan.*

gladstone bag Hand luggage in leather, fabric, or other materials with flexible sides. It is named for William Ewart Gladstone.

glaze To apply a thin coat of material in order to give an article a glossy finish.

glengarry Scottish cap; also a cape coat. In addition, the name Glengarry is given to a kind of British homespun or tweed.

glenurquhart (glen plaid) Scottish tartan of predominantly gray, blue, brown, or greenish casts with multiple colors, in which a group of stripes run vertically and horizontally to form a boxlike pat-

gaiter

galosh

gauntlet

gaucho shirt

guards coat

tern plus an overplaid. Made of various fabrics, including wool, worsted, cotton, polyester, linen, silk, and blends, it is used for apparel and accessories.

glove Covering for the hand in leather or fabric and in a great variety of styles.

glove, button *See* BUTTON GLOVE.

glove, string knit *See* STRING KNIT GLOVE.

goatskin Textured-grain leather from the hide of a goat; used for gloves and leather goods.

gob hat Small shaped hat in white with a narrow band.

golf hose Hose of knee length for wear with knickers or of a shorter length for wear with slacks.

gore shoe Shoe or slipper with elastic insets either at the sides or in front over the instep.

gorge Line where the collar and lapel meet.

goring Elasticized knitted or woven fabric used for insets at the sides of boots or shoes or at the instep of shoes.

gossamer Very thin and sheer fabric such as voile.

grades of men's clothing Categories that range from X through 1, 2, 4 to 6 and 6 plus, depending on the method of tailoring or technique of manufacture.

grain *See* DRAWN GRAIN; PEBBLE GRAIN; SCOTCH GRAIN.

grained leather Leather with a patterned surface, produced by printing, emboss-

ing, or boarding; used for footwear and leather goods.

grandrelle yarn Yarn formed by twisting two contrasting single yarns together, thereby achieving a blended or mixed color effect. It is used mainly in shirtings but also in suitings.

granite cloth Hard-finish material with an irregular pebbled surface, made by weaving tightly twisted yarns of wool or blended fibers.

granite gray Darkish shade of gray suggestive of granite.

grass cloth Loosely woven fabric made in the Far East, often by hand, of vegetable fibers such as ramie or jute. It is used for shirts and sportswear.

gray, granite *See* GRANITE GRAY.

gray (greige) goods Fabric as it comes from the loom before dry or wet finishing. Dry finishing processes may involve sewing, pressing, and mending. Wet finishing includes singeing, dyeing, printing, bleaching, shrinking, and waterproofing.

gray top hat Stiff gray felt hat with a flat-topped, slightly belled crown, a narrow brim, and a dull black band; for wear with formal day clothes.

greatcoat Bulky, heavy overcoat.

Grecian stripes Figured stripes with a Greek fret or similar design, spaced well apart; used as a neckwear pattern.

green, bottle *See* BOTTLE GREEN.

green, hunter *See* HUNTER GREEN.

greige goods *See* GRAY GOODS.

grenadine Fabric with a gauzelike quality made on a jacquard loom with threads crossing from side to side. Figured grenadine is produced by using a closer weave in controlled areas.

Grenfell cloth Closely woven water- and wind-repellent twill-weave cotton, originally used by Sir Wilfred Grenfell and members of his expeditions to Labrador; employed for skiwear and other sportswear.

grommet Eyelet of metal or other material inserted in fabric to provide aeration, to serve as a bushing for cord passed through the fabric, or to form a decoration.

grosgrain Material of silk, rayon, or other fibers with a cotton filling to produce a ribbed effect. It is usually made in a dull finish for trimming on formal evening clothes, neckwear, and accessories.

guanaco Andean mammal of the genus *Lama*. Only the fibers of young guanacos are used for textiles.

guards coat Civilian overcoat patterned after the coat worn by the Grenadier Guards in England. It is a dark-color double-breasted coat with a half belt, an inverted pleat extending from between the shoulder blades to the hem, and deep folds at the sides.

Guayaberra shirt Shirt jacket with a buttoned front and four pockets; originally worn by sugar planters in pre-Castro Cuba.

gummies Casual shoes with thick crepe-rubber soles.

gum twill Name sometimes applied to foulard.

gun-club check Even check pattern with rows of alternating colors and, usually, a white background; for flannel, worsted, cheviot, and tweed.

gun flap Originally an extra piece of fabric at the shoulder of a military trench coat for reinforcement against the stock of a rifle.

gunmetal Deep gray shade similar to the color of the steel of the barrel of a gun; used as a description of the color of fabric or leather.

gusset Piece of fabric, leather, or other material inserted at the seam of a garment to allow extra fullness for easy movement and to serve as a reinforcement.

H

haberdasher Merchant dealing in men's accessories such as shirts, ties, and socks.

hacking jacket Jacket for horseback riding, slightly longer than an ordinary sports jacket, shaped at waist, flared over the hips, and cut by deep center or side vents. It has slanting pockets, known as hacking pockets, with a ticket or change pocket above the lower right-hand pocket.

hacking muffler Muffler of knitted or woven fabric, measuring 72 inches in length. Folded in half, it is wrapped around the neck so that the folded area serves as a loop through which both ends are drawn.

hackling Cleaning and straightening flax fibers with a comb. The process is basically the same as carding and combing in the preparation of cotton.

hacking jacket   hacking muffler

hatband

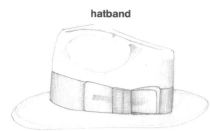

haircloth Stiff fabric made of any fiber, but usually of cotton in the warp and horsehair in the filling. It is used as an interlining or stiffening material.

hair fiber *See* SPECIALTY FIBER.

hairline stripes Very narrow stripes, made by weaving single threads in color to contrast with the background of worsted or other fabrics. They are used mainly in fabrics for men's suits, neckwear, and other apparel.

half belt Belt extending halfway or less around a garment.

half blood Grade of wool, originally implying that the wool was from a half-merino sheep but now merely designating a degree of fineness (grades 60s and 62s).

half hose Socks of short or ankle length.

half sleeve Sleeve of a shirt or other garment extending approximately to the elbow.

half Wellington *See* WELLINGTON BOOT.

hand (handle) Touch or feel of a fabric. An experienced individual can determine the quality and character of a fabric by handling, pulling, stroking, or squeezing it.

hand-blocked Term applied to material printed by hand with a wooden or a wood-and-metal block.

handkerchief Square piece of cotton, linen, silk or blended fabric used for decorative or personal purposes.

handkerchief linen Thin, sheer linen of plain weave.

handle *See* HAND.

handloom Manually operated loom for weaving fabrics.

handpicked Term applied to hand stitching at the edges of a jacket, lapel, or pocket.

hand-rolled hem Edge of a handkerchief, muffler, or other article rolled and stitched by hand. In a necktie the ends are folded under about $\frac{1}{4}$ inch and stitched by hand, producing a soft roll of fabric held by irregular stitching.

handwoven Woven on a loom operated by hand and foot. The finished fabric, such as tweed or homespun, has irregularities that enhance its charm for some people.

hanging Placing coats on shaped hangers and trousers on spring hangers when they are not being worn, thus preserving their fashion.

hank Unit of measure of yarn or thread.

A hank of cotton yarn is 840 yards long; a hank of first-grade woolen yarn, 560 yards long, weighing 1 pound.

happi coat Full-cut garment, made of coarse cotton, originally worn by Japanese coolies and low-rank retainers. This style, with full sleeves and a belt, has been adapted for karate.

hard finish Finish of worsted, woolen, or cotton fabric the surface of which is without nap.

Hargreaves, James English inventor (d. 1778) who created the first machine to spin more than one thread at a time and called it the spinning jenny, after his wife.

harlequin check Pattern of plaid or large blocks in three or more contrasting colors.

harmony (coordination) Pleasing effect achieved by the proper relation of colors, fashion details, and assemblage of clothing and accessories.

harness Frame on a loom that is raised to separate the warp from the filling yarns to allow the shuttle to pass between them. There are at least two harnesses on a loom. More elaborate weaves require more harnesses; for example, a so-called four-harness fabric uses four.

Harris Tweed Trademark of woolen material spun, dyed, and woven by hand by the crofters of Harris and Lewis and other islands of the Outer Hebrides.

harvard cloth Shirting made with a twill weave instead of the plain weave of oxford shirting.

hat Any covering for the head with a crown and a brim.

hatband Strip of fabric in a solid color, stripes, or print wrapped around the

Henley shirt

lower part of the crown of a man's felt, straw, or fabric hat.

Hawaiian print Pattern of tropical leaves, flowers, or the like printed on cotton, acetate, silk, or blended fabrics for men's sportswear.

headband Knitted band of wool or other fibers, $1\frac{1}{2}$ inches or more in width, worn around the head by skiers and other sportsmen to keep the ears warm.

head end First part of a new piece of woven material, invariably marked with the style number or other code identification.

headgear Hat, cap, or other kind of head covering.

heather mixture Blend of yarns in different tones, named for Scottish heather, that is used to achieve a subtle multitoned effect in knitted and woven materials for men's apparel.

heat-setting Applying heat and pressure to a fabric or garment so that it retains its crease.

heddle Twisted wire with an eye, attached to the harness of a loom to guide the warp threads in the weaving process.

heel Piece attached to the sole of the rear part of a shoe or boot, made of leather, rubber, or other material.

Helanca Brand name of nylon or polyester yarn made under license from the Heberlein Patent Corporation. The filaments, which are engineered to have minuscule curls, are heat-set to produce springiness and stretch characteristics.

helmet Head covering with a hard rounded crown and a stiff brim turned down all around.

hem Finish made by turning back the raw edge of material and sewing it by hand or machine.

hem, hand-rolled *See* HAND-ROLLED HEM.

hemp Fiber obtained from inside the bark of a tall Asiatic plant, used in twine, rope, and the soles of certain kinds of footwear.

Henley shirt Collarless, short-sleeved knitted pullover shirt with a buttoned placket front and a contrasting band at the border of the placket and around the neck.

Herculon Registered trademark of an olefin fiber made by Hercules, Inc. It is made from polypropylene pellets derived from propylene gas.

herringbone Ribbed twill fabric in which equal numbers of threads slant right and left to form a pattern similar to that of a fish skeleton; also a chevron design for clothing and accessories.

Hessian boot High boot, usually finished with a tassel at the top, brought to England by the Hessians in the nineteenth century.

hide Raw or dressed pelt of an animal of large size such as a steer or a buffalo.

high-buttoned shoe High shoe with the upper extending above the ankle and closed with buttons at the side. The upper is of leather, box cloth, or other material, and the lower part of plain or patent leather.

high-count fabric Material that is tightly woven.

high fashion Fashion of recent creation, accepted by a limited number of consumers.

high-water pants Pants that reach only to a point slightly above the ankles.

hiking shoe Sturdy shoe, usually in treated leather, with the upper extending above the ankle.

homburg Formal-looking soft felt hat with a tapered crown and a rolled bound-edge brim. In black or dark blue, it may be worn with a dinner jacket; in other colors, with a business suit as well.

The hat is named for Homburg (Bad Homburg), a town near Frankfurt, Germany. For generations people from many parts of the world have come to this center to take health cures or bathe in mineral waters. A regular visitor in his day was King Edward VII, who wore consistently a distinctive kind of hat of Tyrolean origin with a tapered crown and a rolled brim. In the late 1920s men began wearing this style again and referred to it as the homburg because of its fashion background. In gray, brown, soft green, dark blue, and black the homburg was worn with business clothes; in dark blue and black it was later combined with the dinner jacket as the correct formal fashion. Anthony Eden (later Lord Avon) was a consistent wearer of the homburg. Dwight D. Eisenhower wore a dark gray homburg with a formal day outfit of dark coat and striped trousers for his presidential inauguration in 1953.

homespun Material of loose weave, first made by hand and later reproduced by machine. Wool, cotton, linen, rayon, polyester, or blended fibers may be used.

honan Silk fabric made of fibers spun by wild silkworms in Honan Province, China; also a fabric of man-made fibers with a roughish, irregular texture.

honeycomb weave Weave of a fabric, such as piqué for a formal dress shirt, that resembles the design of a honeycomb.

hopsacking Originally a loosely woven burlap carried by pickers of hops; in fashion, an open weave of wool, cotton, or other fibers for men's suits, sports jackets, and other sportswear.

horsehide Tanned and processed skin of a horse, used for work jackets, shoes, gloves, leather goods, and baseballs.

hose, golf See GOLF HOSE.

hose, half See HALF HOSE.

homburg   Hudson Bay coat

huarache

hosiery Knitted socks or stockings.

hot-head press Very hot press for imparting a durable press to apparel. Pressing at a high temperature softens and reshapes synthetic fibers, removing wrinkles and putting creases in the proper place. The heat-set position is permanent, and the fibers tend to return to it after washing.

houndstooth check Check with jagged edges resembling a dog's tooth; used in woven or printed designs of woolen, worsted, cotton, silk, polyester, and other fabrics for sportswear and accessories.

huarache Mexican type of sandal with woven strips of leather at the tip, no counter, and a leather sole.

huarizo Mammal bred from a male llama and a female alpaca; a source of fine fibers.

huckaback Heavy coarse cotton or linen fabric sometimes used for outerwear.

Hudson Bay coat Double-breasted woolen outercoat in white or off-white with two or three colorful wide horizontal stripes around the lower part.

hue Color, differing from black, white, or gray; also the gradation of color.

hunter green Deep shade of green with a faint yellowish cast.

hunter's pink Bright scarlet or a slightly softer shade of red, mellowed by varied weather conditions, of a formal hunting coat.

hunting boot High-laced boot with an all-leather or leather-and-rubber upper and a waterproof sole.

hunting cap Hard round-crown velvet cap with a short visor for wear with formal riding clothes.

hymo Stiff mohair fabric used to shape and reinforce lapels and parts of the body of a jacket or outercoat.

I

ice-cream hat Light-colored felt hat with a telescope shape; an early college man's hat.

imported fabric Any material manufactured abroad and brought to the United States. Since 1965 the Federal Trade Commission has required the inclusion of the country of origin on any label designating a fabric as imported. The leading foreign sources for men's apparel fabrics are Japan, Italy, the United Kingdom, and Hong Kong.

impregnated fabric Fabric made water-repellent by filling the openings between the threads with a chemical compound.

Impregnole Process of the Warwick Chemical Company used to make fabrics spot- and stain-resistant.

in-and-outer Sports shirt of woven or knitted fabric, straight cut across the bottom with side vents, that may be worn inside or outside slacks.

Incas Peruvian Indians who ruled over an empire before the Spanish conquest of South America. They wove cotton, llama wool, and feathers into materials that were technically excellent.

India madras swim shorts Close fitting trunks, with a separate belt or an elasticized waistband, in India madras fabric.

India print Design of Indian subjects

in-and-outer

India madras swim shorts

inverness

printed on cotton or silk, usually hand-blocked.

indigo Plant that was the source of blue dye for fabrics prior to the development of coal-tar dyes.

informal Term applied to clothes suitable for most occasions when a tailcoat or a dinner jacket is not required.

ingrain Material made of yarn dyed prior to weaving or knitting.

initial markup Figure obtained by subtracting the cost from the retail price of merchandise for a given period. It is usually expressed as a percentage of the retail level.

inseam Distance in inches from the crotch to the bottom of the trousers; also a seam on a glove that is sewn inside out.

inset Piece of fabric or other material inserted in a garment as a decoration or as an aid to proper fit.

insignia Emblems or badges of association with an organization, in fabric, metal, or other materials, such as the crest of a club for the chest pocket of a blazer.

insole Part of a shoe between the welt and the outsole.

insulation Protection against low temperatures by, for example, controlled dead air trapped between the fibers of woolen fabric, which shields the wearer's body warmth.

intarsia Italian term for an inlaid mosaic of wood or other materials. In knitting the term is applied to a similar design with the pattern in solid colors on both sides of the fabric.

intensity Degree of brightness of a color, ranging from bright to dull.

interfacing Stiff fabric placed between the shell or outer fabric and the facing to preserve the shape of a garment.

interlining Layer of material between the lining and the shell or outer fabric of a garment.

interlock Term applied to a closely knit fabric produced on a machine with alternating long and short needles.

inverness Single-breasted sleeveless coat with peaked or notched lapels and an attached cape extending to the elbows. It is made in tweeds colorfully patterned for country wear and in dark, smooth fabrics for formal evening wear.

inverted pleat Reverse of a box pleat, with the fullness on the inside.

iridescence Play or reflection of multiple colors attained by using different colors in the warp and filling of a fabric.

Irish linen Thin linen woven of Irish flax, used for handkerchiefs and shirts.

Irish poplin Originally a silk-and-wool material for men's neckwear; also a linen or cotton shirting produced in Ireland.

iron Unit of measure for the thickness of the leather sole of a shoe, equal to $\frac{1}{48}$ inch. A 12-iron sole is $\frac{1}{4}$ inch thick.

Italian cloth Satin material with a wool or cotton back, used mainly for coat and suit linings.

Ivy League Term applied to a suit in which the jacket has natural-width shoulders, is straight-hanging, and has a center vent and the trousers are made without pleats at the waistband and are straight-hanging. The name is registered by Botany Industries.

J

jabot Originally a ruffle on the bosom of a man's shirt; a style of neckwear for formal wear with a neckband and ruffles below it.

jacket Garment with sleeves, opening in front, that varies from waist to hip length. In medieval England a jack was a leather-and-metal protective coat. The modern garment is derived from the somewhat shorter medieval jacket.

jacquard Fabric made on a loom or knitting machine the pattern apparatus of which is controlled by perforated cards; used for clothing, accessories, and sportswear.

jac shirt Short outerwear jacket with a shirt collar and a straight-cut bottom, made in a plaid of heavy woolen or other fabric.

jai alai shoe Low blucher shoe with a white or off-white leather upper and a rubber sole, worn originally by jai alai players and later by sportsmen generally.

jams Long, loose-fitting swim trunks fastened at the waist with a drawstring like that of pajamas.

jaspé Term applied to a neckwear fabric with an arrangement of fine stripes formed by light, medium, and dark

jabot

jerkin

jump suit

jodhpurs

jodhpur boot

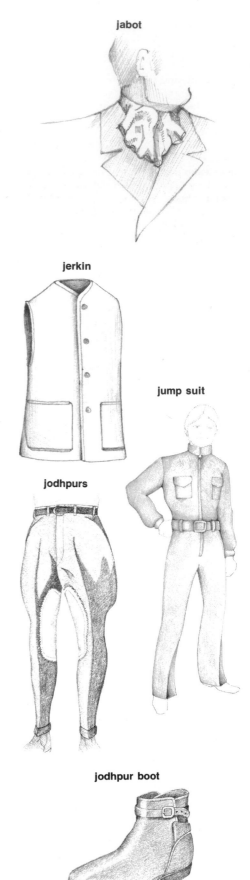

shades of a given color.

jazz suit Post-World War I suit composed of peg-top trousers and a narrow-shouldered jacket with a wasp-waist plain or pinched back having a deep center vent and flared lines and one, two, or three buttons.

jean Twill fabric of cotton or blended fibers for all types of work clothing. Pants made of this fabric are called jeans. The name is derived from "jene fustian," as the English called a coarse fabric first made in Genoa.

jean jacket Waist-length jacket of denim or other twill cotton with panel stitching and patch pockets in front.

jellaba (djellaba) Loose garment with a hood and wide-cut sleeves worn in North Africa.

jenny *See* SPINNING JENNY.

jerkin Close-fitting jacket or waistcoat with a button or zipper closure, made in a woven or knitted fabric, leather, or a combination of fabric and leather.

jersey Knitted fabric with a slight rib on one side, made of wool, cotton, acrylic, polyester, rayon, silk, or blends of fibers for sports shirts, sportswear, and underwear. It derives its name from the island of Jersey, sailors of which first wore sweaters made of this fabric.

jewelry Ornaments such as cuff links, studs, tie holders, and pins in a variety of finishes with precious or imitation stones.

jipajapa Palmlike tree the leaves of which yield fibers that are plaited into hats, known as panama hats; also a broad brimmed planter's style of hat.

jivey Ivy Term applied to a narrow-shouldered jacket with a four-button single-breasted front and snug-fitting pants.

Jockey shorts Specially designed, trim-fitting undershorts, manufactured and registered by Jockey International, a division of Cooper's, Inc.

jodhpur boot Above-ankle leather boot with a strap-and-buckle fastener for wear especially with jodhpur trousers.

jodhpurs Long riding trousers, flared over the hips and narrow from knee to ankle, finished with or without cuffs. Of twill, corduroy, and other fabrics, they are worn with jodhpur boots.

jogger's suit Two-piece knitted suit with a pullover top and elastic-waistband pants designed especially for jogging.

Joinville tie Narrow, straight-cut four-in-hand necktie with straight ends. It is named for the Prince de Joinville (1818–1900), son of Louis Philippe. Early ties were 6 inches wide and 34 inches long.

Joseph's coat Any multicolored striped garment. The name is based on the biblical story of the coat of many colors, given to Joseph as a favor by his father.

josette Strong twill-weave cotton cloth; used for sportswear, slacks, shirts, jackets, and bags.

judo coat Belted cotton coat of fingertip length originally worn by Japanese for judo.

jump suit One-piece garment with long set-in or raglan sleeves and long legs, a zipper or button closure, and a collar, made of wool, cotton, or blended fabric. A short-sleeve, short-leg model is made in terry cloth or crash for beachwear.

jute Bast fiber from a plant grown mainly in the Indian subcontinent. Retted in streams, it is spun into yarns and woven into fabrics.

K

Kabuki robe Short velour kimono-type robe in vibrant colors.

kaftan *See* CAFTAN.

kangaroo leather Tough leather derived from kangaroo skin.

karakul Breed of sheep, originally from Bukhara, with a coarse brown fur; also the curled black fur of a newly born karakul lamb.

karat *See* CARAT.

kashmir *See* CASHMERE.

kemp Wiry, coarse wool fiber.

kepi Military cap with a flat-topped crown and a horizontal visor, worn in the French Army.

kerchief Historically, a head covering; a square or rectangular piece of cotton, silk, or wool fabric in a solid color or a printed or woven pattern.

kersey Closely woven, compact overcoat fabric with a glossy finish. It derives its name from a cloth first woven in Kersey, England, in the eleventh century.

keystone neck Neck opening in the shape of a key, with tapering lines on each side and a horizontal line across the bottom.

khaki Neutral color the name of which is derived from a Hindi word meaning "dust"; also the term applied to military uniforms or sportswear made in twill or other fabrics of this color.

kid Soft leather tanned from the skin of a mature goat, used for footwear; also the tanned skin of a young goat, a soft, flexible leather with a close-textured grain that is thin enough to be used for gloves.

kid mohair Hair of fine quality from a young goat.

kier Pressurized tank in which unfinished cotton is boiled to remove sizing, wax, and other foreign materials.

kilt Knee-length pleated skirt worn primarily by male members of clans in Scotland, particularly in the Highlands.

kiltie (shawl tongue) Tongue of fringed leather that is draped over the instep of

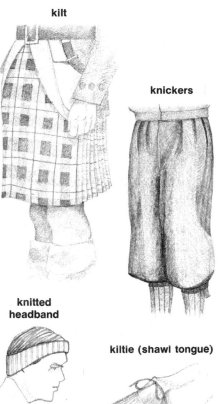

kilt

knickers

knitted headband

kiltie (shawl tongue)

a shoe, covering the laces and eyelets.

kimono Wrap style of robe with full-cut sleeves and a sash, of Japanese origin.

kin Japanese unit of weight for silk: 1 kin = 1.32 pounds, or 756 kin = 1,000 pounds.

kip Undressed hide of a horse, cow, or young steer. In the trade a kip weighs from 15 to 25 pounds.

kipper Wide necktie suggestive of a cured salmon or herring.

knickers (knickerbockers) Loose pants draped over the knee and fastened with a band and buckle above the calf, worn originally for golf and now also for skiing and other sports. They are made in tweed, flannel, gabardine, and washable fabrics.

The name comes from Dietrich Knickerbocker, pretended author of *A History of New York* (1809) by Washington Irving, who was permitted by Harmen Knickerbocker, grandson of the Dutch colonist Harmen Jansen Knickerbocker (1650?–?1716), to use the family name.

knicker suit Suit consisting of a jacket, waistcoat, and knickers in matching fabric.

knit, double *See* DOUBLE KNIT.

knit, plain *See* PLAIN KNIT.

knit, reverse *See* REVERSE KNIT.

knitted headband *See* HEADBAND.

knitted pile fabric Knitted fabric in which one set of yarns forms longer loops than the other set. The loops may be cut, napped, or brushed.

knitted suit Jacket and matching trousers of knitted fabric.

knit terry Plated fabric with two yarns in each stitch, one of which is drawn into a longer loop, producing a terry effect.

knitting Process of producing a fabric by interlocking loops of yarn with needles or wires. There are two main types of knitting. One type is weft knitting, in which a continuous yarn is carried in crosswise rows. Jersey is a weft-knit fabric. The second type is warp knitting, in which a group of yarns form rows running lengthwise by an interlocking process. Warp-knit fabrics are less elastic than weft-knit fabrics. Tricot is an example of a warp knit.

knitting, raschel See RASCHEL KNITTING.

knop (knopped) yarn Yarn in which different-colored small masses of fibers (knops) are mixed with the basic fibers.

knot Fastening or tying together of two ends of a cord, thread, or piece of fabric.

knot, Windsor See WINDSOR KNOT.

Kodel Registered name of a polyester fiber manufactured by Eastman Chemical Products, Inc.

Koroseal Trade name of plasticized vinyl resins, registered by the B. F. Goodrich Co. The name means "seal against corrosion."

Kuron Brand name of stretch material registered by Uniroyal, Inc.

L

lace Openwork material made by bobbins, needles, or hooks.

lace stay Piece of leather sewn to the front of a shoe to strengthen the eyelets or eyelet holes.

lace-to-toe sneaker Sneaker with a blucher front in which the lacing starts over the vamp.

lamb's wool Material made of fibers shorn from lambs up to seven months old. The fibers are soft and have superior spinning properties.

lamé Fabric of silk, polyester, rayon, or other fibers ornamented with flat metal threads in the design or background, usually in a gold or silver coloring.

laminating See BONDING.

lanolin Purified wool grease derived from a sheep's fleece, which is about 80 percent oil by weight. Lanolin is used in cosmetics, creams, and ointments.

lap Lofty compressed layer of fibers as it is rolled out of the carding machine.

lapel Part of the front of a jacket or coat that is turned back on either side of the opening from the collar downward.

lapel, cloverleaf See CLOVERLEAF LAPEL.

lapel, notched See NOTCHED LAPEL.

lapel, peaked See PEAKED LAPEL.

lapin Rabbit fur that has been sheared.

lapis lazuli Rich, deep blue of the semiprecious stone of that name.

last Form of wood or metal, shaped like a foot, over which a shoe is fashioned.

Lastex Brand name registered by Uniroyal, Inc., for an elastic yarn of extruded rubber around which are cotton, silk, nylon, polyester, rayon, or other fibers.

latex Fluid from which rubber is produced.

lawn Fine, sheer cotton or cotton-and-polyester fabric made of combed or carded yarn; used for handkerchiefs and sportswear.

layered look Appearance achieved by wearing a lightweight sweater over a shirt and another sweater or garment over them.

leather Skin of an animal that has been treated chemically, tanned, or otherwise processed for use in apparel, footwear, or other articles.

leather, aniline See ANILINE LEATHER.

leather, buffalo See BUFFALO LEATHER.

leather, crushed See CRUSHED LEATHER.

leather, embossed See EMBOSSED LEATHER.

leather, grained See GRAINED LEATHER.

leather, kangaroo See KANGAROO LEATHER.

leather, ostrich See OSTRICH LEATHER.

leather, patent See PATENT LEATHER.

leather, saddle See SADDLE LEATHER.

leather, sole See SOLE LEATHER.

leather, synthetic See SYNTHETIC LEATHER.

leather patch Piece of leather stitched to the elbow or shoulder of a tweed or other sports jacket.

left-hand twill Twill starting at the lower right and extending upward to the left at an angle of approximately 45 degrees.

legging Shaped covering for the leg, fastened with straps and buckles and laces and hooks, with a strap and buckle under the foot.

leghorn Hat of plaited straw from wheat fibers, named after Leghorn, Italy, from which the straw is exported.

lei Floral wreath worn around the neck in Hawaii; also a hatband made of pheasant and other feathers.

leisure shoe Any soft, comfortable shoe for casual wear.

leno Fabric in a mesh weave formed by twisting two warp yarns around each other. It is made of cotton or cotton and polyester for shirtings or sportswear.

Leonardo da Vinci Italian artist and scientist (1452–1519) who invented the spinning flyer, a device that made it possible to spin yarn continuously. The flyer served as the foundation for the English inventions of the eighteenth century.

leotard Knitted suit with sleeves and legs, worn by acrobats and ballet dancers.

Levi's Trademark of Levi Strauss & Company for heavy denim work pants worn by cowboys, ranchers, and young people generally.

ligne Unit of French origin, equal to $\frac{1}{11}$ inch, used in measuring the width of bands and bindings of hats.

line Style or outline of a garment or of part of a garment.

linen Fabric made of flax fibers; used for handkerchiefs, shirts, underwear, sportswear, and other apparel. Flax fibers may be blended with polyesters. Linen is one of the oldest textiles, dating back to ancient Egypt.

linen, butcher See BUTCHER LINEN.

linen, handkerchief See HANDKERCHIEF LINEN.

linen, Irish see IRISH LINEN.

linen, spun See SPUN LINEN.

linen mesh Open-weave fabric made of flax fibers; used for shirts, sportswear, and underwear.

liner, pile See PILE LINER.

lining Material used to cover partly or completely the interior of a garment or other article, such as a shoe.

links-and-links Term applied to a pattern of purl or fancy knitting stitches produced on a special machine known as a links-and-links machine.

linsey-woolsey Rough fabric with a wool filling and either cotton or linen in the warp. It was worn in different forms by settlers in the American Colonies.

lint Cotton fibers that have been ginned.

linters Short cotton fibers removed from

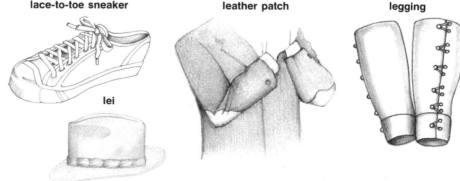

lace-to-toe sneaker

lei

leather patch

legging

loden coat

lumberjack shirt

cottonseed after ginning. Linters may be used to make cellulose sheets for the production of man-made fibers.

lisle Fine quality of tightly twisted long-staple cotton yarn that is passed near a gas flame to remove fuzz and give it a sleek surface; used mainly for men's socks and underwear. It is so called because it was first made in Lisle (now Lille), France.

llama Fleece-bearing mammal of the genus *Lama*, native to the Andes Mountains and related to the alpaca, guanaco, and vicuña; also a fabric made of this wool. Llama hair is sometimes blended with other fibers for outercoatings.

Loafer Brand name of a moccasin-style slip-on shoe registered by Nettleton Shops, Inc.

lock-knot tie Tie with a half Windsor knot.

loden Fleecy type of coating utilizing greasy wool, first made in the Tyrolean Alps. Coats or capes of this fabric are naturally water-repellent.

loden coat Double-breasted coat of loden cloth with a yoke front and back and a wooden toggle or button closure.

loft Resilience, or springiness, of a fabric after it has been subjected to pressure. Big-yarn wool sweaters have good loft.

London-shrunk (shrunk in London) Term applied to a woolen fabric that has been laid in wet blankets to start internal movement, dried in a specially designed room, pressed in hot plates, and finished with a lustrous or dull effect. The cloth is then stable and will not shrink during manufacture into garments or exposure to the elements.

long-roll collar Attached collar, set low in front, with points 4 inches long and with adequate fullness to permit a rolled effect.

long-staple cotton Cotton with fibers at least $1\frac{1}{8}$ inches long.

look *see* BOLD LOOK; CONTINENTAL LOOK; LAYERED LOOK; WET LOOK.

loom Machine on which fabrics are woven. The warp yarns, running lengthwise, are kept taut in a framework. The filling yarns, running at right angles, are interlaced through the warp yarns. After each crosswise movement the yarn is pressed against the previously woven cloth. The process continues until the entire length of the warp has been utilized.

loom, box- *See* BOX-LOOM.

loom, chain *See* CHAIN LOOM.

loom, dobby *See* DOBBY LOOM.

lounge, English *See* ENGLISH DRAPE.

lounge suit *See* SACK SUIT.

lovat Color mixture, a heather blend of hazy blue, soft green, and tan or gray. Of Scottish origin, it suggests blends seen in the landscape of the Highlands.

low-slope collar Attached collar high in back and sloping to low points in front.

lumberjack shirt Heavy shirt of wool, cotton, or a polyester blend in a plaid pattern, worn by workers and skiers. It derives its name from Canadian lumberjacks, who first wore this style.

Lurex Yarn composed of an aluminum base with a plastic coating, manufactured by the Dow Badische Co.

luster Sheen or reflecting quality of a fiber, either natural or man-made. Certain breeds of English sheep yield lustrous long-staple wool that is used for tweed and other husky fabrics. The luster of synthetic fibers can be controlled by special finishing.

Lycra Brand name of a spandex fiber manufactured by Du Pont. Lycra has elasticity and retains its shape.

M

maarad Egyptian cotton developed from American pima seeds.

mac *See* MACKINTOSH.

MacArthur, John Australian pioneer instrumental in bringing merino sheep to New South Wales. In 1797 he got control of a herd of twenty merino sheep that had been refused entry into the Cape Colony. These sheep were the source of the best herds in Australia, and sheep raising became a potent factor in the economy of the Commonwealth.

Macclesfield Open-weave silk fabric in small allover patterns, originally woven in Macclesfield, England. Used mainly for neckwear, it is generally made in contrasting tones such as gray and black or in a solid color with a self-pattern. Macclesfield silk is similar to Spitalfields.

mackinaw Type of heavy napped wool blanket in big stripes or checks used in bartering with the Indians around Fort Mackinac, Michigan, The blanket material was also made into coats for lumbermen. The typical coat, in a double-breasted style with an all around belt, became known as the mackinaw.

mackinaw hat Hat of coarse straw, usually with a flexible brim.

mackintosh Term used in England for a raincoat, called "mac" for short. In 1823 Charles Macintosh, a Scottish chemist, got a patent for a solution of naphtha and crude rubber that he used in cementing two pieces of cloth together to make them waterproof.

macrame Trimming made by knotting the fringed ends of a fabric or by knotting cords.

madder Eurasian plant the root of which was formerly used as a dyestuff. A bright red known as madder red is used for neckwear and sportswear.

madras Plain-weave cotton or blended material in stripes or checks; used for shirts, underwear, and sportswear. It is named for Madras, an early source of textiles.

mackinaw

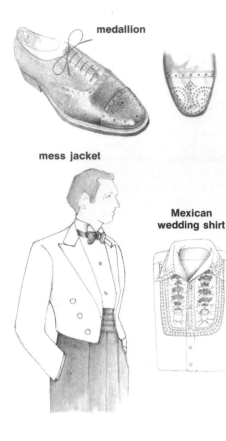

medallion

mess jacket

Mexican wedding shirt

magenta Red shade with a tinge of purple, named for the Battle of Magenta (1859), in which much blood was spilled.

malacca cane Men's cane in a mottled tan tone made from an Asian rattan palm.

mandarin Term applied to a pajama top with a stand-up collar about 1 inch high and a front that is closed with buttons or frogs.

man-made Term applied to rayon, acetate, and other cellulosic materials, which are the products of natural materials such as wood pulp and cotton linters. Although "man-made" and "synthetic" are used interchangeably in the apparel field, "synthetic" applies properly to acrylics and polyesters, which stem from the laboratory.

Manx tweed Woolen material made on the Isle of Man. Usually weighing 15 to 16 ounces to the square yard, it is made in a blend of gray, brown, and green as well as other colors.

Mao jacket Button-front jacket or tunic with a standing collar an inch high or slightly higher, so called because Mao Tse-tung, chairman of the People's Republic of China, has worn it for many years.

marcella Double-twill cotton or linen made of highly twisted yarns; used for formal waistcoats and dress-shirt bosoms.

markup, initial *See* INITIAL MARKUP.

marl Blend of two or more colors in a yarn used primarily in knitted articles such as socks and sweaters but also in woven fabrics such as tweeds.

Marseilles Sturdy raised-weave cotton fabric named for the French city. Similar to cotton piqué, it is used for formal evening dress shirts.

matelassé Figured fabric of cotton, silk, or other fibers made on a jacquard or dobby loom. A French word, matelassé is derived from *matelas* (mattress), which comes from the Arabic *matrah*.

mat (matt, matte) finish Dull finish of smooth-surfaced leather for shoe uppers.

matt Fibro Dull viscose rayon staple fiber manufactured by Courtaulds, Ltd.

maxi Coat length. The word is short for maximum length, reaching just above the ankles.

medallion Design perforated in the leather of a shoe tip or other article.

medium Term applied to wool fiber of grades from about 50s to 58s.

melton Heavy, slightly napped fabric for overcoats, named after Melton Mowbray, a hunting area in England where it was first worn. At first an all-wool material, it is now also made of blends.

melt spinning Process of melting hard nylon, polyester, or glass material so that it can be extruded through the spinneret into fibers.

memory twist *See* FALSE TWIST.

mercerized cotton Smooth, lustrous fabric resulting from the treatment of cotton yarn or fabric under tension with a solution of caustic soda; named after John Mercer, an English calico printer, who originated the process in 1844. Mercerizing strengthens yarns, adds to absorptive qualities, and improves dye penetration. The fabric is used for underwear, pajamas, shirts, and sportswear.

merchandise In commerce, articles of apparel or related items. As a verb, "merchandise" means to transact business, that is, to buy and sell.

merino Breed of sheep that yields the best-quality wool, with a softness resembling that of cashmere. Developed in Spain by the Romans and Arabs, it provided the heritage for all the leading wool breeds and is now the standard of wool quality.

merino, Australian *See* AUSTRALIAN MERINO.

mesh Open woven or knitted fabric of cotton, silk, linen, polyester, or blends of fibers; used for sportswear and underwear.

mesh, linen *See* LINEN MESH.

mess jacket Semiformal waist-length military jacket adapted for civilian wear. Most often made in white, it is seen in pale shades as well.

Mexican wedding shirt White cotton shirt with an attached collar, embroidered in front in white, red, or other colors.

middy Pullover pajama top of woven fabric, with long or short sleeves.

midi Length of an outercoat extending halfway between the knees and the floor.

milan Fine plaited straw hat, named after the Italian city.

mildew-resistant Term applied to material specially processed with chemicals to resist mold and mildew.

Milium Brand name of metal-insulated fabrics registered by Deering Milliken, Inc.

mill end Odd length or unsold piece of material.

mill finish Finish of a worsted fabric with a slightly napped surface.

misti Fleece of a hybrid animal, offspring of a male alpaca and a female llama, of lower grade than that of an alpaca.

mitten Covering for the hand made of knitted fabric, leather, or other material, with one compartment for the thumb and another for the other four fingers and the hand.

mixture *See* BLENDING.

midi

mitten

moccasin

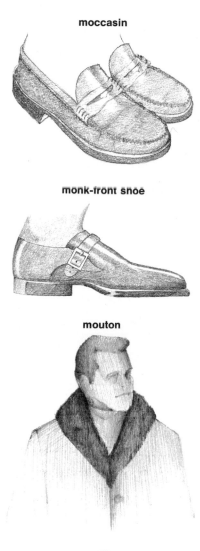

monk-front shoe

mouton

muffler

mukluk

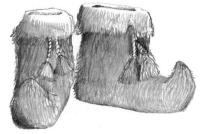

moccasin Originally an Indian type of footwear made of one piece of leather under the foot and at the sides that was sewn to a U-shaped piece over the vamp; also a similar style of modern footwear.

mocha Fine sueded sheepskin for gloves; also a dark grayish brown shade.

mock seam Seam up the back of hose knitted on a tubular form that resembles the seam of full-fashioned hosiery.

modacrylic Term descriptive of a synthetic fiber made up of less than 85 percent and more than 35 percent by weight of acrylonitrile units.

model Garment or outfit created by a designer as a prototype for mass production; also a person who poses for photographs or sketches.

modified rayon Fiber made with additives in the spinning solution to give it wool-like characteristics.

mogador Closely woven, brightly striped silk neckwear fabric with a heavy cord surface.

mohair Sleek, lustrous material made of angora goat fibers; used for suits, coats, evening clothes, and linings.

mohair, kid *See* KID MOHAIR.

moiré Allover watered appearance of silk or other fabrics, achieved with engraved rollers. Moiré taffeta, faille, rayon, and polyester fabrics are used for neckwear, formal evening wear, waistcoats, and scarfs.

moleskin Rugged satin-weave cotton fabric of one-warp, two-filling construction, finished with a soft napped back to resemble mole fur. It is used for outerwear and work clothes.

momme Japanese unit of weight used in the silk industry, equivalent to 0.132 ounce.

monk-front shoe Shoe with a plain tip and a strap and buckle over the instep.

monk's cloth (friar's cloth) Coarse basket-weave fabric of thick cotton or other yarn used for draperies or furniture covering. In lighter weights it is used for sportswear.

monofilament Single filament of a man-made or synthetic material.

Montagnac Overcoating with curls on the surface, weighing from 20 to 36 ounces per yard. The name is a trademark of E. de Montagnac et Fils.

Montego hat Coconut-palm hat originating in Montego Bay, Jamaica.

mordant Chemical that causes a dye to penetrate a fiber quickly and effectively.

morocco Fine-grained goatskin leather used for wallets and other leather goods.

mouton Sheepskin with a short- or medium-length pile, dyed in deep tones for use as collars, linings, and the like for outerwear and sportswear.

muffler Square or long rectangular piece of silk, wool, cashmere, challis, blend, or other fabric worn around the neck as a decorative and protective accessory. Originally mufflers were worn by women to conceal the face or to protect it from wind and sun.

muffler, hacking *See* HACKING MUFFLER.

mufti Civilian apparel as differentiated from a military uniform.

mukluk Sealskin boot with the fur side out, worn originally by Alaskan Eskimos and now also by sportsmen for after-skiing and leisure purposes.

mule Slipper of leather or other material made with coverage over the front and without a counter.

mull Thin, sheer fabric of cotton or cotton and polyester.

multifilament Yarn made up of more than one man-made or synthetic filament.

multiple fabric Material of two or more fabrics bound together as they are woven; for example, a double-faced coating.

musette bag *See* SHOULDER-STRAP BAG.

muslin Plain-weave cotton of thin to coarse texture, used for underwear, shirts, and sportswear. Its name is derived ultimately from Mosul, Iraq, where the fabric was once made.

N

nailhead Small dotted design, suggestive of the head of a nail, used for sharkskin worsted.

nainsook Soft plain-weave cotton fabric similar to muslin, originally made in India. In white, solid colors, or patterns, it is used for underwear and pajamas.

Nandel Certification mark for fabrics of Orlon acrylic rotofil yarn, used in fabrics that meet standards established by Du Pont.

nankeen Sturdy cotton twill fabric originally made in China.

nap Fuzzy fibers on the surface of a material such as flannel or doeskin.

napa Glove leather, originally made in Napa, California, of sheepskin or lambskin tanned by a soap-and-oil method.

napoleon boot High boot of a type worn by Napoleon.

napoleon collar High standing turnover

napoleon collar

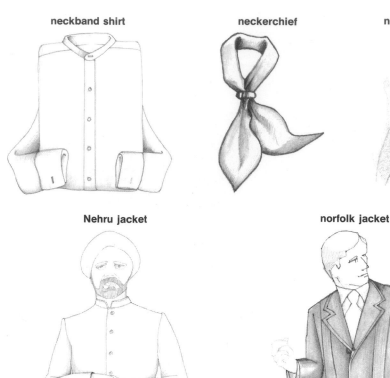

neckband shirt

neckerchief

notched lapel

Nehru jacket

norfolk jacket

collar, worn with wide lapels; adopted by Napoleon.

napping *See* BRUSHING.

natural-shoulder Term applied to a straight-hanging jacket with medium-width, lightly padded shoulders and a center vent. With this style, favored by university men and others, were worn pleatless, trim-cut trousers.

Navajo Indians of the southwestern United States. Originally weavers of cotton, they applied their talents to wool when the Spaniards brought sheep to the area. Their best-known product is the Navajo blanket.

neck *See* BOAT NECK; CREW NECK; KEYSTONE NECK; SCOOP NECK; V NECK.

neckband shirt Shirt with a narrow band circling the neck opening and having buttonholes at the ends.

neckerchief Solid-color or patterned square of silk, cotton, or other material knotted or draped in ascot fashion around the neck.

neckertie Silk square folded and draped around the neck, with the ends tied in a four-in-hand or other knot; worn with a sports shirt.

necktie Two or more thicknesses of fabric sewn in a shaped scarf or band for wear under the collar fold or around the neck and knotted in front. The knot may be a four-in-hand, Windsor knot, half Windsor knot, or any bow style.

neckwear Men's accessory to be worn around neck, such as a cravat, ascot, bow tie, or neckerchief.

negligee Soft woman's dressing gown; also an informal or incomplete outfit. The term was also applied to men's shirts for business wear in the early part of the twentieth century.

Nehru jacket Single-breasted jacket of shapely lines, buttoned high to a standing band collar. It is named for Prime Minister Jawaharlal Nehru.

neoprene Generic term for synthetic rubber manufactured by Du Pont.

nep Unplanned knot or irregularity of a textile fiber. It differs from a slub and a nub, which are planned irregularities used to give fabrics texture.

neutral Term applied to color that contains none of the primary colors. Undyed linen is one example.

Never-Press Registered brand of Wam-

sutta Mills, a division of M. Lowenstein & Sons, Inc.

newmarket Long, double-breasted coat with a seam at the waist, worn at the English racing center Newmarket in the nineteenth century; also a boot with a leg of Irish linen or other material worn for field trials, hacking, and cubbing.

nightshirt Pullover sleeping garment of woven cotton extending to above-ankle length.

noil Short fiber of wool remaining after the carding process; also waste silk fiber.

noncellulosic Term applied to a synthetic fiber not derived from cellulose.

nonsuit Suit similar to an easy suit, with little or no inner construction.

nonwoven Not woven or knitted; term applied to a material made by matting or interlacing fibers and bonding them into a sheet with chemicals.

norfolk jacket Jacket with a box pleat at each side in front, two similar box pleats in back, and an all-around belt.

notched lapel Angle-shaped opening at the point where the collar of a jacket or coat meets the lapel.

novelty yarn Yarn with a planned unevenness, the result of loops or slubs. When such a yarn is woven into fabric, a textured surface is produced.

nub Knot or tangle in yarn planned by a series of increases and decreases of tension during the spinning process. When woven, nubbed yarn gives a desired irregular texture to fabric.

numerical or count system Scale for evaluating the quality of wool, with grades ranging from 80s or higher to 36s or lower. Merino wool ranks as 80s or higher; fine wool, from 64s to 80s.

nutria Fur similar in appearance to beaver.

nylon Synthetic fiber that is spun into yarn and woven or knitted into fabric; used in hosiery, underwear, and sportswear. Nylon is strong, washable, elastic, and resistant to mildew.

nylon 6 Fiber, first manufactured by the Allied Chemical Corporation, that was developed through modifications of the original nylon formula.

O

obi Broad sash worn with traditional Japanese costumes.

obsolescence Process of becoming outmoded, as in the case of a fashion or a machine no longer in use.

OD *See* OLIVE DRAB.

odd waistcoat Waistcoat in a color, pattern, or fabric that does not match the suit or jacket with which it is worn.

oiled silk Soft woven silk treated with boiled linseed oil and dried to make it waterproof for use in rainwear.

odd waistcoat

oilskin

oxford bags

one-piece-top cap

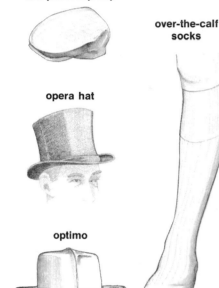

over-the-calf socks

opera hat

optimo

oilskin Raincoat made of a cotton fabric processed with coatings of oil.

olefin Group of synthetic fibers derived from long-chain polymers. One type, called polypropylene, is used mainly for industrial materials. Apparel, particularly hosiery and knitwear, is another olefin use.

olive Soft tone of green with a slight yellowish cast like that of an unripe olive.

olive drab (OD) Grayish olive color of military-uniform fabrics.

ombré Term applied to a fabric woven or dyed in a gradation of shades.

one-end (single-end) bow tie Bow tie with a butterfly shape at one end and a straight band at the other. A single knot is tied, and the band end is pulled over the middle and tucked between the collar and the neck.

one-piece–top cap Cap with a top made of one piece of fabric, without segment seams or center button.

opera hat Collapsible high hat for formal evening wear, covered with silk or other material, with a firm curled brim.

optimo Shape of a panama or other straw hat with a full crown and a ridge extending from front to back.

Orlon Brand name of an acrylic fiber manufactured by Du Pont.

osnaburg Coarse, loosely woven fabric, sometimes made with part waste, that resembles crash; used for work clothing, bags, toweling, and slacks. It is named for Osnabrück, Germany, where it was originally made.

ostrich leather Specialty leather tanned for footwear, luggage, wallets, and accessories.

ottoman Textured, closely woven fabric of raised crosswise ribs, made of silk or other fibers; used for neckwear.

outing flannel Cotton fabric in a plain or twill weave with a napped surface on both sides; used for sportswear and sleepwear.

outseam *See* PRICKSEAM.

overcoat Warm outer garment in single- or double-breasted style, heavier than a topcoat.

overplaid Pattern in which a plaid is placed over a second plaid or other type of design.

over-the-calf socks Men's socks long enough to extend over the calves, knitted of special yarn so that they fit closely at the top.

oxford (1) Low shoe with two or more sets of eyelets for laces, made in bal, blucher, and gillie styles; (2) a very dark shade of gray for fabrics; (3) a plain or basket-weave shirting of cotton or cotton and polyester, used also for summer clothing and sportswear.

oxford, plug *See* PLUG OXFORD.

oxford, saddle *See* SADDLE OXFORD.

oxford bags Full-cut odd trousers of gray flannel or worsted, worn in the mid-1920s, that measured 24 inches at the knees and 21 to 24 inches around the bottoms. They were named for Oxford University, where the fashion originated.

oyster white Very pale shade, just off white, used for rainwear, sportswear, and accessories.

P

paddock-model Term applied to a two-button jacket with the lower button placed above the waistline and the upper button set high, worn by the horsey set in the 1930s.

paisley Intricate allover pattern, woven or printed, resembling the patterns of woolen shawls made in Paisley, Scotland. These in turn were adaptations of cashmere shawls originally made in Kàshmir. Paisley patterns are used in neckwear, mufflers, other accessories, sportswear, and linings.

pajama check Basket weave of yarns woven to achieve a self-check effect.

pajamas Suit consisting of a button-front or pullover top and trousers with a drawstring or an elastic waistband, made of cotton, cotton and polyester, silk, or other fabrics; used primarily for sleepwear but also for lounging and beachwear. The word is of Hindi origin, and the garment was brought back from India by the British.

paletot French term for many styles of overcoats. In American usage, a paletot is an overcoat with flared lines and a waist seam, 52 inches long, sometimes finished with a cape.

palladium Pale bluish-white silver shade

pajamas

parka

pea jacket

peg-top trousers

patch pocket

peaked lapel

suggestive of palladium, a metal in the platinum group. The metal is named for the asteroid Pallas.

Palm Beach cloth   Brand of fabric for summer suits, jackets, slacks, and other articles, registered by the Palm Beach Company.

panama   Type of straw hat first bought by sailors and visitors in the ports of Panama. Originating in Ecuador, Colombia, and Peru, it is plaited from fibers of the jipijapa (toquilla) plant.

panel pattern   Design that has been planned to appear vertically in the center of a necktie.

panne satin   Lustrous silk or synthetic fabric of satin weave, used for facings and other trimmings for evening wear and for high hats.

pants   *See* TROUSERS. The word "pants" is short for "pantaloons," which is derived from Pantalone, a character in the *commedia dell'arte* whose leg covering looked somewhat like present-day trousers.

pants, clamdigger   *See* CLAMDIGGER PANTS.

pants, high-water   *See* HIGH-WATER PANTS.

pants, frontier   *See* FRONTIER PANTS.

pants, skinny   *See* SKINNY PANTS.

parchment   Light beige shade, resembling that of fine paper, used for articles of apparel.

parfait colors   Pale, whitish colors that bring to mind the shades of mixtures of ice cream and berries.

parka   Garment with a hood, similar to that worn by Eskimos, made of nylon, polyester and cotton, cotton, or wool and processed for water repellency; used for winter sports and utility wear.

pastel   Pale tone of a color.

patch, leather   *See* LEATHER PATCH.

patch pocket   Pocket, with or without a flap, made by stitching a piece of fabric on the outside of a garment.

patent leather   Leather with a hard, lustrous finish.

pattern   Guide, usually of cut paper, for cutting pieces of fabric to be made into a garment; also a printed or woven design placed on a fabric according to a plan.

pea coat   *See* PEA JACKET.

Peacock Revolution   Name given to a trend in men's fashions. Many persons and publications have been credited with, or have taken credit for, the creation of this term. It was based on the wearing of exotic colors by a certain segment of the male population in the late 1950s and through the 1960s. First seen in shirts and neckwear, these colors were so surprisingly fresh and new, as compared with the clothes of this conservative era, that the young men wearing them were likened to peacocks. As this custom became more widespread, it became known as the Peacock Revolution.

pea jacket (pea coat)   Heavy, double-breasted dark blue woolen jacket worn by sailors. It derives its name from the Dutch word *pij* for a coarse woolen material. In the early part of the nineteenth century, Count Alfred d'Orsay, a fashion personality, got caught in the rain without a coat and bought such a reefer jacket from a sailor. By the 1850s it had become popular in the United States and Great Britain.

peaked lapel   Lapel cut on an upward slant, coming to a point and leaving only a narrow space between the collar and the lapel.

peau de soie   Soft silk-satin fabric with a slight luster showing fine ribs faintly in the filling. The name means "skin of silk." Fabrics of this type are made also in other fibers or blends.

pebble grain   Regular texture produced on the surface of leather by the embossing process.

pebble-weave   Term applied to material with an irregular texture produced by weaving with shrunken, twisted yarns.

peccary   Soft-textured, fine-grained leather tanned from wild-boar skin; used plain or buffed for gloves and leather goods.

peg-top trousers   Trousers cut full and wide over the hips and tapering to narrow bottoms.

Pellon   Brand name of nonwoven materials, manufactured and registered by the Pellon Corporation, in which natural or man-made fibers or a combination of both are bonded together by chemicals and heat. It is employed in headwear and apparel, usually for its shape-retaining characteristics.

pelt   Skin or hide of an animal with the wool, fur, or hair on it.

pencil stripes   Very fine stripes in men's suit fabric, two or three warps wide, in a color to blend or contrast with the background.

pepper-and-salt   Tweed or other fabric with a speckled effect produced by flecks of black and white, brown and white, blue and white, etc.

percale   Plain-weave, medium-weight cotton or cotton-and-polyester fabric, made in a solid color or a print for shirts,

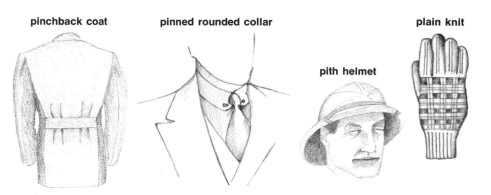

pinchback coat   **pinned rounded collar**   **pith helmet**   **plain knit**

sportswear, and pajamas.

percaline Fine cotton with a glossy or moiré surface; used for linings.

perforation Hole made by punching, as in leather for a shoe upper.

Perkin, Sir William Henry English chemist who, in 1838, at the age of eighteen, in an attempt to make synthetic quinine from coal tar accidentally hit upon the process for producing an aniline dye.

Perlon Trademark of the Perlon Warenzeichenverband for polyamide threads and fibers manufactured by leading firms in Germany.

permanent-press *See* DURABLE-PRESS.

pick *See* FILLING.

pick-and-pick Term applied to a neat-patterned weave with single filling threads in different colors.

picker Machine used to pull apart and separate cotton fibers, which are then shaped into rolls or lofty laps about 45 inches wide.

pick glass Magnifying glass calibrated to enable the viewer to count the warp and filling threads in a square inch of fabric.

picot One of a row of small loops made at the border of a material. A special machine is sometimes utilized.

piece Roll of woven fabric, containing about 100 yards.

piece-dyed Term applied to material that is dyed after it has been woven.

piece goods Materials sold in various lengths by the yard.

pigskin Leather of irregular texture with pits marking the removed bristles, used for gloves and leather goods of many varieties.

pig's whisker Loosely knit sweater that is soft but has fibers with something of a bristle to them.

pile Loops on the surface of a fabric, usually cut but sometimes uncut. Pile fabrics can be made in a plain or a twill weave or with a deep nap. The word "pile" is derived from the Latin *pilus*, meaning "hair."

pile fabric, uncut *See* UNCUT PILE FABRIC.

pile liner Piece of fabric with the furlike appearance of cut pile used for the interior of a garment; made of acrylic, nylon, wool, or other fibers in a pattern or a solid color. The liner, which is zippered or buttoned to the garment, provides insulation and warmth.

pile weave Fabric weave formed with two warp yarns and one filling yarn or with one warp and two filling yarns. The extra warp or filling yarn forms loops that are cut by blades on the loom.

pilling Formation by friction of small tangles or balls on the surface of a fabric. They are attached to the weave and can be removed only by separating them from the weave.

pima Long-staple cotton grown in the Southwest and named after Pima County, Arizona. It was created by crossbreeding Egyptian and American varieties, resulting in fibers that are used in top-quality fabrics for shirts and other articles.

piña (pineapple) cloth Sheer handwoven fabric produced in the Philippines from fibers of the pineapple plant. The fibers are sometimes mixed with silk.

pinchback coat Jacket or coat with pleats and a belt in back to make it fit snugly.

pincheck Small block pattern produced by the end-and-end weave of alternate colored threads; used for suits, sportswear, and accessories.

pinch front Front of the crown of a felt, straw, or cloth hat with indentations at the sides.

pineapple cloth *See* PIÑA CLOTH.

pink Soft shade of red; also, in formal fox-hunting clothes, a scarlet shade, usually faded to some extent.

pink, hunter's *See* HUNTER'S PINK.

pinking Cutting the edge of material in a zigzag design to prevent fraying; also cutting a zigzag edge for the upper of leather footwear.

pinned rounded collar Attached or separate collar with short rounded points held in place with a pin or collar bar.

pinpoint collar Attached collar with straight lines running vertically for about 1 inch, where a point is formed by the lines of the outward spread of the collar.

pin seal Finely grained leather made from sealskin; used for gloves, leather goods, and accessories. The effect is sometimes produced in other leathers by an embossing process.

pinstripes Fine stripes resulting from the use of white, gray, or other yarns in series in the warp of a worsted fabric.

pinwale Term applied to a corduroy material made with narrow ribs or wales.

piping Narrow fold, braid, or cord used to finish or decorate the edges or pockets of a garment.

piqué Fabric of cotton, polyester and cotton, rayon, or silk with ribs running lengthwise, sometimes forming a honeycomb or waffle weave; used for shirts, formal evening wear, accessories, and sportswear.

piqué, bird's-eye *See* BIRD'S-EYE PIQUÉ.

piqué, waffle *See* WAFFLE CLOTH.

pith helmet Lightweight hat made of tissue from the center of the stem of a tropical plant and covered with cloth. Originally worn in the tropics, it has a round crown and a fixed brim slanting downward.

placket Opening in the front of a shirt.

plaid Boxlike design formed by stripes of various widths running vertically and horizontally on a fabric; originally a piece of fabric, usually marked with tartan, worn over the left shoulder by men and women in Scotland.

plaid-back Term applied to an overcoating woven by the double-cloth method in which the underside shows a plaid design.

plain knit Stitch used in a knitted fabric such as jersey in which the yarn is pulled forward to form loops; employed in hosiery, underwear, and gloves.

plain weave Fabric weave in which the filling yarns pass over one warp yarn and under the next warp yarn, continuing alternately across each row.

plaiting Interweaving fibers as in making a straw hat.

pleat Fold of material pressed or stitched so that it is held in place.

pleat, accordion *See* ACCORDION PLEAT.

pleat, bellows *See* BELLOWS PLEAT.

pleat, box *See* BOX PLEAT.

pleat, inverted *See* INVERTED PLEAT.

pleat, reverse *See* REVERSE PLEAT.

pleated bosom Starched or soft shirt

pleated bosom

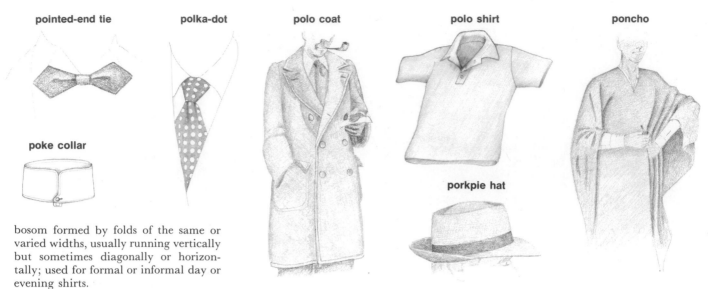

pointed-end tie   **polka-dot**   **polo coat**   **polo shirt**   **poncho**

poke collar

porkpie hat

bosom formed by folds of the same or varied widths, usually running vertically but sometimes diagonally or horizontally; used for formal or informal day or evening shirts.

plissé Cotton or other material with a striped pattern in which some areas are crinkled because the application of caustic soda has caused other areas to shrink.

plug oxford Low-cut shoe with a circular vamp and with the lace stay and forward part of the quarter formed of a separate piece of leather.

plus fours Full-cut knickers that extend 4 inches below the break at the knee. Less well known are plus twos, plus sixes, and plus eights, each name signifying the number of inches below the knee.

plush Pile fabric of silk, cotton, worsted, polyester, or blends of other fibers with a longer or deeper pile than velvet or velour.

ply Strand of a yarn in which two or more strands are twisted together. The term is used as a system of classification: two-ply yarn.

pocket Container formed by sewing one or more pieces of fabric to an outercoat, jacket, trousers, or other garment.

pocket, bellows *See* BELLOWS POCKET.

pocket, change *See* CHANGE POCKET.

pocket, patch *See* PATCH POCKET.

pocket, slash *See* SLASH POCKET.

pocket, ticket *See* TICKET POCKET.

pocketing Twill fabric of strong cotton or other fiber used for the pockets of men's garments.

pointed-end tie Straight-cut or butterfly bow tie with the ends shaped to form points.

pointed-toe Term applied to a shoe with a vamp tapering to a sharp point.

pointing Stitching on the back of a glove made to create raised ridges.

poke collar High standing collar with the upper corners of the ends turned back slightly; intended usually for formal evening wear.

polished cotton Glazed-finish cotton material, usually of plain weave. The glaze is achieved with resin.

polka-dot Term applied to a pattern of small or large dots made by printing, embroidering, or weaving.

Polo, Marco Italian traveler who in 1295 brought back to Venice information about luxurious silks, damasks, and materials of gold and silver from the court of Kublai Khan, Mongol emperor of China.

polo belt Belt of wide coarse-weave webbing or leather worn by polo players.

Polo cloth Brand of coating fabric registered by J. P. Stevens & Co. It is a combination of camel's hair and wool, fortified on the back with fine stripes spaced 3 inches apart.

polo coat Double-breasted or single-breasted outercoat of heavy or light camel's hair or soft fleece with set-in or raglan sleeves, patch pockets with flaps, and a half-belt or all-around belt. It was popularized in the 1920s by polo players, who wore it between chukkers and after matches, and by spectators.

polo shirt Knitted pullover shirt with an attached collar and a buttoned placket in front, first worn by polo players on American and English teams. Originally of knitted wool, it was later made of cotton and other fibers or blends. Although the style has been adopted for other sports and for casual wear, it has continued to be called a polo shirt.

polyamide fiber Name given to natural and synthetic protein fibers and nylon.

polyester Textile fiber produced from ethylene glycol and terephthalic acid. Brand names: Dacron, Fortrel, Kodel, Trevira, Vycron.

polymer Large molecule made by linking many single molecules (monomers). Polymerization is the basis for the creation of such synthetic fibers as polyesters and acrylics.

Polynosic Trademark registered by the American Enka Corporation for a high-modulus rayon fiber.

polypropylene Type of olefin fiber made from propylene gas, a by-product of the petroleum industry.

poncho Loose garment with a slit in the center to be slipped over the head. Made either of a waterproof material or of wool of the types worn in South America, it provides protection for the wearer.

pongee Lightweight, slightly textured silk fabric, in a natural shade, for summer suits, sportswear, pajamas, and underwear.

poplin Corded fabric of cotton, polyester, silk, nylon, wool, or blends of fibers; used for shirts, neckwear, suits, coats, underwear, and pajamas.

poplin, Irish *See* IRISH POPLIN.

porkpie hat Hat of felt or fabric with a flat-topped crown resembling a pork pie in shape.

poromeric material Polyurethane material strengthened by polyester; used for the uppers of shoes, golf bags, cases, and other articles. Brand names: Aztran, Clarino, Corfam, Porvair.

portmanteau Bag or case to carry apparel, originally designed for carrying clothes on horseback.

Porvair Brand of poromeric material registered by the Inmont Corporation.

postboy waistcoat Waistcoat worn originally by a postilion on one of the horses drawing a carriage. It has a five-button single-breasted front, a horizontal lap seam in line with the bottom button, flap pockets on both sides in line with the seam, and long points, either angular or rounded, extending several inches below the bottom button. The back is separated from the front by 6-inch side vents reaching up to the waistline. Fabrics include tattersall-check woolens, yellow or other solid-color box cloth, and billiard cloth.

postcure finish Durable-press finish that is applied to a fabric by the mill but is heat-set or cured by the garment maker after the garment has been completed.

precure finish Durable-press finish that is applied to a fabric and heat-set or cured before the fabric is made into garments.

preshrunk Term applied to a garment of which the fabric has been shrunk in the manufacturing process. However, no degree of shrinkage is indicated by this designation unless the limit is specified.

press, hot-head *See* HOT-HEAD PRESS.

prickseam (outseam) Seam on the outside of a glove with the raw edges showing, sewn with a machine in which the needle moves horizontally instead of vertically in order to form an even edge.

Primatized Trademark of a durable-press process, registered by Deering Milliken, Inc.

Prince Albert Double-breasted black or dark gray frock coat, knee-length or longer, named for Prince Albert Edward (later King Edward VII). It was worn with matching or striped trousers for formal day occasions.

print Fabric on which a pattern has been dyed by means of rollers, blocks, or screens.

print, African *See* AFRICAN PRINT.

print, Hawaiian *See* HAWAIIAN PRINT.

print, India *See* INDIA PRINT.

print, tapestry *See* TAPESTRY PRINT.

print, tone-on-tone *See* TONE-ON-TONE PRINT.

printing *See* BLOCK PRINTING; DISCHARGE PRINTING; RESIST PRINTING; ROLLER PRINTING; SCREEN PRINTING.

postboy waistcoat   **Prince Albert**

puggaree

pump

processed fabric Fabric treated with a chemical to make it water-repellent, stain-resistant, mothproof, shrinkage-proof, etc.

protein fiber Fiber made from a protein such as casein of milk, zein of corn, and peanut protein.

puff cuff Pleated cuff for a shirt sleeve.

puff tie Necktie with two wide ends crossed one over the other and held together with a pin.

puggaree Pleated woven fabric, in a solid color or patterned, for the band of a straw or felt hat. A similar fabric was worn originally in India.

pullman slippers Soft leather slippers with cushioned soles enclosed in a zippered or buttoned case; designed for travel.

pullover Long-sleeved or sleeveless shirt or sweater, with a neck opening only or with a short placket in front and a neck opening, that is pulled over the head.

pump Low-cut slip-on shoe of patent or dull-finish leather or poromeric material with a ribbed ribbon bow in front; used for formal evening wear.

pure-dye Term applied to silk fabric that has only a small amount of weighting.

purl Stitch in knitting in which the yarn is pulled from the face of the fabric toward the back as new loops are formed. The reverse of the plain knit stitch, it produces horizontal rows. In machine knitting purl stitches are produced on a links-and-links machine.

purple Color halfway between blue and red. The purple associated with the garments worn by emperors of ancient Rome was actually crimson.

puttee Band of cloth wound spirally around the leg to form a covering from the ankle to the knee, as worn by soldiers in World War I.

pyjamas British spelling of pajamas.

Q

Qiana Du Pont's registered name for specially processed nylon.

quilting Two pieces of material with a

quilting

raglan

layer of polyester fill, down, or batting inserted between them for insulation. The filling is held in place by stitching it to both pieces in a planned pattern. Quilting is used for ski parkas, jackets, and linings of outercoats or jackets.

R

rabbit Fur of the rabbit, especially the coney; used in the manufacture of felt hats mainly because its fibers have good matting characteristics.

raccoon Long-haired fur, mostly in grayish tones, used for coats.

racking Lateral movements of the needle bed, needles, or both of a knitting machine, which helps make a fabric compact and able to hold its shape.

rack stitch Knitting stitch that produces a herringbone design on one side of the fabric and a ribbed look on the opposite side.

raffia Light-colored fiber derived from the leafstalks of the raffia palm; used for hats.

raglan Loose-fitting coat with full-cut sleeves and a seam extending at an angle from each armhole to the collar in front and in back. It is named after the 1st Baron Raglan, commander of British troops in the Crimea.

raglan, split *See* SPLIT RAGLAN.

raincoat Lightweight coat made of waterproof or water-repellent fabric.

rajah Material somewhat like pongee, manufactured frequently of tussah silk but also of man-made fibers.

Rambouillet Breed of merino sheep that originated in France in the reign of Louis XVI and is now the leader of its type in the United States. It yields wool fibers in the 64s grade.

ramie Bast fiber similar to flax, obtained from a plant grown in eastern Asia and the southern United States; used in sportswear.

raschel knitting Knitting somewhat like tricot.

ratcatcher (1) Informal jacket for riding, walking, or shooting, (2) riding breeches, shirt, or scarf associated with the jacket; (3) folded scarf wrapped around the neck twice and tied with a double knot, as worn by horsemen.

ratiné Rough-surfaced plain-weave fabric of cotton, silk, or other fibers; used for sportswear. The rough texture is created with the use of slub yarns.

rawhide Cattle hide that has been dehaired, limed, and oiled but not tanned.

rayon Textile fiber made from regenerated cellulose by the viscose or cuprammonium process. The word "rayon" was invented in 1924 by Kenneth Lord, who thought the fiber had luster, from "ray" and "on" of cotton.

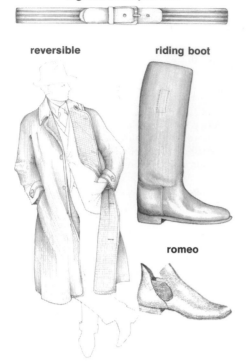

regimental-striped belt

reversible

riding boot

romeo

rayon, modified *See* MODIFIED RAYON.

rayon, spun *See* SPUN RAYON.

rayon, viscose *See* VISCOSE RAYON.

ready-for-the-needle Term applied to wool fabric in a stabilized state after steaming. The fabric holds its shape, and puckering is minimized.

ready-to-wear Term applied to ready-made apparel.

reclaimed (reworked) wool Reprocessed or reused wool.

red, Turkey *See* TURKEY RED.

red Mohr Authentic Scottish district check.

reed Comblike appliance on a loom that keeps the warp yarns apart so that the filling yarns can pass through regularly and pushes the filling thread against the already woven fabric. The separations in the reed are called dents, and the number of dents per inch determines the fineness of the fabric.

reefer Short box coat in a fairly heavy woolen or other cloth, usually double-breasted; also a long oblong muffler, usually of wool.

reel Revolving device or spool on which thread or yarn is wound.

regatta Strong cotton twill fabric, usually in blue-and-white stripes.

Régence *See* CHARVET.

regimental-striped belt Belt made of woven ribbon or webbing or knitted material in the colors of a military regiment.

regimental stripes Colors identified in England with various regiments and used in ties worn by their officers in civilian dress. Not only are authentic

regimental stripes worn, but similar colors and arrangements are used in neckwear in England and the United States.

regulation Term applied to a fabric or a garment accepted as a standard for a specific use such as a military uniform or dress for a special civilian service.

rep (repp) Closely woven ribbed fabric with a transverse cord effect, made of silk, polyester, wool, cotton, rayon, or blends of fibers; used for neckwear, accessories, and sportswear.

repeat Design that appears again and again in a fabric; also the number of threads required to complete one such design.

repp *See* REP.

reprocessed wool Wool fibers that have previously been fabricated but not worn and have been unraveled, restored to fiber form, spun, and woven again into material.

resilience (elasticity) Ability of a fiber or fabric to return to its original shape or position after having been strained or exposed to pressure. Wool and silk have a high degree of resilience, but linen has almost none and cotton has minimal resilience. Some man-made fibers are crimped to give them resilience.

resin finish Finish consisting of phenolic, melamine, or other synthetic resins that is impregnated in a fabric. The fabric is then baked to make it resistant to wrinkling and soiling.

resist-dyeing Method of cross-dyeing fabric by applying a chemical to certain yarns before they are woven and not to others. When the material is dyed, the untreated yarns take the dye and the treated ones resist it. Later the chemical that resists the dye is removed, and the fabric has a colorful pattern.

resist printing Method of printing fabrics. A wax or resinous substance that resists dye is applied to parts of the fabric. When the fabric is dipped in dye, only the uncovered area will take the dye. The wax substance is then removed, and the undyed area forms the design.

resort wear Apparel designed especially for wear at a center of recreation or sports away from the city.

retail Sale of merchandise in small quantities directly to the consumer.

retting Process of soaking vegetable stalks to decompose the gummy material, as in the preparation of flax.

reused wool Wool from garments or other materials used by consumers that has been converted to the fiber state and then spun and woven again.

reversed calf Calf leather with the flesh side on the outside. Excess fiber is removed by buffing to provide a napped surface or suede finish.

reverse knit Flat-knit fabric turned inside out to utilize the inner side for texture or dullness in sweaters, socks, and sportswear.

reverse pleat Pleat at the waistband of trousers that faces outward, in contrast to the normal pleat, which faces inward.

reverse twist Distinctive design created in a fabric by interlacing yarns spun in a counterclockwise direction with yarns spun clockwise.

reversible Term applied to an outercoat with one type of fabric on one side and another on the other side, either of which may be worn on the outside. For example, a coat may be of tweed on one side and cotton poplin on the other.

reworked wool *See* RECLAIMED WOOL.

rib One of a series of cords or ridges in a woven fabric made by using coarser yarns in the filling or warp. Examples of ribbed fabrics are Bedford cord and corduroy.

ribbon belt *See* BELT.

rib-knit Material having lengthwise ribs on both sides, knitted on two sets of opposing needles.

rickrack Edging or braid in a serpentine or zigzag design; used for trimming the borders of garments such as pajamas.

riding boot High leather boot shaped to fit the leg, designed especially for horseback riding.

ring Piece of jewelry in the form of a circle for wear on the finger; also a printed or woven design of this shape.

ring buckle Fastener composed of two rings.

rise Distance from the crotch to the top of the waistband of trousers, as in low-rise slacks and high-rise trousers.

robe (dressing gown) Loose-fitting garment of below-knee length, usually tied at the waist with a sash or cord, for wear in home. Fabrics include wool, silk, cotton, polyester, nylon, and blends.

robe, beach *See* BEACH ROBE.

robe, Kabuki *See* KABUKI ROBE.

roller printing Printing fabrics by means of patterns etched on copper rollers to which inks are applied. The fabrics are run through the roller printing machine at a high rate of speed.

romaine crepe Thin material made of blends such as rayon and wool or polyester and wool for shirts and pajamas.

Roman stripes Bright stripes in groups of contrasting colors, usually running in the warp direction.

romeo Man's fabric or soft leather slipper with a high back, a high front, and elastic insets at the sides.

Romney Breed of sheep that originated in the south of England and is now grown in the United States, Australia, and New Zealand.

rope sole Hemp or braided fibers arranged in the shape of a sole and held

ruffle

together with thread, tar, or adhesive.

roving Drawing cotton or wool fibers out and twisting them slightly.

rubber Substance derived from the latex of tropical plants, characterized by its stretching qualities and resistance to wear; also a synthetic substance resembling natural rubber. Rubber fibers are used in combination with other fibers for stretch materials, for rainwear, and for footwear.

rubber, crepe *See* CREPE RUBBER.

rubberized fabric Material with a coating of rubber on one or both sides to make it waterproof.

rubbers *See* CLOG RUBBERS; STORM RUBBERS.

rucking Wrinkling, folding, or puckering of material.

ruffle Strip of material, gathered or pleated, attached to each side of a shirt front with the outer edge free.

run Piece of fabric manufactured in a continuous operation; also a unit of measure for woolen yarn, a one-run yarn having 1,600 yards to the pound.

run of mill Yarn or fabric that has not been inspected or graded.

Russia Calfskin leather finished with a process involving birch-tar oil that gives it a distinctive aroma; used for footwear.

Russian cord Fabric with two warps, background and fancy. The surface has a raised rib or cable appearance.

Rust, John Daniel and Mack Donald American brothers who invented the Rust cotton-picking machine.

S

sabot Originally a wooden shoe worn by European peasants; in the United States, a wooden-soled slip-on with a leather upper in front, adopted for casual wear.

saddle leather Cowhide treated with vegetable tannage; used for belts, sports shoes, and leather goods.

saddle oxford Laced shoe with a strip of leather over the instep, which may be in the same color as the rest of the shoe or in a contrasting tone such as brown on white.

saddle-shoulder Term applied to a sweater or other knitted garment in which the sleeves are attached with seams extending from the armholes to the collar in front and back, in an effect like that of a raglan coat.

saddle stitch Running stitch in a heavy thread of blending or contrasting color, sewn by hand or by machine in a simulation of handwork; used for gloves and leather goods.

sack suit (lounge suit) Business suit of worsted, flannel, cheviot, tweed, or other fabrics with a loose-fitting single- or double-breasted jacket.

safari jacket *See* BUSH JACKET.

safari suit Suit of lightweight fabric with a belted bush jacket and matching trousers.

saffron Yellowish orange color derived from the dried vegetable plant of the same name or from synthetic dyestuffs.

sailcloth Canvas made of polyester, nylon, cotton, linen, or blends of fibers; used for sails and sportswear.

sailor *See* SENNIT.

sakel Egyptian cotton; one of the leading long-staple types in the world.

Sam Browne belt Wide leather belt with a small strap over the right shoulder, originally worn by British military men and named for an officer, Sir Samuel James Browne.

sandal Footwear consisting of a sole with a strap upper in front and a buckled strap extending from the back over the instep. Sometimes there are crossover or toe straps in front.

sandune Color in which tan and yellow are blended; used for apparel and accessories.

Sanforized Registered brand name of a process of controlling shrinkage in fabrics, owned by the Sanforized Company, a division of Cluett, Peabody & Co.

Sanforized Plus Brand name registered by Cluett, Peabody & Co. for regularly checked standards of performance of wash-and-wear garments. Involved are shrinkage control, smoothness after laundering, crease retention, and tensile strength in accordance with standards set by the Sanforized Company, a subsidiary of the parent company.

Sanitized fabric Material that has been treated with an antiseptic chemical which kills germs and prevents the odor of perspiration. Sanitized is a registered name of the Sanitized Sales Company of America.

sarape (serape) Colorful blanket sometimes worn as an outer garment in Mexico and South America.

sash Band of fabric worn around the waist of a robe or other garment.

sasse yarn Spun yarn made from staple fibers of viscose rayon.

sateen Cotton fabric, often mercerized, in a satin weave; used for linings, pajamas, and sportswear.

satin Closely woven fabric of silk, polyester, or other fibers with a glossy face and a dull-finish back. The lustrous appearance is accentuated by running the material between hot cylinders. Satin is used for neckwear, robes, pajamas, mufflers, waistcoats, cummerbunds, and trimming on formal evening clothes.

satin, panne *See* PANNE SATIN.

Savile Row Street in the West End of London on which many custom tailors were located. The words now connote the fine tailoring and styling of the West End area.

saxony Coating fabric made originally from the wool of merino sheep grown in Saxony; also a lighter-weight fabric with a slightly napped surface similar to flannel, used for suits, jackets, and slacks.

Sayelle Brand name of acrylic fiber, formerly Orlon 21, registered and manufactured by Du Pont.

scarf Originally a sash or band; later a necktie or cravat.

schiffli embroidery Type of embroidery that originated in Switzerland, produced by machine with a side-to-side stitch; used for dress shirts and sportswear.

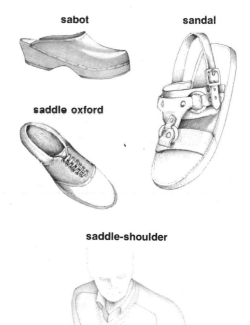

sabot

sandal

saddle oxford

saddle-shoulder

scoop neck Deep oval opening of a sweater or knitted shirt with the appearance of having been scooped out.

Scotchgard Brand name, registered by the 3M Company, of a process for water repellency and stain resistance.

Scotch grain Heavy chrome-tanned side leather with a deeply embossed pebbled surface that is retained after the shoe has been lasted, made originally in Scotland and England and now adopted in the United States. It is used primarily for shoes of the sturdy brogue type.

Scotch tweed Tweed made in a two-up and two-down twill in plain white with a filling of stock-dyed yarns.

scouring Cleansing wool of natural grease, dirt, and dry perspiration.

screen printing Printing fabrics by means of a screen of fine mesh specific areas of which are treated to avoid coloring matter. The coloring material is forced through the screen to the part of the fabric under the untreated areas. Each color in the design requires a separate screen.

scrim Open-weave mesh of cotton or a blend of polyester and cotton; used for shirts, underwear, pajamas, and sportswear.

scutching Use of rollers to break up and separate the woody portions of the flax stem from the retted fiber.

scye *See* ARMSCYE.

Sea Island Variety of long-staple cotton grown on islands off the coast of Florida, Georgia, and South Carolina, along the coast of the mainland, and in the West Indies.

seal, pin *See* PIN SEAL.

sealskin Skin of a seal with soft short hair; used for coats and hats.

seam Area of a garment where two pieces of material are sewn together.

seam, French-felled *See* FRENCH-FELLED SEAM.

seam, mock *See* MOCK SEAM.

seamless-knit fabric *See* CIRCULAR-KNIT FABRIC.

seamless-top shoe Shoe with a one-piece upper, stitched only in back and to the welt.

seconds Yarns, fabrics, or garments that do not meet the manufacturer's standards of quality.

seersucker Washable fabric of polyester and cotton, cotton, silk, or rayon with crinkled stripes made by altering the tension of the warp threads. It comes in woven stripes, plaids, checks, or printed designs for suits, jackets, slacks, pajamas, shorts, shirts, and robes. The word is derived from the Hindi *śīrśakar* (Persian *shīr-o-shakar,* meaning "milk and sugar").

self-pattern Woven design in the same shade as the background of the fabric. Examples: satin stripes, dobby figures.

selvage (selvedge) Either of the edges of a fabric, woven of heavier, special yarns, usually in a bright color, for reinforcement.

sennit (boater; sailor) Stiff straw hat with a flat-top oval crown and a flat brim. The term also referes to a flat natural-colored straw plaited in angles.

serape *See* SARAPE.

serge Smooth-surfaced material in a twill weave with the diagonal rib on both sides. Originally an all-worsted fabric, it is now woven as well in polyester, cotton, rayon, and other fibers or blends; used for suits, slacks, and sportswear.

serge, French-back *See* FRENCH-BACK SERGE.

set-in sleeve Sleeve of a coat, shirt, or other garment sewn in at the armhole.

sett helmet *See* TWEED SHOOTING HELMET.

sevenfold tie Unlined neckwear made with seven folds of fabric.

shade Tone of a color approaching the dark end of the scale.

shag Fabric with a pile or long-nap surface.

shaker sweater Sweater knitted of heavy

shave coat

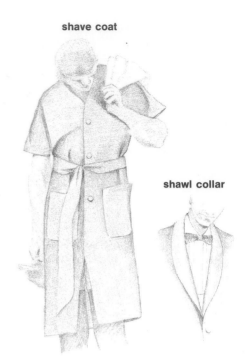

shawl collar

wool yarn in a plain ribbed stitch, so called because members of the Shaker sect originated it. A baby shaker sweater is similar but is knitted in a finer-gauge yarn.

shako High-crowned rigid military headdress with a visor, decorated with a plume. It is the full-dress headgear for the Scottish Highland Light Infantry.

shank Steel-plate or leather reinforcement in a shoe, extending from the heel forward to support the arch.

shantung Nubby fabric similar to pongee, made in silk, polyester, cotton, rayon, or blends of fibers for suits, accessories, and sportswear.

shaper Pattern or curved ruler used as a guide in giving the desired contour to the front of a garment; also a worker who performs this function by trimming the front with shears.

sharkskin Smooth-finished twill-weave material in two tones of yarn, made in worsted for suits and coats and in polyester, rayon, or silk for neckwear and sportswear.

shave coat Wrap style of robe in above-knee length with short sleeves, made of washable fabric with a matching tie belt.

shawl collar Collar extending from the waist around the neck, rolled back without indentations or peaks. Used on formal evening jackets and robes, it may be covered with satin or other facing or be of the same material as the garment.

shawl tongue *See* KILTIE.

shearing Cutting fleece from the body of a sheep with electric clippers; also cutting the nap of a material to an even level.

shearling Skin of a tanned lamb or sheep

scoop neck

seamless-top shoe

sennit (boater; sailor)

set-in sleeve

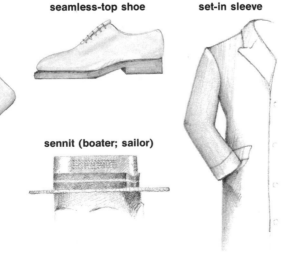

with the wool retained; used for lining material with the wool side in or out, for outerwear, and for gloves.

sheep Animal whose fleece provides wool. There are more than 500 breeds and subbreeds of sheep. Merino sheep yield the finest wool; the leading American merino is known as Delaine.

sheepskin Tanned skin of a sheep, used for linings of shoes and, with the suede side out and the wool side in, for linings of coats and other garments.

sheer Very thin, usually transparent fabric such as voile.

shell Outer fabric of a coat, neckwear, or other article of clothing.

shepherd's check Evenly proportioned check pattern in contrasting colors or shades of a color of a twill-weave fabric of wool, silk, polyester, rayon, or blends of fibers; used for sportswear, other clothing, and accessories.

Sherpa Brand name, registered by Collins and Aikman Corporation, for a pile fabric of acrylic fibers that resembles a shearling.

Shetland Warm, lightweight wool from sheep raised on the Shetland Islands, off the Scottish coast. Similar wools from other parts of the world woven into fabrics to resemble Shetland wool are called Shetland-type wools in the trade.

shirt Close-fitting or loose garment for the upper part of the body, made with short or long sleeves and with or without a collar.

shirting Fabric utilized for the manufacture of shirts, predominantly of polyester and cotton but of other fibers as well.

shirtmaker Person who cuts fabric for and tailors a shirt.

shirt suit Shirt with matching trousers.

shoddy Material made of ground-up rags

sheepskin

---

short-visor cap

silk hat (top hat)

or other reused fabrics, usually of wool or part wool.

shoe Covering for the foot, with a sole, heel, and upper, extending to the ankle or below.

shoehorn Curved implement of metal, wood, or horn used to ease slipping on a shoe.

shoe tree Form of wood or metal to fit inside a shoe in order to keep it in shape when it is not being worn.

shooting coat (shooting jacket) Sports coat or jacket of wool or a processed blended fabric; used for sports including shooting and hunting.

shooting helmet, tweed *See* TWEED SHOOTING HELMET.

short rounded collar Attached or separate shirt collar with rounded points of short length.

shorts (1) Short underwear trousers of a woven or knitted fabric, extending in various lengths to above the knee, with an elastic waistband and a buttoned or a slit front; (2) short-legged, close-fitting garment of woven or knitted fabric, also known as trunks, used for athletic purposes including swimming; (3) outer garment of trousers in twill, poplin, gabardine, flannel, madras, or other fabrics extending to the knee or above, also known as Bermuda shorts because they were first popularized on the island.

shorts, Bermuda *See* BERMUDA SHORTS.

shorts, boxer *See* BOXER SHORTS.

shorts, Jockey *See* JOCKEY SHORTS.

short-visor cap Close-fitting cap of tweed or other cloth with a visor that extends only a short distance in front.

shot silk Silk fabric woven with one color in the warp and another in the filling to achieve an iridescent effect.

shoulder-strap bag Bag of leather or other material with a strap to be worn over the shoulder. Known as a musette bag, it is used especially by men in military service.

---

showerproof Term applied to a fabric or garment treated with a water-repellent finish so that it sheds moisture from a light rainfall.

shrinking Reduction in the dimensions of a fabric after washing or subjection to moisture. To control such shrinkage, the fabric may be treated by a mechanical or chemical process.

shrunken calf Calfskin with a small all-over design developed by shrinking the hide; used mostly for footwear.

shrunk in London *See* LONDON-SHRUNK.

shuttle Implement that moves filling yarns between warp yarns to produce a woven fabric. Persimmon wood, which is shock-resistant, is used for the shuttles of power looms.

sideburns Short whiskers at the sides of the face. The word is derived from "burnsides."

side vent Slit toward the back of either side of a jacket or coat.

silesia Lightweight cotton twill material with a calendered glaze finish; used for linings.

silhouette Outline of a garment or outfit as worn by an individual, such as shapely or flowing lines.

silicone Chemical that makes fabrics water-repellent and stain-resistant. It is derived from silicon, a nonmetallic element found in sand and other parts of the earth's crust.

silk Fiber extruded by the silkworm in forming a cocoon, which is processed and woven into fabric. Silk is resilient and resists wrinkles. It is used for neckwear, shirts, pajamas, robes, and sportswear.

silk, artificial *See* ARTIFICIAL SILK.

silk, oiled *See* OILED SILK.

silk, shot *See* SHOT SILK.

silk, spun *See* SPUN SILK.

silk, tie *See* TIE SILK.

silk, waste *See* WASTE SILK.

silk, weighted *See* WEIGHTED SILK.

silk, wild *See* WILD SILK.

silk floss Short silk fibers in a tangled waste form.

silk hat (top hat) Stiff, high-crowned hat with a stiff, rolled-edge brim, made of lustrous silk plush; used for formal wear.

singeing (gassing) Removing lint or loose threads from the surface of fabric by passing the material over heated plates or gas flames during the finishing process.

single Term applied to one strand of yarn twisted in one direction; also to fabric woven with a single warp and filling.

single-breasted Term applied to a jacket, waistcoat, or outercoat with a single set of buttons sewn a short distance from the edge of one side of the front and buttonholes in the corresponding positions on the other side.

single cuff Cuff of a shirt, either soft or

6 by 3 rib

slipper

skeet-shooting jacket

ski boot

ski cap

slack suit

slacks, flared

starched, of one thickness. It may be fastened with cuff links or buttons.

single-end bow tie *See* ONE-END BOW TIE.

single warp Warp consisting of single strands of yarn, in contrast to two-ply or thicker yarns.

sisal Strong vegetable fiber used in making rope.

6 by 3 rib Term applied to knitting in which six ribs on the outside alternate with three ribs on the inside; used for hosiery, underwear, and other apparel.

size Number or letter designating the dimensions of a ready-made garment or accessory, based on measurements of the chest, waist, inseam, neck, and sleeves.

sizing Finishing process for yarn or fabric, intended to add heft, a smooth surface, or stiffness.

skeet-shooting jacket Jacket of gabardine or other fabric having a leather shoulder pad, designed specifically for skeet shooting.

skein Length of yarn, usually 120 yards, mechanically wrapped around a coil or reel.

skein dyeing Dyeing yarn on a reel.

ski boot High shoe with a single- or dou-

ble-thickness upper or a composition upper, a squarish tip, walled sides, and thick soles for attachment to the binding of a ski.

ski cap Woven fabric cap with a visor and earflaps or a knitted cap for skiing.

skimmer Colloquial term for a sennit straw hat.

skinny pants Separate trousers, cut on trim lines, to fit the legs closely.

skipdent Open-weave fabric for shirts, underwear, and pajamas, produced by skipping dents, the openings between wires in the reed through which the warp ends are drawn.

skive To cut leather in thin layers.

slacks Woven or knitted odd trousers of full or trim cut in wool, wool and polyester, cotton, cotton and polyester, or other fibers. Jeans, bell bottoms, and many other styles are included.

slacks, flared Slacks with trim lines from the waist to just below the knees and widened lines from there to the bottoms.

slack suit Combination of slacks and a shirt or shirt jacket in harmonizing or contrasting colors, generally made in a lightweight fabric for resort, beach, and casual wear.

slash pocket Pocket set into a slash opening, usually vertically or at a slight angle.

Slater, Samuel American industrialist who arrived in the United States from England in 1789. He remembered the details of five vital textile machines, which he built in Pawtucket, Rhode Island. He is regarded as the father of the American textile industry.

sleepcoat Knee-length button-front garment, a modernized version of the night-shirt.

sleeve Part of a shirt, jacket, or coat that covers the arm; made in many different styles including tapered, raglan, set-in, and cuffed.

sleeve, dolman *See* DOLMAN SLEEVE.

sleeve, half *See* HALF SLEEVE.

sleeve, set-in *See* SET-IN SLEEVE.

sleeveless pullover *See* PULLOVER.

sley Number of threads per inch in a woven fabric.

slicker Raincoat of oiled cotton or silk with snap fasteners or buttons and a corduroy-lined standing collar.

slide fastener *See* ZIPPER.

slipover Garment that is put on by slipping it over the head.

slippage Sliding of warp threads over filling threads, or vice versa, as the result of a loose weave or of unevenly matched filling and warp.

slipper Any footwear except a rubber without a fastening that is slipped on the foot and stays there because of tension around the top.

slipper, Faust *See* FAUST SLIPPER.

slippers, pullman *See* PULLMAN SLIPPERS.

slipsole (slip tap) Half sole extending from tip to shank, placed between the outsole and welt or insole of a shoe to provide warmth or improve fit.

sliver Round, untwisted strand of cotton or other fiber removed from the carding or combing machine. The slivers are then drawn and spun into yarn.

slotted collar Attached or separate shirt collar with a stay under each point to prevent it from curling up or down.

slub Irregularity deliberately created in a yarn by tightening and relaxing tension during spinning; also an accidental imperfection.

slug Heavy nail used in the sole of a boot.

smock Loose-fitting garment, made of cotton or other washable material, that is slipped over other clothes to prevent soiling them. An artist wears a smock partly to keep paints from spotting other clothes.

smoking jacket Separate jacket of wool, silk, brocade, velvet, or a blended fabric, worn as an indoor casual jacket. In France a dinner jacket is called "un smoking."

snap-brim hat Felt, straw, or fabric hat with a brim designed to be turned down in front or on one side and up in back.

snap fastener Closure consisting of a metal disc with a springy action and a metal stud to which it may be attached. The two parts are sewn or riveted separately on the edges of the garment to be fastened; used for pajamas, underwear, gloves, and sportswear.

sneaker Laced or slip-on shoe with a

snap-brim hat

sneaker

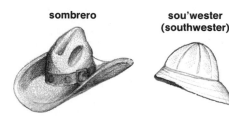

sombrero **sou'wester (southwester)** **spats** **split raglan**

stickpin

canvas upper and a rubber sole; used for tennis and other sports and for casual wear.

sneaker, lace-to-toe *See* LACE-TO-TOE SNEAKER.

socks *See* ABERDEEN SOCKS; CREW SOCKS; CUSHION-FOOT SOCKS; OVER-THE-CALF SOCKS; SUPPORT SOCKS.

soft goods *See* DRY GOODS.

sole, rope *See* ROPE SOLE.

sole leather Heavy leather from cattle hide tanned and finished to create a firm texture for the soles of shoes.

solution dyeing (dope dyeing) Addition of coloring agents to the chemical compound of a man-made fiber before it is extruded through the spinneret. The filament emanating from the spinneret is thus already dyed.

sombrero Big felt or straw hat with a high crown and a wide, deeply rolled brim, worn by Mexican ranchers and others.

soutache Rounded embroidery braid made of silk, cotton, or other fibers, applied as trimming to robes, pajamas, and sportswear.

South African wool Merino wool produced in South Africa in grade 64s to 70s.

sou'wester (southwester) Round-crowned hat of oiled cotton or other waterproof material with a brim widening toward the back.

soybean fiber Protein fiber made from soybeans.

space-dyed yarn Yarn dyed in one color for a certain length and in another color or colors for other lengths, the sequence being repeated. When such a yarn is woven, random effects are achieved.

spandex Synthetic fiber with stretch characteristics. It usually provides the core around which other fibers are wound to enhance wearability.

spats Ankle covering of box cloth, linen, or other materials. Spats extend above the ankles, are fastened at the sides with buckles or buttons, and are held under the shank of the shoes with straps and buckles. The word is an abbreviation of "spatterdashes."

spatterdash Knee-high leg covering formerly used for protection against mud and water.

specialty fiber (hair fiber) Any of a group of fibers that are somewhat similar to wool but are not classed as such. In this category are vicuña, camel's hair, llama, guanaco, cashmere, and angora. Specialty fibers are often blended with wool in woven or knitted materials.

spectrum Colors visible when rays of light pass through a prism, arranged in order of their wavelengths: violet, indigo, blue, green, yellow, orange, red.

spindle Long narrow rod on which spun

thread is twisted and held during the spinning process in a machine or wheel.

spinneret Metal device with tiny holes through which a solution is forced at high speed to make fine filaments, which are solidified in an acid bath.

spinning Drawing and twisting fibers in order to convert them into thread or yarn.

spinning, Bradford *See* BRADFORD SPINNING.

spinning, melt *See* MELT SPINNING.

spinning, wet *See* WET SPINNING.

spinning jenny Machine for spinning cotton with more than one spindle, invented in 1764 by James Hargreaves, who named it after his wife Jenny.

spinning wheel Machine used for spinning yarn in colonial days, now regarded as an antique or a decorator's piece. Modern spinning represents an electrification of the spinning-wheel principle.

Spitalfields Heavy silk in small allover patterns, originally woven in the Spitalfields district of the East End of London; used for neckwear.

splite tie Four-in-hand tie with a center inverted pleat on the apron, or wide end. It generally had a solid-color area for the knot and narrow end and a checked design for the apron.

split raglan Outercoat with the sleeves set in at the front and forming raglan sleeves in the rear, the seams extending at an angle from the collar to the armholes.

sponging Exposing woolen fabric to steam emanating from a perforated cylinder before it is made into garments.

spool *See* BOBBIN.

sporran Traditional pouch of Scottish Highland dress, tied around the waist and hanging in front. It is made of goatskin in black, white, or gray and may be decorated with tassels.

sports shirt Casual shirt with short or long sleeves, often worn without a tie; made of a woven or knitted fabric in a solid color or a figured pattern, check, or plaid.

sports shoe Any of a wide variety of styles of footwear for wear with slacks and sports clothes, made in one color or in a two-tone combination.

sportswear Apparel designed for participants in any sport or for spectators of sporting events.

spot- and stain-resistant Term applied to a fabric treated with chemicals so that

a garment tailored from it will repel spots and stains.

spun glass Glass in the form of textile fibers such as Fiberglas.

spun linen Fine linen woven by hand or machine for use in handkerchiefs and neckwear.

spun rayon Filaments of viscose or cuprammonium rayon cut into controlled lengths (staple) and then twisted into yarn for weaving into fabrics. The short lengths may be blended with other fibers for fabrics used in tailored apparel.

spun silk Short fibers of silk spun into yarn and woven into fabric.

spun yarn Yarn made of fibers of controlled lengths (staple) or of short silk fibers that cannot be reeled.

Stadium Boot Trademark of an above-ankle lined boot.

stain removal Stains should be removed from garments as early as possible. Plain cold water or carbonated water, if applied early, can minimize a stain, and a spot remover can clean most soilage. Dry cleaning is the final answer.

stain-resistant *See* SPOT- AND STAIN-RESISTANT.

staple Mean or average length of a wool, cotton, or other fiber to be utilized in spinning yarn; also any article for which there is a steady demand.

staple, cut *See* CUT STAPLE.

starched (stiff) bosom Set-in shirt front of two or more thicknesses of fabric, laundered with starch to achieve a stiff, smooth surface; intended for formal or business dress. The term also applies to a pleated bosom, usually piqué, that has been starched and pressed.

stickpin *See* TIEPIN.

stiff bosom *See* STARCHED BOSOM.

stitch *See* BLIND STITCH; CABLE STITCH; CREPE STITCH; DROP STITCH; FLOAT STITCH; RACK STITCH; SADDLE STITCH; WHIPSTITCH.

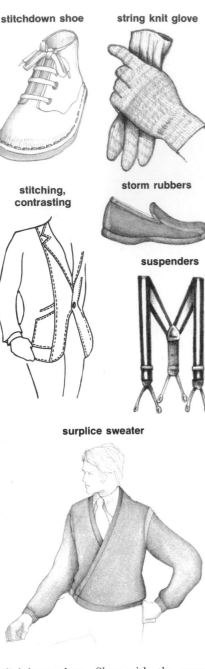

stitchdown shoe

string knit glove

stitching, contrasting

storm rubbers

suspenders

surplice sweater

stitchdown shoe Shoe with the upper extending over the sole at the sides and stitched to it with long, visible stitches.

stitching, contrasting Stitching at seams in white or a color to contrast with the color of a jacket or other article of apparel.

stock Wide band of fabric, either soft or stiffened, worn around the neck and usually fastened with a buckle in back.

stock-dye To place fibers in a chemical color bath before they are spun into yarn, thereby achieving maximum penetration of the dye.

stockinette Knitted fabric of wool or a blend of worsted and cotton, often with a fleece-type back; used for sports jackets and housecoats.

storm rubbers Footwear of rubber-coated material, cut high in front, with sturdy diamond-design molded soles.

straw Vegetable fiber, such as that of wheat or palm, processed and plaited for use in hats or footwear.

straw, coconut *See* COCONUT STRAW.

stretch woven fabric Fabric used originally in ski pants made in Austria and Germany, Elasticity is achieved by the use of special stretch yarns in the warp and worsted in the filling.

stretch yarn Thermoplastic filament yarn texturized so that it can be stretched and make a quick recovery.

string knit glove Glove made of cotton string that is somewhat lighter than cord but much thicker than thread. The knitted texture has a three-dimensional look.

stripes Lines of varying widths, ranging from narrow pin lines to broad, bold bands, used as a fabric design.

stripes, awning *See* AWNING STRIPES.

stripes, Bengal *See* BENGAL STRIPES.

stripes, candy *See* CANDY STRIPES.

stripes, chalk *See* CHALK STRIPES.

stripes, Grecian *See* GRECIAN STRIPES.

stripes, hairline *See* HAIRLINE STRIPES.

stripes, pencil *See* PENCIL STRIPES.

stripes, regimental *See* REGIMENTAL STRIPES.

stripes, Roman *See* ROMAN STRIPES.

stripping Bleaching to remove dye or printed color from portions of a fabric.

stroller Oxford gray or black jacket worn with striped gray trousers for formal day occasions.

stud Fastener with a pin or button back for the bosom of a shirt worn for formal or other occasions. It may be made of plain or tooled metal, pearl, a colored stone, or enamel.

S-twist Yarn twist to the left in which the spirals slant like the middle part of the letter S.

style Distinguishing characteristics in the shape, pattern, material, or color of an article of apparel.

stylist Person who creates ideas for fabrics or garments.

suede Leather of which the flesh side is buffed to a velvet finish. Originally only kidskin was used, but now calfskin is the commonest suede leather. The word is derived from *Suède*, the French name for Sweden, where the process originated.

suede cloth Fabric napped on one side to look like leather; used in sportswear.

Suffolk Breed of British down sheep created by crossing Southdown rams with Norfolk ewes; also the name given to a jacket similar to a norfolk jacket, with two box pleats in front and one in the center of the back.

suit Outfit for men consisting of a jacket and trousers, with or without a vest.

suiting Material of any kind that may be made into a suit.

suiting, tropical *See* TROPICAL SUITING.

sunfast Term applied to a fabric processed with a good dye to resist fading by sunlight.

Sunningdale Style of jacket with fullness across the shoulder blades, 3-inch tucks at the waist spaced about $2\frac{1}{2}$ inches apart, and a one-piece back. It is named for the Sunningdale golf course in England.

Supima Brand name of fabric made of unusually long-staple cotton fibers from the southwestern part of the United States.

support socks Socks made with stretch yarn or with a combination of vertical and horizontal ribbing; worn to provide support for the calves.

surah Soft fabric in a twill weave, made of silk, rayon, polyester, or blends; used for neckwear, mufflers, linings, and sportswear.

surcoat Originally a tunic type of garment worn over armor; now an outercoat worn over a suit.

suri Fine breed of domestic alpaca that yields a very long, silky fiber.

surplice sweater Sweater with a diagonally overlapping front.

surtout Long garment worn as an overcoat.

suspenders Means of supporting trousers, consisting of two straps or bands worn over the shoulders and crossing in back. The British term for suspenders is braces.

swallowtail coat Name for the tailcoat.

swatch Small piece of fabric used to indicate pattern, weave, color, or texture.

sweatband Band, usually of leather, sewn inside a hat where it comes in contact with the head.

sweater Knitted garment, with or without sleeves, in a pullover or jacket style with a button or zipper closure. Made of wool, acrylic, mohair, polyester, cotton, or blends of fibers, it is used for casual wear or active sports.

sweater, belted *See* BELTED SWEATER.

sweater, coat *See* COAT SWEATER.

sweater, Fair Isle *See* FAIR ISLE SWEATER.

sweater, shaker *See* SHAKER SWEATER.

sweater, surplice *See* SURPLICE SWEATER.

sweater, turtleneck *See* TURTLENECK SWEATER.

sweat shirt Knitted pullover shirt of cotton or blends of fibers with a smooth surface on the outside and a napped surface on the inside. It is worn primarily by athletes before and after exercise or participation in sporting events.

swim shorts, India madras *See* INDIA MADRAS SWIM SHORTS.

swimsuit Knitted garment of one or two pieces, designed for swimming.

swivel Additional filling yarn used for clipped woven patterns in a fabric such as dotted swiss.

Syl-Mer Name registered by the Dow Chemical Company for a water-repellent finish of fabrics.

synthetic Term applied to fibers such as nylon, acrylic, and polyester created by scientists from nonfibrous materials to resemble natural fibers. It does not refer to acetate, rayon, or other cellulosic fibers, which are derived from natural products and therefore are known as man-made. However, the two terms are used interchangeably in the apparel field.

synthetic leather Cellulose, rubber-coated material, or paper products fabricated to resemble leather.

synthetic rubber *See* RUBBER.

T

tab Piece of fabric with a buttonhole, as under a collar or at the front of a jacket or coat, for the fastening of a button on the opposite side; also a portion of terry cloth or toweling without pile.

tab collar Shirt collar with slots and stays on the underside of the points that are held in place with tabs buttoning to the neckband button or snapped together.

tabless tab collar Short-point collar resembling a tab collar but lacking tabs or fasteners; often worn with a collar pin to hold the points in place.

tack To baste or stitch temporarily.

taffeta Plain-weave fabric of silk or other fibers that is finished smooth on both sides and has a sheen.

tailcoat Formal evening coat with a shaped upper part and a seam at the waistline from which tails extend in back to the break in the knees. The front has lapels faced with satin or grosgrain that do not meet. Fabrics include lightweight worsted, mohair, and polyester blend in black or midnight blue and, for theatrical appearances, velvet and brocade in maroon, white, or other shades. Matching trousers are finished with braid at the sides.

tailor Person who cuts fabrics and sews pieces into coats, suits, and other apparel.

tails Abbreviated name for a formal evening tailcoat.

tam-o'-shanter Scottish type of cap, usually knitted, with a loose, flat top and a close-fitting headband.

tannage, bark *See* BARK TANNAGE.

tannin (tannic acid) Substance obtained from gallnuts and the bark of trees, especially oak and sumac, used in dyeing textiles and producing leather.

tanning Application of tannin to a raw hide in order to convert it into leather.

There are several types of tanning. Oak-tanned leather is produced after several months in an oak-bark solution, while hemlock leather is produced similarly by utilizing hemlock bark. Union and mongrel tanning are carried out with mixtures of vegetable materials, and chrome tanning with potassium dichromate and muriatic acid.

tapa cloth *See* BARK CLOTH.

tape Band of tightly woven material used for edging or reinforcement.

tape measure Tape, usually at least 60 inches long and $\frac{1}{2}$ inch wide or slightly wider, divided into inches and fractions thereof.

taper Converging lines of a garment, as in trousers that become narrower from the hips or the knees down.

tapestry print Design in colors resembling tapestry printed on a smooth or textured fabric.

tarlatan Thin open-weave muslin used as a stiffening agent to give form to a garment.

tartan Plaid design associated with a specific Scottish clan, made of wool or other fabrics and used for accessories and sportswear; also a woolen cloth in this design, worn over the shoulder by a member of the clan.

Taslan Brand name, registered by Du Pont, for a textured yarn made by the Du Pont bulking process to give it loftiness.

tattersall Checked pattern formed by vertical and horizontal stripes in one or two colors on a light-colored background; used in wool, cotton, and blends of fibers for accessories and sportswear. It is named after a horse market, started by Richard Tattersall in 1766 in London, where sportsmen wore waistcoats of this pattern, which was also prevalent in horse blankets.

teasel Flower head of the fuller's teasel, which has firm barbs when dried. It has long been used to pull and loosen the fibers of fabrics in order to create a soft napped finish. Similar results are achieved by the use of wire brushes.

Tebelized Brand name of a finish applied to fabrics to make them wrinkle-resistant, registered and controlled by Tootal Licensing, English Calico, Ltd.

Teck tie Four-in-hand tie with a ready-made knot and wide ends spread apart; named for the Duke of Teck.

Teflon Brand name of tetrafluoroethylene fiber made by Du Pont.

telescope crown Crown of a felt or straw hat creased with a flat top and an even height at the sides.

Tempra Brand name of industrial rayon yarn manufactured by the American Enka Corporation.

ten-gallon hat *See* COWBOY HAT.

tennis shoe Low shoe with a canvas or leather upper and a rubber or spiked-leather sole.

tensile strength Force, measured in pounds per square inch or other units, that a fabric or fiber can withstand without breaking.

tenterhook Nail used to fasten fabric on a frame known as a tenter so that any alteration in its original measurements that has occurred during the finishing process may be corrected.

Teron Companion fiber to Terylene, made by Imperial Chemical Industries, Ltd., and sold in all parts of the world except the United States.

terra-cotta Reddish orange color associated with baked clay.

territory wool Wool grown in the West, in states that were formerly territories. It is usually lower in quality than bright wool.

terry (terry cloth) Fabric in cotton or cotton and polyester with a looped surface on one or both sides; used for beachwear and sportswear.

terry, knit *See* KNIT TERRY.

Terylene Brand name for polyester, registered and made by Imperial Chemical Industries, Ltd., in England. The word is derived from terephthalate and polyethylene.

textile Any woven, knitted, or felted fabric.

tab collar

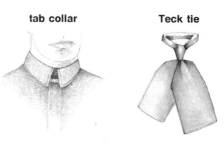

Teck tie

tailcoat

Textralized Trademark of yarn made by a crimping process by Joseph Bancroft & Sons Company.

texture Originally, a woven fabric (the word is derived from the Latin *textura,* meaning "web"); now the surface of a fabric, whether smooth, rough, or irregular.

textured filament yarn Synthetic yarn treated to produce a curled or crimped effect. When such a yarn is woven or knitted, an irregular surface results.

thermal Term applied to knitted material, used mainly for underwear, that keeps the wearer warm by trapping air in the cellular areas between threads.

thermoplastic Term applied to resins and man-made or synthetic fibers that soften at very high temperatures and harden again after cooling. Fabrics or garments made of thermoplastic fibers may be creased or pleated permanently in the softened state.

thibet Piece-dyed heavy suiting, ranging from 12 to 20 ounces per yard, originally made from the wool of sheep raised in Tibet.

thistle-shaped bow tie Straight, narrow bow tie resembling a ribbon-shaped tie.

thong Strip of leather or rawhide used as a fastener.

thread Continuous strand made of ply yarn with many twists per inch, sometimes treated with wax or other coating to produce a smooth surface for sewing.

thread count *See* COUNT.

throat Part of a shoe at the instep where the vamp opens.

ticket pocket Small pocket on the right-hand side of a jacket or coat just above the regular pocket. It provides a conveniently accessible place for tickets or coins.

ticking Twill-weave heavy cotton fabric made without boil-off treatment, usually in white with colored stripes; employed primarily for covering mattresses and furniture and also for sportswear.

tie Short for necktie; also a low laced oxford shoe.

tie, bar-shaped *See* BAR-SHAPED TIE.

tie, bolo *See* BOLO TIE.

tie, bow *See* BOW TIE.

tie, butterfly *See* BUTTERFLY TIE.

tie, court *See* COURT TIE.

tie, Joinville *See* JOINVILLE TIE.

tie, lock-knot *See* LOCK-KNOT TIE.

tie, pointed-end *See* POINTED-END TIE.

tie, puff *See* PUFF TIE.

tie, sevenfold *See* SEVENFOLD TIE.

tie-and-dye (tie dyeing) Method of dyeing fabrics by tying knots so that only certain parts absorb the dye; used for neckwear and sportswear.

tie bar Clip with an ornamental front or chain to hold a tie to the placket of a shirt.

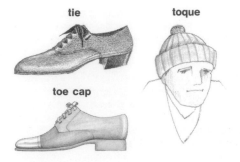

tie   toque

toe cap

tie clasp Metal holder, of a clamp or slip-on type, to keep the lower part of a tie in place.

tie dyeing *See* TIE-AND-DYE.

tiepin (stickpin) Metal pin with a stone, pearl, or other ornament on one end and a point on the other, used as a decoration beneath the knot of a necktie and as a means of holding both ends of the tie in place.

tie silk Twill silk of fine quality used for neckwear and robes.

tie tack Device consisting of two parts: an outer decorative part, backed with a pin, that pierces a necktie and shirt front; and a clamp that attaches to the pin and holds the tie against the shirt.

tint Pale tone of a color, approaching the light end of the scale.

tip, French *See* FRENCH TIP.

tips Ends of suspenders.

tissue Sheer lightweight fabric such as voile and chambray.

toast Soft tan shade of toasted bread.

toboggan cap Long cap of knitted wool or other fibers, worn for tobogganing.

toe, bulb *See* BULB TOE.

toe, bump *See* BUMP TOE.

toe, toothpick *See* TOOTHPICK TOE.

toe box Shaped stiff piece of leather placed inside the tip of a shoe to maintain its contours.

toe cap Outer covering of the tip of a man's shoe, separated from the vamp by a plain or perforated line. It may have a perforated medallion in the center.

toggle Crosspiece of wood, metal, or other material attached to a rope, cord, or chain and designed to be inserted in the loop of a cord, rope, or chain as a closure on a garment; also a hook used to hold leather in a frame after coatings have been applied for patent leather.

toile French term for linen.

tone Quality or value of a color lightened with the addition of white or darkened with the addition of black or gray.

tone-on-tone print Printed design utilizing two or more tones of a color.

tongue Strip of leather sewn to the top of the vamp on the inside of a shoe as a protection under the laces.

tongue, bellows *See* BELLOWS TONGUE.

tongue, shawl *See* KILTIE.

tooth Prickly, wiry feel of a heavy tweed, so called because the fabric gives the impression of a bite.

toothpick toe Very sharply pointed tip of a man's shoe.

top Wool fibers or synthetic staple wrapped in a circular shape resembling a large spool and ready to be spun into yarn; also a knitted pullover or denim shirt or jacket for wear with denim jeans.

topcoat Outercoat made of fabric lighter than that of an overcoat. The maximum weight is 18 ounces per square yard, and most topcoats weigh somewhat less.

topee Helmetlike hat of cork or pith with a cloth covering, worn originally in India as a protection against the sun. When the inner layer is made of pith, it is known also as a pith helmet.

Topel Registered name for cellulosic fiber made by Courtaulds North America, Inc.

top hat *See* GRAY TOP HAT; SILK HAT.

topper Colloquial name for a top hat.

toque Small, close-fitting brimless cap or hat.

torque Force in twisted yarns that produces springiness and soft loftiness in the finished fabric.

toupee Artificial hairpiece; partial wig.

tow Group of continuous filaments loosely held together.

tow coat Three-quarter double-breasted coat in a fleece fabric, fastened with toggles; used for winter sports.

town suit Tailored suit for business wear.

toyo hat Summer hat of man-made fibers resembling paper. The effect is somewhat like that of a panama.

trade Manufacturers and others involved in making apparel and accessories and marketing them to consumers.

trademark Symbol used to identify a product, manufacturer, or source, usually registered with the United States government.

tree *See* BOOT TREE; SHOE TREE.

Tremont hat Felt hat with a tapered crown and a narrow brim, in fashion in the 1950s.

trench coat Double-breasted outercoat patterned after the gabardine coat worn in the trenches by British army officers in World War I. The original had a gun flap, a removable processed lining, an all-around belt, and brass trimming. Most of these details are present in the authentic adaptation for civilians.

trend Movement of fashion in a particular direction.

trews Tight-fitting knitted garment worn by Scotsmen under a kilt; also close-fitting trousers, usually in a tartan-patterned fabric.

triacetate Acetate fiber, so named because the cellulose is acetylated to a greater degree than in other acetates. Employed alone or blended with other fibers, it can be heat-set for use in durable-press garments. The trade name is Arnel, registered by the Celanese Corporation.

tricot Thin, lightweight fabric of the warp-knit type, made of single or fine yarn; used for shirting and other purposes.

tricotine *See* CAVALRY TWILL.

trilby hat Felt hat with a rolled brim, originally worn in England. It derives its name from the dramatic adaptation of the novel *Trilby*.

trilobal Term applied to the cross section of certain textile fibers. The three-lobed shape reflects light and results in fabrics of higher color values.

trimming Ornamental addition to apparel.

tropical suiting Lightweight fabric for men's suits, made in all synthetic fibers or blends.

tropical worsted Worsted suiting weighing from 6 to 11 ounces per yard, made in a variety of weaves with two-ply or single-ply yarns in the warp and filling; used for suits, slacks, and sportswear.

trousering Fabric woven or knitted especially for manufacture into trousers, usually firmer and more compact than suiting.

trousers (pants) Garment covering the lower torso and the two legs separately. Among the early uses of trousers was the covering of silk breeches while riding, much as cowboys employ chaps. The Duke of Wellington exerted some influence in the adoption of trousers by wearing them on ceremonial occasions. After the War of 1812 trousers were widely worn in the United States instead of silk breeches and stockings, which seemed too British.

trousers, peg-top *See* PEG-TOP TROUSERS.

trunks *See* SHORTS.

T-shirt Knitted pullover undershirt with a round or V neck and short sleeves, made of cotton or blends of fibers.

tubular fabric Knitted or, sometimes, woven fabric in a seamless circular form, used for underwear, socks, and sportswear.

tuck Small fold sewn in a garment.

tunic Type of blouse; also a military jacket in a straight-hanging or belted style.

turkey red Bright scarlet dye formerly derived from the madder plant and now made chemically.

turn shoe Shoe with the upper and the sole sewn together on the wrong side and then turned to the right side.

turnup Term used in England for a trouser cuff.

turtleneck sweater Knitted pullover sweater with a long end that is slipped over the head and rolled to fit closely around the neck; made of wool, acrylic, mohair, cotton, or blended fibers.

Tuscan Yellow Italian straw derived from wheat stalks, plaited into various designs for hats.

tussah Wild silk from cocoons gathered in India and China. Fabrics made from such fibers have a nubby texture.

tuxedo Name for a dinner jacket. Until 1886 formal evening wear in the United States consisted of the tailcoat with proper accessories, including a white bow tie and a starched standing collar. That year Griswold Lorillard introduced the tailless evening jacket at Tuxedo Park, New York. This jacket became known as the tuxedo.

TV fold Method of folding a handkerchief so that about ½ inch appears above the line of the chest pocket of a jacket.

tweed Rough-textured woolen fabric appearing in many different patterns in plain and twill weaves; used for sportswear and other apparel. First woven by crofters near the Tweed River in Scotland, it derives its name from *tweel* or *tweed,* the Scottish word for "twill."

tweed, Donegal *See* DONEGAL TWEED.

Tweed, Harris *See* HARRIS TWEED.

tweed, Manx *See* MANX TWEED.

tweed, Scotch *See* SCOTCH TWEED.

tweed shooting helmet (sett helmet) Round-crowned tweed hat with a narrow brim, designed especially for shooting.

twill Basic weave characterized by diagonal lines on the surface of the fabric.

twill, cavalry *See* CAVALRY TWILL.

twill, corkscrew *See* CORKSCREW TWILL.

twill, gum *See* GUM TWILL.

twill, left-hand *See* LEFT-HAND TWILL.

twillette British cotton twill with a soft texture; used mainly in work clothes.

twist Turning of yarn, either to the left (S-twist) or to the right (Z-twist), to prepare it for weaving into a fabric.

twist, false (memory) *See* FALSE TWIST.

Tyrolean hat Hat with a sharply tapered crown, a narrow brim turned up in back and down in front, and a cord type of band decorated with a brush; made of rough-textured felt or velour. It is associated with the Austrian Tyrol.

U

ulster Double-breasted long overcoat with a big convertible collar, wide lapels, and a half or all-around belt; originally worn in Ireland.

ulsterette Double-breasted overcoat similar to an ulster but lighter in weight.

trench coat   **T-shirt**   **tweed shooting helmet (sett helmet)**   **ulster**

turtleneck sweater   **Tyrolean hat**

umbrella Collapsible frame with flexible ribs fastened to a pole and covered with a waterproof material, held with a handle as protection against rain.

unbleached Term applied to cotton or linen fabric in a gray or natural shade.

unconstructed suit Casual or business suit without padding or lining, usually made of double-faced material. The interior seams are either French-felled or bound.

uncut pile fabric Pile fabric woven on a loom with wires that lack cutting edges so that a looped pile appears on the surface.

undershirt Knitted or woven shirt worn next to the skin under a regular shirt.

unfinished worsted Material woven of medium-twisted worsted yarn with a slightly napped surface that conceals a twill weave. Made in plain, striped, checked, and plaid designs, it is used for suits and outercoats.

unhair To remove hair from a hide in making leather.

union cloth Fabric made of two kinds of fiber, as in the case of a cotton warp and a wool filling.

union dye Special coloring used to dye a fabric consisting of two or more different kinds of fiber.

union suit Underwear consisting of a shirt and shorts or pants in one piece.

unisex Term applied to apparel designed to be worn by both men and women.

upland cotton Type of short-staple cotton grown in the southern part of the United States and other areas.

V

vamp Section of the upper part of a shoe extending forward to the toe cap and part or all of the way to the rear seam.

vat dye Dye resulting from the reduction of an insoluble dye to a soluble solution. Vat-dyed fabrics have a high resistance to sunlight and washing.

veal In the leather industry, a large calfskin.

vegetable fiber Any natural fiber of vegetable origin, such as cotton, flax, ramie, and sisal.

Velcro Trademark, registered by the Velcro Corporation, for a hook-and-loop fastener consisting of two mating nylon tapes. The hook, or male, section is covered with little hooks; the loop, or female, section with tiny self-loops. When the two sections are pressed together, they become embedded and hold on with considerable strength until they are peeled apart.

velour Short-pile fabric woven of cotton, silk, spun rayon, polyester, wool, or blends and used for outercoats and sportswear; also a fur felt used for hats.

velvet Fabric with a short, thick-set pile of silk, cotton, or other fibers on a closely woven back of the same or different fibers; used for formal or casual jackets, robes, coats, and sportswear.

velvet, cut See CUT VELVET.

velveteen Short-pile fabric with a cotton filling that resembles velvet; used for trimming and sportswear.

venetian cloth Smooth-textured, warp-faced fabric of wool or cotton. In wool it is used for suits, topcoats, and sportswear; in cotton, for linings.

venetian covert High-grade worsted fabric with a napped surface and a high luster so that the twill weave is hardly discernible.

vent See CENTER VENT; SIDE VENT.

ventilated shoe Shoe with perforations in the upper or cutout areas to allow the free passage of air.

Verel Brand name of a modacrylic staple fiber made by Eastman Chemical Products, Inc.

vermilion Brilliant shade of red.

vest See WAISTCOAT.

vesting Fabric styled especially for tailoring into vests (waistcoats), such as piqué, Bedford cord, and tattersall-check wool.

vest suit Suit consisting of a vest (waistcoat) and matching pants, worn with a long-sleeved shirt, which is usually patterned.

vicuña Fiber from the undercoat of the vicuña, a ruminant related to the llama and found mainly in the high Andes. It is made into a fabric for suits, jackets, robes, and sportswear.

vigoureux printing Method of printing worsted fibers before spinning in order to achieve a mixture of light and dark shades in the finished fabric.

vinyl Polymerized vinyl chloride produced with a peroxide catalyst; used to make textile fibers. When a plasticizer is added, the material is hard and brittle and may be molded.

Vinylite Brand name of the Union Carbide Corporation for a resin made from high-molecular-weight vinyl chloride acetate.

virgin wool Wool used for first time after being clipped from sheep; in other words, wool that has never previously been used in yarn or fabric or for any other purpose.

viscose rayon Rayon filaments or staple produced from cellulose xanthate.

Vivana Nylon fiber registered and manufactured by the Dow Badische Co.

Viyella Registered name of a blend of wool and cotton in woven or knitted fabrics.

V neck Neckline of a pullover sweater or knit shirt forming a point in front.

voile Sheer cotton fabric woven from highly twisted yarn.

Vycron Registered name of a polyester

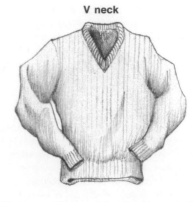

V neck

fiber manufactured by the Beaunit Corporation.

Vyrene Brand of spandex fiber made by Uniroyal, Inc. It is a single-filament polyurethane elastomer with stretch and retractable qualities.

W

wader Waist-high waterproof trousers attached to boots with cleated or corrugated rubber soles; used for wading in streams. The trousers are provided with shoulder straps or with buttons for suspenders.

waffle cloth Fabric of cotton or blended fibers, made in a honeycomb weave and used for formal evening shirts, accessories, and sportswear. Cotton waffle cloth is also known as waffle piqué.

wader

waistband Band around the waist at the top of trousers or shorts, made of non-elastic or elastic material.

waistcoat (vest) Sleeveless single- or double-breasted garment of waist length, fastened with buttons and buttonholes or a zipper; worn under a jacket. Fabrics include wool, silk, linen, flannel, piqué, and blends for business, sports, or formal wear. A waistcoat may or may not match the suit or jacket and trousers with which it is worn.

waistcoat, backless *See* BACKLESS WAIST-COAT.

waistcoat, odd *See* ODD WAISTCOAT.

waistcoat, postboy *See* POSTBOY WAISTCOAT.

waist-seam jacket Jacket with a visible seam around the waistline, sometimes with pleats and vertical panels above the seam. Such a jacket was one of the styles of jazz clothing after World War I.

wale In a woven fabric, a rib or raised cord, as in corduroy; in a knitted fabric, a row of loops running lengthwise.

walking frock suit Suit with a cutaway coat, usually three-buttoned, a matching waistcoat, and close-fitting trousers; in fashion in 1900.

walled-last shoe Shoe with a vertical or boxy line around the tip and front.

wardrobe Clothes possessed by an individual.

warp (end) Yarn that runs lengthwise on a loom. It is under tension as the fabric is being woven.

warp, single *See* SINGLE WARP.

warp knitting *See* KNITTING.

warp print Woven fabric with a shadowy effect produced by the use of printed warp threads and plain filling threads.

washable woolen Wool fabric that can be washed without shrinking to a noticeable degree. To keep the wool fibers from interlocking they are coated with a very thin film of nylon resin.

wash-and-wear *See* AUTOMATIC WASH-AND-WEAR.

waste silk Short filaments of silk remaining on a reel after the long filaments have been taken off. They are used for spun silk.

watch Timepiece worn on the wrist or carried in a pocket.

waterproofing Finishing process designed to make a fabric impervious to water by closing all the openings of the fabric. Rubber, oil, and lacquer compounds are used for this purpose.

water-repellent (water-resistant) Term applied to fabric treated with a chemical or wax finish that sheds water but permits air to circulate through the material. The finish may be renewed from time to time.

wax calf Heavy calfskin finished with wax.

wearable Any article that can be worn.

wear testing Evaluation of a fabric for resistance to abrasion, flexibility, resilience, washability, crease retention, and crease resistance, based on the actual wearing of a garment.

weave *See* BASKET WEAVE; DIAGONAL WEAVE; CHEVRON WEAVE; HONEYCOMB WEAVE; PILE WEAVE; PLAIN WEAVE.

weaving Any method of creating a fabric on a loom by interlacing warp and filling threads with one another. In addition to the basic plain weave, there are innumerable variations suited to different types of materials.

webbing Strong fabric, with or without rubber yarn in the warp, that is used for suspenders, belts, and other articles.

wedge heel Heel of a shoe that fills the space below the shank.

Weejuns Brand name, registered by the G. H. Bass Co., for a moccasin-style shoe.

weft *See* FILLING.

weft knitting *See* KNITTING.

weight *See* COUNT; FABRIC WEIGHT.

weighted silk Silk treated with a metallic solution to add to its weight and give it a rich look.

Wellington, 1st Duke of British soldier (1769–1852) who, after returning to England following his victory over Napoleon, influenced fashion by wearing trousers in public instead of courtly silk breeches and stockings. The Wellington boot is named for him.

Wellington boot Leather boot with a soft upper extending above the knee. The half Wellington is only half as high; it is designed to be worn under trousers or with trousers tucked inside the boot. The name "Wellington" is also given to a type of high rubber boot.

welt Narrow strip of leather stitched to the upper and to the edge of the insole of a shoe. The edge of the strip is then stitched to the outsole.

welt edge Edge of a hat brim that is turned back and stitched or felted by a special process.

welterweight Term applied to suiting of an in-between weight, about 10 or 11 ounces per yard.

Western hat *See* COWBOY HAT.

wet cleaning Using water and soap or detergent to wash soiled garments.

wet look Shiny appearance created by the lustrous, bright surface of vinyl or other materials in garments and footwear.

wet spinning Method of manufacturing man-made and synthetic filaments by extruding the solution of filament-forming material through spinnerets into a coagulating chemical bath.

whangee Yellowish Chinese bamboo used for canes and walking sticks.

whipcord Twill-weave material made of highly twisted worsted yarn; used for

waist-seam jacket

wedge heel

Western hat

suits, topcoats, and sportswear. When used for military uniforms, it is known as elastique.

whipstitch Overcast stitch that is clearly visible.

white Achromatic color at the light end of the black-to-white scale. White is the combination of all colors of the spectrum, ranging in wavelength from the longest to the shortest.

white, oyster *See* OYSTER WHITE.

white-on-white Term applied to a pattern of white figures or stripes on a white broadcloth or other shirt. Made on a dobby or jacquard loom, the patterns are raised above the level of the background.

Whitney, Eli American inventor of the cotton gin (1793), which made the southern part of the United States a world fiber center.

whitney *See* WITNEY.

wholesale Sale of merchandise by a manufacturer or an agent to a retailer instead of to the consumer.

widespread collar Separate or attached shirt collar cut so that there is a wide distance between the points.

wide-wale Term applied to a fabric in which the weave is accentuated by noticeably wide ribs.

wig Covering for the head, made of false hair and a net; worn for style or for concealment of the absence of hair.

wigan Coarse-weave cotton with a stiff finish; used as an interlining.

wild silk Commercial category of silk such as tussah, which is coarse because the caterpillars feed on leaves other than mulberry.

Windbreaker Originally a casual blouse for men; now the name of Windbreaker, Inc., a subsidiary of the Phillips-Van Heusen Corp.

windowpane pattern Design formed by stripes running vertically and horizontally in an arrangement resembling the framework of a window.

Windsor, Duke of Member of the British royal family, who as Prince of Wales, King Edward VIII, and Duke of Windsor exerted a fashion influence from the 1920s to the 1940s. He was credited with popularizing the tab collar, Grenadier Guards tie, snap-brim hat, Windsor-knot tie, brown buckskin shoes, and Fair Isle sweaters.

Windsor collar Attached or separate collar with a wide spread between the points, worn by the Duke of Windsor.

Windsor knot Large necktie knot, tied in a special manner with extra loops, so called because the Duke of Windsor wore large-knot ties in the 1930s and later years.

wing collar Stand-up band collar with folded-back tabs or wings, correct for formal evening or day wear with a tailcoat, cutaway, or dinner jacket or with an oxford-gray jacket and striped trousers.

wing-tip shoe Shoe with a tip shaped like the spread wing of a bird, pointed in the center and extending toward the rear on both sides. It has heavily perforated seams and toe-cap design.

witney (whitney) Soft textured overcoating similar to chinchilla but lacking nubs or knots.

woof *See* FILLING.

wool Fiber from the covering coat of sheep and other animals; also woven, knitted, or felted fabric produced from the fiber.

wool, bright *See* BRIGHT WOOL.

wool, britch (breech) *See* BRITCH WOOL.

wool, chlorinated *See* CHLORINATED WOOL.

wool, crossbred *See* CROSSBRED WOOL.

wool, lamb's *See* LAMB'S WOOL.

wool, reclaimed *See* RECLAIMED WOOL.

wool, reprocessed *See* REPROCESSED WOOL.

wool, reused *See* REUSED WOOL.

wool, reworked *See* RECLAIMED WOOL.

wool, South African *See* SOUTH AFRICAN WOOL.

wool, territory *See* TERRITORY WOOL.

wool, virgin *See* VIRGIN WOOL.

wool-dyed *See* DYED-IN-THE WOOL.

woolen, washable *See* WASHABLE WOOLEN.

woolen system Process of sorting, scouring, blending, oiling, cording, and spinning yarn of short staples, waste, and reworked wool.

worsted Yarn spun from combed long-staple wool fibers; also the closely woven, smooth-surfaced fabric made from this yarn. The name is derived from the village of Worsted (now Worstead), in Norfolk, England, where the fabric was first woven.

worsted, clay *See* CLAY WORSTED.

worsted, clear-face *See* CLEAR-FACE WORSTED.

worsted, tropical *See* TROPICAL WORSTED.

worsted, unfinished *See* UNFINISHED WORSTED.

worsted system Process of carding, combing, gilling, drawing, and spinning worsted fibers into yarn for manufacture into worsted cloth.

wrap coat Full-cut outercoat without a button closure, worn wrapped around the body and held in place by a tied or buckled belt.

wrinkle resistance Characteristic of a fabric in which wrinkling is minimized. Wool or polyester and cotton naturally resist wrinkles. Moreover, a crease-resistant finish may be applied to a fabric or a finished garment.

Wrinkl-Shed Brand name of a wrinkle-resistant process registered by Dan River Mills, Inc.

wristband Band at the end of a long sleeve; also a separate band that covers the wrist.

wristlet Band of knitted or woven fabric, leather, metal, or other material worn around the wrist.

Y

yacht cloth Close-woven unfinished worsted, generally made in navy blue and used for marine clothes.

yachting cap Cap to be worn with yachting clothes. It has a white or navy blue cloth top, black braid running around the sides, insignia in front, and a stiff visor.

yard Unit of measure equal to 36 inches, or 0.914 meter. In Great Britain the yard is the distance between two marks on a rod in the Standards Office at Westminster.

yarn Fibers spun into a continuous strand after being cleaned, drawn, and twisted; used in weaving and knitting. Cotton,

yachting cap

wrap coat

yoke

wool, silk, man-made, synthetic, and other fibers may be made into yarn.

yarn, core-spun *See* CORE-SPUN YARN.

yarn, grandrelle *See* GRANDRELLE YARN.

yarn, novelty *See* NOVELTY YARN.

yarn, sasse *See* SASSE YARN.

yarn, space-dyed *See* SPACE-DYED YARN.

yarn, spun *See* SPUN YARN.

yarn, stretch *See* STRETCH YARN.

yarn, textured filament *See* TEXTURED FILAMENT YARN.

yarn count *See* COUNT.

yarn-dyed Term applied to fabric woven or knitted of yarns that have already been dyed.

yoke Fabric fitted over the shoulders and joined to the lower part of a garment by a visible seam across the chest or back.

yolk Oily matter present in wool after it has been clipped, amounting to about 50 percent by weight. The purified grease, called lanolin, is utilized in toiletries.

Z

Zantrel Brand name of cellulosic rayon manufactured by the American Enka Corporation.

Zefkrome Acrylic fiber made particularly for double-knit fabrics, registered by the Dow Badische Co.

Zefran Basic dyeable acrylic fiber made and registered by the Dow Badische Co.

zein fiber Protein fiber derived from corn.

Zelan Brand name of a water-repellent process registered by Du Pont.

Zepel Trademark of a stain- and water-repellent fluorochemical registered by Du Pont.

zephyr Term applied to a yarn of light-weight worsted, often blended with other fibers, and to a sheer, soft woolen fabric.

Zeset Brand name, registered by Du Pont, for a finish of fabrics of cotton and viscose rayon that may be laundered and bleached.

zigzag Stitching, pattern, or line running alternately from one side to the other in sharply angled turns.

zipper (slide fastener) Flexible device of metal or synthetic material with inter-locking teeth that may be opened or closed by a slide puller. Originally a registered name, zipper is now a generic word for a slide-fastener closure.

zoot suit Suit worn by some young people in 1939 and the early 1940s. The jacket had heavily padded square shoulders and a tapered waist and extended to a few inches above the knees. The trousers were full-cut, measuring 32 inches at knees and tapering sharply to 12 to 15 inches at the bottoms.

Z-twist Yarn twist to the right in which the spirals slant like the middle part of the letter Z.

Index

Italicized page numbers refer to illustrations; boldface page numbers refer to biographies of fashion designers.

D